A Writer's Resource

A Handbook for Writing and Research

Fifth Edition

Elaine P. Maimon
Governors State University

Janice H. Peritz
Queen's College, The City University of New York

Kathleen Blake Yancey
Florida State University

Mc Graw Hill Education

A WRITER'S RESOURCE, FIFTH EDITION

Published by McGraw-Hill Education, 2 Penn Plaza, New York, NY 10121. Copyright © 2016 by McGraw-Hill Education. All rights reserved. Printed in the United States of America. Previous editions © 2012, 2010, 2007. No part of this publication may be reproduced or distributed in any form or by any means, or stored in a database or retrieval system, without the prior written consent of McGraw-Hill Education, including, but not limited to, in any network or other electronic storage or transmission, or broadcast for distance learning.

Some ancillaries, including electronic and print components, may not be available to customers outside the United States.

This book is printed on acid-free paper.

2 3 4 5 6 7 8 9 0 DOC/DOC 1 0 9 8 7 6 5

ISBN 978-0-07-803618-7
MHID 0-07-803618-6

Senior Vice President, Products & Markets: *Kurt L. Strand*
Vice President, General Manager, Products & Markets: *Michael Ryan*
Vice President, Content Design & Delivery: *Kimberly Meriwether David*
Managing Director: *David Patterson*
Director: *Susan Gouijnstook*
Executive Brand Manager: *J. Claire Brantley*
Director, Product Development: *Meghan Campbell*
Executive Market Development Manager: *Nanette Giles*
Senior Marketing Manager: *Brigeth Rivera*
Executive Director of Development: *Lisa Pinto*
Lead Digital Product Analyst: *Janet Smith*
Director, Content Design & Delivery: *Terri Schiesl*
Program Manager: *Jennifer Gehl*
Content Project Manager: *Sandy Wille (core); Samantha Donisi-Hamm (assessment)*
Buyer: *Susan K. Culbertson*
Design: *Matt Backhaus*
Content Licensing Specialists: *Shawntel Schmitt*
Cover Image: © *David Arky Photography*
Compositor: *Laserwords Private Limited*
Printer: *R. R. Donnelley*

All credits appearing on page or at the end of the book are considered to be an extension of the copyright page.

Library of Congress Cataloging-in-Publication Data
Maimon, Elaine P., author.
   A writer's resource : a handbook for writing and research / Elaine P. Maimon, Governors State University; Janice H. Peritz, Queen's College, The City University of New York; Kathleen Blake Yancey, Florida State University.—Fifth Edition.
      pages cm
   Includes bibliographical references and index.
   ISBN 978-0-07-803618-7 (acid-free paper)
   ISBN 0-07-803618-6 (acid-free paper)
   1. English language—Rhetoric—Handbooks, manuals, etc.   2. English language—Grammar—Handbooks, manuals, etc.   3. Report writing—Handbooks, manuals, etc.
I. Peritz, Janice.   II. Yancey, Kathleen Blake, 1950-   III. Title.
   PE1408.M3366 2011
   808'.042—dc23
                                                                            2014019170

The Internet addresses listed in the text were accurate at the time of publication. The inclusion of a website does not indicate an endorsement by the authors or McGraw-Hill Education, and McGraw-Hill Education does not guarantee the accuracy of the information presented at these sites.

www.mhhe.com

About the Authors

Elaine P. Maimon is president of Governors State University in the south suburbs of Chicago, where she is also professor of English. Previously she was chancellor of the University of Alaska Anchorage, provost (chief campus officer) at Arizona State University West, and vice president of Arizona State University as a whole. In the 1970s, she initiated and then directed the Beaver College writing-across-the-curriculum program, one of the first WAC programs in the nation. A founding executive board member of the national Council of Writing Program
Administrators (CWPA), she has directed national institutes to improve the teaching of writing and to disseminate the principles of writing across the curriculum. With a PhD in English from the University of Pennsylvania, where she later helped to create the Writing Across the University (WATU) program, she has also taught and served as an academic administrator at Haverford College, Brown University, and Queens College.

Janice Haney Peritz is an associate professor of English who has taught college writing for more than thirty years, first at Stanford University, where she received her PhD in 1978, and then at the University of Texas at Austin; Beaver College; and Queens College, City University of New York. From 1989 to 2002, she directed the Composition Program at Queens College, where in 1996 she also initiated the college's writing-across-the-curriculum program and the English department's involvement with the Epiphany Project and cyber-composition. She also worked with a
group of CUNY colleagues to develop The Write Site, an online learning center, and more recently directed the CUNY Honors College at Queens College for three years. Currently, she is back in the English department doing what she loves most: full-time classroom teaching of writing, literature, and culture.

Kathleen Blake Yancey is the Kellogg W. Hunt Professor of English, a Distinguished Research Professor, and director of the Graduate Program in Rhetoric and Composition at Florida State University. She is past president of the Council of Writing Program Administrators (CWPA), past chair of the Conference on College Composition and Communication (CCCC), and past president of the National Council of Teachers of English (NCTE). Currently, she co-directs the Inter/National Coalition on Electronic Portfolio Research, which has brought together teachers and researchers from
over 60 institutions around the world to learn together how to use eportfolios to foster learning. She also edits *College Composition and Communication,* the flagship journal for writing studies. She has led many institutes and workshops—focused on electronic portfolios, on service learning and reflection, and on writing and composing with digital technologies. Previously, she taught at UNC Charlotte and at Clemson University, where she directed the Pearce Center for Professional Communication and was the founding director of the Class of 1941 Studio for Student Communication, both of which are dedicated to supporting communication across the curriculum.

A Resource for

A Writer's Resource helps writers identify the fundamental elements of any writing situation—from academic papers to blog posts to 140-character tweets. Its innovative, transferable techniques and practices build confidence for composing across genres, media, and the academic curriculum. And with its numerous examples from a rich cross-section of disciplines, the fifth edition clearly demonstrates that every major, every field of study, and every potential career path depends on written communication.

- *A Writer's Resource* focuses on the most common writing assignments and situations students will encounter today. Its six assignment chapters offer guidelines for writing that informs, analyzes, and argues in different settings. **Three** sample student essays appear in these chapters, including a research report on blogging and an essay arguing for precautions against cyberbullying. Online, *Connect® Composition* offers interactive exercises for practicing MLA and APA styles of documentation with examples representing a range of genres and media.

- Available in *Connect Composition*, *LearnSmart Achieve®* supports *A Writer's Resource* and underscores the importance of the writing situation by helping learners develop a fundamental understanding of writing processes and other basics of composition. *LearnSmart Achieve* offers a personalized learning experience in an adaptive environment, which promotes knowledge transfer by emphasizing metacognitive, reflective understanding. What students learn here, they can apply elsewhere. *LearnSmart Achieve* content spans more than 60 topics and 385 learning outcomes.

- The *Start Smart* feature, exclusive to *A Writer's Resource,* provides guidelines and templates for working through writing situations, reinforcing the idea that there are recognizable landmarks in every writing assignment. In *Connect Composition, Start Smart* launches the process of identifying purpose, audience, and context, and guides users through the eBook for *A Writer's Resource* based on their specific writing situations.

Navigating Any Writing Situation

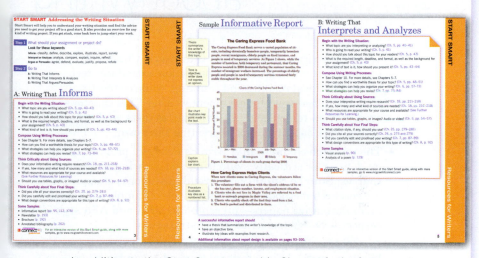

- In addition to the *Start Smart* spread in Chapter 1, the feature set for the fifth edition includes a *Start Smart* box for every section, as well as *Know the Situation, Consider Your Situation, Navigating through College and Beyond, Checklist,* and brand-new *The Evolving Situation* practice boxes throughout the text.

the EVOLVING SITUATION

Personal Writing and Social Media Web Sites

In addition to writing personal essays for class, you may use social media sites like *Facebook* or *Twitter* for personal expression and autobiographical writing. Since these sites are networked, it's important to remember that strangers, including prospective employers, may have access to your profiles and comments.

CHECKLIST Revising Visuals

☐ **Are grid lines needed in tables?** Eliminate grid lines or, if the lines are needed for clarity, lighten them. Tables should not look like nets with every number enclosed. Vertical rules are needed only when space is extremely tight between columns.

A Resource for Thinking Critically about Writing

- Using the writing situation as a framework, Chapter 4, Reading and Writing: The Critical Connection, introduces techniques of critical reading and thinking, while connecting students to resources for argument writing. This chapter shows students how to read actively, summarize texts, and respond to others' work as a precursor to creating their own.

- The research chapters in *A Writer's Resource* provide updated guidelines for critically evaluating and drawing on digital sources. **Source Smart** boxes remind students of appropriate research methods and citation styles. Sample argument and informative papers—presented in MLA and APA styles, respectively—demonstrate these strategies.

- Available in *Connect Composition, Power of Process* offers a hands-on critical thinking tool for reading and writing from any source. Using a recursive and reflective framework to develop essential academic skills such as understanding, analyzing, and synthesizing texts—from either preloaded or uploaded sources—*Power of Process* moves students toward higher order thinking and writing.

SOURCE SMART Deciding to Quote, Paraphrase, or Summarize

Point is eloquently, memorably, or uniquely stated	→	Quote
Details important but not uniquely or eloquently expressed	→	Paraphrase
Long section of material (with many points), main ideas important, details not important	→	Summarize
Part of longer passage is uniquely stated	→	Use quotation inside paraphrased or summarized passage

New to the Fifth Edition

This new edition of *A Writer's Resource* includes an updated focus on the essential elements of the writing process. Using this framework, the fifth edition helps students build a solid set of writing skills that will transfer to the work they will do in other courses, in their communities, and in their professional lives.

- A new feature, **The Evolving Situation,** supports this approach by offering guidance on navigating a variety of writing situations, such as those introduced by new media and technologies.
- New **Start Smart** boxes in every tab provide a quick way to begin and engage with any assignment.

A Writer's Resource, fifth edition, also includes two new sample student papers (visual analysis and poetry analysis) and three revised sample student papers featuring updated content, research, and citations. Here is a quick look at just a few of the changes within the chapters:

Chapter 2, Writing Situations
- Updated coverage of the writing situation, including discussion of new/social media
- Updated coverage of multimodal elements and genres
- Updated discussion of netiquette guidelines

Chapter 5, Planning and Shaping
- Updated examples of free-writing, brainstorming, clustering, and questioning
- New sample outlines on planning a structure
- Sections on visuals and multimedia address new formats for visual presentation, such as Prezi, Camtasia, and Vimeo

Chapter 6, Drafting Text and Visuals
- New discussion of cloud-based tools for saving work
- Updated coverage of visual analogies

Chapter 7, Revising and Editing
- New sample first draft of student text demonstrating revisions for paragraph unity and coherence
- New student sample visual analysis on Dorothea Lange's photo, *Migrant Mother*

Chapter 9, Informative Reports
- Revised student sample informative paper includes updated research and citations

Chapter 10, Interpretive Analogies and Writing about Literature
- New student sample interpretive analysis of Emily Dickinson's "Tell all the Truth . . ."

Chapter 11, Arguments
- Revised student sample proposal includes updated research and citations

Chapter 13, Oral Presentations
- New section 13e on preparing recorded oral presentations

Chapter 14, Multimodal Writing
- New discussion of "The narrative behind the image" includes Pulitzer-prize winning photograph by *New York Times* photographer Tyler Hicks
- New references to resources that offer permission-free material and free server space for hosting Web content

Chapter 17, Writing to Get and Keep a Job
- Updated discussion of sites that replace the standard resume
- New discussion of creating and sharing e-portfolios
- New discussion of importance of assessing one's online presence

Chapter 19, Finding and Managing Print and Online Sources
- New screenshots of research conducted in databases, search engines and online library catalogs

Chapter 23, Plagiarism, Copyright, and Intellectual Property
- Updated coverage of plagiarism, copyright and fair use, and intellectual property

Chapter 24, Working with Sources and Avoiding Plagiarism
- Updated examples of paraphrasing, summarizing, quoting, and synthesizing

MLA Documentation Style
- 8 new examples of in-text citation; 65 new examples of citing sources in a Works Cited list
- Revised student sample research project includes updated research, citations, and annotations

APA Documentation Style
- 9 new examples of APA in-text citation; 54 new examples of APA references
- Revised student sample research includes updated research, citations, and annotations

Chicago and CSE Documentation Styles
- 25 new examples of Chicago Style documentation
- Revised excerpt of student sample paper on blogging
- Updated CSE style coverage; 5 new examples of CSE Style references

Grammar
- New emphasis on basic grammar in **Tips for Multilingual Writers** feature

Why a Digital Solution for Writing Courses?

Connect Composition and *LearnSmart Achieve* ensure students learn the basics of writing through a personalized system that identifies what they already know while providing direct instruction on unfamiliar concepts. Our integrated system constantly adapts and changes as it learns more about each student—their strengths as well as their knowledge gaps. *Connect Composition* provides the kind of support instructors need to focus class time on the highest course expectations: students who truly engage with an assignment, establish themselves as critical thinkers, communicate their ideas effectively, and transfer these skills to different courses and assignments throughout their college experience.

After a one-time simple registration, students have four years of access to all of the tools and activities in *Connect Composition*. McGraw-Hill Education's trusted content includes up-to-date documentation standards and genre models as well as guidance on each step of the writing and research processes. Students benefit from a 14-day courtesy access period during registration.

Connect Composition works seamlessly within any Learning Management System such as BlackBoard, Canvas, or D2L. Assignments as well as data may be integrated, yielding useful reports on a variety of measures. The *Connect* suite of tools includes *LearnSmart Achieve, Outcomes-Based Assessment, Peer Review,* and *Power of Process* (strategies for critical reading and evaluation of sources) in addition to a wide spectrum of writing assignments and activities. Instructors can use all of these tools to make assignments, produce reports, focus discussions, intervene on problem topics, and help at-risk learners.

Connect Composition can also lend a hand in establishing course consistency and assessment transparency while providing data that verifies a program's outcomes are being met. *Connect* can track the progress of individual students or whole sections as it generates easy-to-read reports suitable for program evaluation and accreditation.

Mc Graw Hill Education **connect**®

|COMPOSITION

Connect Composition Tools

Connect Composition offers **four years of access** to comprehensive, reliable writing and research instruction. The following tools and services are available as part of *Connect Composition*:

FEATURE	DESCRIPTION	INSTRUCTIONAL VALUE
Simple LMS Integration	• Seamlessly integrates with every learning management system.	• Students have automatic single sign-on. • *Connect* assignment results sync to LMS's gradebook.
LearnSmart Achieve	• Continuously adapts to a student's strengths and weaknesses, to create a personalized learning environment. • Covers *The Writing Process, Critical Reading, The Research Process, Reasoning and Argument, Multilingual Writers, Grammar and Common Sentence Problems, Punctuation and Mechanics,* and *Style and Word Choice.* • Provides instructors with reports that include data on student and class performance.	• Students independently study the fundamental topics across Composition in an adaptive environment. • Metacognitive component supports knowledge transfer. • Students track their own understanding and mastery and discover where their gaps are.
SmartBook®	• Identifies and highlights topics students have not mastered. The first and only continuously adaptive reading experience <u>available for rhetorics</u>. • Provides instructors with reports that include data on student and class performance.	• The text adapts to the student based on what he or she knows and doesn't know and focuses study time on critical material. • Metacognitive component supports knowledge transfer. • Students track their own understanding and mastery and discover where their gaps are.
Power of Process	Guides students through the critical reading and writing process step-by-step.	• Students demonstrate understanding and develop critical thinking skills for reading, writing, and evaluating sources by responding to short-answer and annotation questions. Students are also prompted to reflect on their own processes. • Instructors or students can choose from a preloaded set of readings or upload their own. • Students can use the guidelines to consider a potential source critically.
Writing Assignments with *Peer Review*	• Allows instructors to assign and grade writing assignments online. • Gives instructors the option of easily and efficiently setting up and managing online peer review assignments for the entire class.	• This online tool makes grading writing assignments more efficient, saving time for instructors. • Students import their Word document(s), and instructors can comment and annotate submissions. • Frequently used comments are automatically saved so instructors do not have to type the same feedback over and over.

Writing **Assignments** *with Outcomes* **Based-Assessment**	• Allows instructors or course administrators to assess student writing around specific learning outcomes. • Generates easy-to-read reports around program-specific learning outcomes. • Includes the most up-to-date Writing Program Administrators learning outcomes, but also gives instructors the option of creating their own.	• This tool provides assessment transparency to students. They can see why a "B" is a "B" and what it will take to improve to an "A." • Reports allow a program or instructor to demonstrate progress in attaining section, course, or program goals.
Connect eBook	• Provides comprehensive course content, exceeding what is offered in print. • Supports annotation and bookmarking.	The eBook allows instructors and students to access their course materials anytime and anywhere.
Connect eReader	Provides access to additional readings that are assignable via *Connect Composition*.	Sample essays provide models for students as well as interesting topics to consider for discussion and writing.
Insight	Provides a quick view of student and class performance with a series of visual data displays that answer the following questions: 1. How are my students doing? 2. How is this student doing? 3. How is my section doing? 4. How is this assignment working? 5. How are my assignments working?	Instructors can quickly check on and analyze student and class performance.
Instructor Reports	• Allow instructors to review the performance of an individual student or an entire section. • Allow instructors or course administrators to review multiple sections to gauge progress in attaining course, department, or institutional goals.	• Instructors can identify struggling students early and intervene to ensure retention. • Instructors can identify challenging topics and adjust instruction accordingly. • Reports can be generated for an accreditation process or a program evaluation
Student Reports	Allow students to review their performance for specific assignments or the course.	Students can keep track of their performance and identify areas they are struggling with.
Pre-& Post-Tests	• Precreated non-adaptive assessments for pre- and post-testing.	Pre-test provides a static benchmark for student knowledge at the beginning of the program. Post-test offers a concluding assessment of student progress.
Tegrity	• Allows instructors to capture course material or lectures on video. • Allows students to watch videos recorded by their instructor and learn course material at their own pace.	• Instructors can keep track of which students have watched the videos they post. • Students can watch and review lectures from their instructor. • Students can search each lecture for specific bits of information.

Support for Digital Success

McGraw-Hill Education provides a variety of ways for instructors to get the help and support they need when incorporating new technology into a writing program. The digital tools in *Connect* were developed by experts to create a teaching and learning environment that engages learners with a wide variety of course assignments, suited for both online as well as hybrid or face-to-face courses. New users of *Connect* have several options for assistance in setting up courses initially as well as throughout the first term.

Digital Faculty Consultants: Experienced instructors are available to offer suggestions, advice, and training for new adopters of *Connect*. To request a Digital Faculty Consultant's assistance, simply e-mail your local McGraw-Hill Education representative.

Learning Technology Consultants: Local McGraw-Hill Education representatives can provide local face-to-face training and support. Find your local rep at www.mhhe.com/rep.

Digital Learning Consultants: These specialists in the field are available to support instructors with initial set-up and training as well as answer questions that may arise throughout the term. DLCs may be contacted directly or by simply asking your local McGraw-Hill Education representative.

Digital Success Team: Team members offer one-on-one training to instructors to demonstrate how *Connect* works while also providing information and guidance on how to incorporate *Connect* into a specific course design and syllabus. Again, ask for a session with a Team Member by writing to your local McGraw-Hill Education representative.

National Training Webinars: McGraw-Hill Education offers an ongoing series of Webinars for instructors to learn and master the *Connect* platform as well as its course-specific tools and features. New Webinars are being scheduled all the time, so be sure to check our online catalog of courses at webinars.mhhe.com.

In general, instructors are encouraged to contact us anytime they need help. Our Customer Support Team is available at 800-331-5094 or online at http://mpss.mhhe.com/contact.php.

Spotlight on Three Tools in *Connect*
LearnSmart Achieve

LearnSmart Achieve helps learners establish a baseline understanding of the language and concepts that make up the critical processes of composition—writing, critical reading, research, reasoning and argument, grammar, mechanics, style, as well as issues surrounding multilingual writers. Across 8 broad units, *LearnSmart Achieve* focuses learners on proficiency in more than 60 topics and 385 learning outcomes.

Outcomes-Based Assessment of Writing

The *Outcomes-Based Assessment* tool in *Connect Composition* is simply a way for any instructor to grade a writing assignment using

UNIT	TOPIC	
THE WRITING PROCESS	The Writing Process Generating Ideas Planning and Organizing	Drafting Revising Proofreading, Formatting, and Producing Texts
CRITICAL READING	Reading to Understand Literal Meaning Evaluating Truth and Accuracy in a Text	Evaluating the Effectiveness and Appropriateness of a Text
THE RESEARCH PROCESS	Developing and Implementing a Research Plan Evaluating Information and Sources	Integrating Source Material into a Text Using Information Ethically and Legally
REASONING AND ARGUMENT	Developing an Effective Thesis or Claim Using Evidence and Reasoning to Support a Thesis or Claim	Using Ethos (Ethics) to Persuade Readers Using Pathos (Emotion) to Persuade Readers Using Logos (Logic) to Persuade Readers
GRAMMAR AND COMMON SENTENCE PROBLEMS	Parts of Speech Phrases, Clauses, and Fragments Sentence Types Fused (Run-on) Sentences and Comma Splices Pronouns Pronoun-Antecedent Agreement	Pronoun Reference Subject-Verb Agreement Verbs and Verbals Adjectives and Adverbs Dangling and Misplaced Modifiers Mixed Constructions Verb Tense and Voice Shifts
PUNCTUATION AND MECHANICS	Commas Semicolons Colons End Punctuation Apostrophes Quotation Marks Dashes	Parentheses Hyphens Abbreviations Capitalization Italics Numbers Spelling
STYLE AND WORD CHOICE	Wordiness Eliminating Redundancies and Sentence Variety Coordination and Subordination	Faulty Comparisons Word Choice Clichés, Slang, and Jargon Parallelism
MULTILINGUAL WRITERS	Helping Verbs, Gerunds and Infinitives, and Phrasal Verbs Nouns, Verbs, and Objects Articles	Count and Noncount Nouns Sentence Structure and Word Order Verb Agreement Participles and Adverb Placement

LearnSmart Achieve **is one of the adaptive learning tools offered in** *Connect Composition.*

a rubric of outcomes and proficiency levels. A pre-loaded rubric is available that uses the Writing Program Administrators (WPA) outcomes for composition courses; however, instructors may adapt any of these outcomes or use their own. Instructors work through a student's piece of writing and assign a score for each outcome, indicating how well the student did on that specific aspect of the writing process. These scores can be useful in assigning an overall grade for the specific assignment and may also be combined with other assignments to get a sense of a student's overall progress. The *Outcomes-Based Assessment* tool offers a range of clear, simple reports that allow instructors to view progress and achievement in a variety of ways. These reports may also satisfy department or college-level requests for data relating to program goals or for accreditation purposes.

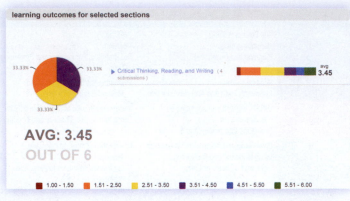

The *Outcomes-Based Assessment* tool offers a range of clear, simple reports that allow instructors to view progress and achievement in a variety of ways.

Power of Process

Power of Process is the newest tool in *Connect Composition. Power of Process* provides strategies that guide students through how to critically read a piece of writing or consider it as a possible source for incorporation into their own work. After they work through the strategies, which include highlighting and annotating a piece of writing, students are encouraged to reflect on their interaction with the reading. Students can print out a summary of their work to use with other projects or to submit alongside their own assignment for grading.

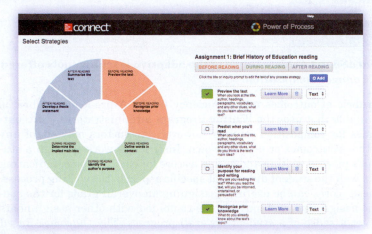

***Power of Process* provides strategies that guide students in reading critically.**

Connect Composition Reports

Connect Composition generates a number of powerful reports and charts that allow instructors to quickly review the performance of a specific student or an entire section. Students have their own set of reports (limited to include only their individual performance) that can demonstrate at a glance where they are doing well and where they are struggling. Here are a few of the reports that are available:

- *Assignment Results Report* – shows an entire section's performance across all assignments.
- *Assignment Statistics Report* – provides quick data on each assignment including mean score as well as high/low scores.
- *Student Performance Report* – focuses on a specific student's progress across all assignments.
- *Learning Outcomes Assessment Report* – for instructors who use the *Outcomes-Based Assessment* Tool to grade a writing assignment, this report provides data on student performance for specific outcomes.
- *At-Risk Report* – provides instructors a dashboard of information that can help identify at-risk students based on low engagement levels.
- *LearnSmart Reports* – focuses on student usage, progress, and mastery of the modules contained within *LearnSmart Achieve, Connect's* highly personalized, adaptive learning resource.

Grade Book Synching

The raw data from the Assignment Results report synchronizes directly with Learning Management Systems so that scores automatically flow from *Connect Composition* into school-specific grade book centers.

Need a *Connect* Account?

Request access to *Connect* from your local McGraw-Hill Education representative (www.mhhe.com/rep) or write to english@mheducation.com and we will be happy to help!

If you have an account already, log in at http://connect.mheducation.com.

Students will have their course materials on the first day of class thanks to a 14-day courtesy access period for *Connect Composition*.

WPA Outcomes Statement for First-Year Composition

Introduction

This Statement identifies outcomes for first-year composition programs in U.S. postsecondary education. It describes the writing knowledge, practices, and attitudes that undergraduate students develop in first-year composition, which at most schools is a required general education course or sequence of courses. This Statement therefore attempts to both represent and regularize writing programs' priorities for first-year composition, which often takes the form of one or more required general education courses. To this end it is not merely a compilation or summary of what currently takes place. Rather, this Statement articulates what composition teachers nationwide have learned from practice, research, and theory.[1] It intentionally defines only "outcomes," or types of results, and not "standards," or precise levels of achievement. The setting of standards to measure students' achievement of these Outcomes has deliberately been left to local writing programs and their institutions.

In this Statement "composing" refers broadly to complex writing processes that are increasingly reliant on the use of digital technologies. Writers also attend to elements of design, incorporating images and graphical elements into texts intended for screens as well as printed pages. Writers' composing activities have always been shaped by the technologies available to them, and digital technologies are changing writers' relationships to their texts and audiences in evolving ways.

These outcomes are supported by a large body of research demonstrating that the process of learning to write in any medium is complex: it is both individual and social and demands continued practice and informed guidance. Programmatic decisions about helping students demonstrate these outcomes should be informed by an understanding of this research.

As students move beyond first-year composition, their writing abilities do not merely improve. Rather, their abilities will diversify along disciplinary, professional, and civic lines as these writers move into new settings where expected outcomes expand, multiply, and diverge. Therefore, this document advises faculty in all disciplines about how to help students build on what they learn in introductory writing courses.

Rhetorical Knowledge

Rhetorical knowledge is the ability to analyze contexts and audiences and then to act on that analysis in comprehending and creating texts. Rhetorical knowledge is the basis of composing. Writers develop rhetorical knowledge

---

[1] This Statement is aligned with the *Framework for Success in Postsecondary Writing,* an articulation of the skills and habits of mind essential for success in college, and is intended to help establish a continuum of valued practice from high school through to the college major.

by negotiating purpose, audience, context, and conventions as they compose a variety of texts for different situations.

By the end of first-year composition, students should
- Learn and use key rhetorical concepts through analyzing and composing a variety of texts
- Gain experience reading and composing in several genres to understand how genre conventions shape and are shaped by readers' and writers' practices and purposes
- Develop facility in responding to a variety of situations and contexts calling for purposeful shifts in voice, tone, level of formality, design, medium, and/or structure
- Understand and use a variety of technologies to address a range of audiences
- Match the capacities of different environments (e.g., print and electronic) to varying rhetorical situations

Faculty in all programs and departments can build on this preparation by helping students learn
- The expectations of readers in their fields
- The main features of genres in their fields
- The main purposes of composing in their fields

Critical Thinking, Reading, and Composing

Critical thinking is the ability to analyze, synthesize, interpret, and evaluate ideas, information, situations, and texts. When writers think critically about the materials they use—whether print texts, photographs, data sets, videos, or other materials—they separate assertion from evidence, evaluate sources and evidence, recognize and evaluate underlying assumptions, read across texts for connections and patterns, identify and evaluate chains of reasoning, and compose appropriately qualified and developed claims and generalizations. These practices are foundational for advanced academic writing.

By the end of first-year composition, students should
- Use composing and reading for inquiry, learning, critical thinking, and communicating in various rhetorical contexts
- Read a diverse range of texts, attending especially to relationships between assertion and evidence, to patterns of organization, to the interplay between verbal and nonverbal elements, and to how these features function for different audiences and situations
- Locate and evaluate (for credibility, sufficiency, accuracy, timeliness, bias and so on) primary and secondary research materials, including journal articles and essays, books, scholarly and professionally established and maintained databases or archives, and informal electronic networks and internet sources
- Use strategies—such as interpretation, synthesis, response, critique, and design/redesign—to compose texts that integrate the writer's ideas with those from appropriate sources

Faculty in all programs and departments can build on this preparation by helping students learn
- The kinds of critical thinking important in their disciplines
- The kinds of questions, problems, and evidence that define their disciplines
- Strategies for reading a range of texts in their fields

Processes

Writers use multiple strategies, or *composing processes*, to conceptualize, develop, and finalize projects. Composing processes are seldom linear: a writer may research a topic before drafting, then conduct additional research while revising or after consulting a colleague. Composing processes are also flexible: successful writers can adapt their composing processes to different contexts and occasions.

By the end of first-year composition, students should
- Develop a writing project through multiple drafts
- Develop flexible strategies for reading, drafting, reviewing, collaborating, revising, rewriting, rereading, and editing
- Use composing processes and tools as a means to discover and reconsider ideas
- Experience the collaborative and social aspects of writing processes
- Learn to give and to act on productive feedback to works in progress
- Adapt composing processes for a variety of technologies and modalities
- Reflect on the development of composing practices and how those practices influence their work

Faculty in all programs and departments can build on this preparation by helping students learn
- To employ the methods and technologies commonly used for research and communication within their fields
- To develop projects using the characteristic processes of their fields
- To review work-in-progress for the purpose of developing ideas before surface-level editing
- To participate effectively in collaborative processes typical of their field

Knowledge of Conventions

Conventions are the formal rules and informal guidelines that define genres, and in so doing, shape readers' and writers' perceptions of correctness or appropriateness. Most obviously, conventions govern such things as mechanics, usage, spelling, and citation practices. But they also influence content, style, organization, graphics, and document design.

Conventions arise from a history of use and facilitate reading by invoking common expectations between writers and readers. These expectations are not universal; they vary by genre (conventions for lab notebooks and discussion-board exchanges differ), by discipline (conventional moves in literature reviews in Psychology differ from those in English), and by occasion (meeting minutes and executive summaries use different registers). A writer's grasp of conventions in one context does not mean a firm grasp in another. Successful writers understand, analyze, and negotiate conventions for purpose, audience, and genre, understanding that genres evolve in response to changes in material conditions and composing technologies and attending carefully to emergent conventions.

By the end of first-year composition, students should
- Develop knowledge of linguistic structures, including grammar, punctuation, and spelling, through practice in composing and revising
- Understand why genre conventions for structure, paragraphing, tone, and mechanics vary
- Gain experience negotiating variations in genre conventions
- Learn common formats and/or design features for different kinds of texts
- Explore the concepts of intellectual property (such as fair use and copyright) that motivate documentation conventions
- Practice applying citation conventions systematically in their own work

Faculty in all programs and departments can build on this preparation by helping students learn
- The reasons behind conventions of usage, specialized vocabulary, format, and citation systems in their fields or disciplines
- Strategies for controlling conventions in their fields or disciplines
- Factors that influence the ways work is designed, documented, and disseminated in their fields
- Ways to make informed decisions about intellectual property issues connected to common genres and modalities in their fields.

Acknowledgments

When we wrote *A Writer's Resource,* we started with the premise that it takes a campus to teach a writer. It is also the case that it takes a community to write a handbook. This text has been a major collaborative effort for all three of us. And over the years, that ever-widening circle of collaboration has included reviewers, editors, librarians, faculty colleagues, and family members.

Let us start close to home. Mort Maimon brought to this project his years of insight and experience as a writer and as a secondary and post-secondary English teacher. Gillian Maimon, Ph.D., first-grade teacher and writing workshop leader contributed special expertise to the fifth edition, especially to the section on literary analysis. Alan Maimon, journalist and author, continues to be a source of encouragement. Elaine also drew inspiration from her young granddaughters, Dasia and Madison Stewart, Annabelle Elaine Maimon, and Lisette Rose Maimon, who already show promise of becoming writers. Rudy Peritz and Lynne Haney reviewed drafts of a number of chapters, bringing to our cross-curricular mix the pedagogical and writerly perspectives of, respectively, a law professor and a sociologist. Jess Peritz, a recent college graduate, was consulted on numerous occasions for her expert advice on making examples both up-to-date and understandable. David, Genevieve, and Matthew Yancey—whose combined writing experience includes the fields of biology, psychology, medicine, computer engineering, mathematics, industrial engineering, and information technology—helped with examples as well as with accounts of their writing practices: completing many kinds of classroom assignments, applying to medical and graduate schools, writing for internships and jobs both inside and outside of the academy.

At Governors State University, Penny Perdue provided research and expert editorial support. Diane Dates Casey was helpful on the role of university libraries. At Arizona State University West, Beverly Buddee worried with us over this project for many years. Our deepest gratitude goes to Lisa Kammerlocher and Dennis Isbell for the guidelines on critically evaluating Web resources in Chapter 18, as well as to Sharon Wilson. Thanks also to C. J. Jeney and Cheryl Warren. ASU West professors Thomas McGovern and Martin Meznar shared assignments and student papers with us.

From Florida State University, we thank the Rhetoric and Composition program and the many good ideas that come from students and faculty alike. Specifically, we thank Liane Robertson—now at William Paterson University of New Jersey—and Kara Taczak—now at the University of Denver—who brought their experiences as excellent teachers of writing to many pages of this book.

Our thanks also go to Judy Williamson and Trent Batson for contributing their expertise on writing and computers as well as for sharing what they learned from the Epiphany Project. Our thanks go out as well to Casey Furlong of Glendale Community College and

Santi Buscemi of Middlesex County College for their excellent contributions to *Connect*. We are grateful to Harvey Wiener and the late Richard Marius for their permission to draw on their explanations of grammatical points in *A Writer's Resource*. We also appreciate the work of Maria Zlateva of Boston University; Karen Batchelor of City College of San Francisco; and Daria Ruzicka, who prepared the ESL materials. Thanks also go to librarians Debora Person, University of Wyoming, Ronelle K. H. Thompson, Augustana College, and Boyd Holmes, who provided us with helpful comments on Tab 5: Researching. Our colleague Don McQuade has inspired us, advised us, and encouraged us throughout the years of this project.

Within the McGraw-Hill Education organization, many wonderful people have been our true teammates on this new fifth edition. We appreciate Claire Brantley's excellent work as executive brand manager. Crucial support came from Susan Gouijnstook, director; David Patterson, managing director for English; Lisa Pinto, lead product developer, and Nanette Giles, executive market development manager. Thanks to Janet Smith, Andrea Pasquarelli, Paula Kepos, Michael O'Loughlin, and Nancy Huebner, all of whom worked diligently on *Connect Composition*. Sandy Wille, content project manager, monitored every detail of production; Matt Backhaus, designer, supervised every aspect of the striking text design and cover; and designer Robin Mouat, was responsible for the stunning visuals that appear throughout the book. Thanks to Diane Kraut for her help in clearing text permissions for this edition. Brigeth Rivera, senior marketing manager, Marisa Cavanaugh, marketing manager, and Ray Kelley, senior field publisher, have worked tirelessly and enthusiastically to market *A Writer's Resource*.

This book has benefited enormously from three extraordinary product developers: David Chodoff, the remarkable Carla Samodulski, and the incredibly talented Elizabeth Murphy. Elizabeth joined the team to shepherd us through the fifth edition and it has been a pleasure working with her. Carla and Elizabeth worked together to strengthen and refine the digital tools available in *Connect* for *A Writer's Resource*.

Finally, many, many thanks go to the reviewers who read chapters from the new edition of one of our handbooks, generously offered their perceptions and reactions to our plans, and had confidence in us as we shaped our texts to address the needs of their students. We wish to thank the following instructors:

Content Consultants and Reviewers

Arizona Western College, Yuma
  Stephen Moore

Baton Rouge Community College
  Shelisa Theus

Bridgewater State University
  Deborah Barshay

Delaware Technical Community College
  Rob Rector

Eastern Illinois University
  Melissa Caldwell
  Dalva Markelis

Front Range Community College
Donna Craine

Hawaii Pacific University
Robert Wilson

Howard University
David Green

Idaho State University
Harold Hellwig

Illinois Central College
Michael Boyd
James Decker

Ivy Tech Community College,
Columbus
John Roberts

Ivy Tech Community College,
Central Indiana
Judith LaFourest
Brenda Spencer

Jacksonville State University
Don Bennett
Christy Burns
Deborah Prickett

West Kentucky Community and
Technical College
Kimberly Russell

Lane College
Unoma Azuah

Lees-McRae College
Kathy H. Olson

Lincoln College
Judy Cortelloni

Lincoln Land Community College
Jason Dockter

McNeese State University
Rita D. Costello

Mercer University
Jonathan Glance

Michigan State University, East
Lansing
Nancy Dejoy

Northwest Arkansas Community
College
Audley Hall
Megan Looney

Palm Beach State College, Lake
Worth
Susan Aguila

Palm Beach State College
Patrick Tierney

Porterville College
Melissa Black

Quinnipiac University
Glenda Pritchett

St. Louis Community College,
Florissant Valley
Lonetta Oliver

Santa Fe College
Akilah Brown

Southern Illinois University
Tara Hembrough

Southwestern Assemblies of God
University
Diane Lewis

Southwestern Illinois College
Judi Quimby

Tarrant County College,
Southeast Campus
Elizabeth Joseph

Texas Christian University
Brad Lucas

Tidewater Community College,
Virginia Beach Campus
Doris Jellig

Tulsa Community College, Metro
Campus
Greg Stone
Jeanne Urie

Tulsa Community College
Ken Clane

The University of Arkansas at
Pine Bluff
Janice Brantley

Union University
David Malone

University of Alabama
Karen Gardiner
Jessica Kidd

The University of Missouri,
Kansas City
  Daniel Mahala

University of Montana
  Amy Ratto-Parks

The University of Toledo
  Anthony Edgington

The University of West Georgia
  Kevin Casper

University of Wisconsin-Stout
  Andrea Deacon

Wayne County Community
College District, Western Campus
  Bakkah Rasheed-Shabazz

Western Technical College
  Pamela Solberg

William Paterson University
  Mark Arnowitz

Freshman Composition Symposia

We are deeply indebted to the following instructors who participated in one of the several composition symposia we hosted in the fall of 2013, and the spring and fall of 2014. Representing the needs and goals of their writing programs and students, they provided vision and guided the McGraw-Hill Education English editors as they made critical decisions concerning *Connect Composition*. Their contributions will result in a rich *Connect Composition* platform for years to come. Thank you.

Arapahoe Community College
  Jamey Trotter

Arizona Western College
  Jana Moore

Brigham Young University–Idaho
  Glenn Dayley

Chemeketa Community College
  Jeremy Trabue

Claflin University
  Reginald Bess

Community College of Baltimore
County
  Evan Balkan

Eastern Washington
University–Cheney
  Tim Roe

Full Sail University
  Danita Berg

Glendale Community College
  Alisa Cooper

Idaho State University
  Susan Swetnam

Indiana University–Purdue
University Fort Wayne
  Steve Amidon

Kaplan University Online
  Kurtis Clements

Lincoln College of New England
  Joyce Doan

Milwaukee Area Technical College
  John Allen

Moraine Valley Community
College
  Tom Dow

West Kentucky Community and
Technical College
  Kimberly Russell

San Jacinto College
  Ann Pearson

Salt Lake Community College
  Brittany Stephenson

Savannah State University
  Michael Lewis

Spokane Falls Community College
  Connie Wasem Scott

St. Louis Community College–
Florissant Valley
Lonetta Oliver

Strayer University
LaRuth Ensley

Texas A&M University
Chris Murray

Texas State University–San
Marcos
Nancy Wilson

University of Arizona
Amy C. Kimme Hea

University of Memphis
Susan L. Popham

University of Miami
Andrew Green

University of South Dakota
Paul Formisano

Vance-Granville Community College
Maureen Walters

Virginia Tech
Sheila Carter-Tod

Washburn University
Melanie Burdick

Research Study Partners and Participants

Our research studies included the Southern California Outcomes
Research in English project (SCORE) and The Writing Situation
Study. Neither would have been possible without the close collaboration and assistance of our instructor-participants and site partners,
to whom we owe special thanks:

Bowling Green State University
Amanda McGuire
Donna Nelson-Beene
Angela Zimmann

Chattanooga State University
Allison Fetters
Brian Hale
Joel Henderson
Jennifer Ontog

Loyola Marymount University
Celeste Amos
Karen Feiner
Wendy Kozak
Ruth Lane
K. J. Peters
Lauren Redwine
Erica Steakley
Shelby Schaefer

Owens Community College
Anita Flynn
Laurence Levy
Ellen Sorg

Santa Ana College
Gary Bennett
Francisco Gomez

Noha Kabaji
Jayne Munoz
Dianne Pearce
Stacey Simmerman
Rachel Sosta

University of California, Irvine
Chieh Chieng
Alberto Gullaba
Lynda Haas
Greg McClure
Ali Meghdadi
Ryan Ridge

University of California, Merced
Cheryl Finley

University of California, Santa
Cruz
Nirshan Perera

University of Toledo
Sheri Benton
Anthony Edgington
Charles Kell

Elaine P. Maimon
Janice H. Peritz
Kathleen Blake Yancey

How to Find the Help You Need in *A Writer's Resource*

A Writer's Resource is a reference for all writers and researchers. When you are writing in any situation, you are bound to come across questions about writing and research. *A Writer's Resource* provides you with answers to your questions.

Begin with Start Smart. If you are responding to an assignment, go to the Start Smart feature at the beginning of Tab 1 to determine the type of writing the assignment requires, along with the steps involved in constructing it and one or more examples. These pages give you an easy means of accessing the many resources available to you within *A Writer's Resource,* from help with finding a thesis to advice on documenting your sources.

Check the table of contents. If you know the topic you are looking for, try scanning the complete contents on the last page and inside back cover, which includes the tab and chapter titles as well as each section number and title in the book. If you are looking for specific information within a general topic (how to correct an unclear pronoun reference, for example), scanning the table of contents will help you find the section you need.

Look up your topic in the index. The comprehensive index at the end of *A Writer's Resource* (pp. I1–I28) includes all of the topics covered in the book. For example, if you are not sure whether to use *I* or *me* in a sentence, you can look up "*I vs. me*" in the index.

Check the documentation resources. By looking at the examples of different types of sources and the documentation models displayed at the opening of each documentation tab, you can determine where to find the information you need to document a source. By answering the questions posed in the charts provided (for MLA style at the beginning of Tab 6 and for APA style at the beginning of Tab 7), you can usually find the model you are looking for.

Look in the grammar tab-opening pages for errors similar to the ones you typically make. Tab 9 opens with a chart of the most common errors students make. Each error includes an example and a reference to the section and page number where you can find a more detailed explanation and examples. Flip through these pages to find a quick reference guide for multilingual writers.

Look up a word in the Glossary of Usage. If you are not sure that you are using a particular word such as *farther* or *further* correctly, try looking it up in the Glossary of Usage on pages FR-3–FR-9.

Refer to Tab 12 if you are a multilingual writer. Chapters 69–72 provide tips on the use of articles, helping verbs, and other problem areas for multilingual writers.

Check the list of Discipline-Specific Resources. In Part 13, Further Resources for Learning (pp. FR-10–FR-12), you will find a comprehensive list of sources that have already been checked for relevance and reliability.

Go to *Connect Composition* for online help with your writing. *Connect Composition* provides individualized instruction and practice with all aspects of writing and research, with immediate feedback on every activity. In addition, a digital version of the handbook gives you the ability to build your own personalized online writing resource.

The **running head** and section number give the topic covered on the page as well as the number of the chapter and section letter in which the topic is discussed.

The **main heading** includes the chapter number and section letter (for example, 51d) as well as the title of the section.

Examples, many of them with hand corrections, illustrate typical errors and how to correct them.

For **Multilingual Writers** boxes provide useful tips and helpful information.

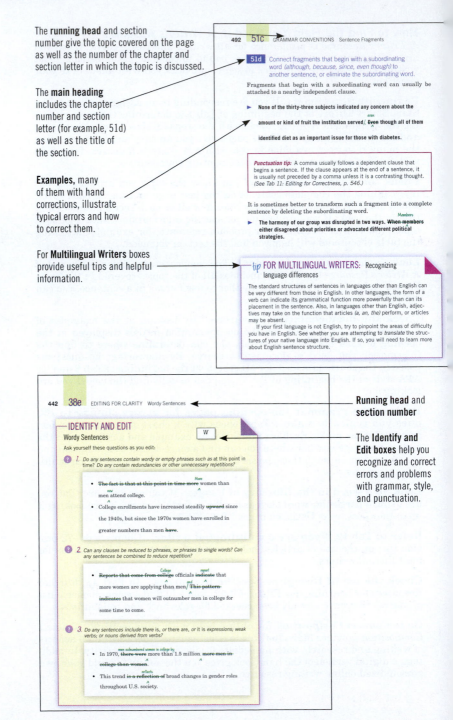

492 51c GRAMMAR CONVENTIONS Sentence Fragments

51d Connect fragments that begin with a subordinating word *(although, because, since, even though)* to another sentence, or eliminate the subordinating word.

Fragments that begin with a subordinating word can usually be attached to a nearby independent clause.

► None of the thirty-three subjects indicated any concern about the amount or kind of fruit the institution served / Even though all of them identified diet as an important issue for those with diabetes.

Punctuation tip: A comma usually follows a dependent clause that begins a sentence. If the clause appears at the end of a sentence, it is usually not preceded by a comma unless it is a contrasting thought. *(See Tab 11: Editing for Correctness, p. 546.)*

It is sometimes better to transform such a fragment into a complete sentence by deleting the subordinating word.

► The harmony of our group was disrupted in two ways. When members either disagreed about priorities or advocated different political strategies. *(correction: Members)*

tip **FOR MULTILINGUAL WRITERS:** Recognizing language differences

The standard structures of sentences in languages other than English can be very different from those in English. In other languages, the form of a verb can indicate its grammatical function more powerfully than can its placement in the sentence. Also, in languages other than English, adjectives may take on the function that articles *(a, an, the)* perform, or articles may be absent.

If your first language is not English, try to pinpoint the areas of difficulty you have in English. See whether you are attempting to *translate* the structures of your native language into English. If so, you will need to learn more about English sentence structure.

442 38e EDITING FOR CLARITY Wordy Sentences

IDENTIFY AND EDIT
Wordy Sentences
Ask yourself these questions as you edit:

? *1.* Do any sentences contain wordy or empty phrases such as at this point in time? Do any contain redundancies or other unnecessary repetitions?

• The fact is that at this point in time more women than men attend college. *(corrections: More; now)*

• College enrollments have increased steadily upward since the 1940s, but since the 1970s women have enrolled in greater numbers than men have.

? *2.* Can any clauses be reduced to phrases, or phrases to single words? Can any sentences be combined to reduce repetition?

• Reports that come from college officials indicate that more women are applying than men / This pattern indicates that women will outnumber men in college for some time to come. *(corrections: College; report; and)*

? *3.* Do any sentences include there is, or there are, or it is expressions; weak verbs; or nouns derived from verbs?

• In 1970, there were more than 1.5 million more men in college than women. *(correction: men outnumbered women in college by)*

• This trend is a reflection of broad changes in gender roles throughout U.S. society. *(correction: reflects)*

Running head and section number

The **Identify and Edit boxes** help you recognize and correct errors and problems with grammar, style, and punctuation.

1

Writing Today

*The adequate study of culture, our own and those on the oppo-
site side of the globe, can press on to fulfillment only as we learn
today from the humanities as well as from the scientists.*

—Ruth Benedict

The compass has long been a tool for explorers and
mapmakers. This book was designed to be a compass
for writing in any discipline.

1 Writing Today

START SMART Addressing the Writing Situation

Start Smart will help you to understand your writing situation and find the advice you need to get your project off to a good start. It also provides an overview for any kind of writing project. If you get stuck, come back here to jump-start your work.

Step 1 What should your assignment or project do?

Look for these keywords

Inform: classify, define, describe, explore, illustrate, report, survey
Interpret or Analyze: analyze, compare, explain, inquire, reflect
Argue or Persuade: agree, defend, evaluate, justify, propose, refute

Step 2 Go to

A: Writing That Informs
B: Writing That Interprets & Analyzes
C: Writing That Argues/Persuades

A: Writing That Informs

Begin with the Writing Situation:
- What topic are you writing about? (Ch. 5, pp. 40–41)
- Who is going to read your writing? (Ch. 5, p. 41)
- How should you talk about this topic for your readers? (Ch. 5, p. 43)
- What is the required length, deadline, and format, as well as the background for your assignment? (Ch. 5, p. 43)
- What kind of text is it; how should you present it? (Ch. 5, pp. 43–44)

Compose Using Writing Processes:
- See Chapter 9. For more details, see Chapters 5–7.
- How can you find a worthwhile thesis for your topic? (Ch. 5, pp. 48–51)
- What strategies can help you organize your writing? (Ch. 6, pp. 57–72)
- What strategies can help you revise? (Ch. 7, pp. 73–84)

Think Critically about Using Sources:
- Does your informative writing require research? (Ch. 18, pp. 211–18)
- If yes, how many and what kind of sources are needed? (Ch. 18, pp. 216–18)
- What resources are appropriate for your course and available? (See Further Resources for Learning)
- Should you use tables, graphs, or images? Audio or video? (Ch. 5, pp. 54–57)

Think Carefully about Your Final Steps:
- Did you cite all your sources correctly? (Ch. 25, pp. 279–81)
- Did you carefully edit and proofread your writing? (Ch. 7, p. 87–89)
- What design conventions are appropriate for this type of writing? (Ch. 8, p. 92)

Some Samples
- Informative report (pp. 95, 112, 378)
- Newsletter (p. 193)
- Brochure (p. 192)
- Annotated bibliography (p. 262)

 For an interactive version of this Start Smart guide, along with more samples, go to www.connect.mheducation.com

Sample Informative Report

The Caring Express Food Bank

Thesis summarizes the writer's knowledge of this topic.

The Caring Express Food Bank serves a varied population of clients, including chronically homeless people, temporarily homeless people, recent immigrants, elderly people on fixed incomes, and people in need of temporary services. As Figure 1 shows, while the number of homeless, both temporary and permanent, that Caring Express assisted in 2008 decreased during the summer months, the number of immigrant workers increased. The percentage of elderly people and people in need of temporary services remained fairly stable throughout the year.

Tone is objective; writer does not express an opinion.

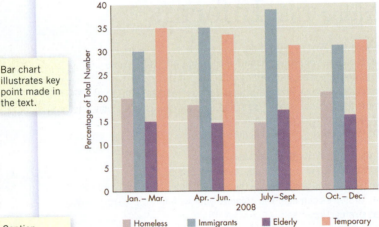

Clients of the Caring Express Food Bank

Bar chart illustrates key point made in the text.

Caption explains bar chart.

Figure 1. Percentage of clients in each group during 2008

How Caring Express Helps Clients

When new clients come to Caring Express, the volunteers follow this procedure:

Procedure illustrates key idea as a numbered list.

1. The volunteer fills out a form with the client's address (if he or she has one), phone number, income, and employment situation.
2. Clients who do not live in Maple Valley are referred to a food bank or outreach program in their area.
3. Clients who qualify check off the food they need from a list.
4. The food is packed and distributed to them.

A successful informative report should
- have a thesis that summarizes the writer's knowledge of the topic.
- have an objective tone.
- illustrate key ideas with examples from research.

Additional information about report design is available on pages 93–100.

B: Writing That
Interprets and Analyzes

Begin with the Writing Situation:
- What topic are you interpreting or analyzing? (Ch. 5, pp. 40–41)
- Who is going to read your writing? (Ch. 5, p. 41)
- How should you talk about this topic for your readers? (Ch. 5, p. 43)
- What is the required length, deadline, and format, as well as the background for your assignment? (Ch. 5, p. 43)
- What kind of text is it; how should you present it? (Ch. 5, pp. 43–44)

Compose Using Writing Processes:
- See Chapter 10. For more details, see Chapters 5–7.
- How can you find a worthwhile thesis for your topic? (Ch. 5, pp. 48–51)
- What strategies can help you organize your writing? (Ch. 6, pp. 57–73)
- What strategies can help you revise? (Ch. 7, pp. 73–84)

Think Critically about Using Sources:
- Does your interpretive writing require research? (Ch. 18, pp. 211–18)
- If yes, how many and what kind of sources are needed? (Ch. 18, pp. 216–18)
- What resources are appropriate for your course and available? (See Further Resources for Learning.)
- Should you use tables, graphs, or images? Audio or video? (Ch. 5, pp. 54–57)

Think Carefully about Your Final Steps:
- What citation style, if any, should you use? (Ch. 25, pp. 279–81)
- Did you cite all your sources correctly? (Ch. 24, pp. 273 and 279)
- Did you carefully edit and proofread your writing? (Ch. 7, pp. 87–89)
- What design conventions are appropriate for this type of writing? (Ch. 8, p. 92)

Some Samples
- Visual analysis (p. 90)
- Analysis of a poem (p. 129)

For an interactive version of this Start Smart guide, along with more samples, go to www.connect.mheducation.com

A Sample Visual Analysis

Diane Chen
Professor Defeo
Art 251: History of Photography
6 December 2014

Inspiring Empathy: Dorothea Lange's *Migrant Mother*

American photographer Dorothea Lange is perhaps best known for her work commissioned by the Farm Services Administration photographing the social and economic effects of the Great Depression. Her arresting portraits of displaced farmers, migrant families, and the unemployed skillfully depict the dire consequences of the Depression for America's working classes. Artful though her photographs are, Lange's technique involved more than artistic skill. Lange considered herself primarily a photojournalist, whose goal was to encourage social action through her work. As a photojournalist who empathetically captured the struggles of her subjects on film, Lange was able to impart compassion to her audience and in turn inspire change.

One of Lange's most famous photographs, *Migrant Mother* (Fig. 1), is an example of her unique ability to document such struggles. *Migrant Mother* is not simply a portrait of one mother's hardship, but is a raw depiction of the plight of thousands of displaced families during the Depression. The mother in this photograph, Florence Owens Thompson, was a migrant worker in Nipomo, California, in 1936, whom Lange encountered sitting outside her tent in a migrant camp. Lange took several exposures of Thompson, moving closer to her subject with each shot. This technique helped her to capture an image that communicated to viewers what poverty looked like at a human level. But the power of Lange's image is not confined to history; even today, *Migrant Mother* remains an iconic reminder of the struggles of the poor.

The photograph's composition reveals Lange's compassion for her subject. Although four figures make up the photograph, the mother, whose face we see in full, is its main subject. She gazes outward, worriedly, as her three children huddle around her. The children frame her figure, two of them with faces hidden behind her shoulders, either out of shyness or shared distress, while the third rests across the mother's lap. The mother's expression conveys a desperate concern, presumably for her children's wellbeing. Her children cling to her, but her own faraway gaze gives evidence that she is too distracted by her worries to give them comfort. Lange emphasizes the mother's expression by making it the focal point of the photograph. In doing so, she encourages viewers to identify with the mother and even to wonder what thoughts pass through her mind.

Fig. 1. Dorothea Lange, **Migrant Mother.**

Annotations:

Topic is identified, followed by statement of a focused, purposeful thesis.

Uses a thoughtful tone.

A description of the image that illustates the main point.

Caption gives the title of the photograph.

A successful visual analysis should

- have a focused and purposeful thesis.
- have a thoughtful tone.
- include a description of the image illustrating the main point.

Full analysis is available (in draft form) on pages 90–92.

C: Writing That
Argues/Persuades

Begin with the Writing Situation:
- What topic are you writing about? (Ch. 5, pp. 40–41)
- Who is going to read your writing? (Ch. 5, p. 41)
- How should you talk about this topic for your readers? (Ch. 5, p. 43)
- What is the required length, deadline, and format, as well as the background for your assignment? (Ch. 5, p. 43)
- What kind of text is it; how should you present it? (Ch. 5, pp. 43–44)

Compose Using Writing Processes:
- See Chapter 11. For more details, see Chapters 5–7.
- How can you find a thesis for your topic? (Ch. 5, pp. 48–51)
- What strategies can help you organize your writing? (Ch. 6, pp. 57–73)
- What strategies can help you revise? (Ch. 7, pp. 73–84)

Think Critically about Using Sources:
- Does your argument require research? (Ch. 18, pp. 211–18)
- If yes, how many and what kind of sources are needed? (Ch. 18, pp. 216–18)
- What resources are appropriate for your course and available? (See Further Resources for Learning.)
- Should you use tables, graphs, or images? Audio or video? (Ch. 5, pp. 54–57)

Think Carefully about Your Final Steps:
- What citation style, if any, should you use? (Ch. 25, pp. 279–81)
- Did you cite all your sources correctly? (Ch. 24, p. 273)
- Did you carefully edit and proofread your writing? (Ch. 7, pp. 87–89)
- What design conventions are appropriate for this type of writing? (Ch. 8, p. 92)

Some Samples
- Arguments (pp. 148, 331)
- Persuasive Web site (p. 9)
- Persuasive PowerPoint/Oral presentation (p. 172)

For an interactive version of this Start Smart guide, along with more samples, go to www.connect.mheducation.com

A Sample Argument

Joseph Honrado

Professor Robertson

English 201

30 November 2013

Cyberbullying: An Alarming Trend for the Digital Age

Before the advent of cell phones and the Internet, bullies would harass their victims on

the playground, the school bus, and in the classroom or lunchroom. In response to these

confrontations, adults would typically advise children to stand up to bullies or to avoid them.

However, in today's digital society, standing up to a bully is much more difficult. According to

PACER's National Bullying Prevention Center, all bullying is typically characterized by an

"imbalance of power" in which the more powerful party "hurts or harms another person

physically or emotionally" ("Bullying Info"). Stopbullying.gov, a website supported by the US

Department of Health and Human Services, updates this definition to include "bullying that takes

place using electronic technology," also known as cyberbullying ("Bullying Definition").

Cyberbullying is a growing problem among today's youth and is especially destructive because

of its immediacy, circulation, and permanence: the humiliation is easily inflicted and can

continue indefinitely before a wide audience. If the problem of cyberbullying is ever to be

overcome, students, parents, educators, and the media must all make efforts to instill guidelines

for online behavior.

Cyberbullying is commonly carried out through text messaging, instant messaging, and

social networking sites like Facebook and Twitter. While cyberbullying can take many forms,

most often it involves the posting of hurtful comments or rumors online, as shown in fig.1. !

Introduces issue of cyberbullying using a reasonable tone.

Presents definition of cyberbullying.

Thesis statement.

Presents a detailed explanation of cyberbullying, followed by a visual (see p. 149) that indicates the extent of the problem.

A successful argument should

- have a reasonable tone.
- include a thesis that clearly states the writer's position.
- identify key points that support and develop the thesis, with evidence for each point.
- use a structure that is appropriate for the content and context of the argument.
- conclude by emphasizing the importance of the position and its implications and by answering the "So what?"

Full argument is available on pages 148–54.

A Sample Persuasive Web Site

MAIN MENU · **MY STORIES: 25** · **FORUMS** · **SUBSCRIBE** · **JOBS**

LAW & DISORDER / CIVILIZATION & DISCONTENTS

Headline highlights key points of article.

Trolling someone online? Bill would slap you with jail time

A new cyberbullying bill aims to punish those who intend to cause "emotional ...

by Jacqui Cheng - May 10 2009, 10:43pm CDT

Text has a reasonable tone.

A recently introduced cyberbullying bill could land us all in jail—that is, if you have ever used an electronic medium to troll someone. HR 1966, the Megan Meier Cyberbullying Prevention Act, is named after the high-profile "MySpace suicide" victim Megan Meier. It's meant to prevent people from using the Internet to "coerce, intimidate, harass, or cause substantial emotional distress to a person." However, as with many bills of this nature, the murky language and vague standards leave much open to interpretation, which has caused critics to call it the Censorship Act instead.

HR 1966 was introduced in April by US Representative Linda Sanchez (D-CA) and it's supported by 14 other members of Congress. According to the text, individuals who bully others via any electronic means could face fines, two years in prison, or both. This, of course, could include those nasty text messages you sent to your ex on Saturday night, the questionable e-mail you sent to your brother, or those forum posts you made in which you called for someone who liked the new *Star Trek* movie to jump off a building.

The bill largely flew under the radar until fairly recently (thanks to NetworkWorld for the heads-up) but criticism has been building. The language in the bill is so vague, it could be interpreted to apply to practically any situation, including blog posts critical of public officials.

UCLA Law Professor Eugene Volokh went into detail on his blog, suggesting that numerous everyday situations could render regular citizens felons if their behavior is considered "severe" enough. "I try to coerce a politician into voting a particular way, by repeatedly blogging (using a hostile tone) about what a hypocrite/campaign promise breaker/fool/etc. he would be if he voted the other way. I am transmitting in interstate commerce a communication with the intent to coerce using electronic means (a blog) 'to support severe, repeated, and hostile behavior'— unless, of course, my statements aren't seen as 'severe,' a term that is entirely undefined and unclear," Volokh wrote.

Link to an expert who supports the writer's position.

A successful Web site should
- include pages that capture and hold interest.
- be readable, with a unified look.
- be easy to access and navigate.

A successful persuasive Web site should
- have a reasonable tone.
- include links to authoritative sources that support the writer's position.
- highlight key points so that readers can spot them quickly.
- use visual cues to establish credibility. Avoid clip art or images/patterns that are cluttered or "cute."

PowerPoints for a
Persuasive Oral Presentation

A compelling opening, clearly presented on the slide.

Cyberbullying: An Alarming Trend for the Digital Age

Cyberbullying Methods

Flaming- using angry/offensive language

Outing- sharing others' secrets

Trickery- getting others to share their secrets

Denigration- spreading rumors/gossip

A focused discussion. Text used sparingly.

Visual aid or source is used to support an important point.

Nearly 20% of students polled admitted to cyberbullying

A persuasive oral presentation should
- have a compelling opening.
- have a clear focus and organization.
- be delivered extemporaneously (avoid reading the slides).
- use visual aids and sources to support key points and highlight content (with text used sparingly).
- conclude memorably.

Tab 1: Learning across the Curriculum

This section will help you answer questions such as the following:

Rhetorical Knowledge

- What is a rhetorical situation, and how can understanding this term help me now and as a writer throughout college and life? (2a)
- How do I respond appropriately to different writing situations? (2a)
- How can belonging to more than one culture help my writing? (3)
- Why is it fine for me to use emoticons and abbreviations in text messages but not in a college assignment? (2e)

Critical Thinking, Reading, and Writing

- How can writing help me learn in all my college courses? (1b)
- How can I plan my time in college? (1c)
- How can writing help me develop fluency in English? (3)

Processes

- What does social media have to do with college writing? (2b)
- How can technology help me work with other students on writing projects? (2b)

Knowledge of Conventions

- What is a discipline? (1a)
- How can I tell what my instructors expect of me in college? (1c, 3a)

For a general introduction to writing outcomes, see 1e, pages 14–16.

CHAPTER 1

Writing across the Curriculum and beyond College

College is a place for exploration, opening new pathways for your life. You will travel through many courses, participating in numerous conversations—spoken and written—about nature, society, and culture. As you navigate your college experience, use this book as your map and guide.

- As a map, this text will help you understand different approaches to knowledge and see how your studies relate to the larger world.

- As a guide, this text will help you write in college—for classes and in exams and research reports—and in other areas of your life: résumés, brochures, complaints, and business correspondence.

As a permanent part of your library, this text can take you where you need to go in college and beyond.

1a   Study the world through a range of academic disciplines.

To some extent, each department in your college represents a specialized territory of academic study, or area of inquiry, called a **discipline.** A discipline has its own history, issues, vocabulary, and subgroups. The discipline of sociology, for example, is concerned with the conditions, patterns, and problems of people in groups and societies. Sociologists collect, analyze, and interpret data connected to that focus; sociologists also debate questions of reliability and interpretation. These debates occur in classrooms with students, in conferences with colleagues, in journals and books that reach national and international academic audiences, and in conversations, presentations, and publications addressing members of the public, including elected officials.

Most college students take courses across a range of disciplines. You may be asked to take one or two courses each in the humanities (the disciplines of literature, music, and philosophy, for example), the social sciences (sociology, economics, and psychology, for example), and the natural sciences (physics, biology, and chemistry, for example). When you write in each discipline—taking notes, writing projects, answering essay-exam questions—you will join the academic conversation, deepen your understanding of how knowledge is constructed, and learn to see and think about the world from different vantage points. You will also discover that courses and assignments overlap in interesting ways. This blurring of disciplinary boundaries provides an opportunity for creativity. Developing the ability to see and interpret experience from different perspectives goes beyond college to success in life. Every day—every hour—the context shifts. Sizing things up, figuring out what is required, and shaping your responses appropriately will help you to manage any situation. Both personally and professionally, empathizing with other points of view, while sustaining the integrity of your own principles, will take you far.

1b   Use writing as a tool for learning.

Writing is a great aid to learning. Think of the way a simple shopping list jogs your memory once you get to the store, or recall the last time you jotted down notes during a meeting. Because of your heightened attention, you undoubtedly knew more about what happened at that meeting than did anyone else in the room. Writing helps you remember, understand, and create.

- **Writing aids memory.** From taking class notes *(see Figure 1.1)* to jotting down ideas for later development, writing helps you to retrieve important information. Many students use an informal outline for lecture notes and then go back to fill in the details after class. Write down ideas inspired by your course work—in any form or order. These ideas can be the seeds for a research project or other types of critical inquiry, or you can apply them to your life outside the classroom.

- **Writing sharpens observations.** When you record what you see, hear, taste, smell, and feel, you increase the powers of your senses. Note the smells during a chemistry experiment, and you will more readily detect changes caused by reactions; record how the aroma of freshly popped popcorn makes you feel, and you will better understand your own moods.

- **Writing clarifies thought.** After composing a draft, carefully reading it helps you pinpoint what you really want to say. The last paragraph of a first draft often becomes the first paragraph of the next draft.

- **Writing uncovers connections.** Maybe a character in a short story reminds you of your neighbor, or an image in a poem makes you feel sad. Writing down the reasons you make these connections can help you learn more about the work and more about yourself.

```
3/17
MEMORY

3 ways to store memory
1.  sensory memory -everything sensed
2.  short term memory STM -15-25 sec.
       -stored as meaning
       -5-9 chunks
3.  long term memory LTM -unlimited
        -rehearsal
        -visualization
* If long term memory is unlimited, why do we forget?
Techniques for STM to LTM
        -write, draw, diagram
        -visualize
        -mnemonics
```

FIGURE 1.1 Lecture notes. Recording the main ideas of a lecture and the questions they raise helps you become a more active listener.

- **Writing improves reading.** When you read, annotating the text—or taking notes on the main ideas—and drafting a brief summary of the writer's points sharpen your reading skills and help you remember what you have read. Because memories are often tinged with emotion, writing a personal reaction to a reading can connect the material to your own life, thereby enhancing both your memory and your understanding. *(For a detailed discussion of critical reading and writing, see Chapter 4.)*

- **Writing strengthens argument.** In academic projects, an argument is not a fiery disagreement, but rather a path of reasoning to a position. When you write an argument supporting a claim, you work out *the connections among your ideas*—uncovering both flaws that force you to rethink your position and new connections that make your position stronger. Through writing, you also address your audience and the objections they might raise. Success in life often depends on understanding opposing points of view and arguing for your own ideas in ways that others can hear. *(For a detailed discussion of argument, see Chapter 11.)*

1c   Take responsibility for reading, writing, and research.

The academic community assumes that you are an independent learner, capable of managing your workload without supervision. For most courses, the syllabus will be the primary guide to what is expected, serving as a contract between you and your instructor. It will tell you what reading you must do in advance of each class, when tests are scheduled, and when formal assignments or stages of projects (for example, topic and research plan, draft, and final project) are due. Use the syllabus to map out your weekly schedule for reading, research, and writing. *(For tips on how to schedule a research paper, see Chapter 18.)*

1d   Recognize that writing improves with practice.

Composition courses are valuable in helping you learn to write at the college level, but your development as a writer only begins there. Writing in all your courses throughout your academic career will prepare you for a lifetime of confidence as a writer, whether you are writing a report in your workplace, a note to your child's teacher, or a blog to express your political views.

1e   Achieve the core outcomes of successful writing.

As you write any project, you will communicate your ideas more effectively if you keep these five outcomes in mind. Although they are presented separately here, these outcomes work together as you

NAVIGATING THROUGH COLLEGE AND BEYOND
Study Skills and Dealing with Stress

Whether academic pursuits are a struggle or come easily to you, whether you are fresh out of high school or are returning to school after many years, college, like all new and challenging experiences, can be stressful. Here are some strategies for dealing with the stress of college and achieving success:

- **Make flexible schedules.** Schedules help you control your time and avoid procrastination by breaking big projects into manageable bits. Be sure to build some flexibility into your schedule, so that you can manage the unexpected.

- **Make the most of your time by setting clear priorities.** Deal with last-minute invitations by saying "no," getting away from it all, and taking control of phone, text, and e-mail interruptions.

- **Take good notes.** The central feature of good note taking, in college and in life, is listening and distilling the important information—not writing down everything that is said.

- **Build reading and listening skills.** When you read, identify and prioritize the main ideas, think critically about the arguments, and explain the writer's ideas to someone else. Listen actively: focus on what is being said, pay attention to nonverbal messages, listen for what is *not* being said, and take notes.

- **Improve your memory.** Rehearsal and making connections are key strategies in remembering important information. Repeat the information, summarize it, and associate it with other concepts or memories.

- **Evaluate the information you gather.** Consider how authoritative the source is, whether the author has potential biases, how recent the information is, and what facts or other evidence is missing from the research. In college, as in life, critical thinking is essential.

- **Take care of yourself.** Eating healthful food, exercising regularly, and getting plenty of sleep are well-known stress relievers. Some people find meditation to be effective. Stopping for a few seconds to take some deep breaths can do wonders.

- **Reach out for support.** If you find it difficult to cope with stress, seek professional help. Colleges have trained counselors on staff as well as twenty-four-hour crisis lines.

Source: Based partly on Robert S. Feldman, *P.O.W.E.R. Learning: Strategies for Success in College and Life,* 2nd ed., New York: McGraw-Hill, 2003.

compose. For example, you will use critical thinking (part of one outcome) as you revise your project (part of another outcome).

- **Rhetorical Knowledge** includes focusing on your purpose for writing and the specific audience you are addressing. It also means using the most appropriate genre and medium to achieve that purpose, employing conventions necessary to the genre, and taking an appropriate rhetorical stance. *See Chapters 2 and 5a.*

- **Critical Thinking, Reading, and Writing** include using writing for inquiry, for thinking about ways to approach a project, and for developing that project, especially as you work with sources. *See Chapters 4, 11b, and 21.*

- **Processes** are flexible strategies for drafting and revising as well as working with others on a writing task, whether through peer review or collaborative writing. *See Chapters 5–7.*

- **Knowledge of Conventions** includes working within the formats that characterize different genres (for example, a résumé or a literary analysis) and using the correct requirements—governing syntax, punctuation, and spelling, for example—expected in every writing project. *See Chapter 8, Tab 4, and Tabs 9–11.*

- **Composing in Electronic Environments** includes composing electronically and publishing your work digitally (for example, on a Web site or social media page) as well as using electronic sources like scholarly databases for researched projects. *See Chapter 14 and Connect Composition.*

Throughout this handbook, Start Smart boxes (like the one that appears at the beginning of this chapter) will help keep you focused on the concerns you are most likely to encounter at each stage of the writing process.

CHAPTER 2

Writing Situations

The **rhetorical situation**—also known as the **writing situation**—refers to the considerations that all writers take into account as they write. When writers think about their situation, they reflect on the following:

- The primary **purpose**
- The **audience(s)** to address
- The **context** in which they are writing

- The **stance,** or authorial tone
- The **genre** and **medium** most appropriate for the purpose, audience, and writing task

Martin Luther King Jr., for example, wrote "A Letter from Birmingham Jail" to achieve a specific purpose, persuading others to rethink their views about achieving racial justice in the South in the 1960s; for a specific audience, those who disagreed with his approach of nonviolent civil disobedience; in a given genre, an *open letter* addressed to a specific group but intended for publication. A student composing a review evaluating a recent film for a newspaper has a different purpose, to provide a recommendation about whether the film is worth seeing; to a given audience, the readers of the newspaper; in the form of a review, another genre. The context for Martin Luther King Jr. was very different from the context for the student writer, of course. A writer's context includes the means of communication, current events, and the environment in which the communication takes place. See an illustration of how these elements are related in Figure 2.1.

2a   View the situation as the framework for approaching any writing task.

All writing tasks are framed by a rhetorical situation. To manage a writing situation successfully, writers must consider their purpose, audience, and context, both before writing and as they compose. By keeping their rhetorical situation in mind, writers find the writing process easier to manage, and the project that results will be stronger and more effective.

1. Understanding your purpose

You write to achieve many different purposes. Sometimes, as when you create electronic research notes, your purpose may seem important only to you: to compose notes allowing you to write a strong research project. At other times, you write for a more directly social purpose, such as when you compose a job application letter or send an e-mail or a text message to inform a family member that you have arrived at your destination safely. Whether your writing **informs**

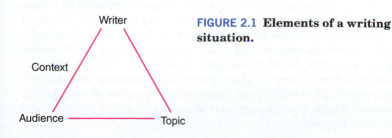

FIGURE 2.1 Elements of a writing situation.

your readers by telling them what you know about a topic or issue, **interprets** and **analyzes** by exploring the meaning of your subject, **argues** or **persuades** by proving a point or supporting an opinion through logic and concrete evidence, or simply **expresses** your feelings, it is always keyed to achieving a given purpose.

2. Thinking about audience

A second, equally important feature of the writing situation is the audience, the readers you are writing to and for. Thinking of your potential readers can help you shape your writing. An exercise program, for example, would look very different if you were to write it as a journal entry for a health class, post it on *Facebook,* or craft it as a press release on a Web site for a business enterprise or community organization. If you were writing about possible changes to Social Security, the examples you would share might vary depending on whether your audience included mostly senior citizens, who are the main beneficiaries of the program now, or people in their twenties, most of whom will not benefit from it for many years. Thinking about the needs of your audience can help you decide what to include in your writing project as you compose—and what medium you use. You would probably write to seniors in print and to the younger readers on a blog, in a tweet, or on *Facebook.*

3. Considering your context

Context, or the larger circumstances surrounding a text, exerts a major influence on the rhetorical situation. Consider how the meaning of a single word can change, depending on the context. For example, a *chair* can be a piece of furniture or someone who leads a committee or department. Likewise, because the contexts differ, writers discussing immigration patterns in an academic context know that their readers expect a balanced and informed discussion of this controversial issue, whereas writers in the context of the Internet or a personal letter may address the same issue in a more personal and impassioned way. Although it is impossible to know the full context of any situation, it is important to identify what you do know and keep that information in mind as you write.

4. Choosing an appropriate stance

A *rhetorical stance* is the attitude a writer takes in relation to a topic and the tone used in addressing the audience. A dignitary giving a commencement address tries to inspire the audience, for example, while a friend consoles another friend on a loss. When you are exploring an issue that could divide your audience, you might take the stance of someone who inquires rather than someone who argues. When creating a résumé, most people take the stance of a competent future employee. Considering your stance carefully is an important part of writing well.

👁 **2b**   Make effective use of multimodal elements and genres.

All writers today have access to digital technologies that widen the possibilities for composing and sharing texts. Through the use of electronic media, people are communicating more than ever before. On Web sites and *blogs* (continuously updated, often topical Web sites), writers combine texts with photos, videos, and audio files—using all of these options to achieve a variety of purposes. Social media sites like *Facebook* and *YouTube* facilitate connections across time and space.

As you plan to compose for a specific writing situation, consider two possibilities for presenting, and sharing, your text:

1. Whether your text will include *electronically multimodal elements* (for example, graphs, hyperlinks, video or audio clips)
2. Which *genre* best suits your purpose

1. Incorporating multimodal elements

Digital technology allows you to include sound files, hyperlinks, and other **multimodal elements** in digital projects to convey ideas more efficiently and powerfully. You can create these elements yourself or import them from other sources. Use multimodal resources to serve your overall purpose, placing a photo, sound file, or link strategically and always citing the source of any item you import into your work. *(See Chapters 23–24 for information on how to do so.)* The source credits for this book, for example, begin at the back on page C-1.

Posting your text online enables you to include an even greater variety of media. You could help your reader hear the music you analyzed by providing a link to an audio file. You could supplement a project about political speeches with a link to a video clip of a politician giving a speech. (*Connect Composition* offers guidelines for constructing effective digital compositions.)

Presentation software such as *PowerPoint* and *Prezi* allows you to integrate audio and visual features into your oral presentations or stand-alone presentations posted online on a site like *SlideShare.* Animation applications literally show certain effects (like the result of a faulty bridge design), but they should always serve a specific and appropriate purpose.

(For details on creating effective visuals and other multimodal elements, see Chapter 5: Planning and Shaping; Chapter 6: Drafting Text and Visuals; and Chapter 7: Revising and Editing. For information on creating oral and multimodal presentations, see Chapter 13: Oral Presentations and Chapter 14: Multimodal Writing. For help with finding appropriate visuals, see Chapter 20: Finding and Creating Effective Visuals, Audio Clips, and Video.)

2. Choosing the best genre

When you know your rhetorical situation, you can select a genre, or kind of writing, that best fits that situation. Poems, stories, and plays are genres of literature, and audiences have different expectations for each. Most of the writing you will be asked to produce in college will be nonfiction, that is, writing about real events, people, and things for the purpose of information, interpretation, or argument. Within nonfiction, however, there are many additional genres of writing such as letters, brochures, case studies, lab reports, and literary analyses. Some types of writing, like the case study, are common in a particular field such as sociology and finance. *(Chapter 5 has additional information on how to choose an appropriate genre for an academic assignment—see p. 43–44.)*

Here are some typical genres for the three purposes you will be using most commonly in academic writing:

- **Informative:** research report, newsletter, lab report, design study, medical record
- **Interpretive:** literary analysis, case study, data analysis, feasibility study, film/music/restaurant review
- **Argument:** editorial, letter to the editor, proposal, position paper, undergraduate thesis

2c Decide on the best medium.

When you know your rhetorical situation, you can select an appropriate medium to support your purpose and communicate with your audience. A **medium** is a means of communication—you can communicate with your audience via print, screen, or network. Print can take various forms: a letter to the editor of a newspaper will probably be published in print and online, whereas a poster for a science presentation is in print, supersized, with images as well as text. A screen composition might consist of a set of *Prezi* slides detailing election results, or it might be a digital photo essay. A composition posted on a computer network could be a blog on athletes' salaries or a video on the issue of abandoned children. Increasingly, all disciplines require that students be able to compose in each of these three media. In some cases, the medium will be determined by the rhetorical situation: a neighborhood improvement campaign would probably call for print posters and flyers. In other cases, you can decide which medium is best.

These questions can help you select the appropriate medium:

1. Does the rhetorical situation provide guidance for which medium to use? What will the audience expect?
2. Does your composition require or should it make use of electronic sources such as an animated graphic or streaming video? Consider a digital or networked medium such as a Web site.

3. What kind of distribution will your composition require? If you plan to send it to a small group, consider print or an e-mail attachment. For a larger distribution, consider a networked medium such as a Web page or social network site such as *Facebook*.

4. How large is your audience, and where is it located? You can reach a small, local audience with a print text such as a flyer. If your audience is large and diversified, consider a networked medium such as a blog.

● **2d**   Become aware of the persuasive power of images.

For many rhetorical situations, carefully chosen visuals—photographs, diagrams, graphs, maps, and other visual types—can help to convey information, illustrate a point, or persuade an audience. If you are reviewing the causes of World War I, you may find it useful to include a map of contested territory. If you are showing how the number of ocean pirates has increased in the past ten years, you could demonstrate that growth with a diagram, and if it were an electronic text, you could connect it to *Google Maps*. When you are defining a rhetorical task, consider whether a photo, diagram, or chart might help to present evidence, illustrate a point, add details, or clarifiy relationships. In a project for a political science course, for example, a photograph like the one shown on page 22 *(Figure 2.2)* can illustrate at a glance how a new generation of protestors has changed the course of world events using social media.

A graph *(see Figure 2.3, p. 22)* can effectively portray important trends for a history assignment. A time line, like the one in *Connect,* can help your readers grasp the relationships among important events. To use images effectively, though, writers need to analyze them with care.

We live in a world of images—in advertising, in politics, in books, and in classrooms. Increasingly, images function together with words, and often without words, to persuade as well as to instruct. Images, like words, require careful, critical analysis. A misleading graph or an altered photograph can easily distort the way readers and viewers perceive a subject. The ability to understand visual information and evaluate its credibility is an essential tool for learning and writing. *(For details on evaluating visuals, see Chapter 4: Reading and Writing, pp. 33–40; for an example of a misleading graph and a revised version that corrects the problem, see Chapter 7: Revising and Editing, p. 85.)*

2e   Take advantage of online and other electronic tools for writing and for learning.

Technology makes it possible to transcend the constraints of the clock and the calendar and to engage in educational activities 24/7: twenty-four hours a day, seven days a week. Different electronic tools work best for different purposes.

FIGURE 2.2 The impact of social media on world events. As this photo vividly illustrates, when protests against the Egyptian government erupted in Cairo in spring 2011, social media such as *Facebook* played a major role in sustaining the rebellion in the face of attempts by officials to shut it down.

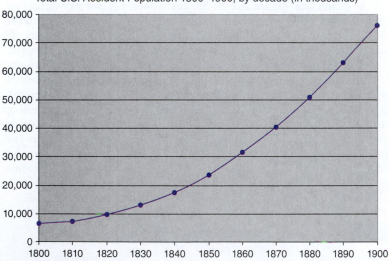

Total U.S. Resident Population 1800–1900, by decade (in thousands)

FIGURE 2.3 A line graph showing trends over time. To learn how to create a graph like this one, see Figure 20.1 on page 235.

- **E-mail. E-mail** is one of the most frequently used forms of written communication. In most classes, you will use e-mail to write to your professor and other students; you may also be able to e-mail a consultant in your school's writing center.

- **Instant messaging.** You can use **instant messaging (IM)** to further your learning in much the same way as e-mail. Some instructors may encourage you to contact them in this way. Otherwise, use IM to save time, and as a complementary tool in a Webinar or on *Facebook*.

- **Text messages. Texting** is especially useful for very short, timely messages. Its abbreviations can also make note taking faster.

- **Course Web sites.** Most courses have accompanying Web sites. **Course Web sites** often distribute abundant information: the class syllabus, class assignments, and readings. You may also be working on this site, posting comments on a discussion board or blog and turning in formal assignments. For more on course Web sites, see page 25–26.

- **Networked classrooms and virtual classrooms.** Many colleges and instructors use **networked classrooms** in which each student works at one of a network of linked computers. Instructors can post daily assignments and discussion topics, and students might be assigned to work collaboratively on a writing project. Computers and the Internet also make it possible for students to engage in distance learning—from almost anywhere in the world—in classes conducted entirely online in **virtual classrooms,** where students interact in writing rather than in spoken discussion, making it easier to save ideas and comments for future use in a first draft.

- **Blogs.** A **blog** is a continually updated site that features dated entries with commentary on a variety of topics, links to Web sites the authors find interesting, links that permit visitors to upload various kinds of multimedia files, and (sometimes) a space for readers to add comments. These readers, as well as the blog's author, may or may not be experts on the topics. *(For information on assessing a blog's credibility, see Chapter 21, pp. 240–47.)* Students sometimes use blogs to summarize and reflect on readings. A class blog may allow students to respond to and analyze readings and comment on one another's drafts. Students may also create their own posts on the blog. Faculty also may use blogs as sites for sharing assignments, where students can access them at any time and ask for clarification. Students can also use a class blog as a site for compiling shared resources. *(See Chapter 14, pp. 183–86.)*

the EVOLVING SITUATION

Netiquette

The term *netiquette* combines the words *Internet* and *etiquette* to form a new word that stands for good manners online. Here are some netiquette guidelines that hold across all electronic rhetorical situations:

- **Remember that you are interacting with real humans,** not machines, and practice kindness, patience, and good humor.
- **Limit e-mails to a single topic, and use accurate subject headers.** Include a sufficient portion of the previous text when responding to an e-mail, or use a dash to keep the conversation flowing and to provide context. **For official e-mails, include your name and contact information at the end of every e-mail you send.**
- **Remember that most forms of electronic communication can be reproduced.** Avoid saying anything you would not want attributed to you or forwarded to others. You should not forward another person's words without consent (although this practice is fairly common).
- **Always seek permission to use other people's ideas,** and acknowledge them properly.
- **Always quote and cite correctly the words of others: do not copy other people's words and present them as your own.** This practice, known as plagiarism, is always wrong. *(See Tabs 6–8 for help with citing Internet sources.)*
- **Bear in mind that without cues such as facial expressions, body language, and vocal intonation, your message can easily be misunderstood.** Be wary of including humor that could be misread as sarcasm. Misunderstandings can escalate quickly into *flaming,* the sending of angry, inflammatory posts characterized by heated language.
- **Avoid ALL CAPS.** Readers will think writers are SHOUTING in such messages.
- **When sending text messages, use abbreviations appropriately.** The standard for acceptable shorthand is determined by the level of familiarity between you and the recipient as well as the subject matter of the text.
- **Consider your tone.** Informality is appropriate when interacting with friends, but remember the need for greater formality in using digital communication for academic and professional purposes.
- **Always keep in mind that, although digital communication looks temporary, its traces can last forever.** When you burn a piece of paper, it's gone. Even if you delete something from cyberspace, it can almost always be recovered.
- **Use words economically** and edit carefully.

- **Podcasts.** Instructors may record their lectures as downloadable audio or video **podcasts,** making them available to the class for repeated listening or viewing on a computer or an MP3 player. Popular radio shows, television shows, and newspapers frequently include podcasts; the *New York Times,* for example, has a print book review section and a podcast of reviews. Reputable podcasts such as these are important sources for research projects.

- **Videos.** Outside school and in some college classes, many students and instructors create short videos, which they may post on video sharing sites such as *YouTube, Vimeo,* or *Vine.* Although writing projects often address a designated audience, many Web sites intend to address anyone on the Web. Creating your own videos will prepare you to analyze informative and persuasive videos in your life outside school, as well as for course assignments.

- **Social media sites.** Sometimes students use collective **social media sites** (like *Facebook*) to discuss writing projects, conduct surveys, and locate experts. Postings may be private, from person to person; or public, from one person to many. As is the case with other social media sites (like your own blog), what you post on these sites is potentially public; is visible to colleagues, family, and prospective employers; and may follow you forever.

- **Wikis.** A **wiki** is a Web site that is created collaboratively, often with interlinking Web pages that, taken together, form databases of information. Because multiple people create and edit pages on a wiki site, college students and instructors often use wikis to create collaborative projects. The popular online encyclopedia *Wikipedia* can be accurate but is not always so because not all the people creating or editing it are experts; therefore, instructors tend to discourage its use as a source. The content of some other wikis is created and monitored by specialists and therefore may be more credible. In college, as in life, you must learn enough about a wiki to assess its credibility. *(See Chapter 21: Evaluating Sources, pp. 240–47).*

- ***Twitter.*** Another social media practice is *tweeting:* composing messages limited to 140 characters that are posted to your *Twitter* page and often to other pages as well (*Facebook,* for example). Like text messages, tweets are condensed messages that can be timely. Some instructors may ask you to use them for academic purposes, for example to raise questions about a reading that you will be discussing in class.

Most colleges offer course management systems (CMS) like Blackboard, Desire to Learn, and Sakai. Although these sites vary, they typically include common features that students can access at any time via a password-protected course Web page. **Chat rooms** are online spaces that permit real-time communication. All participants in a chat see the text of the others as they type. Often the CMS will save a transcript of the chat for future reference.

Some CMS platforms include tools for **peer review,** in which students comment on one another's writing at specific points in the writing process. Specialized software, like the e-book that accompanies this text, makes peer review an efficient, helpful, and accessible writing tool.

If your course has such a home page, take time at the beginning of the semester to become familiar with its features—as well as with any related course requirements. *(For more on chat rooms, see Chapter 5: Planning and Shaping, p. 47 and p. 48.)*

CHAPTER 3

Audience and Academic English

To some extent, all college students, indeed all people, must navigate multiple cultures and languages. To solve a problem with your computer software in Dallas, you may be speaking to a tech support person in India. As you stock shelves in a toy store in Omaha, you may be interacting with a supply chain that originates in Shanghai.

The college environment will introduce you to a wide range of cultural contexts that may be new to you. Each of these contexts presents a rhetorical situation that you must learn to navigate:

- **Social contexts:** Whether you are attending a full-time residential program on campus, commuting to classes at a local community college, or taking classes online, college offers opportunities to join new social groups. These groups may be connected by social action within a community, a shared cultural heritage, a common interest, or simply the residence hall in which you live. They may be connected by social media as friends on *Facebook* or as followers on *Twitter.* Whatever context you find yourself in, you should be aware that colleges are generally gathering places for people from a wide range of cultures and backgrounds, with differences in language, communication practices, and social conventions. Learning to respect, accommodate, and enjoy these differences is an essential part of the college experience.

- **Workplace contexts:** Whether you are working as a barista at the local Starbucks, a home health aid for seniors, or an assistant in the campus library, your job will likely come with new demands and expectations, and you will have an advantage if you can communicate effectively. Chapter 17 will present suggestions for navigating the particular situations involved in trying to get or keep a job.

- **Academic contexts:** Disciplines have distinctive languages and cultural expectations. The language of statistics or anthropology, for example, probably sounds strange and new at first to most students who take those courses. Academic English in general involves conventions and forms that require familiarity for college success. This text presents these conventions, and, although it cannot cover the terminology of every academic discipline, it will prepare you for the vast majority of college courses. *(If you encounter unfamiliar academic terms or expressions, refer to the Selected Terms from across the Curriculum on pp. FR-3–FR-9.)*

In the ways just described, all students are language learners and cultural explorers. In college, however, students who know two or more languages and cultures may find that they have an advantage over those who know only one. Multilingual students can contribute insights about other cultures in a world that is interconnected in ever more complex and sophisticated ways.

This book uses the term *multilingual* to address students from varied cultural, national, and linguistic backgrounds. You may be an international student learning to speak and write English. You may have grown up speaking standard American English at school and another language or dialect at home. Perhaps your family has close ties to another part of the world. You may have moved between the United States and another country more than once. If you came to the United States when young, you may read and write English better than you do your parents' native language. You may speak a blended language such as "Spanglish," a mixture of English and Spanish.

Because the way we talk influences the way we write, blended and other nonstandard forms of English often appear in college students' writing. There is no single "correct" English, but Standard Written English is expected in academic contexts. Academic language is formal, with an expanded vocabulary as well as complex syntax and culturally specific usage patterns. In addition, disciplines have their own language features. Interacting with classmates as you explore together the specialized language of these academic subjects will provide many benefits. Monolingual and multilingual speakers have much to learn from one another.

3a   Become aware of your audience.

If you are familiar with at least two languages and cultures, you already know about multiple ways to interact politely and effectively with other people. All students must carefully assess the classroom situation as a special culture. What does the instructor expect? What counts as evidence? What is polite, and what is not?

1. Joining the academic conversation

In some cultures, asking a question indicates that the student has not done the homework or has not been paying attention. In contrast, instructors in the United States generally encourage students to ask questions and participate in class discussion. The American philosopher Richard Rorty makes the point that the history of philosophy is all about sustaining a lively intellectual conversation, and U.S. classrooms often reflect that principle. Students are usually encouraged to approach the instructor or fellow students outside class to keep the conversation going.

2. Finding out what instructors expect

Just as students are not all the same, neither are instructors. Take advantage of your instructor's office hours—a time designated for further conversation on material discussed in class—to ask questions about assignments as well as other matters.

Instructors in the United States often ask students to form small groups to talk over an issue or solve a problem. All members of such groups are expected to contribute to the conversation and offer ideas. Students usually speak and interact much more informally in these groups than they do with the instructor in class. Peer study groups, whether assigned or formed spontaneously, can be excellent resources for interpreting assignments.

Instructors in different disciplines may use key words in different ways. When biology professors ask for a description of "significant" results, for example, that term may mean something different from what English professors mean when they compare two "significant" fictional characters. Pay attention especially to the terms *analyze, critique,* and *assess* that are used variously. Terms like these are discussed in this book *(see p. 41),* and your instructor and peers can be helpful, too.

3. Determining what your audience expects

Colleges in the United States, and English-speaking culture more generally, emphasize openly exchanging views, clearly stating opinions, and explicitly supporting judgments with examples, observations, and reasons. Being direct is highly valued. Audiences in the United States expect speakers and writers to come to the point and will feel impatient without an identifiable thesis statement. *(See 5c on thesis statements.)* At the same time, to communicate successfully in a global context, you should be aware of differing expectations. If, for example, you are sending business correspondence to a Japanese company, you may accomplish your goals more successfully by spending time on courteous opening remarks. Everything depends on the context.

4. Choosing evidence with care

Different cultures, as well as different academic disciplines, expect varying forms of evidence. Most scientists and mathematicians, for example, are convinced by the application of the scientific method. In that sense, science and math are universal languages, but scientists from different fields rely on different kinds of methods and evidence. Some scientists compare the results from experimental groups and control groups, while others emphasize close observation and quantitative analysis. Likewise, different cultures assign varying degrees of importance to firsthand observations, expert opinion, and quotations from sacred or widely respected sources. Once again, it's essential to figure out the context, the writing situation, and what you are trying to achieve within it.

5. Considering the organization your audience expects

Some texts, such as a laboratory report, are organized according to expectations determined by the discipline. *(See 12b.)* But the organization of other texts can vary. In the classroom, careful study of the assignment and the advice provided in this book will assist you in organizing your project effectively. Practicing this kind of analysis should help in writing to multiple, international audiences as well. Seek guidance by studying effective communication in a particular culture. In addition, it never hurts to ask those familiar with the expectations of readers and listeners in a given situation how to communicate politely and successfully.

6. Choosing an appropriate tone

Writing to strangers is different from writing to friends. Whether you are communicating by e-mail or by formal letterhead stationery, you should use a level of formality when addressing professors, and others who are not your close friends, that you would not use in other writing situations. That attention to tone means typing "Dear Professor Maxell:" even in an e-mail, using full paragraphs, and avoiding abbreviations. "Texting," in contrast, is the ultimate shorthand used by people who know each other well and can literally finish each other's sentences. Once in a while, a professor may invite you to send a text on a simple matter—to confirm, for example, that you have received a message about a classroom relocation. When choosing an appropriate tone, let the writing situation guide you. *(See Chapter 47 for more on tone.)*

3b   Use reading, writing, and speaking to learn more about Academic English.

To develop your facility with Academic English, try using the following strategies:

- **Keep a reading and writing notebook.** Write down thoughts, comments, and questions about the reading assignments in your courses and class discussions. Try to put ideas from the readings into your own words (and note the source). Compare your understanding of a reading with those expressed by your classmates. Make a list of new words and phrases from your reading and from what you overhear. Be alert to idioms, words and phrases that have a special meaning not always included in a simple dictionary definition. Go over these lists with a tutor, a friend, or your writing group.

- **Write a personal journal or blog.** Using English to explore your thoughts, feelings, and questions about your studies and your life in college will help make you feel more at home in the language.

- **Join a study group.** Research shows that nearly all college students benefit from belonging to a study group. Discussing an assignment helps you understand it better. Study groups also provide opportunities to practice some of those new words on your list.

- **Write letters in English.** Letters are a good way to practice the informal style used in conversation. Write to out-of-town acquaintances who do not speak your first language. Write a letter to the college newspaper (though you'll need to be more formal in that situation). You can also write brief notes on paper or through e-mail to instructors, tutors, librarians, secretaries, and other proficient speakers of English.

3c Use learning tools that are available for multilingual students.

The following reference books can also help you as you complete writing tasks for your college courses. You can purchase them in your college's bookstore and find copies in the reference room of your college's library.

ESL dictionary A good dictionary designed especially for second-language students can be a useful source of information about word meanings. Ordinary dictionaries frequently define difficult words with other difficult words. An ESL dictionary defines words more simply.

Thesaurus Look up a word in a thesaurus to find other words with related meanings. The thesaurus can help you expand your vocabulary. However, always look up synonyms in a dictionary before using them because all synonyms differ slightly in meaning.

Dictionary of American idioms An idiom is an expression that is peculiar to a particular language and cannot be understood by looking at the individual words. "To catch a bus" is an idiom.

Desk encyclopedias In the reference room of your college's library and online, you will find brief encyclopedias on every subject from U.S. history to classical or biblical allusions. You may find it useful to look up people, places, and events that are new to you, especially if the person, place, or event is referred to often in U.S. culture.

2

Writing and Designing Texts

I like to do first drafts at night, when I'm tired, and then do the surgical work in the morning when I'm sharp.

—Alex Haley

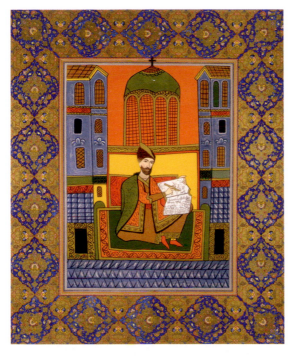

Illuminated manuscripts from the Middle Ages often depict scribes and writers, such as this portrait of the Georgian poet Shota Rustaveli (c. 1160–c. 1220). Then as now, writers transform words and visuals into finished works through careful planning, drafting, revision, and design.

2 Writing and Designing Texts

Section dealing with visual rhetoric. For a complete listing, see the Quick Guide to Key Resources at the back of this book.

— START SMART

Tab 2: Writing and Designing Texts

This section will help you answer questions such as these:

Rhetorical Knowledge

- What is a writing situation? (5a)
- When should I use visuals in my writing? What type of visuals fit my writing situation? (5e)
- What should I *not* put on my blog or social networking page? (14d)
- How can I use presentation software (like PowerPoint) effectively? (13d)

Critical Thinking, Reading, and Writing

- How can annotation and summary help me with reading assignments? (4a)
- How can I analyze photographs and other images? (4a)

Processes

- What are the components of the writing process? (5, 6, 7)
- What is a thesis statement? (5c)
- How should I give feedback on my classmates' work? (7a)
- What steps should I take in planning my Web site? (14c)

Knowledge of Conventions

- How can I make my paragraphs clear and effective? (6b)
- What features of document design can help convey my meaning? (8a)

For a general introduction to writing outcomes, see 1e, pages 14–16.

CHAPTER 4

Reading and Writing: The Critical Connection

Like writing, critical reading is a process that involves moving back and forth, rather than in a straight line. Critical readers, thinkers, and writers get intellectually involved. They recognize that meanings and values are made, not found, so they pose pertinent questions, note significant features, and examine the credibility of various kinds of texts.

┌─CHECKLIST Reading Critically

☐ **Preview** the text before you read it.
☐ **Read** the text for its topic and point.
☐ **Analyze** the *who, what,* and *why* of the text by **annotating** it as you reread it and **summarizing** what you have read.
☐ **Synthesize** through making connections.
☐ **Evaluate** what you've read.

In this context, the word *critical* means "thoughtful." When you read critically, you recognize the literal meaning of the text, make inferences about unstated meanings, and then make your own judgments in response.

Advances in technology have made it easier than ever to obtain information in a variety of ways. It is essential to "read" critically not just written texts but visuals, sounds, video, and other multimodal texts as well. We use the word *text* to refer to works that readers, viewers, or listeners invest with meaning and that can be critically analyzed.

👁 4a Read critically.

1. Previewing

Critical reading begins with **previewing** a text—looking over the information about its author and publication and quickly scanning its contents to gain a sense of its context, purpose, and meaning.

Previewing written texts As you preview a text, ask questions about its approach and claims, and assess the credibility of its evidence and arguments.

- **Author:** Who wrote this piece? What are the writer's credentials? Who is the writer's employer? What is the writer's occupation? Age? What are his or her interests and values?

- **Purpose:** What do the title and first and last paragraphs—which are often the points of greatest emphasis—tell you about the purpose of this piece? Do the headings and visuals provide clues to its purpose? What might have motivated the author to write it? Is the main purpose to inform, to interpret, to argue, to entertain, or is it to accomplish something else?

- **Audience:** Who is the target of the author's information or persuasion? Is the author addressing you or readers like you?

- **Content:** What does the title tell you about the piece? Does the first paragraph include the main point? What do the headings tell you about the gist of the text? Does the conclusion say what the author has focused on or show its significance?

- **Context:** Is the publication date current? Does the date matter? What kind of publication is it? Where and by whom was it published? Does the publisher have biases about the topic? If it was published electronically, was it posted by the author or by an organization with a special interest? Did it undergo a peer review process?

Previewing visuals   You can use most of the previewing questions for written texts to preview visuals. You should also ask some additional questions, however. For example, suppose you were asked to preview the public service advertisement shown in Figure 4.1. Here are some preview questions and possible responses:

- **In what context does the visual appear?** Was it intended to be viewed on its own or as part of a larger work? Is it part of a series of images (for example, a graphic novel, a music video, or a film)? This public service advertisement appeared in several publications targeted to college students. As the

FIGURE 4.1 Peace Corps advertisement. The text superimposed on this photograph reads: "**What happens in Botswana doesn't stay in Botswana.** When you help make a better life for others abroad, you also develop skills and experience that will serve your community back home. Life is calling. How far will you go?"

logo in the lower right-hand corner indicates, the ad was produced by the Peace Corps to recruit volunteers.

- **What does the visual depict? What is the first thing you notice in the visual?** The scene is a bare schoolroom in Botswana. (*Look at the world map in* Connect, *to find Botswana in Africa.*) As sun streams from a window, one young man in the foreground looks on as a younger boy erases a blackboard. On the blackboard, a handwritten poster appears with points of advice, for example, "Accept responsibility for your decision." The sunlight shining directly on the boy at the blackboard draws the viewer's attention to him. (Compare the light in this advertisement with that in Johannes Vermeer's painting *The Geographer* in Tab 13.)

- **Is the visual accompanied by audio or printed text?** Bold text appears in the center of the image, followed by smaller print directly addressed to the viewer. The phone number and Web address for the Peace Corps are printed in the lower left, and another appeal to the viewer, followed by the Peace Corps logo, is printed in the lower right.

—the EVOLVING SITUATION

Evaluating Context in Different Kinds of Publications and Disciplines

Nothing can be understood in isolation. We evaluate meaning in terms of surrounding conditions including types of publications and academic disciplines.

- **For a book:** Are you looking at the original publication or a reprint? What is the publisher's reputation? University presses, for example, are selective and usually publish scholarly works. A vanity press—one that requires authors to pay to publish their work—is not selective at all.

- **For an article in a periodical:** Look at the list of editors and their affiliations. What do you know about the journal, magazine, or newspaper in which this article appears? Are the articles reviewed by experts in a particular field before they are published?

- **For a Web page:** Who created the page? A Web page named for a political candidate, for example, may actually have been put on the Web by opponents.

Whether you are studying a book, an article, or a Web page, consider how the same topic is handled from the perspective of different disciplines. A book on the fall of the Berlin Wall (1989) will differ, for example, depending on whether the author addresses the topic from a historical, a political, or an economic point of view.

2. Reading and recording initial impressions

Read the selection for its literal meaning. Identify the topic and the main point. Note difficult passages to come back to as well as interesting ideas. Look up unfamiliar terms. Record your initial impressions:

- If the text or image is an argument, what opinion is being expressed? Were you persuaded by the argument?
- Did you have an emotional response to the text or image? Were you surprised, amused, or angered by anything in it?
- What was your initial impression of the writer or speaker?
- What key ideas did you take away from the work?

3. Using annotation and summary to analyze a text

Once you understand the literal or surface meaning of a text, you can analyze and interpret it. To **analyze** a text is to break it down into significant parts and examine how those parts relate to each other. Critical readers analyze a text in order to **interpret** it and come to a better understanding of its meanings.

Annotation combines reading with analysis. To annotate a text, read through it slowly and carefully while asking yourself the *who, what, how,* and *why* questions. As you read, underline or make separate notes about words, phrases, and sentences that strike you as significant or puzzling—even if you don't know why at that point— and write down your questions and observations.

SAMPLE ANNOTATED PASSAGE

Opens with a story about his childhood

Both my parents were immigrants from Russia. In my neighborhood, Yiddish was a first and second language. I grew up in the depths of the Great Depression. There were weeks when my father came home with $5 or less. My mother walked blocks to save a few cents on food. *Establishes his authority—he's experienced multiculturalism.*

I went to public school. Some of my friends were sent to the yeshiva—an Orthodox Jewish religious school—but my parents, having experienced the vicious, pervasive anti-Semitism in the Old Country, wanted me to learn what America was all about.

At Boston Latin School and Northeastern University—a working-class college—I took classes that taught a great deal about the fundamental rights and liberties that had to be fought for during this still "unfinished American revolution," as Thurgood Marshall called it. These were required courses, and inspired my lifelong involvement in civil rights and civil liberties. *Essential?? Supreme Court. Does he assume they would inspire everyone?*

—NAT HENTOFF, "Misguided Multiculturalism"

A **summary** conveys the basic content of a text. When you summarize an essay or article, your goal is to condense, without commentary, the text's main points into one paragraph. Even when you are writing a summary of a longer work, use the fewest words possible. A summary should be clear and brief, descriptive and not evaluative. A summary requires getting to the essence of the matter without oversimplification and misrepresentation. *(For specific instructions on how to write a summary, see Chapter 24: Working with Sources and Avoiding Plagiarism, pp. 268–69.)*

Questioning the text   Analysis and interpretation require a critical understanding of the *who, what, how,* and *why* of a text:

- **What is the writer's *stance*, or attitude toward the subject?** Does the writer appear to be objective, or does she or he seem to have personal feelings about the subject?
- **What is the writer's *voice?*** Is it like that of a reasonable judge, an enthusiastic preacher, or a reassuring friend?
- **What assumptions does the writer make about the audience?** Does the writer assume that readers agree, or does the writer try to build agreement? Does the writer choose examples and evidence with a certain audience in mind?
- **What is the writer's primary purpose?** Is it to present findings, offer an objective analysis, or argue for a particular action or opinion?
- **How does the writer develop ideas?** Does the writer define key terms? Include supporting facts? Tell relevant stories? Provide logical reasons?
- **Does the text appeal to emotions?** Does the writer use words, phrases, clichés, images, or examples that are emotionally charged?
- **Is the text fair?** Does the writer consider opposing ideas, arguments, or evidence fairly?
- **Is the evidence strong?** Does the writer provide sufficient and persuasive evidence?
- **Where is the argument strongest and weakest?**
- **Is the text effective?** Have your assumptions on this subject been changed by the text?

Visuals, too, can be subjected to critical analysis, as the comments a reader made on the Peace Corps ad indicate *(see Figure 4.2).*

4. Synthesizing your observations in a critical-response paper

To **synthesize** means to bring together, to make something out of different parts. In the last stage of critical reading, you pull together

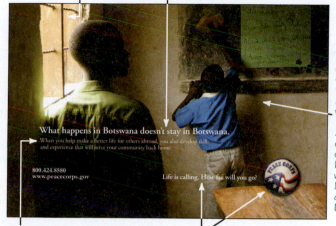

Composition of the photograph like Vermeer's paintings of sunlight illuminating an indoor scene. Subtle appeal to students of art history?

Reference to Las Vegas slogan, "What happens here stays here." Secrets of Las Vegas (superficial fun) stay there because of shame. Working with the Peace Corps (worthwhile life direction) in Botswana illuminates your life—and the world (Reference to sunlight?).

The boy is reaching up to erase or wash something from the blackboard. An older boy watches—also "reaching"? A poster covering part of the board lists principles valuable in Botswana and in the U.S.A.

Smaller print elaborates on win/win opportunity of the Peace Corps vs. odds of losing games in Las Vegas.

The Peace Corps logo combines the globe with the American flag—a global view of patriotism. How far will you go geographically and personally?

FIGURE 4.2 Sample annotations on the Peace Corps ad.

all your thinking—in your summary, analysis, and interpretation—into a coherent whole to support a claim. Whether you realize it or not, you synthesize material every day. When you hear contrasting accounts of a party from two different people, you assess the credibility of each source; you select the information that is most pertinent to you; you evaluate the story that each one tells; and, finally, you create a composite, or synthesis, of what you think really went on. When you synthesize information from two or more texts, you follow the same process.

4b   Write critically.

Sharpening your ability to think critically and to express your views effectively is one of the main purposes of undergraduate study. When you write critically, you gain a voice in the important discussions and decisions of our society. Writing can make a difference.

In college and beyond, you will apply critical-thinking skills to different writing purposes. Tab 3 of this book (*Common Assignments across the Curriculum*) focuses on writing to **inform** (*Chapter 9,* *pp. 107–22),* to **analyze** *(Chapter 10, pp. 122–31),* and to **argue** *(Chapter 11, pp. 131–55).* In each case, you will present evidence that supports a central point, or **thesis.** For your writing to be convincing and effective, you must consider your rhetorical situation: your purpose, audience, and the context of your assignment.

CHAPTER 5

Planning and Shaping

This chapter will help you determine the kind of writing a particular assignment requires and offer strategies for beginning a first draft. After reviewing an assignment, be sure to seek clarification from your instructor. It is far better to ask questions early on rather than to start over later or, even worse, to turn in an assignment that does not do the job.

5a   Learn how to approach assignments.

As a first step toward the goal of completing an assignment successfully, gain a clear understanding of the writing situation, and then make choices based on that knowledge.

1. Understanding the writing situation

Writers respond to **writing situations.** When you write a lab report for a science class, create a flyer for a student government candidate, or send an e-mail inviting a friend for coffee, you shape the communication **(message)** to suit the purpose, audience, and context. The results for each situation will differ. All communication occurs because something is at stake: the **exigence.** The **audience** receives the message. Audience members may be friendly or hostile to the writer's message, and their cultures and backgrounds will influence their reactions. Your **purpose** may be to inform them or to move them to action. Your **context** is the environment in which the communication takes place, including the means of communication available to you and the events that are occurring around you. *(For more on the writing situation, or rhetorical situation, see Chapter 2, pp. 17–18.)*

2. Writing about a question

Most of your academic writing will be in response to assignments that pose a question or ask you to formulate one. The particular course you are taking defines a range of questions that are appropriate within a given discipline. Here are examples of the way your course could help define the questions you might ask if, for example, you are writing about Thomas Jefferson:

U.S. history: How did Jefferson's ownership of slaves affect his public stance on slavery?

Political science: To what extent did Jefferson's conflict with the courts redefine the balance of power among the three branches of government?

Education: Given his beliefs about the relationship between democracy and public education, what would Jefferson think about contemporary proposals for a school voucher system?

3. Being clear about your purpose

What is the kind of assignment you are responding to? Think beyond the simple statement "I have to write an essay." Are you expected to inform, interpret, or argue?

- **Informing:** writing to transmit knowledge. Terms like *classify, illustrate, report,* and *survey* are often associated with the task of informing.

- **Interpreting:** writing to produce understanding. Terms like *analyze, compare, explain,* and *reflect* are more likely to appear when the purpose is interpreting.

- **Arguing:** writing to make a claim or negotiate matters of public debate. Terms like *agree, assess, defend,* and *refute* go with the task of arguing.

Some terms, such as *comment, consider,* and *discuss,* do not point to a particular purpose, but many others do. If you are not clear about the kind of work you are expected to do, ask your professor.

4. Asking questions about your audience

Who makes up your audience? In college, instructors—and sometimes classmates—are usually your primary readers, of course, but they may represent a larger group who have an interest or a stake in your topic. An education professor reads and evaluates a text as a representative of several possible groups—other students in the course, other professors in the program, experts in educational policy, school board members, public school principals, and parents of school-age children, among others.

5. Determining an appropriate rhetorical stance

Your **stance** is determined by the position you take in relationship to your audience and to the evidence. In other words, you might take one stance in your workplace writing as an employee and possibly shift to another stance when you assume leadership responsibilities.

CHECKLIST   Understanding the Writing Situation

Ask yourself these questions as you approach a writing assignment.

Topic *(See 5a.2.)*

☐ What are you being asked to write about?

☐ Have you narrowed your topic to a question that interests you?

☐ What kind of visuals, if any, would be appropriate for this topic?

☐ What types of sources will help you explore this topic? Where will you look for them?

☐ What genre and format would suit this assignment?

Purpose *(See 5a.3.)*

☐ What do you want your writing to accomplish? Are you trying to inform, analyze, or argue? (Which key words in your assignment indicate the purpose?)

☐ Do you want to intensify, clarify, complicate, or change your audience's assumptions or opinions?

Audience, Stance, and Tone *(See 5a.4, 5a.5, and 5a.6.)*

☐ What are your audience's demographics (education level, social status, gender, cultural background, and language)? How diverse is your audience?

☐ What does your audience know about the topic?

☐ What common assumptions and different opinions do these audience members bring to the issue? Are they likely to agree with you, or will you have to persuade them?

☐ What is your relationship to them? How does that relationship influence your rhetorical stance?

☐ What sort of tone would appeal to this audience: informal, entertaining, reasonable, or forceful? Why?

Context *(See 5a.7.)*

☐ Does your topic deal with issues of interest to the public or to members of an academic discipline?

☐ What have other writers said recently about this topic?

☐ How much time do you have to complete the assignment?

☐ What is the desired length (which may be expressed in a specific number of pages or words)?

Genre and Medium *(See 5a.8.)*

☐ What genre would best support your purpose?

☐ What medium are you using (print text, video podcast, Web site, presentation software) and why?

As a college student, your stance is seldom that of an expert, though you can take the stance of a novice who is becoming an expert, someone who is informed, reasonable, and fair.

6. Deciding on your tone

The identity, knowledge level, and needs of your audience will determine the tone of your writing. In speech, the sentence "I am surprised at you" can express anger, excitement, or disappointment depending on your tone of voice. In writing, your content, style, and word choice communicate **tone.** Consider the differences in tone in the following passages on the subject of a cafeteria makeover:

SARCASTIC   "I am special," the poster headline under the smirking face announces. Well, good for you. And I'm *specially* glad that cafeteria prices are up because so much money was spent on motivational signs and new paint colors.

SERIOUS   Although the new colors in the cafeteria are electric and clashing, color in general does brighten the space and distinguish it from the classrooms. But the motivational posters are not inspiring and should be removed.

The tone in the first passage is sarcastic and obviously intended for other students. An audience of school administrators probably would not appreciate the slang or the humor. The second passage is more serious and respectful—the appropriate tone for most college writing—while still offering a critique. *(For more on appropriate language, see Chapter 47.)*

7. Considering the context

The context, or surrounding circumstances, influences how an audience receives your communication. Your assignment goes a long way toward establishing the context in which you write. Your instructor probably has specified a length, due date, and genre. Context also involves broader conversations about your topic. Your course gives you background on what others in the discipline have said and what issues have been debated. Current events, on campus and in society as a whole, provide a context for public writing. You may wish, for example, to e-mail the student newspaper in response to a new school policy or on an issue of general concern.

8. Selecting the appropriate genre and medium

Genre simply means kind of writing. Poems, stories, and plays are genres of literature.

Sometimes an assignment will specify the kind of work, or genre, you are being asked to produce. For example, you may be asked to write a report (an informative genre), a comparative analysis (an interpretive genre), or a critique (an argumentative genre).

Some genres, like the case study, are common in particular fields such as sociology and finance but not in other disciplines. Understanding the genre that is called for is important in completing an assignment successfully. If you are supposed to write a description of a snake for a field guide, you will not be successful if you write a poem—even a very good poem—about a snake. *(See Tab 3: Common Assignments across the Curriculum, pp. 105–86.)* Understanding genre also helps you make decisions about language. For a description of a snake in a field guide, you would use highly specific terms to differentiate one type of snake from another. A poem would incorporate striking images—vivid words and phrases that evoke the senses—and other forms of literary language.

Writers today have wide choices in **medium,** whether in print or online, and many instructors may encourage you to use the appropriate technology for your writing situation. You can ask yourself, for example, what might be the best medium to persuade your college administration to repave the parking lot with materials that protect the environment. Would the print or online medium available in your student newspaper be best, or would it be more effective to use presentation software at a student senate meeting? Or perhaps a Web page or *YouTube* video might make the point more emphatically? In 1964, when Marshall McLuhan coined the now famous aphorism "The medium is the message," he had no idea of the possibilities for expression available today.

5b Explore your ideas.

The following **invention techniques** or **prewriting activities** are designed to help you begin. Remember that what you write at this stage is for your eyes only—no one will be judging your work. You can explore ideas in either a print or digital **journal,** which is simply a place to record your thoughts on a regular basis. *(For more on journals, see p. 47.)* Your class notes constitute a type of academic journal, as do the notes you take on your reading and research.

As you explore, turn off your internal critic and generate as much material as possible.

1. Freewriting

To figure out what you are thinking, try **freewriting,** typically for a limited period of time (five minutes, for example). Just write whatever occurs to you about a topic. If nothing comes to mind, then write "nothing comes to mind" until you do think of something. The trick is to keep pushing forward without stopping or worrying about spelling, punctuation, or grammar. Usually, you will discover some implicit point in your seemingly random writing. You might then try doing some **focused freewriting,** beginning with a point or a specific question to jump-start your thinking. The following is a portion of Diane Chen's freewriting about Dorothea Lange's photograph *Migrant Mother* in response to an assignment to analyze an image.

> I want to talk about what it means to view photographs of poverty, but also to admire the artistic components of such photographs. I feel like those two things shouldn't go together—but my reaction to Dorothea Lange's work inspires me to consider both. In fact, her skill as a photographer makes it harder to look away from the sometimes difficult images she captured.

(You can read the second draft of Chen's essay in Chapter 7 on pp. 90–92.)

2. Listing or Brainstorming

Another strategy is to **brainstorm** by starting with a topic and listing all the words, phrases, images, and ideas that come to mind; again, limiting the time to five minutes or so can "force" ideas. When you brainstorm in this way, don't worry about whether the individual thoughts or ideas are "right." Just get them down on paper or on screen.

Once you have completed your list, go through it looking for patterns and connections. Highlight or connect related ideas, or group related material together. Move apparently extraneous material or ideas to the end of the list or to a separate page. Now zero in on the areas of most interest, and add any new ideas that occur to you. Arrange the items into main points and subpoints if necessary. Later, this material may form the basis of an outline for your paper.

Here is part of a list that Diane Chen produced for her paper about a photograph:

> Documentary photography—photojournalism versus art photography
> Migrant workers—what is the story/history behind this photo?
> Composition communicates information about subject, and the mother's facial expression is significant

3. Clustering

Clustering, sometimes called **mapping,** is a brainstorming technique that generates categories and connections from the beginning. To make an idea cluster, do the following:

- Write your topic in the center of a piece of paper, and circle it.
- Surround the topic with subtopics that interest you. Circle each, and draw a line from it to the center circle. You may also connect the circles to each other.
- Brainstorm more ideas, connecting each one to a subtopic already on the sheet or making it into a new subtopic.

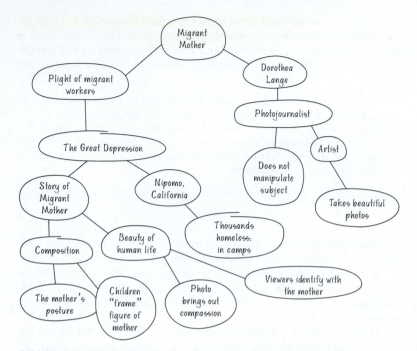

FIGURE 5.1 Diane Chen's cluster about Lange's photograph.

Web sites such as <https://bubbl.us> allow you to use this technique on the computer, alone or in groups. As she explored her ideas about the Dorothea Lange photograph, Diane Chen prepared the cluster that appears in Figure 5.1.

4. Questioning

The journalist's five *w*'s and an *h (who? what? where? when? why?* and *how?)* can help you find specific ideas and details. For example, here are some questions that would apply to the photograph:

- Who is the photographer, who are her subjects, and who is the audience?
- What is the photographer's attitude toward her subjects?
- Where was this picture shot and first exhibited?
- When did these events take place?
- Why are the people in this photograph living in a camp?
- How do I react to this image?

For other examples of what to question and how, you should take note of the problems or questions your professor poses in class discussions. If you are using a textbook in your course, check out the study questions.

5. Reviewing your notes and annotations

Review your notes and annotations on your reading or research. *(For details on annotating, see Chapter 4. For details on keeping a research journal, see Chapter 24.)* If you are writing about something you have observed, review your notes and sketches. These immediate comments and reactions are excellent sources for ideas.

6. Keeping a journal or notebook

Record ideas and questions in a journal or notebook. You might write about connections between your personal life and your academic subjects, connections among your subjects, or ideas touched on in class that you would like to know more about. Jotting down one or two thoughts at the end of class and exploring those ideas at greater length later in the day will help you build a store of ideas for future projects.

> My economics textbook says that moving jobs to companies overseas ultimately does more good than harm to the economy, but how can that be? When the electronics factory closed, it devastated my town.

7. Browsing in the library or searching the Internet

Your college library is filled with ideas—and it can be a great inspiration when you need to come up with your own. Browse the bookshelves containing texts that relate to a topic of interest. Exploring a subject on the Web is the electronic equivalent of browsing in the library. Type keywords related to your topic into a search engine such as *Google,* and visit several sites on the resulting list. *(See Tab 5: Researching, pp. 227–29.)*

8. Exchanging ideas

Writing is a social activity. Most authors thank family members, editors, librarians, and colleagues for help on work in progress. Talking about your writing with your classmates, friends, and family can be a source of ideas.

Online tools offer additional opportunities for collaboration. Discuss your assignments by exchanging e-mail. If your class has a Web site, you might exchange ideas in chat rooms. Other options include instant messaging (IM), text messaging, and blogs. *Facebook* and *Twitter* provide additional opportunities to discuss your work with friends. Keep a list of your interactions so that you can write a note or page of acknowledgment for the help and encouragement you receive.

Writing e-mail   When you work on papers with classmates, you can use e-mail in the following ways:

- To check your understanding of the assignment
- To try out various topics

- To ask each other questions
- To share freewriting, listing, and other exploratory writing
- To respond to each other's ideas

Chatting about ideas   You can use online chat rooms as well as other virtual spaces to share ideas. **Instant messaging (IM)** also permits real-time communication. Exchanging ideas with other writers via IM can help you clarify your thinking on a topic.

Exchanging text messages   **Text messaging**—the exchange of brief messages between cell phones—can be useful to writers in two ways. First, you can text your ideas for an assignment to a classmate (or—with permission—your instructor) for response. In the exchange shown in Figure 5.2, two students use texting to share ideas about volunteerism. Second, you can use abbreviations commonly used in texting for speedier note taking both in class and for outside research. Such shorthand should *never* be used in submitted work.

5c   Develop a working thesis.

The **thesis** or **claim** is the central idea of your project. It should communicate a specific point about your topic and suit the purpose of the assignment. As you explore your topic, ideas for your thesis will begin to emerge. You can focus these ideas by drafting a preliminary or working **thesis statement,** which is typically one or two sentences long. As you draft and revise, you may change your thesis several times to make it stronger.

To develop a thesis, answer a question posed by your assignment. *(For more about questions, see p. 46.)* For example, an assignment in a political science class might ask you to defend or critique "The Limits of the Welfare State," an article by George Will on the conflict between limited government and unlimited human rights. The question your thesis must answer is, "Is George Will's position that government should not be responsible for the economic welfare of its citizens reasonable?"

To create a strong thesis, you will need to think critically, developing a point of view based on reading course materials and doing research. Not all theses can be stated in one sentence, but all strong theses are suitable, specific, and significant.

1. Making sure your thesis is suitable

All theses make an assertion about a topic, but these assertions differ. A thesis for an argument will take a clear position on an issue or recommend an action; a thesis for an informative or interpretive

FIGURE 5.2
**Exchanging ideas
via texting.**

project will often preview the project's content or express the writer's insight into the topic. All the following theses are on the same topic, but each is for a project with a different purpose:

THESIS TO INFORM

James Madison and Woodrow Wilson had different views on the government's role in the economic well-being of its citizens.

THESIS TO INTERPRET

The economic ideas George Will expresses in "The Limits of the Welfare State" are more reactionary than politically conservative.

THESIS TO ARGUE

George Will's contention that government should not be responsible for the economic well-being of its citizens does not adequately take into account the economic complexities of twenty-first century society.

2: Making sure your thesis is specific

Vague theses usually lead to weak, unfocused texts. Avoid thesis statements that simply announce your topic, state an obvious fact about it, or offer a general observation:

ANNOUNCEMENT

I will discuss the article "The Limits of the Welfare State" by George Will. [*What is the writer's point about the article?*]

STATEMENT OF FACT

The article "The Limits of the Welfare State" by George Will is about the need for limited government. [*This thesis gives us information about the article, but it does not make a specific point about it.*]

GENERAL OBSERVATION

George Will's article "The Limits of the Welfare State" is interesting. [*While this thesis makes a point about the article, the point could apply to many articles. What makes this article worth reading?*]

In contrast, a specific thesis signals a focused, well-developed composition.

SPECIFIC

George Will, in his article "The Limits of the Welfare State," is wrong about the government's lack of responsibility for the economic welfare of its citizens. His interpretation of the Constitution is questionable. His reasoning about history is flawed. Above all, his definitions of limits are too narrow.

In this example, the thesis expresses the writer's particular point—there are three reasons to reject Will's argument. It also forecasts the structure of the whole project.

Note: A thesis statement can be longer than one sentence (if necessary) to provide a framework for your main idea. All the sentences taken together, though, should build to one specific, significant point that fits the purpose of your assignment and of the rhetorical situation. (Some instructors may prefer that you limit your thesis statements to one sentence.)

3. Making sure your thesis is significant

A topic that makes a difference to you is much more likely to make a difference to your readers, though you should be sure to connect your interest to theirs. When you are looking for possible theses, be sure to challenge yourself to develop one that you care about.

5d   Plan a structure that suits your assignment.

Every writing project should have the following components:

- A beginning, or **introduction,** that hooks readers and usually states the thesis
- A middle, or **body,** that develops the main idea of the project in a series of paragraphs—each making a point supported by specific details
- An ending, or **conclusion,** that gives readers a sense of completion, often by offering a final comment on the thesis

Typically, you will state your thesis in the introduction. However, in personal, narrative, or descriptive writing, you may instead imply the thesis through the details and evidence you present. Or you may begin with background and contextual material leading up to your thesis. In other cases, the thesis may be most effective at the end. This tactic works well when you are arguing for a position that your audience is likely to oppose.

It is not essential to prepare an outline before you start drafting; indeed, some writers prefer to discover how to connect and develop their ideas as they compose. However, an outline of your first draft will help you spot organizational problems or places where the support for your thesis is weak.

─ *the* EVOLVING SITUATION

Using Presentation Software as a Writing Process Tool

Presentation-software slides provide a useful tool for exploring and organizing your ideas before you start drafting. They can also prompt feedback from peer reviewers and others. Here is a way to begin:

- Far in advance of the due date, create a brief, three- to five-slide presentation—with visuals if appropriate—that previews the key points you intend to make in the paper.
- Present the preview to an audience of friends, classmates, or perhaps even your instructor. Ask for suggestions for improvement and advice for developing the presentation into a completed text.

1. Preparing an informal plan

A **scratch outline** is a simple list of points, without the levels of subordination found in more complex outlines. Scratch outlines are useful for briefer papers. Here is a scratch outline for an analysis of Dorothea Lange's photograph *Migrant Mother:*

- *Migrant Mother* raised awareness of the issue of poverty in America during the Great Depression, and called for social change.
- Lange felt for her subjects; her consideration of them allows her photographs to illustrate the need for social change.
- *Migrant Mother*—describe the subjects, framing, and overall composition, and the emotions it evokes.
- Support Lange's credibility by mentioning her Guggenheim Fellowship.

A **do/say plan** is a more detailed type of informal outline. To come up with such a plan, review your notes and other relevant material. Then write down your working thesis and list what you will say for each of the following "do" categories: introduce, support and develop, and conclude. Here is an example:

Thesis: George Will is wrong about the government's lack of responsibility for the economic welfare of its citizens.

1. **Introduce** the issue and my focus.
   - Use two examples to contrast rich and poor: during the period 2007–2009, the poverty rate increased to 14.3%, a 15-year high (Eckholm). During the same period, the income levels of the wealthiest Americans continued to increase; for example, the top 0.1% had 8% of the total income in the United States in 2008, up from 2% in 1973 (Noah). Say that the issue is how to evaluate increasing economic inequality and its consequences, and introduce Will's article "The Limits of the Welfare State." Summarize Will's argument.
   - Give Will credit for raising issue, but then state thesis: he's wrong about limited government when it comes to citizens' economic well-being.
2. **Support and develop** thesis that Will's argument is wrong.
   - Point out that Will relies on a strict construction of the Constitution in his defense of natural economic rights.
   - Point out one thing that Madison and Wilson would agree on: government should be limited in the exercise of "untrammeled power" over its citizens.
   - Show that government's actions for the well-being of its citizens are appropriate given the natural right of "the pursuit of happiness."

- Say that Will makes fun of those who see the Constitution as a living document in response to evolving times. Will's idea of limited government is too narrow. If government does not focus on economic well-being, then how will U.S. society thrive in times of economic hardship?

3. **Conclude** that Will doesn't ask or answer such key questions because he believes, quoting former British prime minister Margaret Thatcher, that government "always runs out of other people's money." Follow with quote from political analyst James Carvell, "It's the economy, stupid!"?

In outlining his plan, this student has already begun drafting because as he works on the outline, he gets a clearer sense of what he thinks is wrong with Will's argument. He starts writing sentences that he is likely to include in the first complete draft.

2. Preparing a formal outline

A **formal outline** classifies and divides the information you have gathered, showing main points, supporting ideas, and specific details by organizing them into levels of subordination.

A **topic outline** uses single words or phrases; a **sentence outline** states every idea in a sentence. Because the process of division always results in at least two parts, in a formal outline every I must have a II; every A, a B; and so on. Also, items placed at the same level must be of the same kind; for example, if I is London, then II can be New York City but not the Bronx or Wall Street. Items at the same level should also be grammatically parallel; if A is "Choosing screen icons," then B can be "Creating away messages" but not "Away messages."

Here is a formal sentence outline for an analysis of Dorothea Lange's photograph *Migrant Mother:*

Thesis Statement: As a photojournalist who empathetically captured the struggles of her subjects on film, Lange was able to impart compassion to her audience and in turn inspire change.

I. Lange was commissioned to photograph migrant workers and families in the Depression era, and her work in this area is well known.

II. Lange had empathy for her subjects and her consideration of them allows her photographs to illustrate the need for social change.

 A. She showed the public the reality of life for migrant workers.

  1. She was not just an artist, but a photojournalist using documentary techniques.

  2. Lange's work was important in that it provided a perspective on poverty and inspired social change.

B. The photograph *Migrant Mother* is one of Lange's most famous.
  1. The photograph depicts harsh conditions faced by a migrant worker and her three children in Nipomo, California, in 1936.
  2. Lange's technique involved taking many shots, getting closer to the subject as she photographed.
  3. It captures the real-life struggle and allows viewers to see the despair suffered at this time in our history.
  4. The photo remains an iconic representation of poverty and injustice.
C. This photo reveals Lange's compassion for her subjects.
  1. Her three children are gathered around her, with the mother's face as the central focus of the photograph.
  2. The mother's expression looks to the distance and shows evidence of her distress and worry.
  3. Her children cling to her but look away, depicting their need and the mother's helplessness.
  4. The mother's expression tells the story of her despair.
  5. The mother's posture and the hand placed against her face with elbow in her lap suggest deep thought—and possibly depression.
  6. The physical posture of the mother also represents her family's social position.
  7. The ragged and dirty clothes of the children and mother help illustrate the extent of the hardships suffered by migrant workers.
  8. Lange communicates the dire circumstances through these details.
III. *Migrant Mother* and others in Lange's body of work raised awareness of the issue of poverty in America during this time, and called for social change.
  1. In 1941, Lange won a Guggenheim Fellowship for her work.
  2. Lange was recognized as one of the most iconic photographers of the twentieth century.
  3. Her legacy is the photographs like *Migrant Mother,* which opened Americans' eyes to social issues of the time and inspired change.

👁 **5e**   Consider using visuals and multimodal elements, depending on your purpose and audience.

Technology makes it easy to go beyond words to pictures, graphs, sounds, and videos—all with the goal of improving a specific project. Always ask, What do multimodal materials contribute to the project?

When you use graphs, images, audio files, or videos, always credit your source, and be aware that most visuals and other multimodal elements are protected by copyright. If you plan to use a photograph as part of a Web page, for example, you will usually need to obtain permission from the copyright holder. *(For information about finding visuals, audio, and video, see Tab 5: Researching, pp. 233–39.)*

1. Using visuals effectively

Visuals such as tables, charts, and graphs can clarify complex data or ideas. Effective visuals are used for specific purposes, and each type of visual illustrates some kinds of material better than others. *(See "Types of Visuals and Their Uses" on pp. 55–57.)* For example, compare the table and the line graph on pages 55–56. Both present data that show changes over time, but does one strike you as clearer or more powerful than the other?

> *Caution:* Because the use of visual elements is more acceptable in some fields than in others, you may want to ask your instructor for advice before planning to include visuals in your project.

2. Using audio and video effectively

You might use audio elements such as music, interviews, or speeches to present or illustrate your major points. Video elements—clips from films, TV, *YouTube, Vimeo,* or your personal archive—are likewise valuable for clear explanation or powerful argument. *Camtasia* is a useful tool for creating and editing your own demonstration videos by recording what you see on your screen. You should also consider using *Prezi* as a more dynamic alternative to *PowerPoint* as it can incorporate videos.

Types of Visuals and Their Uses

TABLES

Tables organize precise data for readers. Because the measurements in the example include decimals, it would be difficult to plot them on a graph without including very small cells.

Emissions from Waste (Tg CO_2 Eq.)

Gas/Source	1990	2005	2007	2008	2009	2010	2011
CH_4	163.7	129	128.2	130.2	129.8	123.2	119.2
Landfills	147.8	112.5	111.6	113.6	113.3	106.8	103.0
Wastewater treatment	15.9	16.5	16.6	16.6	16.5	16.4	16.2
N_2O	0.5	0.4	0.4	0.4	0.4	0.4	0.4
Incineration of waste	0.5	0.4	0.4	0.4	0.4	0.4	0.4
Total	**164.2**	**129.4**	**128.6**	**130.6**	**130.2**	**123.6**	**119.6**

Note: Totals may not sum due to independent rounding.
SOURCE: U.S. Environmental Protection Agency. "Inventory of U.S. Greenhouse Gas Emissions and Sinks: 1990–2011." *U.S. Environmental Protection Agency, Apr. 2013:27–29.Web. Oct. 2013.*

BAR GRAPHS

Bar graphs highlight comparisons between two or more variables, such as the percentage of men and women employed in various jobs in the nation's newsrooms. They allow readers to see relative sizes quickly.

SOURCE: Data from Table L, "2013: U.S. Newsroom Employment Declines," *ASNE Newsroom Census* (American Society of News Editors; 25 Jun. 2013; Web; 30 Nov. 2013).

PIE CHARTS

Pie charts show the size of parts in relation to the whole. The segments must add up to 100 percent of something, differences in segment size must be noticeable, and there should not be too many segments, as shown in these pie charts illustrating changes in American households over time.

SOURCE: Richard Schaefer, *Sociology in Modules* (New York: McGraw-Hill, 2011; print; 353). Estimate for 2010 based on Bureau of the Census.

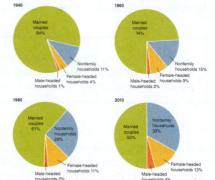

LINE GRAPHS

Line graphs show changes in one or more variables over time. The example shows how the life goals of U.S. college students have changed over a span of thirty-three years.

SOURCE: Richard Schaefer, *Sociology in Modules* (New York: McGraw-Hill, 2011; print; 78).

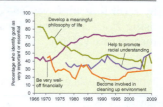

DIAGRAMS

Diagrams show processes or structures visually. Common in technical writing, they include timelines, organization charts, and decision trees. The example shows the factors involved in the decision to commit a burglary.

SOURCE: Clarke and Cornish, "Modeling Offenders' Decisions," in *Crime and Justice*, vol 6, ed. Tonry and Morris, (Chicago: U of Chicago P, 1985; print; 169).

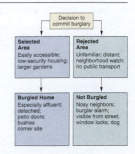

PHOTOS

Photos can reinforce your point by showing readers what your subject actually looks like or how it has been affected. This image could support a portrayal of Occupy Wall Street as a controversial protest movement.

MAPS

Maps highlight locations and spatial relationships and show relationships between ideas. This one shows the routes followed by slaves escaping to freedom in the nineteenth century, prior to the Civil War.

SOURCE: Brigid Harrison and Jean Harris, *A More Perfect Union* (New York: McGraw-Hill: 2011; print; 178).

ILLUSTRATIONS

Like photographs, illustrations make a point dramatically. (*A larger version of this image appears on p. 140.*)

SOURCE: "Absolut AA," *Adbusters*, Adbusters (Web; 3 Aug. 2011).

CHAPTER 6

Drafting Text and Visuals

Think of drafting as an attempt to discover a beginning, a middle, and an end for what you have to say, but remember that a draft is preliminary. Avoid putting pressure on yourself to make it perfect, and leave ample time to revise and edit.

6a   Use electronic tools for drafting.

The following tips will make this process go smoothly:

- **Save your work.** Always protect your hard-won drafts from power surges and other electronic hiccups. Save often, and make backups. Consider using cloud-based tools, such as *Google Drive* and *DropBox* to save your work to the Internet. This will ensure your work is saved should something happen to your computer or external hard drive.

- **Label revised drafts with different file names.** Use a different file name for each successive version of your manuscript. For example, you might save drafts of a project on work as Work1, Work2, Work3, and so on.

6b   Develop ideas using patterns of organization and visuals.

The following strategies can help you develop the ideas that support your thesis into a complete draft. Depending on the purpose of your composition, you may use a few of these patterns throughout or a mix of all of them. For example, for a report about a local issue for your

---

NAVIGATING THROUGH COLLEGE AND BEYOND

Avoiding Writer's Block

Use these tips to get an early start on a first draft:

- **Resist the temptation to be a perfectionist.** For your first draft, do not worry about getting the right word, the stylish phrase, or even the correct spelling.

- **Take it "bird by bird."** Writer Anne Lamott counsels students to break down writing assignments into manageable units and to finish each unit in one session. She passes along her father's advice to her brother, who had procrastinated on a report about birds and was paralyzed by the size of the project: "Bird by bird, buddy. Just take it bird by bird."

- **Start anywhere.** If you are stuck on the beginning, select another section where you know what you want to say. Writers often compose the introduction after drafting a complete text. You can go back later and work out the transitions.

- **Generate more ideas.** If you hit a section where you are drawing a blank, you may need to do more reading, research, or brainstorming. Be careful, though, not to use reading and research as stalling tactics.

- **Set aside time and work in a suitable place.** Many writers find that working undisturbed for at least half an hour at a stretch is helpful.

━ the EVOLVING SITUATION

Using Internet Links as a Writing Process Tool

As you compose, add links to supplemental material that you may—or may not—decide to use in a later draft. For example, you might include a link to additional research, or to a source that refutes an argument, or to interesting information that is not directly relevant to the primary subject. Readers can be helpful in advising you on whether or not to include the linked material in the next draft. Before the final draft, be sure to remove all links.

political science course, you might use narration to provide background and then compare two local officials' differing positions. In the process, you might define key terms that readers need to understand the issue.

Photographs, tables, graphs, and audio and video clips can also support your ideas, as long as they serve the overall purpose of the work and are not used just for fun or decoration. Regardless of the type of visual you use, be sure to discuss it in the body of your text. *(See pp. 55–57 for more on types of visuals and their purposes.)*

1. Illustration

To appeal to readers, showing is better than telling. Detailed examples and well-chosen visuals *(see Figure 6.1)* can make abstractions more concrete and generalizations more specific, as the following paragraph shows:

> As Rubin explains, "for much of the Accord era, the ideal-typical family . . . was composed of a 'stay-at-home-mom,' a working father, and dependent children. He earned wages; she cooked, cleaned, cared for the home, managed the family's social life, and nurtured the family members" (97). Just such an arrangement characterized my grandmother's married life. My grandmother, who had four children, stayed at home with them, while her husband went off to work as a safety engineer. Sadly, when he died, she was left with nothing. She needed to support herself, yet had no work experience, no credit, and little education. But even though society frowned on her for seeking employment, my grandmother eventually found a clerical position—a low-level job with few perks.
>
> —JENNIFER KOEHLER, "Women's Work in the United States: The 1950s and 1990s," student text

FIGURE 6.1 Visuals that illustrate. This advertisement shows an idealized version of the lives of many women in the 1950s and 1960s.

2. Narration

When you narrate, you tell a story. *(See Figure 6.2 for an example of a narrative visual.)* The following paragraph comes from a personal essay on the results of "a lifetime of production":

> My dad changed too. He had come to that job feeling—as I do now—that everything was still possible. He'd served his time in the Air Force during the Korean War. Then, while my mother worked as a secretary to support them, he earned a college degree courtesy of the GI Bill. After graduation, my father painted houses for a season until he was offered a position scheduling the production of corrugated board. He took it, though he has told me that he never planned to stay. It was not something he envisioned as his life's work. I try to imagine what it is like suddenly to look up from a stack of orders and discover that the job you started one December day has watched you age.
>
> —MICHELLE M. DUCHARME, "A Lifetime of Production"

Notice that Ducharme begins with two sentences that state the topic and point of her narration. Then, using the past tense, she recounts in chronological sequence some key events that led to her father's taking a job in the box manufacturing business.

3. Description

To make an object, person, or activity vivid for your readers, describe it in concrete, specific words that appeal to the senses of sight, sound, taste, smell, and touch. *(See Figure 6.3 for an example of a descriptive*

FIGURE 6.2 Visuals that narrate. Images that narrate can reinforce a message or portray events you discuss in your writing. Images like this one help tell one of many stories about work in the United States.

visual.) In the following paragraph, Diane Chen describes her impression of the photograph in Figure 6.3:

> The photograph's composition reveals Lange's compassion for her subject. Although four figures make up the photograph, the mother, whose face we see in full, is its main subject. She gazes outward, worriedly, as her three children huddle around her. The children frame her figure, two of them with faces hidden behind her shoulders, either out of shyness or shared distress, while the third rests across the mother's lap. The mother's expression conveys a desperate concern, presumably for her children's wellbeing. Her children cling to her, but her own faraway gaze gives evidence that she is too distracted by her worries to give them comfort. Lange emphasizes the mother's expression by making it the focal point of the photograph. In doing so, she encourages viewers to identify with the mother and even to wonder what thoughts pass through her mind.

> —DIANE CHEN, "Inspiring Empathy: Dorothea Lange's *Migrant Mother*" student text

FIGURE 6.3 **Visuals that describe.** Pay careful attention to the effect your selection will have on your project. This photograph by Dorothea Lange appeals to the viewer's emotions, evoking sympathy for the migrant workers' plight.

4. Classification

Classification is a useful way of grouping individual entities into identifiable categories. *(See Figure 6.4.)* Classifying occurs in all academic disciplines and often appears with its complement—**division,** or breaking a whole entity into its parts.

In the following passage, Robert Reich first classifies kinds of future work into two broad categories, complex services and person-to-person services. In the next paragraph, he then develops the idea of complex services in more detail, in part by dividing that category into more specific—and familiar—categories like engineering and advertising.

> [M]ost of America's traditional, routinized manufacturing jobs will disappear. So will routinized service jobs that can be done from remote locations, like keypunching of data transmitted by satellite. Instead, you will be engaged in one of two broad categories of work: either complex services, some of which will be sold to the rest of the world to pay for whatever Americans want to buy from the rest of the world, or person-to-person services, which foreigners can't provide for us because (apart from new immigrants and illegal aliens) they aren't here to provide them.
>
> Complex services involve the manipulation of data and abstract symbols. Included in this category are insurance, engineering, law, finance, computer programming, and advertising. Such activities now account for almost 25 percent of our GNP, up from 13 percent in 1950. They have already surpassed manufacturing (down to about 20 percent of GNP).
>
> —ROBERT REICH, "The Future of Work"

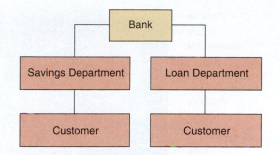

FIGURE 6.4 Visuals that classify or divide. An image can help you make the categories or parts of complex systems or organizations easier to understand. The image shown here, for example, helps readers comprehend the structure of a business.

5. Definition

Define concepts that readers need in order to follow your discussion. *(See Figure 6.5 for an example of a visual that defines.)* Interpretations and arguments often depend on one or two key ideas that cannot be quickly and easily defined. In the following example, an online encyclopedia defines the ionic column:

> Unlike the Greek Doric order, Ionic columns normally stand on a base . . . which separates the shaft of the column from the stylobate or platform. The capital of the Ionic column has characteristic paired scrolling volutes that are laid on the molded cap ("echinus") of the column, or spring from within it. The cap is usually enriched with egg-and-dart. Originally the volutes lay in a single plane . . . ; then it was seen that they could be angled out on the corners. This feature of the Ionic order made it more pliant and satisfactory than the Doric to critical eyes in the 4th century BCE: angling the volutes on the corner columns ensured that they "read" equally when seen from either the front or side facade. The 16th-century Renaissance architect and theorist Vincenzo Scamozzi designed a version of such a perfectly foursided Ionic capital, which became so much the standard, that when a Greek Ionic order was eventually reintroduced, in the later 18th century Greek Revival, it conveyed an air of archaic freshness and primitive, perhaps even republican, vitality.

—WORDIQ.COM

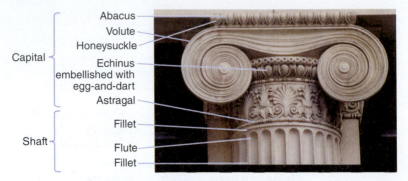

Capital
- Abacus
- Volute
- Honeysuckle
- Echinus embellished with egg-and-dart
- Astragal

Shaft
- Fillet
- Flute
- Fillet

FIGURE 6.5 Visuals that define. Visuals can be effective when used to support a written definition or to identify parts of a whole. This image uses labels and leader lines to identify the characteristics of an Ionic column.

6. Comparison and contrast

When you *compare,* you explore the similarities and differences among various items. When the term *compare* is used along with the term *contrast, compare* has a narrower meaning: "to spell out key similarities." *Contrast* always means "to itemize important differences." *(See Figure 6.6.)*

In the following example, the student writer uses a **subject-by-subject** pattern to contrast the ideas of two social commentators, Jeremy Rifkin and George Will:

> Rifkin and Will have different opinions about unemployment caused by downsizing and the widening income gap between rich and poor. Rifkin sees both the decrease in employment and the increase in income disparity as evils that must be immediately dealt with lest society fall apart: "If no measures are taken to provide financial opportunities for millions of Americans in an era of diminishing jobs, then . . . violent crime is going to increase" (3). Will, on the other hand, seems to believe that both unemployment and income differences are necessary to the health of American society. Will writes, "A society that chafes against stratification derived from disparities of talents will be a society that discourages individual talents" (92). Apparently, the society that Rifkin wants is just the kind of society that Will rejects.
>
> —JACOB GROSSMAN, "Dark Comes before Dawn,"
> student text

Notice that Grossman comments on Rifkin first and then turns to his second subject, Will. To ensure paragraph unity, Rifkin begins with a topic sentence that mentions both subjects.

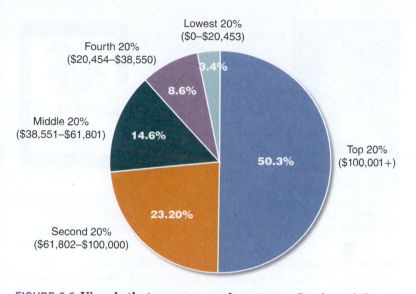

FIGURE 6.6 Visuals that compare and contrast. Graphs and charts are effective for comparing parallel sets of data. This pie chart shows the distribution of U.S. household income in 2009.

In the following paragraph, the student writer organizes her comparison **point by point,** rather than subject by subject. Instead of saying everything about Smith's picture before commenting on the AP photo, she moves back and forth between the two images as she makes and supports two points: (1) that the images differ in figure and scene and (2) that they are similar in theme:

Divided by an ocean, two photographers took pictures that at first glance seem absolutely different. W. Eugene Smith's well-known *Tomoko in the Bath* and the less well-known AP photo *A Paratrooper Works to Save the Life of a Buddy* portray distinctively different settings and people. Smith brings us into a darkened room where a Japanese woman is lovingly bathing her malformed child, while the AP staff photographer captures two soldiers on the battlefield, one intently performing CPR on his wounded friend. But even though the two images seem as different as women and men, peace and war, or life and death, both pictures convey something similar: a time of suffering. It is the early 1970s—a time when the hopes and dreams that modernity promoted are being exposed as deadly to human beings. Perhaps that is why the bodies in both pictures seem humbled. Grief pulls you down onto your knees. Terror impels you to crawl along the ground.

—ILONA BOUZOUKASHVILI, "On Reading Photographs,"
student text

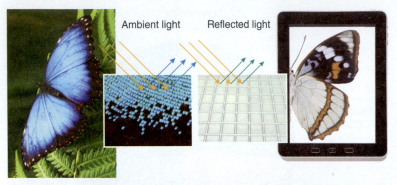

Tiny scales on the butterfly wing diffract and scatter ambient light to create specific, intense colors.

Tiny plates in the Mirasol display for mobile devices scatter ambient light to create vibrant, individual colors for the viewer without using energy-wasting backlight.

FIGURE 6.7 Visuals as analogies. Visual analogies operate in the same way as written analogies. This figure uses the image of a butterfly wing to illustrate how the display on a mobile device works.

7. Analogy

An **analogy** compares topics that at first glance seem quite different (*see Figure 6.7*). A well-chosen analogy can make new or technical information appear more commonplace and understandable:

> The brilliant iridescent blue of the various Morpho species, for example, comes not from pigment, but from "structural color." Those wings harbor a nanoscale assemblage of shingled plates, whose shape and distance from one another are arranged in a precise pattern that disrupts reflective light wavelengths to produce the brilliant blue. To create that same blue out of pigment would require much more energy—energy better used for flying, feeding and reproducing . . . Like the butterfly's wings, "the display is taking the white ambient light around us, white light or sunlight, and through interference is going to send us back a color image," [Brian] Gally says. Unlike conventional LCD screens, the Mirasol doesn't have to generate its own light. "The display brightness just automatically scales with ambient light."
>
> —TOM VANDERBILT, *Smithsonian* magazine

8. Process

When you explain how to do something or show readers how something is done, you use process analysis *(see Figure 6.8),* explaining each step in the process in chronological order, as in the following example:

> The scientific method requires precise preparation in developing useful research. Otherwise, the research data collected

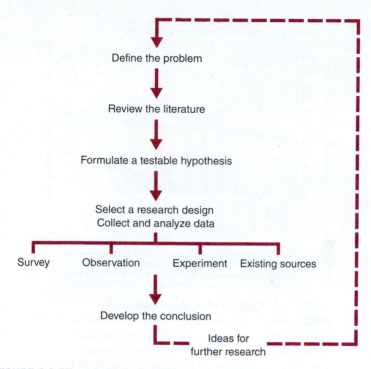

FIGURE 6.8 Visuals that show a process. Flow charts and diagrams are especially useful when illustrating a process. This one shows the scientific method used in disciplines throughout the sciences and social sciences.

may not prove accurate. Sociologists and other researchers follow five basic steps in the scientific method: (1) defining the problem, (2) reviewing the literature, (3) formulating the hypothesis, (4) selecting the research design and then collecting and analyzing the data, and (5) developing the conclusion.

—RICHARD T. SCHAEFER, *Sociology*

9. Cause and effect

This strategy can help you trace the causes of some event or situation, to describe its effects, or both *(see Figure 6.9).* In the following example, Eric Klinenberg explains the possible reasons for the deaths of 739 Chicagoans in the 1995 heat wave:

On July 12, 1995, a dangerous hot-air mass settled over Chicago, producing three consecutive days of temperatures over 99 degrees Fahrenheit, heat indices (which measure the heat

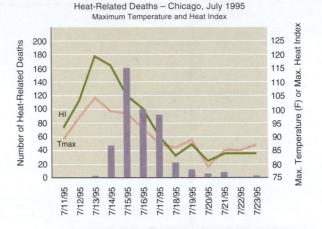

This graph tracks maximum temperature (Tmax), heat index (HI), and heat-related deaths in Chicago each day from July 11 to 23, 1995. The orange line shows maximum daily temperature, the green line shows the heat index, and the bars indicate number of deaths for the day.

FIGURE 6.9 Visuals that show cause and effect. Visuals can provide powerful evidence when you are writing about causes and effects. Although graphs like this one may seem self-explanatory, you still must analyze and interpret them for your readers.

experienced by a typical person) around 120, high humidity, and little evening cooling. The heat wave was not the most extreme weather system in the city's history, but it proved to be Chicago's most deadly environmental event. During the week of the most severe weather, 485 city residents, many of whom were old, alone, and impoverished, died of causes that medical examiners attributed to the heat. Several hundred decedents were never autopsied, though, and after the event the Chicago Department of Public Health discovered that 739 Chicagoans in excess of the norm had perished while thousands more had been hospitalized for heat-related problems.

—ERIC KLINENBERG, "Heat Wave of 1995"

6c Write focused, clearly organized paragraphs.

Paragraphs break the text into blocks for your readers, allowing them to see how your essay builds step by step and establishing a rhythm for their reading. Introductory and concluding paragraphs have special functions, but all paragraphs should have a single, sharp focus and a clear organization. (Paragraphs on the Web tend to be short, with links at the end so readers do not navigate away.)

1. Focusing on one main point or example

In a strong paragraph, the sentences form a unit that explores one main point or elaborates on one main example. When you are drafting, start a new paragraph when you introduce a new reason in support of your thesis, a new step in a process, or a new element in an analysis. New paragraphs also signal shifts in time and place, changing speakers in dialogue, contrasts with earlier material, and changes in level of emphasis. As you draft, bear in mind that each paragraph develops a main point or example.

In the following example, the paragraph focuses on a theory that the writer will refer to later in the essay. The main idea is highlighted:

> Current thinking on the topic of loss and mourning rests on foundations constructed by the British psychiatrist John Bowlby. Using examples from animal and human behavior, Bowlby (1977) posited "attachment theory" as a means of understanding the powerful bonds between humans and the disruption that comes when the bonds are jeopardized or destroyed. The bonds are formed because of a need for security and safety, are developed early in life, are long enduring, and are directed toward a few special individuals. In normal maturation, the child becomes ever more independent, moving away from the figure of attachment, and returning periodically for safety and security. If the bonds are threatened, the individual will try to restore them through crying, clinging, or other types of coercion; if they are destroyed, withdrawal, apathy, and despair will follow.

> The main idea is introduced in the highlighted sentences.

> Details of attachment theory are developed in the rest of the paragraph.

—JONATHAN FAST, "After Columbine:
How People Mourn Sudden Death"

2. Signaling the main idea of your paragraph with a topic sentence

A topic sentence can be a helpful starting point as you draft a paragraph. In the following paragraph, the topic sentence (highlighted) provides the writer with a launching point for a series of details:

> The excavation also revealed dramatic evidence for the commemorative rituals that took place after the burial. Four cattle had been decapitated and their skulls symbolically placed in a ditch enclosing the burial pit. In the soil above the skulls archaeologists found the butchered bones of at least 250 slaughtered cattle, evidence for a huge ceremonial feast. Clearly this

> The topic sentence announces that the paragraph will focus on a certain kind of evidence.

was an expensive way to commemorate a leader. Indeed, the huge quantity of meat suggests that the entire tribe may have gathered at the grave to take part in a ritual feast. Perhaps this was one way the bonds between scattered communities were strengthened.

—DAMIAN ROBINSON, "Riding into the Afterlife"

Sometimes the sentences in a paragraph will lead to a unifying conclusion (highlighted), as in this example:

The nation's community colleges are receiving much deserved attention, from the Oval Office to the family living room. Community colleges in Indiana and Illinois offer great value: high quality at an affordable price. As the academic year moves forward and high school students complete college applications, I recommend that those who intend to continue their education close to home take a look at pathways that lead from the community college to university graduation.

—ELAINE MAIMON, "Students Must Focus on Degree Completion"

If a topic sentence would simply state the obvious, it can be omitted. In the following example, it is not necessary to state that the paragraph is about Igor Stravinsky's preprofessional life:

Stravinsky was born in Russia, near St. Petersburg, grew up in a musical atmosphere, and studied with Nikolai Rimsky-Korsakov. He had his first important opportunity in 1909, when the great impresario Sergei Diaghilev heard his music.

—ROGER KAMIEN, *Music: An Appreciation*

3. Writing paragraphs that have a clear organization

The sentences in your final draft should be clearly related to one another. As you draft, make connections among your ideas and information to move your writing forward. The strategies covered in 6b are suggestions for developing your ideas. Another way to make your ideas work together is to use one of the common organizational schemes for paragraphs, which can also be used for essays as a whole. *(For advice on using repetition, pronouns, and transitions to relate sentences to one another, see Chapter 7, pp. 78–82.)*

- **Chronological organization:** The sentences in a paragraph with a chronological organization describe a series of events, steps, or observations as they occur in time: this happened, then that, and so on.

- **Spatial organization:** The sentences in a paragraph with a spatial organization present details as they appear to a viewer: from top to bottom, outside to inside, east to west, and so on.

- **General-to-specific organization:** As we have seen, paragraphs often start with a general topic sentence that states the main idea and then proceed with specifics that elaborate on that idea. The general topic sentence can include a question that the paragraph then answers or a problem that the paragraph goes on to solve.

- **Specific-to-general organization:** The general topic sentence can come at the end of the paragraph, with the specific details leading up to that general conclusion *(see the paragraph from "Students Must Focus on Degree Completion," p. 70).* This organization is especially effective when you are preparing readers for a revelation.

4. Drafting introductions and conclusions

As you begin your first draft, you may want to skip the introduction and focus on the body of your text. Later you can go back and sketch out the main ideas for your introduction.

To get readers' attention, show why the topic matters. The opening of your text should encourage readers to share your view of its importance. Except for essay exams, it's best not to refer directly to the assignment or to your intentions ("In this paper I will . . ."). Avoid vague general statements ("Jane Austen is a famous author"), and try instead to find a way to arouse readers' interest. Here are some opening strategies:

- Tell a brief story related to the issue your thesis raises.

- Begin with a relevant, attention-getting quotation.

- Begin with a paraphrase of a commonly held view that you immediately question.

- State a working hypothesis.

- Define a key term, but avoid the tired opener that begins, "According to the dictionary . . . ."

- Pose an important question.

For informative reports, arguments, and essays, your opening paragraph or paragraphs will include a thesis statement, usually at the beginning but sometimes near the end of the introduction. If your purpose is interpretive, however, you may instead choose to build up to your thesis. For some types of writing, such as narratives, an explicitly stated thesis may not be needed if the main idea is clear without it.

Just as the opening makes a first impression and motivates readers to continue reading, the closing makes a final impression and motivates readers to think further. While you should not merely repeat the main idea that you introduced at the beginning of the text, you should also avoid overgeneralizing or introducing a completely new topic. Your conclusion should remind readers of your text's significance and satisfy those who might be asking, "So what?" or "What's at stake?" Here are some strategies for concluding:

- Refer to the story or quotation you used in your introduction.
- Answer the question you posed in your introduction.
- Summarize your main point.
- Call for some action on your readers' part.
- Present a powerful image or forceful example.
- Suggest implications for the future.

6d Integrate visuals and multimodal elements effectively.

If you decide to use a table, chart, diagram, photograph, or video or audio file, keep this general advice in mind:

- **Number tables and other figures** consecutively throughout your text: Table 1, Table 2, and so on. Do not abbreviate *Table. Figure* may be abbreviated as *Fig.*

- **Refer to the visual element in your text** before it appears, placing the visual as close as possible to the explanation of the reason for including it. If your project contains complex tables or many other visuals, you may want to group them in an appendix. Always refer to a visual by its label—for example, "See Fig. 1."

- **Give each visual a title and caption** that explains what the visual shows. A visual with its caption should be clear without the discussion in the text, and the discussion of the visual in the text should be clear without the visual itself.

- **Include explanatory notes below the visuals.** If you want to explain a specific element within the visual, use a superscript letter (not a number) both after the specific element and before the note. The explanation should appear directly beneath the graphic, not at the foot of the page or at the end of your paper.

- **Credit sources for visuals and multimodal elements.** You must credit all visuals and multimodal elements that you have imported from other sources. Unless you have specific guidelines to follow, you can use the word *Source,* followed by a colon and complete documentation of the source, including the author, title, publication information, and page number if applicable.

> *Note:* The Modern Language Association (MLA) and the American Psychological Association (APA) provide guidelines for figure captions and crediting sources of visuals that differ from the preceding guidelines. *(See Chapter 29: MLA Style: Paper Format, pp. 329–30, and Chapter 33: APA Style: Paper Format, pp. 376–77.)*

CHAPTER 7

Revising and Editing

To revise means to see something again. In the **revising** stage of the writing process, you review the entire composition, adding, deleting, and moving text as necessary. After you are satisfied with the substance of your draft, **editing** begins. When you edit, you both refine sentences so that you say what you want to say as effectively as possible and correct grammatical and mechanical errors.

This chapter focuses on revising. It also introduces the concepts and principles of editing, which are covered in greater detail in Tabs 9–12.

7a   Get comments from readers.

Asking actual readers to comment on your draft is the best way to get fresh perspectives. (Most professors encourage peer review, but it is wise to check.) Always acknowledge this help, in an endnote, a cover note, a preface, or an acknowledgments page.

1. Using peer review

Peer review involves reading and critiquing your classmates' work while they review yours. You can send your draft to your peer reviewers electronically (also print out a copy for yourself) or exchange drafts in person.

Help your readers help you by giving them information and asking them specific questions. When you share a draft with readers, provide answers to the following questions:

- **What is the assignment?** Readers need to understand the context for your project—especially your intended purpose and audience.

- **How close are you to being finished?** Your answer lets readers know where you are in the writing process and how best to assist you in taking the next step.

┌─NAVIGATING THROUGH COLLEGE AND BEYOND

Re-Visioning Your Work

Revising is a process of "re-visioning"—of looking at your work through the eyes of your audience. Here are some tips for getting a fresh perspective:

- **Get feedback from other readers.** Candid, respectful feedback can help you discover strengths and weaknesses.
- **Let your draft cool.** Try to schedule a break between drafting and revising. A good night's sleep, a movie break, or some physical exercise will help you view your draft as a reader rather than as a writer.
- **Read your draft aloud.** Some find that reading aloud helps them "hear" their words the way their audience will.
- **Use revising and editing checklists.** The checklists in this chapter will assist you in evaluating your work systematically. Even better, create your own editing checklist based on the changes you make to final drafts.

- **What steps do you plan to take to complete the project?** If readers know your plans, they can either question the direction you are taking or give you more specific help, such as the titles of additional sources you might consult.
- **What kind of feedback do you need?** Do you want readers to summarize your main points so you can determine if you have communicated them clearly? Do you want a response to the logic of your argument or the development of your thesis?

Reading other writers' drafts will help you view your own work more objectively, and comments from readers will help you see your own writing as others see it. As you gain more objectivity, you will become more adept at revising your work. In addition, the approaches that you see your classmates taking to the assignment will give you ideas for new directions in your own writing.

2. Responding to readers

While you should consider your readers' suggestions, you are under no obligation to do what they say. Sometimes you will receive contradictory advice: one reader may like a particular sentence that a second reader suggests you eliminate. Is there common ground? Yes. Both readers stopped at that sentence. Ask yourself why—and whether you want readers to pause there.

┌─ CHECKLIST   Guidelines for Giving and Receiving Feedback

Giving Feedback

☐ **Begin with strengths.** Let writers know what you think works well so that they can build on those parts and try similar approaches again.

☐ **Be specific.** Give examples to back up your general reactions.

☐ **Be constructive.** Instead of saying that an example is a bad choice, explain that you did not understand how the example was connected to the main point, and suggest a way to clarify the connection.

☐ **Ask questions.** Jot down any questions that occur to you while reading. Ask for clarification, or note an objection that readers of the final version might make.

(For help giving feedback, see Revising Your Draft for Content and Organization on p. 77.)

Receiving Feedback

☐ **Resist being defensive.** Keep in mind that readers are discussing your draft, not you, and their feedback offers a way for you to see your writing from another angle. Be respectful of their time and effort. Remember that you, not your readers, are in charge of decisions about your work.

☐ **Ask for more feedback if you need it.** Some readers may be hesitant to share all of their reactions, and you may need to do some coaxing.

7b   Use electronic tools for revising.

Even though word-processing programs can make a first draft look finished, it is still a first draft. Check below the surface for problems in content, structure, and style. Move paragraphs around, add details, and delete irrelevant sentences. You may find it easier to revise if you have a printed copy so that you can see the composition as a whole.

To work efficiently, become familiar with the revising and editing tools in your word-processing program:

- **Comments:** Many word-processing programs have a "Comments" feature allowing you to add notes to sections of text. This feature is useful for giving feedback on someone else's draft. Some writers also use it to make notes to themselves.

- **Track changes:** The Track Changes feature allows you to revise and edit a piece of writing while also maintaining the original text. Usually, marginal notes or strike-through marks show what you have deleted or replaced. Because you can still see the original text, you can judge whether a change has improved the draft. If you change your mind, you can restore the deleted text. When collaborating with another writer, save the Track Changes version as a separate file.

You can see the Track Changes and Comments features in the second draft of Diane Chen's analysis on pages 90–92. In addition, many Web-based tools such as *Google Docs* enable work to be shared, edited, and revised online.

7c Focus on the writing situation (topic, purpose, audience, genre, and medium).

As you revise your draft within your selected rhetorical situation, think about your purpose, rhetorical stance, and audience. Is your primary purpose to inform, to interpret, to analyze, or to argue? *(For more on purpose, see Tab 2: Writing and Designing Texts, p. 41.)*

Clarity about your rhetorical situation and writing purpose is especially important when an assignment calls for interpretation, which differs significantly from a description. With this principle in mind, Diane Chen read over her first draft meant to interpret Lange's *Migrant Mother*. Here is a portion of that draft:

FIRST DRAFT

> In addition to the mother's expression, her body language is also important to note. Lange's subject leans an elbow on her lap with a hand touching her face, a gesture of concern. Through her subject's physical position, Lange depicts the poverty in which the mother lives and seems to be reinforcing an important point about the mother's social position. The family's dirty and ragged clothes are proof of the hardships they face and the limited possibilities for escaping those conditions. By capturing this moment in a photograph, Lange shows us important truths about the social implications of poverty.

Keeping the writing situation in mind, Chen realized that she needed to discuss the significance of her observations—to interpret and analyze the details for readers who would see a copy of the photograph incorporated into her online text. Within the framework of a review, she revised to demonstrate how the formal elements of the photograph function.

REVISION

> The mother's posture is also telling of Lange's compassion for her subject. She leans an elbow on her lap with a hand touching her face, a gesture of concern. Through her subject's physical position, Lange seems to be reinforcing an important point about the mother's social position: the same hand that labors in the field also cares for

---

CHECKLIST   Revising Your Draft for Content and Organization

- ☐ **Purpose:** What is the purpose of the text? If it is not clear, what changes would make it apparent?
- ☐ **Thesis:** What is the thesis? Is it clear and specific? What revisions would make it clearer?
- ☐ **Audience:** How does the approach—including evidence and tone— appeal to the intended readers?
- ☐ **Structure:** How does the order of the key points support the thesis? Would another order be more effective? How might overly long or short sections be revised?
- ☐ **Paragraphs:** How might the development, unity, and coherence of each paragraph be improved?
- ☐ **Visuals:** Do visuals communicate the intended meaning clearly, without unnecessary clutter? How might they be improved?

---

and comforts a family. The family's dirty and ragged clothes are proof of the hardships they face and the limited possibilities for escaping those conditions. By capturing this moment in a photograph, Lange communicates important truths about the social implications of poverty and implores her audience to empathize.

7d   Make sure you have a strong thesis.

Remember that a thesis makes an assertion about a topic. It links the *what* and the *why*. Is your thesis evident on the first page of your draft? Before readers get very far along, they expect an answer to the question "What is the point of all this?" If you do not find the point on the first page, its absence is a signal to revise, unless you are deliberately waiting until the end to present your thesis. *(For more on strong theses, see Chapter 5, pp. 48–51.)*

Many writers start with a working thesis, which often evolves into a more specific, complex assertion as they develop their ideas. One of the key challenges of revising is to compose a clear statement of this revised thesis. When she drafted a paper on Germany's economic prospects, Jennifer Koehler stated her working thesis as follows:

WORKING THESIS

Germany is experiencing a great deal of change.

During the revision process, Koehler realized that her working thesis was weak. A weak thesis is predictable: readers read it, agree, and that's that. A strong thesis, on the other hand, stimulates thoughtful inquiry. Koehler's revised thesis provokes questions:

> **REVISED THESIS**
>
> With proper follow-through, Germany can become one of the world's primary sources of direct investment and maintain its status as one of the world's preeminent exporters.

Sometimes writers find that their ideas change altogether, and the working thesis needs to be completely revised.

Your thesis should evolve throughout the draft. Readers need to see a statement of the main idea on the first page, but they also expect a more complex general statement near the end. After presenting evidence to support her revised thesis, Koehler concludes by stating her thesis as a more complex generalization:

> If the government efforts continue, the economy will strengthen over the next decade, and Germany will reinforce its position as an integral nation in the global economy.

7e   Review the structure of your draft.

Does the draft have a beginning, a middle, and an end, with bridges between those parts? When you revise, you can refine and even change this structure so that it supports what you want to say more effectively.

One way to review your structure is by outlining your first draft. *(For help with outlining, see Chapter 5, pp. 51–54.)* Try listing the key points of the draft in sentence form; whenever possible, use sentences that actually appear in the draft. Ask yourself whether the key points are arranged effectively or if another arrangement would work better. The following structures are typical ways of organizing texts:

- **Informative:** Presents the key points of a topic.
- **Exploratory:** Begins with a question or problem and works step-by-step to discover an answer or a solution.
- **Argumentative:** Presents a set of linked reasons plus supporting evidence.
- **Analytic:** Shows how the parts come together to form a coherent whole and makes connections.

7f   Revise for paragraph development, paragraph unity, and coherence.

As you revise, examine each paragraph, asking yourself what role it plays—or should play—in the work as a whole. Keeping this role in mind, check the paragraph for development and unity. You should also read each paragraph for coherence—and consider whether all of the paragraphs together contribute to the work as a whole. Does the length of sections reflect their relative importance? *(For more on paragraphs, see Chapter 6: Drafting Text and Visuals, pp. 68–72.)*

1. Paragraph development

Paragraphs in academic texts are usually about a hundred words long. Consider dividing any that exceed two hundred words or that are especially dense, and develop or combine paragraphs that seem very short. Would more information make the point clearer? Perhaps a term should be defined. Do generalizations need to be supported with examples? Make stylistic choices about paragraph length. In most cases, similar length sets a rhythm for the reader, although you may sometimes use a short paragraph for emphasis.

Note how this writer developed one of her draft paragraphs, adding details and examples to make her argument more effective:

FIRST DRAFT

A 1913 advertisement for Shredded Wheat illustrates Kellner's claim that advertisements sell self-images. The ad suggests that serving Shredded Wheat will give women the same sense of accomplishment as gaining the right to vote.

REVISION

According to Kellner, "advertising is as concerned with selling lifestyles and socially desirable identities . . . as with selling the products themselves" (193). A 1913 ad for Shredded Wheat shows how the selling of self-images works. At first glance, this ad seems to be promoting the women's suffrage movement. In big, bold letters, "Votes for Women" is emblazoned across the top of the ad. But a closer look reveals that the ad is for Shredded Wheat cereal. Holding a piece of the cereal in her hand, a woman stands behind a large bowlful of Shredded Wheat biscuits that is made to look like a voting box. The text claims that "every biscuit is a vote for health, happiness, and domestic freedom." Like the rest of the advertisement, this claim suggests that serving Shredded Wheat will give women the same sense of accomplishment as gaining the right to vote.

—HOLLY MUSETTI, "Targeting Women," student text

2. Paragraph unity

A unified paragraph has a single, clear focus. To check for **unity,** identify the paragraph's topic sentence *(see pp. 69–70),* and make sure everything in the paragraph is clearly and closely related to it. Ideas unrelated to the topic sentence should be deleted or developed into separate paragraphs. Another option is to revise the topic sentence.

Compare the first draft of the following paragraph with its revision, and note how the addition of a topic sentence (in bold in the revision) makes the paragraph more clearly focused and therefore easier for the writer to revise further. Note also that the writer deleted the underlined ideas because they did not directly relate to the paragraph's main point:

FIRST DRAFT

Adelphi University, which has a main campus on Long Island and another in Manhattan, felt the effects of Hurricane Sandy. But perhaps more memorable than the storm's effects were the students' responses. Shortly after the storm, in the course of a single day, university students collected donations, including roughly $1,000 in cash, wrote thank-you cards for first responders, and participated in a blood drive (Peterkin, 2012). <u>Volunteer work continued in many different ways.</u> "Students on Facebook are posting things like 'It's a humbling experience,' and it's positive to see that reaction," said Michael J. Berthel, Senior Assistant Director of Adelphi's Center for Student Involvement (as cited in Peterkin, 2012). <u>This is but one example of student engagement among countless others.</u> There is little doubt that the current generation is doing its part to make the world a better place, in a wide variety of ways (see Figure 1).

REVISION

Historically, college students planning to enter service professions such as nursing or social work have volunteered their time as part of their professional development; however, today all students can make especially valuable contributions in disastrous circumstances, such as the aftermath of Hurricane Sandy. Adelphi University, which has a main campus on Long Island and another in Manhattan, felt the effects of Sandy. But perhaps more memorable than the storm's effects were the students' responses. Shortly after the storm, in a single day, university students collected donations, including roughly $1,000 in cash, wrote thank you cards for first responders, and participated in a blood drive (Peterkin, 2012). Volunteer work continued in many different ways. "Students on Facebook are posting things like 'It's a humbling experience,' and it's positive to see that reaction," said Michael J. Berthel, Senior Assistant Director of Adelphi's Center for Student Involvement (as cited in Peterkin, 2012). This is but one example of student engagement among countless others. There is little doubt that the current generation is doing its part to make the world a better place, in a wide variety of ways (see Figure 1).

—PEGGY GIGLIO, "The New Volunteer: Civic Engagement through Social Media"

3. Coherence

A coherent paragraph flows smoothly, with an organization that is easy to follow and each sentence clearly related to the next. *(See Chapter 6, pp. 58–68, for tips on how to develop well-organized paragraphs.)* You can improve coherence both within and among the paragraphs in your draft by using repetition, pronouns, parallel structure, synonyms, and transitions:

- Repeat key words to emphasize the main idea and provide transition:

  A photograph displays a unique *moment.* To capture that *moment . . .*

- Use pronouns and antecedents to form connections between sentences and avoid unnecessary repetition. In the following example, *it* refers to *Germany* and connects the two sentences:

  Germany imports raw materials, energy sources, and food products. *It* exports a wide range of industrial products, including automobiles, aircraft, and machine tools.

- Repeat sentence structures to emphasize connections:

  Because the former West Germany lived through a generation of prosperity, its people developed high expectations of material comfort. *Because the former East Germany* lived through a generation of deprivation, its people developed disdain for material values.

- Use **synonyms**—words that are close in meaning to words or phrases that have preceded them:

  In the world of photography, critics *argue* for either a scientific or an artistic approach. This *controversy . . .*

- Use transitional words and phrases. One-word transitions and **transitional expressions** link one idea with another, helping readers see the relationship between them. Compare the following two paragraphs, the first version without transitions and the second with transitions (in bold type):

FIRST DRAFT

　　As the credibility of online sources has been called into question, the value of subject experts has increased. Amateur journalists do not guarantee fact checking and do not always have professional experience relevant to the topics they cover. Professional journalist Tony Rogers points out that "most bloggers don't produce news stories on their own. Bloggers comment on news stories already out there— stories produced by journalists." While this is often true, bloggers can also break, or at least advance, a news story. In their report

"Post-Industrial Journalism: Adapting to the Present," C. W. Anderson, Emily Bell, and Shirky contend that the bike-racing blog *NYVelocity* covered the Lance Armstrong performance enhancement story better than the "professional" press (20). Today an event can become news before members of the press begin to cover it, and in fact they may cover it only after their audience has become aware of it another way (Shirky, *Here Comes Everybody* 64–65).

REVISION

As the credibility of online sources has been called into question, the value of subject experts has increased. Amateur journalists do not guarantee fact checking and do not always have professional experience relevant to the topics they cover. Professional journalist Tony Rogers points out that "most bloggers don't produce news stories on their own. **Instead** they comment on news stories already out there—stories produced by journalists." While this is often true, bloggers can also break, or at least advance, a news story. **For example,** in their report "Post-Industrial Journalism: Adapting to the Present," C. W. Anderson, Emily Bell, and Shirky contend that the bike-racing blog *NYVelocity* covered the Lance Armstrong performance enhancement story better than the "professional" press (20). **Furthermore,** today an event can become news before members of the press begin to cover it, and in fact they may cover it only after their audience has become aware of it another way (Shirky, *Here Comes Everybody* 64–65).

—KRIS WASHINGTON, "Breaking News: Blogging's Impact on Traditional and New Media"

- Use **transitional sentences,** which refer to the previous paragraph and move your essay on to the next point, to show how paragraphs in an essay are related to one another:

    The mother in this photograph, Florence Owens Thompson, was a migrant worker in Nipomo, California, in 1936, whom Lange encountered sitting outside her tent in a migrant camp. Lange took several exposures of Thompson, moving closer to her subject with each shot. This technique helped her to capture an image that communicated to viewers what poverty looked like at a human level. But the power of Lange's image is not confined to history; even today, "The Migrant Mother" remains an iconic reminder of the struggles of the poor.

    The photograph's composition reveals Lange's compassion for her subject. Although four figures make up the photograph, the mother . . .

- Avoid confusing shifts between person and number of verbs and pronouns, as well as verb tenses. *(See Tab 9: Editing for Clarity, Chapter 41: Confusing Shifts, pp. 447–50.)*

TRANSITIONAL EXPRESSIONS

- **To show relationships in space:** above, adjacent to, against, alongside, around, at a distance from, at the . . . , below, beside, beyond, encircling, far off, forward, from the . . . , in front of, in the rear, inside, near the end, nearby, next to, on, over, surrounding, there, through the . . . , to the left, up front

- **To show relationships in time:** afterward, at last, before, earlier, first, former, formerly, immediately, in the first place, in the meantime, in the next place, in the last place, later on, meanwhile, next, now, often, once, previously, second, simultaneously, sometime later, subsequently, suddenly, then, third, today, tomorrow, until now, when, years ago, yesterday

- **To show addition or to compare:** again, also, and, and then, besides, further, furthermore, in addition, last, likewise, moreover, next, too

- **To give examples that intensify points:** after all, as an example, certainly, clearly, for example, for instance, indeed, in fact, in truth, it is true, of course, specifically, that is

- **To show similarities:** alike, in the same way, like, likewise, resembling, similarly

- **To show contrasts:** after all, although, but, conversely, differ(s) from, difference, different, dissimilar, even though, granted, however, in contrast, in spite of, nevertheless, notwithstanding, on the contrary, on the other hand, otherwise, still, though, unlike, while this may be true, yet

- **To indicate cause and effect:** accordingly, as a result, because, consequently, hence, since, then, therefore, thus

- **To conclude or summarize:** finally, in brief, in conclusion, in other words, in short, in summary, that is, to summarize

---

7g   Revise visuals and multimodal elements.

If you have used visuals to display data in your paper, return to them during the revision stage to eliminate what scholar Edward Tufte calls **chartjunk,** or distracting visual elements. The checklist on page 84 contains Tufte's suggestions for editing visuals so that your readers will focus on your data rather than your "data containers." Likewise, review multimodal elements—like presentation slides, audio files, and video—to be sure that you have included only what you need; to eliminate distractions, like unnecessary animations on presentation slides; and to provide sufficient context for the viewer.

---CHECKLIST Revising Visuals

☐ **Are grid lines needed in tables?** Eliminate grid lines or, if the lines are needed for clarity, lighten them. Tables should not look like nets with every number enclosed. Vertical rules are needed only when space is extremely tight between columns.

☐ **Are there any unnecessary 3D renderings?** Cubes and shadows can distort the information in a visual. For most charts, including pie charts, a flat image makes it easier for readers to compare parts.

☐ **Are data labeled clearly,** avoiding abbreviations and legends if possible? Does each visual have an informative title?

☐ **Do bright colors focus attention on the key data?** For example, if you are including a map, use muted colors over large areas, and save strong colors for areas you want to emphasize.

☐ **Do pictures distract from the visual's purpose?** Clip art and other decorative elements seldom make data more interesting or substantial.

☐ **Are data distorted?** In the first graph in Figure 7.1 on page 85, each month gets its own point, except for January, February, March, and April, creating a misleading impression of hurricane activity by month. The revision corrects this problem.

7h   Edit sentences.

Tabs 9 and 10 of this handbook address the many specific questions writers have when they are editing for clarity, word choice, and grammatical conventions.

1. Editing for clarity

As you edit, concentrate on sentence style, aiming for clearly focused and interestingly varied writing. A series of short, choppy sentences is like a bumpy ride: consider combining them. An unbroken stream of long, complicated sentences can put readers to sleep. For general audiences, you should strive to vary sentence openings and structure. In the example that follows, notice how the revised version connects ideas for readers and, consequently, is easier to read:

DRAFT

My father was a zealous fisherman. He took his fishing rod on every family outing. He often spent the whole outing staring at the water, waiting for a nibble. He went to the kitchen as soon as he got home. He usually cleaned and cooked the fish the same day he caught them.

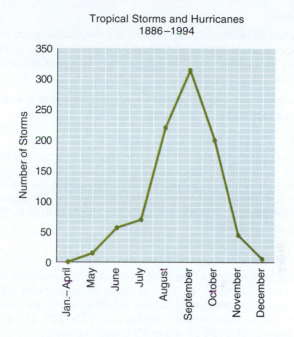

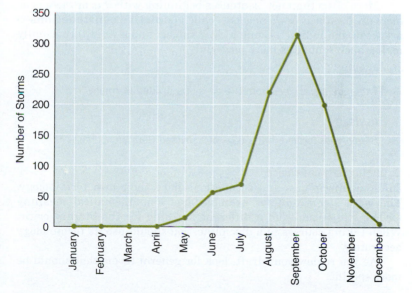

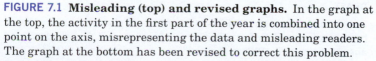

FIGURE 7.1 Misleading (top) and revised graphs. In the graph at the top, the activity in the first part of the year is combined into one point on the axis, misrepresenting the data and misleading readers. The graph at the bottom has been revised to correct this problem.

REVISED

A zealous fisherman, my father took his fishing rod on every family outing. He would often spend the whole afternoon by the shore, waiting for a nibble, and then hurry straight to the kitchen to clean and cook his catch.

You should also condense and focus sentences that are wordy and lack a clear subject and vivid verb:

DRAFT

Although both vertebral and wrist fractures cause deformity and impair movement, hip fractures, which are one of the most devastating consequences of osteoporosis, significantly increase the risk of death, since 12%–30% of patients with a hip fracture die within one year after the fracture, while the mortality rate climbs to 40% for the first two years postfracture.

REVISED

Hip fractures are one of the most devastating consequences of osteoporosis. Although vertebral and wrist fractures cause deformity and impair movement, hip fractures significantly increase the risk of death. Within one year after a hip fracture, 12%–20% of the injured die. The mortality rate climbs to 40% after two years.

More often than not, sentences beginning with *it is* or *there is* or *there are* (or *it was* or *there was*)—called **expletive constructions**—are weak and indirect. Using a clear subject and a vivid verb usually makes such sentences more powerful:

DRAFT

There are stereotypes from the days of a divided Germany.

REVISED

Stereotypes formed in the days of a divided Germany persist.

2. Editing for word choice

Different disciplines and occupations have their own terminology. The word *significant,* for example, has a mathematical meaning for the statistician and a different meaning for the literary critic. When taking courses in a discipline, you should use its terminology accurately.

As you review your draft, look for general terms that should be more specific:

DRAFT

Foreign direct investment (FDI) in Germany will probably remain low because of several *factors.* [Factors *is a general word. To get specific, answer the question* "What *factors?*"]

─CHECKLIST   Editing for Style and Grammar

To create a personalized checklist, fill in the boxes next to your trouble spots, as determined by personal lists you have kept in the past, your instructor's comments, and diagnostic tests.

1. **Clarity** *(Tab 9, Chapters 38–46, pp. 440–65):* Does every sentence communicate the intended meaning in a clear, direct style? Does the text contain any of the following common causes of unclear sentences? Note sections that could be clarified.
   ☐ Wordiness
   ☐ Missing words
   ☐ Mixed constructions
   ☐ Confusing shifts
   ☐ Faulty parallelism
   ☐ Misplaced and dangling modifiers
   ☐ Problem with coordination and subordination
   ☐ Other: _____

2. **Word choice** *(Tab 9, Chapters 47–50, pp. 465–84):* How could the choice of words be more precise, especially given your rhetorical situation? Does the text include slang, biased language, clichés, or other inappropriate usages? Does it misuse any commonly confused words (for example, *advice* vs. *advise*) or use any nonstandard expressions (for example, *could of*)? Are any words at odds with your authorial stance?

3. **Grammatical conventions** *(Tab 10, pp. 487–531):* Does the draft contain any common errors that may confuse or distract readers?
   ☐ Sentence fragments
   ☐ Comma splices
   ☐ Run-on sentences
   ☐ Subject–verb agreement problems
   ☐ Incorrect verb forms
   ☐ Inconsistent verb tenses
   ☐ Pronoun–antecedent agreement problems
   ☐ Incorrect pronoun forms
   ☐ Problems with use of adjectives or adverbs
   ☐ Other: _____

If you are in the process of developing fluency in English, consult Tab 12: Basic Grammar Review for more editing advice.

REVISED

Foreign direct investment (FDI) in Germany will probably remain low because of *high labor costs, high taxation, and government regulation.*

Your search for more specific words can lead you to a dictionary and thesaurus. *(For more on using a dictionary and a thesaurus, see Chapter 49.)*

3. Editing for grammatical conventions

Sometimes, writers will construct a sentence or choose a word form that violates the rules of standard written English:

DRAFT

Photographs of illegal immigrants being captured by the U.S. border patrol, of emotional immigrants on the plane to their new country, and of villagers fleeing rebel gangs. [*This is a sentence fragment because it lacks a verb and omits the writer's point about these images.*]

EDITED SENTENCE

Photographs of illegal immigrants being captured by the U.S. border patrol, of emotional immigrants on the plane to their new country, and of villagers fleeing rebel gangs exemplify the range of migration stories.

A list of common abbreviations and symbols used to note errors in a manuscript can be found at the end of this text. Your instructor and other readers may use these.

7i   Proofread carefully.

Once you have revised your draft at the essay, paragraph, and sentence levels, it is time to give it one last check to make sure that it is free of typos and other mechanical errors.

Even if you are submitting an electronic version of your project, you may still prefer to proofread a printed version. Placing a ruler

─the EVOLVING SITUATION

You Know More Than Grammar and Spell Checkers!

Grammar and spell checkers can help you spot some errors, but they miss many others and may even flag a correct sentence. Consider the following example:

Thee neighbors puts there cats' outsider.

Neither a spelling nor grammar checker detected the five errors in the sentence. (Correct version: *The neighbors put their cats outside.*)

As long as you are aware of the limitations of these checkers, you can use them as you edit your manuscript. Be sure, however, to review your writing carefully yourself.

CHECKLIST Proofreading

☐ Have you included your name, the date, your professor's name, and the paper title? *(See Tabs 6–8 for the formats to use for MLA, APA, Chicago, or CSE style.)*

☐ Are all words spelled correctly? Be sure to check the spelling of titles and headings. *(See Chapter 68, pp. 582–86.)*

☐ Have you used the words you intended, or have you substituted words that sound like the ones you want but have a different spelling and meaning, such as *too* for *to*, *their* for *there*, or *it's* for *its*? *(See Chapter 50, pp. 475–84.)*

☐ Are all proper names capitalized? Have you capitalized titles of works correctly and either italicized them or put them in quotation marks as required? *(See Chapter 63, pp. 568–72, and Chapter 66, pp. 577–79.)*

☐ Have you punctuated your sentences correctly? *(See Tab 12.)*

☐ Are sources cited correctly? Is the works-cited or references list in the correct format? *(See Tabs 6–8.)*

☐ Have you checked anything you changed—for example, quotations and tables—against the original?

---

under each line can make it easier to focus. You can also start at the end and proofread your way backward to the beginning, sentence by sentence. Some students read their drafts aloud. Do not read for content but for form and correctness.

7j   Use campus, Internet, and community resources.

You can call on a number of resources outside the classroom for feedback on your paper.

1. Using the campus writing center

With your instructor's permission, you might ask tutors to read and comment on drafts of your work. They can also help you find and correct problems with grammar and punctuation.

2. Using online writing labs (OWLs)

Most OWLs offer information about writing, including lists of useful online resources that you can access anytime. (Always check with your instructor before accessing this help, and be sure to acknowledge the assistance.) OWLs with tutors can be useful in the following ways:

- You can submit a draft via e-mail for feedback. OWL tutors will return your work, often within forty-eight hours.

- You can post your draft in a public access space where you will receive feedback from more than just one or two readers.
- You can read others' drafts online and learn how they are handling writing issues.

You can learn more about what OWLs have to offer by checking out Purdue University's Online Writing Lab: <http://owl.english.purdue.edu>.

3. Working with experts and instructors

In addition to sharing your work with classmates, through e-mail, or in online environments, you can consult electronically with your instructor or other experts. Your instructor's comments on an early draft are especially valuable. Be sure to think long and hard about the issues your instructor raises and revise your work accordingly.

7k   Learn from one student's revisions.

In the second draft of Diane Chen's analysis of Dorothea Lange's photograph, you can see how she revised to tighten the focus of her descriptive paragraphs and edited to improve clarity, word choice, and grammar. The photograph Chen focuses on appears on p. 91.

Inspiring Empathy: Dorothea Lange's *Migrant Mother*

American photographer Dorothea Lange is ~~most known~~ perhaps best known for her work commissioned by the Farm Services Administration photographing the social and economic effects of the Great Depression. Her arresting portraits of displaced farmers, migrant families, and the unemployed ~~show us how they suffered in the~~ skillfully depict the dire consequences of the Depression for America's working classes. Artful though her photographs are, Lange's technique involved more than artistic skill. Lange considered herself primarily a photojournalist, whose goal was to encourage social action through her work. As a photojournalist who empathetically captured the struggles of her subjects on film, Lange was able to impart compassion to her audience and in turn inspire change.

One of Lange's most famous photographs, *Migrant Mother* (Fig. 1), is an example of ~~the way she showed her audience~~ her unique ability to document such struggles. ~~While~~ *Migrant Mother* is not simply a portrait of one mother's hardship, but is ~~it depicts~~ a raw depiction of the ~~harsh reality for many~~ plight of thousands of displaced families during the Depression. The mother in this photograph, Florence Owens Thompson, was a migrant worker in Nipomo, California, in 1936, whom Lange encountered sitting outside her tent in a migrant camp. Lange took several exposures of Thompson, moving closer to her subject with each shot. This technique helped her to capture an image that communicated to viewers what poverty looked like ~~for real people~~ at a human level. But the power of Lange's image ~~goes beyond the time of the Depression~~ is

Diane Chen 2/4/14 11:38 AM
Comment: Reorganize to first discuss Lange as artist, then expand to her role as photojournalist who inspired change.

not confined to history; even today, *Migrant Mother* remains an iconic reminder of the struggles of the poor.

The photograph's composition reveals Lange's compassion for her subject. Although ~~there are four people in~~ four figures make up the photograph, ~~we mostly see~~ the mother, whose face we see in full, is its main subject. ~~Her expression is worried.~~ She gazes outward, worriedly, as her three children huddle around her. The children frame her figure, two of them with faces hidden behind her shoulders, ~~hiding their shyness and despair~~ either out of shyness or shared distress, while the third rests across the mother's lap. The mother's expression ~~shows~~ conveys a desperate concern, ~~probably~~ presumably for her children's wellbeing. Her children cling to her, but ~~she is suffering her own despair.~~ her own faraway gaze gives evidence that she is too distracted by her worries to give them comfort. Lange ~~displays~~ emphasizes the mother's expression by making it the focal point of the photograph. In doing so, she encourages viewers to identify with the mother and even to wonder what thoughts pass through her mind.

~~In addition to the mother's expression, her body language is also important to note.~~ The mother's posture is also telling of Lange's compassion for her subject. She leans an elbow on her lap with a hand touching her face, a gesture of concern. Through her subject's physical position, Lange ~~depicts the poverty in which the mother lives~~ seems to be reinforcing an important point about the mother's social position: ~~her laborer's hand~~ the same hand that labors in the field also cares for and comforts a family. The family's dirty and ragged clothes are proof of the hardships they face and the limited possibilities for escaping those conditions. By capturing this moment in a photograph, Lange ~~shows us the truth~~ communicates important truths about the social implications of poverty and ~~asks~~ implores her audience to empathize.

As *Migrant Mother* powerfully demonstrates, Lange's work did a great deal to encourage awareness and understanding among her viewers, and in doing so, to inspire social change. Her ability to capture the realities of the Great Depression won Lange a Guggenheim Fellowship in 1941, and helped to solidify her as one of the most iconic photographers of the twentieth century. But perhaps Lange's greatest ~~achievement was~~ legacy is her impact on artists whose work has continued to open our eyes to social issues such as poverty and injustice with the goal of inspiring social change.

> Diane Chen 2/4/14
> 11:45 AM
>
> Comment: Revise wording to objectively analyze the image and how it might be interpreted by all viewers, rather than conveying how you interpret the image.

> Diane Chen 2/4/14
> 12:05 PM
>
> Comment: Add more about Lange's award to illustrate her credibility.

FIG. 1: Dorothea Lange,
Migrant Mother

----------------------[New page]----------------------

Work Cited

Lange, Dorothea. *Migrant Mother.* 1936. Prints and Photographs Div.,
Lib. of Cong. *Dorothea Lange: Photographer of the People.* Web. 5
Jan. 2014.

CHAPTER 8

Designing Academic Texts and Portfolios

A crucial writing task is to format your text so that readers can "see" your ideas clearly. In this chapter, we focus on designing responses to academic writing assignments. *(Multimodal presentations, posters, and Web sites can be found in Chapters 13 and 14 and brochures, newsletters, résumés, and other documents in Chapters 15 and 17.)*

In college and in your professional life, you may wish to showcase your writing and related work in a print or an online portfolio. This chapter offers guidelines for designing effective portfolios.

8a Consider audience and purpose.

As you plan your document, consider your purpose and the needs of your audience. If you are writing an informative project for a psychology class, your instructor—your primary audience—will probably prefer that you follow the guidelines provided by the American Psychological Association (APA). If you are writing a lab report for a biology or chemistry course, you will likely need to follow a well-established format and use the documentation style recommended by the Council of Science Editors (CSE) to cite sources. A history review might call for the use of the Chicago style. Interpretive analyses for language and literature courses usually use the style recommended by the Modern Language Association (MLA). *(For help with these documentation styles, see Tabs 6–8.)*

8b Use the tools available in your word-processing program.

Most word-processing programs provide a range of options for editing, sharing, and, especially, designing your document. For example, if you are using Microsoft Word 2013, you can access groups of commands by clicking on the various tabs at the top of the screen. Figure 8.1 shows the Home tab, which contains basic formatting and editing commands. You can choose different fonts and sizes; add bold, italic, or underlined type; insert numbered or bulleted lists; and so on. Other tabs allow you to add boxes and drawings, make comments, and change the page layout.

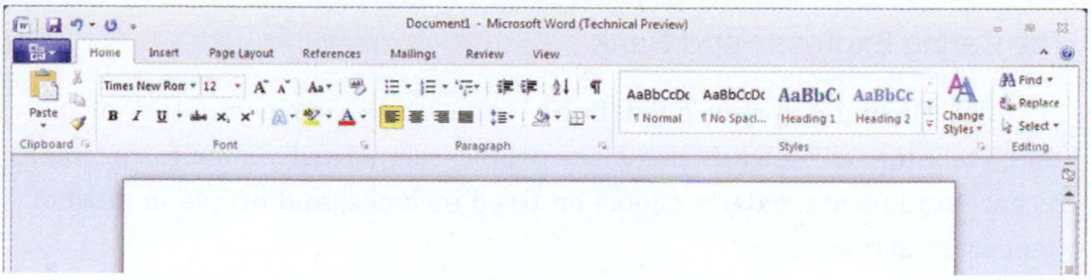

FIGURE 8.1 **The Home Tab in Microsoft Word 2013.**

Word-processing programs vary in their arrangement of options. Some include menus of commands on toolbars instead of on tabs. Take some time to learn the different formatting options available in your program.

8c   Think intentionally about design.

For any document that you create in print or online, whether for an academic course or for a purpose and an audience beyond college, apply the same basic design principles:

- Organize information for readers.
- Choose fonts and use lists and other graphic options to make your text readable and to emphasize key material.
- Format related design elements consistently.
- Include headings to organize long texts.
- Use design elements sparingly and intentionally.
- Meet the needs of all readers, including those with disabilities.

A sample page from a student's report on a local food bank, which includes information that she gathered while serving as a volunteer, illustrates these principles. The content in the sample shown in Figure 8.2 on page 94 is not presented effectively because the author deviated from these principles. By contrast, because of its design, the same material in Figure 8.3 on page 95 is clearer and easier for readers to understand.

1. Organizing information for readers

You can organize information visually and topically by grouping related items, using boxes, indents, headings, spacing, and lists. For example, in this book, headings help to group information for readers, and bulleted and numbered lists like the bulleted list in the Navigating through College and Beyond box on page 97 present related points. These variations in text appearance help readers scan material, locate important information, and dive in when

The Caring Express Food Bank

The Caring Express Food Bank serves a varied population of clients, including chronically homeless people, temporarily homeless people, recent immigrants, elderly people on fixed incomes, and people in need of temporary services.

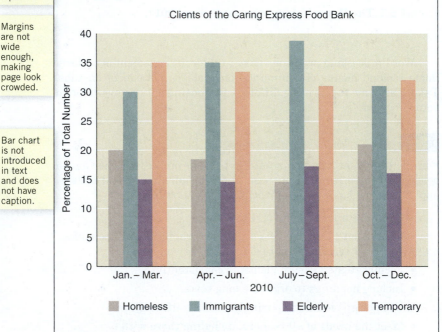

While the number of homeless, both temporary and permanent, that Caring Express assisted in 2010 decreased during the summer months, the number of immigrant workers increased. The percentage of elderly people and people in need of temporary services remained fairly stable throughout the year.

How Caring Express Helps Clients

When new clients come to Caring Express, a volunteer fills out a **form** with their **address** (if they have one), their **phone number,** their **income,** their **employment situation,** and the help they are receiving, if any, from the local department of human services. Clients who do not live in Maple Valley are referred to a food bank or outreach program in their area. Clients who qualify check off the food they need from a list, and then that food is packed and distributed to them.

Margin notes:

Emphasis wrong: title of report is not as prominent as heading within report.

Margins are not wide enough, making page look crowded.

Bar chart is not introduced in text and does not have caption.

Description of procedure is dense, hard to follow.

Bold type and a different typeface are used for no reason.

FIGURE 8.2 Example of a poorly designed report.

The Caring Express Food Bank

The Caring Express Food Bank serves a varied population of clients, including chronically homeless people, temporarily homeless people, recent immigrants, elderly people on fixed incomes, and people in need of temporary services. As Figure 1 shows, while the number of homeless, both temporary and permanent, that Caring Express assisted in 2010 decreased during the summer months, the number of immigrant workers increased. The percentage of elderly people and people in need of temporary services remained fairly stable throughout the year.

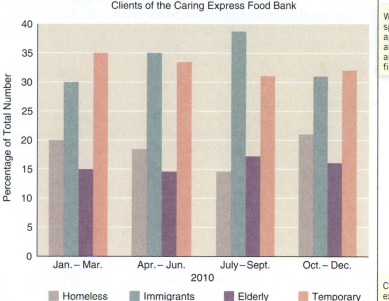

Figure 1. Percentage of clients in each group during 2010

How Caring Express Helps Clients

When new clients come to Caring Express, the volunteers follow this procedure:

1. The volunteer fills out a form with the client's address (if he or she has one), phone number, income, and employment situation.
2. Clients who do not live in Maple Valley are referred to a food bank or outreach program in their area.
3. Clients who qualify check off the food they need from a list.
4. The food is packed and distributed to them.

Title is centered and in larger type than text and heading.

Bar chart is introduced and explained.

White space appears above and below figure.

Caption explains figure.

Heading is subordinate to title.

Procedure is explained in numbered list. Parallel structure used for list entries.

FIGURE 8.3 Example of a well-designed report.

they need to know more about a topic. If a color printer is available to you and your instructor allows you to use color, you have another tool for organizing information. For instance, in this text, headings are in red type and subheadings are in blue type. Use color with restraint, and remember that colors may look different on screen and on paper. Choose colors that display well for all readers *(pp. 99–100).*

White space, areas of a document that do not contain type or graphics, can also help you organize information. Generous margins and plenty of white space above headings and around other elements make the text easier to read.

You should also introduce visuals within your text and position them so that they appear near—but never before—the text reference. Balance your visuals and other text elements; for example, don't try to cram too many visuals onto one page.

2. Using font style and lists to make your text readable and to emphasize key elements

Fonts, or *typefaces,* are designs that have been established by printers for the letters in the alphabet, numbers, punctuation marks, and special characters. For most academic texts, choose a standard, easy-to-read font and a 10- or 12-point size. You can manipulate fonts for effect: for example, 12-point Times New Roman can be **boldfaced,** *italicized,* and <u>underlined.</u> Serif fonts have tiny lines at the ends of letters such as *n* and *y;* sans serif fonts do not have these lines. Standard serif fonts such as the following have traditionally been used for basic printed text because they are easy to read:

Times New Roman	Courier
Bookman Old Style	Palatino

Sans serif fonts like the following are used for headings because they offer a contrast, or for electronic documents because they are more readable on screen. (Some standards may be changing. Calibri, the default font in Microsoft Word 2007, is a sans serif font.)

Calibri	Arial	Verdana

Usually, if the main text of a document is in a sans serif font, headings should be in a serif font, and vice versa. In general, you should not use more than two fonts in a single text.

Many fonts available on your computer are known as *display fonts,* for example:

Curlz	Old English
Lucida Sans	*Monotype Corsiva*

These should be used rarely, if ever, in academic texts, on the screen, or in presentations. They can be used effectively in other kinds of documents, however, such as brochures, flyers, and posters.

Numbered or bulleted lists help you cluster large amounts of information, making the information easier for readers to reference and understand. Because they stand out from your text visually, lists also help readers see that ideas are related. You can use a numbered list to display steps in a sequence, present checklists, or suggest recommendations for action.

Format text as a numbered or bulleted list by choosing the option you want from your word-processing program's formatting commands. Introduce the list with a complete sentence followed by a colon (:); use parallel structure in your list items; and put a period at the end of each item only if the entries are complete sentences.

Putting information in a box provides emphasis and makes it easy to locate for future reference. Most word-processing programs offer several ways to enclose text within a border or box.

3. Formatting related design elements

In design, the key practices are simplicity, contrast, and consistency. If you emphasize an item by putting it in italic or bold type or in color,

---

NAVIGATING THROUGH COLLEGE AND BEYOND

The Basics: Margins, Spacing, Fonts, and Page Numbers

Here are a few basic guidelines for formatting academic texts:

- **First page:** In an assignment under five pages, you can usually place a header with your name, your professor's name, your course and section number, and the date on the first page, above the text. *(See the first page of Joseph Honrado's project on p. 148.)* If your text exceeds five pages, page 1 is often a title page. *(See the first page of Peggy Giglio project, on p. 378.)*

- **Font:** Select a common font and choose the 10- or 12-point size.

- **Margins:** Use one-inch margins on all four sides of the text. Adequate margins make your document easier to read and give your instructor room to write comments and suggestions.

- **Margin justification:** Line up, or justify, the lines of your document along the left margin but not along the right margin. Leaving a "ragged right"—or uneven—right margin, as in this box, enables you to avoid odd spacing between words.

- **Spacing:** Double-space unless you are instructed to do otherwise, and indent the first line of each paragraph five spaces. (Many business documents are single-spaced, with an extra line space between paragraphs, which are not indented.)

- **Page numbers:** Place page numbers in the upper or lower right-hand corner of the page. Some documentation styles require a header next to the page number. *(See Tabs 6–8.)*

or if you use a graphic element such as a box to set it off, consider repeating this effect for similar items so that your document has a unified look. Even a simple horizontal line can be a purposeful element in a long document when used consistently for organization.

4. Using headings to organize long documents

In short texts, headings can be disruptive and unnecessary. In longer texts, though, they can help organize complex information. *(For headings in APA style, see Chapter 33.)*

Effective headings are brief, descriptive, and consistent in grammatical structure and formatting:

PHRASES BEGINNING WITH *-ING* WORDS

Fielding Inquiries

Handling Complaints

NOUNS AND NOUN PHRASES

Customer Inquiries

Complaints

QUESTIONS

How Do I Field Inquiries?

How Do I Handle Complaints?

IMPERATIVE SENTENCES

Field Inquiries Efficiently

Handle Complaints Calmly and Politely

Headings at different levels can be in different forms. For example, the first-level headings in a book might be imperative sentences, while the second-level headings might begin with *-ing* words.

Place and highlight headings consistently throughout the text. If you have not already done so, preparing a formal topic outline will help you decide what your main points and second-level points are and where headings should go. *(For help with topic outlines, see Chapter 5, pp. 51–54.)* You might center all first-level headings, which correspond to the main points in your outline. If you have second-level headings—your supporting points—you might align them at the left margin and underline them. Third-level headings, if you have them, could be aligned at the left margin and set in plain type:

First-Level Heading

<u>Second-Level Heading</u>

Third-Level Heading

If a heading falls at the very bottom of the page, move it to the top of the next page.

5. Using design elements sparingly and intentionally

If you use too many graphics, headings, bullets, boxes, or other elements in a document, you risk making it as "noisy" as a loud radio. Standard fonts have become standard because they are easy on the eye. Bold type, italic type, underlining, and other graphic effects should not continue for more than one sentence at a time.

6. Meeting the needs of readers with disabilities

If your potential audience might include the visually or hearing impaired, take these principles into account:

- **Use a large, easily readable font:** The font should be 14 point or larger; 18 is best, and bold the entire text. Use a sans serif font such as Arial, as readers with poor vision find these fonts easier to read. Make headings larger than the surrounding text (rather than relying on a change in font, bold, italics, or color to set them apart).

- **Use ample spacing between lines:** The American Council of the Blind recommends a line space of at least 1.5.

- **Use appropriate, high-contrast colors:** Black text on a white background is best. If you use color for text or visuals, put light material on a dark background and dark material on a light background. Use colors from different families (such as yellow on purple). Avoid red and green because color-blind readers may have trouble distinguishing them. Do not use glossy paper.

- **Include narrative descriptions of all visuals:** Describe each chart, map, photograph, or other visual in your text. Indicate the key information and the point the visual makes. (This is more important when writing for the Web because individuals may use screen-reader software [*p. 182*].)

— NAVIGATING THROUGH COLLEGE AND BEYOND
Standard Headings and Templates

Some types of documents, such as lab reports and case studies, have standard headings, for example, "Introduction," "Abstract," and "Methods and Materials" for a lab report. *(See Chapter 12, pp. 157–60.)*

Word-processing programs allow you to create **templates,** preformatted styles that establish the structure and settings for a document and apply them automatically. If you make use of a specific format—such as a lab report—on a regular basis, consider creating a template for it.

- **If you include audio or video files in an electronic document, provide transcripts:** Also include a narrative description of what is happening in the video.

For further information, consult the American Council of the Blind (<http://acb.org/accessible-formats.html>), Lighthouse International (<http://www.lighthouse.org/accessibility/design/accessible-print-design/making-text-legible>), and the American Printing House for the Blind (<www.aph.org/edresearch/lpguide.htm>).

8d   Compile an effective print or electronic portfolio.

Students, job candidates, and professionals are often asked to collect their writing in a portfolio. Although most portfolios consist of a collection of texts in print form, many writers create electronic writing portfolios incorporating a variety of media.

Portfolios, regardless of medium, share at least three common features:

- They are a *collection* of work.
- They are a *selection*—or subset—of a larger body of work.
- They are introduced, narrated, or commented on by a text (for example, print or video) that offers *reflections* on the work.

Like any type of writing, portfolios serve a purpose and address an audience—to demonstrate your progress in a course for your instructor, for example, or to present your best work for a prospective employer. Portfolios allow writers to assess their work and set new writing goals.

1. Assembling a print portfolio

Course requirements vary, so always follow the guidelines your instructor provides. You will usually engage in the five activities mentioned below.

Gathering your writing   Create a list, or inventory, of the items that you might include. For a writing course, consider providing exploratory writing, notes, and comments from peer reviewers as well as all drafts for one or more of the selections. Make sure all material includes your name and that your final drafts are error free.

Reviewing written work and making appropriate selections   Keep the purpose of the portfolio in mind as well as the criteria that will be used to evaluate it. If you are assembling a presentation portfolio, select your very best work. If you are demonstrating your improvement as a writer in a process portfolio, select work that shows your development.

Even if no criteria have been provided, consider the audience for the portfolio when deciding which selections will be most appropriate. Who will read it, and what qualities will they be looking for?

Arranging the selections deliberately   If you have not been told how to organize your portfolio—for instance, in the order in which you wrote the pieces—think of it as if it were a single text and decide on an arrangement that will serve your purpose: from weakest item to strongest? From a less important project to a more important one? How will you determine importance? What is the rhetorical situation?

Explain your rationale for this arrangement in a letter to the reader, in a brief introduction, or in annotations in the table of contents.

Writing a reflective essay or letter   The reflective statement may take the form of an essay or a letter, depending on purpose and requirements. Sometimes the reflective essay will be the last one in a portfolio, so the reader can review all the work first and then read the writer's interpretation at the end. Alternatively, a reflective letter can open the portfolio. Regardless of its genre or placement, the reflective text gives you an opportunity to explain something about your writing and about yourself as a writer. Common topics in the reflective text include

- How you developed various assignments
- Which projects you believe are particularly strong and why
- What you learned as you worked on these assignments
- Who you are now as a writer

Follow the stages of the writing process in preparing your reflective essay or letter. Once you have completed it, assemble all the components of your print portfolio in a folder or notebook.

Polishing your portfolio   In the process of writing the reflective letter or essay, you might discover a better way to arrange your work. Or as you arrange the portfolio, you might want to review all your work again. Do not be surprised if you find yourself repeating some of these tasks. As with any writing, peer review will help you revise your portfolio to be most effective.

Most students learn about themselves and their writing as they compile portfolios and write reflections on their work. The process makes them better writers and helps them learn how to demonstrate their strengths to others.

2. Preparing an electronic portfolio

For some courses or professional purposes, you will want to present your work in an electronic format. For example, an education student might be required to provide an electronic portfolio of lesson plans, writing assignments, and other instructional materials. Electronic portfolios can be saved on a CD, DVD, or flash drive, or they can be published on the Web.

The process of creating an electronic portfolio, or e-portfolio, differs somewhat from that of creating a print portfolio. See the Checklist box below for the essential steps.

Gathering your written work as well as your audio, video, and visual texts   Depending on your assignment and purpose, you should consider these four inventories:

- A verbal inventory, consisting of your written work (including any handwritten work, which you should scan)
- A visual inventory (examples: photographs, drawings, presentation slides)
- An audio inventory (examples: speeches, music, podcasts)
- A video inventory (examples: movie clips, videos you have created)

The most important—and typical—components of an electronic portfolio are the verbal and visual texts. Searching for appropriate visuals can help you think about how to describe your work. One writer, for instance, might use images of everyday life in two countries to highlight the inclusion of texts in two languages in her portfolio.

Selecting appropriate texts and making connections among them   Choose works from your inventory based on your portfolio's purpose and audience and the criteria for evaluation. Consider the relationships among your selections as well as external materials. These connections should reveal something about you and your writing. They will become the links that help the reader navigate your digital portfolio. *Internal links* connect items within the portfolio.

CHECKLIST   Creating an Electronic Portfolio

- ☐ Gather all your written work and audio, video, and visual texts.
- ☐ Make selections, and consider connections.
- ☐ Decide on arrangement, navigation, and presentation.
- ☐ Include a reflective essay or letter.
- ☐ Test your portfolio for usability.

For instance, you might link an earlier draft to a later one or link a PowerPoint presentation to a final draft on the same topic. *External links* connect the reader to related files external to the portfolio but relevant to it. If you collaborated with a colleague or a classmate on a project, you might link to that person's electronic portfolio. *(See Chapter 14: Multimodal Writing, pp. 174–86.)*

Deciding on an arrangement, navigation, and presentation
As in a print portfolio, your work can be arranged in a variety of ways, including chronologically or in order of importance. Once you have decided on an arrangement, help your reader navigate the portfolio. Create a storyboard or chart that shows each item in your portfolio and how it is linked to others. *(See Chapter 14: Multimodal Writing, p. 178.)* After you have planned your site's structure, add hyperlinks to your documents. The link text should be clearly descriptive (a link reading "Résumé," for example, should lead to your résumé).

One simple method for helping readers navigate the portfolio is to provide a table of contents with links to the text for each item. Each final draft might link to exploratory writing, drafts in progress, and comments from peer reviewers. Alternatively, you might open with a reflective letter embedded with links that take readers to your written work and other texts. The portfolio in Figure 8.4 on page 104 features a menu of links that appears on each page, as well as links in the reflective text.

Consider how the opening screen will establish your purpose and appeal to your audience. Choose colors and images for the front page and successive pages, as well as fonts that visually present you as a writer and establish a tone appropriate for your purpose.

Writing or videotaping a reflective text
As in a print portfolio, the reflective text explains the selections to readers. A digital environment, however, offers more possibilities for presenting this reflection. You can make it highly visual; for example, you might have it cascade across a series of screens. Another option would be to link to an audio or video file in which you talk directly to the reader.

Testing your electronic portfolio
Make sure your portfolio works—both conceptually and structurally—before releasing it. Navigate through the portfolio yourself, and ask a friend to do so from a different computer. Sometimes links fail to work, or files stored on one machine do not open on another. Your friend will undoubtedly have constructive comments and suggestions about the portfolio's structure and content. Be sure to acknowledge this help in a section of acknowledgments or as part of the introduction.

Process & Product
Reflections

Home

Essays

Reflections

   Process & Product

   Audience & Genre

   Evidence & Analysis

Who is Ken Tinnes?

External Links

Throughout this semester, one of my main goals for this course was to be able to learn how to effectively create and utilize a detailed outline to assist with my writing process in order to ensure good organizational skills. The essay from this semester in which I was best able to achieve this goal was the research project. Due to the abundance of sources, as well as the mere size of the assignment, I knew I would need any organizational help I could get.

Before I could begin writing my paper, or even working on an outline for it, I needed to decide what exactly I wanted to write about, and how I would approach that topic specifically. To do this, I created a thesis statement for my essay. I read and revised my thesis numerous times on my own. I also looked to some of my peers from my dorm floor to revise my thesis as well. After establishing an accurate and detailed thesis summarizing and introducing the content of my essay, I was ready to research and prewrite.

Throughout the entire writing process for the research paper, I was focused on the structure of my essay. When I would find new sources, I would try to automatically classify the topic of that source, and cite it in my outline wherever I found it to be most appropriate. I tried to establish some of my transitions, and extract the exact quotes or information I would be using in my essay. By doing this, I was able to see the progression of my paper before it was even written. I didn't have to worry about rearranging my essay after it had already been written. That was extremely helpful, as there is nothing I find to be more difficult than rearranging full paragraphs, while trying to maintain a rhythmic flow to my paper.

As I wrote my paper, I tried my best to stick to the outline. If I came up with fresh ideas as I was writing, I would put them into my outline first, so that I would know where they would best fit inside my paper. By doing this, I was able to avoid many of the problems I experienced in some of my earlier writings. By filtering everything through my outline first, I was able to think of an intelligent way to convey my information. I would write my main arguments for each source and thought contained in my paper, so that I was able to reconstruct them until they were perfect. In doing this, I created what I like to think of as the most elaborate and detailed passages that I have ever written.

By writing these passages in my outline first, rather than my essay, I was able to avoid the disorganization that comes with a rush of thoughts, and focus on the sole goal of establishing thorough theses and arguments that would have a greater chance of being fully and accurately conveyed by my audience.

Home > Reflections > Process & Product >

© 2006 Ken Tinnes Contact Me

FIGURE 8.4 A screen from a student's electronic portfolio. Note the many links for easy navigation.

3

Common Assignments
across the Curriculum

Anybody who is involved in working across the disciplines is much more likely to have a lively mind and a lively life.

—Mary Field Belenky

Auguste Rodin's sculpture *The Thinker* evokes the psychological complexity of human thought and suggests the spirit of critical inquiry common to all disciplines across the curriculum.

3 Common Assignments

◉ Section dealing with visual rhetoric. For a complete listing, see the Quick Guide to Key Resources at the back of this book.

Tab 3: Common Assignments across the Curriculum

This section will help you answer the following questions about your writing.

Rhetorical Knowledge

- How can I argue persuasively? (11b)
- How can I keep my audience interested in my oral presentation? (13b)
- What should I *not* put on my blog or social media page? (14d)

Critical Thinking, Reading, and Writing

- How do I analyze a literary work? (10b)
- How can I defend my thesis against counterarguments? (11b)

Processes

- What is the best way to prepare for essay exams? (12d)
- How can I use presentation software (such as PowerPoint) effectively? (13c, 14a)
- What steps should I take in planning my Web site? (14c)

Knowledge of Conventions

- What is a review of the literature, and where do such reviews appear? (9d, 12c)
- What disciplines use lab reports and case studies? (12b, c)

For a general introduction to writing outcomes, see 1e, pages 14–16.

Most college courses require writing—from the lab report in chemistry to the policy proposal in economics. This section gives you tips on writing the most common kinds of college assignments and explains the distinctive features of each kind.

CHAPTER 9

Informative Reports

Imagine what the world would be like without records of what others have learned. Fortunately, we have many sources of information to draw on, including informative reports.

9a Understand the assignment.

An **informative report** shares what someone has learned about a topic or issue; it teaches. An informative report gives you a chance to do the following:

- Learn more about an issue that interests you
- Make sense of what you have read, heard, and seen
- Teach others what you have learned

9b Approach writing an informative report as a process.

1. Selecting a topic that interests you

The major challenge in writing informative reports is engaging readers' interest. Selecting a topic that interests you makes it more likely that your report will interest others.

Connect what you are learning in one course with a topic you are studying in another course or with your personal experience. For example, student Peggy Giglio, a political science major, aspired to a career in public affairs. For her topic, she decided to investigate the impact of social media on civic engagement and volunteerism. (*Giglio's essay begins on p. 112.*)

2. Considering what your readers know about the topic

Assume that your readers have some familiarity with the topic but that most of them do not have clear, specific knowledge of it. In her report on volunteering, Giglio assumes that her readers are familiar with social media but may not know much about its civic benefits.

3. Developing an objective stance

A commitment to objectivity gives your report its authority. Present differing views fairly, and do not take sides in a debate. Your voice

---

KNOW THE SITUATION Informative Reports

Purpose: To inform
Audience: Classmates and instructor, other readers on campus interested in the topic, and citizens who may be affected by it.
Stance: Reasonable, informed, objective
Genre: Informative report
Medium: Print, word-processed text, Web page, video, audio, poster
Commonly used: In most disciplines, the workplace, and public life

the EVOLVING SITUATION

Informative Reports

Informative reports are published across print and new media formats and are commonly written by members of humanities, social sciences, and natural sciences disciplines, as these examples indicate:

- In a published article, an anthropologist surveys and summarizes a large body of material on indigenous warfare among the Pueblos before the arrival of the Spanish explorers.
- For an encyclopedia of British women writers, a professor of literature briefly recounts the life and work of Eliza Fenwick, a recently rediscovered eighteenth-century author.
- In an academic journal, two biochemists summarize the findings of more than two hundred recently published articles on defense mechanisms in plants.
- A researcher at the Pew Research Center's *Journalism Project,* a Web site that tracks trends in the news media, reports on the five indicators of sustainability in the nonprofit news sector.

will sound unbiased if you carefully select words that are precise without being emotional.

4. Composing a thesis that summarizes your knowledge of the topic

An informative thesis typically reports the results of the writer's study. Before you commit to a thesis, review the information you have collected. Compose a thesis statement that presents the goal of your paper and forecasts its content. *(For more on thesis statements, see Tab 2: Writing and Designing Texts, pp. 48–51.)*

In the report on social media and volunteering, Giglio develops a general thesis that she supports in the body of her report with information about who is volunteering, in what capacities, and for what specific reasons.

> Certainly, social media have changed *how* students volunteer, but the reasons *why* they volunteer have remained much the same as with the previous generation: The three major reasons students are volunteering are to satisfy their curricular requirements, prepare for the financial success they hope to achieve, and become active members of a community.

Notice how the phrase "three major reasons" forecasts the body of Giglio's report. We expect to learn something about each of the three reasons that students volunteer, and the report is structured to give us that information, subtopic by subtopic.

5. Providing context in your introduction

Informative reports usually begin with a simple introduction to the topic and a straightforward statement of the thesis. Provide relevant context or background, but get to your specific topic as quickly as possible, and keep it in the foreground. *(For more on introductions, see Tab 2: Writing and Designing Texts, pp. 71–72.)*

6. Using classification and division as one way to organize your information

Develop ideas in an organized way by classifying and dividing information into categories, subtopics, or the stages of a process. *(See Tab 2: Writing and Designing Texts, pp. 62–63.)*

7. Illustrating key ideas with examples

Use specific examples to help readers understand your ideas. In her report on volunteerism, Giglio provides many specific examples, including statistical information on student involvement, quotations from administrators at major universities, and a discussion of studies that explore patterns in student civic engagement. Examples make her report interesting as well as educational. *(See Tab 2: Writing and Designing Texts, p. 59, for more advice on using examples.)*

8. Defining specialized terms and spelling out unfamiliar abbreviations

Specialized terms (such as foreign words or discipline-specific terminology) will probably not be familiar to most readers. Explain these terms with a synonym or a brief definition. For example, Giglio provides a definition of the phrase *service learning* in the sixth paragraph of her informative report on volunteerism. *(For more on definition, see Tab 2: Writing and Designing Texts, pp. 63–64.)* Unfamiliar abbreviations like CNCS (Corporation for National and Community Service) are spelled out the first time they are used, with the abbreviation in parentheses.

9. Concluding by answering "so what?"

Conclude by referring to a common idea or an example that speaks to the importance of the information. The conclusion reminds readers of the topic and thesis. It then answers the "so what?" question by giving readers a sense of why they should care about what they have just read.

At the end of her report on social media and volunteerism, for example, Giglio answers the "so what?" question by emphasizing the benefits of civic engagement, not only to the organizations and communities at large, but to the students themselves.

CONSIDER YOUR SITUATION

Author: Peggy Giglio, a political science major, interested in a career in public affairs

Type of writing: Informative report

Purpose: To inform readers about social media and volunteerism

Stance: Reasonable, informed, objective

Audience: Classmates and instructor standing in for U.S. general public

Medium: Print and word-processed text attached to an e-mail

Giglio writes: After writing this informative report, I know a great deal more about how and why students volunteer, and I am eager to share that information with readers.

While students are eager for volunteering opportunities, they likewise want those opportunities to produce meaningful and influential results—for the charities and organizations to which they donate their time, as well as for themselves.

(For more on conclusions, see Tab 2: Writing and Designing Texts, p. 72.)

9c   Student sample: Informative report

In the informative report that follows, Peggy Giglio synthesizes what she has learned about the impact of social media on civic engagement among college students. As you read her report, notice how Giglio provides a context for her topic, cites various sources (using APA documentation style), divides the information into subtopics, and illustrates her ideas with examples, all hallmarks of a clear, carefully developed report. The annotations in the margin point out specific features of the informative report.

> **Note:** For details on the proper formatting of a text in APA style, see Chapter 33 and the student sample that begins on page 378.

SAMPLE STUDENT INFORMATIVE REPORT

Following APA style, Giglio includes a separate title page. Her abstract is given its own page, following the title page. See p. 378 for an example of proper formatting of an abstract in APA style.

The New Volunteer:

Civic Engagement through Social Media

Peggy Giglio

Governors State University

--------------------------------[new page]--------------------------------

Are college students today concerned with helping others? It may not seem so to the previous generation, for whom today's students appear obsessed with social networking, text messaging, and materialistic values. But college students are using social media to actively help others in their communities, and their efforts are having a tangible impact. In fact, studies show that increased

> Topic introduced.

engagement with social media is actually driving students to become more civically involved during college and beyond. Moreover, new technologies allow for an immediacy of action that was unthinkable

> Context provided in introduction.

even ten years ago. Consider the response to the 2013 Boston Marathon bombing. Within minutes of the explosions, people were tweeting about the need to donate blood. A spreadsheet was quickly and widely circulated, listing people who were offering to open their homes to those who might need a place to stay (Hartogs, 2013).

> Source named in signal phrase.

In their book, *Social Change Anytime Everywhere,* Allyson Kapin and Amy Sample Ward (2013) explain that social media have the power to engage not only first responders and the organizations they work for, but also the millions of individuals around the world who check their social media pages as events unfold. Certainly, social media have changed *how* students volunteer, but the reasons *why* they volunteer have remained much the same as with the previous

> Thesis stated.

generation: The three main reasons that students are volunteering are to satisfy their curricular requirements, prepare for the financial success they hope to achieve, and become active members of a community.

Volunteering in America and
Historical Changes in Motivation

According to the Corporation for National and Community Service (CNCS) (2012), 64.3 million people volunteered in 2011, the highest number in the past five years, and a rate that has remained relatively consistent for the past four years. Defining volunteering as "work done through an organization for which there is no pay," DoSomething.org estimates that, in 2011, one quarter of young adults, including college students, volunteered in some capacity (Dosomething.org, 2012). And for many students, volunteering does not end with graduation. In a 2007 study of adult voting and volunteering, Hart, Connelly, Youniss, and Atkins found that "those who participated frequently in community service in high school were more likely to volunteer than were those whose community service was nonexistent or infrequent" (2007, p. 210). While some researchers suggest that this continuation is a product of a difficult job market, others disagree. "I don't think people are just jumping on the bandwagon to do service because the economy is shaky," says Elissa Kim, Executive Vice President of Recruitment for Teach for America, whose organization reports that applications reached an all-time high of 48,000 in 2011 (DiBlasio, 2011, p. D3).

Historically, college students planning to enter service professions such as nursing or social work have volunteered their time as part of their professional development; however, today students in all disciplines choose to make especially valuable contributions in disastrous circumstances, such as the aftermath of Hurricane Sandy. Adelphi University, which has a main campus on Long Island and another in Manhattan, felt the effects of Sandy. But perhaps more memorable than the storm's effects were the students' responses. Shortly after the storm, in the course of a single day, university students collected donations, including roughly $1,000 in cash, wrote thank-you cards for first responders, and participated in a blood drive (Peterkin, 2012). "Students on Facebook are posting things like 'It's a

First use of unfamiliar abbreviation spelled out.

Quotation integrated into writer's sentence.

Development by classification.

humbling experience,' and it's positive to see that reaction," said Michael J. Berthel, Senior Assistant Director of Adelphi's Center for Student Involvement (as cited in Peterkin, 2012, para. 15). There is little doubt that the current generation is doing its part to make the world a better place, in a wide variety of ways (see Figure 1).

In the past, students volunteered to change the status quo and to have an impact on social conditions (Astin, 1998). Today's students report that school, family, and peer groups are among the major motivations to join a volunteer effort (Boyd & Brackmann, 2012; Law, Shek, & Ma, 2013). Unlike their parents, young people seek to effect change with perhaps more practicality than idealism. The 2013 Millennial Impact Report finds that, for young people, "chief motivations for getting involved were: working on a cause they are passionate about (79%), meeting new people who care about the same cause or issue (56%), and being able to lend pro-bono skills and expertise (46%)" (p. 23). In other words, students are thinking about networking and gaining skills useful in the job market, in addition to helping others.

Today it is easier for volunteers to have an impact at the community level than at a national or regional level. Unlike past generations that sought to make a global impact through volunteer efforts, young people today are finding new and creative ways to become involved in their own communities. According to research conducted by Dosomething.org (Dosomething.org Index, 2012), "of young people who volunteered in 2011, 40% did not volunteer with a traditional 'organization' *at all* but instead volunteered with clubs, groups, their family alone, friends alone, or on their own." Increasingly, students are learning that they can make a difference in the local community while also gaining valuable skills and work experience.

Current College Students'
Motivations for Volunteering

One reason that students are volunteering in growing numbers is that civic engagement is now a familiar behavior reinforced in the college environment. In fact, many colleges offer service learning

---

Source information summarized.

Source given for data.

First motivation—introduces subtopic.

courses and service initiatives through campus organizations. Research has shown that these programs not only motivate students' participation in volunteer efforts, but improve their academic performance, as well:

> College students who participate in civic engagement learning activities not only earn higher grade point averages but also have higher retention rates and are more likely to complete their college degree. They also demonstrate improved academic content knowledge, critical thinking skills, written and verbal communication, and leadership skills. Moreover, these students show increased interest in becoming personally and professionally involved in future community enhancement projects (Cress, Burack, Giles, Elkins, & Stevens, 2010, p. 1).

Service learning courses have two objectives: (1) learning in a given content area and (2) learning about citizenship and social policies. CNCS (2010) defines *service learning* as a practice that "engages students in the educational process, using what they learn in the classroom to solve real-life problems" (para. 2). The formal structure of service learning is designed to make student volunteering beneficial not only for the community but also for the students who perform it, increasing their academic development, leadership skills, and community awareness. "Independent of what it does for the community," says Thomas Murphy, chair of anthropology at Edmonds Community College in Washington, "when students are learning in a hands-on situation and their activity has importance and impact on the community, they care more about their assignments than they would if it is make believe" (as cited in McClure, 2013, p. 49). Through service learning initiatives, colleges and universities seek to engage students in civic activities that benefit everyone—community members, local businesses, the students, and even the institutions.

Founded in 1985 by three university presidents, Campus Compact, a national coalition of well over 1,100 colleges and universities, is committed to promoting civic engagement on college

Unfamiliar term defined.

The perspectives of educators are important to this topic, so are quoted directly.

campuses (Campus Compact, 2013a). One of the ways they achieve this goal is through a social media initiative, Connect2Complete. Supported by the Bill and Melinda Gates Foundation, Connect2Complete pairs student volunteers with mentors and peers to encourage service learning and academic success. In their 2012 Annual Member Survey, Campus Compact (2013a) reported that student participation is increasing in the Compact institutions, a fact that stands in marked contrast to the flat or even decreasing rates reported by other sources measuring rates across all institutions (DiBlasio, 2011). The 2012 survey also underscores the important role that colleges play in finding meaningful opportunities for their students. This point has been confirmed by multiple studies showing that "colleges have and can continue to maximize students' civic engagement and ethical learning when both are envisioned as integrated goals straddling students' academic and nonacademic lives and permeating institutional culture" (Boyd & Brackmann, 2012, p. 39). A 2010 study by Prentice and Robinson, and published by The American Association of Community Colleges, "found statistically significant differences between service-learners and non-service-learners on five out of six learning outcomes, including educational success and academic deployment, civic responsibility, critical thinking, communications, and career and teamwork" (Campus Compact, 2013b, p. 9).

A second motivation is market driven. Differences in the ways today's students volunteer reflect the unique challenges they face. Entering the job market has become much more difficult than it was for previous generations. An article published in *The Chronicle of Higher Education* stated that college students need to be "broadly educated and should apply their learning to the real world during college" (Supiano, 2013). Marcy L. Reed, President of National Grid, a Massachusetts gas and electric utility, says, "I have to be sure the people we hire today are fit for tomorrow" (as cited in Supiano, 2013). Students who volunteer gain crucial skills, as well as experience applying what they know to a range of problem-solving efforts. They volunteer for their own personal benefit, motivated partly by the desire

---

Source named in signal phrase.

Second motivation—introduces a subtopic.

to go on to earn a living, perhaps even in the field in which they volunteered. And as Reed's remark confirms, those with volunteer experience are that much more prepared to enter and compete in today's job market.

A third motivation for volunteering is the desire for community. Students today usually turn to social media to connect with others. However, volunteering provides them a much-needed opportunity to interact with others off-line and outside of the classroom. "There seems to be a real longing for students to have hands-on experience and to take what they are learning in school and delve into things they are passionate about," says Maureen Curley, president of Campus Compact (as cited by DiBlasio, 2011). As the Millennial Impact Report states, "Millennials view volunteer opportunities as a way to socially connect with like-minded peers, which moves them beyond technology (social networking) to in-person action" (as cited in Millennial Impact, 2012, p.6). Such potential may particularly motivate college students looking to establish connections within peer groups at their school, or students who want to integrate their daily lives with their academic work. That motivation extends to sharing their skills with a live community, on their college campuses and beyond.

Online collaboration can also fulfill the desire for community interaction. Students often use the Internet to organize support for a cause. For example, students have used *Twitter* and *Facebook* to urge assistance for victims of Hurricane Sandy and survivors of terrorist attacks. The American Red Cross has a social media monitoring center, which, as of March 2012, was the only one if its kind. "This groundbreaking center lets Red Cross staff see more clearly what's happening on the ground . . . and get people the resources they need more quickly" (American Red Cross, 2013, p. 20). Along with K–12 schools, many colleges and universities have Red Cross clubs, over 1,600 as of 2010 (American Red Cross, 2011, p. i). Students get involved in a number of ways. For example, Marissa Miller, a Penn State student, thought to offer students the opportunity to win a $1,000 scholarship by creating and posting

> Third motivation—introduces a subtopic.

> Example given for clarity and interest.

short videos, on *Twitter,* that answer the question, "What do you cross your heart and hope to give?" The Red Cross was happy to use *Twitter* to help spread their message and to acknowledge the substantial donations—6 million units of blood—by college students each year (Red Cross, 2013).

> Paraphrase with a source provided in parenthetical citation.

These social media efforts have a significant impact. Since tweeting was introduced in 2006, an impressive 96% of nonprofits say they use *Twitter* and 97% report using *Facebook* (Barnes, 2011). Social media allow supporters to become actively involved in spreading the message of the organization. For example, a recent search through the New York University NYUService *Twitter* feed and *Facebook* postings turned up plenty of examples of service opportunities and student engagement including: creating cards for veterans and police officers as part of the 9/11 remembrance; a call for students to help rebuild houses destroyed by Hurricane Sandy; and notice of a Service Fair, connecting students to local nonprofits. It is worth noting that student tweets and posts about their own service activities help to raise awareness of these nonprofits and, in turn, motivate more people to volunteer (Kapin & Ward, 2013).

> Examples given for clarity and interest.

An Assessment of College Volunteerism

More and more colleges and universities are joining the Campus Compact and formalizing their programs by opening civic engagement centers and offices, and are even turning to social media to build community encourage students to get involved. After all, most educators would agree that "a democratic system of government needs—and the United States relies on colleges to produce—ethical and engaged citizens" (Boyd & Brackmann, 2012, p. 39). However, college administrators need to remember that, in order for their efforts to be effective, they must keep in mind the motivations and goals of students. While students are eager for volunteering opportunities, they likewise want those opportunities to produce meaningful and impactful results—for the charities and organizations to which they donate their time, as well as for themselves.

> Interpretation provided without bias.

> Point and purpose restated in conclusion.

Despite the variety of their motivations, college students today are making a difference by working together to enrich their communities in myriad ways. Their efforts, largely driven by access to social media, are relevant to their career goals; moreover, they give their time in ways that also benefit their own lives and their own aspirations for the future. What matters is that their commitment to enriching the lives of others, and to enhancing the communities in which they live, is as strong as that of any previous generation.

Restate-ment of thesis at conclusion.

-------------------------------[new page]-------------------------------

References

American Red Cross. (2011). *A comprehensive guide to starting and sustaining a Red Cross school club.* Retrieved from American Red Cross Web site http://www.redcross.org/images/MEDIA_CustomProductCatalog/m4440169_H20978.CIAB_MainDocument.pdf

American Red Cross. (2013). *2012 Annual Report.* Retrieved from American Red Cross website http://www.redcross.org/images/MEDIA_CustomProductCatalog/m16740671_A501-12_AnnualReport_FINAL.pdf

Astin, A. W. (1998). The changing American college student: Thirty-year trends, 1966–1996. *The Review of Higher Education, 21*(2), 115–135. Retrieved from http://www.press.jhu.edu/journals/review_of_higher_education

Barnes, G. N. (2011). *Social media usage now ubiquitous among US top charities, ahead of all other sectors.* Retrieved from University of Massachusetts Dartmouth, Center for Marketing Research website http://www.umassd.edu/cmr/socialmediaresearch/socialmediatopcharities/

Boyd, K. D. & Brackmann, S. (2012). Promoting civic engagement to educate institutionally for personal and social responsibility. *New Directions for Student Services, 2012*(139), 39–50.

References list follows APA style and begins on a new page.

Source: report by a corporate author; retrieved online.

Source: journal article with volume and issue number, retrieved online.

Source: journal article.

Source:
Fact
sheet by a
corporate
author;
retrieved
online.

Corporation for National and Community Service. (2012, December). *Volunteering and civic life in America 2012: Key findings on the volunteer participation and civic health of the nation* [Fact sheet]. Retrieved from http://www.volunteeringinamerica.gov/assets/resources/FactSheetFinal.pdf

Corporation for National and Community Service. (2010, June 15). *What is service learning?* Retrieved from http://www.learnandserve.gov/about/service_learning/index.asp

Source:
Press
release by
corporate
author;
retrieved
online.

Campus Compact. (2013a). *Campus Compact honors 181 community-engaged college students as Newman Civic Fellows* [Press release]. Retrieved from http://www.compact.org/news/campus-compact-honors-181-community-engaged-college-students-as-newman-civic-fellows/24189/?zoom_highlight=dedicated+solely+to

Campus Compact. (2013b). *Creating a culture of assessment: 2012 Campus Compact annual member survey.* Retrieved from http://www.compact.org/wp-content/uploads/2013/04/Campus-Compact-2012-Statistics.pdf

Source:
report by
corporate
author;
retrieved
online.

Cress, C. M., Burack, C., Giles, D. E., Elkins, J., & Stevens, M. C. (2010). A promising connection: Increasing college access and success through civic engagement. Retrieved from Campus Compact website http://www.compact.org/wp-content/uploads/2010/10/Cress_Presidential_Summit_2010.pdf

Source:
print
magazine
article.

DiBlasio, N. (2011, November 29). Longer-term volunteering is the drill for collegians. *USA Today,* p. D3.

Source:
informa-
tion from a
Web site.

Dosomething.org (2012). *The Dosomething.org index on young people and volunteering, 2012: The year of friends with benefits.* Retrieved from http://files.dosomething.org/files/ pictures/blog/2012-Web-Singleview_0.pdf

Source:
journal
article with
volume
and issue
number

Hart, D., Donnelly, T. M., Youniss, J., & Atkins, R. (2007). High school community service as a predictor of adult voting and volunteering. *American Education Research Journal, 44*(1), 197–219. doi:10.3102/0002831206298173

Source:
article on a
Web site.

Hartogs, J. (2013, April 16). *Stories of kindness amid tragedy in Boston marathon bombing.* CBS News. Retrieved from http://www.cbsnews.com/news/stories-of-kindness-amid-tragedy-in-boston-marathon-bombing/

Kapin, A., & Ward, A.S. (2013). *Social change anytime everywhere: how to implement online multichannel strategies to spark advocacy, raise money and engage your community.* San Francisco, CA: Jossey-Bass.

Law, B. M. F., Shek, D. T. L., & Ma, C. M. S. (2013). Validation of family, school, and peer influence on volunteerism scale among adolescents. *Research on social work practice, 23*(4), 458–466. doi: 10.1177/1049731513476144.

McClure, A. (2013, April). Serving the community: Two-year institutions making a bigger commitment to community outreach. *University Business, 16*(4), 49–51. Retrieved from http://www.universitybusiness.com/servingcomm

Millennial Impact. (2013). *The 2013 millennial impact report.* Retrieved from http://cdn.trustedpartner.com/docs/library/AchieveMCON2013/Research%20Report/Millennial%20Impact%20Research.pdf

Peterkin, C. (2012, November 8). A week after Hurricane Sandy, students step up their relief work. *The Chronicle of Higher Education.* Retrieved from http://chronicle.com/article/A-Week-After-Hurricane-Sandy/135686/

Red Cross offers $1,000 scholarship for student's best tweet (2013, September 24). *Penn State News,* n.p. Retrieved from http://news.psu.edu/story/288801/2013/09/23/academics/red-cross-offers-1000-scholarship-student%E2%80%99s-best-tweet

Supiano, B. (2013, April 10). Employers want broadly educated new hires, survey finds. *The Chronicle of Higher Education.* Retrieved from http://chronicle.com/article/Employers-Want-Broadly/138453

Source: book with two authors.

Source: journal article with doi.

Source: journal article; retrieved online.

Source: report by corporate author.

Source: journal article; retrieved online.

Source: article on a Web site.

9d   Write reviews of the literature to survey ideas.

In upper-division courses, instructors sometimes assign a special kind of informative report called a **review of the literature.** Here the term *literature* refers to published research reports—not to novels, poetry, or drama—and the term *review* means a survey of others' ideas, not an evaluation, argument, or opinion. A review presents an organized account of the current state of knowledge in a specific area, something that you and other researchers can use as context for a research question and as a basis for new projects and new directions for research. A review of the literature may also be a subsection within a research report.

The following paragraph is an excerpt from the review of the literature section in an article by psychologists investigating the motivations for suicide.

> One source of information about suicide motives is suicide notes. International studies of suicide notes suggest that women and men do not differ with regard to love versus achievement motives. For example, in a study of German suicide notes, Linn and Lester (1997) found that women and men did not differ with regard to relationship versus financial or work motives. In a study of Hong Kong suicide notes, Ho, Yip, Chiu, and Halliday (1998) reported no gender or age differences with regard to interpersonal problems or financial/job problems. Similarly, in a UK study, McClelland, Reicher, and Booth (2000) found that men's suicide notes did not differ from women's notes in terms of mentioning career failures. In fact, in the UK study, relationship losses were reported more often in men's than in women's suicide notes.
>
> —SILVIA SARA CANETTO AND DAVID LESTER,
> "Love and Achievement Motives in
> Women's and Men's Suicide Notes"

CHAPTER 10

Interpretive Analyses and Writing about Literature

Interpretation means working to understand a written document, literary work, cultural artifact, social situation, or natural event and then explaining what you understand in a meaningful and convincing way to readers.

10a Understand the assignment.

When an assignment asks you to compare, explain, analyze, or discuss something, you are expected to study that subject closely. An **interpretive analysis** moves beyond simple description and examines or compares particular items for a reason: to enhance your readers' understanding of people's conditions, actions, beliefs, or desires.

KNOW THE SITUATION Interpretive Analyses

Purpose: To enhance understanding
Audience: Classmates and instructor, representing readers interested in the topic and the arts
Stance: Thoughtful, inquisitive, open-minded
Genres: Review, critique, blog
Medium: Print, word-processed text, Web page, video, audio
Commonly used: In the arts, humanities, and many other disciplines

---

10b Approach writing an interpretive analysis as a process.

Writing an interpretive analysis typically begins with critical reading. *(See Chapter 4: Reading and Writing: The Critical Connection.)*

1. Discovering an aspect of the subject that is meaningful to you

Think about your own feelings and experiences while you read, listen, or observe. Connecting your own thoughts and experiences to what you are studying can help you develop fresh interpretations.

2. Developing a thoughtful stance

Think of yourself as an explorer. Be thoughtful, curious, and open minded as you discover possible meanings. When you write your analysis, invite your readers to join you on an intellectual journey, saying, in effect, "Come, think this through with me."

3. Using an intellectual framework

To interpret your subject effectively, use a relevant perspective or an intellectual framework. For example, the elements of a work of fiction, such as plot, character, and setting, are often used to analyze stories.

In the student essay that begins on page 129, Gillian Morton does a close reading of Emily Dickinson's "Tell all the Truth. . . ." Morton bases her analysis on word meanings and rhyme patterns. To write her analysis, Morton uses her own interpretive skills rather than researching sources to see what other readers have said.

No matter what framework you use, analysis often entails taking your subject apart, figuring out how the parts make up a cohesive whole, and then putting it all back together. Because the goal of analysis is to create a meaningful interpretation, you need to treat the whole as more than the sum of its parts. Determining meaning is a complex problem with multiple solutions.

┌─ NAVIGATING THROUGH COLLEGE AND BEYOND

Interpretive Analyses

You can find interpretive analyses like the following in professional journals like *PMLA (Publications of the Modern Language Association)* as well as popular publications like the *New Yorker* and the *Atlantic Monthly.* For example, a cultural critic might contrast the way AIDS and cancer are talked about, imagined, and therefore treated, or a musicologist might compare the revised endings of two pieces by Beethoven to figure out what makes a work complete.

Students are often called on to write interpretive analyses such as the following:

- A student in an English course analyzes the poetic techniques in Emily Dickinson's "Tell all the Truth . . ."
- A student majoring in music spells out the emotional implications of the tempo and harmonic progression in Schubert's *Der Atlas.*
- By applying an econometric model of nine variables, a student in an economics course explains that deregulation has not decreased the level of airline safety.

4. Listing, comparing, questioning, and classifying to discover your thesis

To figure out your thesis, it is often useful to explore separate features of your subject. If you are analyzing fiction, you might consider the plot, the characters, the setting, and the tone before deciding to focus your thesis on one character's personality.

Try one or more of the following strategies:

- Annotate the text as you read, or make notes as you experience a movie or concert, and if it helps, write a summary.

- Ask yourself questions about the subject you are analyzing, and write down any interesting answers. Imagine what kinds of questions your instructor or classmates might ask about the artifact, document, or performance you are considering. In answering these questions, try to figure out the thesis you will present and support.

- Name the class of things to which the item you are analyzing belongs (for example, memoirs), and then identify important features of that class (for example, scene, point of view, friends, and turning points).

5. Making your thesis focused and purposeful

To make a point about your subject, focus on one or two key questions. Resist the temptation to describe everything you see. Consider this example of a focused, purposeful thesis for an interpretive analysis of Emily Dickinson's poem, "Tell all the Truth . . ."

In physical terms, a slant acts as a gradual path up or down when a shift in altitude is required. Rather than make the change abruptly, a slant provides a gentler way forward. Employing this logic, Dickinson's poem suggests that indirection is not necessarily a move askew, but can be a safer route toward a difficult destination.

Text continues on page 127.

QUESTIONS FOR ANALYZING LITERATURE

Fiction

Plot and Structure

- What events take place over the course of the work?
- What did you think and feel at different places?
- How do the parts of the work relate to one another?

Characters

- What are the relationships among the people, and how are they portrayed?
- How do they change?
- What does dialogue reveal about their motivations?

Setting

- What is the significance of the time and place?
- What associations does the writer make with the location?

Point of View

- Is there a first-person narrator ("I"), or is the story told by a third-person narrator who reveals what one, all, or none of the characters is thinking?

Tone

- Is the work's tone stern or playful, melancholy, or something else?

Language

- Does the work conjure images that appeal to the senses?
- Does it use **simile** to compare two things directly using *like* or *as (his heart is sealed tight like a freezer door)?*
- Does it use **metaphor** to link two things implicitly *(his ice-hard heart)?*
- What feelings or ideas do individual words suggest?

Theme

- What is at issue in the work?
- What statement is the author making about the issue?

(continued)

QUESTIONS FOR ANALYZING LITERATURE *(continued)*

Poetry

Speaker and Tone

- Who is speaking? Is it a parent, a lover, an adult or a child, a man or a woman?
- What is the speaker's tone—is it stern or playful, melancholy or elated, nostalgic or hopeful?

Connotations

- What feelings or ideas do individual words in the poem connote? Although both *trudge* and *saunter* mean "walk slowly," their connotations (associative meanings) are very different.

Imagery

- Does the poem evoke images that appeal to any of your senses— for example, the shocking feeling of a cold cloth on feverish skin or the sharp smell of a gas station?
- How do the images shape the mood of the poem? What ideas do they suggest?

Figurative Language

- Does the poem use **simile** to directly compare two things using *like* or *as?*
- Does it use **metaphor** to implicitly link one thing to another?
- How does the comparison enhance meaning?

Sound, Rhythm, and Meter

- What vowel and consonant sounds recur through the poem?
- Do the lines of the poem resemble the rhythms of ordinary speech, or do they have a more musical quality? Consider how the sounds of the poem create an effect.

Structure

- Notice how the poem is organized into parts or stanzas, considering spacing, punctuation, capitalization, and rhyme schemes. How do the parts relate to one another?

Theme

- What is the subject of the poem?
- What does the poet's choice of language and imagery suggest about his or her attitude toward that subject?

Although you want your point to be clear, you also want to make sure that your thesis anticipates the "so what?" question and sets up an interesting context for your interpretation. Unless you relate your specific thesis to some more general issue, idea, or problem, your interpretive analysis may seem pointless to readers. *(For more on developing your thesis, see Tab 2: Writing and Designing Texts, pp. 48–51.)*

6. Introducing the general issue, a clear thesis or question, and relevant context

In interpretive analyses, it often takes more than one paragraph to do what an introduction needs to do:

- Identify the general issue, concept, or problem at stake. You can also present the intellectual framework that you are applying.
- Provide relevant background information.
- Name the specific item or items you will focus on.
- State the thesis or pose the main question(s) your analysis will address.

— NAVIGATING THROUGH COLLEGE AND BEYOND

Ideas and Practices for Writing in the Humanities

- **Base your analysis on the work itself.** Works of art affect each of us differently, and any interpretation has a subjective element. There are numerous critical theories about the significance of art. However, the possibility of different interpretations does not mean that any one interpretation is as valid as any other. Your reading of the work needs to be grounded in details from the work itself.

- **Consider how the concepts you are learning in your course apply to the work you are analyzing.** If your course focuses on the formal elements of art, for example, you might look at how those elements function in the painting you have chosen. If your course focuses on the social context of a work, you might look at how the poem or story shares or subverts the belief system and worldview that was common in its time.

- **Use the present tense when writing about the work and the past tense when writing about its history.** Use the present tense to talk about the events that happen within a work: "In Aristophanes' plays, characters frequently *step* out of the scene and *address* the audience directly." Use the past tense, however, to relate historical information about the work or its creator: "Kant *wrote* about science, history, criminal justice, and politics as well as philosophical ideas."

You need not do these things in the order listed. Sometimes it is a good idea to introduce the specific focus of your analysis before presenting either the issue or the background information. Even though you may begin with a provocative statement or a stimulating example, make sure that your introduction does the four things listed in the preceding section. *(For more on introductions, see Tab 2: Writing and Designing Texts, pp. 71–72.)*

7. Planning your analysis so that each point supports your thesis

After you pose a key question or state your thesis, you need to organize your points to answer the question or support your thesis. Readers must be able to follow your train of thought and see how each point you make is related to your thesis. *(For more on developing your ideas, see Tab 2: Writing and Designing Texts, pp. 58–68.)*

As you guide readers through your analysis, you will integrate source material, including important quotations, as Gillian Morton does in her analysis of Emily Dickinson's "Tell all the Truth . . ." on pp. 129–31. When you are writing about a painting or photograph, your pointed description of visual elements will enhance effective communication.

8. Concluding by answering "so what?"

The conclusion of an interpretive analysis needs to answer the "so what?" question by saying why your thesis—as well as the analysis that supports and develops it—is relevant to the larger issue identified in the introduction. What does your interpretation reveal about that issue? *(For information about conclusions, see Tab 2: Writing and Designing Texts, p. 72.)*

10c Student sample: Interpretive analysis

Although literary analysis can never tell us exactly what a poem is saying, it can help us think more deeply about possible meanings.

First read the complete poem without stopping, and then note your initial thoughts and feelings. Re-read the poem several times, paying close attention to the rhythms of the lines (reading aloud helps) and the poet's choice of words. Think about how the poem develops. Do the last lines represent a shift from or fulfillment of the poem's opening? Look for connections among the poem's details, and think about their significance. The questions in the box on page 126 may help guide your analysis.

Use the insights you gain from your close reading to develop a working thesis about the poem. In the student interpretation that begins on page 129, Gillian Morton develops a thesis about the poem "Tell all the Truth . . ." reprinted on page 129. Morton focuses on key words, "truth," "all," and "slant," and then relates the poem's form to its meaning.

─CONSIDER YOUR SITUATION

Author: Gillian Morton

Type of writing: Literary analysis/interpretation

Purpose: To analyze a poem and illuminate its themes

Stance: Reasonable, appreciative, clarifying

Audience: Classmates and instructor representing readers unfamiliar with Emily Dickinson and interested in understanding poetry

Medium: Print, word-processed text, part of e-portfolio

Morton writes: Writing an analysis of Emily Dickinson's poem, "Tell all the Truth . . ." has helped me understand the importance of context and situation in communicating truthful messages. I used to think that telling the truth was simple and straightforward. I now see the importance of one's "slant."

Tell all the Truth . . .
EMILY DICKINSON

Tell all the Truth but tell it slant—
Success in Circuit lies
Too bright for our infirm Delight
The Truth's superb surprise

As Lightning to the Children eased
With explanation kind
The Truth must dazzle gradually
Or every man be blind—

> **Note:** For details on the proper formatting of a text in MLA style, see Chapter 29 and the student sample that begins on page 331.

SAMPLE STUDENT ANALYSIS OF A POEM

Emily Dickinson's "Tell all the Truth . . .":

A Gentle Path to a Difficult Destination

At first glance, the notion of a slanted truth might conjure the distasteful rhetoric of an evasive politician. In fact, Dickinson's "Tell all the Truth but tell it slant" advocates for discourse that is far more subtle and humane. In physical terms, a slant acts as a gradual path up or down when a shift in altitude is required. Rather than make the change abruptly, a slant provides a gentler way forward. Employing this logic, Dickinson's poem suggests that indirection is not necessarily a move askew, but can be a safer route toward a difficult destination.

Thesis of the paper identified.

There is reason to favor a gentle path when we consider the destination Dickinson has in mind, which is not physical but cognitive. She encourages a clear-eyed vision of the world that can be brutal in its reality. After all, her directive is not merely to "Tell the Truth" but to "Tell all the Truth." The line that follows, "Success in Circuit lies," expands upon the nature of this truth. In Dickinson's poem, knowledge has a power analogous to electricity. Just as an electrical current will shock if it is not circuitously wired, truth must be carefully delivered so as not to overwhelm.

Examples provided to illustrate and inter-pret the theme.

Dickinson embraces knowledge that is powerful and unflinching in nature, and she warns that we must be mindful of the process by which this knowledge is shared and received. The "superb surprise" of unadulterated truth might easily overwhelm the "infirm Delight," or delicate sensibilities of a learner. The implications for education are clear. Teachers must never evade. Instead, their job is to put truth into a context "with explanation kind." By doing so, teachers help students to understand the most startling or lightning-like aspects of the world.

Writer interprets the theme in terms of education.

Dickinson's attention to modes of communication has significance for composition as well. In order for the truth to "dazzle gradually," writers must be as mindful of intended audience as they are of their own ideas. To keep their readers from being "blind," or in other words, missing the point, writers must skillfully angle what they say to address what may already be in the reader's mind—sound-bites, preconceived notions, and biases. In this way, Dickinson's slanted truth is the skillful navigation of a writer, whose words must travel from the author's intention to the reader's full understanding.

Writer interprets the poem in terms of com-position/ rhetoric.

Dickinson cannily packages a message about knowledge that was very radical for her time and does so in a fairly traditional poetic structure. There is a pleasant predictability to the A-B-C-B rhyme

Writer demon-strates that poetic technique of rhyme communi-cates the poem's theme.

scheme of the text, which helps to ease communication of Dickinson's truth. In this way, the form of the poem affirms its content. Dickinson has told us all the truth, but has done so through poetic structure that is familiar and reassuring. And so poetic form is the slant Dickinson employs to communicate her unconventional message. Perhaps the intentional structural constraints fundamental to poetry make it uniquely effective circuitry for imparting difficult truths.

Writer reflects on poem as a whole and concludes with a concise statement about poetic structure as way to "Tell all the Truth but tell it slant."

CHAPTER 11

Arguments

In the college classroom and in countless situations outside the classroom, an **argument** makes a reasoned assertion about a debatable issue. In this chapter, we look at how to evaluate arguments presented by others and then how to construct arguments on important issues.

11a Understand the assignment.

In college, opinions based on personal feelings have less weight than reasoned positions expressed as written arguments. When you write an argument, your purpose is not to win but to take part in a discussion by stating and supporting your position on an issue. Written arguments appear in various forms, including critiques, reviews, and proposals:

- **Critiques:** Critiques address the question "What is true?" or "What is accurate?" A critique fairly summarizes someone's position before either refuting or defending it. *Refutations* expose the reasoning of the position as inadequate or present evidence that contradicts the position. *Defenses* clarify the author's key terms and reasoning, present new arguments to support the position, and show that criticisms of the position are unreasonable or unconvincing.

- **Reviews:** Reviews address the question "What is good?" In a review, the writer evaluates an event, an artifact, a practice, or an institution, judging by reasonable principles and criteria. Diane Chen's consideration of a photograph by Dorothea Lange in Chapter 7 *(pp. 90–92)* can be seen as an example of this genre.

- **Proposals, or policy papers:** Proposals, sometimes called policy papers, address the question "What should be done?" They are designed to cause change in the world. Readers are encouraged to see a situation in a specific way and to take action.

⊙ **11b** Learn how to evaluate verbal and visual arguments.

Three common ways to analyze verbal and visual arguments are (1) to concentrate on the type of reasoning the writer is using; (2) to question the logical relation of a writer's claims, grounds, and warrants, using the Toulmin method; and (3) to examine the ways an argument appeals to its audience.

1. Recognizing types of reasoning

Writers of arguments may use either inductive or deductive reasoning. When writers use **inductive reasoning,** they do not prove that the statements that make up the argument are true; instead they convince reasonable people that the argument's assertion is probable by presenting **evidence** (facts and statistics, telling anecdotes, and expert opinions). When writers use **deductive reasoning,** they claim that a conclusion follows necessarily from a set of assertions, or **premises**—if the premises are true and the relationship between them is valid, the conclusion must be true.

Consider the following scenarios.

Inductive reasoning A journalism student writing for the school newspaper makes the following claim:

> As Sunday's game shows, the Philadelphia Eagles are on their way to the playoffs.

Reasoning inductively, the student presents a number of facts—her evidence—that support her claim but do not prove it conclusively.

FACT 1 With three games remaining, the Eagles have a two-game lead over the second-place NY Giants.

FACT 2 The Eagles' final three opponents have a combined record of 15 wins and 24 losses.

FACT 3 The Giants lost their first-string quarterback to a season-ending injury last week.

FACT 4 The Eagles will play two of the last three games at home, where they are undefeated.

A reader would evaluate this student's argument by judging the quality of her evidence, using the criteria listed in the box on page 133.

Inductive reasoning is a key feature of the **scientific method.** Scientists gather data from experiments, surveys, and careful observations to formulate **hypotheses**—statements that can be proved or disproved—that explain the data. They then test their hypotheses by collecting additional information.

Deductive reasoning The basic structure of a deductive argument is the **syllogism.** It contains a **major premise,** or general

── NAVIGATING THROUGH COLLEGE AND BEYOND
Assessing Evidence in an Inductive Argument

- **Is it accurate?** Make sure that any facts presented as evidence are correct and not taken out of context.
- **Is it relevant?** Check to see if the evidence is clearly connected to the point being made.
- **Is it representative?** Make sure that the writer's conclusion is supported by evidence gathered from a sample that accurately reflects the larger population (for example, it has the same proportion of men and women, older and younger people, and so on). If the writer is using an example, make sure that the example is typical and not unique.
- **Is it sufficient?** Evaluate whether there is enough evidence to satisfy questioning readers.

statement; **minor premise,** or specific case; and conclusion, which follows when the general statement is applied to the specific case. Suppose the journalism student were writing about historically great baseball teams and made the following argument.

MAJOR PREMISE	Any baseball team that wins the World Series more than 25 times in 100 years is one of the greatest teams in history.
MINOR PREMISE	The New York Yankees have won the World Series more than 25 times in the past 100 years.
CONCLUSION	The New York Yankees are one of the greatest baseball teams in history.

This is a deductive argument: if the relationship between its premises is valid and both premises are true, the conclusion must be true. The conclusion follows from the premises. For example, it is not accurate to say: "The train is late. Jane is late. Therefore, Jane must be on the train." Jane could be late because her car broke down. However, if the train is late and Jane is on the train, Jane must be late.

If the logical relationship between the premises is valid, a reader must evaluate the truth of the premises themselves. Do you think, for example, that the number of World Series wins is a proper measure of a team's greatness? Or the only measure? If not, you could claim that the major premise is false or suspect and does not support the conclusion.

Deductive reasoning predominates in mathematics and some humanities disciplines, including philosophy. However, you can use both types of reasoning in college courses and in life.

2. Using the Toulmin method to analyze arguments

Philosopher Stephen Toulmin's analysis of arguments is based on **claims** (assertions about a topic), **grounds** (reasons and evidence), and **warrants** (assumptions or principles that link the grounds to the claims).

Consider the following sentence from an argument by a student.

The death penalty should be abolished because if it is not abolished, innocent people could be executed.

This example, like all logical arguments, has three facets.

CLAIM The death penalty should be abolished.

GROUNDS Innocent people could be executed (related stories and statistics).

WARRANT It is not possible to be completely sure of a person's guilt.

1. **The argument makes a claim.** Also known as a *point* or a *thesis,* a **claim** makes an assertion about a topic. A strong claim responds to an issue of real interest to its audience in clear and precise terms. It also allows for some uncertainty by including qualifying words such as *might* or *possibly,* or describes circumstances under which the claim is true. A weak claim is merely a statement of fact or a statement that few would argue with. Because personal feelings are not debatable, they are not an appropriate claim for an argument.

   WEAK CLAIMS The death penalty is highly controversial.

   The death penalty makes me sick.

2. **The argument presents grounds for the claim.** **Grounds** consist of the reasons and evidence (facts and statistics, anecdotes, and expert opinion) that support the claim. As grounds for the claim in the example, the student would present statistics and stories related to innocent people being executed. The box on page 136 should help you assess the evidence supporting a claim.

3. **The argument depends on assumptions that link the grounds to the claim.** When you analyze an argument, be aware of the unstated assumptions, or **warrants,** that underlie both the claim and the grounds that support it. The warrants underlying the example argument against the death penalty include two ideas: (1) it is wrong to execute innocent people; and (2) it is not possible to be completely sure of a person's guilt. Warrants differ from discipline to discipline and from one school of thought to another. If you were studying the topic of bullfighting and its place in Spanish society in a sociology course, for example, you

would probably make different arguments with different warrants than would the writer of a rhetorical analysis of Ernest Hemingway's book about bullfighting, *Death in the Afternoon*. You might argue that bullfighting serves as a safe outlet for its fans' aggressive feelings. Your warrant would be that sports can have socially useful purposes. A more controversial warrant would be that it is acceptable to kill animals for entertainment.

As you read the writing of others and as you write yourself, look for **unstated assumptions.** What does the reader have to assume to accept the reason and evidence in support of the claim? Hidden assumptions sometimes show **bias,** positive or negative inclinations that can manipulate unwary readers. Assumptions also differ across cultures.

3. Analyzing appeals

Arguments support claims by way of three types of appeals to readers, categorized by the Greek words **logos** (logic), **pathos** (emotions), and **ethos** (character):

- **Logical appeals** offer facts, including statistics, as well as reasoning, such as the inductive and deductive arguments on pages 132–33.

- **Emotional appeals** engage an audience's feelings and invoke beliefs that the author and audience share.

- **Ethical appeals** present authors as fair, reasonable, and trustworthy, backed up with the testimony of experts.

Most arguments draw on all three appeals. A proposal for more nutritious school lunches might cite statistics about childhood obesity (a logical appeal). The argument might address the audience's emotions by describing overweight children feasting on junk food available in the cafeteria (an emotional appeal). It might quote a doctor explaining that healthful food aids concentration (a logical appeal) and that all children deserve to have nutritious food available at school (an ethical appeal). When writing an argument, tailor the type and content of appeals to the specific audience you are addressing. For example, school administrators, charged with making decisions about cafeteria food, might be persuaded by statistics demonstrating the relationship of the cost of food to its nutritional value (logical appeal) and the impact of good nutrition on learning (logical appeal).

4. Avoiding fallacies

In their enthusiasm to make a point, writers sometimes commit **fallacies,** or mistakes in reasoning. Fallacies also can be understood as misuses of the three appeals. Learn to identify fallacies when you read and to avoid them when you write.

TYPES OF EVIDENCE FOR CLAIMS

- **Facts and statistics:** Relevant, current facts and statistics can per-suasively support a claim. People on different sides of an issue can **interpret** the same facts and statistics differently, however, or can cite different facts and statistics to prove their point. Facts don't speak for themselves: they must be interpreted to support a claim.
- **Anecdotes:** An anecdote is a brief narrative used as an illustration to support a claim. Because stories appeal to the emotions as well as to the intellect, they can be very effective. Be especially careful to check anecdotes for logical fallacies *(see pp. 136–39)*. Though useful, anec-dotes should be only one of the types of evidence you use.
- **Expert opinion:** The views of authorities in a given field can also be pow-erful support for a claim. Be sure that the expert cited has credentials related to the topic.

Logical fallacies These fallacies involve errors in the inductive and deductive reasoning processes already discussed:

- **Non sequitur:** A conclusion that does not logically follow from the evidence or one that is based on irrelevant evidence.

  EXAMPLE Students don't care about responsibility; they often default on their student loans. [*Students who default on loans could be faced with high medical bills or prolonged unemployment.*]

  Generalizing based on evidence is an important tactic of argu-ment. However, the evidence must be relevant. Non sequiturs also stem from dubious assumptions.

- **False cause or post hoc:** An argument that falsely assumes that because one thing happens after another, the first event was a cause of the second event.

  EXAMPLE I drank green tea and my headache went away; therefore, green tea makes headaches go away. [*How do we know that the headache did not go away for another reason?*]

  Although writers frequently describe causes and effects in argument, fallacies result when writers assume a cause with-out providing sufficient evidence.

- **Self-contradiction:** An argument that contradicts itself.

  EXAMPLE No absolute statement can be true. [*The state-ment itself is an absolute.*]

- **Circular reasoning:** An argument that restates the point rather than supporting it with reasonable evidence.

  EXAMPLE   The wealthy should pay more taxes because taxes should be higher for people with higher incomes. [*The statement does not explain why the wealthy should pay more taxes; it just restates the position.*]

- **Begging the question:** A form of circular reasoning that assumes the truth of a questionable opinion.

  EXAMPLE   The President's poor relationship with the military has weakened the armed forces. [*Does the President really have a poor relationship with the military?*]

  Some claims contain assumptions that must be proven first.

- **Hasty generalization:** A conclusion based on inadequate evidence.

  EXAMPLE   It took me over an hour to find a parking spot downtown. Therefore, the city should build a new parking garage. [*Is this evidence enough to prove this very broad conclusion?*]

- **Sweeping generalization:** An overly broad statement made in absolute terms. When made about a group of people, a sweeping generalization is a **stereotype.**

  EXAMPLE   College students are carefree. [*What about students who work to put themselves through school?*]

  Legitimate generalizations must be based on evidence that is accurate, relevant, representative, and sufficient (*see the box on p. 133*).

- **Either/or fallacy:** The idea that a complicated issue can be resolved by resorting to one of only two options when in reality there are additional choices.

  EXAMPLE   Either the state legislature will raise taxes, or our state's economy will falter. [*Are these really the only two possibilities?*]

  Frequently, arguments consider different courses of action. Authors demonstrate their sense of fairness and their understanding of issues by considering a range of options.

Ethical fallacies   These fallacies undermine a writer's credibility by showing lack of fairness to opposing views and lack of expertise on the subject of the argument.

- **Ad hominem:** A personal attack on someone who disagrees with you rather than on the person's argument.

    EXAMPLE   The district attorney is a lazy political hack, so naturally she opposes streamlining the court system. [*Even if the district attorney usually supports her party's position, does that make her wrong about this issue?*]

    This fallacy stops debate by ignoring the real issue.

- **Guilt by association:** Discrediting a person because of problems with that person's associates, friends, or family.

    EXAMPLE   Smith's friend has been convicted of fraud, so Smith cannot be trusted. [*Is Smith responsible for his friend's actions?*]

    This tactic undermines an opponent's credibility and is based on a dubious assumption: if a person's associates are untrustworthy, that person is also untrustworthy.

- **False authority:** Presenting the testimony of an unqualified person to support a claim.

    EXAMPLE   As the actor who plays Dr. Fine on *The Emergency Room,* I recommend this weight-loss drug because . . . [*Is an actor qualified to judge the benefits and dangers of a diet drug?*]

    Expert testimony can strengthen an argument, as long as the person cited is an authority on the subject. This fallacy frequently underlies celebrity endorsements of products.

Emotional fallacies   These fallacies stir readers' sympathy at the expense of their reasoning.

- **False analogy:** A comparison in which a surface similarity masks a significant difference.

    EXAMPLE   Governments and businesses both work within a budget to accomplish their goals. Just as business must focus on the bottom line, so should government. [*Is the goal of government to make a profit? Does government instead have different goals?*]

    Analogies can enliven an argument and deepen an audience's understanding of a subject, provided the things being compared actually are similar.

- **Bandwagon:** An argument that depends on going along with the crowd, on the false assumption that truth can be determined by a popularity contest.

EXAMPLE   Given the sales of that book, its claims must be true. [*Sales volume does not indicate the truth of the claim. How do we know that a popular book presents accurate information?*]

- **Red herring:** An argument that diverts attention from the true issue by concentrating on an irrelevant one.

EXAMPLE   Hemingway's book *Death in the Afternoon* is unsuccessful because it glorifies the brutal sport of bullfighting. [*Why can't a book about a brutal sport be successful? The statement is irrelevant.*]

5. Reading visual arguments

Like written arguments, visual arguments support claims with reasons and evidence, rely on assumptions, and may contain fallacies. They make logical appeals, such as a graph of experimental data; emotional appeals, such as a photograph of a hungry child; and ethical appeals, such as a corporate logo. Like written works, visual arguments are created by an author to achieve a purpose and to address an audience within a given context. *(See Chapter 2, pp. 17–18.)*

Toulmin's system, as we saw, analyzes arguments based on the claims they make, the grounds (evidence and reasons) for those claims, and the warrants (underlying assumptions) that connect the grounds with the claims. *(See the explanation of Toulmin analysis on pp. 134–35.)* While these elements function similarly in verbal and visual arguments, unstated assumptions play a larger role in visual arguments because we are not used to "reading" visuals and interpreting the implicitly stated claims and grounds.

For example, consider a photograph of a politician with her family members. The image makes a claim (she is a good public servant)

CHECKLIST Reading Visual Arguments Critically

Review the questions for previewing a visual from Chapter 4, pages 35–36, and add the following:

☐ What can you tell about the visual's creator or sponsor?

☐ What seems to be the visual's purpose? Does it promote a product or message?

☐ What features of the visual suggest the intended audience? How?

☐ How do aspects of design such as the size and position of the elements, the colors, and shapes of images affect the visual's message?

☐ What is the effect of any text, audio, or video that accompanies the visual?

and implicitly offers grounds (because she cares for her family). The warrant is that a person's family life indicates how she will perform in office. This assumption may be false.

Advertisements combine text and images to promote a product or message to an audience in a social context. They use the resources of visual design: type of image, position, color, light and shadows, typefaces or fonts, layout, and white space. *(See the questions on previewing a visual in Chapter 4, pp. 35–36 and the discussion of design in Chapter 8, pp. 93–100.)* The public-service ad in Figure 11.1 was developed by the nonprofit advocacy group Adbusters.

The ad's text and format evoke a popular series of ads for a brand of vodka. Its uncluttered design focuses the viewer's attention on the shape of a bottle, the outline of which consists of chairs. The text at the bottom refers to AA: Alcoholics Anonymous. By association, the text and images in this public-service ad remind readers that liquor can lead to alcoholism (and then to AA). In contrast with those it spoofs, this ad evokes an unexpected threat, creating a powerful emotional appeal.

What claims do you think this ad makes? One might be "alcohol is dangerous." The evidence is supplied by the reader's prior knowledge about alcoholism. The argument's assumptions include the viewer's familiarity with both the original liquor campaign and the initials "AA" for Alcoholics Anonymous.

Fallacies frequently occur in visual arguments. For example, celebrity endorsements of products rely on our respect for the celebrity's character. However, a photo of an athlete driving a particular type of car demonstrates false authority, unless the athlete also happens to be an expert on cars. *(See p. 138.)*

FIGURE 11.1 A public-service argument: Adbusters public-service advertisement.

11c   Approach writing your own argument as a process.

Selecting a topic that you care about will give you the energy to think matters through and make cogent arguments. Of course, you will have to go beyond your personal emotions to make the most convincing case. You will also have to empathize with potential readers who may disagree with you about a subject that is important to you.

1. Figuring out what is at issue

Before you can take a position on a topic like noise pollution or population growth, you must figure out what is at issue. Ask questions about your topic. Do you see indications that all is not as it should be? Have things always been this way, or have they changed for the worse? From what different perspectives—economic, social, political, cultural, medical, geographic—can problems like world food shortages be understood? Do people interested in the topic disagree about what is true, what is good, or what should be done?

Based on your answers to such questions, identify the issues your topic raises, and decide what is most important, interesting, and appropriate to write about.

2. Developing a reasonable stance that negotiates differences

When writing arguments, you want your readers to respect your intelligence and trust your judgment. By influencing readers to trust your character, you build **ethos.** Conducting research on an issue can make you well informed; reading other people's views can enhance your thoughtfulness. Pay attention to the places where you disagree with the opinions of others, but also note what you have in

— the EVOLVING SITUATION

Blogs

Weblogs, or *blogs* for short—the continually updated sites linking an author's comments to other sites on the Web—frequently function as vehicles for public debate. For example, online editions of many newspapers include blogs that invite readers to comment on the news of the day and to present dissenting opinions. While online debate can be freewheeling, it's important to search for common ground with your readers. *(For more on blogs, see Chapter 14, pp. 183–85.)*

Looking at blogs can help you learn about an issue or find counterarguments to your position. *(See Chapter 19, p. 232.)* However, evaluate blogs carefully before using them as support for an argument *(see Chapter 21, pp. 240–46).* Many blogs rely heavily on personal opinion, and some are not factually accurate.

KNOW THE SITUATION Arguments

Purpose: To persuade

Audience: Audience members can be close to a writer (for example, classmates) or distant from him or her (for example, citizens of an unfamiliar country), but in either case, keying in on members of that audience is important because reasons, examples, and stories should speak to them.

Stance: Reasonable

Genres: Arguments appear as stand-alone genres and inside other genres like reviews, critiques, and proposals.

Medium: Print, digital, or networked depending on the audience and the topic. (A proposal for a new bridge might be more compelling in a visual medium, for example.)

Commonly used: In most disciplines, the workplace, and public life

common—topical interests, key questions, or underlying values. *(For more on appeals to your audience, see p. 135.)*

Avoid language that may promote prejudice or fear. Misrepresentations of other people's ideas reduce your ethos and weaken your argument, as do personal attacks. Write arguments to expand thinking, your own and that of others. *(See the box on blogs on p. 141.)*

Trying out different perspectives can also help you figure out where you stand on an issue. *(Also see the next section on stating your position.)* Make a list of the arguments for and against a specific position; then compare the lists and decide where you stand, perhaps on one side or the other or somewhere in between. Does one set of arguments seem stronger than the other? Do you want to change or qualify your initial position?

3. Composing a thesis that states your position

A successful argument requires a strong, engaging, arguable thesis. As noted in the section on the Toulmin model of argument, personal feelings and accepted facts cannot serve as an argument's thesis because they are not debatable *(see pp. 134–35)*.

PERSONAL FEELING, NOT A DEBATABLE THESIS

I feel that developing nations should not suffer food shortages.

ACCEPTED FACT, NOT A DEBATABLE THESIS

Food shortages are a growing problem in many developing nations.

DEBATABLE THESIS

Current food shortages in developing nations are in large part caused by climate change and the use of food crops in biofuels.

In proposals and policy papers, the thesis presents a solution in terms of the writer's definition of the problem. The logic behind a thesis for a proposal can be stated like this:

Given these key variables and their underlying cause, one solution to the problem would be . . .

Because this kind of thesis is both complex and qualified, you will often need more than one sentence to state it clearly. Draw on numerous well-supported arguments to make it credible. Readers finally want to know that the proposed solution will not cause more problems than it solves.

4. Identifying key points to support and develop your thesis

A strong, debatable thesis should be supported and developed with sound reasoning and carefully documented evidence. You can think of an argument as a dialogue between writer and readers. The writer states a debatable thesis, and one reader wonders, "Why do you believe that?" Another reader wants to know, "But what about this factor?" Anticipate readers' questions, and answer them by presenting reasons that are substantiated with evidence and by refuting opposing views. Define any abstract terms, such as *freedom,* that figure importantly in your arguments. In his proposal for eliminating cyberbullying, Joseph Honrado defines cyberbullying and shows how it both compares to traditional bullying and differs from it *(pp. 148–54).*

Usually, a well-developed argument includes more than one type of claim and more than one kind of evidence. Employ generalizations based on empirical data or statistics, authoritative reasons based on the opinions of experts, and ethical reasons based on the application of principle. In his argument, Honrado provides data from the Cyberbullying Research Center showing the percentages of teens who have admitted to acts of cyberbullying as well as anecdotal evidence on a teen suicide that helped to raise awareness of the issue.

As you conduct research, note evidence—facts, examples or anecdotes, and expert testimony—that can support each argument for or against your position. Demonstrate your trustworthiness by properly quoting and documenting the information you have gathered from your sources. Joseph Honrado adds credibility to his argument by quoting experts on his topic, integrating the quotation seamlessly into his own sentence:

Trolley and Hanel caution that, beyond guidelines, young people also need to develop a healthy balance of online and offline activities to change the social nature of cyberbullying: "Prevention, primarily through education and process communication, as well as therapeutic intervention, is essential to achieve this proper use of technology" (82).

Also build your credibility by paying attention to **counterarguments,** substantiated claims that do not support your position. Consider whether a reader could reasonably draw different conclusions from your evidence or disagree with your assumptions. Use one of the following strategies to address potential counterarguments:

- Qualify your thesis in light of the counterargument by including a word such as *most, some, usually,* or *likely:* "Students with credit cards *usually* have trouble with debt" recognizes that some do not.

- Add to the thesis a statement of the conditions for or exceptions to your position: "Businesses *with over five hundred employees* saved money using the new process."

- Choose at least one or two counterarguments, and refute their truth or their importance.

Introduce a counterargument with a signal phrase like "Others might contend . . ." *(See Tab 5: Researching, p. 271, for a discussion of signal phrases.)* Refute a counterargument's claim by questioning the author's interpretation of the evidence or the author's assumptions. Honrado acknowledges that teens often don't report instances of cyber bullying, but he refutes the idea that adults can't help by pointing to the example of a high school principal who made a difference by taking quick action.

5. Creating a linked set of reasons

Arguments are most effective when they present a chain—a linked set—of reasons. Honrado states his thesis in the introductory paragraph and then identifies two types of cyberbullying and ways to combat them. Although you can order an argument in many ways, include the following parts (arranged below following **classical structure**):

- An introduction to the topic and the debatable issue, establishing your credibility and seeking common ground with your readers

- A thesis stating your position on the issue

- A point-by-point account of the reasons for your position, including the evidence (facts, examples, authorities) you will use to substantiate each major reason

- A fair presentation and refutation of one or two key counterarguments

- A response to the "so what?" question. Why does your argument matter? If appropriate, include a call to action.

If you expect your audience to disagree with you, consider using a **Rogerian structure:**

- An introduction to the topic and the debatable issue
- An attempt to reach common ground by naming values you share and providing a sympathetic portrayal of your readers' (opposing) position
- A statement of your position and presentation of supporting evidence
- A conclusion that restates your view and suggests a compromise or synthesis

6. Appealing to your audience

You want your readers to see you as *reasonable, ethical,* and *empathetic*—qualities that promote communication among people who have differences. *(For more on appeals, see p. 135.)* When you read your argument, pay attention to the impression you are making. Ask yourself these questions:

- Would a reasonable person be able to follow my logic and acknowledge the evidence I offer in support of my thesis?
- Have I presented myself as ethical and fair? What would readers who have never met me think of me after reading what I have to say?
- Have I expressed my feelings about the issue? Have I been fair in seeking to arouse the reader's emotions?

7. Emphasizing your commitment to dialogue in the introduction

To promote dialogue with readers, look for common ground—beliefs, concerns, and values you share with those who disagree with you and those who are undecided. Sometimes called **Rogerian argument** after the psychologist Carl Rogers, the common-ground approach is particularly important in your introduction, where it builds bridges with readers who might otherwise become too defensive or annoyed to read further. Peggy Giglio includes in her discussion of volunteerism the common perception that young adults today are more interested in socializing through social media than their parents' generation. *See Chapter 34, pp. 378–92, for Peggy Giglio's argument.)* Keep the dialogue open throughout your essay by maintaining a reasonable tone and acknowledging opposing views. If possible, return to that common ground at the end of your argument.

8. Concluding by restating your position and emphasizing its importance

After presenting your reasoning in detail, remind readers of your thesis. To encourage readers to appreciate your argument's importance, make the version of your thesis in your conclusion more complex and qualified than in your introduction. Readers may not agree with you, but they should know why the issue and your argument matter.

9. Using visuals in your argument

Consider including visuals that support your argument's purpose. Each should relate directly to your argument as a whole or to a point within it. Visuals also may provide evidence: a photograph can illustrate an example, and a graph can present statistics that support an argument.

Visual evidence makes emotional, logical, and ethical appeals. The Absolute AA ad on page 140 makes an emotional appeal by substituting a warning against alcoholism for the expected commercial message. The graph of types of cyberbullying in Joseph Honrado's argument *(p. 149)* makes a logical appeal by presenting evidence that supports his claim, demonstrating the depth of his research while at the same time building his ethos.

CHECKLIST Reviewing Your Own and Other Writers' Arguments

First identify what the text is doing well, and find ways to build on those strengths. Then identify parts in the text that are confusing, underdeveloped, or inaccurate, and share ways of addressing those problems:

- [ ] **What makes the thesis strong and arguable?**
- [ ] **Is the thesis supported with a sufficient number of reasons, or are more needed?**
- [ ] **Are the reasons and evidence appropriate for the purpose, audience, and context?**
- [ ] **Does the argument contain mistakes in logic?** Refer to pages 136–39 to check for logical fallacies.
- [ ] **How is each reason developed?** Is the reason clear? Where are its key terms defined? Is the supporting evidence sufficient?
- [ ] **Does the argument quote or paraphrase from sources accurately and document them properly?** *(For more on quoting, paraphrasing, and documenting sources, see Tab 5 Researching, and Tabs 6-8, which cover commonly used documentation styles.)*
- [ ] **Has at least one significant counterargument been addressed?** How have opposing views been treated?
- [ ] **In what way does each visual support the thesis?** How are the visuals tailored to the audience?
- [ ] **Are logical, ethical, and emotional appeals used consistently and effectively?**

┌───

CONSIDER YOUR SITUATION

Author: Joseph Honrado

Type of writing: Argument in the form of a proposal

Purpose: To show (1) that cyberbullying is a new form of bullying and (2) that if it is to be stopped, students, parents, and educators must work together to create guidelines for online behavior

Stance: Informed and reasonable

Audience: Students, parents, and educators

Medium: This argument is developed in two media: print and slides.

Honrado writes: As I worked on this argument, I was at first dismayed that the wonders of technology have opened up new opportunities for emotional violence. But then I realized the importance of calling upon students, parents, and educators to address the issue.

└───

Consider how your audience is likely to react to your visuals. Non-specialists will need more explanation of charts, graphs, and other visuals. When possible, have members of your target audience review your argument and visuals. Provide specific captions that identify each visual, showing how it supports your argument. Mention each image in your text. Make sure charts and graphs are free of distortion or chartjunk *(see Chapter 7: Revising and Editing, p. 83)*. Also acknowledge data from other sources and obtain permission when needed. *(See pp. 233–39.)*

10. Reexamining your reasoning
After you have completed the first draft of your argument, take time to reexamine your reasoning for errors. Step outside yourself, and assess your argument objectively. Peer review can be especially helpful in testing your reasoning and persuasive powers.

11d   Student sample: Proposal

In an English course, Joseph Honrado conducted research on cyberbullying and then constructed a policy paper (sometimes called a proposal) to address the question, "What should be done?" In the humanities, as well as in other disciplines, arguments like Joseph Honrado's are designed to bring about change. Honrado documents the impact of cyberbullying, evaluates its negative consequences, and then argues that students, parents, and educators must take action.

> **Note:** For details on the proper formatting of a text in MLA style, see Chapter 29 and the sample research report that begins on page 331.

SAMPLE STUDENT ARGUMENT

Joseph Honrado

Professor Robertson

English 201

30 November 2013

Cyberbullying: An Alarming Trend for the Digital Age

Before the advent of cell phones and the Internet, bullies would harass their victims on the playground, the school bus, and in the classroom or lunchroom. In response to these confrontations, adults would typically advise children to stand up to bullies or to avoid them. However, in today's digital society, standing up to a bully is much more difficult. According to PACER's National Bullying Prevention Center, all bullying is typically characterized by an "imbalance of power" in which the more powerful party "hurts or harms another person physically or emotionally" ("Bullying Info"). Stopbullying.gov, a Web site supported by the US Department of Health and Human Services, updates this definition to include "bullying that takes place using electronic technology," also known as cyberbullying ("Bullying Definition"). Cyberbullying is a growing problem among today's youth and is especially destructive because of its immediacy, circulation, and permanence: the humiliation is easily inflicted and can continue indefinitely before a wide audience. If the problem of cyberbullying is ever to be overcome, students, parents, educators, and the media must all make efforts to instill guidelines for online behavior.

Cyberbullying is commonly carried out through text messaging, instant messaging, and social networking sites like Facebook and Twitter. While cyberbullying can take many forms, most often it involves the posting of hurtful comments or rumors online, as shown in Fig. 1. Cyberbullying is especially dangerous because technology is so ubiquitous. As a recent article in *USA Today* explains, "Today's

Margin annotations:

Introduces issue of cyberbullying.

Presents definition of cyberbullying.

Thesis statement.

Presents a detailed explanation of cyberbullying, followed by a visual that indicates the extent of the problem.

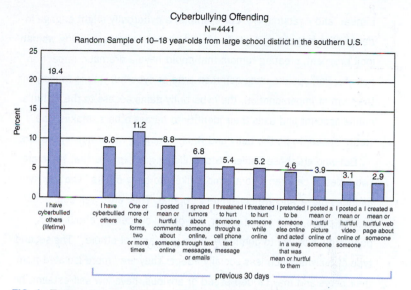

FIG. 1. Percentages of 10- to 18-year-olds who admitted to cyberbullying. Hinduja, Sameer, and Justin W. Patchin. "Cyberbullying Fact Sheet: Identification, Prevention, and Response." Cyberbullying Research Center, 2010. Web. 17 Nov. 2013.

cyberbullying is more extreme than the bullying anyone over 30 remembers. Before such abuse went digital, victims at least had escape routes—at home, in an activity, or when they changed schools" ("Use New Tools"). The hurtful messages can be targeted to one person privately or posted publicly for the target's peers to see. Insults and threats posted to social media, for instance, are not easily retracted and can be reposted by others. This permanent and potentially uncontrollable content is often disseminated far and wide before the victim can do anything to mitigate its effects.

Some common cyberbullying tactics include *flaming* (using angry language in an online "fight"), *harassment* (repeated online messages that insult or offend), *outing* (sharing secrets online, including embarrassing images or information), *trickery* (deliberate deception or tricking someone into sharing secrets widely), *denigration* (malicious spreading of gossip or a rumor), *cyber stalking* (aggressive online behavior that intimidates or threatens a person's safety), and *exclusion* (from online groups, lists, or activities) (Kowalski,

Establishes the nature of the problem with examples and demonstrates its seriousness.

Limber, and Agatston 47). For example, a cyberbully might engage in *denigration* by posting digitally altered photos to make a young woman look pregnant, creating rumors that could have a dramatic impact on her life. Perhaps the most common type of cyberbullying is *trickery* in the form of impersonation: the cyberbully gains access to the victim's online account and uses their identity to harass others, making the victim appear to be the bully and thus damaging his or her reputation.

But who are these bullies? Stopbullying.gov explains that there are two types of children who are more likely to bully others. The first type includes those who are considered popular. They are "well connected to their peers, have social power, are overly concerned about their popularity, and like to dominate or be in charge of others." The second type of bully is much less socially adept. They are "more isolated from their peers and may be depressed or anxious, have low self-esteem, be less involved in school, be easily pressured by peers, or not identify with the emotions or feelings of others" ("Risk Factors"). Though the ages of cyberbullies and their victims range from young children to college students, cyberbullying may be most destructive to younger teens because they lack the maturity to handle such situations and rarely seek help from adults. A recent Pew survey reported that 78% of teens have cell phones (almost half of which are smart phones) and 93% have computers or access to them (Madden et al. 2, 5). When unsupervised, technology use among young children can breed the inappropriate digital behaviors researchers warn about.

Whether due to their age or personality types, some cyberbullies seem to not comprehend the gravity of their actions. One of the most famous cases of cyberbullying resulted in the victim, Rutgers student Tyler Clementi, taking dire action. His roommate, Dharun Ravi, set up a webcam in their dorm room in order to secretly live stream to their peers Clementi's dates with another man (Gendar, Sandoval, and McShane). This hurtful invasion of Clementi's privacy is a perfect example of *outing* as described above. After Clementi realized he was a victim of cyberbullying, he committed suicide. When sentencing Ravi after the trial, the judge stated, "I haven't heard you apologize

Provides factual support indicating who the cyberbullies are.

Summarizes research on the causes of the problem of cyberbullying.

Provides anecdotal support (emotional appeal).

once" (qtd. in Susman). The judge went on to say that he did not think Ravi was homophobic but that "he acted out of colossal insensitivity" (Susman). Ravi later admitted that some of his actions were wrong but stated, "I wasn't the one who caused him to jump off the bridge" (qtd. in Gomstyn). Ravi's lack of remorse for his actions is a strong characteristic of a bully. Without an understanding of the consequences of cyberbullying, bullies are unlikely to end their harmful behavior.

Presents quotation from a person engaged in this behavior.

Evidence of the serious consequences of cyberbullying is mounting quickly. In her article "Cyberbullying," Jennifer Holladay quotes a study by Sameer Hinduja, which shows that "cyberbullying victims were nearly twice as likely to attempt suicide compared with students not targeted with online abuse" (5). Other effects of cyberbullying are much more common and leave lasting, devastating impacts. In their article "High-Tech Cruelty," Hinduja and Justin W. Patchin report a "link between cyberbullying and low self-esteem, family problems, academic problems, school violence, and delinquent behaviors" for victims. In addition, they claim that "those who have been cyberbullied are more likely to struggle with these emotional, psychological, and behavioral problems than those who have not" (50). Since cyberbullying is relatively new, there are few long-term studies on victims. However, one such long-term study, originally published in *JAMA Psychiatry in America,* associates cyberbullying with "an elevated risk of psychiatric problems that extends into adulthood" (qtd. in Louise 5). Scott Freeman, Director of the Cybersmile Foundation, agrees. In fact, he believes that "we're going to have a delayed mental health issue with cyberbullying. . . . There are going to be long-term problems" (qtd. in Louise 5).

Provides factual support (logical appeal).

While students may not appreciate the potential for "pranks" to lead to tragedy and long-term mental anguish, many parents are starting to comprehend the dangers. Louise notes that while parents tend to restrict the physical places their children can go—to the mall or the movies, for example—too often they are not paying attention to their activities on the Internet (8). Stopbullying.gov encourages parents

Establishes that parents are becoming more aware of the problem and the need to take action.

to talk to their children, making sure they understand bullying and feel comfortable bringing issues to their parents. Trolley and Hanel caution that, beyond guidelines, young people also need to develop a healthy balance of online and offline activities to change the social nature of cyberbullying: "Prevention, primarily through education and process communication, as well as therapeutic intervention, is essential to achieve this proper use of technology" (82). Families can begin to achieve that cyber balance by placing the computer in a common area and establishing guidelines for behavior when a family member is using the computer or a cell phone.

Integrates expert testimony to support the argument.

Educators have also become more involved in both identifying cases of cyberbullying and responding to specific incidents. Highline Academy, a charter school in Denver, sprang into action when "a conflict fueled by Facebook posts ultimately led to a physical altercation" (Holladay 6). School officials ordered a 48-hour moratorium on Facebook activity at home and called the parents of each student involved. "Numerous parents came back to us and said, 'I had no idea'—no idea what their child was doing online," said Highline's principal, Greg Gonzales (qtd. in Holladay 6). Schools are also being proactive by creating programs designed to prevent cyberbullying and to give their students a forum for discussion, a step that Hinduja and Patchin believe is critical to solving the problem of cyberbullying ("Fact Sheet").

Establishes that educators are becoming more aware of the problem and the need to take action.

Mass media and social media outlets can also be powerful advocates for cyberbullying prevention. In 2010, MTV.com launched its "A Thin Line" campaign to raise awareness about teen digital abuse and to help teens recognize and handle it. As part of that campaign, every two years MTV partners with the Associated Press to conduct a survey of digital abuse among 14- to 24-year-olds. Their 2011 study found that over half of the respondents had been the victims of digital abuse, and half of those reported frequent encounters with discriminatory language over social media ("MTV-AP Digital Abuse Study"). Facebook has also taken on the problem by creating a cyberbullying prevention hub, "arming bullying victims with information on what they can do when they see harassing content" (Risen).

In spite of the best efforts of parents and school officials, many children still don't talk about their experiences as victims of cyberbullying. Louise notes that one reason kids don't report abuse is because of their age: teenage years are a time "when a child separates from his or her parents and becomes their own person," and when "one's peers mean more than anyone else" (3). Stopbullying. gov offers several other reasons for remaining quiet, including that victims may fear being seen as "weak" or a "tattletale," fear retaliation by their bullies, or believe that "no one cares or could understand" ("Warning Signs"). Though these concerns are warranted, if students don't report instances of bullying, authority figures can do little to stop it.

If cyberbullying is ever to be diminished, students, parents, educators, and the media must work together to establish guidelines for proper online behavior, or "netiquette." With increasing awareness of the impact of cyberbullying on its victims, families and schools can mitigate those effects by balancing technology use with common sense and by preparing children to understand and report incidents of cyberbullying before they result in tragedy. Trolley and Hanel suggest victims adopt a "Stop, Save, and Share" approach to cyberbullying. They offer simple tips that families can implement: children should stop and consider consequences before reacting to a cyberbully attack, save the information as proof, and share the information with a trusted adult (79). Websites like Stopbullying.gov also offer a wide variety of resources for dealing with cyberbullies, including counselling services, community outreach, workshops, and a helpline. Through these measures, the very technology that has allowed cyberbullying to exist can also be a large part of the solution.

-------------------------------[new page]-------------------------------

Works Cited

"Bullying Definition." *Stopbullying.gov.* Stopbullying.gov, n.d. Web. 17 Nov. 2013.

"Bullying Info and Facts." *PACER's National Bullying Prevention Center.* Pacer.org, n.d. Web. 17 Nov. 2013.

Sidebar (margin note 1): Emphasizes common ground ("these concerns are warranted"), but provides evidence that adult intervention can work to refute the counterargument.

Sidebar (margin note 2): List of works cited begins on a new page and is formatted according to MLA style.

Gendar, Alison, Edgar Sandoval, and Larry McShane. "Rutgers Freshman Kills Self After Classmates Use Hidden Camera to Watch His Sexual Activity." *Nydailynews.com*. NY Daily News, 30 Sept. 2010. Web. 18 Nov. 2013.

Gomstyn, Alice. "Rutgers' Ravi: 'I Wasn't the One Who Caused Him to Jump'." *ABC News*. ABC News Network, 22 Mar. 2012. Web. 19 Nov. 2013.

Hinduja, Sameer, and Justin W. Patchin. "Cyberbullying Fact Sheet: Identification, Prevention, and Response." Cyberbullying Research Center, 2010. Web. 17 Nov. 2013.

———. "High-Tech Cruelty." *Educational Leadership* 68.5 (2011): 48–52. Web. 17 Nov. 2013.

Holladay, Jennifer. "Cyberbullying." *Education Digest* 76.5 (2011): 4–9. Web. 18 Nov. 2013.

Kowalski, Robin M., Susan P. Limber, and Patricia W. Agatston. *Cyber Bullying: Bullying in the Digital Age*. Malden: Blackwell, 2008. Print.

Louise, France. "Cyberbullying and Its Teenage Victims." *Thetimes. co.uk*. The Times (United Kingdom), 15 Jun. 2013: 22–28. Web. 17 Nov. 2013.

Madden, Mary, et al. "Teens and Technology 2013." Pew Research Center, 13 Mar. 2013. Web. 18 Nov. 2013.

"MTV-AP Digital Abuse Study." *A Thin Line*. MTV.com, Sept. 2011. Web. 22 Nov. 2013.

Risen, Tom. "Facebook Adds Online Bullying Prevention Hub." *USNews.com*. U.S. News, 6 Nov. 2013. Web. 18 Nov. 2013.

"Risk Factors." *Stopbullying.gov*. Stopbullying.gov, n.d. Web. 18 Nov. 2013.

Susman, Tina. "Dharun Ravi Sentenced to Jail in Rutgers Webcam Case." *Latimes.com*. Los Angeles Times, 21 May 2012. Web. 18 Nov. 2013.

Trolley, Barbara C., and Constance Hanel. *Cyber Kids, Cyber Bullying, Cyber Balance*. Thousand Oaks: Corwin, 2010. Print.

"Use New Tools to Combat New Forms of Bullying." *USAToday.com*. USA Today, n.d. Web. 17 Nov. 2013.

"Warning Signs." *Stopbullying.gov*. Stopbullying.gov, n.d. Web. 19 Nov. 2013.

CHAPTER 12

Other Kinds of Assignments

12a   Personal essays

The personal essay is a literary form. Like a poem, a play, or a story, it should feel meaningful to readers and relevant to their lives. A personal essay should speak in a distinctive voice and be both compelling and memorable.

1. Making connections between your experiences and those of your readers

When you write a personal essay, you are exploring your experiences, clarifying your values, and composing a public self. Since the writing situation involves an audience of strangers who will be more interested in your topic than in you, it is important to make distinctions between the personal and the private. Whether you are writing a personal essay about a tree in autumn, a trip to Senegal, or an athletic event, your purpose is to engage readers in what is meaningful to you—and potentially to them—in these objects and experiences.

When we read a personal essay, we expect to learn more than the details of the writer's experience; we expect to see the connections between that experience and our own.

2. Turning your essay into a conversation

Personal essayists usually use the first person (*I* and *we*) to create a sense of open-ended conversation between writer and reader. Your rhetorical stance—whether you appear shy, belligerent, or friendly in this conversation, for example—will be determined by the details you include in your essay as well as the connotations of the words you use. Consider how actress and writer Tina Fey represents herself in the following excerpt from "Confessions of a Juggler," which appeared in the *New Yorker* in February 2011:

> My daughter recently checked out a book from the preschool library called *My Working Mom*. It had a cartoon witch on the cover. "Did you pick this book out all by yourself?" I asked her, trying to be nonchalant. Yes. We read the book, and the witch mother was very busy and sometimes reprimanded her daughter for messing things up near her cauldron. She had to fly away to a lot of meetings, and the witch's child said something like "It's hard having a working mom, especially when she enjoys her work." In the heartwarming conclusion, the witch mother makes it to the child's school play at the last second, and the

---

the EVOLVING SITUATION

Personal Writing and Social Media Web Sites

In addition to writing personal essays for class, you may use social media sites like *Facebook* or *Twitter* for personal expression and autobiographical writing. Since these sites are networked, it's important to remember that strangers, including prospective employers, may have access to your profiles and comments.

---

witch's child says she doesn't like having a working mom but she can't picture her mom any other way. I didn't love it. I'm sure the *two men* who wrote this book had the absolute best intentions, but this leads me to my point. The topic of working moms is a tap-dance in a minefield.

3. Structuring your essay like a story

There are three common ways to narrate events and reflections:

- **Chronological sequence:** uses an order determined by clock time; what happened first is presented first, followed by what happened second, then third, and so on.

- **Emphatic sequence:** uses an order determined by the point you want to make; for emphasis, events and reflections are arranged from either least to most or most to least important.

- **Suspenseful sequence:** uses an order determined by the emotional effect the writer wants the essay to have on readers. To keep readers engaged, the essay may begin in the middle with a puzzling event, then flash back or go forward. Some essays may even begin with the end and then flash back to recount how the writer came to that insight.

4. Letting details tell your story

It is through the details that the story takes shape. The details you emphasize, the words you choose, and the characters you create communicate the point of your essay.

Consider, for example, the following passage by Gloria Ladson-Billings:

Mrs. Harris, my third-grade teacher, was quite a sharp dresser. She wore beautiful high-heeled shoes. Sometimes she switched to flats in the afternoon if her feet got tired, but every morning began with the click, click, click of her high heels as she greeted us up and down the rows. I wanted to dress the way Mrs. Harris did. I didn't want to wear old-lady

> comforters like Mrs. Benn's, and I certainly didn't want to
> wear worn-out loafers like those of my first-grade teacher,
> Miss Schwartz. I wanted to wear beautiful, shiny, high-heeled
> shoes like Mrs. Harris's. That was the way a teacher should
> look, I thought.
>
> —GLORIA LADSON-BILLINGS, *The Dreamkeepers: Successful*
> *Teachers of African-American Children*

Ladson-Billings uses details to make her idea of a good teacher come
alive for the reader. At one level—the literal—the "click, click, click"
refers to the sound of Mrs. Harris's shoes. At another level, it represents the glamorous teacher. And at the most figurative level, the
"click, click, click" evokes the kind of feminine power that the narrator both longs for and admires.

5. Connecting your experience to a larger issue

To demonstrate the significance of a personal essay to readers, writers usually connect their individual experience to a larger issue.
Here, for example, are the closing lines of Fey's essay:

> That night, as I was putting the witch book in my daughter's
> backpack to be returned to school, I asked her, "Did you pick
> this book because your mommy works? Did it make you feel
> better about it?" She looked at me matter-of-factly and said,
> "Mommy, I can't read. I thought it was a Halloween book."

Notice how Fey surprises readers by switching to the child's perspective, emphasizing that the bad feeling associated with juggling family and career was a problem for the mother, not for the daughter. Fey
thereby connects her personal story to the larger issue of mothers
working and to the psychology of family relationships.

12b   Lab reports in the experimental sciences.

Scientists form hypotheses (tentative answers to research questions
that can be proved true or false) and plan new experiments as they
observe, read, and write. When they work in the laboratory, they
keep detailed notebooks. They also write and publish lab reports to
share their discoveries with other scientists.

Lab reports usually include the following sections: Abstract,
Introduction, Methods and Materials, Results, Discussion, Acknowledgments, and References. Begin drafting the report, section by section, while your experiences in the lab are still fresh in your mind.

Follow the scientific conventions for abbreviations, symbols, and
numbers (often listed in your textbook). Use numerals for dates, time,
pages, figures, tables, and standard units of measurement. Spell out
numbers between one and nine that are not part of a series of larger
numbers.

1. Abstract

An **abstract** is a one-paragraph summary of your lab report. It answers these questions:

- What methods were used in the experiment?
- What variables were measured?
- What were the findings?
- What do the findings imply?

2. Introduction

In the introduction, state your topic, summarize prior research, and present your hypothesis.

Employ precise scientific terminology *(α-amylase),* and spell out the terms that you will later abbreviate *(gibbelleric acid [GA]).* Use the passive voice when describing objects of study, which are more important than the experimenter. *(For a discussion of active and passive voices, see Tab 9: Editing for Clarity, pp. 463–65.)* Use the present tense to state established knowledge ("the rye seed *produces*"); use the past tense to summarize the work of prior researchers ("Haberlandt *reported*"). The writer of the excerpt below cites sources using a superscript number system. *(For information about CSE style, see pp. 419–30.)*

> According to studies by Yomo[1], Paleg[2], and others[3,4], barley seed embryos produce a gibbelleric acid (GA) which stimulates the release of hydrolytic enzymes, especially α-amylase. These enzymes break down the endosperm, thereby making stored energy sources available to the germinating plant. What is not evident is how GA actually works on the molecular level to stimulate the production of hydrolytic enzymes. As several experiments[5–8] have documented, GA has an RNA-enhancing effect. Is this general enhancement of RNA synthesis just a side effect of GA's action, or is it directly involved in the stimulation of α-amylase?

The first sentence names both a general topic, barley seed embryos, and a specific issue, GA's stimulation of hydrolytic enzymes. The last sentence poses a question that prepares readers for the hypothesis by focusing their attention on the role enhanced RNA synthesis plays in barley seed germination.

3. Methods and materials

Select the details that other scientists will need to replicate the experiment. Using the past tense, recount in chronological order what was done with specific materials.

4. Results

In this section, tell readers about the results that are relevant to your hypothesis, especially those that are statistically significant. Results may be relevant even if they are different from what you expected.

You might summarize results in a table or graph. For example, the graph in Figure 12.1, which plots the distance (in centimeters, y-axis) covered by a glider over a period of time (in seconds, x-axis), was used to summarize the results of an engineering assignment.

Every table and figure you include in a lab report must be referred to in the text. Point out relevant patterns the table or figure reveals. If you run statistical tests on your findings, do not make the tests themselves the focus of your writing. Reserve interpretations for the Discussion section.

Note: Like the terms *correlated* and *random,* the term *significant* has a specific statistical meaning for scientists and should therefore be used in a lab report only in relation to the appropriate statistical tests.

---

5. Discussion

In discussing your results, interpret your major findings by explaining how and why each finding does or does not confirm the original hypothesis. Connect your work with prior scientific research, and look ahead to potential future research.

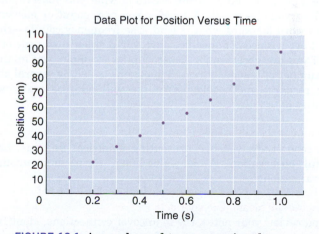

FIGURE 12.1 A graph used to summarize the results of an engineering assignment.

6. Acknowledgments

In professional journals, most reports of experimental findings include a brief statement acknowledging those who assisted the author(s).

7. References

Include at the end of your report a listing of all manuals, books, and journal articles you consulted during the research and writing process. Use one of the citation formats developed by the Council of Science Editors (CSE style), unless your instructor prefers another format. *(See Tab 8: Chicago and CSE Documentation Styles.)*

12c Case studies in the social sciences.

Social scientists are trained observers and recorders of individual and group behavior. They write to see clearly and remember precisely what they observe and then to interpret its meaning.

1. Choosing a topic that raises a question

In writing or conducting a case study, your purpose is to connect what you observe with issues and concepts in the social sciences. Choose a topic, and turn it into a research question. Write down your hypothesis—a tentative answer to your research question. Record types of behavior and other categories (for example, appearance) to guide your research in the field.

2. Collecting data

Make a detailed and accurate record of what you observe and when and how you observe it. Whenever you can, count or measure, and record word-for-word what is said. Use frequency counts—the number of occurrences of specific, narrowly defined instances of behavior. If you are observing a classroom, for example, you might count the number of teacher-directed questions asked by several children. Your research methodologies course will address many ways to quantify data.

3. Assuming an unbiased stance

In a case study, you are presenting empirical findings, based on careful observation. Avoid value-laden terms and unsupported generalizations.

4. Discovering meaning in your data

As you review your notes, try to uncover connections, identify inconsistencies, and draw inferences. For example, ask yourself why a subject behaved in a specific way, and consider different explanations for the behavior. Draw on the techniques for quantitative analysis that you have learned in a statistics course.

┌─NAVIGATING THROUGH COLLEGE AND BEYOND
Case Studies

Social scientists publish their findings in such journals as the *American Sociological Review, Harvard Business Review,* and *Journal of Marriage and the Family.* For example, a developmental psychologist might study conflict resolution in children by observing a group of four-year-olds in a day care center and publish her findings in a journal. As a student, you will find case studies used in a number of social science disciplines:

- **In sociology:** You may be asked to analyze a small group to which you have belonged or belong now. Your study will address such issues as the group's norms and values, cultural characteristics, and stratification and roles. Your audience will be your professor, who wants to see how your observations reflect current theories on group norms.

- **In nursing:** For a nursing class, you may note details of patient care that corroborate or differ from the norm. Your audience is the supervising nurse, who is interested in the patient's progress and your interactions with the patient.

- **In education:** As a student teacher, you may closely observe and write about students in the context of their socioeconomic and family backgrounds. Your audience will be the cooperating teacher, who seeks greater insight into students' behavior.

5. Presenting your findings in an organized way

There are two basic ways to present your findings in the body of a case study: as stages of a process and in analytic categories. Using stages of a process, a student studying gang initiation organized her observations chronologically into appropriate stages. If you organize your study this way, be sure to transform the minute-by-minute history of your observations into a pattern with distinct stages. Using analytic categories, a student observing the behavior of a preschool child organized his findings according to three categories from his textbook: motor coordination, cognition, and socialization.

6. Including a review of the literature, a statement of your hypothesis, and a description of your methodology in your introduction

The introduction presents the framework, background, and rationale for your study. Begin with the topic, and review related research, working your way to the specific question that the study addresses. Follow that opening with a statement of your hypothesis, accompanied by a description of your **methodology**—how, when, and where you made your observations and how you recorded them.

> **Note:** *Develop stages or categories while you are making your observations.* In your analysis, be sure to illustrate these stages or categories with material drawn from observations—with descriptions of people, places, and behavior, as well as with well-chosen quotations.

7. Discussing your findings in the conclusion

The conclusion of your case study should answer these three questions: (1) Did you find what you expected? (2) What do your findings show, or what is the bigger picture? and (3) What should researchers explore further?

12d Essay exams.

Spending time in advance thinking about writing essay exams will reduce stress and increase success.

1. Preparing with the course and your instructor in mind

Consider the specific course as your writing context and the course's instructor as your audience:

- What questions or problems did your instructor explicitly or implicitly address? What frameworks did your instructor use to analyze topics?
- What key terms did your instructor repeatedly use during lectures and discussions?

2. Understanding your assignment

Essay exams are designed to test your knowledge and understanding, not just your memory. Make up some essay questions that require you to do the following:

- **Explain** what you have learned in a clear, well-organized way. *(See question 1 in the box on p. 163.)*
- **Connect** what you know about one topic with what you know about another topic. *(See question 2 in the box on p. 163.)*
- **Apply** what you have learned to a new situation. *(See question 3 in the box on p. 163.)*
- **Interpret** the causes, effects, meanings, value, or potential of something. *(See question 4 in the box on p. 163.)*
- **Argue** for or against some controversial statement about what you have learned. *(See question 5 in the box on p. 163.)*

Almost all these directions require you to synthesize what you have learned from your reading, class notes, and projects.

─NAVIGATING THROUGH COLLEGE AND BEYOND

Essay Exam Questions across the Curriculum

During finals week, you may be asked to respond to essay questions like the following:

1. Discuss the power of the contemporary presidency as well as the limits of that power. [*from a political science course*]

2. Compare and contrast the treatment of labor supply decisions in the economic models proposed by Greg Lewis and Gary Becker. [*from an economics course*]

3. Describe the observations that would be made in an alpha-particle scattering experiment if (a) the nucleus of an atom were negatively charged and the protons occupied the empty space outside the nucleus and (b) the electrons were embedded in a positively charged sphere. [*from a chemistry course*]

4. Examine the uses of caesura and enjambment in the following poem, and analyze their effect on the poem's rhythm. [*from a literature course*]

5. In 1800, was Thomas Jefferson a "dangerous radical" as the Federalists claimed? Define key terms, and support your position with evidence from specific events and documents. [*from an American history course*]

3. Planning your time

Quickly look through the whole exam, and determine how much time you will spend on each part. You will want to move as quickly as possible through the questions with lower point values and spend the bulk of your time responding to those that are worth the greatest number of points.

4. Responding to short-answer questions by showing the significance of the information

The most common type of short-answer question is the identification question: Who or what is X? In answering questions of this sort, present just enough information to show that you understand X's significance within the context of the course. For example, if you are asked to identify "Federalists" on an American history exam, don't just write, "political party that opposed Thomas Jefferson." Instead, craft one or two sentences that identify the Federalists as a party that supported the Constitution over the Articles of Confederation but then evolved, under the influence of Alexander Hamilton, into support for an elite social establishment.

5. Responding to essay questions tactically

Keep in mind that essay questions usually ask you to do something specific with a topic. Begin by determining precisely what you are being asked to do. Before you write anything, read the question—all of it—and circle key words.

> (Explain) (two) ways in which Picasso's *Guernica* evokes (war's) terrifying (destructiveness.)

To answer this question, you need to focus on two of the painting's features, such as color and composition, not on Picasso's life.

6. Using the essay question to structure your response

Usually, you can transform the question itself into the thesis of your answer. If you are asked to agree or disagree with the Federalists' characterization of Thomas Jefferson in the election of 1800, you might begin with this thesis.

> In the election of 1800, the Federalists characterized Jefferson as a dangerous radical. Although Jefferson's ideas were radical for the times, they were not dangerous to the republic.

Take a minute or two to list evidence for each of your main points, and then write the essay.

7. Checking your work

Save a few minutes to read quickly through your completed answer, looking for words you might have omitted or key sentences that make no sense. Make corrections neatly.

SAMPLE ESSAY TEST RESPONSE

A student's response to an essay question in an art appreciation course appears below. Both the question and the student's notes are provided.

QUESTION

Both of these buildings (Figure 1 and Figure 2) feature dome construction. Identify the buildings, and discuss the differences in the visual effects created by the different dome styles.

STUDENT'S NOTES

Fig 1: Pantheon. Plain outside-concrete, can barely see dome. Dramatic inside-dome opens up huge interior space. Oculus to sky: light, air, rain. Coffered ceiling.

Fig 2: Taj Mahal. Dramatic exterior-dome set high, marble, reflecting pool, exterior lines go up. Inside not meant to be visited.

STUDENT'S ANSWER

The Pantheon (Figure 1) and the Taj Mahal (Figure 2) are famous for their dome construction. The styles of the domes are dramatically different, however, resulting in dramatically different visual effects.

FIGURE 1

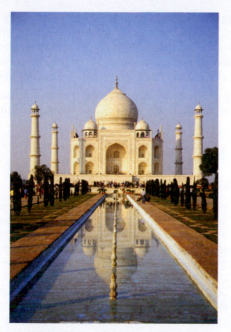

FIGURE 2

The Pantheon, which was built by the Romans as a temple to the gods, looks very plain on the exterior. The dome is barely visible from the outside, and it is made of a dull grey concrete. Inside the building, however, the dome produces an amazing effect. It opens up a huge space within the building, unobstructed by interior supports. The sides of the dome are coffered, and those recessed rectangles both lessen the weight of the dome and add to its visual beauty. Most dramatically, the top of the dome is open to the sky, allowing sun or rain to pour into the building. This opening is called the oculus, meaning "eye" (to or of Heaven).

The Taj Mahal, which was built by a Muslim emperor of India as a tomb for his wife, is the opposite of the Pantheon–dazzling on the outside and plain on the inside. The large central dome is set up high on the base so that it can be seen from far away. It is made of white marble, which reflects light beautifully. The dome is surrounded by other structures that frame it and draw attention to its exterior–a long reflecting pond and four minarets. Arches and smaller domes on the outside of the building repeat the large dome's shape. Because the Taj Mahal's dome is tall and narrow, however, it does not produce the kind of vast interior space of the shorter, squatter Pantheon dome. Indeed, the inside of the Taj Mahal is not meant to be visited. Unlike the Pantheon, the dome of the Taj Mahal is intended to be admired from the outside.

12e Coauthored projects.

A project is coauthored when more than one person is responsible for producing it. In many fields, working collaboratively is essential. Here are some suggestions to help you make the most of this challenge:

- Working with your partners, decide on some ground rules, including meeting times, deadlines, and ways of reconciling differences. Will the majority rule, or will some other principle prevail? Is there an interested and respected third party who can be consulted if the group's dynamics break down?

- Will the group meet primarily online or in person? See the box above for guidelines for online communication.

the EVOLVING SITUATION

Coauthoring Online

Computer networks make it easy for two or more writers to coauthor texts. Wikis, a type of writing environment that is supported by *cloud technology,* allow writers to contribute to a common structure and edit one another's work. Other cloud technologies like *Google Docs* may be available to make coauthoring even easier. Most courseware (such as Blackboard) includes chat rooms and public space for posting and commenting on drafts and programs like *Skype* and *Google Hangout* can facilitate real-time meetings. Word-processing software also allows writers to make tracked changes in files.

If your group meets online, make sure a transcript of the discussion is saved. If you exchange ideas via e-mail, you automatically will have a record of how the piece developed and how well the group worked together. Archive these transcripts and e-mails into designated folders. In all online communications, be especially careful with your tone. Without the benefit of facial expressions and other cues, which e-mails and text messages lack, writers can easily misinterpret even the most constructive criticism.

- Divide the work fairly so that everyone has a part to contribute to the project. Keep in mind that each group member should do some researching, drafting, revising, and editing. Responsibility for taking notes at meetings should rotate.

- In your personal journal, record, analyze, and evaluate the intellectual and interpersonal workings of the group as you see and experience them. If the group's dynamics begin to break down, seek the assistance of a third party.

- After each group member has completed his or her assigned part or subtopic, gather the whole group face to face or online to weave the parts together and create a focused piece of writing with a consistent voice. At this point group members usually need to negotiate with one another. Although healthy debate is good for a project, tact is essential.

CHAPTER 13

Oral Presentations

Preparing an oral presentation, like preparing any text, is a process. Consider your rhetorical situation—your audience, purpose, and context—as you determine focus and level of communication. Gather information, decide on the main idea, think through the organization, and choose visuals that support your points.

13a   Plan and shape your oral presentation.

Effective oral presentations seem informal, but that effect is the result of careful planning and strategic shaping of the material.

1. Considering the interests, background knowledge, and attitudes of your audience

Find out as much as you can about your listeners before you prepare the speech. What does the audience already think about your topic? Do you want to intensify your listeners' commitment to already existing views, provide new and clarifying information, provoke more analysis and understanding, or change listeners' beliefs?

If you are addressing an unfamiliar audience, ask the people who invited you to speak to fill you in on the audience's interests and expectations. You also can adjust your speech once you get in front of the actual audience, making your language more or less technical, for example, or offering additional examples to illustrate points.

2. Working within the time allotted to your presentation

Gauge how many words you speak per minute by reading a passage aloud at a conversational pace (about 120 to 150 words per minute is ideal). Be sure to time your presentation when you practice it.

👁 **13b** Draft your presentation with the rhetorical situation in mind.

1. Making your opening interesting

A strong opening puts the speaker at ease and gains the audience's confidence and attention. During rehearsal, try out several approaches to your introduction to see what gets the best reactions. Stories, brief quotations, striking statistics, and surprising statements are good attention getters. Try crafting an introduction that lets your listeners know what they have to gain from your presentation—for example, new information or new perspectives on a subject of common interest.

2. Making the focus and organization of your presentation explicit

Select two or three ideas that you most want your audience to hear—and remember. Make these ideas the focus of your presentation, and let your audience know what to expect by previewing the content of your presentation—"I will make three points about fraternities on campus"—and then listing the three points.

The phrase "to make three points" signals a topical organization. Other common organizational patterns include chronological *(at first . . . later . . . in the end),* causal *(because of that . . . then this follows),* and problem-solution *(given the situation . . . then this set of proposals).* A question-answer format also works well, either as an overall strategy or as part of another organizational pattern.

3. Being direct

What your audience hears and remembers has as much to do with how you speak as it does with what you say. Use a direct, simple style:

- Choose basic sentence structures.
- Repeat key terms.
- Pay attention to the pace and rhythm of your speech.
- Don't be afraid to use the pronouns *I, you,* and *we.*

Notice how applying these principles transforms the following written sentence into a group of sentences appropriate for oral presentation.

WRITTEN

Although the claim that the position of the stars can help people predict the future has yet to be substantiated by either an ample body or an exemplary piece of empirical research, advocates of astrology persist in pressing the claim.

ORAL

Your sign says a lot about you. So say advocates of astrology. But what evidence do we have that the position of the stars helps people predict the future? Do we have lots of empirical research or even one really good study? The answer is, "Not yet."

4. Using visual aids: Posters and presentation software

Slides, posters, objects, video clips, and music help make your focus explicit. Avoid oversimplifying your ideas to fit them on a slide. Make sure the images, videos, or music fit your purpose and audience. Presentation software such as PowerPoint and *Prezi* can help you stay focused while you are speaking. *(For more on using presentation software to incorporate multimodal elements into a presentation, see Section 13c.)*

When preparing a poster presentation, keep the poster simple with a clear title, bullets listing key points, and images that support your purpose. Be sure that text can be read from several feet away. *(For more on design principles, see Chapter 8: Designing Academic Texts and Portfolios, pp. 92–104.)*

5. Concluding memorably

Make your ending memorable: return to that surprising opener, play with the words of your opening quotation, look at the initial image from another angle, or reflect on the story you have told. Make sure your listeners are aware that you are about to end your presentation, using such signal phrases as "in conclusion" or "let me end by saying," if necessary. Keep your conclusion short to hold the audience's attention.

13c   Use presentation software to create multimodal presentations.

Presentation software makes it possible to incorporate audio, video, and animation into a talk. This software can also be used to create multimodal compositions that viewers can review on their own.

1. Using presentation software for an oral presentation

Presentation slides that accompany a talk should identify major points and display information in a visually effective way.

Remember that slides support your talk; they do not replace it. Limit the amount of information on each slide to as few words as possible, and plan to show each slide for about one minute. Use bulleted lists and phrases keyed to your major points rather than full sentences. Make fonts large enough to be seen by the person in the last row of your audience: titles should be in 44-point type or larger, subheads in 32-point type or larger. High-contrast color schemes and sufficient blank space between slide elements will also increase the visibility of your presentation.

2. Using presentation software to create independent projects

With presentation software, you can also create projects that run on their own or at the prompting of the viewer. This capability is especially useful in distance learning settings, where students attend class and share information electronically.

3. Preparing a slide presentation

The following guidelines will help you prepare effective slides.

Decide on a slide format   Begin thinking about slides while you plan what you are going to say because the slides and the words will inform each other. As you decide on the words for your talk or independent project, you will think of visuals that support your points, and, as you work out the visuals, you are likely to see additional points you can make—and adjust your presentation as a result. Every feature of your slides—fonts, images, and animations—should support your purpose and appeal to your audience.

Before you create your slides, establish their basic appearance. What background color will they have? What font or fonts? What design elements, such as borders and icons? Will the templates provided by the software suit your talk, or should you modify a template to suit your needs? Since the format you establish will be the canvas for all your slides, avoid distractions and make sure that it complements the images and words you intend to display.

Incorporate images into your presentation   Include images when appropriate. To summarize quantitative information, you might use a chart or graph. To show geographical relationships, you would likely use a map. You can also add photographs that illustrate your points. In all cases, select appropriate, relevant images that support your purpose.

Incorporate relevant audio, video, and animation   Slides can also include audio files, which can provide background information for each slide in an independent composition project. For a presentation on music, you can insert audio files to show how a type of music has developed over time.

Video files and animated drawings and diagrams can also be useful. An animated diagram of the process of cell division could help illustrate a presentation on cellular biology. If you are using audio, video, or animation files that belong to others, cite the source. If you plan to make your presentation publicly available online, provide citations or obtain permission to use these items from the copyright holder. *(For more on finding and citing multimodal elements, see Chapter 20, Finding and Creating Effective Visuals, pp. 233–39.)*

Incorporate hypertext links You might use an internal link within a slide sequence to jump to another slide that illustrates or explains a particular point or issue or an external link to a site on the Internet. For instance, for a presentation on insects, you might include a hyperlink to a slide about insects specific to the part of the country in which you live, complete with an image of one of them. You can also create external links to resources about insects on the Web. Be careful not to rely too much on external links, however, because they can undermine the coherence of a presentation and can sometimes take a long time to load.

4. Reviewing a slide presentation

Once you have the text of your presentation in final form and the multimodal elements in place, you should carefully review your slides to make sure they work together coherently:

- **Check how slides in your software's slide sorter window move one to the next.** Do you have an introductory slide? Should you add transitional effects that reveal the content of a slide gradually or point by point? Use transitional effects to support your rhetorical situation. For example, would audio help make your point? Do you have a concluding slide?

- **Make sure that the slides are consistent with the script of the talk you plan to deliver.** If the slides are to function independently, do they include enough information in the introduction, an adequate explanation of each point, and a clear conclusion?

- **Check the arrangement of your slides.** Try printing them and spreading them out over a large surface, rearranging them if necessary, before implementing needed changes on the computer.

- **Be sure the slides have a unified look.** For example, do all the slides have the same background? Do they all use the same fonts in the same way? Are headers and bullets consistent?

For an example of a slide presentation created to accompany a talk about the issue of cyberbullying, see Figure 13.1 on page 172.

Caution: If you plan to make external links part of your presentation, make sure that you have a functioning Web browser on your computer and that a fast connection to the Internet is available where you will be giving the presentation. If possible, do a practice run of your presentation on site so you can be sure that your links work.

FIGURE 13.1 Sample PowerPoint slides for a presentation on the topic of cyberbullying.

Cyberbullying: An Alarming Trend for the Digital Age

Cyberbullying

Bullying that takes place using electronic technology (texting, **IMing**, social media sites, etc.) in the form of hurtful comments or physical threats

Nearly 20% of students polled admitted to cyberbullying

Cyberbullying Methods

Flaming- using angry/offensive language

Outing- sharing others' secrets

Trickery- getting others to share their secrets

Denigration- spreading rumors/gossip

Who Bullies?

- "The Popular Bully"- well connected to peers and likes to dominate others

- "The Isolated Bully"- not well connected to peers, has low self-esteem, and may not identify with others' feelings

Impact of Cyberbullying

Victims often experience
- Low self-esteem
- Family problems
- Academic problems from avoiding school
- Depression sometimes leading to suicide

Cyberbullying Resources

www.athinline.org
www.stopbullying.gov
www.cyberbullying.us
www.stopcyberbullying.org

13d   Prepare for your presentation.

Your oral presentation will have the appropriate effect on an audience if you make certain crucial decisions in advance.

1. Deciding whether to use notes or a written script

When giving your talk, make eye contact with your listeners to monitor their responses and adjust your message accordingly. For most occasions, it is inappropriate to write out everything you want to say and then read it word for word, nor do you want to read from the slides. Instead, speak from an outline or bullet points, and write out only those parts of your presentation where precise wording counts, such as quotations.

In some scholarly or formal settings, precise wording may be necessary, especially if your oral presentation is to be published or if your remarks will be quoted by others. Sometimes the setting for your presentation may be so formal or the audience may be so large that a script feels necessary. In such instances, do the following:

- Triple-space the typescript of your text.
- Avoid carrying sentences over from one page to another.
- Mark your manuscript for pauses, emphasis, and the pronunciation of proper names.

2. Rehearsing, revising, and polishing

Whether you are using an outline or a script, practice your presentation aloud. Revise transitions that don't work, points that need further development, and sections that are too long. After you have settled on the content of your speech and can present it comfortably, polish delivery. Ask your friends to watch and listen to your rehearsal. Check that your body posture is straight but relaxed, that your voice is loud enough and clear, that you keep your hands away from your face, and that you make eye contact around the room. Time your final rehearsals, adding and cutting material as necessary.

3. Accepting nervousness as normal

The adrenaline surge you feel before a presentation can actually invest your talk with positive energy. Practice and revise your presentation until it flows smoothly, and make sure that you have a strong opener to get you through the first, most difficult moments. Remember that other people cannot always tell that you are nervous.

13e   Prepare a version of TED talks.

TED is a nonprofit organization, founded in 1984, devoted to "Ideas Worth Spreading." TED stands for Technology, Entertainment, Design—the original topics of the conference that gave TED its name.

The TED talk—strictly limited to no more than eighteen minutes—has become a new genre for effective oral communication—delivered concisely and without notes. Take a look at the TED Web site for further information and sample talks: http://www.ted.com/pages/about.

CHAPTER 14

Multimodal Writing

Multimodal writing combines words with images, video, or audio into a single composition. The most common form of multimodal writing—discussed in many chapters of this handbook—is a combination of words and still visuals such as photographs, maps, charts, or graphs. Another form is an oral presentation with any kind of visual support from a diagram on a Smartboard to a *Prezi* slide show *(see Chapter 13, Oral Presentations)*. Digital technology also allows writers to combine written words with sound, video, and animation. On social media Web sites such as *Facebook,* users integrate text, images, and other multimodal elements.

Like any form of composition, multimodal writing is governed by the rhetorical situation; you use multimodal resources to convey a message effectively to a particular audience for a particular purpose: to inform, to interpret, or to persuade. A video or audio segment—like a photograph, map, or recording—must support your purpose and be appropriate for the audience to whom you are writing.

14a   Learn about tools for creating multimodal texts.

Multimodal writing can take a variety of forms and can be created with a variety of software tools. Here are a few options:

- Most word-processing programs permit you to insert still images into a word document, and many also make it possible to create a composition that links to various files—including audio, image, and video files *(see 14b and 14c)*.

- Most presentation software allows you to include audio and video files in your presentation as well as still visuals *(see 13c, pp. 169–72)*.

- A variety of programs and Web-based tools allow you to create your own **Web pages** and **Web sites,** which can include a wide range of multimodal features *(see 14c)*.

- You can create a **Weblog (blog)** on which, in addition to your written entries, you can post multimodal files and links to files on other blogs and Web sites. You also can collaborate with other writers on a **wiki.** *(See 14d.)*

👁 **14b**   Combine text and image using a word-processing program to analyze images.

Two types of assignments you might be called on to write are an image analysis and a narrative that explains an image.

1. Composing an image analysis

You may be asked to analyze a single image such as a piece of art from a museum (possibly viewed online), as Diane Chen does in her analysis of the Dorothea Lange photograph in Chapter 7 *(see pp. 91–92)*. In an image analysis, you have two tasks: (1) describe the picture as carefully as possible, using adjectives, comparisons, and words that help readers focus on the picture and the details that compose it; and (2) analyze the argument the image seems to be making.

2. The narrative behind the image

Sometimes a writer tries to imagine the story behind an evocative photograph. Often the story is as much an expression of the writer as it is a statement about the photograph.

Some photographs, like the one in Figure 14.1 by photojournalist Tyler Hicks, fulfill Emily Dickinson's mandate to "Tell all the Truth but tell it slant—." Hicks's photograph of the 2013 terrorist attack on a Kenyan shopping mall is literally pictured on a slant. But Hicks tells "all the truth"—the horror of destruction, the worst of humanity—in the context of the best—a mother's protective love, "with explanation kind," as Dickinson says. But there is nothing sentimental about the photograph. Everyday objects—cups, toasters, all

FIGURE 14.1 **A mother and her children hide during the 2013 terrorist attack on a Kenyan shopping mall.**

in disarray—surround the family as they hide from the evil thrust upon them.

Those of you who know the Greek myth of Perseus slaying the monster Medusa will have a deeper understanding of Dickinson's and Hicks's impulse to "Tell all the Truth but tell it slant—." In Figure 14.2, Perseus is shown after he has beheaded Medusa—quite a feat, since anyone who looked upon the mythical monster directly was turned to stone. Perseus used his shield as a mirror to capture Medusa's reflection so that he could behead her. In the statue, after the act, Perseus does not look directly at Medusa. His gaze is on a slant.

Many interpret Perseus's shield to be the mirror of art, which allows people to experience "all the truth" without turning to unfeeling stone or becoming blind to human suffering. In your own experience, has art—photography, sculpture, painting, poetry, fiction, or drama—helped you to experience what Gillian Morton calls, "a clear-eyed vision of the world that can be brutal in its reality"?

Tell all the Truth . . .
EMILY DICKINSON

Tell all the Truth but tell it slant—
Success in Circuit lies
Too bright for our infirm Delight
The Truth's superb surprise

FIGURE 14.2 Bronze statue of Perseus holding the head of Medusa, in Piazza della Signoria, Florence, Italy.

As Lightning to the Children eased
With explanation kind
The Truth must dazzle gradually
Or every man be blind—

👁 **14c**   Create a Web site.

Thanks to Web editing software, it is now almost as easy to create a Web site and post it on the Internet as it is to write a print text using word-processing software. Many Web-based businesses like *Google,* *Weebly,* and *Wix* provide free server space for hosting sites and offer tools for creating Web pages. Many schools also make server space available for student Web sites.

To be effective, a Web site must be well designed and serve a well-defined purpose for its audience. In creating a Web site, plan the site, draft its content, and select its visuals; then revise and edit as you would for any other composition. *(See Tab 2: Writing and Designing Texts.)* The following sections offer guidelines for composing a Web site.

1. Planning a structure for your site

Like most print documents, a Web site can have a hierarchical, linear structure, where one page leads to the next. Because of the hyperlinked nature of this medium, however, a site can also be organized in a hub-and-spoke structure, with a central page leading to other pages. The diagrams in Figure 14.3 on page 178 illustrate these two structures. To choose the structure that will work best, consider how users will want to access information or opinion on the site. For example, visitors intrigued by the topic of Tyler County's historic buildings may want to explore the topic further. Caregivers visiting

---

⌐ KNOW THE SITUATION   Web Sites

Purpose: To inform or persuade

Audience: Audience members for the Web can be people who need information about your topic (and may be knowledgeable themselves) or those who are only mildly interested. Writing for the Web is often more complicated than other types of situations because of the wide range of audiences that may read a site.

Stance: Knowledgeable

Genres: Web sites often host several genres, for instance, reports, reviews, and opinion pieces

Medium: Digital and networked

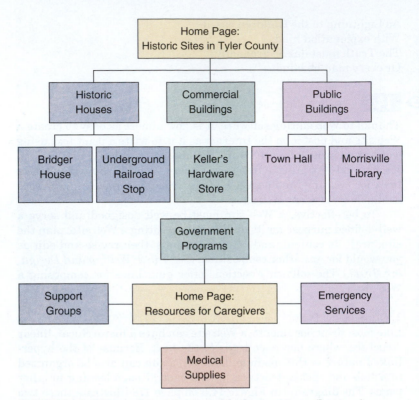

FIGURE 14.3 Hierarchical (top) and hub structure (bottom).

a site offering them professional resources will want to find specific information quickly.

To determine your site's structure, try mapping the connections among its pages by arranging them in a storyboard. Represent each page with an index card, and rearrange the pages on a flat surface, experimenting with different possible arrangements. Alternatively, use Post-it notes on a whiteboard, and draw arrows connecting them. Also begin planning the visual design of your site. For consistency, establish a template page, including background color and fonts. Choose a uniform location (for example, at the top, in the middle) for material that will appear on each such as site title, page title, navigation links, a repeated visual or theme unifying all the pages, and your contact information. *(See pp. 180–81 on designing a site with a unified look.)*

2. Gathering content for your site

The content for a Web site will usually consist of written work along with links and graphics. Depending on the situation, you might also provide audio files, video files, and even animation.

CHECKLIST Planning a Web Site

When you begin your Web composition, consider these questions about this writing situation:

☐ What is your purpose?

☐ Who are your viewers, and what are their needs? Will the site be limited by password protection to a specific group of viewers, or should you plan for a broader audience?

☐ What type of content will you include on your site: images, audio files, video files?

☐ Will you need to get permission to use visuals or other files that you obtain from outside sources?

☐ What design elements will appeal to your audience and complement your purpose and content?

☐ Given your technical knowledge, amount of content, and deadline, how much time should you allot to each stage of building your site?

☐ Will the site be updated, and, if so, how frequently?

Follow these special requirements for written content on a Web site:

- Usually readers do not want lengthy text explanations; they expect chunks of information—short paragraphs—delivered quickly.

- Chunks for each topic or point should fit on one screen. Avoid long passages that require readers to scroll.

- Use links to connect your interests with those of others and to provide extra sources of credible and relevant information. Integrate links into your text, and give them descriptive names, such as "Historic Houses" for one of the Web sites in Figure 14.3. Place links at the end of a paragraph so readers do not navigate away in the middle.

As you prepare your written text, gather the graphics, photographs, and audio and video files that you plan to include. Some sites allow you to download images, and some images, including many of the historical photographs available through the Library of Congress, are in the public domain. Another useful site for visual, audio, and video files is *Creative Commons* (search.creativecommons.org), which directs you to material licensed for specific types of use, and all the images on *Wikipedia* are *Creative Commons,* so approved for use as well. Check the license of the material to see what is permitted, and always provide acknowledgments.

Always cite any material that you do not generate yourself. If your Web text will be public, request permission for use of any material not in the public domain unless the site says permission is not needed. Check for a credit in the source, and if the contact information of the creator is not apparent, e-mail the sponsor of the site and ask for it. *(For citation formats see Tabs 6–8.)*

3. Designing Web pages to capture and hold interest

On reader-friendly Web sites, you will find such easy-to-follow links as "what you'll find here," FAQs (frequently asked questions), or "list of those involved." In planning the structure and content of your site, keep your readers' needs in mind.

4. Designing a readable site with a unified look

The design of your site should suit its writing situation, in the context of its purpose and intended audience: a government site to inform users about copyright law will present a basic, uncluttered design that focuses attention on the text. A university's **home page** might feature photographs of young people and sun-drenched lawns to entice prospective students. Readers generally appreciate a site with a unified look. "Sets" or "themes" are readily available at free graphics sites offering banners, navigation buttons, and other design elements. You also can create visuals with a graphics program, scan your own art, and scan or upload personal photographs. Design your home page to complement your other pages, or your readers may lose track of where they are in the site—and lose interest in staying:

- Use a design template—a preformatted style with structure and headings established—to keep elements of page layout consistent across the site.
- Align items such as text and images.
- Consider including a site map—a Web page that serves as a table of contents for your entire site.
- Select elements such as buttons, signs, and backgrounds with a consistent design suited to your purpose and audience. Use animations and sounds sparingly.
- Use colors that provide adequate contrast, white space, and sans serif fonts to make text easy to read. Pages that are too busy are not visually compelling and too much white space makes the site feel empty. *(For more on design, see Tab 2: Writing and Designing Texts, pp. 93–100.)*
- Limit the width of your text; readers find wide lines of text difficult to process.
- Leave time to find appropriate image, audio, and video files created by others and to obtain permission to use them.
- Always check your Web site to be sure all the pages and links load as planned.

the EVOLVING SITUATION

Understanding Web Jargon

- **Browser:** software that allows you to access and view material on the Web. When you identify a site you want to see on the Web by typing in a URL (see below), your browser (*Microsoft Internet Explorer, Mozilla Firefox, Google Chrome,* or *Safari,* for example) tells a distant com-puter—a **server**—to allow you to access it.

- **JPEG and GIF:** formats for photographs and other visuals that are recog-nized by browsers. Photographs that appear on a Web site should be saved in JPEG (pronounced "*jay-peg*") format, which stands for Joint Photographic Experts Group. The file extension is .jpg or .jpeg. Clip art should be saved as GIF files (Graphics Interchange Format, pronounced like *gift* without the *t.*)

- **HTML/XML:** hypertext markup language/extensible markup language. These languages tag or code text so that your browser can rebuild a doc-ument from the compressed files that travel through the Internet. It is not necessary to learn HTML or XML to publish on the Web. Programs such as *Publisher, Dreamweaver, Wix.com,* and *Mozilla* provide a WYSIWYG (What You See Is What You Get) interface for creating Web pages. Most word-processing programs have a "Save as HTML" option.

- **URL:** uniform resource locator or Web address. When you type or paste a URL into your Web browser, you are sending a request through your browser to another computer, asking it to allow you access.

The home page and interior page shown in Figure 14.4 on page 182 illustrate some of these design considerations.

5. Designing a Web site that is easy to access and navigate
Help readers find their way to the areas of the site they want to visit. Make it easy for them to take interesting side trips without wasting their time or losing their way:

- **Identify your Web site on each page, and provide a link to the home page.** Remember that readers will not always enter your Web site through the home page. Give the title of the site on each page, and provide an easy-to-spot link to your home page.

- **Provide a navigation bar on each page. A navigation bar** can be a simple line of links that you copy and paste at the top or bottom of each page. A navigation bar on each page makes it easy for visitors to move from the site's home page to other pages and back again.

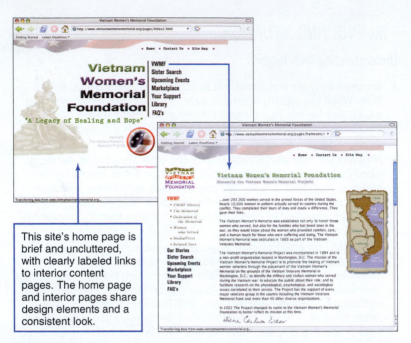

This site's home page is brief and uncluttered, with clearly labeled links to interior content pages. The home page and interior pages share design elements and a consistent look.

FIGURE 14.4 Home page and an interior page from the Web site of the Vietnam Women's Memorial Foundation.

- **Use graphics that load quickly.** Limit the size of your images to no more than 40 kilobytes so that they will load faster.

- **Use graphics judiciously.** Your Web site should not depend on graphics alone to make its message clear and interesting. Graphics should reinforce your purpose. The designers of the Library of Congress Web site *(Figure 14.5)* use icons such as musical notation and a map to help visitors navigate the site. Avoid clip art, which often looks unprofessional.

- **Be aware of the needs of visitors with disabilities.** Provide alternate ways of accessing visual and auditory information. Include text descriptions of visuals, media files, and tables (for users of screen-reader software or text-only **browsers**). All audio files should have captions and full transcriptions. For more information, visit *Webmonkey* <www.webmonkey.com>. *(See Chapter 8, Designing Academic Texts and Portfolios, pp. 99–100.)*

FIGURE 14.5
**The home
page of the
Web site of
the Library
of Congress.**

6. Using peer feedback to revise your Web site

Before publishing your site, to be read by anyone in the world, proof-read your text carefully, and ask friends to look at your site in different browsers and share their responses with you. Make sure your site reflects favorably on your abilities.

14d   Create and interact with blogs and wikis.

Weblogs or **blogs** are Web sites that can be continually updated. They often invite readers to post comments on entries. Some blogs provide a space where a group of writers can discuss one another's work and ideas. In schools, students blog to discuss issues, organize work, develop sources, compile portfolios, and gather and store material and commentary. Figure 14.6 depicts a blog for a writing course.

Blogs are important as vehicles for public discussion and commentary. Most presidential campaigns in 2012 maintained blogs on their Web sites, and nearly all conventional news sources, like the *New York Times,* link to their own blogs. Compared to other types of publications and academic writing, blogs have an informal tone that combines information, entertainment, and personal opinion. Blogs provide excellent sites for students to discuss class readings, plan a group project, or share a draft in process.

FIGURE 14.6 The blog for a writing course.

A **wiki** is another kind of Web-interfaced database that can be updated easily. One well-known wiki is the online encyclopedia *Wikipedia (see Chapter 19, p. 221)*. Many instructors do not consider Wikipedia a credible source for research because almost anyone can create or edit its content. Although changes are reviewed before appearing on the site, the reviewers may not have the requisite expertise. Verify that the information provided is correct by confirming it with another source. Some other wikis, such as Citizendium, rely on experts in a discipline to write and edit articles.

---CHECKLIST Setting up a Blog

When you begin your blog, consider these questions about your writing situation:

☐ What is your purpose? How will your blog's visual design reflect that purpose? What other multimodal elements can contribute to your purpose?

☐ To whom will you give access? Should the blog be public for all to see or be limited to a specific group of viewers?

☐ Do you want to allow others to post to your blog, comment on your posts, or both?

☐ Do you want to set up a schedule of postings or a series of reminders that will cue you to post?

☐ Do you know others with blogs? Do you want to link to their sites? Should they link to yours and comment on it?

1. Creating your own blog

To begin blogging, set up a blog site with a server such as *Blogger* (blogger.com) or *WordPress* (wordpress.org). Be sure about your writing situation, especially regarding purpose, which may be very specifically focused on a single issue or, alternatively, provide space for opinions on a range of issues.

Some social media sites such as *NING* will, for a charge, allow users to create blogs. These blogs can sometimes be used to explore a topic or find an expert on a particular subject. For example, if school policy permits, you might informally survey your friends on a campus issue or set up a group to discuss the topic.

Caution: Blogs and profiles on social media sites are more or less public depending on the level of access they allow. Do not post anything (including photographs and videos) that you would not want family members, teachers, and prospective employers to view.

CHECKLIST Setting Up a Wiki

When you begin your wiki, consider these questions related to your writing situation:

☐ What is your purpose?

☐ Who is the audience, and to whom will you give access? Will the wiki have broad participation, or is it designed for a specific group of participants?

☐ Given the tasks that participants will work on, do you want to set up a schedule of deadlines or post reminders to the group?

☐ What design elements will appeal to the participants and to your audience?

☐ Do you have a preference for the specific content? Should participants contribute images? Audio files? Video files?

☐ Will you need to get permission to use any visuals or other files that you obtain from other sources?

☐ Given your technical knowledge, the amount of content you anticipate, and your deadline, how much time should you allot to each stage of building your site?

☐ Will the site be updated, and if so how frequently?

2. Setting up a wiki

A wiki is an updateable Web site for sharing and coauthoring content. In addition to using wikis to conduct research together, students often use them simply to share their writing and various kinds of information—for instance relevant videos or Web sites related to a common research topic. Coauthors and peer reviewers find wikis useful because they provide a history of the revisions in any document. To create a wiki, begin by identifying the writing situation and the platform you will use, probably one like *wikispaces.com* or *pbwiki,* which provides set-up tools and directions.

Like blogs, wikis can have a limited number of participants or be open to the world.

4

Writing Beyond College

The aim of education must be the training of independently acting and thinking individuals, who, however, see in the service of the community their highest life problem.

—Albert Einstein

Health-care professionals write frequently to record their observations and update their colleagues. Writing is an integral part of the world of work as well as of our civic lives.

4 Writing Beyond College

👁 Section dealing with visual rhetoric. For a complete listing, see the Quick Guide to Key Resources at the back of this book.

Tab 4: Writing beyond College

This section will help you answer questions such as the following:

Rhetorical Knowledge

- How can I design brochures and newsletters to reach a particular community? (15b)

Critical Thinking, Reading, and Writing

- What is the best way to make my voice heard on an issue in the community? (16a)
- How can I write a letter of complaint that will help me as a consumer? (16b)

Processes

- How do I apply for a job? (17b, c, d)
- What are some online resources for job-hunting? (17e)

Knowledge of Conventions

- What should go on my résumé? (17b)
- How should I format my résumé and cover letter? (17b, c)
- How do I organize a business memo? (17e)
- What do I need to consider when writing professional e-mail? (17e)

For a general introduction to writing outcomes, see 1e, pages 14–16.

Although college may be unfamiliar territory to the newcomer, it is part of the larger world. Writing represents an access road—a way of connecting classroom, workplace, and community.

CHAPTER 15

Service Learning and Community-Service Writing

Your ability to research and write can be of great value to organizations that serve the community. Courses at every level of the university, as well as extracurricular activities, offer opportunities to work with organizations such as homeless shelters, tutoring centers, and environmental groups.

15a Address the community to effect change.

You may be assigned or volunteer to assist in a homeless shelter, tutoring center, hospice, or other not-for-profit with the goal of helping to communicate with various audiences. Your first task will be to understand the writing situation. Members of each organization have a particular way of talking about issues. As someone coming from the outside, you will have opportunities to converse with insiders and then assist the group in achieving its purposes by drafting newsletters, press releases, or funding proposals.

Writing on behalf of a community organization almost always involves negotiation and collaboration. A community organization may revise your draft to fit its needs, and you will have to live with those revisions. In these situations, having a cooperative attitude is as important as having strong writing skills.

Even if you are not writing on behalf of a group, you can write in your own name to raise an issue of concern in a public forum—for example, a newspaper editorial or a letter to a public official.

15b Design posters, brochures, and newsletters with an eye to purpose and audience.

If you are participating in a service learning program or an internship, you may design posters to create awareness and promote events and brochures and newsletters for wide distribution. To create an effective poster, brochure, or newsletter, you will need to integrate your skills in document design with what you have learned about purpose and audience.

Here are a few tips:

- Consider how readers will access the pages of the brochure or newsletter. How will it be mailed or distributed? What are the implications for the overall design? For instance, can you create a newsletter with space on the back page for the organization's address?

- Sketch the design in pencil or on a whiteboard before using the computer.

- Make decisions about photographs, illustrations, type fonts, and design in general to create the sponsoring organization's overall image.

- If the organization has a logo, include it; if not, suggest designing one. A **logo** is a small visual symbol, like the Nike "swoosh" or the distinctive font used for Coca-Cola.

- Create a template for the poster, brochure, or newsletter so that you can easily produce future versions. In word-processing and document design programs, a **template** is a blank document that includes all the necessary formatting and codes. When you use a template, you add new copy and visuals since the format and design are already done.

Notice, for example, how the poster "Cyberspace: The New Bully in Town?" in Figure 15.1 directs the eye to the large mobile phone that dominates the space. The screen displays an important message about responding to cyberbullying, summarized in the acronym "REACT."

The brochure, "Stop Cyberbullies in Their Tracks" *(Figure 15.2 on p. 192),* carefully defines terms *(bully, cyberbullying),* reviews consequences, and suggests countermeasures.

On the second page, a photo of a young woman standing alone in a hallway evokes isolation and victimhood; the red text in the top left corner encourages her to REACT, a response to bullying that is summarized in the panel to the right. The complementary image and the text are elegant in their simplicity and impact.

The newsletter from The Coalition for Internet Safety also has a simple, clear design *(Figure 15.3, p. 193).* The designer uses a shaded

FIGURE 15.1 **Example of a well-designed poster.**

The purpose of the brochure is to be informative by providing a definition of cyberbullying and giving advice. The audience is high school students.

Don't fall victim to being cyberbullied:

Educate yourself
Take preventative measures
Have zero tolerance

REACT

For more information on how to educate and protect yourself from cyberbullying, visit the following Web sites:

http://www.stopbullying.gov/cyberbullying

http://www.cyberbullying.us

STOP CYBERBULLIES IN THEIR TRACKS:

Recognize and **REACT**

NO BULLY ZONE

Are You Being Bullied?

What Is a Bully?
A bully is someone who makes you feel uncomfortable, often in a threatening way. It is the person who won't leave you alone and says mean and nasty things to you.

What Is a Cyberbully?
A cyberbully uses digital technologies like text messaging and Internet communication to threaten or scare someone else. Cyberbullies can be more dangerous than a traditional bully because they can hide behind digital technology and because their threats or intimidations can be dispersed to a wider audience through social media.

Consequences of Being Bullied
Victims are more likely to feel anxious and depressed. They think that because one person is mean to them, lots of people will be mean to them. Even when the bullying stops, victims can be haunted by negative memories. Do not let yourself become a victim: **REACT!** Now.

A brochure is meant to inform the audience about the topic. It's important to present straightforward facts and examples and use clean lines and spacing.

What You Can Do:

Educate yourself—understand what a cyberbully is and the consequences of being bullied.

Take preventative measures against cyberbullies—let your family and friends know what you are doing on the computer (the people you are talking to and what they are saying to you).

Have zero tolerance—if you believe you are being bullied, don't wait to take action.

REACT

REACT

Recognize you are being bullied
Notice the signs of bullying: the use of angry language or insults, the sharing of embarrassing images or information, the spreading of gossip or rumors, and being threatened.

Eliminate contact with the bully
Eliminating contact depends on the situation you are facing. If it is a face-to-face bully, create situations where you are always with other people. If it is a cyberbully, either de-friend the bully or create a new profile.

Ask someone in authority for help
Seek help from a parent, a teacher, an older brother or sister, or someone you trust. Ask this person to give you guidance on how to deal with being bullied and to help you do something about the person who is bullying you.

Compliment yourself for seeking help
Dealing with bulling is not easy. By getting help, you have taken the first step toward no longer being a victim.

Tell others your story
By sharing your story, you could help prevent others from becoming victims.

FIGURE 15.2 Example of a well-designed brochure.

The Coalition for Internet Safety

Volume 13.2   June 2010

Internet Safety: Tips for Keeping Kids Safe Online

- Don't allow kids to have computers in their bedrooms – keep computers in the kitchen or family room where you can supervise their use.

- Have house rules and post them near the computer.

- Go online with kids to see who their "friends" are and what they are viewing regularly.

- Regulate kids' computer time to ensure they enjoy offline activities and friends.

- Beware of late night computer use, which may indicate a child is keeping secrets.

- Watch out for any changes in self-esteem or unusual behavior – it may indicate a problem in kids' virtual life.

- Talk to kids about Internet safety on an ongoing basis.

Internet Safety: It Takes a Village

Staying safe on the Internet isn't always easy; even adults have to watch out for scams, traps that can lead to identity theft, computer viruses, malware, annoying spam, and simple information overload. Kids can be more susceptible to trouble online because they may not be able to distinguish between honest communication, a sales pitch, and predatory behavior. They may mistake someone posing as a friend for a genuine friend and communicate with that person under this misapprehension.

Parents are often way behind their children when it comes to knowledge about the Internet and what dangers can lurk there. Even tech-savvy parents may not realize how kids can inadvertently put themselves at risk. Information or photos posted publicly on social networking sites can give predators clues about a child's interests or after-school activities, for example. Even information shared online with a known friend can end up as public knowledge, an action not easily undone that can sometimes lead to tragic consequences. For example, posting a private photograph online intended only for a friend to see can quickly become an embarrassment if that friend in turn posts it more publicly. Intentionally or not, such public exposure can cause what can feel to its subject like an insurmountable level of anxiety and distress.

Helping young children stay safe online may seem easy to parents at first. Parents and teachers can set rules and monitor children's online activities. But once older children become more familiar with the Internet and begin using social-networking sites, as well as cell phones for texting, protecting them from danger becomes more difficult. Rather than one-time instruction on Internet safety, children need constant mentoring about online behavior. To keep children safe in a digital environment, adults need to make an ongoing commitment to understanding privacy and other concerns for different applications and in a growing variety of situations, and they need to be diligent. Parents, older siblings, and educators can all play a role in fostering appropriate digital behavior.

Parental Online Awareness

The greatest challenge for parents in monitoring their children's online behavior is a lack of familiarity with the Internet itself or with the ways in which their kids interact with others online. The best way to understand and prevent the potential online dangers your child might be exposed to is to use the Internet in the same way they do. Create a profile on the social networking sites they use and go there regularly so that you understand their virtual world and can see their online friends. Monitor text messages and limit cell phone time so that your children are preoccupied with homework rather than texting. Learn the shorthand that young people use online or while texting, such as POS (parent over shoulder), so you won't miss warning signs for potentially dangerous situations, such as inappropriate online communication with an unknown person.

Internet Safety Awareness Seminar
Detective Marc Rivera, Cybercrimes Unit
June 25, 5:00 – 7:00 p.m.
Griffin Middle School Auditorium

Intro to Social Networking Workshop
Collier County Community College
July 1, 6:30 – 9:00 p.m.
Hutchins Building, 230–A

The Coalition for Internet Safety

p. 2

Internet Safety: Online Resources for Parents and Children

- MTV recently launched athinline.org to help teens understand how easily the line between appropriate and inappropriate online behavior can be crossed. Parents will also find this resource helpful in understanding the peer pressures and challenges their children face online (www.athinline.org).
- Worried about cyber bullying? Check out the Cyber Bullying Research Center, which hosts a wealth of information on everything from awareness and prevention to contacting authorities for help (www.cyberbullyingresearchcenter.org).
- The FBI produces an online Parent's Guide to Internet Safety that is updated regularly and describes how to keep your child safe from Internet predators (http://www.fbi.gov/publications/pguide/pguidee.htm).
- i–SAFE Inc. is a nonprofit organization endorsed by Congress that is dedicated to protecting kids online. It features a classroom curriculum, community outreach initiatives, and information for students, parents, law enforcement, educators and any others concerned with keeping children safe online (www.isafe.org).
- For parents concerned with monitoring online activity, companies like InternetSafety.com provide products designed to prevent danger, including Internet filters that block selected sites and mobile phone locators (www.internetsafety.com).

Report to Congress Outlines Latest Safety Concerns and Solutions

SafeKids.com recently prepared a report to Congress that advocates civility and respect online. The report also recommends increased media literacy among youth using the Internet and those protecting their interests. Youth Safety on a Living Internet "points to the growing importance of online citizenship and media-literacy education, in addition to what has come to be seen as online safety education, as solutions to youth risk online" (Magid).

The report looks at the previous 20 years of online safety, but also considers the newest research on the use of social media among today's youth. The report calls for kids themselves to become more responsible for online actions and to become more aware of the risky behavior that may lead to unfortunate consequences. Today, young people are just as likely to create online content as they are to consume it; this requires responsibility and a respect for "the living entity that is the Internet today" (Magid). The report can be viewed online at SafeKids.com or downloaded in PDF format. The site also features a wide range of helpful tools for encouraging safe online behavior (www.safekids.com).

Magid, Larry. "Study has good news about kids' online behavior." SafeKids.com. Larry Magid. 26 June 2010. Web. 5 July 2010.

Privacy Settings Workshop Hits Home

Dr. Pat Carroll has been recognized numerous times for her scholarship and teaching excellence at Collier County Community College. In May she hosted a workshop for parents of area students, providing information on the latest trends in online behavior of tweens and teens and helping parents understand how to keep a handle on what kids are doing online.

Photo credit: Emily Baker (2008)

Dr. Carroll's workshop hit home with Lisa Brooks, mother to 14-year-old twin girls, who worries about what her kids do online. "I don't really understand what they're doing most of the time, even if I'm looking at the screen," she explains. "My girls know much more about using the Internet than I do, but this workshop helped me understand how to better understand what they're up to online." Parents worry that they are invading their children's privacy by closely monitoring online activity. Dr. Carroll advises parents to tell their children that when they use privacy settings or monitor their online activity, it is for their own protection. She compares letting young people use the Internet unsupervised to a parent dropping children off in Times Square at midnight without adult supervision.

FIGURE 15.3
Example of a well-designed newsletter.

area on the left side of the front page to summarize tips for keeping kids safe online. The box with the heading "Internet Safety: Online Resources for Parents and Children" on the second page includes Web addresses for further information.

(For more information about document design, see Chapter 8, Designing Academic Texts and Portfolios, pp. 92–104.)

CHAPTER 16
Letters to Raise Awareness and Share Concern

Your ability to write and your willingness to share your opinions and insights can influence community actions and affect the way an organization treats you. A letter to a local politician about a current issue or to a corporation about customer service can accomplish much if clearly argued, concisely phrased, and appropriately directed.

16a Write about a public issue.

Your task in writing to a newspaper, community organization, or public figure is to present yourself as a polite, engaged, and reasonable person who is invested in a particular issue and can offer a compelling case for a particular course of action.

Most publications, corporations, and not-for-profit organizations include forms, links, or e-mail addresses on their Web sites for submitting letters or comments. Whenever possible, use online options instead of writing a print letter. Here are some guidelines:

- Address the appropriate person or department by name. Consult the organization's Web site for this information.

- Concisely state your area of concern in the subject line.

- Never include an attachment to your e-mail: an organization's server may screen out your message as spam.

- Keep it brief. Many community organizations and corporations receive millions of e-mails each week. Most publications post specific word-count limits for letters to the editor or comments.

- Follow the conventions of professional e-mail *(see pp. 204–7)*. Use capital letters, where appropriate, and standard punctuation.

- Keep your tone polite and professional (neither combative nor overly chatty).

- In the first paragraph, concisely state the matter you wish to address and why it is important to you. For example, if you are writing to your local school board, you might state that you are the parent of a child at the local school.

- In the second paragraph, provide clear and compelling evidence for your concern. If relevant, propose a solution.

- In your conclusion, thank the reader for considering your thoughts. Repeat any request for specific action, for example, having an item added to the agenda of the next school board meeting. If you want a specific response, politely request an e-mail or telephone call. If you intend to follow up on your correspondence, note that you will be calling or writing again within an appropriate time frame.

16b   Write as a consumer.

Writing is a powerful tool for accomplishing goals in everyday life.

1. Writing a letter of complaint

Suppose a product you ordered from an online store as a gift arrived too late, despite a guaranteed delivery date. Following the Customer Service link on the Web site, you compose an e-mail letter of complaint like the one in Figure 16.1. In writing such a letter, present

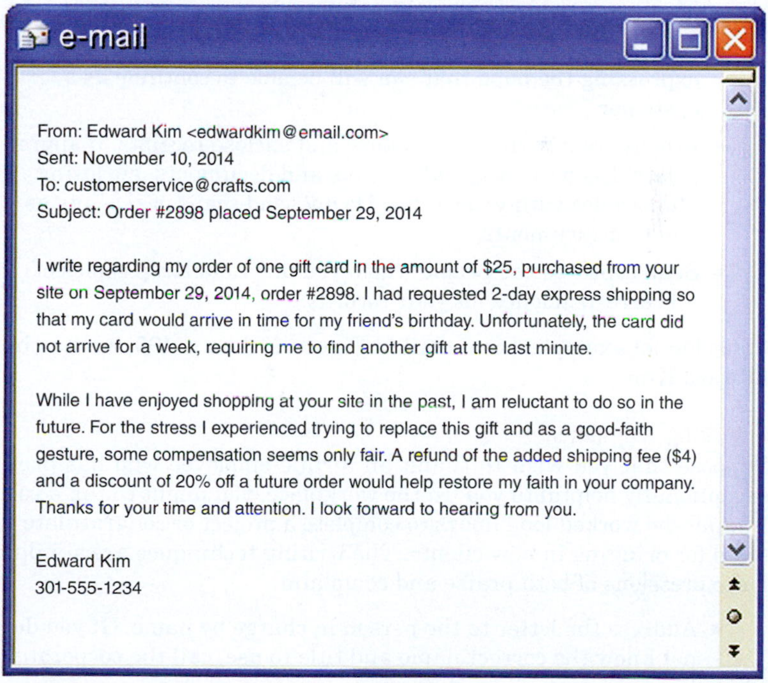

e-mail

From: Edward Kim <edwardkim@email.com>
Sent: November 10, 2014
To: customerservice@crafts.com
Subject: Order #2898 placed September 29, 2014

I write regarding my order of one gift card in the amount of $25, purchased from your site on September 29, 2014, order #2898. I had requested 2-day express shipping so that my card would arrive in time for my friend's birthday. Unfortunately, the card did not arrive for a week, requiring me to find another gift at the last minute.

While I have enjoyed shopping at your site in the past, I am reluctant to do so in the future. For the stress I experienced trying to replace this gift and as a good-faith gesture, some compensation seems only fair. A refund of the added shipping fee ($4) and a discount of 20% off a future order would help restore my faith in your company. Thanks for your time and attention. I look forward to hearing from you.

Edward Kim
301-555-1234

FIGURE 16.1 Sample letter of complaint.

yourself as a reasonable person who has experienced unfair treatment. If you are writing as a representative of your company, state that fact calmly and propose a resolution.

Here are some guidelines for writing a letter of complaint:

- If the company's Web site specifies procedures for complaints, follow those instructions.

- If possible, send the complaint via e-mail unless you must submit supporting documentation (such as receipts).

- If you are sending a print letter, use the business format on pages 204–7.

- In the first paragraph, concisely state the problem and the action you request.

- In the following paragraphs, explain clearly and objectively what happened. Refer to details such as the date and time of the incident so that the person you are writing to can follow up.

- Recognize those who tried to help you as well as those who did not.

- Mention previous positive experiences with the organization, if you can. Your protest will have more credibility if you come across as a person who does not usually complain.

- Conclude by thanking the person you are addressing and expressing the hope that you will be able to continue as a customer.

- Propose reasonable recompense and enclose receipts, if appropriate. Keep the original receipts and documents, enclosing photocopies with your letter. Do *not* send scans of receipts as e-mail attachments.

- Send copies to the people whom you mention. Keep copies of all correspondence for your records.

Consider, for example, the e-mail in Figure 16.1 on p. 195, written by Edward Kim.

2. Writing compliments

Suppose that you wish to thank an airline employee who has been exceptionally helpful to you. In the workplace, you might thank a colleague who worked long hours to complete a project or congratulate a team for bringing in new clients. The writing techniques are similar for expressions of both praise and complaint:

- Address the letter to the person in charge by name. (If you do not know the correct name and title to use, call the corporate headquarters.)

- If you are sending a print letter, use the format for a business letter *(see pp. 204–7)*.
- In the first paragraph, concisely state the situation and the help that was provided.
- In the following paragraphs, narrate what happened, referring to details such as the date and time of the incident so that the person you are writing to can follow up with the person who helped you.
- Conclude by thanking the person you are writing to for his or her time and expressing your intention to continue doing business with the company.
- Send copies to the people whom you mention.
- Whenever possible, for the speediest response, use the format provided on the company's Web site.

CHAPTER 17

Writing to Get and Keep a Job

Many students work on or off campus in jobs, as interns, or as volunteers for community organizations. Writing is one way to connect your work, your other activities, and your studies. Strong writing skills will also help you find a good job once you leave college and advance in your chosen career.

17a   Explore internship possibilities, and keep a portfolio of career-related writing.

An internship, in which you do work in your chosen field, is a vital connection between the classroom and the workplace, allowing you to gain academic credit for integrating the theoretical and the practical. Writing and learning go together. During your internship, keep a journal or notebook to record and analyze your experiences, as well as a file of writing you do on the job. With permission, your final project for internship credit could be an analysis of this file.

   On-the-job writing, clippings of articles and editorials you have written for the student newspaper, brochures you have created for a community organization—these and other documents demonstrate your ability to apply intellectual concepts to real-world demands. Organized into a portfolio, especially into an electronic portfolio (e-portfolio), this material displays your marketable skills. Your campus career resource center may offer assistance, keep your portfolio on file, if it is print, and send it to future employers or graduate schools. *(For advice on assembling an e-portfolio, see Chapter 8, pp. 100–4.)*

17b Keep your résumé up-to-date and available on a flash drive or zip drive or post it online.

A **résumé** is a brief summary of your education and your work experience that you send to prospective employers. Expect the person reviewing your résumé to give it no more than sixty seconds. Make that first impression count. Design a document that is easy to read, attractively formatted, and flawlessly edited.

1. Guidelines for writing a résumé

Always include the following *necessary* categories in a résumé:

- Heading (name, address, phone number, e-mail address)
- Education (in reverse chronological order; do not include high school)
- Work experience (in reverse chronological order)
- References (often included on a separate sheet; for many situations, you can substitute the line "References available upon request" instead)

Include the following *optional* categories in your résumé as appropriate:

- Objective or Goals
- Honors and awards
- Internships
- Activities and service
- Special skills

Some career counselors still recommend that you list a career objective right under the heading of your résumé, but others discourage you from including something so specific and counsel you instead to incorporate goals into your cover letter. If you do include an objective or goals, be sure you know what the prospective employer is looking for and tailor your résumé accordingly.

2. Two sample résumés

Laura Amabisca has organized the information in her résumé *(see p. 199)* by date and by categories. Within each category, she has listed items from most to least recent. This reverse chronological order gives appropriate emphasis to what she is doing now and has most recently done. Because she is applying for jobs in public relations, she has highlighted her internship in that field by placing it at the top of her experience section.

The résumé on page 199 reflects appropriate formatting for print. Note the use of a line rule, alignment of text, bullet points, and bold and italic type. These elements organize the information visually, directing the reader's eye appropriately.

Laura Amabisca
20650 North 58th Avenue, Apt. 15A
Glendale, AZ 85308
623-555-7310
lamabisca@peoplelink.com

Education	**Arizona State University West,** Phoenix
	• Bachelor of Arts, History, Minor in Global Management (May 2014)
	• Senior Thesis: Picturing the Hopi, 1920-1940: A Historical Analysis
	Glendale Community College, Glendale, AZ (2010–2012)

Experience   **Public Relations Office, Arizona State University West** *Intern* (Summer 2013)
• Researched and reported on university external publications.
• Created original content for print and Web.
• Assisted in planning fundraising campaigns and events.

Sears, Bell Road, Phoenix, AZ
Assistant Manager, Sporting Goods Department (2012–present)
• Supervise team of sales associates.
• Ensure quality customer service.

Sales Associate, Sporting Goods Department (2009–2012)
• Recommended products to meet customer needs.
• Processed sales and returns.

Stock Clerk, Sporting Goods Department (2007–2009)
• Received, sorted, and tracked incoming merchandise.
• Stocked shelves to ensure appropriate supply on sales floor.

Special Skills   *Language:* Bilingual: Spanish/English
Computer: Windows, Mac OS, MS Office, HTML

Activities   **America Reads**
Tutor, Public-Relations Consultant (2013)
• Taught reading to first-grade students.
• Created brochure to recruit tutors.

Multicultural Festival, Arizona State University West *Student Coordinator* (2013)
• Organized festival of international performances, crafts, and community organizations.

Writing Center, Glendale Community College
Tutor (2010–2012)
• Met with peers to help them with writing assignments.

References   Available upon request to Career Services, Arizona State University West

Amabisca's entire résumé is just one page. A brief, well-organized résumé is more attractive to potential employers than a rambling, multipage one.

The résumé features active verbs such as *supervise.*

Amabisca uses a simple font and no bold or italic type, ensuring that the résumé will be scannable.

Asterisks replace bullets.

Amabisca includes keywords (high-lighted here) to catch the eye of a potential employer or match desired positions in a database. Amabisca knows that a position in public relations requires computer skills, communication skills, and experience working with diverse groups of people. Keywords such as *sales, bilingual, HTML,* and *public relations* are critical to her résumé.

LAURA AMABISCA
20650 North 58th Avenue, Apt. 15A
Glendale, AZ 85308
623-555-7310
lamabisca@peoplelink.com

EDUCATION Arizona State University West, Phoenix
* Bachelor of Arts, History, Minor in Global Management (May 2014)
* Senior Thesis: Picturing the Hopi, 1920–1940: A Historical Analysis

Glendale Community College, Glendale, AZ (2010–2012)

EXPERIENCE
Public Relations Office, Arizona State University West (Summer 2014)
Intern
* Researched and reported on university external publications.
* Created original content for print and Web.
* Assisted in planning fundraising campaigns and events.

Sears, Bell Road, Phoenix, AZ
Assistant Manager, Sporting Goods Department (2012–present)
* Supervise team of sales associates.
* Ensure quality customer service.

Sales Associate, Sporting Goods Department (2009–2012)
* Recommended products to meet customer needs.
* Processed sales and returns.

Stock Clerk, Sporting Goods Department (2007–2009)
* Received, sorted, and tracked incoming merchandise.
* Stocked shelves to ensure appropriate supply on sales floor.

SPECIAL SKILLS
Language: Bilingual: Spanish/English
Computer: Windows, Mac OS, MS Office, HTML

ACTIVITIES
America Reads (2013)
Tutor, Public-Relations Consultant
* Taught reading to first-grade students.
* Created brochure to recruit tutors.

Multicultural Festival, Arizona State University West (2014)
Student Coordinator
* Organized festival of international performances, crafts, and community organizations.

Writing Center, Glendale Community College (2010–2012)
Tutor
* Met with peers to help them with writing assignments.

REFERENCES
Available upon request to Career Services, Arizona State University West

the EVOLVING SITUATION

Electronic and Scannable Résumés

Many employers now request résumés by e-mail and electronically scan print résumés. Here are some tips for using electronic technology to submit your résumé:

- Contact the human resource department of a potential employer and ask whether your résumé should be scannable.
- If so, be sure to use a clear, common typeface in an easy-to-read size. Do not include any unusual symbols or characters.
- If the employer expects the résumé as an e-mail attachment, save it in a widely readable form such as rich text format (RTF) or PDF. Use minimal formatting and no colors, unusual fonts, or decorative flourishes.
- Configure your e-mail program to send you an automated reply when your e-mail has been successfully received.
- Include specific keywords that allow employers to locate your electronic résumé in a database. See the résumé section of Monster.com at http://resume.monster.com for industry-specific advice on appropriate keywords and other step-by-step advice.

17c   Write a tailored application letter.

A clear and concise **application letter** should always accompany a résumé. Before drafting the letter, do some research about the organization you are contacting. For example, even though Laura Amabisca was already familiar with the Heard Museum, she found out the name of the director of public relations. *(Amabisca's application letter appears on p. 202.)* If you are unable to identify an appropriate name, it is better to direct the letter to "Dear Director of Public Relations" or "Dear Director of Personnel" than to "Dear Sir or Madam."

Here are some additional guidelines:

- **Tailor your letter.** A form letter accompanied by a generic résumé is not an effective way of getting a job interview. Before writing an application letter or preparing a résumé, you should consider the overall situation. What exactly is the employer seeking? How might you draw on your experience to address the employer's needs?

- **Use business style.** Use the block form shown on page 202. Type your address at the top of the page, with each line starting at the left margin; place the date at the left margin two lines above the recipient's name and address; use a colon (:)

20650 North 58th Avenue, Apt. 15A
Glendale, AZ 85308
August 17, 2014

Amabisca writes to a specific person and uses the correct salutation (*Mr., Ms., Dr.,* etc.). Never use someone's first name in an application letter, even if you are already acquainted.

Ms. Jaclyn Abel
Director of Public Relations
Heard Museum
2301 North Central Avenue
Phoenix, AZ 85004

Dear Ms. Abel:

I am writing to apply for the position of Public Relations Assistant that you recently advertised in the *Arizona Republic.* I believe that my experience and qualifications fit well with your needs at the Heard, a museum that I have visited and loved all my life.

Amabisca briefly sums up her work experience. This information is also available on her résumé, but she makes evident in her cover letter why she is applying for the job. Without this explanation, a potential employer might not even look at her résumé.

As the attached résumé indicates, I have experience in the public relations field. While at Arizona State University West, I worked as an intern in the Public Relations Office, where I was responsible for analyzing and reporting on the image projected by the university's external publications. I also had a hand in creating the brochure for the University-College Center and participated in planning ASU West's "Dream Big" campaign. In addition I assisted in organizing an opening convocation attended by 800 people. This work in the not-for-profit sector has prepared me well for employment at the Heard.

My undergraduate major in U.S. history has also helped me understand the rich heritage of Native Americans. In my senior thesis, which received the Westmarc Writing Award, I studied the history of the relationship between the Hopis and the Anglo population as reflected in photographs taken from 1920 to 1940. Although my thesis focuses on a specific tribe, I have been interested for many years in Native American culture and have often made use of resources in the Heard. I think that I would do a superior job of presenting the Heard as the premier museum of Native American culture.

Amabisca demonstrates her familiarity with the museum to which she is applying. This shows her genuine interest in joining the organization.

Confidential reference letters are available from ASU West Career Services. I sincerely hope that we will have an opportunity to talk further about the Heard Museum and its outstanding cultural contributions to the Phoenix metropolitan area. Please contact me at 623-555-7310 or at lamabisca@peoplelink.com.

Sincerely,

Laura Amabisca

Laura Amabisca

Enc.

after the greeting; double-space between single-spaced paragraphs; use a traditional closing *(Sincerely, Sincerely yours, Yours truly);* and make sure that the inside address and the address on the envelope match exactly.

- **Be professional.** Your letter should be crisp and to the point. Be direct as well as objective in presenting your qualifications, and maintain a courteous and dignified tone toward the prospective employer. Your résumé should contain only education and work-related information. It is better not to include personal information (such as ethnicity, age, or marital status).

- **Limit your letter to three or four paragraphs.** Focus clearly and concisely on what the employer needs to know. In the first paragraph, identify the position you are applying for, mention how you heard about it, and briefly state that you are qualified. In the following one or two paragraphs, explain your qualifications, elaborating on the most pertinent items in your résumé. Because Amabisca was applying for a public relations job at a museum of Native American culture, she chose to highlight her internship and her thesis. In another application letter, however, this time for a management position at American Express, she made different choices. In that letter, she emphasized her work experience at Sears, including the fact that she had progressed through positions of increasing responsibility.

- **State your expectation for future contact.** Conclude with a one- or two-sentence paragraph informing the reader that you are anticipating a follow-up to your letter.

- **Use *Enc.* if you are enclosing additional materials.** Decide whether it is appropriate to enclose supporting materials other than your résumé, such as samples of your writing. Amabisca decided to do so because she was applying for her ideal job and had highly relevant materials to send. If you have been instructed to send a cover letter and résumé as attachments to an e-mail, include the word *Attachments* after your e-mail "signature."

17d   Prepare in advance for the job interview.

Many campus career centers offer free seminars on interviewing skills and can also arrange for you to role-play an interview with a career guidance counselor.

Here are some additional guidelines for job interviews:

- Call to confirm your interview the day before it is scheduled. Determine how much time you will need to get there. A late appearance at an interview can count heavily against you.

- Dress professionally.
- Bring an additional copy of your résumé and cover letter.
- Expect to speak with several people—perhaps someone from human resources as well your potential supervisor and other people in the department.
- *Always* send a personalized thank-you note or e-mail to everyone who took the time to meet you. In each, mention an interesting point that the person made and your interest in working with him or her. Send these notes within twenty-four hours of your interview.

17e   Apply what you learn in college to your on-the-job writing.

Once you get a job, writing is a way to establish and maintain lines of communication with your colleagues and clients. When you write in the workplace, you should imagine a reader who is pressed for time and wants you to get to the point immediately.

1. Writing e-mail and memos in the workplace

In the workplace, you will do much of your writing online, in the form of e-mail. *(For more on e-mail, see Tab 1: Learning across the Curriculum, pp. 23–24.)* Most e-mail programs set up messages in memo format, with "From," "To," "Sent," and "Subject" lines, as in Figure 17.1.

E-mail in the workplace requires a more formal style than the e-mail you send to family and friends. In an e-mail for a business occasion—communication with colleagues, a request for information, or a thank-you note after an interview—you should observe the same care with organization, spelling, and tone that you would in a business letter:

- Use a concise subject line to cue the reader as to the intent of the e-mail. When replying to messages, replace subject lines that do not clearly reflect the topic.
- Maintain a courteous tone. Avoid joking, informality, and sarcasm since not everyone reading the memo will know you well enough to understand your intent.
- Make sentences brief and to the point. Use short paragraphs.
- Use special formatting such as italics sparingly since not all readers may be able to view it.
- Use standard punctuation and capitalization.
- Close with your name and contact information. *(See the example in Figure 17.1.)*

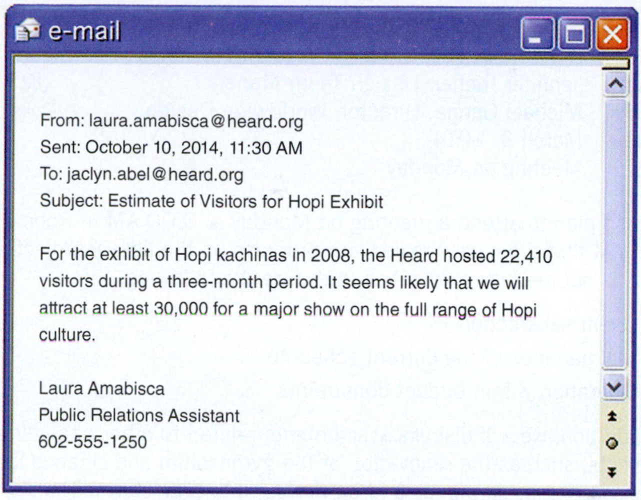
e-mail

From: laura.amabisca@heard.org
Sent: October 10, 2014, 11:30 AM
To: jaclyn.abel@heard.org
Subject: Estimate of Visitors for Hopi Exhibit

For the exhibit of Hopi kachinas in 2008, the Heard hosted 22,410 visitors during a three-month period. It seems likely that we will attract at least 30,000 for a major show on the full range of Hopi culture.

Laura Amabisca
Public Relations Assistant
602-555-1250

FIGURE 17.1 Sample workplace e-mail.

- Particularly when you do not know the recipient, use the conventions of letter writing, such as opening with "Dear" and ending with "Sincerely."

Business memos are used for communication with others within an organization and are usually sent electronically. Memos, written in a professional tone, are concise and formal and may be used to set up meetings, summarize information, or make announcements. *(See the example on p. 206.)* They generally contain the following elements:

- A header at the top that identifies recipient, author, date, and subject
- Block paragraphs that are single-spaced within the paragraph and double-spaced between paragraphs
- Bulleted lists and other design elements (such as headers) to set off sections of longer memos
- A section at the top or bottom that indicates other members of the organization who have received copies of the memo

Whether you are sending your memo by e-mail or interoffice mail, consider both the content and the appearance of the document. For example, presenting your information as a numbered or bulleted list surrounded by white space aids readability and allows you to highlight important points and to emphasize crucial ideas. *(For more help with document design, see Tab 2: Writing and Designing Texts, pp. 93–100.)*

To: Sonia Gonzalez, Grace Kim, Jonathan Jones
From: Jennifer Richer, Design Team Manager   *JR*
cc: Michael Garcia, Director, Worldwide Design
Date: March 3, 2014
Re: Meeting on Monday

Please plan to attend a meeting on Monday at 9:00 AM in Room 401. At that time, we'll review our progress on the library project as well as outline future activities to ensure the following:

- Client satisfaction
- Maintenance of the current schedule
- Operation within budget constraints

In addition, we will discuss assignments related to other upcoming projects, such as the renovation of the gymnasium and science lab. Please bring design ideas and be prepared to brainstorm. Thanks.

FIGURE 17.2 Sample memo.

2. Writing in other business genres

Conventional forms of business writing also increase readability because readers have built-in expectations for the genre and therefore know what to look for. Besides the memo, there are a number of common business genres:

- **Business letters:** Use business letters to communicate formally with people outside an organization. Typically, letters in business format have single-spaced block paragraphs with double spacing between the paragraphs. *(See the example on p. 202.)*

- **Business reports and proposals:** Like college research projects, business reports and proposals can be used to inform, analyze, and interpret. An abstract, sometimes called an **executive summary,** is almost always required. Tables and graphs should be included when appropriate. *(For more about these visual elements, see Tab 2: Writing and Designing Texts, pp. 54–57.)*

- **Evaluations and recommendations:** You might need to evaluate a person, or you might be called on to evaluate a product or a procedure and recommend whether the company should buy or use it. Like the reviews and critiques that college writers compose, workplace evaluations should

— *the* EVOLVING SITUATION

E-Mail in the Workplace

Anything you write using a company's or an organization's computers or computer systems is considered company property. If you want to gossip with a co-worker, do so over lunch. If you want to e-mail your best friend about your personal life, do so from your home computer. The following guidelines will help you use e-mail wisely:

- When you are replying to an e-mail that has been sent to several people (the term *cc* means "carbon copy"), determine whether your response should go to all of the original recipients or just to the original sender. Avoid cluttering other people's in-boxes.
- Open attachments from known senders only.
- File your e-mail as carefully as you would paper documents. Create separate folders in your e-mail program for each client, project, or co-worker. Save any particularly important e-mails as separate files.
- While it may be acceptable for you to browse news and shopping sites during your breaks and lunchtime, do not visit sites that would embarrass you if a colleague or your supervisor suddenly looked over your shoulder, and remember that all sites you have visited are cached—or stored—on that computer.

be reasonable as well as convincing. Always support your account of both strengths and weaknesses with specific illustrations or examples.

- **Presentations:** In many professions, information is presented informally and formally to different groups of people. You might suddenly be asked to offer an opinion in a group meeting, or you might be given a week to prepare a formal presentation, with visuals, on an ongoing project. *(For more information about oral presentations, including PowerPoint and other presentation tools, see Tab 3: Common Assignments, pp. 167–74.)*

5

Researching

For all knowledge and wonder (which is the seed of knowledge)
is an impression of pleasure in itself.

–Francis Bacon

The Hubble Space Telescope, which has helped astronomers view the far reaches of the universe, provided this image of a blast wave caused by a stellar explosion that occurred approximately 15,000 years ago.

5 Researching

 Sections dealing with visual rhetoric. For a complete listing, see the Quick Guide to Key Resources at the back of this book.

─START SMART
Tab 5: Researching

This section will help you answer questions such as the following:

Rhetorical Knowledge
- What writing situation does my assignment specify? (18c)

Critical Thinking, Reading, and Writing
- What is the difference between primary and secondary research? (19)
- How can I tell if sources are worth including? (21)
- How do I present my ideas along with those of my sources? (24c, e)
- How should I evaluate sources that I find on the Web? (21b)

Processes
- How can I think of a topic for my research project? (18d)
- How should I plan my research project? (18e)
- When and how should I use visuals in my project? (20)
- Where can I find appropriate images from online sources? (20b)

Knowledge of Conventions
- What is an annotated bibliography, and how do I create one? (24b)
- What is a documentation style? Which one should I use? (25c)

For a general introduction to writing outcomes, see 1e, pages 14–16.

CHAPTER 18

Understanding Research

Your campus library provides valuable resources for almost any kind of research. These libraries offer not only books, magazines, and journals, but also specialized online databases and the expert guidance of research librarians.

Doing research in the twenty-first century includes using the library but is not limited to it. In seconds, the Internet provides direct access to an abundance of information unimaginable to earlier generations of students. The results of Internet searches, however, can sometimes provide an overwhelming flood of sources, many of questionable legitimacy.

The goal of the research section of this book *(Chapters 18–25)* is to help you learn about the research process, manage the information you discover within it, and use that information to write research projects.

18a Understand primary and secondary research.

Doing **primary research** means working in a laboratory, in the field, or with an archive of raw data, original documents, and authentic artifacts to make firsthand discoveries. *(For more information about primary research, see Chapter 22, pp. 247–52.)* Doing **secondary research** means looking to see what other people have learned and written about a topic.

Knowing how to identify facts, interpretations, and evaluations is key to good secondary research:

- **Facts** are objective. Like your body weight, facts can be measured, observed, or independently verified.

- **Interpretations** spell out the implications of facts. Are you as thin as you are because of your genes, because you exercise every day, or both? The answer to this question is an interpretation.

- **Evaluations** are debatable judgments based on a set of facts or a situation. The assertion that "one can never be too rich or too thin" is an evaluation.

Once you are up to date on the facts, interpretations, and evaluations in a particular area, you will be able to design a research project that adds your *perspective* on the sources you have found and read:

- Given all that you have learned about the topic, what strikes you as important or interesting?

- What patterns do you see, or what connections can you make between one person's work and another's?

- Where is the research going, and what problems still need to be explored?

Putting together all the facts, interpretations, and evaluations—**synthesis**—requires time and thought. Since in research writing you are not just stitching sources together but using them to support your own thesis, try beginning the process by focusing on a question you want to answer.

18b Recognize the connection between research and writing in college and beyond.

In one way or another, research informs all writing. But some tasks require more rigorous and systematic research than do others. These **research projects** require that you go beyond course readings and more casually selected sources—to find and read both classic and current material on a specific issue. A research paper constitutes your contribution to the ongoing conversation on the topic.

Research is a key component of much workplace and public writing. A sound business proposal will depend on research to identify best practices. A public commentary on the value of charter schools will require research into their performance. Engaging in academic research provides an excellent opportunity to prepare for writing situations that you will encounter throughout life.

When you are assigned research writing, the project may seem overwhelming at first. If you break it into phases, however, and allow enough time for each phase, you can manage your work and prepare a project that contributes to an ongoing conversation.

18c   Understand the research assignment.

Consider the rhetorical situation of the research project. Think about your project's audience, purpose, voice/stance/tone, genre, context, and scope *(see Tab 2: Writing and Designing Texts, pp. 40–44)*.

1. Audience

Although your *audience* may include only your instructor and your classmates, thinking critically about the needs and expectations of your readers will help you to plan an effective research strategy and create a schedule for writing your project.

Ask yourself the following questions about your audience:

- What do they already know about my subject? How much background information and context should I provide? (Your research should include *facts*.)

- Might they find my conclusions controversial or challenging? How should I accommodate and acknowledge different perspectives and viewpoints? (Your research should include *interpretations,* which balance opposing perspectives.)

- Do I expect the audience to take action based on my research? (Your research should include *evaluations,* carefully supported by facts and interpretations, which demonstrate clearly why readers should adopt a course of action or point of view.)

2. Purpose

Your *purpose* for writing a research project depends on both the specifics of the assignment as set by your instructor and your own interest in the topic. Your purpose might be **informative**—to educate your audience about an unfamiliar subject or point of view *(see Chapter 9: Informative Reports, p. 107)*. Your purpose might be **interpretive**—to reveal the meaning or significance of a work of art, a historical document, a literary work, or a scientific study *(see Chapter 10: Interpretive Analyses and Writing about Literature, p. 122)*. Your purpose might be **persuasive**—to convince your audience, with logic and evidence, to accept your point of view on a controversial

---

NAVIGATING THROUGH COLLEGE AND BEYOND
Classic and Current Sources

Classic sources are well-known and respected older works that made such an important contribution to a discipline or a particular area of research that contemporary researchers use them as touchstones for further research in that area. In many fields, sources published within the past five years are considered current. However, sources on topics related to medicine, recent scientific discoveries, or technological change must be much more recent to be considered current.

---

issue or to act on the information in your project *(see Chapter 11: Arguments, p. 131)*. Review your assignment for keywords that signal its purpose. Note, however, that some terms can signal more than one type of assignment, depending on the context. Here are some examples:

- **Informative:** Explain, describe, define, review
- **Interpretive:** Analyze, compare, explain, interpret
- **Persuasive:** Assess, justify, defend, refute, determine

3. Voice/stance/tone
Your stance in a research project—reflected in your voice and tone—should be that of a well-informed, helpful individual. Even though you will have done extensive work on the topic, it is important to avoid sounding like a know-it-all; instead, you are sharing with others who want to be informed.

4. Genre/medium
Research projects prepared for different purposes will reflect characteristics of various genres and may be expressed in different media. Your research on charter schools, for example, may take the form of a proposal or an informative report. Either genre could be communicated in print or on a Web site. In addition, some projects are shared in more than one medium: you may present the findings of your research in class with presentation software, share a brief summary of it on the Web, and submit the full study to the teacher in print.

5. Context
The overall situation will affect the presentation of your project. State cuts in public school funding will affect your presentation of a proposal to expand charter schools, even if you have full confidence in the research you have synthesized. Recent scientific research may change your attitude about the role of taking daily vitamins in maintaining health.

6. Scope

A project's scope includes the expected length of the paper, the deadline, and any other requirements such as number and type of sources. Are primary sources appropriate? Should you include visuals, and is any type (for example, photos, maps, graphs) specified?

18d   Choose an interesting research question for critical inquiry.

Approach your assignment in a spirit of critical inquiry. *Critical* in this sense does not mean "fault finding," "skeptical," "cynical," or even "urgent." Rather, it refers to a receptive, but reasonable and discerning, frame of mind. Choosing an interesting topic will make the results of your inquiry meaningful—to yourself and your readers.

1. Choosing a question with personal significance

Even though you are writing for an academic assignment, you can still get personally involved in your work. Begin with the wording of the assignment, analyzing the project's required audience, purpose, and scope *(see Section 18c, pp. 213–15)*. Then browse through the course readings and your class notes, looking for a match between your interests and topics, issues, or problems in the subject area.

For example, suppose you are assigned to write a report on a selected country's global economic prospects. If you have visited Mexico, you might find it interesting to explore that country's economic future.

2. Making your question specific

The more specific your question, the more your research will have direction and focus. To make a question more specific, use the "five *w*'s and an *h*" strategy by asking about the *who, what, where, why, when,* and *how* of a topic *(see Tab 2: Writing and Designing Texts, p. 46)*.

After you have compiled a list of possible research questions, choose one that is specific, or rewrite a broad one to make it more specific and therefore answerable. For example, as Peggy Giglio developed a topic for a research report for a sociology course on the reasons young adults volunteer, she rewrote the following broad question to make it answerable:

TOO BROAD	How has the volunteerism of young people affected the United States?
ANSWERABLE	Why do today's college students choose to volunteer?

(Giglio's finished paper appears in Chapter 34, pp. 378–92.)

3. Finding a challenging question

If a question can be answered with a yes or no, a dictionary-like definition, or a textbook presentation of information, choose another question or rework it to make it more challenging.

─ *the* EVOLVING SITUATION

Typical Lines of Inquiry in Different Disciplines

Research topics and questions—even when related to a single broad issue such as volunteerism—differ from one discipline to another. The following examples show the distinctions:

- **History:** How important were volunteers in the creation of lending libraries in nineteenth-century America?
- **Marketing:** What marketing strategies have successfully persuaded busy adults that they should volunteer?
- **Political Science:** What role did volunteers play in the election of national political candidates in the early twenty-first century?
- **Anthropology:** How have volunteers contributed to the creation of archives?

NOT CHALLENGING	Do college students volunteer?
CHALLENGING	What motivates college students to give of their "time and treasure" when they get no material reward for such efforts?

4. Speculating about answers

Sometimes it can be useful to speculate on the answer to your research question so that you have a **hypothesis** to work with during the research process. Don't forget, though, that a hypothesis is a tentative answer that must be tested and revised based on the evidence you turn up in your research. Be aware of the assumptions embedded in your hypothesis or research question. Consider, for example, the following.

HYPOTHESIS	College students volunteer for more than one reason.

This hypothesis assumes that because college students differ from one another in many ways, they have more than one reason for volunteering. But assumptions are always open to question. Researchers must be willing to adjust their ideas as they learn more about a topic.

As the preceding example demonstrates, your research question must allow you to generate testable hypotheses. Assertions about your personal beliefs and feelings cannot be tested.

18e   Create a research plan.

Your research will be more productive if you create both a general plan and a detailed schedule immediately after you receive your assignment. A general plan ensures that you understand the full scope of the assignment. A detailed schedule helps you set priorities and meet deadlines.

Use the table in Figure 18.1, which outlines the steps in a research project, as a starting point, adjusting the time allotments based on the amount of time you have to complete the assignment. Consider what you already know about the topic as well as what you must learn through your research.

Scheduling Your Research Project

Task	Date

Phase I

- Complete general plan for research.
- Decide on topic and research question.   _____
- Consult reference works and reference librarians.   _____
- Make a list of relevant keywords for online searching
  (see Chapter 19, pp. 221–22).   _____
- Compile a **working bibliography** (see Chapter 24, p. 258-61).   _____
- Sample some items in bibliography.   _____
- Make arrangements for primary research (if necessary).   _____

Phase II

- Locate, read, and evaluate selected sources.   _____
- Take notes, write summaries and paraphrases.   _____
- Cross-check notes with working bibliography.   _____
- Conduct primary research (if necessary).   _____
- Find and create visuals.   _____
- Confer with instructor or writing center (optional).   _____
- Develop thesis and outline or plan organization of project.   _____

Phase III

- Write first draft, deciding which primary and secondary source
  materials to include.   _____
- Have peer review (optional).   _____
- Revise draft.   _____
- Confer with instructor or writing center (optional).   _____
- Do final revision and editing.   _____
- Create works-cited or references page.   _____
- Proofread and check spelling.   _____

Due date   _____

FIGURE 18.1 Sample schedule for a research project. Use this table to determine how much time you will need to complete each stage of your own research projects.

—**SOURCE SMART** Planning Your Search

Your research plan should include where you expect to find your sources. For example, you may have to visit the library to view print materials that predate 1980; you will need to consult a subscription database online or at the library for recent scientific discoveries; you may need to access archives for historical research; and you may need to conduct field research, such as interviewing fellow students.
Set priorities to increase your efficiency in each location (library, archive, field, online).

CHAPTER 19

Finding and Managing Print and Online Sources

To conduct a meaningful search through the vast amount of available information, focus on the following three activities:

- Collecting keywords from reference works
- Using library databases
- Finding material in the library and on the Web

19a Use the library in person and online.

Librarians know what is available at your library and how to obtain material from other libraries. They can also show you how to access the library's computerized book catalog, periodical databases, and electronic resources and how to use the Internet to find information relevant to your research. At many schools, reference librarians are available for online chats, and some even take queries via text message. Your library's Web site may also have links to subscription databases or important reference works available on the Internet, as shown in Figure 19.1.

In addition, **help sheets** or online tutorials at most college libraries give the location of both general and discipline-specific periodicals and noncirculating reference books, along with information about the book catalog, special databases, indexes, Web resources, and library policies.

FIGURE 19.1 A page from the Web site of Governors State University. The Web page provides links to a variety of Web-based reference sources.

19b Consult various kinds of sources.

You should always consult more than one source and usually more than one *kind* of source. Your assignment may specify how many print and electronic sources you are expected to consult and cite. Here are some of the available resources:

- **General reference works (for overview and keywords)**

  Encyclopedias, annuals, almanacs

  Computer databases, bibliographies, abstracts

- **Specialized reference works (for overview and keywords)**

  Discipline-specific encyclopedias, almanacs, and dictionaries

- **Books**
- **Periodical articles**

  In scholarly and technical journals

  In newspapers

In magazines

On the Web

- **Specialized databases**
- **Web sites**
- **Other online sources**
- **Virtual communities**

MOOs (multiuser object-oriented dimensions)

- **Government documents, pamphlets, census data**
- **Primary sources**

Original documents like literary works, art objects, performances, manuscripts, letters, and personal journals

Museum collections; maps; photo, film, sound, and music archives

Field notes, surveys, interviews

Results of observation and lab experiments

19c Use printed and online reference works for general information.

Reference works provide an overview of a subject area and typically are less up-to-date than the specialized knowledge found in academic journals and scholarly books. If your instructor approves, you may start your research by consulting a general or discipline-specific encyclopedia, but for college research you must explore your topic in more depth. Often, the list of references at the end of an encyclopedia article can lead you to useful sources on your topic.

Reference books do not circulate, so take notes and make photocopies of the pages you may need to consult later. Check your college library's home page for access to online encyclopedias.

Here is a list of some other reference materials available in print, on the Internet, or both:

ALMANACS	*Almanac of American Politics* *Information Please Almanac* *World Almanac*
BIBLIOGRAPHIES	*Bibliographic Index* *Bibliography of Asian Studies* *MLA International Bibliography*
BIOGRAPHIES	*African American Biographical Database* *American Men and Women of Science* *Dictionary of American Biography* *Dictionary of Literary Biography:* *Chicano Writers*

Dictionary of National Biography
Webster's New Biographical Dictionary
Who's Who

DICTIONARIES   *American Heritage Dictionary of the*
English Language
Concise Oxford Dictionary of Literary Terms
Dictionary of American History
Dictionary of Philosophy
Dictionary of the Social Sciences
Oxford English Dictionary (OED)

19d   Understand keywords and keyword searches.

Most online research—whether conducted in your library's catalog, in a specialized database, or on the Web—requires an understanding of **keyword searches.** In this context, a **keyword** is a term (or terms) you enter into a **search engine** (searching software) to find sources that have information about a particular subject.

As you focus more clearly on your topic, you must also refine your search terms. Although search engines vary, the following guidelines for refining keyword searches should work for many.

- **Group words together.** Put quotation marks or parentheses around the specific phrase you are looking for, for example, "traditional news media."

- **Use Boolean operators.**
  AND (+)   Use AND or + when you need sites with both of two or more words: "New York Times" + blogs.
  OR   Use OR when you want sites with either of two or more terms: blogs OR "online journalism."
  NOT   Use NOT in front of words that you do not want to appear together in your results: Rogers NOT Tony.

- **Use a root word plus a "wildcard."** For more results, combine part of a keyword with an asterisk (*) used as a wildcard: blog* (for "blogger," "blogging," "blogs," and so forth).

the EVOLVING SITUATION

Wikipedia

The online encyclopedia Wikipedia offers information on almost any subject, and it can be a good starting place for research. However, you should evaluate its content critically. Volunteers (who may or may not be experts) write Wikipedia's articles, and almost any user can edit any article. While the site has some mechanisms to maintain accuracy, always check findings with another source (and cite that source, if you use the information).

─NAVIGATING THROUGH COLLEGE AND BEYOND

Sources: Popular or Scholarly?

A source's audience and purpose determine whether it should be considered *popular* or *scholarly*. You may begin your inquiry into a research topic with popular sources, but to become fully informed you must consult scholarly sources.

Popular sources

- Are widely available on newsstands and in retail stores (print)
- Are printed on magazine paper with a color cover (print)
- Accept advertising for a wide range of consumer goods or are themselves widely advertised (in the case of books)
- Are published by a commercial publishing house or media company (such as Time Warner)
- May include a wide range of topics in each issue, from international affairs to popular entertainment
- Usually do not contain bibliographic information
- Have a URL that likely ends in .com (online)

Scholarly sources

- Are usually found in libraries, not on newsstands (print)
- Usually list article titles and authors on the cover (print)
- Have few advertisements
- Are published by a scholarly or nonprofit organization, often in association with a university press
- Focus on discipline-specific topics
- Include articles by authors who typically are affiliated with colleges, museums, or other scholarly institutions
- Include articles with extensive citations and bibliographies
- Have a URL that likely ends in .edu or .org (online)
- Are **refereed** (peer reviewed), which means that each article has been reviewed, commented on, and accepted for publication by other scholars in the field

- **Search the fields.** Some search engines permit you to search within fields, such as the title field of Web pages or the author field of a library catalog. Thus, TITLE + "News media" will give you all pages that have "News Media" in their title.

Look for advanced search features that help with the refining process.

19e   Use print indexes and online databases to find articles in journals and other periodicals.

Indexes and online databases are essential tools for researching in journals and other periodicals.

1. Periodicals

Newspapers, magazines, and scholarly journals that are published at regular intervals are classified as **periodicals.** The articles in scholarly and technical journals, written by experts and based on up-to-date research, are more credible than articles in popular newspapers and magazines. Ask your instructor or librarian which periodicals are considered important in the discipline you are studying.

2. Indexes and databases

Articles published in periodicals are cataloged in general and specialized **indexes.** Indexes are available on subscription-only **databases** and as print volumes. If you are searching for articles that are more than twenty years old, you may use print indexes or an appropriate electronic index. Print indexes can be searched by author, subject, or title. Electronic databases can also be searched by date and keyword and will provide a list of articles that meet your search criteria. Each entry in the list will include the information you need to find and cite the article.

You can find databases on your library's Web site. When selecting a database, consult its description on your library's site (often labeled "Info") to see the types of sources included, subjects covered, and number of periodicals from each subject area. Would your topic be best served by a general database (such as EBSCO Academic Search Premier) or by one that is discipline specific (such as PsycINFO)? Also consider the time period the database spans.

Some of the major online databases are listed below, and the screen shots in Figures 19.2 and 19.3 on pages 224–25 illustrate a search on one of them, EBSCOhost.

When searching a database, you will encounter either abstracts or full-text articles (in certain cases both). Full-text articles may be available in either PDF or HTML format:

- **Abstract:** An abstract is a brief summary of a full-text article. Abstracts appear at the beginning of articles in some scholarly journals and are used in databases to summarize complete articles. Do not mistake an abstract for a full-text source.

- **Full text:** When an article is listed as "full text," the database provides a link to the complete text. Full-text articles retrieved through databases do not always include accompanying photographs or other illustrations, however.

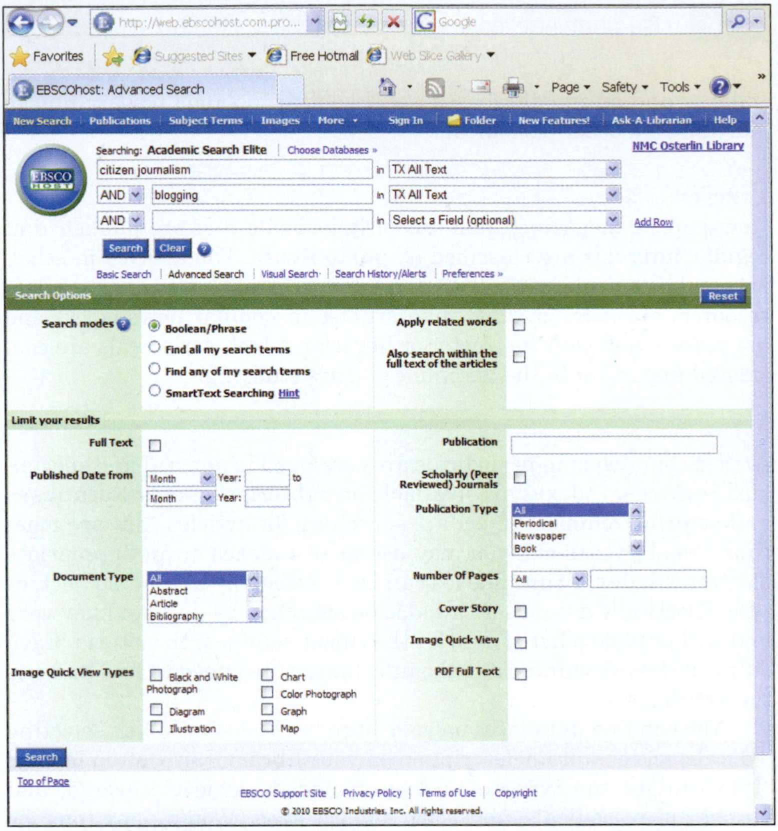

FIGURE 19.2   EBSCOhost's Advanced Search page

- **PDF** and **HTML:** Articles in databases and other online sources may be in either PDF or HTML format (or both). Documents in HTML (hypertext markup language) have been formatted to read as Web pages and may directly link to related sources. PDF (portable document format) documents appear as a facsimile of the original pages. To read a PDF document, download *Adobe Acrobat Reader* for free at <www.adobe.com>.

Keep in mind that not all libraries subscribe to all databases. But here we provide a list of some common databases to which your library is likely to subscribe.

- *ABC-CLIO:* This service offers access to numerous history-related databases including *American History* and *American Government* as well as databases on

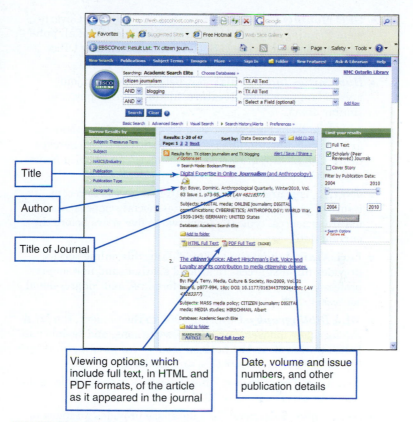

Title

Author

Title of Journal

Viewing options, which include full text, in HTML and PDF formats, of the article as it appeared in the journal

Date, volume and issue numbers, and other publication details

FIGURE 19.3 Partial results of the search started in Figure 19.2.

African American, American Indian, and Latino American experience, pop culture, war, social history, geography, and world history.

- **EBSCOhost:** The *Academic Search Premier* database provides full-text coverage for more than 8,000 scholarly publications and indexes articles in all academic subject areas.

- **ERIC:** This database lists publications in the area of education.

- **Factiva:** This database offers access to the Dow Jones and Reuters news agencies, including newspapers, magazines, journals, newsletters, and Web sites.

- **General Science Index:** This index is general rather than specialized. It lists scholarly and popular articles by biologists, chemists, and other scientists.

- *GPO Monthly Catalogue:* Updated monthly, the Government Printing Office Catalogue contains records of all publications printed by the U.S. Government Printing Office since 1976.

- *Humanities Index:* This index lists articles from journals in language and literature, history, philosophy, and similar areas.

- *InfoTrac Web:* This Web-based service searches bibliographic and other databases such as the *General Reference Center Gold, General Business File ASAP,* and *Health Reference Center.*

- *JSTOR:* This archive provides full-text access to recent issues of journals in the humanities, social sciences, and natural sciences, typically from two to five years before the current date.

- *LexisNexis Academic:* Updated daily, this online service provides full-text access to around six thousand newspapers, professional publications, legal references, and congressional sources.

- *MLA Bibliography:* Covering 1963 to the present, the *MLA Bibliography* indexes journals, dissertations, and serials published worldwide in the fields of modern languages, literature, literary criticism, linguistics, and folklore.

- *New York Times Index:* This index lists major articles published by the *Times* since 1913.

- *Newspaper Abstracts:* This database provides an index to fifty national and regional newspapers.

- *PAIS International:* Produced by the Public Affairs Information Service, this database selectively indexes literature on public policy, social policy, and the social sciences from 1972 to the present.

- *Periodical Abstracts:* This database indexes more than two thousand general and academic journals covering business, current affairs, economics, literature, religion, psychology, and women's studies from 1987 to the present.

- *ProQuest:* This database provides access to dissertations; newspapers and journals; information on sources in business, general reference, the social sciences, and humanities; and historical sources dating back to the nineteenth century.

- *PsycInfo:* Sponsored by the American Psychological Association (APA), this database indexes and abstracts books, scholarly articles, technical reports, and dissertations in psychology and related disciplines from the 1800s.

- *PubMed:* The National Library of Medicine publishes this database, which indexes and abstracts fifteen million journal articles in biomedicine and provides links to related databases.

- *Sociological Abstracts:* This database indexes and abstracts articles from more than 2,600 journals, as well as books, conference papers, and dissertations.

- *Social Science Index:* This index lists articles from such fields as economics, psychology, political science, and sociology.

- *WorldCat:* This is a catalog of books and other resources available in libraries worldwide.

19f   Use search engines and subject directories to find Internet sources.

To find information that has been published in Web pages, use more than one Internet search engine, since each searches the Web in its own way. Some of the more popular Internet search engines include general search engines, meta search engines, and mediated search engines:

General search engines: These sites allow for both category and keyword searches:

- *AltaVista* <www.altavista.com>
- *Google* <www.google.com>
- *Bing* <www.bing.com>
- *Yahoo!* <www.yahoo.com>
- *Ask* <www.ask.com/>

Meta search engines: These sites search several different search engines at once:

- *Dogpile* <www.dogpile.com>
- *Internet Public Library* <www.ipl.org>
- *Ixquick* <www.ixquick.com>
- *Library of Congress* <www.loc.gov/index.html>
- *MetaCrawler* <www.metacrawler.com>
- *WebCrawler* <www.webcrawler.com>

Mediated search engine: This site has been assembled and reviewed by people who sometimes provide annotations and commentary about topic areas and specific sites:

- *About.com* <www.about.com>

Each search engine's home page provides a link to advice on efficient use as well as help in refining a search. Look for a link labeled "search help," "about us," or something similar.

Some Internet search engines allow you to conduct specialized searches—for images, for example *(see Chapter 20)*. *Google Book Search* can help locate books on your topic. *Google Scholar* locates only scholarly sources in response to a search term. At this point, it offers incomplete information, so you should not rely on it alone.

Many Internet search engines also include sponsored links—links that a commercial enterprise has paid to make appear in response to specific search terms. These links are usually clearly identified as such.

To find relevant results, carefully select the words for Internet keyword searches. For example, a search of *Google* using the keywords *citizen journalism* yields a list of more than 49 million Web sites. Altering the keywords to make them more specific narrows the results (Figure 19.4). The most relevant matches will appear at the beginning of the results page.

Most search engines have an advanced search option. This option allows you to search for exact phrases, to exclude a specific term, to search only for pages in a certain language, and to refine searches in other ways.

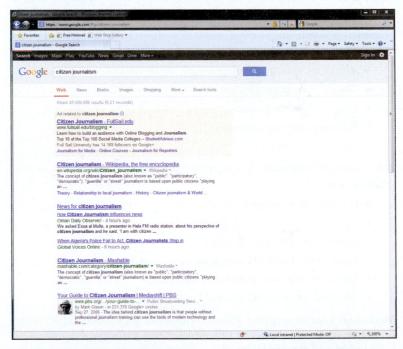

FIGURE 19.4 Refining the search. Adding the key terms *blogging, social media, newspapers,* and *reporting* reduces the number of hits to two million from more than 49 million.

In addition to keyword searches, many Internet search engines offer a **subject directory**—a listing of broad categories. Clicking through this hierarchy of choices eventually brings you to a list of sites related to a specific topic.

Some Web sites, such as *the Internet Public Library* (<www.ipl .org/>), provide content-specific subject directories designed for research in a particular field. These sites are often reviewed or screened and are excellent starting points for academic research.

Other online tools can help organize sources and keep track of your Web research. Save the URLs of promising sites to your browser's Bookmarks or Favorites. Your browser's history function can allow you to retrace your steps if you forget how to find a particular site. The box at the bottom of this page includes additional online resources.

19g   Use your library's catalog to find books.

Books in most libraries are shelved by **call numbers** based on the Library of Congress classification system. The *Library of Congress Subject Headings (LCSH)* shows you how your research topic is classified and provides you with a set of key terms that you can use in your search. In this system, books on the same topic have similar call numbers and are shelved together. You will need the call number to locate the actual book on the library's shelves. Therefore, when consulting a library catalog, be sure to jot down (or print out) the call numbers of books you want to consult.

You can conduct a keyword search of most online library catalogs by author, by title, or by subject. Subject terms appear in the *LCSH*, which provides a set of key terms that you can use in your search for sources. Keyword searches of many catalogs also include publisher, notes, and other fields.

the EVOLVING SITUATION

Online Tools for Research

- *Zotero* <www.zotero.org>: Compatible with the *Mozilla Firefox* browser (version 2.0 and higher), this program automatically saves citation information for many types of online sources (text and images) via your browser. It creates formatted references in multiple styles and helps you organize your sources by assigning tags (categories based on keywords) to them.

- *DiRT (Digital Research Tools)* <https://digitalresearchtools.pbworks .com/w/page/17801672/FrontPage>: This site links to online tools that help researchers in the humanities and social sciences perform many tasks, such as collaborating with others, finding sources, and visualizing data.

Card catalogs are rarely used except by archives and specialized libraries. Cards are usually filed by author, title, and subject (based on the *LCSH*).

The results of a keyword search of a library's online catalog will provide a list comprised mostly of books. The search of the Governors State University online catalog depicted in figures 19.5 and 19.6, shows how you can alter the terms of a search to restrict the formats to a specific medium.

As with any keyword search, getting what you really need—a manageable number of relevant sources—depends on your choice of keywords. If your search terms are too broad, you will get too many hits; if they are too narrow, you will get few or none.

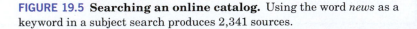

FIGURE 19.5 Searching an online catalog. Using the word *news* as a keyword in a subject search produces 2,341 sources.

FIGURE 19.6 Changing a search term. A keyword search using the search term *citizen journalism* produces thirty results, a manageable number.

19h Take advantage of printed and online government documents.

The U.S. government publishes an enormous amount of information and research every year, most of which is available online. The *GPO Monthly Catalogue* and the *U.S. Government Periodicals Index* are available as online databases. The Government Printing Office's own Web site, *The Federal Digital System* <www.gpo.gov/fdsys>, available through Lexis-Nexis, is an excellent resource for identifying and locating federal government publications. Other useful online government resources include:

- *FedWorld Information Network* (maintained by the National Technical Information Service) <www.fedworld.gov>
- *FirstGov* (the U.S. government's "Official Web Portal") <http://firstgov.gov>
- *The National Institutes of Health* <www.nih.gov>
- *U.S. Census Bureau* <www.census.gov>

─ **SOURCE SMART** Organizing Your Sources

List your sources alphabetically. For each source, include citation information *(see pp. 258–59)*, key points, and its relevance to your topic. Does the source support or detract from your claim? Is it an early source or a more recent one? Does it agree or disagree with other sources you have read? Do other sources refer to this one? You might color-code your list to indicate related ideas that appear in a number of your sources. Include useful quotations and their page numbers.

19i Explore online communication.

Usenet news groups, electronic mailing lists, blogs, and social networking offer opportunities to converse regularly with people who have common interests. Carefully evaluate information from these sources *(see Chapter 21: Evaluating Sources, pp. 240–47)*. Participants will have different levels of expertise—or possibly no expertise at all. Online sites can help you with research in the following ways:

- You can get ideas for your writing by identifying topics of general concern and becoming aware of general trends in thinking about the topic.
- You can zero in on a very specific or current topic.
- You can query an expert in the field about your topic via e-mail or a social networking site.

Caution: Since the credibility of online sites varies widely, use your library or department Web site to find scholarly forums for purposes of comparison and assessment.

Social networking sites like *Facebook* and *Twitter* help people form online communities. **Blogs** *(see Chapter 14)* can be designed to allow readers to post their own comments and questions on a wide range of views on a topic under debate. However, many blog postings consist of unsupported opinion, and they may not be monitored closely for accuracy. **Wikis,** sites designed for online collaboration, allow people both to comment on and to modify one another's contributions. When evaluating information from a wiki, check to see who can update content and whether experts review the changes. If content is not monitored by identified experts, verify your findings with another source.

Unlike electronic mailing lists, **Usenet news groups** are posted to a *news server*—a computer that hosts the news group and distributes postings to participating servers. You must subscribe to read postings, which are not automatically distributed by e-mail.

Podcasts are downloadable digital audio or video recordings, updated regularly. The Smithsonian produces credible podcasts on many topics <www.si.edu/Connect/Podcasts>.

RSS (Really Simple Syndication) **feeds** deliver the latest content from continuously updated Web sites to your browser or home page. You can use RSS feeds to keep up with information on your topic, once you identify relevant Web sites.

Synchronous communication includes **chat rooms** organized by topic, where people can carry on real-time discussions. **Instant messaging (IM)** links only those who have agreed to form a conversing group. Other formats include virtual worlds such as multiuser dimensions (MUDs) and object-oriented multiuser dimensions (MOOs). These can be used for collaborative projects. However, you will want to check with your instructor before using such materials in an assignment.

CHAPTER 20

Finding and Creating Effective Visuals, Audio Clips, and Videos

Visuals can support a writer's thesis, enhance an argument, and sometimes constitute the complete argument. Relief organizations, for example, may post a series of compelling visuals on their Web sites to persuade potential donors to contribute money following a catastrophic event.

For some writing situations, you will prepare or provide your own visuals. You may, for example, make your own sketch of an experiment or create a bar graph from data that you have collected. In other situations, however, you may decide to create a visual from data that you have found in a source, or you may search in your library or on the Internet for a visual to use.

In an online text, an audio clip or a video can provide support for an argument or add an engaging note to a personal Web site.

20a   Find quantitative data and display it visually.

Research writing in many disciplines—especially in business, math, the sciences and social sciences, and engineering, as well as other technical fields—almost always requires reference to quantitative information. That information generally has more impact when it is displayed visually in a chart, graph, or map than as raw numbers alone. Pie charts, for instance, show percentages of a whole. Bar graphs are often used to compare groups over time. Line graphs also show trends over time, such as the impact of wars on immigration rates and population movements. Visual displays of information are also tools of analysis.

Think through the writing situation as you decide about when and what types of visuals are appropriate to include. Consider your readers' expectations for presentations of numerical relationships that words alone cannot convey. Since digital technology makes it relatively easy to find and create visual images, your audience will have higher expectations for visual communication when you are working online.

(For examples of graphs and charts, and a discussion of what situations to use them in, see Tab 2: Writing and Designing Texts, pp. 54–57.)

1. Finding existing graphs, charts, and maps

As you search for print and online sources *(see Chapter 19)*, take notes on useful graphs, charts, or maps with proper acknowledgment that you might incorporate (with proper acknowledgment) into your text. If your source is available in print only, you may be able to use a scanner to capture and digitize it.

2. Creating visuals from quantitative data

Sometimes you may find data presented in writing or in tables that would be more effective as a chart or graph. Using the graphics tool available in spreadsheet or other software, you can create your own visual.

For example, suppose you are drafting a research project about population trends in the United States in the nineteenth century and want to illustrate the country's population growth in that period with a line graph, using data from the U.S. Census Bureau, which are in the public domain. Most census data, however, appear in tables like the one shown in Figure 20.1. If you transfer data from a table to a spreadsheet program or a word-processing program, you can use them to create graphs that you can insert into a project, as in Figure 20.1.

SOURCE SMART Citing Data

Make citations of data specific. Indicate the report and page number or Web address(es) where you found the information, as well as any other requirements of your documentation style. If you analyze the data, refer to any analysis in the source before presenting your own interpretation.

Caution: Whether you are using data from a source to create an image or incorporating an image made by someone else, you must give credit to the source of the data or image. Furthermore, if you plan to publish this visual on a Web site or in another medium, you must obtain permission to use it from the copyright holder unless the source specifically states that such use is allowed or it is in the public domain.

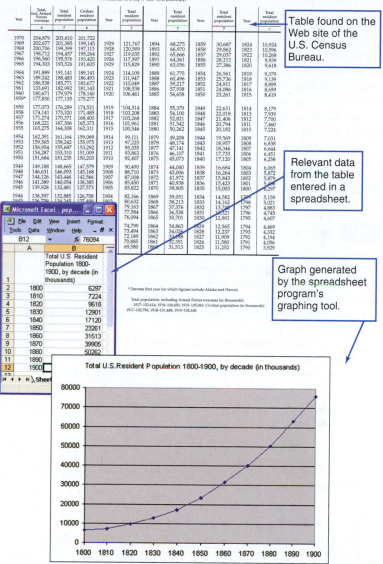

Series A 6–8. Annual Population Estimates for the United States: 1790 to 1970
In thousands. As of July 1, 1960–1970, preliminary;

Table found on the Web site of the U.S. Census Bureau.

Relevant data from the table entered in a spreadsheet.

Graph generated by the spreadsheet program's graphing tool.

FIGURE 20.1 Using a spreadsheet program to create a graph from data in a table.

3. Displaying the data accurately

Display data in a way that is consistent with your purpose and not misleading to viewers. For example, Nancy Kaplan has pointed out distortions in a graph from a National Endowment for the Arts report on reading practices (Figure 20.2). The NEA graph presents the years 1984 to 2004, showing a sharp decline in reading. However, the source for the graph, the National Center for Educational Statistics (NCES), presents a less alarming picture in Figure 20.3. Here, reading levels are plotted over a longer period of time, from 1971 to 2004. In addition, the NEA graph is not consistent in its units: the four-year period from 1984 to 1988 takes up the same amount of space as the two-year period from 1988 to 1990. In selectively displaying and distorting data, the NEA graph stacks the deck to argue for the reality of a reading crisis.

Avoid intentionally or unintentionally distorting data. Plot the axes of line and bar graphs so that they do not misrepresent data. *(See Tab 2: Writing and Designing Texts, pp. 84–85.)* Do not use photo editing software to alter photographs.

20b Search for appropriate images in online and print sources.

Photographs, pictures of artwork, drawings, diagrams, and maps can provide visual support for many kinds of texts, particularly in subjects like history, English and other languages, philosophy, music, theater, and other performing arts. As with the display of quantitative data, you might *choose* an image from another source, or you might *create* one. If you were writing or creating a report comparing the way different corporations are organized, for example, you might use organizational charts that appear in corporate reports. Alternatively, you could use your word processor's drawing feature to create

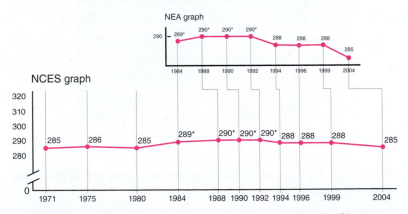

FIGURE 20.2 A distorted display of reading practices indicates a decline.

FIGURE 20.3 An accurate display of reading practices shows only mild fluctuations.

┌─CHECKLIST   Deciding When to Use an Image in Your Project

Consider these questions as you look for visuals:

- ☐ What contribution will each image make to the text?
- ☐ What contribution do the images taken as a whole make to the text?
- ☐ How many images do you need?
- ☐ Where will each image appear in the text?
- ☐ Does the audience have enough background information to interpret each image in the way you intend?
- ☐ If not, what additional information should you include?
- ☐ What information should be in the caption?
- ☐ Have you reviewed your own text (and perhaps asked a friend to review it as well) to see how well the image is working in terms of appropriateness, location, and context?

---

your own organizational charts based on information you find in the corporate reports. When using an image from another source, be sure to cite it correctly. If the image will appear on a public Web site, consult the copyright holder for permission.

The following are three sources of images that you can draw on:

- **Online library and museum image collections and subscription databases:** Several libraries and other archives maintain collections of images online. See Figure 20.4 on page 238 for the URLs of image collections. Follow the guidelines for usage posted on these sites. Your library also may subscribe to an image database such as the Associated Press *AP Multimedia Archive.*

- **Images on the Internet:** Many search engines have the ability to search the Web for images. You can conduct an image search on *Google,* for example, by clicking on the "images" option, entering the key term, and then clicking "search." Image- and media-sharing sites such as *Flickr* and *YouTube* can serve as sources as well. Read the information on the site carefully to see what uses of the material are permitted. The Creative Commons site (<www.creativecommons .org>) lets you search for material with a Creative Commons license, which describes the uses of the content that are allowed. The material shown can be used or altered for noncommercial purposes, as long as it is cited. All the images accompanying Wikipedia are licensed through Creative Commons, so that is another source. Assume that copyright applies to material on the Web unless the site says otherwise. If your project will be published or placed on a public Web

—CHECKLIST Deciding What Kind of Chart or Graph to Use

In deciding the kind of chart or graph to use, consider these questions:

- [ ] Who are my readers, and what are their expectations?
- [ ] What information is most important to show, and why?
- [ ] What options do I have for displaying the information?
- [ ] How much context is necessary to include, and why?
- [ ] How many charts or graphs will contribute to achieving my purpose, based on readers' expectations, academic discipline, medium, and genre?
- [ ] How detailed should each visual be, and why?
- [ ] Will my visual project into the future or report on the past?
- [ ] What information will be left out or minimized, and how important is that omission?
- [ ] What other information—an introduction, an explanation, a summary, an interpretation—will readers need to make sense of the graphed information?

site, you must obtain permission to use this material. *(See Chapter 23: Plagiarism, Copyright, and Intellectual Property, pp. 252–57.)*

- **Images scanned from a book or journal:** You can use a scanner to scan some images from books and journals into a paper but, as always, only if you are sure your use is within fair-use guidelines. Also, be sure to credit the source.

- *Art Institute of Chicago* (selected works from the museum's collection)
- *The Library of Congress* <www.loc.gov/index.html> Various images and documents from American history
- *National Archives Digital Classroom* (documents and photographs from American history) <www.archives.gov/digital_classroom/index.html>
- *National Aeronautics and Space Administration* (images and multimodal features on space exploration) <www.nasa.gov/multimedia/imagegallery/index.html>
- *National Park Service Digital Image Archive* (thousands of public domain photographs of U.S. national parks) <www.nps.gov/photosmultimedia/photogalleries.htm>
- *New York Public Library* <http://www.nypl.org/collections/articles-databases/nypl-digital-gallery> Maps, posters, photographs, and documents
- *Schomburg Center for Research in Black Culture* <www.nypl.org/research/sc/sc.html> Articles, books, and images representing the African diaspora and African American history
- *VRoma: A Virtual Community for Teaching and Learning Classics* (images and other resources related to ancient Rome) <www.vroma.org/images/image_search.html>

FIGURE 20.4 Online image collections.

> *Caution:* The results of Internet image searches, like those of any Internet search, must be carefully evaluated for relevance and credibility. *(See Chapter 21: Evaluating Sources, pp. 240–47.)* Make sure you have proper source information for any images you use that you find in this way.

20c   Search for or create appropriate audio clips and videos.

Some writing situations call for audio or video clips. A history of the ways that Franklin Delano Roosevelt managed his paralyzed legs might include a video showing him leaning against a podium to give a talk. Video of the *Challenger* explosion in 1986 could underscore the constant danger faced by astronauts. The sounds made by locusts would help explain how quickly these insects consume everything in their path.

When deciding to use a video or audio clip, you have two choices: you can use material that is available elsewhere, crediting it appropriately, or create your own. A rich stock of material is available on the Web, as the University of Illinois library's Web site shows, including those listed in Figure 20.5. You can begin by searching in general categories such as *Google* Video Search or *Yahoo* video search or in more specific categories like CNN video or the National Science Foundation's *NSF Science Nation.* Likewise, you can find audio clips at large databases like the Library of Congress *American Memory* Web site and on DIY (Do It Yourself) Web sites like *Pandora* and *Spotify,* where you can create your own playlist.

For some projects, you might include video and audio clips that you create yourself. Audio interviews with students engaged in volunteer activities can allow them to "speak" to the experience and provide details supporting your claim about student volunteerism. A video of a student discussing his or her award-winning artwork—with the artwork visible—helps your reader see both the artist and the art. Whenever you create an audio or video file, be sure to ask your subjects for permission.

- *Google Video Search* <http://video.google.com/?ie=UTF8&hl=enj&tab=wv>: A good place to search for videos on a wide range of subjects.

- *CNN Video* <www.cnn.com/video/>: Provides free video news about national and international events.

- *MTV Music Videos* <www.mtv.com/music/videos/#/music/video>: Allows you to search for your favorite artist or music video; however, will play a short MTV ad before the video.

- *American Memory Project* <http://memory.loc.gov/ammem /browse/index.html>: Provided by the Library of Congress; provides access to historical materials that document the American experience. Select "Motion Pictures" in the Browse Collections Containing section.

FIGURE 20.5 Online sources of audio and video clips, from the University of Illinois library's Web site.

CHAPTER 21

Evaluating Sources

Never before in the history of the planet has information been more readily available. The catch is that a good deal of this information is misleading or downright false. Your major task is to evaluate the information that you find for credibility, accuracy, reasonableness, and support (CARS).

Digital technologies give you fast access to a tremendous variety of sources, but it is then up to you to pose questions. Is the source relevant: does it pertain to your research topic? Is the source **trustworthy:** does it provide credibility, accuracy, reasonableness, and support?

21a Question print sources.

Just because something is in print does not make it relevant or true. How can you determine whether a print source is likely to be both credible and useful? Before assessing a source's credibility, make sure it is relevant to your topic. The Checklist on page 242 provides some questions to ask about any source you are considering.

Relevance can be a tricky matter, requiring careful analysis of the writing situation. What sources will be particularly meaningful or persuasive to your anticipated audience? For an audience opposed to gun control legislation, an acknowledgment that certain types of weapons should be regulated will be more relevant and persuasive from a source that usually supports the NRA (National Rifle Association). Relevance is also associated with the academic discipline that forms the context for your work. Your sociology instructor will expect you to give special preference to sociological sources in a project on the organization of the workplace. Your business management instructor will expect you to use material from that field in a project on the same topic. Be prepared to discover that some promising sources turn out to be less relevant than you first thought.

21b Question Internet sources.

Although the questions in the Checklist on page 242 should be applied to online sources, Web resources also require additional methods of ensuring the credibility of information presented. Most of the material in the library has been evaluated to some extent for credibility. Editors and publishers have reviewed the content of books, magazines, journals, and newspapers, and journals and many books are reviewed by scholars as well. Some presses and publications are more reputable than others. Subscription databases generally compile articles that originally appeared in print, and librarians try to purchase the most reliable databases. While you should still evaluate all sources, you can have some confidence that most of the material you find in a college library is credible, at least to some degree.

In contrast, anyone can create a Web site that looks attractive but contains nonsense. Similarly, the people who post to blogs, discussion lists, and news groups may not be experts or even marginally well informed. Some information on the Web is valuable and timely, but much of it is not, so you must assess its credibility carefully. Consult the Checklist box on page 242, and consider the following questions when determining whether online information is reliable:

1. Who is hosting the site? Is the site hosted by a university or by a government agency (such as the National Science Foundation or the National Endowment for the Humanities)? In general, sites hosted by institutions with scholarly credentials are more likely to be trustworthy. However, they remain open to critical inquiry (as exemplified by the NEA graph on page 236).

2. Who is speaking on the site? A nationally recognized biologist is likely to be more credible on biological topics than a politician with no scientific background. If you cannot identify the author, who is the editor or compiler? If you cannot identify an author, editor, compiler, or sponsoring organization, do not use the source.

3. What links does the site provide? If it is networked to sites with obviously unreasonable or inaccurate content, you must question the credibility of the original site.

4. Is the information on the site supported with documentation from scholarly or otherwise credible sources (for example, government reports)?

Consider these factors as well:

- **Authority and credibility:** Are the author and sponsor of the Web site identifiable? Does the author include biographical information? Is there any indication that the author has relevant expertise on the subject? Look for information about the individual or organization sponsoring the site. The following extensions in the Web address, or uniform resource locator (URL), can help you determine the type of site (which often tells you something about its purpose):

.com commercial (business)	**.edu** educational	**.mil** military
.org nonprofit organization	**.gov** U.S. government	**.net** network

―CHECKLIST Relevance and Credibility of Sources

Relevance

☐ **Do the source's title and subtitle indicate that it addresses your specific research question?**

☐ **What is the publication date?** Is the material up to date, classic, or historic? The concept of "up to date" depends on discipline and topic. Ask your instructor how recent sources should be for your project.

☐ **Does the table of contents indicate that it contains useful information?**

☐ **If the source is a book, does it have an index?** Scan the index for keywords related to your topic.

☐ **Does the abstract at the beginning or the summary at the end of an article suggest it will be useful?** An abstract or a summary presents the main points made in the article.

☐ **Does the work contain headings?** Skim the subheadings to see whether they indicate that the source contains useful information.

Credibility

☐ **What information can you find about the writer's credentials?** Obtain biographical information about the writer by checking the source itself, consulting a biographical dictionary, or conducting an Internet search of the writer's name. Is the writer affiliated with a research institution that contributes knowledge about an issue? Is the writer an expert on the topic? Is the writer cited frequently in other sources about the topic?

☐ **Who is the publisher?** University presses and academic publishers are considered more scholarly and therefore more credible than the popular press.

☐ **Does the work include a bibliography of works consulted or cited?** Trustworthy writers cite a variety of sources and document their citations properly. Does this source do so? Does the source include a variety of citations?

☐ **Does the work argue reasonably for its position and treat opposing views fairly?** What tone does the author use? Is the work objective or subjective? Are the writer's arguments clear and logical? What is the author's point of view? Does he or she present other views fairly? *(For more on evaluating arguments, see Tab 2: Writing and Designing Texts, pp. 132–40.)*

- A tilde (~) followed by a name in a URL usually means the site is a personal home page not affiliated with any organization.

- **Audience and purpose:** How does the appearance of the site, along with the tone of any written material, suggest its intended audience? A site's purpose also influences the way it presents information and the credibility of that information. Is the site's main purpose to promote a cause, raise money, adver-tise a product or service, deliver factual information, present research results, provide news, share personal information, or offer entertainment? Always try to view the site's home page; delete everything after the first slash in the URL to do so.

- **Objectivity and reasonableness:** Look carefully at the purpose and tone of the text. Nearly all sources express a point of view or bias. You should consult sources that repre-sent a range of opinions on your topic. However, unreasonable sources have no place in academic debate. Clues that indicate a lack of reasonableness include an intemperate tone, broad claims, exaggerated statements of significance, conflicts of interest, no recognition of opposing views, and strident attacks on differing opinions. *(For more on evaluating argu-ments, see Tab 2: Writing and Designing Texts, pp. 132–40.)*

- **Relevance and timeliness:** In what ways does the information from an online source specifically support (or refute) your thesis or topic? Do the site's intended audience and purpose include an academic audience? Does the site indicate how recently it has been updated, and are most of the included links still working?

- **Context:** Do others' comments on a blog or posts to a discus-sion list make your source appear more credible or undermine the writer's credibility?

the EVOLVING SITUATION

Using the CARS Checklist to Evaluate Web Sites

Use your understanding of the writing situation to evaluate sources on the Web. For example, before judging a Web site to be credible or accurate, give sufficient consideration to its purpose and authorial stance. A Web site that is **c**redible, **a**ccurate, **r**easonable, and **s**upported (CARS) should meet the following criteria:

Credibility
The source is trustworthy; you would consider a print version to be authori-tative (for example, an online edition of a respected newspaper or major news magazine).

- The argument and use of evidence are clear and logical.
- The author's or sponsor's credentials are available (visit the home page and look for a link that says "About Us").
- Quality control is evident (spelling and grammar are correct; links are functional).

(continued)

─*the* EVOLVING SITUATION *(continued)*

- The source is a known or respected authority; it has organizational support (such as a university, a research institution, or a major news publication).

Accuracy

- The site is updated frequently, if not daily (and includes "last-updated" information).
- The site is factual, not speculative, and provides evidence for its assertions.
- The site is detailed; text appears in full paragraphs.
- The site is comprehensive, including archives, links, and additional resources. A search feature and table of contents or tabs allow users to quickly find the information they need.
- The site's purpose includes completeness and accuracy.

Reasonableness

- The site is fair, balanced, and objective. (Look at comments on a blog or related messages on a news group.)
- The site makes its purpose clear. (Is it selling something? Prompting site visitors to sign a petition? Promoting a new film?)
- The site contains no conflicts of interest.
- The site content does not include fallacies or a slanted tone *(for more on fallacies, see Chapter 11: Arguments, pp. 135–39)*.

Support

- The site lists sources for its information, providing links where appropriate.
- The site clarifies the content it is responsible for and which links are created by unrelated authors or sponsors.
- The site provides contact information for its authors and/or sponsors.
- If the site is an academic resource, it follows the conventions of a specific citation style (for example, MLA or APA).

Consider a student writing a report on the reintroduction of gray wolves in the western United States following their near extinction. Many environmentalists have favored this program, while farmers and ranchers have worried about the impact of wolves on livestock.

The student conducts an online keyword search and finds the site in Figure 21.1. This site focuses on the gray wolf population in the United States and its status under the Endangered Species Act, making it relevant to the student's topic. The URL indicates that the site belongs to a U.S. government agency, suggesting its credibility (although such sites are not immune from politics and bias).

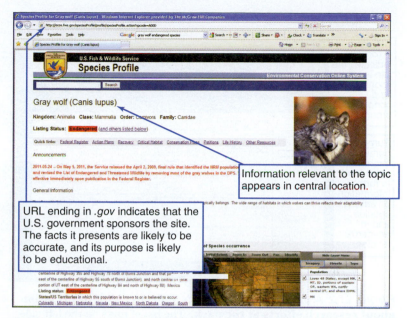

FIGURE 21.1 **U.S. Fish & Wildlife Service Endangered Species Program site on the gray wolf.** This government site provides information on the efforts to preserve and rebuild the gray wolf population in the United States.

Information on the site appears in a simple, easy-to-follow format, indicating an educational purpose. It links to other government sites. Scrolling down, the student sees the site has been updated recently. This site's apparent authority, credibility, and purpose make it a good candidate for use as a source.

Next, the student finds the site in Figure 21.2. Following the link that says "About Us," the student learns that the site is sponsored by Wolf Park, a nonprofit organization in Indiana dedicated to the preservation and study of wolves. The site's purpose appears to be educational and persuasive; it includes information about wolves and conservation efforts on their behalf. The page shown in Figure 21.2 describes research at the park and includes a link to papers with clearly documented sources, suggesting that the site is credible.

After further research the student reaches the site in Figure 21.3 on page 246, which presents apparently accurate and impartial information about wolves. Scrolling down, the student sees that the site also features advertisements, which do not appear in most scholarly sources. The site does not state the author's credentials, nor does it include documentation for its information. For these reasons, the student should confirm its statements with another source before using them in an academic report.

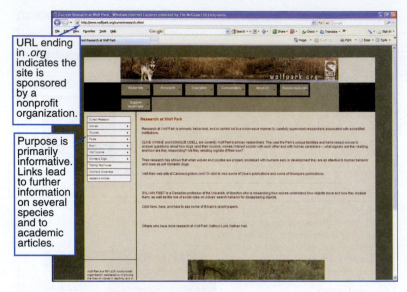

URL ending in *.org* indicates the site is sponsored by a nonprofit organization.

Purpose is primarily informative. Links lead to further information on several species and to academic articles.

FIGURE 21.2 A page from Wolf Park's Web site, with information about research efforts at the park. The list of links on the left side of the page includes a link to academic articles.

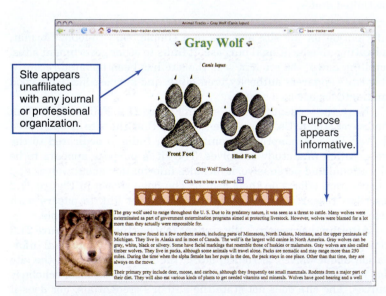

Site appears unaffiliated with any journal or professional organization.

Purpose appears informative.

FIGURE 21.3 Animal Tracks gray wolf site. This site's information appears to be accurate, but it does not document its sources or present the author's credentials.

21c   Evaluate a source's arguments.

As you read the sources you have selected, continue to assess their credibility. Look for arguments that are qualified, supported with evidence, and well documented. Avoid sources that appeal mostly to emotions or promote one-sided agendas instead of inquiry and discussion. A fair-minded researcher must read and evaluate sources on many sides of an issue, including relevant primary sources if they exist.

CHAPTER 22

Doing Research in the Archive, Field, and Lab

Research involves more than **secondary research**—finding answers to questions in books and other print and online resources. When you conduct **primary research**—looking up old maps, consulting census records, polling community members about a current issue—you participate in the discovery of knowledge.

The three kinds of primary research discussed in this chapter are archival research, field research, and laboratory research.

- **Archival research:** An **archive** is a cataloged collection of documents, manuscripts, and other materials, possibly including receipts, wills, photographs, sound recordings, and other kinds of media.

- **Field research:** Field research takes you out into the world to gather and record information.

- **Laboratory research:** Every science course will most likely involve a laboratory component. In the laboratory, you work individually or as a team to record each step of an experiment carefully.

22a   Adhere to ethical principles when doing primary research.

In the archive, field, or lab, you are working directly with something precious and immediate: an original record, a group of people, or special materials. An ethical researcher shows respect for materials, experimental subjects, fellow researchers, and readers. Here are some guidelines for ethical research:

- Handle original documents and materials with great care, always leaving sources and data available for other researchers.

- Accurately report your sources and results.
- Follow proper procedures when working with human participants.

Researchers who work with human participants should also adhere to the following basic principles:

- **Confidentiality:** People who fill out surveys, participate in focus groups, or respond to interviews should be assured that their names will not be used without their permission.
- **Informed consent:** Before participating in a study, all participants must sign a statement affirming that they understand the general purpose of the research.
- **Minimal risk:** Participants in research should not incur any risks greater than they do in everyday life.
- **Protection of vulnerable groups:** Researchers must be held strictly accountable for research done with the physically disabled, prisoners, people who are mentally impaired or incompetent, minors, the elderly, and pregnant women.

NAVIGATING THROUGH COLLEGE AND BEYOND

Primary Research in the Disciplines

Primary research is almost always impressive because you are working with authentic documents to discover new ideas. As always, the overall situation is essential to your decisions. If your purpose is to summarize research done by others, you would be overstepping the boundaries of the genre by inserting a survey of your own. Always keep in mind the constraints and opportunities of the situation.

Different forms of primary research characterize different disciplines. Here are some examples:

- **Archival research:** Languages and literature; education; music and the performing arts; visual arts; media and popular culture; social sciences. For a report on how different sections of the country were represented by the photographers of the 1930s, a historian might research the images of Dorothea Lange housed in the Library of Congress.
- **Field research:** Social sciences; marketing and advertising; media and communication. For a proposal on developing a new brand identity, a marketing researcher might survey current users of the brand.
- **Laboratory research:** Life sciences; physical sciences; computer science; engineering. To find out whether fish that swim in schools connect more readily with fish of their own species, a scientist could create a controlled environment in a laboratory to test the hypothesis.

22b   Prepare yourself for archival research.

Archives are found in libraries, museums, other institutions and private collections, and on video and audiotape. Your own attic may contain family archives—letters, diaries, and photographs that could have value to a researcher. Some archival collections are accessible through the Internet; others you must visit in person (*see Figure 22.1* for a list of Internet resources that will help you locate and make use of a range of archives). The more you know about your area of study, the more likely you will be to see the significance of an item in an archival collection.

Archives generally require that you call or e-mail to arrange a time for your visit, and some are restricted in terms of access. If you find an archive on the Internet that you would like to visit, phone or e-mail well in advance to find out if you will need references, a letter of introduction, or other qualifying papers. Archives often will not allow you to browse; instead, use finding aids (often available online) to determine which records you need to see.

Archives also generally require you to present a photo identification and to leave personal items in a locker or at a coat check. They have strict policies about reproducing materials and rarely allow anything to leave the premises. The more you know about the archive's policies and procedures before you visit, the more productive your visit will be. When you are finished, thank the archivist for the help you have received.

22c   Plan your field research carefully.

Field research involves recording observations, conducting interviews, and administering surveys. To conduct field research at a particular site, such as a place of business or a school, you must obtain permission. Explain the nature of your project, the date and time you would like to visit, and how much time you will need. Will you be observing? Interviewing people? Taking photographs? Also ask for a confirming letter or e-mail. Always write a thank-you note after you have concluded your research.

1. Observing and writing field notes

College assignments offer opportunities to conduct systematic observations. For a sociology class, you might observe the behavior of students in the cafeteria, taking notes on who sits with whom in terms of race, class, and social status. Such primary research will help you to look and observe throughout your life.

When you use direct observation, keep careful records to retain the information you gather. Here are some guidelines to follow:

- Be systematic in your observations, but be alert to unexpected behavior.
- Record what you see and hear as objectively as possible: describe; don't evaluate.

- *American Memory* <http://memory.loc.gov/ammem/index.html>: This site offers access to more than seven million digital items from over a hundred collections of material on U.S. history and culture.
- *Radio Program Archive* <https://umdrive.memphis.edu /mbensman/public/>: This site lists radio archives available from the University of Memphis and explains how to obtain cassettes of programs.
- *Repositories of Primary Sources* <www.uiweb.uidaho.edu /special-collections/Other .Repositories.html>: This site lists more than 4,800 Web sites describing holdings of manuscripts, rare books, historical photographs, and other archival materials.
- *Television News Archive* <http://tvnews.vanderbilt.edu>: This site provides summaries of television news broadcasts and information on how to order videocassettes.
- *U.S. National Archives and Records Administration* (NARA) <www.archives.gov/index .html>: Learn how to use the National Archives at this page <www.archives.gov/ research/>, and then search the site for the documents you want.
- *Virtual Library Museums Page* <www.museumlink.com /virtual.htm>: This site lists online museums throughout the world.
- *Women Writers Project* <www.wwp.brown.edu/>: This site lists archived texts—by pre-Victorian women writers—that are available through the project.

FIGURE 22.1 **Online information about archives that can lead you to a wide range of archival sources.**

- Take more notes than you think you will need.
- When appropriate, categorize the types of behavior you are looking for, and devise a system for counting instances of each type.
- When you have recorded data over a substantial period of time, group your observations into categories for careful study.

(For advice on conducting direct observations for a case study, see Tab 3: Common Assignments across the Curriculum, pp. 160–62.)

2. Conducting interviews

Interviews are useful in a wide variety of writing situations: finding out what students think about the university logo; gathering ideas to promote recycling on campus; talking with a family member about memories of a historical figure. Interviews can be conducted in person, by phone, or online. Like other research tools, interviews require systematic preparation and implementation:

- Identify appropriate people for your interviews.
- Do background research, and plan a list of open-ended questions.
- Take careful notes and, if possible, tape-record the interview (but be sure to obtain your subject's permission if you use audiotape or videotape). Verify quotations.

SOURCE SMART Quoting from Interviews

Before an interview, obtain permission to quote the interviewee. If the interview is not being recorded (or captured on a transcript if online), use oversized quotation marks to enclose direct quotations in your notes. Record the interviewee's name and the location and date of the interview in your research notebook. Afterward, verify quotations with your interviewee.

- Follow up on vague responses with questions that get at specific information. Do not rush interviewees.
- Politely probe inconsistencies and contradictions.
- Write thank-you notes to interviewees, and later send them copies of your report.

3. Taking surveys

Surveys are useful in numerous situations when it is important to go beyond individual impressions to a more systematic basis for forming conclusions. Do students and alumni at Governors State University prefer the old tagline, "Empower Yourself," or a new one, "Success by Degrees"? But even a straightforward question like that, which can be administered online through a site such as *Survey Monkey,* requires careful design.

Conducted either orally or in writing, **surveys** are made up of structured questions. Written surveys are called **questionnaires.** Many colleges have offices that must review and approve student surveys. Check to see what guidelines your school may have. The following suggestions will help you prepare informal surveys:

- Define your purpose and your target population—the people who are relevant to the purpose of your interview. Are you trying to gauge attitudes, learn about typical behaviors, or both?
- Write clear directions and questions. For example, if you are asking multiple-choice questions, make sure that you cover all possible options and that your options do not overlap.
- Make sure that your questions do not suggest a preference for one answer over another.
- Make the survey brief and easy to complete.

22d Keep a notebook when doing lab research.

Firsthand observations in the controlled environment of the laboratory are at the heart of the scientific method and define the situation for scientific research.

To provide a complete and accurate account of your laboratory work, keep careful records in a notebook. The following guidelines will help you take accurate notes on your research:

- Record immediate, on-the-spot, accurate notes on what happens in the lab. Write down as much detail as possible. Measure precisely; do not estimate. Identify major pieces of apparatus, unusual chemicals, and laboratory animals in enough detail so that, for example, a reader can determine the size or type of equipment you used. Use drawings, when appropriate, to illustrate complicated equipment setups. Include tables, when useful, to present results.

- Follow a basic format. Present your results in a format that allows you to communicate all the major features of an experiment. The five basic sections that must be included are title, purpose, materials and methods, results, and conclusions. *(For more advice on preparing a lab report, see Tab 3: Common Assignments across the Curriculum, pp. 157–60.)*

- Write in complete sentences, even if you are filling in answers to questions in a lab manual. Resist the temptation to use shorthand to record your notes. Later, the complete sentences will provide a clear record of your procedures and results. Highlight connections in your sentences by using the following transitions: *then, next, consequently, because,* and *therefore.* Cause-effect relationships should be clear.

When necessary, revise and correct your laboratory notebook in visible ways. If you make a mistake in recording laboratory results, correct it as clearly as possible, either by erasing or by crossing out and rewriting on the original sheet. If you make an uncorrectable mistake in your notebook, simply fold the sheet lengthwise and mark *omit* on the face side. Unanticipated results often occur in the lab, and you may find yourself jotting down notes on a convenient piece of scrap paper. Attach these notes to your notebook.

CHAPTER 23

Plagiarism, Copyright, and Intellectual Property

When we draw on the words and ideas of others, integrity and honesty require us to acknowledge their contributions. Otherwise, we are committing plagiarism. Some forms of plagiarism are obvious, such as buying a term paper from an online paper mill or "borrowing" a friend's completed assignment. Others are more subtle and may even be inadvertent. Since ignorance is no excuse, it is important to learn appropriate ways to paraphrase or summarize another writer's material. *(See Chapter 24: Working with Sources and Avoiding Plagiarism, pp. 264–70, for more on paraphrasing and summarizing.)*

Penalties for plagiarism are serious. Journalists who are caught plagiarizing are publicly exposed and fired by the publications they write for. Those publications must then work hard to repair their credibility. Scholars who fail to acknowledge the words and ideas of others lose their professional credibility and often their jobs. Students who plagiarize might receive a failing grade for an assignment or course and face other disciplinary action—including expulsion. Be sure to read your campus's written policy on plagiarism and its consequences.

The Internet has made many types of sources available, and it can be unclear what, when, and how to cite. For example, bloggers and other Web authors often reproduce material from other sites, while some musicians make their music available for free download. Although the line between "original" and "borrowed" appears to be blurring in our society, you should review the following guidelines for crediting sources appropriately.

23a   Understand how plagiarism relates to copyright and intellectual property.

Related to plagiarism are the concepts of copyright and intellectual property. **Copyright** is the legal right to control the reproduction of any original work—a piece of writing, a musical composition, a play, a movie, a computer program, a photograph, a work of art. A copyrighted work is the **intellectual property** of the copyright holder,

---

—SOURCE SMART Determining What Is "Common Knowledge"

Information that an audience could be expected to know from many sources is considered common knowledge. You do not need to cite common knowledge if you use your own wording and sentence structure. Common knowledge can take various forms, including at least these four:

- Folktales with no particular author (for example, Little Red Riding Hood outsmarted the wolf)
- Common sense (for example, property values in an area fall when crime rises)
- Historical facts and dates (for example, the United States entered World War II in 1941)
- Information found in many general reference works (for example, the heart drives the body's circulation system)

Maps, charts, graphs, and other visual displays of information are not considered common knowledge. Even though everyone knows that Paris is the capital of France, if you reproduce a map of France in your paper, you must credit the map's creator.

─the EVOLVING SITUATION

Learning More about Plagiarism, Copyright and Fair Use, and Intellectual Property

It is important to approach all writing assignments with consideration for your sources and your audience. Using the resources provided in the links below, learn more about the meaning of copyright and fair use, as well as the details constituting intellectual property.

- **Plagiarism:** For more information about plagiarism, see the Council of Writing Program Administrator's "Defining and Avoiding Plagiarism: The WPA Statement on Best Practices" <http://wpacouncil.org/positions/WPAplagiarism.pdf>. Educators at Indiana University offer tips on avoiding plagiarism at <www.Indiana.edu/~wts/pamphlets/plagiarism.shtml>. Georgetown University's Honor Council offers an example of a campus honor code pertaining to plagiarism and academic ethics at <gervaseprograms.georgetown.edu/honor/system/53377.html>.

- **Copyright and fair use:** For information and discussion of fair use, see Copyright and Fair Use at <http://fairuse.stanford.edu> and the U.S. Copyright Office at <www.copyright.gov>. The University of Texas posts guidelines for fair use and multimodal projects at <http://copyright.lib.utexas.edu/ccmcguid.html>.

- **Intellectual property:** For information about what constitutes intellectual property and related issues, see the World Intellectual Property Organization Web site at <www.wipo.int>. For a legal perspective, the American Intellectual Property Law Association offers information and overviews of recent cases at <www.aipla.org>.

whether that entity is a publisher, a record company, an entertainment conglomerate, or the individual creator of the work. Here is some additional information on these important legal concepts:

- **Copyright:** A copyrighted text cannot be reproduced legally (in print or online) without the written permission of the copyright holder. The copyright protects the right of authors and publishers to benefit from their productions.

- **Fair use:** The concept of **fair use** protects most academic use of copyrighted sources. Under this provision of copyright law, you can legally quote a brief passage from a copyrighted text for an academic purpose without infringing on copyright. Of course, to avoid plagiarism you must identify the passage as a quotation and cite it properly. *(See page 257 for more information.)*

- **Intellectual property:** In addition to works protected by copyright, intellectual property includes patented inventions, trademarks, industrial designs, and similar intellectual creations that are protected by other laws.

─SOURCE SMART   What Must Be Acknowledged?

You **do not** have to acknowledge

- common knowledge expressed in your words and sentence structure *(see the box on page 253),*
- your independent thinking, or
- your original field observations, surveys, or experimental results.

You **must** acknowledge

- concepts you learned from a source, whether or not you copy the source's language,
- interviews other than surveys,
- abstracts,
- visuals,
- statistics, including those you use to create your own visuals *(see Chapter 20, pp. 233–36),* and
- your own work for another assignment (use only with your instructor's permission).

Acknowledge the source each time you cite from the material, regardless of the length of the selection. If you use multiple sources in a paragraph, make clear which ideas are from which sources. *(See Tab 6: MLA Documentation Style, p. 284, and Tab 7: APA Documentation Style, p. 344.)*

23b   Take steps to avoid plagiarism.

When people are under pressure, they sometimes make poor choices. Inadvertent plagiarism occurs when busy students take notes carelessly, forgetting to record the source of a paraphrase or accidentally inserting material downloaded from a Web site into a paper. Deliberate plagiarism occurs when students "borrow" a paper from a friend or copy and paste portions of an online article into their own work. Even though you may be tired or pressured, careful planning and adherence to the following guidelines can help you avoid plagiarism:

- When you receive an assignment, write down your thoughts and questions before you begin looking at sources. Use this record to keep track of changes in your ideas.

- As you proceed with your research, record your ideas in one color and those of others in a different color.

- As you continue researching and taking notes, keep accurate records. If you do not know where you got an idea or a piece of information, do not use it until you find out.

- When you take notes, put quotation marks around words, phrases, or sentences taken verbatim from a source and note the pages. If you use any of those words, phrases, or sentences when

CHECKLIST Avoiding Plagiarism

☐ Is my thesis my own idea, not something I found in one of my sources?

☐ Have I used a variety of sources, not just one or two?

☐ Have I identified each source clearly?

☐ Do I fully understand and explain all words, phrases, and ideas in my paper?

☐ Have I acknowledged all ideas that are based on neither my original thinking nor common knowledge?

☐ Have I properly integrated material from sources, using paraphrases, summaries, or quotations *(see Chapter 24, pp. 264–70)*?

☐ If I am planning to publish my text online, have I received all necessary permissions?

summarizing or paraphrasing the source, put them in quotation marks. Changing a word here and there while keeping a source's sentence structure or phrasing still constitutes plagiarism even if you credit the source for the ideas. *(See pp. 264–70 for examples.)*

- Do not rely too much on one source, or you may easily slip into using that person's thoughts as your own.

- Cite the source of all ideas, opinions, facts, and statistics that are not common knowledge.

- Choose an appropriate documentation style, and use it consistently and properly. *(See Tabs 6–8 for information about the most common documentation styles for academic writing.)*

When working with electronic sources, keep in mind the following guidelines:

- Print or save to your computer any online source you consult. Note the date on which you viewed it, and be sure to keep the complete URL in case you need to view the source again. Some documentation styles require you to include the URL in your citation *(see Tabs 6–8)*.

- If you copy and paste a passage from a Web site into a word-processing file, use a different font to identify that material as well as the URL and the access date.

- Acknowledge all sites you use as sources, including those you access via links on another site.

- As a courtesy, request the author's permission before quoting from blogs, news group postings, or e-mails.

- Acknowledge any audio, video, or illustrated material that has informed your research.

It may be tempting to copy and paste material from the Internet without acknowledgment, but instructors can easily detect that form of plagiarism by using a search engine to locate the original.

Posting material on a publicly accessible Web site is usually considered the legal equivalent of publishing it in print format. (Password-protected sites generally are exempt.) Before posting on a public site, seek copyright permission from all your sources. *(See the box on p. 254 and the following guidelines for fair use.)*

23c   Use copyrighted materials fairly.

All original works, including student projects, graphics, and videos, are covered by copyright even if they do not bear an official copyright symbol. A copyright grants its owner—often the creator—exclusive rights to the use of a protected work, including reproducing, distributing, and displaying the work. The popularity of the Web as a venue for publication has led to increased concerns about the fair use of copyrighted material. Before you publish your work on the Web or produce a multimodal presentation that includes audio, video, and graphic elements copied from a Web site, make sure that you have used copyrighted material fairly by considering these four questions:

- **What is the purpose of the use?** Educational, nonprofit, and personal use are more likely to be considered fair than is commercial use.

- **What is the nature of the work being used?** In most cases, imaginative and unpublished materials can be used only if you have the permission of the copyright holder.

- **How much of the copyrighted work is being used?** The use of a small portion of a text for academic purposes is more likely to be considered fair than the use of a whole work for commercial purposes. While no clear legal definition of "a small portion" exists, one conservative guideline is that you can quote up to fifty words from an article (print or online) and three hundred words from a book. It is safest to ask permission to quote an entire work or a substantial portion of a text (be cautious with poems, plays, and songs). Images and multimodal clips are considered entire works. Also, you may need permission to link your Web site to another.

- **What effect would this use have on the market for the original?** The use of a work is usually considered unfair if it would hurt sales of the original.

When in doubt, ask permission.

CHAPTER 24

Working with Sources and Avoiding Plagiarism

Once you have a research question, an idea about what the library and Internet have to offer, and some credible, appropriate sources in hand, you are ready to begin working with your sources. If you pay attention to detail and keep careful records at this stage, you will stay organized, save time, and credit sources appropriately.

24a Maintain a working bibliography.

As you research, compile a **working bibliography**—a list of those books, articles, pamphlets, Web sites, and other sources that seem most likely to help you answer your research question. Maintain an accurate and complete record of all sources you consult so that you can find and cite all sources accurately.

While the exact bibliographic information you will need depends on your documentation style, the following list includes the major elements of most systems *(see Tabs 6–8 for the requirements of specific documentation styles):*

Book

- Call number (so you can find the source again; not required for documentation)
- Names of all authors, editors, and translators
- Title of chapter
- Title and subtitle of book
- Edition (if not the first), volume number (if applicable)
- Publication information (city, publisher, date)
- Medium (print)

Periodical article

- Names of authors
- Title and subtitle of article
- Title and subtitle of periodical
- Date, edition or volume number, issue number
- Page numbers
- Medium (print)

Article from database (in addition to the preceding)

- Name of database
- Date you retrieved source

- URL of database's home page (if online)
- Medium (Web, CD-ROM, or DVD-ROM)

Internet source (including visual, audio, video)

- Names of all authors, editors, or creators
- Title and subtitle of source
- Title of larger site, project, or database (if applicable)
- Version or edition, if any
- Publication information, if available, including any about a version in another medium (such as print, radio, or film)
- Date of electronic publication or latest update, if available
- Sponsor of site
- Date you accessed site
- URL of site
- Any other identifying numbers, such as a Digital Object Identifier (DOI)

Other sources

- Name of author or creator
- Title
- Format (for example, photograph or lecture)
- Title of larger publication, if any
- Publisher, sponsor, or institution housing the source
- Date of creation or publication
- Any identifying numbers

You can record bibliographic information on note cards or in a word-processing file; you can print out or e-mail to yourself bibliographic information obtained from online searches in databases and library catalogs; you can use an app on your cell phone to send a citation to yourself; or you can record bibliographic information directly on photocopies of source material. You can also save most Web pages and other online sources to your own computer.

1. Using note cards or a word processor

One classic method for taking notes is still useful: using three-by-five-inch or four-by-six-inch note cards to compile the working bibliography, with each potential source getting a separate card, as in Figure 24.1. You can also use the cards to include all information necessary for documentation, to record brief quotations, and to note your own comments (carefully marked as yours). Because each source has its own card, this method can help you rearrange information when you are

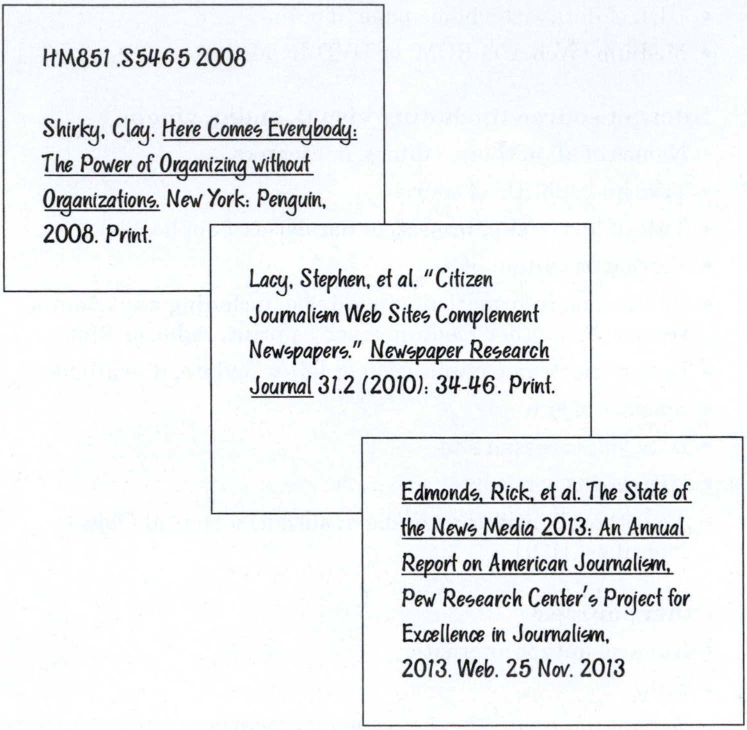

HM851 .S5465 2008

Shirky, Clay. <u>Here Comes Everybody:</u>
<u>The Power of Organizing without</u>
<u>Organizations.</u> New York: Penguin,
2008. Print.

Lacy, Stephen, et al. "Citizen
Journalism Web Sites Complement
Newspapers." <u>Newspaper Research</u>
<u>Journal</u> 31.2 (2010): 34-46. Print.

<u>Edmonds, Rick, et al. The State of</u>
<u>the News Media 2013: An Annual</u>
<u>Report on American Journalism,</u>
Pew Research Center's Project for
Excellence in Journalism,
2013. Web. 25 Nov. 2013

FIGURE 24.1 Three sample bibliography note cards in MLA style. The cards are for a book (top), for a journal article (middle), and for a Web site (bottom).

deciding how to organize your paper, and it can then help you create your list of citations. Instead of handwriting on cards, you can record bibliographic information in a computer file.

2. Printing the results of online searches in databases and library catalogs

The results of searches in online indexes and databases usually include bibliographic information about the sources they list. *(See the example of a database search in Chapter 19, p. 224.)* You can print these results directly from your browser or, in some cases, save them to a flash drive and transfer them to a Word file. Be sure also to record the name of the database and the date of your search.

You can similarly print out or save bibliographic information from the results of searches in online library catalogs. Some college libraries make it possible for you to compile a list of sources and e-mail it to yourself.

—SOURCE SMART   The Uses and Limits of Bibliographic Software

Programs such as *Microsoft Word 2013* allow you to store source data, automatically insert citations in common documentation styles, and generate a list of references. These programs might not incorporate the most recent updates to documentation styles, however, nor do they accommodate all types of sources. Talk to your instructor before using bibliographic software, and check your citations carefully against the models in Tabs 6–8. Also check references that a database creates for you.

Caution: If you download the full text of an article from a database and refer to it in your paper, your citation may require information about the database (depending on your documentation style) as well as bibliographic information about the article itself. *(See Tabs 6–8.)*

3. Using photocopies and printouts from Web sites

If you photocopy articles, essays, or pages of reference works from a print or a microfilm source, noting the bibliographic information on the photocopy can save you time later. Similarly, if you print out a source you found on a Web site or copy it to your computer, be sure to note the site's author, name, sponsor, date of publication, complete URL, and the date you visited the site.

24b   Create an annotated bibliography.

An annotated bibliography can be useful to you in your research. You will need the full citation, correctly formatted, for your works-cited or references list. The annotation for each source should include a summary of major points, your evaluation of the source's relevance and credibility, and your thoughts on what the material contributes to your project and where it might fit in *(see Figure 24.2)*.

24c   Take notes on your sources.

Taking notes helps you think through your research question and read both digital and print sources more systematically. Consult a table of contents or other introductory parts to find the most relevant sections. As you work, annotate photocopies, and make note of useful ideas and powerful quotations. See whether categories emerge that can help you organize your project.

Lacy, Stephen, et al. "Citizen Journalism Web Sites Complement
    Newspapers." *Newspaper Research Journal* 31.2 (2010): 34-46. Print.
This scholarly study compares the purpose of citizen journalism websites to
that of newspaper websites. It includes a discussion of the theoretical
framework behind the study, a review of the literature on citizen journalism,
and extensive notes on the research that informed the study. The article
concludes that citizen journalism sites cannot sufficiently replace, but should
instead accompany, newspaper sites.

Shirky, Clay. *Here Comes Everybody: The Power of Organizing without
    Organizations*. New York: Penguin, 2008. Print.
Aimed at a popular audience, Shirky's book describes the impact of group
communications, such as blogs, and predicts the far-reaching benefits of such
forms of social media. Shirky also compares traditional media to new media
and explains how and why this transition is necessary. Shirky's book supports
my ideas about the need for journalists to adopt forms of new media.

FIGURE 24.2 Sample annotated bibliography. A section of Kris
Washington's annotated bibliography. *(To read "Breaking News: Blogging's Impact on Traditional and New Media," Washington's final
research report on this topic, see Chapter 30.)*

1. Annotating

One way to take notes is to annotate photocopied articles and print-
outs from online information services or Web sites. See Figure 24.3
for an example. (Do this for sources you save to your computer by
using the Comments feature in your word processor.) As you read, do
the following:

- On the first page, write down complete bibliographic information for the source.
- Record questions, reactions, and ideas in the margins.
- Comment on ideas that agree with or differ from those you
  have already learned about.
- Put important and difficult passages into your own words by
  paraphrasing or summarizing them in the margins. *(For help
  with paraphrasing and summarizing, see pp. 264–69.)*

Highlight statements that you may want to quote because they
are especially well expressed or are key to readers' understanding of
the issue.

2. Taking notes in a research journal or log

A **research journal** or **research log** is a tool for keeping track
of your research. It can be a spiral or loose-leaf notebook, a box of

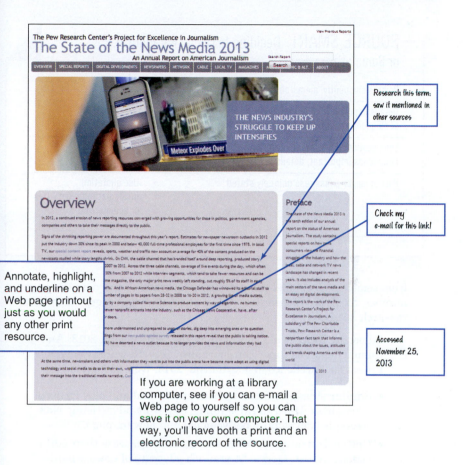

FIGURE 24.3 An annotated Web page printout.

note cards, a word-processing document on a laptop computer, or a blog—whatever form you are most comfortable with. Use the journal to write down leads for sources and to record ideas and observations about your topic as they occur to you. If you use a blog, you can use it to link to potential sources.

When you have finished annotating a photocopy, printout, or electronic version of an article, use your research journal to explore the comments, connections, and questions you recorded. If you do not have a copy of the material to annotate, take notes directly in your research journal.

Enclose in quotation marks any exact words from a source. If you think you may forget that the phrasing, as well as the idea, came

---

SOURCE SMART Deciding to Quote, Paraphrase, or Summarize

Point is eloquently, memorably, or uniquely stated	→	Quote
Details important but not uniquely or eloquently expressed	→	Paraphrase
Long section of material (with many points), main ideas important, details not important	→	Summarize
Part of longer passage is uniquely stated	→	Use quotation inside paraphrased or summarized passage

---

from someone else, label the passage a "quotation" and note the page number, as Kris Washington did in the following excerpt from her research notebook:

> Edmonds, Rick, et al. The State of the News Media 2013: An Annual Report on American Journalism, Pew Research Center's Project for Excellence in Journalism, 2013. Web. 25 Nov. 2013.
>
> • Similar struggles faced by both traditional and new forms of journalism. Hard to raise funds, esp. from advertising. New strategies developing between old and new (n. pag.).
>
> • One such strategy is for news outlets to reassess their editorial strengths. Quote: "A staunch advocate of news organizations focusing editorial muscle in key areas where they can bring real value and distinction, Gilbert told the Pew Research Center that in the digital age, news outlets have to be differentiated. 'Invest where you can be the best in the world,' he explained" (n. pag.).

Unless you think you might use a particular quotation in your project, it is usually better to express the author's ideas in your own words by using a paraphrase or a summary.

24d Take stock of what you have learned as you paraphrase, summarize, quote, and synthesize your sources.

When you take stock, remember your writing situation. As you synthesize what you have learned from the sources you are consulting, think about how these sources relate to one another. Where do they agree, and where do they disagree? Where do you stand relative to these sources? Did anything you read surprise or disturb you, and how will it affect your audience? Writing down your responses to such questions can help you clarify what you have learned and decide how that information fits in with your own claim as you are developing it.

The credibility of your work depends on the relevance and reliability of your sources as well as the scope and depth of your reading and observation. College research projects usually require multiple sources and viewpoints. A project on the impact of blogging on traditional news, for example, is unlikely to be credible if it relies on only one source of information. An argument about an issue in the social sciences will not be taken seriously if it cites research on only one side of the debate.

As the context and kind of writing change, so too do the requirements for types and numbers of sources. As a general rule, however, you should consult more than two sources and use only sources that are both credible and respected by people working in the field. To determine whether you have located appropriate and sufficient sources, ask yourself the following questions:

- Are your sources trustworthy? *(See Chapter 21, pp. 240–47, for more on evaluating sources.)*

- If you have developed a tentative answer to your research question, have your sources provided you with sufficient facts, examples, and ideas to support that answer?

- Have you used sources that examine the issues from several different perspectives?

- Upon examination of the sources, can my tentative answer be legitimately reversed or otherwise changed?

1. Paraphrasing information from sources

When you **paraphrase,** you put someone else's statement into your words and sentence structures. Paraphrase when a passage's details are important to your topic but its exact words are not memorable, or when you need to reorder a source's ideas or clarify complicated information. A paraphrase should be about the same length and level of detail as the original. Cite the original writer, and put quotation marks around any exact phrasing from the source.

In the first unacceptable paraphrase that follows, the writer has done a word-for-word translation, using synonyms for some terms but retaining phrases from the original (highlighted) and failing to enclose them in quotation marks ("few-to-few, one-to-one, and many-to-many," "attentive publics"). Notice also how close the sentence structures in the first faulty paraphrase are to the original.

SOURCE

The media used to work in a one-to-many pattern—that is, by broadcasting. The Internet, though it can be used for one-to-many transmission, is just as well suited for few-to-few, one-to-one, and many-to-many patterns. Traditionally, the media connected audiences "up" to centers of power, people of influence, and national spectacles. The Internet does all that, but it is equally good at connecting us laterally—to peers, to colleagues, and to strangers who share our interests. When experts and power players had something to communicate to the attentive publics they wished to address, they once had to go through the media. Now they can go direct.

—JAY ROSEN, "The New News"

UNACCEPTABLE PARAPHRASE: PLAGIARISM

The news was previously transmitted from one to many. Online media, although they can function in this way, can also follow a few-to-few, one-to-one, and many-to-many pattern. In the past, traditional news outlets connected audiences up to those in a position of power. Online media can do that as well, but they also succeed in connecting us laterally to others who share our interests. If those in a position of power wanted to reach their attentive publics, traditional news outlets used to be their only method. Currently, they can communicate directly with their audiences (Rosen).

In the second example of a faulty paraphrase (following), the writer has merely substituted synonyms for the original author's words (such as "individual-to-individual" instead of "one-to-one") and kept the source's sentence structure. Because it relies on the sentence structure of the original source, the paraphrase is too close to the original and constitutes **plagiarism.**

UNACCEPTABLE PARAPHRASE (SENTENCE STRUCTURE OF SOURCE): PLAGIARISM

The news was previously transmitted from single corporations to several individuals. Online media, although they can function in this way, can also follow a group-to-group, organization-to-organization, and individual-to-individual model. In the past, traditional news outlets linked consumers upward to those in a position of authority. Online media can do that as well, but they also succeed in linking us to one another, including others with whom we have something in common. If those in a position of authority wanted to reach their captive audiences, traditional news outlets used to be their only method. Currently, they can communicate right with their audiences (Rosen).

—**SOURCE SMART** Guidelines for Writing a Paraphrase

- **Read the passage carefully.** Focus on its sequence of ideas and important details.
- **Be sure you understand the material.** Look up any unfamiliar words.
- **Imagine addressing an audience that has not read the material.**
- **Without looking at the original passage, write down its main ideas and key details.**
- **Use clear, direct language.** Express complicated ideas as a series of simple ones.
- **Check your paraphrase against the original.** Make sure your text conveys the source's ideas accurately without copying its words or sentence structures. Add quotation marks around any phrases from the source or rewrite them.
- **Note the citation information.** List author and page number after every important point.

The third unacceptable paraphrase (following) alters the sentence structure of the source but plagiarizes by using some of the original wording (highlighted in the example) without quotation marks.

UNACCEPTABLE PARAPHRASE (WORDING FROM SOURCE): PLAGIARISM

In contrast to traditional news outlets, which functioned in a one-to-many pattern, online media use other patterns to engage audiences, such as few-to-few, one-to-one, and many-to-many (Rosen).

The acceptable paraphrase expresses all ideas from the original using different words and phrasing. Although it quotes a few words from the source, the writer has used quotation marks and indicates where the paraphrase begins.

ACCEPTABLE PARAPHRASE

According to Rosen, the shift away from expert reporting to citizen journalism has opened doors for those who both produce and consume the news. No longer at the mercy of those in a position to seek out and select what makes the news, citizens now have more authority, through the power of the Internet, to investigate and publicize the events that matter to us. As a result, we are linked to other informed citizens like never before.

Note that all paraphrases require a citation.

In the following two paraphrases of an article, note that the unacceptable version copies words and phrasing from the source.

SOURCE

Many reporters, especially those at the largest news organizations, have followed their beats for years. So whether it's a Washington bureau chief writing about White House politics, or a longtime sports columnist covering the latest draft picks, chances are they can write with authority because they know the subject.

—TONY ROGERS, "Can Bloggers Replace Professional Journalists?"

UNACCEPTABLE PARAPHRASE: PLAGIARISM

Having followed their beats for years, many reporters for the larger news organizations are able to write with a great deal of authority.

ACCEPTABLE PARAPHRASE

As Tony Rogers notes in his article "Can Bloggers Replace Professional Journalists?" reporters tend to earn credibility over time by covering a particular subject with frequency.

2. Summarizing information from sources

When you **summarize,** you state the main point of a piece, condensing paragraphs into sentences, pages into paragraphs, or a book into a few pages. As you work with sources, you will summarize more frequently than you will quote or paraphrase. Summarizing works best when the passage is very long and the central idea is important but the details are not.

Following are two summaries of a passage on journalism by Clay Shirky, which is reprinted first.

SOURCE

For the next few decades, journalism will be made up of overlapping special cases. Many of these models will rely on amateurs as researchers and writers. Many of these models will rely on sponsorship or grants or endowments instead of revenues. Many of these models will rely on excitable 14-year-olds distributing the results. Many of these models will fail. No one experiment is going to replace what we are now losing with the demise of news on paper, but over time, the collection of new experiments that do work might give us the journalism we need.

—CLAY SHIRKY, "Newspapers and Thinking the Unthinkable"

The unacceptable summary is simply a restatement of Shirky's thesis using much of his phrasing (highlighted).

UNACCEPTABLE SUMMARY: PLAGIARISM

The journalism of the future will be made up of overlapping special cases, some of which will rely on novice reporters and new

SOURCE SMART Guidelines for Writing a Summary

- **Read the material carefully.** Locate relevant sections.
- **If the text is longer than a few paragraphs, divide it into sections, and sum up each section in one or two sentences.** Compose a topic sentence for each of these sections.
- **Be sure you understand the material.**
- **Imagine explaining the points to an audience that has not read this content.**
- **Identify the main point of the source, in your own words.** Compose a sentence that names the text, the writer, what the writer does (reports or argues), and the most important point.
- **Note any other points that relate to your topic.** State each one (in your words) in one sentence or less. Simplify complex language.
- **Combine your sentence stating the writer's main point with your sentences about secondary points or those summarizing the text's sections.**
- **Check your summary against the original** to see whether it makes sense, expresses the source's meaning, and does not copy any wording or sentence structure.
- **Note all the citation information for the source.**

revenue models. Although many of these models will fail, they will, collectively, help to give us the journalism we need.

The acceptable summary states Shirky's main point in the writer's own words. Note that the acceptable summary still requires a citation.

ACCEPTABLE SUMMARY

According to Shirky, partnerships between traditional and citizen journalism will take several forms. Although many wonder whether new forms can offer information that is as reliable as traditional news, as they evolve they may usher in a new era of journalism that is better able to serve our needs ("Newspapers" 29).

3. Quoting your sources directly

Sometimes the writer of a source will say something so eloquently and perceptively that you will want to include that writer's words as a **direct quotation** in your work.

In general, quote these types of sources:

- Primary sources (for example, in a text about Rita Dove, a direct quotation from her or a colleague)
- Sources containing very technical language that cannot be paraphrased

- Literary or historical sources, when you analyze the wording
- An authority in the field whose words support your thesis
- Debaters explaining their different positions on an issue

To avoid inadvertent plagiarism, be careful to indicate that the content is a direct quotation when you copy it onto your note cards or into your research notebook. Try to keep quotations short, and always place quotation marks around them. You might also use a special color to indicate direct quotations or deliberately make quotation marks oversized.

When referring to most secondary sources, paraphrase or summarize instead of quoting. Your readers will have difficulty following a text with too many quotations, and your own voice and ideas may not be heard. In some instances you may use paraphrase, summary, and quotation together. You might summarize a long passage, paraphrase an important section of it, and directly quote a short part of that section.

Note: If you have used more than one quotation every two or three paragraphs, convert most of the quotations into paraphrases *(see pp. 265–68).*

24e Integrate quotations, paraphrases, and summaries properly and effectively.

Ultimately, you will use some of the paraphrases, summaries, and quotations you have collected during the course of your research to support and develop the ideas you present in your paper. Here are some guidelines for integrating them properly and effectively into the body of your text. (Examples in this section represent MLA format for in-text citations and block quotations.)

1. Integrating brief quotations

Be selective about the quotations you include. Brief quotations can be effective if they are especially well phrased and make a significant point. But take a moment to think about your own interpretation, which might actually be better than the exact wording of the source.

Short quotations should be enclosed in quotation marks and well integrated into your sentence structure. Set off longer quotations in blocks *(see p. 274).* The following example from Kris Washington's text on the impact of blogging on traditional news shows the use of a short quotation:

EFFECTIVE QUOTATION

Contrary to Rogers' value of professional journalism, Anderson, Bell, and Shirky claim, "The way news is most effectively and reliably relayed is by those with a combination of deep knowledge of the subject and a responsiveness to audience requirements" (20).

The quotation is effective because it provides a concise explanation of the main factors that contribute to good news reporting. Washington integrates the quotation effectively by introducing the name of the source (*Anderson, Bell, and Shirky*) and then blending the quotation into the structure of her own sentence. By contrast, the following poorly integrated quotation is not set up for the reader in that way:

POORLY INTEGRATED QUOTATION

Amateur journalists do not guarantee fact checking and do not always have professional experience relevant to the topics they cover. "Most bloggers don't produce news stories on their own. Instead they comment on news stories already out there—stories produced by journalists" (Rogers).

When you are integrating someone else's words into your writing, use a **signal phrase** that indicates whom you are quoting. The signal phrase "Anderson, Bell, and Shirky claim," identifies Anderson, Bell, and Shirky as the source of the quotation in the effective passage above.

A signal phrase clearly indicates where your words end and the source's words begin. The first time you quote a source, include the author's full name and credentials, such as, "New York University professor and media consultant Clay Shirky explains. . . ." You may also include the title of the work for context: "For example, in their article "Post-Industrial Journalism: Adapting to the Present," C. W. Anderson, Emily Bell, and Clay Shirky contend . . ."

When you introduce a brief quotation with a signal phrase, you have three basic options:

- Use a complete sentence followed by a colon.
- Use a phrase.
- Make the source's words part of your own sentence structure.

A complete sentence followed by a colon   Introducing a quotation with a complete sentence allows you to provide context for the quotation. Use a colon (:) at the end of this introductory sentence.

COMPLETE SENTENCE	New York University professor and media consultant Clay Shirky explains how the proliferation of blogs is affecting news: "The change isn't a shift from one kind of news institution to another, but rather in the definition of news" (*Here Comes Everybody* 65–66).

An introductory or explanatory phrase, followed by a comma. Phrases move the reader efficiently to the quotation.

PHRASE   As New York University Professor Clay Shirky
           explains, "The change isn't a shift from one kind of
           news institution to another, but rather in the defi-
           nition of news" (*Here Comes Everybody* 65–66).

Instead of introducing a quotation, the signal phrase can follow
or interrupt it.

FOLLOWS   "The change isn't a shift from one kind of news
           institution to another, but rather in the definition
           of news," explains New York University Professor
           Clay Shirky (*Here Comes Everybody* 65–66).

INTERRUPTS "The change isn't a shift from one kind of news
           institution to another," explains New York Univer-
           sity Professor Clay Shirky, "but rather in the defi-
           nition of news" (*Here Comes Everybody* 65–66).

Part of your sentence structure   When you can, integrate the
quotation as part of your own sentence structure without any punctuation between your words and the words you are quoting. By doing
so, you will clearly connect the quoted material with your own ideas.

QUOTATION   New York University Professor Clay Shirky
INTEGRATED   notes that this transformation "isn't a shift from
             one kind of news institution to another, but
             rather in the definition of news" (*Here Comes
             Everybody* 65–66).

The verb you use in a signal phrase, such as *refutes* or *summarizes,* should show how you are using the quotation in your text. If
your source provides an example that strengthens your argument,
you could say, "Mann *supports* this line of reasoning." *(For more on
varying signal phrases, see the box on p. 275.)*

MLA style places signal phrase verbs in present tense *(Johnson
writes)* while APA uses past tense *(Johnson wrote). (See Chapter 25,
p. 279–81, for more on these documentation styles.)* When a quotation,
paraphrase, or summary in MLA or APA style begins with a signal
phrase, the ending citation includes the page number (unless the
work lacks page numbers). You can quote without a signal phrase if
you give the author's name in the parenthetical citation.

Brackets and ellipses are important tools for integrating quotations into your text:

- **Brackets within quotations** Sentences that include quotations must make sense grammatically. Sometimes you may
  have to adjust a quotation to make it fit your sentence. Use
  brackets to indicate any such minor adjustments. For example, *over* has been changed to *Over* to make the quotation fit
  in the following sentence.

"[O]ver time," Shirky writes, "the collection of new experiments that do work might give us the journalism we need" ("Newspapers" 29).

- **Ellipses within quotations** Use ellipses (. . .) to indicate that words have been omitted from the body of a quotation, but be sure that what you omit does not significantly alter the source's meaning:

Shirky sees the cooperation between professionals and amateurs as necessary to the survival of journalism: "Many of these models will fail. . . . [O]ver time, the collection of new experiments that do work might give us the journalism we need" ("Newspapers" 29).

(For more on using ellipses, see Tab 11: Editing for Correctness, pp. 566–67.)

CHECKLIST Paraphrasing, Summarizing, and Quoting Sources

Paraphrases

☐ Have I used my own words and sentence structure for all paraphrases?
☐ Have I maintained the original meaning?

Summaries

☐ Do all my summaries include my own wording and sentence structure? Are they shorter than the original text?
☐ Do they accurately represent the content of the original?

Quotations

☐ Have I enclosed in quotation marks any uncommon terms, distinctive phrases, or direct quotations from a source?
☐ Have I checked all quotations against the original source?
☐ Do I include ellipsis marks and brackets where I have altered the original wording and capitalization of quotations?

Documentation

☐ Have I indicated my source for all quotations, paraphrases, summaries, statistics, and visuals either within the text or in a parenthetical citation?
☐ Have I included page numbers as required for all quotations, paraphrases, and summaries?
☐ Does every in-text citation have a corresponding entry in the list of works cited or references?

2. Using long quotations in block format

Quotations longer than four lines should be used rarely because they tend to break up the text and make readers impatient. Research projects should consist primarily of your own analysis of sources. Always tell your readers why you want them to read a long quotation, and afterward comment on it.

If you use a verse quotation longer than three lines or a prose quotation longer than four typed lines, set the quotation off on a new line and indent each line one inch (ten spaces) from the left margin. *(This is MLA style; for APA style, see Tab 7.)* Double-space above and below the quotation. If the quotation is more than one paragraph, indent the first line of each new paragraph a quarter inch. Do not use quotation marks. Writers often introduce a block quotation with a sentence ending in a colon. *(For examples of block quotations, see the sample student papers in Chapter 30, p. 336, and Chapter 34, p. 383.)*

3. Integrating paraphrases and summaries

The principles for integrating paraphrases and summaries into your text are similar to those for including direct quotations. Make a smooth transition between a source's point and your own voice, accurately attributing the information to the source. Use signal phrases to introduce ideas you have borrowed from your sources.

Besides crediting others for their work, signal phrases make ideas more interesting by giving them a human face. Include a citation after the paraphrase or summary. Here are some examples.

> *Further, Anderson, Bell, and Shirky explain* that blogs and other forms of social media allow for "superdistribution," meaning that stories—including those published by smaller outlets—can reach a wider audience than ever before, and at very little expense (14).

In the preceding passage, Kris Washington uses the signal phrase *Further, Anderson, Bell, and Shirky explain* to identify Anderson, Bell, and Shirky as the source of the paraphrased information about "superdistribution."

> *According to their comprehensive study comparing the purpose of citizen journalism Web sites to that of newspaper Web sites, journalism experts Stephen Lacy, Margaret Duffy, Daniel Riffe, Esther Thorson, and Ken Fleming conclude* that citizen journalism cannot sufficiently replace, but should instead accompany, newspaper sites (42).

The preceding passage in Washington's text about blogging uses the signal phrase *According to their comprehensive study comparing the purpose of citizen journalism Web sites to that of newspaper Web sites, journalism experts Stephen Lacy, Margaret Duffy, Daniel Riffe, Esther*

— NAVIGATING THROUGH COLLEGE AND BEYOND

Varying Signal Phrases

To keep your work interesting, to show the original writer's purpose (*Martinez describes* or *Lin argues*), and to connect the quote to your reasoning (*Johnson refutes . . .),* use appropriate signal verbs such as the following:

according to	contends	points out
acknowledges	denies	proposes
adds	describes	proves
admits	emphasizes	refutes
argues	explains	rejects
asks	expresses	remarks
asserts	finds	reports
charges	holds	responds
claims	implies	shows
comments	insists	speculates
complains	interprets	states
concedes	maintains	suggests
concludes	notes	verifies
considers	observes	warns

Thorson, and Ken Fleming conclude to lead into a summary of the source's conclusions about this type of Web site.

> In a recent report, *the Pew Research Center's Project for Excellence in Journalism points out* print advertising is consistently declining with each year.

In the preceding passage, Washington uses the phrase *points out* to signal her paraphrase of a report. She directly names the source (The Pew Research Center), so she does not need additional parenthetical documentation.

CHAPTER 25

Writing the Text

You have chosen a challenging research question and have located, read, and evaluated a variety of sources. It is now time to develop a thesis that will allow you to share your perspective on the issue and make use of all that you have learned.

👁 **25a** Plan and draft your paper.

Begin planning by recalling the context and purpose of your paper. If you have an assignment sheet, review it to see if the paper is primarily supposed to inform, interpret, or argue. Think about the academic discipline or disciplines that shape the perspective of your work, and think through the special genres within those disciplines. Consider how much your audience is likely to know about your topic. Keep your overall situation in mind—purpose, audience, and context—as you decide on a thesis to support and develop.

1. Deciding on a thesis

Consider the question that guided your research as well as others provoked by what you have learned during the process. Revise the wording of these questions, and summarize them in a central question that is interesting and relevant to your audience *(see Chapter 18: Understanding Research, pp. 215–16)*. After you write down this question, compose an answer that you can use as your working thesis, as Kris Washington does in the following example.

WASHINGTON'S FOCAL QUESTION

What are some of the fundamental differences between traditional and new media?

WASHINGTON'S WORKING THESIS

To survive, journalism must continue to look for ways to blend traditional forms of reporting with other methods to get news out into the world instantaneously and universally.

2. Outlining a plan for supporting and developing your thesis

Guided by your tentative thesis, outline a plan that uses your sources in a purposeful way. Decide on an organization to support your thesis—chronological, problem-solution, or thematic—and develop your support by choosing facts, examples, and ideas drawn from a variety of sources. A chronological organization presents examples from earliest to most recent, and a problem-solution structure introduces an issue and a means of addressing it. A thematic organization orders examples from simple to complex, specific to general, or in another logical way. *(See Chapter 6: Drafting Text and Visuals, p. 58–68, for more on these organizational structures.)*

For her research project on new forms of journalism, Washington decided on a thematic organization, an approach structured around raising and answering a central question:

- Introduce some of the fundamental differences between traditional and new media.

- To survive, journalism must continue to look for ways to blend traditional forms of reporting with blogs, tweets, and other methods that get news and opinions out into the world instantaneously and universally.

- Offer background information on blogging and social media and how it has changed journalism.

- Introduce the concept of *citizen journalism,* and explain the shift from expert to novice reporting.

- Discuss how mainstream journalism and citizen journalism have merged, and then give examples of the benefits of this relationship.

- Illustrate what the relationship between traditional and new media outlets looks like and how it functions.

- Discuss how this relationship will continue to develop as people continue to demand reporting that is both reliable and instantaneous.

- Describe the benefits of blogs to the field of journalism.

- Conclude: The evolution of journalism toward citizen-driven news has led to a more open, more immediate, more widespread, and more emphatic experience of world issues and events.

To develop this outline, Washington would need to list supporting facts, examples, or ideas for each point as well as indicate the sources of this information. Each section should center on her original thinking, backed by her analysis of sources. *(For more on developing an outline, see Chapter 5, pp. 51–54.)*

3. Organizing and evaluating your information

Your note-taking strategies will determine how you collect and organize your information. Whether you have taken notes in a research journal, in a blog, or on note cards, group them according to topic and subtopic. For example, Kris Washington could have used the following categories to organize her notes:

Characteristics—traditional reporting

Characteristics—blogging and social media

Evolution of journalism—general info

Citizen journalism—benefits

Relationship betw. old and new—examples

Sorting index cards into stacks that match up topics and subtopics allows you to see what you have gathered. A small stack of cards for a particular subtopic might mean that the subtopic is not as important as you originally thought—or that you need to do additional research focused on that specific subtopic.

If your notes are primarily on your computer, you can create a new category heading for each topic and subtopic and then copy and paste to move information to the appropriate category.

4. Writing a draft that you can revise, share, and edit

When you have a tentative thesis and a plan, you are ready to write a draft. Many writers present their thesis or focal question at the end of an introductory, context-setting paragraph or two. The introduction should interest readers.

As you write beyond the introduction, be prepared to reexamine and refine your thesis. When drawing on ideas from your sources, be sure to quote and paraphrase properly. *(For advice on quoting and paraphrasing, see Chapter 24, pp. 264–68.)*

Make your conclusion as memorable as possible. You may need to review the draft as a whole before writing the conclusion. In the final version of Washington's text, on pages 331–41, note how she uses the idea of the audience becoming both consumers and producers of the news to end her argument. In doing so, she enhances her concluding point—that new forms of media are changing, and enhancing, older forms.

Washington came up with the last line of her work as she revised her first draft. Often writers will come up with fresh ideas at this stage—an excellent reason to spend time revising and editing your text. *(For more on revising, see Tab 2, pp. 73–92. For help with editing, see Tabs 9–12.)*

5. Integrating visuals

Well-chosen visuals like photographs, drawings, charts, graphs, and maps can sometimes help illustrate your argument. In some cases, a visual might itself be a subject of your analysis. Kris Washington uses a line graph that illustrates how the newsroom workforce has decreased in recent years, and continues to drop. She integrates this visual into her research project.

When integrating visuals, be sure to give careful attention to figure numbers and captions:

- **Figure numbers:** Both MLA and APA style require writers to number each image in a research paper. In MLA style, the word "figure" is abbreviated to "Fig." In APA style, the full word "Figure" is written out.

- **Captions:** Each visual that you include in your paper must be followed by a caption that includes the title of the visual (if given; otherwise, a brief description will do) and its source. In MLA style, each caption begins with the figure number and a period after the number (Fig. 1.); in APA style, use italics for the figure number *(Figure 1.).*

25b   Revise your draft.

You may prefer to revise a print copy of your draft by hand, or you might find it easier to use the Track Changes feature in your word-processing program. Either way, be sure to keep previous versions of your drafts. It is useful to have a record of how your work evolved—especially if you need to hunt down a particular source or want to reincorporate something you used earlier in the process.

25c   Document your sources.

Be sure to acknowledge information, ideas, or words that are not your own. As noted in the box on page 253, the only exception to this principle is when you use information that is common knowledge, such as the chemical composition of water or the names of the thirteen original states in the U.S. When you tell readers what sources you have consulted, they can more readily understand your text as well as the conversation you are participating in by writing it.

The mode of documentation depends on the overall situation. How sources are documented varies by field and discipline. Choose a documentation style that is appropriate for the particular course you are taking, and use it properly and consistently.

Specific documentation styles meet the needs of different disciplines. Literature and some other humanities disciplines use MLA style. Researchers in these disciplines use many historic texts including multiple editions of certain sources. The author's name and page number, but not the year, appear in the in-text citation. The edition of the source appears in the works-cited list. The author's full name appears at the first mention of the work, and sources are referred to in present tense (because writing exists in the present).

APA style, often used by practitioners of the social sciences, places the date of a work in the in-text citation. The currency of sources matters in these disciplines. References to past research appear in the past tense, and researchers are referred to by last name only.

Chicago, or CMS, style, used by other humanities disciplines, has two forms. The first minimizes the in-text references to sources by using footnotes or endnotes indicated by superscript numerals. Disciplines that use it, such as history, tend to use many sources. An alternative form of CMS resembles APA style.

CSE style, used by the sciences, has different forms. Name-year style shares important features with APA style, while citation-sequence and citation-name style use endnotes. The prevalence of abbreviations in CSE style indicates that researchers are expected to know the major texts in their fields.

If you are not sure which of the four styles covered in this handbook to use, ask your instructor. If you are required to use an

CHECKLIST Revising and Editing a Research Paper

Consider these questions as you read your draft and gather feedback from your instructor and peers *(see also Checklist for Avoiding Plagiarism, Chapter 23, p. 256):*

Thesis and structure

☐ How does my project address the topic and purpose given in the assignment?

☐ Who are my readers, and how much can I assume that they know about the topic?

☐ What are the conventions of the academic discipline or disciplines in which I am working?

☐ Do I communicate in an informed, thoughtful tone, without condescension?

☐ How well does my thesis fit my evidence and reasoning?

☐ Is the central idea of each section based on my own thinking and backed with evidence from my sources?

☐ How have I dealt with the most likely critiques of my thesis?

☐ Do the transitions from section to section assist the reader in moving from one topic to the next?

☐ What evidence do I use to support each point? Is it sufficient?

Editing: Use of sources

☐ Do my paraphrases and summaries alter the wording and sentence structure, but not the meaning, of the original text?

☐ Have I checked all quotations for accuracy and used ellipses or brackets where necessary?

☐ Do signal phrases set off and establish context for quotations, paraphrases, and summaries?

☐ Have I provided adequate in-text citation for each source?

☐ Do my in-text citations match my works-cited or references page?

☐ Do all my illustrations have complete and accurate captions?

(See also the checklists Revising Content and Organization, p. 77, Editing for Style and Grammar, p. 87, and Proofreading, p. 89.)

alternative, discipline-specific documentation style, consult the list of manuals in Figure 25.1.

For her research project on blogging and its effect on traditional news, Kris Washington used the MLA documentation style. *(The final draft of the text appears in Tab 6: MLA Documentation, on pp. 331–41.)*

SPECIFIC DISCIPLINE	POSSIBLE STYLE MANUAL
Chemistry	Coghill, Anne M., and Lorrin R. Garson, eds. *The ACS Style Guide: A Manual for Authors and Editors.* 3rd ed. Washington, DC: American Chemical Society, 2006.
Geology	Bates, Robert L., Rex Buchanan, and Marla Adkins-Heljeson, eds. *Geowriting: A Guide to Writing, Editing, and Printing in Earth Science.* 5th ed. Alexandria, VA: American Geological Institute, 1995.
Government and law	Garner, Diane L., and Diane H. Smith, eds. *The Complete Guide to Citing Government Information Resources: A Manual for Writers and Librarians.* Rev. ed. Bethesda, MD: Congressional Information Service, 1993.
	Harvard Law Review et al. *The Bluebook: A Uniform System of Citation.* 18th ed. Cambridge, MA: Harvard Law Review Assn., 2005.
Journalism	Goldstein, Norm, ed. *Associated Press Stylebook, 2008.* Revised and updated ed. New York: Associated Press, 2008.
Linguistics	Linguistic Society of America. "LSA Style Sheet." *LSA Bulletin.* Published annually in the December issue.
Mathematics	American Mathematical Society. *AMS Author Handbook: General Instructions for Preparing Manuscripts.* Providence, RI: AMS, 2007.
Medicine	Iverson, Cheryl, ed. *American Medical Association Manual of Style: A Guide for Authors and Editors.* 10th ed. New York: Oxford University Press, 2007.
Political science	American Political Science Association. *Style Manual for Political Science.* Rev. ed. Washington, DC: APSA, 2006.

FIGURE 25.1 **Style manuals for specific disciplines.**

6

MLA
Documentation
Style

Next to the originator of a good sentence is the first quoter of it.
—Ralph Waldo Emerson

Built near the site of the Great Library of Alexandria, Egypt, an ancient storehouse of knowledge that was destroyed by fire in the fourth century C.E., the new Bibliotheca Alexandrina offers a variety of collections and programs, including books, rare manuscripts, and a science museum.

6 MLA Documentation Style

MLA style requires writers to provide bibliographic information about their sources in a works-cited list. To format works-cited entries correctly, you need to know first of all what kind of source you are citing. The directory on pages 303–5 will help you find the appropriate sample to use as your model. As an alternative, you can use the charts on the pages that follow. Answering the questions provided in the charts will usually lead you to the sample entry you need. If you cannot find what you are looking for, consult your instructor for help.

Sections dealing with visual rhetoric. For a complete listing, see the Quick Guide to Key Resources at the back of this book.

The Elements of an MLA Works-Cited Entry:
Book

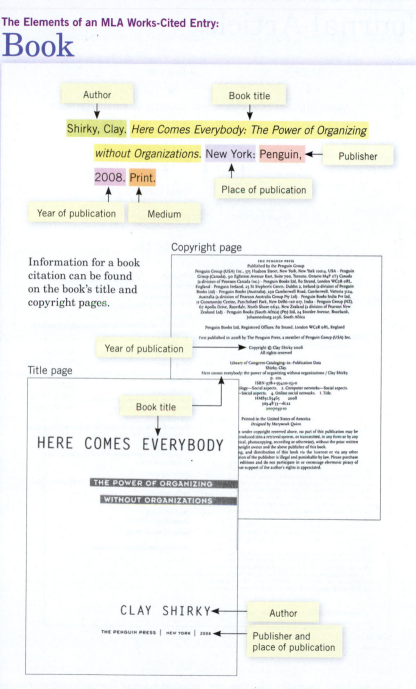

Author

Book title

Shirky, Clay. *Here Comes Everybody: The Power of Organizing without Organizations.* New York: Penguin, 2008. Print.

Publisher

Place of publication

Year of publication

Medium

Information for a book citation can be found on the book's title and copyright pages.

Copyright page

THE PENGUIN PRESS
Published by the Penguin Group
Penguin Group (USA) Inc., 375 Hudson Street, New York, New York 10014, USA · Penguin Group (Canada), 90 Eglinton Avenue East, Suite 700, Toronto, Ontario M4P 2Y3 Canada (a division of Pearson Canada Inc.) · Penguin Books Ltd, 80 Strand, London WC2R 0RL, England · Penguin Ireland, 25 St Stephen's Green, Dublin 2, Ireland (a division of Penguin Books Ltd) · Penguin Books (Australia), 250 Camberwell Road, Camberwell, Victoria 3124, Australia (a division of Pearson Australia Group Pty Ltd) · Penguin Books India Pvt Ltd, 11 Community Centre, Panchsheel Park, New Delhi–110 017, India · Penguin Group (NZ), 67 Apollo Drive, Rosedale, North Shore 0632, New Zealand (a division of Pearson New Zealand Ltd) · Penguin Books (South Africa) (Pty) Ltd, 24 Sturdee Avenue, Rosebank, Johannesburg 2196, South Africa

Penguin Books Ltd, Registered Offices: 80 Strand, London WC2R 0RL, England

First published in 2008 by The Penguin Press, a member of Penguin Group (USA) Inc.

Year of publication

Copyright © Clay Shirky 2008
All rights reserved

Library of Congress Cataloging-in-Publication Data
Shirky, Clay.
Here comes everybody: the power of organizing without organizations / Clay Shirky.
p. cm.
ISBN 978-1-59420-153-0
1. [Techno]logy—Social aspects. 2. Computer networks—Social aspects. [Social aspects.] 4. Online social networks. I. Title.
HM851.S5465 2008
303.48'33—dc22
2007035110

Printed in the United States of America
Designed by Marysarah Quinn

[Except as] under copyright reserved above, no part of this publication may be [repr]oduced into a retrieval system, or transmitted, in any form or by any [mechani]cal, photocopying, recording or otherwise), without the prior written [consent of the cop]yright owner and the above publisher of this book.
[The scanni]ng, and distribution of this book via the Internet or via any other [means without the permis]sion of the publisher is illegal and punishable by law. Please purchase [only authorized] editions and do not participate in or encourage electronic piracy of [copyrightable materials. Yo]ur support of the author's rights is appreciated.

Title page

Book title

HERE COMES EVERYBODY

THE POWER OF ORGANIZING

WITHOUT ORGANIZATIONS

CLAY SHIRKY

Author

THE PENGUIN PRESS | NEW YORK | 2008

Publisher and place of publication

The Elements of an MLA Works-Cited Entry:

Journal Article

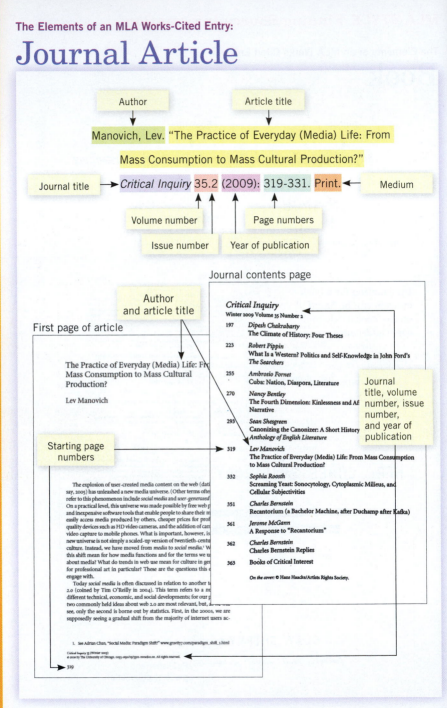

Author

Article title

Manovich, Lev. "The Practice of Everyday (Media) Life: From Mass Consumption to Mass Cultural Production?"

Journal title → *Critical Inquiry* 35.2 (2009): 319-331. Print. ← Medium

Volume number

Issue number   Year of publication

Page numbers

Journal contents page

Author and article title

First page of article

The Practice of Everyday (Media) Life: Fr[...]
Mass Consumption to Mass Cultural Production?

Lev Manovich

Starting page numbers

Journal title, volume number, issue number, and year of publication

Critical Inquiry
Winter 2009 Volume 35 Number 2

197 Dipesh Chakrabarty
     The Climate of History: Four Theses

223 Robert Pippin
     What Is a Western? Politics and Self-Knowledge in John Ford's
     The Searchers

255 Ambrosio Fornet
     Cuba: Nation, Diaspora, Literature

270 Nancy Bentley
     The Fourth Dimension: Kinlessness and Af[...]
     Narrative

293 Sean Shesgreen
     Canonizing the Canonizer: A Short History[...]
     Anthology of English Literature

319 Lev Manovich
     The Practice of Everyday (Media) Life: From Mass Consumption
     to Mass Cultural Production?

332 Sophia Roosth
     Screaming Yeast: Sonocytology, Cytoplasmic Milieus, and
     Cellular Subjectivities

351 Charles Bernstein
     Recantorium (a Bachelor Machine, after Duchamp after Kafka)

361 Jerome McGann
     A Response to "Recantorium"

362 Charles Bernstein
     Charles Bernstein Replies

363 Books of Critical Interest

On the cover: © Hans Haacke/Artists Rights Society.

The explosion of user-created media content on the web (dati[...]
say, 2005) has unleashed a new media universe. (Other terms ofte[...]
refer to this phenomenon include *social media* and *user-generated*[...]
On a practical level, this universe was made possible by free web p[...]
and inexpensive software tools that enable people to share their m[...]
easily access media produced by others, cheaper prices for prof[...]
quality devices such as HD video cameras, and the addition of cam[...]
video capture to mobile phones. What is important, however, is[...]
new universe is not simply a scaled-up version of twentieth-centu[...]
culture. Instead, we have moved from *media* to *social media.* W[...]
this shift mean for how media functions and for the terms we u[...]
about media? What do trends in web use mean for culture in gen[...]
for professional art in particular? These are the questions this e[...]
engage with.

Today *social media* is often discussed in relation to another t[...]
2.0 (coined by Tim O'Reilly in 2004). This term refers to a nu[...]
different technical, economic, and social developments; for our p[...]
two commonly held ideas about web 2.0 are most relevant, but, as [...]
see, only the second is borne out by statistics. First, in the 2000s, we are
supposedly seeing a gradual shift from the majority of internet users ac-

1. See Adrian Chan, "Social Media: Paradigm Shift?" www.gravity7.com/paradigm_shift_1.html

Critical Inquiry 35 (Winter 2009)
© 2009 by The University of Chicago. 0093-1896/09/3502-0000$10.00. All rights reserved.

319

Some academic journals, like this one, provide most of the information needed for a citation on the first page of an article as well as, like others, on the cover or contents page. You will need to look at the article's last page for the last

page number.

The Elements of an MLA Works-Cited Entry:

Journal Article from an
Online Database

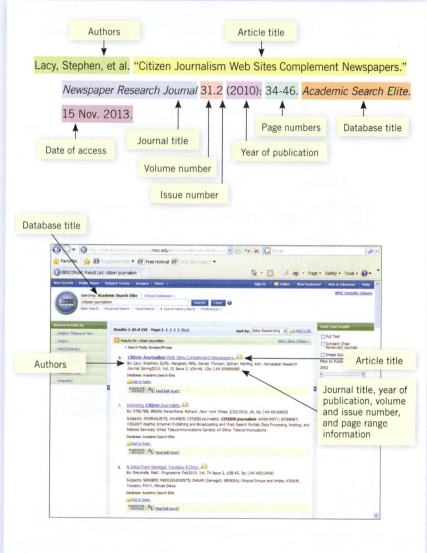

Authors

Article title

Lacy, Stephen, et al. "Citizen Journalism Web Sites Complement Newspapers."

Newspaper Research Journal 31.2 (2010): 34-46. *Academic Search Elite.*

15 Nov. 2013.

Date of access

Journal title

Volume number

Issue number

Page numbers

Year of publication

Database title

Database title

Authors

Article title

Journal title, year of publication, volume and issue number, and page range information

A citation for an article obtained from an online database includes information about the database, the medium, and the date of access in addition to information about the print version of the article. Information about the date of access comes from the researcher's notes. When a work has more than three authors, you have the option of using the abbreviation *et al.* (meaning "and others") after the first name.

The Elements of an MLA Works-Cited Entry:

Short Work on a
Web Site

Author

Title of short work

Sponsor or publisher

Starkman, Dean. "A New Consensus on the Future of News." Reuters.

Columbia Journalism Review, 28 February 2014. Web. 25 Nov. 2013.

Title of web site

Date of publication or most recent update

Medium

Date of access

Title of web site

Title of short work

Date of publication or most recent update

Author

COLUMBIA JOURNALISM REVIEW
The future of media is here

THE **Audit**
on the business press

A new consensus on the future of news
The future isn't what it used to be, and that's a good thing

By Dean Starkman

Just a couple of years ago, although it feels like a lot longer, the media world was embroiled in something like a gigantic family argument over the idea of whether it was good idea to charge readers for news online. Among aficionados, this was known as the "paywall debate."

The angry fracas was part of a much larger argument about the future of news itself. On one side, a new generation of technology-centered journalists trumpeted a new, decentered news system of networks, news shared and even gathered by volunteers, a more, informal, "iterative," approach (posting news now and fixing mistakes along the way), less concern about separating business and editorial functions, and, of course, free online news for all. The other side, my side, which resisted the name "old guard," argued about the importance of news institutions and professional newsgathering, traditional standards (or many of them), longform storytelling, reporter impartiality, strict separation of the news "church" and the business-side "state," and paywalls. (One thing we old guarders did not insist on, by the way, was the survival of print.)

When I wrote critically about what I called the "future of news (FON) consensus" in the CJR in the fall of 2011, the technologists' views were in ascendance and predicting, if not hastening, the death of newspapers. The intra-journalism debate that has unfurled over the last couple years has been heated and often angry, sometimes surprisingly enlightening, sometimes deeply stupid.

But now, it shows signs of abating. I see a consensus taking hold, one that, all in all, is much, much healthier for public-interest reporting than the old one. Is this inside media baseball? Most definitely! But the reality is that such debates can have an alarmingly large impact on the actual news the public will get. They matter. What was damaging about the old consensus, particularly, was its fealty to the god of clicks—digital ads revenue generated by high traffic volumes, which, in turn, require high quantities of new posts, often of indifferent quality. This side also believed that newspapers, under no circumstances, should charge readers for news online. This created what I called the

ALSO BY DEAN STARKMAN
The Financial Times breaks the law of large numbers — Digital subscriptions soar, putting paid circulation at a record

South African welfare queens gorge on lamb and macaroni as anecdotal Bloomberg fails data test — The wire misses badly

NEW CJR ISSUE
March-April
Read the Stories →

MOST POPULAR   MOST COMMENTED   TWITTER

A letter from death row backfires on Gawker (UPDATED)

Strange bedfellows: Climate change deniers, newspapers partner in a FOIA fight

The NYT preps its paywall part deux

Diversity—or lack thereof—in journalism startups, cont.

Two local papers have accepted money from City Hall in 2014. Is this a thing now?

If you cannot find the source's author or sponsor, look for a link that says "About us" or "Contact us." If the source has an edition or version number, place it after the site title. See page 323 for online scholarly journals and page 320 for works existing online and in another medium (e.g., print or film).

Entries in a Works-Cited List:

Books

Check the next panel or the directory on pages 303–05 or consult your instructor.

Print
Periodicals or Other Print Sources

? Is Your Source from a Journal, a Magazine, or a Newspaper?

NO   YES

Go to this entry on page

Is it from an academic journal?

Does the journal have a volume number?	**25**	310
Does the journal have an issue number but no volume number?	**26**	311
Is your source an abstract (a brief summary) of an article?	**32**	312

Is it from a magazine?

Is the magazine published monthly?	**27**	311
Is the magazine published weekly?	**27**	311
Is your source a letter to the editor?	**33**	312
Is it a review (e.g., a review of a book or film)?	**30**	311
Is it an interview?	**40**	313

Is it from a newspaper?

Is it an article?	**28**	311
Is it an interview?	**40**	313
Is it an editorial?	**31**	312
Is it a letter to the editor?	**33**	312
Is it a review (e.g., a review of a book or film)?	**30**	311

Is the author unknown?   **29** 311

? Is it a Print Source but Not a Book, a Part of a Book, or an Article in an Academic Journal, a Magazine, or a Newspaper?

NO   YES

Go to this entry on page

Is it published by the government or a nongovernment organization?

Is it a pamphlet or other type of document?	**34, 35**	312, 313
Is it a court case or other legal document?	**48**	315
Is it from the *Congressional Record*?	**69**	320

Is it an academic work?

Is it an unpublished dissertation?	**38**	313
Is it an abstract of a dissertation?	**39**	313
Is it an unpublished essay?	**47**	315

Is it a personal letter or a letter from an archive?   **46, 47** 315

Is it a visual text or an advertisement?

Is it a map or chart?	**41**	314
Is it a cartoon?	**42**	314
Is it a photograph?	**42**	314
Is it a reproduction of a work of visual art?	**43**	314
Is it an advertisement?	**44**	314

Is it stored in an archive?   **47** 315

Is it published in more than one medium (e.g., a book and a CD-ROM)?   **106** 328

Check the directory on pages 303–05 or consult your instructor.

Entries in a Works-Cited List:

Electronic or Other Nonprint Sources

? Did You Find Your Nonprint Source Online?

NO **YES**

Go to this entry on page

Did you find your source using an online database (e.g., InfoTrac)?
Is it an article from a scholarly journal?	**85**	324
Is it an abstract (a brief summary of an article from a scholarly journal)?	**85**	324
Is it a newspaper or magazine article?	**84**	324

Is it from an online scholarly journal?
Is it an article?	**81**	323
Is it a review (e.g., a book review)?	**83**	323
Is it an editorial or letter to the editor?	**82**	323

Is it from an online magazine or newspaper?
Is it an article?	**54**	317
Is it an editorial or a letter to the editor?	**55, 56**	317
Is it a review?	**57**	318
Is it an interview?	**58**	318

Does your online source also exist in print or another medium?
Is it a book or part of a book?	**70, 71**	321
Is it a doctoral dissertation?	**72**	321
Is it a pamphlet or brochure?	**73**	321
Is it a map or chart?	**74**	321
Is it a cartoon?	**75**	322
Is it a work of art (e.g., painting, drawing, photograph)?	**76**	322
Is it an online broadcast interview?	**79**	322
Is it an online radio or TV program?	**78**	322
Is it an online video or film?	**77**	322
Is it archival material?	**80**	323

Is your source sponsored by or related to the government? **68, 69** 320

Does your source exist only online?
Is it an entire Web site or independent work?
Is it a personal Web site?	**49**	316
Is it an entire blog?	**53**	316
Is it a home page for a course or an academic department?	**51**	316
Is it a page on a social networking site?	**52**	316
Is it another independent Web site or source?	**49**	316

Is it part of a larger online work?
Is it a blog entry?	**53**	316
Is it part of a wiki or another reference work?	**59, 60**	319
Is it an online visual (e.g., map, chart, or photograph)?	**61**	319
Is it an online slide show?	**62**	319
Is it an online advertisement?	**63**	319
Is it an audio or video podcast?	**64**	319
Is it an online video (Web original)?	**65**	319
Is it another short work from a Web site?	**50**	316

Is it an online communication?
Is it a posting to a news group, online forum, or discussion list?	**66**	320
Is it a synchronous (real-time) communication?	**67**	320
Is it an e-mail communication?	**86**	324
Is it an e-mail interview?	**103**	327

Go to the next panel.

? Is it a Computer-Based Source Not Found Online?

NO   YES

↓ ————————————————————————→   Go to this entry on page

Is it a digital file stored on your computer?
Is it a text file?	**87**	324
Is it a PDF file?	**88**	324
Is it an audio file (e.g., an MP3)?	**89**	325
Is it an image?	**90**	325

Is it a CD-ROM or DVD-ROM?   **91, 92** 325

Is it computer software?   **93** 325
| Is it a video game? | **94** | 325 |

? Is it Another Nonprint Source?

NO   YES

↓ ————————————————————————→   Go to this entry on page

Is it a film, DVD, or Blu-ray?   **95, 96** 326

Is it a personal or an archival video or audio recording?   **97** 326

Is it a broadcast interview?   **99** 326

Is it a radio or TV program?   **98** 326

Is it a personal or telephone interview?   **103** 327

Is it a sound recording, musical composition, or work of art?   **100–102** 326, 327

Is it a lecture, speech, or performance?   **104, 105** 327, 328

Do its components include multiple media (e.g., a book with a CD-ROM)?   **106** 328

Check the directory on pages 303–05 or consult your instructor.

MLA MLA MLA MLA MLA MLA MLA MLA MLA MLA MLA MLA MLA MLA MLA MLA MLA MLA MLA

START SMART

Tab 6: MLA Documentation Style

This section will help you answer questions such as the following:

Rhetorical Knowledge

- Which disciplines use MLA style? (26)
- When should I use explanatory notes in MLA style? (28)

Critical Thinking, Reading, and Writing

- Why do I need to document my sources? (26)

Processes

- How do I create a works-cited list? (27)
- How should I position and label visuals? (29)

Knowledge of Conventions

- What are correct formats for in-text citations (26), works-cited list entries (27) and notes (28)?
- How do I cite electronic sources such as databases, Web sites, and podcasts? (27)
- What kind of spacing and margins should I use? (29)
- How do I cite a Web site or a blog in the text of my paper? (26) In my list of works cited? (27)

For a general introduction to writing outcomes, see 1e, pages 14–16.

The documentation style developed by the Modern Language Association (MLA) is used by many researchers in the arts and humanities, especially by those who write about language and literature. The guidelines presented here are based on the seventh edition of the *MLA Handbook for Writers of Research Papers* (New York: MLA, 2009).

College texts include information, ideas, and quotations from sources that must be accurately documented. Documentation allows others to see the path you have taken in researching and writing your paper. *(For more on what to document, see Tab 5: Researching, pp. 258–75.)*

The MLA documentation style has three parts:

- In-text citations
- List of works cited
- Explanatory notes and acknowledgments

In-text citations and a list of works cited are mandatory; explanatory notes are optional.

CHAPTER 26

MLA Style: In-Text Citations

In-text citations let readers know that they can find full bibliographical information about your sources in the list of works cited at the end of your paper.

1. Author named in sentence In your first reference, give the author's full name as the source presents it. Afterward, use the last name only, unless two or more of your sources have the same last name *(see no. 6)* or unless two or more works by the same author appear in your works-cited list *(no. 3)*.

signal phrase

> In his book, *Here Comes Everybody: The Power of Organizing without Organizations,* New York University professor and media consultant Clay Shirky explains how the proliferation of blogs is affecting news: "The change isn't a shift from one kind of news institution to another, but rather in the definition of news" (65-66).

The parenthetical page citation comes after the closing quotation mark but before the period.

2. Author named in parentheses If you do not name the source's author in your sentence, then you must provide the name in the parentheses. (Give the full name if the author of another source has the same last name.)

> Furthermore, today an event can become news before members of the press begin to cover it, and in fact they may cover it only after their
> *no comma after author's name*
> audience has become aware of it another way (Shirky 64-65).

There is no comma between the author's name and the page number. If you cite two or more distinct pages, however, separate the numbers with a comma: (Shirky 64, 67).

3. Two or more works by the same author If you use two or more works by the same author, you must identify which work you are citing, either in your sentence or in an abbreviated form in parentheses: (Shirky, *Here Comes Everybody* 66).

> Shirky sees the cooperation between professionals and amateurs as necessary to the survival of journalism: "Many of these models will fail. . . . [O]ver time, the collection of new experiments that do work
> *article title is abbreviated*
> might give us the journalism we need" ("Newspapers" 29).

MLA IN-TEXT CITATIONS: Directory to Sample Types

(See pp. 302–28 for works-cited examples.)

4. Two or three authors of the same work If a source has up to three authors, you should name them all either in your text, as the next example shows, or in parentheses: (Anderson, Bell, and Shirky 14).

> In a report published online, C. W. Anderson, Emily Bell, and Clay Shirky explain that blogs and other forms of social media allow for "superdistribution," meaning that stories—including those published by smaller outlets—can reach a wider audience than ever before, and at very little expense (14).

5. More than three authors If a source has more than three authors, either list all the authors, or give the first author's last name followed by *et al.* (not italicized), meaning "and others" (note that *et,* which means "and," is fine as is, but *al.,* which is an abbreviation for *alia,* needs a period). Do the same in your works-cited list.

Changes in social regulations are bound to produce new forms of subjectivity (Henriques et al. 275).

6. Authors with the same last name If the authors of two or more of your sources have the same last name, include the first initial of the author you are citing (R. Campbell 63); if the first initial is also shared, use the full first name, as shown in the following example.

In the late nineteenth century, the sale of sheet music spread rapidly in a Manhattan area along Broadway known as Tin Pan Alley (Richard Campbell 63).

7. Organization as author Treat the organization as the author. If the name is long, put it in a signal phrase.

The Centre for Contemporary Cultural Studies claims that "there is nothing inherently concrete about historiography" (10).

─MLA IN-TEXT CITATIONS

- Name the author, either in a signal phrase such as "Shirky compares" or in a parenthetical citation.
- Include a page reference in parentheses. No "p." precedes the page number; if the author is named in the parentheses, there is no punctuation between the author's name and the page number.
- Place the citation as close to the material being cited as possible and before any punctuation marks that divide or end the sentence except in a block quotation, where the citation comes one space after the period or final punctuation mark. See no. 12 for quotations ending with a question mark or an exclamation point.
- Italicize the titles of books, magazines, and plays. Place quotation marks around the titles of articles and short poems.
- For Internet sources, follow the same general guidelines as for print sources. Keep the parenthetical citation simple, providing enough information for your reader to find the full citation in your works-cited list. Cite either the author's name or the title of the site or article. Begin the parenthetical citation with the first word of the corresponding works-cited list entry.
- For works without page or paragraph numbers, give the author or title only. Often it is best to mention the author or title in your sentence, in which case no parenthetical citation is needed.

8. Unknown author   When no author is given, cite a work by its title, using either the full title in a signal phrase or an abbreviated version in the parentheses. When abbreviating the title, begin with the word by which it is alphabetized in your works-cited list.

title of article

"Squaresville, USA vs. Beatsville" makes the Midwestern small-town

home seem boring compared with the West Coast artist's "pad" (31).

The Midwestern small-town home seems boring compared with the

West Coast artist's "pad" ("Squaresville" 31).

9. Entire work   Acknowledge an entire work in your text, not in a parenthetical citation. Include the work in your list of works cited, and include in the text the word by which the entry is alphabetized.

Sidney J. Furie's film *Lady Sings the Blues* presents Billie Holiday as a

beautiful woman in pain rather than as the great jazz artist she was.

10. Paraphrased or summarized source   If you include the author's name in your paraphrase or summary, include only the page number or numbers in your parenthetical citation. Signal phrases clarify that you are paraphrasing or summarizing.

For example, in their report "Post Industrial Journalism: Adapting to

signal phrase

the Present," Anderson, Bell, and Shirky contend that the bike-racing

blog *NYVelocity* covered the Lance Armstrong story better than the

"professional" press (20).

11. Source of a long quotation   For a quotation of more than four typed lines of prose or three of poetry, do not use quotation marks. Instead, indent the material you are quoting by one inch. Following the final punctuation mark of the quotation, allow one space before any parenthetical information.

Shirky describes what this trend toward "pro-am" reporting might

look like:

> For the next few decades, journalism will be made up of
>
> overlapping special cases. Many of these models will rely on
>
> amateurs as researchers and writers. Many of these models
>
> will rely on sponsorship or grants or endowments instead

of revenues. Many of these models will rely on excitable

14-year-olds distributing the results. Many of these models

ellipses and brackets indicate an omission from the quotation

will fail. . . . [O]ver time, the collection of new experiments

that do work might give us the journalism we need.

("Newspapers" 29)

12. Source of a short quotation   Close the quotation before the parenthetical citation. If the quotation concludes with an exclamation point or a question mark, place the closing quotation mark after that punctuation mark, and place the sentence period after the parenthetical citation.

Encyclopaedia Britannica defines a *blog,* short for *Web log,* as an

"online journal where an individual, group, or corporation presents a

record of activities, thoughts, or beliefs" ("Blog").

Shakespeare's Sonnet XVIII asks, "Shall I compare thee to a summer's

day?" (line 1).

13. One-page source   You need not include a page number in the parenthetical citation for a one-page printed source.

14. Government publication   To avoid an overly long parenthetical citation, name the government agency that published the source within your text.

According to a report issued by the Bureau of National Affairs, many

employers in 1964 needed guidance to apply new workplace rules

that ensured fairness and complied with the Civil Rights Act of

1964 (32).

15. Photograph, map, graph, chart, or other visual

VISUAL APPEARS IN YOUR TEXT

An aerial photograph of Manhattan (fig. 3), taken by the United

States Geographical Survey, demonstrates how creative city planning

can introduce parks and green spaces within even the most densely

populated urban areas.

If the caption you write for the image includes all the information found in a works-cited list entry, you need not include it in your list.

VISUAL DOES NOT APPEAR IN YOUR TEXT

An aerial photograph of Manhattan taken by the United States Geographical Survey demonstrates how creative city planning can introduce parks and green spaces within even the most densely populated urban areas (TerraServer-USA).

Provide a parenthetical citation that directs your reader to information about the source of the image in your works-cited list.

16. Web site or other online electronic source   If you cannot find the author of an online source, then identify the source by title or sponsor, either in your text or in a parenthetical citation. Because most online sources do not have set page, section, or paragraph numbers, they must usually be cited as entire works.

organization cited as author

The Pew Research Center's Project for Excellence in Journalism points out that print advertising is consistently declining with each year.
page number not provided

17. Work with numbered paragraphs or sections instead of pages   To distinguish them from page numbers, use the abbreviation *par(s).* or the type of division such as *section(s)* or *screen(s)*.

Rothstein suggests that many German Romantic musical techniques may have originated in Italian opera (par. 9).

Give the paragraph or section number(s) after the author's name and a comma in a parenthetical citation: (Rothstein, par. 9).

18. Work with no page or paragraph numbers   When citing an electronic or print source without page, paragraph, or other reference numbers, try to include the author's name in your text instead of in a parenthetical citation.

In "Gap-Year Travel Brings Students Back to Learning," reporter
author's name
John Ross cites recent research and explains how a gap year might positively or negatively affect the college experience.

19. Multivolume work   When citing more than one volume of a multivolume work in your paper, include with each citation the volume number, followed by a colon, a space, and the page number.

Scott argues that today people tend to solve problems "by turning to the Web" (2: 5).

If you consult only one volume of a multivolume work, then specify that volume in the works-cited list *(see p. 309),* but not in the parenthetical citation.

20. Literary works

Novels and literary nonfiction books Include the relevant page number, followed by a semicolon, a space, and the chapter number.

> Jenkins states that because Harry Potter's fandom involves both adults and children, it's a "space where conversations could occur across generations" (216; ch. 5).

If the author is not named in your sentence, add the name in front of the page number: (Jenkins 216; ch. 5).

Poems Use line numbers, not page numbers.

> In "Ode on a Grecian Urn," Keats asks, "What men or gods are these? What maidens loth? / What mad pursuit? What struggle to escape?" (lines 8-9). He can provide no answer, but he notes that the lucky lovers pictured on the urn are "for ever young; / All breathing human passion far above" (27-28).

Note that the word *lines* (not italicized), rather than *l.* or *ll.,* is used in the first citation to establish what the numbers in parentheses refer to; subsequent citations need not use the word *lines.*

Plays and long, multisection poems Use division (act, scene, canto, book, part) and lines, not page numbers. In the following example, notice that Arabic numerals are used for act and scene divisions as well as for line numbers: (*Ham.* 2.3.22-27). The same is true for canto, verse, and lines in the following citation of Byron's *Don Juan:* (*DJ* 1.37.4-8). (The *MLA Handbook* lists abbreviations for titles of certain literary works.)

21. Religious text
Cite material in the Bible, Upanishads, or Koran by book, chapter, and verse, using an appropriate abbreviation when the name of the book is in the parentheses rather than in your sentence. Name the edition from which you are citing.

> As the Bible says, "The wise man knows there will be a time of judgment" (*Holy Bible, Rev. Stand. Vers.,* Eccles. 8.5).

Note that titles of scriptural writings are not italicized.

22. Historical document   For familiar documents such as the Constitution and the Declaration of Independence, provide the document's name and the numbers of the parts you are citing.

> Judges are allowed to remain in office "during good behavior," a
>
> vague standard that has had various interpretations (US Const., art. 3,
>
> sec. 1).

23. Indirect source   When you quote or paraphrase a quotation you found in someone else's work, put *qtd. in* (not italicized, meaning "quoted in," with a period after the abbreviation) before the name of your source.

> Advertising agencies try to come up with ways to "interrupt" people so
>
> that "they pay attention to one-way message[s]" (qtd. in Scott 7).

In your list of works cited, list only the work you consulted, in this case the indirect source by Scott.

24. Two or more sources in one citation   When you credit two or more sources for the same idea, use a semicolon to separate the citations.

> The impact of blogging on human knowledge, communication, and
>
> interactions has led to improvements in our daily lives. We are not
>
> only more up to date on the latest goings-on in the world, but we are
>
> also connected to other informed citizens like never before (Ingram;
>
> Shirky).

25. Two or more sources in one sentence   Include a parenthetical reference after each idea or quotation you have borrowed.

> Ironically, Americans lavish more money each year on their pets
>
> than they spend on children's toys (Merkins 21), but the feral cat
>
> population—consisting of abandoned pets and their offspring—is at
>
> an estimated 70 million and growing (Mott).

26. Work in an anthology   When citing a work in a collection, give the name of the specific work's author, not the name of the editor of the whole collection.

> "Exile marks us like a talisman or tattoo. It teaches us how to endure
>
> long nights and short days" (Agosin 273).

Here, Agosin is cited as the source, even though his work appears in a collection edited by Ringoberto Gonzalez. Note that the list of works cited must include an entry for Agosin.

27. E-mail, letter, or personal interview Cite by name the person you communicated with, using either a signal phrase or parentheses.

> Blogging is a beneficial tool to use in the classroom because it allows
>
> students to keep up with new media trends (Carter).

In the works-cited list, after giving the person's last name you will need to identify the kind of communication and its date *(see pp. 314–15, 324, and 327)*.

CHAPTER 27

MLA Style: List of Works Cited

MLA documentation style requires a works-cited page with full bibliographic information about your sources. The list of works cited should appear at the end of your research project, beginning on a new page entitled "Works Cited." Include only those sources you cite, unless your instructor tells you to prepare a "Works Consulted" list.

Books

1. Book with one author Italicize the book's title. Generally only the city, not the state, is included in the publication data. Conclude with the medium (e.g., Print). In MLA style, abbreviations are suggested for most publishers, for instance, *Wayne State UP* for *Wayne State University Press,* and *Random* for *Random House.* For books published by a division within a publishing company, known as an imprint, put a hyphen between the imprint and publisher, like so: Knopf-Random.

> Shirky, Clay. *Here Comes Everybody: The Power of Organizing without*
>
> *Organizations.* New York: Penguin, 2008. Print.

2. Two or more works by the same author(s) Give the author's name in the first entry only. For subsequent works authored by that person, replace the name with three hyphens and a period. Alphabetize by title.

> Shirky, Clay. *Here Comes Everybody: The Power of Organizing without*
>
> *Organizations.* New York: Penguin, 2008. Print.
>
> ---. "Newspapers and Thinking the Unthinkable." *Risk Management*
>
> May 2009: 24-29. *Academic Search Elite.* Web. 21 Apr. 2010.

MLA WORKS-CITED ENTRIES: Directory to Sample Types

(See pp. 294–302 for examples of in-text citations.)

(continued)

MLA WORKS-CITED ENTRIES *(continued)*

3. Book with two or three authors Name the two or three authors in the order in which they appear on the title page, putting the last name first for the first author only.

> Ottolenghi, Yotam, and Sami Tamimi. *Jerusalem: A Cookbook.*
>
> Berkeley: Ten Speed, 2012. Print.

4. Book with four or more authors When a work has more than three authors, you may list them all or use the abbreviation *et al.* (meaning "and others") to replace the names of all authors except the first.

> Schaffner, Ingrid, et al. *Maira Kalman: Various Illuminations (Of a Crazy*
>
> *World).* New York: Prestel, 2010. Print.

5. Organization as author Consider as an organization any group, commission, association, or corporation whose members are not identified on the title page.

> Centre for Contemporary Cultural Studies. *Women Take Issue: Aspects*
>
> *of Women's Subordination.* London: Routledge, 2007. Print.

6. Book by an editor or editors If the title page lists an editor instead of an author, begin with the editor's name followed by the abbreviation *ed.* with a period (not italicized). Use *eds.* when more than one editor is listed. Only the first editor's name should appear in reverse order. When a book's title contains the title of another book (as this one does), do not italicize the title-within-a-title (here, *Dr. Who*).

title in title not italicized

Leitch, Gillian, ed. Dr. Who *in Time and Space: Essays on Themes,*

Characters, History and Fandom. Jefferson, NC: McFarland,

2013. Print.

7. Book with an author and an editor Put the author and title first, followed by the abbreviation *Ed.* (not italicized, for "edited by") and the name of the editor. However, if you cite something written by the editor, see no. 15.

James, Henry. *The Portrait of a Lady.* Ed. Robert D. Bamberg. New

York: Norton, 1975. Print.

8. Work in an anthology or textbook or chapter in an edited book List the author and title of the selection, followed by the title of the anthology, *Ed.* (not italicized) and the editor's name, publication data, page numbers of the selection, and medium. The first example cites a reading from a textbook.

Brodkey, Linda. "On the Subjects of Class and Gender in 'The Literacy

Letters.'" *Cross-Talk in Comp Theory.* Ed. Victor Villanueva.

Urbana: NCTE Press, 2003. 677-96. Print.

Fisher, Walter R. "Narration, Knowledge, and the Possibility of

Wisdom." *Rethinking Knowledge: Reflections across the*

Disciplines. Eds. Robert F. Goodman and Walter R. Fisher. Albany:

SUNY Press, 1995. 169-92. Print.

9. Two or more items from one anthology Include a complete entry for the anthology beginning with the name of the editor(s). Each selection should have its own entry in the alphabetical list that includes only the author, title of the selection, editor, and page numbers.

entry for the anthology

Jacobs, Jonathan, Ed. *Open Game Table: The Anthology of Roleplaying*

place of publication unknown, see no. 10

in Game Blogs. Vol. 2. N.p.: Open Game Table, 2010. Print.

entry for a selection from the anthology

Jones, Jeremy. "Gaming Roots and Reflections." Jacobs 11-35.

10. Book without publication information or pagination If a book has no page numbers, as in the first example, use *N. pag.* instead. Or, if the place of publication is unknown, as in the second example, indicate *N.p.* (not italicized).

Barber, Tiki, and Ronde Barber. *By My Brother's Side.* New York:

Simon, 2004. N. pag. Print.

Kaplan, Harold. *A Memoir of Being Human.* N.p.: Lulu, 2013. Print.

MLA LIST OF WORKS CITED

- Begin on a new page with the centered title "Works Cited."
- Include an entry for every source cited in your text.
- Include author, title, publication data, and medium (such as print, Web, radio), if available for each entry. Use a period to set off each of these elements from the others. Leave one space after the periods.
- Do not number the entries.
- Put entries in alphabetical order by author's or editor's last name. If the work has more than one author, see nos. 3 and 4 *(p. 305).* (If the author is unknown, use the first word of the title, excluding the articles *A, An,* or *The.*)
- Italicize titles of books, periodicals, long poems, and plays. Put quotation marks around titles of articles, short stories, and short poems.
- Capitalize the first and last and all important words in all titles and subtitles. Do not capitalize articles, prepositions, coordinating conjunctions, and the *to* in infinitives unless they appear as the first or last word in the title. Place a colon between title and subtitle unless the title ends in a question mark or an exclamation point.
- In the publication data, abbreviate months and publishers' names (Dec. rather than December; Oxford UP instead of Oxford University Press), and include the name of the city in which the publisher is located but not the state (unless the city is obscure or ambiguous): Ithaca: Cornell UP. Use *n.p.* in place of publisher or location information if none is available. If the date of publication is not given, provide the approximate date, enclosed in brackets: [c. 1975]. If you cannot approximate the date, write *n.d.* for "no date."
- Do not use *p., pp.,* or *page(s).* Use *n. pag.* (not italicized) if the source lacks page or paragraph numbers or other divisions. When page citations over one hundred have the same first digit, do not repeat it for the second number: 243-47.
- Abbreviate all months except May, June, and July.
- For articles and other print sources that skip pages, provide the page number for the beginning of the article followed by a plus (+) sign.
- Use a hanging indent: Start the first line of each entry at the left margin, and indent all subsequent lines of the entry five spaces (or one-half inch in a word-processing program).
- Double-space throughout the works cited.

11. Signed article in an encyclopedia or another reference work   Cite the author's name, title of the entry (in quotation marks), title of the reference work (italicized), edition, publication information, and medium. Omit page numbers if entries appear in alphabetical order.

> Hirsch, E. D. "Idioms." *Dictionary of Cultural Literacy.* 2nd ed. Boston:
>
> Houghton, 1993. 59. Print.

12. Unsigned entry in an encyclopedia or another reference work   Start the entry with the title. For well-known reference works, omit the place and publisher.

> "Godiva, Lady." *Dictionary of Cultural Literacy.* 2nd ed. Boston:
>
> Houghton, 1993. 199. Print.

13. Article from a collection of reprinted articles

> Haney-Peritz, Janice. "Monumental Feminism and Literature's
>
> Ancestral House: Another Look at 'The Yellow Wallpaper.'"
>
> *abbreviation for 'reprinted'*
> *Women's Studies* 12.2 (1986): 113-28. Rpt. in *The Captive*
>
> *Imagination: A Casebook on "The Yellow Wallpaper."* Ed. Catherine
>
> Golden. New York: Feminist, 1992. 261-76. Print.

14. Anthology

> Moehringer, J. R., ed. *The Best American Sports Writing 2013.* New
>
> York: Mariner, 2013. Print.

15. Preface, foreword, introduction, or afterword   When the writer of some part of a book is different from the author of the book, use the word *By* after the book's title and cite the author's full name. If the book's sole author wrote the part and the book has an editor, use only the author's last name after *By*. If there is no editor and the author wrote the part, cite the complete book.

> *name of part of book*
> Kraemer, Harry M. Jansen, Jr. Foreword. *Master the Matrix: 7*
>
> *Essentials for Getting Things Done in Complex Organizations.* By
> *author of the book*
> Susan Z. Finerty. Minneapolis: Two Harbors, 2012. 1. Print.

16. Translation   The translator's name goes after the title, with the abbreviation *Trans.*

> Oz, Amos. *Scenes from Village Life.* Trans. Nicholas de Lange. New
>
> York: Mariner, 2012. Print.

17. Edition other than the first   Include the number of the edition: *2nd ed., 3rd ed.* (not italicized), and so on. Place the number after the title, or if there is an editor, after that person's name.

> Wood, Ethel. *AP World History: An Essential Coursebook.* 2nd ed.
>
> > Germantown, NY: WoodYard, 2011. Print.

18. Religious text   Give the version, italicized; the editor's or translator's name (if any); and the publication information including medium.

> *ESV New Classic Reference Bible.* Wheaton: Crossway, 2011. Print.
>
> *The Bhagavad Gita.* Trans. Eknath Easwaran. Tomales: Nilgiri,
>
> > 2005. Print.

19. Multivolume work   The first example indicates that the researcher used more than one volume of the work; the second shows that only the second volume was used *(to cite an individual article or chapter in a multivolume work or set of reference books, refer to nos. 8 or 11).*

> Manning, Martin J., and Clarence R. Wyatt. *Encyclopedia of Media*
>
> > *and Propaganda in Wartime America.* 2 vols. Santa Barbara:
> >
> > ABC-CLIO, 2010. Print.
>
> Manning, Martin J., and Clarence R. Wyatt. *Encyclopedia of Media*
>
> > *and Propaganda in Wartime America.* Vol. 1. Santa Barbara:
> >
> > ABC-CLIO, 2010. Print.

20. Book in a series   After the medium, put the name of the series and, if available on the title page, the number of the work.

> Wimmer, Roger D., and Joseph R. Dominick. *Mass Media Research:*
>
> > *An Introduction (with InfoTrac).* Boston: Wadsworth, 2005. Print.
> >
> > *name of series not italicized*
> > Contributions in Wadsworth Ser. in Mass Comm. and Journalism.

21. Republished book   Put the original date of publication, followed by a period, before the current publication data.

> *original publication date*
> Wheatley, Dennis. *The Forbidden Territory.* 1970. London: Bloomsbury,
>
> > 2013. Kindle file.

22. Unknown author   The citation begins with the title. In the list of works cited, alphabetize the citation by the first important word, excluding the articles *A, An,* and *The.*

> *Webster's College Dictionary.* New York: Random; New York: McGraw,
>
> 1991. Print.

Note that this entry includes both of the publishers listed on the dictionary's title page; they are separated by a semicolon.

23. Book with illustrator List the illustrator after the title with the abbreviation *illus.* (not italicized). If you refer primarily to the illustrator, put that name before the title instead of the author's.

> Carroll, Lewis. *Alice's Adventures in Wonderland and through the*
>
> *Looking-Glass.* Illus. John Tenniel. New York: Modern Library-
>
> Random, 2002. Print.

> Tenniel, John, illus. *Alice's Adventures in Wonderland and through*
>
> *the Looking-Glass.* By Lewis Carroll. New York: Modern Library-
>
> Random, 2002. Print.

24. Graphic novel or comic book Cite graphic narratives created by one person as you would any other book or multivolume work. For collaborations, begin with the person whose work you refer to most, and list others in the order in which they appear on the title page. Indicate each person's contribution. *(For part of a series, see no. 20.)*

> L'Engle, Madeleine, writer. *A Wrinkle in Time.* Illus. Hope Larson. New
>
> York: Farrar, Straus and Giroux, 2012. Print.

> Fetter-Vorm, Jonathan. *Trinity: A Graphic Novel of the First Atomic*
>
> *Bomb.* New York: Hill and Wang, 2013. Print.

Periodicals

Periodicals are published at set intervals, usually four times a year for scholarly journals, monthly or weekly for magazines, and daily or weekly for newspapers. Between the author and the publication date are two titles: the title of the article, in quotation marks; and the title of the periodical, italicized. *(For online versions of print periodicals and periodicals published only online, see pp. 316–19 and 323–24.)*

25. Article in a journal with volume numbers Most journals have a volume number corresponding to the year and an issue number for each publication that year. The issue may be indicated by a month or season. Put the volume number after the title. Follow it with a period and the issue number. Give the year of publication in parentheses, followed by a colon, a space, and the page numbers of the article. End with the medium.

MLA MLA MLA MLA MLA MLA MLA MLA MLA MLA MLA MLA MLA MLA MLA MLA MLA MLA MLA MLA

Lacy, Stephen, et al. "Citizen Journalism Web Sites Complement

Newspapers." *Newspaper Research Journal* 31.2 (2010):

34-46. Print.

26. Article in a journal with issue numbers only   Give only the issue number.

Wyile, Herb. "I Questioned Authority and the Question Won." *Canadian*

Literature 216 (2013): 67-83. Print.

27. Article in a popular magazine   For a monthly magazine, provide the month and year, abbreviating all months except May, June, and July. For a weekly publication, include the complete date: day, month, and year.

Newman, Catherine. "My Friend Belittles My Job!" *Real Simple* Mar.

2013: 67. Print.

Frazier, Ian. "Hidden City." *New Yorker* 28 Oct. 2013: 38-49. Print.

28. Article in a newspaper   Provide the day, month, and year. If an edition is named on the top of the first page, specify the edition— *natl. ed.* or *late ed.* (without italics), for example—after the date. If the section letter is part of the page number, see the first example. Give the title of an unnumbered section with *sec.* (not italicized). If the article appears on nonconsecutive pages, put a plus (+) sign after the first page number.

Davey, Monica. "In Detroit, Mayor's Race Is One Piece of a Puzzle."

New York Times 3 Nov. 2013, natl. ed.: A15+. Print.

Carr, Nicholas. "Attention Must Be Paid." *New York Times* 3 Nov.

2013, natl. ed., Book Review sec.: 16. Print.

29. Unsigned article in a magazine or newspaper   The citation begins with the title and is alphabetized by the first word, excluding articles such as *A, An,* or *The.*

"Harper's Index." *Harper's* Apr. 2013: 15. Print.

"Salem: Curse Victims, Meet Adam Smith." *Boston Globe* 2 Nov.

2013: A10. Print.

30. Review   Begin with the name of the reviewer and, if there is one, the title of the review. Add *Rev. of* (without italics, meaning "review of") and the title plus the author or performer of the work being reviewed.

> Wyman, Bill. "The Pale King." Rev. of *Untouchable: The Strange Life and Tragic Death of Michael Jackson,* by Randall Sullivan. *New Yorker* 24 & 31 Dec. 2012: 133-38. Print.

31. Editorial   Treat editorials as articles, but add the word *Editorial* (not italicized) after the title. If the editorial is unsigned, begin with the title.

> Shaw, Theodore M. "The Debate over Race Needs Minority Students' Voices." Editorial. *Chronicle of Higher Education* 25 Feb. 2000: A72. Print.

32. Abstract of a journal article   Collections of abstracts from journals can be found in the library's reference section. Include the publication information for the original article, followed by the title of the publication that provides the abstract, the volume, the year in parentheses, the item or page number, and the medium.

> Theiler, Anne M., and Louise G. Lippman. "Effects of Mental Practice and Modeling on Guitar and Vocal Performance." *Journal of General Psychology* 122.4 (1995): 329-43. *Psychological Abstracts* 83.1 (1996): item 30039. Print.

33. Letter to the editor

> Patterson, James T. Letter. *New York Review of Books* 5 Dec. 2013: 58. Print.

Other print sources

34. Government document   Either the name of the government and agency or the name of the document's author comes first. If the government and agency name come first, follow the title of the document with the word *By* for a writer, *Ed.* for an editor, or *Comp.* for a compiler (if any), and give the name. Publication information and medium come last.

> United States. Bureau of Natl. Affairs. *The Civil Rights Act of 1964: Text, Analysis, Legislative History; What It Means to Employers, Businessmen, Unions, Employees, Minority Groups.* Washington: BNA, 1964. Print.

(For the format to use when citing the Congressional Record, *see no. 69.)*

35. Pamphlet or brochure   Treat it as a book. If the pamphlet or brochure has an author, list his or her name first; otherwise, begin with the title.

The Digital Derry Strategy. Donegal: PIKE, 2009.

36. Conference proceedings   Cite as you would an edited book, but include information about the conference if it is not in the title.

Mendel, Arthur, Gustave Reese, and Gilbert Chase, eds. *Papers Read*

at the International Congress of Musicology Held at New York

September 11th to 16th, 1939. New York: Music Educators' Natl.

Conf. for the American Musicological Soc., 1944. Print.

37. Published dissertation   Cite as you would a book. After the title, add *Diss.* (not italicized) for "dissertation," the name of the institution, the year the dissertation was written, place of publication, publishing institution, year, and medium.

Fraser, Wilmot Alfred. *Jazzology: A Study of the Tradition in Which Jazz*

Musicians Learn to Improvise. Diss. U of Pennsylvania, 1983. Ann

Arbor: UMI, 1987. Print.

38. Unpublished dissertation   Begin with the author's name, followed by the title in quotation marks, the abbreviation *Diss.* (not italicized), the name of the institution, the year the dissertation was written, and the medium.

Price, Deidre Dowling. "Confessional Poetry and Blog Culture in the

Age of Autobiography." Diss. Florida State U, 2010. Print.

39. Abstract of a dissertation   Use the format for an unpublished dissertation. After the dissertation date, give the abbreviation *DA* or *DAI* (for *Dissertation Abstracts* or *Dissertation Abstracts International*), then the volume number, the issue number, the date of publication, the page number, and the medium.

Quinn, Richard Allen. "Playing Together: Improvisation in Postwar

American Literature and Culture." Diss. U of Iowa, 2000. *DAI*

61.6 (2001): 2305A. Print.

40. Published interview   Name the person interviewed, and give the title of the interview or the descriptive term *Interview* (not italicized), the name of the interviewer (if known and relevant), the publication information, and the medium.

MLA MLA MLA MLA MLA MLA MLA MLA MLA MLA MLA MLA MLA MLA MLA

King, Gayle. "Watch the Throne." Interview by Andrew Goldman. *New York Times Magazine* 27 May 2012: 10. Print.

41. Map or chart Cite as you would a book with an unknown author. Italicize the title of the map or chart, and add the word *Map* or *Chart* (not italicized) following the title.

Streetwise Brooklyn. Map. Sarasota: Streetwise, 2013. Print.

42. Cartoon or photograph in a print work Include the artist's name, the title of the image (in quotation marks for cartoons, italicized for photographs), the publication information, and the medium. Include the word *Cartoon* or *Photograph* (not italicized) after the title.

Chast, Roz. "Recipes from the Jean-Paul Sartre Cookbook." Cartoon. *New Yorker* 23 Sept. 2013. Print.

Herbert, Gerald. *President Obama Touched on a Range of Issues Friday at the Port of New Orleans.* Photograph. *Philadelphia Inquirer* 9 Nov. 2013: A4. Print.

43. Reproduction of artwork Treat a photograph of a work of art in another source like a work in an anthology *(no. 8)*. Italicize the titles of both the artwork and the source, and include the institution or collection and city where the work can be found prior to information about the source in which it appears.

Sargent, John Singer. *Venice: Under the Rialto Bridge.* 1909. Museum of Fine Arts: Boston. *MFA Preview,* Nov./Dec. 2013. 10. Print.

44. Advertisement Name the item or organization being advertised, include the word *Advertisement* (not italicized), and indicate where the ad appeared.

Geico. Advertisement. *Sports Illustrated* 11 Nov. 2013: 45. Print.

45. Published letter Treat like a work in an anthology, but include the date. Include the number, if one was assigned by the editor. If you use more than one letter from a published collection, follow the instructions for cross-referencing in no. 9.

Hughes, Langston. "To Arna Bontemps." 17 Jan. 1938. *Arna Bontemps–Langston Hughes Letters 1925-1967.* Ed. Charles H. Nichols. New York: Dodd, 1980. 27-28. Print.

46. Personal letter   To cite a letter you received, start with the writer's name, followed by the descriptive phrase *Letter to the author* (not italicized), the date, and *MS* (manuscript).

> Cogswell, Michael. Letter to the author. 15 Mar. 2008. MS.

To cite someone else's unpublished personal letter, see no. 47.

47. Manuscripts, typescripts, and material in archives   Give the author, a title or description *(Letter, Notebook),* the date, the form (*MS* if handwritten, *TS* if typed), any identifying number, and the name and location of the institution housing the material. (Do not italicize any part of the citation.)

> Arendt, Hannah. Thinking and Moral Considerations: A Lecture.
> *date uncertain*
> [c. 1971]. TS. Library of Congress Manuscript Div., Washington.

> Pollack, Bracha. "A Man ahead of His Time." 1997. TS.

48. Legal source (print or online)   To cite a specific act, give its name, Public Law number, its Statutes at Large number, page range, the date it was enacted, and the medium.

> Patient Protection and Affordable Care Act. Pub. L. 111-48. 24 Stat.
>
> 119-1024. 23 Mar. 2010. Print.

To cite a law case, provide the name of the plaintiff and defendant, the case number, the court that decided the case, the date of the decision, and the medium.

PRINT

> United States v. Windsor. 12-307. Supreme Court of the US. 2013. Print.

WEB

> United States v. Windsor. 12-307. Supreme Court of the US. 2013.
>
> *Supreme Court Collection.* Legal Information Inst., Cornell U Law
>
> School, n.d. Web. 28 June 2013.

For more information about citing legal documents or from case law, MLA recommends consulting *The Bluebook: A Uniform System of Citation,* published by the Harvard Law Review Association.

Online sources

The examples that follow are based on guidelines for the citation of electronic sources in the seventh edition of the *MLA Handbook for Writers of Research Papers* (2009).

For scholarly journals published online, see no. 81. For periodical articles from an online database, see no. 84. Cite most other Web sources according to nos. 49 and 50. For works that also exist in another medium (for example, print), the MLA recommends including information about the other version in your citation. See nos. 70 through 80.

Basic Web sources

49. Web site or independent online work   Begin with the author, editor (*ed.*), compiler (*comp.*), director (*dir.*), performer (*perf.*), or translator (*trans.*), if any, of the site. Give the title (italicized), the version or edition (if any), the publisher or sponsor (or *n.p.*), publication date (or last update, or *n.d.*), medium, and your access date. (Use italics for the title only.) Citations 50 through 69 follow this format. The following examples are of a government-sponsored Web site, a professional site, and a personal site.

> *Cyber Crimes Center.* U.S. Immigration and Customs Enforcement,
>
> 2010. Web. 18 Dec. 2010.

> Garrett, Chris. *The Business of Blogging and New Media.* Headway,
>   *no date*
> n.d. Web. 20 Dec. 2010.

>   *no publisher*
> Johnson, Steven. *StevenBerlinJohnson.com.* N.p., 2002. Web. 19 Dec.
>
> 2010.

50. Page, selection, or part of a Web site or larger online work   Give the title of the part in quotation marks. If no title is available, use a descriptive term such as "Home page."

> Oliver, Rachel. "All About: Forests and Carbon Trading." *CNN.com.*
>
> Cable News Network, 11 Feb. 2008. Web. 14 Mar. 2008.

51. Course Web page   After the instructor's name, list the site title, then the department and school names.
                                          web site title
> Stilwell, Robynn. *Gateway to Film and Media Studies.* Dept. of Film
>
> Studies. Georgetown U, 27 Aug. 2014. Web. 20 Sept. 2014.

52. Personal page on a social networking site

> Kron, Susan. "Susan Kron." *Facebook.* Facebook, 24 Nov. 2013. Web.
>
> 25 Nov. 2013.

53. Blog   The first example cites an entire blog; the second refers to a specific entry from one.

McLennan, Doug. *Diacritical.* ArtsJournal, 2013. Web. 12 Mar. 2014.

McLennan, Doug. "Are Arts Leaders 'Cultural' Leaders?" *Diacritical.*
    ArtsJournal, 10 Aug. 2013. Web. 12 Mar. 2014.

54. Article in an online magazine or newspaper

di Giovanni, Janine. "Baby You Can Drive My Car." *Newsweek.com.* 8
    Nov. 2013. Web. 20 Feb. 2014.

Loveday, Morris. "Syrian Opposition Agrees to Peace Talks, with
    Conditions." *Washington Post.* Washington Post, 11 Nov. 2013.
    Web. 22 Dec. 2013.

sponsor

55. Online editorial   Include the word *Editorial* (not italicized) after the published title of the editorial.

"Saner Gun Laws." Editorial. *New York Times.* New York Times, 22
    Jan. 2011. Web. 23 Jan. 2011.

sponsor

56. Online letter to the editor   Include the word *Letter* (not italicized) after the name of the letter writer.

Garcia, Art. Letter. *ABQJournal.* Albuquerque Journal, 8 Nov. 2013.
    Web. 29 Dec. 2013.

sponsor

—the EVOLVING SITUATION

Web Addresses in MLA Citations

Include the URL (Web address) of an online source in a citation only if your reader would be unable to find the source without it (via a search engine). For example, basic citation information might not sufficiently identify your source if multiple versions of a document exist online without version numbers. Place a URL at the end of your citation in angle brackets, and end with a period.

Raeburn, Bruce Boyd, ed. *William Ransom Hogan Archive of New*
    Orleans Jazz. Tulane U, 13 Apr. 2006. Web. 11 May 2013.
    <http://jazz.tulane.edu/>.

If you need to divide a URL between lines, do so after a slash or double slash, and do not insert a hyphen. If the URL is long (more than one line of your text), give the URL of the site's search page. Do not make the URL a hyperlink.

CITING ELECTRONIC SOURCES IN MLA STYLE

- Begin with the name of the writer, editor, compiler, translator, director, or performer.
- Put the title of a short work in quotation marks.
- If there is no title, identify the genre of your source, such as *editorial* or *comment* (not italicized).
- Italicize the name of the publication or Web site. The online versions of some print magazines and newspapers have different titles than the print versions.
- Cite the date of publication or last update.
- For an online magazine or newspaper article or a Web original source, give the source (in quotation marks), the site title (italicized), version (if any), publisher or sponsor, date of publication, medium (Web), and access date. *(See p. 316.)*
- You may cite online sources that also appear in another medium with information about the other version *(see pp. 320-23)*. (Do not cite online versions of print newspapers and magazines in this way.)
- For a journal article, include the article title (in quotation marks), periodical title (italicized), volume and issue numbers, and inclusive page numbers or *n. pag.* (not italicized). Conclude with the medium (Web) and access date. *(See pp. 323-24.)*
- To cite a periodical article from an online database, provide the print publication information, the database title (italicized), the medium, and your access date.
- If the source is not divided into sections or pages, include *n. pag.* (not italicized) for "no pagination." Give the medium (Web).
- Include your most recent date of access to the specific source (not the general site).
- Conclude the citation with a URL only if readers may have difficulty finding the source without it *(see the Evolving Situation box on p. 317)*.

57. Online review

> Kot, Greg. "Gaga Aims for 'Artpop' but Falls Short." Rev. of *Artpop,* by Lady Gaga. *Chicago Tribune.* Chicago Tribune, 8 Nov. 2013. Web. 12 Nov. 2013.

sponsor

58. Online interview   See no. 40 for a print interview.

> Springsteen, Bruce. Interview by David Fricke. *Rollingstone.com.* Rolling Stone, 20 June 2013. Web. 22 June 2013.

59. Article in an online encyclopedia or other reference work Begin with the author's name if any is given.

> Greene, Brian R. "String Theory." *Encyclopaedia Britannica Online.*
>
> > Britannica, 2012. Web. 20 Nov. 2013.

60. Entry in a wiki A wiki is a collaborative creation, so no author should be listed. Begin with the title of the entry or file, the wiki name, the sponsor, the date of latest update, the medium, and your access date. Check with your instructor before using a wiki as a source.

> "Prince George of Cambridge." *Wikipedia.* The Wikimedia Foundation,
>
> > 27 June 2013. Web. 13 Dec. 2013.

61. Online visual (map, chart, or photograph—Web only) Include the genre—*Map, Chart,* or similar term—unless the image is a photograph (do not italicize). Begin with the artist's name, if one is given.

> "Freehold, New Jersey." Map. *Google Maps.* Google. 23 Sept. 2013.
>
> > Web. 3 Oct. 2013.
>
> Mazur, Kevin. "Taylor Swift Attends the 2013 American Music Awards
>
> > Powered in Los Angeles, California." *Rolling Stone.* Rolling Stone,
> >
> > 24 Nov. 2013. Web. 2 Jan. 2014.

62. Online slide show

> *Typhoon in the Philippines.* Slide program. *New York Times.* New York
>
> > Times, 11 Nov. 2013. Web. 2 Dec. 2013.

63. Online advertisement

> The Hermitage Club. Advertisement. *Pandora Internet Radio.* Web. 4
>
> > Apr. 2014.

64. Audio or video podcast

> Isbell, Jason. "Jason Isbell Locates His Musical Compass on
>
> > 'Southern.'" Interview by Terry Gross. *Fresh Air.* Natl. Public
> >
> > Radio. WHYY, Philadelphia, 17 July 2013. Web. 12 Nov. 2013.

65. Online video (Web original)

> Wesch, Michael. "Smile Because It Happened." *Digital Ethnology.*
>
> > Kansas State U, 14 June 2013. Web. 11 Feb. 2014.

For material posted online from a film, TV series, or other non-Web source, see nos. 77–80.

66. Posting to a news group, electronic forum, or e-mail discussion list Treat an archived posting as a Web source. Include the author and use the subject line as the title of the posting. If there is no subject, substitute *Online posting* (not italicized).

> Harbin, David. "Furtwangler's Beethoven 9 Bayreuth." *Opera-L*
>
> Archives. City U of New York, 3 Jan. 2008. Web. 12 May 2008.
>
> Pomeroy, Leslie K., Jr. "Racing with the Moon." *Rec.music.bluenote.*
>
> N.p., 4 May 2008. Web. 12 May 2008.

67. Synchronous (real-time) communication Cite the online transcript of a synchronous communication as you would an online lecture or shorter work on a Web site.

> Curran, Stuart, and Harry Rusche. "Discussion: Plenary Log 6.
>
> Third Annual Graduate Student Conference in Romanticism."
>
> *Prometheus Unplugged: Emory MOO.* Emory U, 20 Apr. 1996.
>
> Web. 4 Jan. 1999.

68. Online government publication other than the *Congressional Record* Begin with the name of the country, followed by the name of the sponsoring department, the title of the document, and the names (if listed) of the authors.

> United States. National Commission on Terrorist Attacks upon the
>
> United States. *The 9/11 Commission Report.* By Thomas H. Kean,
>
> et al. 5 Aug. 2004. Web. 12 May 2008.

69. *Congressional Record* (online or print) The *Congressional Record* has its own citation format, which is the same for print and online (apart from the medium and access date). Abbreviate the title, and include the date and page numbers. Give the medium (print or Web).

> *Cong. Rec.* 23 Sept. 2013: H5805-H5806. Web. 29 Oct. 2013.

Web sources also available in another medium

If an online work also appears in another medium (for example, print), the MLA recommends (but does not require) that your citation include information about the other version of the work. (Information about the editor or sponsor of the Web site or database is optional in this model.) If the facts about the other version of the source are not available, cite it as a basic Web source *(see nos. 49 and 50)*. (Articles on the Web sites of newspapers and magazines are never cited with print publication information. *For academic journals, see nos. 81–83 and 85.*)

70. Online or electronic book (e-book)   Cite a book you download from a database such as *Bartleby.com* as a print book *(no. 1)*. Instead of ending with *Print* (not italicized), give the Web site or database, the medium (Web), and your access date.

> Arter, Jared Maurice. *Echoes from a Pioneer Life.* Atlanta: Caldwell,
>
> *name and location (optional) of Web publisher*
> 1922. *Documenting the American South.* U of North Carolina,
>
> Chapel Hill. Web. 21 May 2008.

For an e-book that you download from an online bookseller or library, use the same format as a print book *(no. 1)*, but change the medium from *Print* to the kind of e-book (for example, *Kindle file*).

> McCann, Colum. *TransAtlantic.* New York: Random House, 2013.
>
> Kindle e-book file.

71. Selection from an online book   Add the title of the selection after the author. If the online version of the work lacks page numbers, use *n. pag.* instead (capitalize the *n* in *n. pag.* when it follows a period).

> Sandburg, Carl. "Chicago." *Chicago Poems.* New York: Holt, 1916.
>
> N. pag. *Bartleby.com.* Web. 11 May 2014.

72. Online dissertation   Give the Web site or database, the medium (Web), and your access date. Or cite as a basic Web source *(see nos. 49 and 50)*.

> Kosiba, Sara A. "A Successful Revolt? The Redefinition of Midwestern
>
> Literary Culture in the 1920s and 1930s." Diss. Kent State U,
>
> 2007. *OhioLINK.* Web. 12 May 2008.

73. Online pamphlet or brochure (also in print)   Cite as a book. Give the title of the Web site or database, the medium (Web), and your access date. Or cite as a basic Web source *(see no. 49 and 50)*.

> United States. Federal Trade Commission. Bureau of Consumer
>
> Protection. *Choosing a College: 8 Questions to Ask.* Washington:
>
> GPO, 2013. *US Federal Trade Commission.* Web. 4 Jan. 2014.

74. Online map or chart (also in print)   See no. 41 for a print map. Remove the medium; add the title of the database or Web site, the medium (Web), and your access date. *(See no. 61 for a Web-only map.)* Or cite as a basic Web source *(see nos. 49 and 50)*.

MTA New York City Subway. New York: Metropolitan Transit Authority,

2013. *MTA New York City Transit.* Web. 26 Dec. 2013.

75. Online cartoon (also in print)   See no. 42 for a cartoon. Remove the medium; add the database or site, the medium (Web), and your access date. Or cite as a basic Web source *(see nos. 49 and 50).*

Maslin, Michael. "The Weekend Can't Come Fast Enough." *New Yorker*

14 Oct. 2013: 50. *Cartoonbank.com.* Web. 13 Dec. 2013.

76. Online rendering of visual artwork   Cite as you would the original *(no. 102).* Remove the medium; add the database or Web site, the medium (Web), and your access date. Or cite as a basic Web source *(see nos. 49 and 50).*

Modigliani, Amedeo. *Reclining Nude.* 1919. Museum of Mod. Art, New

York. *MoMA.org.* Web. 8 Aug. 2013.

77. Online video or film (also on film or DVD)   See nos. 96 and 97 for a film or video. Remove the medium; add the database or site, the medium (Web), and your access date. Or cite as a basic Web source *(see nos. 49 and 50).*

Enron: The Smartest Guys in the Room. Dir. Alex Gibney. Magnolia

Pictures, 2005. *Internet Archive.* Web. 6 May 2014.

78. Online radio or television program   See no. 98 for a radio or television program. Remove the medium; add the database or site, the medium (Web), and your access date. Or cite as a basic Web source *(see nos. 49 and 50).*

"Bill Evans: 'Piano Impressionism.'" *Jazz Profiles.* Narr. Nancy Wilson.

Natl. Public Radio. WGBH, Boston, 27 Feb. 2008. *NPR.org.* Web.

16 Mar. 2014.

episode (not series)   *director of episode*   *series*   *performer in series*

"Local Ad." Dir. Jason Reitman. *The Office.* Perf. Steve Carrell. NBC.

WNBC, New York, 12 Dec. 2007. *NBC.com.* Web. 12 May 2014.

79. Online broadcast interview   See no. 99 for a broadcast interview. Remove the medium; add the database or site and the medium (Web), and give your access date. Or cite as a basic Web source *(see nos. 49 and 50).*

Ottolenghi, Yotam, and Sami Tamimi. Interview by Melissa Block. *All*

Things Considered. Natl. Public Radio. WBUR, Boston, 15 Oct.

2012. *NPR.org.* Web. 5 Apr. 2014.

80. Online archival material   Provide the information for the original. Add the Web site or database, the medium (Web), and your access date. Otherwise, cite as a basic Web source *(see nos. 49 and 50).*

> *date uncertain*
> Whitman, Walt. "After the Argument." [c. 1890]. The Charles E.
>
> Feinberg Collection of the Papers of Walt Whitman, Lib. of Cong.
>
> *The Walt Whitman Archive.* Web. 13 May 2013.

Works in online scholarly journals

Use the same format for all online journals, including those with print editions.

81. Article in an online journal   Give the author, the article title (in quotation marks) or a term such as *Editorial* (not italicized), the journal title (italicized), the volume number, issue number, date, and the inclusive page range (or *n. pag.*—not italicized—if the source lacks page numbers). Conclude with the medium (Web) and your access date.

> Neal, Michael, Katherine Bridgman, and Stephen J. McElroy.
>
> "Making Meaning at the Intersections: Developing a Digital
>
> Archive for Multimodal Research." *Kairos* 17.3 (2013): 1-6.
>
> Web. 4 May 2014.

82. Editorial or letter to the editor in an online journal

> Heitmeyer, Wilhelm, et al. "Letter from the Editors." Editorial.
>
> *International Journal of Conflict and Violence* 1.1 (2007): n. pag.
>
> Web. 14 May 2013.
>
> Destaillats, Frédéric, Julie Moulin, and Jean-Baptiste Bezelgues. Letter.
>
> *Nutrition & Metabolism* 4.10 (2007): n. pag. Web. 14 May 2013.

83. Review in an online journal

> Friedman, Edward H. Rev. of *Transnational Cervantes,* by William
>
> Childers. *Cervantes: Bulletin of the Cervantes Society of America*
>
> 27.2 (2007): 41-43. Web. 13 May 2008.

Works from online databases

In addition to information about the print version of the source, provide the title of the database (in italics), the medium (Web), and your access date.

84. Newspaper or magazine article from an online database

Blumenfeld, Larry. "House of Blues." *New York Times* 11 Nov. 2007:
A33. *Academic Universe.* Web. 31 Dec. 2013.

Farley, Christopher John. "Music Goes Global." *Time* 15 Sept. 2001:
4+. *General OneFile.* Web. 31 Dec. 2013.

85. Journal article or abstract from an online database

Nielson, Aldon Lynn. "A Hard Rain." *Callaloo* 25.1 (2002): 135-45.
Academic Search Premier. Web. 17 Mar. 2014.

Dempsey, Nicholas P. "Hook-Ups and Train Wrecks: Contextual
Parameters and the Coordination of Jazz Interactions." *Symbolic
Interaction* 31.1 (2008): 57-75. Abstract. *Academic Search
Premier.* Web. 17 Mar. 2014.

86. E-mail Include the author, the subject line (if any) in quotation
marks, the descriptive term *Message to* (not italicized), and the name
of the recipient, the date of the message, and the medium.

Morgan, Rocky. "Re: Summer Arts Walk." Message to T. Martinez.
11 July 2013. E-mail.

Other electronic (non-Web) sources

87. A digital file stored on your computer Record the file format as
the medium (for example, *XML file*). If the format is unclear, use the
designation *Digital file.* Do not italicize the medium. Use the citation
format of the most closely related print or nonprint source. Cite local
word-processor documents as manuscripts *(see no. 47),* and note the
date last modified if you wish to cite a specific version.

McNutt, Lea. "The Origination of Avian Flight." 2008. *Microsoft Word* file.

Hoffman, Esther. "Louis Armstrong and Joe Glaser: More Than Meets
the Eye." File last modified on 9 May 2008. *Microsoft Word* file.

88. A PDF Treat local PDFs as published, and follow the closest
print model.

United States. Social Security Administration. *Disability Benefits
for Wounded Warriors.* Washington: US Social Security
Administration, 2013. PDF file.

89. An audio file   Use the format for a sound recording *(see no. 100)*. Record the file format as the medium.

> Holiday, Billie. "God Bless the Child." *God Bless the Child.* Columbia,
>
> > 1936. MP3 file.

90. A visual file   Cite local image files as works of visual art *(see no. 102)*. Record the file format as the medium.

> Gursky, Andreas. *Times Square, New York.* 1997. Museum of Mod. Art,
>
> > New York. JPEG file.

91. CD-ROM or DVD-ROM published periodically   If a CD-ROM or DVD-ROM is revised on a regular basis, include in its citation the author, title of the work, any print publication information, medium, title of the CD-ROM or DVD-ROM (if different from the original title), vendor, and date of electronic publication.

> Ross, Alex. "Separate Worlds, Linked Electronically." *New York Times*
>
> > 29 Apr. 1996, late ed.: A22. CD-ROM. *New York Times Ondisc.*
> >
> > UMI-ProQuest. Dec. 1996.

92. CD-ROM or DVD-ROM not published periodically   Works on CD-ROM or DVD-ROM are usually cited like books or parts of books if they are not revised periodically. The medium and the name of the vendor (if different from the publisher) appear after the publication data. For a work that also exists in print, give the print publication information followed by the medium, electronic publisher, and date of electronic publication.

> *print publisher omitted for pre-1900 work*
>
> Jones, Owen. *The Grammar of Ornament.* London, 1856. CD-ROM.
>
> > Octavo, 1998.

If there are multiple discs, list the total number of discs at the end of the entry, or give the number of the disc you reviewed if you used only one.

93. Computer software   Include the title, version, publisher, and date in your text or in an explanatory note. Do not include an entry in your works-cited list.

94. Video game   In your entry, include the title, version, publisher, date of publication, and medium.

> *Guardians of Middle-earth.* Burbank: Warner Bros. Interactive
>
> > Entertainment, 2013. Digital file.

Audiovisual and other nonprint sources

95. Film   Begin with the title (italicized) unless you want to highlight a particular contributor. For a film, cite the director and the featured performer(s) or narrator (*Perf.* or *Narr.,* neither italicized), followed by the distributor and year. Conclude with the medium.

> *The Big Lebowski.* Dir. Joel Coen and Ethan Coen. Perf. Jeff Bridges, John
>
> Goodman, and Julianne Moore. Gramercy Pictures, 1998. Film.

96. DVD or Blu-Ray   See no. 95. Include the original film's release date if relevant. Conclude with the medium (for example, DVD, Blu-Ray).

> *Lawrence of Arabia.* Dir. David Lean. Perf. Peter O'Toole and Omar
>
> Sharif. 1962. Sony, 2012. Blu-Ray.

97. Personal or archival video or audio recording   Give the date recorded and the location of the recording.

> Adderley, Nat. Interview by Jimmy Owens. Schomburg Center for
>
> Research in Black Culture, New York Public Lib. 2 Apr. 1993.
>
> Videocassette.

98. Radio or television program   Give the episode title (in quotation marks), the program title (italicized), the name of the series (if any), the network (call letters), the city, the broadcast date, and the medium (*Radio* or *Television,* neither italicized). Name individuals if relevant.

> "Scientists Turn to Crowdfunding for Research." *Here and Now.* Natl.
>
> Public Radio, KUOW, Seattle, 17 Sept. 2013. Radio.
>
> *episode [not series]   director of episode   series   performer in series*
> "Game On." Dir. David Nutter. *Homeland.* Perf. Morgan Saylor.
>
> Showtime. SHOW, New York, 20 Oct. 2013. Television.

99. Broadcast interview   Give the name of the person interviewed, followed by the word *Interview* (not italicized) and the name of the interviewer if you know it. End with information about the broadcast and the medium.

> Sotomayor, Sonia. Interview by Jon Stewart. *The Daily Show with Jon*
>
> *Stewart.* Comedy Central, 21 Jan. 2013. Television.

100. Sound recording   Start with the composer, conductor, or performer, depending on your focus. Include the following information: the work's title (italicized); the artist(s), if not already mentioned; the manufacturer; the date of release; and the medium. In the first example, an individual song on a recording is noted (in quotation marks) before the album title.

> Frank Turner. "The Way I Tend to Be." *Tape Deck Heart*. BMG Rights,
>
> 2013. MP3 file.

> Foxes. *Glorious.* Sign of the Times/Sony Music, 2014. CD.

101. Musical composition   Include only the composer and title, unless you are referring to a published score (see the third example). Published scores are treated like books except that the date of composition appears after the title. Titles of instrumental pieces are not italicized when known only by form and number, unless the reference is to a published score.

> Ellington, Duke. *Satin Doll.*

> Haydn, Franz Josef. Symphony No. 94 in G Major.
>
> *reference to a published score*
> Haydn, Franz Josef. *Symphony No. 94 in G Major.* 1791. Ed. H. C.
>
> Robbins Landon. Salzburg: Haydn-Mozart, 1965. Print.

102. Artwork   Provide the artist's name, the title of the artwork (italicized), the date (if unknown, write *n.d.*), the medium, and the institution or private collection and city (or *n.p.*) in which the artwork can be found. For anonymous collectors, write *Private collection,* and omit city (do not write *n.p.*).

> Palley, Diane. *Choose Life.* 1994. Papercut. Private collection, Boston.

103. Personal, telephone, or e-mail interview   Begin with the person interviewed, followed by *Personal interview, Telephone interview,* or *E-mail interview* (not italicized) and the date of the interview. *(See no. 40 for a published interview.)*

> Greene, Gigi. Personal interview. 7 May 2013.

104. Lecture or speech   Give the speaker, the title (in quotation marks), the name of the forum or sponsor, the location, and the date. Conclude with a description such as *Speech, Lecture,* or *Presentation* (not italicized). If you access the speech online, include that information and replace the medium *Speech* with *Web.*

> Beaufort, Anne. "All Talk, No Action? Or, Does Transfer Really Happen
>
> after Reflective Practice?" Conference on College Composition
>
> and Communication. Hilton San Francisco. 13 March 2009.
>
> Presentation.

105. Live performance   To cite a play, opera, dance performance, or concert, begin with the title; followed by the authors *(By)*; information such as the director *(Dir.)* and major performers; the site; the city; the performance date; and the word *Performance* (not italicized).

> *Kinky Boots.* By Harvey Fierstein and Cyndi Lauper. Dir. Jerry Mitchell.
>
> Al Hirschfeld Theatre, New York. 18 July 2013. Performance.

106. Publication in more than one medium   If you are citing a publication that consists of several different media, list alphabetically all of the media you consulted. Follow the citation format of the medium you used primarily (which is "print" in the example).

> Black, Christopher, and Mark Anest. *McGraw-Hill's SAT 2014 Edition.*
>
> New York: McGraw, 2013. Kindle, print, Web.

CHAPTER 28

MLA Style: Explanatory Notes and Acknowledgments

Explanatory notes are used to cite multiple sources for borrowed material or to give readers supplemental information. You can also use explanatory notes to acknowledge people who helped you with research and writing. Acknowledgments are a courteous gesture. If you acknowledge someone's assistance in your explanatory notes, be sure to send that person a copy of your research project.

The example that follows is a note that provides additional information—examples of blogs run by companies and organizations.

TEXT

This definition points out an important aspect of blogs: some are run by companies and organizations, such as the *New York Times* and *Chicago Tribune.*[1]

NOTE

1. The *Tribune*'s blogs offer a wide range of topics. Some examples include "Julie's Health Club," "The Theater Loop," the sports blog "The Red Card," and the news blog "Voice of the People" (www.chicagotribune.com).

CHAPTER 29

MLA Style: Format

The following guidelines will help you prepare your research project in the format recommended by the seventh edition of the *MLA Handbook for Writers of Research Papers*. For an example of a research paper that has been prepared using MLA style, see pages 331–41.

Materials   Back up your final draft on a flash drive, CD, DVD, or on one of the many cloud-based sites often available for free or by subscription. Use a high-quality printer and high-quality, white 8½-by-11-inch paper. Put the printed pages together with a paper clip.

Heading and title   Include a separate title page if your instructor requires one. In the upper left-hand corner of the first page of the paper, one inch from the top and side, enter on separate, double-spaced lines your name, your instructor's name, the course number, and the date. Double-space between the date and the title and between the title and the first line of text, as well as throughout your paper. The title should be centered and properly capitalized *(see p. 331)*. Do not italicize the title or put it in quotation marks or bold type.

If your instructor requires a title page, prepare it according to his or her instructions. If your instructor requires a final outline, place it between the title page and the first page of the paper.

Margins and spacing   Use one-inch margins all around, except for the top right-hand corner, where the page number goes. Your right margin should be ragged (not "justified," or even).

Double-space lines throughout, including in quotations, notes, and the works-cited list. Indent the first word of each paragraph one-half inch (or five spaces) from the left margin. For block quotations, indent one inch (or ten spaces) from the left.

Page numbers   Put your last name and the page number in the upper right-hand corner of the page, one-half inch from the top and flush with the right margin.

Visuals   Place visuals (tables, charts, graphs, and images) close to the place in your text where you refer to them. Label and number tables consecutively *(Table 1, Table 2),* and give each one an explanatory caption; put this information above the table. The term *Figure* (abbreviated *Fig.*) is used to label all other kinds of visuals, except for musical illustrations, which are labeled *Example* (abbreviated *Ex.*). Place a figure or an example caption below each visual. Below all visuals, cite the source of the material, and provide explanatory notes as needed. *(For more on using visuals effectively, see Chapter 6: Drafting Text and Visuals.)*

the EVOLVING SITUATION

Electronic Submission of Assignments

Some instructors may request that you submit your project electronically. Keep these tips in mind:

- Confirm the appropriate procedure for submission.
- Find out in advance your instructor's preferred format for the submission of documents. *Always ask permission before sending an attached document to anyone.*
- If you are asked to send a document as an attachment, save your document as a "rich text format" (.rtf) file or in PDF format.
- As a courtesy, run a virus scan on your file before sending it electronically or submitting it on a disk or CD-ROM.

CHAPTER 30

Sample Research Project in MLA Style

As a first-year college student, Kris Washington wrote the following research project for her composition course. She knew very little about blogging before beginning her research.

CONSIDER YOUR SITUATION

Author: Kris Washington

Type of writing: Research report

Purpose: To investigate the effect of blogging on traditional forms of news reporting

Stance: Informed and reasonable

Audience: Students, instructors, consumers of both types of media

Medium: Print, as text attachment, part of e-portfolio

Washington writes: Although I didn't know very much about blogging as I began this project, as I worked on this research report, I learned about the effects it has had—and continues to have—on traditional journalism. You can see the impact of my research in the information I have shared.

1"   ½"

Kris Washington

1"

Professor Spaulding

English 120

7 December 2013

Place your name, your professor's name, your course title, and the date at the left margin, double-spaced.

Breaking News:

Blogging's Impact on Traditional and New Media

Title centered, not italicized.

In previous decades, when people wanted to know what was happening in the world, they turned to the daily newspaper, the radio, or their television sets. Today, we are more likely to go online where a simple *Google* search on any subject can produce thousands of hits and open doors to seemingly limitless sources of information; or, with even less effort, we may receive tweets or email alerts with embedded links that lead us to news reports. While there are still many online news sources, much of our information comes from online journals known as blogs, which have redefined the concept of news and increased the speed with which we receive it. In the blogosphere—the vast assortment of these individual Web sites on the Internet—a wide range of voices provides us with news and opinion, which has led to a movement of citizen journalism, or news for and by the people. Bloggers frame a single event, such as a devastating storm or a politician's blunder, according to various political, geographical, economic, and philosophical positions and are often able to publish or post their reportage within minutes. In fact, multimedia corporations have come to depend on bloggers to deliver the most recent developments on global events and increasingly have found ways to incorporate information from blogs, tweets, and other social media into

Double-spaced throughout.

Establishes a context for argument.

Note use of transitional expression.

Washington 2

traditional news reports. To survive, journalism must blend
traditional forms of reporting with blogs, tweets, and other
new methods that get news and opinion to the people
instantaneously and universally.

Thesis statement.

Encyclopaedia Britannica defines a *blog,* short for *Web log,*
as an "online journal where an individual, group, or corporation
presents a record of activities, thoughts, or beliefs" ("Blog").
This definition points out an important aspect of blogs: some
are run by companies and organizations, such as the *New York
Times* and the *Chicago Tribune;*[1] however, many are
maintained by people not necessarily affiliated with traditional
news outlets. In his book, *Here Comes Everybody: The Power
of Organizing without Organizations,* New York University
professor and media consultant Clay Shirky explains how the
proliferation of blogs is affecting news: "The change isn't a
shift from one kind of news institution to another, but rather in
the definition of news" (65-66). Blogging has ushered in a
new set of consumer expectations for immediate news
coverage distributed widely on a broad range of topics.

Online encyclopedia definition; development by definition (see pp. 63–64).

Superscript number indicates an explanatory note.

Development by classification (see p. 62).

Bloggers are able to decide what is newsworthy and they have
the ability to spread that information globally at very little
cost. In a report published online, C. W. Anderson, Emily Bell,
and Shirky explain that blogs and other forms of social media
allow for "superdistribution," meaning that stories—including
those published by smaller outlets—can reach a wider
audience than ever before and at very little expense (14).
Rather than pay subscription fees to print newspapers,
magazines, and journals, many people are turning to the
Internet for free and immediate information.

Paraphrase of a source mixed with a direct quotation of the phrase "superdistribution." Signal phrase names authors and adds brief description of source, enhancing authors' credibility.

Washington 3

With the rise of blogs and the abundance of free online information, media companies are finding it increasingly difficult to maintain funding for traditional news reporting. This dramatic increase of free information online is reflected in the alarming numbers with which newspapers have been cutting staff. According to Pew Research Center's Project for Excellence in Journalism, newsroom employment is down 30% since 2000 (see fig. 1) (4). Newspapers were slow to make their content available on mobile devices, and advertising revenue has also been slow to follow. Without that revenue, traditional news companies will be limited in their abilities to print and distribute news and hire staff. Alternatively, the proliferation of user-generated content introduces what media scholar Lev Manovich refers to as "a new economics of media," which means that even when produced on a much smaller scale, new media hold the potential to generate higher revenues than more traditional outlets (320). Anderson, Bell, and Shirky suggest that news organizations "should master working with amateurs, crowds, machines or other partners to keep cost low and leverage high" and "should assume that cost control is the central discipline" (116). Clearly, a partnership between traditional and new media is essential to the future of journalism.

If the public is receiving more and more of its news from blogs and other electronic means, why does the loss of newsroom employees matter so much? Traditional forms of reporting, such as newspapers and televised news broadcasts, have always depended on the objectivity and credibility of their journalists, the reliability of their sources,

> Support by key fact and reference to visual.

> Page number provided at the end of quotation; source's names are included in the introduction to the quotation so no need to restate their names in the parenthetical citation.

> Restatement of thesis.

> Focus introduced.

Washington 4

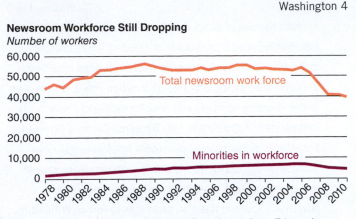

Fig. 1 Newsroom Workforce Still Dropping. Graph from Edmonds, Rick, Emily Guskin, Mark Jurkowitz, and Amy Mitchell, "The State of the News Media 2013" (Pew Research Center's Project for Excellence in Journalism, 18 July 2013; Web; 25 Nov. 2013).

Figure number and caption explaining information in the visual, followed by information about its source.

and the extensive research and fact checking that inform every news story. Blogs are a fast and convenient way to publicize current issues and events, but it's questionable if blogs can offer information as reliable as that of traditional news organizations. For example, on the *New York Times* blog *The Choice,*[2] high-school senior Leobardo Espinoza, Jr. reported on his post-graduate plans in a post titled "Gap Year Now or Study Abroad Later?" While the sources he cites—family and friends who have weighed in on his choice—have valid opinions, none are education experts. Neither his posting nor the comments are backed by the comprehensive, objective research that informed an Australian newspaper article on the same subject. In "Gap-Year Travel Brings

Signal phrase introduces quotation; title is used in parenthetical citation because source does not include an author's name; no page reference is needed because source is a single page.

Development by contrast (see pp. 64–65).

SOURCE: American Society of News Editors, Newsroom Employment Census, 2010. NOTE: ASNE dates its data according to the release date. Pew Research presents the data according to the year the data were compiled. Minorities include Native Americans. African Americans, Latinos, and Asian Americans.

Washington 5

Students Back to Learning," reporter John Ross cites recent research and explains how a gap year may positively or negatively affect the college experience. As an Australian editorial recently stated, "Hard-core media values—truth, accuracy, fairness, balance, perspective, objectivity— are being lost at precisely the wrong time, as the news media faces the challenges of falling revenue, distracted audiences and a loss of skilled practitioners" ("Lost in the Twitterverse"). This shift away from expert reporting to citizen journalism means that audiences must be more discerning when deciding what to believe.

As the credibility of online sources has been called into question, the value of subject experts has increased. Amateur journalists do not guarantee fact checking and do not always have professional experience relevant to the topics they cover. Professional journalist Tony Rogers points out that "most bloggers don't produce news stories on their own. Instead they comment on news stories already out there— stories produced by journalists." While this is often true, bloggers can also break, or at least advance, a news story. For example, in their report "Post-Industrial Journalism: Adapting to the Present," Anderson, Bell, and Shirky contend that the bike-racing blog *NYVelocity* covered the Lance Armstrong performance enhancement story better than the "professional" press (20). Furthermore, today an event can become news before members of the press begin to cover it, and in fact they may cover it only after their audience has become aware of it another way (Shirky, *Here Comes Everybody* 64-65). Rogers does not discount all blogs, but he

MLA in-text citation: author (Shirky) named in parentheses because his name is not included in a signal phrase; title identifies which one of two works by Shirky is cited.

Washington 6

recognizes the effort professional journalists make to become field experts:

> Many reporters, especially those at the largest news organizations, have followed their beats for years. So whether it's a Washington bureau chief writing about White house politics, or a longtime sports columnist covering the latest draft picks, chances are they can write with authority because they know the subject. Now, some bloggers are experts on their chosen topic as well. But many more are amateur observers who follow developments from afar.

Contrary to Rogers's value of professional journalism, Anderson, Bell, and Shirky claim, "The way news is most effectively and reliably relayed is by those with a combination of deep knowledge of the subject and a responsiveness to audience requirements" (20). This definition not only applies to professionals but to knowledgeable bloggers, as well. They offer the example of the infamous Bernie Madoff Ponzi scheme as a missed opportunity. Investor Harry Markopolos provided the Securities and Exchange Commission with "detailed and accurate warnings of wrongdoing," which the SEC failed to act on (qtd. in Anderson, Bell, and Shirky 20). Later, investment blogger Ray Pellecchia wondered in a blog post if Markopolos could have stopped Madoff with a blog of his own. Such a question speaks powerfully to the role that blogging increasingly plays in breaking news stories that traditional reporters then carry forward. Whatever opinion one holds on credibility in reporting, most everyone can agree that journalism is no longer a specialized field.

Block quotation is introduced by a complete sentence, ending in a colon; quotation is indented one inch; page reference is not needed for reference from one-page work.

Anderson et al. is the source of the second quotation, so it is not necessary to repeat those names in the parenthetical citation.

Support by anecdote (see p. 136).

Washington 7

As news producers become more widespread and less specialized, the line between mainstream journalism and citizen journalism has become increasingly blurred. Mainstream media companies, such as *Newsweek,* BBC, and CNN, have started their own blogs and have even adopted other forms of media like *Twitter* in an effort to expand their audience base.[2] FOX News Chicago's Web page even asks viewers to "[b]ecome a member of the FOX 32 News team" by sending in photos or videos of breaking news, which experienced newscasters then weave into their broadcasts.[3] No longer at the mercy of those in a position to seek out and select what makes the news, citizens now have more authority, through the power of blogging, to investigate and publicize the events they feel deserve attention.

> Presents a claim plus supporting evidence.

In one of the most comprehensive studies to date comparing the purpose of citizen journalism Web sites to that of newspaper Web sites, journalism experts Stephen Lacy, Margaret Duffy, Daniel Riffe, Esther Thorson, and Ken Fleming conclude that citizen journalism cannot sufficiently replace, but should instead accompany, newspaper sites (42). The relationship between traditional and new media outlets will develop as people continue to demand up-to-the-minute reporting on a vast array of issues. Bloggers and other social media users might post the first reports of a news story, but these reports often require additional fact checking. When newspapers and news stations pick up these stories, they must carefully review them in order to distinguish facts from rumors. While bloggers and amateur reporters recognize the need for credibility, mainstream

Washington 8

media corporations also value amateurs' ability to create and spread news quickly. Increasingly, both groups are realizing that they need to work together by expanding on the other's stories. Shirky sees the cooperation between professionals and amateurs as necessary to the survival of journalism: "Many of these models will fail. . . . [O]ver time, the collection of new experiments that do work might give us the journalism we need" ("Newspapers" 29).

The evolution of journalism toward citizen-driven news has opened doors for those who both produce and consume the news. In the waning years of the newspaper, traditional news outlets have learned a harsh reality: consumers want the news now, and they want it in an interactive format. Blogging has proved to be a valuable tool for breaking news, but it has also been responsible for spreading invalid information to the public. Though traditional news sources are extremely valuable, corporations have long controlled how much the public knows. With the onset of the digital age, blogs have been instrumental in this shift toward a freer, more immediate, widespread, and comprehensive experience of world events. The integration of fast-paced digital production with the carefully edited and fact-checked print news would allow traditional news corporations to stay afloat while citizens participate in the gathering and dissemination of the news.

Period followed by three ellipsis points indicates omission in the quotation. Capitalization of the first word following the ellipses is adjusted with brackets (see pp. 566–67). Parenthetical citation precedes the period.

Conclusion with qualified version of thesis.

Notes

1. The *Tribune*'s blogs offer a wide range of topics. Some examples include "Julie's Health Club," "The Theater Loop," the sports blog "The Red Card," and the news blog "Voice of the People" (www.chicagotribune.com).

2. A recent post titled "*The Choice* Blog's Valediction" reported that *The Choice* was recently discontinued. However, it will "continue to serve student readers at *The Learning Network,* a blog dedicated to teaching and learning."

3. Similar statements can be found on most news Web sites.

New page, title centered; first line of each note indented one-half inch.

Cites additional sources, by way of example.

Cites by title additional source that provides supplemental information.

Cites information supplemental to the essay.

Title centered; entries
in alphabetical order
by author's last name
or, if no author, by
first important word in
the title.

Source: online
report by three
authors.

Source: online
encyclopedia.

Source: online
report by more
than three
authors.

Source: blog.

Source: jour-
nal article by
more than
three authors,
in online
database.

Source: one-
page newspa-
per article.

Source: jour-
nal article in
print.

Source: one-
page article on
a Web site.

Source: news-
paper article.

Washington 10

Works Cited

Anderson, C. W., Emily Bell, and Clay Shirky. *Post-Industrial
    Journalism: Adapting to the Present.* New York: Tow Center for
    Digital Journalism, Columbia University, n.d. Web. 25 Nov. 2013.

"Blog." *Encyclopaedia Britannica Online.* Encyclopaedia
    Britannica, 2010. Web. 22 Nov. 2013.

Edmonds, Rick, et al. *The State of the News Media 2013: An
    Annual Report on American Journalism.* Pew Research
    Center's Project for Excellence in Journalism, 2013. Web. 25
    Nov. 2013.

Espinoza, Leobardo, Jr. "Gap Year Now or Study Abroad
    Later?" *The Choice.* New York Times, 21 Mar. 2013. Web.
    25 Nov. 2013.

Lacy, Stephen, et al. "Citizen Journalism Web Sites Complement
    Newspapers." *Newspaper Research Journal* 31.2 (2010):
    34-46. *Academic Search Elite.* Web. 15 Nov. 2013.

"Lost in the Twitterverse." Editorial. *The Australian.* News Corp
    Australia, 13 Nov. 2013. Web. 22 Nov. 2013.

Manovich, Lev. "The Practice of Everyday (Media) Life: From
    Mass Consumption to Mass Cultural Production?" *Critical
    Inquiry* 35.2 (2009): 319-31. Print.

Pellecchia, Ray. "Could a Markopolos Blog Have Stopped
    Madoff?" *Seeking Alpha.* Seeking Alpha, 4 Feb. 2009. Web.
    24 Nov. 2013.

Rogers, Tony. "Can Bloggers Replace Professional Journalists?"
    About.com Journalism. About.com, n.d. Web. 25 Nov. 2013.

Ross, John. "Gap-Year Travel Brings Students Back to Learning."
    The Australian. News Corp Australia, 17 Apr. 2013. Web. 25
    Nov. 2013.

Washington 11

Shirky, Clay. *Here Comes Everybody: The Power of Organizing without Organizations.* New York: Penguin, 2008. Print.

---. "Newspapers and Thinking the Unthinkable." *Risk Management* May 2009: 24-29. *Academic Search Elite.* Web. 21 Nov. 2013.

"Upload Your Photos and Videos." FOX 32 News, n.d. Web. 25 Nov. 2013.

Source: entire book.

Source: magazine article in online database; three hyphens are used instead of repeating author's name.

7

APA
Documentation Style

*Take the whole range of imaginative literature, and we
are all wholesale borrowers. In every matter that relates to
invention, to use, or beauty or form, we are borrowers.*

–Wendell Phillips

This detail of a Mayan vase shows a scribe at work. Scribes—who documented the
deeds of rulers—were esteemed in the great Mayan cities that flourished on the
Yucatan Peninsula from around 100 to 900 C.E.

7 APA Documentation Style

APA style requires writers to provide bibliographic information about their sources in a list of references. To format entries for the list of references correctly, it is important to know what kind of source you are citing. The directory on pages 360–361 will help you find the appropriate sample to use as a model. Alternatively, you can use the charts on the pages that follow. Answering the questions in the charts will usually lead you to the sample entry you need. If you cannot find what you are looking for, consult your instructor.

 Sections dealing with visual rhetoric. For a complete listing, see the Quick Guide to Key Resources at the back of this book.

The Elements of an APA Reference Entry:

Book

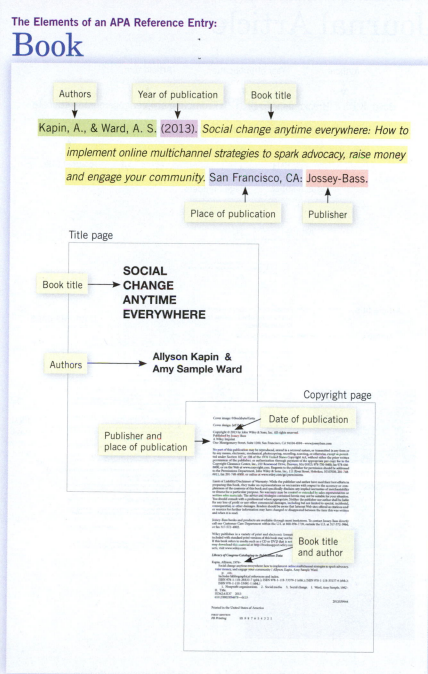

> Authors | Year of publication | Book title
>
> Kapin, A., & Ward, A. S. (2013). *Social change anytime everywhere: How to implement online multichannel strategies to spark advocacy, raise money and engage your community.* San Francisco, CA: Jossey-Bass.
>
> Place of publication | Publisher

Title page

Book title ➤ SOCIAL CHANGE ANYTIME EVERYWHERE

Authors ➤ Allyson Kapin & Amy Sample Ward

Copyright page

Date of publication

Publisher and place of publication

Book title and author

Information for a book citation can be found on the book's title and copyright pages.

The Elements of an APA Reference Entry:

Journal Article

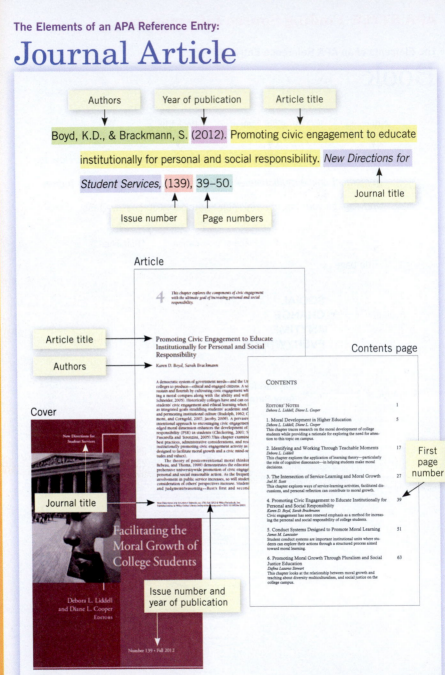

Authors → Year of publication → Article title

Boyd, K.D., & Brackmann, S. (2012). Promoting civic engagement to educate institutionally for personal and social responsibility. *New Directions for Student Services,* (139), 39–50.

Journal title

Issue number   Page numbers

Article

4 *This chapter explores the components of civic engagement with the ultimate goal of increasing personal and social responsibility.*

Article title →

Promoting Civic Engagement to Educate Institutionally for Personal and Social Responsibility

Authors →

Karen D. Boyd, Sarah Brackmann

Contents page

CONTENTS

EDITORS' NOTES   1
Debora L. Liddell, Diane L. Cooper

1. Moral Development in Higher Education   5
Debora L. Liddell, Diane L. Cooper
This chapter traces research on the moral development of college students while providing a rationale for exploring the need for attention to this topic on campus.

2. Identifying and Working Through Teachable Moments   17
Debora L. Liddell
This chapter explores the application of learning theory—particularly the role of cognitive dissonance—in helping students make moral decisions.

3. The Intersection of Service-Learning and Moral Growth   27
Joel H. Scott
This chapter explores ways of service-learning activities, facilitated discussions, and personal reflection can contribute to moral growth.

4. Promoting Civic Engagement to Educate Institutionally for Personal and Social Responsibility   39
Karen D. Boyd, Sarah Brackmann
Civic engagement has seen renewed emphasis as a method for increasing the personal and social responsibility of college students.

5. Conduct Systems Designed to Promote Moral Learning   51
James M. Lancaster
Student conduct systems are important institutional units where students can explore their actions through a structured process aimed toward moral learning.

6. Promoting Moral Growth Through Pluralism and Social Justice Education   63
Dafina Lazarus Stewart
This chapter looks at the relationship between moral growth and teaching about diversity multiculturalism, and social justice on the college campus.

First page number →

Cover

New Directions for Student Services

Journal title →

Facilitating the Moral Growth of College Students

Debora L. Liddell and Diane L. Cooper
EDITORS

Issue number and year of publication →

Number 139 • Fall 2012

In this journal, the information needed for a citation appears on the first page of an article. Some journals list their contents and publication information on the cover.

The Elements of an APA Reference Entry:

Online

Journal Article with DOI Assigned

Authors — Plummer, C. A., Ai, A. L., Lemieux, C., Richardson, R., Dey, S., Taylor, P., . . .

Year of publication — Hyun-Jun, K (2008).

Article title — Volunteerism among social work students during Hurricanes Katrina and Rita.

Journal title — Journal of Social Service Research

Volume number / Issue number — 34(3),

Page numbers — 55–77.

Database title — doi:10.1080/01488370802086328.

If the article has a DOI (Digital Object Identifier), the citation does not require a URL. This article lists the DOI beneath the volume and issue numbers. For journals paginated by issue, include the issue number in parentheses after the volume number. For an article with more than seven authors, list the first six, followed by an ellipsis mark (three spaced periods) and the last author's name.

The Elements of an APA Works-Cited Entry:

Short Work on a
Web Site

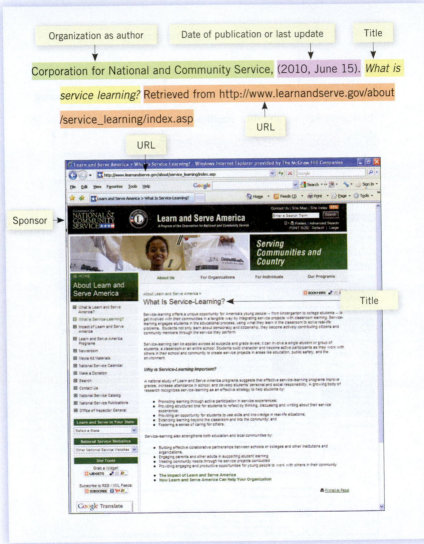

Organization as author

Date of publication or last update

Title

Corporation for National and Community Service, (2010, June 15). *What is service learning?* Retrieved from http://www.learnandserve.gov/about /service_learning/index.asp

URL

URL

Sponsor

Title

The above citation derives from the APA model for an online report. You may need to search on a site to find author, date, and other information. List an individual author's last name first. If no date is given, include *n.d.* Supplemental information about format may follow the title. Here, the author is also the Web site sponsor (Corporation for National and Community Service). When the author is not the sponsor, name the sponsor after "Retrieved from" (see no. 56 on p. 372). Include the home page URL for magazine, newspaper, and journal articles (lacking a DOI). Give the full URL for other sources.

APA STYLE Identifying and Documenting Sources

Entries in a List of References:

Books

❓ Is Your Source a Complete Book?

NO **YES**

Go to this entry on page

Is it a complete book with one named author?

Is it the only book by this author that you are citing?	**1** 358
Are you citing more than one book by this author?	**4** 359
Does it also have an editor or translator?	**5, 9,** 359, 362

Is it a complete book with more than one named author? — **2** 359

Is it a complete book without a named author or editor?

Is the author an organization?	**3** 359
Is the author anonymous or unknown?	**12** 362

Is it a complete book with an editor or a translator?

Is there an editor instead of an author?	**5** 359
Is it a translation?	**9** 362
Is it an entire reference work?	**11** 362

Is it a complete book with a volume or an edition number?

Is it part of a multivolume work (e.g., Volume 3)?	**14** 362
Does it have an edition number (e.g., Second Edition)?	**13** 362

Is it a republished work (e.g., a classic study)? — **15** 363

❓ Is Your Source Part of a Book?

NO **YES**

Go to this entry on page

Is it a work from an anthology or a chapter in an edited book?	**6** 359
Is it an article in a reference work (e.g., an encyclopedia)?	**10** 362
Is it a published presentation from a conference?	**27** 366
Is it an introduction, preface, foreword, or afterword?	**8** 362
Is it a published letter?	**30** 367

Check the next panel or the directory on pages 360–61 or consult your instructor.

Entries in a List of References:

Print
Periodicals or Other Print Sources

? Is Your Source from a Journal, a Magazine, or a Newspaper?

NO   YES

Go to this entry on page

Is it from an academic journal?

Does the journal have a volume number?	**16**	363
Is your source an abstract (a brief summary) of an article?	**18**	364

Is it from a magazine?

Is the magazine published monthly?	**20**	365
Is the magazine published weekly?	**20**	365
Is your source a letter to the editor?	**22**	365
Is it a review (e.g., a review of a book or film)?	**24**	365
Is it an interview?	**42**	369

Is it from a newspaper?

Is it an article?	**21**	365
Is it an interview?	**42**	369
Is it an editorial?	**22**	365
Is it a letter to the editor?	**22**	365
Is it a review (e.g., a review of a book or film)?	**24**	365

Is the author unknown? **23** 365

? Is it a Print Source but Not a Book, a Part of a Book, or an Article in an Academic Journal, a Magazine, or a Newspaper?

NO   YES

Go to this entry on page

Is it published by the government or a nongovernment organization?

Is it a government document?	**25**	366
Is it a report or a working paper?	**26**	366
Is it a brochure, pamphlet, fact sheet, or press release?	**29**	367
Is it from the *Congressional Record?*	**64**	373

Is it an unpublished conference presentation? **27** 366

Is it a dissertation or dissertation abstract? **28** 366

Check the directory on pages 360–61 or consult your instructor.

Entries in a List of References:

Electronic or Other Nonprint Sources

Go to the next panel.

❓ Is it a Computer-Based Source Not Found Online?

NO   YES

	Go to this entry on page
Is it computer software or a video game?	77 375
Is it a film or DVD?	31 367
Is it a TV series or episode?	34, 35 367, 368
Is it a radio broadcast?	33 367
Is it a CD or audio recording?	32 367
Is it a live performance?	39 368
Is it a musical composition?	40 368
Is it a lecture, speech, or address?	41 368
Is it a map or chart?	38 368
Is it an image, a photograph, or a work of art?	37 368
Is it an advertisement?	36 368
Is it a personal interview?	42 369

Check the directory on pages 360–61 or consult your instructor.

—START SMART

Tab 7: APA Documentation Style

This section will help you answer questions such as the following:

Rhetorical Knowledge

- Which disciplines use APA style? (31)

Critical Thinking, Reading, and Writing

- Why do I need to document my sources? (31, 32)

Processes

- How should I position and label visuals? (33)
- What information should an abstract contain? (33)

Knowledge of Conventions

- How do I cite sources in the text of my paper? (31)
- How do I create a list of references? (32)
- What kind of spacing and margins should my paper have? (33)
- What is a Digital Object Identifier (DOI), and how is it used? (32)
- How do I cite electronic sources, such as Web sites, podcasts, and online articles with DOIs? (32)

For a general introduction to writing outcomes, see 1e, pages 14–16.

Instructors of courses in psychology, sociology, political science, communications, education, and business usually prefer a documentation style that emphasizes the author and the year of publication.

The information in Chapters 31 through 34 is based on the sixth edition of the American Psychological Association's *Publication Manual* (Washington: APA, 2010). For updates, check the APA-sponsored Web site at <www.apastyle.org>.

APA documentation style has two mandatory parts:

- In-text citations
- List of references

CHAPTER 31

APA Style: In-Text Citations

In-text citations let readers know that they can find full information about the source of an idea you have paraphrased or summarized, or the source of a quotation, in the list of references at the end of your project.

1. Author named in sentence   Follow the author's name with the year of publication (in parentheses).

signal phrase

In their book, *Social Change Anytime Everywhere,* Allyson Kapin and Amy Sample Ward (2013) explain that social media have the power to engage not only first responders and the organizations they work for, but also the millions of individuals around the world who check their social media pages as events unfold.

2. Author named in parentheses   If you do not name the source's author in your sentence, then you must include the name in the parentheses, followed by the date and, if you are giving a quotation or a specific piece of information, the page number. Separate the name, date, and page number with commas.

Since tweeting was introduced in 2006, an impressive 96% of nonprofits say they use *Twitter* and 97% report using *Facebook* (Barnes, 2011).

3. Two to five authors   If a source has five or fewer authors, name all of them the first time you cite the source.

APA IN-TEXT CITATIONS: DIRECTORY to SAMPLE TYPES

(See pp. 358–76 for examples of references entries.)

1. Author named in sentence   *354*
2. Author named in parentheses   *354*
3. Two to five authors   *354*
4. Six or more authors   *355*
5. Organization as author   *356*
6. Unknown author   *356*
7. Two or more authors with the same last name   *356*
8. Two or more works by the same author in the same year   *356*
9. Two or more sources cited at one time   *357*
10. E-mail, letters, and conversations   *357*
11. Specific part of a source   *357*
12. Indirect (secondary) source   *357*
13. Electronic source   *357*
14. Two or more sources in one sentence   *358*
15. Sacred or classical text   *358*

> In a 2007 study of adult voting and volunteering, Hart, Connelly, Youniss, and Atkins (2007) found that "those who participated frequently in community service in high school were more likely to volunteer than were those whose community service was nonexistent or infrequent" (p. 210).

If you put the names of the authors in parentheses, use an ampersand *(&)* instead of *and*.

> After all, most educators would agree that "a democratic system of government needs—and the United States relies on colleges to
> *Ampersand used within parentheses*
> produce—ethical and engaged citizens" (Boyd & Brackmann, 2012, p. 39).

After the first time you cite a work by three or more authors, use the first author's name plus *et al.* (as an abbreviation, the *al.* has a period following it): (Hart et al., 2007). Always use both names when citing a work by two authors.

4. Six or more authors   For in-text citations of a work by six or more authors, always provide the first author's name plus *et al.* In the

APA IN-TEXT CITATIONS

- Identify the author(s) of the source, either in the sentence or in a parenthetical citation.
- Indicate the year of publication of the source following the author's name, either in parentheses if the author's name is part of the sentence or, if the author is not named in the sentence, after the author's name and a comma in the parenthetical citation.
- Include a page reference for a quotation or specific piece of information. Put "p." before the page number. If the author is named in the text, the page number appears in the parenthetical citation following the borrowed material. Page numbers are not necessary when you are summarizing the source as a whole or paraphrasing an idea found throughout a work. *(For more on summary, paraphrase, and quotation, see Chapter 24: Working with Sources and Avoiding Plagiarism, pp. 258–75.)*
- If the source does not have page numbers (as with many online sources), do your best to direct readers. If the source has no page or paragraph numbering or easily identifiable headings, just use the name and date. *(See no. 13 on p. 357 and the note on p. 358.)*

reference list, however, list up to seven author names. For more than seven authors, list the first six authors' names, followed by an ellipsis mark (three spaced periods) and the last author's name *(see p. 364)*.

> In a retrospective study, Çevik et al. (2013) evaluated the various characteristics of lung and liver hydatid disease in children.

5. Organization as author Treat the organization as the author, and spell out its name the first time the source is cited. If the organization is well known, you may use an abbreviation thereafter.

> According to the Corporation for National and Community Service (CNCS) (2012), 64.3 million people volunteered in 2011, the highest number in the past five years, and a rate that has remained relatively consistent for the past four years.

> Anxiety disorders affect nearly twice as many women as men (National Institute of Mental Health [NIMH], 2013).

In subsequent citations, only the abbreviation and the date need to be given: (NIMH, 2013).

6. Unknown author Give the first one or two important words of the title. Use quotation marks for titles of articles, chapters, or Web pages, and italics for titles of books, periodicals, or reports.

> The transformation of women's lives has been hailed as "the single most important change of the past 1,000 years" ("Reflections," 1999, p. 77).

7. Two or more authors with the same last name If the authors of two or more sources have the same last name, always include their first initial, even if the year of publication differs.

> M. Smith (2008) showed how Mexican migrants with dual citizenship display active civic engagement in U.S. and Mexican politics.

8. Two or more works by the same author in the same year Alphabetize the works by their titles in your reference list, and assign a letter in alphabetical order (for example, *2012a, 2012b*). Use that same year-letter designation in your in-text citation.

> J. P. Agarwal (1996b) described the relationship between trade and foreign direct investment (FDI).

9. Two or more sources cited at one time   Cite the authors in the order in which they appear in the list of references, separated by a semicolon.

> Today's students report that school, family, and peer groups are
>
> among the major motivations to volunteer (Boyd & Brackmann, 2012;
>
> Law, Shek, & Ma, 2013).

10. E-mails, letters, and conversations   To cite information received from unpublished forms of personal communication—such as conversations, letters, notes, and e-mail messages—give the source's first initial or initials and last name, and provide as precise a date as possible. Because readers do not have access to them, do not include personal communications in your reference list.

> According to scholar T. Williams (personal communication, June 10,
>
> 2010), many students volunteer because they believe in giving back to
>
> the community they grew up in.

11. Specific part of a source   Include the chapter *(Chapter),* page *(p.),* figure, or table number.

> Although social media have had a positive impact on the messaging
>
> capabilities of nonprofits, 62% of Americans reported they are
>
> very likely to support causes they learn about through in-person
>
> communication channels (Kapin & Ward, 2013, Chapter 1).

12. Indirect (secondary) source   When referring to a source that you know only from reading another source, use the phrase *as cited in* followed by the author of the source you actually read and its year of publication.

> Marcy L. Reed, president of National Grid, a Massachusetts gas and
>
> electric utility, says, "I have to be sure the people we hire today are fit
>
> for tomorrow" (as cited in Supiano, 2013).

The work by Supiano would be included in the reference list, but the work by Marcy L. Reed would not.

13. Electronic source   Cite the author's last name or the name of the site's sponsor (if an author's name is not available) and the publication date. If the document is a PDF (portable document format) file with stable page numbers, cite the page number. If the source has paragraph numbers instead of page numbers, use *para.* instead of *p.*

CNCS (2010) defines *service learning* as a practice that "engages students in the educational process, using what they learn in the classroom to solve real-life problems."

> **Note:** If the specific part lacks page or paragraph numbering, cite the heading and the number of the paragraph under that heading where the information can be found. If the heading is long, use a short version in quotation marks. If you cannot determine the date, use the abbreviation *n.d.* in its place: (*CNCS, n.d.*).

14. Two or more sources in one sentence   Include a parenthetical reference after each fact, idea, or quotation you have borrowed.

In its 2012 Annual Member Survey, Campus Compact (2013a) reported that student participation is increasing in the Compact institutions, a fact that stands in marked contrast to the flat or even decreasing rates reported by other sources measuring rates across all institutions (DiBlasio, 2011).

15. Sacred or classical text   Cite these within your text only, and include the version you consulted as well as any standard book, part, or section numbers.

The famous song sets forth a series of opposites, culminating in "a time to love, and a time to hate; a time of war, and a time of peace" (Eccles. 3:8, King James Bible).

CHAPTER 32

APA Style: References

APA documentation style requires a list of references where readers can find complete bibliographical information about the sources referred to in your project. The list should appear at the end of your research project, beginning on a new page titled "References."

Books

1. Book with one author

Sagawa, S. (2010). *The American way to change: How national service and volunteers are transforming America.* San Francisco, CA: Jossey-Bass.

2. Book with two or more authors   Precede the final name with an ampersand *(&)*.

> Kapin, A., & Ward, A. S. (2013). *Social change anytime everywhere:*
>
> > *How to implement online multichannel strategies to spark*
> >
> > *advocacy, raise money and engage your community.* San
> >
> > Francisco, CA: Jossey-Bass.

For more than seven authors, list the first six, an ellipsis mark (three spaced periods), and the final author *(see no. 17)*.

3. Organization as author   When the publisher is the author, use *Author* instead of repeating the organization's name as the publisher.

> Oxfam America. (2013). *Dashed expectations.* Boston, MA: Author.

4. Two or more works by the same author   List the works in publication order, with the earliest one first. If a university publisher's name includes the state, do not repeat it.

> Kapin, A., & Ward, A. S. (2013). *Social change anytime everywhere:*
>
> > *How to implement online multichannel strategies to spark*
> >
> > *advocacy, raise money and engage your community.* San
> >
> > Francisco, CA: Jossey-Bass.

If the works were published in the same year, put them in alphabetical order by title and add a letter *(a, b, c)* to the year to distinguish each entry in your in-text citations *(see no. 19)*.

5. Book with editor(s)   Add *(Ed.)* or *(Eds.)* after the name. If a book lists an author and an editor, treat the editor like a translator *(see no. 9)*.

> Oseland, James (Ed.). (2013). *A fork in the road: Tales of food, pleasure*
>
> > *and discovery on the road.* Melbourne, Australia: Lonely Planet.

6. Selection in an edited book or anthology   The selection's author, year of publication, and title come first, followed by the word *In* and information about the edited book. The page numbers of the selection are placed in parentheses after the book's title.

> Angell, M. (2012). The crazy state of psychiatry. In Brooks, D. (Ed.),
>
> > *The best American essays 2012* (pp. 6–28). New York, NY:
> >
> > Houghton Mifflin.

APA REFERENCE ENTRIES: DIRECTORY to SAMPLE TYPES

(See pp. 353–58 for examples of in-text citations.)

7. Selection from a work also listed in references   Include all information for the larger work (see second example) preceded by that for the specific selection.

Cole, D. (2011). Don't just stand there. In B. F. Clouse (Ed.), *Patterns for a purpose: A rhetorical reader* (pp. 311–315). New York, NY: McGraw-Hill.

Clouse, B. F. (Ed). (2011). *Patterns for a purpose: A rhetorical reader.* New York, NY: McGraw-Hill.

8. Introduction, preface, foreword, or afterword   List the author and the section cited.

> Folger, T. (2012). Foreword. In D. Ariely (Ed.), *The best American science and nature writing 2012*. New York, NY: Houghton Mifflin.

9. Translation   After the title of the translation, put the name(s) of the translator(s) in parentheses, followed by the abbreviation *Trans.*

> Yan, Mo (2012). *Shifu, you'll do anything for a laugh* (H. Goldblatt, Trans.). New York, NY: Arcade.

10. Article in an encyclopedia or another reference work   Begin with the author of the selection, if given. If no author is given, begin with the selection's title.

> *title of the selection*
> Arawak. (2000). In *The Columbia encyclopedia* (6th ed., p. 2533). New York, NY: Columbia University Press.

11. Entire dictionary or reference work   Unless an author or editor is indicated on the title page, list dictionaries by title, with the edition number in parentheses. (The in-text citation should include the title or a portion of the title.) *(See no. 10 on citing an article in a reference book and no. 12 on alphabetizing a work listed by title.)*

> *The American heritage dictionary of the English language* (5th ed.). (2012). Boston, MA: Houghton Mifflin.
>
> Hinson, M. (2004). *The pianist's dictionary.* Bloomington: Indiana University Press.

12. Unknown author or editor   Start with the title. When alphabetizing, use the first important word of the title (excluding articles such as *The, A,* or *An*).

> *Give me liberty.* (1969). New York, NY: World.

13. Edition other than the first

> Ferris, J., & Worster, L. (2013). *Music: The art of listening* (9th ed.). New York, NY: McGraw-Hill.

14. One volume of a multivolume work   If the volume has its own title, put it before the title of the whole work. No period separates the title and parenthetical volume number.

> Strategic management. (2014). In *Wiley encyclopedia of management* (Vol. 12). Hoboken, NJ: Wiley.

APA LIST OF REFERENCES

- Begin on a new page with the centered title "References."
- Include a reference for every in-text citation except personal communications and sacred or classical texts *(see in-text citations no. 10 on p. 357 and no. 15 on p. 358).*
- Put references in alphabetical order by author's last name.
- Give the last name and first or both initials for each author. If the work has more than one author, see no. 2 *(p. 359)* or no. 17 *(p. 364).*
- Put the publication year in parentheses following the author or authors' names.
- Capitalize only the first word and proper nouns in titles. Also capitalize the first word following the colon in a subtitle.
- Use italics for titles of books but not articles. Do not enclose titles of articles in quotation marks.
- Include the city and publisher for books. Give the state or country. If a university publisher's name includes the state, do not repeat it (e.g., Berkeley, rather than Berkeley, CA).
- Include the periodical name and volume number (both in italics) as well as the page numbers for a periodical article.
- End with the DOI, if any *(see nos. 16 and 43 and the box on p. 369).*
- Separate the author's name or authors' names, date (in parentheses), title, and publication information with periods.
- Use a hanging indent: Begin the first line of each entry at the left margin, and indent all subsequent lines of an entry (five spaces).
- Double-space within and between entries.

15. Republished book   In-text citations should give both years: "As Goodman (1956/2012) pointed out . . ."

> Goodman, P. (2012). *Growing up absurd.* New York, NY: NYRB
>
> Classics. (Original work published 1956).

Periodicals

16. Article in a journal (paginated by volume or issue)   Italicize the periodical title and the volume number. Provide the issue number—*not* italicized—in parentheses after the volume number, with no space between them. A DOI ends the entry if available *(also see no. 43).*

> Masters, K., & Hooker, S. (2013). Religiousness/spirituality,
>
> cardiovascular disease, and cancer: Cultural integration for health
>
> research and intervention. *Journal of Consulting and Clinical*
>
> *Psychology, 81*(2), 206–216. doi:10.1037/a0030813

17. Article with three to seven authors or with more than seven authors   If a work has up to seven authors, list them all (see first example); if it has more than seven authors, list the first six followed by a comma, an ellipsis mark (three spaced periods), and the final author's name (see second example).

> Çevik, M., Eser, I., & Boleken M. (2013). Characteristics and outcomes
>
> of liver and lung hydatid disease in children. *Tropical Doctor,*
>
> *43*(3), 93–95. doi:10.1177/0049475513493415

> Plummer, C. A., Ai, A. L., Lemieux, C., Richardson, R., Dey,
>
> S., Taylor, P., . . . Hyun-Jun, K. (2008). Volunteerism
>
> among social work students during Hurricanes Katrina and
>
> Rita. *Journal of Social Service Research, 34*(3), 55–71.
>
> doi:10.1080/01488370802086328

18. Abstract   For an abstract that appears in the original source, add the word *Abstract* in brackets after the title. If the abstract appears in a printed source that is different from the original publication, first give the original publication information for the article, followed by the publication information for the source of the abstract. If the dates of the publications differ, cite them both, with a slash between them, in the in-text citation: Murphy (2003/2004).

> Burnby, J. G. L. (1985, June). Pharmaceutical connections: The Maw's
>
> family [Abstract]. *Pharmaceutical Historian, 15*(2), 9–11.

> Murphy, M. (2003). Getting carbon out of thin air. *Chemistry &*
>
> *Industry, 6,* 14–16. Abstract retrieved from *Fuel and Energy*
>
> *Abstracts, 45*(6), 389.

19. Two or more works in one year by the same author   Alphabetize by title, and attach a letter to each entry's year of publication, beginning with *a*. In-text citations must use the letter as well as the year.

> Agarwal, J. P. (1996a). *Does foreign direct investment contribute*
>
> *to unemployment in home countries? An empirical survey*
>
> (Discussion Paper No. 765). Kiel, Germany: Institute of World
>
> Economics.

Agarwal, J. P. (1996b). Impact of Europe agreements on FDI in

developing countries. *International Journal of Social Economics,*

23(10/11), 150–163.

20. Article in a magazine   After the year, add the month for magazines published monthly or the month and day for magazines published weekly. Note that the volume and issue numbers are also included.

McLean, B. (2014, January). Yahoo's geek goddess. *Vanity Fair,* 641, 68.

21. Article in a newspaper   Use *p.* or *pp.* (not italicized) with the section and page number. List all page numbers, separated by commas, if the article appears on discontinuous pages: pp. C1, C4, C6. If there is no identified author, begin with the title of the article.

Fitzsimmons, E. G. (2013, December 8). Winter storms grip U.S.,

knocking out power and grounding flights. *The New York Times,*

p. N23.

22. Editorial or letter to the editor   Note the use of brackets to identify the genre.

Glaeser, E. L. (2013, October 31). High value in unpaid internships

[Opinion]. *The Boston Globe,* p. A15.

23. Unsigned article   Begin the entry with the title, and alphabetize it by the first important word (excluding articles such as *The, A,* or *An*).

Lessons of Newtown. (2013, December 13). *Forward,* p. 8.

24. Review   If the review is untitled, use the bracketed description in place of a title.

Lane, A. (2013, September 16). How they roll [Review of the motion

picture *Wadjida,* 2013]. *The New Yorker,* pp. 72, 74.

Calhoun, A. (2013, December 8). The Chelsea [Review of the book

Inside the dream palace: The life and times of New York's

legendary Chelsea Hotel by S. Tippins]. *The New York Times Book*

Review, p. 84.

Other Print and Audiovisual Sources

25. Government document   When no author is listed, use the government agency as the author.

> U.S. Bureau of the Census. (1976). *Historical statistics of the United States: Colonial times to 1970*. Washington, DC: Government Printing Office.

For an enacted resolution or piece of legislation, see no. 64.

26. Report or working paper   If the issuing agency numbered the report, include that number in parentheses after the title.

> Forbes, K. J., & Klein, M. W. (2013). *Pick your poison: The choices and consequences of policy responses to crises*. (MIT Sloan Research Paper No. 5062-13). Cambridge, MA: Sloan School of Management.

27. Conference presentation   Treat published conference presentations as a selection in a book *(no. 6)*, as a periodical article *(no. 16)*, or as a report *(no. 26)*, whichever applies. For unpublished conference presentations, provide the author, the year and month of the conference, the italicized title of the presentation, and the presentation's form, forum, and place.

> Manka, K. (2012, January). *Hollywood vs. Silicon Valley*. Keynote address presented at the Davos World Economic Forum 2012, Davos, Switzerland.

> Merkel, A. (2012, January). *Do we dare more Europe?* Opening speech presented at the Davos World Economic Forum 2012, Davos, Switzerland.

28. Dissertation or dissertation abstract   Use this format for an unpublished dissertation. For a published dissertation accessed via a database, see no. 48.

> Lederman, J. (2011). *Critical, third-space phenomenology as a framework for validating college composition placement*. (Unpublished doctoral dissertation). Indiana University, Indiana, PA.

If you used an abstract from *Dissertation Abstracts International,* treat the entry like a periodical article.

APA APA APA APA APA APA APA APA APA APA APA APA APA APA APA APA APA

Leger-Rodriguez, T. N. (2011). Paraprofessional preparation and

 supervision in special education. *Dissertations Abstracts*

 International, 71, 2846.

29. Brochure, pamphlet, fact sheet, or press release   If there is no date of publication, put *n.d.* in place of the date. If the publisher is an organization, list it first, and name the publisher as *Author* (not italicized).

U.S. Postal Service. (1995). A consumer's guide to postal services and

 products [Brochure]. Washington, DC: Author.

Union College. (n.d.). The Nott Memorial: A national historic landmark

 at Union College [Pamphlet]. Schenectady, NY: Author.

30. Published letter   Begin with the letter writer's name, treating the addressee as part of the title *(Letter to . . .).* The following example is published in a collection of letters, so it is also treated as a selection within a larger book.

Lewis, C. S. (1905). Letter to his brother. In Walter Hooper (Ed.), *The*

 collected letters of C. S. Lewis: Vol 1. Family letters, 1905–1931

 (pp. 2–3). New York, NY: HarperCollins.

31. Film or DVD   Begin with the cited person's name and, if appropriate, a parenthetical notation of his or her role. After the title, identify the medium, followed by the country and name of the distributor. *(For online video, see no. 75.)*

Goldsman, A. (Writer), Goldsman, A. (Director), & Goldsman, A., Platt,

 E., Tadross, M., & Allard, T. (Producers). (2014). *Winter's tale*

 [Motion picture]. United States: Warner Brothers Pictures.

32. CD or audio recording   See no. 72 for an MP3 or no. 73 for an audio podcast.

title of piece
Springsteen, B. (2014). 41 shots [Recorded by B. Springsteen]. On
title of album
 High hopes [CD]. New York, NY: Columbia Records.

33. Radio broadcast   See no. 73 for an audio podcast.

Van Zandt, S. (Host). (2012, April 10). *Underground garage* [Radio

 broadcast]. Washington, DC: WKGO Radio.

34. TV series   For an entire TV series or specific news broadcast, treat the producer as author.

Ashford, Michelle (Producer). (2013). *Masters of sex* [Television series]. New York, NY: Showtime.

35. Episode from a TV series Treat the writer as the author and the producer as the editor of the series. See no. 74 for a podcast TV series episode.

Bensinger, T. (Writer), & Fywell, T. (Director). (2013). *All together now* [Television series episode]. In M. Ashford (Producer), *Masters of sex*. New York, NY: Showtime.

36. Advertisement Include the word *advertisement* within brackets.

Progressive Insurance. (2014, February 18). [Advertisement]. Atlantic City, NJ: WMGM-TV.

37. Image, photograph, or work of art If you have reproduced a visual, give the source information with the caption. See no. 57 for online visuals.

Smith, W. E. (1950). *Guardia Civil, Spain* [Photograph]. Minneapolis, MN: Minneapolis Institute of Arts.

38. Map or chart If you have reproduced a visual, give the source information with the caption *(for an example, see p. 392)*. Also include a reference-list entry. See no. 57 for online visuals.

Colonial Virginia [Map]. (1960). Richmond: Virginia Historical Society.

39. Live performance

Parker, T., Stone, M., & Lopez, R. (Authors), Nicholaw, C., & Parker T. (Directors). (2014, March 4). *The Book of Mormon* [Theatrical performance]. Eugene O'Neill Theatre, New York, NY.

40. Musical composition

Salonen, E. (2010). *NYX* [Musical composition].

41. Lecture, speech, or address List the speaker; the year, month, and date (if available); and the italicized title of the presentation. Include location information when available. (For online versions, add "Retrieved from," the Web site sponsor, and the URL.)

Saunders, G. (2013, May 11). *Becoming kinder.* Commencement address given at Syracuse University, Syracuse, NY.

APA ELECTRONIC REFERENCES

- Many print and online books and articles have a Digital Object Identifier (DOI), a unique alphanumeric string. Citations of online documents with DOIs do not require the URL. Do not place a period after a DOI.
- Include a retrieval date only for items that probably will change (such as a wiki).
- Do not include information about a database or library subscription service in the citation unless the work is difficult to find elsewhere (for example, archival material).
- Include the URL of the home page for journal, magazine, and newspaper articles lacking a DOI.
- Include the full URL for all other items lacking a DOI. Do not place a period after a URL.
- For nonperiodicals, name the site sponsor in the retrieval statement unless the author is the sponsor *(see no. 56)*. This format derives from the APA model for an online report.

author
Salisbury, C. (2013, December 23). Jaguars in Argentine Chaco on

Web site sponsor
verge of local extinction. Retrieved from Mongabay.com website:

http://news.mongabay.com/2013/1223-salisbury-argentine-chaco-

jaguars-verge-extinction.html

author as Web site sponsor
Oxfam International. (2012). *FAQs*. Retrieved from http://oxfam/en/

about/faqs

42. Personal interview   Like other unpublished personal communications, personal interviews are not included in the reference list. See in-text citation entry no. 10 *(p. 357)*.

Electronic Sources

43. Online journal article with a Digital Object Identifier (DOI)   If your source has a DOI, include it at the end of the entry; URL and access date are not needed.

Brown, T. S. (2013). The sixties in the city: Avant-gardes and urban

rebels in New York, London, and West Berlin. *Journal of social*

history, 46(4), 817–842. doi:10.1093/jsh/sht007

44. Online journal article without a DOI   Include the URL of the journal's home page.

Zhang, P., & McLuhan, E. (2013). Media ecology: Illuminations.

Canadian Journal of Communication, 38(4). Retrieved from http://
www.cjc-online.ca

45. Abstract from an online journal article   Treat much like a journal article, but include the word *Abstract* before retrieval information.

Chen, Y. (2013). Partnership and performance of community-based

organizations: A social network study of Taiwan. *Journal of Social*

Service Research, 39(5). Abstract doi:10.1080/01488376.2013

.829164

46. Journal article from an online, subscription, or library database Include database information only if the article is rare or found in just a few databases. *(Otherwise, see nos. 43 and 44.)* Give the URL of the database's home page.

Gore, W. C. (1916). Memory, concept, judgment, logic (theory).

Psychological Bulletin, 13, 355–358. Retrieved from

PsycARTICLES database: http://psycnet.apa.org

47. Abstract from database as original source

O'Leary, A., & Wolitski, R. J. (2009). Moral agency and the sexual

transmission of HIV. *Psychological Bulletin, 135,* 478–494.

Abstract retrieved from PsycINFO database: http://psycnet.apa.org

48. Published dissertation from a database   Include the dissertation file number at the end of the entry.

Gorski, A. (2007). *The environmental aesthetic appreciation of cultural*

landscapes (Doctoral dissertation). Available from ProQuest

Dissertations and Theses database. (UMI No. 1443335)

49. Newspaper or magazine article from a database   Include database information for archival material not easily found elsewhere. Give the URL of the database's home page. *(Otherwise, see no. 50 for an online newspaper article or no. 51 for an online magazine article.)*

Culnan, J. (1927, November 20). Madison to celebrate arrival of first air

mail plane. *Wisconsin State Journal,* p. A1. Retrieved from Wisconsin

Historical Society database: http://www.wisconsinhistory.org/WLHBA

50. Article in an online newspaper

Streitfeld, D. (2013, December 16). Amazon strikers take their fight

to Seattle. *The New York Times*. Retrieved from http://www

.nytimes.com

51. Article in an online magazine   Include the volume and issue numbers after the magazine title.

Courage, K. (2013, December 9). Genetic cures for the gut. *Scientific*

American, 309(6). Retrieved from http://www.sciam.com

52. Supplemental online magazine content   A description in brackets such as *online exclusive* indicates that the material is distributed only in online venues.

Kluger, J. (2013, December 4). *Top 10 new species* [Online exclusive].

Time. Retrieved from http:/www.time.com

53. Review from an online publication

Solow, R. (2013, December 16). Alan Greenspan is still trying to

justify his bad decisions. [Review of the book *The Map and the*

territory: Risk, human nature, and the future of forecasting, by

A. Greenspan]. *New Republic*. Retrieved from www.newrepublic.com.

54. In-press article   Include the designation *in press* (not italicized) in place of a date.

Schwartz, S., & Correll, C. (in press). Efficacy and safety of atomoxetine in

children and adolescents with attention-deficit/hyperactivity disorder:

Results from a comprehensive meta-analysis and metaregression.

Journal of the American Academy of Child & Adolescent Psychiatry.

Retrieved from http://www.jaacap.org/inpress

55. Article in an online newsletter   Give the full URL.

Latour, M. (2013, September 3). From farm to closet: Do

you know where your wool comes from? *Conservancy*

Talk Newsletter, The Nature Conservancy. Retrieved

from http://blog.nature.org/conservancy/2013/09/03/

farm-to-closet-do-you-know-where-your-wool-comes-from/

56. Document or report on a Web site Include the Web site sponsor in the retrieval statement unless the author of the work is also the sponsor. Here, the author is the World Health Organization, and the sponsor is BPD Sanctuary.

> World Health Organization. (1992). *ICD-10 criteria for borderline*
>
> *personality disorder.* Retrieved from BPD Sanctuary website:
>
> http://www.mhsanctuary.com/borderline/icd10.htm

57. Visual on a Web site If you have used a graph, chart, map, or image, give the source information following the figure caption *(for an example, see p. 392)*. Also include a reference-list entry.

> Chicago [Map]. (2013). Retrieved from http://www.mapquest.com

58. Document on a university's Web site Include relevant information about the university and department in the retrieval statement.

> Tugal, C. (2002). Islamism in Turkey: Beyond instrument and meaning.
>
> *Economy and Society, 31,* 85–111. Retrieved from University
>
> of California–Berkeley, Department of Sociology website: http://
>
> sociology.berkeley.edu/public_sociology_pdf/tugal.pps05.pdf

59. Electronic version of a print book Provide a DOI, if it is available, instead of the URL.

> Mill, J. S. (1869). *On liberty.* (4th ed.). Retrieved from http://books
>
> .google.com/books

> Shariff, S. (2009). Confronting cyber-bullying: What schools need
>
> to know to control misconduct and avoid legal consequences.
>
> [Cambridge Books Online]. doi:10/1017/CBO9780511551260

60. Chapter from an electronic book

> Owen, S., & Kearns, R. (2006). Competition, adaptation and resistance:
>
> (Re)forming health organizations in New Zealand's third sector. In
>
> Milligan, C., & Conradson, D. (Eds.), *Landscapes of voluntarism:*
>
> *New spaces of health, welfare and governance* (pp. 115–134).
>
> Retrieved from http://books.google.com.proxy.lib.fsu.edu

61. Electronic book, no print edition

Stevens, K. (n.d.). *The dreamer and the beast.* Retrieved from http://
www.onlineoriginals.com/showitem.asp?itemID=321

62. Online brochure

Corporation for National & Community Service. (2010). *A guide to
working with the media* [Brochure]. Retrieved from http://www
.nationalservice.gov/pdf/Media_Guide.pdf

63. Online government document other than the *Congressional Record*

National Commission on Terrorist Attacks upon the United States.
(2004). The 9/11 Commission report. Retrieved from Government
Printing Office website: http://www.gpoaccess.gov/911/index.html

64. *Congressional Record* (online or in print)   For enacted resolutions or
legislation, give the number of the congress after the number of the
resolution or legislation, the *Congressional Record* volume number,
the page number(s), and year, followed by *(enacted).*

H. Res. 2408, 108th Cong., 150 Cong. Rec. 1331–1332 (2004)
(enacted).

Give the full name of the resolution or legislation when citing it
within your sentence, but abbreviate the name when it appears in a
parenthetical in-text citation: *(H. Res. 2408, 2004).* 368, 2013

65. Online policy brief or white paper

Cramer, K., Shelton, L., Dietz, N., Dote, L., Fletcher, C.,
Jennings, S., . . . Silsby, J. (2010). *Volunteering in America
2010: National, state, and city information.* Retrieved from
Corporation for National and Community Service website:
http://www.volunteeringinamerica.gov/assets/resources/
IssueBriefFINALJune15.pdf

66. Online document lacking either a date or an author   Place the title
before the date if no author is given. Use the abbreviation *n.d.* (no
date) for any undated document.

Center for Science in the Public Interest. (n.d.). *Food additives to*

avoid. Retrieved from Mindfully.org website: http://www.mindfully

.org/Food/Food-Additives-Avoid.htm

67. Article in an online reference work   Begin with the author's name, if given, followed by the publication date. If no author is given, place the title before the date. Include the full URL.

Attribution theory. (2013). In *Encarta*. Retrieved from http://encarta

.msn.com/encyclopedia_761586848/Attribution_Theory.html

68. Wiki article   Wikis are collaboratively written Web sites. Most are updated regularly, so include the access date in your citation. Check with your instructor before using a wiki article as a source.

Social media. (2014, February 11). Retrieved from Citizendium

website: http://en.citizendium.org/wiki/Social_media

69. Blog posting   This model is for a blog post. For an example of a video blog post, see the second example; use the description "video file." For a comment, use the same format but substitute "Blog comment" for "Blog post."

Kashin, K. (2013, March 25). App stats: Fowler and Hall on "Do

legislators cater to the priorities of their constituents?" [Blog

post]. Retrieved from Social Science Statistics Blog website:

http://www.iq.harvard.edu/blog/sss

Freeman, M. (2013, July 19). *Christian Science Monitor*

staff photographer. [Video file] Retrieved from Christian

Science Monitor website: http://www.csmonitor.com/

Mandela-and-Africa-in-the-American-imagination

70. Post to an electronic mailing list, newsgroup, or discussion forum Provide the message's author, its date, and its subject line as the title. For a post to a mailing list, provide the description *Electronic mailing list message* in brackets. For a post to a newsgroup or discussion forum, give the identifying information *Online forum comment* in brackets. Conclude either entry with the words *Retrieved from,* followed by the URL of the archived message.

Phaltan, N. (2013, December 13). NY Times article on what fuel poor

need. [Electronic mailing list message]. Retrieved from http://lists

.bioenergylists.org/pipermail/stoves_lists.bioenergylists.org/

2013-December/007752.html

Reysa, G. (2014, January 1). Stealing heat from a woodstove for water

heating. [Online forum comment]. Retrieved from http://lists

.bioenergylists.org/pipermail/greenbuilding_lists.bioenergylists.org/

2014-January.txt

71. E-mail or instant message (IM)   E-mail, instant messages, or other nonarchived personal communication should be cited in the body of your text but not given in the references list *(see in-text citation entry no. 10, on p. 357).*

72. MP3 or other digital audio file   Use brackets to identify the file type.

Mars, B. (2012). Locked out of heaven. On *Unorthodox jukebox* [MP3].

New York, NY: Atlantic Records.

73. Audio podcast

Glass, I. (Host). (2013, November 8). The seven things you're not

supposed to talk about. *This American life* [Audio podcast].

Retrieved from http://www.thisamericanlife.org

74. Video podcast

Reitman, J. (Director), & Novak, B. J. (Writer). (2007). Local ad

[Television series episode]. In S. Carrell, M. Kaling, L. Eisenberg,

& G. Stupnitsky (Producers), *The office* [Video podcast]. Retrieved

from http://www.nbc.com/the_office/video/episodes.shtml

75. Online video   For an online speech, see no. 41.

Orr, M. (2013, December 20). The soul of the square [Video file].

Retrieved from www.nytimes

76. Online advertisement

Acura. (2014, April) [Advertisement]. Retrieved from www.nytimes.com

77. Computer software or video game   Cite only specialized software. Familiar software such as Microsoft Word doesn't need to be cited.

A hat in time. (2014). [Video game]. Copenhagen, Denmark: Gears for

breakfast.

78. Presentation slides

Volunteering Australia Inc. (2009). Volunteering: What's it all

about? [PowerPoint slides]. Retrieved from http://www

.volunteeringaustralia.org/files/WZ7KOVWICM/Volunteering%20

what_s%20it%20all%20about.ppt

CHAPTER 33

APA Style: Format

The following guidelines are recommended by the *Publication Manual of the American Psychological Association,* sixth edition. For an example of a research project that has been prepared using APA style, see pages 378–92.

Materials   Back up your final draft. Use a high-quality printer and high-quality white 8½-by-11-inch paper. Do not justify your text or hyphenate words at the right margin; it should be ragged.

Title page   The first page of your research report should be a title page. Center the title between the left and right margins in the upper half of the page, and put your name, the name of your course, your instructor's name, and the date on separate lines below the title. *(See p. 378 for an example.)*

Margins and spacing   Use one-inch margins all around, except for the upper right-hand corner, where the page number goes, and the upper left-hand corner, where the running head goes.

Double-space lines throughout, including in the abstract, within any notes or captions, and in the list of references. Indent the first word of each paragraph one-half inch (or five spaces).

For quotations of more than forty words, use block format, and indent five spaces from the left margin. Double-space the quoted lines.

Page numbers and abbreviated titles   All pages, including the title page, should have a short version of your title in uppercase letters. On the title page, preface this with the words "Running head" and a colon. Put this information in the upper left-hand corner of each page, about one-half inch from the top. Put the page number in the upper right-hand corner.

Abstract   Instructors sometimes require an abstract—a summary of your paper's thesis, major points or lines of development, and conclusions. The abstract appears on its own numbered page, entitled "Abstract," right after the title page. It should not exceed 150 to 250 words.

Headings Primary headings should be boldfaced and centered. All key words in the heading should be capitalized.

Secondary headings should be boldfaced and appear flush against the left-hand margin. Do not use a heading for your introduction, however. *(For more on headings, see Chapter 8: Designing Academic Texts and Portfolios, p. 98.)*

Visuals Place each visual (table, chart, graph, or image) on its own page following the reference list and any content notes. Tables precede figures. Label each visual as a table or a figure, and number each kind consecutively (Table 1, Table 2). Provide an informative caption for each visual. Cite the source of the material, and provide explanatory notes as needed. *(For more on using visuals effectively, see Chapter 6: Drafting Text and Visuals, pp. 57–73.)*

CHAPTER 34

Sample Research Project in APA Style

Peggy Giglio researched the topic of student volunteerism and wrote a report about it for her introductory sociology course. Her sources included books, journal articles, and Web documents.

CONSIDER YOUR SITUATION

Author: Peggy Giglio

Type of writing: Research report

Purpose: To report on motivations for student volunteerism

Stance: Objective

Audience: Students, instructors, sociologists

Medium: Print, as text attachment, part of e-portfolio

Giglio writes: As I did my research for this topic, I was surprised about the impact that social media has on volunteering.

All pages: short title and page number; on title page only: "Running head."

Running head: THE NEW VOLUNTEER   1

The New Volunteer:

Civic Engagement Through Social Media

Peggy Giglio

Sociology 101

Professor Morgan

May 15, 2014

Title appears in full and centered on separate page with student's name, course information, and date.

THE NEW VOLUNTEER   2

Abstract appears on a new page after the title page. The first line is not indented.

Abstract

College students today are volunteering in large numbers. Research indicates that today's youth are just as committed to community service as the young Americans of the 1960s, who are often perceived as the most civic-minded of American generations. However, current college students have reasons for volunteering beyond the desire to do good. Today, volunteerism is built into the academic curriculum, aids career development, and provides a sense of community. While the motivations for and methods of volunteering may vary from one generation to another, the fact remains that today's students are committed to service in their communities and making their world a better place for all.

Research report is concisely and objectively summarized—key points included, but not details or statistics.

Paragraph should be between 150 and 250 words.

THE NEW VOLUNTEER   3

Full title is repeated on first page only.

The New Volunteer:

Civic Engagement through Social Media

Are college students today concerned with helping others? It may not seem so to the previous generation, for whom today's students appear obsessed with social networking, text messaging, and materialistic values. But college students are using social media to actively help others in their communities, and their efforts are having a tangible impact. In fact, studies show that increased engagement with social media is actually driving students to become more civically involved during college and beyond. Moreover, new technologies allow for an immediacy of action that was unthinkable even ten years ago. Consider the response to the 2013 Boston Marathon bombing. Within minutes of the explosions, people were tweeting about the need to donate blood. A spreadsheet was quickly and widely circulated, listing people who were offering to open their homes to those who might need a place to stay (Hartogs, 2013, April 16). In their book, *Social Change Anytime Everywhere,* Allyson Kapin and Amy Sample Ward (2013) explain that social media have the power to engage not only first responders and the organizations they work for, but also the millions of individuals around the world who check their social media pages as events unfold. Certainly, social media have changed *how* students volunteer, but the reasons *why* they volunteer have remained much the same as with the previous generation: the three major reasons that students are volunteering are to satisfy their curricular requirements,

Paraphrase from a book; first citation from this source, so authors are named in the text and the date follows their names in parentheses.

THE NEW VOLUNTEER   4

prepare for the financial success they hope to achieve, and become active members of a community.

Volunteering in America and
Historical Changes in Motivation

According to the Corporation for National and Community Service (CNCS) (2012), 64.3 million people volunteered in 2011, the highest number in the past five years, and a rate that has remained relatively consistent for the past four years. Defining volunteering as "work done through an organization for which there is no pay," DoSomething.org estimates that, in 2011, one quarter of young adults, including college students, volunteered in some capacity (Dosomething.org Index, 2012). And for many students, volunteering does not end with graduation. In a 2007 study of adult voting and volunteering, Hart, Connelly, Youniss, and Atkins (2007) found that "those who participated frequently in community service in high school were more likely to volunteer than were those whose community service was nonexistent or infrequent" (p. 210). While some researchers suggest that this continuation is a product of a difficult job market, others disagree. "I don't think people are just jumping on the bandwagon to do service because the economy is shaky," says Elissa Kim, executive vice president of Recruitment for Teach for America, whose organization reports that applications reached an all-time high of 48,000 in 2011 (as cited in DiBlasio, 2011, p. D3).

Margin annotations:

Thesis statement.

Heading in bold type, centered.

Source is a fact sheet with a corporation as its author; spelled out at first mention with abbreviation in parentheses.

Four names in a source joined by *and* in running text, not by an ampersand *(&)*; direct quote from a source; page number is included in parenthetical citation.

Source is a newspaper article; for print newspapers, include page numbers in citation.

THE NEW VOLUNTEER   5

Historically, college students planning to enter service professions such as nursing or social work have volunteered their time as part of their professional development; however, today students in all disciplines choose to make especially valuable contributions in disastrous circumstances, such as the aftermath of Hurricane Sandy. Adelphi University, which has a main campus on Long Island and another in Manhattan, felt the effects of Sandy. But perhaps more memorable than the storm's effects were the students' responses. Shortly after the storm, in the course of a single day, university students collected donations, including roughly $1,000 in cash, wrote thank-you cards for first responders, and participated in a blood drive (Peterkin, 2012). "Students on Facebook are posting things like 'It's a humbling experience,' and it's positive to see that reaction," said Michael J. Berthel, Senior Assistant Director of Adelphi's Center for Student Involvement (as cited in Peterkin, 2012). There is little doubt that the current generation is doing its part to make the world a better place, in a wide variety of ways (see Figure 1).

In the past, students volunteered to change the status quo and to have an impact on social conditions (Astin, 1998). Today's students report that school, family, and peer groups are among the major motivations to join a volunteer effort (Boyd & Brackmann, 2012; Law, Shek, & Ma, 2013). Unlike their parents, young people seek to effect change with perhaps more practicality than idealism. The 2013 Millennial Impact Report finds that, for young people,

Illustration by anecdote (see p. 136).

Development by illustration (see p. 59); figure reference provided. Figure appears after the list of references.

Summary of research reported by two different sources is grouped in a parenthesis sources are listed alphabetically; two authors and three authors, respectively.

THE NEW VOLUNTEER   6

"chief motivations for getting involved were: working on a cause they are passionate about (79%), meeting new people who care about the same cause or issue (56%), and being able to lend pro-bono skills and expertise (46%)" (p. 23). In other words, students are thinking about networking and gaining skills useful in the job market, in addition to helping others.

Today it is easier for volunteers to have an impact at the community level than at a national or regional level. Unlike past generations that sought to make a global impact through volunteer efforts, young people today are finding new and creative ways to become involved in their own communities. According to research conducted by Dosomething.org (Dosomething.org Index, 2012), "of young people who volunteered in 2011, 40% did not volunteer with a traditional 'organization' *at all* but instead volunteered with clubs, groups, their family alone, friends alone, or on their own." Increasingly, students are learning that they can make a difference in the local community while also gaining valuable skills and work experience.

Current College Students' Motivations for Volunteering

One reason that students are volunteering in growing numbers is that civic engagement is now a familiar behavior reinforced in the college environment. In fact, many colleges offer service learning courses and service initiatives through campus organizations. Research has shown that these programs not only motivate students' participation in

The first motivation for volunteering; from the thesis.

THE NEW VOLUNTEER   7

volunteer efforts, but improve their academic performance,
as well:

> College students who participate in civic engagement
> learning activities not only earn higher grade point
> averages but also have higher retention rates and
> are more likely to complete their college degree.
> They also demonstrate improved academic content
> knowledge, critical thinking skills, written and verbal
> communication, and leadership skills. Moreover, these
> students show increased interest in becoming personally
> and professionally involved in future community
> enhancement projects (Cress, Burack, Giles, Elkins, &
> Stevens, 2010, p. 1).

Service learning courses have two objectives: (1)
learning in a given content area and (2) learning about
citizenship and social policies. CNCS (2010) defines
service learning as a practice that "engages students in the
educational process, using what they learn in the classroom
to solve real-life problems." The formal structure of service
learning is designed to make student volunteering beneficial
not only for the community but also for the students
who perform it, increasing their academic development,
leadership skills, and community awareness. "Independent
of what it does for the community," says Thomas Murphy,
chair of anthropology at Edmonds Community College in
Washington, "when students are learning in a hands-on
situation and their activity has importance and impact on the
community, they care more about their assignments than

Quotations of more than forty words are indented one-half inch from margin. Source with five names, so all five are included in the first parenthetical citation; page number is included because the source is quoted.

THE NEW VOLUNTEER   8

they would if it is make believe" (as cited in McClure, 2013, p. 49). Through service learning initiatives, colleges and universities seek to engage students in civic activities that benefit everyone—community members, local businesses, the students, and even the institutions.

Founded in 1985 by three university presidents, Campus Compact, a national coalition of well over 1,100 colleges and universities, is committed to promoting civic engagement on college campuses (Campus Compact, 2013a). One of the ways the organization achieves this goal is through a social media initiative, Connect2Complete. Supported by the Bill and Melinda Gates Foundation, Connect2Complete pairs student volunteers with mentors and peers to encourage service learning and academic success. In its 2012 Annual Member Survey, Campus Compact (2013b) reported that student participation is increasing in the Compact institutions, a fact that stands in marked contrast to the flat or even decreasing rates reported by other sources measuring rates across all institutions (DiBlasio, 2011). The 2012 survey also underscores the important role that colleges play in finding meaningful opportunities for their students. This point has been confirmed by multiple studies showing that "colleges have and can continue to maximize students' civic engagement and ethical learning when both are envisioned as integrated goals straddling students' academic and nonacademic lives and permeating institutional culture" (Boyd & Brackmann, 2012, p. 39). A 2010 study by Prentice and Robinson, and published by The American Association

Source has two authors, so names are separated by an ampersand (&); because there are only two names, both names are included in subsequent citation; page number is included because the source is quoted.

THE NEW VOLUNTEER   9

of Community Colleges, "found statistically significant differences between service-learners and non-service-learners on five out of six learning outcomes, including educational success and academic deployment, civic responsibility, critical thinking, communications, and career and teamwork" (as cited in Campus Compact, 2013b, p. 9).

> Name of corporate author included in its entirety in parenthetical citation.

   A second motivation is market driven. Differences in the ways today's students volunteer reflect the unique challenges they face. Entering the job market has become much more difficult than it was for previous generations. An article published in *The Chronicle of Higher Education* stated that college students need to be "broadly educated and should apply their learning to the real world during college" (Supiano, 2013). Marcy L. Reed, president of National Grid, a Massachusetts gas and electric utility, says, "I have to be sure the people we hire today are fit for tomorrow" (as cited in Supiano, 2013). Students who volunteer gain crucial skills, as well as experience applying what they know to a range of problem-solving efforts. They volunteer for their own personal benefit, motivated partly by the desire to go on to earn a living, perhaps even in the field in which they volunteered. And as Reed's remark confirms, those with volunteer experience are that much more prepared to enter and compete in today's job market.

> The second motivation for volunteering; from the thesis.

> There are no page numbers given—this appears online only: http://chronicle.com/article/Employers-Want-Broadly/138453

> Secondary source; no page number is given for the location of the quotation in the Supiano article, because it appears online only.

   A third motivation for volunteering is the desire for community. Students today usually turn to social media to connect with others. However, volunteering provides them a much-needed opportunity to interact off-line and outside of

> The third motivation for volunteering; from the thesis.

THE NEW VOLUNTEER   10

the classroom. "There seems to be a real longing for students to have hands-on experience and to take what they are learning in school and delve into things they are passionate about," says Maureen Curley, president of Campus Compact (as cited in DiBlasio, 2011). As the Millennial Impact Report (2012) states, "Millennials view volunteer opportunities as a way to socially connect with like-minded peers, which moves them beyond technology (social networking) to in-person action" (p. 6). Such potential may particularly motivate college students looking to establish connections within peer groups at their school, or students who want to integrate their daily lives with their academic work. That motivation extends to sharing their skills with a live community, on their college campuses and beyond.

Online collaboration can also fulfill the desire for community interaction. Students often use the Internet to organize support for a cause. For example, students have used *Twitter* and *Facebook* to urge assistance for victims of Hurricane Sandy and survivors of terrorist attacks. The American Red Cross has a social media monitoring center, which, as of March 2012, was the only one if its kind. "This groundbreaking center lets Red Cross staff see more clearly what's happening on the ground . . . and get people the resources they need more quickly" (American Red Cross, 2013, p. 20). Along with K–12 schools, many colleges and universities have Red Cross clubs, over 1,600 as of 2010 (American Red Cross, 2011, p. i). Students get involved in a number of ways. For example, Marissa Miller, a Penn State

THE NEW VOLUNTEER   11

student, thought to offer students the opportunity to win a

$1,000 scholarship by creating and posting short videos, on

Twitter, that answer the question, "What do you cross your

heart and hope to give?" The Red Cross was happy to use

Twitter to help spread its message and to acknowledge the

substantial donations—6 million units of blood—by college

students each year ("Red Cross," 2013).

These social media efforts have a significant impact.

Since tweeting was introduced in 2006, an impressive 96%

of nonprofits say they use *Twitter* and 97% report using

Facebook (Barnes, 2011). Social media allow supporters

to become actively involved in spreading the message of

the organization. For example, a recent search through

the New York University NYUService *Twitter* feed and

Facebook postings turned up plenty of examples of service

opportunities and student engagement including: creating

cards for veterans and police officers as part of the 9/11

remembrance; a call for students to help rebuild houses

destroyed by Hurricane Sandy; and notice of a Service Fair,

connecting students to local nonprofits. It is worth noting

that student tweets and posts about their own service

activities help to raise awareness of these nonprofits and,

in turn, motivate more people to volunteer (Kapin & Ward,

2013, p. 6).

An Assessment of College Volunteerism

More and more colleges and universities are joining the

Campus Compact and formalizing their programs by opening

> Quotation and para-phrase; source is an article with no author named, so short form of title, in quotation marks, is used in parentheses.

> Authors' names are not needed in text because this is the second in-text citation of the source.

THE NEW VOLUNTEER   12

civic engagement centers and offices, and they are even turning to social media to build community and encourage students to get involved. After all, most educators would agree that "a democratic system of government needs—and the United States relies on colleges to produce—ethical and engaged citizens" (Boyd & Brackmann, 2012, p. 39). However, college administrators need to remember that, in order for their efforts to be effective, they must keep in mind the motivations and goals of students. While students are eager for volunteering opportunities, they likewise want those opportunities to produce meaningful and influential results— for the charities and organizations to which they donate their time, as well as for themselves.

Despite the variety of their motivations, college students today are making a difference by working together to enrich their communities in myriad ways. Their efforts, largely driven by access to social media, are relevant to their career goals; moreover, students give their time in ways that also benefit their own lives and their own aspirations for the future. What matters is that their commitment to enriching the lives of others, and to enhancing the communities in which they live, is as strong as that of any previous generation.

Restate-
ment of
thesis at
conclusion.

THE NEW VOLUNTEER   13

References

American Red Cross. (2011). *A comprehensive guide to starting and sustaining a Red Cross school club.* Retrieved from American Red Cross website http://www.redcross.org/images/MEDIA_CustomProductCatalog/m4440169_H20978.CIAB_MainDocument.pdf

American Red Cross. (2013). *2012 Annual Report.* Retrieved from American Red Cross website http://www.redcross.org/images/MEDIA_CustomProductCatalog/ m16740671_A501-12_AnnualReport_FINAL.pdf

Astin, A. W. (1998). The changing American college student: Thirty-year trends, 1966–1996. *The Review of Higher Education, 21*(2), 115–135. Retrieved from http://www.press.jhu.edu/ journals/review_of_higher_education

Barnes, G. N. (2011). Social media usage now ubiquitous among US top charities, ahead of all other sectors. Retrieved from University of Massachusetts Dartmouth Center for Marketing Research website http://www.umassd.edu/cmr/socialmediaresearch/socialmediatopcharities/

Boyd, K. D., & Brackmann, S. (2012). Promoting civic engagement to educate institutionally for personal and social responsibility. *New Directions for Student Services,* 2012(139), 39–50.

Campus Compact. (2013a). Campus Compact honors 181 community-engaged college students as Newman Civic Fellows [Press release]. Retrieved from http://www.compact.org/news/campus-compact-honors-181-community-engaged-college-students-as-newman-civic-fellows/24189/?zoom_highlight=dedicated+solely+to

New page, title centered. Entries are in alphabetical order by author's last name or, if no author, by first important word in the title.

Source: Report by a corporate author; retrieved online.

Source: Journal article with volume and issue number; retrieved online.

Source: Journal article.

Source: Press release by corporate author; retrieved online.

THE NEW VOLUNTEER   14

Campus Compact. (2013b). *Creating a culture of assessment:
        2012 Campus Compact annual member survey.* Retrieved
        from http://www.compact.org/wp-content/uploads/2013/04/
        Campus-Compact-2012-Statistics.pdf

Corporation for National and Community Service. (2012, December).
        *Volunteering and civic life in America 2012: Key findings on
        the volunteer participation and civic health of the nation* [Fact
        sheet]. Retrieved from http://www.volunteeringinamerica.gov/
        assets/resources/FactSheetFinal.pdf

Corporation for National and Community Service. (2010, June
        15). *What is service learning?* Retrieved from http://www
        .learnandserve.gov/about/service_learning/index.asp

Cress, C. M., Burack, C., Giles, D. E., Elkins, J., & Stevens, M. C.
        (2010). A promising connection: Increasing college
        access and success through civic engagement. Retrieved
        from Campus Compact website http://www.compact
        .org/wp-content/uploads/2010/10/Cress_Presidential_
        Summit_2010.pdf

DiBlasio, N. (2011, November 29). Longer-term volunteering is
        the drill for collegians. *USA Today,* p. D3.

Dosomething.org (2012). *The* Dosomething.org *index on young
        people and volunteering, 2012: The year of friends with
        benefits.* Retrieved from http://files.dosomething.org/files/
        pictures/blog/2012-Web-Singleview_0.pdf

Hart, D., Donnelly, T. M., Youniss, J., & Atkins, R. (2007). High
        school community service as a predictor of adult voting and
        volunteering. *American Education Research Journal, 44*(1),
        197–219. doi:10.3102/0002831206298173

Source:
Fact sheet
by a cor-
porate
author;
retrieved
online.

Source:
Report by
corporate
author;
retrieved
online.

Source:
Print
newspaper
article.

Source:
Informa-
tion from a
Web site.

Source:
Journal
article with
volume and
issue num-
ber; doi
included.

THE NEW VOLUNTEER   15

Hartogs, J. (2013, April 16). Stories of kindness amid tragedy
     in Boston marathon bombing. CBS News. Retrieved from
     http://www.cbsnews.com/news/stories-of-kindness-amid-
     tragedy-in-boston-marathon-bombing/

Kapin, A., & Ward, A. S. (2013). *Social change anytime
     everywhere: How to implement online multichannel
     strategies to spark advocacy, raise money and engage your
     community.* San Francisco, CA: Jossey-Bass.

Law, B. M. F., Shek, D. T. L., & Ma, C. M. S. (2013). Validation
     of family, school, and peer influence on volunteerism scale
     among adolescents. *Research on social work practice,
     23*(4), 458–466. doi:10.1177/1049731513476144

McClure, A. (2013, April). Serving the community: Two-year
     institutions making a bigger commitment to community
     outreach. *University Business, 16*(4), 49–51. Retrieved
     from http://www.universitybusiness.com/servingcomm

Millennial Impact. (2013). *The 2013 millennial impact report.*
     Retrieved from http://cdn.trustedpartner.com/docs/library/
     AchieveMCON2013/Research%20Report/Millennial%20
     Impact%20Research.pdf

Peterkin, C. (2012, November 8). A week after Hurricane
     Sandy, students step up their relief work. *The Chronicle
     of Higher Education.* Retrieved from http://chronicle.com/
     article/A-Week-After-Hurricane-Sandy/135686/

Red Cross offers $1,000 scholarship for student's
     best tweet (2013, September 24). *Penn State
     News,* n.p. Retrieved from http://news.psu.
     edu/story/288801/2013/09/23/academics/

Source:
Article on
a Web site.

Source:
Book
with two
authors.

Source:
Journal
article with
doi.

Source:
Journal
article;
retrieved
online.

Source:
Report by
corporate
author.

Source:
Article in
an online
newspaper.

Source:
Online
news
article with
no author,
listed
alpha-
betically by
title.

red-cross-offers-1000-scholarship-student%E2%80%99s-

best-tweet

Supiano, B. (2013, April 10). Employers want broadly educated

new hires, survey finds. *The Chronicle of Higher*

Education. Retrieved from http://chronicle.com/article/

Employers-Want-Broadly/138453

Source: Article in an online newspaper.

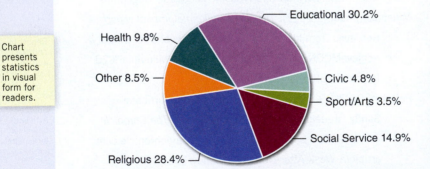

Where People Volunteer

Educational 30.2%

Health 9.8%

Other 8.5%

Civic 4.8%

Sport/Arts 3.5%

Social Service 14.9%

Religious 28.4%

Numbers in the chart may not add up to 100% because of rounding

Figure 1. Where millennials volunteer, by percentage. Reported in *Volunteering and Civic Life in America* by Corporation for National and Community Service, 2011. Retrieved from http://www.volun-teeringinamerica.gov/special/Millennials

Chart presents statistics in visual form for readers.

Figure number in italics, followed by figure title and source information, appears below the figure.

8

Other Documentation Styles
Styles
Chicago & CSE

Nothing gives an author so much pleasure as to find his works respectfully quoted by other learned authors.

–Benjamin Franklin

With concerns scientists have cited about the harm that the use of fossil fuels can cause to the environment, the United States and other countries throughout the world are increasingly turning to alternative energy sources such as this wind energy plant in Altamont, California.

8 Other Documentation Styles

—START SMART

Tab 8: Other Documentation Styles

This section will help you answer questions such as the following:

Rhetorical Knowledge
- Which disciplines use Chicago style? (35)
- Which disciplines use CSE style? (37)
- What are the three forms of CSE style? (37)

Critical Thinking, Reading, and Writing
- Why do I need to document my sources? (35, 37)

Knowledge of Conventions
- How do I cite sources in the text of my paper in Chicago and CSE style? (35, 36, 37)
- What formats are used for a bibliography or works-cited list in Chicago style? (35, 36)
- What is appropriate formatting for a list of references in CSE style? (37)
- How do I cite electronic sources, such as Web sites, podcasts, and online articles with DOIs? (35, 37)

For a general introduction to writing outcomes, see 1e, pages 14–16.

There are many documentation styles besides those developed by the Modern Language Association *(see Tab 6)* and the American Psychological Association *(see Tab 7)*. In this section, we cover the style presented in *The Chicago Manual of Style* and the three styles developed by the Council of Science Editors. To find out where you can learn about other style types, consult the list of style manuals on page 281. If you are not sure which style to use, ask your instructor.

CHAPTER 35

Chicago Documentation Style: Elements

The note and bibliography style presented in the sixteenth edition of *The Chicago Manual of Style* (Chicago: University of Chicago Press, 2010) is used in many disciplines, including history, art, philosophy, business, and communications. This style has three parts:

- Numbered in-text citations
- Numbered footnotes or endnotes
- A bibliography of works consulted

The first two parts are necessary; the third is optional, unless your instructor requires it. (Chicago also has an alternative author-date system that is similar to APA style.) For more information on this style, consult the *Chicago Manual of Style*. For updates and answers to frequently asked questions about this style, go to the "*Chicago Manual of Style* Web site" at <http://www.chicagomanualofstyle.org/tools_citationguide.html>.

35a   Use numbered in-text citations and notes.

Whenever you use information or ideas from a source, you need to indicate what you have borrowed by putting a superscript number in the text ([1]) at the end of the borrowed material. These superscript numbers are placed after all punctuation marks except for the dash.

> In his book, *Here Comes Everybody: The Power of Organizing without Organizations,* New York University professor and media consultant Clay Shirky explains how the proliferation of blogs is affecting news: "The change isn't a shift from one kind of news institution to another, but rather in the definition of news."[2]

If a quotation is fairly long, you can set it off as a block quotation. Indent it five spaces or one-half inch from the left margin, and double-space the quotation, leaving an extra space above and below it. Place the superscript number after the period that ends the quotation.

Each in-text superscript number must have a corresponding note either at the foot of the page or at the end of the text. Indent the first line of each footnote like a paragraph. Footnotes begin with the number and are single-spaced, with a double space between notes.

If you are using endnotes instead of footnotes, they should begin after the last page of your text on a new numbered page titled "Notes." The list of endnotes can be double-spaced, unless your instructor prefers that you make them single-spaced.

The first time you cite a source in either a footnote or an endnote, you should include a full citation. Subsequent citations require less information.

FIRST REFERENCE TO SOURCE

2. Clay Shirky, *Here Comes Everybody: The Power of Organizing without Organizations* (New York: Penguin, 2008), 65–66.

ENTRY FOR SOURCE ALREADY CITED

6. Shirky, 80.

If several pages pass between references to the same title, include a brief version of the title to clarify the reference.

ENTRY FOR SOURCE ALREADY CITED IN LONGER PAPER

7. Shirky, *Here Comes Everybody*, 99–100.

If you quote from the same work immediately after providing a full footnote, use the abbreviation *Ibid.* (Latin for "in the same place"), followed by the page number.

8. Ibid., 135.

35b   Prepare a separate bibliography or list of works cited if your instructor requires one.

Some instructors require a separate list of works cited or of works consulted. If you are asked to provide a works-cited list, do so on a separate, numbered page titled "Works Cited." If the list should include all works you consulted, title it "Bibliography." Here is a sample entry.

Shirky, Clay. *Here Comes Everybody: The Power of Organizing without Organizations.* New York: Penguin, 2008.

CHICAGO STYLE: DIRECTORY TO SAMPLE TYPES

(continued)

CHICAGO STYLE:
DIRECTORY TO SAMPLE TYPES *(continued)*

35c   Use the correct Chicago style for notes and bibliography entries.

Books

1. Book with one author

NOTE

> 1. Paul Bloom, *Just Babies: The Origin of Good and Evil* (New York: Crown, 2013), 32.

BIBLIOGRAPHY ENTRY

> Bloom, Paul. *Just Babies: The Origin of Good and Evil.* New York: Crown, 2013.

2. Multiple works by the same author   After providing complete information in the first footnote, include only a shortened version of the title with the author's last name and the page number in any subsequent footnotes. In the bibliography, list entries in alphabetical order by title; in the references list, list by date, from earliest to most recent. After the first listing, replace the author's name with a "three-em" dash (type three hyphens in a row).

NOTES

2. Shirky, *Cognitive Surplus,* 15.

3. Shirky, *Here Comes Everybody,* 65–66.

BIBLIOGRAPHY ENTRIES

Shirky, Clay. *Cognitive Surplus: Creativity and Generosity in a Connected Age.* New York: Penguin, 2010.

———. *Here Comes Everybody: The Power of Organizing without Organizations.* New York: Penguin, 2008.

3. Book with two or more authors   In notes, you can name up to three authors. When there are three authors, put a comma after the first name and a comma plus *and* after the second.

NOTE

4. Joelle Reeder and Katherine Scoleri, *The IT Girl's Guide to Blogging with Moxie* (Hoboken, NJ: Wiley, 2007), 45.

BIBLIOGRAPHY OR REFERENCES LIST IN CHICAGO STYLE

- Begin on a new page.
- Begin with the centered title "References" if you are including only works referred to in your research project. Use the title "Bibliography" if you are including every work you consulted.
- List sources alphabetically by author's (or editor's) last name.
- Capitalize the first and last words in titles as well as all important words and words that follow colons.
- Indent all lines except the first of each entry five spaces, using your word processor's hanging indent feature.
- Use periods between author and title as well as between title and publication data.
- Double-space both within each entry and between entries, unless your instructor prefers that you make the entries single-spaced.

BIBLIOGRAPHY ENTRY

Reeder, Joelle, and Katherine Scoleri. *The IT Girl's Guide to Blogging with Moxie.* Hoboken, NJ: Wiley. 2007.

When more than three authors are listed on the title page, use *et al.* (meaning "and others") after the first author's name in the note.

NOTE

5. Julian Henriques et al., *Changing the Subject: Psychology, Social Regulation and Subjectivity* (New York: Methuen, 1984), 275.

BIBLIOGRAPHY ENTRY

Henriques, Julian, Wendy Holloway, Cathy Urwin, Couze Venn, and Valerie Walkerdine. *Changing the Subject: Psychology, Social Regulation and Subjectivity.* New York: Methuen, 1984.

Give all author names in bibliography entries.

4. Book with an author and an editor or a translator (or both)   Put the author's name first, and add the editor's *(ed.)* or translator's *(trans.)* name after the title. Spell out *Edited* or *Translated* in the bibliography entry.

NOTE

6. Jorge Luis Borges, *Professor Borges: A Course on English Literature,* eds. Martin Arias and Martin Hadis, trans. Katherine Silver (New York: New Directions, 2013).

BIBLIOGRAPHY ENTRY

Borges, Jorge Luis. *Professor Borges: A Course on English Literature.* Edited by Martin Arias and Martin Hadis. Translated by Katherine Silver. New York: New Directions, 2013.

5. Anthology or other book with an editor in place of an author   Put the editor's name first, followed by the abbreviation *ed.* Otherwise, use the same format as for an author-based note.

NOTE

7. Elizabeth Strout, ed., *The Stories of Frederick Busch* (New York: Norton, 2013).

BIBLIOGRAPHY ENTRY

Strout, Elizabeth, ed. *The Stories of Frederick Busch.* New York: Norton, 2013.

6. Organization as author   Treat the organization as the author, and use the same format as for an author-based note.

NOTE

8. United Nations, *World Investment Report 2013: Global Value Chains—Investment and Trade for Development* (New York: United Nations, 2013), 15.

BIBLIOGRAPHY ENTRY

United Nations. *World Investment Report 2013: Global Value Chains—Investment and Trade for Development.* New York: United Nations, 2013.

7. Work in an anthology or part of an edited book   Begin with the author and title of the specific work or part.

NOTES

9. Louise Erdrich, "Fleur," in *The Oxford Book of American Short Stories,* ed. Joyce Carol Oates (New York: Oxford University Press USA, 2012), 761.

10. Alice Waters, Foreword to *An Everlasting Meal: Cooking with Economy and Grace,* by Tamar Adler (New York: Scribner, 2011).

BIBLIOGRAPHY ENTRIES

Erdrich, Louise. "Fleur." In *The Oxford Book of American Short Stories,* edited by Joyce Carol Oates, 761. New York: Oxford University Press, 2012.

Waters, Alice. Foreword to *An Everlasting Meal: Cooking with Economy and Grace,* by Tamar Adler. New York: Scribner, 2011.

In notes, descriptive terms such as *introduction* are not capitalized. In bibliography entries, these descriptive terms are capitalized.

8. Article in an encyclopedia or a dictionary   For well-known reference works, publication data can be omitted from a note, but the edition or copyright date should be included. There is no need to include page numbers for entries in reference works that are arranged alphabetically; the abbreviation *s.v.* (meaning "under the word") plus the entry's title can be used instead.

NOTES

11. Robert E. Buswell, "Abhirati," in *The Princeton Dictionary of Buddhism,* by Robert E. Buswell and Donald S. Lopez. (Princeton: Princeton University Press, 2013) 10.

12. *Webster's New College Dictionary,* 5th ed., s.v. "Cognitive."

Reference works are not listed in the bibliography unless they are unusual or crucial to your project.

BIBLIOGRAPHY ENTRY

Robert E. Buswell. "Abhirati." In *The Princeton Dictionary of Buddhism.* By Robert E. Buswell and Donald S. Lopez. Princeton: Princeton University Press, 2013.

9. The Bible Abbreviate the name of the book, and use Arabic numerals for chapter and verse, separated by a colon. Name the version of the Bible cited, and do not include the Bible in your bibliography.

NOTE

13. Eccles. 8:5 (Jerusalem Bible).

10. Edition other than the first Include the number of the edition after the title or, if there is an editor, after that person's name.

NOTE

14. Ann Majchrzak and M. Lynne Markus, *Methods for Policy Research: Taking Socially Responsible Action,* 2nd ed. (Thousand Oaks, CA: Sage, 2013), 73.

BIBLIOGRAPHY ENTRY

Majchrzak, Ann, and Markus, M. Lynne. *Methods for Policy Research: Taking Socially Responsible Action.* 2nd ed. Thousand Oaks, CA: Sage, 2013.

11. Reprint of an older book Include the original publication date and other publication details if they are relevant. If referencing page numbers, be sure to note the date of the cited edition.

NOTE

15. Ernest Hemingway, *The Sun Also Rises* (1926; repr., New York: Scribner, 2006), 94.

BIBLIOGRAPHY ENTRY

Hemingway, Ernest. *The Sun Also Rises.* New York: Scribner, 1926. Reprint, New York: Scribner, 2006. Page references are to the 2006 edition.

12. Multivolume work In ·the note, include the volume number in Arabic numerals followed by a colon, before the page number.

NOTE

16. Jean-Michel Kornprobst, *Encyclopedia of Marine Natural Products* (Hoboken, NJ: Wiley-Blackwell, 2014), 3:30–32.

BIBLIOGRAPHY ENTRY

Kornprobst, Jean-Michel. *Encyclopedia of Marine Natural Products.* Vol. 3. Hoboken, NJ: Wiley-Blackwell, 2014.

13. Work in a series   Include the name of the series as well as the book's series number, if available. The series name should not be italicized or underlined.

NOTE

17. Lauren Kessler and Duncan McDonald, *When Words Collide,* Contributions in Wadsworth Series in Mass Communication and Journalism (Stamford, CT: Cengage, 2013).

BIBLIOGRAPHY ENTRY

Kessler, Lauren, and McDonald, Duncan. *When Words Collide.* Contributions in Wadsworth Series in Mass Communication and Journalism. Stamford, CT: Cengage, 2013.

14. Unknown author   Cite anonymous works by title, and alphabetize them by the first word, ignoring *A, An,* or *The.*

NOTE

18. *The British Album* (London: John Bell, 1790), 2:43–47.

BIBLIOGRAPHY ENTRY

The British Album. Vol. 2. London: John Bell, 1790.

15. Book with a title within a title   Place the title of any short-form or long-form work (regardless of how it would otherwise be formatted) appearing within a larger title in quotation marks.

NOTE

19. Robert W. Lewis, *"A Farewell to Arms": The War of the Words* (New York: Twayne Publishers, 1992).

BIBLIOGRAPHY ENTRY

Lewis, Robert W. *"A Farewell to Arms": The War of the Words.* New York: Twayne Publishers, 1992.

16. Source quoted in another source   Quote a source within a source only if you are unable to find the original source. List both sources in the entry.

NOTE

20. Peter Gay, *Modernism: The Lure of Heresy* (New York: Norton, 2007): 262, quoted in Terry Teachout, "The Cult of the Difficult," *Commentary* 124, no. 5 (2007): 66–69.

BIBLIOGRAPHY ENTRY

Gay, Peter. *Modernism: The Lure of Heresy.* New York: Norton, 2007. Quoted in Terry Teachout. "The Cult of the Difficult." *Commentary* 124, no. 5 (2007): 66–69.

Periodicals

17. Article in a journal paginated by volume   When journals are paginated by yearly volume, your citation should include the following: author, title of article in quotation marks, title of journal, volume number and year, and page number(s).

NOTE

21. Frank Tirro, "Constructive Elements in Jazz Improvisation," *Journal of the American Musicological Society* 27 (1974): 300.

BIBLIOGRAPHY ENTRY

Tirro, Frank. "Constructive Elements in Jazz Improvisation." *Journal of the American Musicological Society* 27 (1974): 285–305.

18. Article in a journal paginated by issue   If the periodical is paginated by issue rather than by volume, add the issue number, preceded by the abbreviation *no* followed by a period.

NOTE   *title within title enclosed in single quotations*

22. Jeffrey Meyers, "Plath's 'Lady Lazarus,'" *Notes on Contemporary Literature* 42, no. 3 (2012): 33.

BIBLIOGRAPHY ENTRY

Meyers, Jeffrey. "Plath's 'Lady Lazarus.'" *Notes on Contemporary Literature* 42, no. 3 (2012): 33–35.

19. Article in a magazine   Identify magazines by week (if available) and month of publication. If the article cited does not appear on consecutive pages, do not put any page numbers in the bibliography entry. You can, however, give specific pages in the note. In Chicago style, the month precedes the date, and months are not abbreviated.

NOTE

23. Robin Raisfeld and Rob Patronite. "Vanishing," *New York,* December 23, 2013, 96.

BIBLIOGRAPHY ENTRY

Raisfeld, Robin, and Rob Patronite. "Vanishing." *New York,* December 23, 2013.

20. Article in a newspaper   Provide the author's name (if known), the title of the article, the name of the newspaper, and the date of publication. Do not give a page number. Instead, give the section number or title if it is indicated. If applicable, indicate the edition (for example, *national edition*) before the section number.

NOTE

24. Callum Borchers, "Want to Share Workspace? The Menu's a Big One." *Boston Globe,* January 6, 2014, sec. B.

Newspaper articles cited in the text of your paper do not need to be included in a bibliography or works-cited list. If you are asked to include articles in the list, however, or if you did not provide full citation information in the essay or the note, format the entry as follows.

BIBLIOGRAPHY ENTRY

Borchers, Callum. "Want to Share Workspace? The Menu's a Big One," *Boston Globe,* January 6, 2014, sec. B.

21. Unsigned article or editorial in a newspaper   Begin the note with the name of the article, and if you provide a bibliography or works-cited list entry, begin it with the name of the newspaper.

NOTE

25. "Who Says Math Has to Be Boring?" *New York Times,* December 7, 2013.

Other Sources

22. Review   If the review is untitled, start with the author's name (if any) and *review of* for a note or *Review of* for a bibliography entry.

NOTE

26. Jonathan Rosen, review of *A Feathered River Across the Sky: The Passenger Pigeon's Flight to Extinction,* by Joel Greenberg, *New Yorker,* January 6, 2014, 62.

BIBLIOGRAPHY ENTRY

Rosen, Jonathan. Review of *A Feathered River Across the Sky: The Passenger Pigeon's Flight to Extinction,* by Joel Greenberg. *New Yorker,* January 6, 2014, 62–67.

23. Interview   Treat published print interviews like articles *(see no. 19).* However, unless an interview has a given title (such as "Talking with the Dead: An Interview with Yiyun Li"), start with the name of the person interviewed. If a record of an unpublished interview exists, note the medium and where it may be found; the first example here is for a broadcast interview. Only interviews accessible to your readers are listed in the bibliography; the second example shown here, for a personal interview, would require only a note.

NOTES

27. Bob Woodruff, interview by Jon Stewart, *The Daily Show with Jon Stewart,* Comedy Central, November 4, 2013.

28. Susan Horowitz, personal interview by author, March 15, 2014, audio recording, Cincinnati.

BIBLIOGRAPHY ENTRY

Woodruff, Bob. Interview by Jon Stewart. *The Daily Show with Jon Stewart,* Comedy Central. November 4, 2013.

24. Published letter For a letter published in a collection, begin the entry with the letter writer's name, followed by *to* and the name (or in this case, the relationship) of the addressee. An approximate date for when the letter was written can be prefaced with the abbreviation *ca.* for *circa*. Follow information about the letter with publication information about the source it appears in.

NOTE

29. C. S. Lewis to his brother, ca. November 1905, in *The Collected Letters of C. S. Lewis, Vol. 1: Family Letters, 1905–1931,* ed. Walter Hooper (New York: Harper Collins, 2004), 2–3.

BIBLIOGRAPHY ENTRY

Lewis, C. S. C. S. Lewis to his brother, ca. November 1905. In *The Collected Letters of C. S. Lewis, Vol. 1: Family Letters, 1905–1931,* edited by Walter Hooper. New York: HarperCollins, 2004.

25. Personal letter or e-mail Do not list a letter that readers could not access in your bibliography.

NOTES

30. Daniel Clemons, letter to author, January 11, 2014.

31. Patricia Tyrell, e-mail message to author, May 29, 2012.

26. Government document If it is not already obvious in your text, in your bibliography, name the country first.

NOTE

32. Bureau of National Affairs, *The Civil Rights Act of 1964: Text, Analysis, Legislative History; What It Means to Employers, Businessmen, Unions, Employees, Minority Groups* (Washington, DC: BNA, 1964), 22–23.

BIBLIOGRAPHY ENTRY

U.S. Bureau of National Affairs. *The Civil Rights Act of 1964: Text, Analysis, Legislative History; What It Means to Employers, Businessmen, Unions, Employees, Minority Groups.* Washington, DC: BNA, 1964.

27. Unpublished document or dissertation Include a description of the document as well as information about where it is available. If more than one item from an archive is cited, include only one entry for the archive in your bibliography.

NOTES

33. Joe Glaser to Lucille Armstrong, September 28, 1960, Louis Armstrong Archives, Rosenthal Library, Queens College CUNY, Flushing, NY.

34. Deidre Dowling Price, "Confessional Poetry and Blog Culture in the Age of Autobiography." (PhD diss., Florida State University, 2010), 20–22.

BIBLIOGRAPHY ENTRIES

Glaser, Joe. Letter to Lucille Armstrong. Louis Armstrong Archives. Rosenthal Library, Queens College CUNY, Flushing, NY.

Price, Deidre Dowling. "Confessional Poetry and Blog Culture in the Age of Autobiography." PhD diss., Florida State University, 2010.

28. Conference presentation   When citing a presentation or lecture, include the location where it was given after the title; in the note, this information should be parenthetical. Also include a description, as in this example.

NOTE

35. Susan Jarratt, Katherine Mack, Alexandra Sartor, and Shevaun Watson. "Pedagogical Memory and the Transferability of Writing Knowledge: An Interview-Based Study of Juniors and Seniors at a Research University" (presentation, Writing Research across Borders Conference, Santa Barbara, CA, February 22, 2008).

BIBLIOGRAPHY ENTRY

Jarratt, Susan, Katherine Mack, Alexandra Sartor, and Shevaun Watson. "Pedagogical Memory and the Transferability of Writing Knowledge: An Interview-Based Study of Juniors and Seniors at a Research University." Paper presented at the Writing Research across Borders Conference, Santa Barbara, CA, February 22, 2008.

29. DVD or other form of recorded video   Include the original release date before the publication information if it differs from the release date for the DVD.

NOTE

36. *Behind the Candelabra,* directed by Steven Soderbergh (2013; New York: HBO Home Video), DVD.

BIBLIOGRAPHY

Behind the Candelabra. Directed by Steven Soderbergh. 2013. New York: HBO Home Video. DVD.

30. Sound recording   Begin with the composer or other person or group responsible for the content.

NOTE

37. Gaslight Anthem, *Handwritten.* Mercury Records, 2012, compact disc.

Chicago Chicago Chicago Chicago Chicago Chicago Chicago Chicago Chicago

BIBLIOGRAPHY ENTRY

Gaslight Anthem. *Handwritten.* Mercury Records, 2012. compact disc.

31. Artwork   Begin with the artist's name, and include both the name and the location of the institution holding the work. Italicize the name of any photograph or work of fine art. Works of art are usually not included in the bibliography.

NOTE

38. Andy Warhol, *Campbell's Soup Can* (oil on canvas, 1962, Saatchi Collection, London).

32. CD-ROM or other electronic non-Internet source   Indicate the format after the publication information.

NOTE

39. Owen Jones, *The Grammar of Ornament* (London, 1856; repr., Oakland: Octavo, 1998), CD-ROM.

BIBLIOGRAPHY ENTRY

Jones, Owen. *The Grammar of Ornament.* London, 1856. Reprint, Oakland: Octavo, 1998. CD-ROM.

Online Sources

The sixteenth edition of *The Chicago Manual of Style* specifically addresses the documentation of electronic and online sources. In general, citations for electronic sources include all of the information required for print sources, in addition to a URL (universal resource locator) or DOI (direct object identifier) and, in some cases, the date of access. There are three key differences between Chicago- and MLA-style online citations:

- Chicago recommends URLs or DOIs (preferring the latter when available) for all online sources. They should not be enclosed in angle brackets.
- Months are not abbreviated, and the date is usually given in the following order: month, day, year (September 13, 2014).
- Chicago recommends including dates of access only for sources that do not disclose a date of publication or revision. However, many instructors require students to include access dates for all online sources. Ask your instructor for his or her policy. If access dates are required, include them *before* the URL or DOI.

Use a period after any URL or DOI. If the URL or DOI has to be broken across lines, the break should occur *before* a slash (/), a period, a hyphen, an underscore, or a tilde (~). However, a break should occur *after* a colon.

33. Electronic book   Online versions of books are available either free of charge on the Web (often older titles that are in the public domain and out of print) or in versions that can be downloaded from a library or bookseller and also exist in a print version. For an older book you have accessed on the Web, include the date of access before the URL—or DOI if it is available—if your instructor requires it, as in the following example.

NOTE

40. Carl Sandburg, *Chicago Poems* (New York: Henry Holt, 1916), accessed March 18, 2008, http://www.bartleby.com/165/index.html.

BIBLIOGRAPHY ENTRY

Sandburg, Carl. *Chicago Poems.* New York: Henry Holt, 1916. Accessed March 18, 2008. http://www.bartleby.com/165/index.html.

For an electronic book you have purchased or obtained from a library, follow the guidelines for citing a print book *(see nos. 1–6),* but indicate the format at the end of the citation (for example, *Kindle edition, PDF e-book*). Because page numbers can vary, use the chapter number, section number, or another means of referring your reader to a specific part of the text.

NOTE

41. Stacy Schiff, *Cleopatra: A Life* (New York: Little Brown, 2010), Kindle edition, chap. 3.

BIBLIOGRAPHY

Schiff, Stacy. *Cleopatra: A Life.* New York: Little, Brown, 2010. Kindle edition.

34. Partial or entire Web site   Identify as many of the following as you can: author (if any), title of short work or page (if applicable), title or sponsor of site, and URL.

NOTES

42. Chris Garrett, "How I Use My Blog as a Fulcrum and You Can Too," *The Business of Blogging and New Media,* accessed January 28, 2011, http://www.chrisg.com/fulcrum/.

43. Chris Garrett, *The Business of Blogging and New Media,* last modified January 16, 2011, http://www.chrisg.com/.

44. Will Allison's Facebook page, last modified January 29, 2011, http://www.facebook.com/profile.php?id=591079933#!/profile.php?id=519407651.

Chicago Chicago Chicago Chicago Chicago Chicago Chicago Chicago Chicago

BIBLIOGRAPHY ENTRIES

Garrett, Chris. "How I Use My Blog as a Fulcrum and You Can Too." *The Business of Blogging and New Media.* Accessed January 28, 2011. http://www.chrisg.com /fulcrum/.

Garrett, Chris. *The Business of Blogging and New Media.* Last modified on January 16, 2011. http://www.chrisg.com/.

35. Article in an online reference work (dictionary or encyclopedia) Widely used reference works are usually cited in notes, not bibliographies, and most publication information can be omitted. Signed entries, however, should include the entry author's name.

NOTE

45. *Encyclopedia of World Biography,* s.v. "Nelson Mandela," accessed March 3, 2014, http://www.notablebiographies.com/Lo-Ma/Mandela-Nelson.html.

36. Article from an online periodical (with a DOI) Whenever a DOI is available for an article, use it instead of the URL. Include the date of access before the DOI if required.

NOTE

46. Diana S. Ali, et al., "'I Became a Mom': Identity Changes in Mothers Receiving Public Assistance," *Journal of Social Service Research* 39, no. 5 (2013): 587–605, doi:10.1080/01488376.2013.801391.

BIBLIOGRAPHY ENTRY

Diana S. Ali, M. Elizabeth Lewis Hall, Tamara L. Anderson, and Michele M. Willingham. "'I Became a Mom': Identity Changes in Mothers Receiving Public Assistance." *Journal of Social Service Research* 39, no. 5 (2013): 587–605. doi:10.1080/01488376. 2013.801391.

37. Article from an online journal, magazine, or newspaper (with no DOI) When no DOI is available, provide the source's direct URL.

NOTES

47. Jay Rosen, "The New News," *Technology Review,* January/February 2010, http://www.technologyreview.com/communications/24175/?a=f.

48. Michelle Castillo, "FCC Passes Ruling To Protect Net Neutrality." *Time.com,* December 21, 2010, http://techland.time.com/2010/12/21/fcc-passes-ruling-to-protect-net-neutrality/.

49. Larry Magid, "FCC Network Neutrality Rules Neither Socialism nor Sellout," *Huffington Post,* December 21, 2010, http://www.huffingtonpost.com/larry-magid/fcc-network-neutrality-ru_b_799999.html.

BIBLIOGRAPHY ENTRIES

Rosen, Jay. "The New News," *Technology Review,* January/
February 2010. http://www.technologyreview.com/
communications/24175/?a=f.

Castillo, Michelle. "FCC Passes Ruling to Protect Net Neutrality."
Time.com. December 21, 2010. http://techland.time.com/
2010/12/21/fcc-passes-ruling-to-protect-net-neutrality/.

Magid, Larry. "FCC Network Neutrality Rules Neither Socialism
nor Sell-out." *Huffington Post.* December 21, 2010. http://
www.huffingtonpost.com/larry-magid/fcc-network-neutrality-
ru_b_799999.html.

**38. Journal, magazine, or newspaper article from a library subscription
database**   Give the name of the database after information about the
article. An access date is required only if items do not include a publication or revision date. If a stable/permanent URL is provided for the
source, include it, but otherwise provide the name of the database. If
an identifying reference number is provided for the source, include it
in parentheses (between the database name and the closing period).

NOTE

50. Lacy, Stephen, et al. "Citizen Journalism Web Sites
Complement Newspapers." *Newspaper Research Journal* 31, no. 2
(Spring 2010): 34–46. Academic Search Elite.

BIBLIOGRAPHY ENTRY

Lacy, Stephen, Margaret Duffy, Daniel Riffe, Esther Thorson, and
Ken Fleming. "Citizen Journalism Web Sites Complement
Newspapers." *Newspaper Research Journal* 31, no. 2 (Spring
2010): 34–46. Academic Search Elite.

39. Blog posting   Individual blog posts are cited in the notes, along
with the description *blog* in parentheses after the larger blog's title. A
frequently cited blog can also be cited in the works-cited list or bibliography, as in this example.

NOTE

51. Dan Piepenbring, "Siri Hates Her and Other News," *On
the Shelf* (blog), January 7, 2014, http://www.theparisreview.org/
blog/2014/01/07/siri-hates-her-and-other-news.html.

BIBLIOGRAPHY ENTRY

Piepenbring, Dan. *On the Shelf* (blog). http://www.theparisreview.org/
blog/.

40. Posting to an electronic mailing list   Give the URL if the posting
is archived. If included, the name or number of a posting should be
noted after the date. Do not create a bibliography entry.

NOTE

> 52. Roland Kayser to Opera-L mailing list, January 3, 2008, http://listserv.bccls.org/cgi-bin/wa?A2=ind0801A&L=OPERA-L&D=0&P=57634.

41. Podcast The note should include any important name(s); the title; the source; the description, such as *podcast audio;* and the date. Bibliographic items follow the same sequence.

NOTE

> 53. Margaret Atwood, "Readings from Her Recent Work," *Southeast Review Online,* podcast audio, February 2010, http://southeastreview.org/2010/02/margaret-atwood.html.

BIBLIOGRAPHY ENTRY

Atwood, Margaret. "Readings from Her Recent Work." *Southeast Review Online.* Podcast audio. February 2010. http://southeastreview.org/2010/02/margaret-atwood.html.

42. Online video Notes for online videos include the relationship of the video to another source.

NOTE

> 54. Steven Johnson, "Where Good Ideas Come From," YouTube video, 4:07, as a trailer for Johnson's book *Where Good Ideas Come From,* posted by "RiverheadBooks," September 17, 2010, http://www.youtube.com/watch?v=NugRZGDbPFU.

BIBLIOGRAPHY ENTRY

Johnson, Steven. "Where Good Ideas Come From." YouTube video, 4:07. Posted September 17, 2010. http://www.youtube.com/watch?v=NugRZGDbPFU.

43. Online broadcast interview

NOTE

> 55. Malala Yousafzai, Interview by Jon Stewart, *The Daily Show with Jon Stewart,* Comedy Central video posted October 9, 2013, http://www.thedailyshow.com/watch/tues-october-8-2013/exclusive---malala-yousafzai-extended-interview-pt--1.

BIBLIOGRAPHY ENTRY

Yousafzai, Malala. "Interview with Malala Yousafzai." By Jon Stewart. *The Daily Show with Jon Stewart,* Comedy Central video. Posted October 9, 2013. http://www.thedailyshow.com/watch/tues-october-8-2013/exclusive---malala-yousafzai-extended-interview-pt--1.

CHAPTER 36

Chicago Documentation Style: Sample from a Student Research Project

The following brief excerpt from Kris Washington's project on blogging's impact on new media has been adapted and put into Chicago style so that you can see how citation numbers, endnotes, and a works-cited list work together. *(Washington's entire paper, in MLA style, can be found on pages 331–41.)*

   The Chicago Manual of Style is primarily a guide for publishers or those who wish to submit work to be published. To prepare a research project using Chicago documentation style, you can use the guidelines provided in pages 395–412 or check with your instructor. The formatting of the following sample pages is consistent with the guidelines found in Turabian's *Manual for Writers*.

1

In previous decades, when people wanted to know what was happening in the world, they turned to the daily newspaper, the radio, or their television sets. Today, we are more likely to go online where a simple *Google* search on any subject can produce thousands of hits and open doors to seemingly limitless sources of information; or, with even less effort, we may receive tweets or email alerts with embedded links that lead us to news reports. While there are still many online news sources, much of our information comes from online journals known as blogs, which have redefined the concept of news and increased the speed with which we receive it. . . . In fact, multimedia corporations have come to depend on bloggers to deliver the most recent developments on global events and increasingly have found ways to incorporate information from blogs, tweets, and other social media into traditional news reports. To survive, journalism must blend traditional forms of reporting with blogs, tweets, and other new methods that get news and opinion to the people instantaneously and universally.

Encyclopaedia Britannica defines a *blog,* short for *Web log,* as an "online journal where an individual, group, or corporation presents a record of activities, thoughts, or beliefs" ("Blog").[1] This definition points out an important aspect of blogs: some are run by companies and organizations, such as the *New York Times* and the *Chicago Tribune;* however, many are maintained by people not necessarily affiliated with traditional news outlets. In his book, *Here Comes Everybody: The Power of Organizing without Organizations,* New York University professor and

2

media consultant Clay Shirky explains how the proliferation of blogs is affecting news: "The change isn't a shift from one kind of news institution to another, but rather in the definition of news."[2] Blogging has ushered in a new set of consumer expectations for immediate news coverage distributed widely on a broad range of topics. Bloggers are able to decide what is newsworthy and they have the ability to spread that information globally at very little cost. Anderson, Bell, and Shirky explain that blogs and other forms of social media allow for "superdistribution," meaning that stories—including those published by smaller outlets—can reach a wider audience than ever before and at very little expense.[3] Rather than pay subscription fees to print newspapers, magazines, and journals, many people are turning to the Internet for free and immediate information.

With the rise of blogs and the abundance of free online information, media companies are finding it increasingly difficult to maintain funding for traditional news reporting. . . . Newspapers were slow to make their content available on mobile devices, and advertising revenue has also been slow to follow. Without that revenue, traditional news companies will be limited in their abilities to print and distribute news and hire staff. Alternatively, the proliferation of user-generated content introduces what media scholar Lev Manovich refers to as "a new economics of media," which means that even when produced on a much smaller scale, new media hold the potential to generate higher revenues than more traditional outlets.[4] Anderson, Bell, and Shirky suggest that news organizations "should master working

3

with amateurs, crowds, machines or other partners to keep cost low and leverage high" and "should assume that cost control is the central discipline."[5] Clearly, a partnership between traditional and new media is essential to the future of journalism.

Traditional forms of reporting, such as newspapers and televised news broadcasts, have always depended on the objectivity and credibility of their journalists, the reliability of their sources, and the extensive research and fact checking that inform every news story. Blogs are a fast and convenient way to publicize current issues and events, but it's questionable if blogs can offer information as reliable as that of traditional news organizations. For example, in the *New York Times* blog *The Choice,* high-school senior Leobardo Espinoza Jr. reported on his postgraduate plans in a post titled "Gap Year Now or Study Abroad Later?"[6] While the sources he cites—family and friends who have weighed in on his choice—have valid opinions, none are education experts. Neither his posting nor the comments are backed by the comprehensive, objective research that informed an Australian newspaper article on the same subject. In "Gap-Year Travel Brings Students Back to Learning," reporter John Ross cites recent research and explains how a gap year may positively or negatively affect the college experience.[7] As an Australian editorial recently stated, "Hard-core media values—truth, accuracy, fairness, balance, perspective, objectivity—are being lost at precisely the wrong time, as the news media faces the challenges of falling revenue, distracted audiences and a loss of skilled practitioners[8].". . .

Notes

1. *Encyclopaedia Britannica Online,* s.v. "Blog," accessed November 22, 2013, http://www.britannica.com/EBchecked/topic/869092/blog.

2. Clay Shirky, *Here Comes Everybody: The Power of Organizing without Organizations* (New York: Penguin, 2008), 64–65.

3. C. W. Anderson, Emily Bell, and Clay Shirky, "Post-Industrial Journalism: Adapting to the Present," *Tow Center for Digital Journalism,* n.d., http://towcenter.org/research/post-industrial-journalism/.

4. Lev Manovich, "The Practice of Everyday (Media) Life: From Mass Consumption to Mass Cultural Production?" *Critical Inquiry* 35, no. 2 (2009): 319–31.

5. Anderson, et al.

6. Leobardo Espinoza Jr., "Gap Year Now or Study Abroad Later?" *New York Times* (blog), March 21, 2013, http://thechoice.blogs.nytimes.com/2013/03/21/envelope-please-leobardo-espinoza-jr-9/?_r=0.

7. John Ross, "Gap-Year Travel Brings Students Back to Learning," *The Australian,* April 17, 2013, http://www.theaustralian.com.au/higher-education/gap-year-travel-brings-students-back-to-learning/story-e6frgcjx-1226621972703.

8. "Lost in the Twitterverse," *The Australian,* November 13, 2013, http://www.theaustralian.com.au/opinion/editorials/lost-in-the-twitterverse/story-e6frg71x-1226758522447.

Works Cited

Anderson, C. W., Emily Bell, and Clay Shirky. *Post Industrial Journalism: Adapting to the Present.* New York: Tow Center for Digital Journalism, Columbia University, n.d. Accessed November 25, 2013, http://towcenter.org/research/post-industrial-journalism/.

Edmonds, Rick, Emily Guskin, Mark Jurkowitz, and Amy Mitchell. *The State of the News Media 2013: An Annual Review of American Journalism,* July 18, 2013. Pew Research Center's Project for Excellence in Journalism. Accessed December 12, 2013, http://stateofthemedia.org/2013/newspapers-stabilizing-but-still-threatened.

Espinoza, Leobardo. *The Choice: Demystifying College Admissions and Aid* (blog). http://thechoice.blogs.nytimes.com/2013/03/21/envelope-please-leobardo-espinoza-jr-9/?_r=0.

Lacy, Stephen, Margaret Duffy, Daniel Riffe, Esther Thorson, and Ken Fleming. "Citizen Journalism Web Sites Complement Newspapers." *Newspaper Research Journal* 31, no. 2 (Spring 2010): 34–46. Academic Search Elite.

CHAPTER 37
CSE Documentation Style

The Council of Science Editors (CSE) endorses three documentation styles in the eighth edition of *Scientific Style and Format: The CSE Manual for Authors, Editors, and Publishers* (Chicago, IL: Univ. of Chicago Press, 2014):

- The **name-year style** includes the last name of the author and year of publication in the text. In the list of references, sources are in alphabetical order and unnumbered.
- The **citation-sequence style** includes a superscript number or a number in parentheses in the text. In the list of references, sources are numbered and appear in order of citation.
- The **citation-name style** also uses a superscript number or a number in parentheses in the text. In the list of references, however, sources are numbered and arranged in alphabetical order.

Learn your instructor's preferred style and use it consistently within a research project. Also ask your instructor about line spacing, headings, and other design elements, which the CSE manual does not specify.

37a   CSE in-text citations.

Name-year style   Include the author's last name and the year of publication.

According to Gleeson (1993), a woman loses 35% of cortical bone and 50% of trabecular bone during her lifetime.

In epidemiologic studies, small increases in BMD and decreases in fracture risk have been reported in individuals using NSAIDS (Raisz 2001; Carbone et al. 2003).

Citation-sequence or citation-name style   Insert a superscript number immediately after the relevant name, word, or phrase and before any punctuation. Put a space before and after the superscript unless a punctuation mark follows.

As a group, American women over 45 years of age sustain approximately 1 million fractures each year, 70% of which are due to osteoporosis.[1]

That number now belongs to that source, and you should use it if you refer to that source again in your paper.

According to Gleeson,[6] a woman loses 35% of cortical bone and 50% of trabecular bone over her lifetime.

Credit more than one source at a time by referring to each source's number. Separate the numbers with a comma.

According to studies by Yomo,[2] Paleg,[3] and others,[1,4] barley seed embryos produce a substance that stimulates the release of hydrolytic enzymes.

If more than two numbers are in sequence, however, separate them with a hyphen.

As several others[1-4] have documented, GA has an RNA-enhancing effect.

37b CSE list of references.

Every source cited in your project must correspond to an entry in your list of references, which should be prepared according to the guidelines in the box on page 422.

Books, reports, and papers

In *name-year style,* include the author(s), last name first; publication year; title; place; and publisher. In *citation-sequence* or *citation-name style,* include the same information, but put the year after the publisher.

1. Book with one author If a work has no named author, begin with the title. *(See nos. 17 and 18 for examples.)*

NAME-YEAR

Reinhard T. 2014. Superfoods: the healthiest foods on the planet. Ontario (CA): Firefly Books.

CITATION-SEQUENCE OR CITATION-NAME

1. Reinhard T. Superfoods: the healthiest foods on the planet. Ontario (CA): Firefly Books; 2014.

2. Book with two or more authors List up to ten authors; if there are more than ten, use the first ten names with the phrase *et al.* or *and others* (not italicized).

NAME-YEAR

Pinna K, Rolfes SR, Whitney E. 2014. Understanding normal and clinical nutrition. 10th ed. Stamford (CT): Cengage Learning.

CSE STYLE: DIRECTORY TO SAMPLE TYPES

Books, Reports, and Papers

Periodicals

Online and Multimodal Sources

CITATION-SEQUENCE OR CITATION-NAME

2. Pinna K, Rolfes SR, Whitney E. 2014. Understanding normal and clinical nutrition. 10th ed. Stamford (CT): Cengage Learning; 2014.

3. Two or more cited works by the same author(s) published in the same year   This structure is not necessary in the citation-sequence style because entries are arranged and numbered by the order in which they appear.

NAME-YEAR

Yancey KB. 2008a. A place of our own: spaces and materials for composing in the new century. In: Tassoni J, Powell D, editors. Composing other spaces. Creskill (NJ): Hampton.

Yancey KB. 2008b. The literacy demands of entering the university. In: Christenbury L, Bomer R, Smagorinsky P, editors. Handbook on adolescent literacy. New York: Guilford.

CSE LIST OF REFERENCES

- Begin on a new page after your text but before any appendices, tables, and figures.
- Use the centered title "References."
- Include only references that are cited in your paper.
- For citation-sequence and citation-name styles, begin each entry with a superscript number.
- Start each entry with the author's last name, followed by initials for first and middle names. Add no spaces or periods between initials.
- Abbreviate periodical titles as shown in the CSE manual, and capitalize major words.
- Use complete book and article titles; capitalize the first word and any proper nouns or proper adjectives.
- Do not use italics, underlining, or quotation marks to set off any kind of title.
- List the extent of a source (number of pages or screens) at the end of the entry if your instructor requires it.
- When a URL must be broken across lines of text, break it before or after a slash or other punctuation.

Name-Year Style
- Always put the date after the author's name.
- List the references in alphabetical order, but do not number them.

Citation-Sequence Style
- Put the date after the name of the book publisher or periodical.
- List and number the references in the order they first appear in the text.

Citation-Name Style
- Put the date after the name of the book publisher or periodical.
- List and number the references in alphabetical order. Make the numbering of your in-text citations match.

4. Book with organization as author   In name-year style, start the entry with the organization's abbreviation, but alphabetize by the full name.

NAME-YEAR

[NIH] National Institutes of Health (US). 1993. Clinical trials supported by the National Eye Institute (US): celebrating vision research. Bethesda (MD): US Dept. of Health and Human Services.

CITATION-SEQUENCE OR CITATION-NAME

3. National Institutes of Health (US). Clinical trials supported by the National Eye Institute (US): celebrating vision research. Bethesda (MD): US Dept. of Health and Human Services; 1993.

5. Chapter in a book   In both styles, the chapter number and title and the pages follow the publication information.

NAME-YEAR

O'Connell C. 2007. The elephant's secret sense: the hidden life of the wild herds of Africa. New York: Free Press. Chapter 9, Cracking elephant Morse code; p. 119–126.

CITATION-SEQUENCE OR CITATION-NAME

4. O'Connell C. The elephant's secret sense: the hidden life of the wild herds of Africa. New York: Free Press; 2007. Chapter 9, Cracking elephant Morse code; p. 119–126.

6. Reprint of an older book   Indicate the copyright date (the date of the first publication) just after the date of the reprint in name-year style and following the original publisher in the other two styles.

NAME-YEAR

Hamaker JI. 2010, c1913. The principles of biology. Charleston (SC): Forgotten Books. 474 p.

CITATION-SEQUENCE OR CITATION-NAME

5. Hamaker JI. The principles of biology. Philadelphia (PA): P. Blakiston's Son; 1913. Charleston (SC): Forgotten Books; 2010. 474 p.

7. Book with editor(s)   If there is no identifiable author, begin with the editor's name, followed by the word *editor*.

NAME-YEAR

Mukherjee S, Folger T, editors. 2013. The best American science and nature writing 2013. New York: Mariner.

CITATION-SEQUENCE OR CITATION-NAME

6. Mukherjee S, Folger T, editors. The best American science and nature writing 2013. New York: Mariner; 2013.

8. Selection in an edited book In the name-year style, begin with the author, the date, and then the title of the selection, followed by the name of the editor or editors and the publication information. When using the citation-sequence or citation-name style, put the date between the publisher and the pages.

NAME-YEAR

Bohus B, Koolhaas JM. 1993. Psychoimmunology of social factors in rodents and other subprimate vertebrates. In: Ader R, Felten DL, Cohen N, editors. Psychoneuroimmunology. San Diego (CA): Academic Press. p. 807–830.

CITATION-SEQUENCE OR CITATION-NAME

7. Bohus B, Koolhaas JM. Psychoimmunology of social factors in rodents and other subprimate vertebrates. In: Ader R, Felten DL, Cohen N, editors. Psychoneuroimmunology. San Diego (CA): Academic Press; 1993. p. 807–830.

9. All volumes of a multivolume work Provide the number of volumes followed by the abbreviation *vol.*

NAME-YEAR

Bittar EE. 1992. Fundamentals of medical cell biology. Cambridge (MA): Elsevier Science. 4 vol.

CITATION-SEQUENCE OR CITATION-NAME

8. Bittar, EE. Fundamentals of medical cell biology. Cambridge (MA): Elsevier Science; 1992. 4 vol.

10. Technical report or government document Include the name of the sponsoring organization or agency as well as any report or contract number.

NAME-YEAR

Bolen S, Wilson L, Vassy J, Feldman L, Yeh J, Marinopoulos S, Wilson R, Cheng D, Wiley C, Selvin E, et al. (Johns Hopkins University Evidence-based Practice Center, Baltimore, MD). 2007. Comparative effectiveness and safety of oral diabetes medications for adults with type 2 diabetes. Comparative effectiveness review No. 8. Rockville (MD): Agency for Healthcare Research and Quality (US). Contract No.: 290-02-0018. Available from: AHRQ, Rockville, MD; AHRQ Pub. No. 07-EHC010-1.

CITATION-SEQUENCE OR CITATION-NAME

9. Bolen S, Wilson L, Vassy J, Feldman L, Yeh J, Marinopoulos S, Wilson R, Cheng D, Wiley C, Selvin E, et al. (Johns Hopkins University Evidence-based Practice Center, Baltimore, MD). Comparative effectiveness and safety of oral diabetes medications for adults with type 2 diabetes. Comparative effectiveness review No. 8. Rockville (MD): Agency for Healthcare Research and Quality (US); 2007. Contract No.: 290-02-0018. Available from: AHRQ, Rockville, MD; AHRQ Pub. No. 07-EHC010-1.

11. Paper in conference proceedings   For name-year style, begin with the name and the year of publication of the proceedings (preceded by a *c*), and include the paper title, the name of the editor or editors, the title of the proceedings, and the conference date and year. In the citation-sequence and citation-name styles, the conference date appears after the publication title, and the publication date appears between the publisher and the pages.

NAME-YEAR

De Jong E, Franke L, Siebes A. c2007. On the measurement of genetic interactions. In: Berthold MR, Glen RC, Feelders AJ, editors. Proceedings of the AIP 940. 3rd International Symposium on Computational Life Science; 2007 Oct 4–5; Utrecht (NL). Melville (NY): American Institute of Physics. p. 16–25.

CITATION-SEQUENCE OR CITATION-NAME

10. De Jong E, Franke L, Siebes A. On the measurement of genetic interactions. In: Berthold MR, Glen RC, Feelders AJ, editors. Proceedings of the AIP 940. 3rd International Symposium on Computational Life Science; 2007 Oct 4–5; Utrecht (NL). Melville (NY): American Institute of Physics; c2007. p. 16–25.

12. Dissertation   Include *dissertation* in brackets and the location of the institution granting the dissertation, also in brackets, followed by a colon and the university.

NAME-YEAR

Bertrand KN. 2007. Fishes and floods: stream ecosystem drivers in the Great Plains [dissertation]. [Manhattan (KS)]: Kansas State University.

CITATION-SEQUENCE OR CITATION-NAME

11. Bertrand KN. Fishes and floods: stream ecosystem drivers in the Great Plains [dissertation]. [Manhattan (KS)]: Kansas State University; 2007.

Periodicals

When listing most periodical articles, include the author(s); year; title of article; title of journal (abbreviated); number of the volume; number of the issue, if available (in parentheses); and page numbers. In name-year style, put the year after the author(s). In citation-sequence or citation-name style, put the year after the journal title.

Up to ten authors can be listed by name. If you cannot determine the article's author, begin with the title. If both an author and an organization or affiliation are listed, use only the author's name.

13. Article in a journal that uses only volume numbers Include only the volume number before the pages.

NAME-YEAR

Devine A, Prince RL, Bell R. 1996. Nutritional effect of calcium supplementation by skim milk powder or calcium tablets on total nutrient intake in postmenopausal women. Am J Clin Nutr. 64:731–737.

CITATION-SEQUENCE OR CITATION-NAME

12. Devine A, Prince RL, Bell R. Nutritional effect of calcium supplementation by skim milk powder or calcium tablets on total nutrient intake in postmenopausal women. Am J Clin Nutr. 1996;64:731–737.

14. Article in a journal that uses volume and issue numbers Include the issue number in parentheses after the volume number.

NAME-YEAR

Hummel-Berry K. 1990. Obstetric low back pain, a comprehensive review, part 2: evaluation and treatment. J Ob Gyn PT. 14(2):9–11.

CITATION-SEQUENCE OR CITATION-NAME

13. Hummel-Berry K. Obstetric low back pain, a comprehensive review, part 2: evaluation and treatment. J Ob Gyn PT. 1990;14(2):9–11.

15. Article in a magazine Indicate the year, month, and day (if available) of publication.

NAME-YEAR

Specter M. 2014 Jan 6. The gene factory. New Yorker. 34–43.

CITATION-SEQUENCE OR CITATION-NAME

14. Specter M. The gene factory. New Yorker. 2014 Jan 6:34–43.

16. Article in a newspaper Indicate the year, month, and day of publication.

NAME-YEAR

Fountain H. 2011 Mar 8. The reinvention of silk. New York Times. Sect. D:1 (col. 4).

CITATION-SEQUENCE OR CITATION-NAME

15. Fountain H. The reinvention of silk. New York Times. 2011 Mar 8;Sect. D:1 (col. 4).

17. Article with no named author When there is no named author, begin with the title.

NAME-YEAR

Senate repeals military gay ban. 2010 Dec 19. Times (St. Petersburg, FL). Sect A:1 (col. 2).

CITATION-SEQUENCE OR CITATION-NAME

16. Senate repeals military gay ban. Times (St. Petersburg, FL). 2010 Dec 19;Sect. A:1 (col. 2).

18. Editorial Editorials usually do not have signed authors, so begin with the title, followed by *[editorial]*.

NAME-YEAR

Blogs gone bad [editorial]. 2005. New Atlantis 8:106–109.

CITATION-SEQUENCE OR CITATION-NAME

17. Blogs gone bad [editorial]. New Atlantis 2005;8:106–109.

19. Review A note following the page number can give additional, optional information about the article in the CSE system.

NAME-YEAR

Wang C. 2007 Spring. Where old and new media collide. Spectator. 101–103. Review of Jenkins H, Convergence culture.

CITATION-SEQUENCE OR CITATION-NAME

18. Wang C. Where old and new media collide. 2007 Spring. Spectator. 101–103. Review of Jenkins H, Convergence culture.

Online and multimodal sources

Include information on author, title, and so forth, as with print works. Follow these special guidelines:

- Include in brackets the date of the most recent update (if any) and the date you accessed the source.
- List the publisher or the sponsor, or use the bracketed phrase *[publisher unknown]* (not italicized).
- To include length of a document without page numbers, use designations such as *[16 paragraphs]* or *[4 screens]* (neither italicized).
- List the URL at the end of the reference. Do not put a period after a URL unless it ends with a slash.

The following examples are in the citation-sequence or citation-name style. For name-year style, list the publication date after the author's name and do not number your references.

20. Online book (monograph)   Provide the year and date accessed (in brackets) followed by the URL.

19. Kohn LT, Corrigan JM, Donaldson MS, editors. To err is human: building a safer health system. Washington (DC): National Academy Press; 2000 [accessed 2007 Oct 19]. http://www .nap.edu/books/0309068371/html

21. Article in an online journal   Include the journal issue and page numbers after the bracketed access date and before the URL.

20. Krieger D, Onodipe S, Charles PJ, Sclabassi RJ. Real time signal processing in the clinical setting. Ann Biomed Engn. 1998 [accessed 2007 Oct 19];26(3):462–472. http://www .springerlink.com/content/n31828q461h54282

22. Articles on the Internet (print versions available)   Insert in brackets the date of access; provide the URL after the print page number.

21. Wald ML. EPA says it will press on with greenhouse gas regulation. New York Times. 2010 [accessed 2010 Dec 23];A:16. http://www.nytimes.com/2010/12/24/science/earth/24epa .html?ref=science

23. Material from a library subscription database   CSE does not specify a format. Give the information for a print article with database title and publication information.

CSE CSE CSE CSE CSE CSE CSE CSE CSE CSE CSE CSE CSE CSE CSE CSE CSE CSE

22. Baccarelli A, Zanobetti A, Martinelli I, Grillo P, Lifang H, Lanzani G, Mannucci PM, Bertazzi PA, Schwartz, J. Air pollution, smoking, and plasma homocysteine. Environ Health Perspect. 2007 Feb [accessed 2007 Oct 23];115(2):176–181. Health Source: Nursing/ Academic Edition. Birmingham (AL): EBSCO. http://www.ebsco.com

24. Material from a Web site

23. Hutchinson JR. Vertebrate flight. University of California— Berkeley. 2005 Sep 9 [accessed 2008 Jan 15]. http://www .ucmp.berkeley.edu/vertebrates/flight/flightintro.html

25. Message posted to a discussion list   Include the name, the header for the message, the list name, an identification of the list in brackets, the group or institution responsible for the list, the date of the posting, the date of citation, and the URL.

24. Parfitt M. Inquiry vs. argument: your thoughts. WPA-L [discussion list]. Tempe (AZ): Council of Writing Program Administrators; 2010 Dec 22 [accessed 2010 Dec 22]. http://wpa-l.asu .edu<mailto:wpa-l@asu.edu>/.

26. Videos or podcasts

25. Johnson S. Where good ideas come from [video on the Internet]. Riverhead Books 2010 Sep 17, 4:07. [accessed 2010 Dec 19]. http://www.youtube.com/watch?v=NugRZGDbPFU

27. Slide set or presentation slides   For a slide set, substitute the label *slides*. This particular presentation was downloaded from an online source, so retrieval information is also included.

26. Volunteering: what's it all about? [PowerPoint slides]. Sydney, AU: Volunteering Australia Inc.; 2009. 24 slides. [accessed 2014 Aug 7] http://www.volunteeringaustralia.org/files/WZ7KOVWICM/ Volunteering%20what_s%20it%20all%20about.ppt

28. Audio or video recording

27. Planet Earth: the complete BBC series [DVD]. London (UK): BBC; c2007. 4 DVDs: 550 mins, sound, color.

29. Document on a CD-ROM or DVD-ROM

28. Jones O. The grammar of ornament [CD-ROM]. London (UK): Octavo; 1998.

30. Map   The physical description of the map is optional.

29. GIS mapping of boom locations and other information needed for Tampa Bay oil spill contingency program [marine survey map]. St. Petersburg (FL): NOAA and Tampa Bay National Estuary Program; 1996. 51 x 66 in., b&w, scale 1:24,000.

37c Sample references list: CSE name-year style

The following is the first part of a list of references in CSE name-year style for a student research report on the origins of avian flight.

References

Anderson, A. 1991. Early bird threatens archaeopteryx's perch. Science. 253(5015):35.

Geist N, Feduccia A. 2000. Gravity-defying behaviors: identifying models for protoaves. Am Zoologist. 40(4):664–675.

Goslow GE, Dial KP, Jenkins FA. 1990. Bird flight: insights and complications. Bioscience. 40(2):108–116.

37d Sample references list: CSE citation-name style

Here are the same references as in 37c but in citation-name style, listed and numbered in alphabetical order. Citation-sequence style would look the same, but entries would be in the order in which they were cited in the paper.

References

1. Anderson, A. Early bird threatens archaeopteryx's perch. Science. 1991;253(5015):35.

2. Geist N, Feduccia A. Gravity-defying behaviors: identifying models for protoaves. Am Zoologist. 2000;40(4):664–675.

3. Goslow GE, Dial KP, Jenkins FA. Bird flight: insights and complications. Bioscience. 1990;40(2):108–116.

CSE CSE CSE CSE CSE CSE CSE CSE CSE CSE CSE CSE CSE CSE

9

Editing for Clarity

I . . . believe that words can help us move or keep us para-
lyzed, and that our choices of language and verbal tone have
something—a great deal—to do with how we live our lives
and whom we end up speaking with and hearing.

–Adrienne Rich

The Palais des Congrés in downtown Montreal features an impressive window display made of more than three hundred glass panels. Sunlight brings out the clarity of the window's design; and, in turn, the design transforms the light.

9 Editing for Clarity

✓ Sections referenced in Resources for Writers: Identifying and Editing Common Problems
(following Tab 9).

—**START SMART**

Tab 9: Editing for Clarity

This section will help you answer questions such as the following:

Rhetorical Knowledge

- Is my writing too formal or too informal for college assignments? (47b)
- How can I avoid sexist language such as *mankind* and the generic use of *he?* (47e)

Critical Thinking, Reading, and Writing

- How can subordination clarify relationships between ideas? (44b)
- How can I choose between two words with similar meanings? (48a, 49a, b)

Processes

- Can my word processor's grammar checker help me edit for clarity? (38, 40a, 41, 43a, 43e, 45, 46)
- Can a grammar checker help me find mixed constructions, shifts, and misplaced and dangling modifiers in my writing? (40a, 41, 43a, e)

Knowledge of Conventions

- What's wrong with the comparison *I like texting more than John?* (39c)
- What's wrong with saying *the reason . . . is because?* (40c)
- Should I use *their, there,* or *they're* in this sentence? (50)

For a general introduction to writing outcomes, see 1e, pages 14–16.

GRAMMAR Identifying and Editing Common Problems

If you are having difficulty finding the advice you need in *A Writer's Resource*, consult the chart of students' most common errors below. Once you have identified the issue giving you trouble, turn to the indicated section of this book for more explanation and examples. This icon [✓] marks each of those sections in the text. A list of these sections also appears in the Quick Guide to Key Resources at the back of this book.

Editing for Clarity

TAB 9

(Style, Voice, and Tone)

Mia was neither surprised *by* nor happy with her grade on the exam. | inc

Missing Word — Ch. 39a, p. 443

~~When~~ Juan knew the test was canceled because the classroom was empty. | mix

Mixed construction — Ch. 40a, p. 445

If students want to use the lounge, ~~you~~ *they* have to sign up in advance. | shift

Beethoven was completely deaf when he ~~writes~~ *wrote* his last symphony. | shift

Confusing shifts (person and verb tense) — Ch. 41a, 41b, and p. 450

During vacation I plan to relax, sleep late, and ~~I will~~ spend time with my family. | //

Faulty parallelism — Ch. 42a and p. 452

Following the recipe carefully, ~~the cake went~~ *I put* the cake in the oven for an hour. | dm

Dangling modifier — Ch. 43e, p. 457

Sean was distracted by the ~~incredulous~~ *incredible* news and did not ~~rely~~ *really* hear his instructor's question. | ww ww

Wrong words — Ch. 48f, p. 472

Editing for Grammar Conventions

TAB 10

GRAMMAR

(Sentence Structure and Cohesion)

My car won't start, which

~~Which~~ means I'll be late for work.
^

	frag

Sentence fragment

Ch. 51, p. 487

---

but

The Internet has increased the speed of people's communications, it
has not improved the quality.
^

	cs

They

Some people send text messages while driving. ~~they~~ often
get distracted.
^

	run-on

Comma splices and run-ons

Ch. 52, p. 493

Each of Gloria's clocks shows a different time.
^

	agr

Subject-verb agreement

Ch. 53, p. 498

---

eating [OR after he or she eats]

Each person who sits at this table must clean up after ~~they eat~~.
^

	agr

Pronoun-antecedent agreement

Ch. 55a and p. 518

Ellen

Ellen and her sister argued after ~~she~~ went to the party alone.
^

	ref

Unclear pronoun reference

Ch. 55b, p. 519

---

me

John drove my friend and ~~I~~ to the hockey game.
^

	case

Pronoun case

Ch. 55d and p. 552

Editing for Correctness

TAB 11

(Punctuation, Mechanics, and Spelling)

If I don't feed my dog in the morning, she will bark all day long.

Comma needed to set off introductory word group   Ch. 57a, p. 536

Jaime was going to meet us, but his flight was delayed.

Comma needed before coordinating conjunction   Ch. 57c, p. 538

Neil Armstrong's moon landing, which millions watched, inspired many people.

Commas needed for nonrestrictive word group   Ch. 57e, p. 539

Sonia's dog likes to chase it's tail.

Incorrect use of apostrophe with possessive pronoun   Ch. 60c, p. 555

My ~~english~~ class comes right after my biology class.

Incorrect capitalization   Ch. 63a, p. 568

their
The boys took ~~there~~ time on the way home.

Spelling error (*homonym*)   Ch. 68b, p. 585

Nouns and Pronouns

(**Ch. 69b,** p. 595; **Ch. 69c,** p. 599; **Ch. 70a,** p. 610)

Count and Noncount Nouns

Count nouns name persons, places, or things that can be counted. Count nouns can be singular or plural.

Noncount nouns name a class of things. Usually, noncount nouns have only a singular form.

COUNT	NONCOUNT	COUNT	NONCOUNT
cars	information	child	humanity
table	furniture	book	advice

Pronouns

Common Problem: Personal pronoun restates subject.

INCORRECT	My sister, she works in the city.
CORRECT	My sister works in the city.

Pronouns replace nouns. They stand for persons, places, or things and can be singular or plural.

Personal pronouns act as subjects, objects, or words that show possession.
Subject pronouns: I, we, you, he, she, it, one, they, who
Object pronouns: me, us, you, him, her, it, one, them, whom
Possessive pronouns: my, mine, our, ours, your, yours, his, her, hers, its, their, theirs, whose

Relative pronouns introduce dependent clauses.
Relative pronouns: that, whatever, which, whichever, who, whoever, whom, whomever, whose

EXAMPLE	His sister, who lives in Canada, came to visit.

Sentence Structure

(**Ch. 70,** p. 610)

Subjects and Verbs

English requires both a subject and a verb in every sentence or clause.

   S   V   S   V
She slept.   He ate.

Direct and Indirect Objects

Verbs may be followed by direct or indirect objects. A direct object receives the action of the verb.

   S   V   DO
He drove the car.

An indirect object is the person or thing to which something is done.

   S   V   IO   DO
She gave her sister a birthday gift.

GRAMMAR

Resources for Writers

Articles

Common Problem: Article is omitted.

INCORRECT	Water is cold. I bought watch.
CORRECT	The water is cold. I bought a watch.

Using Articles with Count and Noncount Nouns

Definite article (the): used for specific reference with all types of nouns.

> *The* car I bought is red. [*singular count noun*]
> *The* dogs howled at the moon. [*plural count noun*]
> *The* furniture makes the room appear cluttered. [*noncount noun*]

Do not use *the* before most singular proper nouns, such as the names of people, cities, languages, and so on.

> ~~The~~ Dallas is a beautiful city.

Indefinite articles (a, an): used with singular count nouns only.

Use *a* before a word that begins with a consonant sound.
> *a* pencil
> *a* sports car
> *a* tropical rain forest

Use *an* before a word that begins with a vowel sound.
> *an* orange
> *an* hour
> *an* instrument

Do not use an indefinite article with a noncount noun.

> *Water*
> ~~A water~~ is leaking from the faucet.

No article: Plural count nouns and noncount nouns do not require indefinite articles. Plural count nouns and noncount nouns do not need definite articles when they refer to all of the items in a group.

Plural count nouns and noncount nouns

> Every night I hear ~~a~~ dogs barking.

> I needed to find ~~an~~ information in the library.

Plural count nouns

SPECIFIC ITEM	The dogs next door never stop barking.
ALL ITEMS IN A GROUP	Dogs make good pets.

Noncount nouns

SPECIFIC ITEM	The jewelry she wore to the party was beautiful.
ALL ITEMS IN A GROUP	Jewelry is expensive.

Verbs

(Ch. 54f, p. 510; Ch. 69a, p. 590; Ch. 70b, p. 613)

Common Problem: *be* verb is left out.

INCORRECT	He sleeping now. She happy.
CORRECT	He is sleeping now. She is happy.

Verb Tenses

Tense refers to the time of action expressed by a verb.

Present tense (**base form or form with -s ending**): action taking place now. I *sleep* here. She *sleeps*. We *sleep* late every weekend.

Past tense (**-d or -ed ending**): past action. I *laughed*. He *laughed*. They *laughed* together.

Future tense (***will* + base form**): action that is going to take place. I *will go* to the movie. He *will run* in the marathon. You *will write* the paper.

Present perfect tense (***have* or *has* + past participle**): past action that was or will be completed. I *have spoken*. He *has washed* the floor. We *have made* lunch.

Past perfect tense (***had* + past participle**): past action completed before another past action. I *had spoken*. She *had been* busy. They *had noticed* a slight error.

Future perfect tense (***will* + *have* + past participle**): action that will begin and end in the future before another action happens. I *will have eaten*. She *will have danced* in the recital by then. You *will have taken* the train.

Present progressive tense (***am, are,* or *is* + present participle**): continuing action. I *am writing* a novel. He *is working* on a new project. They *are studying* for the test.

Past progressive tense (***was* or *were* + present participle**): past continuing action. I *was cleaning* the house. She *was working* in the yard. You *were making* dinner.

Future progressive tense (***will* + *be* + present participle**): future continuing action. I *will be traveling* to Europe. She *will be sightseeing* in New York. They *will be eating* together tonight.

Present perfect progressive tense (***have* or *has* + *been* + present participle**): past action that continues in the present. I *have been practicing*. He *has been sleeping* all morning. They *have been coming* every weekend.

Past perfect progressive tense (***had* + *been* + present participle**): continuous action completed before another past action. I *had been driving* for six hours. She *had been reading* when I arrived. They *had been singing*.

Future perfect progressive tense (***will* + *have* + *been* + present participle**): action that will begin, continue, and end in the future. I *will have been driving* for ten hours. He *will have been living* there for three years. You *will have been* for the test all afternoon.

CHAPTER 38

Wordy Sentences

A sentence does not have to be short and simple to be concise, but every word must count.

Wordiness and Grammar Checkers

Most computer grammar checkers recognize wordy structures inconsistently. One flagged most passive verbs and some *it is* and *there are* (expletive) constructions, but not others. It also flagged the redundant expression *true fact,* but it missed *round circle* and the empty phrase *it is a fact that.*

38a Eliminate redundancies.

Redundancies are meaningless repetitions that result in wordiness. Eliminate common redundancies like *first and foremost, full and complete, final result, past histories, round in shape,* and *refer back.*

► **Students living ~~in close proximity~~ in the dorms need to cooperate ~~together if they want~~ to live in harmony.**

Sometimes, modifiers such as *very, rather,* and *really* and intensifiers such as *absolutely, definitely,* and *incredibly* do not add meaning to a sentence. Instead, they are redundant.

► **That film was ~~really~~ hard to watch, but ~~absolutely~~ worth seeing.**

► **The ending ~~definitely~~ shocked us ~~very much~~.**

38b Do not repeat words unnecessarily.

Although repetition is sometimes used for emphasis, unnecessary repetitions weaken sentences and should be removed.

► **The children enjoyed watching television more than ~~they enjoyed~~ reading books.**

► **They watched cartoons in the morning and ~~cartoons~~ again in the afternoon.**

ALTERNATIVES FOR WORDY PHRASES

Wordy Phrases	*Concise Alternatives*
at this point in time	now
at the present time	now
in the not-too-distant future	soon
in close proximity to	near
is necessary that	must
is able to	can
has the ability to	can
due to the fact that	because
for the reason that	because
in spite of the fact that	although
in the event that	if
in the final analysis	finally
in order to	to
for the purpose(s) of	to

38c   Avoid wordy phrases.

Make your sentences more concise by eliminating wordy phrases or replacing them with one-word alternatives.

> *Tests must now*
> ▶ ~~It is necessary at this point in time that tests~~ be run ~~for the purposes of~~ *to measure*
>
> ~~measuring~~ the switch's strength.

> ▶ ~~What I mean to say is that~~ Wordsworth's poetry inspired many other
>
> writers of the Romantic period.

38d   Reduce clauses and phrases.

For conciseness and clarity, simplify your sentence structure by turning modifying clauses into phrases.

> ▶ The film *The Social Network,* ~~which was~~ directed by David Fincher,
>
> portrays the turbulent founding of *Facebook.*

Also look for opportunities to reduce phrases to single words.

> ▶ David Fincher's film *The Social Network* portrays the turbulent founding
>
> of *Facebook.*

IDENTIFY AND EDIT

Wordy Sentences

W

Ask yourself these questions as you edit:

? *1. Do any sentences contain wordy or empty phrases such as* at this point in time? *Do any contain redundancies or other unnecessary repetitions?*

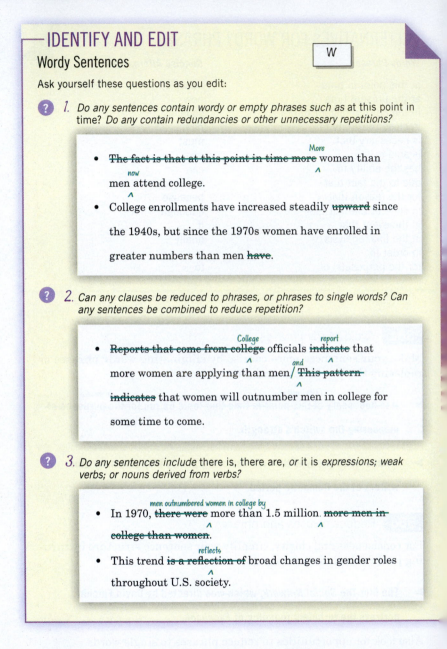

- ~~The fact is that at this point in time more~~ **More** women than now men attend college.

- College enrollments have increased steadily ~~upward~~ since the 1940s, but since the 1970s women have enrolled in greater numbers than men ~~have~~.

? *2. Can any clauses be reduced to phrases, or phrases to single words? Can any sentences be combined to reduce repetition?*

- ~~Reports that come from college~~ **College** officials ~~indicate~~ **report** that more women are applying than men **and** / ~~This pattern indicates~~ that women will outnumber men in college for some time to come.

? *3. Do any sentences include* there is, there are, *or* it is *expressions; weak verbs; or nouns derived from verbs?*

- In 1970, ~~there were~~ **men outnumbered women in college by** more than 1.5 million. ~~more men in college than women~~.

- This trend ~~is a reflection of~~ **reflects** broad changes in gender roles throughout U.S. society.

38e Combine sentences.

Sometimes, you can combine several short, repetitive sentences into a single, more concise, sentence.

▶   *'s torrential rains devastated*

Hurricane Ike ~~had a devastating effect on~~ **our town**/, ~~The destruction~~

                                         ing

~~resulted from torrential rains. Flooding~~ **submerged Main Street under**

                     and   *ing*

eight feet of water. ~~The rain also~~ **triggered mudslides that destroyed two**

nearby towns.

38f Make your sentences straightforward.

Eliminate expletive constructions like *there is, there are,* and *it is,* and replace the static verbs *to be* and *to have* with active verbs. *(For more on active verbs, see pp. 463–65.)* Change passive voice *(The book was read by Miguel)* to active voice *(Miguel read the book).*

ROUNDABOUT

There are stylistic similarities between "This Lime-Tree Bower" and "Tintern Abbey," which are indications of the influence that Coleridge had on Wordsworth.

STRAIGHTFORWARD

The stylistic similarities between "This Lime-Tree Bower" and "Tintern Abbey" indicate that Coleridge influenced Wordsworth.

Eliminating the expletive *There are* makes the main subject of the sentence—*similarities*—clearer. To find the action in the sentence, ask what *similarities* do here; they *indicate*. Find the noun *(indications)* that can become the verb *(indicate).* Do the same for the sentence's other subject, *Coleridge,* by asking what he did: *Coleridge . . . influenced.*

CHAPTER 39

Missing Words

When editing, make sure you have not omitted any words readers need to understand your meaning.

✓ 39a Add words needed to make compound structures complete and clear.

For conciseness, you can sometimes omit words from compound structures (which then are called *elliptical structures*): *His anger is extreme and his behavior [is] violent.*

    Do not leave out part of a compound structure unless both parts of the compound are the same, however.

                                     with

▶ **The gang members neither cooperated nor listened to the authorities.**

39b Include *that* when needed for clarity.

The word *that* can often be omitted, especially when the clause it introduces is short and the sentence's meaning is clear: *Carrie Underwood sings the kind of songs many women love.* You should add it, though, if doing so makes the sentence clearer.

                       that

▶ The attorney argued ^ men and women should receive equal pay for

equal work.

39c Make comparisons clear.

To be clear, comparisons must be complete. If you have just said, "Peanut butter sandwiches are boring," you can say immediately afterward, "Curried chicken sandwiches are more interesting." Saying only "Curried chicken sandwiches are more interesting" does not give your audience enough information. Name who or what completes the comparison.

To clarify comparisons, add the missing words.

                                  did

▶ I loved my grandmother more than my sister. ^

                             I loved

▶ I loved my grandmother more than ^ my sister.

When you use *as* to compare people or things, be sure to use it twice.

                       as

▶ Napoleon's temper was ^ volatile as a volcano.

Include *other* or *else* to indicate that people or things belong to the group with which they are being compared.

▶ High schools and colleges stage *The Laramie Project* more than any

other play.

▶ Professor Koonig wrote more books than anyone *else* in the department.

Use a possessive form when comparing attributes or possessions.

                                        Aristotle's.

▶ Plato's philosophy is easier to read than ~~that of Aristotle.~~ ^

39d Add articles *(a, an, the)* where necessary.

In English, omitting an article usually makes an expression sound odd, unless you omit the same article from a series of nouns.

▶ A dog that bites should be kept on leash.
  ^a

▶ He gave me books he liked best.
  ^{the}

▶ The classroom contained a fish tank, birdcage, and rabbit hutch.

Note: If the articles in a series are *not* the same, include all of them.

▶ The classroom contained an aquarium, birdcage, and rabbit hutch.
  ^a   ^a

(For more information about the use of articles, multilingual writers should consult Tab 12: Basic Grammar Review, pp. 598–99.)

CHAPTER 40

Mixed Constructions

Sentence parts that do not fit grammatically or logically confuse readers; revise them to clarify meaning.

40a Untangle mixed sentence structures.

Mixed constructions occur when writers change grammatical direction midway through a sentence. The following sentence begins with a prepositional phrase (a phrase introduced by a preposition such as *at, by, for, in,* or *of*), which the writer then tries to make into the subject. A prepositional phrase cannot be the subject of a sentence. Eliminating *For* makes it clear that *family members* is the subject of the verb *choose.*

▶ ~~For family~~ members who enjoy one another's company often choose a
  ^{Family}

vacation spot together.

In the following example, the dependent clause *when a Curandero is consulted* cannot serve as the subject of the sentence. Transforming this dependent clause into an independent clause with a subject and **predicate**—a complete verb plus its object or complement—solves the problem.

▶ In Mexican culture, ~~when~~ a Curandero ~~is~~ consulted ~~can address~~ spiritual
                              ^{can be}   ^{for}

or physical illness.

Sometimes you may need more than one sentence to clarify your ideas. The following sentence tries to do two things at once: contrast

England and France in 1805 and define the difference between an oligarchy and a dictatorship. Using two sentences instead makes both ideas clear.

> **MIXED UP**
>
> In an oligarchy like England was in 1805, a few people had the power rather than a dictatorship like France, which was ruled by Napoleon.
>
> **REVISED**
>
> In 1805, England was an oligarchy, a state ruled by the few. In contrast, France was a dictatorship, a state ruled by one man: Napoleon.

Mixed Constructions and Grammar Checkers

Computer grammar checkers are unreliable at detecting mixed constructions. One failed to highlight the three examples of mixed-up sentences in Section 40a.

40b Make sure predicates fit their subjects.

A predicate (complete verb) must connect logically to a sentence's subject to avoid faulty predication.

► ~~The best kind of education for me would be a~~ university with both a
         would be best for me.
school of music and a school of government.

A university is an institution, not a type of education.

40c Edit sentences with *is when, is where,* and *the reason . . . is because* to make the subject clear.

The phrases *is where* and *is when* may sound logical, but they usually result in faulty predication.

the production of carbohydrates from the interaction of
► Photosynthesis is ~~where~~ carbon dioxide, water, and chlorophyll ~~interact~~

in the presence of sunlight. ~~to form carbohydrates.~~

Photosynthesis is not a place, so *is where* is illogical.

Although *the reason . . . is because* may seem logical, it creates an awkward sentence. Change *because* to *that,* or change the subject of the sentence:

▶ The reason the joint did not hold is ~~because~~ *that* the coupling bolt broke.

or

▶ ~~The reason the~~ *The* joint did not hold ~~is~~ because the coupling bolt broke.

CHAPTER 41

Confusing Shifts

When you are editing, eliminate jarring shifts to make your sentences consistent.

Confusing Shifts and Grammar Checkers

Computer grammar checkers rarely flag sentences with confusing shifts in verb tense and voice like this:

▶ The teacher entered the room, and then roll is called.

Although it shifts confusingly from past to present tense and from active to passive voice, at least one grammar checker failed to highlight it.

✓ **41a** Make your point of view consistent.

Writers can choose from three points of view:

- First person *(I or we)* emphasizes the writer and is used in personal writing.
- Second person *(you)* focuses attention on readers and is used to give orders, directions, or advice.
- Third person *(he, she, it, one, or they)* is topic oriented and prevalent in academic writing.

Once you choose a point of view, use it consistently. For example, the writer of the following sentence shifted confusingly from third person *(students)* to second *(you).*

▶ Students will have no trouble getting a good seat if ~~you~~ *they* arrive at the theater before 7 o'clock.

Do not switch from singular to plural or plural to singular for no reason. When editing such shifts, choose the plural to avoid using *his or her* or introducing gender bias *(see Tab 10: Editing for Grammar Conventions, p. 516–17).*

▶ ~~A person is~~ *People are* often surprised when they are complimented.

✓ 41b Keep your verb tenses consistent.

Verb tenses show the time of an action as it relates to other actions. Choose a time frame—present, past, or future—and use it consistently, changing tense only when the meaning requires it.

Confusing shifts in time may occur when you are narrating events that are still vivid in your mind.

▶ The wind was blowing a hundred miles an hour when suddenly there ~~is~~ *was* a big crash, and a tree ~~falls~~ *fell* into the living room.

You may also introduce inconsistencies when using the present perfect tense, perhaps because the past participle causes you to slip from present tense to past tense.

▶ She has admired many strange buildings at the university but ~~thought~~ *thinks* the new Science Center ~~looked~~ *looks* out of place.

41c Avoid unnecessary shifts in mood and voice.

Verbs have three basic moods: (1) the **indicative,** used to state or question facts, acts, and opinions; (2) the **imperative,** used to give commands or advice; and (3) the **subjunctive,** used to express wishes, conjectures, and hypothetical conditions. Unnecessary shifts in mood can confuse and distract readers.

⌐NAVIGATING THROUGH COLLEGE AND BEYOND

Present Tense and Literary Works

By convention—because as long as a book is read, it is "alive"— we use the present tense to write about the content of literary works.

▶ David Copperfield describes villains such as Mr. Murdstone and heroes such as Mr. Micawber in unforgettable detail. But Copperfield ~~was~~ *is* not himself an especially interesting person.

> *could go*
> If he ~~goes~~ to night school, he would take a course in accounting.
> ^

> The sign says that in case of emergency passengers should follow the
> *should not*
> instructions of the train crew and ~~don't~~ leave the train unless instructed
> ^
> to do so.

Most verbs have two voices. In the **active voice,** the subject does the acting; in the **passive voice,** the subject is acted on. Abrupt shifts in voice often indicate awkward changes in subject.

> *They favored violet,*
> The Impressionist painters hated black. ~~Violet,~~ green, blue, pink, and
> ^
> red. ~~were favored by them.~~
> ^

The revision uses *they* to make "the Impressionist painters" the subject of the second sentence as well as the first.

41d Avoid awkward shifts between direct and indirect quotations and questions.

Indirect quotations report what others wrote or said without repeating their words exactly. **Direct quotations** report the words of others exactly and should be enclosed in quotation marks. *(For more on punctuating quotations, see Tab 11: Editing for Correctness, pp. 556–61.)* Do not shift from one form of quotation to the other within a sentence.

> In his inaugural speech, President Kennedy called on Americans not to
> *to*   *they could*
> ask what their country could do for them but instead ⁁ask what ~~you can~~
> ^   ^
> *their*
> do for ~~your~~ country."
> ^

The writer could have included the quotation in its entirety: *In his inaugural speech, President Kennedy said, "My fellow Americans, ask not what your country can do for you; ask what you can do for your country."*

Similarly, do not shift from an indirect to a direct question.

> *whether*
> The performance was so bad the audience wondered ~~had~~ the performers
> *had*   ^
> ⁁ever rehearsed.
> ^

As an alternative, the writer could ask the question directly: *Had the performers ever rehearsed? The performance was so bad that the audience wasn't sure.*

IDENTIFY AND EDIT

Confusing Shifts

To avoid confusing shifts, ask yourself these questions as you edit:

? *1. Does the sentence shift from one point of view to another, for example, from third person to second?*

- Over the centuries, millions of laborers helped build and
  maintain the Great Wall of China, and ~~if you were one, you~~
  ^*most of them*^
  ~~probably~~ suffered great hardship as a result.

? *2. Are the verbs consistent in the following ways:*

In tense (past, present, or future)?

- Historians call the period before the unification of China the
  Warring States period. It ~~ends~~ when the ruler of the Ch'in
  ^*ended*^
  state conquered the last of his independent neighbors.

In mood (statements vs. commands or hypothetical conditions)?

- If a similar wall ~~is~~ built today, it would cost untold
  ^*were*^
  amounts of time and money.

In voice (active vs. passive)?

- The purpose of the wall was to protect against invasion,
  but commerce. ~~was promoted by it also.~~
  ^*it also promoted*^

? *3. Are quotations and questions clearly phrased in either direct or indirect form?*

- The visitor asked the guide ~~when~~ did construction of the
  ^*, "When*^
  Great Wall begin?^*"*^

- The visitor asked the guide when ~~did~~ construction of the
  Great Wall ~~begin?~~
  ^*began.*^

CHAPTER 42

Faulty Parallelism

Parallel constructions present equally important ideas in the same grammatical form. The following sentence presents three prepositional phrases:

▶ At Gettysburg in 1863, Lincoln said that the Civil War was being fought

to make sure that government *of the people*, *by the people*, and *for the*

people might not perish from the earth.

If paired ideas or items in a series do not have the same grammatical form, edit to make them parallel. Put items at the same level in an outline or items in a list in parallel form.

✓ **42a** Edit items in a series to make them parallel.

A list or series of equally important items should be parallel in grammatical structure.

▶ The Census Bureau classifies people as employed if they receive

payment for any kind of labor, are temporarily absent from their jobs, or

work
~~working~~ at least fifteen hours as unpaid laborers in a family business.
    ^

In the next example, the writer changed a noun to an adjective. Repeating the word *too* makes the sentence more forceful and memorable.

too
▶ My sister obviously thought I was too young, ignorant, and ~~a~~
                                       ^
too troublesome.
~~troublemaker.~~
    ^

42b Edit paired ideas to make them parallel.

Paired ideas connected with a coordinating conjunction (*and, but, or, nor, for, so, yet*), a correlative conjunction (*not only . . . but also, both . . . and, either . . . or, neither . . . nor*), or a comparative expression (*as much as, more than, less than*) must have parallel grammatical form.

both   *challenge their students.*
▶ Successful teachers must inspire ~~students~~ and ~~challenging them is also~~
                                  ^   ^

~~important.~~

IDENTIFY AND EDIT
Faulty Parallelism

// ✓

To avoid faulty parallelism, ask yourself these questions:

? *1.* *Are the items in a series in parallel form?*

> • The senator stepped to the podium, ~~an angry glance~~ ^glanced angrily at^ ~~shooting toward~~ her challenger, and began to refute his charges.

? *2.* *Are paired items in parallel form?*

> • Her challenger, she claimed, ~~had~~ not only ^had^ accused her falsely of accepting illegal campaign contributions, but ~~his contributions were from illegal sources.~~ ^had accepted illegal contributions himself.^

? *3.* *Are the items in outlines and lists in parallel form?*

FAULTY PARALLELISM

She listed four reasons for voters to send her back to Washington:

1. Ability to protect the state's interests
2. Her seniority on important committees
3. Works with members of both parties to get things done
4. Has a close working relationship with the President

REVISED

She listed four reasons for voters to send her back to Washington:

1. *Her ability* to protect the state's interests
2. *Her seniority* on important committees
3. *Her ability* to work with members of both parties to get things done
4. *Her* close working *relationship* with the President

> *winning*
> ► I dreamed not only of getting the girl but also of the gold medal.
> ᴧ

> ► Many people find that having meaningful work is more important
>
> *earning*
> than high pay.
> ᴧ

42c   Repeat function words as needed to keep parallel structures clear.

Function words give information about a word or indicate the relationships among words in a sentence. They include:

- Articles *(the, a, an)*
- Prepositions (for example, *to, for,* and *by*)
- Subordinating conjunctions (for example, *although* and *that*)
- The word *to* in infinitives

You can omit repeated function words whenever the parallel structure is clear without them, as in the first example. Otherwise, include them, as in the second example.

> ► Her goals for retirement were to travel, ~~to~~ study art history, and ~~to~~ write
>
> a book about Michelangelo.

> ► The project has three goals: to survey the valley for Inca-period sites,
>
> *to*   *to*
> ᴧexcavate a test trench at each site, and ᴧexcavate one of those sites
>
> completely.

The added *to* makes it clear where one goal ends and the next begins.

CHAPTER 43

Misplaced and Dangling Modifiers

For a sentence to make sense, its parts must be arranged appropriately. When a modifying word, phrase, or clause is misplaced or dangling, readers get confused.

43a Put modifiers close to the words they modify.

For clarity, modifiers should usually come immediately before or after the words they modify. In the following sentence, the clause *after the police arrested them* modifies *protesters,* not *destroying.*

> *After the police had arrested them, the*
> ▶ ~~The~~ protesters were charged with destroying college property ~~after the~~
>
> ~~police had arrested them.~~

Misplaced Modifiers and Grammar Checkers

Some grammar checkers will reliably highlight split infinitives *(see 43d)* but only occasionally highlight other types of misplaced modifiers. One grammar checker, for example, missed the misplaced modifier *with a loud crash* in this sentence.

> ▶ The valuable vase *with a loud crash* fell to the floor and broke into hundreds of pieces.

The following sentence was revised to clarify that the hikers were watching the storm from the porch.

> *From the cabin's porch, the*
> ▶ ~~The~~ hikers watched the storm gathering force ~~from the cabin's porch.~~

43b Clarify ambiguous modifiers.

Adverbs modify words that precede or follow them. When they are ambiguously placed, they are called **squinting modifiers.** The following revision shows that the objection is vehement, not the argument.

> *vehemently*
> ▶ Historians who object to this account ~~vehemently~~ argue that the
>
> presidency was never endangered.

Problems can occur with **limiting modifiers** such as *only, even, almost, nearly,* and *just.* In the following sentence, does the writer mean that vegetarian dishes are the only dishes served at dinner, or that dinner is the only time vegetarian dishes are available? Place the modifier immediately before the modified word or phrase.

AMBIGUOUS

The restaurant *only offers* vegetarian dishes for dinner.

REVISED

The restaurant *offers only* vegetarian dishes for dinner.

or

The restaurant *offers* vegetarian dishes *only* at dinner.

Misplacing the limiting modifier *not* can create an inaccurate sentence:

Not all
► ~~All~~ the vegetarian dishes are ~~not~~ low in fat and calories.
   ^

43c Move disruptive modifiers.

When a lengthy modifying phrase or clause separates grammatical elements that belong together, a sentence can be difficult to read. With the modifying phrase at the beginning, the edited version of the following sentence restores the connection between subject and verb.

Despite their similar conceptions of the self,
► Descartes and Hume~~, despite their similar conceptions of the self,~~
   ^

deal with the issue of personal identity in different ways.

43d Check split infinitives for ambiguity.

An **infinitive** couples the word *to* with the present tense of a verb. In a **split infinitive,** one or more words intervene between *to* and the verb form. Avoid separating the parts of an infinitive with a modifier unless keeping them together results in an awkward or ambiguous construction.

In the following example, the modifier *successfully* should be moved. The modifier *carefully* should stay where it is, however, even though it splits the infinitive *to assess:*

successfully,
► To ~~successfully~~ complete this assignment/ students have to carefully
   ^

assess projected economic benefits.

Putting *carefully* after *assess* would cause ambiguity because readers might think it modifies *projected economic benefits.*

✓ 43e Fix dangling modifiers.

A **dangling modifier** is a descriptive phrase that implies an actor different from the sentence's subject. When readers try to connect the modifying phrase with the actual subject, the results may be humorous as well as confusing. To fix a dangling modifier, you must name

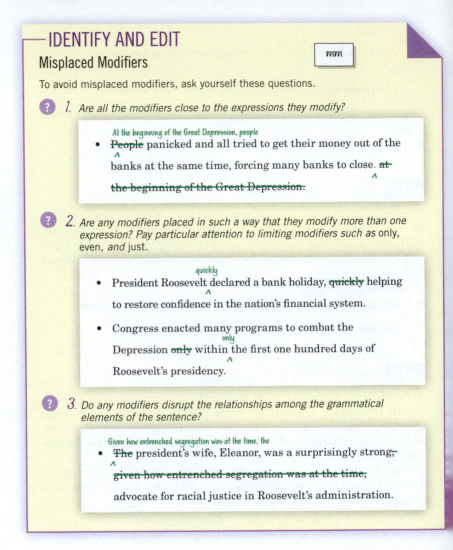

IDENTIFY AND EDIT

Misplaced Modifiers

mm

To avoid misplaced modifiers, ask yourself these questions.

? *1.* *Are all the modifiers close to the expressions they modify?*

- ~~People~~ *At the beginning of the Great Depression, people* ∧ panicked and all tried to get their money out of the banks at the same time, forcing many banks to close. ~~at the beginning of the Great Depression.~~ ∧

? *2.* *Are any modifiers placed in such a way that they modify more than one expression? Pay particular attention to limiting modifiers such as* only, even, *and* just.

- President Roosevelt declared a bank holiday, *quickly* ~~quickly~~ helping ∧ to restore confidence in the nation's financial system.

- Congress enacted many programs to combat the Depression ~~only~~ *only* within the first one hundred days of ∧ Roosevelt's presidency.

? *3.* *Do any modifiers disrupt the relationships among the grammatical elements of the sentence?*

- ~~The~~ *Given how entrenched segregation was at the time, the* ∧ president's wife, Eleanor, was a surprisingly strong~~,~~ ~~given how entrenched segregation was at the time,~~ advocate for racial justice in Roosevelt's administration.

its implied actor explicitly, either as the subject of the sentence or in the modifier itself:

DANGLING MODIFIER   *Swimming toward the boat on the horizon,* the crowded beach felt as if it were miles away.

REVISED   Swimming toward the boat on the horizon, *I* felt as if the crowded beach were miles away.

or

As *I swam* toward the boat on the horizon, the crowded beach seemed miles away.

IDENTIFY AND EDIT
Dangling Modifiers

✓

dm

To avoid dangling modifiers, ask yourself these questions when you see a descriptive phrase at the beginning of a sentence:

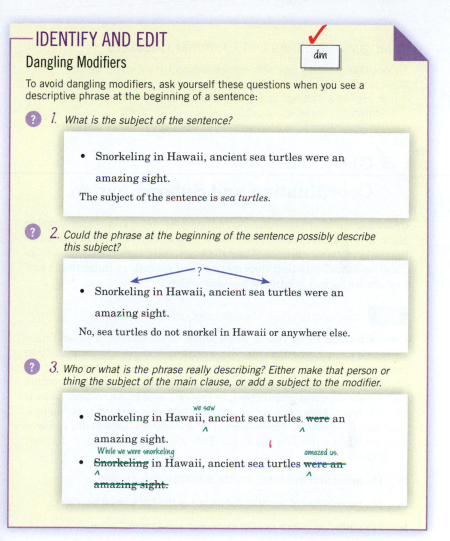

? *1.* *What is the subject of the sentence?*

- Snorkeling in Hawaii, ancient sea turtles were an

  amazing sight.

  The subject of the sentence is *sea turtles*.

? *2.* *Could the phrase at the beginning of the sentence possibly describe this subject?*

- Snorkeling in Hawaii, ancient sea turtles were an

  amazing sight.

  No, sea turtles do not snorkel in Hawaii or anywhere else.

? *3.* *Who or what is the phrase really describing? Either make that person or thing the subject of the main clause, or add a subject to the modifier.*

- Snorkeling in Hawaii, ancient sea turtles. *we saw* ~~were~~ an

  amazing sight.

- ~~Snorkeling~~ *While we were snorkeling* in Hawaii, ancient sea turtles ~~were an~~ *amazed us.*

  ~~amazing sight.~~

Simply moving a dangling modifier will not fix the problem. To make the meaning clear, you must make the implied actor in the modifying phrase explicit.

DANGLING MODIFIER   *After struggling for weeks in the wilderness,* the town pleased them mightily.

REVISED   After struggling for weeks in the wilderness, *they were pleased to come upon the town.*

or

After *they had struggled* for weeks in the wilderness, the town appeared in the distance.

Dangling Modifiers and Grammar Checkers

Computer grammar checkers cannot distinguish a descriptive phrase that properly modifies the subject of the sentence from one that implies a different actor. As a result, they do not flag dangling modifiers.

CHAPTER 44

Coordination and Subordination

Coordination and subordination allow you to combine and develop ideas in ways that readers can follow and understand. Use coordination only when two or more ideas deserve equal emphasis. Use subordination to indicate that information is of secondary importance and to show its logical relation to the main idea.

44a   Use coordination to express equal ideas.

Coordination gives two or more ideas equal weight. To coordinate parts within a sentence, join them with a coordinating conjunction (*and, but, or, for, nor, yet,* or *so*) or a correlative conjunction (*either . . . or, both . . . and*). To coordinate two or more sentences, use a comma plus a coordinating conjunction, or insert a semicolon. A semicolon is often followed by a conjunctive adverb such as *moreover, nevertheless, however, therefore,* or *subsequently*. *(For more on conjunctive adverbs and correlative conjunctions, see Tab 12: Basic Grammar Review, pp. 608–10.)*

► The auditorium was huge, *and* the acoustics were terrible.

► The tenor bellowed the aria, *but* no one in the back could hear him.

► The student was *both* late for class *and* unprepared.

► Jones did not agree with her position on health care; *nevertheless,* he supported her campaign for office.

44b   Use subordination to express unequal ideas.

Subordination makes one idea depend on another and is therefore used to combine ideas that are not of equal importance. The main idea is expressed in an independent clause, and the secondary ideas are expressed in subordinate clauses or phrases. Subordinate clauses start with a relative pronoun (*who, whom, that, which, whoever, whomever, whose*) or a subordinating conjunction (*after, although, because, if, since, when, where*).

▶ The blue liquid, *which will be added to the beaker later,* must be kept at room temperature.

▶ Christopher Columbus discovered the New World in 1492, *although he never understood just what he had found.*

▶ *After writing the opening four sections,* Wordsworth put the work aside for two years.

Note: Commas often set off subordinate ideas, especially when the subordinate clause or phrase opens the sentence. *(For more on using commas, see Tab 11: Editing for Correctness, pp. 536–48.)*

44c   Do not subordinate major ideas.

Major ideas belong in main clauses, not in subordinate clauses or phrases. The writer revised the following sentence to emphasize the definition of literacy because that topic was the focus of the essay.

INEFFECTIVE SUBORDINATION

Literacy, which has been defined as the ability to talk intelligently about many topics, is highly valued by businesspeople as well as academics.

REVISION

Highly valued by businesspeople as well as academics, literacy has been defined as the ability to talk intelligently about many topics.

44d   Combine short, choppy sentences.

Short sentences are easy to read, but several of them in a row can become so monotonous that meaning gets lost.

CHOPPY

My cousin Jim is not an accountant. But he does my taxes every year. He suggests various deductions. These deductions reduce my tax bill considerably.

Use subordination to put the idea you want to emphasize in the main clause, and use subordinate clauses and phrases for the other ideas. In this revision, the main clause is italicized.

REVISED

Even though he is not an accountant, *my cousin Jim does my taxes every year,* suggesting various deductions that reduce my tax bill considerably.

If a series of short sentences includes two major ideas of equal importance, use coordination for the two major ideas and subordinate the secondary information.

CHOPPY

Bilingual education is designed for children. The native language of these children is not English. Smith supports expanding bilingual education. Johnson does not support expanding bilingual education.

REVISED

Smith supports bilingual education for children whose native language is not English; Johnson, however, does not.

44e Avoid overloading sentences with excessive subordination.

Separate an overloaded sentence into two or more sentences.

OVERLOADED

Big-city mayors, who are supported by public funds, should be cautious about spending taxpayers' money for personal needs, such as furnishing official residences, especially when municipal budget shortfalls have caused extensive job layoffs, angering city workers and the general public.

REVISED

Big-city mayors should be cautious about spending taxpayers' money for personal needs, especially when municipal budget shortfalls have caused extensive job layoffs. They risk angering city workers and the general public by using public funds for furnishing official residences.

CHAPTER 45

Sentence Variety

Enliven your prose and keep your readers interested by using a variety of sentence patterns.

Sentence Variety and Grammar Checkers

Monotony is not a grammatical error; sentence variety is an issue of style, not syntax, and the type of sentences a writer uses also depends on the writing situation. A computer grammar checker might flag a very long sentence, but it cannot decide whether the sentence is *too* long.

45a Vary your sentence openings.

When all the sentences in a passage begin with the subject, you risk losing readers' attention. Vary your sentences by moving a modifier to the beginning. The modifier may be a single word, a phrase, or a clause.

► *Eventually,*
Louis Armstrong's innovations on the trumpet ~~eventually~~ became the standard.

► *In at least two instances, this*
~~Armstrong's~~ money-making strategy backfired ~~in at least two instances.~~

► *After Glaser became his manager,*
Armstrong no longer had to worry about business ~~after Glaser became his manager.~~

A **participial phrase** begins with an *-ing* verb (*driving*) or a past participle (*moved, driven*) and serves as a modifier. You can move it to the beginning of a sentence for variety, but make sure it describes the explicit subject of the sentence or you will end up with a dangling modifier (*see p. 455–58*).

► *Pushing the other children aside,*
Joseph~~, pushing the other children aside,~~ demanded that the teacher give him a cookie first.

► *Stunned by the stock market crash in 1929, many*
~~Many~~ brokers~~, stunned by the stock market crash in 1929,~~ committed suicide.

45b Vary the length and structure of your sentences.

Short, simple sentences (under ten words) will keep your readers alert, but only if your work also includes longer, complex sentences.

As you edit, see whether you have overused one kind of sentence structure. Are most of your sentences short and simple? If so, use subordination to combine some of them (*see p. 458–59*). But if most of your sentences are long and complex, put at least one of your ideas into a short, simple sentence. Your goal is to achieve a good mix.

DRAFT

I dived quickly into the sea. I peered through my mask at the watery world. It turned darker. A school of fish went by. The distant light glittered on their bodies, and I stopped swimming.

I waited to see whether the fish might be chased by a shark. I was satisfied that there was no shark and continued down.

REVISED

I dived quickly into the sea, peering through my mask at a watery world that turned darker as I descended. A school of fish went by, the distant light glittering on their bodies. I stopped swimming and waited. Perhaps the fish were being chased by a shark? Satisfied that there was no shark, I continued down.

(For more information about sentence types, see Tab 12: Basic Grammar Review, pp. 620–21. For more on sentence variety, see Tab 2: Writing and Designing Texts, pp. 84–88.)

45c   Include a few cumulative and periodic sentences and rhetorical questions.

Cumulative sentences add a series of descriptive participial or absolute phrases to the basic subject-plus-verb pattern, making your writing forceful and detailed. *(See Tab 12: Basic Grammar Review, pp. 616–17 for more on these phrases.)* You can also use them to add details, as this example shows:

► The motorcycle spun out of control, *plunging down the ravine, crashing through the fence,* and *coming to rest on its side.*

Another way to increase the force of your writing is to use a few **periodic sentences,** in which the key word, phrase, or idea appears at the end, where readers are most likely to remember it.

In 1946 and 1947, young people

► ~~Young people fell in love with the jukebox in 1946 and 1947 and~~ turned

and fell in love with the jukebox.

away from the horrors of World War II.

Asking a question invites your readers to participate more actively in your work. Because you do not expect an answer, this kind of question is called a **rhetorical question.**

► Athletes injured at an early age too often find themselves without a job, a college degree, or their health. Is it any wonder that a few turn to drugs and alcohol?

Rhetorical questions work best in the middle or at the end of a long, complicated passage. They can also help you make a transition from one topic to another. Use them selectively, however, and do not begin with a broad rhetorical question such as "How did the Peace Corps begin?"

45d   Try an occasional inversion.

Occasionally, try using an inverted sentence pattern or another sentence type, such as a rhetorical question or an exclamation, to vary the normal sentence pattern of subject plus verb plus object. *(For more on sentence types, see Tab 12: Basic Grammar Review, pp. 620–21.)*

You can create an **inversion** by putting the verb before the subject. Because many inversions sound odd, use them infrequently and carefully. In a passage on the qualities of various contemporary artists, the following inversion makes sense and adds interest.

▶ **Characteristic of Issey Miyake's work are bold design and original thinking.**

45e   Use exclamation points sparingly and appropriately.

Exclamations are rare in academic writing, so if you decide to use one for special effect, be sure that strong emotion is appropriate.

▶ **Wordsworth completed the thirteen-book Prelude in 1805, after seven years of hard work. Instead of publishing his masterpiece, however, he devoted himself to revising it—for more than thirty years! The poem, in a fourteen-book version, was finally published in 1850, after he had died.**

CHAPTER 46

Active Verbs

Active verbs such as *run, shout, write,* and *think* are more direct and forceful than forms of the *be* verb *(am, are, is, was, were, been, being)* or passive-voice constructions. The more active your verbs, the stronger and clearer your writing will be.

Active Verbs and Grammar Checkers

Computer grammar checkers generally do not flag weak uses of the *be* verb. A grammar checker did not flag the sentence *The paper was an argument for a stronger police presence* because it is grammatically correct, although it is stronger as *The paper argued . . .*

Some grammar checkers do flag most passive-voice sentences *(see 46b),* but their suggestions for revising them can sometimes make the sentence worse.

46a Consider alternatives to some *be* verbs.

Although it is not a strong verb, *be* does a lot of work in English.

As a linking verb:

▶ Germany *is* relatively poor in natural resources.

▶ Decent health care *is* a necessity, not a luxury.

As a helping verb:

▶ Macbeth *was* returning from battle when he met the three witches.

Be verbs are so useful that they get overworked. Consider using active verbs in place of *be* verbs and clunky, abstract nouns made from verbs (like *is a demonstration of*). (See also Chapter 38: *Wordy Sentences, pp. 440–43.*)

▶ The mayor's refusal to meet with our group ~~is a demonstration of~~ his *demonstrates*

lack of respect for us, as well as for the environment.

46b When writing for a general audience, prefer the active voice.

Transitive verbs, which connect an actor with something that receives the action, can be in the active or passive voice. In the **active voice,** the subject of the sentence acts; in the **passive voice,** the subject is acted on:

ACTIVE   The Senate finally passed the bill.

PASSIVE   The bill was finally passed by the Senate.

The passive voice downplays the actors as well as the action, so much so that the actors are often left out of the sentence.

PASSIVE   The bill was finally passed.

─NAVIGATING THROUGH COLLEGE AND BEYOND

Passive Voice in Scientific Writing

The passive voice is often used in scientific reports to keep the focus on the experiment and its results rather than on the experimenters.

▶ The bacteria were treated carefully with nicotine and stopped reproducing.

The active voice is more forceful, and readers usually want to know who or what does the acting, particularly in nontechnical genres.

PASSIVE   Polluting chemicals were dumped into the river.

ACTIVE   Industrial Products Corporation dumped polluting chemicals into the river.

When the recipient of the action is more important than the doer of the action, however, the passive voice is the more appropriate choice.

► **After her heart attack, my mother was taken to the hospital.**

Mother and the fact that she was taken to the hospital are more important than who took her there.

CHAPTER 47

Appropriate Language

Language is appropriate when it fits your writing situation: your topic, purpose, and audience. Whether you are preparing to write about literature or natural science or history, take some time to read how writers in the field have handled your topic.

47a   In college writing, avoid slang, regional expressions, and nonstandard English.

Slang, regional sayings, and nonstandard English appear often in conversation but are too informal for college writing—unless that writing is literary or is reporting conversation. Slang words also change frequently. In college writing, avoid slang and the informal tone that goes with it.

SLANG   In *Heart of Darkness,* we hear a lot about a *dude* named Kurtz, but we don't see the *guy* much.

REVISED   In *Heart of Darkness,* Marlow, the narrator, talks continually about Kurtz, but we meet Kurtz himself only at the end.

Like slang, regional and nonstandard expressions such as *y'all, hisself,* and *don't be doing that* are fine in conversation, but not in formal college writing. In U.S. colleges, professions, and businesses, the dominant dialect is Standard Written English. Most of your instructors will expect you to write in this dialect, unless you have a good reason not to. *(See the Glossary of Usage for common nonstandard expressions, pp. 475–84.)*

47b Use an appropriate level of formality.

College writing assignments usually call for a style that avoids extremes of stuffy and casual, pretentious and chatty. Revise passages that veer toward one or the other extreme.

PRETENTIOUS	Romantic lovers are characterized by a preoccupation with a deliberately restricted set of qualities in the love object that are viewed as means to some ideal end.
REVISED	People in love see what they want to see, usually by idealizing the beloved.

Prefer clear, concise language to inflated words.

Pretentious	Simple
ascertain	find out
commence	begin
endeavor	try
finalize	finish
impact (as verb)	affect
optimal	best
parameters	limits
prior to	before
reside	live
utilize	use

47c Avoid jargon.

When specialists communicate with each other, they often use technical or specialized language called **jargon.** Jargon has its place, but you should not use terms appropriate for specialists when writing for a nonspecialist audience.

JARGON	Pegasus Technologies developed a Web-based PSP system to support standard off-line brands in meeting their loyalty-driven marketing objectives via the social media space.
REVISED	Pegasus Technologies developed a system that helps businesses create media sites to run promotions for their customers.

If you must use technical terms when writing for nonspecialists, be sure to provide definitions.

▶ **Armstrong's innovative singing style featured "scat," a technique that combines "nonsense syllables [with] improvised melodies" (Robinson 515).**

—NAVIGATING THROUGH COLLEGE AND BEYOND

Discourse Communities

People who share certain interests, knowledge, and customary ways of communicating constitute a **discourse community.** Book collectors, for example, talk and write about *marginalia, foxing,* and *provenance,* terms that are probably unfamiliar to people outside the community. The more familiar you are with a discourse community, the more you will know about the language appropriate in it.

47d   Avoid most euphemisms and all doublespeak.

Euphemisms and doublespeak have one goal: to cover up the truth. **Euphemisms** substitute words like *correctional facility* and *passing away* for such harsh realities as *prison* and *death.*

Doublespeak is used to obscure facts and evade responsibility.

DOUBLESPEAK	Pursuant to the environmental protection regulations enforcement policy of the Bureau of Natural Resources, special management area land use permit issuance procedures have been instituted.
REVISED	The Bureau of Natural Resources has established procedures for issuing land use permits.

47e   Do not use biased or sexist language.

Biased or sexist language can undermine your credibility with readers.

1. Recognizing biased language

Watch for stereotypes—rigid, unexamined generalizations that demean, ignore, or patronize people on the basis of gender, race, religion, national origin, ethnicity, physical ability, sexual orientation, occupation, age, or any other human condition. Revise for inclusiveness.

For example, do not assume that Irish Catholics have large families.

▶ Although the Browns are Irish Catholics, there are only two children in the family.

The ... *an* ... *Catholic family with*

Remember that a positive stereotype is still an overgeneralization, which readers find patronizing, that is, as coming from someone who believes she or he is superior.

▶ ~~Because Asian students are whizzes at math, we~~ ^{We} all wanted ~~them~~ ^{math whizzes} in our study group.

Do not assume that readers will share your background. Be careful about using *we* and *they*.

Refer to groups as they refer to themselves (for example, *Asian* not *Oriental*). Refer to someone's ethnicity, religion, age, or other circumstances only when the writing situation requires it.

Avoid language that demeans or stereotypes women and men. Many labels and clichés imply that women are not as able or mature as men. Consider the meaning of words and phrases like *the fair sex, acting like a girl, poetess, maiden name,* and *coed*.

2. Revising sexist language

Avoiding bias means avoiding even subtle stereotypes. For example, not all heads of state are or have to be men.

BIASED	Wives of heads of state typically choose to promote a charity that benefits a cause they care about.
REVISED	Spouses of heads of state typically choose to promote a charity that benefits a cause they care about.

Traditionally, the pronoun *he* was used to represent either gender. Today, however, the use of *he* or *man* or any other masculine noun to represent people in general is considered offensive.

BIASED	Everybody had his way.
REVISED	We all had our way.
BIASED	It's every man for himself.
REVISED	All of us have to save ourselves.

Follow these simple principles to eliminate gender bias from your writing:

- Replace terms that indicate gender with their gender-free equivalents:

No	Yes
chairman	chair, chairperson
congressman	representative, member of Congress
forefathers	ancestors
male nurse	nurse
man, mankind	people, humans, humankind
manmade	artificial
policeman	police officer
spokesman	spokesperson
woman doctor	doctor

- Refer to men and women in parallel ways: *ladies and gentlemen* [not *ladies and men*], *men and women, husband and wife.*

  BIASED   D. H. Lawrence and Mrs. Woolf met, but Lawrence did not like the Bloomsbury circle that revolved around Virginia.

  REVISED   D. H. Lawrence and Virginia Woolf met, but Lawrence did not like the Bloomsbury circle that revolved around Woolf.

- Replace the masculine pronouns *he, him, his,* and *himself* when they are being used generically to refer to both women and men. One way to replace masculine pronouns is to use the plural.

  ▶   ~~Each senator~~ Senators returned to ~~his district~~ their districts during the break.

    Some writers alternate *he* and *she* and *him* and *her.* This strategy may be effective in some writing situations, but it can also be distracting. The constructions *his or her* and *he or she* are acceptable as long as they are not used more than once in a sentence:

  AWKWARD   Each student in the psychology class was to choose a different book according to *his or her* interests, to read the book overnight, to do without *his or her* normal sleep, to write a short summary of what *he or she* had read, and then to see whether *he or she* dreamed about the book the following night.

  REVISED   Every student was to choose a book, read it overnight, do without sleep, write a short summary of the book the next morning, and then see whether *he or she* dreamed about the book the following night.

The constructions *his/her* and *s/he* are not acceptable.

Note: Using the neuter impersonal pronoun *one* can sometimes help you avoid masculine pronouns, but it can make your writing sound stuffy.

  STUFFY   The American creed holds that if one works hard, one will succeed in life.

  REVISED   The American creed holds that those who work hard will succeed in life.

(For more on editing to avoid the generic use of he, him, his, *or* himself, *see Tab 10: Editing for Grammar Conventions, pp. 516–18.)*

CHAPTER 48

Exact Language

To convey your meaning clearly, you need to choose the right words. As you revise, look for problems with diction: Is your choice of words as precise as it should be?

48a　Choose words with suitable connotations.

Words have denotations and connotations. **Denotations** are their primary meanings, while **connotations** are the feelings and images associated with a word.

Consider, for example, the following three statements:

Murdock *ignored* the no-smoking rule.

Murdock *disobeyed* the no-smoking rule.

Murdock *flouted* the no-smoking rule.

Even though the three sentences depict the same event, each sentence describes Murdock's action somewhat differently. If Murdock *ignored* the rule, he may simply not have known or cared about it. If he *disobeyed* the rule, he must have known about it and consciously decided not to follow it, but what if he *flouted* the rule? Well, there was probably a look of disdain on his face as he made sure that others would see him puffing a cigarette.

As you revise, consider replacing any word whose connotations do not exactly fit what you want to say.

> ▶ The players' union should ~~request~~ demand that the NFL amend its pension plan.

If you cannot think of a more suitable word, consult a thesaurus *(see p. 475)* for **synonyms**—words with similar meanings. Keep in mind, however, that most words have connotations that allow them to work in some contexts but not in others. To find out more about a synonym's connotations, look up the word in a dictionary.

48b　Include specific and concrete words.

In addition to general and abstract terms, effective writers use specific and concrete words.

General words name broad categories of things, such as *trees, books, politicians,* and *students.* **Specific words** name particular kinds of things or items, such as *pines* and *college sophomores.*

Abstract words name qualities and ideas that do not have physical properties, such as *charity, beauty, hope,* and *radical.*

Concrete words name things we can sense by touch, taste, smell, hearing, and sight, such as *velvet, vinegar, smoke, screech,* and *sweater.*

By creating images that appeal to the senses, specific and concrete words make writing more precise.

VAGUE   The trees were affected by the bad weather.

PRECISE   The tall pines shook in the gale.

As you edit, make sure you have developed your ideas with specific and concrete details. Also check for overused, vague terms—such as *factor, thing, good, nice,* and *interesting*—and replace them with specific and concrete alternatives.

> ▶ The protesters were charged with ~~things~~ they never ~~did~~. *crimes* *committed*

48c Use standard idioms.

Idioms are habitual ways of expressing ideas. They are not always logical and can be hard to translate. Often they involve selecting the right preposition: we do not go *with* the car but *in* the car or simply *by* car; we do not abide *with* a rule but *by* a rule. If you are not sure which preposition to use, look up the main word in a dictionary. *(For more on idioms and multilingual writers, see Tab 12: Basic Grammar Review, pp. 606–07.)*

Some verbs, called **phrasal verbs,** include a preposition to make their idiomatic meaning complete:

Henry *made up* with Gloria.

Henry *made off* with Gloria.

Henry *made out* with Gloria.

(For more on phrasal verbs, see pp. 607–08.)

48d Avoid clichés.

A **cliché** is an overworked expression. If someone says, "She was as mad as a _____," we expect the next word to be *hornet.* We have heard this expression so often that it no longer creates a vivid picture in our imagination. It is usually best to rephrase clichés in plain language.

CLICHÉ   When John turned in his project three weeks late, he had to *face the music.*

BETTER   When John turned in his project three weeks late, he had to *accept the consequences.*

Here are some common clichés to avoid:

agony of suspense	flat as a pancake	sadder but wiser
beat a hasty retreat	give 110 percent	sink or swim
beyond a shadow of	green with envy	smart as a whip
a doubt	heave a sigh of relief	sneaking suspicion
blind as a bat	hit the nail on the	straight and narrow
calm, cool, and	head	tired but happy
collected	last but not least	tried and true
cold, hard facts	the other side	ugly as sin
cool as a cucumber	of the coin	untimely death
crazy as a loon	pale as a ghost	white as a sheet
dead as a doornail	pass the buck	worth its weight in
deep, dark secret	pretty as a picture	gold
depths of despair	quick as a flash	
few and far between	rise to the occasion	

48e Create suitable figures of speech.

Figures of speech make writing vivid, most often by using a comparison to supplement the literal meaning of words. A **simile** is a comparison that contains the word *like* or *as*.

▶ **Hakim's smile was like sunshine after a rainstorm.**

A **metaphor** is an implied comparison. It treats one thing or action, such as a politician's speech, as if it were something else (a drive on a familiar road in this instance).

▶ **The senator's speech rolled along a familiar highway, past the usual landmarks: taxes and foreign policy.**

Because it is compressed, a metaphor is often more forceful than a simile.

Comparisons can make your prose more vivid, but only if they suit your subject and purpose. Do not mix metaphors; if you use two or more comparisons together, make sure they are compatible.

MIXED	His presentation of the plan was such a *well-constructed tower of logic* that we immediately decided *to come aboard.*
REVISED	His clear presentation of the plan immediately convinced us to come aboard.

✓ 48f Avoid misusing words.

Avoid mistakes with new or unfamiliar words by always consulting a dictionary whenever you include an unfamiliar word in your writing.

> *exhibited*
> The artistocracy ~~exuded~~ numerous vices including greed and ~~license~~. *licentiousness*

Always think critically about the suggestions made by your word-processing program's spell checker. In the example, the writer mistyped the word *instate* as *enstate* and received the incorrect suggestion *estate.*

> *instate*
> We needed approval to ~~estate~~ the change.

As you edit, read carefully to make sure you have the right word in the right place.

CHAPTER 49

The Dictionary and the Thesaurus

A dictionary and a thesaurus are essential tools for all writers.

49a   Make using the dictionary a habit.

A standard desk dictionary contains 140,000 to 180,000 entries. Dictionaries also provide information such as the correct spellings of important place names, the official names of countries, correct forms of address, and conversion tables for weights and measures. Dictionaries of varying size also appear in most word-processing software programs and on Web sites.

All dictionaries include guides to their use. The guides explain the terms and abbreviations that appear in the entries as well as special notations such as *slang, nonstandard,* and *vulgar.*

An entry from the *Random House Webster's College Dictionary* follows. The labels point to the kinds of information discussed in the following sections.

Phonetic symbols showing pronunciation.

Word endings and grammatical abbreviations.

Dictionary entry.

com•pare (kəmpâr'), *v.,* **-pared, -par • ing,** *n.* —*v.t.* **1.** to examine (two or more objects, ideas, people, etc.) in order to note similarities and differences. **2.** to consider or describe as similar; liken: *"Shall I compare thee to a summer's day?"* **3.** to form or display the degrees of comparison of (an adjective or adverb). —*v.i.* **4.** to be worthy of comparison: *Whose plays can compare with Shakespeare's?* **5.** to be in similar standing; be alike: *This recital compares with the one he gave last year.* **6.** to appear in quality, progress, etc., as specified: *Their development compares poorly with that of neighbor nations.* **7.** to make comparisons. —*n.* **8.** comparison: *a beauty beyond compare.* —**Idiom.** **9. compare notes,** to exchange views, ideas, or impressions. [1375–1425; late ME < OF *comperer* < L *comparāre* to place together, match, v. der. of *compar* alike, matching (see COM-, PAR)] —**com•par'er,** *n.* —**Usage.** A traditional rule states that COMPARE should be followed by *to* when it points out likenesses between unlike persons or things: *she compared his handwriting to knotted string.* It should be followed by *with,* the rule

Definitions as transitive verb (*v.t.*).

Definitions as intransitive verb (*v.i.*).

Special meaning.

Definition as noun (n.).

Etymology (word origin)

Usage note.

says, when it examines two entities of the same general class for similarities or differences: *She compared his handwriting with mine.* This rule, though sensible, is not always followed, even in formal speech and writing. Common practice is to use *to* for likeness between members of different classes: *to compare a language to a living organism.* Between members of the same category, both *to* and *with* are used: *Compare the Chicago of today with* (or *to*) *the Chicago of the 1890s.* After the past participle COMPARED, either *to* or *with* is used regardless of the type of comparison.

1. Spelling, word division, and pronunciation

Entries in a dictionary are listed in alphabetical order according to their standard spelling. In the *Random House Webster's College Dictionary,* the verb *compare* is entered as **com•pare.** The dot separates the word into its two syllables.

Phonetic symbols in parentheses follow the entry and show its correct pronunciation. The second syllable of *compare* receives the greater stress when you pronounce the word correctly: "com-PARE." In this dictionary, an accent mark (′) appears after the syllable that receives the primary stress. Online dictionaries often include a recording of the pronunciation.

Plurals of nouns are usually not given if they are formed by adding an *s,* unless the word is foreign *(gondolas, dashikis).* Irregular plurals—such as *children* for *child*—are noted.

Some dictionaries list alternate spellings, always giving the preferred spelling first or placing the full entry under the preferred spelling only.

2. Word endings and grammatical labels

The abbreviation *v.* immediately after the pronunciation tells you that *compare* is most frequently used as a verb. The next abbreviation, *n.,* indicates that *compare* can sometimes function as a noun, as in the phrase *beyond compare.*

Here is a list of common abbreviations for grammatical terms:

adj.	adjective	*prep.*	preposition
adv.	adverb	*pron.*	pronoun
conj.	conjunction	*sing.*	singular
interj.	interjection	*v.*	verb
n.	noun	*v.i.*	intransitive verb
pl.	plural	*v.t.*	transitive verb
poss.	possessive		

The *-pared* shows the simple past and past participle form of the verb; the present participle form, *-paring,* follows, indicating that *compare* drops the final *e* when *-ing* is added.

3. Definitions and word origins

In the sample entry on pp. 473–74, the definitions begin after the abbreviation *v.t.,* indicating that the first three meanings relate to *compare* as a transitive verb. A little further down in the entry, *v.i.*

introduces definitions of *compare* as an intransitive verb. Next, after *n.*, comes the definition of *compare* as a noun. Finally, the word *Idiom* signals a special meaning not included in the previous definitions.

Included in most dictionary entries is an **etymology**—a brief history of the word's origins—set off in brackets. *Compare* came into the English language between 1375 and 1425 and was derived from the Old French word *comperer,* which came from Latin.

4. Usage

Some main entries in the dictionary conclude with examples of and comments about the common usage of the word. These might include labels like *slang* (very informal), *nonstandard, regional,* and *obsolete* (out-of-date).

49b   Consult a thesaurus for words that have similar meanings.

A **thesaurus** is a dictionary of synonyms. Several kinds are available, many called *Roget's* after Peter Mark Roget (pronounced ro-ZHAY), who published the first one in 1852. Today, thesauruses are included in most word-processing software packages.

Consider the connotations as well as the denotations of the words you find in the thesaurus. Do not choose a word just because it sounds smart or fancy.

CHAPTER 50

Glossary of Usage

The following words and expressions are often confused (such as *advice* and *advise*), misused (such as *etc.*), or considered nonstandard (such as *could of*).

Consulting this list will help you use these words precisely.

a, an   Use *a* with a word that begins with a consonant sound: *a cat, a dog, a one-sided argument* (*one* begins with a consonant sound), *a house* (*h* is pronounced). Use *an* with a word that begins with a vowel sound: *an apple, an X-ray, an honor* (*h* is silent).

accept, except   *Accept* is a verb meaning "to receive willingly": *Please accept my apologies. Except* usually is a preposition meaning "but": *Everyone except Julie saw the film.* Except can be a verb meaning "to exclude": *We must except present company from the contest.*

adapt, adopt   *Adapt* means "to adjust or become accustomed to": *They adapted to the customs of their new country. Adopt* means "to take as one's own": *We adopted a puppy.*

advice, advise   *Advice* is a noun meaning "suggestion"; *advise* is a verb meaning "suggest": *I took his advice and deeply regretted it. I advise you to disregard it, too.*

affect, effect As a verb, *affect* means "to influence": *Inflation affects our sense of security.* As a noun, *affect* means "a feeling or an emotion": *To study affect, psychologists probe the unconscious.* As a noun, *effect* means "result": *Inflation is one of the many effects of war.* As a verb, *effect* means "to make or accomplish": *Inflation has effected many changes in the way we spend money.*

aggravate While *aggravate* colloquially means "irritate," in formal writing it means "intensify" or "worsen": *The need to refuel the plane aggravated the delay, which irritated the passengers.*

agree to, agree with *Agree to* means "consent to"; *agree with* means "be in accord with": *They will agree to a peace treaty, even though they do not agree with each other on all points.*

ain't A slang contraction for *is not, am not,* or *are not, ain't* should not be used in formal writing or speech.

all ready, already *All ready* means "fully prepared"; *already* means "previously": *I was all ready to go out when I discovered that Jack had already ordered a pizza.*

all right, alright *Alright* is nonstandard. Use *all right. He told me it was all right to miss class tomorrow.*

all together, altogether *All together* expresses unity or common location; *altogether* means "completely": *At the casino, it was altogether startling to see so many kinds of gambling all together in one place.*

allude, elude, refer to *Allude* means "to refer indirectly": *He alluded to his miserable adolescence. Elude* means "to avoid" or "to escape from": *She eluded the police for nearly two days.* Do not use *allude* to mean "to refer directly": *The teacher referred* [not *alluded*] *to page 468 in the text.*

almost, most *Almost* means "nearly." *Most* means "the greater part of." Do not use *most* when you mean *almost: He wrote to me about almost* [not *most*] *everything he did. He told his mother about most things he did.*

a lot *A lot* is always two words. Do not use *alot.*

A.M., AM, a.m. These abbreviations mean "before noon" when used with numbers: 6 A.M., 6 a.m. Be consistent, and do not use the abbreviations as a synonym for *morning: In the morning* [not *the a.m.*]*, the train is full.*

among, between Generally, use *among* with three or more nouns, and *between* with two: *The distance between Boston and Knoxville is a thousand miles. The desire to quit smoking is common among those who have smoked for a long time.*

amoral, immoral *Amoral* means "neither moral nor immoral" and "not caring about moral judgments"; *immoral* means "morally wrong": *Unlike such amoral natural disasters as earthquakes and hurricanes, war is intentionally violent and therefore immoral.*

amount, number Use *amount* for quantities you cannot count; use *number* for quantities you can count: *The amount of oil left underground in the United States is a matter of dispute, but the number of oil companies losing money is tiny.*

an See a, an.

anxious, eager *Anxious* means "fearful": *I am anxious before a test. Eager* signals strong interest or desire: *I am eager to be done with that exam.*

anymore, any more   *Anymore* means "no longer." *Any more* means "no more." Both are used in negative contexts: *I do not enjoy dancing anymore. I do not want any more peanut butter.*

anyone/any one, anybody/any body, everyone/every one, everybody/every body   *Anyone, anybody, everyone,* and *everybody* are singular in definite pronouns: *Anybody can make a mistake.* When the pronoun *one* or the noun *body* is modified by the adjective *any* or *every,* the words should be separated by a space: *A good mystery writer accounts for every body that turns up in the story.*

as   Do not use *as* as a synonym for *since, when,* or *because*: *I told him he should visit Alcatraz since* [not *as*] *he was going to San Francisco. When* [not *as*] *I complained about the meal, the cook said he did not like to eat there himself. Because* [not *as*] *we asked her nicely, our teacher decided to cancel the exam.*

as, like   In formal writing, avoid the use of *like* as a conjunction: *He sneezed as if* [not *like*] *he had a cold. Like* is perfectly acceptable as a preposition that introduces a comparison: *She handled the reins like an expert.*

at   Avoid the use of *at* to complete the notion of *where*: not *Where is Michael at?* but *Where is Michael?*

awful, awfully   Use *awful* and *awfully* to convey terror or wonder (awe-full): *The vampire flew out the window with an awful shriek.* In formal writing, do not use *awful* to mean "bad" or *awfully* to mean "very" or "extremely."

awhile, a while   *Awhile* is an adverb: *Stay awhile with me* [but not *for awhile with me*]. *A while* consists of an article and a noun and can be used with or without a preposition: *A while ago I found my red pencil. I was reading under the tree for a while.*

bad, badly   *Bad* is an adjective used after a linking verb such as *feel*; *badly* is an adverb: *She felt bad about playing the piano badly at the recital.*

being as, being that   Do not use *being as* or *being that* as synonyms for *since* or *because*: *Because* [not *being as*] *the mountain was there, we had to climb it.*

belief, believe   *Belief* is a noun meaning "conviction"; *believe* is a verb meaning "to have confidence in the truth of ": *Her belief that lying was often justified made it hard for us to believe her story.*

beside, besides   *Beside* is a preposition meaning "next to" or "apart from": *The ski slope was beside the lodge. She was beside herself with joy. Besides* is both a preposition and an adverb meaning "in addition to" or "except for": *Besides a bicycle, he will need a tent and a pack.*

better   Avoid using *better* in expressions of quantity: *Crossing the continent by train took more than* [not *better than*] *four days.*

between   *See* among, between.

bring, take   Use *bring* when an object is being moved toward you, and *take* when it is being moved away: *Please bring me a new flash drive, and take the old one home with you.*

but that, but what   In expressions of doubt, avoid writing *but that* or *but what* when you mean *that*: *I have no doubt that* [not *but that*] *you can learn to write well.*

can, may   *Can* refers to ability; *may* refers to possibility or permission: *I see that you can Rollerblade without crashing into people; nevertheless you may not Rollerblade on the promenade.*

can't hardly   This double negative is ungrammatical and self-contradictory: *I can* [not *can't*] *hardly understand algebra. I can't understand algebra.*

capital, capitol   *Capital* can refer to wealth or resources or to a city; *capitol* refers to a building where lawmakers meet: *Protesters traveled to the state capital to converge on the capitol steps.*

censor, censure   *Censor* means "to remove or suppress material"; *censure* means "to reprimand formally." (Both can also be nouns.) *The Chinese government has been censured by the U.S. Congress for censoring Web access.*

cite, sight, site   The verb *cite* means "to quote or mention": *Be sure to cite all your sources in your bibliography.* As a noun, the word *sight* means "view": *I cringed at the sight of him. Site* is a noun meaning "a particular place" as well as "a location on the Internet."

compare to, compare with   Use *compare to* to point out similarities between two unlike things: *She compared his singing to the croaking of a wounded frog.* Use *compare with* to assess differences or likenesses between two things in the same general category: *Compare Shakespeare's* Antony and Cleopatra *with Dryden's* All for Love.

complement, compliment   *Complement* is a verb meaning "to go well with" or a noun describing "something that goes well with or completes something else": *I consider sauerkraut the perfect complement to sausages. Compliment* is a noun or verb meaning "praise": *She received many compliments on her thesis.*

conscience, conscious   The noun *conscience* means "a sense of right and wrong": *His conscience bothered him.* The adjective *conscious* means "awake" or "aware": *I was conscious of a presence in the room.*

continual, continuous   *Continual* means "repeated regularly and frequently": *She continually checked her Blackberry for new e-mail. Continuous* means "extended or prolonged without interruption": *The car alarm made a continuous wail in the night.*

could care less   *Could care less* is nonstandard; use *does not care at all* instead: *She does not care at all about her physics homework.*

could of, should of, would of   Avoid these nonstandard forms of *could have, should have,* and *would have.*

criteria, criterion   *Criteria* is the plural form of the Latin word *criterion,* meaning "standard of judgment": *The criteria are not very strict. The most important criterion is whether you can do the work.*

data   *Data* is the plural form of the Latin word *datum,* meaning "fact." Although informally used as a singular noun, *data* should be treated as a plural noun in writing: *The data indicate that recycling has gained popularity.*

differ from, differ with   *Differ from* expresses a lack of similarity: *The ancient Greeks differed greatly from the Persians. Differ with* expresses disagreement: *Aristotle differed with Plato on some important issues.*

different from, different than   Use *different from: The east coast of Florida is very different from the west coast.*

discreet, discrete   *Discreet* means "tactful" or "prudent." *Discrete* means "separate" or "distinct." *What's a discreet way of telling them that these are two discrete issues?*

disinterested, uninterested   *Disinterested* means "impartial": *We expect members of a jury to be disinterested. Uninterested* means "indifferent": *Most people today are uninterested in alchemy.*

don't, doesn't   *Don't* is the contraction for *do not* and is used with *I, you, we, they,* and plural nouns; *doesn't* is the contraction for *does not* and is used with *he, she, it, one,* and singular nouns: *You don't know what you're talking about. He doesn't know what you're talking about either.*

each and every   Use one of these words but not both: *Every cow came in at feeding time. Each one had to be watered.*

each other, one another   Use *each other* in sentences having two subjects and *one another* in sentences having more than two: *Husbands and wives should help each other. Classmates should share ideas with one another.*

eager   *See* anxious, eager.

effect   *See* affect, effect.

either, neither   Both *either* and *neither* are singular: *Neither of the two girls has played the game. Either of the two boys is willing to show you the way home.* When used as an intensive, *either* is always negative: *She told him she would not go either. (For* either . . . or *and* neither . . . nor *constructions, see p. 501.)*

elicit, illicit   The verb *elicit* means "to draw out"; the adjective *illicit* means "unlawful": *The detective was unable to elicit any information about other illicit activities.*

elude   *See* allude, elude, refer to.

emigrate, immigrate   *Emigrate from* means "to move away from one's country": *My father emigrated from Vietnam in 1980. Immigrate to* means "to move to another country and settle there": *Father immigrated to the United States.*

eminent, imminent, immanent   *Eminent* means "celebrated" or "well known": *Many eminent Victorians were melancholy. Imminent* means "about to happen" or "about to come": *In August 1939, many Europeans sensed that war was imminent. Immanent* refers to something invisible but dwelling throughout the world: *Medieval Christians believed God's power was immanent through the universe.*

etc.   The abbreviation *etc.* stands for the Latin *et cetera,* meaning "and others" or "and other things." Because *and* is included in the abbreviation, do not write *and etc.* In a series, a comma comes before *etc.,* just as it would before the coordinating conjunction that closes a series: *He brought tofu, beans, soymilk, etc.* In most college writing, it is better to end a series of examples with a final example or the words *and so on.*

everybody/every body, everyone/every one   *See* anyone/any one.

except, accept   *See* accept, except.

expect, suppose   *Expect* means "to hope" or "to anticipate": *I expect a good grade on my final paper. Suppose* means "to presume": *I suppose you didn't win the lottery on Saturday.*

explicit, implicit *Explicit* means "stated outright"; *implicit* means "implied, unstated": *Her explicit instructions were for us to go to the party without her, but the implicit message she conveyed was disapproval.*

farther, further *Farther* describes geographical distances: *Ten miles farther on is a hotel. Further* means "in addition" when geography is not involved: *He said further that he didn't like my attitude.*

fewer, less *Fewer* refers to items that can be counted individually; *less* refers to general amounts: *Fewer people signed up for indoor soccer this year than last. Your argument has less substance than you think.*

firstly *Firstly* is common in British English but not in the United States. *First, second, third,* and so on are the accepted forms.

flaunt, flout *Flaunt* means "to wave" or "to show publicly" with delight or even arrogance: *He flaunted his wealth by wearing many gold chains. Flout* means "to scorn" or "to defy," especially publicly, without concern for the consequences: *She flouted the traffic laws by running through red lights.*

former, latter *Former* refers to the first and *latter* to the second of two things mentioned previously: *Mario and Alice are both good cooks; the former is fonder of Chinese cooking, the latter of Mexican.*

further *See* farther, further.

get In formal writing, avoid colloquial uses of *get,* as in *get with it, get it together, get-up-and-go, get it,* and *that gets me.*

good, well *Good* is an adjective and should not be used in place of the adverb *well: He felt good about doing well on the exam.*

hanged, hung People are *hanged* by the neck until dead. Pictures and all other things that can be suspended are *hung.*

hopefully *Hopefully* means "with hope." It is often misused to mean "it is hoped": *We waited hopefully for our ship to come in* [not *Hopefully, our ship will come in,* but *We hope our ship will come in*].

if . . . then Avoid using these words in tandem. Redundant: *If I get my license, then I can drive a cab.* Better: *If I get my license, I can drive a cab. Once I get my license, I can drive a cab.*

if, whether Use *whether* instead of *if* when expressing options: *If we go to the movies, we don't know whether we'll see a comedy or a drama.*

illicit *See* elicit, illicit.

imminent *See* eminent, imminent, immanent.

immigrate *See* emigrate, immigrate.

immoral *See* amoral, immoral.

implicit *See* explicit, implicit.

imply, infer *Imply* means "to suggest without stating directly": *By putting his fingers in his ears, he implied that she should stop singing. Infer* means "to draw a conclusion": *When she dozed off during his declaration of love, he inferred that she did not feel the same way about him.*

in, in to, into *In* refers to a location inside something: *Charles kept a snake in his room. In to* refers to motion with a purpose: *The resident manager came in to capture it. Into* refers to movement from outside to inside or from separation to contact: *The snake escaped by crawling into a drain.*

incredible, incredulous   *Incredible* stories and events cannot be believed; *incredulous* people do not believe: *Kaitlyn told an incredible story of being abducted by a UFO over the weekend. We were all incredulous.*

inside of, outside of   The "of" is unnecessary in these phrases: *He was outside the house.*

ironically   *Ironically* means "contrary to what was or might have been expected" in a sense that implies the unintentional or foolish: *Ironically, the peace activists were planning a "War against Hate" campaign.* It should not be confused with *surprisingly* ("unexpectedly") or with *coincidentally* ("occurring at the same time or place").

irregardless   This construction is a double negative because both the prefix *ir-* and the suffix *-less* are negatives. Use *regardless* instead.

it's, its   *It's* is a contraction, usually for *it is* but sometimes for *it has*: *It's often been said that English is a difficult language to learn. Its* is a possessive pronoun: *The dog sat down and scratched its fleas.*

kind(s)   *Kind* is singular: *This kind of house is easy to build. Kinds* is plural and should be used only to indicate more than one kind: *These three kinds of toys are more educational than those two kinds.*

kind of, sort of   These constructions should not be used to mean *somewhat* or *a little*: *I was somewhat tired after the party.*

lay, lie   *Lay* means "to place." Its main forms are *lay, laid,* and *laid.* It generally has a direct object, specifying what has been placed: *She laid her book on the steps and left it there. Lie* means "to recline" and does not take a direct object. Its main forms are *lie, lay,* and *lain: She often lay awake at night.*

less   *See* fewer, less.

like   *See* as, like.

literally   *Literally* means "actually" or "exactly as written": *Literally thousands gathered along the parade route.* Do not use *literally* as an intensive adverb when it can be misleading or even ridiculous: *His blood literally boiled.*

loose, lose   *Loose* is an adjective that means "not securely attached." *Lose* is a verb that means "to misplace." *Better tighten that loose screw before you lose the whole structure.*

may   *See* can, may.

maybe, may be   *Maybe* is an adverb meaning "perhaps": *Maybe he can get a summer job as a lifeguard. May be* is a verb phrase meaning "is possible": *It may be that I can get a job as a lifeguard, too.*

moral, morale   *Moral* means "lesson," especially a lesson about standards of behavior or the nature of life: *The moral of the story is, do not drink and drive. Morale* means "attitude" or "mental condition": *Employee morale dropped sharply after the president of the company was arrested.*

more important, more importantly   Use *more important.*

most   *See* almost, most.

myself (himself, herself, and so on)   Pronouns ending with *-self* refer to or intensify other words: *Jack hurt himself. Standing in the doorway was the man himself.* When you are unsure whether to use *I* or *me, she* or *her, he* or *him* in a compound subject or object, you may be tempted to substitute one of the *-self* pronouns. Don't do it: *The quarrel was between her and me* [not *myself*]. *(Also see Tab 10: Problems with Pronouns, beginning on p. 515.)*

neither *See* either, neither

nohow, nowheres These words are nonstandard for *anyway, in no way, in any way, in any place,* and *in no place.* Do not use them in formal writing.

number *See* amount, number.

off of Omit the *of: She took the painting off the wall.*

one another *See* each other, one another.

outside of *See* inside of, outside of.

plus Avoid using *plus* as a coordinating conjunction (use *and*) or a transitional expression (use *moreover*): *He had to walk the dog, empty the garbage, and* [not *plus*] *write a term paper.*

precede, proceed *Precede* means "come before;" *proceed* means "go forward": *Despite the heavy snows that preceded us, we managed to proceed up the hiking trail.*

previous to, prior to Avoid these wordy and pompous substitutions for *before.*

principal, principle *Principal* is an adjective meaning "most important" or a noun meaning "the head of an organization" or "a sum of money": *Our principal objections to the school's principal are that he is a liar and a cheat. Principle* is a noun meaning "a basic standard or law": *We believe in the principles of honesty and fair play.*

proceed *See* precede, proceed.

raise, rise *Raise* means "to lift or cause to move upward." It takes a direct object—someone raises something: *I raised the windows in the classroom. Rise* means "to go upward." It does not take a direct object—something rises by itself: *We watched the balloon rise to the ceiling.*

real, really Do not use the word *real* when you mean *very: The cake was very* [not *real*] *good.*

reason . . . is because, reason why These are redundant expressions. Use either *the reason is that* or *because: The reason he fell on the ice is that he cannot skate. He fell on the ice because he cannot skate.*

refer to *See* allude, elude, refer to.

respectfully, respectively *Respectfully* means "with respect": *Treat your partners respectfully. Respectively* means "in the given order": *The three Williams she referred to were Shakespeare, Wordsworth, and Yeats, respectively.*

rise *See* raise, rise.

set, sit *Set* is usually a transitive verb meaning "to establish" or "to place." It takes a direct object, and its principal parts are *set, set,* and *set: DiMaggio set the standard of excellence in fielding. She set the box down in the corner. Sit* is usually intransitive, meaning "to place oneself in a sitting position." Its principal parts are *sit, sat,* and *sat: The dog sat on command.*

shall, will Today, most writers use *will* instead of *shall* in the ordinary future tense for the first person: *I will celebrate my birthday by throwing a big party. Shall* is still used in questions: *Shall we dance?*

should of   *See* could of, should of, would of.

site   *See* cite, sight, site.

sort of   *See* kind of, sort of.

stationary, stationery   *Stationary* means "standing still": *Our spinning class uses stationary bicycles. Stationery* is writing paper: *That stationery smells like a rose garden.*

suppose   *See* expect, suppose.

sure   Avoid confusing the adjective *sure* with the adverb *surely: The dress she wore to the club was surely bizarre.*

sure and   *Sure and* is often used colloquially. In formal writing, *sure to* is preferred: *Be sure to* [not *be sure and*] *get to the wedding on time.*

take   *See* bring, take.

than, then   *Than* is a conjunction used in comparisons: *I am taller than you. Then* is an adverb referring to a point in time: *We will sing and then dance.*

that, which   Use *that* for restrictive (that is, essential) clauses and *which* for nonrestrictive (that is, nonessential) clauses: *The bull that escaped from the ring ran through my china shop, which was located in the square. (Also see Commas, pp. 539–42, in Tab 11.)*

their, there, they're   *Their* is a possessive pronoun: *They gave their lives. There* is an adverb of place: *Takesha was standing there. They're* is a contraction of *they are: They're reading more poetry this semester.*

theirself, theirselves, themself   Use *themselves.*

this here, these here, that there, them there   Avoid these nonstandard forms in writing.

to, too, two   *To* is a preposition; *too* is an adverb; *two* is a number: *The two of us got lost too many times on our way to his house.*

try and   *Try to* is the standard form: *Try to* [not *try and*] *understand.*

uninterested   *See* disinterested, uninterested.

unique   *Unique* means "one of a kind." Do not use any qualifiers with it.

utilize   *Use* is preferable because it is simpler: *Use five sources in your project.*

verbally, orally   To say something *orally* is to say it aloud: *We agreed orally to share credit for the work, but when I asked Andrea to confirm it in writing, she refused.* To say something *verbally* is to use words: *Quinn's eyes flashed anger, but he did not express his feelings verbally.*

wait for, wait on   People *wait for* those who are late; they *wait on* tables.

weather, whether   The noun *weather* refers to the atmosphere: *She worried that the weather would not clear up in time for the victory celebration. Whether* is a conjunction referring to a choice between options: *I can't decide whether to go now or next week.*

well   *See* good, well.

whether   *See* if, whether, *and* weather, whether.

which, who, whose, that   *Which* is used for things, and *who* and *whose* for people: *My fountain pen, which I had lost last week, was found by a child who had never seen any pens except ballpoints.* Use *that* for things and groups of people: *The committee that makes hiring decisions meets on Friday.*

who, whom Use *who* with subjects and their complements. Use *whom* with objects of verbs and prepositions: *The person who will fill the position is Janelle, whom you met last week.* (Also see Problems with Pronouns in Tab 10, p. 525.)

will *See* shall, will.

would of *See* could of, should of, would of.

your, you're *Your* is a possessive pronoun: *Is that your new car? You're* is a contraction of *you are: You're a lucky guy.*

CHECKLIST Editing for Clarity and Word Choice

As you revise, check your writing for clarity and be sure you used words correctly by asking yourself these questions:

☐ Are all sentences complete, concise, and straightforward? *(See Chapter 38: Wordy Sentences, pp. 440–43 and Chapter 39: Missing Words, pp. 443–45.)*

☐ Do the key parts of each sentence fit together well, or are there mismatches in person, number, or grammatical structure? *(See Chapter 41: Confusing Shifts, pp. 447–50, and Chapter 42: Faulty Parallelism, pp. 451–53.)*

☐ Are the parts of each sentence clearly and closely connected, or are some modifiers separated from what they modify? *(See Chapter 43: Misplaced and Dangling Modifiers, pp. 453–58.)*

☐ Are the focus, flow, and voice of the sentences clear, or do some sentences have ineffective coordination and subordination? *(See Chapter 44: Coordination and Subordination, pp. 458–60.)*

☐ Do sentence patterns vary sufficiently? Is there a mixture of long and short sentences? *(See Chapter 45: Sentence Variety, pp. 460–63.)*

☐ Are all verbs strong and emphatic, or are the passive voice, the verb *to be,* or other weak or too-common verbs overused? *(See Chapter 46: Active Verbs, pp. 463–65.)*

☐ Do you have a dictionary at hand for unfamiliar words you encounter? Do you have a thesaurus at hand to find the most appropriate word to convey your meaning? *(See Chapter 49: The Dictionary and the Thesaurus, pp. 473–75.)*

☐ Is your language appropriate to the assignment? Does it include any euphemisms, doublespeak, slang, or jargon? Have you used any stereotyping, biased, or sexist expressions? *(See Chapter 47: Appropriate Language, pp. 465–69.)*

☐ Have you chosen words with the appropriate connotations? Have you confused words that have similar denotations? *(See Chapter 48: Exact Language, pp. 470–73, and Chapter 50: Glossary of Usage, pp. 475–84.)*

☐ Have you used specific and concrete words and suitable figures of speech? Have you avoided clichés? *(See Chapter 48: Exact Language, pp. 470–73.)*

10

Editing for
Grammar
Conventions

*There is a core simplicity to the English language and
its American variant, but it's a slippery core.*

–Stephen King

This detail from a first century C.E. wall painting in the ancient Roman
city of Pompeii shows a woman writing on a wax-covered tablet.
Working on tablets like this, Roman writers could smooth over words
and make corrections with ease.

10 Editing for Grammar Conventions

10 | Editing for Grammar Conventions

✓ Sections referenced in Resources for Writers: Identifying and Editing Common Problems (following Tab 9).

Tab 10: Editing for Grammar Conventions

This section will help you answer questions such as the following:

Rhetorical Knowledge

- Are sentence fragments ever acceptable in any kind of writing? (51b)

Critical Thinking, Reading, and Writing

- What's wrong with *A student should enjoy their college experience?* How can I fix it without sounding sexist? (55a)

Processes

- How can I recognize and fix sentence fragments when I edit? (51a–d)
- Can my word processor's grammar checker help me edit for grammar conventions? (51–56)

Knowledge of Conventions

- When should I use *lie* or *lay?* (54b)
- Is it ever correct to say *I feel good?* (56b)

For a general introduction to writing outcomes, see 1e, pages 14–16.

When you edit, your purpose is to make the sentences in your text both clear and strong. The preceding section of the handbook focused on editing for clarity. This section focuses on editing for common grammatical problems.

CHAPTER 51

Sentence Fragments

A **sentence fragment** is an incomplete sentence treated as if it were complete. It may begin with a capital letter and end with a period, a question mark, or an exclamation point, but it lacks one or more of the following:

- A complete verb
- A subject
- An independent clause

Although writers sometimes use them intentionally, fragments are rarely appropriate for college assignments.

✓ **51a**   Learn how to identify sentence fragments.

Identify fragments in your work by asking three questions:

- Do you see a complete verb?
- Do you see a subject?
- Do you see *only* a dependent clause?

1. Do you see a complete verb?   A **complete verb** consists of a main verb and helping verbs needed to indicate tense, person, and number. *(See Chapter 54: Problems with Verbs, pp. 509–10.)* A group of related words without a complete verb is a phrase fragment, not a sentence.

FRAGMENT	The ancient Mayas were among the first to develop many mathematical concepts. *For example, the concept of zero.* [no verb]
SENTENCE	The ancient Mayas were among the first to develop many mathematical concepts. *For example, they developed the concept of zero.*

2. Do you see a subject?   The **subject** is the *who* or *what* that a sentence is about. *(See Tab 12: Basic Grammar Review, pp. 610–13.)* A group of related words without a subject or complete verb is a phrase fragment, not a sentence.

FRAGMENT	The ancient Mayas were accomplished mathematicians. *Developed the concept of zero, for example.* [no subject]
SENTENCE	The ancient Mayas were accomplished mathematicians. *They developed the concept of zero, for example.*

3. Do you see *only* a dependent clause?   An **independent clause** has a subject and complete verb and can stand on its own as a sentence. A **dependent** or **subordinate clause** also has a subject and complete verb, but it begins with a subordinating word such as *although, because, that,* or *which.* Dependent clauses function within sentences as modifiers or nouns, but they cannot stand as sentences on their own. *(See Tab 12: Basic Grammar Review, pp. 618–19.)*

FRAGMENT	The ancient Mayas deserve a place in the history of mathematics. *Because they were among the earliest people to develop the concept of zero.*
SENTENCE	The ancient Mayas deserve a place in the history of mathematics *because they were among the earliest people to develop the concept of zero.*

Fragments and Grammar Checkers

Grammar checkers identify some fragments, but they will not tell you what the fragment is missing or how to edit it. Grammar checkers can also miss fragments that lack subjects but that could be interpreted as commands, such as *Develop the concept of zero, for example.*

51b   Learn how to edit sentence fragments.

You can repair sentence fragments by editing them in one of two ways:

- Transform them into sentences.

> ► Many people feel threatened by globalization. ~~Because they~~ ^{They} think it will undermine their cultural traditions.

- Attach them to a nearby independent clause.

> ► Many people feel threatened by globalization/ ^{because} ~~Because~~ they think it will undermine their cultural traditions.

Your solution is a stylistic decision. Sometimes one approach may be clearly preferable, and sometimes both are effective.

51c   Connect a phrase fragment to another sentence, or add the missing elements.

Often unintentional fragments are **phrases**—word groups that lack a subject or a complete verb or both and usually function as modifiers or nouns.

1. Watching for verbals   Phrase fragments frequently begin with **verbals**—words derived from verbs, such as *putting* or *to put.* They do not change form to reflect tense and number. *(For more on verbals, see pp. 616–17.)*

> **FRAGMENT**   That summer, we had the time of our lives. *Swimming in the mountain lake each day and exploring the nearby woods.*

One way to fix this fragment is to transform it into an independent clause with its own subject and verb.

> ► That summer, we had the time of our lives. ~~Swimmi~~ng ^{We swam} in the mountain lake each day and ~~exploring~~ ^{explored} the nearby woods.

IDENTIFY AND EDIT
Sentence Fragments

✓ frag

? *1.* *Do you see a complete verb?*

Yes | **No → FRAGMENT**

FRAGMENT — For example, the concept of zero.

SENTENCE — For example, they <u>were</u> among the first to develop the concept of zero.
(subj verb)

? *2.* *Do you see a subject?*

Yes | **No → FRAGMENT**

FRAGMENT — Developed the concept of zero, for example.

SENTENCE — <u>They</u> <u>developed</u> the concept of zero, for example.
(subj verb)

? *3.* *Do you see only a dependent clause?*

No | **Yes → FRAGMENT**

FRAGMENT — Because they were among the earliest people to develop the concept of zero.

SENTENCE — The Mayas deserve a place in the history of mathematics because they were among the earliest people to develop the concept of zero.

SENTENCE

Notice that the two *-ing* verbals in the fragment need to be changed to keep the phrases in the new sentence parallel. *(For more on parallelism, see Tab 9: Editing for Clarity, pp. 451–53.)*

The fragment can also be attached to the part of the preceding sentence that it modifies (in this case, *the time of our lives*).

─ *the* EVOLVING SITUATION

Intentional Fragments

Advertisers often use attention-getting fragments: "Hot deal! Big savings! Because you're worth it." In everyday life, we often speak in fragments: "You okay?" "Fine." As a result, people who write fiction and drama use fragments to create realistic dialogue, and people who write popular nonfiction often use them for emphasis and variety. Keep in mind, however, that advertising, literary writing, and college writing have different contexts and purposes. In formal writing, use intentional sentence fragments sparingly, if at all.

► That summer, we had the time of our lives./ ~~Swimming~~ *, swimming* in the mountain lake each day and exploring the nearby woods.

2. Watching for preposition fragments   Phrase fragments can also begin with one-word prepositions such as *as, at, by, for, from, in, of, on,* or *to.* Attach these fragments to a nearby sentence.

► Impressionist painters often depicted their subjects in everyday

situations./ ~~At~~ *, at* a restaurant, perhaps, or by the seashore.

3. Watching for transitional phrases   Some fragments start with two- or three-word prepositions that function as transitions, such as *as well as, as compared with,* or *in addition to.*

► For the past sixty-five years, the growth in consumer spending has been

both steep and steady./ ~~In~~ *, in* contrast with the growth in gross domestic

product (GDP), which fluctuated significantly between 1929 and 1950.

4. Watching for words and phrases that introduce examples   Check word groups beginning with expressions that introduce examples—such as *for example* or *such as.* If they are fragments, edit to make them into sentences, or attach them to an independent clause.

► Elizabeth I of England faced many dangers as a princess. For example,

~~falling~~ *she fell* out of favor with her sister, Queen Mary, and ~~being~~ *was* imprisoned in

the Tower of London.

5. Watching for appositives An **appositive** is a noun or noun phrase that renames a noun or pronoun.

▶ In 1965, Lyndon Johnson increased the number of troops in Vietnam/ A former French colony in Southeast Asia.

, a

6. Watching for fragments that consist of lists You can connect a list to the preceding sentence using a colon or a dash.

▶ In the 1930s, three great band leaders helped popularize jazz/: Louis Armstrong, Benny Goodman, and Duke Ellington.

7. Watching for fragments that are parts of compound predicates A **compound predicate** is made up of at least two verbs as well as their objects and modifiers, connected by a coordinating conjunction such as *and, but,* or *or.* The parts of a compound predicate have the same subject and should be in one sentence.

▶ The group gathered at dawn at the base of the mountain/ And assembled their gear in preparation for the morning's climb.

and

51d Connect fragments that begin with a subordinating word *(although, because, since, even though)* to another sentence, or eliminate the subordinating word.

Fragments that begin with a subordinating word can usually be attached to a nearby independent clause.

▶ None of the thirty-three subjects indicated any concern about the

amount or kind of fruit the institution served/. Even though all of them

even

identified diet as an important issue for those with diabetes.

> ***Punctuation tip:*** A comma usually follows a dependent clause that begins a sentence. If the clause appears at the end of a sentence, it is usually not preceded by a comma unless it is a contrasting thought. *(See Tab 11: Editing for Correctness, p. 546.)*

It is sometimes better to transform such a fragment into a complete sentence by deleting the subordinating word.

▶ The harmony of our group was disrupted in two ways. When members either disagreed about priorities or advocated different political strategies.

Members

CHAPTER 52

Comma Splices and Run-on Sentences

Comma splices and run-on sentences are sentences with improperly joined independent clauses. Recall that an independent clause has a subject and a complete verb and can stand on its own as a sentence. *(See page 488.)*

✓ **52a**   Learn how to identify comma splices and run-on sentences.

A **comma splice** is a sentence with two independent clauses joined by only a comma:

COMMA SPLICE	The media influence people's political views, the family is another major source of ideas about the proper role of government.

A **run-on sentence,** sometimes called a **fused sentence,** does not have even a comma between the independent clauses.

RUN-ON	Local news shows often focus on crime stories network and cable news broadcasts cover national politics in detail.

Writers may mistakenly join two independent clauses with only a comma or create a run-on sentence in three situations:

- When a transitional expression like *as a result* or *for example* or a conjunctive adverb like *however* links the second clause to the first. *(A list of conjunctive adverbs and transitional expressions appears on p. 497.)*

COMMA SPLICE	Rare books can be extremely valuable, *for example,* an original edition of Audubon's *Birds of America* is worth over a million dollars.

RUN-ON	Most students complied with the new policy *however* a few refused to do so.

- When the second clause specifies or explains the first.

RUN-ON	The economy is still recovering from the financial crisis that began in 2007 Bear Stearns was the first large investment bank to experience problems that year.

- When the second clause begins with a pronoun.

COMMA SPLICE	President Garfield was assassinated, he served only six months in office.

1. Checking for transitional expressions and conjunctive adverbs Check those sentences that include transitional expressions or conjunctive adverbs like *however (see p. 497)*. If a comma precedes one of these words or phrases, you may have found a comma splice. If no punctuation precedes one of them, you may have found a run-on sentence. Can the word groups that precede and follow the conjunctive adverb or transitional expression both stand alone as sentences? If so, you have found a comma splice or a run-on sentence.

2. Reviewing sentences with commas Check sentences that contain commas. Can the word groups that appear on both sides of the comma stand alone as sentences? If so, you have found a comma splice.

Comma Splices, Run-on Sentences, and Grammar Checkers

Computer grammar checkers are unreliable at identifying run-on sentences and comma splices. One grammar checker, for example, correctly flagged this sentence for incorrect comma usage: *Many history textbooks are clear, some are hard to follow.* It failed, however, to flag this longer alternative: *Many history textbooks are clear and easy to read, some are dense and hard to follow.*

52b Learn five ways to edit comma splices and run-on sentences.

- Join the two clauses with a comma and a coordinating conjunction *(and, but, or, nor, for, so, yet) (52c, p. 496)*.

  ▶ The media influence people's political views, *and* the family is another major source of ideas about the proper role of government.

- Join the two clauses with a semicolon *(52d, p. 496)*.

  ▶ Local news shows often focus on crime stories; network and cable news broadcasts cover national politics in detail.

  You can also add an appropriate conjunctive adverb or transitional expression, followed by a comma.

  ▶ Local news shows often focus on crime stories; *however,* network and cable news broadcasts cover national politics in detail.

- Separate the clauses into two sentences *(52e, pp. 497–98)*.

  ▶ Salt air corrodes metal easily ~~therefore~~ *. Therefore,* automobiles in coastal regions require frequent washing.

IDENTIFY AND EDIT
Comma Splices and Run-ons

These questions can help you spot comma splices and run-on sentences:

? *1. Does the sentence contain only one independent clause?*

No ↓

Yes → **Not a run-on or comma splice**

? *2. Does it contain two independent clauses joined by a comma and a coordinating conjunction (and, but, or, not, for, so, or yet)?*

No ↓

Yes → **Not a run-on or comma splice**

? *3. Does it contain two independent clauses joined by a semicolon, a semicolon and a transitional expression, a colon, or a dash?*

No ↓

Yes → **Not a run-on or comma splice**

	├─────independent clause─────┤
RUN-ON	Football and most other team sports have a time limit
	├───independent clause───┤
	baseball has no time limit.
COMMA SPLICE	Football and most other team sports have a time limit, baseball has no time limit.
REVISED: COMMA AND COORDINATING CONJUNCTION	Football and most other team sports have a time limit, but baseball has no time limit. [*See 52c.*]
REVISED: SEMICOLON	Football and most other team sports have a time limit; baseball has no time limit. [*See 52d.*]
REVISED: TWO SENTENCES	Football and most other team sports have a time limit. Baseball has no time limit. [See 52e.]
REVISED: SUBORDINATION	Although football and most other team sports have a time limit, baseball has none. [*See 52f.*]
REVISED: ONE INDEPENDENT CLAUSE	Baseball, unlike football and most other team sports, has no time limit. [*See 52g.*]

- Turn one of the independent clauses into a dependent clause *(52f, p. 498). For more on dependent clauses, see pages 618–19.*

  ▶ **Treasure hunters shopping in thrift stores and at garage sales**

  because
  should be realistic/ valuable finds are extremely rare.
    ^

- Transform the two clauses into a single independent clause *(52g, p. 498).*

  and
  ▶ **The best history books are clear/ they also tell a compelling story.**
    ^

52c Join the two clauses with a comma and a coordinating conjunction such as *and, but, or, nor, for, so,* or *yet.*

If you decide to correct a comma splice or run-on sentence by joining the two clauses, make sure the two ideas are equally important, and choose the coordinating conjunction that most clearly expresses the logical relationship between them. A comma *must* precede the conjunction, or the sentence remains a run-on.

so
▶ **Julio is a very stubborn person, I had a hard time convincing him to let me take the wheel.**
                                   ^

, but
▶ **My stepmother teaches at Central State I go to Eastern Tech.**
                                           ^

52d Join the two clauses with a semicolon (or a colon or dash).

A semicolon tells readers that two closely related clauses are logically connected. However, it does not spell out the logic of the connection.

▶ **Most students complied with the new policy/; a few refused to do so.**
                                             ^

To show the logic of the connection, you can add a conjunctive adverb or transitional expression.

; however,
▶ **Most students complied with the new policy/ a few refused to do so.**
                                             ^

When the first independent clause introduces the second one, use a colon instead of a semicolon. A colon is also appropriate if the second clause expands on the first one in some way or introduces a quotation. *(See Tab 11: Editing for Correctness, pp. 553–54.)* A dash may be appropriate for informal writing situations to highlight a list, explanation, or shift in tone. *(See Tab 11: Editing for Correctness, pp. 563–64.)*

Note: The conjunctive adverb or transitional expression is usually followed by a comma when it appears at the beginning of the second clause (as in the preceding example). It can also appear in the middle of a clause, set off by two commas, or at the end, preceded by a comma.

► Most students complied with the new policy/. a few refused to do so.
   , however,

► Most students complied with the new policy/. a few refused to do so.
   , however

► Professor Kim then revealed his most important point. the paper would count for half my grade.

52e Separate the clauses into two sentences.

The simplest way to correct comma splices and run-on sentences is to turn the clauses into separate sentences. This solution is not always best, however, especially if the result is two short, simple sentences. The simplest solution works in the next example because the second sentence is a compound sentence.

► I realized that it was time to choose/. Either either I had to learn how to drive, or I had to move back to the city.

CONJUNCTIVE ADVERBS AND TRANSITIONAL EXPRESSIONS

also	incidentally	nonetheless
as a result	indeed	now
besides	in fact	of course
certainly	in other words	on the contrary
consequently	instead	otherwise
finally	in the meantime	similarly
for example	likewise	still
for instance	meanwhile	then
furthermore	moreover	therefore
however	nevertheless	thus
in addition	next	undoubtedly

When the two independent clauses are part of a quotation, with a phrase such as *he said* or *she noted* between them, each clause should be a separate sentence.

▶ "This was the longest day of my life," she said, <u>"unfortunately</u>, it's not over yet."

Unfortunately,

52f   Turn one of the independent clauses into a dependent clause.

In editing the following sentence, the writer chose to make the clause about *a few* her main point and the clause about *most* a subordinate idea. Readers will expect subsequent sentences to tell them more about the subject of the main clause.

▶ *Although most* <u>Most</u> students complied with the new policy, <u>however</u> a few refused to do so.

52g   Transform the two clauses into one independent clause.

Transforming two clauses into one clear and correct independent clause is often worth the effort.

▶ I realized that it was time <u>to choose,</u> either <u>I had</u> to learn how to drive or <u>I had</u> to move back to the city.

Sometimes you can change one of the clauses to a phrase and place it next to the word it modifies.

▶ Baseball cards are an obsession among some collectors, <u>the cards were first printed in the nineteenth century.</u>

, first printed in the nineteenth century,

CHAPTER 53

Subject-Verb Agreement

All verbs must agree with their subjects in person (first, second, or third—*I, we; you; he, she, it, they*) and in number (singular or plural).

✓ 53a   Learn the standard subject-verb combinations.

For regular verbs, add the present tense *-s* or *-es* ending to the verb if its subject is third-person singular; otherwise, the verb has no ending. Most verbs have one past-tense form. Note, however, that the verb *be* has irregular forms in both the present and the past tense.

The irregular verbs *be, have,* and *do* have the following forms in the present and past tenses:

Verb Tenses (Present and Past)

	READ (REGULAR)	BE	HAVE	DO
SINGULAR				
First person (*I*)	read (*read*)	am (*was*)	have (*had*)	do/don't (*did/didn't*)
Second person (*you*)	read (*read*)	are (*were*)	have (*had*)	do/don't (*did/didn't*)
Third person (*he, she, it*)	reads (*reads*)	is (*was*)	has (*had*)	does/doesn't (*did/didn't*)
PLURAL				
First person (*we*)	read (*read*)	are (*were*)	have (*had*)	do/don't (*did/didn't*)
Second person (*you*)	read (*read*)	are (*were*)	have (*had*)	do/don't (*did/didn't*)
Third person (*they*)	read (*read*)	are (*were*)	have (*had*)	do/don't (*did/didn't*)

Problems with subject-verb agreement tend to occur when writers do the following:

- Lose sight of the subject *(53b, pp. 499–500)*
- Use compound, collective, or indefinite subjects *(53c–e, pp. 500–4)*
- Have a subject that follows the verb *(53f, p. 504)*
- Confuse a subject complement with the subject *(53g, p. 504)*
- Use a relative pronoun as the subject of a dependent clause *(53h, pp. 504–5)*
- Use a phrase beginning with an *-ing* verb or infinitive (*to* followed by the base form of the verb) as the subject *(53i, p. 505)*
- Use titles, company names, or words considered by themselves *(53j, p. 505)*

53b Do not lose sight of the subject when a word group separates it from the verb.

To locate the subject of a sentence, find the verb, and then ask the *who* or *what* question about it ("Who is?" "What is?"). Does that subject match the verb in number?

▶ **The leaders of the trade union** *oppose* ~~opposes~~ **the new law.**
         ^

The answer to the question "Who opposes?" is *leaders,* a plural noun, so the verb should be in the plural form: *oppose.*

> *Note:* If a word group beginning with *as well as, along with,* or *in addition to* follows a singular subject, the subject does not become plural.
>
> ▶ My teacher, as well as other faculty members, ~~oppose~~ the new
>   school policy. *opposes*

Subject-Verb Agreement and Grammar Checkers

A grammar checker failed to flag this sentence for correction: *The candidate's position on foreign policy issues trouble some voters.* The subject is the singular noun *position,* so the verb should be *troubles.* Apparently, however, the grammar checker interpreted the word *issues* as the subject.

53c Treat most compound subjects—connected by *and, or, nor, both . . . and, either . . . or,* or *neither . . . nor*—as plural.

Compound subjects are made up of two or more parts joined by either a coordinating conjunction *(and, or, nor)* or a correlative conjunction *(both . . . and, either . . . or, neither . . . nor).*

1. Treating most compound subjects as plural   Most subjects joined by *and* should be treated as plural.

▶ *The king and his advisers* were shocked by this turn of events.

▶ This poem's *first line and last word* have a powerful effect on the reader.

2. Treating some compound subjects as singular   There are exceptions to the rule that subjects joined by *and* are plural.

- The two subjects refer to the same entity.

  ▶ *My best girlfriend and most dependable adviser* is my mother.

- The two subjects are considered as a single unit.

  ▶ *Forty acres and a mule continues* to be what is needed.

- The two subjects are preceded by the word *each* or *every.*

  ▶ *Each* man, woman, and child *deserves* respect.

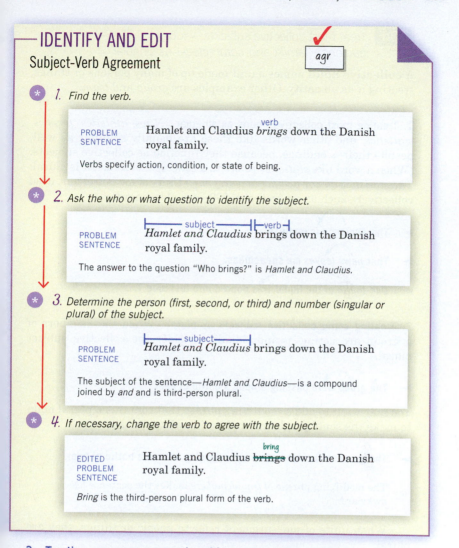

IDENTIFY AND EDIT
Subject-Verb Agreement

agr ✓

1. *Find the verb.*

PROBLEM
SENTENCE

verb
Hamlet and Claudius *brings* down the Danish royal family.

Verbs specify action, condition, or state of being.

2. *Ask the who or what question to identify the subject.*

PROBLEM
SENTENCE

├── subject ──┤├─verb─┤
Hamlet and Claudius brings down the Danish royal family.

The answer to the question "Who brings?" is *Hamlet and Claudius.*

3. *Determine the person (first, second, or third) and number (singular or plural) of the subject.*

PROBLEM
SENTENCE

├── subject ──┤
Hamlet and Claudius brings down the Danish royal family.

The subject of the sentence—*Hamlet and Claudius*—is a compound joined by *and* and is third-person plural.

4. *If necessary, change the verb to agree with the subject.*

EDITED
PROBLEM
SENTENCE

bring
Hamlet and Claudius ~~brings~~ down the Danish royal family.

Bring is the third-person plural form of the verb.

3. Treating some compound subjects as either plural or singular
Compound subjects connected by *or, nor, either . . . or,* or *neither . . . nor* can take either a singular or a plural verb, depending on which subject is closer to the verb.

SINGULAR   **Either the children or their mother is to blame.**

PLURAL   **Neither the experimenter nor her subjects were aware of the takeover.**

Sentences often sound less awkward with the plural subject closer to the verb.

53d Treat most collective subjects—subjects like *audience, family,* and *committee*—as singular.

A **collective noun** names a unit made up of many persons or things, treating it as an entity. Other examples are *group* and *team.*

1. Treating most collective nouns as singular *News, athletics, physics, statistics,* and other words like these are usually singular as well, despite their *-s* endings, because they function as collective subjects. (When a word like *statistics* refers to a collection of items, it is plural: *The statistics on car accidents worry me.*) Units of measurement used collectively, such as *six inches* or *20%,* are also singular.

▶ The *audience is* restless.

▶ That *news leaves* me speechless.

▶ *One-fourth* of the liquid *was* poured into test tube 1.

2. Treating some collective subjects as plural When the members of a group are acting as individuals, consider the collective subject plural.

▶ The *group were* passing around a bottle of beer.

You may want to add a modifying phrase that contains a plural noun to make the sentence clearer and avoid awkwardness.

▶ The *group of troublemakers were* passing around a bottle of beer.

The modifying phrase *of troublemakers* makes the sentence less awkward.

When units of measurement refer to people or things, they are plural.

▶ *One-fourth* of the students in the class *are* failing the course.

3. Distinguishing between *a number* and *the number* *A number* takes a plural verb, while *the number* takes a singular verb.

▶ *A number* of shoppers *prefer* Brand X.

▶ *The number* of people who shop online *is* growing.

53e   Treat most indefinite subjects—subjects like *everybody, no one, each, all,* and *none*—as singular.

Indefinite pronouns such as *everybody* and *no one* do not refer to a specific person or item.

1. Recognizing that most indefinite pronouns are singular   The following indefinite pronouns are always singular: *anybody, anyone, anything, each, either, everybody, everyone, everything, neither, nobody, none, no one, nothing, one, somebody, someone,* and *something.*

▶   **Everyone** in my hiking club **is** an experienced climber.

None and *neither* are singular when they appear by themselves.

▶   In the movie, five men set out on an expedition, but **none returns.**

▶   **Neither sees** a way out of this predicament.

If a prepositional phrase that includes a plural noun or pronoun follows *none* or *neither,* the indefinite pronoun seems to have a plural meaning. Although some writers treat *none* or *neither* as plural in such situations, others maintain that these two pronouns are always singular. It is a safe bet to consider them singular.

▶   In the movie, five men set out on an expedition, but **none** of them **returns.**

▶   **Neither** of the hikers **sees** a way out of this cave.

2. Recognizing that some indefinite pronouns are always plural   A handful of indefinite pronouns *(both, few, many, several)* are always plural because by definition they mean more than one. *Both,* for example, always indicates two.

▶   **Both** of us **want** to go to the rally for the environment.

▶   **Several** of my friends **were** very happy about the outcome of the election.

3. Recognizing that some indefinite pronouns can be either plural or singular   Some indefinite pronouns *(some, any, all, most)* can be either plural or singular, depending on whether they refer to a plural or a singular noun in the sentence.

▶   **Some** of the **book is** missing, but **all** the **papers are** here.

4. Treating phrases beginning with question words as singular or revising to avoid awkwardness

▶ *How you do on the exam* **counts** for half your grade.

| AWKWARD | *What we need is* new clothes. |
| BETTER | *We need* new clothes. |

53f   Make sure the subject and verb agree when the subject comes after the verb.

In most English sentences, the verb comes after the subject. Sometimes, however, a writer will switch this order. In the following sentence, you can locate the subject by asking, "Who or what stand?" The answer is the sentence's subject: *an oak and a weeping willow.* Because the subject is a compound subject (two subjects joined by *and*), the verb must be plural.

▶ Out back behind the lean-to *stand an old oak tree and a weeping willow.*

In sentences that begin with *there is* or *there are,* the subject always follows the verb.

▶ There *is* a worn wooden *bench* in the shade of the two trees.

In questions, the helping verb agrees with the subject.

▶ *Do you* understand her?

53g   Make sure the verb agrees with its subject, not the subject complement.

A **subject complement** renames and specifies the sentence's subject. It follows a **linking verb**—a verb, often a form of *be,* that joins the subject to its description or definition: *children* <u>are</u> *innocent.* In the following sentence, the singular noun *gift* is the subject. *Books* is the subject complement. Therefore, *are* has been changed to *is* to agree in number with *gift.*

▶ One gift that gives her pleasure *~~are~~* books.
    is

53h   *Who, which,* and *that* (relative pronouns) take verbs that agree with the subject they replace.

When a relative pronoun such as *who, which,* or *that* is the subject of a dependent clause, it is taking the place of a noun that appears earlier in the sentence—its **antecedent.** The verb that goes with *who, which,* or *that* must agree with this antecedent. In the following sentence, the relative pronoun *that* is the subject of the dependent clause *that has dangerous side effects. Disease,* a singular noun, is the antecedent of *that;* therefore, the verb in the dependent clause is singular.

▶   Measles is a childhood *disease that has* dangerous side effects.

The phrase *one of the* implies more than one and so is plural. *Only one of the* implies just one, however, and is singular. Generally, use the plural form of the verb when the phrase *one of the* comes before the antecedent. Use the singular form of the verb when *only one of the* comes before the plural noun.

PLURAL   Tuberculosis is one of the diseases *that have* long, *tragic* histories in many parts of the world.

SINGULAR   Barbara is the *only one of the* scientists *who has a* degree in physics.

53i   Phrases beginning with *-ing* verbs or infinitives take the singular form of the verb when they are subjects.

A **gerund phrase** is an *-ing* verb form followed by objects, complements, or modifiers. When a gerund phrase is the subject in a sentence, it is singular.

▶   *Experimenting with drugs is* a dangerous practice.

Infinitive phrases *(see Tab 12: Basic Grammar Review, p. 617)* are singular subjects.

▶   *To win medals is* every competitor's dream.

53j   Titles, company names, and words considered as words are singular.

                            is
▶   *The Two Gentlemen of Verona* ~~are~~ considered the weakest of Shakespeare's comedies.

                        includes
▶   The company I work for ~~include~~ many different divisions.

                                        has
▶   In today's highly partisan politics, *moderates* ~~have~~ come to mean "wishy-washy people."

CHAPTER 54

Problems with Verbs

Verbs report action and show time. They change form to indicate person, number, voice, and mood.

54a Learn the principal forms of regular and irregular verbs.

All English verbs have five main forms, except for the *be* verb, which has eight. *(For examples, see pp. 498–99 and pp. 590–91.)*

- The **base form** is the form found in a dictionary. *(For irregular verbs, other forms are given as well. See p. 507 for a list.)*

- The **present tense** form indicates an action occurring at the moment, habitually, or at a set future time and also introduces quotations, literary events, and scientific facts *(54f, p. 510, and 54h, pp. 512–13)*. The third-person singular present tense is the *-s* form.

- The **past tense** indicates an action completed at a specific time in the past *(54f, p. 510)*.

- The **past participle** is used with *have, has,* or *had* to form the perfect tenses *(54f, p. 511)*; with a form of the *be* verb to form the passive voice; and as an adjective (the *polished* silver).

- The **present participle** is used with a form of the *be* verb to form the progressive tenses *(54f, p. 511)*. It can also serve as a noun (the *writing* is finished) and as an adjective (the *smiling* man).

1. Learning about common irregular verbs **Regular verbs** always add *-d* or *-ed* to the base verb to form the past tense and past participle. **Irregular verbs,** in contrast, do not form the past tense or past participle in a consistent way. The box on page 507 lists the principal forms of common irregular verbs, which you can find in the dictionary.

2. Using the correct forms of irregular verbs that end in *-en* The forms of irregular verbs with past tenses that end in *-e* and past participles that end in *-n* or *-en*, such as *ate/eaten* and *rode/ ridden*, are sometimes confused.

► He had ~~ate~~ the apple. *(eaten)*

► They had ~~rode~~ the whole way on the bus. *(ridden)*

COMMON IRREGULAR VERBS

Base	Past tense	Past participle	Base	Past tense	Past participle
awake	awoke	awoke/awakened	hang	hanged	hanged (for people)
arise	arose	arisen	have	had	had
be	was/were	been	hear	heard	heard
beat	beat	beaten	know	knew	known
become	became	become	lose	lost	lost
begin	began	begun	pay	paid	paid
blow	blew	blown	raise	raised	raised
break	broke	broken	ride	rode	ridden
bring	brought	brought	ring	rang	rung
buy	bought	bought	rise	rose	risen
catch	caught	caught	say	said	said
choose	chose	chosen	see	saw	seen
cling	clung	clung	set	set	set
come	came	come	shake	shook	shaken
do	did	done	sit	sat	sat
draw	drew	drawn	spin	spun	spun
drink	drank	drunk	steal	stole	stolen
drive	drove	driven	spend	spent	spent
eat	ate	eaten	strive	strove/strived	striven/strived
fall	fell	fallen	swear	swore	sworn
fight	fought	fought	swim	swam	swum
fly	flew	flown	swing	swung	swung
forget	forgot	forgotten/forgot	take	took	taken
forgive	forgave	forgiven	tear	tore	torn
freeze	froze	frozen	tread	trod	trod/trodden
get	got	gotten/got	wear	wore	worn
give	gave	given	weave	wove	woven
go	went	gone	wring	wrung	wrung
grow	grew	grown	write	wrote	written
hang	hung	hung (for things)			

3. Using the correct forms of *went* and *gone* and *saw* and *seen* *Went* and *saw* are the past tense forms of the irregular verbs *go* and *see*. *Gone* and *seen* are the past participle forms.

► I had ~~went~~ there yesterday.
(gone)

► We ~~seen~~ the rabid dog and called for help.
(saw)

54b Distinguish between *lay* and *lie*, *rise* and *raise*, and *sit* and *set*.

Even experienced writers confuse the verbs *lay* and *lie*, *rise* and *raise*, and *sit* and *set*. The correct forms are given in the following table.

Often-Confused Verbs and Their Principal Forms

BASE	-S FORM	PAST	PAST PARTICIPLE	PRESENT PARTICIPLE
lay (to place)	lays	laid	laid	laying
lie (to recline)	lies	lay	lain	lying
lie (to speak an untruth)	lies	lied	lied	lying
rise (to go/get up)	rises	rose	risen	rising
raise (to lift up)	raises	raised	raised	raising
sit (to be seated)	sits	sat	sat	sitting
set (to put on a surface)	sets	sat	set	setting

One verb in each of these groups *(lay, raise, set)* is **transitive**: an object receives the action of the verb. The other verbs *(lie, rise, sit)* are **intransitive** and cannot take an object. You should use a form of *lay, raise,* or *set,* if you can replace the verb with *place* or *put*. *(See Tab 12: Basic Grammar Review, pp. 615–16 for more on transitive and intransitive verbs.)*

▶ The dog *lays a bone* at your feet and then *lies* down and closes his eyes.

    direct object

▶ As the flames *rise,* the heat *raises the temperature* of the room.

    direct object

▶ The technician *sits* down and *sets the samples* in front of her.

    direct object

Lay (to place) and *lie* (to recline) are also confusing because the past tense of the irregular verb *lie* is *lay (lie, lay, lain)*. Always double-check the verb *lay* in your writing.

    laid

▶ He washed the dishes carefully and ~~lay~~ them on a clean towel.

54c Add an *-s* or *-es* ending when necessary.

In the present tense, almost all verbs add an *-s* or *-es* ending if the subject is third-person singular. *(See pp. 498–99 for more on standard subject-verb combinations.)* Third-person singular subjects can be nouns *(woman, Benjamin, desk),* pronouns *(he, she, it),* or indefinite pronouns *(everyone).*

    rises

▶ The stock market ~~rise~~ when economic news is good.

If the subject is in the first person *(I)*, the second person *(you)*, or the third-person plural *(people, they)*, the verb does *not* add an *-s* or *-es* ending.

► You invests your money wisely.

► People needs to invest wisely.

54d   Add a *-d* or an *-ed* ending when necessary.

When speaking, people sometimes leave the *-d* or *-ed* ending off certain verbs such as *asked, fixed, mixed, supposed to,* and *used to.* However, in writing, include the endings on all regular verbs in the past tense and all past participles of regular verbs.

► The driving instructor ~~ask~~ *asked* the student driver to pull over to the curb.

► After we had ~~mix~~ *mixed* the formula, we let it cool.

Also check for missing *-d* or *-ed* endings on past participles used as adjectives.

► The ~~concern~~ *concerned* parents met with the school board.

Verb Forms and Grammar and Spelling Checkers

A grammar checker flagged the incorrect form in this sentence: *She had chose to go to the state college.* It also suggested the correct form: *chosen.* However, the checker missed the misuse of *set* in this sentence: *I am going to set down for a while.*

Spelling checkers will not highlight a verb form that is used incorrectly in a sentence.

54e   Make sure your verbs are complete.

A **complete verb** consists of the main verb and any helping verbs needed to express the tense *(see pp. 509–10)* or voice *(see p. 594).* **Helping verbs** include forms of *be, have,* and *do* and the modal verbs *can, could, may, might, shall, should, will, ought to, must,* and *would. (For more on modals, see Tab 12: Basic Grammar Review, pp. 594–95.)* Helping verbs can be part of contractions *(He's running, we'd better go),* but they cannot be left out of the sentence entirely.

► They *will* be going on a field trip next week.

Do not use *of* in place of *have.*

► I could ~~of~~ *have* finished earlier.

Also avoid *could've* in formal writing.

A **linking verb,** often a form of *be,* connects the subject to a description or definition of it: *Cats are mammals.* Linking verbs can be part of contractions *(She's a student),* but they should not be left out entirely.

► Montreal a major Canadian city.
          is ^

54f Use verb tenses accurately.

Tenses show the time of a verb's action. English has three basic time frames—present, past, and future—and each tense has simple, perfect, progressive, and perfect progressive verb forms to indicate the time span of the actions taking place. *(For a review of the present tense forms of a typical verb and of the verbs* be, have, *and* do, *see 53a, p. 499; for a review of the principal forms of regular and irregular verbs, which form tenses, see 54a, pp. 506–7.)*

1. The simple present and past tenses These two tenses do not use a helping verb or verbs. The **simple present tense** describes actions occurring at the moment, habitually, or at a set future time. The **simple past tense** describes actions completed at a specific time in the past.

> **SIMPLE PRESENT**
>
> Every May, she *plans* next year's marketing strategy.
>
> **SIMPLE PAST**
>
> In the early morning hours before the office opened, she *planned* her marketing strategy.

2. The simple future tense The **simple future tense** takes *will* plus the verb. It is used for actions that have not yet begun.

> **SIMPLE FUTURE**
>
> In May, I *will plan* next year's marketing strategy.

3. Perfect tenses The **perfect tenses** take a form of *have (has, had)* plus the past participle. They indicate actions that were or will be completed by the time of another action or a specific time. The present perfect also describes actions that continue into the present. *(For more on the past participle, see p. 506.)*

> **PRESENT PERFECT**
>
> She *has* already *planned* next year's marketing strategy. She *has planned* the marketing strategy for the past five years.
>
> **PAST PERFECT**
>
> By the time she resigned, Maria *had* already *planned* next year's marketing strategy.

FUTURE PERFECT

By May 31, she *will have planned* next year's marketing strategy.

When the verb in the past perfect is irregular, be sure to use the proper form of the past participle.

▶ By the time the week was over, both plants had ~~grew~~ five inches.

grown

4. Progressive tenses   The **progressive tenses** take a form of *be (am, are, was, were)* plus the present participle. The progressive forms of the simple and perfect tenses indicate ongoing action.

PRESENT PROGRESSIVE

She *is planning* next year's marketing strategy now.

PAST PROGRESSIVE

She *was planning* next year's marketing strategy when she started to look for another job.

References to planned events that didn't happen take *was/were going to* plus the base form.

She *was going to plan* the marketing strategy, but she left the company.

FUTURE PROGRESSIVE

During the month of May, she *will be planning* next year's marketing strategy.

5. Perfect progressive tenses   The **perfect progressive tenses** take *have* plus *be* plus the verb. These tenses indicate an action that takes place over a specific period of time. The present perfect progressive tense describes actions that start in the past and continue to the present; the past and future perfect progressive tenses are used for actions that ended or will end at a specified time or before another action.

PRESENT PERFECT PROGRESSIVE

She *has been planning* next year's marketing strategy since the beginning of May.

PAST PERFECT PROGRESSIVE

She *had been planning* next year's marketing strategy when she was offered another job.

FUTURE PERFECT PROGRESSIVE

By May 18, she *will have been planning* next year's marketing strategy for more than two weeks.

54g Use the past perfect tense to indicate an action completed at a specific time or before another event.

When a past event was ongoing but ended before a particular time or another past event, use the past perfect rather than the simple past.

▶ Before the Johnstown Flood occurred in 1889, people in the
  had
  area expressed their concern about the safety of the dam on the

  Conemaugh River.

  People expressed their concern before the flood occurred.

If two past events happened simultaneously, however, use the simple past, not the past perfect.

▶ When the Conemaugh flooded, many people in the area ~~had~~ lost their lives.

  Do not use *would have* in *if* (conditional) clauses.

  had
▶ If the students ~~would have~~ come to class, they would have known the material.

54h Use the present tense for literary events, scientific facts, and introductions to quotations.

If the conventions of a discipline require you to state what your paper does, do so in the present, not the future, tense.

▶ In this paper, I *describe* the effects of increasing NaCl concentrations on the germination of radish seeds.

─NAVIGATING THROUGH COLLEGE AND BEYOND

Reporting Research Findings

Although we see a written work as always existing in the present, we think of research findings as having been collected at one time in the past. Use the past or present perfect tense to report the results of research.

  responded
▶ Three of the compounds (nos. 2, 3, and 6) ~~respond~~ positively by turning purple.

  has reviewed
▶ Clegg (1990) ~~reviews~~ studies of workplace organization focused on

  struggles for control of the labor process.

Here are some other special uses of the present tense:

- By convention, events in a novel, short story, poem, or other literary work are described in the present tense.

  ▶ **Even though Huck's journey down the river ~~was~~ *is* an escape from**

  society, his relationship with Jim ~~was~~ *is* a form of community.

- Like events in a literary work, scientific facts are considered to be perpetually present, even though they were discovered in the past.

  ▶ **Mendel discovered that genes ~~had~~ *have* different forms, or alleles.**

  (Theories proven false should appear in the past tense.)

- The present tense introduces a quotation, paraphrase, or summary of someone else's writing.

  ▶ **William Julius Wilson ~~wrote~~ *writes* that "the disappearance of work has**

  become a characteristic feature of the inner-city ghetto" (31).

Note: When using APA style, introduce others' writing or research findings with the past tense (for example, Wilson *wrote*) or past perfect tense (Johnson *has found*).

54i   Make sure infinitives and participles fit with the tense of the main verb.

Infinitives and participles are **verbals**—words formed from verbs that have various functions within a sentence. Verbals can form phrases by taking objects, modifiers, or complements. Because they express time, verbals need to fit with the main verb in a sentence.

1. Using the correct tense for infinitives   An **infinitive** has the word *to* plus the base verb *(to breathe, to sing, to dance)*. The perfect form of the infinitive is *to have* plus the past participle *(to have breathed, to have sung, to have danced)*. If the action of the infinitive happens at the same time as or after the action of the main verb, use the present tense.

▶ **I hope to *sing and dance* on Broadway next summer.**

If the action of the infinitive happened before the action of the main verb, use the perfect form.

▶ **My talented mother would like *to have sung and danced* on Broadway as a young woman, but she never had the chance.**

2. Using the correct tense for participles that are part of phrases Participial phrases can begin with the present participle *(breathing, dancing, singing),* the present perfect participle *(having breathed, having danced, having sung),* or the past participle *(breathed, danced, sung).* If the action of the participle happens simultaneously with the action of the sentence's verb, use the present participle.

▶ *Singing one hour a day together,* **the chorus developed perfect harmony.**

If the action of the participle happened before the action of the main verb, use the present perfect or past participle form.

▶ *Having breathed* **the air of New York, I exulted in the possibilities for my life in the city.**

▶ *Tinted* **with a strange green light, the western sky looked threatening.**

54j Use the subjunctive mood for wishes, requests, and conjecture.

The **mood** of a verb indicates the writer's attitude. Use the **indicative mood** to state or question facts, acts, and opinions *(Our collection is on display. Did you see it?).* Use the **imperative mood** for commands, directions, and entreaties. The subject of an imperative sentence is always *you,* but the *you* is usually understood, not written out *(Shut the door!).* Use the **subjunctive mood** to express a wish or a demand or to make a statement contrary to fact *(I wish I were a millionaire).* The mood that writers have the most trouble with is the subjunctive.

Verbs in the subjunctive mood may be in the present tense, past tense, or perfect tense. Present tense subjunctive verbs do not change form to signal person or number. The only form used is the verb's base form: *accompany* or *be,* not *accompanies* or *am, are, is.* Also, the verb *be* has only one past tense form in the subjunctive mood: *were.*

1. Using the subjunctive mood to express a wish

> WISH

> **I wish I *were* more prepared for this test.**

Note: In everyday conversation, most speakers use the indicative rather than the subjunctive when expressing wishes *(I wish I was more prepared for this test).*

---

2. Using the subjunctive mood for requests, recommendations, and demands Because requests, recommendations, and demands have not yet happened, they—like wishes—are expressed in the subjunctive mood. Words such as *ask, insist, recommend, request,* and *suggest* indicate the subjunctive mood; the verb in the *that* clause that follows should be in the subjunctive.

DEMAND

I insist that all applicants *find* their seats by 8:00 a.m.

3. Using the subjunctive in statements that are contrary to fact   Often such statements contain a subordinate clause that begins with *if*: the verb in the *if* clause should be in the subjunctive mood.

CONTRARY-TO-FACT STATEMENT

He would not be so irresponsible if his father *were* [not *was*] still alive.

Note: Some common expressions of conjecture are in the subjunctive mood, including *as it were, come rain or shine, far be it from me,* and *be that as it may.*

CHAPTER 55

Problems with Pronouns

A **pronoun** (*he/him, it/its, they/their*) takes the place of a noun. The noun that the pronoun replaces is called its **antecedent.** In the following sentence, snow is the antecedent of the pronoun *it.*

▶   The *snow* fell all day long, and by nightfall *it* was three feet deep.

Like nouns, pronouns are singular or plural.

SINGULAR   The *house* was dark and gloomy, and *it* sat in a grove of tall cedars.

PLURAL   The *cars* swept by on the highway, all of *them* doing more than sixty-five miles per hour.

A pronoun needs an antecedent to refer to and agree with, and a pronoun must match its antecedent in number (*plural/singular*) and gender (*he/his, she/her, it/its*). A pronoun must also be in a form, or case, that matches its function in the sentence.

✓ **55a**   Make pronouns agree with their antecedents.

Problems with pronoun-antecedent agreement tend to occur when a pronoun's antecedent is an indefinite pronoun, a collective noun, or a compound noun. Problems can also occur when writers try to avoid the generic use of *he.*

Pronoun Problems and Grammar Checkers

Do not rely on grammar checkers to alert you to problems in pronoun-antecedent agreement or pronoun reference. One grammar checker, for example, missed the case error in the following sentence: *Ford's son Edsel, who [should be* whom*] the auto magnate treated very cruelly, was a brilliant automotive designer. (See p. 525 for a discussion of the proper use of* who *and* whom.*)*

1. Indefinite pronouns   **Indefinite pronouns** such as *someone, anybody,* and *nothing* refer to nonspecific people or things. They sometimes function as antecedents for other pronouns. Most indefinite pronouns are singular *(anybody, anyone, anything, each, either, everybody, everyone, everything, much, neither, nobody, none [meaning* not one*], no one, nothing, one, somebody, something).*

ALWAYS SINGULAR	Did *either* of the boys lose *his* bicycle?

Some writers and instructors consider *none* plural in certain circumstances *(see p. 503),* but it is safest to use it as singular.

The indefinite pronouns *both, few, many,* and *several* are plural.

ALWAYS PLURAL	*Both* boys lost *their* bicycles.

The indefinite pronouns *all, any, more, most,* and *some* can be either singular or plural, depending on the noun to which they refer.

PLURAL	The *students* debated, *some* arguing that *their* positions on the issue were in the mainstream.
SINGULAR	The *bread* is on the counter, but *some* of *it* has already been eaten.

Problems arise when writers attempt to make indefinite pronouns agree with their antecedents without introducing gender bias. There are three ways to avoid gender bias when correcting a pronoun agreement problem such as the following.

FAULTY	None of the great Romantic writers believed that their achievements equaled their aspirations.

- If possible, change a singular indefinite pronoun to a plural pronoun, editing the sentence as necessary.

         All

▶ ~~None of~~ the great Romantic writers believed that their

            fell short of

  achievements ~~equaled~~ their aspirations.

- Reword the sentence to eliminate the indefinite pronoun.

  ▶   ~~None of the~~ *The* great Romantic writers believed that their

  achievements ~~equaled~~ *fell short of* their aspirations.

- Substitute *he or she* or *his or her* (but never *his/her*) for the singular pronoun. Change the sentence as necessary to avoid using this construction more than once.

  ▶   None of the great Romantic writers believed that ~~their~~

  ~~achievements equaled their~~ *his or her* aspirations *had been realized*.

2. Generic nouns

A **generic noun** represents anyone and everyone in a group—a typical doctor, the average voter. Because most groups consist of both males and females, using male pronouns to refer to generic nouns is usually considered sexist. To fix agreement problems with generic nouns, use one of the three options suggested in the previous section.

▶   ~~A college student~~ *College students* should have ~~a~~ mind*s* of their own.

▶   A college student should have ~~a mind of their own.~~ *an independent point of view.*

▶   A college student should have a mind of ~~their~~ *his or her* own.

3. Collective nouns

Collective nouns such as *team, family, jury, committee,* and *crowd* are treated as singular unless the people in the group are acting as individuals.

▶   The crowd burst through the door, trampling everything in ~~their~~ *its* path.

The activity of bursting through a door as a group indicates that this crowd is acting as a collection of individuals.

▶   The committee left the conference room and returned to ~~its~~ *their* offices.

In this case, the members of the committee are acting as individuals: each is returning to an office.

If you are using a collective noun that has a plural meaning, consider adding a plural noun to clarify the meaning.

▶   The *committee members* left the conference room and returned to *their* offices.

IDENTIFY AND EDIT

Pronoun-Antecedent Agreement and Gender Bias

 ✓ *agr*

Try these three strategies for avoiding gender bias when an indefinite pronoun or generic noun is the antecedent in a sentence:

1. *If possible, change the antecedent to a plural indefinite pronoun or a plural noun.*

- ~~Each~~ ^{All} of us should decide ~~their~~ ^{our} vote on issues, not personality.
- ^{Responsible citizens decide} ~~The responsible citizen decides~~ their vote on issues, not personality.

2. *Reword the sentence to eliminate the pronoun.*

- Each of us should ~~decide their~~ vote on issues, not personality.
- The responsible citizen ~~decides their vote~~ ^{votes} on issues, not personality.

3. *Substitute he or she or his or her (but never his/her) for the singular pronoun to maintain pronoun-antecedent agreement.*

- Each of us should decide ~~their~~ ^{his or her} vote on issues, not personality.
- The responsible citizen decides ~~their~~ ^{his or her} vote on issues, not personality.

Caution: Use this strategy sparingly. Using *he* or *she* or *his* or *her* several times in quick succession makes for tedious reading.

4. Compound antecedents Compound antecedents joined by *and* are almost always plural.

▶ To remove all traces of the crime, James put the book and the

magnifying glass back in ~~its~~ ^{their} place.

When a compound antecedent is joined by *or* or *nor,* the pronoun should agree with the closest part of the compound antecedent. If one part is singular and the other is plural, the sentence will be smoother and more effective if the plural antecedent is closest to the pronoun.

PLURAL   Neither *the child nor the parents* shared *their* food.

If the compound antecedent consists of a male and a female, however, the rule does not apply. Revise the sentence to avoid this situation.

▶   ~~Neither~~ José ~~nor~~ Laura ~~could make it to her~~ appointment ~~on time~~.

When the two parts of the compound antecedent refer to the same person, or when the word *each* or *every* precedes the compound antecedent, use a singular pronoun.

SINGULAR   Being *a teacher and a mother* keeps *her* busy.

SINGULAR   *Every* poem and letter by Keats has *its* own special power.

✓ **55b**   Make pronoun references clear.

If a pronoun does not clearly refer to a specific antecedent, readers can become confused. Two common problems are ambiguous references and implied references.

1. Ambiguous pronoun references   If a pronoun can refer to more than one noun in a sentence, the reference is ambiguous.

VAGUE   The friendly banter between Hamlet and Horatio
          eventually provokes him to declare that his world-
          view has changed.

To clear up the ambiguity, eliminate the pronoun and use the appropriate noun.

CLEAR   The friendly banter between Hamlet and Horatio
          eventually provokes Hamlet to declare that his
          worldview has changed.

Sometimes the ambiguous reference can be cleared up by rewriting the sentence.

VAGUE   Jane Austen and Cassandra corresponded regu-
          larly when she was in London.

CLEAR   When Jane Austen was in London, she corre-
          sponded regularly with Cassandra.

2. Implied pronoun references   The antecedent that a pronoun refers to must be present in the sentence, and it must be a noun or another pronoun, not a word that modifies a noun. Possessives and verbs cannot be antecedents in college writing, although this usage is common in speech and informal contexts.

▶ In ~~Wilson's~~ essay "When Work Disappears," ~~he~~ proposes a four-point

      his   *Wilson*

plan for the revitalization of blighted inner-city communities.

Replacing *he* with *Wilson* gives the pronoun *his* an antecedent that is stated explicitly, not just implied. Note that in the revised sentence, the antecedent follows the pronoun.

▶ Every weekday afternoon, my brothers skateboard home from school,

              their skateboards
and then they leave ~~them~~ in the driveway.

In the original sentence, *skateboard* is a verb, not a noun, and cannot act as a pronoun antecedent.

3. References for *this, that,* and *which*   The pronouns *this, that,* and *which* often refer vaguely to ideas expressed in preceding sentences. To make the sentence containing the pronoun clearer, either change the pronoun to a specific noun or add a specific antecedent or clarifying noun.

▶ As government funding for higher education decreases, tuition

                                 these higher costs
increases. Are we students supposed to accept ~~this~~ without protest?

▶ As government funding for higher education decreases, tuition

                                 situation
increases. Are we students supposed to accept this without protest?

4. References for *you, they,* and *it*   The pronouns *you, they,* and *it* should refer to definite, explicitly stated antecedents. If the antecedent is unclear, replace the pronoun with an appropriately specific noun, or rewrite the sentence to eliminate the pronoun.

                          the government pays
▶ In some countries, such as Canada, ~~they pay~~ for such medical procedures.

                     students
▶ According to college policy, ~~you~~ must have a permit to park a car
on campus.

  The
▶ ~~In the~~ textbook, ~~it~~ states that borrowing to fund the purchase of financial

assets results in a double-counting of debt.

In college writing, use *you* only to address the reader: *Turn left when you reach the corner.*

Note: Writers sometimes use *one* as a generic pronoun. This practice usually seems pompous, however, and is best avoided.

55c Make your pronouns consistent within a sentence or passage.

Keep the same point of view (first, second, or third person) and number (singular or plural) within a sentence or series of related sentences.

▶ **Once you discover how easy it can be to buy downloadable music, you**

You   *as well as*

will be hooked. ~~One~~ can easily find any type of music, ~~and I have found~~

a number of services that offer a good selection.

(For more on confusing shifts, see Tab 9: Editing for Clarity, pp. 447–50.)

✓ **55d** Make pronoun cases match their function (for example, *I* vs. *me*).

When a pronoun's form, or **case,** does not match its function in a sentence, readers will feel that something is wrong.

- Pronouns in the subjective case are subjects or subject complements: *I, you, he, she, it, we, they, who, whoever.*
- Pronouns in the objective case are objects of verbs or prepositions: *me, you, him, her, it, us, them, whom, whomever.*
- Pronouns in the possessive case show ownership: *my, mine, your, yours, his, hers, its, our, ours, their, theirs, whose.* Adjective forms (*her* room, *our* office) appear before nouns. Noun forms stand alone (that room is *hers; mine* is on the left). When noun forms act as subjects, the verb agrees with the antecedent *(room).*

1. Compound structures **Compound structures** (words or phrases joined by *and, or,* or *nor*) can appear as subjects or objects. If you are not sure which form of a pronoun to use in a compound structure, treat the pronoun as the only subject or object, and note how the sentence sounds.

                                  I
SUBJECT   **Angela and ~~me~~ were cleaning up the kitchen.**

IDENTIFY AND EDIT

✓

case

Pronoun Case

Follow these steps to decide on the proper form of pronouns in compound structures:

1. *Identify the compound structure (a pronoun and a noun or other pronoun joined by and, but, or, or nor) in the problem sentence.*

> *compound structure*
>
> PROBLEM SENTENCE   [Her or her roommate] should call the campus technical support office and sign up for broadband Internet service.

> *compound structure*
>
> PROBLEM SENTENCE   The director gave the leading roles to [my brother and I].

2. *Isolate the pronoun that you are unsure about, then read the sentence to yourself without the rest of the compound structure. If the result sounds wrong, change the case of the pronoun (subjective to objective, or vice versa), and read the sentence again.*

> PROBLEM SENTENCE   [Her ~~or her roommate~~] should call the campus technical support office and sign up for broadband Internet service.

Her should call the campus technical support office sounds wrong. The pronoun should be in the subjective case: *she.*

> PROBLEM SENTENCE   The director gave the leading roles to [~~my brother and~~ I]

The director gave the leading role[s] to I sounds wrong. The pronoun should be in the objective case: *me.*

3. *If necessary, correct the original sentence.*

- ~~Her~~ **She** or her roommate should call the campus technical ⋀ support office and sign up for broadband Internet service.

- The director gave the leading roles to my brother and ~~I~~. **me** ⋀

If you treat the pronoun as the only subject, the original sentence is clearly wrong: *Me [was] cleaning up the kitchen.*

OBJECT My parents waited for an answer from John and ~~I~~.
(me)

If you treat the pronoun as the only object, the original sentence is clearly wrong: *My parents waited for an answer from I.*

> **Note:** Do not substitute a reflexive pronoun for the pronoun you are unsure of: *Angela and I [not myself] were cleaning up the kitchen. (For more on reflexive and intensive pronouns, see Tab 12: Basic Grammar Review, p. 602.)*

---

2. Subject complements   A **subject complement** renames and specifies the sentence's subject. It follows a **linking verb**—a verb, often a form of *be,* that links the subject to its description or definition: *Children* <u>are</u> *innocent.*

SUBJECT Mark's best friends are Jane and ~~me~~.
(I)

You can also switch the order to make the pronoun into the subject: *Jane and I are Mark's best friends.*

3. Appositives   **Appositives** are nouns or noun phrases that rename nouns or pronouns. They appear right after the word they rename and have the same function in the sentence that it has.

SUBJECTIVE The two weary travelers, Ramon and ~~me~~, finally found shelter.
(I)

OBJECTIVE The police arrested two protesters, Aliyah and ~~I~~.
(me)

4. *We* or *us*   When *we* or *us* comes before a noun, it has the same function in the sentence as the noun it precedes and renames.

SUBJECTIVE ~~Us~~ students never get to decide such things.
(We)

OBJECTIVE Things were looking desperate for ~~we~~ campers.
(us)

5. Comparisons with *than* or *as*   In comparisons, words are often left out of the sentence because the reader can guess what they would be. When a pronoun follows *than* or *as,* make sure you are using the correct form by mentally adding the missing word or words.

▶ Megan is quicker than she [is].

▶ We find ourselves remembering Maria as often as [we remember] her.

Sometimes the correct form depends on intended meaning:

▶ **My brother likes our dog more than *I* [do].**

▶ **My brother likes our dog more than [he likes] *me*.**

If a sentence with a comparison sounds too awkward or formal, add the missing words: *Megan is quicker than she is.*

6. Pronoun as the subject or the object of an infinitive   An infinitive has the word *to* plus the base verb *(to breathe, to sing, to dance)*. Whether a pronoun functions as the subject or the object of an infinitive, it should be in the objective case.

subject   object
▶ **We wanted our lawyer and *her* to defend *us* against this charge.**

Note that in the example the subject of the infinitive is a compound noun. If a compound functioning as the subject or object of an infinitive has two pronouns, both should be in the objective case: *The police officer told her and me to move along.*

7. Noun or pronoun with an *-ing* noun (a gerund)   When a noun or pronoun appears before a **gerund** (an *-ing* verb form functioning as a noun), it should usually be treated as a possessive. Possessive nouns are formed by adding *'s* to singular nouns *(the teacher's desk)* or an apostrophe only *(')* to plural nouns *(three teachers' rooms). (See Tab 11: Editing for Correctness, pp. 553–54.)*

     animal's
▶ **The ~~animals~~ fighting disturbed the entire neighborhood.**
     ^

     their
▶ **Because of ~~them~~ screeching, no one could get any sleep.**
     ^

When the *-ing* word is functioning as a modifier, not a noun, use the subjective or objective case for the pronoun that precedes it. Consider these two sentences:

▶ **The teacher punished their cheating.**

Cheating is the object of the sentence, modified by the possessive pronoun *their.*

▶ **The teacher saw them cheating.**

Them is the object of the sentence, modified by *cheating.*

Note: Possessive pronouns never contain an apostrophe and an *s*. Pronouns that appear with an apostrophe and an *s* are always part of a contraction. Be especially careful to use *its,* not *it's,* when the possessive form is called for: *The cat finally stopped its* [not *it's*] *screeching.*

55e   Distinguish between *who* and *whom.*

The relative pronouns *who, whom, whoever,* and *whomever* are used to introduce dependent clauses and in questions. Their case depends on their function.

- Subjective: *who, whoever*
- Objective: *whom, whomever*

1. Determining the pronoun's function in a clause If the pronoun is functioning as a subject and is performing an action, use *who* or *whoever.* If the pronoun is the object of a verb or preposition, use *whom* or *whomever.* (Note that *whom* usually appears at the beginning of the clause.)

▶ **Henry Ford, *who* started the Ford Motor Company, was autocratic and stubborn.**

Who, which refers to *Henry Ford,* is performing an action in the dependent clause: starting a company.

▶ **Ford's son Edsel, *whom* the auto magnate treated cruelly, was a brilliant automobile designer.**

Whom, which refers to *Edsel,* is the object of the verb *treated,* although it precedes the verb and the subject, *the auto magnate.* You can check the pronoun by changing the order within the clause: *The auto magnate treated whom [him] cruelly.*

Phrases such as *I think* or *they say* do not affect pronoun case.

▶ **Ford, *who* many say was a visionary, pioneered use of the assembly line.**

2. Determining the pronoun's function in a question To choose the correct form for the pronoun, answer the question with a personal pronoun:

▶ ***Who* founded the General Motors Corporation?**

The answer could be *He founded it. He* is in the subjective case, so *who* is correct.

▶ ***Whom* did Chrysler turn to for leadership in the 1980s?**

The answer could be *It turned to him. Him* is in the objective case, so *whom* is correct.

Note: Infinitives take the objective case, *whom,* as a subject or object: *Ford could not decide whom* [not *who*] *to trust.*

CHAPTER 56

Problems with Adjectives and Adverbs

Adjectives and **adverbs** are words that qualify—or modify—the meanings of other words. Adjectives modify nouns and pronouns. Adverbs modify verbs, adjectives, and other adverbs.

> **56a** Use adverbs to modify verbs, adjectives, other adverbs, and whole clauses.

Adverbs tell where, when, why, how, how often, how much, or to what degree.

▶ The authenticity of the document is *hotly* contested.

▶ The water was *brilliant* blue and *icy* cold.

▶ Dickens mixed humor and pathos *better* than any other English writer after Shakespeare.

▶ *Consequently,* Dickens is still read by millions.

(For information on the placement of adverbs in sentences, see Tab 12: Basic Grammar Review, pp. 604–05.)

Adjectives, Adverbs, and Grammar Checkers

Computer grammar checkers are sensitive to some problems with adjectives and adverbs but miss far more than they catch. A grammar checker failed to flag the errors in the following sentences: *The price took a suddenly plunge* [should be *sudden*] and *The price plunged sudden* [should be *suddenly*].

> **56b** Use adjectives to modify nouns or as subject complements.

Adjectives modify nouns and pronouns; they do not modify any other kind of word. Adjectives tell what kind or how many and may come before or after the noun or pronoun they modify.

▶ *Ominous gray* clouds loomed over the lake.

▶ The *looming* clouds, *ominous* and *gray,* frightened the children.

Some proper nouns have adjective forms. Proper adjectives, like the proper nouns they are derived from, are capitalized: *Victoria/Victorian, Britain/British, America/American, Shakespeare/Shakespearean.*

In some cases, a noun is used as an adjective without a change in form.

▶ *Cigarette* smoking harms the lungs and is banned in offices.

Occasionally, descriptive adjectives function as if they were nouns.

▶ The *unemployed* should not be equated with the *lazy.*

(For information about compound adjectives such as "well known," see Tab 11: Editing for Correctness, pp. 580–81.)

1. Avoiding incorrect use of adjectives   In common speech, we sometimes treat adjectives as adverbs. In writing, avoid this informal usage.

▶ He hit that ball ~~real good~~. (really well)

> Both *real* and *good* are adjectives, but they are used as adverbs in the original sentence, with *real* modifying *good* and *good* modifying the verb *hit.*

Note that *well* can function as an adjective and subject complement with a linking verb to describe a person's health.

▶ After the treatment, the patient felt *well* again.

▶ She ~~sure~~ made me work hard for my grade. (certainly)

> In the original sentence, the adjective *sure* tries to do the work of an adverb modifying the verb *made.*

2. Using adjectives after linking verbs   **Linking verbs** connect the subject of a sentence to its description. The most common linking verb is *be.* Descriptive adjectives that modify a sentence's subject but appear after a linking verb are called **subject complements.**

▶ During the winter, both Emily and Anne *were sick.*

▶ The road *is long, winding,* and *dangerous.*

Linking verbs are related to states of being and the five senses: *appear, become, feel, grow, make, prove, look, smell, sound,* and *taste.*

Verbs related to the senses can be either linking or action verbs, depending on the meaning of the sentence.

ADJECTIVE　The dog smelled *bad*.

Bad modifies the noun *dog*. The sentence indicates that the dog needed a bath.

ADVERB　The dog smelled *badly*.

Badly modifies the verb *smelled,* an action verb in this sentence. The sentence indicates that the dog had lost its sense of smell.

Good and *bad* appear after *feel* to describe emotional states.

▶　**I feel *bad* [not *badly*] for her because she does not feel well.**

3. Recognizing that some adjectives and adverbs are spelled alike　In most instances, *-ly* endings indicate adverbs; however, words with *-ly* endings can sometimes be adjectives *(the lovely girl)*. In standard English, many adverbs do not require the *-ly* ending, and some words are both adjectives and adverbs: *fast, only, hard, right,* and *straight.* Note that *right* also has an *-ly* form as an adverb: *rightly.* When in doubt, consult a dictionary.

56c　Use positive, comparative, and superlative adjectives and adverbs correctly.

Most adjectives and adverbs have three forms: positive *(dumb),* comparative *(dumber),* and superlative *(dumbest).* The simplest form of the adjective is the positive form.

1. Distinguishing between comparatives and superlatives　Use the comparative form to compare two things and the superlative form to compare three or more things.

▶　**In total area, New York is a *larger* state than Pennsylvania.**

▶　**Texas is the *largest* state in the Southwest.**

2. Learning when to use *-er/-est* endings and when to use *more/most,* or *less/least*　To form comparatives and superlatives of short adjectives, add the suffixes *-er* and *-est (brighter/brightest).* With longer adjectives (three or more syllables), use *more* or *less* and *most* or *least (more dangerous/most dangerous).* (A dictionary will tell you whether an adjective takes *-er/-est.*)

▶　Mercury is the ~~most near~~ planet to the sun.
　　　　　　　　　　nearest

A few short adverbs have *-er* and *-est* endings in their comparative and superlative forms *(harder/hardest).* Most adverbs, however, including all adverbs that end in *-ly,* use *more* and *most* in their comparative and superlative forms. Negative comparatives and superlatives are formed with *less* and *least: less funny/least funny.*

▶   She sings *more loudly* than we expected.

Two common adjectives—*good* and *bad*—form the comparative and superlative in an irregular way: *good, better, best* and *bad, worse, worst.*

▶   He felt ~~badder~~ worse as his illness progressed.

These and other irregular adjectives and adverbs are listed in the box on page 530. When in doubt, consult a dictionary.

3. Watching out for double comparatives and superlatives   Use either an *-er* or an *-est* ending or *more/most* to form the comparative or superlative, as appropriate; do not use both.

▶   Since World War II, Britain has been the most closest ally of the United States.

4. Recognizing concepts that cannot be compared   Do not use comparative or superlative forms with adjectives such as *unique, infinite, impossible, perfect, round, square,* and *destroyed.* These concepts are *absolutes.* If something is unique, for example, it is the only one of its kind, making comparison impossible.

▶   You will never find a ~~more unique~~ another restaurant ~~than~~ like this one.

5. Making sure your comparison is complete   Unless the context of your sentence makes the comparison clear, be sure to include both items you are comparing.

▶   Charles Dickens had more popular successes. than any other British writer of his time

(For more on making comparisons complete, see Tab 9, Editing for Clarity, p. 444.)

56d   Avoid double negatives.

The words *no, not,* and *never* can modify the meaning of nouns and pronouns as well as other sentence elements.

NOUN	You are *no* friend of mine.
ADJECTIVE	The red house was *not* large.
VERB	He *never* ran in a marathon.

However, it takes only one negative word to change the meaning of a sentence from positive to negative. When two negatives are used together, they cancel each other, resulting in a positive meaning. Unless you want your sentence to have a positive meaning *(I am not unaware of your feelings in this matter),* edit by changing or eliminating one of the negative words.

COMPARISON IN ADJECTIVES AND ADVERBS

Examples of Regular and Irregular Forms

REGULAR ADJECTIVES

	POSITIVE	COMPARATIVE	SUPERLATIVE
One-syllable adjectives	red	redder, less red	reddest, least red
Two-syllable adjectives ending in -*y*	lonely	lonelier, less lonely	loneliest, least lonely
Other adjectives of two or more syllables	famous	more/less famous	most/least famous

REGULAR ADVERBS

	POSITIVE	COMPARATIVE	SUPERLATIVE
One-syllable adverbs	hard	harder, less hard	hardest, least hard
Most other adverbs	truthfully	more/less truthfully	most/least truthfully

IRREGULAR ADJECTIVES

	POSITIVE	COMPARATIVE	SUPERLATIVE
	good	better	best
	bad	worse	worst
	little	less, littler	least, littlest
	many	more	most
	much	more	most
	some	more	most

IRREGULAR ADVERBS

	POSITIVE	COMPARATIVE	SUPERLATIVE
	badly	worse	worst
	well	better	best

▶ They don't have ~~no~~ *any* reason to go there.

▶ He ~~can't~~ *can* hardly do that assignment.

Note that *hardly* has a negative meaning and cannot be used with *no, not,* or *never.*

CHECKLIST Editing for Grammar Conventions

To detect grammatical problems in your writing, ask yourself the following questions:

☐ Is each sentence grammatically complete, or is some necessary part missing? Does each sentence include a subject, a complete verb, and an independent clause? *(See Chapter 51, Sentence Fragments, pp. 487–92.)*

☐ Does any sentence seem like two or more sentences jammed together without a break? If a sentence has more than one independent clause, are those clauses joined in an acceptable way? *(See Chapter 52, Comma Splices and Run-on Sentences, pp. 493–98.)*

☐ Do the key parts of each sentence fit together well, or are the subjects and verbs mismatched in person and number? *(See Chapter 53, Subject-Verb Agreement, pp. 498–505.)*

☐ Is the time frame of events represented accurately, conventionally, and consistently, or are there problems with verb form, tense, and sequence? *(See Chapter 54, Problems with Verbs, pp. 506–15.)*

☐ Do the pronouns in every sentence clearly refer to a specific noun or pronoun and agree with the nouns or pronouns they replace? *(See Chapter 55, Problems with Pronouns, pp. 515–25.)*

☐ Does the form of each modifier match its function in the sentence? *(See Chapter 56, Problems with Adjectives and Adverbs, pp. 526–31.)*

11

Editing for Correctness

Punctuation, Mechanics, and Spelling

It wasn't a matter of rewriting but simply of tightening up all the bolts.
—Marguerite Yourcenar

Question marks and exclamation points signal the type of sentence that they conclude. Like the other punctuation marks covered in this part, they convey important information for readers.

11 Editing for Correctness

✓ Sections referenced in Resources for Writers: Identifying and Editing Common Problems (following
Tab 9).

START SMART

Tab 11: Editing for Correctness

This section will help you answer questions such as the following:

Rhetorical Knowledge

- Should I use contractions such as *can't* or *don't* in my college work? (60b)
- Which numbers should be spelled out in my technical report? (65c)

Critical Thinking, Reading, and Writing

- How should I set off words I have added to a quotation? (62f)
- How do I use ellipses ethically to indicate omissions from quotations? (62g)

Processes

- What are some strategies for proofreading my work? (68)
- What are the strengths and limitations of my word processor's spelling checker? (60, 68)
- Can my word processor's grammar checker help me edit for punctuation and mechanics? (57–59, 61–64)

Knowledge of Conventions

- When should I set off a word or phrase with commas? (57e)
- What is the difference between *its* and *it's?* (60c)

For a general introduction to writing outcomes, see 1e, pages 14–16.

CHAPTER 57

Commas

COMMON USES OF THE COMMA

You may have been told that commas are used to mark pauses, but that is not an accurate general principle. To indicate meaning, commas are used to set off sentence elements. They are also used in other conventional ways.

✓ **57a** Use a comma after an introductory word group that is *not* the subject of the sentence.

A comma both attaches an introductory word, phrase, or clause to and distinguishes it from the rest of the sentence.

▶ **Finally, the speeding car careened to the right.**

▶ **Reflecting on her life experiences, Washburn attributed her successes to her own efforts.**

▶ **Until he noticed the handprint on the wall, the detective was frustrated by the lack of clues.**

When the introductory phrase is shorter than five words and there is no danger of confusion without a comma, the comma can be omitted.

▶ **For several hours we rode on in silence.**

Do not add a comma after a word group that functions as the subject of the sentence. Be especially careful with word groups that begin with *-ing* words.

▶ **Persuading constituents,/ is one of a politician's most important tasks.**

Commas and Grammar Checkers

Computer grammar checkers usually will not highlight missing commas following introductory elements or between independent clauses joined by a coordinating conjunction such as *and,* and they cannot decide whether a sentence element is essential or nonessential.

57b   Use commas between items in a series.

A comma should appear after each item in a series.

▶ **Three industries that have been important to New England are shipbuilding, tourism, and commercial fishing.**

—the EVOLVING SITUATION

Styles within Disciplines

The rules for capitalizing, abbreviating, and italicizing terms, as well as conventions for using numbers and hyphens, can vary from one course or discipline to another. If you are not sure about the conventions for a discipline, see what rules your course textbook follows. If you cannot figure out the accepted practice from your text, ask your instructor for help, use the general rules presented in this book, or consult a style manual from the list on page 281.

Commas clarify which items are part of the series. In the following example, the third comma clarifies that the hikers are packing lunch *and* snacks, not chocolate and trail mix meant for lunch.

CONFUSING	For the hiking trip, we needed to pack lunch, chocolate and trail mix.
CLEAR	For the hiking trip, we needed to pack lunch, chocolate, and trail mix.

If items in the series contain internal commas or other punctuation, separate the items with a semicolon *(see Chapter 58, pp. 548–51)*.

> **Note:** If you are writing for a journalism course, you may be required to leave out the final comma that precedes *and* in a series, just as magazines and newspapers sometimes do.

✓ **57c** Use a comma in front of a coordinating conjunction that joins independent clauses.

When a coordinating conjunction *(and, but, for, nor, or, so, yet)* joins clauses that could each stand alone as a sentence, put a comma before the coordinating conjunction.

▶ **Injuries were so frequent that he began to worry, and his style of play became more cautious.**
^

If the word groups you are joining are not independent clauses, do not add a comma. *(See 57m on p. 546.)*

Exception: If you are joining two short clauses, you may leave out the comma unless it is needed for clarity.

▶ **The running back caught the ball and the fans cheered.**

57d Add a comma between coordinate adjectives not joined by *and,* but do not separate cumulative adjectives with a comma.

Use a comma between coordinate adjectives that precede a noun and modify it independently *(a brave, intelligent, persistent woman)*. Adjectives are coordinate if they can be joined by *and* (brave *and* intelligent *and* persistent) or if their order can be changed *(a persistent, brave, intelligent woman)*.

▶ **This brave, intelligent, persistent woman was the first female to earn a**
^   ^
Ph.D. in psychology.

If you cannot add *and* between the adjectives or change their order, they are cumulative, with each one modifying the ones that follow it, and should not be separated with a comma or commas.

▶ **Andrea Boccelli, the world-famous Italian tenor, has performed in concerts and operas.**

> *World-famous* modifies *Italian tenor,* not just the noun *tenor.* You could not add *and* between the adjectives (world-famous *and* Italian tenor) or change their order *(Italian world-famous tenor).*

✓ **57e**   Use commas to set off nonessential additions to a sentence, but do not set off essential elements.

Nonessential, or **nonrestrictive,** words, phrases, and clauses add information to a sentence but are not required for its basic meaning to be understood. Nonrestrictive additions are set off with commas.

NONRESTRICTIVE

Mary Shelley's best-known novel, *Frankenstein or the Modern*

Prometheus, was first published in 1818.

> The sentence would have the same basic meaning without the title *(Mary Shelley's best-known novel was first published in 1818).*

Restrictive words, phrases, and clauses are essential to a sentence because they identify exactly who or what the writer is talking about. Restrictive additions are not set off with commas.

RESTRICTIVE

Mary Shelley's novel *Frankenstein or the Modern Prometheus* was first published in 1818.

> Without the title, the reader would not know which novel the sentence is referring to, so *Frankenstein or the Modern Prometheus* is restrictive.

Often, the context determines whether to enclose a word, phrase, or clause with commas. In the following examples, notice how a preceding sentence can affect the meaning and determine whether commas are needed around the participial phrase:

▶ **Two customers with angry looks on their faces approached the check-out counter. The customers, demanding a refund, lined up by the register.**

▶ **The store opened at the usual time. The customers demanding a refund lined up by the register.**

Three types of additions to sentences often cause problems: adjective clauses, adjective phrases, and appositives.

IDENTIFY AND EDIT
Commas with Nonrestrictive Words or Word Groups

Follow these steps if you have trouble deciding whether a word or word group should be set off with a comma or commas:

1. *Identify the word or word group that may require commas. Pay special attention to words that appear between the subject and verb.*

> **PROBLEM SENTENCE**
>
>   subj   verb
> Joan Didion [a native of California] has written essays and screenplays as well as novels.

> **PROBLEM SENTENCE**
>
>   subj   verb
> Her book [*The Year of Magical Thinking*] is a description of the experience of grief.

2. *Read the sentence to yourself without the word or word group. Does the basic meaning stay the same, or does it change? Can you tell what person, place, or thing the sentence is about?*

> **SENTENCE WITHOUT THE WORD GROUP**
>
> Joan Didion has written essays and screenplays as well as novels.
>
> The subject of the sentence is identified by name, and the basic meaning of the sentence does not change.

> **SENTENCE WITHOUT THE WORD GROUP**
>
> Her book is a description of the experience of grief.
>
> Without the words *The Year of Magical Thinking,* we cannot tell what book the sentence is describing.

3. *If the meaning of the sentence stays the same without the word or word group, set it off with commas. If the meaning changes, the word or word group should not be set off with commas.*

> • Joan Didion, a native of California, has written essays and screenplays as well as novels.
>
> • Her book *The Year of Magical Thinking* is a description of the experience of grief.
>
> The sentence is correct. Commas are not needed to enclose *The Year of Magical Thinking.*

1. Adjective clauses Adjective clauses begin with a relative pronoun or an adverb—*who, whom, whose, which, that, where,* or *when*—and modify a noun or pronoun within the sentence. Adjective clauses can be either nonrestrictive or restrictive.

NONRESTRICTIVE

With his tale of Odysseus, *whose journey can be traced on modern maps,* Homer brought accounts of strange and alien creatures to the ancient Greeks.

RESTRICTIVE

The contestant *whom he most wanted to beat* was his father.

> **Note:** Use *that* only with restrictive clauses. Many writers prefer to use *which* only with nonrestrictive clauses.

2. Adjective phrases Like an adjective clause, an adjective phrase also modifies a noun or pronoun in a sentence. Adjective phrases begin with a preposition (for example, *with, by, at,* or *for*) or a verbal (a word formed from a verb). Adjective phrases can be either nonrestrictive or restrictive.

NONRESTRICTIVE

Some people, *by their faith in human nature or their general good will,* bring out the best in others.

The phrase does not specify which people are being discussed. The sentence would have the same meaning without it.

RESTRICTIVE

People *fighting passionately for their rights* can inspire others.

The phrase indicates which people the writer is talking about and therefore is restrictive. It is not set off with commas.

3. Appositives Appositives are nouns or noun phrases that rename nouns or pronouns and appear right after the word they rename.

NONRESTRICTIVE

One researcher, *the widely respected R. S. Smith,* has shown that a child's performance on IQ tests can be inconsistent.

Because the word *one* already restricts the word *researcher,* the researcher's name is not essential to the meaning of the sentence.

RESTRICTIVE

The researcher *R. S. Smith* has shown that a child's performance on IQ tests can be inconsistent.

The name *R. S. Smith* tells readers which researcher is meant.

57f Use a comma or commas with transitional and parenthetical expressions, contrasting comments, and absolute phrases.

1. Transitional expressions Transitional expressions show the relationship between ideas in a sentence. Conjunctive adverbs *(however, therefore, moreover)* and other transitional phrases *(for example, on the other hand)* are usually set off by commas when used at the beginning, in the middle, or at the end of a sentence. *(For a list of transitional expressions, see Tab 10: Editing for Grammar Conventions, p. 497.)*

▶ Brian Wilson, for example, was unable to cope with the pressures of touring with the Beach Boys.

▶ As a matter of fact, he had a nervous breakdown shortly after a tour.

▶ He is still considered one of the most important figures in rock and roll, however.

When a transitional expression connects two independent clauses, use a semicolon before and a comma after it.

▶ The Beatles were a phenomenon when they toured the United States in 1964; subsequently, they became the most successful rock band of all time.

> **Note:** Short expressions such as *also, at least, certainly, instead, of course, then, perhaps,* and *therefore* do not always need to be set off with commas.
>
> ▶ I found my notes and *also* got my story in on time.

2. Parenthetical expressions The information that parenthetical expressions provide is relatively insignificant and could easily be left out. Therefore, these expressions are set off with a comma or commas.

▶ Human cloning, so they say, will be possible within a decade.

▶ The experiments would take a couple of weeks, more or less.

3. Contrasting comments Contrasting comments beginning with words such as *not, unlike, while, although, even though,* or *in contrast to* should be set off with commas.

▶   Adam Sandler is famous as a comedian, not a tragedian.
                                              ^
▶   Comedy, unlike tragedy, often lacks critical respect.
         ^   ^

4. Absolute phrases   Absolute phrases usually include a noun *(sunlight)* followed by a participle *(shining)* and are used to modify whole sentences. Do not separate the noun and participle with a comma.

▶   The snake slithered through the tall grass, the sunlight,/ shining now and
    then on its green skin.   ^

57g   Use a comma or commas to set off words of direct address, *yes* and *no,* mild interjections, and tag sentences.

Words that interrupt a sentence are set off by commas because they are not essential to the sentence's meaning.

▶   Thank you, Mr. Rao, for your help.
             ^   ^
▶   Yes, I will meet you at noon.
       ^
▶   Of course, if that's what you want, we'll do it.
             ^   ^
▶   We can do better, don't you think?
                    ^

57h   Use a comma or commas to separate a direct quotation from the rest of the sentence.

▶   Irving Howe declares, "Whitman is quite realistic about the place of the
                        ^
    self in an urban world" (261).

▶   "Whitman is quite realistic about the place of the self in an urban world,"
    declares Irving Howe (261).   ^

   Note that the comma appears inside the closing quotation mark.

Use commas to set off words that interrupt quotations.

▶   "When we interpret a poem," DiYanni says, "we explain it to ourselves
                             ^
    in order to understand it."

If you are quoting more than one sentence and interrupting the quotation between sentences, the interrupting words should end with a period.

▶   "But it is not possible to give to each department an equal power of self

    defense," James Madison writes in *The Federalist No. 51.* "In republican
                                                            ^
    government the legislative authority, necessarily, predominates."

A comma is not needed to separate an indirect quotation or a paraphrase from the words that identify its source. It is also not needed when a direct quotation is integrated into your sentence.

▶ **Irving Howe notes,/ that Whitman realistically depicts the urban self as free to wander (261).**

▶ **Stanley Fish maintains that teaching content,/ "is a lure and a delusion."**

(For more on quotations, see Chapter 61, pp. 556–61.)

57i   Use commas with parts of dates, letters, and addresses; with people's titles; and in numbers.

- **Dates.** Use paired commas in dates when the month, day, and year are included. Do not use commas when the day of the month is omitted or when the day appears before the month.

  ▶ **On March 4, 1931, she traveled to New York.**

  ▶ **She traveled to New York in March 1931.**

  ▶ **She traveled to New York on 4 March 1931.**

- **Parts of letters.** Use a comma following the greeting in an informal letter and following the closing in any type of letter. (In a business letter, use a colon following the greeting.)

  ▶ **Dear Marta,   Sincerely yours,**

- **Addresses.** Use commas to set off the parts of an address or the name of a state, but do not use a comma preceding a zip code.

  ▶ **At Cleveland, Ohio, the river changes direction.**

  ▶ **My address is 63 Oceanside Drive, Apt. 2A, Surf City, New Jersey 08008.**

- **People's titles or degrees.** Put a comma between the person's name and the title or degree when it comes after the name, followed by another comma.

  ▶ **Luis Mendez, MD, gave her the green light to resume her exercise regimen.**

If an abbreviation such as *Jr.* or a roman numeral such as *II* follows a name, setting it off with a comma is optional: *Milton Clark Jr.* or *Milton Clark, Jr.* (Consult your discipline's style manual.)

- **Numbers.** When a number has more than four digits, use commas to mark off the numerals by hundreds—that is, by groups of three, beginning at the right.

  ▶ **Andrew Jackson received 647,276 votes in the 1828 election.**

- If the number is four digits long, the comma is optional.

▶   **The survey had 1856 [or 1,856] respondents.**

Exceptions: Street numbers, zip codes, telephone numbers, page numbers (p. 2304), and years (1828) do not include commas.

57j   Use a comma to take the place of an omitted word or phrase or to prevent misreading.

When a writer omits one or more words from a sentence to create a special effect, a comma is often needed to make the meaning of the sentence clear for readers.

▶   **Under the tree he found his puppy, and under the car, his cat.**

The second comma substitutes for the phrase *he found.*

Commas are also used to keep readers from misunderstanding a writer's meaning when words are repeated or might be misread.

▶   **Many birds that sing, sing early in the morning, before the sun rises.**

▶   **Any items that can be, are sold at auction Web sites.**

It is often better, however, to revise the sentence and avoid the need for the clarifying comma: *Many songbirds sing first thing in the morning.*

COMMON MISUSES OF THE COMMA

Commas should *not* be used in the following situations.

57k   Do not use commas to separate major elements in an independent clause.

Do not use a comma to separate a subject from a verb, a verb from its object, or a preposition from its object.

▶   **Reflecting on your life,/ is necessary for emotional growth.**

The subject, *reflecting on your life,* should not be separated from the verb, *is.*

▶   **Washburn decided,/ that her own efforts were the key to her success.**

The verb *decided* should not be separated from its direct object, the subordinate clause *that her own efforts were the key to her success.*

▶   **Although he is a famous actor he is in,/ emotional limbo.**

The preposition *in* should not be separated from its object, *emotional limbo.*

> **Note:** If a nonessential phrase appears between the subject and verb, it should be set off with a pair of commas *(see 57e on p. 539)*.

57l Do not add a comma before the first or after the final item in a series.

Use commas to separate items in a series but never before or after the series.

▶ **Employees in the United States work longer hours than,/ German, French, or British workers,/ are expected to work.**

Commas should never be used after *such as* or *like (see p. 548)*.

57m Do not use commas to separate compound word groups unless they are independent clauses.

A comma should not be used between word groups joined with a coordinating conjunction such as *and* unless the groups are both full sentences.

▶ **Injuries were so frequent that he became worried,/ and started to play more cautiously.**

In this sentence *and* joins two verbs *(became* and *started)*.

▶ **He is worried that injuries are more frequent,/ and that he will have to play more cautiously to avoid them.**

In this sentence *and* joins two subordinate clauses beginning with *that*.

57n Do not use commas to set off restrictive modifiers, appositives, or slightly parenthetical words or phrases.

If a word, phrase, or clause in a sentence is necessary to identify the noun or pronoun that precedes it, it is restrictive and should not be set off with commas. *(See pp. 539–42.)*

▶ **The applicants *who had studied for the admissions test* were restless and eager for the exam to begin.**

Because only those applicants who had studied were eager for the test to begin, the clause *who had studied for the admissions test* is restrictive and should not be set off with commas.

1. Appositives identifying nouns and pronouns An appositive is a noun or noun phrase that renames a noun or pronoun and appears right after the word it renames.

▶ The director,/ Alfred Hitchcock,/ was responsible for many classic thrillers and horror films, including *Psycho.*

2. Concluding adverb clauses

Adverb clauses beginning with *after, as soon as, before, because, if, since, unless, until,* and *when* are usually essential to a sentence's meaning.

RESTRICTIVE

I am eager to test the children's IQ again *because significant variations in a child's test scores indicate that the test itself may be flawed.*

Clauses beginning with *although, even though, though,* and *whereas* present a contrasting thought and are usually nonrestrictive.

NONRESTRICTIVE

IQ tests can be useful indicators of a child's abilities, *although they should not be taken as the definitive measurement of a child's intelligence.*

Note: An adverb clause that appears at the beginning of a sentence is usually followed by a comma: *Until we meet, I'm continuing my work on the budget (see pp. 536–37).*

---

3. Words and phrases that are slightly parenthetical

If setting off a brief parenthetical remark with commas *(see p. 542)* would draw too much attention to the remark and interrupt the flow of the sentence, the commas can be left out.

▶ Science is *basically* the last frontier.

57o   Correct other common comma errors.

- **Remove commas between cumulative adjectives** *(see p. 538–39).*

  ▶ Three,/ well-known,/ U.S. writers visited the artist's studio.

- **Remove a comma that appears between an adjective and a noun.**

  ▶ An art review by a celebrated, powerful,/ writer would be guaranteed publication.

- **Remove a comma that appears between a noun and participle in an absolute phrase.**

  ▶ My favorite singer,/ having lost the contest, I stopped paying attention.

- **Remove a comma that appears between an adverb and an adjective.**

  ▶ The artist's studio was delightfully,/ chaotic.

- **Remove a comma that appears after a coordinating conjunction** *(and, but, or, nor, for, so, yet).*

  ▶ The *duomo* in Siena was begun in the thirteenth century, and,/ it was used as a model for other Italian cathedrals.

- **Eliminate a comma after *although, such as,* or *like.***

  ▶ Stage designers can achieve many unusual effects, such as,/ the helicopter that landed onstage in *Miss Saigon.*

- **Eliminate a comma before *than.***

  ▶ An appointment to the Supreme Court has more long-range consequences,/ than any other decision a President makes.

- **Remove a comma before a parenthesis.**

  ▶ When in office cubicles,/ (a recent invention), workers need to be considerate of others.

- **Remove a comma with a question mark or an exclamation point that ends a quotation** *(also see Chapter 61, p. 560).*

  ▶ "Where are my glasses?,/" she asked in a panic.

CHAPTER 58

Semicolons

Semicolons are used to join ideas that are closely related and grammatically equivalent.

58a Use a semicolon to join independent clauses.

A semicolon should join two related independent clauses when they are not joined by a comma and a coordinating conjunction *(and, but, or, nor, for, so, yet).*

Semicolons and Grammar Checkers

Grammar checker programs will catch some comma splices that can be corrected by adding a semicolon between the two clauses. They will also catch some incorrect uses of the semicolon. They will not tell you when a semicolon *could* be used for clarity, however, nor whether the semicolon is the best choice.

▶ **Before 8000 B.C.E. wheat was not the luxuriant plant it is today; it was**
   ^

   merely a wild grass that spread throughout the Middle East.

Sometimes, the close relationship is a contrast.

▶ **Philip had completed the assignment; Lucy had not.**
   ^

> **Note:** When a semicolon appears next to a quotation mark, it is always placed outside the quotation mark: *My doctor advised me to "get plenty of rest"; my supervisor had other ideas.*

An occasional semicolon adds variety to your writing, but too many can make it seem monotonous. If you have used three or more semicolons in a paragraph, revise to eliminate most of them.

> **Note:** If a comma is used between two clauses without a coordinating conjunction, the sentence is a comma splice, a serious error. One way to correct a comma splice is by changing the comma to a semicolon. *(For more help with correcting comma splices and run-on sentences, see Tab 10: Editing for Grammar Conventions, pp. 493–98.)*

58b   Use semicolons with transitional expressions that connect independent clauses.

Transitional expressions, including transitional phrases *(for example, in addition, on the contrary)* and conjunctive adverbs *(consequently, however, moreover, nevertheless, then, therefore)*, indicate the relationship between two clauses. When a transitional expression appears between two clauses, it is preceded by a semicolon and usually followed by a comma. Using a comma instead of a semicolon creates a comma splice. *(For a list of transitional expressions, see Tab 10: Editing for*

Grammar Conventions, p. 497. For help with correcting comma splices, see pp. 493–98.)

▶ Sheila had to wait until the plumber arrived; consequently, she was late for the exam.

Coordinating conjunctions *(and, but, or, nor, for, so, yet)* also indicate the way clauses are related. Unlike transitional expressions, however, they are preceded by a comma, not a semicolon, when they join two independent clauses.

Note: The semicolon always appears between the two clauses, even when the transitional expression is in another position within the second clause. Wherever it appears, the transitional expression is usually set off with a comma or commas.

▶ My friends are all taking golf lessons; my roommate and I, however, are more interested in tennis.

58c Use a semicolon to separate items in a series or clauses when the items or clauses contain commas.

Because the following sentence contains a series with internal commas, the semicolons are needed for clarity.

▶ The committee included Dr. Curtis Youngblood, the county medical examiner; Roberta Collingwood, director of the bureau's criminal division; and Darcy Coolidge, the chief of police.

If two independent clauses are joined by a coordinating conjunction *(and, but, for, nor, or, so, yet)* and at least one of them already contains several internal commas, a semicolon can help readers locate the point where the clauses are separated.

▶ The closing scenes return to the English countryside, recalling the opening; but these scenes are bathed in a different, cooler light, suggesting that memories of her marriage still haunt her.

58d Correct common semicolon errors.

- **Use a comma, not a semicolon, to join a dependent clause or a phrase to an independent clause.**

  ▶ Professional writers need to devote time every day to their writing; although doing so takes discipline.

  ▶ Seemingly tame and lovable; housecats can be fierce hunters.

- **Use a comma, not a semicolon, to join most independent clauses linked by a coordinating conjunction (*and, but, or, nor, for, so, yet*);** if the clauses contain several internal commas, a semicolon is acceptable *(see 58c).*

  ▶ Nineteenth-century women wore colorful clothes;/, but their

  attire looks drab in the black-and-white photographs of the era.

- **Use a colon, not a semicolon, to introduce a series, an explanation, or a quotation.**

  ▶ My day was planned;/: a morning walk, an afternoon in the

  library, dinner with friends, and a great horror movie.

  ▶ The doctor diagnosed the problem;/: a sinus infection.

  ▶ Boyd warns of the difficulty in describing Bach;/: "Even his

  physical appearance largely eludes us."

CHAPTER 59

Colons

Colons draw attention to what they introduce. They also have other conventional uses. A colon always follows an independent clause, but unlike the semicolon *(see pp. 548–51),* the element that follows it need not be an independent clause.

Colons and Grammar Checkers

A grammar checker may point out when you have used a colon incorrectly, but since colons are usually optional, most of the time you must decide whether a colon is your best choice.

59a Use a colon after a complete sentence to introduce a list, an appositive, or a quotation.

A colon is used after a complete sentence (independent clause) to introduce lists, appositives (nouns or noun phrases that appear right after the word they rename), and quotations.

independent clause   *list*
▶ Several majors interest me: biology, chemistry, and art.

independent clause   *appositive*
▶ She shared with me her favorite toys: a spatula and a pot lid.

If you use *that is* or *namely* with an appositive, it should follow the colon: *She showed me another toy: namely, her mother's keys.*

independent clause   *quotation*
► He said the dreaded words: "Let's just be friends."

When you use a colon to introduce a sentence element, make sure the colon is preceded by an independent clause.

                      are
► Three kinds of futility dealt with in the novel: pervasive poverty, lost
                    ^
love, and inescapable aging.

The words *the following* or *as follows* often appear at the end of the introductory clause.

59b   Use a colon when a second closely related independent clause elaborates on the first one.

Use a colon when you want to emphasize the second clause.

► I can predict tonight's sequence of events: my brother will arrive late,
                                          ^
talk loudly, and eat too much.

59c   Use colons after salutations in business documents, to indicate ratios, to indicate times of day, to provide city and publisher citations in bibliographies, and to separate titles and subtitles.

► Dear Mr. Worth: To:
► The ratio of armed to unarmed members of the gang was 3:1.
► He woke up at 6:30 in the morning.
► New York: McGraw-Hill, 2015
► *Possible Lives: The Promise of Public Education in America*

> **Note:** If you introduce a quotation with a signal phrase such as *he said* or *Morrison comments* instead of a complete sentence, you should use a comma, not a colon. *(For more on introducing quotations, see pp. 556–61.)*

59d   Correct common colon errors.

- **Remove a colon that appears between a verb and its object or complement.**

  ► The elements of a smoothie are: yogurt, fresh fruit, and honey.

- **Remove a colon that appears between a preposition and its object or objects.**

  ▶ Many feel that cancer can be prevented by a diet of/ fruit, nuts, and vegetables.

- **Remove a colon that appears after *such as, for example,* or *including.***

  ▶ I am ready for a change, such as/ a vacation.

Note: When a complete sentence follows a colon, the first word may begin with either a capital or a lowercase letter. Be consistent throughout your document.

- **Edit to remove more than one colon in a sentence.**

  ▶ He was taken in by ~~a new con:~~ the Spanish lottery scam: victims are told they have won a prize and are asked to send financial information to a fake Spanish company.

CHAPTER 60

Apostrophes

Apostrophes show possession *(the dog's bone)* and indicate omitted letters in contractions *(don't)*.

To determine whether a particular noun should be in the possessive form rather than plural, reword the sentence using the word *of (the bone of the dog).*

Apostrophes and Spelling Checkers

A spelling checker will sometimes highlight *its* used incorrectly (instead of *it's*) or an error in a possessive (for example, *Englands' glory*), but this identification is not consistent. Double-check all words that end in *-s* in your work.

60a   Use apostrophes with nouns and indefinite pronouns to indicate possession.

For a noun to be possessive, two elements are usually required: a possessor; and a thing, person, or attribute that is possessed. Sometimes the thing possessed precedes the possessor: *The motorcycle is the student's.*

Sometimes the sentence may not name the thing possessed, but its identity is clearly understood by the reader: *I saw your cousin at Nick's.*

1. Deciding whether to use an apostrophe and an *s* or only an apostrophe

To form the possessive of all singular nouns, add an apostrophe plus -*s* to the ending: *baby's.* Even singular nouns that end in -*s* form the possessive by adding -*'s: bus's.*

If a singular noun with more than two syllables ends in -*s* and adding -*'s* would make the word sound awkward, it is acceptable to use only an apostrophe to form the possessive: *Socrates'.* Be consistent.

- To form the possessive of a plural noun that ends in -*s,* add only an apostrophe: *subjects', babies'.*

- To form the possessive of a plural noun that does not end in -*s,* add an apostrophe plus -*s: men's, cattle's.*

- To form the possessive of most indefinite pronouns, such as *no one, everyone, everything,* or *something,* add an apostrophe plus -*s: no one's, anybody's.*

2. Using the apostrophe in tricky situations

To express joint ownership, use the possessive form for the last name only; to express individual ownership, use the possessive form for each name.

► **Felicia and Elias' report**

► **The city's and the state's finances**

To form the possessive of compound words, add an apostrophe plus *s* to the last word in the compound.

► **My father-in-law's job**

To form the possessive of proper names, follow the rules given above *(Elisa's advice; Microsoft's program),* with some exceptions. Place names that include a possessive noun generally lack an apostrophe, and many organizational names do as well: *Pikes Peak; Department of Veterans Affairs.*

60b   Use apostrophes to form contractions.

In a contraction, the apostrophe substitutes for omitted letters.

we've = we have	won't = will not (irregular)
weren't = were not	don't = do not
here's = here is	can't = cannot

In informal writing, apostrophes can substitute for omitted numbers in a decade: *the '50s*. Spell out the name of the decade in formal writing: *the fifties*.

> **Note:** Although the MLA and APA style manuals allow contractions in academic writing, some instructors think they are too informal. Check with your instructor before using contractions.

✓ **60c**   Distinguish between contractions and possessive pronouns.

The following pairs of **homonyms** (words that sound alike but have different meanings) often cause problems for writers. Note that the apostrophe is used only in the contraction.

CONTRACTION	POSSESSIVE PRONOUN
it's (it is or it has)	its
It's too hot.	The dog scratched *its* fleas.
you're (you are)	your
You're a lucky guy.	Is that *your* new car?
who's (who is)	whose
Who's there?	The man *whose* dog was lost called us.
they're (they are)	their*
They're reading poetry.	They gave *their* lives.

*The adverb *there* is also confused with *their*: She was standing *there* [not *their*].

60d   Using an apostrophe with *s* to form plural letters and words used as words is optional.

An apostrophe plus *s* (*'s*) can be used to show the plural of a letter. Underline or italicize single letters but not the apostrophe or the *s*. (Do not italicize letter grades.)

▶ **Committee has two *m*'s, two *t*'s, and two *e*'s.**

If a word is used as a word rather than as a symbol of the meaning it conveys, it can be made plural by adding an apostrophe plus *s*. The word should be italicized or underlined, but the *'s* should not be. If the word is in quotation marks, you should always use *'s* when you are forming the plural.

▶ **There are twenty-five *no*'s [or "no's"] in the first paragraph.**

60e Watch out for common misuses of the apostrophe.

Never use an apostrophe with *s* to form a plural noun.

teachers
▶ The ~~teacher's~~ asked the girls and boys for their attention.

(See pp. 584–85 for more on forming plural nouns.)

Never use an apostrophe with *s* to form the present tense of a verb paired with a third-person singular subject (*he, she, it,* or a singular noun).

needs
▶ A professional singer ~~need's~~ to practice a lot.

Never use an apostrophe with the possessive form of a pronoun such as *hers, ours,* or *theirs.*

ours
▶ That cat of ~~our's~~ is always sleeping!

(See 60c for advice on distinguishing contractions [it's] from possessive pronouns [its].)

Never use an apostrophe with *s* to form the plural of a surname.

Clintons
▶ The ~~Clinton's~~ made history when Hillary was elected to the Senate

during the same year Bill left the White House.

MLA and APA style recommend against using an apostrophe to form plurals of numbers and abbreviations. You may see that usage elsewhere.

2s *5s*
▶ He makes his ~~2's~~ look like ~~5's.~~

PhDs
▶ Professor Sanchez has two ~~PhD's.~~

CHAPTER 61

Quotation Marks

Quotation marks enclose words, phrases, and sentences that are quoted directly; titles of short works such as poems, articles, songs, and short stories; and words and phrases used in a special sense.

> **Note:** Citations and formatting instructions in this chapter follow MLA style. See Tabs 7 and 8 for examples of APA, Chicago, and CSE styles.

Quotation Marks and Grammar Checkers

A grammar checker can alert you to the lack of an opening or closing quotation mark, but it cannot determine where a quotation should begin and end. Grammar checkers also may not point out errors in the use of quotation marks with other marks of punctuation. For example, a grammar checker did not highlight the error in the placement of the period at the end of the following sentence *(see 61f, pp. 559–60).*

INCORRECT

▶ **Barbara Ehrenreich observes, "There are no Palm Pilots, cable channels, or Web sites to advise the low-wage job seeker".**

61a   Use quotation marks to indicate the exact words of a speaker or writer.

Direct quotations from written material may include whole sentences or only a few words or phrases. They can lend immediacy to your writing.

▶ **In *Angela's Ashes,* Frank McCourt writes, "Worse than the ordinary miserable childhood is the miserable Irish childhood" (11).**

▶ **Frank McCourt believes that being Irish worsens what is all too "ordinary"—a "miserable childhood" (11).**

Use quotation marks to enclose everything a speaker says in written dialogue. If the quoted sentence is interrupted by a phrase like *he said,* enclose just the quotation in quotation marks. When another person begins to speak, start a new paragraph to indicate a change in speaker.

"I don't know what you're talking about," he said. "I did listen to everything you told me."

"If you had been listening, you would have known what I was talking about."

If a speaker continues for more than a paragraph, begin each subsequent paragraph with an opening quotation mark, but do not insert a closing quotation mark until the end of the quotation.

Note: Do not use quotation marks to set off an indirect quotation, which reports what a speaker said but does not use the exact words.

▶ **He said that ⟋he didn't know what I was talking about.⟍**

Two or three lines of poetry may be run in to your text, much like any other *short* quotation. Line breaks are shown with a slash. Leave a space before and after the slash. *(See also 62h, pp. 567–68.)*

▶ **Wordsworth writes of the weary acquisitiveness of our modern age: "The world is too much with us; late and soon, / Getting and spending, we lay waste our powers" (lines 1–2).**

> *Note:* In MLA style, line numbers appear in parentheses following the quotation. The word *lines* should precede the numbers the first time the poem is quoted.

61b Set off long quotations in indented blocks.

Set off a quotation that is longer than four typed lines as a block quotation. *(For instructions on formatting block quotations, see Tab 5: Researching, p. 274.)* A block quotation is *not* surrounded by quotation marks. If the text you are quoting includes another direct quotation, however, use quotation marks to set those words off.

61c Enclose a quotation within a quotation with single quotation marks.

Use single quotation marks to set off a quotation within a quotation.

▶ **In response to alumni, the president of the university said, "I know you're saying to me, 'We want a winning football team.' But I'm telling you that I want an honest football team."**

61d Use quotation marks to enclose titles of short works such as articles, poems, and stories.

The titles of long works, such as books, are usually put in italics (or underlined). *(See Chapter 66, pp. 577–78.)* The titles of book chapters, essays, most poems, and other short works are usually put in quotation marks. Quotation marks are also used for titles of unpublished works, including student writing, theses, and dissertations.

Works That Should Be Enclosed in Quotation Marks

- **Essays:** "Once More to the Lake"
- **Songs:** "Seven Nation Army"
- **Short poems:** "Daffodils"
- **Short stories:** "The Tell-Tale Heart"

- **Articles in periodicals:** "Scotland Yard of the Wild" (from *American Way*)

- **Book chapters or sections:** "Microcredit: The Financial Revolution" (Chapter 11 of *Half the Sky*)

- **Episodes of radio and television programs:** "I Can't Remember" (on *48 Hours*)

- **Titles of unpublished works,** including student works, theses, and dissertations: "Breaking News: Blogging's Impact on Traditional and New Media" (Do not use quotation marks to enclose the title of your own work on its title page.)

If quotation marks are needed within the title of a short work, use single quotation marks: "The 'Animal Rights' War on Medicine."

61e   Use quotation marks to indicate that a word or phrase is being used in a special way.

Put quotation marks around a word or phrase that someone else has used in a way that you or your readers may not agree with. These quotation marks function as raised eyebrows do in conversation and should be used sparingly.

▶   The "worker's paradise" of Stalinist Russia included slave-labor camps.

Words cited as words can also be put in quotation marks, although the more common practice is to italicize them.

▶   The words "compliment" and "complement" sound alike but have different meanings.

Definitions and translations should appear in quotation marks.

▶   *Agua* means "water" in Spanish.

61f   Place punctuation marks within or outside quotation marks, as convention and your meaning require.

As you edit, check all closing single and double quotation marks and the marks of punctuation that appear next to them to make sure that you have placed them in the right order.

1. Periods and commas   Always place the period or comma before the final quotation mark, even when the quotation is brief.

▶   "Instead of sharing an experience the spectator must come to grips with things," Brecht writes in "The Epic Theatre and Its Difficulties."

However, place the period or comma after a parenthetical reference.

▶   Brecht wants the spectator to "come to grips with things" (23).

2. Question marks and exclamation points Place a question mark or an exclamation point after the final quotation mark if the quoted material is not itself a question or an exclamation.

▶ How does epic theatre make us "come to grips with things"?

Place a question mark or an exclamation point inside the final quotation mark when it is part of the quotation. No additional punctuation is needed, unless you are adding a parenthetical citation in MLA style (see the third example following).

▶ "Are we to see science in the theatre?" he was asked.

▶ Brecht was asked, "Are we to see science in the theatre?"

▶ Brecht was asked, "Are we to see science in the theatre?" (27).

3. Colons and semicolons Place colons and semicolons after the final quotation mark.

▶ Dean Wilcox cited the items he called his "daily delights": a free parking space for his scooter at the faculty club, a special table in the club itself, and friends to laugh with after a day's work.

4. Dashes Place a dash outside either an opening or a closing quotation mark if the dash precedes or follows the quotation or outside both if two dashes are used to set off the quotation.

▶ One phrase—"time is running out"—haunted me.

Place a dash inside either an opening or a closing quotation mark if it is part of the quotation.

▶ "Where is the—" she called. "Oh, here it is. Never mind."

(For more on integrating quotations into your sentences, see Chapter 24, Working with Sources and Avoiding Plagiarism, pp. 270–75.)

61g Edit to correct common errors in using quotation marks.

- **Avoid using quotation marks to distance yourself from slang, clichés, and trite expressions.** Instead, stay away from overused or slang expressions in college writing. If your writing situation permits slang, however, do not enclose it in quotation marks.

  ▶ Californians are so ⁄"laid back."⁄

- Revising the sentence is usually a better solution.

  ▶ Many Californians have a carefree attitude.

- **Do not use quotation marks for indirect quotations.**
  Watch out for errors in pronoun reference as well. *(See Tab 10: Editing for Grammar Conventions, pp. 519–21.)*

  ▶   He told his boss that /the company had lost its largest account./

- Another way to correct this sentence is to change to a direct quotation.

  ▶   He said to his boss, "We just lost our largest account."

- **Do not add another question mark or exclamation point to the end of a quotation that already ends in one of these marks.**

  ▶   What did Juliet mean when she cried, "O Romeo, Romeo! Wherefore art thou Romeo?"/

- If you quote a question within a sentence that makes a statement, place a question mark before the closing quotation mark and a period at the end of the sentence.

  ▶   "What was Henry Ford's greatest contribution to the Industrial Revolution?" he asked.

- **Do not enclose the title of your own essay on the title page or above the first line of the text in quotation marks.**

  ▶   /Edgar Allan Poe and the Paradox of the Gothic/

- If you use a quotation or a title of a short work in your title, though, put quotation marks around it.

  ▶   Edgar Allan Poe's "The Raven" and the Paradox of the Gothic

CHAPTER 62

Other Punctuation Marks

Punctuation and Grammar Checkers

Your grammar checker might highlight a period used instead of a question mark at the end of a question. However, grammar checkers will not tell you when you might use a pair of dashes or parentheses to set material off in a sentence or when you need a second dash or parenthesis to enclose parenthetical material.

62a Use a period to end sentences and with some abbreviations.

Use a period to end all sentences apart from direct questions or exclamations.

STATEMENT

This book contains more than one thousand periods.

STATEMENT CONTAINING AN INDIRECT QUESTION

She asked me where I had gone to college.

POLITE REQUEST

Please read Chapter 5 for next week.

A period or periods are conventionally used with the following common abbreviations, which end in lowercase letters.

Mr.	Mrs.	i.e.	Mass.
Ms.	Dr.	e.g.	Jan.

If the abbreviation is made up of capital letters, however, the periods are optional. Do not put a space after an internal period.

RN (or R.N.)	BA (or B.A.)
MD (or M.D.)	PhD (or Ph.D.)

Periods are omitted in abbreviations for organizations, famous people, states in mailing addresses, and acronyms (words made up of initials).

FBI	JFK	MA	NATO
CIA	LBJ	TX	NAFTA

When in doubt, consult a dictionary.

When an abbreviation ends a sentence, the period at the end of the abbreviation serves as the period for the sentence. If a question mark or an exclamation point ends the sentence, place it *after* the period in the abbreviation.

► When he was in the seventh grade, we called him "Stinky," but now he is William Percival Abernathy, Ph.D.!

62b Use a question mark after a direct question.

► Who wrote *The Old Man and the Sea*?

Occasionally, a question mark changes a statement into a question.

► You expect me to believe a story like that?

When questions follow one another in a series, each one can be followed by a question mark even if they are not all complete sentences. Question fragments may begin with a capital or lowercase letter.

► **What will you contribute? Your time? Your talent? Your money?**

Use a question mark in parentheses to indicate a questionable date, number, or word, but do not use it to convey an ironic meaning.

► **Chaucer was born in 1340 (?) and lived until 1400.**

► **His dog had graduated from obedience ~~(?)~~ training.**

Do not use a question mark after an indirect question.

► **He asked her whether she would be at home later~~?~~.**

Do not use a period or comma after a question mark that ends a direct quotation.

► **She asked, "What is the word count?"~~.~~**

62c   Use exclamation points sparingly to convey shock, surprise, or some other strong emotion.

► **Stolen! The money was stolen! Right before our eyes, somebody snatched my purse and ran off with it.**

Using numerous exclamation points throughout a document actually weakens their force. Try to convey emotion with your choice of words and your sentence structure.

► **Jefferson and Adams both died on the same day in 1826, exactly fifty years after the signing of the Declaration of Independence~~!~~.**

The fact the sentence reports is surprising enough without the addition of an exclamation point.

Do not use a period or comma after an exclamation point that ends a direct quotation.

62d   Use the dash to emphasize the words that precede or follow.

A typeset dash, sometimes called an *em dash,* is a single, unbroken line about as wide as a capital M. Most word-processing programs provide the em dash as a special character or will convert two hyphens to an em dash as an automatic function. Otherwise, you can make a dash by typing two hyphens in a row with no space between them. Do not put a space before or after the dash.

1. Highlighting an explanation or a list   A dash indicates a strong pause and emphasizes what comes immediately before or after it.

▶   **Coca-Cola, potato chips, and brevity—these are the marks of a good study session.**

▶   **I think the Comets will win the tournament for one reason—their goalie.**

A colon could also be used in the second example. *(See Chapter 59, pp. 551–53.)*

    If an appositive consists of a list of items, use dashes to set it off more clearly for readers.

▶   **The symptoms of hay fever⫽ sneezing, coughing, itchy eyes⫽ can be**

    controlled with over-the-counter medications.

Do not separate a subject and verb with a dash, however.

▶   **Haydn, Mozart, and Beethoven—are famous composers.**

2. Setting off a nonessential phrase or independent clause within a sentence

▶   **All finite creations—including humans—are incomplete and contradictory.**

▶   **The first rotary gasoline engine—it was made by Mazda—burned 15 percent more fuel than conventional engines.**

3. Indicating a sudden change in tone or idea

▶   **Breathing heavily, the archaeologist opened the old chest in wild anticipation and found—an old pair of socks and an empty soda can.**

Caution: The dash can make your writing disjointed if overused.

▶   **After we found the puppy—shivering under the porch—, we**

    brought her into the house—into the entryway, actually—and

    wrapped her in an old towel—to warm her up.

62e   Use parentheses for nonessential information.

Parentheses should be used infrequently and only to set off supplementary information, a digression, or a comment that interrupts the flow of thought within a sentence or paragraph.

▶   **The tickets (ranging in price from $10 to $50) go on sale Monday.**

When parentheses enclose a whole sentence, the sentence begins with a capital letter and ends with a period before the final parenthesis. A sentence that appears inside parentheses *within a sentence* should neither begin with a capital letter nor end with a period.

▶ **Folktales and urban legends often reflect the concerns of a particular era. (The familiar tale of a cat accidentally caught in a microwave oven is an example.)**

▶ **Angela Merkel (she is the first female chancellor of Germany) formed a coalition government following her election in 2005.**

If the material in parentheses is at the end of an introductory or nonessential word group followed by a comma, place the comma after the closing parenthesis. A comma should never appear before the opening parenthesis.

▶ **As the soloist walked onstage,/ (carrying her famous violin), the audience rose to its feet.**

Parentheses enclose numbers or letters that label items in a list.

▶ **He says the argument is nonsense because (1) university presidents don't work as well as machines, (2) university presidents don't do any real work at all, and (3) universities should be run by faculty committees.**

Parentheses also enclose in-text citations in many systems of documenting sources. *(For more on documenting sources, see Tabs 6–8.)*

62f When quoting, use brackets to set off material that is not part of the original quotation.

Use brackets to set off information you add to a quotation.

▶ **Samuel Eliot Morison has written, "This passage has attracted a good deal of scorn to the Florentine mariner [Verrazano], but without justice."**

In this sentence, the writer places the name of the "Florentine mariner"—Verrazano—in brackets so readers will know his identity.

You can also place brackets around words you insert within a quotation to make it fit the grammar or style of your own sentence. If you replace a word with your own word in brackets, you do not need ellipses.

▶ **At the end of *Pygmalion,* Henry Higgins confesses to Eliza Doolittle that he has "grown accustomed to [her] voice and appearance."**

To make the quotation fit properly into the sentence, the bracketed word *her* is inserted in place of *your.*

Use brackets to enclose the word *sic* (Latin for "thus") after a word in a quotation that was incorrect in the original. If you are following MLA style, the word *sic* should not be underlined or italicized.

▶ **The critic noted that "the battle scenes in _The Patriot_ are realistic, but the rest of the film is historically inacurate [sic]."**

Use _sic_ sparingly because it can appear condescending.

If you change the first letter of a word in a quotation to a capital or lowercase letter, enclose the letter in brackets: _Ackroyd writes, "[F]or half a million years there has been in London a pattern of habitation and hunting, if not settlement."_

If you need to set off words within material that is already in parentheses, use brackets: _(I found the information on a Web site published by the National Institutes of Health [NIH].)_

Note: MLA style calls for brackets around ellipses that you insert to show omission from a source that already contains ellipses in the original.

62g Use ellipses to indicate that words have been omitted.

Use three spaced periods, called ellipses or an ellipsis mark, to show readers that you have omitted words from a passage you are quoting. Some instructors suggest that you use brackets to enclose any ellipses you add. _(See the note above regarding MLA style.)_

FULL QUOTATION FROM A WORK BY WILKINS

In the nineteenth century, railroads, lacing their way across continents, reaching into the heart of every major city in Europe and America, and bringing a new romance to travel, added to the unity of nations and fueled the nationalist fires already set burning by the French Revolution and the wars of Napoleon.

EDITED QUOTATION

In his account of nineteenth-century society, Wilkins argues that "railroads . . . added to the unity of nations and fueled the nationalist fires already set burning by the French Revolution and the wars of Napoleon."

If you are leaving out the end of a quoted sentence, the three ellipsis points are preceded by a period to end the sentence.

EDITED QUOTATION

In describing the growth of railroads, Wilkins pictures them "lacing their way across continents, reaching into the heart of every major city in Europe and America. . . ."

When you need to add a parenthetical reference after the ellipses at the end of a sentence, place it after the quotation mark but before the final period: . . ." (253).

Ellipses are usually not needed to indicate an omission when only a word or phrase is being quoted.

▶ Railroads brought "a new romance to travel," according to Wilkins.

To indicate the omission of an entire line or more from the middle of a poem, insert a line of spaced periods.

> Shelley seems to be describing nature, but what's really at issue is the
> seductive nature of desire:
>
>> See the mountains kiss high Heaven,
>>
>> And the waves clasp one another;
>>
>> . . . .
>>
>> What is all this sweet work worth
>>
>> If thou kiss not me? (1-2, 7-8)

Use ellipses only as a means of shortening a quotation, never as a device for changing its fundamental meaning or emphasis.

You can use ellipses at the end of a sentence if you mean to leave a thought hanging. In the following passage, Dick Gregory uses an ellipsis to suggest there was no end to his worries.

▶ Oh God, I'm scared. I wish I could die right now with the feeling I have because I know Momma's gonna make me mad and I'm going to make her mad, and me and Presley's gonna fight . . . "Richard, you get in here and put your coat on. Get in here or I'll whip you."

Ellipses also indicate pauses or interruptions in speech.

62h   Use slashes according to convention.

Use the slash to show divisions between lines of poetry when you quote more than one line of a poem as part of a sentence. Add a space on either side of the slash. When you are quoting four or more lines of poetry, use a block quotation instead *(see p. 274 and the preceding discussion).*

▶ In "Tell all the Truth..." Dickinson insists "The truth must dazzle gradually / Or every man be blind" (275).

The slash is sometimes used between two words that represent choices or combinations. Do not add spaces around the slash when you use it in this way.

▶ The college offers three credit/noncredit courses.

Slashes (called *forward slashes*) also mark divisions in online addresses (URLs): http://www.georgetown.edu/crossroads/navigate .html.

Some writers use the slash as a marker between the words *and* and *or,* or between *he* and *she* and *his* and *her* to avoid sexism. Most writers, however, consider such usage awkward. It is usually better to rephrase the sentence. *(See also Tab 10: Editing for Grammar Conventions, pp. 515–19.)*

▶ A bill can originate in the House of Representatives, ~~and/or~~ the Senate.
                                                        in   *, or both*

CHAPTER 63

Capitalization

Many rules for the use of capital letters have been fixed by custom, such as the convention of beginning each sentence with a capital letter, but the rules change all the time. A recent dictionary is a good guide to capitalization.

✓ **63a** Capitalize proper nouns (names), words derived from them, brand names, certain abbreviations, and call letters.

Proper nouns are the names of specific people, places, or things. Capitalize proper nouns, words derived from proper nouns, brand names, abbreviations of capitalized words, and call letters of radio and television stations.

> **Proper nouns:** Ronald Reagan, the Transamerica Pyramid
>
> **Words derived from proper nouns:** Reaganomics, Siamese cat *but* french fries, simonize

Capitalization and Grammar Checkers

Grammar checkers will flag some words that should be capitalized or lowercased by convention, but they won't flag proper nouns unless the noun is stored in the program's dictionary, and they may not flag a noun that can be either proper or common depending on the context.

> **Brand names:** Apple, Kleenex, *but* eBay
>
> **Abbreviations:** FBI (government agency), A&E (cable television station)
>
> **Call letters:** WNBC (television), WMNR (radio)

> **Note:** Seasons, such as *summer,* and the days of the month given as numbers are not capitalized when they are spelled out: *Valentine's Day falls in the middle of* <u>winter,</u> *on the* <u>fourteenth</u> *of February.*

63b Capitalize titles when they appear before a proper name but not when they are used alone or after the name.

Family members: Aunt Lou, *but* my aunt, Father (name used alone) *or* my father

Political Figures: Governor Andrew Cuomo, Senator Olympia Snowe, *but* the governor, my senator

Most writers do not capitalize the title *president* unless they are referring to the President of the United States: *The* president *of this university has seventeen honorary degrees.*

63c Capitalize titles of works of literature, works of art, and musical compositions.

Capitalize the important words in titles and subtitles. Do not capitalize articles *(a, an,* and *the),* the *to* in infinitives, or prepositions and coordinating conjunctions unless they begin or end the title or subtitle. Capitalize both parts of a hyphenated word. In MLA style, capitalize subordinating conjunctions *(Because).* Capitalize the first word after a colon or semicolon in a title. Capitalize titles of major divisions of a work, such as chapters.

Book: *Water for Elephants*
Play: *The Importance of Being Earnest*
Building: the Eiffel Tower
Ships, aircraft: the *Titanic,* the *Concorde*
Painting: the *Mona Lisa*
Article or essay: "Next-Generation Scientists"
Poem: "Stopping by Woods on a Snowy Evening"
Music: "The Star-Spangled Banner"
Chapter: "Capitalization" in *A Writer's Resource*

63d Capitalize names of areas and regions.

Names of geographic regions are generally capitalized if they are well established, like *the Midwest* and *Central Europe.* Names of directions, as in the sentence *Turn south,* are not capitalized.

CORRECT   *East* meets *West* at the summit.

CORRECT   You will need to go *west* on Sunset.

PROPER AND COMMON NOUNS

- **People:** Helena Bonham Carter, Sonia Sotomayor, Bill Gates
- **Nationalities, ethnic groups, and languages:** English, Swiss, African Americans, Arabs, Chinese, Turkish
- **Places:** the United States of America, Tennessee, the Irunia Restaurant, the Great Lakes, *but* my state, the lake
- **Organizations and institutions:** Phi Beta Kappa, Republican Party (Republicans), Department of Defense, Cumberland College, the North Carolina Tarheels, *but* the department, this college, our hockey team
- **Religious bodies, books, and figures:** Jews, Christians, Baptists, Hindus, Roman Catholic Church, the Bible, the Koran *or* Qur'an, the Torah, God, Holy Spirit, Allah, *but* a Greek goddess, a biblical reference
- **Scientific names and terms:** *Homo sapiens, H. sapiens, Acer rubrum, A. rubrum,* Addison's disease (*or* Addison disease), Cenozoic era, Newton's first law, *but* the law of gravity
- **Names of planets, stars, and other astronomical bodies:** Earth (as a planet) *but* the earth, Mercury, Polaris *or* the North Star, Whirlpool Galaxy, *but* a star, that galaxy, the solar system
- **Computer terms:** the Internet, the World Wide Web *or* the Web, *but* search engine, a network, my browser
- **Days, months, and holidays:** Monday, Veterans Day, August, the Fourth of July, *but* yesterday, spring and summer, the winter term, second-quarter earnings
- **Historical events, movements, periods, and documents:** World War II, Impressionism, the Renaissance, the Jazz Age, the Declaration of Independence, the Magna Carta, *but* the last war, a golden age, the twentieth century, the amendment
- **Academic subjects and courses:** English 101, Psychology 221, a course in Italian, *but* a physics course, my art history class

The word *western,* when used as a general direction or the name of a genre *(the western* High Noon), is not capitalized except when it is part of the name of a specific region: *I visited Western Europe last year.*

63e Follow standard practice for capitalizing names of races, ethnic groups, and sacred things.

The words *black* and *white* are usually not capitalized when they refer to members of racial groups because they are adjectives that substitute for the implied common nouns *black person* and *white person.* However, names of ethnic groups and races are capitalized: *African Americans, Italians, Asians, Caucasians.*

> **Note:** In accordance with current APA guidelines, most social scientists capitalize the terms *Black* and *White,* treating them as proper nouns.

Many religious terms, such as *sacrament, altar,* and *rabbi,* are not capitalized. The word *Bible* is capitalized (though *biblical* is not), but not when used as a metaphor for an essential book.

▶ His book *Winning at Stud Poker* used to be the bible of gamblers.

63f Capitalize the first word of a quoted sentence but not the first word of an indirect quotation.

▶ She cried, "Help!"

▶ He said that jazz was one of America's major art forms.

The first word of a quotation from a printed source is capitalized if the quotation is introduced with a phrase such as *she notes* or *he concludes.*

▶ Jim, the narrator of *My Ántonia,* concludes, "Whatever we had missed, we possessed together the precious, the incommunicable past" (324).

When a quotation from a printed source is treated as an element in your sentence and not as a sentence on its own, the first word is not capitalized.

▶ Jim took comfort in sharing with Ántonia "the precious, the incommunicable past" (324).

If you need to change the first letter of a quotation to fit your sentence, enclose the letter in brackets.

▶ The lawyer noted that "[t]he man seen leaving the area after the blast was not the same height as the defendant."

If you interrupt the sentence you are quoting with an expression such as *he said,* the first word of the rest of the quotation should not be capitalized.

▶ "When I come home an hour later," she explained, "the trains are usually less crowded."

When quoting a text directly, reproduce the capitalization used in the original source, whether or not it is correct by today's standards.

▶ Blake's marginalia include the following comment: "Paine is either a Devil or an Inspired Man" (603).

63g　Capitalize the first word of a sentence.

A capital letter is used to signal the beginning of a new sentence.

▶ **Robots reduce human error, so they produce uniform products.**

Sentences in parentheses also begin with a capital letter unless they are embedded within another sentence:

▶ **Although the week began with the news that he was hit by a car, by Thursday we knew he was going to be all right. (It was a terrible way to begin the week, though.)**

▶ **Although the week began with the news that he was hit by a car (it was a terrible way to begin the week), by Thursday we knew he was going to be all right.**

63h　Capitalizing the first word of an independent clause after a colon is optional.

If the word group that follows a colon is not a complete sentence, do not capitalize it. If it is a complete sentence, you may capitalize it or not, but be consistent throughout your document. (See whether your instructor or style guide prefers one option.)

▶ **The question is serious: do you think peace is possible?**

or

▶ **The question is serious: Do you think peace is possible?**

CHAPTER 64

Abbreviations and Symbols

Unless you are writing a scientific or technical report, spell out most terms and titles, except in the cases discussed in this chapter. You may also want to consult your discipline's style manual for guidelines.

Abbreviations and Grammar Checkers

Computer grammar or spelling checkers may flag an abbreviation, but they generally will not tell you if your use is acceptable or consistent within a piece of writing.

64a   Abbreviate familiar titles that always precede or follow a person's name.

Some abbreviations appear before a person's name *(Mr., Ms., Mrs., Dr.)*, and some follow a proper name *(Jr., Sr., MD, Esq., PhD)*. When an abbreviation follows a person's name, place a comma between the name and the abbreviation. Many writers consider the comma before *Jr.* and *Sr.* to be optional. Spell out religious, government, and professional titles such as Rev. (Reverend) in academic writing and when they appear with only the last name.

- **Before names:** Mrs. Jean Bascom; Dr. Epstein
- **After names:** Robert Robinson Jr. or Robert Robinson, Jr.; Elaine Less, CPA, LL.D.

Do not use two abbreviations that represent the same thing: *Dr. Peter Joyce, MD.* Use either *Dr. Peter Joyce* or *Peter Joyce, MD.*

Spell out titles used without proper names, and do not capitalize them.

▶ **Mr. Carew asked if she had seen the ~~dr.~~** *doctor.*
                                          ^

64b   Use abbreviations only when you know your readers will understand them.

If you use a technical term or the name of an organization in a report, you may abbreviate it as long as your readers are likely to be familiar with the abbreviation. For example, a medical writer might use PT *(physical therapy)* in a medical report or professional newsletter. Abbreviations of three or more capital letters generally do not use periods: *CBS, EPA, IRS, NAACP, USA.*

FAMILIAR ABBREVIATION	The EPA has had a lasting impact on the air quality of this country.
UNFAMILIAR ABBREVIATION	After you have completed them, take these *the Human Resources and Education Center* forms to ~~HREC~~. ^

Note: In the body of a paper, you can use *U.S.* as an adjective *(U.S. Constitution)* but not as a noun *(I grew up outside the United States).*

─NAVIGATING THROUGH COLLEGE AND BEYOND
Scientific and Latin Abbreviations

Most abbreviations used in scientific or technical writing, such as those related to measurement, should be given without periods: *mph, lb, dc, rpm.* If an abbreviation looks like an actual word, however, you can use a period to prevent confusion: *in., Fig.* In some types of scholarly writing, Latin abbreviations are acceptable (in parenthetical statements and notes).

Write out an unfamiliar term or name the first time you use it, and give the abbreviation in parentheses.

▶ **The Student Nonviolent Coordinating Committee (SNCC) was far to the left of other civil rights organizations. However, SNCC quickly burned itself out and disappeared.**

64c Abbreviate words typically used with times, dates, and numerals, as well as units of measurement in charts and graphs.

Use abbreviations or symbols associated with numbers only when they accompany a number: *3 p.m.,* not *in the p.m.; $500,* not *How many $ do you have?* The abbreviation B.C. ("Before Christ") follows a date; A.D. ("in the year of our Lord") precedes the date. The alternative abbreviations B.C.E. ("Before the Common Era") and C.E. ("Common Era") can be used instead of B.C. and A.D., respectively; both of these follow the date.

6:00 p.m. or 6:00 P.M. or 6 PM	9:45 a.m. or 9:45 A.M. or 9:45 AM
498 B.C. or 498 BC or	A.D. 275 or AD 275
498 B.C.E. or 498 BCE	or 275 C.E. or 275 CE
6,000 rpm	271 cm

In charts and graphs, abbreviations and symbols such as = for *equals, in.* for *inches,* % for *percent,* and *$* with numbers are acceptable because they save space.

> **Note:** Be consistent. If you use *a.m.* in one sentence, do not switch to *A.M.* in the next sentence.

64d Avoid Latin abbreviations in formal writing.

In formal writing, it is usually a good idea to avoid even common Latin abbreviations (*e.g., et al., etc.,* and *i.e.*). Instead of *e.g. (exempli gratia),* use *such as* or *for example.*

cf.	compare *(confer)*
et al.	and others *(et alia)*
etc.	and so forth, and so on *(et cetera)*
i.e.	that is *(id est)*
N.B.	note well *(nota bene)*
viz.	namely *(videlicet)*

64e   Avoid inappropriate abbreviations and symbols.

Days of the week *(Sat.)*, places *(TX* or *Tex.)*, the word *company (Co.)*, people's names *(Wm.)*, disciplines and professions *(econ.)*, parts of speech *(v.)*, parts of written works *(ch., p.)*, symbols *(@)*, and units of measurement *(lb)* are all spelled out in formal writing.

▶ The *environmental* (not *env.*) engineers from the Paramus Water Company (not *Co.*) are arriving in *New York City* (not *NYC*) this *Thursday* (not *Thurs.*) to correct the problems in the *physical education* (not *phys. ed.*) building in time for *Christmas* (not *Xmas*).

If an ampersand (&) or an abbreviation such as *Inc., Co.,* or *Corp.* is part of a company's official name, however, you can use it in formal writing: *Apple Inc. announced these changes in late December.*

Use -*s*, not -'*s*, to make abbreviations plural (two *DVDs*).

CHAPTER 65

Numbers

65a   In nontechnical writing, spell out numbers up to one hundred, and round numbers greater than one hundred.

▶ Approximately *two hundred fifty* students passed the exam, but *twenty-five* students failed.

When you are using a great many numbers, or when a spelled-out number would require more than three or four words, use numerals.

▶ This regulation affects nearly *10,500* taxpayers, substantially more than the *200* originally projected. Of those affected, *2,325* filled out the papers incorrectly, and another *743* called the office for help.

Round numbers larger than one million are expressed in numerals and words: 8 million, 2.4 trillion.

Use all numerals rather than mixing numerals and spelled-out words for the same type of item in a passage.

▶ We wrote to 132 people but only ~~sixteen~~ 16 responded.

Exceptions: When two numbers appear together, spell out one, and use numerals for the other: *two 20-pound bags.*

65b Spell out a number that begins a sentence.

If a numeral begins a sentence, reword the sentence, or spell out the numeral.

▶ **Twenty-five children are in each elementary class.**

65c In technical and business writing, use numerals for exact measurements and all numbers greater than ten.

▶ **The endosperm halves were placed in each of 14 small glass test tubes.**

▶ **Sample solutions with GA$_3$ concentrations ranging from O g/mL to 10^5 g/mL were added, one to each test tube.**

▶ **With its $1.9 trillion economy, Germany has an important trade role to play.**

65d Use numerals for dates, times of day, addresses, and similar kinds of conventional quantitative information.

- **Dates:** October 9, 2009; 1558–1603; A.D. 1066 (*or* AD 1066); *but* October ninth, May first
- **Time of day:** 6 A.M. (*or* AM *or* a.m.), a quarter past eight in the evening, three o'clock in the morning
- **Addresses:** 21 Meadow Road, Apt. 6J, Grand Island, NY 14072
- **Percentages:** 73 percent, 73%
- **Fractions and decimals:** 21.84, 6½, two-thirds (*not* 2-thirds), a fourth
- **Measurements:** 100 miles per hour (*or* 100 mph), 9 kilograms (*or* 9 kg), 38°F, 15°Celsius, 3 tablespoons (*or* 3 T), 4 liters (*or* 4 L), 18 inches (*or* 18 in.)
- **Volume, chapter, page:** volume 4, chapter 8, page 44
- **Scenes in a play:** *Hamlet,* act 2, scene 1, lines 77–84
- **Scores and statistics:** 0 to 3, 98–92, an average age of 35
- **Amounts of money:** 10¢ (*or* 10 cents), $125, $2.25, $2.8 million (*or* $2,800,000)
- **Serial or identification numbers:** batch number 4875, 105.5 on the AM dial
- **Surveys:** 9 of 10
- **Telephone numbers:** (716) 555-2174

To make a number plural, add *-s.*

> **Note:** In nontechnical writing, spell out the names of units of measurement *(inches, liters)* in text. Use abbreviations *(in., L)* and symbols *(%)* in charts and graphs to save space.

CHAPTER 66

Italics (Underlining)

Italics, characters in a typeface that slants to the right, are used to set off certain words and phrases. If italics are not available or if your instructor prefers, however, you may <u>underline</u> words that would be typeset in italics. MLA style requires italics.

▶ Daniel Day-Lewis gives one of his best performances in *There Will Be Blood.*

▶ Daniel Day-Lewis gives one of his best performances in <u>There Will Be Blood.</u>

66a   Italicize (or underline) titles of lengthy works or separate publications.

Italicize (or underline) titles of long works or works that are not part of a larger publication.

Works That Should Be Italicized (or Underlined)

- **Books (including textbooks):** *The Color of Water, The Art of Public Speaking*
- **Magazines and journals:** *Texas Monthly, College English*
- **Newspapers:** *Chicago Tribune*
- **Comic strips:** *Dilbert*

the EVOLVING SITUATION

Italics and Underlining

Italics may not be available in online environments. To indicate underlining, put an underscore mark or an asterisk before and after what you would italicize in a manuscript: Daniel Day-Lewis gives one of his best performances in _There Will Be Blood_.

On the Web, underlining indicates a hypertext link. If your work is going to be posted online, use italics instead of underlining for titles to avoid confusion.

- **Plays, films, television series, radio programs:** *Death of a Salesman, On the Waterfront, American Idol, Car Talk*
- **Long musical compositions:** Beethoven's *Pastoral Symphony* (*But* Beethoven's Symphony No. 6—the title consists of the musical form, a number, and/or a key.)
- **Choreographic works:** Balanchine's *Jewels*
- **Artworks:** Edward Hopper's *Nighthawks*
- **Web sites:** *Slate*
- **Software:** *Microsoft PowerPoint*
- **Long poems:** *Odyssey*
- **Pamphlets:** *Gorges: A Guide to the Geology of the Ithaca Area*
- **Electronic databases:** *Academic Search Premier*

In titles of lengthy works, *a, an,* or *the* is capitalized and italicized (or underlined) if it is the first word, but *the* is not generally treated as part of the title in names of newspapers and periodicals in MLA or Chicago style: the *New York Times.* If you are following APA or CSE style, however, you should treat *the* as part of the title.

> **Note:** Do not use italics or underlining when referring to the Bible and other sacred books.

Court cases may also be italicized or underlined, but legal documents and laws are not: the Constitution.

▶ In ***Brown v. Board of Education of Topeka*** (1954), the U.S. Supreme Court ruled that segregation in public schools is unconstitutional.

▶ He obtained a writ of habeas corpus.

Do not italicize or underline punctuation marks that follow a title unless they are part of the title: I finally finished reading *Moby Dick*!

Quotation marks are used for the titles of short works—essays, newspaper and magazine articles and columns, short stories, short poems, and individual Web pages. Quotation marks are also used for titles of unpublished works when they are referred to within a text, including student writing, theses, and dissertations. *(See Chapter 61, pp. 558–59, for more on quotation marks with titles.)*

66b Italicize (or underline) the names of ships, trains, aircraft, and spaceships.

Queen Mary 2   *Montrealer*   *Spirit of St. Louis*   *Apollo 11*

Do not italicize abbreviations used with the name, such as HMS or SS. Model names and numbers (such as Boeing 747) are not italicized.

66c Italicize (or underline) foreign terms.

▶ **In the Paris airport, we recognized the familiar no-smoking sign:**
Défense de fumer.

Many foreign words have become so common in English that everyone accepts them as part of the language, and they require no italics or underlining: rigor mortis, pasta, and sombrero, for example. (These words appear in English dictionaries.)

66d Italicize (or underline) scientific names.

The scientific (Latin) names of organisms, consisting of the **genus** and **species**, are always italicized. The genus is capitalized.

▶ **Most chicks are infected with *Cryptosporidium baileyi,* a parasite typical of young animals.**

66e Italicize (or underline) words, letters, and numbers referred to as themselves.

For clarity, italicize words or phrases used as words rather than for the meaning they convey. (You may also use quotation marks for this purpose.)

▶ **The term *romantic* does not mean the same thing to the Shelley scholar that it does to the fan of Danielle Steel's novels.**

Letters and numbers used alone should also be italicized.

▶ **The word *bookkeeper* has three sets of double letters: double *o,* double *k,* and double *e.***

▶ **Add a *3* to that column.**

66f Use italics (or underlining) sparingly for emphasis.

An occasional word in italics helps you make a point. Too much emphasis, however, may mean no emphasis at all.

| WEAK | You don't mean that your teacher *told the whole class* that *he* did not know the answer *himself?* |
| REVISED | Your teacher admitted that he did not know the answer? That is amazing. |

If you add italics or underlining to a quotation, indicate the change in parentheses following the quotation.

▶ **Instead of promising that no harm will come to us, Blake only assures us that we "need not *fear* harm" (emphasis added).**

CHAPTER 67

Hyphens

67a   Use hyphens for compound words and for clarity.

A hyphen joins two nouns to make one compound word. Scientists speak of a *kilogram-meter* as a measure of force, and professors of literature talk about the *scholar-poet*. The hyphen lets us know that the two nouns work together as one.

A dictionary is the best resource when you are unsure about whether to use a hyphen. If you cannot find a compound word in the dictionary, spell it as two separate words. Whatever spelling you choose, be consistent throughout your document.

67b   Use hyphens to join two or more words to create compound adjective or noun forms.

A noun can also be linked with an adjective, an adverb, or another part of speech to form a compound adjective.

accident-prone   quick-witted

Use hyphens as well in nouns designating family relationships and compounds of more than two words.

brother-in-law   stay-at-home

Compound nouns with hyphens generally form plurals by adding *-s* or *-es* to the most important word.

attorney general/attorneys general
mother-in-law/mothers-in-law

Some proper nouns that are joined to make an adjective are hyphenated.

the Franco-Prussian war   of Mexican-American heritage

Hyphens often help clarify adjectives that come before the word they modify. Modifiers that are hyphenated when placed *before* the word they modify are usually not hyphenated when placed *after* the word they modify.

▶   It was a *bad-mannered* reply.

▶   The reply was *bad mannered.*

Do not use a hyphen to connect *-ly* adverbs to the words they modify. Similarly, do not use a hyphen with *-er* or *-est* adjectives and adverbs.

▶   **They explored the newly/discovered territories.**

▶   **This dress is better/looking in red.**

In a pair or series of compound nouns or adjectives, add suspended hyphens after the first word of each item.

▶   **The child care center accepted three-, four-, and five-year-olds.**

67c   Use hyphens to spell out fractions and compound numbers.

Use a hyphen when writing out fractions or compound numbers from twenty-one to ninety-nine.

three-fourths of a gallon   thirty-two

> **Note:** In MLA style, use a hyphen to show inclusive numbers: *pages 100-40.*

67d   Use a hyphen to attach some prefixes and suffixes.

Use a hyphen to join a prefix and a capitalized word or a number.

un-American   pre-Columbian   pre-1970
mid-August   neo-Nazi

A hyphen is sometimes used to join a capital letter and a word.

T-shirt   V-six engine

The prefixes *all-, ex-, quasi-* and *self-*, and the suffixes *-elect, -odd,* and *-something,* generally take hyphens.

all-purpose   president-elect
ex-convict   fifty-odd
quasi-scientific   thirty-something
self-sufficient

Most prefixes, however, are not attached by hyphens, unless a hyphen is needed to show pronunciation, avoid double letters *(anti-immigration),* or distinguish the word from the same word without a hyphen: *recreate* (play) versus *re-create* (make again). Check a dictionary to be sure you are using the standard spelling.

67e   Use hyphens to divide words at the ends of lines.

The *MLA Handbook for Writers of Research Papers* advises writers to turn off the automatic-hyphenation function in their word-processing

─ *the* EVOLVING SITUATION

Dividing Internet Addresses

If you need to divide an Internet address between lines, divide it after a slash. Do not divide a word within the address with a hyphen; readers may assume the hyphen is part of the address. Break an e-mail address after @. Check your style manual for specific guidelines.

programs. In this way, you will avoid breaking words at the ends of lines. When you must divide words, do so between syllables. Pronunciation alone cannot always tell you where to divide a word, however. If you are unsure about how to break a word into syllables, consult your dictionary.

▶   My writing group had a very fruitful *collab-*
    oration. [not *colla-boration*]

Never leave just one or two letters on a line.

▶   He seemed so sad and vulnerable and so *discon-*
    nected from his family. [not *disconnect-ed*]

Compound words such as *hardworking, rattlesnake,* and *book-case* should be broken only between the words that form them: *hard-working, rattle-snake, book-case.* Compound words that already have hyphens, like *brother-in-law,* are broken only after the hyphens.

> **Note:** Never hyphenate an abbreviation, a contraction, a numeral, or a one-syllable word.

CHAPTER 68

Spelling

Proofread your writing carefully. Misspellings creep into the prose of even the best writers. Use the following strategies to help you improve your spelling:

- Become familiar with major spelling rules *(68a).*
- Keep a list of words that give you trouble.
- If you are not sure how a word is spelled, look it up in the dictionary.

Spelling Checkers

Computer spell checkers are helpful tools. Remember, however, that a spell checker cannot tell *how* you are using a particular word. If you write *their* but mean *there,* a spell checker cannot point out your mistake. Spell checkers also cannot point out many misspelled proper nouns.

68a   Learn the rules that generally hold for spelling, as well as their exceptions.

1. Use *i* before *e* except after *c* or when sounded like *a,* as in *neighbor* and *weigh.*

- ***i* before *e*:** believe, relieve, chief, grief, wield, yield
- **Except after *c*:** receive, deceive, ceiling, conceit

  Exceptions: seize, caffeine, weird, height, science, species

2. Prefixes do not change a word's spelling when attached.

- **Examples:** preview, reconnect, unwind, deemphasize

3. Suffixes change a word's spelling depending on the suffix or the final letter(s) of the root word.

- **Final silent *e*:**

  Drop it if the suffix begins with a vowel: *force/forcing, remove/removable, surprise/surprising*

  Keep it if the suffix begins with a consonant: *care/careful.*

  Exceptions: argue/argument, true/truly, change/changeable, judge/judgment, acknowledge/acknowledgment

> **Note:** Keep the silent *e* if it is needed to clarify the pronunciation or if the word would be confused with another word without the *e.*
>
> dye/dyeing (to avoid confusion with *dying*)
> hoe/hoeing (to avoid mispronunciation)

- **Final *y*:**

  Keep it when adding the suffix *-ing: enjoy/enjoying, cry/crying*
  Keep or change it when adding other suffixes:

  - **When *y* follows a consonant, change to *i* or *ie*:** happy/happier, marry/married
  - **When *y* follows a vowel, keep it:** defray/defrayed, enjoy/enjoying

- **Final consonant:**

  Double it if the root word ends in a single vowel + a consonant and is only one syllable long or has an accent on the final syllable: *grip/gripping, refer/referred*

  For other types of root words, do not double the consonant: *crack/cracking, laundering*

  Exceptions: bus/busing, focus/focused

- **-ly with words that end in -ic:**

  Add *-ally:* logic/logically, terrific/terrifically

  Exception: public/publicly

- **Words ending in *-able/-ible, -ant/-ent,* and *-ify/-efy:***

  Consult a dictionary for the correct spelling of words ending in these frequently confused suffixes.

4. Forming plurals Most plurals are formed by adding *-s*. Some are formed by adding *-es*.

- **Words ending in *-s, -sh, -x, -z,* "soft" *-ch* (add *-es*):** bus/buses, bush/bushes, fox/foxes, buzz/buzzes, peach/peaches

- **Words ending in a consonant + *o* (add *-es*):** hero/heroes, tomato/tomatoes, *but* solo/solos

- **Words ending in a consonant + *y* (change *y* to *i* and add *-es*):** beauty/beauties, city/cities, *but* the Kirbys (a family's name)

- **Words ending in *-f* or *-fe* (change *f* to *v* and add *-s* or *-es*):** leaf/leaves, knife/knives, wife/wives, *but* staff/staffs, roof/roofs

Most plurals follow standard rules, but some have irregular forms *(child/children, tooth/teeth),* and some words with foreign roots create plurals in the pattern of the language they come from, as do these words:

alumna/alumnae	datum/data
alumnus/alumni	medium/media
analysis/analyses	stimulus/stimuli
criterion/criteria	thesis/theses

> ***Note:*** Some writers now treat *data* as though it were singular, but the preferred practice is still to recognize that *data* is plural and takes a plural verb: *The data are clear on this point: the pass/fail course has become outdated.*

Some nouns with foreign roots have regular and irregular plural forms *(appendix/appendices/appendixes)*. Be consistent in using the spelling you choose.

Compound nouns with hyphens generally form plurals by adding *-s* or *-es* to the most important word:

brother-in-law/brothers-in-law

For some compound words that appear as one word, the same rule applies *(passersby);* for others, it does not *(cupfuls)*. Consult a dictionary if you are not sure.

If both words in the compound are equally important, add *-s* to the second word: *singer-songwriters*.

A few words, such as *fish* and *sheep,* have the same forms for singular and plural. To indicate that the word is plural, you need to add a word or words that specify quantity: *five fish, a few sheep*.

68b   Learn to distinguish words pronounced alike but spelled differently.

Homonyms sound alike but have different meanings and different spellings. The following is a list of common homonyms as well as words that are almost homonyms. For more complete definitions, consult the Glossary of Usage *(Chapter 50, pp. 475–84)* and a dictionary.

accept: to take willingly
except: to leave out (verb); but for (preposition)

affect: to influence (verb); a feeling or an emotion (noun)
effect: to make or accomplish (verb); result (noun)

all ready: prepared
already: by this time

cite: to quote or refer to
sight: spectacle, sense
site: place

it's: contraction for *it is* or *it has*
its: possessive pronoun

loose: not tight
lose: to misplace

precede: to come before
proceed: to go forward

principal: most important (adjective); the head of an organization *or* a sum of money (noun)
principle: a basic standard or law (noun)

their: possessive pronoun
there: adverb of place
they're: contraction for *they are*

to: indicating movement
too: also
two: number

who's: contraction for *who is*
whose: possessive of *who*

your: possessive pronoun
you're: contraction for *you are*

┌─ CHECKLIST Editing for Sentence Punctuation, Mechanics, and Spelling

As you revise, check your writing for proper punctuation and spelling by asking yourself these questions:

☐ Are commas used appropriately to separate or set off introductory sentence elements; coordinated independent clauses; items in a series and coordinate adjectives; nonessential sentence elements; direct quotations; and the parts of dates, addresses, titles, and numbers? *(See Chapter 57: Commas, pp. 536–45.)* Are any commas mistakenly used with sentence elements that should not be separated or set off? *(See Chapter 57: Commas, pp. 545–48.)*

☐ Are semicolons used appropriately to join independent clauses and to separate items in a series when the items contain commas? *(See Chapter 58: Semicolons, pp. 548–51.)*

☐ Are colons used appropriately after a complete sentence to introduce a list, an appositive, or a quotation; after one independent clause to introduce a second that elaborates on the first; and in business letters, ratios, and bibliographic citations? *(See Chapter 59: Colons, pp. 551–53.)*

☐ Are quotation marks used appropriately with other punctuation to identify brief direct quotations, dialogue, and the titles of short works? Are single quotation marks used appropriately to identify quotations within quotations? *(See Chapter 61: Quotation Marks, pp. 556–61.)*

☐ Are periods used appropriately at the end of sentences and in abbreviations? Are question marks and exclamation points used appropriately at the end of sentences and within quotations? Are brackets and ellipses used correctly to identify words added to and omitted from quotations? Are dashes and parentheses used appropriately to insert or highlight nonessential information within a sentence? *(See Chapter 62: Other Punctuation Marks, pp. 561–68.)*

☐ Are words and letters capitalized according to convention and context? *(See Chapter 63: Capitalization, pp. 568–72.)*

☐ Are abbreviations capitalized and punctuated in a consistent way? Are Latin abbreviations and nonalphabetic symbols used appropriately? *(See Chapter 64: Abbreviations and Symbols, pp. 572–75.)*

☐ Are numbers either spelled out or represented with numerals according to the conventions of the type of writing (nontechnical or technical) you are engaged in? *(See Chapter 65: Numbers, pp. 575–77.)*

☐ Are italics (or is underlining) used appropriately for emphasis and to identify the titles of works, foreign words, and words used as words? *(See Chapter 66: Italics [Underlining], pp. 577–79.)*

☐ Are apostrophes used appropriately to indicate possession and to form contractions? *(See Chapter 60: Apostrophes, pp. 553–56.)*

12

Basic Grammar Review

With Tips for Multilingual Writers

Grammar and rhetoric are complementary. . . .
Grammar maps out the possible; rhetoric narrows
the possible down to the desirable or effective.

–Francis Christensen

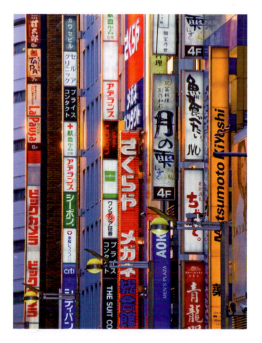

Shinjuku's Skyscraper District in Tokyo—featured in the film *Lost in Translation*—caters to an international, multilingual populace with signs in Japanese, English, Chinese, and Korean.

12   Basic Grammar Review

tips FOR MULTILINGUAL WRITERS

Tab 12: Basic Grammar Review

This section will help you answer questions such as the following:

Rhetorical Knowledge

- How does sentence structure in some other languages differ from that of English? (70)
- How does a sentence's purpose affect its type? (72b)

Critical Thinking, Reading, and Writing

- When might I use a simple sentence rather than a compound or complex sentence? (72a)

Processes

- During editing, should I add a comma after an *-ing* verb phrase? (72b)

Knowledge of Conventions

- How do nouns function in a sentence? What are count and noncount nouns? (69b)
- What are the five common sentence patterns in English? (70b)
- How do verb tenses work with *if* (conditional) clauses? (71e)

For a general introduction to writing outcomes, see 1e, pages 14–16.

— NAVIGATING THROUGH COLLEGE AND BEYOND
What Was the Language of Your Ancestors?

Your native language or even the language of your ancestors may influence the way you use English. Even if English is your first language, you may be part of a group that immigrated generations ago but has retained traces of other grammatical structures. For example, the slang contraction *ain't*, brought here by Scottish settlers, may have meant *am not* at one time. Take note of the Tips for Multilingual Writers in this section. Some might help native speakers as well.

Written language, although based on the grammar of spoken language, has its own logic and rules. The chapters that follow explain the basic rules of standard written English.

┌───┐

tip FOR MULTILINGUAL WRITERS: Recognizing language differences

The standard structures of sentences in languages other than English can be very different from those in English. In other languages, the form of a verb can indicate its grammatical function more powerfully than can its placement in the sentence. Also, in languages other than English, adjectives may take on the function that articles *(a, an, the)* perform, or articles may be absent.

If your first language is not English, try to pinpoint the areas of difficulty you have in English. See whether you are attempting to *translate* the structures of your native language into English. If so, you will need to learn more about English sentence structure.

└───┘

CHAPTER 69

Parts of Speech

English has eight primary **parts of speech:** verbs, nouns, pronouns, adjectives, adverbs, prepositions, conjunctions, and interjections. All English words belong to one or more of these categories. Particular words can belong to different categories, depending on the role they play in a sentence. For example, the word *button* can be a noun *(the button on a coat)* or a verb *(Button your jacket now).*

69a Verbs

Verbs carry a lot of information. They report action *(run, write),* condition *(bloom, sit),* or state of being *(be, seem).* Verbs also change form to indicate person, number, tense, voice, and mood. To do all this, a **main verb** is often preceded by one or more **helping verbs,** thereby becoming a **verb phrase.**

                mv

▶ The play *begins* at eight.

    hv   *mv*   *hv* *mv*

▶ I *may change* seats after the play *has begun.*

1. Main verbs

Main verbs change form **(tense)** to indicate when something has happened. If a word does not indicate tense, it is not a main verb. All main verbs have five forms, except for *be,* which has eight.

      BASE FORM   *(talk, sing)*

      PAST TENSE   Yesterday I *(talked, sang).*

PAST PARTICIPLE	In the past, I have *(talked, sung)*.
PRESENT PARTICIPLE	Right now I am *(talking, singing)*.
THIRD-PERSON SINGULAR (OR *-S* FORM)	Usually he/she/it *(talks, sings)*.

(For more on subject-verb agreement and verb tense, see Tab 10: Editing for Grammar Conventions, pp. 498–99 and pp. 506–8, and the list of common irregular verbs on p. 507.)

---

tip FOR MULTILINGUAL WRITERS: Using verbs followed by gerunds or infinitives

Verbs in English differ as to whether they can be followed by a gerund, an infinitive, or either. Some verbs, like *avoid,* can be followed by a gerund but not an infinitive. These constructions often express facts.

►   *climbing*
     We avoided ~~to climb~~ the mountain during the storm.

Other verbs, like *attempt,* can be followed by an infinitive but not a gerund. Often these constructions convey intentions.

►   *to reach*
     We attempted ~~reaching~~ the summit when the weather cleared.

Others can be followed by either a gerund or an infinitive with no change in meaning.

►   **We began climbing.**

►   **We began to climb.**

Still others have a different meaning when followed by a gerund than they do when followed by an infinitive. Compare these examples.

►   **She stopped eating.** [She was eating but she stopped.]

►   **She stopped to eat.** [She stopped what she was doing before in order to eat.]

The following lists provide common examples of each type of verb.

Some Verbs That Take Only an Infinitive

appear	fail	need	seem
ask	intend	plan	threaten
claim	learn	prepare	want
decide	manage	promise	wish
expect	mean	refuse	would like

(continued)

tip FOR MULTILINGUAL WRITERS: *(continued)*

Some Verbs That Take Only a Gerund

admit	forgive	regret
avoid	imagine	resist
consider	mention	risk
defend	mind	suggest
deny	practice	support
discuss	quit	tolerate
enjoy	recommend	understand
finish		

Some Verbs That Can Take Either a Gerund or an Infinitive

An asterisk (*) indicates those verbs for which the choice of gerund or infinitive affects meaning.

begin	like	start
continue	love	*stop
*forget	prefer	*try
hate	*remember	

> **Note:** For some verbs, such as *allow, cause, encourage, have, persuade, remind,* and *tell,* a noun or pronoun must precede the infinitive: *I reminded my sister to return my sweater.* For a few verbs, such as *ask, expect, need,* and *want,* the noun may either precede or follow the infinitive, depending on the meaning you want to express: *I want to return my sweater to my sister. I want my sister to return my sweater.*
>
> *Make, let,* and *have* are followed by a noun or pronoun plus the base form without *to: Make that boy come home on time.*

To make a verb followed by an infinitive negative, add *not* or *never* before the verb or before the infinitive. The location of *not* sometimes affects meaning:

▶ **He did not promise to write the report.** [He may or may not write the report since he made no promises.]

▶ **He promised not to write the report.** [He said he would not write the report.]

Verbs followed by a gerund always take the negative word before the gerund: *She regrets not finishing the assignment.*

2. Helping verbs that show time

Some helping verbs—mostly forms of *be, have,* and *do*—function to signify time *(will have been playing, has played)* or emphasis *(does play). (See Tab 10: Editing for Grammar Conventions, pp. 510–11.)*

Forms of *do* are also used to ask questions *(Do you play?).* Here are other such helping **(auxiliary)** verbs:

be, am, is	being, been	do, does, did
are, was, were	have, has, had	

The helping verb *do* and its forms *does* and *did* combine with the base form of a verb to ask a question or to emphasize something. Any helping verb can also combine with the word *not* to create an emphatic negative statement.

QUESTION	*Do* you hear those dogs barking?
EMPHATIC STATEMENT	I *do* hear them barking.
EMPHATIC NEGATIVE	I *do not* want to have to call the police about those dogs.

The helping verb *have* and its forms *has* and *had* combine with a past participle (usually ending in *-d, -t,* or *-n*) to form the *perfect tenses.* Do not confuse the simple past tense with the present perfect tense (formed with *have* or *has*), which is distinct from the simple past because the action can continue in the present. *(For a review of perfect tense forms, see Tab 10: Editing for Grammar Conventions, pp. 510–12.)* To form a negative statement, add *not* after the helping verb.

SIMPLE PAST	Those dogs *barked* all day.
PRESENT PERFECT	Those dogs *have barked* all day.
	Those dogs *have not barked* all day.
PAST PERFECT	Those dogs *had barked* all day.

Forms of *be* combine with a present participle (ending in *-ing*) to form the *progressive tenses,* which express continuing action. Do not confuse the simple present tense or the present perfect with these progressive forms. Unlike the simple present, which indicates an action that occurs frequently and might include the present moment, the present progressive form indicates an action that is going on right now. In its past form, the progressive tense indicates actions that were going on simultaneously. *(For a review of progressive tense forms, see Tab 10: Editing for Grammar Conventions, p. 511.)*

SIMPLE PRESENT	Those dogs *bark* all the time.
PRESENT PROGRESSIVE	Those dogs *are barking* all the time.
PAST PROGRESSIVE	Those dogs *were barking* all day while I *was trying* to study.

When *be* is used as a helping verb, it is preceded by a modal verb such as *can* or *may: I may be leaving tomorrow.* When *been* is the helping verb, it is preceded by a form of *have: I have been painting my room all day.*

Forms of *be* combine with the past participle (which usually ends in *-d, -t,* or *-n*) to form the passive voice, which is often used to express a state of being instead of an action.

BE + PAST PARTICIPLE

PASSIVE The dogs *were scolded* by their owner.

PASSIVE I *was satisfied* by her answer.

When *be, being,* or *been* is the helping verb, it needs another helping verb to be complete.

MODAL VERB The dogs *will be scolded* by their owner.

ANOTHER FORM The dogs *were being scolded* by their owner.
OF *BE*

FORM OF *HAVE* The dogs *have been scolded* by their owner.

3. Modals

Other helping verbs, called **modals,** express an attitude toward the action or circumstance of a sentence:

can	ought to	will
could	shall	would
may	should	must
might		

Modal verbs share several characteristics:

- They do not change form to indicate person or number.
- They do not change form to indicate tense.
- They are followed directly by the base form of the verb without *to.*
- Sometimes they are used with *have* plus the past participle of the verb to indicate the past tense.

▶   We must ~~to~~ study now.

▶   He *must* have studied hard to do so well.

Some verbal expressions ending in *to* also function as modals, including *have to, be able to,* and *be supposed to.* These **phrasal modals** behave more like ordinary verbs than true modals, changing form to indicate tense and agree with the subject. Modals are used to express the following:

FUNCTION	PRESENT/FUTURE	PAST
Permission	*may, might, can, could* *May* I come at five o'clock?	*might, could* My instructor said I *could* hand in my paper late.
Polite request	*would, could* *Would* you please open the door?	

FUNCTION	PRESENT/FUTURE	PAST
Ability	*can, am/is/are able to* I *can (am able to)* take one piece of luggage.	*could, was/were able to* I *could (was able to)* take only one piece of luggage on the plane yesterday.
Possibility	*may, might* She *may (might)* try to return this afternoon.	*might + have + past participle* His train *may (might) have* arrived already.
Expectation	*should* I have only one more chart to create, so I *should* finish my project today.	*should + have + past participle* The students *should have* finished the project by now.
Necessity	*must (have to)* I *must (have to)* pass this test.	*had to + base form* She *had to* study hard to pass.
Prohibition	*must + not* You *must not* go there.	
Logical deduction	*must (has to)* He *must (has to)* be there by now.	*must + have + past participle* You *must have* left early to make the noon bus.
Intention	*will, shall* I *will (shall)* go today.	*would* I told you I *would* go.
Speculation *(past form implies that something did not happen or is contrary to fact)*	*would, could, might* If she learned her lines, she *could* play the part.	*would (could/might) + have + past participle* If she had learned her lines, she *might have* gotten the part.
Advisability *(past form implies that something did not happen)*	*should (ought to)* You *should (ought to)* water the plant every day.	*should + have + past participle* You *should have* listened to the directions more carefully.
Habitual past action		*would (used to) + base form* When I was younger, I *would* ride my bike to school every day.

Nouns name people (*Shakespeare, actors, Englishman*), places (*Manhattan, city, island*), things (*Kleenex, handkerchief, sneeze, cats*), and ideas (*Marxism, justice, democracy, clarity*).

▶   **Shakespeare** lived in *England* and wrote *plays* about the human *condition*.

1. Proper and common nouns

Proper nouns name specific people, places, and things and are always capitalized: *Aretha Franklin, Hinduism, Albany, Microsoft*. All other nouns are **common nouns:** *singer, religion, capital, corporation*.

2. Count and noncount nouns

A common noun that refers to something specific that can be counted is a **count noun.** Count nouns can be singular or plural, like *orange* or *suggestion* (*four oranges, several suggestions*). **Noncount nouns** are nonspecific; these common nouns refer to categories of people, places, or things and cannot be counted. They do not have a plural form. (*The orange juice is delicious. His advice was useful.*)

Count Nouns		Noncount Nouns	
cars	tools	transportation	equipment
computers	machines	Internet	machinery
facts	suggestions	information	advice
clouds	earrings	rain	jewelry
stars		sunshine	

---

tip FOR MULTILINGUAL WRITERS: Using quantifiers with count and noncount nouns

Consult an ESL dictionary if you have trouble determining whether a word is a count or noncount noun. If a word is a noncount noun, it will not have a plural form.

> *Note:* Many nouns can be either count or noncount depending on the context in which they appear.
>
> ▶ **Baseball** [the game: noncount] **is never played with two baseballs** [the object: count] **at the same time.**

Count and noncount nouns are often preceded by **quantifiers,** words that tell how much or how many. Quantifiers are a type of determiner. *(See pp. 598–99 for a discussion of determiners.)* Following is a list of some quantifiers for count nouns and for noncount nouns, as well as a few quantifiers that can be used with both:

- **With count nouns only:** *several, many, a couple of, a number of, a few, few, each, every*
- **With noncount nouns only:** *a great deal of, much, not much, little, a little, less,* a word that indicates a unit *(a bag of sugar)*
- **With either count or noncount nouns:** *all, any, some, a lot of, no, enough, more*

> *Note:* The quantifiers *a few* and *few* for count nouns and *a little* and *little* for noncount nouns all indicate a small quantity. In contrast to *a few* and *a little,* however, *few* and *little* have the negative connotation of *hardly any.*
>
> ▶ **The problems are difficult, and we have few options for solving them.** [The outlook for solving the problems is gloomy.]
>
> ▶ **The problems are difficult, but we have a few options for solving them.** [The outlook for solving the problems is hopeful.]

—tip **FOR MULTILINGUAL WRITERS:** *(continued)*

▶ **We have little time to find a campsite before sunset.** [The campers might spend the night in the open by the side of the trail.]

▶ **We have a little time to find a campsite before sunset.** [The campers will probably find a place to pitch a tent before dark.]

(For help using articles with count and noncount nouns, see the section on pp. 598–99.)

3. Concrete and abstract nouns

Nouns that name things that can be perceived by the senses are called **concrete nouns**: *boy, wind, book, song.* **Abstract nouns** name qualities and concepts that do not have physical properties: *charity, patience, beauty, hope. (For more on using concrete and abstract nouns, see Tab 9: Editing for Clarity, pp. 470–71.)*

4. Singular and plural nouns

Most nouns name things that can be counted and are singular or plural. Singular nouns typically become plural by adding *-s* or *-es: boy/boys, ocean/oceans, church/churches, agency/agencies.* Some have irregular plurals, such as *man/men, child/children,* and *tooth/ teeth.* Noncount nouns like *intelligence* and *electricity* do not form plurals.

5. Collective nouns

Collective nouns such as *team, family, herd,* and *orchestra* are treated as singular. They are not noncount nouns, however, because collective nouns can be counted and can be made plural: *teams, families. (Also see Tab 10: Editing for Grammar Conventions, pp. 502 and 517.)*

6. Possessive nouns

When nouns are used in the **possessive case** to indicate ownership, they change their form. To form the possessive case, singular nouns add an apostrophe plus *s ('s)*, whereas plural nouns ending in *-s* just add an apostrophe *('). (Also see Tab 11: Editing for Correctness, pp. 553–56.)*

SINGULAR	insect	insect's sting
PLURAL	neighbors	neighbors' car

7. Determiners used with nouns

Determiners precede and specify nouns: *a* desk, *five* books. They include articles *(a, an, the)*, possessives *(my, neighbors')*, demonstrative pronouns used as adjectives *(this, that, these, those)*, and numbers as well as quantifiers *(see pp. 596–97)*. A singular count noun must have a determiner.

---

tip FOR MULTILINGUAL WRITERS: *Using articles* (a, an, the) *appropriately*

Articles in English express three basic meanings: indefinite (indicating nonspecific reference), definite (indicating specific reference), and generic (indicating reference to a general category).

Indefinite and definite meaning

A noun has an indefinite meaning, or a nonspecific reference, when it is first mentioned. To express an indefinite meaning with count nouns, use the **indefinite article** (*a* before consonant sound, *an* before vowel sound) for singular forms and no article for plural forms.

▶   I bought *a* new computer.

▶   I sold *an* old computer.

▶   I bought new computers.

> **Note:** Unless they are qualified (e.g., a knowledge of science), noncount nouns *never* take the indefinite article.
>
> *Knowledge*
> ▶   ~~A knowledge~~ is a valuable commodity.

To express a definite meaning or a specific reference, use the **definite article** *(the)* with both noncount nouns and singular and plural count nouns. A noun has a definite meaning or a specific reference in a variety of situations:

- **When the noun identifies something previously mentioned.**

  I was driving along Main Street when *a* car [nonspecific reference] pulled up behind me. *The* car [specific reference to the previously mentioned car] swerved into the left lane and sped out of sight.

- **When the noun identifies something familiar or known from the context.**

  We could not play today because *the* soccer field was wet.

- **When the noun identifies a unique subject.**

  The moon will be full tonight.

—tip FOR MULTILINGUAL WRITERS: *(continued)*

- **When the noun is modified by a superlative adjective.**

  We adopted *the* most economical strategy.

- **When information in modifying phrases and clauses makes the noun definite.**

  The goal *of this discussion* is to explain article use.

Generic meaning

A noun is used generically when it is meant to represent all the individuals in the category it names. Singular count nouns used generically can take either an indefinite article or a definite article depending on the context.

▶ *A student* **can use the Internet to research** *a topic* **efficiently.**

▶ *The university* **is an institution with roots in ancient times.**

Noncount nouns and plural count nouns used generically take no article.

▶ *Television* **may be harmful to young children.**

▶ *Psychologists* **believe that** *children* **should reduce the amount of time they spend watching television.**

Articles and proper nouns

Most proper nouns are not used with articles.

▶ ~~The~~ **Arizona is a dry state.**

Some proper nouns, however, do take the definite article.

▶ *The* **Civil War was a watershed event in American history.**

Some other exceptions are the names of structures *(the White House)*, names that include the word of *(the Fourth of July)*, plural proper nouns *(the United States)*, and many countries with names that are two or more words long *(the Dominican Republic)*.

Whenever you encounter an unfamiliar proper noun, determine whether it is used with a definite article. (A dictionary may help you.)

69c   Pronouns

A **pronoun** takes the place of a noun. The noun that the pronoun replaces is called its **antecedent.** Some pronouns function as adjectives. *(For more on pronoun-antecedent agreement, see Tab 10: Editing for Grammar Conventions, pp. 515–21.)*

▶ **The** *snow* **fell all day long, and by nightfall** *it* **was three feet deep.**

The box on p. 602 summarizes the different kinds of pronouns.

1. Personal pronouns

The **personal pronouns** *I, me, you, he, his, she, her, it, we, us, they,* and *them* refer to specific people or things and vary in form to indicate person, number, gender, and case. *(For more on pronoun reference and case, see Tab 10: Editing for Grammar Conventions, pp. 519–25.)*

▶   *You* told *us* that *he* gave Jane a lock of *his* hair.

2. Possessive pronouns

Like possessive nouns, **possessive pronouns** indicate ownership. However, unlike possessive nouns, possessive pronouns do not add apostrophes: *my/mine, your/yours, her/hers, his, its, our/ours, their/theirs.*

▶   Brunch is at *her* place this Saturday.

3. Reflexive and intensive pronouns

Pronouns ending in *-self* or *-selves* are either reflexive or intensive. **Reflexive pronouns** refer back to the subject and are necessary for sentence sense.

▶   Many of the women blamed *themselves* for the problem.

Intensive pronouns add emphasis to the nouns or pronouns they follow and are grammatically optional.

▶   President Harding *himself* drank whiskey during Prohibition.

4. Relative pronouns

The **relative pronouns** *who, whom, whose, that,* and *which* relate a dependent clause—a word group containing a subject and verb and a subordinating word—to an antecedent noun or pronoun in the sentence.

dependent clause

▶   In Kipling's story, Dravot is the man *who* would be king.

The form of a relative pronoun varies according to its **case**—the grammatical role it plays in the sentence. *(For more on pronoun case, see Tab 10: Editing for Grammar Conventions, pp. 521–25.)*

5. Demonstrative pronouns

The **demonstrative pronouns** *this, that, these,* and *those* point out nouns and pronouns that come later.

▶   *This* is the book literary critics have been waiting for.

Sometimes these pronouns function as adjectives: <u>*This*</u> *book won the Pulitzer.* Sometimes they are noun equivalents: <u>*This*</u> *is my book.*

6. Interrogative pronouns

Interrogative pronouns such as *who, whatever,* and *whom* are used to ask questions.

▶   *Whatever* **happened to you?**

The form of the interrogative pronouns *who, whom, whoever,* and *whomever* indicates the grammatical role they play in a sentence. *(See Tab 10: Editing for Grammar Conventions, p. 525.)*

7. Indefinite pronouns

Indefinite pronouns such as *someone, anybody, nothing,* and *few* refer to a nonspecific person or thing and do not change form to indicate person, number, or gender.

▶   *Anybody* **who cares enough to come and help may take** *some* **home.**

Most indefinite pronouns are always singular *(anybody, everyone).* Some are always plural *(many, few),* and a handful can be singular or plural *(any, most). (See Tab 10, pp. 503–4 and 516–17.)*

8. Reciprocal pronouns

Reciprocal pronouns such as *each other* and *one another* refer to the separate parts of their plural antecedent.

▶   **My sister and I are close because we live near** *each other.*

69d   Adjectives

Adjectives modify nouns and pronouns by answering questions like *Which one? What kind? How many? What size? What color? What condition?* and *Whose?* They can describe, enumerate, identify, define, and limit *(one person, that person).* When articles *(a, an, the)* identify nouns, they function as adjectives.

Sometimes proper nouns are treated as adjectives; the proper adjectives that result are capitalized: *Britain/British.* Pronouns can also function as adjectives *(his green car),* and adjectives often have forms that allow you to make comparisons *(great, greater, greatest).*

▶   **The** *decisive* **and** *diligent* **king regularly attended meetings of the council.** [What kind of king?]

▶   *These four artistic* **qualities affect how an advertisement is received.** [Which, how many, what kind of qualities?]

▶   *My little blue* **Volkswagen died** *one icy winter morning.* [Whose, what size, what color car? Which, what kind of morning?]

Like all modifiers, adjectives should be as close as possible to the words they modify. *(See Tab 9: Editing for Clarity, pp. 453–58.)* Most

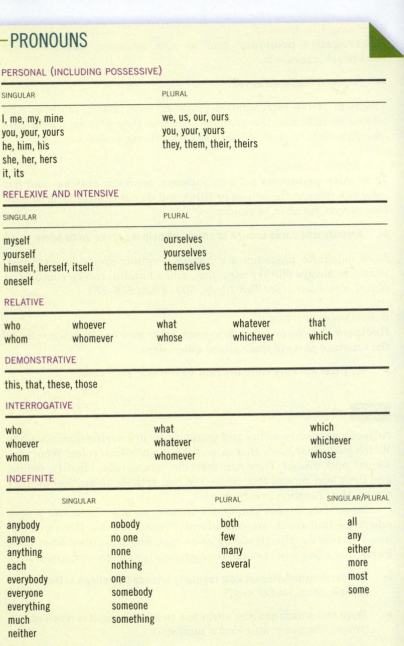

PRONOUNS

PERSONAL (INCLUDING POSSESSIVE)

SINGULAR	PLURAL
I, me, my, mine	we, us, our, ours
you, your, yours	you, your, yours
he, him, his	they, them, their, theirs
she, her, hers	
it, its	

REFLEXIVE AND INTENSIVE

SINGULAR	PLURAL
myself	ourselves
yourself	yourselves
himself, herself, itself	themselves
oneself	

RELATIVE

who	whoever	what	whatever	that
whom	whomever	whose	whichever	which

DEMONSTRATIVE

this, that, these, those

INTERROGATIVE

who	what	which
whoever	whatever	whichever
whom	whomever	whose

INDEFINITE

SINGULAR		PLURAL	SINGULAR/PLURAL
anybody	nobody	both	all
anyone	no one	few	any
anything	none	many	either
each	nothing	several	more
everybody	one		most
everyone	somebody		some
everything	someone		
much	something		
neither			

RECIPROCAL

each other, any other, one another

often, adjectives appear before the noun they modify, but **descriptive adjectives**—adjectives that designate qualities or attributes—may come before or after the noun or pronoun they modify for stylistic reasons. Adjectives that describe the subject and follow linking verbs (*be, am, is, are, was, being, been, appear, become, feel, grow, look, make, prove, taste*) are called **subject complements.**

BEFORE SUBJECT

The *sick* and *destitute* poet no longer believed that love would save him.

AFTER SUBJECT

The poet, *sick* and *destitute,* no longer believed that love would save him.

AFTER LINKING VERB

No longer believing that love would save him, the poet was *sick* and *destitute.*

---

tip FOR MULTILINGUAL WRITERS:
Using adjectives correctly

English adjectives do not change form to agree with the number and gender of the nouns they modify.

▶ Juan is an *attentive* father. Alyssa is an *attentive* mother. They are *attentive* parents.

As noted above, though adjectives usually come before a noun, they can also occur after a linking verb: *The food at the restaurant was* delicious. The position of an adjective can affect its meaning, however. The phrase *my old friend,* for example, can refer to a long friendship (*a friend I have known for a long time*) or an elderly friend (*my friend who is eighty years old*). In the sentence, *My friend is old,* in contrast, *old* has only one possible meaning—elderly.

Adjective order

When two or more adjectives modify a noun cumulatively, they follow a sequence—determined by their meaning—that is particular to English logic:

1. Determiner/article: *the, his, my, that, some*
2. Adjectives that express subjective evaluation: *cozy, intelligent, outrageous, elegant, original*
3. Adjectives of size and shape: *big, small, huge, tiny, tall, short, narrow, thick, round, square*
4. Adjectives expressing age: *old, young, new*
5. Adjectives of color: *yellow, green, pale*

(continued)

─tip **FOR MULTILINGUAL WRITERS:** *(continued)*

6. Adjectives of origin and type: *African, Czech, Gothic*
7. Adjectives of material: *brick, plastic, glass, stone*
8. Nouns used as adjectives: *dinner [menu], computer [keyboard]*
9. Noun modified

Here are some examples.

▶ **the small red brick cottage**

▶ **the tall African statues**

▶ **its striking arched Gothic stained-glass window**

Present and past participles used as adjectives
Both the present and past participle forms of verbs can function as adjectives. To use them properly, keep the following in mind:

• Present participle adjectives usually modify nouns that are the agent of an action.

• Past participle adjectives usually modify nouns that are the recipient of an action.

▶ **This problem is *confusing*.**

The present participle *confusing* modifies *problem,* which is the agent, or cause, of the confusion.

▶ **The students are *confused* by the problem.**

The past participle *confused* modifies *students,* who are the recipients of the confusion the problem is causing.

The following are some other present and past participle pairs that often cause problems:

amazing/amazed	frightening/frightened
annoying/annoyed	interesting/interested
boring/bored	satisfying/satisfied
depressing/depressed	shocking/shocked
embarrassing/embarrassed	surprising/surprised
exciting/excited	tiring/tired
fascinating/fascinated	concerned/concerning

69e Adverbs

Adverbs often end in *-ly* (*beautifully, gracefully, quietly*) and usually answer such questions as *When? Where? How? How often? How much? To what degree?* and *Why?*

▶ **The authenticity of the document is *hotly* contested.** [How is it contested?]

Adverbs modify verbs, other adverbs, and adjectives. Like adjectives, adverbs can be used to compare *(less, lesser, least)*. In addition to modifying individual words, they can be used to modify whole clauses. Adverbs can be placed at the beginning or end of a sentence or before the verb they modify, but they should not be placed between the verb and its direct object. Generally, they should appear as close as possible to the words they modify.

▶   **The water was *brilliant* blue and *icy* cold.** [The adverbs intensify the adjectives *blue* and *cold*.]

▶   **Dickens mixed humor and pathos *better* than any other English writer after Shakespeare.** [The adverb compares Dickens with other writers.]

▶   ***Consequently,* he is still read by millions.**

Consequently is a conjunctive adverb that modifies the independent clause that follows it and shows how the sentence is related to the preceding sentence. *(For more on conjunctive adverbs, see the material on conjunctions, p. 610.)*

   No, not, and *never* are among the most common adverbs. *Never* should not appear at the end of a sentence.

   It takes only one negator *(no/not/never)* to change the meaning of a sentence from positive to negative. In fact, when two negatives are used together, they cancel each other.

▶   **They don't have ~~no~~ ^{any} reason to go there.**

69f   Prepositions and prepositional phrases

Prepositions *(on, in, at, by)* usually appear as part of a **prepositional phrase.** Their main function is to allow the noun or pronoun in the phrase to modify another word in the sentence. Prepositional phrases always begin with a preposition and end with a noun,

---

—tip FOR MULTILINGUAL WRITERS: Putting adverbs in the correct place

Although adverbs can appear in almost any position within a sentence, they should not separate a verb from its direct object.

▶   **Juan found ^{quickly} ~~quickly~~ his cat.**

The negative word *not* usually precedes the main verb and follows the first helping verb in a verb phrase.

▶   **I have been ^{not} ~~not~~ sick lately.**

pronoun, or other word group that functions as the **object of the preposition** (in *time,* on the *table*).

A preposition can be one word *(about, despite, on)* or a word group *(according to, as well as, in spite of).* Place prepositional phrases as close as possible to the words they modify. Adjectival prepositional phrases usually appear right after the noun or pronoun they modify and answer questions like *Which one?* and *What kind of?* Adverbial phrases can appear anywhere in a sentence and answer questions like *When? Where? How?* and *Why?*

AS ADJECTIVE	Many species *of birds* nest there.
AS ADVERB	The younger children stared *out the window.*

Every language uses prepositions idiomatically in ways that do not match their literal meaning. In English, prepositions combine with other words in such a variety of ways that the combinations can be learned only with repetition and over time. For example, you would *arrive in* a city or country *(I arrived in Paris)* but *arrive at* an event at a specific location *(I arrived at the museum at ten o'clock). (See* Connect *for a list of these combinations and their meanings.)*

1. Idiomatic uses of prepositions indicating time and location

The prepositions that indicate time and location are often the most idiosyncratic in a language. Here are some common ways in which the prepositions *at, by, in,* and *on* are used.

TIME

AT	The wedding ceremony starts *at two o'clock.* [a specific clock time]
BY	Our honeymoon plans should be ready *by next week.* [a particular time]
IN	The reception will start *in the evening.* [a portion of the day]
ON	The wedding will take place *on May 1.* The rehearsal is *on Tuesday.* [a particular date or day of the week]

LOCATION

AT	I will meet you *at the zoo.* [a particular place]
	You need to turn right *at the light.* [a corner or an intersection]
	We took a seat *at the table.* [near a piece of furniture]
BY	Meet me *by the fountain.* [a familiar place]
IN	Park your car *in the parking lot* and give the money to the attendant *in the booth.* [a space of some kind or inside a structure]
	I enjoyed the bratwurst *in Chicago.* [a city, state, or other geographic location]
	I found that article *in this book.* [a print medium]

PREPOSITIONS AND COMPOUND PREPOSITIONS

about	behind	in addition to	through
above	below	in case of	to
according to	beside	including	toward
across	between	in front of	under
after	beyond	in place of	underneath
against	by	in regard to	until
along	by means of	inside	up
along with	by way of	instead of	upon
among	down	into	up to
apart from	during	like	via
as	except	near	with
as to	except for	of	within
as well as	excluding	on	without
at	following	on account of	with reference to
because of	from	over	with respect to
before	in	since	

ON   An excellent restaurant is located *on Mulberry Street.* [a street, avenue, or other thoroughfare (not an exact address)]

I spilled milk *on the floor.* [a surface]

I watched the report *on television.* [an electronic medium]

2. Prepositions plus gerunds *(-ing)*

A gerund is the *-ing* form of a verb acting as a noun. A gerund can occur after a preposition *(thanks for coming)*, but when the preposition is *to,* be careful not to confuse it with the infinitive form of a verb. If you can replace the verbal with a noun, use the gerund.

►   I look forward to ~~win~~ at Jeopardy.
    _{winning}

3. Using direct objects with two-word verbs

A two-word verb, or *verb phrasal,* is a combination of a verb and a preposition that has a meaning different from the meaning of the verb alone. Here is a list of common verb phrasals; an asterisk (*) indicates a separable particle (preposition):

break down: stop functioning	**give up:* surrender; stop work on
*call off: cancel	**leave out:* omit
*fill out: complete	*look into:* research
*find out: discover	**look up:* check a fact
get over: recover	*turn down:* reject

If a two-word verb has a direct object, the preposition (particle) may be either separable *(I filled the form out)* or inseparable *(I got over the shock).* If the verb is separable, the direct object can also follow the preposition if it is a noun *(I filled out the form).* If the direct object is a pronoun, however, it must appear between the verb and preposition.

► I filled out ~~it.~~ *it*

69g Conjunctions

Conjunctions join words, phrases, or clauses and indicate their relation to each other.

1. Coordinating conjunctions

The common **coordinating conjunctions** (or **coordinators**) are *and, but, or, for, nor, yet,* and *so.* Coordinating conjunctions join elements of equal weight or function.

► She was strong *and* healthy.

► The war was short *but* devastating.

► They must have been tired, *for* they had been climbing all day long.

2. Correlative conjunctions

Correlative conjunctions also link sentence elements of equal value, but they always come in pairs: *both . . . and, either . . . or, neither . . . nor, not only . . . but also,* and *whether . . . or.*

► *Neither* the doctor *nor* the police believe his story.

3. Subordinating conjunctions

Common **subordinating conjunctions** (or **subordinators**) link sentence elements that are not of equal importance. They include the following words and phrases:

Subordinating Words

after	once	until
although	since	when
as	that	whenever
because	though	where
before	till	wherever
if	unless	while

Subordinating Phrases

as if	even though	in that
as soon as	even when	rather than
as though	for as much as	sooner than
even after	in order that	so that
even if	in order to	

Because subordinating conjunctions join unequal sentence parts, they are used to introduce dependent, or subordinate, clauses in a sentence.

▶ **The software will not run properly *if* the computer lacks sufficient memory.**

—*tip* FOR MULTILINGUAL WRITERS: Using coordination and subordination appropriately

Do not use both subordination and coordination to combine the same two clauses, even if the subordinating and coordinating words are similar in meaning. Some examples include *although* or *even though* with *but* and *because* with *therefore*.

▶ **Although I came early, ~~but~~ the tickets were already sold out.**

or

▶ **~~Although~~ I came early, but the tickets were already sold out.**

▶ **Because Socrates is human, and humans are mortal, ~~therefore~~ Socrates is mortal.**

or

▶ **~~Because~~ Socrates is human, and humans are mortal/. therefore. Socrates is mortal.**

When you use a coordinating conjunction *(and, but, or, for, nor, yet, so)*, make sure you use the conjunction that expresses the relationship between the two clauses that you want to show.

but
▶ **My daughter's school is close to my house, ~~and~~ my office is far away.**

In the revised version, *but* shows the contrast the writer is describing.

When you use a subordinating conjunction, make sure you attach it to the clause that you want to subordinate, not to the main idea. For example, if the main point is that commuting to work takes too much time, then the following sentence is unclear.

| MAIN POINT OBSCURED | Although commuting to work takes two hours out of every day, I use the time to catch up on my reading. |
| MAIN POINT CLEAR | Commuting to work takes two hours out of every day, although I use the time to catch up on my reading. |

(For help in punctuating sentences with conjunctions, see Tab 11: Editing for Correctness, pp. 538 and 547.)

4. Conjunctive adverbs

Conjunctive adverbs indicate the relation between two clauses, but unlike conjunctions *(and, but),* they are not grammatically strong enough on their own to hold the clauses together. A period or semicolon is also needed.

▶ Swimming is an excellent exercise for the heart and muscles; *however,* swimming does not help a person control weight as well as jogging does.

Common Conjunctive Adverbs

accordingly	hence	now
also	however	otherwise
as a result	indeed	similarly
besides	instead	specifically
certainly	likewise	still
consequently	meanwhile	subsequently
finally	moreover	then
furthermore	nevertheless	therefore

69h Interjections

Interjections are forceful expressions that often occur alone (as in the first example following). They are rarely used in academic writing except in quotations of dialogue.

▶ *"Wow!"* Davis said. "Are you telling me that there's a former presidential adviser who hasn't written a book?"

▶ Tell-all books are, *alas,* the biggest sellers.

CHAPTER 70

Parts of Sentences

Every complete sentence contains at least one **subject** (a noun and its modifiers) and one **predicate** (a verb and its objects, complements, and modifiers) that fit together to make a statement, ask a question, or give a command.

       subject   *predicate*
▶ The *children solved* the puzzle.

70a Subjects

The **simple subject** is the word or words that name the topic of the sentence; it is always a noun or pronoun. To find the subject, ask who or what the sentence is about. The **complete subject** is the simple subject plus its modifiers.

─tip **FOR MULTILINGUAL WRITERS:** Putting sentence parts in the correct order for English

In some languages (such as Spanish), it is acceptable to omit subjects. In others (such as Arabic), it is acceptable to omit certain kinds of verbs. Other languages (such as Japanese) place verbs last, and still others (such as Hebrew) allow verbs to precede the subject. English has a distinct order for sentence parts that most sentences follow.

MODIFIERS + SUBJECT → VERB + OBJECTS, COMPLEMENTS, MODIFIERS

▶   *mod   subj   verb   mod   obj   obj comp*
   The playful kitten batted the crystal glasses on the shelf.

Changing a **direct quotation** (someone else's exact words) to an **indirect quotation** (a report on what the person said or wrote) often requires changing many sentence elements. When the quotation is a declarative sentence, however, the subject-before-verb word order does not change.

DIRECT QUOTATION	The instructor said, "You have only one more week to finish your papers."
INDIRECT QUOTATION	The instructor told the students that they had only one more week to finish their papers.

> **Note:** In the direct quotation, the verb *have* is in the present tense, but in the indirect quotation it changes to the past tense *(had)*.

Changing a direct question to an indirect question, however, does require a word-order change—from the verb-subject pattern of a question to the subject-verb pattern of a declarative sentence.

DIRECT QUESTION	The instructor always asks, "Are you ready to begin?"
INDIRECT QUESTION	The instructor always asks [us] if we are ready to begin.

In an indirect quotation of a command, a pronoun or noun takes the place of the command's omitted subject, *you,* and is followed by the infinitive *(to)* form of the verb.

DIRECT QUOTATION: COMMAND	The instructor always says "*[you]* Write down the assignment before you leave."
INDIRECT QUOTATION: COMMAND	The instructor always tells us to write down the assignment before we leave.

In indirectly quoted negative imperatives, the word *not* comes before the infinitive.

DIRECT	The instructor said, "Do not forget your homework."
INDIRECT	The instructor reminded us not to forget our homework.

simple subject

▶ Did *Sir Walter Raleigh* give Queen Elizabeth I complete obedience?

[Who gave the queen obedience?]

complete subject

simple subject

▶ *Three six-year-old children* solved the puzzle in less than five minutes.

[Who solved the puzzle?]

A **compound subject** contains two or more simple subjects connected with a conjunction such as *and, but, or,* or *neither . . . nor.*

compound

simple   *simple*

▶ *Original thinking* and *bold design* characterize her work.

In **imperative sentences,** which give directions or commands, the subject *you* is usually implied, not stated. A helping verb is needed to transform an imperative sentence into a question.

---

tip FOR MULTILINGUAL WRITERS: *Including only one subject or* there *or* it *in the subject position*

All English sentences and clauses except commands require an explicitly stated subject.

                                                            She said

▶ The teacher told us to review sentence structure. ~~Said~~ we would have a
                                                            ^

  quiz on it next class.

> **Note:** In commands, or imperative sentences, the subject, which is always *you,* is omitted.
>
> ▶ [*You*] Read the instructions before using this machine.

Unlike in some other languages, however, a pronoun cannot duplicate the subject.

▶ The teacher ~~she~~ told us to review sentence structure.

If the subject follows the verb, then the expletive *there* or *it* is needed in the subject position.

There is

▶ ~~Is~~ a new independent radio station in our city.
   ^

—*tip* FOR MULTILINGUAL WRITERS: *(continued)*

There indicates existence or locality. The verb *is* agrees with the subject *(radio station)*, which follows the verb.

▶   It is
   ~~Is~~ hard to find doctors who are willing to move to rural areas.
   ^

> **Note:** The pronoun *it* can also be the subject of a sentence about weather or environmental conditions *(It is cold in this house)*, time *(It is three o'clock)*, or distance *(It is five miles to the next filling station)*. *There* is an expletive or adverb and cannot be used as a subject.

▶   [*You*] Keep this advice in mind.

▶   *Would you* keep this advice in mind?

In sentences beginning with *there* or *here* followed by some form of *be,* the subject comes after the verb.

▶   *simple subject*
   Here are the *remnants* of an infamous empire.

In questions, the subject may precede the verb (*Who* will go?), follow the verb (*Are you* very busy?), or appear between the helping verb and main verb (Will *you* go?).

70b   Verbs and their objects or complements

In a sentence, the **predicate** says something about the subject. The verb constitutes the **simple predicate.** The verb plus its object or complement make up the **complete predicate.**

Verb functions in sentences

Based on how they function in sentences, verbs are linking, transitive, or intransitive. The kind of verb determines what elements the complete predicate must include and therefore determines the correct order of sentence parts. Most meaningful English sentences use one of five basic sentence patterns:

- **SUBJECT + LINKING VERB + SUBJECT COMPLEMENT**
  New Yorkers are busy people.
- **SUBJECT + TRANSITIVE VERB + DIRECT OBJECT**
  The police officer caught the jaywalker.

─ tip **FOR MULTILINGUAL WRITERS:** Including a complete verb

Verb structure, as well as where the verb is placed within a sentence, varies dramatically across languages, but in English each sentence needs to include at least one complete verb. *(See Chapter 69, pp. 590–95.)* The verb cannot be an infinitive—the *to* form of the verb—or an *-ing* form without a helping verb.

▶   The caterer ~~to bring~~ dinner.
       is bringing

▶   Children running in the park.
      are

In some languages, linking verbs (verbs like *be, seem, look, sound, feel, appear,* and *remain*) may sometimes be omitted, but not in English.

▶   They happy.
    look

- **SUBJECT + TRANSITIVE VERB + INDIRECT OBJECT + DIRECT OBJECT**
  The officer gave the jaywalker a ticket.
- **SUBJECT + TRANSITIVE VERB + DIRECT OBJECT + OBJECT COMPLEMENT**
  The ticket made the jaywalker unhappy.
- **SUBJECT + INTRANSITIVE VERB**
  She sighed.

Linking verbs and subject complement   A **linking verb** joins a subject to information about the subject that follows the verb. That information is called the **subject complement.** The subject complement may be a noun, a pronoun, or an adjective.

      subj   *lv*   *comp*
▶   Ann Yearsley was *a police officer.*

The most frequently used linking verb is the *be* verb *(is, are, was, were),* but verbs such as *seem, look, appear, feel, become, smell, sound,* and *taste* can also function as links between a sentence's subject and its complement.

      subj   *lv*   *comp*
▶   That new hairstyle *looks* beautiful.

Transitive verbs and direct objects   A **transitive verb** identifies an action that the subject performs or does to somebody or something else—the receiver of the action, or **direct object.** To complete its meaning, a transitive verb needs a direct object, usually a noun, pronoun, or word group that acts like a noun or pronoun.

NOUN	I threw *the ball*.
PRONOUN	I threw *it* over a fence.
WORD GROUP	I put *what I needed* into my backpack.

Most often, the subject is doing the action, the direct object is being acted on, and the transitive verb is in the **active voice.**

ACTIVE *Parents* sometimes *consider* their *children* unreasonable.

If the verb in a sentence is transitive, it can be in the **passive voice.** In the following revised sentence, the direct object *(children)* has become the subject; the original subject *(parents)* is introduced with the preposition *by* and is now part of a prepositional phrase.

PASSIVE Children are considered unreasonable by their parents.

Transitive verbs, indirect objects, and direct objects **Indirect objects** name to whom an action was done or for whom it was completed and are most commonly used with verbs such as *give, ask, tell, sing,* and *write.*

subj   v   ind obj   dir obj

► **Coleridge wrote *Sara* a heartrending letter.**

Note that indirect objects appear after the verb but before the direct object.

Transitive verbs, direct objects, and object complements In addition to a direct object and an indirect object, a transitive verb can take another element in its predicate: an **object complement.** An object complement describes or renames the direct object it follows.

dir obj   obj comp

► **His investment in a plantation made Johnson *a rich man*.**

—tip FOR MULTILINGUAL WRITERS: Including only one direct object

In English, a transitive verb must take an explicit direct object. For example, *Take it!* is a complete sentence but *Take!* is not, even if *it* is clearly implied. Be careful not to repeat the object, especially if the object includes a relative adverb *(where, when, how)* or a relative pronoun *(which, who, what),* even if the relative pronoun does not appear in the sentence but is only implied.

► **Our dog guards the house *where* we live ~~there~~.**

Intransitive verbs   An **intransitive verb** describes an action by a subject that is not done directly to anything or anyone else. Therefore, an intransitive verb cannot take an object or a complement. However, adverbs and adverb phrases often appear in predicates built around intransitive verbs. In the sentence that follows, the complete predicate is in italics and the intransitive verb is underlined.

► **As a recruit, I *complied* with the order mandating short hair.**

Some verbs, such as *cooperate, assent, disappear,* and *insist,* are always intransitive. Others, such as *increase, grow, roll,* and *work,* can be either transitive or intransitive.

TRANSITIVE   I *grow* carrots and celery in my victory garden.

INTRANSITIVE   My son *grows* taller every week.

Your dictionary will note if a verb is *v.i.* (intransitive), *v.t.* (transitive), or both.

CHAPTER 71

Phrases and Dependent Clauses

A **phrase** is a group of related words that lacks either a subject or a predicate or both. Phrases function within sentences but not on their own. A **dependent clause** has a subject and a predicate but cannot function as a complete sentence because it begins with a subordinating word.

71a   Noun phrases

A **noun phrase** consists of a noun or noun substitute plus all of its modifiers. Noun phrases can function as a sentence's subject, object, or subject complement.

SUBJECT   *The old, dark, ramshackle house* collapsed.

OBJECT   Greg cooked *an authentic, delicious haggis* for the Robert Burns dinner.

SUBJECT COMPLEMENT   Tom became *an accomplished and well-known cook.*

71b   Verb phrases and verbals

A **verb phrase** is a verb plus its helping verbs. It functions as the predicate in a sentence: *Mary should have photographed me.* **Verbals** are words derived from verbs. They function as nouns, adjectives, or adverbs, not as verbs.

VERBAL AS NOUN	*Crawling* comes before walking.
VERBAL AS ADJECTIVE	Chris tripped over the *crawling* child.
VERBAL AS ADVERB	The child began *to crawl.*

Verbals may take modifiers, objects, and complements to form **verbal phrases.** There are three kinds of verbal phrases: participial, gerund, and infinitive.

1. Participial phrases

A **participial phrase** begins with either a present participle (the *-ing* form of a verb) or a past participle (the *-ed* or *-en* form of a verb). Participial phrases always function as adjectives. They can appear before or after the word they modify.

▶ *Working in groups,* the children solved the problem.

▶ *Insulted by his remark,* Elizabeth refused to dance.

▶ His pitching arm, *broken in two places by the fall,* would never be the same again.

2. Gerund phrases

A **gerund phrase** uses the *-ing* form of the verb, just as some participial phrases do. But gerund phrases always function as nouns, not adjectives.

▶ *Walking one hour a day* will keep you fit.
    [subj]

▶ The instructor praised *my acting in both scenes.*
    [dir obj]

3. Infinitive phrases

An **infinitive phrase** is formed using the infinitive, or *to* form, of a verb: *to be, to do, to live.* It can function as an adverb, an adjective, or a noun and can be the subject, subject or object complement, or direct object in a sentence. In constructions with *make, let,* or *have,* the *to* is omitted.

▶ *To finish his novel* was his greatest ambition.
    [noun/subj]

▶ He made many efforts *to finish his novel* for his publisher.
    [adj/obj comp]

▶ He needed *to finish his novel.*
    [adv/dir obj]

▶ Please let me *finish my novel.*
    [adv/dir obj]

71c Appositive phrases

Appositives rename nouns or pronouns and appear right after the word they rename.

noun   appositive
▶   One researcher, *the widely respected R. S. Smith,* has shown that a child's performance on such tests can be very inconsistent.

71d   Absolute phrases

Absolute phrases modify an entire sentence. They include a noun or pronoun, a participle, and their related modifiers, objects, or complements. They may appear almost anywhere in a sentence.

▶   The sheriff strode into the bar, *his hands hovering over his pistols.*

71e   Dependent clauses

Although **dependent clauses** (also known as **subordinate clauses**) have a subject and predicate, they cannot stand alone as complete sentences. They are introduced by subordinators—either by a subordinating conjunction such as *after, in order to,* or *since (for a more complete listing, see pp. 608–9)* or by a relative pronoun such as *who, which,* or *that (for more, see the box on p. 602).* They function in sentences as adjectives, adverbs, or nouns.

1. Adjective clauses

An **adjective clause** modifies a noun or pronoun. Relative pronouns *(who, whom, whose, which,* or *that)* or relative adverbs *(where, when)* are used to connect adjective clauses to the nouns or pronouns they modify. The relative pronoun usually follows the word that is being modified and also points back to the noun or pronoun. *(For help with punctuating restrictive and nonrestrictive clauses, see Tab 11, pp. 539–40 and 546–47.)*

▶   Odysseus's journey, *which can be traced on modern maps,* has inspired many works of literature.

In adjective clauses, the direct object sometimes comes before rather than after the verb.

dir obj subj   v
▶   The contestant *whom he most wanted to beat* was his father.

2. Adverb clauses

An **adverb clause** modifies a verb, an adjective, or an adverb and answers the same questions adverbs answer: *When? Where? What? Why?* and *How?* Adverb clauses are often introduced by subordinators *(after, when, before, because, although, if, though, whenever, where, wherever).*

▶   *After we had talked for an hour,* he began to get nervous.

▶   He reacted *as if he already knew.*

3. Noun clauses

A **noun clause** is a dependent clause that functions as a noun. In a sentence, a noun clause may serve as the subject, object of a verb or preposition, or complement and is usually introduced by a relative pronoun (*who, which, that*) or a relative adverb (*how, what, where, when, why.*)

SUBJECT	*What he saw* shocked him.
OBJECT	The instructor found out *who had skipped class.*
COMPLEMENT	The book was *where I had left it.*

As in an adjective clause, in a noun clause the direct object or subject complement can come first, violating the typical sentence order.

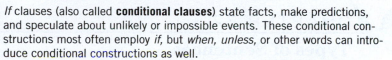

► The doctor wondered *to whom he* should send the bill.

---

tip FOR MULTILINGUAL WRITERS: Understanding the purposes and constructions of *if* clauses

If clauses (also called **conditional clauses**) state facts, make predictions, and speculate about unlikely or impossible events. These conditional constructions most often employ *if,* but *when, unless,* or other words can introduce conditional constructions as well.

- Use the present tense for facts. When the relationship you are describing is usually true, the verbs in both clauses should be in the same tense.

  STATES FACTS

  If people *practice* doing good consistently, they *have* a sense of satisfaction. When Meg *found* a new cause, she always *talked* about it incessantly.

- In a sentence that predicts, use the present tense in the *if* clause. The verb in the independent clause is a modal plus the base form of the verb.

  PREDICTS POSSIBILITIES

  If you *practice* doing good through politics, you *will have* a greater effect on your community.

- If you are speculating about something that is unlikely to happen, use the past tense in the *if* clause and *could, should,* or *would* plus the base verb in the independent clause.

  SPECULATES ON THE UNLIKELY

  If you *were* less over-committed, you *would volunteer* for that good cause.

- Use the past perfect tense in the *if* clause if you are speculating about an event that did not happen. In the independent clause, use *could have, might have,* or *would have* plus the past participle.

(continued)

---

tip FOR MULTILINGUAL WRITERS: *(Continued)*

SPECULATES ON SOMETHING THAT DID NOT HAPPEN

If you *had volunteered* for the Peace Corps when you were young, you *would have been* a different person today.

- Use *were* in the *if* clause and *could, might,* or *would* plus the base form in the main clause if you are speculating about something that could never happen.

SPECULATES ABOUT THE IMPOSSIBLE

If Lincoln *were* alive today, he *would fight* for equal protection under the law.

- Do not use *will* in *if* clauses.

▶   If you ~~will~~ study, you will do well.

CHAPTER 72

Types of Sentences

Classifying by how many clauses they contain and how those clauses are joined, we can categorize sentences into four types: simple, compound, complex, and compound-complex. We can also classify them by purpose: declarative, interrogative, imperative, and exclamatory.

72a   Sentence structures

A clause is a group of related words that includes a subject and a predicate. **Independent clauses** can stand on their own as complete sentences. **Dependent, or subordinate, clauses** cannot stand alone. They function in sentences as adjectives, adverbs, or nouns. The presence of one or both of these two types of clauses, and their relation to each other if there is more than one, determines whether the sentence is simple, compound, complex, or compound-complex.

1. Simple sentences

A simple sentence has only one independent clause. Simple does not necessarily mean short, however. Although a simple sentence does not include any dependent clauses, it may have several embedded phrases, a compound subject, and a compound predicate.

INDEPENDENT CLAUSE

The bloodhound is the oldest known breed of dog.

INDEPENDENT CLAUSE: COMPOUND SUBJ + COMPOUND PRED

Historians, novelists, short-story writers, and playwrights write about characters, design plots, and usually seek the dramatic resolution of a problem.

2. Compound sentences

A compound sentence contains two or more independent clauses but no dependent clause. The independent clauses may be joined by a comma and a coordinating conjunction or by a semicolon with or without a conjunctive adverb.

▶   **The police arrested him for drunk driving, *so* he lost his car.**

▶   **The sun blasted the earth; *therefore,* the plants withered and died.**

3. Complex sentences

A complex sentence contains one independent clause and one or more dependent clauses.

independent clause   *dependent clause*

▶   He consulted the dictionary *because he did not know how to pronounce the word.*

4. Compound-complex sentences

A compound-complex sentence contains two or more coordinated independent clauses and at least one dependent clause (italicized in the example).

▶   **She discovered a new world of international finance, but she worked so hard investing other people's money *that she had no time to invest any of her own.***

72b   Sentence purposes

When you write a sentence, your purpose helps you decide which sentence type to use. If you want to provide information, you usually use a declarative sentence. If you want to ask a question, you usually use an interrogative sentence. To make a request or give an order (a command), you use the imperative. An exclamatory sentence emphasizes a point or expresses strong emotion.

DECLARATIVE	He watches *Seinfeld* reruns.
INTERROGATIVE	Does he watch *Seinfeld* reruns?
IMPERATIVE	Do not watch reruns of *Seinfeld*.
EXCLAMATORY	I'm really looking forward to watching *Seinfeld* reruns with you!

┌─ CHECKLIST Self-Editing for Multilingual Writers

This checklist will help you identify the types of errors that can confuse your readers. Check the rules for those items that you have trouble with, and study them in context.

As you edit a sentence, ask yourself these questions:

☐ Do the subject and verb agree? *(See Chapters 53: Subject-Verb Agreement and 54: Problems with Verbs.)*

☐ Is the form of the verb or verbs correct? *(See Chapters 53: Subject-Verb Agreement and 54: Problems with Verbs, as well as the coverage of verbs in Chapters 69 and 70 and verb phrases in Chapter 71.)*

☐ Is the tense of the verb or verbs appropriate and correctly formed? *(See Chapters 53: Subject-Verb Agreement and 54: Problems with Verbs, as well as the coverage of verbs in Chapter 69.)*

☐ Do all pronouns agree with their referents, and are the referents unambiguous? *(See Chapter 55: Problems with Pronouns, as well as the coverage of pronouns in Chapter 69.)*

☐ Is the word order correct for the sentence type (for example, declarative or interrogative)? Is the word order of any reported speech correct? *(See Chapter 72 for sentence types and Chapter 70 for word order.)*

☐ Is the sentence complete (not a fragment)? Is the sentence a run-on or a comma splice? *(See Chapters 51: Sentence Fragments and 52: Comma Splices and Run-on Sentences.)*

☐ Are articles and quantifiers used correctly? *(See Chapter 69.)*

☐ Is the sentence active or passive? *(See Chapter 46: Active Verbs.)*

☐ Are the words in the sentence well chosen? *(See Chapters 47: Appropriate Language and 48: Exact Language.)*

☐ Is the sentence punctuated correctly? *(See the chapters in Tab 11: Editing for Correctness.)*

13

Further Resources for Learning

To be able to be caught up into the world of thought—that is to be educated.

–Edith Hamilton

Dutch painter Johannes Vermeer captured the spirit of intellectual discovery in his masterpiece *The Geographer,* created c. 1668–1669. The image suggests a man with an active mind and a habit of inquiry, qualities possessed by scholars in every age.

13   Further Resources for Learning

Selected Terms from across the Curriculum

*Here is a sampling of terms that commonly appear in academic **discourse**. Each of the words printed in bold has its own entry. (A more complete list can be found online at mcgrawhillconnect.com)*

alienation Being estranged from one's society or even from oneself. First used in psychology, the term was adapted by Karl Marx (1818–1883) in his writings on the relationship of workers to the products of their labor. In the twentieth century, existentialist philosophers used the word to mean an individual's loss of a sense of self, his or her *authenticity,* amid the pressures of modern society. *See also* **Marxism.**

archetype A model after which other things are patterned. The psychoanalyst Carl Jung (1875–1961) used the term to denote a number of universal symbols—such as the Mother or the universal Creator—that inhabit the collective unconscious, the elements of the unconscious that are common to all people.

Aristotelian Relating to the writings of Aristotle (384–322 B.C.E.), Greek philosopher and author of works on logic, ethics, rhetoric, and the natural sciences. Aristotle established a tradition that values **empirical** observation, **deductive reasoning,** and science. This tradition can be contrasted with **Platonic idealism.**

bell curve In statistics and science, a graph in which the greatest number of results are grouped in the middle. If a math test is graded on a bell curve, for instance, most students will receive C's, whereas only a few will receive A's or F's. Plotted on a graph, the curve will evoke the shape of a bell.

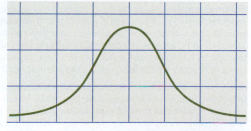

A bell curve.

bourgeois Of or relating to the middle **class.** The term is used in **Marxist** analysis to represent the capitalist class. *Bourgeois* commonly connotes an excessive concern with respectability and material goods.

canon Originally referring to a code of laws established by the church, the canon now typically refers to a collection of books deemed necessary for a complete education. Current debate tends to focus on the exclusion from the canon of works by and about women and people of color. *See also* **multiculturalism.**

case study An intensive investigation and analysis of a person or group; often the object of study is proposed as the model of a certain phenomenon. Originally used

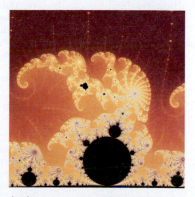

An image generated from the Mandelbrot set, an aspect of chaos theory.

in medicine, the term is now also common in many fields, including education, sociology, composition studies, psychology, and business.

chaos theory A branch of mathematics used to describe highly complex phenomena such as weather or the flow of blood through the body. Chaos theory starts with the recognition that minute changes in a system can have large and unpredictable results.

class *See* **Marxism.**

classical Originally used to describe the artistic and literary conventions of ancient Greece and Rome. *Classical* (or *classicism/neoclassicism*) is also used for periods and products in the sciences, social sciences, philosophy, and music marked by straightforwardly rational models that describe the workings of the universe and human society as logical and ultimately harmonious. *See also* **modernism, postmodernism.**

colonialism A policy by which a nation extends and maintains political and military control over a territory, often reducing it to a state of dependence. *Postcolonial* refers to a state (or a cultural product or even a state of mind) that reflects former colonial occupation. *See also* **imperialism.**

construct (*noun*) Something that is shaped by culture ("constructed") but sometimes assumed to be "natural." For example, sociologists maintain that the idea of gender ("maleness" and "femaleness") is a construct rather than an essential or inborn quality, in contrast to a person's sex.

Darwinism British naturalist Charles Darwin's (1809–1882) theory of the historical evolution of species based on *natural selection.*

deconstruction A method of literary criticism whose best-known theorist, Jacques Derrida (1930–2004), postulated that texts rest on binary oppositions such as *nature/culture, subject/object,* and *spirit/matter* that have been incorrectly assumed to be true; in exposing this fallacy, Derrida revealed the illogic of texts thought to be logical and coherent. In more common usage, to *deconstruct* something is to analyze it intensively, exposing it as (perhaps) something unexpected.

deductive reasoning Reasoning to a conclusion based on a previously held principle. *Inductive reasoning,* on the other hand, is the process of deriving a conclusion based on data. **Empiricism** holds that all knowledge is derived from sense experience by induction, whereas *rationalism* claims that knowledge can be deduced from certain a priori (presumptive) claims.

dialectic In philosophy, history, and the humanities, the use of logical oppositions as a means of arriving at conclusions about ideas or events. *Dialectical reasoning* is most often associated with the philosophies of Georg Hegel (1770–1831) and Karl Marx (1818–1883). According to Hegel, any human idea or *thesis* (for example, the sun circles the earth) naturally gives rise to an opposing idea or *antithesis* (the earth circles the sun), and these ideas resolve into a new idea or *synthesis* (the earth revolves around the sun but in an ellipse).

discipline A field of study with common research methods, approaches to creating knowledge, and written genres: for example, sociology, chemistry, art history. Sometimes, members of multiple disciplines come together to address a complex issue, such as global warming, from different perspectives.

discourse *Discourse* is most often used in English to denote writing and speech. *Discourse* can also refer to habits of expression characteristic of a particular community or to the content of that expression ("The *discourse* of experimental science does not often allow the use of the personal pronoun *I*").

discourse community People who participate in the same field, taking up similar questions, agreeing on what counts as evidence, and composing in the same genres.

ecosystem A principal unit of study in ecology, the science of the relationships between organisms and their environments. All parts of an ecosystem are interdependent, and even small changes to one part can have profound effects on all of the other parts.

empiricism (from the Greek *empierikos,* "experienced") A philosophical trend, developed in large part by the philosophers John Locke (1632–1704) and David Hume (1711–1776), that data derived from experience or the senses are the ultimate source of knowledge, as opposed to reason, tradition, or authority. *Empirical* data are data gained through observation or experiment.

Enlightenment An intellectual movement committed to secular views based on reason that established itself in Europe in the eighteenth century (ca. 1688–1790).

epistemology The study of the nature of knowledge, its foundations and limits.

ethos (Greek for "character, a person's nature or disposition") The spirit or code of behavior peculiar to a specific person or group of people. Ethos is one of Aristotle's three kinds of rhetorical appeals (**ethos-logos-pathos**): in order to argue effectively, a speaker or writer must communicate a credible **persona** and a coherent perspective.

fascism A name for the form of government established by Benito Mussolini (1883–1945) in Italy and Adolf Hitler (1889–1945) in Germany. Arising in response to economic and political upheaval in Europe after World War I, both governments centralized authority under a dictator, exerted strong economic controls, suppressed opposition through censorship and terror, and implemented belligerent nationalist and racist policies.

Mussolini and Hitler.

feminism The principle that women should enjoy equal political, economic, social, and cultural rights and opportunities. Mary Wollstonecraft's *A Vindication of the Rights of Woman* (1792) was a pioneering feminist work. The *suffrage movement,* which demanded that women be granted the right to vote, emerged following the first women's rights convention in Seneca Falls, New York, in 1848, and had achieved its goal in the United States and Europe by the early twentieth century. The *women's movement* that began in the 1960s initiated a new wave of feminism that focused on rectifying political, economic, social, and cultural inequalities between women and men.

Freudian Relating to the theories of Sigmund Freud (1856–1939), the Viennese neurologist who invented psychoanalysis. A Freudian interpretation focuses on the unconscious emotional dynamics that are played out in a particular situation; in the study of literature, a Freudian interpretation focuses on such dynamics as they are represented in the **text.**

game theory (also sometimes called *decision theory*) A mathematical method for analyzing situations of conflict or competition so as to determine a winning strategy. Game theory is useful not only in *true games* such as poker but also in business management, economics, and military strategy.

genre The kind of text a writer composes. For example, movie critics often write reviews, which are one example of a genre. A genre is both a way of writing and of engaging in action.

globalization The process by which communication and transportation technologies have made the world seem more interconnected. In economics, *globalization* refers to the way these advances have made national borders far less relevant in determining markets.

humanism (also *secular humanism*) A movement traditionally associated with Renaissance philosophers who deemphasized the role of religion or God in society while celebrating the achievements of human beings.

hypothesis A statement that can be shown to be true or false either experimentally (in science) or through the use of logic (in other disciplines).

icon In **semiotics,** a sign that looks like what it refers to. A picture of the globe used to signify the earth or a line drawing of a suitcase indicating where to go to get your luggage at an airport are icons.

idealism In philosophy and psychology, the notion that the mind determines ultimate reality, an idea that can be traced to Plato (428–347 B.C.E.).

ideology A set of beliefs about the world (and often how it can be changed) espoused by an individual, group, or organization; a systematized worldview. Capitalism, for example, is an ideology.

imperialism One country's imposition of political and economic rule on other countries. The British annexation of several countries in Africa in the nineteenth century is an example of this brand of imperialism. Today the term has been broadened to include the exportation of dominant cultural products and values. For example, some people in Europe and other parts of the world see the influx of American films into their markets as a form of *cultural imperialism. See also* **colonialism.**

inductive reasoning *See* **deductive reasoning.**

logos (Greek for "word") In Aristotle's system of rhetorical appeals, the topic of the argument, the argument itself, or the argument's logic.

longitudinal A study in which the same group of subjects is examined over a long period of time. A *longitudinal study* could, for example, be conducted to test the rate of obesity over time among a certain group of schoolchildren.

Marxism The economic and political doctrine put forth by Karl Marx (1818–1883) and Friedrich Engels (1820–1895). It centers on the **class** struggle between the proletariat (the working class) and the **bourgeoisie** (capitalists, those who own the *means of production*). Marxism predicts that the working class will wrest the means of production from the bourgeoisie and cede them to the state, which will distribute goods equitably.

materialism In philosophy, the belief that physical matter is all that exists and that so-called higher phenomena—for example, thought, feeling, mind, will—are wholly dependent on and determined by physical processes. Since the **Enlightenment,** almost all scientists have been materialists.

modernism Often used in opposition to classicism or neoclassicism when denoting periods in the sciences, social

Virginia Woolf.

sciences, philosophy, and music, *modernism* as a trend in thought represents a break with the certainties of the past, among them a confidence that everything can be known. *Modern* science has been characterized by highly counterintuitive theories such as **relativity** and **quantum physics.** In literature, the **stream of consciousness** and/or *free association* style of *modernist* writers like Virginia Woolf (1882–1941) and James Joyce (1882–1941) broke decisively with the story-telling conventions of the late-nineteenth-century, or Victorian, novel. Thus, some critics believe that **postmodernism** is really only the development of a trend begun in the modernist era.

multiculturalism The view that many cultures, not just the dominant one, should be given attention in the classroom and in broader society. The debate on multiculturalism is related to the debate on the **canon.**

nature-nurture controversy A debate about whether genetic (*nature*) or environmental (*nurture*) factors have the upper hand in determining human behavior. This debate pervades countless topics studied in the social sciences, among them questions of gender difference, intelligence, poverty, crime, and childhood development.

object/subject In philosophy and psychology, the *subject* does the observing or experiencing, while the *object* is that which is observed or experienced. In **Freudian** and post-Freudian psychology, an *object* is an external person or thing that gratifies an infant and is therefore loved.

objective Pertaining to that which is independent of perception or observation, as opposed to *subjective*, which pertains to that which is determined by perception, observation, or judgment.

ontology Generally, the study of being and human consciousness.

paradigm A theoretical framework that serves as a foundation for a field of study or branch of knowledge. Darwinian evolution, Newtonian physics, and Aristotle's chemistry are all examples of scientific paradigms. *Paradigm shifts* designate the transition from one paradigm to another, usually with a profoundly transformative effect.

pathos (Greek for "suffering, experience, emotion") In Aristotle's system of rhetorical appeals, the feelings evoked in the audience by an argument.

persona (Latin for "mask") An assumed or public identity, as distinct from the *inner self;* a character adopted for a particular purpose; in literature, the voice or character of the speaker.

Platonic Following the teachings of the Greek philosopher Plato (428–347 B.C.E.), Platonic **idealism** is a system that attempts to show a rational relationship between the individual, the state, and the universe, governed by what is good, true, and beautiful. It can be contrasted with the **Aristotelian** tradition, which values empirical observation and scientific reasoning. In common usage, a *platonic relationship* is a close friendship that does not have a sexual component.

pluralism In everyday language, a condition of society in which multiple religions, ethnicities, and subcultures coexist peacefully.

postcolonial *See* **colonialism.**

postmodernism A cultural trend that seeks to expose the artificiality of the **constructs** that defined earlier periods of cultural production while confessing—indeed, in some cases even boasting of—an inability to replace them with an authentic substitute. *See also* **modernism.**

praxis Often used as a substitute for *practice* in ordinary usage, and opposed to **theory.**

qualitative research Research that focuses on observing what people say and do. Qualitative research methods include observation, interviews, surveys, and focus groups. In contrast, *quantitative research* depends on numerical data.

quantitative research *See* **qualitative research.**

quantum physics A theoretical branch of physics that deals with the behavior of atoms and subatomic particles. The work of such pioneers as Max Planck (1858–1947), Niels Bohr (1885–1962), and later Werner Heisenberg (1901–1976) has had a profound impact on the way we understand such things as the relationships between matter and energy. *See also* **relativity.**

relativism The belief that the meaning and value of all things are determined by their *context*—their relationship to other things in that time and place—rather than that things have inherent or absolute meaning or worth. *Moral relativism* is the idea that different people, groups, nations, or cultures have differing ideas about what constitutes good and evil and that those differences must be respected.

Albert Einstein.

relativity In physics, the theory expounded by Albert Einstein (1879–1955), which states that all motion is relative and that energy and matter are convertible.

rhetoric In classical times, the art of public speaking. Currently, the term more broadly encompasses *language* or *speech,* often in a derogatory context (as in "The mayor's speech was so much empty *rhetoric*"), as well as the study of writing and the effective use of language.

rhetorical situation The context for writing, the stance of the author, the audience, and the topic all contribute to the rhetorical situation, also known as the writing situation.

rhetorical triangle Aristotle's description of the context of argument, consisting of **ethos** (the character of the speaker), **logos** (the topic of the argument or the argument itself), and **pathos** (feelings evoked in the audience).

scientific method A process involving observations of phenomena and the conducting of experiments to test ideas suggested by those observations. The development of the scientific method, a specialized form of trial and error, ushered in the scientific revolution of the seventeenth century. Francis Bacon (1561–1626), René Descartes (1596–1650), and especially Galileo Galilei (1564–1642) are most often credited with developing its constituent procedures: (1) choosing a question or problem; (2) developing a **hypothesis;** (3) conducting observations and experiments; (4) examining and interpreting the data; (5) affirming, revising, or rejecting the hypothesis; and (6) deriving further experiments and hypotheses from it.

secular Not having to do with religion or the church; deriving its authority from nonreligious sources. *See also* **humanism.**

semiotics The theory and study of signs and symbols. According to semiotics, meaning is never inherent but is always a product of social conventions, and **culture** can be analyzed as a series of sign systems. *See also* **structuralism.**

Socratic method Repeated questioning to arrive at implicit truths, a teaching method used by the Greek philosopher Socrates (470?–399? B.C.E.), who influenced Plato.

solipsism Philosophical theory that the self is the only thing that can be known and verified and therefore is the only reality.

stream of consciousness A **modernist** literary technique in which the writer renders the moment-by-moment progress of a character's or narrator's thoughts. Among those writers who have used the technique are James Joyce (1882–1941) in *Ulysses,* and Virginia Woolf (1882–1941) in *Mrs. Dalloway.*

structuralism An analytical method, today often subsumed under **semiotics,** that is used in the social sciences, the humanities, and the arts to examine underlying deep structures in a **text** by close investigation of its constituent parts (often termed *signs*). *See also* **semiotics, deconstruction.**

subjective *See* **objective.**

symbiosis In biology, a prolonged association and interdependence of two or more organisms, usually to their mutual benefit.

taxonomy Any set of laws and principles of classification. Originating in biology, taxonomy includes the theory and principles governing the classification of organisms into categories such as species and phyla. Today a literary critic might compose a "taxonomy of literary styles."

text In academic usage, anything undergoing rigorous intellectual examination and analysis. Texts may be oral works such as speeches, visual works such as paintings, everyday objects like toys, and even human behavior. Analysis is often called "reading the text," even if the text is not a written work.

theory A statement devised to explain a collection of facts or observations; also, the systematic organization of such statements. Theory is commonly contrasted with *practice* or **praxis.**

trope A figure of speech. In literary criticism, the term is often used to refer to any technique that recurs in a **text.** Comparing women's faces to flowers is a common trope in Renaissance poetry.

uncertainty principle An important theory in **quantum physics** formulated by German physicist Werner Heisenberg (1901–1976) that places an absolute, theoretical limit on the accuracy of certain pairs of simultaneously recorded measurements. This principle prevents scientists from making absolute predictions of the future state of certain systems. Heisenberg's principle has been applied to philosophy, where it is called the *indeterminacy principle.*

Discipline-Specific Resources

The list that follows will help you get started doing research in specific disciplines. Print sources appear before electronic sources. Remember that Web addresses change frequently, so if you cannot access a site, try using a search engine.

Anthropology
Abstracts in Anthropology
Annual Review of Anthropology
Dictionary of Anthropology
Encyclopedia of World Cultures
American Anthropology Association
    <http://www.aaanet.org>
National Anthropological Archives
    <http://www.nmnh.si.edu/naa/>
Anthropology Resources on the Internet
    <http://www.anthropologie.net>

Art and Architecture
Art Abstracts
Art Index
BHA: Bibliography of the History of Art
Encyclopedia of World Art
McGraw-Hill Dictionary of Art
    Artcyclopedia
    <http://www.artcyclopedia.com>
The Louvre <http://www.louvre.fr/>
The Metropolitan Museum of Art (New
    York) <http://www.metmuseum.org>
Voice of the Shuttle Art History and
    Architecture <http://vos.ucsb.edu/
    index.asp>

Biology
Biological Abstracts
Biological and Agricultural Index
Encyclopedia of the Biological Sciences
Henderson's Dictionary of Biological
    Terms
Zoological Record
Biology Online
    <http://www.biology-online.org/>
Harvard University Biology Links
    <https://www.mcb.harvard.edu/mcb/
    p/library-links/>
National Science Foundation: Biology
    <http://www.nsf.gov/news/overviews/
    biology/index.jsp>

Business
ABI/Inform
Accounting and Tax Index
Business and Industry
Business Periodicals
Encyclopedia of Business Information
    Sources
Newslink Business Newspapers
    <http://newslink.org/biznews.html>

Chemistry
Chemical Abstracts (CASEARCH)
McGraw-Hill Dictionary of Chemistry

Van Nostrand Reinhold Encyclopedia of
    Chemistry
American Chemical Society
    <http://www.chemistry.org>
Sheffield ChemDex
    <http://www.chemdex.org>
WWW Virtual Library: Chemistry
    <http://www.liv.ac.uk/chemistry/
    links/links.html>

Classics
Oxford Classical Dictionary
Princeton Encyclopedia of Classical Sites
Perseus Digital Library
    <http://www.perseus.tufts.edu>

Communications and Journalism
Communication Abstracts International
Encyclopedia of Communications
Journalism Abstracts
Journalism and Mass Communications
Mass Media Bibliography
American Communication Association
    <http://www.americancomm.org>
The Poynter Institute
    <http://www.poynter.org>

Computer Science and Technology
Computer Abstracts
Dictionary of Computing
Encyclopedia of Computer Science
McGraw-Hill Encyclopedia of Science
    and Technology
FOLDOC (Free Online Dictionary of
    Computing) <http://foldoc.org/>
MIT Computer Science and Artificial
    Intelligence Laboratory
    <http://www.csail.mit.edu/>

Cultural Studies, American and Ethnic Studies
Dictionary of American Negro Biography
Encyclopedia of World Cultures
Gale Encyclopedia of Multicultural
    America
Mexican American Biographies
National Museum of the American Indian
    <http://www.nmai.si.edu>
Schomburg Center for Research in
    Black Culture <http://www.nypl.org/
    locations/schomburg>
Smithsonian Center for Folklife and
    Cultural Heritage <http://www
    .folklife.si.edu/>

Economics
EconLit
PAIS: Public Affairs Information Service
Internet Resources for Economists
  <http://www.oswego.edu/~economic/
  econweb.htm>
Resources for Economists on the Internet
  <http://www.rfe.org>

Education
Dictionary of Education
Education Index
Encyclopedia of Educational Research
*International Encyclopedia of
  Education*
Resources in Education
The Educator's Reference Desk
  <http://www.eduref.org>
EdWeb <http://edwebproject.org>
U.S. Department of Education
  <http://www.ed.gov>

Engineering
Applied Science and Technology Index
Engineering Index
*McGraw-Hill Encyclopedia of
  Engineering*
IEEE Spectrum
  <http://www.spectrum.ieee.org>

Environmental Sciences
Dictionary of the Environment
*Encyclopedia of Energy, Technology, and
  the Environment*
Encyclopedia of the Environment
Environment Abstracts
Environment Index
Envirolink <http://envirolink.org>
U.S. Environmental Protection Agency
  <http://www.epa.gov>

Film
Dictionary of Film Terms
The Film Encyclopedia
Film Index International
Film Literature Index
Internet Movie Database
  <http://www.imdb.com>

Geography
Geographical Abstracts
Longman Dictionary of Geography
*Modern Geography: An Encyclopedic
  Survey*
CIA World Factbook <https://www.cia
  .gov/library/publications/the-world-
  factbook/index.html>

Geology
Bibliography and Index of Geology
Challinor's Dictionary of Geology
*The Encyclopedia of Field and General
  Geology*

American Geological Institute
  <http://www.agiweb.org>
U.S. Geological Survey
  <http://www.usgs.gov>

Health and Medicine
*American Medical Association
  Encyclopedia of Medicine*
Cumulated Index Medicus
*Medical and Health Information
  Directory*
Nutrition Abstracts and Reviews
U.S. National Library of Medicine
  <http://www.nlm.nih.gov>
World Health Organization
  <http://www.who.int>

History
America: History and Life
Dictionary of Historical Terms
Encyclopedia of American History
An Encyclopedia of World History
Historical Abstracts
Electronic Documents in History
  <http://www2.tntech.edu/history/
  edocs.html>
History World
  <http://www.historyworld.net/>
NARA Archival Research Catalog
  <http://www.archives.gov/research_
  room/arc/index.html>

Languages, Linguistics, and Rhetoric
Cambridge Encyclopedia of Language
International Encyclopedia of Linguistics
*LLBA: Linguistics and Language
  Behavior Abstracts*
Center for Applied Linguistics
  <http://www.cal.org>
CompPile <http://comppile.org>
SIL International Linguistics
  <http://www.sil.org/linguistics>
Silva Rhetoricoe
  <http://humanities.byu.edu/rhetoric/
  Silva.htm>

Literature
*Concise Oxford Dictionary of Literary
  Terms*
MLA International Bibliography
*The New Princeton Encyclopedia of
  Poetry and Poetics*
Project Gutenberg
  <http://www.gutenberg.org>

Mathematics
American Statistics Index
Facts on File Dictionary of Mathematics
*International Dictionary of Applied
  Mathematics*
Mathematical Reviews (MathSciNet)
American Mathematical Society
  <http://www.ams.org>
Math Forum <http://mathforum.org>

Music
Music Index
New Grove Dictionary of Music and Musicians
New Oxford Companion to Music
New Oxford Dictionary of Music
RILM Abstracts of Musical Literature
All Music <http://allmusic.com>

Philosophy
Dictionary of Philosophy
Philosopher's Index
Routledge Encyclopedia of Philosophy
American Philosophical Association <http://www.apaonline.org>
EpistemeLinks.com <http://www.epistemelinks.com>

Physics
Dictionary of Physics
McGraw-Hill Encyclopedia of Physics
Physics Abstracts
American Institute of Physics <http://aip.org>
American Physical Society <http://www.aps.org>
Physics World <http://physicsworld.com>

Political Science
Almanac of American Politics
Congressional Quarterly Almanac
Encyclopedia of Government and Politics
International Political Science Abstracts
Public Affairs Information Service (PAIS)
Thomas: Legislative Information on the Internet <http://thomas.loc.gov>
United Nations <http://www.un.org>

Psychology
International Dictionary of Psychology
Psychological Abstracts

American Psychological Association <http://www.apa.org>
American Psychological Society <http://www.psychologicalscience.org>
Encyclopedia of Psychology <http://www.psychology.org/>
PsychWeb <http://www.psywww.com>

Religion
ATLA Religion
Dictionary of Bible and Religion
Encyclopedia of Religion
Religion Index
Religions and Scriptures <http://www.wright-house.com/religions>

Sociology
Annual Review of Sociology
Encyclopedia of Social Work
Encyclopedia of Sociology
Sociological Abstracts
American Sociological Association <http://asanet.org>

Theater and Dance
International Encyclopedia of the Dance
McGraw-Hill Encyclopedia of World Drama
The WWW Virtual Library: Theater and Drama <http://vl-theatre.com>

Women's Studies
Women Studies Abstracts
Women's Studies: A Guide to Information Sources
Women's Studies Encyclopedia
Feminist Majority Foundation Online <http://www.feminist.org>
National Women's History Project <http://www.nwhp.org>

Index

Index for Multilingual Writers

Credits

Text / Line Art Credits

Chapter 1: p. 15: Based partly on Robert S. Feldman, *Power Learning*: *Strategies for Success in College and Life*, 2/e Copyright © 2010 The McGraw-Hill Companies. Reprinted with permission.

Chapter 2: Fig. 2.1: From Elaine P. Maimon, et al., *McGraw-Hill Handbook*, 2nd Ed. Copyright © 2010 The McGraw-Hill Companies, Inc. Reproduced with permission by The McGraw-Hill Companies.

Chapter 4: p. 42 Checklist: Checklist from Maimon, Elaine, Peritz., Janice H., Yancey, Kathleen, *The New McGraw-Hill Handbook*. Copyright © 2007 The McGraw-Hill Companies, Inc. **p. 37:** Nat Hentoff, "Misguided Multiculturalism" *The Village Voice*, July 19–25, 2000, pp. 29–30. Copyright © 2000, Village Voice Media. Reprinted with the permission of The Village Voice and Nat Hentoff, staff Writer, Village Voice/author, *The War on the Bill of Rights and the Gathering Resistance* (7 Stories Press).

Chapter 5: p. 56 Bar graph: Richard Schaefer, *Sociology in Modules* Copyright © 2011 The McGraw-Hill Companies. Reprinted with permission. **p. 56 Pie chart:** Richard Schaefer, *Sociology in Modules* Copyright © 2011 The McGraw-Hill Companies. Reprinted with permission. **p. 56 Diagram:** From Clarke & Cornish, "Modeling Offenders' Decisions" in *Crime and Justice*, Vol. 6, Torry & Morris (eds.) p. 169. Copyright © 1985 University of Chicago Press. Used by permission of the publisher, University of Chicago Press. **p. 57 Map:** Brigit Harrison and Jean Harris, *A More Perfect Union* Copyright © 2011 The McGraw-Hill Companies. Reprinted with permission.

Chapter 6: p. 60 text: Quote from: Michalle M. Ducharme, "A Lifetime of Production; like Many Workers, Dad's Skill and Dedication Helped His Firm Flourish in Good and Bad Years" *Newsweek*, September 9, 1996. Copyright © 1996. Reprinted by permission of the author. **Fig. 6.4:** 'William Galle, Business Communication: A Technology Based Approached. Copyright © 2000. Reprinted by permission of the McGraw-Hill Companies, Inc. **p. 62 text:** Robert Reich, "The Future of Work" *Harper's* April, 1989. Copyright © 1989. Reprinted by permission of the author. **Fig. 6.7:** Tom Vanderbilt, "How Biochemistry Is Inspiring Human Innovation" *Smithsonian Magazine*, September 2012. Copyright © 2012. Reprinted with permission. **p. 67 text:** Richard Schaefer, *Sociology in Modules* Copyright © 2011 The McGraw-Hill Companies. Reprinted with permission. **pp. 67–68 text:** Eric Klinenberg, "Heat Wave of 1995" Reprinted by permission of the author. **p. 69 text:** Excerpt from Jonathan Fast, "After Columbine: How Peole Mourn Sudden Death" in *Social Work*, Vol. 48(4) October 2003 Copyright © 2003 National Association of Social Workers, Inc. Reprinted by permission of Oxford University Press on behalf of National Association of Social Workers, Inc. **pp. 69–70 text:** Excerpt from Damian Robinson, "Riding into the Afterlife" *Archaeology*, Volume 57(2) March/April 2004. Copyright © 2004. Reprinted with permission. **p. 70:** Elaine Maimon, "Students Must Focus on Degree Completion" *The Times of Northwest Indiana*, 11/7/10/ Copyright © 2010. http://www.nwitimes.com/news/opinion/gues-commentary/article_b738b4c3-c318-5b9b-bca4-26ed7075968c.html.

Chapter 7: Fig. 7.1: Mathematics: Applications and Connections - Course 2 © 1998. Reprinted by permission of the McGraw-Hill Companies.

Chapter 8: Fig. 8.1: © Copyright 2014 Microsoft Corporation. **pp. 100–03 text:** Maimon, Elaine, Peritz., Janice H., Yancey, Kathleen, The New McGraw-Hill Handbook. Copyright © 2008 Reprinted by permission of the McGraw-Hill Companies. **Fig. 8.4:** Reprinted by permission of Ken Tinnes.

Chapter 9: p. 122 text: Canetto, Silvia Sara and David Lester. "Love and Achievement Motives in Women's and Men's Suicide Notes." *The Journal of Psychology.*

Chapter 10: p. 123 poem: Reprinted by permission of the publishers and Trustees of Amherst College from *The Poems of Emily Dickinson: Variorum Edition,* edited by Ralph W. Franklin, Cambridge, Mass.: The Belknap Press of Harvard University Press. Copyright © 1998 by the President and Fellows of Harvard College. Copyright © 1951, 1955, 1979, 1983 by the President and Fellows of Harvard College.

Chapter 12: pp. 155–56 text: Excerpt from Tina Fey, *Bossypants* © 2013 Regan Arthur/Little Brown co. **p. 156–57 text:** Excerpt from Gloria Ladson-Billings, *The Dreamkeepers: Successful Teachers of African-American Children* Copyright © 2009 John Wiley & Sons, Inc.

Chapter 13: p. 149 Graph: Hinduja, Sameer, and Justin W. Patchin, "Research"; *Cyberbullying Research Center* (www.cyberbullying.us, 2010 Web; 31, May 2010). Copyright 2010. Reprinted by permission.

Chapter 14: Fig. 14.4: Vietnam Women's Memorial, Washington, D.C. Copyright 1993, Vietnam Women's Memorial Foundation, Inc., Glenna Goodacre, Sculptor. **Fig. 14.6:** Courtesy of Kati Blake Yancey, Florida State University.

Chapter 19: Fig. 19.1: Reprinted by permission of Governors State University. **Fig. 19.2:** © EBSCO Information Services. All rights reserved. **Fig. 19.4:** Google and the Google logo are registered trademarks of Google Inc., used with permission. **Fig. 19.5:** Reprinted by permission of Governors State University. **Fig. 19.6:** Reprinted by permission of Governors State University.

Chapter 21: Fig. 21.2: Reprinted by permission of Wolf Park. **Fig. 21.3:** Reprinted by permission of the International society for Professional Trackers.

Chapter 24: Fig. 24.3: Pew Research Center's Project for Excellence in Journalism © 2013.

Chapter 30: p. 334, Fig. 1: Pew Research Center's Project for Excellence in Journalism © 2013.

Start Smart Resource: © ARS Technica/Jacqui Cheng/Conde Nast.

MLA Resource: From *Here Comes Everybody: The Power of Organizing Without Organizations* by Clay Shirky, copyright © 2008 by clay Shirky. Used by permission of The Penguin Press, a division of Penguin Group (USA) LLC; Reprinted by permission University of Chicago Press; Artwork © Hans Haacke/Artist Rights Society (ARS), New York/VG Bild-Kunst, Bonn; Reprinted by permission of EBSCOhost; Reprinted by permission of Columbia Journalism Review (www.cjr.org).

APA Resource: Social Change Everywhere: How to implement online multichannel strategies to spark advocacy, raise money, and engage your community by Kaplan, Allyson, Ward, Amy Sample. Reproduced with permission of Jossey-Bass in the format Republish in a book via Copyright Clearance Center; "Promoting civic engagement to educate institutionally for personal and social responsibility" in SS/New Directions for Student Services by Boyd, K. D. & Brackmann, S. Copyright © Reprinted by permission of John Wiley & Sons, Ltd.; Taylor & Francis, www.tandfonline.

Photo Credits

Tab 1: © iStock Vectors/Getty Images RF; **p. 6:** Library of Congress Prints and Photographs Division [LC-DIG-fsa-8b29516]; **p. 22:** © Manoocher Deghati/AP Images

How to find what you need in *The Writer's Handbook*:

If you know what part you want to look at in *The Writer's Handbook*, then use the **color-coded tabbed dividers** to open to that section.

If you want to know more about what's in a particular chapter or part, then open the back cover of the handbook and consult the **Detailed Contents**.

If you want to look up a very specific word or problem, then use the **Index** on pp. 559–581.

There are more resources at the back of *The Writer's Handbook* that can help you find answers to your questions:

- A handy list of **Common Errors** on the inside back cover flap, which tells you where to find answers to the most common grammar, punctuation, and mechanics questions.

- A **Glossary** with basic grammatical and usage terms, on pp. 547–558.

- A **Revision Guide** of editing and proofreading symbols, on the last page.

D0205106

THE WRITER'S HANDBOOK

SIXTH EDITION

LESTER FAIGLEY
University of Texas at Austin

330 Hudson Street, NY NY 10013

VP & Portfolio Manager: Eric Stano
Development Editor: Anne Stameshkin
Marketing Manager: Nick Bolte
Program Manager: Rachel Harbour
Project Manager: Lois Lombardo, Cenveo®
    Publisher Services

Cover Designer: Pentagram
Cover Illustration: Anuj Shrestha
Manufacturing Buyer: Roy L. Pickering, Jr.
Printer/Binder: LSC Communications
Cover Printer: Phoenix Color

Acknowledgments of third-party content appear on pages 583–584, which constitute an extension of this copyright page.

PEARSON, ALWAYS LEARNING, and Revel are exclusive trademarks in the United States and/or other countries owned by Pearson Education, Inc., or its affiliates.

Unless otherwise indicated herein, any third-party trademarks that may appear in this work are the property of their respective owners and any references to third-party trademarks, logos, or other trade dress are for demonstrative or descriptive purposes only. Such references are not intended to imply any sponsorship, endorsement, authorization, or promotion of Pearson's products by the owners of such marks, or any relationship between the owner and Pearson Education, Inc., or its affiliates, authors, licensees, or distributors.

Library of Congress Cataloging-in-Publication Data

Names: Faigley, Lester, date- author.
Title: The Writer's handbook / Lester Faigley.
Other titles: Brief Penguin handbook
Description: Sixth edition. | Boston : Pearson, [2017] | Includes index. |
  Previously published as: The Brief Penguin Handbook 5e.
Identifiers: LCCN 2016050999 | ISBN 9780134571331 (Student Edition) | ISBN
  0134571339 (Student Edition) | ISBN 9780134573946 (A la Carte) | ISBN
  0134573943 (A la Carte)
Subjects: LCSH: English language--Rhetoric--Handbooks, manuals, etc. |
  English language--Grammar--Handbooks, manuals, etc. | Report
  writing--Handbooks, manuals, etc.
Classification: LCC PE1408 .F243 2017 | DDC 808/.042--dc23
LC record available at https://lccn.loc.gov/2016050999

The Writer's Handbook was previously published under the title *The Brief Penguin Handbook*.

Copyright © 2018, 2015, 2012 by Pearson Education, Inc. All Rights Reserved. Printed in the United States of America. This publication is protected by copyright, and permission should be obtained from the publisher prior to any prohibited reproduction, storage in a retrieval system, or transmission in any form or by any means, electronic, mechanical, photocopying, recording, or otherwise. For information regarding permissions, request forms and the appropriate contacts within the Pearson Education Global Rights & Permissions Department, please visit www.pearsoned.com/permissions/.

1 16

www.pearsonhighered.com

Pearson

Student Edition ISBN 10: 0-13-457133-9
Student Edition ISBN 13: 978-0-13-457133-1
A la Carte ISBN 10: 0-13-457394-3
A la Carte ISBN 13: 978-0-13-457394-6

Preface

The *Writer's Handbook* continues a long tradition started by the previous editions of *The Brief Penguin Handbook*. While having a name change, the book still grows out of my experiences as a writing teacher at a time when the tools for writing, the uses of writing, and the nature of writing itself are undergoing astounding and rapid transformation in an era of multimedia. Yet the traditional qualities of good writing—clarity, brevity, readability, consistency, effective design, accurate documentation, freedom from errors, and a human voice—are prized more than ever.

Each edition of *The Writer's Handbook* has started with the question: How do students learn best? Stated simply, the answer is that students learn best when they can find the right information when they need it without being overwhelmed with detail. Complicated subjects are broken down into processes, giving students strategies for dealing with problems in their writing. Many thousands of students have become better writers with the help of *The Writer's Handbook*.

What's new in this edition?

- Expanded discussions of critical thinking, critical reading, and academic writing.
- Updated section on Writing in the Disciplines.
- More on digital and multimodal composition.
- More on incorporating sources and avoiding plagiarism.
- Revised MLA chapter reflects the major changes introduced in the eighth edition of the *MLA Handbook* (2016).

Revel™

Educational Technology Designed for the Way Today's Students Read, Think, and Learn

This edition of *The Writer's Handbook* also comes in a Revel version. When students are engaged deeply, they learn more effectively and perform better in their courses. This simple fact inspired the creation of Revel: an interactive learning environment designed for the way today's students read, think, and learn. Revel enlivens course content with media interactives and assessments—integrated directly within the author's narrative—that provide opportunities for students to read, practice, and study in one

continuous experience. This immersive educational technology replaces the textbook and is designed to measurably boost students' understanding, retention, and preparedness. Learn more about Revel at http://www.pearsonhighered.com/revel/.

Instructor's Resource Manual and Answer Key

The *Instructor's Resource Manual* offers guidance to new and experienced teachers for using the handbook to the best advantage. A separate *Answer Key* to accompany the exercises included in this handbook is also available to instructors.

Acknowledgments

The scope and complexity of a handbook require a talented, experienced team, and I have been blessed to work with the best. I much appreciate the guidance of Anne Stameshkin, Development Editor, and Alice Batt, Program Coordinator of the University Writing Center at Texas, for their many contributions in bringing this book to fruition. They are my coauthors. Writing a handbook is a lonely journey, and having supportive companions is invaluable.

Cynthia Cox, managing editor at Ohlinger Publishing Services, along with the rest of the team at Ohlinger have contributed their wisdom and experience to this handbook; Lois Lombardo of Cenveo provided excellent project management that guided the text through production; and Stephanie Magean contributed fine copyediting skills. I have been fortunate to teach extraordinary students at the University of Texas at Austin, who produced the splendid work that is included in this edition.

Over the years I've learned and continue to learn from colleagues around the country. I am fortunate to have an expert group of reviewers, who were not only perceptive in their suggestions but could imagine a handbook that broke new ground. They are Crystal Bickford, Southern New Hampshire University; Nancy Henschel, Lakeshore Technical College; Veronda R. Hutchinson, Johnston Community College; Kristy Ingram, Olivet Nazarene University; Sam Pritchard, Des Moines Area Community College—Boone; Alison Reynolds, University of Florida—Gainesville; Pam Solberg, Western Technical College—La Crosse.

As always, my greatest debt of gratitude is to my wife, Linda, who makes it all possible.

Lester Faigley

WRITING PROCESS MAP

Understand how to think like a college writer

- College readers expect specific claims or proposals supported by evidence and in-depth analysis. Go to 1a.
- College writers keep in mind their intended audience, their credibility, and their purposes for writing. Go to 1b–1f.
- College writers think about their genre, their medium, and their tone. Go to 1g-1i.

Analyze your writing task and develop a plan

- Often your assignment will direct your purpose. Go to 2a.
- Write a working thesis. Go to 2c.
- Plan a strategy. Go to 2d.

Write a draft

- Use your plan to compose and link paragraphs. Go to 3a, 3b, and 3c.
- Write effective beginning and concluding paragraphs. Go to 3e.

Revise, edit, and proofread

- Evaluate your draft, starting with the big picture. Does your project fulfill the assignment? Go to 4a.
- Make a plan for your revision. Go to 4b.
- Revise using your instructor's comments. Go to page 37.
- Edit for style and proofread carefully. Go to 4c and 4d.

Respond to other writers' drafts

- Go to 4e.

PART 1 Planning, Drafting, and Revising

1 | Think as a Writer

After reading this chapter, you should be able to . . .

- Recognize the demands of writing in college (1a)
- Recognize how to think critically (1b)
- Identify how to persuade your readers (1c)
- Identify your audience (1d)
- Recognize credibility (1e)
- Identify your purposes for writing (1f)
- Identify your genre (1g)
- Identify your medium (1h)
- Identify your tone (1i)

1a Think About What College Readers Expect

Writing in college varies considerably from course to course. A lab report for a biology course looks quite different from a paper in your English class, just as a classroom observation in an education course differs from a case study report in an accounting class.

Nevertheless, some common expectations about arguments in college writing extend across disciplines. Setting out a specific proposal or claim supported by reasons and evidence is at the heart of most college writing, no matter what the course. Some expectations of arguments (such as including a thesis statement) may be familiar to you, but others (such as finding opposing views on a subject) may be unfamiliar.

EXPECTATIONS OF COLLEGE WRITERS		
College writers are expected to . . .	**College writing . . .**	
State explicit claims	Has a main claim, often called a thesis.	see 2c
Support claims with reasons	Expresses reasons after making a claim (We should do something *because* _____).	see 10a
Base reasons on evidence	Provides evidence for reasons.	see 10a and 10b

(Continued on next page)

1

EXPECTATIONS OF COLLEGE WRITERS *(Continued)*		
College writers are expected to . . .	**College writing . . .**	
Consider opposing positions	Helps readers understand why there are disagreements about issues.	see 9c
Analyze with insight	Provides in-depth analysis.	see 7a–7b
Investigate complexity	Explores the complexity of a subject by asking "Have you thought about this?"	see 7c
Organize information	Makes the main ideas evident to readers.	see 2d and 2e
Signal relationships of parts	Indicates logical relationships clearly.	see 3b and 3c
Document sources carefully	Provides the sources of information.	see Part 6

1b Think Critically

The expectations listed above of college writers have one thing in common: critical thinking. Critical thinking involves using evidence and logic to support what we think, say, or write. When we think critically, we move beyond the question "What do I think or believe?" to "Why do I think or believe this?" and "Is my thinking on this subject reasonable?"

This kind of thinking puts us in the position of investigators. It asks us to consider a range of ideas, many of which are different from our own. It prompts us to look at evidence we may not have considered and to think carefully about where that evidence came from and how it was collected. It forces us to consider the reasons why someone might have a very different position on a topic than we do.

Sometimes critical thinking leads us to find solid support for an idea we already believe. Other times, it challenges us by pointing out the weaknesses in our thinking. When that happens, we delve for better reasons and evidence to support our position. If we can't find them, we modify our position to make it consistent with the evidence at hand. Being a college writer requires this kind of open-mindedness and commitment to logic.

Critical thinking is the cornerstone of good writing. It plays a role at every stage of the writing process. When we first receive an assignment, we apply critical thinking to *analyze* it. We ask questions: What does my instructor expect? How much ground should I try to cover in a

paper this long? What kind of research will I need to do? How long will the research and writing take? Where do I start, and how should I proceed from there?

Later in the writing process, critical thinking helps us *evaluate* sources of information. We ask how recent and relevant an article or book is, what kind of review process it underwent before it was published, and whether the author or editor has a particular bias. When we know these things, we are better prepared to choose the best evidence for our arguments.

We also think critically when we *pinpoint holes in logic*. Have you ever felt like a writer was trying to get you to choose between two options when you knew there was a third? Or maybe you noticed when a writer seemed to be leaving out something important to the topic being discussed? In both cases, your critical thinking skills were hard at work, helping you find the weak points in someone else's argument. You can also use critical thinking to find weaknesses in drafts of your own arguments.

EXAMPLES OF CRITICAL THINKING ARE . . .	
Recognizing verbal fallacies	5d
Recognizing visual fallacies	5f
Analyzing a piece of writing	7a, 7b, 7c
Recognizing what counts as evidence	11b, 12b
Analyzing a research task	17a
Drafting a thesis or narrowing a topic	7b, 8b, 9b, 10a, 17c, 17e
Evaluating sources	19a–19d, 21b, 21d, 21h
Using sources as points of departure	22c

1c Think About How to Persuade Others

The process of communication involves the interaction of three essential elements: the writer or speaker, the audience, and the subject. These three elements interact with one another.

The ancient Greeks represented the dynamic nature of communication with the **rhetorical triangle**. The most important teacher of rhetoric in ancient Greece, Aristotle (384–323 BCE), defined *rhetoric* as the art of finding the best available means of persuasion in any situation. He set out three primary tactics of persuasion: appeals based on the trustworthiness of the speaker (*ethos*); appeals to the emotions and deepest-held values of the audience (*pathos*); and appeals to logic, reasoning, and evidence (*logos*).

Ethos
appeals to the character and expertise of the writer or speaker

Pathos
appeals to the beliefs and values of the audience

Logos
appeals based on logic, reasoning, and evidence concerning the subject

Figure 1.1   The rhetorical triangle

1d   Think About Your Audience

Readers of college writing expect more than what they can find out on *Wikipedia* or from a *Google* search. Facts are easy to obtain online. Readers want to know how these facts are connected. Good college writing also involves an element of surprise. If readers can predict exactly where a writer is going, even if they fully agree, they will either skim to the end or stop reading. Readers expect you to tell them something that they don't know already.

To make sure you understand your audience, ask yourself a few questions:

WRITING SMART

Understand your audience

- Who is most likely to read what you write?
- How much does your audience know about your subject? Are there any key terms or concepts that you will need to explain?
- How interested is your audience likely to be? If they lack interest in your subject, how can you engage them?
- What is their attitude likely to be toward your subject? If they hold attitudes different from yours, how can you get them to consider your views?
- What would motivate your audience to want to read what you write?

1e Think About Your Credibility

Some writers begin with a strong ethos because of who they are; they have immediate credibility. Most writers, however, have to convince their readers to keep reading by demonstrating knowledge of their subject and concern with their readers' needs. Furthermore, no matter how much you know about a subject or how good your ideas are, your credibility is destroyed if readers in college, in the workplace, or in public life find your writing poor in quality, especially if it is full of errors and sloppy sentences.

Before you get too far into any writing project, consider how you can build your credibility:

WRITING SMART

Build your credibility

- How can you convince your audience that you are knowledgeable about your subject? Do you need to do research?

- How can you convince your audience that you have their interests in mind?

- What strategies can you use that will enhance your credibility? Should you cite experts on your subject? Can you acknowledge opposing positions, indicating that you've taken a balanced view on your subject?

- Does the appearance, accuracy, and clarity of your writing give you credibility?

1f Think About Your Purpose

The starting point for effective writing is determining in advance what you want to accomplish. Knowing your purpose shapes everything else you do as a writer—your choice of the kind of writing, your subject matter, your organization, and your style. The purposes of academic writing can vary widely depending on the class. If you are unsure of your purpose, consider these questions:

WRITING SMART

Identify your purposes for writing

- Are you analyzing a verbal or visual text to understand how it persuades readers? (See Chapter 7.)

(Continued on next page)

WRITING SMART   *(Continued)*

- Are you writing to report information, to explain a process, to explore questions and problems, or to analyze patterns? (See Chapter 8.)
- Are you arguing for a position on a controversial issue? (See Chapter 9.)
- Are you arguing to convince people to take a particular course of action? (See Chapter 10.)

1g   Think About Your Genre

College writers also pay attention to genre. *Genre* is another word for category. All academic writing is classified into different types: scholarly articles, essays, reviews, research reports, blogs, and so on. Of course, there are many sub-genres within these broad genres. Different genres may require different formats, types of evidence, and ways of citing sources. Usually your assignment will explain these differences. You can also learn more about them in Part 3.

Here are two examples of genres:

A Research Report

A new study by researchers at NASA and the University of California, Irvine, finds a rapidly melting section of the West Antarctic Ice Sheet appears to be in an irreversible state of decline, with nothing to stop the glaciers in this area from melting into the sea.

The study presents multiple lines of evidence, incorporating 40 years of observations that indicate the glaciers in the Amundsen Sea sector of West Antarctica "have passed the point of no return," according to glaciologist and lead author Eric Rignot, of UC Irvine and NASA's Jet Propulsion Laboratory (JPL) in Pasadena, California. The new study has been accepted for publication in the journal *Geophysical Research Letters*.

These glaciers already contribute significantly to sea level rise, releasing almost as much ice into the ocean annually as the entire Greenland Ice Sheet. They contain enough ice to raise global sea level by 4 feet (1.2 meters) and are melting faster than most scientists had expected.

Source: Rassmusen, Carol. "NASA-UCI Study Indicates Loss of West Antarctic Glaciers Appears Unstoppable." *NASA*, 12 May 2014, www.nasa.gov/press/2014/may/nasa-uci-study-indicates-loss-of-west-antarctic-glaciers-appears-unstoppable/#.VzTcshUrLFQ.

Blog

BLOG | Posted at 4:18 p.m.   3 comments

Why Are the East Coast and Gulf of Mexico Hotspots of Sea Level Rise?

Global average sea level has increased 8 inches since 1880. Several locations along the East Coast and Gulf of Mexico have experienced more than 8 inches of local level rise in only the past 50 years.

The rate of local sea level rise is affected by global, regional, and local factors.

Along the East Coast and Gulf of Mexico, changes in the path and strength of ocean currents are contributing to faster-than-average sea level rise.

In parts of the East Coast and Gulf regions, land is subsiding, which allows the ocean to penetrate farther inland.

Source: "Global Warming." *Union of Concerned Scientists.* 30 Apr. 2014, www.ucsusa.org/global_warming/science_and_impacts/impacts/infographic-sea-level-rise-global-warming.html#.VzTehBUrLFQ.

1h Think About Your Medium

A medium is a channel of communication. All humans communicate by talking (oral or sign language) and through body language. Across centuries analog media were gradually added to the human repertoire—handwriting, print, telephone, radio, and film. Analog media have increasingly been supplanted by new digital media.

Today we are never far from a wireless or mobile network signal, social media, e-mail, texting, photo services, online mapping services, and audio and video sites. We're accustomed to using an app for whatever we want to read, see, or hear. The challenge now is when to use what media:

- Would a chart, graph, or diagram help to explain your message?
- Would one or more photographs allow your readers to see what you are discussing?
- Would a video support your presentation?
- Would an audio recording add to your presentation?

You'll find more about multimedia composing in Part 4.

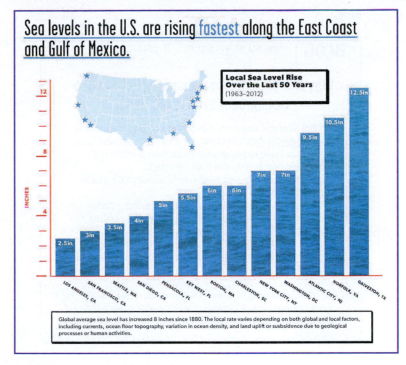

Figure 1.2   The Union of Concerned Scientists created this infographic on the rise of sea levels along the coasts of the United States. It was published as part of the blog post in 1g.

1i   Think About Your Tone

Tone is the attitude conveyed through the writer's words. The tone of academic writing is generally formal and serious because the purpose is serious. Consider the research report and blog in 1g. In each, the purpose is to convey information related to rising sea levels, a subject that causes readers concern because it affects coastlines and the populations that inhabit them.

Both present lots of facts, and the research report cites an expert from NASA's Jet Propulsion Laboratory. (The blog does not cite experts, because it is written by experts presenting their own findings.) The writers' choice of words, such as "irreversible state of decline" and "faster-than-average sea level rise," convey a sense that the topic must be taken seriously.

But serious and formal are not the only tones you'll encounter in college writing. Depending on the assignment, a certain amount of playfulness, warmth, urgency, or even scathing satire may be appropriate. Some assignments, such as those for creative arts courses, may encourage an informal tone. Thinking carefully about audience and purpose before you start writing will help you select an appropriate tone.

2 | Plan and Draft

QUICK*TAKE*

After reading this chapter, you should be able to . . .
- Establish your goals (2a)
- Explore your topic (2b)
- Compose a working thesis (2c)
- Plan a strategy (2d)
- Compose a draft (2e)

2a Establish Your Goals

Your instructor will give you specific suggestions about how to think about your audience and topic. There are two ways to make your task simpler.

- Be sure you are responding to the assignment appropriately.
- Select a topic that both fits the assignment and appeals to you strongly enough to make you want to write about it.

Look carefully at your assignment

When your instructor gives you a writing assignment, look closely at what you are asked to do. Often the assignment will contain key words such as *analyze, define, describe, evaluate,* or *propose* that will assist you in determining what direction to take. If you are unclear about what the assignment calls for, talk with your instructor.

- **Analyze:** Find connections among a set of facts, events, or readings and make them meaningful.
- **Define:** Make a claim about how something should be defined, according to features that you set out.
- **Describe:** Observe carefully and select details that create a dominant impression.
- **Evaluate:** Argue that something is good, bad, best, or worst in its class, according to criteria that you set out.
- **Propose:** Identify a particular problem and explain why your solution is the best one.

Find a topic you care about

If you do not have an assigned topic, a good way to find one is to look first at the materials for your course. You may find something that interests you in the readings for the course or in a topic that came up in class discussion.

If your assignment gives you a wide range of options, you might write more than one list, starting with your personal interests. Think also about campus topics, community topics, and national topics that intrigue you.

After you make a list or lists, you should review it.

- Put a checkmark beside the topics that look most interesting or the ones that mean the most to you.
- Put a question mark beside the topics that you don't know very much about. If you choose one of these topics, you will have to do research.
- Select the two or three topics that look the most promising.

2b Explore Your Topic

Once you have identified a potential topic, the next step is to determine what you already know about that topic and what you need to find out. Experienced writers use many strategies for exploring their knowledge of a topic and how interesting it really is to them. Here are a few.

Ask questions

These classic reporter's questions will assist you in thinking through a topic.

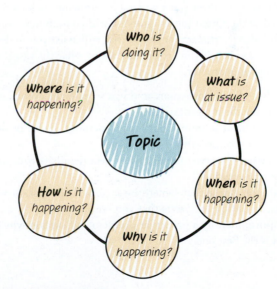

Figure 2.1   The reporter's questions

Freewrite

Another way to find out how much you know about a topic is to **freewrite**: Write as quickly as you can without stopping for a set time, usually 5 or 10 minutes. The goal of freewriting is to get as much down as possible. Don't stop to correct mistakes. The constant flow of words should generate ideas—some useful, some not.

If you get stuck, write the same sentence over again, or write about how hungry you are, or how difficult freewriting is, until thoughts on your selected topic reappear. After you've finished, read what you have written and single out any key ideas. The following freewrite was composed by Mariela Martinez on a student free speech case that wound up before the United States Supreme Court in March 2007. In 2002 in Juneau, Alaska, high school senior Joseph Frederick was suspended for ten days by principal Deborah Morse after he displayed a banner off of school property during the Winter Olympics Torch Relay. You can read Martinez's essay in 9d.

Freewrite on Morse v. Frederick

I did dumb stuff when I was a senior in high school. I can imagine Joe Frederick sitting around with his friends after they found out that the Winter Olympics Torch Relay would pass by his school. I can imagine what happened. Someone said it would be really cool if we held up a banner that said Bong Hits 4 Jesus in front of the cameras. Everyone else said awesome! But what happens next? That's what Joe and his friends didn't think through. And when it happened, the principal didn't think it through either, but give her credit, she had to react on the spot. She did what she thought was right at the time, but she fell right into the trap. The bottom line is when do stupid statements become illegal? A lot of adults and high school students make stupid statements, but unless they are racist, profane, or libelous, they don't get punished. Joe did get punished. He was outside on a public sidewalk. And school was called off that afternoon because of the parade. So he was just a high school student doing something dumb, not something illegal. Joe made the principal look bad, but he embarrassed his school and his parents, and my guess is that if he had it to do over again, he wouldn't do it. Still, he shouldn't have

*been punished. He didn't make a serious argument in favor
of doing drugs. Or ridicule Christians. The real argument is
about the limits of free speech.*

Ideas to Use

1. *Joe's banner was in poor taste, but poor taste doesn't meet
   the legal requirement for censorship.*
2. *The principal was embarrassed and made a knee-jerk reaction without thinking.*
3. *The real issue is what free speech rights do young people have.*

You may want to use a key word or idea as a starting point for a second
freewrite. After two or three rounds, you will discover how much you
already know about your topic and possible directions for developing it.

Brainstorm

An alternative method of discovery is to **brainstorm**. The end result of
brainstorming is usually a list—sometimes of questions, sometimes of
statements. You might come up with a list of observations and questions
such as these for the free speech case.

- *The student wasn't in the school at the time of the incident.*
- *The principal overreacted.*
- *Drugs are an excuse to give authorities more control.*
- *What is the recent history of free speech cases involving
  high school students?*
- *Student's citing of Jefferson resulted in more punishment—
  WHY???*
- *Isn't there protection for satire?*

Make an idea map

Still another strategy for exploring how much you know about a potential
topic is to make an **idea map**. Idea maps are useful because they let you see
everything at once, and you can begin to make connections among the different aspects of an issue—definitions, causes, effects, proposed solutions,
and your personal experience. A good way to get started is to write down
ideas on sticky notes. Then you can move the sticky notes around until you
figure out which ideas fit together. Figure 2.2 shows what an idea map on
the freedom of speech case involving Joseph Frederick might look like.

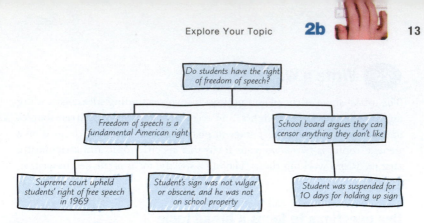

Figure 2.2 Idea map on the Juneau, Alaska, freedom of speech case

Respond to something you've read

Most of the writing you do in college will be linked to texts you are reading. Find time to read about your topic before writing about it. Select a book or an article that you find to be a powerful statement about your topic.

Imagine you are sitting down face-to-face with the author. Find places where you can write things like the following:

- *"I agree with your general point, but did you think of this other example? What would you do with it?"*
- *"Here you seem to be arguing for one side, but later you seem to contradict yourself and give credit to the other side."*
- *"I don't agree with this claim because your evidence doesn't support your assertion."*

Talking back to a text can help you find your own position: "While X sees it this way, I look at it a different way."

■ You can get one-on-one help in developing your ideas, focusing your topic, and revising your paper at your writing center.

2c Write a Working Thesis

The initial stage of the planning process involves finding ideas, expanding and broadening your thoughts, and recording ideas from written sources and conversations. The next stage of planning, after you have decided on a general topic, is *narrowing* your focus to a specific topic and articulating that focus as a working thesis. Having a specific focus is the key to writing a strong essay.

Use questions to focus a broad topic

Ask questions that will turn a big topic into one that is manageable. Start with broad questions and then make them more specific, as in the flowchart in Figure 2.3.

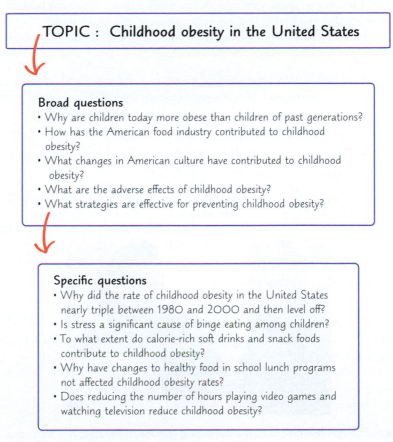

Figure 2.3   Focusing a topic

Turn your topic into a thesis statement

Your **thesis** states your main idea. Much of the writing that you will do in college and later in your career will have an explicit thesis, usually stated near the beginning. The thesis announces your topic and indicates what points you want to make about that topic.

Your thesis should be closely tied to your purpose—to reflect on your own experience, to explain some aspect of your topic, or to argue for a position or course of action.

Reflective thesis	*I became aware of the psychological effects of childhood obesity while growing up with an overweight younger brother who was constantly teased by classmates and even members of his family, leading to his low self-esteem and depression.*
Informative thesis	*The greatest risk factor for childhood obesity is the obesity of parents, which suggests that childhood obesity results from an interplay of genetic and environmental factors.*
Persuasive thesis	*Just as the United States has had success in addressing other teenage health problems such as smoking, drug use, and teen pregnancy, we need to take similar proactive steps to reverse the trend of rising childhood obesity, including restricting marketing of junk food to children, increasing education about food, and promoting healthy lifestyles with more exercise.*

What makes an effective thesis statement?

A thesis should not be a question. The thesis is your answer to your research question. Along with being specific, manageable, and interesting, your thesis should also tell *what* you plan to argue and indicate *how* you plan to argue without simply offering a list. Announce how you will be weighing and arranging the points in your argument.

Uninteresting	*High gasoline prices, dissatisfaction with air service, and traffic congestion in the*

Northeast Corridor have increased the number of Americans using Amtrak.
{the typical boring five-paragraph organization: high gas prices, yada yada; bad air service, yada yada; traffic, yada yada}

Better
Although high gasoline prices no doubt have led more Americans to take the train rather than drive, new routes serving cities outside the Northeast Corridor and improved services like WiFi and electronic ticketing are major factors in Amtrak's steadily increasing ridership.
[arguing that one or two elements are more important breaks out of the five-paragraph formula]

Another way to narrow a potential thesis is to think about possible counterarguments and then to make sure you address these in your argument.

Better
Although Amtrak's taxpayer subsidy has long been a target of politicians, highways are subsidized at a much higher percentage than Amtrak, which actually makes money in the heavily traveled Northeast Corridor and which has paid off most of its outstanding debt.

A thesis should never be combative or confrontational.

Combative
Because Americans in general are clueless about how government works, dishonest politicians take advantage of the public's ignorance of how Amtrak is funded.

STAYING ON TRACK

Evaluate your working thesis

Ask yourself these questions about your working thesis.

1. Is it specific?
2. Is it manageable in its length and the time I have?
3. Is it interesting to my intended readers?

Consider the following examples.

Example 1

Eating disorders remain a serious problem on college campuses.

Specific? The thesis is too broad. Exactly who suffers from eating disorders? Is the problem the same for men and women?

Manageable? Because the thesis is not limited to a particular aspect of eating disorders, it cannot be researched adequately.

Interesting? The topic is potentially interesting, but most people know that many college students suffer from eating disorders. If you choose this topic, what can you tell your readers that they don't know already?

Revised thesis

Glamorous images of ultrathin people in the fashion industry, the movie industry, and other media are a contributing cause of eating disorders on college campuses because they influence young people to believe they are fat when in fact their weight is normal.

Example 2

The United States entered World War II when the Japanese bombed Pearl Harbor on December 7, 1941.

Specific? The thesis is too narrow. It states a commonly acknowledged fact.

Manageable? A known fact is stated in the thesis, so there is nothing to research. The general topic of the attack on Pearl Harbor is too large for essay-length treatment.

Interesting? The attack on Pearl Harbor remains interesting to Americans (witness a recent Hollywood film that deals with the subject), but there is no topic to work from.

Revised thesis

Although combat between the United States and Japan began at Pearl Harbor, the unofficial war began when President Roosevelt froze Japanese assets in the United States in July 1940 and later declared a commercial embargo.

These examples suggest that the key to writing an effective thesis is finding a topic that is neither too vast nor too narrow—and not obvious. You may have to adjust your working thesis more than once as you plan and begin drafting.

2d Plan a Strategy

People who write frequently on the job or who make their living by writing have many different ways of producing a successful piece of writing. Some may plan extensively in advance, either individually or as a team, specifying exactly what will go in each section. Other writers find that putting ideas into words often changes the ideas and generates new ones. These writers know that writing drafts is a way of discovering their subject, and they count on one or two or more rewrites to get their document into shape.

Consider making an outline

At some point in school, you may have been required to produce an outline to submit along with a paper. A **formal outline** typically begins with the thesis statement, which anchors the entire outline. Each numbered or lettered item clearly supports the thesis, and the relationship among the items is clear from the outline hierarchy.

> Thesis statement: The United States needs to take concrete steps to reduce obesity in children.

> I. A disturbing aspect of the trend of fatter Americans is that children are increasingly obese.
>   A. More than one-third of children 10–17 are obese.
>   B. Obese children suffer many serious health problems today.
>   C. America has had some success in addressing other teenage health problems, including smoking, drug use, and teen pregnancy.

> II. Many causes have been proposed for overweight America.
>   A. One proposed cause is the move to the suburbs, but the population shift to the suburbs occurred before the rapid rise in weight gain.
>   B. The couch potato argument is countered by increases in exercise and participation in athletics.
>   C. The simple answer is that Americans consume about twice as many calories per day as they need.

Consider using a working outline

A working outline is more like an initial sketch of how you will arrange the major sections. Jotting down main points and a few subpoints before you begin can be a great help while you are writing. You can read the complete essay that Ashley Walker developed from these outlines in Section 10c.

Addressing Childhood Obesity

Section 1: Begin with a description of the problem, including statistics on the rising number of obese children.

Section 2: Discuss the causes that have been proposed for childhood obesity.

Section 3: Discuss how the eating patterns of Americans have changed during the last thirty years and how portions served have increased.

Section 4: Examine how food is being marketed to children.

Section 5: Look at the role of parents and why parents often don't control much of the environment where children eat.

Section 6: Describe solutions: (1) Restrict marketing of food to children, (2) educate parents and children, (3) promote healthier lifestyles.

Section 7: Discuss how these solutions can be implemented.

2e Compose a Draft

Skilled writers aim at producing a good draft—not a perfect draft. They know that they can go back and revise later.

Essays typically contain an introduction, body, and conclusion. You do not have to write these parts in that order, though. In your **introduction**, you can offer a short example that illustrates the problem being discussed. You can state a surprising fact. You can begin with a fascinating quotation. Your aim is to interest the reader.

The **body** of the essay consists of the primary discussion. Remember to guide readers through the discussion by letting them know where you are going. Your readers need road signs to tell them where the discussion is taking them. Road signs are transition words and phrases such as *consequently*, *the third reason is . . . ,* and *on the other hand*.

The last section, the **conclusion**, often repeats what has already been said. If the essay has been long and complex, sometimes this repetition is necessary, but usually the repetition is just that—annoying redundancy. The final paragraph does not have to repeat the main point. It can give a compelling last example or propose a course of action. It can ponder the larger significance of the subject under discussion. It can pose an important question for the reader to think about.

2f Write as a Member of a Team

Almost without exception, people in occupations that require a college education write frequently on the job, and much of that writing is done in
collaboration rather than alone. The better you understand how to write
effectively with other people, the more enjoyable and more productive the
process will be for you.

Determine the goals and identify tasks and roles

- Write down the goals as specifically as you can and discuss them as
  a team.
- Determine what tasks are required to meet those goals. Write
  down the tasks and arrange them in the order in which they need
  to be completed.
- If the team does not possess the necessary skills and resources,
  adjust the goals to what you can realistically expect to accomplish.

Make a work plan

- Make a time line that lists the dates when specific tasks need to be
  completed and distribute it to all team members. Charts are useful
  tools for keeping track of progress.
- Assign tasks to team members.
- Set up specific dates for review and assign team members to be responsible for reviewing work that has been done.

Understand the dynamics of a successful team

- Teamwork requires some flexibility. Keep talking to each other
  along the way.
- It may be desirable to rotate roles during the project.

Deal with problems when they come up

- If a team member is not participating, find out why.
- Get the team together if you are not meeting the deadlines you
  established in the work plan and devise a new plan, if necessary.

3 | Compose Paragraphs

QUICK*TAKE*

After reading this chapter, you should be able to . . .

- Create focused paragraphs (3a)
- Organize your paragraphs (3b)
- Establish paragraph coherence (3c)
- Determine paragraph length (3d)
- Compose effective beginning and concluding paragraphs (3e)

3a Focus Your Paragraphs

Readers expect sentences in a paragraph to be closely related to one another. Often writers will begin a paragraph with one idea, but other ideas will occur to them while they are writing. Paragraphs confuse readers when they go in different directions. When you revise your paragraphs, check for focus.

In the following example, notice how much stronger the paragraph becomes when we remove the sentences in burgundy. They distract us from the subject, Royal Chitwan National Park in Nepal and how it is different from Western national parks.

> Like everything else in Nepal, Royal Chitwan National Park is different from Western notions of a park. It is a jungle between two rivers, with grass 20 to 25 feet tall growing in the swampy land along the rivers. Several rare or endangered species live in the park, including leopards, crocodiles, royal Bengal tigers, and the greater one-horned Asian rhinoceros. **In fact, we saw several rhinos during our weeklong visit to the park. To my relief we saw all but one from the safety of an elephant's back.** But the boundaries of the park restrict neither the Nepalis nor the animals. The Nepalis cross the river into the park to gather firewood and the tall grass, which they use to make their houses. Some even live within the park. The rhinos and deer raid the Nepalis' fields at night, and the leopards prey on their dogs and livestock. To keep the truce between these competitors, the army patrols the park, mostly to prevent poachers from killing the tigers and rhinos. But confrontations do occur; the animals lose habitat, and the Nepalis lose their crops and lives.

When to use explicit topic sentences

You were probably taught to begin a paragraph with a topic sentence. Topic sentences alert readers to the focus of a paragraph and help writers stay on topic. Topic sentences should explain the focus of the paragraph and situate it in the larger argument. However, topic sentences do not have to begin paragraphs, and they need not be just one sentence. You will decide what placement and length will best suit your subject.

Topic sentences at the beginning of a paragraph will quickly orient readers, preparing them for the sentences to come. Each sentence that follows elucidates the topic sentence.

Topic sentence at the beginning

We live in a world of risks so much beyond our control that it is difficult to think of anything that is risk free. Even the most basic human acts involve risk—having sex in an era of AIDS, eating in an era of genetically altered food, walking outdoors in an ozone-depleted atmosphere, drinking water and breathing air laden with chemicals whose effects we do not understand. Should we eat more fish in our daily diet? Nutritionists tell us that eating fish reduces the risk of heart disease. Other scientists, however, tell us that fish are contaminated with a new generation of synthetic chemicals.

When a paragraph builds to make a particular point, the topic sentence is more effective at the end of the paragraph.

Topic sentence at the end

We are continually being summoned to change ourselves for the better—through fitness programs, through various kinds of instruction, through advice columns, through self-help books and videos—and somehow we never quite measure up. The blame always comes back on us. If we had eaten better, or exercised more, or paid more attention to our investments, or learned a new skill, or changed our oil every 3,000 miles, then things would have turned out better. Very rarely do we ask how a different social organization might have made things better. **Our society incorporates critical thinking without being much affected by the consequences of that thinking.**

When to use implicit topic sentences

In some cases, particularly in narrative prose, writers omit explicit topic sentences because they would clash with the tone or style of the paragraph. Instead, these paragraphs use tightly connected, focused sentences to make the topic implicitly clear.

Implicit topic sentence

By the mid-1970s in the United States, the temporary advantage of being the only major power with its industries undamaged following World War II had evaporated, and rust-belt industries failed one after the other against competition from a revived Europe and an emergent Asia. The United States seemed to be going the way of other historical world powers, where efficient trading nations beat out bloated military regimes. Japan appeared to be the model for a fast and light capitalism that the rest of the world would imitate. Just a few years later, however, the American decline reversed. The United States again became the economic leader of the world in the 1990s.

The implicit topic sentence is something like "The United States' economy appeared to be in rapid decline in the 1970s, only to bounce back to world leadership in the 1990s."

3b Organize Your Paragraphs

Well-organized paragraphs in essays usually follow a pattern similar to that of a well-organized paper, but in miniature. Chances are you'll use a combination of these strategies in order to get your point across.

Description

Description is a common strategy for informative and narrative writing. Providing concrete details—sights, sounds, smells, textures, and tastes—gives the reader a sensory memory of your subject.

Topic sentence

Details convey a dominant impression.

The airport at Kathmandu resembles one-gate airports in the United States, with a small waiting room and baggage area, except that it is deluged with international tourists. Busloads of young people lug bright nylon rucksacks and duffle bags emblazoned with names like "Australian Wilderness Adventures" and "South Korean Dhaulagiri Winter Expedition." Mingled with them are traders from India and Nepal—some dressed in suits, some in peasant clothes—carrying bulky goods like folding chairs, drums of cooking oil, and boxes of medicine.

This descriptive paragraph relies on a comparison to a place U.S. readers will probably recognize.

The example paragraphs about Nepal are adapted from Lester Faigley, "Nepal Diary: Where the Global Village Ends." *North Dakota Quarterly*, vol. 57, no. 3, 1989, pp. 106–29.

Narration or process

Narrative paragraphs tell a story for a reason. Organized by time, narratives relate a series of events in the order in which they occur. This approach is

useful when the temporal order of ideas or events is essential to their logic, such as in how-to writing.

Verbs establish the sequence of events to orient the reader in time.

The ascent goes easier than they expected. In two hours they reach the yak pastures where they will make the high camp. The view from the high camp is spectacular, with Dhaulagiri in clouds above them and the three sunlit summits of Nilgiri across the valley, with snow plumes blowing from their tops. Jim and Lester drop their packs at the campsite and continue walking to scout the route above the camp that they will follow in the darkness of early morning the next day. They find a steep path that parallels

Narrative paragraphs often include description to orient the reader in space.

a fern-lined gorge, now rich in fall color. It is the lushest forest they have seen in Nepal. They congratulate each other on their decision to attempt the climb to the Dhaulagiri icefall, unaware that they will soon experience the mountain's furious weather, even on its lower slopes.

Comparison and contrast

Paragraphs of comparison assess one subject in terms of its relation to others, usually highlighting what they have in common. Contrasting paragraphs analyze differences between things.

You can organize a comparison or a contrast in two ways: by describing one thing and then describing another, or by moving back and forth between the two items point by point. Often the latter strategy highlights contrasts, as the following paragraph illustrates.

Establishes the terms of the comparison.

Each phrase shows the medieval "heart" and the "thin overlay" of Western culture.

Nepal was closed to Europeans from 1843 to 1949 and missed the colonial influences of the British. Consequently, Kathmandu remains a medieval city at heart, with a thin overlay of the last two decades of trendy Western culture: Tibetan women dressed in traditional clothes weave rugs on antique looms while humming Sting tunes; a traffic jam on Kathmandu's only wide street is caused by bulls fighting in an intersection; restaurants play U2 and serve tough buffalo steak under the name *chateau briande*; coffee houses serve cappuccino across the street from women drying rice by lifting it into the air with hoes; nearly naked children wearing burlap sacks grab cake slices out of the hands of gawking tourists emerging from a Viennese pastry shop.

This comparison/contrast also uses a cause/effect pattern to help organize it. The word *consequently* in the second line is the transition from the cause to the effect.

Definition

Much writing in college depends on establishing the definitions of key terms. Consequently, writers often use entire paragraphs for definitions. Paragraphs organized by definition usually begin with the term and then go on to list its distinguishing features, sometimes using examples. Writers may begin with a standard definition and then qualify or add to that definition in unexpected ways.

Definitions are critical to persuasive writing. If your audience accepts your definitions of key terms, usually you will be convincing.

Tranquility in Western countries is usually equated with getting away from it all. Its synonyms are *calmness, serenity,* and *peace of mind,* and no wonder: We live in a world where it is increasingly difficult to get completely away from human-produced noise. In the Hindu and Buddhist traditions, however, tranquility is thought of as an internal quality that is gained when a person no longer is controlled by worldly desires. While this definition of tranquility may seem foreign to us, the internal state of tranquility is evident when you are in the presence of someone who possesses it.

Usual definition

Extended definition adds a new dimension.

Examples and illustrations

If you want to prove a point or bring an issue to life, an organization based on examples and illustrations may work well. This structure usually begins with the main idea or point, then moves to a vivid explanation of one or two examples that illustrate the main idea. Examples and illustrations also can work well in opening and concluding paragraphs.

Point

Illustration

When religious principles clash with practical realities, ingenuity often comes to the rescue. Upon entering Braga, a Buddhist village built into a cliffside high in the Himalayas, Jim and Lester noticed that the men of the village surrounded two yaks, wrestled them to the ground, and tied their feet together. By a stone wall on the side of the field, an old bearded man read from a holy book while the yaks were stabbed in the heart. They lay panting, bleeding little, taking a long time to die. Three young men poured water down the throats of the yaks, while the other men chanted in their Tibetan dialect. As Buddhists, the people of Braga are forbidden to kill animals, yet the environment demands that they eat meat to survive. They resolve the dilemma by helping the animal to assume a higher form when it is reincarnated.

Cause and effect

Cause-and-effect paragraphs are structured in two basic ways. The paragraph can begin with a cause or causes, then state its effects, or it can begin with an effect, then state its causes. Insightful analysis often requires you to look beyond the obvious to the underlying causes.

Effects

Obvious cause

Underlying cause 1

Underlying cause 2

The loss of the world's forests affects every country through global warming, decreased biodiversity, and soil erosion, but few suffer its impact more than Nepal. Deforestation in Nepal has led to economic stagnation and further depletion of forest resources. The immediate cause of deforestation is the need for more fuel and more farmland by an increasing population. The loss of trees in Nepal, however, has been accelerated by government policies. During the eighteenth and nineteenth centuries, Nepal taxed both land and labor. Farmers could avoid these high taxes for three years if they converted forests to farmland. Others could pay their taxes in firewood or charcoal. While these taxes were reduced in the twentieth century, the government required farmers to register their land, which encouraged clearing of trees to establish boundaries. Furthermore, the stagnant

economy led to families' wanting more children to help **Underlying cause 3**
in the fields at home and to send abroad to find jobs as
another source of income.

3c Make Your Paragraphs Coherent

You've no doubt heard that good writing should "flow," but what exactly does flow mean? Writing that flows is coherent, which means readers understand how sentences fit together. Repeating key phrases and signaling relationships with transitional terms help in building coherence.

Reiterate key terms and phrases

In the following paragraph, notice how the writer keeps the focus on *Facebook*, *privacy*, and *personal information* by repeating key terms.

> The value of **Facebook** as a corporate entity is based on its potential for advertising revenue. In November 2007, **Facebook** launched Beacon, an advertising system that sent targeted advertising and tracked activities of **Facebook** members on partner Web sites, even when the members were not logged in on **Facebook**. **Facebook** retreated to an opt-in **privacy** policy only after large-scale protests brought negative publicity, but activists discovered that **Facebook** was still collecting **personal information** from those who had opted out. In August 2008, the activists filed a class-action lawsuit against **Facebook** and its corporate marketing partners, alleging that **Facebook's** selling of members' **personal information** is a violation of federal and state **privacy** laws. Even though **Facebook** has shut down Beacon, there are no certain safeguards to protect **privacy**. The BBC program *Click* demonstrated that anyone with a basic knowledge of Web programming could gain access to restricted **personal details** on **Facebook**. Furthermore, the **information** does not go away. **Facebook** friends are literally friends forever because social networking sites are archived on servers.

Signal relationships with transitional terms

Transitional terms act like warning signs for readers, preparing them for what is around the bend. Notice how transitional terms signal the relationship of one sentence to the next.

> Critics of Web 2.0, including Tim Berners-Lee, who is credited with inventing the Web, dismiss the term as jargon, pointing out that the Web has always been about connecting people. **Indeed**, in the late 1970s and early 1980s, e-mail and hobby bulletin boards were the

most popular features of the ARPANET, the predecessor of the Internet. **More accurately**, Web 2.0 marked a revival of the mid-1990s ebullience about the Internet as one of the greatest achievements in human history. **For example**, Kevin Kelly speaks of Web 2.0 in terms of religious transcendence: "The Machine provided a new way of thinking (perfect search, total recall) and a new mind for an old species. It was the Beginning."

STAYING ON TRACK

Use transitional terms

Be sure to use transitional terms accurately in order to signal the relationships between your sentences.

- **To enumerate:** again, also, and, as well, finally, furthermore, first, second, third, in addition, last, moreover, next, too
- **To generalize:** commonly, in general, for the most part, on the whole, usually, typically
- **To offer an example:** for example, for instance, indeed, in fact, of course, specifically, such as, the following
- **To situate in time:** after a month, afterward, as long as, as soon as, at the moment, at present, at that time, before, earlier, followed by, in the meantime, in the past, lately, later, meanwhile, now, preceded by, presently, since then, so far, soon, subsequently, suddenly, then, this year, today, until, when, while
- **To situate in space:** above, below, beyond, close to, elsewhere, far from, following, here, near, next to, there
- **To conclude:** as a result, hence, in conclusion, in short, on the whole, therefore, thus
- **To contrast:** although, but, even though, however, in contrast, conversely, in spite of, instead, nevertheless, nonetheless, on the one hand, on the contrary, on the other hand, still, though, yet
- **To compare:** again, also, in the same way, likewise, similarly
- **To signal cause or effect:** as a result, because, consequently, for this reason, hence, if, so, then, therefore, thus
- **To sum up:** as I said, as we have seen, as mentioned earlier, in conclusion, in other words, in short, in sum, therefore, thus
- **To concede a point:** certainly, even though, granted, in fairness, in truth, naturally, of course, to be fair, while it's true

3d Consider Paragraph Length

Paragraph breaks can signal various kinds of shifts.

- A new concept
- The next step in an argument
- The end of the introduction
- The beginning of the conclusion
- A new speaker in dialogue
- A shift in time or place
- A logical pause that gives the reader a breather

What is the ideal length for a paragraph? It depends on what sort of paragraphs you are writing. Business letter writers strive for short paragraphs so their readers can see the essential information at a glance. Academic writers need space to make and support arguments in depth. As a general rule, readers' eyes glaze over when they see paragraphs in an essay that stretch beyond one page. Nevertheless, too many short paragraphs are a sign that the piece lacks either weighty ideas or sufficient development.

3e Write Effective Beginning and Ending Paragraphs

Beginning and ending paragraphs of essays should behave like a smart suitor meeting "the parents" for the first time: Dress well; start with a firm handshake; show you are thoughtful and personable; close on a strong note. Because readers are more likely to remember beginning and ending paragraphs, they are your best opportunity to make a good impression.

Understand what beginning paragraphs do

Effective beginning paragraphs convince the reader to read on. They capture the reader's interest and set the tone for the piece. In essays they often state the thesis and briefly map out the way the writing will progress from paragraph to paragraph. Sometimes the work of the beginning paragraph might be carried through three or four paragraphs. A writer might start with a memorable example, then use the example to launch the rest of the essay.

Start beginning paragraphs with a bang

Getting the first few sentences of an essay down on paper can be daunting. Begin with one of the following strategies to get your reader's attention.

A question

How valuable are snow leopards? The director of a zoo in Darjeeling, India, was fired when its snow leopard caught a cold and died.

A hard-hitting fact

Poaching is big business—to be exact, a six-billion-dollar business. The only illegal trade that's larger is drugs.

A pithy quotation

"That the snow leopard is," writes Peter Matthiessen, "that it is here, that its frosty eyes watch us from the mountains—that is enough." And it has to be enough because, while snow leopards are here now, they may not be here much longer.

Images

Tons of animal pelts and bones sit in storage at Royal Chitwan National Park in Nepal. The mounds of poached animal parts confiscated by forest rangers reach almost to the ceiling. The air is stifling, the stench stomach-churning.

An anecdote

The snow leopard stood so still in the frosty bushes, it wasn't until the goat squealed that we saw it. Its mottled white fur was now spattered with the goat's blood. Steam rose from the animal's wounds. We fumbled for our cameras, hoping to capture this terrible beauty.

A problem

Ecologists worry that the construction of a natural gas pipeline in Russia's Ukok Plateau will destroy the habitat of endangered snow leopards, argali mountain sheep, and steppe eagles.

A concisely stated thesis

If the governments of China and Russia don't act decisively soon, snow leopards will be extinct in a few years.

A contradiction or paradox

Snow leopards are tremendously versatile animals, strong enough to kill a horse and fast enough to chase down a hare. What they can't do is hide from poachers in Nepal and India. And this may be their downfall.

An odd, ridiculous, or unbelievable fact

Caterpillar fungus is a hot commodity. Traditional healers and their clients are willing to pay handsomely for illegally harvested ingredients for their treatments. As a result, demand for the fungus, along with other poached items like rhinoceros horns and snow leopard bones, drives a lucrative and destructive black market in endangered species.

Understand what ending paragraphs do

Ending paragraphs remind readers where they've been and invite them to carry your ideas forward. Use the ending paragraph to touch on your key points but do not merely summarize. Leave your readers with something that will inspire them to continue to think about what you have written.

Conclude with strength

The challenge in ending paragraphs is to leave the reader with something provocative, something beyond pure summary of the previous paragraphs. The following are strategies for ending an essay.

Issue a call to action

Although ecological problems in Russia seem distant, students like you and me can help protect the snow leopard by joining the World Wildlife Fund campaign.

Discuss the implications of your argument

Even though the extinction of snow leopards would be a sad event, their end is not the fundamental problem. Instead, their precarious position is a symptom of a larger dilemma: Environmental damage throughout developing nations in Asia threatens their biodiversity.

Explain the applications of your argument

This study of snow leopard breeding behavior can inform captive breeding programs in zoos.

Make recommendations

Russia's creditors would be wise to sign on to the World Wildlife Fund's proposal to relieve some of the country's debt in order to protect the snow leopard habitat. After all, if Russia is going to be economically viable, it needs to be ecologically healthy.

Speculate about the future

Unless Nepali and Chinese officials devote more resources to snow leopard preservation, these beautiful animals will be gone in a few years.

Tell an anecdote that illustrates a key point

Poachers are so uncowed by authorities that they even tried to sell a snow leopard skin to a reporter researching a story on endangered species.

Describe a key image

As they watched the pile of confiscated furs and bones burn, Nepali forest rangers flashed proud smiles that seemed to say, "This time we mean business."

Offer a quotation that expresses the essence of your argument

Too often, developed nations impose their high-flown priorities, like protecting snow leopards and tigers, on developing nations. A Russian farmer summed up the disjunction succinctly. Tigers ate two cows in his herd of fifty. When he was compensated for the two, he asked, "What's this? Can't the tiger come back and eat the remaining forty-eight?"

Ask a rhetorical question

Generally, the larger and more majestic (or better yet, cute) an endangered animal is, the better its chances of being saved. Bumper stickers don't implore us to save blind cave insects; they ask us to save the whales, elephants, and tigers. But snow leopards aren't cave bugs; they are beautiful, impressive animals that should be the easiest of all to protect. If we can't save them, do any endangered species stand a chance?

4 | Rewrite, Edit, and Proofread

QUICK *TAKE*

After reading this chapter, you should be able to . . .

- Evaluate your draft by reading critically (4a)
- Identify strategies for rewriting (4b)
- Apply edits for structure and style (4c)
- Demonstrate careful proofreading (4d)
- Compose responses to other writers' drafts (4e)

4a Switch from Writer to Reader

Even the best writers often have to revise several times to get the result they want. To be able to revise effectively, you have to plan your time. You cannot revise effectively if you wait until the last minute to begin working. Allow at least a day to let what you write sink in. With a little time, you will gain enough distance to "re-see" it, which, after all, is what *revision* means.

You must also have effective strategies for revising if you're going to be successful. The biggest trap you can fall into is starting off with the little stuff first. *Don't sweat the small stuff at the beginning.* When you see a word that's wrong or a misplaced comma, the great temptation is to fix it. But if you start searching for errors, it's hard to get back to the larger concerns.

Begin your revision by pretending you are someone who is either uninformed about your subject or holds an opposing view. If possible, think of an actual person and pretend to be that person. Read your draft aloud, all the way through. When you read aloud, you will probably hear clunky phrases and outright errors, but do no more at this stage than put checks in the margins so you can find these things later. Once again, you don't want to get bogged down with the little stuff.

Use the following questions to evaluate your draft. Note any places where you might make improvements.

Does your paper or project meet the assignment?

- Look again at your assignment, especially at the key words, such as *analyze*, *define*, *evaluate*, and *propose*. Does your paper or project do what the assignment asks?
- Look again at the assignment for specific guidelines, including length, format, and amount of research. Does your work meet these guidelines?

Does your writing have a clear focus?

- Does your project have an explicitly stated thesis? If not, is your thesis clearly implied?
- Is each paragraph related to your thesis?
- Do you get off the track at any point by introducing other topics?

Are your main points adequately developed?

- Can you add more examples and details that would help to support your main points?
- Would additional research fill in gaps or make your case stronger?

Is your organization effective?

- Are there any places where you find abrupt shifts or gaps?
- Are there sections or paragraphs that could be rearranged to make your draft more effective?

Do you consider your potential readers' knowledge and points of view?

- Do you give enough background if your readers are unfamiliar with your subject?
- Do you acknowledge opposing views that readers might have?

Do you represent yourself effectively?

- To the extent you can, forget for a moment that you wrote what you are reading. What impression do you have of you, the writer?
- Has "the writer" done his or her homework?

Do you conclude emphatically?

- Conclusions that only summarize tend to bore readers. Does your conclusion offer more than a review of ideas you have already fully discussed?
- Could you conclude by making recommendations for change or improvement, or by urging readers to take action?

When you finish, make a list of your goals for the revision. You may have to write another draft before you move to the next stage.

4b Understand Strategies for Rewriting

Now it's time to go through your draft in detail. You should work on the goals you identified in your review.

Get off to a fast start	• Revise your title to get your readers interested in your topic. • Reread each of your paragraphs' opening sentences. Think of ways you can make them more engaging.
Sharpen your focus wherever possible	• Revise your thesis and supporting paragraphs to make them more specific.
Develop your ideas	• Explain in more detail key points and ideas. • Find opportunities to add more supporting evidence.
Check links between paragraphs	• Signal the relationship between each paragraph. • Rewrite when you encounter an abrupt shift.
Strengthen your conclusion	• End with something interesting and provocative. Give your readers something to think about.

4c   Edit for Particular Goals

In your final pass through the text of your paper, you should concentrate on style and eliminate as many errors as you can.

1. Check the connections between sentences.   Notice how your sentences are connected. If you need to signal the relationship from one sentence to the next, use a transitional word or phrase.

2. Check your sentences.   If you notice that a sentence is hard to read or doesn't sound right when you read your paper aloud, think about how you might rephrase it. Often you can pick up problems with verbs (see Chapters 34 and 35), pronouns (see Chapter 36), and modifiers (see Chapter 37) by reading aloud. If a sentence seems too long, you might break it into two or more sentences. If you notice a string of short sentences that sound choppy, you might combine them. If you notice run-on sentences or sentence fragments, fix them (see Chapter 33).

3. Eliminate wordiness.   Writers tend to introduce wordiness in drafts. Look for long expressions that can easily be shortened (*at this point in time* to *now*) and unnecessary repetition. Remove unnecessary qualifiers (*rather, very, somewhat, little*). See how many words you can take out without losing the meaning (see Chapter 28).

4. Use active verbs.   Any time you can use a verb other than a form of *be* (*is, are, was, were*) or a verb ending in *-ing,* take advantage of the opportunity to make your style more lively. Sentences that begin with *There is (are)* and *It is* often have better alternatives.

> **Draft**   It is true that exercising a high degree of quality control in the manufacture of our products will be an incentive for increasing our market share.

> **Revised**   If we pay attention to quality when we make our products, more people will buy them.

Notice too that the use of active verbs often cuts down on wordiness (see Chapter 28).

5. Use specific and inclusive language.   As you read, stay alert for any vague words or phrases (see Chapter 30). Check to make sure that you have used inclusive language throughout (see Chapter 31).

Writer at Work

Gabriella Lopez received both global and local comments from her instructor. Gabriella first dealt with the global comments; she did additional research before adding the amplification shown in green. (Gabriella's final version of her project is in 23k.)

Returned draft with comments (opening paragraph)

> As concern about the environment grows, colleges and universities are beginning to incorporate sustainability into their programs. Environmental studies classes and majors are growing and diversifying.

Can you give examples here?

Gabriella's revision

> As concern about the environment grows, colleges and universities are beginning to incorporate sustainability into their programs. Environmental studies classes and majors are growing and diversifying. Students can now get MBAs in sustainable-business practices and train to build and operate wind turbines, among other things (Berman). In the area of public policy, a major in this field is also becoming more valuable. The *New York Times Magazine* notes this cultural trend: "Time was, environmental studies majors ran campus recycling programs. Now they run national campaigns" ("Learn").

Then Gabriella moved on to the local comments, including the following example.

Returned draft with comments (body paragraphs)

Some schools, most notably Yale University, have even established farms and gardens on or near campus that serve as living classrooms for environmental studies and provide food for students as well as the community.

Make a smoother transition to the next paragraph.

For those reasons, many schools, including our own, are finding it difficult to move beyond campus-wide recycling programs to other initiatives such as increasing the amount of local organic foods in the dining halls.

Gabriella added a sentence to connect the paragraphs.

Gabriella's revision

Some schools, most notably Yale University, have even established farms and gardens on or near campus that serve as living classrooms for environmental studies and provide food for students as well as the community.

"Going green" is not easy; nor is it inexpensive. For those reasons, many schools, including our own, are finding it difficult to move beyond campus-wide recycling programs to other initiatives such as increasing the amount of local organic foods in the dining halls.

4d Proofread Carefully

To proofread effectively, you have to learn to slow down. Some writers find that moving from word to word with a pencil slows them down enough to allow them to find errors. Others read backward to force themselves to concentrate on each word.

1. Know what your spelling checker can and cannot do.   Spelling checkers are the greatest invention since peanut butter. They turn up many typos and misspellings that are hard to catch. But spelling checkers do not catch wrong words (e.g., *to much* should be *too much*), missing endings (*three dog*), and other, similar errors. You still have to proofread carefully to eliminate misspellings.

2. Check for grammar and mechanics.   Nothing hurts your credibility with readers more than a text with numerous errors. Many job application letters get tossed in the reject pile because an applicant made a single glaring error. Issues of grammar are treated in Chapters 32–37. The conventions for using punctuation, capitalization, italics, abbreviations, acronyms, and numbers can be found in Chapters 38–47. Get into the habit of referring to these chapters.

4e Respond to Other Writers' Drafts

Your instructor may ask you to review your classmates' drafts. If you feel like you don't know enough to make useful comments, remember that you are charged only with letting the writer know how you—one of many potential readers—react.

1. Read the first time through without stopping.   When you finish you should have a good sense of the writer's main idea and purpose.

2. Read through a second time and pay attention to content, organization, and completeness.

- **Introduction:** Does the writer's first paragraph effectively introduce the topic and engage your interest? What might the writer do differently?
- **Thesis:** Where exactly is the writer's thesis? Draw a line under the thesis.
- **Audience:** Who is the writer's intended audience? What does the writer assume the audience knows and believes?

- **Focus:** Does the writer maintain focus on the topic? Note any places where the writer seems to wander off to another topic.
- **Organization:** Are the sections and paragraphs ordered effectively? Do any paragraphs seem to be out of place? Do you note any abrupt shifts? Can you suggest a better order for the paragraphs?
- **Completeness:** Do any sections and paragraphs lack key information or adequate development? Where do you want to know more?
- **Tone:** Is the tone appropriate for the writer's purpose and audience? Is the tone consistent throughout the draft? Are there places where another word or phrase might work better?
- **Sources:** If the draft uses outside sources, are they cited accurately? If there are quotations, are they used correctly and worked into the fabric of the draft?

3. Read the paper a third time, paying attention to style and sentence-level problems.

- **Make comments in the margins.** If you find a sentence hard to read, let the writer know. If you think a sentence is repetitive, let the writer know. If you think a word was left out, say so in the margin. Also let the writer know when a sentence is especially successful.

  Word missing here?
  Same point as sentence 1?
  Can you join this sentence with the previous sentence?
  Vivid description!

- **Use symbols to indicate possible problems.** Draw a wavy line under any phrase or sentence where you think there may be a problem. Even if you are not sure what the problem is, you can ask the writer to look carefully at a particular sentence. If you think a word is misspelled, draw a circle around it. If you think words can be deleted, put parentheses around them.

4. Write a note to the writer.
Summarize your comments and let the writer know about any issues that need to be addressed. Be specific and refer to paragraphs by number. When you finish, answer these two questions:

- What does the writer do especially well in the draft?
- What one or two things would most improve the draft in a revision?

WRITING SMART

Standard proofreading symbols

Advanced editing requires learning standard proofreading symbols. Authors, editors, and printers use proofreaders' marks to indicate changes. These marks are used in pairs: One mark goes in the text where the change is to be made, and the other goes in the margin, close to the change.

Mark in the margin	Mark in the text
ℯ	Delete: take it out
⌢	Close up: foot ball
∧	Caret: insert here
#	Insert a space: a word
ⓣⓡ	Transpose: the in beginning
⌃	Add a comma: moreover we
⌄	Add an apostrophe: Ellens books
⌄/⌄	Add double quotation marks: James Joyce's Clay
:	Add a colon: 3:45 p.m.
;	Add a semicolon: concluded however, we
⊙	Add a period: last call Next we
¶	Begin a new paragraph
No¶	No new paragraph
sp	Spell out: 7 dwarfs => seven dwarfs
stet	Ignore correction: in the beginning

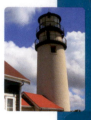

PART 2 Analyzing, Informing, Arguing

READING CRITICALLY AND WRITING FOR PURPOSES MAP

Understand what is involved in critical reading and viewing	• Read verbal texts critically and recognize verbal fallacies. Go to 5a–5d. • View visual texts critically and recognize visual fallacies. Go to 6a–6b.

Write an analysis	• Interpret a text or event to find connections and reach conclusions. Go to Chapter 7.

Write an informative essay	• Report information or explain a concept or idea. Go to Chapter 8.

Write a position argument	• Take a position on an issue. Go to Chapter 9.

Write a proposal argument	• Propose a solution to a problem that you identify. Go to Chapter 10.

5 | Read with a Critical Eye

QUICK*TAKE*

After reading this chapter, you should be able to . . .

- Demonstrate critical reading (5a)
- Demonstrate active reading (5b)
- Compose summaries and paraphrases of readings (5c)
- Recognize verbal fallacies (5d)
- Recognize how critical reading leads to writing (5e)

5a Become a Critical Reader

Critical thinking begins with critical reading. For most of what you read, one time through is enough. When you start asking questions about what you are reading, you are engaging in **critical reading**.

You've head the phrase "Don't believe everything you read." In part, this is what critical readers do. They don't take anything for granted. They want to know why something was written, who it is written for, and what bias might affect the writer's choice of sources and facts. They also pay attention to the choices the author made about word choice and organization, and how these choices affect readers.

Critical reading is a four-part process. First, begin by asking where a piece of writing came from and why it was written. Second, read the text carefully to find the author's central claim or thesis and the major points. Third, decide if you can trust the author. Fourth, read the text again to understand how it works.

Where did it come from?

- Who wrote this material?
- Where did it first appear? In a book, newspaper, magazine, or online?
- What else has been written about the topic or issue?
- What do you expect after reading the title?

What does it say?

- What is the topic or issue?
- What is the writer's thesis or overall point?
- Does the writer state the main point, or are you expected to infer it?

- What reasons or evidence does the writer offer?
- Who are the intended readers? What does the writer assume the readers know and believe?

Can you trust the writer?

- Does the writer have the necessary knowledge and experience to write on this subject?
- Do you detect a bias in the writer's position?
- Can you trust the writer's facts? Where did the facts come from?
- Are the sources reliable?
- Does the writer acknowledge opposing views and unfavorable evidence? Does the writer deal fairly with opposing views?

How does a text work?

- How is the piece of writing organized? How are the major points arranged?
- How does the writer conclude? Does the conclusion follow from the evidence the writer offers? What impression does the reader take away?
- How would you characterize the style? Describe the language that the writer uses.
- How does the writer represent herself or himself?

5b Read Actively

Critical readers are active readers: They put down the highlighter and read with a pen or pencil in hand. They take notes and map out the author's ideas so they can remember them easily. They list the questions they have about a reading so they can think about them later.

If you own what you are reading, make notes in the margins. If not, start a reading journal where you can record first impressions, note any ideas you find stimulating or useful, explore relationships, and write down questions.

Connect with what you read

You'll read more thoroughly if you consider how what you're reading matches up with what you already know or believe.

- Imagine that the author is with you. What points does the writer make that you would respond to in person?
- What questions would you ask the author? These indicate what you might need to look up.

- What ideas do you find that you might develop or interpret differently?

Annotate what you read

Using annotating strategies will make your effort more rewarding.

- **Mark major points and key concepts.** Sometimes major points are indicated by headings, but often you will need to locate them.
- **Connect passages.** Notice how ideas connect to each other. Draw lines and arrows. If an idea connects to something a few pages before, write a note in the margin with the page number.
- **Ask questions.** Note anything that puzzles you, including words to look up.
- **Pay attention to the outside sources the writer uses.** Are they current, relevant, and trustworthy?

Sample: Critical response

What really makes Portland unusual is how it has chosen to grow. While most American cities were building more highways, Portland invested in transit and biking. While most cities were reaming out their roadways to speed traffic, Portland implemented a Skinny Streets program. While most American cities were amassing a spare tire of undifferentiated sprawl, Portland instituted an urban growth boundary. These efforts and others like them, over several decades—a blink of the eye in planner time—have changed the way that Portlanders live.

This par. talks about how Portland became walkable. What is this program?

This change is not dramatic—were it not for the roving hordes of bicyclists, it might be invisible—but it is significant. While almost every other American city has seen its residents drive farther and farther every year and spend more and more of their time stuck in traffic, Portland's vehicle miles traveled per person peaked in 1996. Now, compared to other major metropolitan areas, Portlanders on average drive 20 percent less (Cortright 1).

Speck uses a lot of info from this source.

Small change? Not really: according to Cortright, this 20 percent (four miles per citizen per day) adds up to $1.1 billion of savings each year, which equals fully 1.5 percent of all personal income earned in the region. And that number ignores time not wasted in traffic: peak travel times have actually fallen from 54 minutes per day to 43 minutes per day (1-2). Cortright calculates this improvement at another $1.5 billion. Add those two dollar amounts together and you're talking real money.

What are the savings mentioned here? Gas money? What else? Check Cortright.

—Jeff Speck, "The Walkability Dividend." From *Walkable City: How Downtown Can Save America, One Step at a Time,* Farrar, Straus and Giroux, 2012.

Sample: Map of structure

Effects of Skinny Streets Program

Skinny Streets program ➔ Portlanders drive 20% less than other metro drivers ➔ Cortright says they save $1.1 billion annually

Identify the rhetorical situation

Remember that it's always helpful to understand the rhetorical situation when you are working with a reading. Use search tools to explore the larger conversation about the issue your author identifies.

Outline a reading

Another strategy that you can use to better understand a text that you're reading is to outline it. Creating a working (or informal) outline that describes what a reading says, paragraph by paragraph, will help you see how a reading is organized and how the different ideas in the reading relate to each other and to the main thesis. When outlining a reading, you'll want to include the main thesis of the reading as well as a sentence or phrase that recaps each paragraph of the reading.

The following is a working outline for the opening paragraphs from the "The Walkability Dividend" by Jeff Speck.

> *Thesis: There are real benefits to living in a walkable city*
>
> *1. How is Portland different from other cities [Background info]*
>
> *2. How are Portland's urban growth strategies different from those in other cities [Background info]*
>
> *3. Today, Portlanders drive 20% less than people in other cities [Why Portland is used as the example in this reading]*
>
> *4. Billions of dollars saved from driving less in Portland [Evidence to support main thesis]*
>
> *5. Where does saved money go? Above-average spending on recreation in Portland*

5c Summarize and Paraphrase

Write a summary

A summary should be concise but thorough.

- Begin your summary with the main point.
- Then report the key ideas. Represent the author's argument in miniature as accurately as you can, quoting exact words for key points (see 21e and 21f for how to quote and integrate an author's words into your summary).
- Your aim is to give your readers an understanding of what the author is arguing for. Withhold judgment even if you think the author is dead wrong. Do not insert your opinions and comments. Stick to what the author is saying and what position the author is advocating.

Usually summaries are no longer than 150 words. Note the following example.

> Jeff Speck argues that Portland's commitment to being walkable has benefited the city in many ways. Drawing on a report by Joe Cortright entitled "Portland's Green Dividend," he notes that Portland's decision to invest in transit and biking, rather than build more highways, has resulted in Portlanders driving 20 percent less than people in other metro areas.
>
> The result is a savings of approximately $2.6 billion dollars that gets reinvested locally, either in entertainment (according to

Cortland) or in their homes (according to Christopher Leinberger, *The Option of Urbanism: Investing in a New American Dream*). Speck also notes that residents of walkable cities suffered less when gas prices increased and the housing bubble burst. Other benefits of walkability include the creation of jobs improving transit and bicycle facilities, the influx of knowledge-based jobs, and the influx of college-educated workers. Cortland concludes that "creating a higher quality of life is the first step to attracting new residents and jobs" (qtd. in Speck 29).

Speck, Jeff. "The Walkability Dividend." *Walkable City: How Downtown Can Save America, One Step at a Time*, Farrar, Straus and Giroux, 2012.

Write a paraphrase

When you paraphrase, you represent the ideas articulated in a source in your own words at about the same length as the original. If you use the exact words from the source, then you will need to put them within quotation marks and cite the page number. Also cite the page number for the source of any facts you include. Read the following example.

In "The Walkability Dividend," Jeff Speck examines the economic benefits that Portland enjoys from reducing the vehicle miles driven per person by 20 percent since 1996 (29). Drawing on statistics from Joe Cortright, Speck concludes that the people of Portland save over $2.6 billion by driving less. Furthermore, Speck argues that the money saved on cars and gasoline—money that now leaves the city—gets invested in housing, which Speck says is "about as local as it gets" (29).

Decide when to summarize and when to paraphrase

When you want to discuss a text that you've read, you'll need to decide if you should summarize or paraphrase or even quote from the reading. In general, if you want to discuss the details of a reading or some particular part of an argument, then it works best to paraphrase or quote from the reading. However, if you want to mention only the basic argument or main point of a reading, or if you want to broadly compare one reading with another, then it works best to use a short summary.

5d Recognize Verbal Fallacies

Reasoning depends less on proving a claim than it does on finding evidence for that claim that readers will accept as valid. The kinds of faulty reasoning called *logical fallacies* reflect failures to provide sufficient evidence for a claim that is being made.

Fallacies of logic

- **Begging the question.** *People who take 8:00 a.m. classes are crazy because no sane person would choose to get up that early.* The fallacy of begging the question occurs when the claim is restated and passed off as evidence.

- **Cherry-picking the evidence.** Our car's gas mileage is best in class. Auto manufacturers are notorious for exaggerating fuel economy on data from the most favorable conditions—special software settings, tailwinds, and wrong tire sizes.

- **Either-or.** *Either fraternities must be forced to cancel all parties, or the university will never be able to control its underage drinking problem.* The either-or fallacy suggests that there are only two choices in a complex situation. Rarely, if ever, is this the case. (In this example, the writer ignores the fact that some students under 21 drink when they are not at a fraternity party.)

- **False analogies.** *Permitting children to play computer games in school is like giving them ice cream for watching television.* Analogies always depend on the degree of resemblance of one situation to another. In this case, the analogy fails to consider the content of the computer games and what children might be learning.

- **Hasty generalization.** *We have been in a drought for three years; that's a sure sign of climate change.* A hasty generalization is a broad claim made on the basis of a few occurrences. Climate cycles occur regularly over spans of a few years; climate trends must be observed over centuries.

- **Non sequitur.** *Janet Jackson's "wardrobe malfunction" during the 2004 Super Bowl shows how far contemporary morals have sunk.* A non sequitur (which is a Latin term meaning "it does not follow") ties together two unrelated ideas. In this case, one person's behavior is not indicative of society's morals.

- **Oversimplification.** *If the federal income tax were doubled for all wage brackets, then we could easily provide comprehensive health care for all citizens.* This claim may be true, but the argument would be unacceptable to most citizens. More complex, if less definitive, solutions are called for.

- ***Post hoc* fallacy.** *The stock market goes down when the AFC wins the Super Bowl in even years.* The *post hoc* fallacy (from the Latin *post hoc ergo propter hoc,* which means "after this, therefore because of this") assumes that things that follow in time have a causal relationship.

- **Rationalization.** *I could have finished my paper on time if my printer was working.* People frequently come up with excuses and weak

explanations for their own and others' behavior that avoid actual causes.

- **Slippery slope.** *If the government were to legalize a gateway drug like marijuana, there would be a huge increase in the use of hard drugs like cocaine and heroin.* The slippery slope fallacy maintains that one thing inevitably will cause something else to happen.

Fallacies of emotion and language

- **Bandwagon appeals.** *Since all the power hitters in baseball use steroids, I'll have to use them too if I want to be able to compete.* This argument suggests that everyone is doing it, so why shouldn't you? But on close examination, it may be that everyone really isn't doing it—and in any case, it may not be the right thing to do.

- **Name calling.** Name calling is frequent in politics and among competing groups (*radical, tax-and-spend liberal, racist, fascist, right-wing ideologue*). Unless these terms are carefully defined, they are meaningless.

- **Polarization.** *Feminists are all man haters.* Polarization, like name calling, exaggerates positions and groups by representing them as extreme and divisive.

- **Straw man.** *Liberals want America to lose the war on terror so that our country will have less influence on global affairs.* A straw man argument is a diversionary tactic that sets up another's position in a way that can be easily rejected.

5e   Move from Critical Reading to Writing

In college writing, you will be asked to make a contribution to an ongoing conversation about a topic. But you can't say anything new until you know what the conversation is about. That's why critical reading is important. When you read critically and use active reading techniques, you fully engage another writer's ideas about a topic. Engaging ideas will help you find out what you think about the topic yourself and what you'd like to write about it.

The first step is to gain a basic *understanding* of what the other writer has said. You may find yourself looking up unfamiliar words or doing research, especially if the writer refers to people or events you don't know. You will also need to *interpret* what you read. Interpretation is reading between the lines to figure out what the writer really means.

When people hear the word *interpret*, they typically think of interpreting symbols in a poem or short story. But interpretation is important in

reading nonfiction, too. Sometimes writers don't state their main point directly. When that happens, you will have to look carefully at what they *do* say and *how* they say it, and draw your own conclusions about what they mean.

Once you have a basic understanding of what a writer has said, you can begin *analyzing* a piece of writing more completely. Analysis is breaking the whole down into its parts and considering how the pieces fit together. For instance, if you want to know how a politician persuades an audience, you consider several pieces: how the politician builds credibility with listeners, how she appeals to their emotions and emphasizes shared values, and what claims she makes and what reasons she offers in support of them. Looking at these pieces can give you a sense of how the speech works as a whole.

As you read, you also *evaluate* what a writer says. Perhaps some of her reasons seem weaker than others, or he offers examples that are no longer relevant. Perhaps the data he uses is out of date or comes from unreliable sources. Or perhaps the opposite is true: Her points are clear and well supported. Seeing the weaknesses and strengths of another writer's argument can give you ideas about where you can contribute to the discussion.

Interpretation, analysis, and evaluation make up the groundwork for *synthesis*, or putting the pieces together in a new way. If you read carefully and critically, you will be well prepared to synthesize what you've read with what you know and to create something original when you write.

6 | View with a Critical Eye

QUICKTAKE

After reading this chapter, you should be able to . . .
- Analyze images by reading them critically and actively (6a)
- Identify visual fallacies (6b)

6a Become a Critical Viewer

Critical viewing is similar to critical reading. An image such as a photograph doesn't float in space but instead has a specific location—in a book with a caption, in a family photo album, in a magazine advertisement, on a Web page—that tells us a great deal about why the photograph was taken and what purpose it is intended to serve. But even without the external context, there are often clues within a photograph that suggest its origins.

We could guess the approximate date of the photograph on the following page by the content of the billboard. By the end of the 1950s, long-distance travel by passenger train was being replaced by airline travel, so the picture must have been taken before then. The name of the railroad, Southern Pacific, along with the barren landscape, indicates that the photograph was taken in the southwestern United States. In fact, this photograph was taken in 1937 by Dorothea Lange (1895–1955), who gave it the title "Toward Los Angeles, California."

One approach to critical viewing is to examine a photograph in terms of its **composition**. In Lange's photograph the lines of the shoulder of the road, the highway, and the telephone poles slope toward a vanishing point on the horizon, giving the image a sense of great distance. At the same time, the image divides into ground and sky with the horizon line in the center. The two figures in dark clothing walking away contrast to a rectangular billboard with a white background and white frame.

Another approach to critical viewing is to **analyze the content**. In 1937 the United States was in the midst of the Great Depression and a severe drought, which forced many small farmers in middle America to abandon their homes and go to California in search of work. The luxury portrayed on the billboard contrasts with the two walking figures, who presumably do not have bus fare, much less enough money for a luxury train. By placing the figures and the billboard beside each other (a visual relationship called **juxtaposition**), Lange is able to make an ironic commentary on the lives of well-off and poor Americans during the depression.

No one set of questions can cover the great variety of images, but a few general questions can assist you in developing a critical response.

- What kind of an image or visual is it?
- Who created this image (movie, advertisement, television program, and so on)?
- What is it about? What is portrayed in the image?
- Where did it first appear? Where do you usually find images like this one?
- When did it appear?

The following questions are primarily for still images. For animations, movies, and television, you also have to ask questions about how the story is being told.

- What attracts your eye first? If there is an attention-grabbing element, how does it connect with the rest of the image?
- What impression of the subject does the image create?
- How does the image appeal to the values of the audience? (For example, politicians love to be photographed with children.)
- How does the image relate to what surrounds it?
- Was it intended to serve purposes other than art and entertainment?

6b Recognize Visual Fallacies

Misleading images and videos

The era of digital imaging has made it possible to create images of lifelike dinosaurs chasing humans, interactions between people now living and those long dead, and human feats that defy human limits and the laws of physics.

■ Can't afford a vacation to Egypt? *Photoshop* can take you there.

Almost from the beginnings of photography, images were staged and negatives were manipulated. In the twentieth century, the technicians in Hitler's and Stalin's darkrooms became experts in removing from photographs people who had fallen out of favor.

The difference in the digital era is that anyone can do it. Perhaps there's nothing wrong with using *Photoshop* to add absent relatives to family photographs or remove ex-boyfriends and ex-girlfriends. Few people complain when a photographer shaves off a few pounds with the *Photoshop* liquefy filter. More doubtful is the routine practice of fashion magazines giving already thin models unnatural shapes or adding muscles to male stars, yet we accept that anything goes in advertising.

But where should we draw the line? Not only do many videos on *YouTube* use outright deception, but newsmagazines and networks have also been found guilty of these practices. Ask questions about what you view.

- Who created the image or video? What bias might the creator have?
- Who published the image or video? What bias might the publisher have?
- Who is the intended audience? For example, political videos often assume that the viewers hold the same political views as the creators.
- What is being shown, and what is not being shown? For example, a video ad promoting tourism for the Gulf of Mexico will look very different from a video showing sources of pollution.
- Who is being represented, and who is not being represented? Who gets left out is as important as who gets included.
- In images, how does the caption influence the interpretation? In videos, how does the voiceover narration shape the meaning?

Misleading charts

A special category of visual fallacies is misleading charts. For example, the fictitious company Glitzycorp might use the chart in Figure 6.1 to attract investors. The chart shows what looks like remarkable growth from 2014 to 2016 and projects additional sales for 2017. But is the picture quite as rosy as it is painted?

Notice that the bars in this bar chart start at 20 rather than at 0. The effect is to make the $22 million sales in 2015 appear to double the $21 million sales of 2014, even though the increase was less than 5 percent. Three years is also a short span to use to project a company's future profits. Figure 6.2 shows the sales of Glitzycorp over seven years, and it tells quite a different story. The big growth years were in 2011 and 2012, followed by a collapse in 2013 and slow growth ever since.

Glitzycorp's sales charts illustrate how facts can be manipulated in visual presentations.

Figure 6.1   Misleading.
The starting point on the y-axis is $20 million, not 0.

Figure 6.2   Accurate.
The actual increase from 2014 to 2016 was less than 5%.

7 | Write an Analysis

QUICK*TAKE*

After reading this chapter, you should be able to . . .

- Analyze a text rhetorically (7a)
- Analyze texts in context (7b)
- Organize and write a rhetorical analysis (7c)
- Analyze a sample rhetorical analysis (7d)
- Analyze images and other kinds of visual texts (7e)

7a Understand the Goal of a Rhetorical Analysis

The goal of a **rhetorical analysis** is to understand how a particular act of writing or speaking influenced particular people at a particular time. Rhetorical analysis is not limited to speaking and writing. The tools of rhetorical analysis have been applied to understanding how meaning is made by art, buildings, photographs, dance, memorials, Web sites, music, advertisements—any kind of symbolic communication.

Writing a rhetorical analysis (also called "critical analysis" or "textual analysis") is frequently an assignment in college. A rhetorical analysis requires you to step back from a text and consider it from multiple perspectives. Writing a rhetorical analysis can give you a heightened awareness of a text and a better appreciation of what the author has accomplished.

Understanding how communication works or fails to work is a worthy goal by itself, but rhetorical analysis has other benefits. It enables you to think about a text in more depth, to better understand the arguments it makes, and to appreciate how it is put together. In turn, this knowledge helps you in writing your own text. You will have a much better sense of what has been said and written about your subject and where you have opportunities to contribute your own ideas.

7b Analyze the Context and the Text

A rhetorical analysis begins with a text to analyze. If your instructor does not assign a text, select a text that has significance for you, either because it was important when it was written or because it is about a subject that is important to you.

Think of your analysis as running on a continuum between considering the **context**—the relationship between the piece of writing or speaking and the larger society surrounding it—and the **text** itself—what it is about and how it is designed. We can think of the context, which lies at one end of the continuum, in two senses. First, the **immediate context** refers to where the

The Gettysburg Address

■ Text

■ Broader context

■ Immediate context

text was written and read or heard. For example, Abraham Lincoln delivered his 10-sentence, 272-word Gettysburg Address on November 19, 1863, at the dedication ceremony of a national cemetery, where he followed a speaker who had talked for 2 hours. Second, the **broader context** refers to the larger cultural and historical circumstances in which a text is produced and read. The broader context of the Gettysburg Address was, of course, the American Civil War, which had taken thousands of lives and was far from over at the time Lincoln spoke. Lincoln's brief remarks have been immortalized because he could envision an end to the war and a healing process.

At the other end of the continuum lies the text itself. We can consider a text as if it were a piece in a museum, where we closely scrutinize it. For example, if you look carefully at the language of the Gettysburg Address, you'll begin to appreciate Lincoln's tactics and skill. He says of his purpose: "We have come to dedicate a portion of that field, as a final resting place for those who here gave their lives that that nation might live."

But then he immediately turns this purpose on its head: "But in a larger sense, we can not dedicate—we can not consecrate—we can not hallow—this ground. The brave men, living and dead, who struggled here, have consecrated it, far above our poor power to add or detract." Lincoln's words become powerful because they defy expectation: We cannot consecrate the field because the field is already consecrated. Lincoln does not once refer to "the enemy" in the Gettysburg Address. Instead he says, "The brave men, living and dead, who struggled here." Even though the cemetery was a burying ground for Union soldiers, Lincoln's language invokes the heroism and sacrifice of both sides.

Often in the back-and-forth movement between text and context, you gain surprising insights about how a text achieves certain effects. The following questions will help you get started in composing a rhetorical analysis.

Analyze the immediate context
Examine the author

- What is the author's purpose: to change beliefs? to inspire action? to teach about a subject? to praise or blame? to amuse?
- How did the author come to this subject?
- What else did the author write?

Examine the audience

- Who was the intended audience?
- What were their attitudes and beliefs about the subject?
- What were their attitudes and beliefs about the author?
- What does the author assume about the audience?

Analyze the broader context
Examine the larger conversation

- Why did this text appear at this particular time?
- What else has been said or written about this subject?
- What was going on at the time that influenced this text?

Examine the larger society

- What social, political, and economic influences can you find in the text?

Analyze the text
Examine the kind of text

- What kind of text is it: speech? essay? letter? editorial? advertisement?
- What is the medium: print? online? voice recording?

Summarize the content

- What is the author's main claim or main idea?
- How is the main claim or main idea supported?
- How is the text organized?

Examine the appeals

- *Ethos:* How does the author represent himself or herself? How does the author build or fail to build trust?
- *Logos:* What kinds of facts and evidence does the author use?
- *Pathos:* How does the author appeal to values shared with the audience?

Examine the language and style

- Is the style formal? informal? academic?
- Does the author use humor or satire?
- What metaphors are used?

7c   Organize and Write a Rhetorical Analysis

When you have completed your initial analysis, you are ready to begin writing. Expect to discover additional ideas you can use in the analysis while you are writing and when you read the text again.

1 **Before you write**

Take stock of your initial analysis
- If your selected text isn't working for the assignment, find one that works better.
- Look at your notes on the author, the audience, the circumstances of original publication or delivery, what other texts the author was responding to, and what else was going on at the time.
- Spend some time thinking about how to organize your analysis.

Think about your readers
- How much do readers know about your text? the author? the events surrounding the text? other texts like it?
- What will readers gain from reading your analysis?

2 **Write an introduction**

Begin your analysis by giving the necessary background
- Inform your readers about the author and why the author selected this particular topic.
- Tell readers about the original audience and the conversation about the topic that was going on at the time the text was written.

Make a claim
- Make a claim about how the text you are analyzing uses rhetoric for particular purposes.

3 **Organize and write the body of your paper**

Support your claim with your detailed analysis of the text and context
- Give examples from the text to show how the author builds credibility with the audience, appeals to their values and beliefs, and convinces them with facts and evidence.
- Analyze the author's style, tone, and language, including metaphors.
- Analyze how the author responded to the immediate context and to the broader context.

4 **Write a conclusion**

End with more than a summary
- Draw larger implications from your analysis.
- End with a vivid example from the text.

5 **Revise, revise, revise**

Evaluate your draft
- Make sure your analysis meets the requirements of the assignment.
- Consider where you might provide more information about the context.
- Consider where you might provide more evidence supporting your claim about the text.
- When you have finished revising, edit and proofread carefully.

7d **Sample Rhetorical Analysis**

Jackson 1

Samantha Jackson

Professor Janis

English 100

3 May 2016

Rhetorical Strategies in Sojourner Truth's

"Ain't I a Woman?"

Sojourner Truth was born into slavery in 1797 and given the name Isabella Baumfree. Between 1797 and her escape from slavery in 1827, Isabella was "owned" by five different masters. Her last owner, John Dumont, sometimes bragged that she could "do a good family's washing in the night and be ready to go into the field the next morning, where she would do as much raking and binding as his best hands" (Washington 15). However, in 1817, the New York Legislature had passed a law that slavery in New York would end ten years later, on July 4, 1827. With this date fast approaching, Dumont decided to strike a deal with Isabella: he would release her one

Jackson's opening provides background to help readers understand why Truth's personal history is relevant.

Jackson 2

year early if she worked hard throughout 1826. Isabella
agreed, but at the end of the year Dumont refused
to release her. Enraged, Isabella escaped. After
experiencing mystical visions from God on June 1, 1843,
at the age of forty-six, Isabella changed her name to
Sojourner Truth and pledged to "'sojourn' the land and
speak the 'truth' of God's word" (Washington 15).

This paragraph uses examples to show how slavery and the Women's Suffrage movement shaped the rhetorical situation.

As debates over slavery raged, Sojourner was
sometimes harassed. Once she was told that a building
she was scheduled to speak in would be burned down if
she lectured there. She replied, "Then I will speak to
the ashes" (Washington 11). As the Women's Suffrage
movement became more popular in the late 1840s,
Truth took notice. In 1851 she traveled to Akron, Ohio,
to attend a women's rights convention aimed at getting
Ohio to add more rights for women in its state
constitution. Many Ohioans were against this goal.
Many local men, including several ministers, attended
the convention just to heckle speakers. Sojourner Truth

In these sentences, Jackson makes a claim about the persuasive power of Truth's speech.

delivered her famous "Ain't I a Woman?" speech in this
intense atmosphere. In her spontaneous lecture, Truth
used her own physical and intellectual credibility to
make powerful emotional appeals and convincing
logical claims. Her arguments redefined the word
"womanhood" and made direct connections between
women's rights and the abolition of slavery for an all-
white audience. Her powerful speech was so successful
that her words are the main reason this convention is
remembered today.

Jackson 3

When Truth began to speak, her words displayed her experience and wisdom. Rather than addressing her audience as "Ladies and gentlemen," or, "Members of the convention," Truth begins this way: "Well children, when there is so much racket there must be something out of kilter" (268). By using the word "children" to address her adult, white audience, Truth draws attention to her age and wisdom, and at the same time proves that she is equal to, not subservient to, these white adults. She also refers to the heated arguments between the women and men attending the convention as "so much racket," a statement that takes her out of the arguments she is witnessing and therefore makes her seem like a voice of reason in a chaotic environment.

> Jackson demonstrates how Truth established her relationship to her audience in the opening of her speech.

Another reason Truth was such an effective speaker at this convention was how she used humor to break down arguments against women's rights. Just after she notes that the convention has become a "racket," she offers a tongue-in-cheek observation: "I think that 'twixt the negroes of the South and the women at the North, all talking about rights, the white men will be in a fix pretty soon" (268). Although Truth is making the serious point that when white women and African Americans get equal rights, white men will be less powerful, she uses humor to break up some of the tension of the moment.

> Jackson discusses the humor employed by Truth to defuse tension and put her audience at ease.

Once Truth has her audience listening through this light tone, she begins to use her status as a former slave woman to bring out feelings of guilt and shame in her audience. She builds her argument slowly.

First, she shows the fallacy in the argument that women do not need rights because male chivalry protects them from harm and guarantees them protection. Truth restates this argument: "That man over there says that women need to be helped into carriages, and lifted over ditches, and to have the best place everywhere." She points out that as a poor, black woman, she is excluded from this definition of womanhood: "Nobody ever helps me into carriages, or over mud puddles, or gives me any best place! And ain't I a woman?" (268).

She next shows the connection between women's rights and abolition by referring to the unique horrors of womanhood under slavery:

> I could work as much and eat as much as a man—when I could get it—and bear the lash as well! And ain't I a woman? I have borne thirteen children, and seen them most all sold off to slavery, and when I cried out with a mother's grief none but Jesus heard me. (268-69)

By using emotional appeals to produce shame in her audience, Truth connects women's rights and abolition. She argues that people who believe women should be protected and treated to "the best" are obliged to treat all women, black and white, with "chivalry."

Although Truth is appealing to her audience's shame here, and asking them to reconsider their positions on women's rights and abolition, her main way of arguing is through logic. Truth tries to expose the flaws in arguments

This paragraph demonstrates how Truth built her argument by drawing on personal experience and by using emotional appeals to her audience's sense of shame.

Jackson analyzes Truth's use of logic to expose fallacies in common arguments against women's rights.

Jackson 5

against women's rights, and also in arguments against equal rights for African Americans. First, Truth points out that claiming that chivalry makes rights unnecessary for women is illogical because her audience's definition of "woman" is flawed. Women, she argues, are not only people who need assistance getting into fancy carriages, or those who wear expensive clothes that must be protected from mud puddles. Women are also people like her, who "have ploughed and planted, and gathered into barns" (268).

Truth's most powerful logical argument for this audience of mostly religious men is her argument about God, Eve, and women's rights. She first restates their argument: that "women can't have as much rights as men, 'cause Christ wasn't a woman." Then she exposes the flaws in that argument: she asks, "Where did your Christ come from?" and answers, "From God and a woman. Man had nothing to do with Him." Then, turning to her audience's argument that women should not have rights because of Eve's sins, she asks, "If the first woman God ever made was strong enough to turn the world upside down all alone, these women together ought to be able to turn it back, and get it right side up again!" She is arguing here that if these men credit the first woman, Eve, with such a huge amount of power, then they should see that other women are equally powerful and should be given equal rights. If Eve turned the world upside down, these women can turn it right-side up again. Truth argues: "And now they is asking to do it, the men better let them."

Jackson describes the process Truth used to counter arguments that the Bible authorized male supremacy.

Jackson 6

Finally, Truth addresses the topic of intelligence: "Then they talk about this thing in the head; what's this they call it?" (269). An audience member reminds her that the word is "intellect," and she replies, "That's it, honey." She then asks, "What's that got to do with women's rights or negro's rights?" (269). This question is deceptive. Although at first it seems like Truth is agreeing with sexist notions when she characterizes women's minds as capable of "hold[ing] but a pint" while male minds can "hold a quart," it becomes clear that she is using flattery as a manipulative tool: "if my cup won't hold but a pint, and yours holds a quart, wouldn't you be mean not to let me have my little half measure full?" Clearly, a speaker who can develop such convincing logical arguments is just as intelligent as the audience members whose arguments she exposed as flawed. It is for this reason that Sojourner Truth's "Ain't I a Woman?" speech made such an impression then, and continues to do so today.

> Jackson concludes with a powerful example of Truth's wit.

Jackson 7

Works Cited

Truth, Sojourner. "Ain't I a Woman?" *Argument in America: Essential Issues, Essential Texts*, edited by Jack Selzer, Longman Publishers, 2004, pp. 268-69.

Washington, Margaret, editor. *The Narrative of Sojourner Truth*. Random House, 1993.

7e Analyze Images and Other Visual Texts

The word *text* typically brings to mind words on a printed page. But in the sense that anything that can be "read" can be a text, then nearly everything is a text. We see hundreds of visual texts every day distributed on television, the Web, films, newspapers, advertisements, product labels, clothing, signs, buildings—indeed, on nearly everything. We can analyze how these images create meaning by the same means we use to analyze verbal texts— by examining the relationship between the text and its contexts.

Some culturally significant images, significant at least at the time they were created, are public art and public sculpture. On the south bridge house of the Michigan Avenue Bridge crossing the Chicago River in downtown Chicago is a large relief sculpture depicting the massacre of settlers fleeing Fort Dearborn in 1812. The size of the sculpture and its placement on the busiest and most famous street in Chicago attests to its significance at the time it was commissioned.

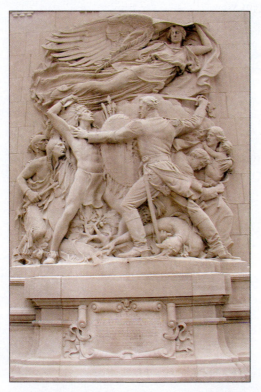

■ Relief sculpture of the Fort Dearborn Massacre, on the Michigan Avenue Bridge, Chicago

Two central figures—an American soldier and a Potawatomi Indian—battle as an angel hovers above. On the left another Indian is stealthily approaching, crouched with a tomahawk in hand. On the right a man shields a woman and a child from the threat. The sculpture uses a familiar stereotype of American Indians to make a visual argument: The Indians are attacking because they are bloodthirsty and sneaky; the innocent settlers bravely resist. The sculpture does not speak to the circumstances of the massacre: The Potawatomis allied with the British during the War of 1812 to resist settlers who were taking their land, and the settlers waited too long to evacuate Fort Dearborn in the face of growing numbers of Indians surrounding the fort.

It's not surprising that the sculpture represents the settlers as heroic. The bridge and monument were part of a grand plan, begun in 1909, to enhance Chicago's waterfront. Thus, the monument plays its part in obscuring the actual history of the area. Viewers who are unaware of the facts may feel a sense of patriotic pride in the actions of the soldier and the woman. Viewers who are familiar with the whole story may take a different view.

8 | Write an Informative Essay

QUICK_TAKE_

After reading this chapter, you should be able to . . .
- Select a topic that explains or explores questions and problems (8a)
- Construct a thesis statement from a narrowed topic (8b)
- Organize and write an informative essay (8c)

8a Find an Informative Topic

Many of the writing tasks assigned in college are informative—from lab reports and essay exams to analyses of literature, research papers, and case studies. Look at your assignment for key words such as _study, analyze, explain_, and _explore_, which indicate what kind of writing you are expected to produce (see 2a). Informative writing has four primary functions: to report new or unfamiliar information; to analyze for meaning, patterns, and connections; to explain how to do something or how something works; and to explore questions and problems.

Reporting information

Reporting information takes many forms, ranging from reports of experimental research and reports of library research to simple lists of information. In one sense, writing to persuade (Chapters 9 and 10) also reports information. The main difference is that the focus of a report and other informative kinds of writing is on the subject, not on the writer's reflections or on changing readers' minds or on getting them to take action. Writers of reports usually stay in the background and keep their language as neutral as possible.

Analyzing meaning, patterns, and connections

Writers not only report what they read and observe; they also often construct meaning through selecting what and what not to include and in organizing that information. Sometimes this construction of meaning is made explicit as **analysis**. The complexity of the world we live in requires making connections. For example, advertisers know that certain kinds of ads (for example, ads that associate drinking beer with social life) sell the product, but often they do not know exactly how these ads work or why some ads are more effective than others.

Explaining how

Often what you know well is difficult to explain to others. You may know how to solve certain kinds of difficult problems, such as how to fix a problem in your car's electrical system, but if you have to tell a friend how to do it over the phone, you may quickly become very frustrated. Often you have to break down a process into steps that you can describe in order to explain it. Explaining a process sometimes requires you to think about something familiar in a new way.

Exploring questions and problems

Not all informative writing is about topics with which you are familiar or ones that you can bring to closure. Often college writing involves issues or problems that perplex us and for which we cannot come to a definitive conclusion. The goal in such writing is not the ending but the journey. Tracing the turns of thought in a difficult intellectual problem can result in writing far beyond the ordinary. Difficult issues often leave us conflicted; readers appreciate it when we deal honestly with those conflicts.

Finding a topic

When your general subject is specified in your assignment, you can make your work more enjoyable by choosing a specific topic that is either more familiar to you or that you find particularly interesting. Your level of engagement in a topic can have a real impact on your readers' level of interest. Here are guidelines you can use when choosing a topic.

- Choose a topic you will enjoy writing about.
- Choose a topic that readers will enjoy reading about.
- Choose a topic for which you can make a contribution of your own, perhaps by viewing something familiar in a new way.
- If you choose an unfamiliar topic, you must be strongly committed to learning more about it.

8b Narrow Your Topic and Write a Thesis

A central difficulty with writing to inform is determining where to stop. For any large subject, even a lifetime may be insufficient. The key to success is to limit the topic. Find a topic you can cover thoroughly in the space you have. Broad, general topics are nearly impossible to cover in an essay of five pages. Look for ways of dividing large topics, such as *the use of steroids among college students*, into smaller

categories and select one that is promising. *Why college athletes ignore the risks of steroids* is a topic that you are more likely to be able to cover in a short paper.

Often your readers will lack initial interest in your topic. If you ignore their lack of interest, they in turn will likely ignore you. Instead, you can take your readers' knowledge and interest into account when you draft your thesis. For example, someone who knows a lot about birds in the parks of your city might write this informative thesis:

> Watching birds in urban areas is interesting because unusual birds often show up in city parks.

It doesn't sound like a topic that most college students would find as interesting as the writer does. But if the writer puts the audience's attitude in the foreground, challenging them to consider a subject they have likely not thought much about, a college audience might read beyond the title.

> Although most college students think of bird watching as an activity for retired people, watching birds gives you a daily experience with nature, even in urban areas.

This thesis also gives the writer a stance from which to approach the topic.

8c Organize and Write an Informative Essay

Successful reporting of information requires a clear understanding of the subject and a clear presentation. How much information you need to include depends on your readers' knowledge of and potential interest in your topic. You might not follow this order, as writing is often a back-and-forth process.

---

1 **Before you write**

Think about your readers
- What do your readers already know about the subject?
- What questions or concerns might they have about your subject?
- What is their attitude toward the subject? If it is different from yours, how can you address the difference?

Review your thesis and scope
- When you learn more about your topic, you should be able to identify one aspect or concept that you can cover thoroughly.

2 Write an introduction

Engage your readers quickly
- Write a title and an introduction that will make readers take an interest in your topic.

3 Organize and write the body of your paper

Think about your main points
- Use an idea map to organize your main points (see 2b).
- Make a working outline to identify your main points and the relationships among them.

Decide how your points are best ordered
- Chronological organization often works best for a topic that occurs over time.
- Conceptual organization focuses on how important concepts are related.
- Compare and contrast organization helps to show how two things are similar or different.

4 Write a conclusion

End with more than a summary
- Make a point that readers can take away.
- Raise an interesting question.
- End with a vivid example.

5 Revise, revise, revise

Evaluate your draft
- Examine the order of your ideas and reorganize if necessary.
- Add detail or further explanation where needed.
- When you have finished revising, edit and proofread carefully.

8d Sample Informative Essay

Haddad 1

Akilah Haddad

Professor Swift

English 1102

25 February 2016

Protecting Your Privacy on the Internet:

Is There an App for That?

Users of social media daily submit massive volumes
of data to these sites, and increasingly the corporations
that own these sites have looked for ways to make them
even more profitable. No site has registered more users
or become more profitable than Facebook. Launched in
2004 and opened to all adults in 2006, Facebook had
gained 1.59 billion active users by the end of 2015 and
earned revenue totaling nearly $18 billion in 2015,
growing a remarkable 44% a year (Rosenfeld).

The incredible growth of Facebook, however, has
also brought controversy and an ongoing battle over
privacy concerns. As Facebook has grown, it has
become able to aggregate user data from a wider
range of sites. It has also expanded the sort of user
information it collects and the way it uses that
information. Consequently, growing numbers of users
have become concerned that it is violating their
privacy. That concern increased in 2013, when it
became known that "the National Security Agency uses
Facebook and other social media profiles to create
maps of social connections—including those of

> Haddad's title,
> given as a
> question,
> piques reader
> interest.

American citizens" (Simpson). More recently, in 2015, users in Illinois created a class-action lawsuit against the company because of its "faceprint" technology, which allows users to "tag" friends in photos. They argued that faceprinting violates the state's Biometric Information Privacy Act, which provides clear rules about how biometric images, including scans of facial features, should be collected and how long they should be kept. Earlier in the year, the Belgian Privacy Commission accused Facebook of violating laws that protect European consumers. They cited a report about Facebook by law scholars and information studies scholars from iMinds, an information technology research institute in Belgium. The authors concluded "Facebook only offers an opt-out system for its users in relation to profiling for third-party advertising purposes. The current practice does not meet the requirements for legally valid consent" (Van Alsenoy). Executives at Facebook claimed that their policies are consistent with the law. But since then, Belgian authorities have succeeded in forcing Facebook to stop unauthorized tracking of nonusers' activity. French regulators are demanding the same limits, and also wish to stop some transfers of data to the United States. These events revive the fear that, as the *Economist* puts it, "online privacy is being trampled underfoot as Internet behemoths race to grab as much data as possible" ("Dicing"). And the behemoths want these data because of the potential for huge profits,

Haddad's thesis is given in the last two sentences of the second paragraph.

Haddad 3

especially for Facebook, which generates most of its
revenue from targeted advertisements based on users'
demography (Robinson).

The debates about Internet privacy are nothing new;
they have been raging since websites started leaving
"cookies" on users' hard drives to trace their Internet
behavior. At the center of this debate has been the
question of who is responsible for making sure that
information collected by websites is not misused—the
government, the Internet companies, or consumers
themselves. Vice President Albert Gore was an early
advocate of government intervention, and he announced
an "Electronic Bill of Rights" in 1998, defining privacy as
a basic human right protected by the Constitution and
numerous federal laws (Broder). In light of the Facebook
scandals, other people, such as social-networking expert
Danah Boyd, are again thinking that the Internet should
be regulated by the government, perhaps as a utility.

Advocates of self-regulation believe that since
Internet companies are financially motivated to make
consumers feel secure about their Internet use, they
should be trusted to police themselves. However, if self-
regulation is to work, there have to be consequences for
bad behavior, which leads to the next question: How can
self-regulation be enforced? TRUSTe, a program operated
by a nonprofit that grants certificates to websites posting
a privacy statement that meets TRUSTe's standards and
submitting to an audit, was created as a partial solution
to this issue ("Tailed").

**Haddad provides
an analysis of
the problems of
regulating the
Internet.**

Haddad 4

In addition, companies have to recognize their culpability, which they are often reluctant to do. The CEO of Facebook, Mark Zuckerberg, was reluctant to accept blame for his company's actions, arguing that Facebook should be entirely public. He believes that most users are agreeable to Facebook being open by default because, as he says, "people have really gotten comfortable not only sharing more information and different kinds, but more openly and with more people. That social norm is just something that has evolved over time" (Kirkpatrick).

These controversies have spurred discussion about whether or not the idea of privacy itself has changed, and consequently, how responsible consumers are for protecting themselves. Like Zuckerberg, Facebook's Barry Schnitt believes that the world is becoming more open, as evidenced by Twitter, Myspace, and reality TV (Kirkpatrick). In his book *Delete*, Viktor Mayer-Schönberger warns of the costs of what he calls the "digital panopticon," in which every move and decision is recorded into digital memory, incapable of being forgotten. Thus, compromising photos, candid statements about our jobs, embarrassing searches, and controversial acts can be used against us in a variety of contexts (11). Since users voluntarily disclose information about themselves every day, "in that strict sense, they bear responsibility for the consequences of their disclosures" (5). However, there are also times when users disclose without knowing, as is the case with recent Facebook privacy scandals. Most Facebook users,

A conceptual organization has been used to explain the threats to privacy and how Facebook has responded to critics of the policies.

Haddad 5

for example, did not know that their Facebook time lines always had been public until Facebook clarified their policy in December 2012 (Rosenblatt).

More recently, in 2015, Facebook changed its search function, suddenly allowing searches of approximately 2 trillion posts marked public. Previously users could only see these posts if they were friends with the poster or had liked the page (Constantine).

These questions still consider privacy a matter of culture, however. Issues become more thorny when privacy enters the legal realm. Helen Nissenbaum in *Privacy in Context* argues that the changes to the Internet have happened too fast for us to be able to accurately assess how harmful the aggregation and dissemination of information will be. In particular, increasing sophistication of both software and users has made what was once rather boring and disconnected information gathering dust in databases vulnerable to being "remixed" into full, recognizable profiles of individuals by savvy programmers and hackers (17). In addition, some of Google's Map features have raised unexpected questions in law enforcement. Specifically, why do you need a warrant to search a property for drugs when Google Earth and Street View can show you what's growing in someone's yard? And is evidence gathered in this way admissible in court (Morozov)?

As the Internet continues to grow and change, these debates over responsibility will continue. Regarding government intervention, experts agree that it is unlikely

Haddad 6

that the Internet will be regulated as a utility since sites such as Facebook and Google are not essential services, nor do they enjoy a monopoly. In addition, regulating the Internet in this way could restrict further innovation ("Dicing"). As for the companies themselves, it is in their best interest to keep consumers happy, which was certainly the case for Facebook. In fact, according to Tom Spring in *PC World* magazine, on several other occasions from 2007 to the present, public pressure has led Facebook to change policies and page layouts. But the problem still remains that, despite these lessons, Facebook continues to engage in practices that enrage consumers. As Spring points out, Facebook would be "well served to be more proactive about communicating changes to its terms and services rather than reactive." Until that happens, it remains the user's job to police what is being made of his or her information online.

Haddad concludes with a key point for readers to take away—namely, it is up to each of us to safeguard our privacy on the Internet.

Haddad 7

Works Cited

Boyd, Danah. "Facebook Is a Utility; Utilities Get Regulated." *Apophenia*, 15 May 2010, www.zephoria.org/thoughts/archives/2010/05/15/facebook-is-a-utility-utilities-get-regulated.html.

Broder, John M. "Gore to Announce 'Electronic Bill of Rights' Aimed at Privacy." *The New York Times*, 14 May 2010, p. 16.

Haddad 8

Constantine, Josh. "Facebook Expands Search to All 2
Trillion Posts, Surfacing Public Real-Time News."
Tech Crunch, 22 Oct. 2015, techcrunch.com/2015/
10/22/facebook-search/.

"Dicing with Data: Facebook, Google and Privacy." *The
Economist*, 22 May 2010, p. 16.

Kirkpatrick, Marshall. "Facebook's Zuckerberg Says
That the Age of Privacy Is Over." *ReadWriteWeb*,
9 Jan. 2010, readwrite.com/2010/01/09/
facebooks_zuckerberg_says_the_age_of_privacy_
is_ov/.

Mayer-Schönberger, Viktor. *Delete: The Virtue of Forgetting in the Digital Age*. Princeton UP, 2009.

Morozov, Evgeny. "E-outed." Review of *Privacy in Context*,
by Helen Nissenbaum. *The Times Literary Supplement*, 12 Mar. 2010, p. 8.

Nissenbaum, Helen. *Privacy in Context: Technology,
Policy, and the Integrity of Social Life*. Stanford UP,
2009.

Robinson, James. "Facebook Users Revolt Against Mark
Zuckerberg Over Privacy." *The Guardian*, 23 May
2010, www.theguardian.com/technology/2010/
may/23/facebook-network-begins-to-unravel.

Rosenfeld, Everett. "Facebook Smashes Street's Highest
Estimates on Revs and EPS." *CNBC*, 27 Jan. 2016,
www.cnbc.com/2016/01/27/facebook-q4-earnings.
html.

Rosenblatt, Seth. "Facebook Voting Is Gone, but Privacy
Issues Just Get Worse." *CNET*, CBS Interactive,

Haddad 9

12 Dec. 2012, www.cnet.com/news/facebook-
voting-is-gone-but-privacy-issues-just-get-worse/.

Simpson, David, and Pamela Brown. "NSA Mines Data for
Connections, Including Americans' Profiles." *CNN*,
20 Sept. 2013, edition.cnn.com/2013/09/30/us/
nsa-social-networks/index.html?hpt=ibu_c2.

Spring, Tom. "Quit Facebook Day Was a Success Even as It
Flopped." *PC World*, 1 June 2010, www.pcworld.
com/article/197686/Quit_Facebook_Day_was_a_
Success_Even_as_it_Flopped.html.

Van Alsenoy, Brendan, et al. *From Social Media Service to
Advertising Network: A Critical Analysis of Facebook's
Revised Policies and Terms*. Version 1.3, 25 Aug.
2015. *Ku Loiven*, law.kuleuven.be/citip/en/news/
item/facebooks-revised-policies-and-terms-v1-3.
pdf.

"You Are Being Tailed." *The Economist*, 27 June 1998,
p. 62.

9 | Write a Position Argument

QUICK*TAKE*

After reading this chapter, you should be able to . . .
- Explain the characteristics of written arguments (9a)
- Select a topic and develop a claim with reasons (9b)
- Organize and write a position argument (9c)

9a Position Arguments and Proposal Arguments

When you imagine an argument, you might think of two people with different views, engaged in a heated debate—maybe even shouting slogans. In college courses, in public life, and in professional careers, written arguments are meant to persuade readers who refuse to accept a **claim** when it is expressed as a slogan.

Written arguments

- offer evidence and reasons,
- examine the assumptions on which the evidence and reasons are based,
- explore opposing arguments, and
- anticipate objections.

You may want to convince your readers to change their thinking about an issue or perhaps get them to consider the issue from your perspective. Or you may want your readers to take some course of action based on your argument. These two kinds of arguments can be characterized as **position arguments** (this chapter) and **proposal arguments** (see Chapter 10).

9b Find an Arguable Topic and Make a Claim

In a position argument, you make a claim about a controversial issue. You

- define or rebut the issue,
- take a clear position,
- make a convincing argument, and
- acknowledge opposing views.

Position arguments often take two forms—definition arguments and rebuttal arguments.

Definition arguments

People argue about definitions (for example, is graffiti vandalism or is it art?) because of the consequences of something being defined in a certain way. If you can get your audience to accept your definition, then usually your argument will be successful. **Definition arguments** take the form shown here.

> Something is (or is not) _____ because it has (or does not have) Criteria A, Criteria B, and Criteria C (or more).

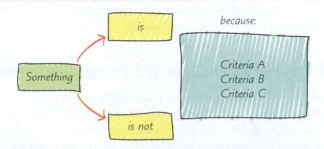

Graffiti is art because it is a means of self-expression, it shows an understanding of design principles, and it stimulates both the senses and the mind.

Rebuttal arguments

Rebuttal arguments take the opposite position. You can challenge the criteria a writer uses to make a definition or you can challenge the evidence that supports the claim. Often the evidence presented is incomplete or wrong. Sometimes you can find counterevidence.

Rebuttal arguments take this form.

> The opposing argument has serious shortcomings that undermine the claim because
>
> flawed reason 1
> flawed reason 2

The great white shark gained a false reputation as a "man eater" from the 1975 movie Jaws, but in fact attacks on humans are rare and most bites have been "test bites," which is a common shark behavior with unfamiliar objects.

Finding an arguable topic

Probably you know people who will argue about almost anything. Some topics, however, are much better suited than others for writing an extended argument. One way to get started is to make a list of topics you care about. Below are examples of other starting points.

Think about issues that are debated on your campus

- Should admissions decisions be based solely on academic achievement?
- Should varsity athletes get paid for playing sports that bring in revenue?

Think about issues that are debated in your community

- Should people who ride bicycles and motorcycles be required to wear helmets?
- Should public schools be privatized?

Think about national and international issues

- Should advertising be banned on television shows aimed at pre-school children?
- Should capital punishment be abolished?

Read about your issue

- What are the major points of view on your issue?
- Who are the experts on this issue? What do they have to say?
- What major claims are being offered?
- What reasons are given to support the claims?
- What kinds of evidence are used to support the reasons?
- How can you add to what has been said about your subject?

Supporting claims with reasons

The difference between a slogan, such as *Oppose candidate X*, and an arguable claim, such as *Oppose candidate X because she will not lower taxes and not improve schools*, is the presence of a reason linked to the claim. A reason is typically offered in a ***because* clause**, a statement that begins with the word *because* and provides a supporting reason for the claim. The word *because* signals a **link** between the reason and the claim.

Making claims specific and contestable

In addition to being supported by reasons that are appropriately linked to it, your claim must also be *specific*. Broad general claims, such as *The United States has become too crowded*, are nearly impossible to argue effectively. Often general claims contain more restricted claims that can be argued, such as *The United States should increase its efforts to reduce illegal immigration* or *The amount of land in national parks should be doubled to ensure adequate wild spaces for future generations*.

Your claim must also be contestable. A claim that you like sour cream on a baked potato is specific but not contestable. No matter how often you are told that a baked potato is less fattening without sour cream, the fact that you like sour cream won't change. You may stop eating the sour cream, but you won't stop wanting to eat it.

9c Organize and Write a Position Argument

Thinking of reasons to support a claim is not hard. What *is* hard is convincing your audience that your reasons are good ones. Imagine you will have critical readers. Whenever you put forward a reason, they will ask *So what?* You will have to have evidence, and you will have to link that evidence to your claim in ways they will accept if they are to agree that your reason is a good reason. Be open to new ideas while you are writing. Often you will go back and forth in developing a position argument.

1 | Before you write

Think about your readers

- What do your readers already know about the subject?
- What is their attitude toward the subject? If it is different from your position, how can you address the difference?
- What are the chances of changing the opinions and beliefs of your readers? If your readers are unlikely to be moved, can you get them to acknowledge that your position is reasonable?
- Are there any sensitive issues you should be aware of?

2 | Write an introduction

Engage your readers quickly

- Get your readers' attention with an example of what is at stake.
- Define the subject or issue.
- State your thesis to announce your position.

3 Organize and write the body of your paper

Develop reasons
• Can you argue from a definition? Is _____ a _____?

EXAMPLES
Are cheerleaders athletes?
Are zoos guilty of cruelty to animals?

• Can you compare and contrast? Is _____ like or unlike _____?

• Can you argue that something is good (better, bad, worse)?

• Can you argue that something caused (or may cause) something else?

• Can you refute objections to your position?

Support reasons with evidence
• Can you support your reasons by going to a site and making observations?

• Can you find facts, statistics, or statements from authorities to support your reasons?

Consider opposing views
• Acknowledge other stakeholders for the issue and consider their positions.

• Explain why your position is preferable.

• Make counterarguments if necessary.

4 Write a conclusion

End with more than a summary
• Think of a strong way to end by offering more evidence in support of your thesis, reinforcing what is at stake, or giving an example that gets at the heart of the issue.

5 Revise, revise, revise

Evaluate your draft
• Make sure your position argument meets the assignment requirements.

• Can you sharpen your thesis to make your position clearer?

• Can you add additional reasons to strengthen your argument?

• Can you supply additional evidence?

• Examine your language for bias and emotionally loaded words and reword if needed.

• When you have finished revising, edit and proofread carefully.

Sample Position Argument

Martinez 1

Mariela Martinez

Professor Barnes

English 102

13 April 2016

Should Students Have the Right
of Freedom of Speech?

In January 2002, students at Juneau-Douglas High
School in Juneau, Alaska, were dismissed from classes
for a parade for the Winter Olympic Torch Relay, which
passed in front of the school. Across the street and off of
school grounds, high school senior Joseph Frederick and
his friends waited until the torch and cameras
approached. They then unfurled a banner that read
"Bong Hits 4 Jesus." The outraged school principal,
Deborah Morse, ran across the street and seized the
banner. She then suspended Frederick for ten days
(Mears).

Frederick appealed to the Superintendent and the
Juneau School Board, which denied his appeal. He then
filed suit against Morse and the school board, claiming
they had violated his First Amendment right to freedom
of speech. The federal district court ruled in favor of
Morse and the school board. The United States Court of
Appeals for the Ninth Circuit, however, reversed the
district court in a unanimous decision, ruling that
Frederick's right to freedom of speech had been violated
(Hussain). The Juneau School Board then took the case

These paragraphs give the background of an issue that likely is unfamiliar to most readers.

Martinez 2

to the United States Supreme Court, which heard oral arguments on March 19, 2007. Kenneth Starr, the Whitewater prosecutor during the Clinton administration, presented the case for the school board.

At first glance the incident seems blown enormously out of proportion, certainly unworthy of consuming many hours of a federal judge's time. Frederick's banner was a stupid prank done in poor taste by an adolescent. He is far from the ideal poster child for free speech. But the underlying issue is huge. I maintain that there is no reason to restrict the First Amendment rights of students when they are not disrupting the school. To give school authorities the right to control anything a student says anywhere far exceeds any reasonable interpretation of our Constitution.

> Martinez gives her interpretation that the event was not worthy of the attention it received. Then she states her thesis that students' rights to freedom of speech should be protected.

Attorney Kenneth Starr argued before the Supreme Court that Morse's censorship of Frederick was justified because of the precedent set in *Bethel School District v. Fraser*. In that 1986 case, the Supreme Court ruled that public schools could limit student speech at a school assembly. Vulgar or obscene speech could be censored. The court decided that

> [T]he undoubted freedom to advocate unpopular and controversial views in schools and classrooms must be balanced against the society's countervailing interest in teaching students the boundaries of socially appropriate behavior.

But that case involved a school assembly on school property. Starr argued that *Frederick v. Morse* is

> Martinez examines the opposing position. She concludes that the evidence cited by the opposition does not apply to the Juneau case.

Martinez 3

comparable because students had been collectively
released from school to watch the Olympic torch pass by
and were accompanied by their teachers.

The case *Frederick v. Morse* is not, as Starr
maintained, about protecting young people from "the
scourge of drugs." The drug reference is a red herring.
Frederick described the words as nonsense meant to get
the attention of the television cameras (Biskupic). The
banner was not pornographic or obscene. The banner did
not incite violence. The only violent act was the
principal's seizing the banner. Neither could it be
interpreted as attacking Christianity. Organizations that
litigate on behalf of the religious right, including the
Christian Legal Society and the American Center for Law
and Justice, founded by the Rev. Pat Robertson, have
sided with Frederick (Greenhouse).

Instead the case is an effort by school administrators
supported by their professional organizations to get the
Supreme Court to allow them to censor anything they
disagree with. This effort is chilling because they currently
have the power to censor obscene, violent, and libelous
speech. It is an attempt to use the public's fear about illegal
drugs to justify heavy-handed authoritarian control of
student expression, whether on or off campus. Morse and
Starr may not like to admit it, but the First Amendment does
apply in our nation's public schools. The U.S. Supreme Court
decided in 1969, in the case of *Tinker et al. v. Des Moines
Independent Community School District*, that students do
have the right of political expression. The court ruled that as

---

Martinez argues that Frederick's banner neither broke any laws nor insulted Christian organizations because the religious right sided with Frederick.

Martinez supplies evidence that students do have the right of political expression when they are not disruptive.

Martinez 4

long as the student's expression does not disrupt the educational environment, officials cannot suppress it (Haynes). The Supreme Court has long maintained that speech that is unpleasant or uncomfortable is nonetheless protected.

Frederick's prank was stupid and boorish, but imagine that Frederick held up a banner protesting racial segregation in the South in 1961. We would now see his act as courageous. Indeed, students were at the forefront of the Civil Rights movement, and many school administrators opposed their actions. Principal Morse was not wrong to disagree with Frederick's message, but she was wrong to censor it. The Supreme Court declared in its Tinker ruling in 1969 that students do not "shed their constitutional rights to freedom of speech or expression at the 'schoolhouse gate.'" The First Amendment is fundamental to our sense of what the United States is about, and we should always be vigilant when those in power seek to limit freedom of speech.

In her conclusion, Martinez reiterates that she does not think Frederick's prank was a good idea, but the principal was wrong to deny his right to freedom of speech off of school property. She gives additional evidence that the Supreme Court has ruled in the past that students do have freedom of speech.

Martinez 5

Works Cited

Biskupic, Joan. "Justices Debate Student's Suspension
for Banner." *USA Today,* 20 Mar. 2007, p. 3A.

"Freedom of Speech: General." *Bill of Rights Institute,* 2016,
www.billofrightsinstitute.org/educate/educator-
resources/landmark-cases/freedom-of-speech-general/.

Martinez 6

Greenhouse, Linda. "Free Speech Case Divides Bush and
	Religious Right." *The New York Times*, 18 Mar. 2007,
	p. A22.

Haynes, Charles C. "T-shirt Rebellion in the Land of the
	Free." *First Amendment Center,* Vanderbilt Univer-
	sity, 14 Mar. 2004, www.firstamendmentcenter.
	org/t-shirt-rebellion-in-the-land-of-the-free.

Hussain, Murad. "The 'Bong' Show: Viewing Frederick's
	Publicity Stunt Through Kulmeier's Lens." *Yale Law
	Journal Pocket Parts*, 9 Mar. 2007, www.yalelawjournal.
	org/forum/the-qbongq-show-viewing-fredericks-
	publicity-stunt-through-kuhlmeiers-lens.

Mears, Bill. "'Bong Hits 4 Jesus' Case Limits Student
	Rights." *CNN*, 26 June 2007, www.cnn.com/2007/
	LAW/06/25/free.speech/.

United States Supreme Court. *Bethel School District v. Fraser,
	478 US 675*. 1986. *Supreme Court Collection*, Legal
	Information Institute, Cornell University Law School,
	www.law.cornell.edu/supremecourt/text/478/675.

—. *Tinker et al. v. Des Moines Independent Community
	School District, 393 US 503*. 1969. *Supreme Court
	Collection*, Legal Information Institute, Cornell U
	Law School, www.law.cornell.edu/supremecourt/
	text/393/503.

10 | Write a Proposal Argument

QUICK**TAKE**

After reading this chapter, you should be able to . . .

- Select a topic and propose a solution (10a)
- Organize and write a proposal argument (10b)

10a Find an Arguable Topic and Make a Proposal

Every day we hear and read arguments that some action should be taken. We even make these arguments ourselves: We should eat better; we should exercise more; we should change our work habits. Convincing others to take action for change is always harder. Other people may not see the problem that you see, or they may not think it is important. Nevertheless, most people aren't satisfied with doing nothing about a problem that they think is important. The problem we face in persuading others is not so much that people are resistant to change but that they need to be convinced that the change we propose is the right one and worthy of their efforts to make it happen.

In a proposal argument, you present a course of action in response to a recognizable problem. The proposal says what can be done to improve the situation or change it altogether. You

- define the problem,
- propose a solution or solutions, and
- explain why the solution will work and is feasible.

Proposal arguments take the form shown here.

SOMEONE should (or should not) do SOMETHING because _____

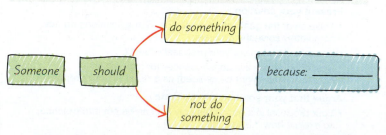

91

For more on finding an arguable topic, supporting claims with reasons, and evaluating your claims to ensure they are specific and contestable, see 9b.

10b Organize and Write a Proposal Argument

Writing an effective proposal argument takes time. Often you start out with something that bothers you but that no one seems to be doing much about. Writing about the problem can inspire you to learn more about what causes it and how the solution you are proposing might actually be put into practice.

1 Before you write

Think about your readers

- How much are your readers affected by the problem you are addressing?
- Do your readers agree that the problem you are addressing is important?
- If your readers are unaware of the problem, how can you make them think that solving the problem is important?

2 Write an introduction

Identify the problem

- Do background research on what has been written about the problem and what solutions have been attempted.
- Summarize the problem for your readers and identify whose interests are at stake.
- Describe what is likely to happen if the problem isn't addressed.

3 Organize and write the body of your paper

Describe other solutions that have been attempted or proposed

- Explain why other solutions don't solve the problem or are unrealistic.

Present your solution

- Make clear the goals of your solution. Some solutions do not completely solve the problem.
- Describe the steps of your proposal in detail.
- Describe the positive consequences (or how negative consequences might be avoided) as a result of your proposal.

Argue that your solution can be done

- Your proposal is a good idea only if it can be put into practice, so explain how it is feasible.
- If your proposal requires money, explain where the money will come from.
- If your proposal requires people to change their present behavior, explain how they can be convinced to change.

4 Write a conclusion

End with a call to action

- Think about shared community values—such as fairness, justice, or clean air and water—that you might raise with your readers.
- Put your readers in a position that if they agree with you, they will take action.
- Explain exactly what they need to do.

5 Revise, revise, revise

Evaluate your draft

- Make sure your proposal argument meets the requirements of the assignment.
- Can you better explain the problem or provide more evidence about it?
- Can you add additional evidence that your proposal will solve the problem?
- Can you supply additional evidence that your proposal can be implemented?
- Do you explain why your solution is better than other possible solutions?
- When you have finished revising, edit and proofread carefully.

10c Sample Proposal Argument

Walker 1

Ashley Walker

Professor Avalos

English 102

3 December 2016

Preventing Obesity in Children

Americans are among the fattest people on the planet and continue to expand. According to results from the 2011-2012 National Health and Nutrition Examination Survey (NHANES), of adults over the age of

Walker 2

20, 33.9% are overweight, 35.1% are obese, and 6.4%
are extremely obese (United States). Excess weight is not
just a matter of looks. Obesity magnifies the risk of heart
disease, diabetes, high blood pressure, and other
ailments—already overtaking tobacco as the leading
cause of chronic illness (Brownell and Horgen 4). An
especially disturbing aspect of this trend is that obesity
among children is at an all-time high. Approximately
17% of youth aged 2-19 in the United States are obese
(Ogden et al. 2402-03). Obese children have a 70%
chance of becoming obese adults with a much higher risk
of serious illness than those of normal weight (Brownell
and Horgen 46). Pediatricians now routinely treat
atherosclerosis and type II diabetes, diseases that used
to be frequent only among older people (Tyre 38).
Today's children are among the first generation in
American history who may die at earlier ages than their
parents.

     For most people in the United States, obesity is a
matter of individual choice and old-fashioned willpower
(Lee and Oliver). The usual advice for overweight people
is to eat less and exercise more, but how applicable is
this advice for children unless they have strong guidance
from adults? How can children make intelligent choices
about eating in an environment where overeating is
normal and where few adults know what's in the food
they eat? The United States has been successful in
addressing teenage health problems: drug use has
dropped, teenage pregnancy has been reduced, and teen

Walker uses the first two paragraphs to give factual support to her argument. She places her thesis statement in the last sentence in paragraph 2.

Walker 3

smoking has declined. We need to take a similar proactive response by taking concrete steps to reverse the trend toward more obese children.

Many have blamed the rise in obesity on a more sedentary lifestyle, including the move to the suburbs, where people drive instead of walk, and increased viewing of television and playing of video games. No doubt that children who exercise less tend to weigh more, but the couch potato argument does not explain why the enormous weight gains have occurred over the past twenty-eight years. The move to the suburbs and the widespread viewing of television began in the 1950s.

The simple answer to why Americans of all ages have steadily gained weight over the past three decades is that we're consuming more food high in calories and high in fat than ever before—about 350 more per child per day and about 500 more per adult per day than in the 1970s. Counteracting this increase with exercise is also not realistic as a child would have to walk 150 more minutes per day and an adult would have to walk 110 more minutes per day (Shute).

Patterns of eating in America have changed over the past three decades. With more people working longer hours and fewer staying at home, annual spending in adjusted dollars at restaurants increased by a factor of more than ten between 1970 and 2010, from $42.8 billion to $586.7 billion ("2016 Restaurant Industry"). The growth was most rapid among fast-food chains. According to Eric Schlosser, in 1970, Americans spent

about $6 billion on fast food; in 2001, they spent more than $110 billion (3).

As the restaurant business became more competitive, fast-food chains realized that the cost of the food they served was small in comparison to the costs of buildings, labor, packaging, and advertising, so they began increasing the size of portions. Amanda Spake and Mary Brophy Marcus note:

> When McDonald's opened, its original burger, fries, and 12-ounce Coke provided 590 calories. Today, a supersize Extra Value Meal with a quarter pounder with cheese, supersize fries, and a supersize drink is 1,550 calories. (44)

Large portions may represent good value for the dollar, but they are not good value for overall health.

Another significant change in the American diet beginning in the 1970s has been the introduction of high-fructose corn syrup into many foods. Listed at the top of food labels today are fructose, dextrose, maltrose, or a similar name—all corn syrup products—in foods like peanut butter, crackers, and ketchup not associated with high levels of sugar. Food producers found that sweetness is an important component of taste, and they have been dumping in sweet corn syrup ever since. High-fructose corn syrup is cheap to produce and enjoys government subsidies, enabling soft drink manufacturers to increase size without increasing cost. The 8-ounce soft drink bottle of the 1950s has been replaced with the 12-ounce can, 20-ounce bottle, and 32-ounce

Walker 5

fountain drink. Harvard researcher David Ludwig has found that food high in sugar makes people hungrier in a short time because it creates a spike in blood sugar followed by a crash, triggering overeating (Uhlenhuth). In other words, one cookie does lead to another.

Also contributing to the rise of obesity is the widespread availability of food. Stores that formerly did not sell food, such as drugstores and gas stations, now have aisles of food. Gas stations have been replaced by mini-marts. Vending machines are found nearly everywhere, particularly in cash-strapped schools. And food companies have produced an endless line of good-tasting snack foods for consumption at home and at work. When we eat food high in sugar and feel hungry two hours later, usually food is close by.

Walker summarizes the problem for her readers and provides useful background information in the first several paragraphs of her essay.

These factors have contributed to a general rise in obesity, but they do not explain why the rate of obesity among children has skyrocketed. One prominent cause is the huge increase in marketing food to children, which has not only doubled since 1992 but also become increasingly sophisticated. An average child in the United States who watches television now sees a food ad on Saturday morning every five minutes and a total of over 10,000 a year, overwhelmingly ads for high-sugar and high-fat food (Brownell and Horgen 101-02). Restaurant and food companies spend $15 billion marketing to children each year with sophisticated advertising campaigns that include product tie-ins (Barboza C1).

Walker 6

Obesity in children is a health crisis comparable to the illnesses caused by smoking. The crisis for children is analogous to secondhand smoke. To blame children for choosing to be fat is like blaming a baby for being born to parents who smoke. Most children lack the knowledge to make intelligent food choices, and they often have no access to healthy food. Parents can make a difference, but parents do not control much of the environment where children eat, including school lunch programs and vending machines in schools. Furthermore, the majority of adults have inadequate skills for controlling their weight.

Some changes have begun to occur. Several states have passed laws banning junk food in vending machines in schools. McDonald's and other fast-food companies have begun to offer healthier alternatives to their fat-laden foods. Also, the Health Care Bill requires chain restaurants to display nutrition information on menus, menu boards, and drive-throughs (Goldstein). But these are small steps in addressing the biggest health crisis of the twenty-first century.

Walker presents her solution in three steps that clearly outline what action is needed.

The first major step in reducing obesity in children is to restrict marketing of junk food to children. When the American public realized how effective Joe Camel ads were in reaching children, their outrage led to a ban on many forms of cigarette advertising. The food industry has no such restrictions and uses popular cartoon characters and actors to pitch their products. Other countries including Belgium, Greece, Norway, and

Walker 7

Sweden now limit advertising directed toward children (Brownell and Horgen 123). The United States should join these nations.

The second major step is to develop a campaign to educate children and parents about healthy and unhealthy food. Children and their parents need to know more about the health risks of obesity and how to follow healthier eating habits. Parents play an important role in selecting what children eat, but children also need to be able to make good choices about eating on their own.

The third major step is to promote a healthy lifestyle through more exercise. Exercise, like eating, is not simply a matter of personal choice. Many schools cannot afford to provide physical education programs and activities that encourage exercise, and many communities lack public space and facilities where people can exercise. More exercise for children needs to be made a priority in schools and communities.

Step one can be accomplished either by voluntary restriction of marketing to children or by legislation, and steps two and three have already received some attention. In February 2010, Michelle Obama launched the "Let's Move" initiative to combat childhood obesity by promoting more nutrition information, physical activity, access to healthier foods, and personal responsibility (Givhan). This initiative has faced controversy, however. Some, such as Margo Wootan of the consumer advocacy group Center for Science in the Public Interest, feel that Obama needs to use her power

Walker acknowledges opposing viewpoints to the "Let's Move" initiative.

to eliminate junk food from schools and junk food advertising from children's television programming. Others say that childhood obesity should not be a priority in tough economic times when school budgets are already stretched thin (Travers).

Alternative proposals are the so-called "fat taxes" on fattening foods and beverages. These food tax proposals have been extremely controversial. The Center for Consumer Freedom, a group supported by the restaurant and food industry, has launched ads against "fat taxes" and legal actions against junk food, arguing that healthy food is a choice ("You Are Too Stupid"). The choice argument, however, is more difficult to make for children.

If food taxes are the best way to promote healthier eating and more exercise among children, would Americans support such a tax? A 2003 opinion poll sponsored by the Harvard Forums on Health found that Americans are overwhelmingly in favor of measures to fight obesity in children including banning vending machines that sell unhealthy foods in schools and providing healthier school lunches (Robinson and Killen 266). The poll indicates that the majority of Americans are willing to pay higher taxes for government-sponsored programs to promote healthy eating and exercise, although the majority opposed specific taxes on junk food. Just as Americans eventually woke up to the risks of smoking among young people and took decisive action, they are gradually becoming aware of the threat of obesity to their children's future and, more important, starting to do something about it.

Walker cites another opposing viewpoint to show how she has carefully considered other solutions.

Walker's concluding statement ends with strength. By comparing her proposal to the stop smoking efforts, she signals the likelihood of success in curbing childhood obesity.

Walker 9

Works Cited

Barboza, David. "If You Pitch It, They Will Eat." *The New York Times*, 3 Aug. 2003, p. C11.

Brownell, Kelly D., and Katherine Battle Horgen. *Food Fight: The Inside Story of the Food Industry, America's Obesity Crisis, and What We Can Do About It*. McGraw-Hill Education, 2004.

Givhan, Robin. "First Lady Michelle Obama: 'Let's Move' and Work on Childhood Obesity Problem." *The Washington Post*, 10 Feb. 2010, www.washingtonpost.com/wp-dyn/content/article/2010/02/09/AR2010020900791.html.

Goldstein, Katherine. "Calorie Count Disclosure and the Health Care Bill. Will This Lead to a Food Revolution?" *The Huffington Post*, 23 Mar. 2010, www.huffingtonpost.com/2010/03/23/calorie-count-disclosure_n_509964.html.

Lee, Taeku, and J. Eric Oliver. "Public Opinion and the Politics of America's Obesity Epidemic." *Faculty Research Working Paper Series*, RWP02-017, John F. Kennedy School of Government/Harvard University, May 2002, papers.ssrn.com/sol3/papers.cfm?abstract_id=313824.

Ogden, Cynthia L., et. al. "Prevalence of Childhood and Adult Obesity in the United States, 2011-2012." *JAMA*, vol. 311, no. 8, 2014, pp. 806-14, doi:10.1001/jama.2014.732.

Robinson, Thomas N., and Joel D. Killen. "Obesity Prevention for Children and Adolescents." *Body Image, Eating Disorders, and Obesity in Youth: Assessment, Prevention, and Treatment*, edited by J. Kevin Thompson and Linda Smolak, APA, 2001, pp. 261-92.

Walker 10

Schlosser, Eric. *Fast Food Nation: The Dark Side of the All-American Meal*. Harper Perennial, 2002.

Shute, Nancy. "Today's Kids Are Fat. Why? They Eat More." *U.S. News & World Report*, 11 May 2009, health.usnews.com/health-news/blogs/on-parenting/2009/05/11/todays-kids-are-fat-why-they-eat-more.

Spake, Amanda, and Mary Brophy Marcus. "A Fat Nation." *U.S. News & World Report*, 19 Aug. 2002, pp. 40-47.

Travers, Karen. "First Lady Michelle Obama Says 'Let's Move' to Fight Childhood Obesity, Encourage Healthy Eating." *ABC News.com*, 9 Feb. 2010, blogs.abcnews.com/politicalpunch/2010/02/first-lady-michelle-obama-says-lets-move-to-fight-childhood-obesity-encourage-healthy-living-.html.

"2016 Restaurant Industry Pocket Factbook." *2016 Restaurant Industry Forecast*, National Restaurant Association, 2016, www.restaurant.org.

Tyre, Peg. "Fighting 'Big Fat.'" *Newsweek*, 5 Aug. 2002, pp. 38-40.

Uhlenhuth, Karen. "Spoonful of Sugar Makes Appetites Go Up." *Advertiser*, 19 Jan. 2003, p. 39.

United States, Department of Health and Human Services, Centers for Disease Control and Prevention. "Prevalence of Overweight, Obesity, and Extreme Obesity among Adults: United States, Trends 1976-1980 through 2005-2006." *NCHS E-Stats*, Dec. 2008, www.cdc.gov/nchs/data/hestat/overweight/overweight_adult.pdf.

"You Are Too Stupid." *ConsumerFreedom.com*, Center for Consumer Freedom, 2011, www.consumerfreedom.com/downloads/ads/print/print_nyc_toostupid.pdf.

PART **3** # Writing in the Disciplines

11 Write About Literature and the Humanities 103

12 Write in the Sciences and Social Sciences 117

13 Compose for the Workplace 126

WRITING IN COLLEGE DISCIPLINES MAP

Understand what is involved in writing about literature and in the humanities	• Analyze and interpret texts and works of art. Go to 11a and 11b. • Become a critical reader of literature. Go to 11c and 11d. • Write a literary analysis. Go to 11e and 11f. • Write an essay exam. Go to 11g.
Understand what is involved in writing in the sciences and social sciences	• Recognize the genres, purposes, and documentation styles of science and social science disciplines. Go to 12a and 12b. • Write an observation. Go to 12c. • Write a case study. Go to 12d. • Write a lab report. Go to 12e.
Understand what is involved in writing in the workplace	• Write a letter of application. Go to 13a. • Write a résumé. Go to 13b. • Write a proposal. Go to 13c. • Write a business e-mail. Go to 13d.

11 Write About Literature and the Humanities

QUICK*TAKE*

After reading this chapter, you should be able to . . .

- Describe the purposes and genres of disciplines in the humanities (11a)
- Identify the types of evidence required in humanities disciplines (11b)
- Analyze literature (11c)
- Construct an interpretation (11d)
- Compose a literary analysis (11e)
- Compose an essay exam (11g)

11a What Are the Humanities?

Researchers and writers in the humanities write to explore, explain, and interpret aspects of the human experience. Most of this chapter deals with writing about literature and writing essay exams, beginning with Section 11c, but the general approach of analyzing and interpreting texts and works of art is shared across humanities and fine arts disciplines. The texts you read in the humanities may include novels, poems, plays, philosophical treatises, historical documents, paintings, or films to be analyzed and interpreted as primary sources. Researchers and writers in the humanities also rely on secondary sources, including books and articles that present the interpretations of others.

The groupings can vary from one institution to another, but the chart that follows shows the most common fields and majors within the humanities and fine arts. Note, however, that there is significant overlap and sharing of knowledge among various fields. For example, archaeology is often housed in humanities programs, yet the study of ancient civilizations combines many of the scientific methods used in natural sciences like paleontology.

Ask your instructor for advice and for examples of the writing genres common in your field. Some genres, such as case studies, vary considerably from discipline to discipline, so locate an example from your field.

DISCIPLINES, PURPOSES, AND GENRES				
Discipline	**Common fields or majors**	**Purposes**	**Genres**	**Preferred documentation style**
Fine Arts	Theater, dance, studio art, art history, music	Creation of artwork; history and reception of art	Essay, critique, review, visual analysis, iconography, research paper, grant proposal, creative writing	MLA and CMS (see Chs. 23 and 25)
Humanities	Literature, history, classics, languages, philosophy, education	Interpreting, appreciating, and imagining the human experience	Essay, research paper, abstract, case study, grant proposal, oral history, ethnography	Primarily MLA, but also APA and CMS (see Chs. 23, 24, and 25)

11b What Counts as Evidence in the Humanities?

What counts as acceptable evidence to make a point or build an argument in one field may be less persuasive to experts in a different field. The types of evidence noted below are those that carry the most weight in the humanities.

FIELDS OF STUDY AND TYPES OF EVIDENCE										
Field	Controlled experimental data	Nonparticipatory observation	Participatory observation	Material data (fossil record, human artifacts, material properties)	Historical records (letters, maps)	Literary texts	Man-made artifacts: buildings, paintings	Preexisting, gathered statistics	Interviews, surveys	Articles by other experts
Archaeology				✓	✓	✓	✓			✓
Literature					✓	✓				✓
Classics					✓	✓	✓			✓
History	✓				✓	✓	✓	✓	✓	✓
Fine Arts		✓	✓		✓	✓	✓			✓

Look for key words and phrases in the assignment that signal what you should use as evidence (see 2a for a list of key words in assignments). For example, if in an American history class you are asked to *describe with examples* a trend in the United States from 1850 to 1900, you will need to use the *ProQuest Historical Newspapers*, which includes the *New York Times* from 1851 onward with an index (see 18b for more on using databases). If you have any doubts about the kind of evidence to use, you should always check with your instructor.

Experts in the various disciplines look for different kinds of evidence because they are trying to solve different problems. For example, here are questions the experts in five fields might ask as they begin to explore the topic of global climate change.

Field	Possible questions
History	What percentage of recorded famines might be attributable in part to global climate change?
Classics	What ancient texts describe possible effects of global climate change, and what can these texts tell us about humans' response to such change?
Literature	How do literary descriptions of climate-related catastrophes (floods, drought, hurricanes) change over time?
Fine Arts	How might a performance piece utilizing dance and music demonstrate the impact of global climate change on human beings?
Archaeology	What effect did global climate change have on ancient human population and migration patterns?

11c Become a Critical Reader of Literature

Reading literature requires a set of practices different from those you might use while reading the Sunday paper or a magazine article. Think of yourself as an active critical observer. Carry on a dialogue with the text using marginal notes. Keeping a record of your reading will force you to engage with a text; being an active reader is practice toward being a thoughtful reader. And marginal comments will be your best resource to use in generating a paper's topic.

As you read, make notes, using the following list as a guide.

- Study the plot of the story. Determine how the events in the story relate to each other. What is the conflict, and how is it resolved?
- Examine the principal characters in the story. What are their most defining characteristics? Are there minor characters? What purpose do they serve?

- Describe the setting of the story. What role does it play?
- Identify the point of view—the perspective from which the story is told. Does a major character relay the events? Does a minor character? Or a fly on the wall?
- Look for shifts in the tone, style, and language of the story.
- Look for symbols, imagery, and interesting metaphors. Are sounds, images, or motifs repeated? What role do they play?
- Identify the story's central theme or main idea. Consider the title of the story and how the main characters fit the theme.

When reading poetry also pay attention to the following.

- Identify the rhyme scheme. For example, when the first and third lines rhyme and the second and fourth do, the rhyme scheme is *abab*.
- Listen to the meter. The most common meter in English is *iambic*, where an unstressed syllable is followed by a stressed syllable (for example, "To swell the gourd, and plump the hazel shells," from John Keats, "To Autumn").
- Listen for alliteration, the repetition of initial consonant sounds (for example, *M*arch *m*adness, *r*oad *r*age, *B*ed *B*ath and *B*eyond).
- Note the stanza, the unit of poetry. The shortest stanza is the two-line couplet.

11d Develop an Interpretation

Assignments for English classes tend to be more open-ended than writing assignments in other disciplines so you can focus on an aspect of the text that interests you. Develop an original idea. Ideally your audience will see the text differently after reading your interpretation.

Opinion versus interpretation

Papers about literature are often called *critical analyses*. Don't let the term trip you up. *Critical* in this sense doesn't mean judgmental. The fact is, your understanding of the text is much more interesting to a reader than whether you like it or not. Avoid making an argument about your opinion of a text unless the assignment specifically asks for one. Instead, develop an interpretation that illuminates some aspect of the text.

Develop your thesis

Ask *what*, *how*, and *why* questions. These questions will lead you from observation, to exploration, to an interpretation.

Observation: What's going on in the text?

What did you observe in the text that was unexpected, odd, powerful, or central? What questions did you ask? Wonderful interpretations frequently evolve from a question or confusion about the text.

> Why does the concluding scene of *Pride and Prejudice* feature the Gardiners, two secondary characters?

Although you won't have an interpretation yet, answering *why* questions will help you narrow your focus to a potentially fruitful topic for interpretation.

Exploration: How does the text do what it's doing?

The answer to this question may consider technical, stylistic, or thematic aspects of the text. At this point you'll begin to develop the first stages of your interpretation.

> How does Austen feature the Gardiners in the last scene of *Pride and Prejudice*? Throughout the novel Austen shows us strained or broken marriages, but the Gardiners are an exception. She presents them as a well-matched, well-adjusted couple.

Analysis and interpretation: Why does the text do what it's doing?

Consider to what end or for what purpose the text functions as it does. What are the ultimate implications of this feature of the text? Frequently answers will fall into one of the following lines of inquiry.

- It advances or complicates a major theme of the text.
- It engages in commentary about larger political, social, philosophical, or literary issues of the author's day.
- It reflects the influence of another writer or text.
- It advances the plot or adds depth to a character.
- It's attempting to be technically innovative. It highlights a capability or limitation in the author's choice of theme, genre, structure, stylistic elements, or narrative technique.

> Why does the end of *Pride and Prejudice* feature two secondary characters, the Gardiners? The Gardiners exemplify successful marriage. By ending the novel with them, Austen lends a note of hope for Elizabeth and Darcy's union. The novel, then, is not a condemnation of marriage as an institution but of the social forces that promote bad matches. We can analyze Austen's characterization of the Gardiners to better understand the kind of marriage making she wants to advocate.

11e   Write a Literary Analysis

Keep your audience in mind when writing a literary analysis. Those who have already read the work will be bored by plot summary. Quote or paraphrase passages that advance your interpretation. Never use the text as evidence without analyzing it. Your analysis should explain how the text you've chosen illustrates your interpretation.

1 Before you write

Read and analyze closely

- Go through your text line by line, annotating your responses.
- Develop a thesis for your interpretation that might start with a question and turn into a claim.
- When you have a thesis, reread the text to look for evidence.

2 Write an introduction

Engage your reader

- Raise what is at stake in your literary text. Many literary texts speak to large issues, whether about art or about life. What issues does your text raise?

3 Organize and write the body of your paper

Use literary concepts to examine your text

- Take into account literary concepts such as character, setting, theme, motif, symbol, point of view, or imagery to express your ideas.
- Your analysis will likely answer such questions as who are the characters, what is the setting and what role does it play, what are themes or motifs in the text, from what point of view is the work told, what language choices are made, and what is the significance of the title?

Support your interpretation

- Cite the precise passages in the text that support your interpretation.
- Attribute every direct quotation and explain its significance.
- If your instructor asks you to use secondary sources, either literary criticism or biographical information about the author, decide where these sources are relevant.

4 | **Write a conclusion**

End with something other than a summary
- Draw larger implications from your analysis.
- End with a vivid example from the text.

5 | **Revise, revise, revise**

Evaluate your draft
- Make sure your analysis meets the requirements of the assignment.
- Make sure your thesis is specific and significant. If you identify a pattern but say nothing about why it is important, your reader will ask "So what?" What does the pattern contribute to an overall interpretation?
- Make sure your evidence and examples are relevant to your thesis. Explain the significance of the evidence for your thesis.
- When you have finished revising, edit and proofread carefully.

Incorporating critical strategies

Your instructor might ask you to use particular critical strategies, such as to consider a literary work from a feminist approach. Ask your instructor to recommend major critical books, journal articles, and other sources that deal with your topic. Then consider ways you can advance or revise the conversation about your topic. Does your interpretation of the text advance or complicate an existing critical perspective? Is there a scene or an aspect of the text that the critics don't consider but should? By developing original responses to these questions, you enter the critical conversation.

STAYING ON TRACK

Use the literary present tense

The disciplinary convention in English is to employ the **literary present tense**. The literary present tense requires the use of present tense when analyzing any literary text such as a poem, a play, or a work of fiction. Also use the present tense when discussing literary criticism.

Incorrect In *Song of Myself*, Walt Whitman **tempered** his exuberant language with undercurrents of doubt about whether language **could** do all he **asked** of it.

Correct In *Song of Myself*, Walt Whitman **tempers** his exuberant language with undercurrents of doubt about whether language **can** do all he **asks** of it.

11f   Sample Literary Analysis

The following student paper responds to the assignment "Analyze how W. B. Yeats's poem 'A Prayer for My Daughter' uses poetic language to describe a father's ambitions for his child's future. What does the speaker's 'prayer' tell us about his own conceptions of femininity?"

Include your last name and page number as the header on each page.

Include name, instructor, course number, and date.

Center the title.

Samuel 1

Renee Samuel

Professor Reitz

Literature and Culture

2 April 2016

Yeats's Conception of Womanhood in

"A Prayer for My Daughter"

Whether or not they ever speak their hopes out loud, parents dream of brilliant futures for their children: high school valedictorian? law school? the ballet? the White House? Although these dreams are usually well-intentioned, often a parent's definition of his or her child's "brilliant future" is filtered through that parent's own desires, fears, and prejudices. The speaker in W. B. Yeats's 1919 poem "A Prayer for My Daughter" is a father who at first seems to have his daughter's best interests at heart. As his child sleeps in her cradle, immune to a raging storm outside, the speaker "walk[s] and pray[s] for this young child" for hours on end (9). But despite such protective behavior, the father's prayers contain old-fashioned and conservative notions about femininity. By describing the kind of woman he hopes his daughter

Samuel 2

will one day become, Yeats's speaker also gives the reader a definition of his "perfect woman." By analyzing this definition, we learn more about how this father's past has influenced his ideas about women than we do about his concern for his daughter's future.

> Thesis statement appears at end of first paragraph.

This father's first prayer for his daughter concerns ideal beauty. He prays, "May she be granted beauty and yet not / Beauty to make a stranger's eye distraught, / Or hers before a looking glass" (17-19). The speaker wants his daughter to be beautiful, but not *too* beautiful, because "being . . . beautiful overmuch" might allow her to slide by on her beauty and "consider beauty a sufficient end" (20-21). The father fears that this vanity will lead to other life problems: She will "lose natural kindness," miss out on "heart-revealing intimacy," and worst of all, "never find a friend" (12-24).

> The interpretation is supported by quotations from the poem.

> Line numbers are given in parentheses for each quotation from the poem.

By "a friend" the speaker means a husband, and Yeats makes this clear in the next stanza when the speaker declares that he wants his less-than-beautiful daughter "chiefly learned" in the art of "courtesy" (33), because "Hearts are not had as a gift but hearts are earned / By those that are not entirely beautiful" (34-35). According to the speaker, men who have been seduced by and "played the fool" for "beauty's very self" (37) will eventually prefer a woman with "glad kindness" instead of "charm" (40). The father also prays that his daughter will not be too intellectual

Samuel 3

or opinionated, because such women are unattractive and "choked with hate" (52). He states that "Intellectual hatred is the worst" (57) and prays that his daughter will grow up to "think opinions are accursed" (58). In this way she will avoid becoming like a woman her father once knew, who

> Because of her opinionated mind
>
> Barter[ed] that horn and every good
>
> By quiet natures understood
>
> For an old bellows full of an angry wind? (61-64)

If his daughter follows this definition of ideal womanhood (ideal women are courteous rather than too beautiful and avoid the bitterness caused by intellect and opinion), this father believes she will marry well, live in "a house / where all's accustomed, ceremonious" and "be happy" (73-74, 72).

This father's prayer for his daughter is not all bad; surprisingly, this poem's speaker idolizes nonperfect women and believes that true love should come from courtesy and kindness rather than just lust. As Elizabeth Cullingford argues, "It is refreshing to be offered the 'not-entirely-beautiful' woman as an ideal. . . . Pleasing, too, is the notion of love as a gradual development rather than a thunderbolt" (136). However, behind this open-mindedness is anger over how he was treated by beautiful, opinionated women in his past and anxiety over the dying out of old traditions. This anger and anxiety leads to some sexist ideas about femininity.

A secondary source is introduced to supply a context for the interpretation.

Samuel 4

For most of his early life, Yeats was in love with Maud Gonne, a beautiful, smart, opinionated, and political woman who rejected his affection. However, Yeats felt that she used her beauty to manipulate him into writing beautiful poetry about her. In 1917, Yeats finally married a less beautiful but also less independent woman: Georgie Hyde-Lees. When the poem's speaker prays that his daughter will be "not entirely beautiful," he is also wishing that she will be more gentle and kind, and less opinionated, than Maud Gonne with her "opinionated mind" and "angry wind" (61, 64). Here we see the father's protective sexism: He would selfishly prefer a submissive daughter over a smart one who would remind him of the "loveliest woman born" for whom he once "played the fool" (57, 36).

Furthermore, this kind of daughter will be less likely to "dance to [the] frenzied drum" of modern womanhood (15). Instead, she will carry on old traditions and "live like some green laurel / Rooted in one dear perpetual place" (47-48). Here, the speaker shows his desire to keep his daughter protected against the modern violence of the twentieth century (which Yeats symbolizes through images of "howling," "roof-leveling" storms and "flooded," "murderous" seas) by hiding her away in past traditions. The father prays that his daughter will marry into a family rooted in old aristocratic tradition, and he chooses this "hypothetical son-in-law" not because he is a good

Samuel 5

If the author of a secondary source is not mentioned, include the author's last name and page number in the in-text citation.

match for his daughter but "because of his aristocratic social status and ownership of landed property" (Cullingford 138). The father is so anxious about the future that he prays his daughter will give up her individual identity and free will to become an "innocent," "beautiful" ambassador of tradition (Cullingford 76).

Even though the speaker in "A Prayer for My Daughter" selfishly projects his own past onto his daughter's future, Yeats does not seem to want us to think we are hearing the prayer of an unreliable narrator. Although Yeats believed in gender equality, this poem "marks a regression in Yeats's acceptance of changing gender roles" (Cullingford 136). Perhaps the point, though, is just this: When it comes to their children's futures, even open-minded parents sometimes become conservative and reactionary.

Samuel 6

Center heading on new page.

Works Cited

Secondary source

Cullingford, Elizabeth. *Gender and Sexuality in Yeats's Love Poetry*. Syracuse UP, 1996.

Poem

Yeats, W. B. "A Prayer for My Daughter." *The Collected Poems of W. B. Yeats*, edited by Richard J. Finneran, Collier Books, 1989.

11g Write an Essay Exam

Instructors use essay exams to test your understanding of course concepts and to assess your ability to analyze ideas independently.

Elements of an exam essay

Introduction	Briefly restate the question, summarizing the answer you will provide.
	EXAMPLE
	The letter Lydia Bennett leaves after eloping highlights several of her most important character traits: her failure to take her own mistakes seriously, her casual attitude toward morality, and her disregard for the pain she causes others.
Body paragraphs	Each paragraph should address a major element of the question. Order your main points so the reader can tell how you are responding to the question.
	EXAMPLE
	Of the many factors leading to the downfall of Senator Joseph McCarthy, the Army-McCarthy hearings were the most important.
Conclusion	*Briefly* restate your answer to the question, not the question itself.
	EXAMPLE
	Thus, the three things all responsible creditors assess before making a loan are the borrower's capacity, credit history, and collateral.

What you need to do

- Actively respond with the kinds of information and analysis the question asks you to provide; don't just write generally about the topic.
- Plan your response before you begin writing. Note how much time you have to write your response.
- Respond to each element of the question, providing support and being as specific as possible.
- Save a few minutes to read over your essay, correcting errors and adding information where needed.

Sample essay exam

HIS 312: Early American History Describe the economic, cultural, and political variables that led to the establishment of slavery in the American South.

Amy Zhao began her response to the essay question by jotting down ideas for each of the three categories mentioned. Her outline also served as a map for the structure of her essay.

<u>*economic*</u>	<u>*cultural*</u>	<u>*political*</u>
plantation economy	*racist ideologies*	*elite leadership of southern colonies*
trade with Europe	*divide with indentured servants*	*legislature limited to large landowners*

Amy uses the key terms from the question to indicate where she is addressing that element of the question.

Multiple variables in economics, culture, and politics combined to help institutionalize slavery in the American South. Most important among these variables were the plantation economy, racist ideologies, conflict among the lowest social classes, and the stranglehold of elite landowners on the legislative process. **Economic variables** arose primarily from the Southern colonies' unique geographical situation. Physically isolated from the large markets of Europe but blessed with huge quantities of arable land, the region required cheap labor in order to exploit its full economic potential. Relatively wealthy white colonists secured large tracts of land and strongly resisted any forces that pushed for the breakup of these plantations into smaller, individually owned farm holdings. The concentrated wealth and power of the plantation owners allowed them to arrange conditions to protect their land. Slavery came to be seen as the best way to maintain their power.

12 | Write in the Sciences and Social Sciences

QUICK*TAKE*

After reading this chapter, you should be able to . . .

- Explain the purposes and genres of science and social science disciplines (12a)
- Identify the types of evidence required in science and social science disciplines (12b)
- Compose an observation (12c)
- Compose a case study (12d)
- Compose a lab report in the sciences (12e)

12a What Are the Sciences and Social Sciences?

In the sciences and social sciences, good writing is likely to exhibit some standard qualities—it will be clear, concise, and logical, supplying appropriate evidence in sufficient amounts to persuade the audience. But because the individual disciplines have different purposes, they use different vocabularies, formats, and evidence to make and support claims.

Social sciences and *sciences* are broad cover terms for an array of specific fields. Social sciences include fields like psychology, government, sociology, and anthropology, but the many fields in education and communication also are often classified as social sciences. At the core of the sciences are fields like physics, mathematics, biology, astronomy, chemistry, and geology, but engineering, computer science, nursing, medicine, and other health fields are often grouped with the sciences. With so many different fields involved, it's no wonder that a common genre like a lab report is written in many different formats.

	DISCIPLINES, PURPOSES, AND GENRES			
Discipline	**Common fields or majors**	**Purposes**	**Genres**	**Preferred documentation style**
Education	Curriculum and instruction, education administration	Training teachers and developing effective teaching methods	Lesson plan, literature review, abstract, case study, grant proposal	APA (see Ch. 24)

(Continued on next page)

117

	DISCIPLINES, PURPOSES, AND GENRES *(Continued)*			
Discipline	Common fields or majors	Purposes	Genres	Preferred documentation style
Media/ Communi- cations	Journalism, radio/ television/film studies, advertising, information management	Informing and entertaining the public, promot- ing commerce, and effecting the exchange of information	Article, analysis, advertising, scripts, screenplays	APA and CMS (see Chs. 24 and 25)
Social Sciences	Psychology, sociology, anthropology, geography, social work, government, human ecology	Exploring human behavior in individuals and groups— both in the past and the present—with a strong desire to learn to predict human behavior in the future	Literature review, abstract, case study, oral his- tory, grant pro- posal, poster presentation	Primarily APA (see Ch. 24)
Natural Sciences	Physics, math, astronomy, biology (bot- any, zoology, marine sci- ence), geol- ogy, ecology, chemistry	The study of living things, inanimate mat- ter, systems, and processes	Literature review, lab report, abstract, grant proposal, poster presentation	APA and CSE (see Chs. 24 and 26); some sciences, like chemistry and physics, have their own style guides
Engineering	Civil, industrial, chemical, petroleum, aerospace, biomedical, mechanical, electrical	Practical application of science and technology to improve human civilization	Case study, design report, progress report, lab report, proposal	Primarily CSE (see Ch. 26)
Health Sciences	Nursing, phar- macy, kinesiol- ogy, premed, veterinary medicine	Improving health and well-being	Lab report, case study, poster presentation	APA and CSE (see Chs. 24 and 26)

	Common fields or majors			Preferred documentation style
DISCIPLINES, PURPOSES, AND GENRES (*Continued*)				
Discipline		Purposes	Genres	
Computer Science and Technology	Information management, technical communications, computer engineering	Building, maintaining, and optimizing electronic communications systems and databases	User manuals, support documentation, technical reports, journal articles	CSE (see Ch. 26) and IEEE (Institute of Electrical and Electronics Engineers)

12b **What Counts as Evidence in the Sciences and Social Sciences?**

Experts in most fields ask particular kinds of questions that require certain types of evidence. Experts in the various disciplines look for different kinds of evidence because they are trying to solve different problems. For example, here are questions the experts in ten fields might ask when beginning to explore the topic of global climate change.

Field	Possible questions
Geography	What constitutes a "normal" range of global climate conditions?
Psychology	How has the "clean energy" movement changed individuals' norms regarding fossil fuels?
Sociology	How does a community's assumptions about socioeconomic values affect its response to the threat of global climate change?
Economics	What burdens do carbon dioxide emissions controls impose on large businesses versus small businesses?
Geology	What do worldwide coal deposits tell us about the global Paleolithic climate?
Astronomy	What can humans' impact on Earth's atmosphere and climate teach us about making other planets habitable?
Biology	Is recent deforestation responsible for an increase in CO_2 in the Earth's atmosphere?
Chemistry	To what extent has the reduced production of chlorofluorocarbons "solved" the problem of ozone depletion?
Engineering	How can engineers protect coastal urban areas from the stronger hurricanes associated with global warming?
Government	How might rising sea levels affect the stability of governments in coastal third-world nations?

12c   Write an Observation

Observations are common in the sciences and in the social sciences. Observations begin as notes taken firsthand by the writer as he or she observes an event, phenomenon, or place and should include as many relevant and specific details as possible.

Elements of an observation

Title	Include a precise title.
	EXAMPLE
	Doppler Profile of the Structure of Tornadoes Near Attica, Kansas, on 12 May 2013
Description and context	Be specific about what or whom you are observing. How did you limit your site or subject? What background information do readers need?
	EXAMPLE
	Eleven mixed-breed puppies six weeks old were observed during feeding and play periods over a five-week period. Each puppy's tendency to exhibit alpha- or omega-dog behaviors changed relatively little over this period.
Record of observations	Report what you observed in some logical order: chronologically, from most obvious features to least obvious, or some other pattern.
	EXAMPLE
	On the second day of observation, between 8:00–11:00 a.m., a significantly higher number of migratory birds were seen in the feeding area.
Conclusion or summary	Give your readers a framework in which to understand your observations. What conclusions can you draw from them? What questions are left unanswered?
	EXAMPLE
	It appears that the toddlers observed were often aware of social expectations even when they were unable to meet those expectations in their own behavior. This indicates that an awareness of norms probably develops independently from an individual's ability to control impulsive behavior.

What you need to do

- Carry a notebook and make extensive field notes. Provide as much information as possible about the situation in which your observations occurred.
- Record in your notebook exactly when you arrived and left, where you were, and exactly what you saw and heard.
- Analyze your observations before you write about them. Identify patterns and organize your report according to those patterns.

Sample observation

Animal Activity in Barton Springs Pool
from 15 April to 22 April 2016

Barton Springs Pool is a 225-meter-long, natural spring-fed pool in a limestone creek bed in Austin, Texas. It is both a wildlife habitat and a busy hub of human activity. Because of the constant flow from the springs, the water temperature is constant at 68°F (20°C), allowing swimmers to use the pool year-round.

My first observation was on 15 April from 1:45–4:00 p.m. on a warm sunny day with the air temperature at 74°F (23°C). I used a mask and snorkel to observe below the water. It was remarkable how oblivious people and wildlife were of each other. While from forty to fifty-five Austinites splashed on the surface, many fish (mostly smallmouth bass with two large channel catfish on the bottom) swam below them, and large numbers of crayfish crept along the rocky portion of the pool's bottom. Eight small turtles (red-eared sliders) alternately swam at the surface or dove below near the dam at the deep end. Twelve endangered Barton Springs salamanders (*Eurycea sosorum*), ranging in color from bright orange to paler yellow, were active by the larger spring at the center of the pool.

At the times when humans are not present or nearly absent, animal activity noticeably increases. From the side of the pool on 16 April (clear, 72°) from 7:25 p.m. until closing at 8 p.m., I observed smallmouth bass schooling near the dam and feeding on mosquitoes and mayflies. Nine ducks (seven lesser scaup and two mallards) landed on the pool at 7:40 p.m. and remained when I left. (Lesser scaup migrate to the area in large numbers in the winter; the mallards are likely domesticated ducks.) A pair of wood ducks (male and female) were also on the cliff above the shallow end.

Specific times, weather conditions, numbers of individual species, and behaviors are recorded.

12d Write a Case Study

Case studies are used in a wide range of fields such as nursing, psychology, business, and anthropology. Their exact structure can vary from discipline to discipline, so be sure to get instructions from your professor. Case studies are narrow in focus. Rather than giving the "big picture" about phenomena, they provide a rich, detailed portrait of a specific event or subject.

Elements of a case study

Introduction	Explain the purpose of your study and how or why you selected your subject. Use language appropriate to your discipline and specify the boundaries of your study.
Methodology	Explain the theories or formal process that guided your observations and analysis during the study. **EXAMPLE** A face-to-face survey methodology was used, where interviewers asked respondents a set of prepared questions and noted answers on the survey sheet.
Observations	Describe the "case" of the subject under study by writing a narrative, utilizing interviews, research, and other data to provide as much detail and specificity as possible. **EXAMPLE** The subject reported a lengthy history of heart trouble, beginning at age thirty-seven, involving multiple trips to the emergency room.
Discussion	Explain how the variables in your case might interact. Don't generalize from your case to a larger context; stay within the limits of what you have observed.
Conclusion	What is implied, suggested, or proven by your observations? What new questions arise?
References	Using the appropriate format, cite all the outside sources you have used. (See Chapter 24 for APA documentation and Chapter 26 for CSE documentation.)

What you need to do

- Understand the specific elements of your assignment. Ask your instructor if you aren't sure about the focus, context, or structure your case study should have.
- Use careful observations and precise, detailed descriptions to provide a complex picture with a narrow focus.
- Write your observations in the form of a narrative, placing yourself in the background (avoid using *I* or *me*).
- Analyze your findings and interpret their possible meanings, but draw your conclusions from the observed facts.

Sample case study

Underage Drinking Prevention Programs
in the Radisson School District

Introduction

This study examines the effect of Smith and Bingham's
drinking-prevention curriculum on drinking rates in the Radisson
School District, 2009–2013. Prior to 2011, the Radisson School
District offered no formal drinking-prevention education. In
2009, as part of a state initiative, the district proposed several
underage drinking education curricula for possible adoption.
After substantial debate and input from parents, Smith and
Bingham's curriculum was chosen for implementation in ninth
through twelfth grades. This study tracks student drinking rates
from 2009 to 2013, and compares the results after introduction
of the curriculum to district rates prior to implementation.

Discussion

The data from this study showed no correlation between the
curriculum and student drinking rates. Drinking rates remained
unchanged before, during, and after the implementation of the
curriculum. Additionally, survey data indicate that levels of student
drinking remained constant as well. Therefore, in this case, it
cannot be said that Smith and Bingham's curriculum had any
measurable effect on changing students' drinking behavior.

Conclusion

In terms of reducing student drinking, Smith and Bingham's
curriculum does not appear to be any more effective than no
drinking-prevention education at all. Since no measurable
results were obtained, the strong administrative support for
the curriculum in the school district cannot be attributed to its
success. A possible explanation for that support may be the
approval expressed by parents who preferred it to the other
curricula proposed. Further studies might usefully expand the
scope of this study and compare multiple school districts' use of
Smith and Bingham's curriculum to identify variables that might
alter its effectiveness.

Some disciplines
require title
pages. See 24i for
an example of an
APA title page.

The introduction
identifies both
the problem and
the particular
subject of the
case study.

The conclusion
sums up what
has been
observed. Many
case studies do
not give defini-
tive answers
but rather raise
further ques-
tions to
explore.

12e Write a Lab Report in the Sciences

Lab reports follow a strict structure, enabling specialists in a given field to assess quickly the experimental methods and findings in any report. Though the basic elements are usually the same, details of formatting can vary among disciplines in the sciences. Check with your instructor for the specific elements needed in your report.

Elements of a lab report

Title	The title of a lab report should state exactly what was tested, using language specific to the field.
Abstract	The abstract briefly states the questions and the findings in the report.
Introduction	The introduction gives the full context of the problem, defining the hypothesis being tested.
Methods	Describe the materials used, as well as the method of investigation. Your methods and procedure sections should be specific enough to allow another researcher to replicate your experiment. **EXAMPLE** A double-blind structure was used so the investigators did not know which subjects received placebos.
Procedure	Step-by-step, narrate exactly what you did and what happened. In most fields, use the passive voice to avoid distracting the reader with references to yourself. **EXAMPLE** The salts were dissolved in distilled water to achieve a salinity level of 3 percent.
Results	State the outcomes you obtained, providing well-labeled charts and graphics as needed. **EXAMPLE** The tempered glass plates resisted fracture 2.3 times better than the standard glass plates.
Discussion	State why you think you got the results you did, using your results to explain. If there were anomalies in your data, note them as well. **EXAMPLE** Since all of the plants grew normally, it appears that the high acidity levels in the soil were not harmful to their early development. However, the low fruit yields indicate that high acidity is detrimental to reproduction.

(Continued on next page)

Conclusion	Briefly, what was learned from this experiment? What still needs to be investigated?
References	Using the appropriate format, cite all the outside sources you have used. (See Chapter 24 for psychology lab reports and Chapter 26 for science lab reports.)

What you need to do

- Understand the question you are researching and the process you will use before you begin.
- Take thorough notes at each step of your process. You may be asked to keep a lab notebook with a specific format for recording data. Review your notes before you begin drafting your report.
- Don't get ahead of yourself. Keep methods, procedure, discussion, and conclusion sections separate. Remember that other scientists will look at specific sections of your report expecting to find certain kinds of information. If that information isn't where they expect it to be, your report will not make sense.
- Write your abstract last. Writing all the other sections of the report first will give you a much clearer picture of your findings.

Sample abstract from a lab report

Wave interference in visible light using the double-slit method

Abstract

Filtered light was projected through one slit in a piece of cardboard, producing a single bar of light, brightest in the center and shaded darker toward the edges, on the wall behind the cardboard. When a second slit was added to the cardboard, the projected image changed to alternating bands of bright light and darkness. The conclusion reached is that wavelength patterns in the light cancelled or reinforced one another as they reached the wall, increasing or decreasing the observed light. These results are consistent with the wave theory of light.

For an example of how to format a lab report, see 26e.

13 | Compose for the Workplace

QUICK*TAKE*

After reading this chapter, you should be able to . . .

- Compose effective letters of application (13a)
- Construct effective résumés (13b)
- Compose effective proposals (13c)
- Compose effective business e-mails (13d)

13a Write a Letter of Application

Successful letters of application, or cover letters, place the reader's needs first and show why you are the best candidate. Great jobs attract many applicants. Convince your readers that you are worthy of an interview. A well-written letter of application gets your foot in the door.

Elements of a letter of application

Inside address and salutation	Use the name and title of the person doing the hiring whenever possible. If you don't know the name, call the organization for the person's name and official title.
First paragraph	Name the position for which you are applying.
Body	Explain why your education, experience, and skills make you a good candidate for the position.
Conclusion	Mention that you've attached your résumé and your contact information.

What you need to do

- Limit yourself to one page.
- Find out as much as you can about the organization or company.
- Don't fall into the trap of emphasizing why the job would be good for you; instead, show why you are well suited for the employer's needs.
- List in your résumé the qualifications and work experience that make you well suited for the position.
- If you are applying by e-mail, name the position you are applying for in the subject line (*Application for production assistant position*).

Sample letter of application

609 McCaslin Lane
Manitou Springs, CO 80829

November 2, 2016

Ann Darwell
100 Pine Street
Colorado Springs, CO 80831

Dear Ms. Darwell:

Please consider my application for Fox 45's *Kids' Hour* production assistant position.

During my senior year at Boston College, I interned for the Emmy-winning children's program *Zoom*. Through the internship I learned not only the technical skills necessary to produce a weekly, hour-long show but also the finesse required to manage an all-child cast.

My experience as the producer of *All the News* also gave me intensive training in the skills of a successful producer. Under my direction, a staff of fifteen crew members and reporters regularly broadcast creative campus news pieces. Because I produced this weekly show for three years, I would need little initial supervision before being able to make significant contributions to *Kids' Hour*.

After one year at *Zoom*, I want to continue production work in a position that offers more responsibility in the field of children's television. My work at *Zoom*, particularly my authoring and producing a series of spots to teach children Spanish, has given me hands-on experience in creating the kind of innovative television for which *Kids' Hour* is known.

Thank you for considering my application. Attached is my résumé. I would be happy to send my references if you wish to see them. You can reach me at (719) 555-0405 or c.popolo@hotmail.com. I look forward to speaking with you about the production assistant position.

Sincerely,

Christian Popolo

Christian Popolo

13b Write a Résumé

Finding the right job depends on writing a successful résumé, one of the most important pieces of writing that you will ever compose. The secret of a successful résumé is understanding its purpose—to place you in the small group of candidates to be interviewed.

Elements of a résumé

Objective section	Target the objective section to the position you are applying for. Be as specific as possible.
	EXAMPLE
	Special education teacher in the greater Atlanta area specializing in brain-injured patients and requiring familiarity with coordinating ARDS and completing IED documentation.
Overview section	List your education in reverse chronological order, beginning with certificates or degrees earned. List work experience in reverse chronological order, focusing on your more recent jobs and including details of your duties.
	EXAMPLE
	Reviewed real estate investments and loan portfolios for documentation, structure, credit analysis, risk identification, and credit scoring.

What you need to do

- Focus on the employer's needs. Imagine you are the person hiring. List the qualifications and work experience an ideal candidate would have.
- Make a list of your qualifications and work experience.
- Compare the two lists. What qualifications and work experience do you have that make you well suited for the position? Put checks beside the items on your list that you find are most important for the position.
- Create two printed résumés—a scannable résumé and a traditional résumé. Many companies now scan résumés and store the information in a database. Make your scannable résumé simple and clean, and avoid any graphics such as bulleted points and lines.

Sample résumé

Christian Popolo
609 McCaslin Lane
Manitou Springs, CO 80829
(719) 555-0405
c.popolo@hotmail.com

OBJECTIVE
Production assistant position for an innovative Colorado television program requiring prior experience in children's television and a strong technical background.

SUMMARY OF SKILLS
On-location production, studio-based production, news production, children's television, management, fund-raising, animation, AVID Media Composer, AVID Xpress DV, MS Word, MS Office, fluent Spanish, detail-oriented, articulate, excellent writer

EDUCATION
Bachelor of Arts in Communications, Boston College, May 2016 GPA: 3.65/4.0

WORK EXPERIENCE
Producer, All the News, BCTV Campus Television, Chestnut Hill, MA, August 2013–May 2016. Produced a weekly, half-hour campus news program. Supervised seven studio staffers and eight reporters. Spearheaded successful initiative to increase Student Services funding of the program by 15 percent.
Intern, Zoom, Boston, MA, May 2015–May 2016. Interned in the production department of award-winning national children's television program. Wrote and produced three 2-minute "Hablamos" segments, designed to teach Spanish phrases.
Technician, Communications Media Lab, Chestnut Hill, MA, August 2013–April 2015. Maintained over $300,000 worth of the latest filming and editing technology.

HONORS
Presidential Scholar, August 2013–May 2016
BCTV Excellence Award, May 2014 and May 2015

REFERENCES
Available upon request from the Career Center, Boston College, Southwell Hall, Chestnut Hill, MA 02467 at (617) 555-3430.

13c Write a Proposal

Successful proposals use good reasons to convince readers that if they act, something positive will happen. In an *internal proposal*, people in a company try to persuade those in charge to get something done (to start a new project, etc.). In a *business proposal*, a person or group tries to convince bankers or investors to fund a new business or business expansion. In a *grant proposal*, a nonprofit organization appeals to a potential donor to get support for the work it does.

ELEMENTS OF A PROPOSAL	
Introduction (sometimes called an *executive summary*)	A brief statement that describes the problem, your proposed solution, and what you seek from the person reading the proposal.
Description of problem	Fully describe the problem, what causes it, and whom it affects.
Solution	Explain how your solution will work. Address any possible arguments that it will not work. If necessary, show that your solution is affordable and feasible.
Conclusion	Recap the benefits of your proposal. Conclude with a call to action.

What you need to do

- Understand the required parts and format of the proposal before you begin. Long proposals tend to require a title page, table of contents, executive summary, time line, and budget. Short proposals often take the form of a letter.
- Help readers feel the problem. Describe it in a way that lets them empathize with the people affected by it.
- Do research. Provide facts, statistics, and examples to describe the problem and support your solution.
- Anticipate readers' questions. Will they wonder if the solution will really solve the problem? Or if your group has the experience to solve it? If so, provide the reasons or evidence that will put these concerns (or others) to rest.

Sample proposal

In this e-mail proposal, a PTA president encourages a local business owner to donate funds for a special project.

🗑 ⚑ ↩ ⏪ ➡   ✉ Re: Supporting fitness at Mill Valley Elementary School   🖨 ⚑ ▾

Paige Wheeler
To: Julia.kane@funfitness.com
RE: Supporting fitness at Mill Valley Elementary School

Dear Ms. Kane,

On behalf of the staff, students, and families at Mill Valley Elementary School, I would like to ask your support for a project that affects the well-being of the children in our community. Specifically, I encourage you to contribute $500 toward a playground cover at our school, which will support the health of our students.

There's no denying that physical activity is important for children. According to guidelines published on health.gov, children and adolescents should get at least an hour of exercise daily. A combination of aerobic, muscle-strengthening, and bone-strengthening exercise helps prevent risk factors for disease and increases the likelihood that children will grow up physically and mentally healthy. Recent studies also show a connection between exercise and learning. A study published in *Journal of Pediatrics* in 2013 showed that better fitness correlates to higher grades on standardized tests.

At Mill Valley, we are committed to helping every child get enough exercise, and we are fortunate to have playground equipment to help us reach that goal. Unfortunately, during four months of the school year, the equipment is too hot to touch for most of the day. Concerns about sun damage also prevent us from letting our students play outside for long periods of time. Being stuck inside for recess is frustrating for students and teachers alike.

For these reasons, we are asking community leaders to help us purchase a playground cover. By making our playground equipment usable and preventing excess sun exposure, the sun cover will help us ensure that our students get the exercise they need.

Teachers and students at Mill Valley have long enjoyed working with you on other fitness-related projects. We hope we can count on your support for this one.

Best,

Paige Wheeler
President
Mill Valley Elementary PTA

In an e-mail proposal, you can link directly to sources. The passages underlined in blue include embedded links to, respectively, http://health.gov/paguidelines/guidelines/chapter3.aspx and http://dx.doi.org/10.1016/j.jpeds.2013.01.006.

13d Write a Business E-mail

E-mail is now the preferred form for most day-to-day communication in the business world. An e-mail is faster than a letter and, unlike a phone call, leaves a record of the conversation between sender and recipient. It's important to remember that e-mail is easily shared and forwarded. You should never assume that e-mails you send will remain private.

Elements of a business e-mail

Addresses **To:** **Cc:** **Bcc:**	Use the address line for the primary recipient or recipients—those you address directly in your salutation. Use the "Cc:" field for addresses of people who also need to know about the issue. "Bcc:" recipients receive a copy but are hidden from the main recipient.
Subject line	Always provide a subject. Make it informative and specific. Avoid words and phrases that are likely to trigger a recipient's junk mail filter, such as "Opportunity," "Credit," "Loans," or "Please read—URGENT."
Salutation	Always include a formal salutation, especially when e-mailing someone from a different company or organization.
Body	Keep business e-mails as short as possible. Skip a line between paragraphs instead of indenting the first line.
Signature	Many e-mail programs allow you to automate your signature, so your name, title, and contact information appear at the bottom of every e-mail. You should always "sign" your name at the end of an e-mail.

What you need to do

- Keep an e-mail brief, and limit it to one topic. If you need to communicate about more than one issue, send another e-mail.
- The subject line is critical in a business e-mail to reference the contents. Business projects often produce hundreds of messages.
- Be specific about what you want the recipient to do and when. Make deadlines, dates, and desired actions clear and prominent.
- Use a professional, straightforward tone. Proofread messages for grammar and punctuation errors.

PART 4

4 Multimedia and Online Composing

HOW TO COMPOSE IN MULTIMEDIA AND ONLINE GENRES

Understand multimedia composing and principles of document design

- Understand how words and visuals work together. Go to 14b.
- Create a photo essay. Go to 14c.
- Understand principles of document design. Go to 14d.
- Understand principles of selecting type. Go to 14e.
- Create tables, charts, and graphs. Go to 14f.

Design and deliver an effective presentation

- Know how to plan an effective presentation. Go to 15a.
- Design visuals for a presentation. Go to 15b.
- Deliver an effective presentation. Go to 15c.

Understand what is involved in composing in online genres

- Create a Web page. Go to 16a.
- Create a podcast. Go to 16b.
- Create a video. Go to 16c.
- Create a discussion post. Go to 16d.

14 | Communicate in Multimedia

QUICK*TAKE*

After reading this chapter, you should be able to . . .
- Compose in multimedia (14a)
- Use verbal and visual texts effectively (14b)
- Compose a photo essay (14c)
- Design documents (14d)
- Select typefaces and other effects (14e)
- Create tables, charts, and graphs (14f)

14a Multimedia Composing

Digital technologies now make it possible for an individual to create multimedia projects that formerly required entire production staffs. You can publish multimedia projects on the Internet (either as Web sites or as downloadable files), as stand-alone media, or in print with posters, brochures, and essays with images.

Start with the audience

Most college assignments specify the medium, such as a printed paper or a downloadable file that you submit to the instructor. In the workplace and in life outside college, the choice of medium often isn't immediately evident. For example, if you want to address a neighborhood issue, would a brochure or a social media site be more effective?

College viewers and listeners have the same expectations of multimedia projects that they do of essays and research papers. They expect

- your project to be well organized and free of errors,
- your claims to be supported with evidence,
- your analysis to be insightful,
- your sources to be documented, and
- your work clearly to be distinguished from the work of others.

Create multimedia projects

If you decide to create a multimedia project, find out what resources are available for students on your campus. Many colleges and universities have digital media labs, which offer workshops and can provide video and audio studios, technical assistance, equipment, and software. Look for links to digital media services on your college's Web site.

133

14b ## Think About Verbal and Visual Relationships

Knowing when to use audio, video, images, and graphics and when to use words requires you to think about them as **media**—as different means of conveying information and ideas. The word *writing* makes us think of words, yet in our daily experience reading newspapers, magazines, advertisements, posters, Web sites, social media, and signs, we find words combined with images and graphics. On the flip side, television uses words extensively (think of the words you see on commercials when you have the sound off or the text running across the bottom of the screen on news, sports, and financial programs).

Think about what an image communicates

What are the expectations of your audience?

- Most essays don't use images. Most Web sites, social media, brochures, and instructions do use images.
- Think about the purpose of including an image. Does it communicate a concept? Does it show something that is hard to explain in words alone?
- Think about the focus of the image. You may need to crop the image.
- Provide an informative caption for the images you include and refer to them in your text.

■ Sometimes images are used in place of words.

■ Sometimes words bring images to mind.

14c ## Create a Photo Essay

A combination of words and images often works best to help your readers understand an unfamiliar subject. Christine Vasquez received an assignment to create a photo essay about an environmentally threatened place in her environmental studies class.

A native of Ecuador, Christine knew she wanted to submit a photo essay on the Cotacachi Cayapas Ecological Reserve in central Ecuador, a tropical cloud forest where she had volunteered in past summers and had taken numerous photos. She realized, however, that most of her classmates had never been to a cloud forest and had no idea where they existed. Thus she had to inform her audience what a cloud forest is and why cloud forests are an important ecosystem before she stated the threat they face.

Protecting the Cloud Forest: Cotacachi Cayapas Ecological Reserve
Christine Vasquez

■ The first slide should have a descriptive title. It should give a strong visual introduction to the content of the photo essay. Christine chose a photo that shows both the mountain environment and the cloud forest.

The Cotacachi Reserve is located in the mountains of northern Ecuador, near the border with Colombia. Source: © Google, Inc. All rights reserved.

■ Maps are critical when a place is unfamiliar.

Cloud forests have persistent, low-level cloud cover with an abundance of ferns and mosses.

■ An explanation of the subject should come early in a photo essay.

Over 500 species of birds live in the reserve including this Toucan Barbet.

■ Details should follow after the subject is introduced.

Over 2,000 types of flora have been identified in the reserve.

■ People who are environmentally concerned understand threats to wildlife, but few are aware of the enormous loss of plant life or that many of those plants can provide benefits to people, such as medicine. Photographs allow people to see rare plants.

Only 5% of Ecuador's cloud forest remains. Much land has been cleared for growing crops, and illegal mining within the Cotacachi Reserve causes great environmental destruction because of erosion.

■ Christine waited until the end to present the current threat to the Cotacachi Reserve because she had to establish first why the reserve is a valuable environmental asset.

14d Design Documents

MLA style (the major style in the humanities and fine arts) and APA style (the major style in the social sciences and education) both provide extensive guidelines for formatting papers. See the sample paper for MLA in 23k and the sample paper for APA in 24i.

Use color effectively

Color can provide contrast to draw attention to headings and emphasized words. We are surrounded by so much color that sometimes the strongest effects are created by using color in minimal ways. Limited use of warm colors—yellow, orange, and especially red—can make an impact.

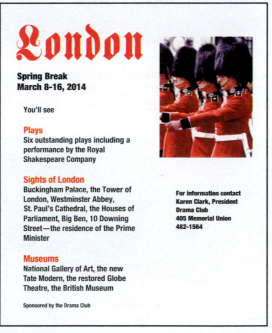

■ The red used in the titles and headings both matches and balances the red uniforms in the image.

Design brochures and other documents

With today's easy-to-use software, you can produce a professional-looking project. Handsome brochures are one example. Templates take care of the

basic layout, allowing you to focus on the content and design. If you are creating a brochure, select the size of paper you want, fold the sheet of paper, and number the panels. Make a sketch of what you want to appear on each panel, including headings, text, images, and graphics.

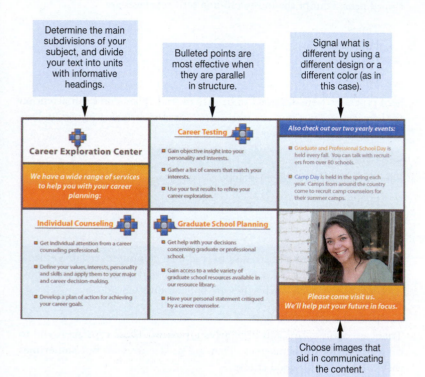

Determine the main subdivisions of your subject, and divide your text into units with informative headings.

Bulleted points are most effective when they are parallel in structure.

Signal what is different by using a different design or a different color (as in this case).

Choose images that aid in communicating the content.

■ The inside panels of a three-panel brochure fold out to show the services offered by the Career Exploration Center.

14e Choose Type

Writing on a computer enables you to use dozens of different typefaces and fonts. (A particular style of type is called a **typeface**, such as Times New Roman or Arial. A specific kind of typeface, such as Verdana bold, is called a **font**.) At first, typefaces may all appear similar, but when you pay attention to various typefaces, you will notice how they differ.

Use typefaces effectively

Serif type

Serif and **sans serif** are major categories of typefaces. Serifs are the little wedge-shaped ends on letter forms, which scribes produced with wedge-tipped pens. Four of the most common serif typefaces are

> Times
> Palatino
> Bookman
> Garamond

Serif typefaces were designed to be easy to read. They don't call attention to themselves. Thus they are well suited for long stretches of text and are used frequently.

Sans serif type

Popular sans serif typefaces include

> Helvetica
> Arial
> Verdana

Some sans serif typefaces are easy to read on a computer screen. Verdana, Helvetica, and Arial are sans serif typefaces that most computers now have installed, which is why they are popular on Web sites.

Script and decorative type

There are many script and decorative typefaces. These typefaces tend to draw attention to themselves. They are harder to read, but sometimes they can be used for good effects.

Popular script typefaces include Nuptial Script and Dorchester Script:

> *When you want only the very best*
>
> *Snead, Potter, and Jones, Attorneys at Law*

Some decorative typefaces, including Lazyvermont and ComicStrip Classic, are informal, almost irreverent:

> *That's a no brainer.*
>
> TOTALLY AWESOME!

Use a readable type size

It's easy to change the size of type when you compose on a computer. For long stretches of text, use at least 10- or 12-point type. Use larger type for headings and for text that will be read on a screen.

Use other effects as needed

Finally, use font formats such as **boldface**, *italics*, and underlining for emphasis.

14f Create Tables, Charts, and Graphs

Tables, charts, and graphs are easy to create in editing and presentation software, and they can be imported from one program (e.g., Excel) to another (e.g., Word). While software does much of the formatting of tables, charts, and graphs, you still have to supply the labels for the different parts of the graphic and an accurate title or caption.

STAYING ON TRACK

Use and evaluate tables

When to use tables

- To present a summary of several factors
- To present exact numbers
- To give an orderly arrangement so readers can locate and compare information

Evaluating tables

- Does the table have a clear purpose?
- Does the title indicate the purpose?
- What units do the numbers represent (dollars, people, voters, percentages, and so on)?
- What is the source of the data?
- Is the table clearly organized?
- Is the table clearly labeled?

Sample table format

Name of item	Factor 1	Factor 2	Factor 3
AAA	000	00	0
BBB	00	0	000
CCC	0	000	00

Like any graphic, tables, charts, and graphs can be used to mislead readers. Small differences can be exaggerated, for example, or relevant differences concealed (see 6b). You have an ethical responsibility to create accurate tables, charts, and graphs.

Tables

Extensive statistical data can be dull or cumbersome to communicate in sentences and paragraphs. Readers can more quickly and easily grasp data when they are displayed in a table. A table allows readers to view an entire set of data at once or to focus only on relevant aspects (see Table 14.1).

Table 14.1   U.S. Population by Sex and Age, 2000–2008

	2000 (April)	2005	2006	2007	2008
Resident population (1,000)	281,425	295,561	298,363	301,290	304,060
Male (1,000)	138,056	145,465	146,946	148,466	149,925
Female (1,000)	143,368	150,096	151,417	152,824	154,135
Under 5 years old (1,000)	19,176	20,301	20,436	20,730	21,006
5 to 17 years old (1,000)	53,119	53,077	53,158	53,129	52,936
18 to 44 years old (1,000)	112,184	112,665	112,737	112,891	113,190
45 to 64 years old (1,000)	61,954	72,765	74,768	76,598	78,058
65 years old and over (1,000)	34,992	36,752	37,264	37,942	38,870

Source: United States. Census Bureau. *The 2012 Statistical Abstract: USA Statistics in Brief.* 2012, 23 Sept. 2013, www.census.gov/library/publications/2011/compendia/statab/131ed/brief.html.

Bar charts

Bar charts are useful for comparing data.

Declining Crime Rates

According to the FBI's latest Preliminary Semiannual Uniform Crime Report, violent crime in the nation dropped 3.5 percent and property crime declined 2.5 percent during the first six months of 2008, compared to the same period in 2007.

Murder −4.4
Forcible Rape −3.3
Robbery −2.2
Aggravated Assault −4.1
Burglary −0.8
Larceny-Theft −1.2
Motor Vehicle Theft −12.6
Arson −5.6

Source: United States, Department of Justice, Federal Bureau of Investigation. *Some Good News: Crime Is Declining.* 12 Jan. 2009, www.fbi.gov/news/stories/2009/january/ucr_stats011209.

Line graphs

Line graphs are well suited for displaying changes in data across time. Line graphs can have one line, or two or more sets of data can be displayed on different lines, emphasizing the comparative rates of change.

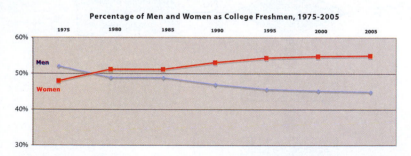

Percentage of Men and Women as College Freshmen, 1975-2005

Source: United States, Census Bureau. *Statistical Abstract of the United States: 2007.* Government Printing Office, 2007, p. 177.

Pie charts and flowcharts

Pie charts are commonly used to represent the relationship of parts to a whole. You must have data in percentages to use a pie chart, and the slices of the pie must add up to 100 percent. If the slices are too small, a pie chart becomes confusing. Six or seven slices are about the limit for a pie chart that is easy to interpret.

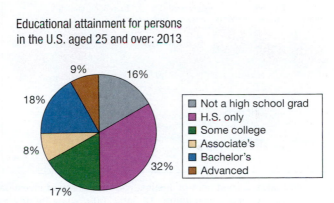

Educational attainment for persons
in the U.S. aged 25 and over: 2013

Legend:
- Not a high school grad
- H.S. only
- Some college
- Associate's
- Bachelor's
- Advanced

■ Pie charts display the relationship of parts to a whole.

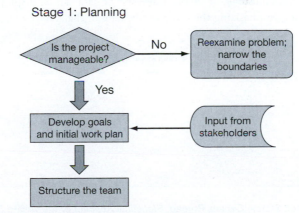

Stage 1: Planning

■ Flowcharts are useful for representing steps in a process.

STAYING ON TRACK

Use and evaluate charts

When to use charts

- To direct readers to what is important
- To give evidence for claims
- To show factual information visually
- To show statistical relationships more clearly than either words or numbers alone permit

Selecting the right chart

	Bar charts	Make comparisons in particular categories
	Line graphs	Show proportional trends over time
	Pie charts	Show the proportion of parts in terms of the whole
	Flowcharts	Show the steps in a process

Evaluating charts

- Does the chart have a clear purpose?
- Does the title indicate the purpose?
- What do the units represent (dollars, people, voters, percentages, and so on)?
- What is the source of the data?
- Is the type of chart appropriate for the information presented?
- Is there any distortion of information?

15 | Design Presentations

QUICK*TAKE*

After reading this chapter, you should be able to . . .
- Plan an effective presentation by putting the audience first (15a)
- Design simple slides (15b)
- Construct and deliver an effective presentation (15c)

15a Plan a Presentation

If you are assigned to give a presentation, look carefully at the assignment for guidance on finding a topic. The process for finding a topic is similar to that for a written assignment (see Chapter 2). If your assignment requires research, you will need to document the sources of information just as you do for a research paper (see Chapters 17–22).

Start with your goal in mind

What is the real purpose of your presentation? Are you informing, persuading, or motivating? Take the elevator test. Imagine you are in an elevator with the key people who can approve or reject your ideas. Their schedule is very tight. You have only 30 seconds to convince them. Can you make your case?

This scenario is not far-fetched. One executive demanded that every new idea had to be written in one sentence on the back of a business card. What's your sentence?

It's all about your audience

Who is your audience? In college your audience is often your instructor and fellow students—an audience you know well. Many times you will not have this advantage. Take a few minutes to answer these questions.

My audience
Will they be interested in the topic?
Why does it matter to them?
What are they likely to know and believe about the topic?
What are they likely to not know?
Where are they likely to disagree?

What do I want them to do?
How much time do I have?
If they remember only one thing, what should it be?

Get organized

Start with pen and paper before you begin creating slides. Sticky notes are another useful planning tool.

- **Make a list of key points.** Think about the best order for your major points.
- **Plan your introduction.** Your success depends on your introduction. You must gain the attention of your audience, introduce your topic, indicate why it's important, and give a sense of where you are headed. It's a tall order, but if you don't engage your audience in the first 2 minutes, you will lose them.
- **Plan your conclusion.** You want to end on a strong note. Stopping abruptly or rambling on only to tail off leaves your audience with a bad impression. Give your audience something to take away, a compelling example or an idea that captures the gist of your presentation.

Build content

Content alone does not make a presentation successful, but you cannot succeed without solid content. Support your major points with relevant evidence. Consider creating a handout so your audience can refer to important facts, statistics, and quotations.

- **Facts.** Speakers who know their facts build credibility.
- **Statistics.** Effective use of statistics can give the audience the impression that you have done your homework. Statistics can also indicate that a particular example is representative.
- **Statements by authorities.** Quotations from credible experts can support key points.
- **Narratives.** Narratives are brief stories that illustrate key points. Narratives can hold the attention of the audience, but keep them short or they will become a distraction.

15b Design Visuals for a Presentation

With slides, less is more. One text-filled slide after another is mind-numbingly dull. Presentations using slides can be better than a series of slides with bulleted points, one after the other seemingly forever.

Keep it simple

Compare the following examples.

Food Crisis in the United States

- The U.S. Department of Agriculture reported that over 50 million Americans lived with reduced-quality food or reduced food intake in 2011.

- The 2011 survey reports that over 20% of all households with children were food insecure.

- Over 8 million children lacked a healthy diet and at times did not have enough to eat.

FOOD CRISIS
8.6 million U.S. children lacked a healthy diet or enough to eat in 2011

8.6 million children

■ Which slide makes the point most effectively?

Simple design rules!
> *One point per slide*
> *Very few fonts*
> *Quality photos, not clip art*
> *Less text, more images*
> *Easy on the special effects*

U.S. households by food security status, 2011

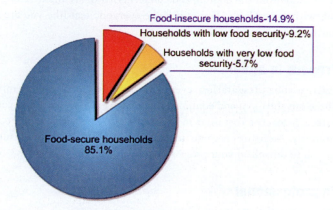

■ Charts and graphs make statistics easier to understand in a presentation.
Source: United States Department of Agriculture. *Food Security in the U.S.*
4 Sept. 2012, www.ers.usda.gov/media/884525/err141.pdf.

But what if you have a lot of data to show? Make a handout that the audience can study later. They can make notes on your handout, which gives them a personal investment. Keep your slides simple and emphasize the main points in the presentation.

Use effective charts

Again, simpler is better. Limit your charts to only the details you need to make the point. If you have a complicated table or chart, distribute it as a handout.

Use audio and video clips strategically

Short audio and video clips can offer concrete examples and add some variety to your presentation. An audience appreciates hearing and even seeing the people you interview. *PowerPoint, Keynote, Prezi,* and other presentation software make it simple to embed the files within a presentation. Be careful, however, in using the built-in sound effects such as canned applause. Most sound effects are annoying and make you come off as inexperienced.

15c Deliver an Effective Presentation

If you are not passionate about your subject, you will never get your audience committed to your subject, no matter how professional looking your slides are. Believe in what you say; enthusiasm is contagious.

It's all about you

The audience didn't come to see the back of your head in front of slides. Move away from the podium and connect with them. Make strong eye contact with individuals. You will make everyone feel like you are having a conversation instead of giving a speech.

Prepare in advance

Practice your presentation, even if you have to speak to an empty chair. Check out the room and equipment in advance. If you are using your laptop with a projector installed in the room, make sure it connects. Begin promptly. Audiences become impatient if they have to wait several minutes for you to download your presentation.

Be professional

Pay attention to the little things.

- **Proofread carefully.** A glaring spelling error can destroy your credibility.
- **Be consistent.** If you randomly capitalize words or insert punctuation, your audience will be distracted.
- **Pay attention to the timing of your slides.** Stay in sync with your slides. Don't leave a slide up when you are talking about something else.
- **Use the "B" key.** If you get sidetracked, press the "B" key, which makes the screen go blank so the audience can focus on you. When you are ready to resume, press the "B" key again and the slide reappears.
- **Involve your audience.** Invite response during your presentation where appropriate and leave time for questions at the end.
- **Add a bit of humor.** Humor can be tricky, especially if you don't know your audience well. But if you can get your audience to laugh, they will be on your side.
- **Slow down.** When you are nervous, you tend to go too fast. Stop and breathe. Let your audience take in what's on your slides.
- **Finish on time or earlier.** Your audience will be grateful.

16 | Compose in Online Genres

QUICK*TAKE*

After reading this chapter, you should be able to . . .
- Create Web pages (16a)
- Create podcasts (16b)
- Create videos (16c)
- Create a discussion post (16d)

16a Create a Web Page

Readers approach Web pages differently than they do older media like books and newspapers. Readers of Web pages expect to be able to move through your site according to their own interests, rather than starting on the first page and reading straight through to the last.

Elements of a Web page

Title and subheadings	The title of your Web page should appear in the page itself and at the top of the reader's browser window. Use subheadings to divide your information into readable sections.
Navigation menu	Navigation elements are the "table of contents" for a Web site. They should be clear and easy to find but should not distract readers from the main content of the page.
Content	"Content" refers to the text, images, embedded videos, sound files, and all other material on your page.
Affiliation and credentials	Let your readers know who sponsors the Web site. If the site is for an organization or business, provide an "About" page and a link to the page in the main menu.

What you need to do

- Capture your readers' attention and don't waste their time. Unlike readers of books, readers of Web pages can, with the click of their mouse, leave your page for thousands of other entertaining and

informative sites. You must give them a reason to spend time on your site.

- Avoid large blocks of unbroken text. Divide your information into chunks, and if it runs longer than a page, consider dividing it between two or more Web pages.
- Build navigation into your content. Think about where people will need to go next after they read your page.
- Provide links to sources.
- Proofread carefully for mechanics, grammar, and spelling; they can make or break your credibility with readers.

Sample Web page for a student organization

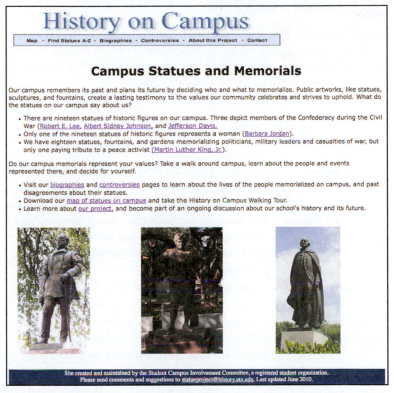

■ Campus organizations, like nearly all organizations, create Web sites to publicize their mission and activities.

WRITING SMART

Evaluate the design of a Web site

You can learn a great deal about effective Web design by keeping these criteria in mind when you visit Web sites.

1. **Audience and purpose:** How does the site identify its intended audience? Why was the site created?
2. **Content:** How informative is the content? Has the site been updated recently? What do you want to know more about?
3. **Readability:** Is there sufficient contrast between the text and the background to make it legible? Are there paragraphs that go on too long and need to be divided? Are headings inserted in the right places, and if headings are used for more than one level, are the levels indicated consistently?
4. **Visual design:** Does the site have a consistent visual theme? Do the images contribute to the visual appeal, or do they detract from it?
5. **Navigation:** Does the first page indicate what else is on the site? How easy or difficult is it to move from one page to another on the site? Are there any broken links?

16b Create a Podcast

Podcasts are easy to create using your own audio editor and your Web site, or you can create them in a multimedia lab and post them on a third-party site. For a podcast with high audio quality, you'll need a headset with a noise-canceling microphone, a portable voice recorder, and podcasting software. All these may be available from your campus multimedia lab.

The process for creating a podcast

Identify your purpose	What exactly do you want to accomplish?
Plan your content	Do you want to conduct interviews about a subject or an issue? Do a documentary of an event? Give practical advice or instructions? Give a history or an analysis? Make a persuasive argument?
Compose your audio	Arrange and record interviews. Write a script.

Know the law	If you use music created by someone else, you likely will have to pay for the right to broadcast that music. If someone agrees to be your guest, you have the right to broadcast that person's voice.
Record your podcast	Reserve a campus audio production lab or record on your computer. Create an audio file by combining the interviews with your narration.
Edit your podcast	Your multimedia lab may have instructions or consultants for using audio editing software. Allow ample time for editing.
Publish your podcast	Export the audio into a format such as WAV or MP3 that you can put on the Web or share as a downloadable file.

■ Free open-source editors are available for Windows, Mac, and Linux.

16c Create a Video

The cost and technical barriers for creating a video have been significantly reduced. Phones and PDAs can now record video along with simple-to-use camcorders. Most new computers come with video editors installed, including Apple's *iMovie* or Windows' *MovieMaker*. *YouTube* and other video-sharing Web sites make it easy to publish your video.

Nonetheless, making a high-quality video requires a great deal of effort. In addition to the technical demands, producing quality videos requires the hard work of planning and revising that extended writing tasks demand.

The process for creating a video

Identify your subject and purpose	What exactly do you want to accomplish?
Decide on your approach	Do you want to conduct interviews? Do a documentary of an event? Make an announcement? Reenact a past event?

Plan your content	Will all the video be original? Will you incorporate other video such as *YouTube* clips? Will you include still images? Maps or graphs? Music? Voiceover?
Draft a script and a storyboard	A storyboard is a shot-by-shot representation of your project that will help you organize your shooting schedule.
Make a schedule and plan your locations	Quality videos take many hours to shoot and edit. Visit all locations in advance to take into account issues such as lighting and noise.
Arrange for your equipment	At minimum you will need video and sound recording equipment and an editing suite. Find out what is available from your campus multimedia lab.
Compose your video	You can create a more dynamic video by using techniques of still photographers. You can add movement by using the zoom feature on your camera.
Capture audio	The microphone installed in your camera is usually not the best option. Your multimedia lab may have external microphones that will give you better quality. Microphones record ambient noises—such as the wind noise, traffic, and computer fans—which you need to minimize.
Edit your video	Editing software allows you to combine video clips and edit audio. Your multimedia lab may have instructions or consultants for using video editing software. Allow ample time for editing.
Publish your video	Export the video into a format such as *Quick-Time* that you can put on the Web or share as a downloadable file.

16d Create a Discussion Post

Productive writers often use discussion forums, e-mail, blogs, and instant messaging to communicate and discuss ideas. Your instructor will likely give specific instructions for how often you are required to participate in online discussion forums and may also specify the number and kinds of posts you must make.

When you are posting the first entry in a discussion thread, give your post a clear, specific subject line that lets readers know what you are writing about before they open it. For new or response posts, offer the context (the assignment or reading name), the date and name of a previous post, or other background.

When you reply to other students' posts, use a respectful tone and keep your language clear and to the point. Think about the voice your writing creates and how classmates and your instructor will hear it. Follow commonsense rules of etiquette and avoid posting angry or personal attacks, taking special care to be respectful when you disagree. Finally, take time to reread and edit your work before posting.

Discussion post assignment

Discussion #2: Visual signs

Think of some clothing or style that is popular among friends of yours: tattoos, baseball caps, piercings, jewelry, sneakers, and so on. Interview a friend who wears the item and photograph him or her, focusing on the item. Upload the photo to the discussion board. Write a post of 250–400 words about the significance of the item and what it says about the generation who values it.

Sample discussion post

Clear subject line repeats assignment language.

Thread: Style or clothing? Magenta Chucks with Cartoon Laces

Author: Lindsey Rodriguez

Posted Date: Thursday, January 27, 2016 4:54:31 PM CST

Edited Date: Thursday, January 27, 2016 4:58:23 PM CST

Shoes are a versatile type of clothing because the wearer can consciously choose the size of the statement they make. People can pick a pair of subtle shoes that complement their outfit or wear a pair for their functionality. Alternatively, shoes may also serve as a statement—accessories that make a jarring contrast

against the rest of the outfit or even serve as the focal point.

Photograph responds to assignment and shows details described in post.

For example, a pair of well-worn, magenta Converse sneakers with mismatching laces can only be meant to generate intrigue as a clothing choice. While a magenta pair of Converses with Hello-Kitty and Spiderman laces would seem odd for the typical male, Rick Wang's closet is a sea of black, white, and shades of purple with the occasional ironic or vintage T-shirt lying on the floor. Rick is unlike any person I've ever met. For his senior yearbook portrait, he wore the same rented tux that was required for all guys with one exception: after much convincing of the photographer, on his shoulder sat the turtle beanie-baby he named Cornelius Alfonso Laramy Galileo III Esq. His eighteenth birthday party was held at Chuck E. Cheese's, where he gallivanted around with the cape and Chuck E. Cheese mask given to all birthday children. Like many of his generation, the shoes convey his embrace of the strange, fun, and colorful

Post relates results of interview.

without any regard to dignity. The cartoon shoelaces are a display of his eccentricity and still lively inner child.

Post length is appropriate to assignment.

As the technological revolution gave power and prestige to nerds, Converse's "Chucks" became popular among the generation that values socially awkward yet intelligent and quirky individuals. Crazy-colored shoes have also grown in popularity because they express creativity and individualism for a generation that resists becoming boring.

Research Map 1: Conducting Research (see the back of this divider)

RESEARCH MAP 1: CONDUCTING RESEARCH

College research writing requires that you

- determine your goals,
- find a topic,
- ask a question about that topic,
- find out what has been written about that topic,
- evaluate what has been written about that topic, and
- make a contribution to the discussion about that topic.

Here are the steps in planning research and finding sources.

1 | Plan the research project

First, analyze what you are being asked to do and set a schedule.
Go to 17a and 17b.

Ask a question about a topic that interests you and narrow that topic. Go to 17c.

Determine what kinds of research you will need: research using secondary sources and field research. Go to 17d.

Conduct field research if it is appropriate for your project. See strategies for

- **CONDUCTING INTERVIEWS**;
  go to 20b.
- **ADMINISTERING SURVEYS**;
  go to 20c.
- **MAKING OBSERVATIONS**;
  go to 20d.

2 | Draft a working thesis

Draft a working thesis. Go to 17e.

Create a working bibliography.
Go to 17f.

If you are assigned to create an annotated bibliography, go to 17g.

You'll see in Parts 5 and 6 the process Gabriella Lopez used to produce her research project. Gabriella's final version of her project is in 23k.

See Research Map 2 at the beginning of Part 6 for guidance on incorporating and documenting sources.

Find and track sources

nsult with a research librarian if ssible and determine where and how start looking for sources.

d sources online and in print:

- for sources in **DATABASES**, go to 18b.
- for **ONLINE SOURCES**, go to 18c.
- for **MULTIMEDIA** sources, go to 18d.
- for **PRINT** sources, go to 18e.

ep track of sources. Go to 18f.

---

4 | Evaluate sources

Decide which sources are going to be useful for your project. For each source you'll need to determine:

- **RELEVANCE** to your research question; go to 19a.
- **QUALITY** for your purposes; go to 19b.

Evaluate the different types of sources you are using:

- **DATABASE** and **PRINT SOURCES**; go to 19c.
- **ONLINE SOURCES**; go to 19d.

17 | Plan Your Research

QUICK*TAKE*

After reading this chapter, you should be able to . . .

- Plan your research project (17a)
- Organize a schedule (17b)
- Identify a topic (17c)
- Identify what kind of research is needed (17d)
- Compose a working thesis (17e)
- Create a working bibliography (17f)
- Create an annotated bibliography (17g)

17a Analyze the Research Task

Research is a creative process, which is another way of saying it is messy. However, your results will improve if you keep the big picture in mind. When you get a research assignment, look at it closely.

Look for words that signal what is expected

Often the assignment will tell you what is expected.

- An *analysis* or *examination* asks you to look at an issue in detail, explaining its history, the people and places affected, and what is at stake.
- A *review of scholarship* requires you to summarize what key scholars and researchers have written about the issue.
- An *evaluation* requires you to make critical judgments.
- An *argument* requires you to assemble evidence in support of a claim you make.

Identify your potential readers

- How familiar are your readers with your subject?
- What background information will you need to supply?
- If your subject is controversial, what opinions or beliefs are your readers likely to hold?
- If some readers are likely to disagree with you, how can you convince them?

Assess the project's length, scope, and requirements

- What kind of research are you being asked to do?
- What is the length of the project?

- What kinds and number of sources or field research are required?
- Which documentation style—such as MLA (see Chapter 23) or APA (see Chapter 24)—is required?

Writer at Work

Gabriella Lopez made notes on her assignment sheet.

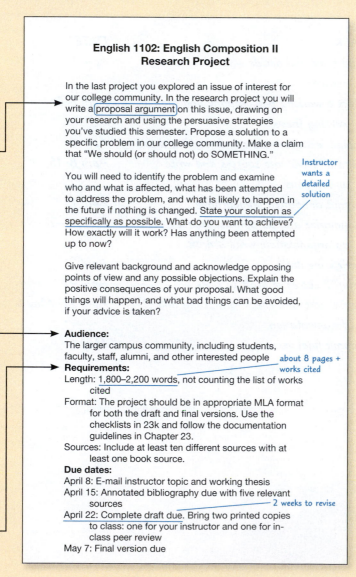

**English 1102: English Composition II
Research Project**

In the last project you explored an issue of interest for our college community. In the research project you will write a proposal argument on this issue, drawing on your research and using the persuasive strategies you've studied this semester. Propose a solution to a specific problem in our college community. Make a claim that "We should (or should not) do SOMETHING."

Instructor wants a detailed solution

You will need to identify the problem and examine who and what is affected, what has been attempted to address the problem, and what is likely to happen in the future if nothing is changed. State your solution as specifically as possible. What do you want to achieve? How exactly will it work? Has anything been attempted up to now?

Give relevant background and acknowledge opposing points of view and any possible objections. Explain the positive consequences of your proposal. What good things will happen, and what bad things can be avoided, if your advice is taken?

Audience:
The larger campus community, including students, faculty, staff, alumni, and other interested people   *about 8 pages + works cited*
Requirements:
Length: 1,800–2,200 words, not counting the list of works cited
Format: The project should be in appropriate MLA format for both the draft and final versions. Use the checklists in 23k and follow the documentation guidelines in Chapter 23.
Sources: Include at least ten different sources with at least one book source.
Due dates:
April 8: E-mail instructor topic and working thesis
April 15: Annotated bibliography due with five relevant sources   *2 weeks to revise*
April 22: Complete draft due. Bring two printed copies to class: one for your instructor and one for in-class peer review
May 7: Final version due

17b Set a Schedule

Writer at Work

Gabriella used the assignment to create her work schedule.

TASK	DATE
Find topic and decide what research is needed	April 1
Start a working bibliography and draft a working thesis	April 1–8
E-mail instructor topic and working thesis	April 8
Read and evaluate sources and write annotations	April 8–15
Submit annotated bibliography	April 15
Summarize and paraphrase sources; plan an organization; write a draft	April 15–21
Review my draft	April 21
Bring 2 copies of draft to class	April 22
Revise, edit, and check formatting and documentation	April 22–May 5
Submit final version	May 6

17c Find and Narrow a Topic

If you ask meaningful questions, research will be enjoyable. Your courses may give you ideas about questions to ask, or you may simply want to pursue an interest of your own. One good way to begin is by browsing, which may also show you the breadth of possibilities included in a topic and possibly lead you to new topics.

You might begin browsing by doing one or more of the following.

- **Visit "Research by Subject" on your library's Web site.** Clicking on a subject such as "African and African American Studies" will take you to a list of online resources. Often you can find an e-mail link to a reference librarian who can assist you.

- **Look for topics in your courses.** Browse your course notes and readings. Are there any topics you might want to explore in greater depth?

- **Browse an online subject directory.** Subject directories are useful when you want to narrow a topic or learn what subcategories a topic might contain. Additionally, the Library of Congress *Virtual Reference Shelf* (www.loc.gov/rr/askalib/virtualref.html) may help you identify sites relevant to your topic.

- **Consult a specialized encyclopedia.** Specialized encyclopedias focus on a single area of knowledge, go into more depth about a subject, and often include bibliographies. Check if your library database page has a link to the Gale Virtual Reference Library, which offers entries from many specialized encyclopedias and reference sources.

- **Look for topics as you read.** When you read actively, you ask questions and respond to ideas in the text. Review what you wrote in the margins or the notes you have made about something you read that interested you. You may find a potential topic.

Writer at Work

Gabriella Lopez knew immediately that she wanted to write about the general topic of sustainable food on campus. Gabriella was personally aware of the difficulty of healthy eating on campus, and she had voiced concerns in her dormitory about the few options for eating organic food. But she was also aware that many students, including herself, were struggling to pay for college and didn't want to pay more for campus food. She drew different possibilities she might pursue and what objections might be raised.

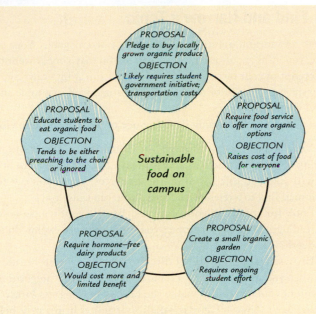

Two possibilities looked promising: creating a student organization to pledge to buy fresh, locally grown produce and creating a small organic garden on campus. She decided to go with the garden because the idea was simpler to implement.

STAYING ON TRACK

Decide if a topic is manageable

It can be tricky to find a balance between what you want to say about a topic and the amount of space you have to say it in. Usually your instructor will suggest a length for your project, which should help you decide how to limit your topic. If you suspect your topic is becoming unmanageable and your project may be too long, look for ways to narrow your focus.

Off track	A five-page paper on European witch hunts
On track	A five-page paper tracing two or three major causes of the European witch hunts of the fifteenth and sixteenth centuries
Off track	A ten-page paper on accounting fraud
On track	A ten-page paper examining how a new law would help prevent corporate accounting fraud

17d Determine What Kind of Research You Need

When you begin your research, you will have to make a few educated guesses about where to look. Ask these questions before you start.

- How much information do you need? The assignment may specify the number of sources you should consult.
- Are particular types of sources required? If so, do you understand why those sources are required?
- How current should the information be? Some assignments require you to use the most up-to-date information you can locate.
- Do you need to consider point of view? Argument assignments sometimes require you to consider opposing viewpoints on an issue.

Secondary research

Most people who do research rely partly or exclusively on the work of others as sources of information. Research based on the work of others is called **secondary research.** In the past this information was contained almost exclusively in collections of print materials housed in libraries, but today enormous amounts of information are available on the Internet and in various recorded media. Chapters 18 and 19 explain in detail how to find and evaluate database, online, and print sources.

Primary research

Much of the research done at a university creates new information through **primary research:** experiments, data-gathering surveys and interviews, detailed observations, and the examination of historical documents. If you are researching a campus issue such as the problem of inadequate parking for students, you may need to conduct interviews, make observations, and take a survey. Or, if you are training in a field where primary research is important, you may be required to conduct research in order to learn research methods. Chapter 20 explains how to plan and conduct three types of field research: interviews (20b), surveys (20c), and observations (20d).

17e Draft a Working Thesis

If you ask a focused and interesting research question, your answer will be your **working thesis.** This working thesis will be the focus of the remainder of your research and ultimately your research project.

Ask questions about your topic

When you have a topic that is interesting to you, manageable in scope, and possible to research using sources or doing field research, then your next task is to ask researchable questions.

Explore a definition

- While many (most) people think X is a Y, can X be better thought of as a Z?

  Most people think of deer as harmless animals that are benign to the environment, but their overpopulation devastates young trees in forests, leading to loss of habitat for birds and other species that depend on those trees.

Evaluate a person, activity, or thing

- Can you argue that a person, activity, or thing is either good, better, or best (or bad, worse, or worst) within its class?

  Fender Stratocasters from the 1950s remain the best electric guitars ever made because of their versatility, sound quality, and player-friendly features.

Examine why something happened

- Can you argue that while there were obvious causes of Y, Y would not have occurred had it not been for X?

  College students are called irresponsible when they run up high credit card debts that they cannot pay off, but these debts would not have occurred if credit card companies did not aggressively market cards and offer high lines of credit to students with no income.

- Can you argue for an alternative cause rather than the one many people assume?

  The defeat of the Confederate Army at the Battle of Gettysburg in July 1863 is often cited as the turning point in the Civil War, but in fact the South was running out of food, equipment, and soldiers, and it lost its only real chance of winning when Great Britain failed to intervene on its side.

Counter objections to a position

- Can the reverse or opposite of an opposing claim be argued?

  New medications that relieve pain are welcomed by runners and other athletes, but these drugs also mask signals that our bodies send us, increasing the risk of serious injury.

Propose a solution to a problem

- Can you propose a solution to a local problem?

   The traffic congestion on our campus could be eased by creating bike lanes on College Drive, which would encourage more students, faculty, and staff to commute by bicycle.

Turn your answers into a working thesis

Topic	Reading disorders
Researchable question	Why do some people learn to read top-to-bottom Chinese characters more easily than left-to-right alphabetic writing?
Working thesis	The direction of text flow may be an important factor in how an individual learns to read.

Writer at Work

Garbriella's working thesis answered her research question.

TOPIC	*Sustainable food on our campus*
RESEARCHABLE QUESTION	*How can our campus increase the amount of locally grown food that students eat without adding to the cost they pay and increase student awareness of environmental stewardship?*
WORKING THESIS	*Establishing a small organic garden can provide both fresh, healthy food and a low-cost way to support our school's environmental mission.*

17f Create a Working Bibliography

When you begin to collect your sources, make sure you get full bibliographic information for everything you might want to use in your project: articles, books, Web sites, and other materials. Decide which documentation style you will use. If your instructor does not tell you which style is appropriate, ask. (The major documentation styles—MLA, APA, CMS, and CSE—are dealt with in detail in Chapters 23–26.)

Find the necessary bibliographic information

Section 18f gives instructions on what information you will need to collect for each kind of source. In general, as you research and develop a working bibliography, the rule of thumb is to write down more information rather than less. You can always delete unnecessary information when it comes time to format your citations according to your chosen documentation style (APA, MLA, CMS, or CSE), but it is time-consuming to go back to sources to find missing bibliographic information.

Record bibliographic information

There are many ways to record and organize your sources. You can record each source's bibliographic information on individual note cards; you can print out or photocopy relevant pages from each source; you can e-mail articles to yourself from library databases; and you may be able to use your library's bibliographic software to manage citations (but be aware that the software often does not get everything you need). Whichever way you choose, always check that you have complete and accurate publication information for each source.

Alternatives to copying from a source are cutting and pasting into a file (for online sources) or making photocopies (for a print source). Both methods ensure accuracy in copying sources, but in either case make sure you attach full bibliographic information to the file or photocopy.

If you are not careful about putting quotation marks around material you cut and paste, you can get confused about where the material came from and plagiarize unintentionally (see Chapter 21 for information on incorporating sources and avoiding plagiarism). In Chapter 23 you'll find detailed instructions on how to find the information you need for MLA documentation. See Chapter 24 for APA, Chapter 25 for CMS, and Chapter 26 for CSE documentation.

Writer at Work

Gabriella was careful to distinguish her notes from material she quoted directly. She identified by page number any quoted material.

> *Pollan, Michael. <u>The Omnivore's Dilemma: A Natural History of</u>*
> *<u>Four Meals</u>. Penguin Books, 2006.*
>
> *Pollan sums up the big problem I want to write about.*
>
> *"Our ingenuity in feeding ourselves is prodigious, but at*
> *various points our technologies come into conflict with*
> *nature's way of doing things, as when we seek to maximize*
> *efficiency by planting crops or raising animals in vast*
> *monocultures. This is something nature never does, always*
> *and for good reason practicing diversity instead." (9)*

17g Create an Annotated Bibliography

A working bibliography is an alphabetized list of sources with complete publication information that you collect while researching your topic. An **annotated bibliography** builds on the basic citations of a working bibliography by adding a brief summary or evaluation of each source. Annotated bibliographies must include

- a complete citation in the documentation style you are using (MLA, APA, CMS, CSE) and
- a concise summary of the content and scope.

In addition, your instructor may ask you to include one or more of the following.

- A comment on the relevance of the source to your research topic
- An evaluation of the background and qualifications of the author
- A comparison to another work on your list

Writer at Work

Gabriella Lopez

Professor Kimbro

English 1102

15 Apr. 2016

Annotated Bibliography

Bartholomew, Mel. *All New Square Foot Gardening: Grow
More in Less Space*. Cool Spring Press, 2006. Mel
Bartholomew is the expert on square foot
gardening. This book explains everything you need
to know about constructing and maintaining a
square-foot garden. It will help me show not only
how to create small campus gardens but also
all of the options available and how easy and
inexpensive it will be.

Berman, Jillian. "Sustainability Could Secure a Good
Future: College Students Flock to 'Green' Degrees,
Careers." *USA Today,* 3 Apr. 2009, p. 7D. This
article describes how the growth in "green" jobs is
making students seek colleges that provide them
with opportunities to learn about sustainability.
This trend will be useful in helping me argue that
our college needs to offer students opportunities
to learn about sustainability in real ways.

Lewington, Jennifer. "Lean Green Campus Machines:
Students Are at the Forefront of a Grassroots
Environmental Revolution As They Coax—and
Sometimes Embarrass—Administrators into

Walking the Walk with Them." *The Globe and Mail*,
23 Oct. 2008, p. 14. This article talks about how
students in Canada are getting administrators to
support sustainability. It shows how a new kind of
collaborative student activism works.

Rozin, Paul, et al. "Food and Life, Pleasure and Worry,
among American College Students: Gender
Differences and Regional Similarities." *Journal of
Personality and Social Psychology*, vol. 85, no. 1,
2003, pp. 132–41. *PsycARTICLES*, doi: 10.1037/
0022-3514.85.1.132. This scientific article
describes a study of how students think about
food. It not only complements Michael Pollan's
argument that we have developed an unhealthy
relationship with food, but it also shows how
important the college years are for establishing
that relationship.

Samadzadeh, Nozlee. "Farm Update: The Third Annual
Jack Hitt Annual Last Day of Classes Pig Roast."
Yale Sustainable Food Project, 3 May 2010,
yalesustainablefoodproject.wordpress.
com/2010/05/03/farm-update-the-third-annual-
jack-hitt-annual-last-day-of-classes-pig-roast/.
This article reminds readers that going green does
not necessarily mean going vegetarian. The writer,
a student member of the Yale Sustainable Food
Project, describes the process of obtaining and
preparing ethically raised pork.

18 | Find Sources

QUICK*TAKE*

After reading this chapter, you should be able to . . .
- Use effective search strategies (18a)
- Use library databases to find sources (18b)
- Use search techniques to find online sources (18c)
- Apply research skills to find multimedia sources (18d)
- Use strategies to find print sources (18e)
- Apply techniques like note-taking to keep track of sources (18f)

18a Develop Strategies for Finding Sources

Libraries still contain many resources not available online. Even more important, libraries have professional research librarians who can help you locate sources quickly.

Determine where to start looking

Searches using *Google* or *Bing* turn up thousands of items, many of which are often not useful for research. Considering where to start is the first step.

Scholarly books and articles in scholarly journals often are the highest quality sources, but the lag in publication time makes them less useful for very current topics. Newspapers cover current issues, but often not in the depth of books and scholarly journals. Government sites and publications are often the best for finding statistics and are also valuable for researching science and medicine.

Learn the art of effective keyword searches

Keyword searches take you to the sources you need. Start with your working thesis and generate a list of possible keywords for researching your thesis.

First, think of keywords that make your search **more specific**. For example, a search for sources related to youth voter participation might focus more specifically on young adults *and*

> voter registration
> historical participation rates
> voter turnout

WRITING SMART

Find the right kinds of sources

Type of source	Type of information	How to find them
Scholarly books	Extensive and in-depth coverage of nearly any subject	Library catalog
Scholarly journals	Reports of new knowledge and research findings by experts	Online library databases
Trade journals	Reports of information pertaining to specific industries, professions, and products	Online library databases
Popular magazines	Reports or summaries of current news, sports, fashion, and entertainment subjects	Online library databases
Newspapers	Recent and current information; foreign newspapers are useful for international perspectives	Online library databases
Government publications	Government-collected statistics, studies, and reports; especially good for science and medicine	Library catalog and city, state, and federal government Web sites
Videos, audio sources, documentaries, maps	Information varies widely	Library catalog, online library databases, open Internet

Also think about **more general** ways to describe what you are doing—what synonyms can you think of for your existing terms? Instead of relying on "young adult," try keywords like

under 30
millennials
college students

You can even search using terms that refer to related people, events, or movements that you are familiar with

>Rock the Vote
>MTV voter registration drive

Many databases have a thesaurus that can help you find more keywords.

WRITING SMART

Adjust searches to improve results

If your search turns up hundreds or thousands of hits, consider the following options.

- Try more specific search terms.
- Use a phrase within quotation marks or specify "the exact phrase."
- Specify NOT for terms you are not interested in finding.
- Limit your search by a date range.
- Limit the search by domain name (site:.edu, site:.gov).

If your search turns up fewer than ten hits, you can use these options.

- Check your spelling.
- Try broader search terms.
- Try another index or search engine.

Writer at Work

Gabriella Lopez wanted the most recent information she could locate about student-run farms, so she searched the *LexisNexis Academic* database, which is an excellent tool for searching newspapers. She first used "campus farms" as her keywords, but this search produced over 2,000 sources, most off her topic. She next tried "college organic farm" and limited the search to the last five years, which produced a more manageable sixteen sources.

LexisNexis® *Academic* — Home

General Searching	Power Search	Help Clear
▸ Easy Search™	**Use of this service is subject to Terms and Conditions**	
▸ Power Search		

Tip: Click the headings below to view links to specialized search forms and other useful features.

Search Type: ● Terms & Connectors ○ Natural Language

Search Terms: college organic farm   **Search**

Specify Date: Previous 5 years

18b Find Sources in Databases

Sources found through library databases have already been filtered for you by professional librarians. They will include some common sources like popular magazines and newspapers, but the greatest value of database sources are the many journals, abstracts, studies, e-books, and other writing produced by specialists whose work has been scrutinized and commented upon by other experts. When you read a source from a library database, chances are you are hearing an informed voice in an important debate.

Locate databases

You can find databases on your library's Web site. Sometimes you will find a list of databases. Sometimes you select a subject, and then you are directed to databases. Sometimes you select the name of a database vendor such as EBSCO or ProQuest. The vendor is the company that provides databases to the library.

![The University of Kansas Libraries Articles and Databases web page screenshot]

The University of Kansas Libraries

Articles and Databases

Libraries Home

Articles & Databases
Catalog: books & more
E-journals
Research by Subject
Course Reserves
Library Pages A-Z

Images
KU ScholarWorks
» more Digital Collections

Hours
My Account
Request Materials
Friends & Benefactors
Suggestions

ask a librarian

Quick Search for Articles

[Search]
» Quick Search in more databases

You are searching these databases:
• Academic Search Premier
• Project MUSE
• Wilson OmniFile full text select

Find Articles by Citation

Databases

By Title
A B C D E F G H I J K L M N O P Q R S T U V W X Y Z 0-9

By Subject
To see more specific subjects, expand the list of broad subjects.

☑ Show all subjects
☐ Collapse subjects

⊞ Area and Cultural Studies
⊞ Arts and Humanities
⊞ Business
⊞ General and Reference
⊞ History
⊞ Languages and Literature
⊞ Medicine and Health
⊞ Science and Engineering
⊞ Social Sciences

Help
Selecting Sources
Searching Databases
Search Strategies
Importing Citations - EndNote
Citing sources
Save Searches / Alerts
Ask a Librarian

Related
Off-campus Access
New Database Trials
New and Updated Databases
Databases by Platform

■ You can find a link to your library's database collection on the library's home page.

WRITING SMART

Know the advantages of subscription database versus free access online sources

	Library database sources	Open online sources
Speed	✓ Users can find information quickly	✓ Users can find information quickly
Accessibility	✓ Available 24/7	✓ Available 24/7
Organization	✓ Materials are organized for efficient search and retrieval	Users must look in many different places for related information
Consistency and quality	✓ Librarians review and select resources	Anyone can claim to be an "expert," regardless of qualifications
Comprehensiveness	✓ Collected sources represent a wide and representative body of knowledge	No guarantee that the full breadth of an issue will be represented
Permanence	✓ Materials remain available for many years	Materials can disappear or change in an instant
Free of overt bias	✓ Even sources with a definite agenda are required to meet certain standards of documentation and intellectual rigor	Sources are often a "soapbox" for organizations or individuals with particular agendas and little knowledge or experience
Free of commercial slant	✓ Because libraries pay for their collections, sources are largely commercial-free	Sources are often motivated primarily by the desire to sell you something

Use databases

Your library has a list of databases and indexes by subject. If you can't find this list on your library's Web site, ask a reference librarian for help. Follow these steps to find articles.

1. Select a database appropriate to your subject. (For example, if you are researching multiple sclerosis, you might start with *Health Reference Center*, *MEDLINE*, *PsycINFO,* or *PubMed.*)
2. Search the database using your list of keywords. (You could start with "multiple sclerosis" and then combine "MS" with other terms to narrow your search.)
3. Once you have chosen an article, print or e-mail to yourself the complete citation to the article. Look for the e-mail link after you click on the item you want.
4. Print or e-mail to yourself the full text if it is available. The full text is better than cutting and pasting because you might lose track of which words are yours, leading to unintended plagiarism.
5. If the full text is not available, check the online library catalog to see if your library has the journal.

Your library will probably have printed handouts or information online that tells you which database to use for a particular subject. Ask a librarian who works at the reference or information desk to help you.

If you wish to get only full-text articles, you can check that option. Full-text documents give you the same text you would find in print. Sometimes the images are not reproduced in the HTML versions, but the PDF versions show the actual printed copy.

Results of articles in the PDF format are scans of the printed text with page numbers. Get the PDF version if it is available. Articles in HTML format usually do not contain the page numbers.

Writer at Work

Gabriella did a full-text search for "sustainable farm" on *Academic Search Complete*.

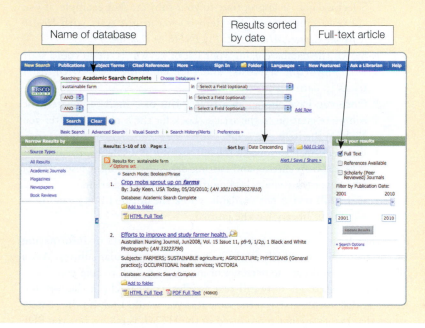

Name of database

Results sorted by date

Full-text article

Common Databases

Academic OneFile	Indexes periodicals from the arts, humanities, sciences, social sciences, and general news, with full-text articles and images. (Formerly *Expanded Academic ASAP*)
Academic Search Premier and Complete	Provides full-text articles for thousands of scholarly publications, including social sciences, humanities, education, computer sciences, engineering, language and linguistics, literature, medical sciences, and ethnic-studies journals.
ArticleFirst	Indexes journals in business, the humanities, medicine, science, and social sciences.
Business Search Premier	Provides full-text articles in all business disciplines.

EBSCOhost Research Databases	Is a gateway to a large collection of EBSCO databases, including *Academic Search Premier* and *Complete, Business Source Premier* and *Complete, ERIC,* and *Medline.*
Factiva	Provides full-text articles on business topics, including articles from the *Wall Street Journal.*
Google Books	Allows you to search within books and gives you snippets surrounding search terms for copyrighted books. Many books out of copyright have the full text. Available for everyone.
Google Scholar	Searches scholarly literature according to criteria of relevance. Available for everyone.
General OneFile	Contains millions of full-text articles about a wide range of academic and general-interest topics.
JSTOR	Provides scanned copies of scholarly journals.
LexisNexis Academic	Provides full text of a wide range of newspapers, magazines, government and legal documents, and company profiles from around the world.
ProQuest Databases	Like *EBSCOhost, ProQuest* is a gateway to a large collection of databases with over 100 billion pages, including the best archives of doctoral dissertations and historical newspapers.

WRITING SMART

Why Database Searches Are Often Better Than the First Ten Hits on *Google*

If you did a *Google* search for *oil spill* in summer 2010, the first link you would see on the list would be a site that issued BP press releases giving their spin on the oil spill. BP paid *Google* a large sum to have their site show up first. Similarly, a search for *oil spill lawsuits* would produce three law firms looking for business at the top of the list for the same reason—the law firms paid to be first.

There's nothing wrong with *Google* making money through advertising, but the first hits on *Google* searches are often of limited value for research. Library databases are supported by subscriptions from libraries, not through advertising, and you don't have to wade through the commercial clutter.

18c Find Sources on the Web

Because anyone can publish online, there is no overall quality control and there is no system of organization—two strengths we take for granted in libraries. Nevertheless, the Web offers you some resources for current topics that would be difficult or impossible to find in a library. The key to success is knowing where you are most likely to find current and accurate information about the particular question you are researching, and knowing how to access that information.

Use search engines wisely

Search engines designed for the Web work in ways similar to library databases and your library's online catalog but with one major difference. Databases typically do some screening of the items they list, but search engines potentially take you to everything on the Web—millions of pages in all. Consequently, you have to work harder to limit searches on the Web, or you can be deluged with tens of thousands of items.

Kinds of search engines

A search engine is a set of programs that sort through millions of items at incredible speed. There are four basic kinds of search engines.

1. **Keyword search engines** (e.g., *Bing, Google, Yahoo!*). Keyword search engines give different results because they assign different weights to the information they find.
2. **Meta-search engines** (e.g., *Dogpile, MetaCrawler, Surfwax*). Meta-search engines allow you to use several search engines simultaneously. While the concept is sound, meta-search engines are limited because many do not access *Google* or *Yahoo!*
3. **Web directories** (e.g., *Britannica.com*). Web directories classify Web sites into categories and are the closest equivalent to the cataloging system used by libraries. On most directories professional editors decide how to index a particular Web site. Web directories also allow keyword searches.
4. **Specialized search engines** are designed for specific purposes:
   - Regional search engines (e.g., *Baidu* for China)
   - Medical search engines (e.g., *iMediSearch*)
   - Legal search engines (e.g., *Lexis*)
   - Job search engines (e.g., *Indeed*)
   - Property search engines (e.g., *Zillow*)
   - Comparison-shopping search engines (e.g., *Froogle*)

Advanced searches

Search engines often produce too many hits and are therefore not always useful. If you look only at the first few items, you may miss what is most valuable. The alternative is to refine your search. Most search engines offer you the option of an advanced search, which gives you the opportunity to limit numbers.

Google searches can be focused by using the "Search tools" option. You can specify the time range from the past hour to the past year to a custom date range. You can also specify that *Google* finds the exact phrase you type in with the Verbatim option under "All results." Another useful way of limiting searches is to specify the domain, e.g., **site:.gov.**

■ The "Search tools" option on *Google* allows you to specify a date range.

Source: © Google, Inc. All rights reserved.

The **OR** operator is useful if you don't know exactly which term will get the results you want, especially if you are searching within a specific site. For example, you could try this search: "face-to-face OR f2f site: webworkerdaily.com."

You can also exclude terms with the − operator. If you want to search for social network privacy, but not *Facebook*, try "social network privacy − Facebook."

WRITING SMART

Keep track of online research

One of the easiest ways to return to Web sites you find useful for your research is to use the **Add to Favorites** or **Add Bookmark** command on your browser. You can arrange the sites you mark in folders and even download them onto a keychain drive or other storage device so you can retrieve the Web sites on other computers.

You can also use the **History** menu on your browser to obtain a list of sites you have visited. Most allow you to go back a few days, so if you remember a site you visited but didn't add to your favorites list, you can probably find it again.

Find online government sources

The federal government has made many of its publications available on the Web. Also, many state governments now publish important documents on the Web. Often the most current and most reliable statistics are government statistics. Among the more important government resources are the following.

- **Bureau of Labor Statistics** (www.bls.gov/). Source for official U.S. government statistics on employment, wages, and consumer prices
- **Census Bureau** (www.census.gov/). Contains a wealth of links to sites for population, social, economic, and political statistics, including the *Statistical Abstract of the United States* (www.census. gov/compendia/statab/)
- **Centers for Disease Control** (www.cdc.gov/). Authoritative and trustworthy source for health statistics
- **CIA World Factbook** (www.cia.gov/library/publications/the-world-factbook/). Resource for geographic, economic, demographic, and political information on the nations of the world
- **Library of Congress** (www.loc.gov/). Resources from the largest library in the world.
- **National Institutes of Health** (www.nih.gov/). Extensive health information, including *MedlinePlus* searches

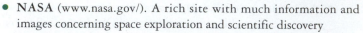

- **NASA** (www.nasa.gov/). A rich site with much information and images concerning space exploration and scientific discovery
- **Thomas** (thomas.loc.gov/). The major source of legislative information, including bills, committee reports, and voting records of individual members of Congress
- **USA.gov** (www.usa.gov/). The place to start when you are not sure where to look for government information

Find online reference sources

Your library's Web site has a link to **reference sites**, either on the main page or under another heading like **research tools.**

Reference sites are usually organized by subject, and you can find resources under the subject heading.

- **Business information** (links to business databases and sites like *Hoover's* that profile companies)
- **Dictionaries** (including the *Oxford English Dictionary* and various subject dictionaries and language dictionaries)
- **Education** (including *The College Blue Book* and others)
- **Encyclopedias** (including *Britannica Online* and others)
- **Government information** (links to federal, state, and local Web sites)
- **Reference books** (commonly used books like atlases, almanacs, biographies, handbooks, and histories)
- **Statistics and demographics** (links to federal, state, and local government sites; *FedStats* [www.fedstats.gov/] is a good place to start)

Find and explore archives

An archive is traditionally a physical place where historical documents, such as manuscripts and letters, are stored. Recently the term has come to mean any collection of documents, typically preserved for educational purposes, and many are now available online.

For example, if you want to do a research project on how people living at the time of the American Civil War understood the war, you will need to look at documents written at the time—letters, diaries, newspapers, speeches, and sermons. *The Valley of the Shadow* project has made available on the Web thousands of documents written at the time of the Civil War from Augusta County, Virginia, and Franklin County, Pennsylvania (valley. vcdh.virginia.edu/).

Other extensive archive sites include the following.

- **American Memory** (memory.loc.gov/ammem/). Library of Congress site offering over 11 million digital items from more than a hundred historical collections.

- **A Chronology of U.S. Historical Documents** (www.law.ou.edu/hist/). Sponsored by the University of Oklahoma College of Law, this site contains chronologically ordered primary sources ranging from the Federalist Papers to recent presidential addresses.
- **JSTOR: The Scholarly Journal Archive** (www.jstor.org). Electronic archive of the back issues of over a hundred scholarly journals, mainly in the humanities and social sciences.
- **University of Michigan Documents Center** (www.lib.umich.edu/government-documents-center/). Huge repository of local, state, federal, foreign, and international government information; includes an extensive subject directory.

Search interactive media

The Internet allows you to access other people's opinions on thousands of topics. Millions of people post messages on discussion lists and groups, *Facebook* groups, blogs, RSS feeds, *Twitter*, and so on. Much of what you read on interactive media sites is undocumented and highly opinionated, but you can still gather important information about people's attitudes and get tips about other sources, which you can verify later.

Several search engines have been developed for interactive media. *Facebook* and *Twitter* also have search engines for their sites.

Discussion list search engines

- **Big Boards.** Tracks over 2,000 of the most active discussion forums

---

WRITING SMART

Know the limitations of *Wikipedia*

Wikipedia is a valuable resource for current information and for popular culture topics that are not covered in traditional encyclopedias. You can find out, for example, that SpongeBob SquarePants's original name was "SpongeBoy," but it had already been copyrighted.

Nevertheless, many instructors and the scholarly community in general do not consider *Wikipedia* a reliable source of information for a research project. The fundamental problem with *Wikipedia* is stability, not whether the information is correct or incorrect. *Wikipedia* and other wikis constantly change. The underlying idea of documenting sources is that readers can consult the same sources that you consulted. To be on the safe side, treat *Wikipedia* as you would a blog. Consult other sources to confirm what you find on *Wikipedia* and cite those sources.

- **Google Groups.** Archives discussion forums dating back to 1981
- **Yahoo Groups.** A directory of groups by subject

Blog search engines

- **Google Blog Search.** Searches blogs in several languages besides English
- **IceRocket.** Searches blogs, *MySpace*, and *Twitter*
- **Technorati.** Searches blogs and other user-generated content

18d Find Multimedia Sources

A variety of multimedia resources—from podcasts and audio files to streaming video—are now available online. For example, the Hubble Space Telescope discovered a planet being devoured by a star in 2010. A search for "hubble star eats planet" turns up the image below on NASA's Web site.

■ The Hubble Space Telescope finds a star eating a planet (www.nasa.gov/mission_pages/hubble/science/planet-eater.html).

Find images

The major search engines for images include the following:

- Bing Images
- Google Image Search
- Picsearch
- Yahoo! Image Search

Libraries and museums also offer large collections. For example, the *American Memory* collection in the Library of Congress offers an important visual record of the history of the United States. Sites like *Instagram* and *Flickr* may also have some excellent offerings.

Find videos

- Bing Videos
- blinkx
- Google Videos
- Vimeo
- YouTube

Find podcasts

- iTunes Podcast Resources
- PodcastDirectory.com

Find charts, graphs, and maps

You can find statistical data represented in charts and graphs on many government Web sites.

- Statistical Abstract of the United States
- Google Earth
- Perry Casteñada Map Collection, University of Texas

Respect copyright

Just because images, videos, and other multimedia files are easy to download does not mean that everything is available for you to use. Look for the creator's copyright notice and suggested credit line. This notice will tell you if you can reproduce the multimedia file.

For example, the Cascades Volcano Observatory makes its images available to all: "The maps, graphics, images, and text found on our website, unless stated otherwise, are within the Public Domain. You may download and use them. Credit back to the USGS/Cascades Volcano Observatory is appreciated." Most images on government Web sites can be reproduced, but check the copyright restrictions. You should acknowledge the source of any image you use.

In many cases you will find a copyright notice that reads, "Any use or retransmission of text or images in this website without written consent of the copyright owner constitutes copyright infringement and is prohibited." You must write to the creator to ask permission to use an image from a site that is not in the public domain, even if you cannot find a copyright notice.

18e Find Print Sources

Print sources may seem "old fashioned" if you grew up with the Internet. You might even feel a little bit intimidated by them. But they are the starting point for much of the research done by experts. In college and beyond, they are indispensable. No matter how current the topic you are researching, you will likely find information in print sources that is simply not available online.

Print sources have other advantages as well:

- Books are shelved according to subject, allowing easy browsing.
- Books often have bibliographies, directing you to other research on the subject.
- You can search for books in multiple ways: author, title, subject, or call letter.
- The majority of print sources have been evaluated by scholars, editors, and publishers, who decided whether they merited publication.

Find books

Nearly all libraries now shelve books according to the Library of Congress Classification System, which uses a combination of letters and numbers to give you the book's unique location in the library. The Library of Congress call number begins with a letter or letters that represent the broad subject area into which the book is classified.

Writer at Work

Gabriella found this book by doing a subject search for "farming" **AND** "sustainability."

> Author, title, and publication information

Brief Record

Author	Pollan, Michael
Title	The omnivore's dilemma: a natural history of four meals
Published	New York: Penguin, 2006.
Description	450 p.; 25 cm.
Subjects	Agriculture
	Farming
	Food Habits
	Food Preferences
	Nutrition
	Sustainability
ISBN	1594200823
OCLC Number	62290639
Call Number and Location	GT 2850 C6 P65 2006 Main Library Stacks

> Subject terms can help you find other books on the same topic

> The call number can help you find a print book in the stacks; it can also help you locate or order a source from another library.

Locating books in your library

The floors of your library where books are shelved are referred to as the stacks. The call number will enable you to find the item in the stacks. You will need to consult the locations guide for your library, which gives the level and section where an item is shelved.

■ The signs in the stacks guide you to the books you are looking for.

Locating e-books

Use your library's online catalog to find e-books the same way you find printed books. You'll see on the record "e-book" or "electronic resource." Click on the link and you can read the book and often download a few pages or even the entire book.

| SUBJECT | organic farm | ALL Locations | System Sorted | Sort |

Search
☐ *Limit to available items*
Limited to: MATERIAL type "EBOOKS"

Save All to Clipboard   Save to My Lists

SUBJECTS (1-19 of 19)

1   **Agrarian Dreams : The Paradox of Organic Farming in California. [electronic resource]**
Electronic   2004
Material   Guthman, Julie.
Berkeley : University of California Press, 2004.
Electronic Resource

Save to Clipboard

■ Books are increasingly becoming available in electronic form through your library's online catalog.

Locating book reviews

Book Review Digest is available in the print version in your library's reference room, or else your library's Web site has a link to the online version, *Book Review Digest Plus*. Library databases also contain reviews.

- **Academic OneFile** (Search for the title or author and add the word *review* [for example, *The Omnivore's Dilemma* and review].)
- **Academic Search Complete** (Enter the title of the book and limit the *Document Type* to "Book Review.")

Find journal articles

Like books, scholarly journals provide in-depth examinations of subjects. The articles in scholarly journals are written by experts, and they usually contain lists of references that can guide you to other research on a subject.

Popular magazines are useful for gaining general information. Articles in popular magazines are usually short with few, if any, source references and are typically written by journalists. Some instructors frown on using popular magazines, but these journals can be valuable for researching current opinion on a particular topic. (See 19b for more on scholarly journals and popular magazines.)

Many scholarly journals and popular magazines are available on your library's Web site. Find them the same way you look for books, using your library's online catalog. Databases increasingly contain the full text of articles, allowing you to read and copy the contents onto your computer. If the article you are looking for isn't available online, the paper copy will be shelved with the books in your library.

18f Keep Track of Sources

As you begin to collect your sources, make sure you get full bibliographic information for everything you might want to use in your project. Decide which documentation style you will use. (The major documentation styles—MLA, APA, CMS, and CSE—are dealt with in detail in Chapters 23–26.)

Locate elements of a citation in database sources

For any sources you find on databases, MLA style requires you to provide the full print information, the name of the database in italics, and the URL or DOI (digital object identifier) of the article. Note that when you give citation information for a periodical, you do not need to list the publisher.

Author's name	Ingraham, Christopher
Title of article (your source)	"U.S. Data Shows a Surge in Drinking Related Deaths"
Title of periodical (container)	*The Washington Post*
Publication Date	23 Dec. 2015
Page number (location)	A3
Name of database (second container)	*LexisNexis Academic*
DOI or, as in this example, URL (location)	www.lexisnexis.com.ezproxy.lib.utexas.edu/lnacui2api/api/version1/getDocCui?oc=00240&.

The citation would appear as follows in an MLA-style works-cited list (see 23g).

> Ingraham, Christopher. "U.S. Data Shows a Surge in Drinking Related Deaths." *The Washington Post*, 25 Dec. 2015, p. A3. *LexisNexis Academic*, www.lexisnexis.com.ezproxy.lib.utexas.edu/lnacui2api/api/version1/getDocCui?oc=00240&.

APA style no longer requires listing the names of common databases or listing the date of access, unless the content is likely to change (see Section 24g). If you name the database, do not list the URL.

> Ingraham, C. (2015, December 23). U.S. data shows a surge in drinking related deaths. *The Washington Post*, p. A3.

Locate elements of a citation in online sources

As you conduct your online research, make sure you collect the necessary bibliographic information for everything you might want to use as a source. Because of the potential volatility of online sources (they can and do disappear overnight), their citations require extra information. Depending on the citation format you use, you'll arrange this information in different ways.

Collect the following information about a Web site.

Author's name, if available (if not, use the associated institution or organization)	Samadzadeh, Nozlee
Title of article	"Farm Update: The Third Annual Jack Hitt Annual Last Day of Classes Pig Roast"
Name of site or online journal	*Yale Sustainable Food Project Student Blog*
Publisher or sponsor of the site (for MLA style, but only if the sponsor is notably different from the site's name and/or creator.)	(The sponsor for this site, Yale Sustainable Food Project, is similar to the site's name, so it should not be included.)
Date of publication (for an article) or of site's last update	3 May 2010
URL (location)	yalesustainablefoodproject.wordpress.com/2010/05/03/farm-update-the-third-annual-jack-hitt-annual-last-day-of-classes-pig-roast/

An MLA works-cited entry for this article would look like this:

Samadzadeh, Nozlee. "Farm Update: The Third Annual Jack Hitt Annual Last Day of Classes Pig Roast." *Yale Sustainable Food Project Student Blog*, 3 May 2010, yalesustainablefoodproject.wordpress.com/2010/05/03/farm-update-the-third-annual-jack-hitt-annual-last-day-of-classes-pig-roast/.

In an APA references list, the citation would look like this:

Samadzadeh, N. (2010, May 3). Farm update: The third annual Jack Hitt Annual Last Day of Classes Pig Roast. Retrieved from http://yalesustainablefoodproject.wordpress.com/2010/05/03/farm-update-the-third-annual-jack-hitt-annual-last-day-of-classes-pig-roast/

You can find more examples of how to cite online sources in MLA style (23g) and APA style (24g).

Locate elements of a citation in print sources

For books you will need, at minimum, the following information, which can typically be found on the front and back of the title page.

Author's name	Ojito, Mirta
Title of the book (source)	*Finding Mañana: A Memoir of a Cuban Exile*
Name of publisher	Penguin
Date of publication	2005

Here's how the book would be cited in an MLA-style works-cited list.

> Ojito, Mirta. *Finding Mañana: A Memoir of a Cuban Exile*. Penguin
> Books, 2005.

Here's the APA citation for the same book. Note that APA requires the place of publication, while MLA does not.

> Ojito, M. (2005). *Finding mañana: A memoir of a Cuban exile*. New
> York, NY: Penguin.

You will also need the page numbers if you are quoting directly or referring to a specific passage, and the title and author of the individual chapter if your source is an edited book with contributions by several people.

For journals you will need the following.

Author's name	Romano, Susan
Title of article	"'Grand Convergence' in the Mexican Colonial Mundane: The Matter of Introductories"
Publication information	
Name of journal	*Rhetoric Society Quarterly*
Volume number and issue number	MLA: vol. 40, no. 1
	APA: *40*(1)
Date of publication	2010
Page numbers of the article	pp. 71–93
Digital object identifier (DOI) if available, or a stable URL if there is no DOI.	10.1080/02773940903413407

An entry in an MLA-style works-cited list would look like this.

> Romano, Susan. "'Grand Convergence' in the Mexican Colonial Mundane: The Matter of Introductories." *Rhetoric Society Quarterly*, vol. 40, no. 1, 2010, pp. 71–93. doi:10.1080/02773940903413407.

And in APA style, the same entry would look like this.

> Romano, S. (2010). "Grand convergence" in the Mexican colonial mundane: The matter of introductories. *Rhetoric Society Quarterly*, *40*, 71–93. doi:10.1080/02773940903413407

19 | Evaluate Sources

QUICK*TAKE*

After reading this chapter, you should be able to . . .
- Evaluate the relevance of sources (19a)
- Evaluate the quality of sources (19b)
- Evaluate database and print sources (19c)
- Evaluate Web sources (19d)

19a Determine the Relevance of Sources

Whether you use print or online sources, a successful search will turn up many more items than you can expect to use in your final product. You have to make a series of decisions as you evaluate your material. Use your research question and working thesis to create guidelines for yourself about importance and relevance.

For example, if your research question asks why the Roman Empire declined rapidly at the end of the fourth and beginning of the fifth centuries CE, you may find older sources to be as valuable as new ones. Edward Gibbon's three-volume history, *The Decline and Fall of the Roman Empire*, remains an important source even though it was published in 1776 and 1781.

But if you ask a research question about contemporary events—for example, why Chinese businesses are thriving in African nations at a time when the Western presence is dwindling—you will need to find current information. Statistics such as the growth of Chinese trade with Africa to

$160 billion in 2011 or the fact that over a million Chinese live and work in Africa describe the trend, but statistics alone do not explain why. An article on the new popularity of Chinese food in some African cities might be interesting, but it is not relevant. Relevant articles will discuss China's willingness to invest in factories and businesses in Africa while Western investment in the continent has decreased.

Use these guidelines to determine the importance and relevance of your sources to your research question.

- Does your research question require you to consult primary or secondary sources?
- Does a source you have found address your question?
- Does a source support or disagree with your working thesis? (You should not throw out work that challenges your views. Representing opposing views accurately enhances your credibility.)
- Does a source add significant information?
- Is the source current? (For most topics try to find the most up-to-date information.)
- What indications of possible bias do you note in the source?

19b Determine the Quality of Sources

In the Internet era, we don't lack for information, but we do lack filters for finding quality information. Two criteria will help you to make a beginning assessment of quality: individual vs. edited sources and popular vs. scholarly sources.

Distinguish individual and anonymous sources from edited sources

Anyone with access to the Internet can put up a Web site. Furthermore, a person can put up sites anonymously or under an assumed name. It's no wonder that there are so many sites that contain misinformation or are intentionally deceptive.

In general, sources that have been edited and published in scholarly journals, scholarly books, major newspapers, major online and print magazines, and government Web sites are considered of higher quality than what an individual might put on a personal Web site, a *Facebook* page, a user review, or a blog. Nevertheless, people tend to believe reports from individuals. Corporations are well aware that blogs and user reviews on sites like Amazon are now more trusted than newspaper and magazine articles, and they regularly send bloggers information about new products and pay them for favorable mentions. Some corporations have gone even further, hiring public relations firms to write favorable reviews and favorable blogs.

Edited sources can have biases, and indeed some are quite open about their perspectives. *National Review* offers a conservative perspective, *The Wall Street Journal* is pro-business, and *The Nation* is a liberal voice. The difference from individual and anonymous sites is that we know the editorial perspectives of these journals, and we expect the editors to check the facts. On self-published sites and in self-published books, anything goes.

Distinguish popular sources from scholarly sources

Scholarly books and **scholarly journals** are published by and for experts. Scholarly books and articles published in scholarly journals undergo a **peer review** process in which a group of experts in a field reviews them for their scholarly soundness and academic value. Scholarly books and articles in scholarly journals include

- the author's name and academic credentials and
- a list of works cited.

Newspapers, popular books, and **popular magazines** vary widely in quality. Newspapers and popular magazines range from highly respected publications such as *The Los Angeles Times*, *Scientific American*, and *The Atlantic Monthly* to the sensational tabloids at grocery-store checkouts. Popular sources are not peer reviewed and require more work on your part to determine their quality.

POPULAR VS. SCHOLARLY SOURCES			
	Popular books and magazines	**Newspapers**	**Scholarly books and journals**
Author	staff writers, journalists	journalists	scholars, researchers
Audience	general public	general public	scholars, college students
Reviewed by	professional editor	professional editor	other scholars and researchers
Purpose	entertain, express an opinion	entertain, express an opinion, inform	share information with the scholarly community
Documentation	usually none	usually none	extensive, with lists of works cited or footnotes
Advertisements	frequent in magazines	frequent	a few ads for scholarly products
Evidence of bias	usually some bias	usually some bias	little bias

	Popular books and magazines	Newspapers	Scholarly books and journals
Examples	[book] Elizabeth Gilbert, *The Signature of All Things*; Colson Whitehead, *The Underground Railroad* [magazines] *Cosmopolitan, GQ, Rolling Stone, Sports Illustrated, Time*	*The New York Times, Toronto Globe and Mail, The Independent* (London), *The Washington Post*	[book] Robert Putnam, *Bowling Alone: The Collapse and Revival of American Community*; [journals] *College English, JAMA: Journal of the American Medical Association*

Distinguish primary sources from secondary sources

Another key distinction for researchers is primary versus secondary sources. In the humanities and fine arts, **primary sources** are original, creative works and original accounts of events written close to the time they occurred. **Secondary sources** interpret creative works and primary sources of events.

In the sciences, **primary sources** are the factual results of experiments, observations, clinical trials, and other factual data. **Secondary sources** analyze and interpret those results.

PRIMARY VS. SECONDARY SOURCES		
Examples	Humanities and fine arts	Sciences
Primary sources	• Novels, short stories, poems, plays, music • Paintings, sculpture, photographs, maps • Speeches • Diaries, letters, journals • Interviews with witnesses and participants • Government records	• Published results • Collections of data • Collections of observations
Secondary sources	• Histories • Biographies • Literary criticism • Reviews	• Publications interpreting the results of experiments and clinical trials • Reviews of several studies or experiments

Read sources critically

Evaluating sources requires you to read critically, which includes the following.

- Identifying the source, which is not always easy online
- Identifying the author and assessing the author's credentials
- Understanding the content—what the text says
- Recognizing the author's purpose—whether the author is attempting to reflect, inform, or persuade
- Recognizing how the purpose influences the choices of words, examples, and structure
- Recognizing biases in the choices of words, examples, and structure
- Recognizing what the author does not include or address
- Developing an overall evaluation that takes into account all of the above

(For more on critical reading, see Chapters 5–6.)

Evaluate the quality of visual sources

Evaluating the quality of visual sources involves skills similar to critical reading. Similar to critical reading, you should

- identify and assess the source,
- identify the creator,
- identify the date of creation,
- describe the content,
- assess the purpose, and
- recognize how the purpose influences the composition of the image, graphic, or video.

For graphics including charts and graphs, pay attention to the source of any data presented and that the data are presented fairly. (For more on the evaluation of visual sources, see 6a and 6b.)

19c Evaluate Database and Print Sources

Books are expensive to print and distribute, so book publishers generally protect their investment by providing some level of editorial oversight. Printed and online materials in your library undergo another review by professional librarians who select them to include in their collections. Library database collections, which your library pays to access, also are screened, which eliminates many poor-quality sources.

This initial screening doesn't free you, however, from the responsibility of evaluating the quality of the sources. Many printed and database sources contain their share of inaccurate, misleading, and biased information. Also, all sources carry the risk of becoming outdated if you are looking for current information.

WRITING SMART

Checklist for evaluating database and print sources

Over the years librarians have developed a set of criteria for evaluating sources, and you should apply them in your research.

1. **Source.** Who published the book or article? Enter the publisher's name on *Google* or another search engine to learn about the publisher. Scholarly books and articles in scholarly journals are generally more reliable than popular magazines and books, which tend to emphasize what is sensational or entertaining at the expense of accuracy and comprehensiveness.

2. **Author.** Who wrote the book or article? What are the author's qualifications? Enter the author's name on *Google* or another search engine to learn more about him or her. Does the author represent an organization?

3. **Timeliness.** How current is the source? If you are researching a fast-developing subject such as treating ADHD, then currency is very important, but even historical topics are subject to controversy or revision.

4. **Evidence.** Where does the evidence come from—facts, interviews, observations, surveys, or experiments? Is the evidence adequate to support the author's claims?

5. **Biases.** Can you detect particular biases of the author? How do the author's biases affect the interpretation offered?

6. **Advertising.** For print sources, is advertising a prominent part of the journal or newspaper? How might the ads affect the credibility or the biases of the information that gets printed?

19d Evaluate Web Sources

Researching online has been compared to drinking from a fire hose. The key to success is not only getting the torrent down to the size of a glass but also making sure the water in the glass is pure enough to drink.

Pay attention to domain names

Domain names can give you clues about the quality of a Web site.

- **.com** *Commercial site.* The information on a .com site may be about a product or company, but anyone can register to use and purchase a .com domain. The purpose of a commercial site is to sell a product or service.
- **.edu** *Educational institution.* The suffix tells you the site is on a school server, ranging from kindergarten to higher education. If the information is from a department or research center, it is generally credible, but if the site belongs to an individual (student, staff, or faculty member), treat it as you would other kinds of self-published information.
- **.gov** *Government.* If you see this suffix, you're viewing a federal government site. Most government sites are considered credible sources. However, keep in mind that materials from political candidates, agencies, and administrations may also be biased.
- **.org** *Nonprofit organization.* Initially, nonpartisan organizations like the Red Cross used this domain, but increasingly partisan political groups and commercial interests have taken the .org suffix. Treat this domain with scrutiny.
- **.mil** *Military.* This domain suffix is owned by the various branches of the armed forces.
- **.net** *Network.* As with .com, anyone can purchase and use a .net address to create a site.

Be alert for biased Web sites

Nearly every large company and political and advocacy organization has a Web site. We expect these sites to represent the company or the point of view of the organization. Many sites on the Web, however, are not so clearly labeled.

For example, if you do a search for "Sudden Infant Death Syndrome (SIDS)" and "vaccines," you'll find near the top of the list an article titled "Vaccines and Sudden Infant Death Syndrome (SIDS): A Link?" The article concludes that vaccines cause SIDS. If you look at the home page, you'll find that the site's sponsor, Global Vaccine Institute, opposes all vaccinations of children.

Always look for other objective sources for verification of your information. The U.S. Centers for Disease Control and Prevention publishes fact

sheets with the latest information about diseases and their prevention. The fact sheet on SIDS and vaccines reports that people associate sudden infant death syndrome with vaccinations because babies begin vaccinations between two and four months, the same age babies die of SIDS. There is no scientific evidence that vaccines cause SIDS.

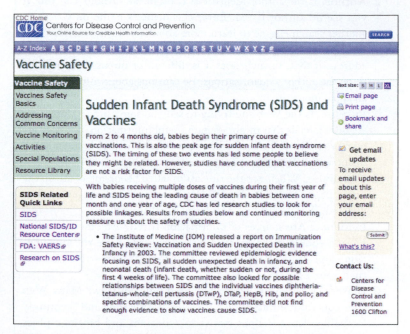

■ FAQ on vaccines and SIDS from the Centers for Disease Control (www.cdc.gov/vaccinesafety/Concerns/sids_faq.html)

WRITING SMART

Checklist for evaluating online sources

Online sources present special challenges for evaluation. When you find a Web page by using a search engine, you will often go deep into a complex site without having any sense of the context for that page. To evaluate the credibility of the site, you would need to examine the home page, not just the specific page you get to first.

Use these criteria for evaluating online sources.

1. **Source.** What organization sponsors the site? Look for the site's owner at the top or bottom of the home page or in the URL. Enter

(Continued on next page)

WRITING SMART *(Continued)*

the owner's name on *Google* or another search engine to learn about the organization. If a Web site doesn't indicate ownership, then you have to make judgments about who put it up and why.

2. **Author.** Is the author identified? Look for an "About Us" link if you see no author listed. Enter the author's name on *Google* or another search engine to learn more about the author. Often Web sites give no information about their authors other than an e-mail address, if that. In such cases it is difficult or impossible to determine the author's qualifications. Be cautious about information on an anonymous site.

3. **Purpose.** Is the Web site trying to sell you something? Many sites are infomercials that might contain useful information, but they are no more trustworthy than other forms of advertising. Is the purpose to entertain? To inform? To persuade?

4. **Timeliness.** When was the site last updated? Look for a date on the home page. Many Web pages do not list when they were last updated; thus you cannot determine their currency.

5. **Evidence.** Are sources of information listed? Any factual information should be supported by indicating where the information came from. Reliable sites that offer information will list their sources.

6. **Biases.** Does the site offer a balanced point of view? Many Web sites conceal their attitude with a reasonable tone and seemingly factual evidence such as statistics. Citations and bibliographies do not ensure that a site is reliable. Look carefully at the links and sources cited, and peruse the "About Us" link if one is available.

Writer at Work

Gabriella Lopez's topic, college gardens, focuses on a quite recent development and has been treated in few scholarly books and scholarly articles. She had to expand her searches to include popular books, newspapers, and online sources. One of the books she found was Mel Bartholomew's *All New Square-Foot Gardening*. Here is her evaluation.

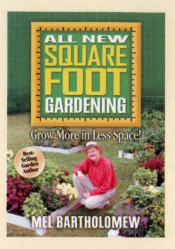

Source:	popular book; Cool Springs Press, according to its Web site, is the largest publisher of gardening books
Author:	Mel Bartholomew has published on this topic for 30 years and has a Web site
Purpose:	persuade people to move to square-foot gardening and to inform how to do it
Timeliness:	published in 2006
Evidence:	almost all the author's experience
Biases:	author strongly committed to his method but isn't trying to sell anything
Conclusion:	book is repetitive but author is convincing about the subject; published reviews and user reviews on Amazon are strongly favorable

20 Plan Field Research

QUICK*TAKE*

After reading this chapter, you should be able to . . .
- Identify the goals of field research (20a)
- Complete informative interviews (20b)
- Construct and administer focused surveys (20c)
- Demonstrate detailed observations (20d)

20a Know What You Can Obtain from Field Research

Even though much of the research you do for college courses will be secondary research conducted at a computer or in the library, some topics do call for primary research, requiring you to gather information on your own. Field research of this kind can be especially important for exploring local issues. It is also used extensively in professions that you may be joining after college.

Be aware that the ethics of conducting field research require you to inform people about what you are doing and why you are gathering information. If you are uncertain about the ethics of doing field research, talk to your instructor.

Three types of field research that can usually be conducted in college are **interviews, surveys,** and **observations.**

- **Interviews.** College campuses are a rich source of experts in many areas, including those on the faculty and in the surrounding community. Interviewing experts on your research topic can help build your knowledge base. You can use interviews to discover what the people most affected by a particular issue are thinking and feeling.
- **Surveys.** Extensive surveys that can be projected to large populations, like the ones used in political polls, require the effort of many people. Short surveys, however, often can provide insight on local issues.
- **Observation.** Local observation can be a valuable source of data. For example, if you are researching why a particular office on your campus does not operate efficiently, observe what happens when students enter and how they are handled by the staff.

20b Conduct Interviews

Before you contact anyone to ask for an interview, think carefully about your goals; knowing what you want to find out through your interviews will help you determine whom you need to interview and what questions you need to ask.

- Decide what you want or need to know and who best can provide that for you.
- Schedule each interview in advance and let the person know why you are conducting the interview.
- Plan your questions in advance. Write down a few questions and have a few more in mind. Listen carefully so you can follow up on key points.
- Come prepared with a tablet, laptop, or paper notebook for taking notes and jotting down short quotations. Record the date, time, place, and subject of the interview. If you want to make an audio recording, ask for permission in advance.
- When you are finished, thank your subject and ask his or her permission to get in touch again if you have additional questions.
- When you are ready to incorporate the interview into a paper or project, think about what you want to highlight from the interview and which direct quotations to include.

20c Administer Surveys

Use surveys to find out what large groups of people think about a topic (or what they are willing to admit they think). Surveys need to be carefully designed. There are two important components: the survey instrument itself—which is the list of questions you will ask—and the place, time, and way in which the survey will be administered.

- Write a few specific questions. Make sure that they are unambiguous. People will fill out your survey quickly, and if the questions are confusing, the results will be meaningless. To make sure your questions are clear, test them on a few people before you conduct the survey.
- Include one or two open-ended questions, such as "What do you like about X?" "What don't you like about X?" Open-ended questions can be difficult to interpret, but sometimes they turn up information you had not anticipated.
- Decide whom you need to survey and how many people to include. If you want to claim that the results of your survey represent the

views of residents of your dormitory, your method of selecting respondents should give all residents an equal chance to be selected. Don't select only your friends.

- Decide how you will contact participants in your survey. If you are going to e-mail your survey, include a statement about what the survey is for and a deadline for returning it. You may need to get permission to conduct a survey on private property such as a mall.

- Think about how you will interpret your survey. Multiple-choice formats make data easy to tabulate, but often they miss key information. Open-ended questions will require you to figure out a way to analyze responses.

- When writing about the results, be sure to include information about who participated in the survey, how the participants were selected, and when and how the survey was administered.

20d Make Observations

Simply observing what goes on in a place can be an effective research tool. Your observations can inform a controversy or topic by providing a vivid picture of real-world activity.

- Choose a place where you can observe with the least intrusion. The less people wonder about what you are doing, the better.

- Carry a tablet, laptop, or paper notebook and write extensive field notes. Get down as much information as you can and worry about analyzing it later.

- Record the date, exactly where you were, exactly when you arrived and left, and important details like the number of people present.

At some point you have to interpret the data. When you analyze your observations, think about what constitutes normal and unusual activities for this place. What can you determine about the purposes of these activities?

PART

6 Incorporating and Documenting Sources

Research Map 2: Working with Sources (see the back of this divider)

RESEARCH MAP 2: WORKING WITH SOURCES

Using sources effectively requires that you

- decide when to include quotations from a source and when to paraphrase,
- integrate quotations, summaries, paraphrases, and visuals,
- avoid plagiarism in taking notes, summarizing, and paraphrasing,
- write and revise your research project, and
- document all sources using the format of a major documentation style.

Here are the steps in incorporating and documenting sources.

1 | Use sources effectively

Understand the purposes of sources; go to 21a.

Decide when to quote and when to paraphrase; go to 21b.

Take notes effectively; go to 21c.

Use quotations effectively; go to 21d.

Use summaries and paraphrases effectively; go to 21f.

2 | Avoid plagiarism

Understand exactly how plagiarism is defined; go to 21h.

Understand what you are required to acknowledge; go to 21h.

Parts 5 and 6 illustrate the process Gabriella Lopez used to produce her research project. Gabriella's final version of her project is in 23k.

See Research Map 1 (on the back of the divider for Part 5) for guidance on planning research and finding sources.

3 | Write and revise

ke stock of your research; go to 22a.

se sources to provide evidence and points of departure; go to 22b and c.

an your organization by creating a rking outline; go to 22d.

gin your draft by writing a specific e, an introduction, and a conclusion; to 22e.

view your project and revise, begin-ng with high-level issues of content d organization; go to 22f.

4 | Document sources

Decide which documentation style you will use:

- **MODERN LANGUAGE ASSOCIATION (MLA);** go to Chapter 23.

- **AMERICAN PSYCHOLOGICAL ASSOCIATION (APA);** go to Chapter 24.

- **CHICAGO MANUAL OF STYLE (CMS);** go to Chapter 25.

- **COUNCIL OF SCIENCE EDITORS (CSE);** go to Chapter 26.

21 Use Sources Effectively and Avoid Plagiarism

QUICK*TAKE*

After reading this chapter, you should be able to . . .

- Identify the purposes of sources (21a)
- Determine when to quote and when to paraphrase (21b)
- Create effective notes (21c)
- Use quotations effectively (21d)
- Use and integrate quotations correctly in your writing (21e)
- Use summaries and paraphrases effectively (21f)
- Identify what plagiarism is (21h)

21a Understand the Purposes of Sources

Documenting sources can seem like learning Latin—something obscure and complicated that has little use in daily life. You don't see footnotes or lists of works cited in magazines and newspapers, so you may wonder why they are so important in college writing. Careful documentation of sources, however, is essential to developing knowledge and allows scholars and researchers to build on the work of other scholars and researchers.

Sources build knowledge

Knowledge is built through ongoing conversations that take place in writing as well as talking. The practice of citing sources provides a disciplinary map, indicating the conversation in which the writer is participating. Often knowledge building does not move in a straight line but reflects wrong turns and backtracking. Tracing these movements would be extremely difficult if writers did not acknowledge their sources.

Sources must be accurate

Accurate referencing of sources allows you or any reader the opportunity to consult those sources. For example, historians who write about the distant past must rely on different kinds of evidence, including letters, records, public documents, newspaper articles, legal manuscripts, and other material from that time; they also take into account the work of contemporary scholars. Other historians working in the same area must be able to find and read these primary sources to assess the accuracy of the interpretation. Research using sources requires that summaries and paraphrases be

accurate, that words taken from the original be set off in quotation marks, and that full information be provided to locate the source.

Sources and fairness

Another basic issue is fairness. When historians draw on the interpretations of other historians, they should give those historians credit. In this respect citing sources builds community with writers of both the present and the past. When you begin to read the published research in an academic discipline, your awareness of that community takes shape. But the issue of fairness also is part of the much larger issues of intellectual property and scholastic honesty—issues that need to be considered carefully when you use sources.

21b Decide When to Quote and When to Summarize and Paraphrase

Use sources to support what you say; don't expect them to say it for you. Next to plagiarism, the worst mistake you can make with sources is to string together a series of long quotations. This strategy leaves your readers wondering whether you have anything to say. Relying too much on quotations from others also makes for a bumpy read. Think about how each source relates to your thesis.

When to quote and when to paraphrase

The general rule in deciding when to include direct quotations and when to paraphrase lies in the importance of the original wording.

- If you want to refer to an idea or fact and the original wording is not critical, make the point in your own words and cite the source.

  The residents of New York City, which is often imagined as an ecological nightmare, in fact use less gasoline than those of any other American city because 82 percent walk, bike, or take public transportation to their workplaces (Owen 2). [Here the facts are important, not the original wording.]

- Save direct quotations for language that is memorable or conveys the character of the source.

  Edward Glaesner argues that "if you love nature, stay away from it. The best means of protecting nature is to live in the heart of a city" (18). [Here the original language gives the core argument.]

21c Take Notes Effectively

The most important thing when you are taking notes is to take care to distinguish source words from your own words. Don't mix words from the source with your own words. Create a folder for your research project and clearly label the files.

- **Create a working bibliography and make separate files for content notes.** Create a file for each source. If you work on paper, use a separate page for each source. Also write down all the information you need for a list of works cited or a list of references in your working bibliography (see 18f).
- **If you copy anything from a source when taking notes, place those words in quotation marks and note the page number(s) where those words appear.** If you copy words from an online source, take special care to note the source. You could easily copy online material and later not be able to find where it came from.
- **Print out the entire source so you can refer to it later.** Having photocopies or complete printed files allows you to double-check later that you haven't used words from the source by mistake and that any words you quote are accurate.

21d Use Quotations Effectively

Effective research writing builds on the work of others. You can summarize or paraphrase the work of others, but often it is best to let authors speak in your text by quoting their exact words. Indicate the words of others by placing them inside quotation marks and giving a citation to the source.

Use quotation marks for direct quotations

Gabriella Lopez decided to include the highlighted words from the original below in her text.

Writer at Work

Original text

Questionnaires on food attitudes and behavior were completed by 2,200 American undergraduates from 6 regionally dispersed college campuses. Results indicate that a substantial minority of women and a much smaller minority of men have major concerns about eating and food with respect to both weight and health.

Source citation

Rozin, Paul, et al. "Food and Life, Pleasure and Worry, among American College Students: Gender Differences and Regional Similarities." *Journal of Personality and Social Psychology*, vol. 85, no. 1, 2003, p. 132. *PsycARTICLES*, doi:10.1037/0022-3514.85.1.132.

Above, see her works-cited entry for the source.

Below, see how Gabriella referenced this source in the body of her paper. She placed quotation marks around the words taken from the source. She also included an in-text citation with the lead author's name (so readers could identify the source in her list of works cited) and the page number where she found the words (so readers could find them in the original source). Notice that the in-text citation is after the closing quotation mark but before the period.

According to a survey of 2,200 American college students, a significant number of women and a smaller group of men "have major concerns about eating and food with respect to both weight and health" (Rozin et al. 132).

Attribute each quotation

The alternate way Gabriella could have acknowledged the source of the words is by mentioning the authors in her text. If the author or authors' names appear in the sentence, cite only the page number in parentheses.

Writer at Work

According to a survey of 2,200 American college students conducted by Paul Rozin, Rebecca Bauer, and Dana Catanese, a significant number of women and a smaller group of men "have major concerns about eating and food with respect to both weight and health" (132).

Writer at Work

For background for her proposal to create a campus garden, Gabriella Lopez wanted to cite two ideas from Michael Pollan's *In Defense of Food*—that food has meanings beyond nutrition and that the industrialization of food production has led to less variety in the American diet with negative consequences for health.

Pollan, Michael. In Defense of Food: An Eater's Manifesto. Penguin Books, 2008.

We forget that, historically, people have eaten for a great many reasons other than biological necessity. Food is also about pleasure, about community, about family and spirituality, about our relationship to the natural world, and about expressing our identity. As long as humans have been taking meals together, eating has been as much about culture as it has been about biology.

That eating should be foremost about bodily health is a relatively new and, I think, destructive idea—destructive not just of the pleasure of eating, which would be bad enough, but paradoxically of our health as well. Indeed, no people on earth worry more about the health consequences of their food choices than we Americans do—and no people suffer from as many diet-related health problems. We are becoming a nation of orthorexics: people with an unhealthy obsession with healthy eating.
. . .

All of our uncertainties about nutrition should not obscure the plain fact that the chronic diseases that now kill most of us can be traced directly to the industrialization of our food: the rise of highly processed foods and refined grains; the use of chemicals to raise plants and animals in huge monocultures; the superabundance of cheap calories of sugar and fat produced by modern agriculture; and the narrowing of the biological diversity of the human diet to a tiny handful of staple crops, notably wheat, corn, and soy. These changes have given us the Western diet that we take for granted: lots of processed foods and meat, lots of added fat and sugar, lots of *every*thing—except vegetables, fruits, and whole grains.

QUOTE SENTENCE
"Food is also about pleasure, about community, about family and spirituality, about our relationship to the natural world, and about expressing our identity" (8).

PARAPHRASE
This promotion of discrete nutrients over whole food has led to industrialization of food production— more processed foods, more artificial grains, more chemicals to raise animals and vegetables in vast "monocultures," more sugars and fats, and less variety in our diet that has been reduced to a glut of wheat, corn, and soy (Pollan 10).

Source: From *In Defence of Food: An Eater's Manifesto* by Michael Pollan, copyright © 2008 by Michael Pollan. Used by permission of Penguin Press, an imprint of Penguin Publishing Group, a division of Penguin Random House LLC.

21e Integrate Quotations

All sources should be well integrated into the fabric of your project. Introduce quotations by attributing them in your text.

> Even those who fought for the United States in the U.S.-Mexican War of 1846 were skeptical of American motives: "We were sent to provoke a fight, but it was essential that Mexico should commence it" (Grant 68).

The preceding quotation is used correctly, but it loses the impact of the source. Compare it with the following.

> Many soldiers who fought for the United States in the U.S.-Mexican War of 1846 were skeptical of American motives, including Civil War hero and future president Ulysses S. Grant, who wrote: "We were sent to provoke a fight, but it was essential that Mexico should commence it" (68).

Use signal phrases

Signal verbs often indicate your stance toward a quotation. Introducing a quotation with "X says" or "X believes" tells your readers nothing. Find a livelier verb that suggests how you are using the source. For example, if you write "X contends," your reader is alerted that you likely will disagree with the source. Be as precise as possible.

Signal phrases that report information or a claim

> X argues that . . .
> X asserts that . . .
> X claims that . . .
> X observes that . . .
> As X puts it, . . .
> X reports that . . .
> As X sums it up, . . .

Signal phrases when you agree with the source

> X affirms that . . .
> X has the insight that . . .
> X points out insightfully that . . .
> X theorizes that . . .
> X verifies that . . .

Signal phrases when you disagree with the source

X complains that . . .
X contends that . . .
X denies that . . .
X disputes that . . .
X overlooks that . . .
X rejects that . . .
X repudiates that . . .

Signal phrases in the sciences

Signal phrases in the sciences often use the past tense, especially for interpretations and commentary.

X described . . .
X found . . .
X has suggested . . .

Introduce block quotations

Long direct quotations, called **block quotations**, are indented from the margin instead of being placed in quotation marks. In MLA style, a quotation in prose longer than four lines, or in poetry, longer than three lines, should be indented one-half inch. A quotation of forty words or longer is also indented one-half inch in APA style. In both MLA and APA styles, long quotations are double-spaced, using the same spacing as in the rest of the paper. You still need to integrate a block quotation into the text of your project by mentioning who wrote or said it.

- No quotation marks appear around the block quotation.
- Words quoted in the original retain the double quotation marks.
- The page number appears after the period at the end of the block quotation.

It is a good idea to include at least one or two sentences following the quotation to describe its significance to your thesis.

Double-check quotations

Whether they are long or short, you should double-check all quotations you use to be sure they are accurate and that all words belonging to the original are set off with quotation marks or placed in a block quotation. If you wish to leave out words from a quotation, indicate the omitted words with ellipses (. . .) but make sure you do not alter the meaning of the original quote (see 44e). If you need to add words of your own to a quotation to make the meaning clear, place your words in square brackets (see 44d).

WRITING SMART

Use quotations effectively

Quotations are a frequent problem area in research projects. Review every quotation to ensure that each is used effectively and correctly.

- **Check that each quotation is supporting your major points rather than making major points for you.** If the ideas rather than the original wording are what's important, paraphrase the quotation and cite the source.

- **Check that each quotation is introduced and attributed.** Each quotation should be introduced and the author or title named. Check for verbs that signal a quotation: Smith *claims*, Jones *argues*, Brown *states*.

- **Check that each quotation is properly formatted and punctuated.** Prose quotations longer than four lines (MLA) or forty words (APA) should be indented one-half inch. Shorter quotations should be enclosed within quotation marks.

- **Limit the use of long quotations.** If you have more than one block quotation on a page, look closely to see if one or more can be paraphrased or summarized. Use direct quotations only if the original wording is important.

- **Check that you cite the source for each quotation.** You are required to cite the sources of all direct quotations, paraphrases, and summaries.

- **Check the accuracy of each quotation.** It's easy to leave out words or mistype a quotation. Compare what is in your project with the original source. If you need to add words to make the quotation grammatical, make sure the added words are in brackets. Use ellipses to indicate omitted words.

- **Read your project aloud to a classmate or a friend.** Each quotation should flow smoothly when you read your project aloud. Put a check beside rough spots as you read aloud so you can revise later.

21f Use Summaries and Paraphrases Effectively

In many cases you will want to include the ideas and facts from a source, but the exact words from the source are not especially important. You still need to cite the source, but you put the ideas and facts into your own words.

Summaries

A summary states the major ideas of an entire source or part of a source in a paragraph or perhaps even a sentence. The key is to put the summary in your own words. If you use words from the source, you have to put those words within quotation marks.

Gabriella Lopez wanted to establish that many college students are becoming more aware of the benefits of healthy and sustainable food. She wanted to document that a trend is occurring by citing sources. She summarized an article in *USA Today* in one sentence (see 23k).

Writer at Work

> According to a 2006 article in *USA Today*, students are increasingly interested in schools with "green" practices, which offer local, sustainable, and organic options in their food service (Horovitz).

Paraphrases

Paraphrases represent the ideas in a source in your own words at about the same length as the original. You still need to include an in-text citation to the source. If you take words from the source, put them within quotation marks.

Gabriella wanted to give specifics about square-foot gardening in her research project. She paraphrased the discussion from Mel Bartholomew's *All New Square Foot Gardening*. The facts about square-foot gardening were important for her, but not the wording from the source.

Writer at Work

> I propose that we establish a campus garden following the very simple principles of organic "square-foot" gardening. Square-foot gardening is raised-bed gardening that takes place in 6- to 12-inch-deep frames that have been segmented into a grid (see fig. 1). The size of each square in the grid depends on what plants are planted there; certain plants require larger and deeper grids (Bartholomew 15-16). The main benefit of square-foot gardening is that one can grow the same amount of produce in a 140-square-foot grid that is typically grown in the average 700-square-foot, single-row garden (42).

21g Use Visuals Effectively

Like quotations, visuals should not be dropped in without introductions.

- Place all visuals as close as possible to the related text.
- Introduce each visual in your text.
- In MLA style give each visual a figure number (abbreviated *Fig.*) and a caption.
- Give complete information about the source in the caption.
- If the source is not mentioned in the text, you do not need to include it in the list of works cited.

In April 1947 Jackie Robinson became the first African American to play baseball in the major leagues in the twentieth century, ending the segregation practice that restricted black players to the Negro leagues. Robinson's superior athletic ability quickly became evident, and he won the Most Valuable Player award in the National League in 1949. His success made him a popular culture icon at the time, with a hit song written about him, a Hollywood movie about his life in 1950 (sixty-three years before the film *42*), and even a comic book. (See Fig. 3.)

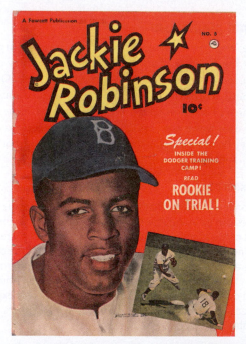

Fig. 3. Front cover of a Jackie Robinson comic book. "By Popular Demand: Jackie Robinson and Other Baseball Highlights, 1860s–1960s." *American Memory*, Library of Congress, 1951, lccn.loc.gov/97519504.

21h What Is Plagiarism?

Plagiarism means claiming credit for someone else's intellectual work no matter whether it's to make money or get a better grade. Intentional or not, plagiarism has dire consequences. Reputable authors have gotten into trouble through carelessness by copying passages from published sources without acknowledging those sources. A number of famous people have had their reputations tarnished by accusations of plagiarism, and several prominent journalists have lost their jobs and careers for copying the work of other writers and passing it off as their own.

Deliberate plagiarism

If you buy a paper on the Web, copy someone else's paper word for word, or take an article off the Web and turn it in as yours, it's plain stealing, and people who take that risk should know that the punishment can be severe—usually failure for the course and sometimes expulsion. Deliberate plagiarism is easy for your instructors to spot because they recognize shifts in style, and it is easy for them to use search engines to find the sources of work stolen from the Web.

Unintentional plagiarism

The use of the Web has increased instances of plagiarism in college. Some students view the Internet as a big free buffet where they can grab anything, paste it in a file, and submit it as their own work. Other students intend to submit work that is their own, but they commit plagiarism because they aren't careful in taking notes to distinguish the words of others from their own words (see 21c). Sometimes students do use their own words, but they commit plagiarism by presenting an author's ideas in the same order, without giving credit to the author.

Original source

The economic advantage that has already begun to accrue to the walkable places can be attributed to three key factors. First, for certain segments of the population, chief among them young "creatives," urban living is simply more appealing; many wouldn't be caught dead anywhere else. Second, massive demographic shifts occurring right now mean that these pro-urban segments of the population are becoming dominant, creating a spike in demand that is expected to last for decades. Third, the choice to live the walkable life generates considerable savings for these households. . . .

Source: Speck, Jeff. *Walkable City: How Downtown Can Save America One Step at a Time.* Farrar, Straus, and Giroux, 2012.

Patch plagiarism

The economic advantage gained by walkable places can be attributed to three key factors. First, for certain segments of the population, chief among them young "creatives," urban living is simply more appealing; many wouldn't be caught dead anywhere else. Second, young urban professionals are becoming dominant, creating a spike in demand that is expected to last for decades. Third, young professionals have figured out that they can save money by not owning a car. [Here phrases and an entire sentence highlighted in red are lifted from the original without quotation marks or acknowledgment of the source.]

Structural plagiarism

Three elements contribute to the financial gains walkable cities are beginning to enjoy. First, artists and other talented youth find city life alluring and would never want to live in a nonurban environment. Second, the convergence of these would-be urbanites upon cities is creating a demand that is not expected to end anytime soon. Third, these populations are discovering the financial benefits of a life without car payments and gas costs. [Here the words are new, but the structure of the ideas is the same as in the original. Note that this paragraph would not be considered plagiarism if the student had written "According to Jeff Speck" at the beginning.]

Strategies for avoiding plagiarism

1. **Draw from a variety of sources on your topic.** The more articles or chapters you read, the less likely you'll be to rely too heavily on one.
2. **Separate reading and summarizing.** Read thoroughly first. Then close the book (or click away from the article) and start summarizing. If you don't have the original handy, you'll be more likely to put the writer's ideas in your own words. When you finish, look back at the original and make sure the words you used were actually your own.
3. **Map the conversation.** On a sheet of paper (or using mind-mapping software), write your topic inside a circle at the middle of the page. Then create a branch off of that circle for each writer you are reading. Next to each writer's name, summarize what he or she wrote. Seeing writers' names next to their ideas makes it easier to remember to give them credit. It can also help you figure out what they haven't said yet and what you can add to the discussion.
4. Put quotations around quoted material as you draft. Don't expect to go back and put them in later.

5. When you finish drafting a paragraph that includes quotes, stop and reread it. Make sure you have included signal phrases and names for each author you quoted. Make sure it is easy to tell whose ideas are whose.

What you are not required to acknowledge

Fortunately, common sense governs issues of academic plagiarism. The standards of documentation are not so strict that the source of every fact you cite must be acknowledged. You do not have to document the following.

- **Facts available from many sources.** For example, many reference sources report that the death toll of the sinking of the *Titanic* on April 15, 1912, was around 1,500.
- **Results of your own field research.** If you take a survey and report the results, you don't have to cite yourself. You do need to cite individual interviews.

What you are required to acknowledge

The following sources should be acknowledged with an in-text citation and an entry in the list of works cited (MLA style) or the list of references (APA style).

- **Quotations.** Short quotations should be enclosed within quotation marks, and long quotations should be indented as a block. See 21e for how to integrate quotations with signal phrases.
- **Summaries and paraphrases.** Summaries represent the author's argument in miniature as accurately as possible (see 5c). Paraphrases restate the author's argument in your own words.
- **Facts that are not common knowledge.** For facts that are not easily found in general reference works, cite the source.
- **Ideas that are not common knowledge.** The sources of theories, analyses, statements of opinion, and arguable claims should be cited.
- **Statistics, research findings, examples, graphs, charts, and illustrations.** As a reader you should be skeptical about statistics and research findings when the source is not mentioned. When a writer does not cite the sources of statistics and research findings, there is no way of knowing how reliable the sources are or whether the writer is making them up.

STAYING ON TRACK

Plagiarism in college writing

If you find any of the following problems in your academic writing, you may be guilty of plagiarizing someone else's work. Because plagiarism is usually inadvertent, it is especially important that you understand what constitutes using sources responsibly. Avoid these pitfalls.

- **Missing attribution.** Make sure the author of a quotation has been identified. Include a lead-in or signal phrase that provides attribution to the source and identify the author in the citation.

- **Missing quotation marks.** You must put quotation marks around material quoted directly from a source.

- **Inadequate citation.** Give a page number to show where in the source the quotation appears or where a paraphrase or summary is drawn from.

- **Paraphrase relies too heavily on the source.** Be careful that the wording or sentence structure of a paraphrase does not follow the source too closely.

- **Distortion of meaning.** Don't allow your paraphrase or summary to distort the meaning of the source and don't take a quotation out of context, resulting in a change of meaning.

- **Missing works-cited entry.** The list of works cited must include all the works cited in the project.

- **Inadequate citation of images.** A figure or photo must appear with a caption and a citation to indicate the source of the image. If material includes a summary of data from a visual source, an attribution or citation must be given for the graphic being summarized.

22 | Write and Revise the Research Project

QUICK*TAKE*

After reading this chapter, you should be able to . . .

- Revisit your research (22a)
- Use sources to provide evidence (22b)
- Use sources to provide points of departure (22c)
- Plan your organization (22d)
- Compose a draft of a research project (22e)
- Review and revise (22f)

22a Revisit Your Research

Before you begin writing your project, review the assignment and your goals (see Chapter 17). Your review of the assignment will remind you of your purpose (analysis, review, survey, evaluation, argument), your potential readers, your stance on your subject, and the length and scope you should aim for.

Take stock of your research

Gather the source material and any field research you have generated (see Chapters 18, 19, and 20). Often additional questions come up in the course of your research. Group your notes by subject. Ask yourself the following:

- Which sources provide evidence that supports your thesis or main points?
- Which sources turned out not to be relevant?
- Which ideas or points lack adequate sources? You may need to do additional research before starting to write your project.

Revise your working thesis

Often you will find that one aspect of your topic turned out to be more interesting and produced more information. If you have ample material, narrowing your subject is a benefit. At this stage in the writing process, your working thesis may be rough and may change as you write your draft, but having a working thesis will help keep your project focused (see 2c).

Revise or write out your working thesis.

I plan to (analyze, review, survey, evaluate, argue) that _____.
This subject matters to my readers because _____.

222

22b Use Sources to Provide Evidence

A common saying is that 88 percent of all statistics (or whatever percentage) are made up on the spot, which of course is an example of the error it describes. Readers expect to see evidence to support claims, and they want to know where the evidence came from. For example, polls and studies are often funded by those who have an interest in the outcome.

Your obligation is to find the most reliable evidence and to document the sources of that evidence. Let's consider an example of a student, George Abukar, writing on the topic of identity theft. Abukar has a friend whose driver's license was stolen. The thief then applied for a credit card in Abukar friend's name and made thousands of dollars of fraudulent purchases. None of the people who could have stopped the thief did so: The credit card company did not bother to verify the friend's identity, and the three major credit card reporting agencies did not remove the information about unpaid bills from her file, leaving her with a bad credit rating. Abukar's thesis proposes that the United States Congress pass federal legislation making credit-reporting agencies liable for damages when their actions or negligence leads to loss from identity theft.

Sources can help you build a case for why your claim matters. To argue for his thesis, Abukar had to establish first that the problem affected many more people besides his friend. He found statistics in the Federal Trade Commission's *Consumer Sentinel Data Book, January-December 2009* and included them in his paper.

Readers expect evidence to support claims and reasons. The Federal Trade Commission (FTC) reports that of 1.3 million complaints received in 2009, the number one complaint category was identity theft with 21% of the total (3). The number of identity theft complaints rose from 31,140 in 2000 to 278,078 in 2009 (5).

22c Use Sources as Points of Departure

All good research writing responds to sources. Every significant issue has an extensive history of discussion with various points of view.

Keep your voice when using sources

Your task as a researcher is to enter ongoing discussions by "talking" to your sources. Just as you would in a conversation with several people who hold different views, you may disagree with some people, agree with some, and agree with others only up to a point and then disagree.

Think about assuming roles in relation to your sources:

- the **skeptic**, who disagrees with a source,
- the **contributor**, who agrees with a source and has another point to add, or
- the **analyst**, who agrees with a source up to a point but has reservations.

George Abukar uses all three strategies to position his sources in relation to his argument.

Take the role of the skeptic

You can use this template.

A common way of thinking about this issue is _____, but this view is mistaken because _____.

George Abukar argues that there are inadequate safeguards against identity theft because credit card companies and reporting agencies have no financial interest in preventing identity theft and in some ways even profit from it. He needed to establish that a common view is that individuals are responsible for identity theft. He found a Federal Trade Commission Web site that puts forth this view and included a quotation from the site in his paper.

Abukar quotes common sense advice from the FTC Web site.

Mostly, consumers are being told to protect themselves. The Federal Trade Commission has an entire Web site devoted to telling consumers how to minimize their risk of identity theft. Some of their advice is obvious, like "Keep your purse or wallet in a safe place at work." Some tips are more obscure: "Treat your mail and trash carefully." Some assume that people have a lot more time, patience, and knowledge than they really do:

Ask about information security procedures in your workplace or at businesses, doctor's offices, or other institutions that collect your personally identifying information. Find out who has access to your personal information and verify that it is handled securely. Ask about the disposal procedures for those records as well. Find out if your information will be shared with anyone else. If so, ask how your information can be kept confidential. ("Deter")

Abukar points out how impractical the FTC advice is.

However, not many people are prepared to spend 20 minutes grilling the checkout person at Old Navy when she asks for their phone number.

Take the role of the contributor

You can use this template.

I agree with _____ because my experience confirms that _____ .

Sources should not make your argument for you. Indicate exactly how they support your position by making an additional point.

> The credit-reporting agencies are not content with letting consumers and banks foot the bill for their sloppy handling of our digital identities. They want to make more money off the insecurity they have created. Kevin Drum reports in *Washington Monthly*:

The source describes how credit card reporting agencies make money off the fear of identity theft, supporting Abukar's claim.

> > For their part, the major credit-reporting bureaus—Experian, Equifax, and TransUnion—don't seem to care much about the accuracy of their credit reports. In fact, they actually have a positive incentive to let ID theft flourish. Like mobsters offering "protection" to frightened store owners, credit-reporting agencies have recently begun taking advantage of the identity-theft boom to offer information age protection to frightened consumers. For $9.95 a month, Equifax offers "Credit Watch Gold," a service that alerts you whenever changes are made to your credit report. Experian and TransUnion offer similar services. In effect, customers are being asked to pay credit agencies to protect them from the negligence of those same agencies.

Abukar makes an additional point that builds on his source.

> Unlike consumers, who usually at least try to act responsibly to protect their credit rating, credit-reporting agencies avoid responsibility for, and profit from, identity theft. Therefore, the most important step to take in reducing identity theft is to implement legislation that holds credit-reporting agencies responsible for the damage their actions or inactions cause consumers.

Take the role of the analyst

You can use this template.

I agree with _____ up to a point, but I disagree with the conclusion _____ because _____ .

Incorporating sources is not a matter of simply agreeing or disagreeing with sources. Often you will agree with a source up to a point, but you will object to the conclusions. Or you may agree with the conclusions but not with the reasoning.

Abukar used a source with which he was in basic agreement, but he found one part of the argument in the source much stronger than the other part.

Abukar summarizes the position of his source.	In his book *The Digital Person: Technology and Privacy in the Information Age*, Daniel J. Solove proposes that the way to reduce identity theft is to change the structure, or "architecture," of the systems we use to collect and store personal information. He recommends giving individuals more control over their personal information and requiring the companies that use that information to inform
Abukar goes on to argue that the source misses how the solution proposed might be implemented.	people whenever something unusual happens to their files. While Solove's plan sounds good, he neglects the key for implementing the solution. Solove says that any new system should be "premised on the notion that the collection and use of personal information is an activity that carries duties and responsibilities" (121). This statement is an indirect way of saying, "Companies that handle personal information ought to be held liable for damages caused by identity theft." I would argue that if you make companies responsible to consumers by making them liable (the second half of Solove's plan), then they will automatically give consumers more control over their own information (the first half).

WRITING SMART

Determine the relationship of each source to your thesis

Gather the list of sources you have found in your research. You may have assembled these sources in a working bibliography or an annotated bibliography. Examine each source in relation to your working thesis. Note beside each source how it relates to your argument, using the "skeptic," "contributor," and "analyst" strategy.

- Does the source provide evidence for your claim or your reasons?
- Do you disagree with the source, and can you use it as a jumping-off point for your argument?
- Do you agree with the source and find you can expand on it?
- Do you agree with the source up to a point, and can you use it to show how your argument is different and perhaps better?

22d Plan Your Organization

After you have drafted a thesis, look back over your notes and determine how to group the ideas you researched. Decide what your major points will be and how those points support your thesis. Group your research findings so that they match up with your major points.

Now it is time to create a working outline. Always include your thesis at the top of your outline as a guiding light. Some writers create formal outlines with roman numerals and the like; others compose the headings for the paragraphs of their project and use them to guide their draft; still others may start writing and then determine how they will organize their draft when they have a few paragraphs written (see 2e).

Writer at Work

Gabriella Lopez made a working outline for her project.

Establishing a Campus Garden

Thesis: Establishing a small organic campus garden is a low-cost, high-yield way to support our school's mission, our students, the local community, and the global environment.

Section 1 Give background on why students are increasingly interested in sustainability and where campus farms have been established

Section 2 Propose establishing a campus garden as the least expensive way our campus can "go green"

Section 3 Argue that gardening can promote a healthy relationship with food at a time many students suffer from eating disorders

Section 4 Argue for the social, environmental, and educational benefits

Section 5 Explain the specifics for making the garden

Section 6 Explain how support for the garden can be generated and maintained

Section 7 Conclude by returning to the importance of sustainability for the future

22e Write a Draft

Some writers begin by writing the title, first paragraph, and concluding paragraph.

Write a specific title

A bland, generic title says to readers that you are likely to be boring.

Generic   Good and Bad Fats

Specific titles are like tasty appetizers; if you like the appetizer, you'll probably like the main course.

Specific   The Secret Killer: Hydrogenated Fats

Write an engaging introduction

Get off to a fast start. If, for example, you want to alert readers to the dangers of partially hydrogenated oils in the food we eat, you could begin by explaining the difference in molecular structure between natural unsaturated fatty acids and trans fatty acids. And you would probably lose your readers by the end of the first paragraph.

Instead, let readers know what is at stake along with giving some background and context (see 3e). State your thesis early on. Then go into the details in the body of your project.

> Americans today are more heath conscious than ever before, yet most are unaware that they may be ingesting high levels of dangerous fat in the form of partially hydrogenated oils. Hydrogenation is the process of passing hydrogen bubbles through heated oil, which makes the oil taste like butter. Nearly all processed food contains some level of hydrogenated oils. The food tastes good, but the oil it contains will make you fat and can eventually kill you.

Write a strong conclusion

The challenge in writing ending paragraphs is to leave the reader with something provocative, something beyond pure summary of the previous paragraphs. Connect back to your thesis and use a strong concluding image, example, question, or call to action to leave your readers with something to remember and think about (see 3e).

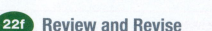

22f Review and Revise

After you've finished your first draft, you'll want to get comments from other writers. A good source of help is fellow students. Your instructor may include a peer review session as part of the assignment.

Reading another student's project

It is usually best to read through a project twice, looking at different levels (see Chapter 4). The first time you read through a project, concentrate on comprehension and overall impressions. See if you can summarize the project after reading it once.

Once you've read through the project a second time, write concluding suggestions and comments about how the writer could improve the project. Be specific. Saying "I liked your project" or "It's a good first draft" does not help the writer. Comments like "You need to cite more sources" or "You might consider switching paragraphs 2 and 4" give the writer specific areas to concentrate on in the revision.

Reading your own project

Reading your project aloud to yourself will help you find rough places. Parts that are difficult for you to speak aloud are going to be hard for your readers to get through. Try to imagine yourself as a reader who does not know much about your subject or who holds a viewpoint different from yours. What could you add that would benefit that reader?

Revise, Revise, Revise

After you've gone through the peer editing process, received comments from your instructor, or assessed your own draft, sit down with your project and consider the changes you need to make. (You can see how Gabriella Lopez responded to her instructor's comments in 4c.) Start from the highest level, reorganizing paragraphs and possibly even cutting large parts of your project and adding new sections. If you make significant revisions, you will likely want to repeat the overall evaluation of your revised draft when you finish.

When you feel your draft is complete, begin the editing phase. Use the guidelines in 4c to revise style and grammatical errors. Finally, proofread your project, word by word, checking for mistakes (see 4d). After you print out the final project, check each page for formatting errors (see 23k for MLA-style formatting and 24i for APA-style formatting).

STAYING ON TRACK

Check for missing documentation

When you reach the proofreading stage, make one pass through your draft to check for missing documentation. Print your draft and your works-cited list, and then place them beside each other.

1. Check that every parenthetical citation and every mention of an author's name in your text has an entry in your works-cited list. Put a check beside each when you find they match and note what is missing.

2. Read your text carefully for missing citations. For example, if you find a sentence similar to the following, you'll need to insert a parenthetical citation.

Off track   One critic of the exuberance over Web 2.0 writes, "Today's amateur monkeys can use their networked computers to publish everything from uninformed political commentary, to unseemly home videos, to embarrassingly amateurish music, to unreadable poems, reviews, essays and novels."

On track   One critic of the exuberance over Web 2.0 writes, "Today's amateur monkeys can use their networked computers to publish everything from uninformed political commentary, to unseemly home videos, to embarrassingly amateurish music, to unreadable poems, reviews, essays and novels" **(Keen 3)**.

3. Check for missing page numbers for sources that have pagination.

Off track   Andrew Keen describes *Wikipedia* as "an online encyclopedia where anyone with opposable thumbs and a fifth-grade education can publish anything on any topic from AC/DC to Zoroastrianism."

On track   Andrew Keen describes *Wikipedia* as "an online encyclopedia where anyone with opposable thumbs and a fifth-grade education can publish anything on any topic from AC/DC to Zoroastrianism" **(3)**.

Remember: Faulty documentation hurts your credibility as a researcher and can be a cause of plagiarism.

MLA

23 **MLA Documentation**   **231**

MLA Documentation Map (see the back of this divider)

MLA

23 | MLA Documentation

QUICK*TAKE*

After reading this chapter, you should be able to . . .

- Recognize in-text citations in MLA style (23a)
- Create and format in-text citations (23b)
- Recognize works-cited entries in MLA style (23c)
- Create and format works-cited entries (23d)
- Create citations for periodicals (23e)
- Create citations for books (23f)
- Create citations for online-only and digital sources (23g)
- Create citations for visual and multimedia sources (23h)
- Create citations for other source types (23i)
- Construct informational notes (23j)
- Use MLA formatting for a paper (23k)

MLA DOCUMENTATION MAP

1 | Collect the right information

For every source you need to have

- the name of the author or authors,
- the full title, and
- complete publication information.

For instructions go to the illustrated examples in 23d of three frequently used source types:

- **PRINTED BOOK**
- **ARTICLE IN A DATABASE**
- **ARTICLE ON A WEB SITE**

For other kinds of sources such as visual and multimedia sources, see the index of works-cited entries at the end of 23d and the examples in 23h.

2 | Cite sources in two places

Remember, this is a two-part process.

You will learn **how to cite sources in your project** from a Writer at Work in 23a.

To create citations

(1) in the **body of your paper**; go to 23a and 23b.
(2) in a **list of works cited at the end of your paper**; go to 23c and 23d.

Research writing requires you to document the sources of all of your information that is not common knowledge. The style developed by the Modern Language Association (MLA) requires you to document each source in two places: an in-text citation in the body of your project and a list of works cited at the end. If your readers want to find the source of a fact or quotation in your project, they can use your in-text citation to find the full information about a source in your works-cited list.

If you have questions that the examples in this chapter do not address, consult the *MLA Handbook*, eighth edition (2016), or the *MLA Style Center* at style.mla.org/.

---

3 | Find the right model citations

You'll find **illustrated examples of sources** in 23d.

Once you match your source to one of those examples, you can move on to more specific examples:

- **PERIODICAL (print, online, or database);** go to 23e.
- **BOOK** or parts of a book; go to 23f.
- **ONLINE:** was the source
  (1) found only online? Go to 23g.
  (2) from **another visual or multimedia source?** Go to 23h.

A complete list of examples is found in the index of works-cited entries at the end of 23d.

---

4 | Format your paper

You will find a **sample research paper** and instructions on formatting the body of your paper and your works-cited list in 23k.

A note about footnotes:
MLA style does not use footnotes for documentation. Use in-text citations instead (see 23a and 23b). The only use of footnotes in MLA style is for providing additional information, as you will see in 23j.

Writer at Work

Gabriella Lopez chose to make a proposal argument for a campus garden as her research project. She wanted to argue that the garden is important for her school for reasons beyond providing a few fresh vegetables and that college students are increasingly concerned about eating healthy foods. You can see the complete paper in 23k at the end of this chapter.

How to quote and cite a source in the text of an MLA-style paper

Gabriella searched for an article on the *PsycARTICLES* database using the search terms "food," "college students," and "health attitudes." She found the article below, and she printed a copy.

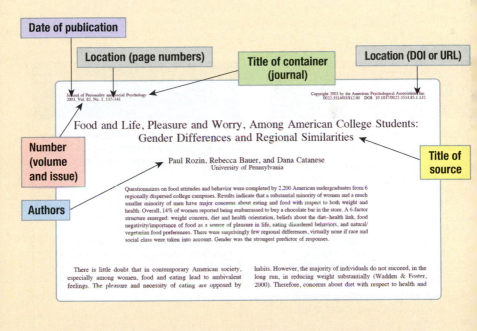

To support her argument that many students are concerned about what they eat, she decided to include a short quotation that points to the benefits of a healthy relationship with food.

If a paper has one or two authors, the writer can (1) mention them in the text of the paper with a signal phrase or (2) place the author's names inside parentheses following the quotation. Because this article has more than two authors, Gabriella should refer to them as Paul Rozin et al. Either with or without the signal phrase, in most cases she must include the page number where she found the quotation inside parentheses.

Author's name in signal phrase

> Paul Rozin et al. found in a survey of 2,200 American college students that a significant number of women and a smaller group of men have "major concerns about eating and food with respect to both weight and health" (132).

OR

Author's name in parenthetical citation

> According to a survey of 2,200 American college students, a significant number of women and a smaller group of men have "major concerns about eating and food with respect to both weight and health" (Rozin et al. 132).

If Gabriella includes a quotation that is longer than four lines, she must double-space and indent the quotation in her paper a half inch (see example in the student paper in 23k).

Include in-text citations for summaries and paraphrases

To argue for the feasibility of the garden proposal, Gabriella supplied specific details of how square-foot gardens work. She used information from a book by Mel Bartholomew, who is an expert on square-foot gardening. The wording was not especially important, so Gabriella summarized Bartholomew's recommendations and gave the page numbers from her source.

> The size of each square in the grid depends on what plants are planted there; certain plants require larger and deeper grids (Bartholomew 15-16). The main benefit of square-foot gardening is that one can grow the same amount of produce in a 140-square-foot grid that is typically grown in the average 700-square-foot, single-row garden (42).

23b In-Text Citations in MLA Style

Paraphrase, summary, or short quotation

A short quotation of prose occupies four lines or fewer in your paper; a short quotation or poetry is three lines or fewer.

> The computing power of networked technology is growing at an accelerating rate, prompting some visionaries to argue that the Internet "may actually become self-aware sometime in the next century" (Johnson 114).

Here, the author's name is provided in the parenthetical reference.

> Science writer and cultural critic Steven Johnson poses the question this way: "Is the Web itself becoming a giant brain?" (114).

Note that the period goes *after* the parentheses.

The author of the quotation is named in this sentence, so only a page number is needed in the parenthetical reference.

Quotations longer than four lines

The sentence introducing the quotation names the author, so only the page number needs to appear in the parenthetical reference.

> Technology writer and cultural commentator Steven Johnson relates how he often responded to questions about whether or not networked computers would ever be able to think or develop awareness:
>
> > For there to be a single, global consciousness, the Web itself would have to be getting smarter, and the Web wasn't a single, unified thing—it was just a vast sum of interlinked data. You could debate whether the Web was making us smarter, but that the Web itself might be slouching toward consciousness seemed ludicrous. (114)
>
> Despite his initial skepticism, however, Johnson slowly began to change his mind about the idea of artificial consciousness or intelligence.

Note that the period appears *before* the parentheses in an indented block quotation.

WHEN DO YOU PROVIDE A PAGE NUMBER?

- Provide the page number for each quotation, paraphrase, and summary. If the source is longer than one page, provide inclusive page numbers.

  (e.g., 313-15)

- If an online source includes paragraph numbers rather than page numbers, use *par.* with the number.

  (Cello, par. 4)

- If the source does not include page numbers, consider citing the work and the author in the text rather than in parentheses.

  In a hypertext version of James Joyce's *Ulysses,* . . .

Index of in-text citations

Include in-text citations as you are writing your project rather than waiting until you finish. Use this index to determine the right format.

Sample in-text citations for sources in general

1. **Author named in a signal phrase**

   Put the author's name in a signal phrase in your sentence.

   > Sociologist Daniel Bell called this emerging U.S. economy the "postindustrial society" (3).

2. **Author not named in your text**

   > In 2015, the Gallup poll reported that 76% of adults in the United States think secondhand smoke is "very harmful," compared with only 36% in 1994 (Saad 4).

3. **Work by one author**

   The author's last name comes first, followed by the page number. There is no comma.

   > (Bell 3)

4. **Work by two authors**

   The authors' last names follow the order of the title page. Join the names with *and*.

   > (Vaughn and Lynn 7)

5. **Work by three or more authors**

   Use the phrase *et al.* (meaning "and others") for all names but the first.

   > (Abrams et al. 1653)

6. **Author unknown**

   Use a shortened version of the title that includes at least the first important word. Your reader will use the shortened title to find the full title in the works-cited list.

   > A review in *The New Yorker* of Ryan Adams's new album focuses on the artist's age ("Pure" 25).

   Notice that "Pure" is in quotation marks because it is the shortened title of an article. If it were a book, the short title would be in italics.

7. **Work by a group or organization**

   Treat the group or organization as the author. Try to identify the group author in the text and place only the page number in parentheses.

   > According to the *Irish Free State Handbook*, published by the Ministry for Industry and Finance, the population of Ireland in 1929 was approximately 4,192,000 (23).

8. **Quotations longer than four lines**

NOTE: When using indented ("block") quotations that are longer than four lines, the period appears *before* the parentheses enclosing the page number. Indent the quotation a half inch, the same indentation afforded to the first line of new paragraphs.

> In her article "Art for Everybody," Susan Orlean attempts to explain the popularity of painter Thomas Kinkade:
>> People like to own things they think are valuable. . . . The high price of limited editions is part of their appeal: it implies that they are choice and exclusive, and that only a certain class of people will be able to afford them. (128)
>
> This same statement could also explain the popularity of phenomena like PBS's *Antiques Roadshow*.

If the source is longer than one page, provide the page number for each quotation, paraphrase, and summary.

9. **Two or more works by the same author**

Use the author's last name and then a shortened version of the title of each source.

> The majority of books written about coauthorship focus on partners of the same sex (Laird, *Women* 351).

Note that *Women* is italicized because it is the title of a book.

10. **Different authors with the same last name**

If your list of works cited contains items by two or more different authors with the same last name, include the initial of the first name in the parenthetical reference. Note that a period follows the initial.

> Web surfing requires more mental involvement than channel surfing (S. Johnson 107).

11. **Two or more sources within the same sentence**

Place each citation directly after the statement it supports.

> Many sweeping pronouncements were made in the 1990s that the Internet is the best opportunity to improve education since the printing press (Ellsworth xxii) or even in the history of the world (Dyrli and Kinnaman 79).

12. **Two or more sources within the same citation**

If two sources support a single point, separate them with a semicolon.

(McKibbin 39; Gore 92)

13. **Work quoted in another source**

When you do not have access to the original source of the material you wish to use and only an indirect source is available, put the abbreviation *qtd. in* ("quoted in") before the information about the indirect source.

National governments have become increasingly what Ulrich Beck, in a 1999 interview, calls "zombie institutions"—institutions which are "dead and still alive" (qtd. in Bauman 6).

Sample in-text citations for particular kinds of sources

14. **One-page source**

A page reference is unnecessary if you are citing a one-page work.

Economists agree that automating routine work is the broad goal of globalization (Lohr).

15. **Online sources, including Web pages, blogs, podcasts, tweets, social media, wikis, videos, and other multimedia sources**

MLA prefers that you mention the author in your text instead of putting the author's name in parentheses.

Andrew Keen ironically used his own blog to claim that "blogs are boring to write (yawn), boring to read (yawn), and boring to discuss (yawn)."

If you cannot identify the author, mention the title in your text.

The podcast "Catalina's Cubs" describes the excitement on Catalina Island when the Chicago Cubs came for spring training in the 1940s.

16. **Source in time-based media**

When possible, include time stamps when citing audio or video materials.

In her Ted Talk entitled "The Power of Vulnerability," Brene Brown muses, "Maybe stories are just data with a soul" (00:01:13).

17. **Work in an edited anthology**

Cite the name of the author of the work within an anthology, not the name of the editor of the collection. For example, Melissa Jane Hardie published the chapter "Beard" in *Rhetorical Bodies*, a book edited by Jack Selzer

and Sharon Crowley. Note that Hardie, not Selzer and Crowley, is named in a parenthetical citation.

> (Hardie 278-79)

18. Work in more than one volume

Give the volume number in the parenthetical reference before the page number, with a colon and a space separating the two.

> (Walther and Metzger 2: 647).

19. Poems, plays, and classic works

Poems

If you quote all or part of two or three lines of poetry that do not require special emphasis, put the lines in quotation marks and separate the lines using a slash (/) with a space on each side. To cite them, put the line numbers in parentheses. Write "line" or "lines" before the numbers.

> John Donne's "The Legacy" associates the separation of lovers with death: "When I died last, and, Dear, I die / As often as from thee I go" (lines 1-2).

Plays

Give the act, scene, and line numbers when the work has them, or the page numbers when it does not. Abbreviate titles of famous works (e.g., *Hamlet*).

> (*Ham.* 3.2.120-23).

Classic Works

To supply a reference to classic works, you sometimes need more than a page number from a specific edition. Readers should be able to locate a quotation in any edition of the book. Give the page number from the edition that you are using, then a semicolon and other identifying information.

> "Marriage is a house" is one of the most memorable lines in *Don Quixote* (546; pt. 2, bk. 3, ch. 19).

20. Sacred texts

Cite a sacred text such as the Bible or the Qur'an the first time with the name of the edition you use along with the book, chapter, and verse. In subsequent citations you need to give only the book, chapter, and verse. Abbreviate the names of books with five or more letters (e.g., *Prov.* for *Proverbs*).

> The memorable phrase from the Vietnam War, "hearts and minds," actually comes from the New Testament (*New Oxford Annotated Bible*, Phil. 4.7).

23c Creating the List of Works Cited

Core elements of a works-cited entry

MLA style is based on the idea that most sources have several characteristics in common, known as the core elements. This is true whether you find the source in print or online, or experience it in a public space, such as a museum or lecture hall.

To write a works-cited entry in MLA style, identify and list as many of these core elements as the source provides. (The examples in 23d–23i provide additional instructions and exceptions according to a variety of specific source types.)

Core Elements	Description
Author	The person or group chiefly responsible for creating the source. It might be an individual, group of individuals, company, organization, or government agency.
Title of source	The name of the article, book, Web page, lecture, artwork, company or government report, or other item you are citing.
Title of container	The larger whole that contains your source. If the source is a chapter, the container may be a book or anthology (print or online). If the source is an article, the container is likely a journal or magazine (print or online).
Other contributors	Other people who helped create the work. They may be editors, translators, illustrators, directors, adaptors, or performers.
Version	The edition of the source that you are citing. Look for these phrases: 2nd edition, revised edition, director's cut, expanded edition, updated edition, unabridged version. For journals, look for the volume number.
Number	Works in a multivolume set are numbered, as are articles in journals. If a journal publishes several times a year, the articles in it have a volume and a number (volume 6, number 2). Journals that prefer not to publish in volumes will just have a number.
Publisher	The organization that has primary responsibility for making the source available. Sometimes a source has more than one publisher. When that happens, list them both, separated by a forward slash (/).

Core Elements	Description
Publication date	The date the source became publically available. Some sources have more than one publication date. In cases like these, indicate the date of the version you used. If you wish to include the original date of publication, place it directly after the title.
Location	Information to help readers find the work. For a print work, provide page numbers. For a Web site, provide the URL (minus *http://*). For an artwork, lecture, or performance, provide the place where you experienced it.

Not every element appears in every works-cited entry, but every element always appears in a fixed order and ends with the same punctuation.

Format of works-cited entry by element

Author. Title of source. Container, Other contributors, Version, Number, Publisher, Publication date, Location.

Secondary containers

Sometimes a container will be nested within another container. For example, an article in a journal (primary container) might be contained in an online database (secondary container). When a source has more than one container, provide complete information about the first container before mentioning the second. Separate containers with a period. (See the Writer at Work example that follows and p. 246.)

For a secondary container, you will usually find distinctive information on only a few core elements—for instance, the name of the container and the location, and possibly a different publication date. For digital containers, click around to see if you can provide a DOI or a permalink URL for the source. (*DOI* stands for *digital object identifier*, which is a permanent unique number assigned to an online document.) If neither of these options is available, provide the full, direct URL, minus http://.

Writer at Work

Gabriella is ready to create an entry for the list of works cited at the end of her paper. Gabriella kept a copy of this screenshot from her library database and made notes about the proper information to create the works-cited entry.

Copyright:	American Psychological Association. 2003
Digital Object Identifier:	http://dx.doi.org.ezproxy.lib.utexas.edu/10.1037/ 0022-3514.85.1.132
PMID:	12872889

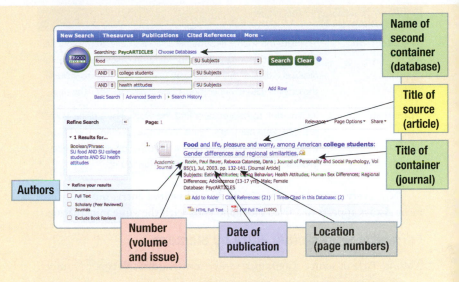

Gabriella asked herself a series of questions to create an entry for this source in her list of works cited.

1. What information do I need to pull from this screenshot?

For a source like this article from an online database, she needs to know several things: (1) the author; (2) the title of the source (article); (3) the title of the container (journal), (4) the number (volume and issue), (5) the date of publication (year), (6) the location (page numbers), and (7) the name of the secondary container (database). She will also need to find (8) the secondary container's location (DOI).

2. I know this is from my library's online database, but that could be one of several different types of sources. What kind of source is this?

The kinds of sources you'll find in a database are an article from a periodical (newspaper or a scholarly journal), a business or financial report, a legal case, or an abstract. Gabriella selected the database *PsycARTICLES* for her search; thus she knew that her source type would be an article.

3. Now how do I find the author's name?

Look for a bold heading that says something like "AUTHOR" or "BYLINE." If two authors are listed, take note of both. If there are more than two authors, you will need to name only the first.

4. What is the title of my source?

If the title is not immediately evident, look for a heading that says "TITLE" or "HEADLINE."

5. Where do I find the publication information?

The name and date of the periodical are usually listed at the top of the page but sometimes are found at the bottom.

6. Where do I find the name of the database and the DOI?

For databases distributed by EBSCO, you have to look for the name of the database. EBSCO is the vendor who sells access to many databases such as *Academic Search Complete*. To find the DOI, you may need to click on the title of the source and scroll down. Or you can search for any source's DOI at the Web site crossref.org. If a source has no DOI, use the URL.

Gabriella listed the information.

AUTHORS.	Rozin, Paul, et al.
TITLE OF SOURCE.	"Food and Life, Pleasure and Worry, among American College Students: Gender Differences and Regional Similarities."
TITLE OF CONTAINER (journal),	*Journal of Personality and Social Psychology,*
NUMBER (volume, issue),	vol. 52, no. 1,
DATE OF PUBLICATION (year),	2003,
LOCATION (page numbers).	pp. 132–41.
SECONDARY CONTAINER (database),	*PsycARTICLES,*
LOCATION (DOI or URL).	doi:10.1037/ 00223514.85.1.132.

Then she used the instructions on page 247 to format her citation. You can see Gabriella's complete list of works cited on pages 277–279 at the end of this chapter.

Works Cited

Rozin, Paul, et al. "Food and Life, Pleasure and Worry, among American College Students: Gender Differences and Regional Similarities." *Journal of Personality and Social Psychology*, vol. 85, no.1, 2003, pp. 132-41. *PsycARTICLES*, doi:10.1037/0022-3514.85.1.132.

23d Illustrated Samples and Index of Works Cited in MLA Style

Printed book

Use your library's online catalog to locate printed books on your library's shelves. Find the copyright date on the copyright page, which is on the back of the title page. Use the copyright date for the date of publication, not the date of printing.

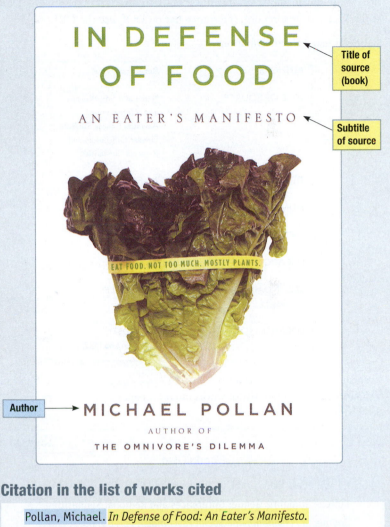

IN DEFENSE OF FOOD — Title of source (book)

AN EATER'S MANIFESTO — Subtitle of source

EAT FOOD. NOT TOO MUCH. MOSTLY PLANTS.

Author → MICHAEL POLLAN

AUTHOR OF
THE OMNIVORE'S DILEMMA

Citation in the list of works cited

Pollan, Michael. *In Defense of Food: An Eater's Manifesto.*
Penguin Books, 2008.

Elements of the citation

Author's or Editor's Name

The author's last name comes first, followed by a comma and the first name.

For edited books, put the word *editor* after the name, preceded by a comma:

Kavanagh, Peter, editor.

Book Title

Use the exact title, as it appears on the title page (not the cover).

Italicize the title.

Publisher

For university presses, use *UP*:
New York UP

Otherwise spell out full publisher names, including words like *Press* or *Books* but not corporate words or abbreviations like *Inc.* or *Company*.

If two different publishers are equally responsible for producing the book, name them both with a forward slash (/) between them.

When the title page shows three publisher names—a parent company, a division, and an imprint—include only the division. When the title page shows two publisher names—a parent publisher and an imprint—use the imprint.

Publication Date

Give the year as it appears on the copyright page.

If no year of publication is given, but it can be approximated, put a *c.* ("circa") and the approximate date in brackets: [c. 1999].

Find the right example as your model (you may need to refer to more than one model)

How many authors are listed?
- One, two, or more authors: see examples #1–3.
- Unknown author: see example #13.
- Group or organization as the author: see example #24.

Do you have a book with an editor, translator, or illustrator?
- For a focus on the editor, see example #28.
- For a focus on the author of an edited book, see example #29.
- For a book with a translator, see example #30.
- For an illustrated book, see example #32.

Do you have only a part of a book?
- For an introduction, foreword, preface, or afterword, see example #34.
- For a selection in an anthology or edited collection, see example #35.
- For more than one selection in an anthology or edited collection, see example #36.

Do you have two or more books by the same author?
- See example #20.

Article accessed through a database

You can access library databases through your library's Web site. A few databases, including *Google Scholar*, are available to everyone, but most library databases are password protected if you access them off campus.

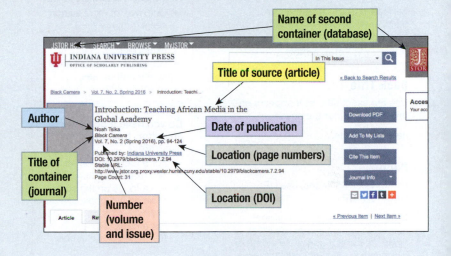

Citation in the list of works cited

Berry, Scott M., et al. "Bridging Different Eras in Sports." *Journal of the American Statistical Association,* vol. 94, no. 447, 1999, pp. 661–76. *JSTOR,* doi:10.2307/2669973.

Elements of the citation

Start the citation with the exact format of a print citation.

Author's Name

The author's last name comes first, followed by a comma and the first name. For two or more works by the same author, see example #20.

Title of Source (article)

Use the exact title and put it inside quotation marks. If a book title is part of the article's title, italicize the book title.

Title of Container (periodical)

Provide the entire title, without abbreviations. If the item includes an article, such as *The*, include it. Be sure to italicize the name of a journal or newspaper.

Number (volume and issue)

List the same information you would for a print item.

Publication Date

List the year of publication. If you have the full date, list the day first, then month and year.

Location (page numbers)

Include the complete range of pages.

Title of Secondary Container (database)

Italicize the name of the database, followed by a comma.

Location (DOI or URL)

Provide a DOI or a stable, direct URL (permalink) for the article.

Find the right example as your model (you may need to refer to more than one model)

Most databases allow you to search by document type, such as scholarly journal, newspaper article, financial report, legal case, or abstract. Use these categories to identify the type of publication.

What kind of publication do you have?

- For an article in a scholarly journal, see example #6.
- For a magazine article, see examples #7–11.
- For a newspaper article, see examples #12–18.
- For a legal case, see example #69.
- For a company report, see example #78.

Do you have a publication with an unknown author?

- See example #13.

Online publication

Title of container (Web site)

Location (URL)

Date of publication

Title of source (article)

Author

Citation in the list of works cited

Granath, Bob. "Gemini IX Crew Found 'Angry Alligator' in Earth's Orbit." *NASA*, 1 June 2016, www.nasa.gov/feature/gemini-ix-crew-found-angry-alligator-in-earth-orbit/.

Elements of the citation

Author's Name

Authorship is sometimes hard to discern for online sources. If you know the author or creator, follow the rules for books and journals.

If the only authority you find is a group or organization, begin the entry with the title of the source. List the organization as the publisher, before the date of publication.

Title of Source

Place the title of the work inside quotation marks if it is part of a larger Web site.

Title of Container

Italicize the name of the overall site if it is different from the work. The name of the overall Web site will usually be found on its index or home page.

Version

Some Web sites are updated, so list the version if you find it (e.g., *version 1.2*).

Number

If the source lists a volume number, provide it with *vol.* before it and a comma after; if a source lists an issue number, provide it next with *no.* before it and a comma after: vol. 27, no. 7,

Publisher

List the publisher's name, if available, followed by a comma.

Location

Provide the URL where the source can be found.

Date of Publication

List the date of publication by day, month, and year if available. Some sources will provide only the year. Others will provide the exact time; include this information after the year and a comma: **25 Oct. 2015, 1:36 p.m.**

Find the right example as your model (you may need to refer to more than one model)

Do you have a Web page or an entire Web site?

- For an entire Web site, see example #40.
- For a page on a Web site, see example #41.

What kind of publication do you have, and who is the author?

- For a known author, see example #42.
- For a group or organization as the author, see example #43.
- For an article in an online scholarly journal, newspaper, or magazine, see examples #5, 10, and 14.
- For a government publication accessed online, see example #68.
- For a posting on social media, see example #46.

Index of Works-Cited Entries

 **Other Sources   263**

23e   Periodicals

JOURNAL ARTICLES

1. **Article by one author**

> Ekotto, Frieda. "Against Representation: Countless Hours for a Professor." *PMLA,* vol. 127, no. 4, 2012, pp. 968-72.

2. **Article by two authors**

The second author's name is printed first name first. Notice that a comma separates the authors' names.

> Condon, William, and Carol Rutz. "A Taxonomy of Writing across the Curriculum Programs: Evolving to Serve Broader Agendas." *CCC,* vol. 64, no. 2, 2012, pp. 357-82.

3. **Article by three or more authors**

Use the phrase *et al.* (meaning "and others") for all authors but the first. Use the same method in the in-text citation.

> Breece, Katherine E., et al. "Patterns of mtDNA Diversity in Northwestern North America." *Human Biology,* vol. 76, no. 5, 2004, pp. 33-54.

4. Article with a title within a title

If the title of the article contains the title of another short work, include it in single quotation marks. Italicize the title or a word that would normally be italicized.

> Happel, Alison, and Jennifer Esposito. "Vampires, Vixens, and Feminists: An Analysis of *Twilight*." *Educational Studies,* vol. 46, no. 5, 2010, pp. 524-31.

5. Article in a scholarly journal online

Some scholarly journals are published online only. List articles by author, title, name of journal in italics, volume, issue number, and date of publication. Provide information about the article's digital location. Ideally, this should be a DOI (digital object identifier). If a DOI is not available, provide a direct permalink or stable URL, omitting *http://*.

> Stolley, Karl. "The Lo-Fi Manifesto, 2.0." *Kairos,* vol. 20, no. 2, 2016, kairos.technorhetoric.net/20.2/inventio/stolley/index.html.

6. Scholarly journal article from a library database

If you locate an article in a database, treat the database as a second container. List the article by author, title, name of journal in italics, volume, issue number, date of publication, and page numbers (if available). Then add the name of the database in italics. You may have to click around on the record in the database until you find the article's DOI or a stable URL.

> Anjali Jain. "Fighting Obesity: Evidence of Effectiveness Will be Needed to Sustain Policies." *The BMJ,* vol. 328, no. 7452, 5 June 2004, pp. 1327-28. *JSTOR,* doi:10.1136/bmj.328.7452.1327.

MAGAZINE ARTICLES

7. Monthly or seasonal magazines or journals

For magazines and journals identified by the month or season of publication, use the month (or season) and year in place of the volume and number. If the volume and number are available, place the season after them, set off by commas. Abbreviate the names of all months except May, June, and July.

> Huang, Yasheng. "China's Other Path." *Wilson Quarterly,* Spring 2010, pp. 58-64.

8. **Weekly or biweekly magazines**

For weekly or biweekly magazines, give both the day and month of publication, as listed on the issue.

> Thurman, Judith. "Ask Betty." *The New Yorker,* 11 Nov. 2012,
>   pp. 40-43.

9. **Article by an unknown author**

Begin the entry with the title.

> "Light Box." *Time,* 28 Jan. 2013, pp. 6-7.

10. **Article in a popular magazine online**

Provide a permalink or stable direct URL at the end of your works-cited entry. Sometimes you will have to explore the page to find one. The following permalink came from the e-mail function on the page where the article appeared.

> Begley, Sarah. "Sean Parker to Donate $250 Million to Cancer
>   Immunotherapy Research." *Time,* 13 Apr. 2016, time.com/
>   4291890/sean-parker-to-donate-250-million-to-cancer-
>   immunotherapy-research/.

11. **Magazine article from a library database**

> Mitchell, Robert L. "Tom Mitchell; This Carnegie Mellon Researcher
>   Predicts a Revolution in Psychology and Neuroscience. What's
>   on His Mind Is Learning What's on Yours." *Computerworld,* 22
>   Feb. 2010. *Academic OneFile,* go.galegroup.com/ps/i.do?id=
>   GALE%7CA221023352&v=2.1&u=cuny_hunter&it=r&p=
>   AONE&sw=w&asid=20c01a3b928e4fa1041475cdc86cb77a.

NEWSPAPER ARTICLES

12. **Article by one author**

> Rojas, Rick. "For Young Sikhs, a Tie That Binds Them to Their Faith."
>   *The Washington Post,* 20 June 2010, p. C03.

13. **Article by an unknown author**

Begin the entry with the title.

> "Missile Launcher Turns Up at Buyback." *Austin American-Statesman,*
>   21 Jan. 2013, p. A7.

14. **Online newspaper article**

List the name of the author, last name first, followed by a period. Then place the name of the article in quotation marks and the newspaper in italics, each followed by a comma. Provide the date of publication and the URL last. Only include the publisher's name if it is markedly different from the publication's.

> Brown, Patricia Leigh. "Australia in Sonoma." *The New York Times*, 3 July 2008. www.nytimes.com/2008/07/03/garden/03australia.html.

15. **Newspaper article accessed from a library database**

> Jervis, Rick. "Mardi Gras keeps marching on; New Orleans' numerous parades and parties still rolling, despite the nation's tough economic times." *USA Today*, 23 Feb. 2009, p. 3A. *LexisNexis Academic*, www.lexisnexis.com.ezproxy.lib.utexas.edu/lnacui2api /api/version1/getDocCui.

REVIEWS, EDITORIALS, AND LETTERS TO THE EDITOR

16. **Review**

List the reviewer's name and the title of the review. Then include the prefix *Review of* followed by the title of the work, the word *by*, and the author's name. If there is no title, just name the work reviewed. For film reviews, name the director.

> Mendelsohn, Daniel. "The Two Oscar Wildes." Review of *The Importance of Being Earnest,* directed by Oliver Parker. *The New York Review of Books,* 10 Oct. 2002, pp. 23-24.

> Garner, Dwight. "Violence Expert Visits Her Dark Past?" Review of *Denial: A Memoir of Terror,* by Jessica Stern. *The New York Times,* 25 June 2010, p. 28.

17. **Editorial**

For an editorial, add the word *Editorial* (with no italics or quotation marks) after the title (or in place of one if the piece is untitled). If it is unsigned, begin with the title.

> "Stop Stonewalling on Reform." Editorial. *Business Week*, 17 June 2002, p. 108.

18. **Letter to the editor**

Add the description *Letter to the Editor* after the name of the author.

> Patai, Daphne. Letter to the Editor. *Harper's Bazaar*, Dec. 2001, p. 4.

23f Books

19. Book by one author

> Mayer-Schönberger, Viktor. *Delete: The Virtue of Forgetting in the Digital Age*. Princeton UP, 2009.

20. Two or more books by the same author

In the entry for the first book, include the author's name. In the second entry, substitute three hyphens and a period for the author's name. List the titles of books by the same author in alphabetical order.

> Krakauer, Jon. *Into the Wild*. Villard Books, 1996.
>
> ---. *Where Men Win Glory: The Odyssey of Pat Tillman*. Doubleday, 2009.

21. Book by two authors

The second author's name appears first name first.

> Burger, Edward B., and Michael Starbird. *Coincidences, Chaos, and All That Math Jazz*. W. W. Norton, 2006.

22. Book by three or more authors

Use the phrase *et al.* (meaning "and others") for all authors but the first. Use the same method in the in-text citation.

> North, Stephen M., et al. *Refiguring the Ph.D. in English Studies*. National Council of Teachers of English, 2000.

23. Book by an unknown author

Begin the entry with the title.

> *Encyclopedia of Americana*. Somerset, 2001.

24. Book by a group or organization

Treat the group as the author of the work.

> United Nations. *The Charter of the United Nations: A Commentary*. Oxford UP, 2000.

25. Title within a title

If the title contains the title of another book or a word normally italicized, do not italicize that title or word.

> Higgins, Brian, and Hershel Parker. *Critical Essays on Herman Melville's* Moby-Dick. G. K. Hall, 1992.

26. E-book (online)

If you include the original date of publication, place it after the book title.

> Stoker, Bram. *Dracula*. 1897. *Project Gutenberg*, 2013, www.gutenberg.org/
> files/345/345-h/345-h.htm.

27. E-book (Kindle, iPad, or another device)

The URL can provide information about the format, in this case Kindle.

> Morrison, Toni. *Home*. Kindle ed., Vintage Books, 2013.

EDITIONS, TRANSLATIONS, AND ILLUSTRATED BOOKS

28. Book with an editor—focus on the editor

> Lewis, Gifford, editor. *The Big House of Inver*. By Edith Somerville and
> Martin Ross, A. and A. Farmar, 2000.

29. Book with an editor—focus on the author

> Somerville, Edith, and Martin Ross. *The Big House of Inver*. Edited by
> Gifford Lewis, A. and A. Farmar, 2000.

30. Book with a translator

If the book is translated, you have two options. If the book itself is the subject of your writing, list the author first. If the translation is the subject of your writing, list the translator first.

> Mallarmé, Stéphane. *Divagations*. Translated by Barbara Johnson.
> Harvard UP, 2007.

> Johnson, Barbara, translator. *Divagations*. By Stéphane Mallarmé,
> Harvard UP, 2007.

31. Second or subsequent edition of a book

> Hawthorn, Jeremy, editor. *A Concise Glossary of Contemporary
> Literary Theory*. 3rd ed., Hodder Arnold, 2001.

32. Illustrated book or graphic narrative

After the title of the book, give the illustrator's name, preceded by *Illustrated by*.

> Strunk, William, Jr., and E. B. White. *The Elements of Style Illustrated*. Illustrated by Maira Kalman, Penguin Books, 2005.

If the emphasis is on the illustrator's work, place the illustrator's name before the title, followed by the word *illustrator*, and list the author after the title, preceded by the word *By*.

> Kalman, Maira, illustrator. *The Elements of Style Illustrated*. By William Strunk, Jr., and E. B. White, Penguin Books, 2005.

33. Sacred texts

Names of scriptural texts in general are not italicized, but specific editions are. Treat them as you would treat any other book title.

> *The New Oxford Annotated Bible*. Edited by Bruce M. Metzger and Roland E. Murphy, Oxford UP, 1991.

PARTS OF BOOKS

34. Introduction, foreword, preface, or afterword

Write the name of the part of the book after the author. Do not italicize it.

> Benstock, Sheri. Introduction. *The House of Mirth*, by Edith Wharton, Bedford, 2002, pp. 3-24.

35. Selection in an anthology or edited collection

> Sedaris, David. "Full House." *The Best American Nonrequired Reading 2004*, edited by Dave Eggers, Mariner Books, 2004, pp. 350-58.

36. More than one selection from an anthology or edited collection

Multiple selections from a single anthology can be handled by creating a complete entry for the anthology and shortened cross-references for individual works in that anthology.

> Adichie, Chimamanda Ngozi. "Half of a Yellow Sun." Eggers, pp. 1-17.
> Eggers, Dave, editor. *The Best American Nonrequired Reading 2004*. Mariner Books, 2004.
> Sedaris, David. "Full House." Eggers, pp. 350-58.

37. Article in a reference work

When the reference work is arranged alphabetically, no page numbers are needed.

"Utilitarianism." *The Columbia Encyclopedia*, 6th ed., 2001.

PARTS OF SERIES OR MULTIVOLUME WORKS

38. One volume of a multivolume work

After the title, include the volume you have used.

Samuel, Raphael. *Theatres of Memory*. Vol. 1, Verso, 1999.

39. Book in a series

Give the series name after the publishing information. If the book has a number, include it after the series name.

Watson, James. *William Faulkner: Self-Presentation and Performance*. U of Texas P, 2000. Literary Modernism.

23g Online-Only and Digital Sources

40. Page on a Web site

The basic format for citing a Web page includes the author or editor, the title of the page, the title of the site (in italics), the sponsor or publisher of the site, the date of publication, and the URL (minus *http://*). If the name of the publisher and the name of the Web site are essentially the same, skip the name of the publisher.

Boerner, Steve. "Compositions." *The Mozart Project*, 24 Sept. 2011, www.mozartproject.org/compositions/index.html.

41. Entire Web site

Boerner, Steve. *The Mozart Project*. 24 Sept. 2011, www.mozartproject.org.

42. Publication by a known author

Provide as many publication details as you can find in the source.

Davis, Diane. *DDD's Dossier: Embrace Your Rhetoricity*. 2016, faigley.dwrl.utexas.edu/davis/.

43. **Publication by a group or organization**

If a work is published by a group that is separate from the publisher, list it as the author.

> Cornell Lab of Ornithology. "State of the Birds 2014." U.S. Fish and
>   Wildlife Service, 2014, www.stateofthebirds.org/.

44. **Scholarly project or archive**

Give the name of the editor if available, the name of the scholarly project or archive in italics, and the publisher or sponsor followed by a comma. If the project was developed over time, give the range of dates and the location.

> McGann, Jerome J., editor. *The Rossetti Archive*. IATH/NINES,
>   1993-2008, www.rossettiarchive.org/.

45. **Document within a scholarly project or archive**

Give the name of the author if available, the title of the source, the year of publication, and relevant location information. Follow with the title of the scholarly project or archive in italics, and relevant details about publication and location.

> "New York Quiet." *Franklin Repository,* 5 Aug. 1863, p. 1. *Valley of
>   the Shadow*, U of Virginia, valley.lib.virginia.edu/news/fr1863/
>   pa.fr.fr.1863.08.05.xml.

46. **Social media posting**

To help readers find the posting, include a time stamp along with the date.

> The Metropolitan Museum of Art. "Immerse yourself in this 360° video
>   capturing dawn to dusk in the Temple of Dendur." *Facebook,* 31 Mar.
>   2016, 11:37 a.m., www.facebook.com/metmuseum/?fref=nf.

23h Visual and Multimedia Sources

VISUAL SOURCES

47. **Cartoon or comic strip**

Give the author's name, the title of the cartoon or comic strip in quotation marks, the paper in which it appeared (if applicable), and the date of publication.

> Trudeau, G. B. "Doonesbury." *The Washington Post,* 21 Apr. 2013, p. C15.

48. Cartoon or comic strip on the Web

Tomorrow, Tom. "Modern World." *Daily Kos*, 11 Apr. 2016,
   www.dailykos.com/blog/Tom%20Tomorrow.

49. Advertisement

Begin with the name of the advertiser or product, then the word *Advertisement.*

Nike. Advertisement. ABC, 8 Oct. 2013.

50. Map, graph, or chart

If the format is not apparent in the name of the source, container, or publisher, and if it is important to the citation, note a description (*Map, Chart,* or similar) directly after the title. If a map is published as a stand-alone item, its title should be italicized. If it is published as part of a larger source, its title should be placed in quotation marks.

Greenland. International Travel Maps, 2004.

51. Map online

"Existing Land Use: Design Lansing 2012 Comprehensive Plan."
   Map. *City of Lansing: Where Michigan Works*, www.lansingmi.gov/
   media/view/ExistingLandUseMap/7906.

52. Table reproduced in your text

This is how a table might appear in your text:

In *The Republic*, Plato explains how the three parts of the individual soul should be repeated in the structure of the ideal city-state (see Table 1).

Table 1   Plato's Politics

Soul	Reason	Courage	Appetites
State	Elite Guardians	Soldiers	Masses

Source: Richard Osborne, *Philosophy for Beginners*. Writers and Readers, 1992, p. 15.

53. Painting, sculpture, or photograph

Give the artist's name if available, the title of the work in italics, its date of creation, the name of the institution that houses the work, and the city. In the text, mentioning the work and the artist is preferable to a parenthetical citation.

Manet, Edouard. *Olympia*. 1863, Musée d'Orsay, Paris.

54. Work of art online

Mapplethorpe, Robert. *Self Portrait*. 1972. *Robert Mapplethorpe Foundation*, www.mapplethorpe.org/portfolios/self-portraits/.

55. Photograph on the Web

Swansburg, John. *The Illinois Monument at the Vicksburg National Military Park. Slate*, 2010, www.slate.com/articles/life /welltraveled/features/2010/civil_war_road_trip/the_genius_ of_grants_vicksburg_campaign.html.

56. Photograph from an archive

List the photographer, the title of the source, and the year of publication. Follow with the title of the archive (in italics) and relevant details about the publisher and location.

Parks, Gordon. *Washington, D.C. Government Charwoman*. 1942. *America from the Great Depression to World War II: Photographs from the FSA-OWI, 1935-1945,* Prints and Photographs Division, Library of Congress, www.loc.gov/pictures/item/fsa1998023725/PP/.

VIDEO SOURCES

57. Film

If you are focusing on a particular person's contribution to the film, list that name in the author position, along with a description of that person's role.

Bekmambetov, Timur, director. *Wanted*. Universal Studios, 2008.

If not, list the film title first, followed by the main contributor; then list the publisher and date.

Wanted. Directed by Timur Bekmambetov, Universal Studios, 2008.

58. Television program or series

Many people are involved in creating a television program or series. If you are focusing on a key character, name the actor and the writer who created the character. If the episode is in a series, give the season and episode numbers.

"Kaisha." *The Sopranos,* created by Terence Winter, performances by James Gandolfini, Lorraine Bracco, and Edie Falco, season 6, episode 12, HBO, 2006.

If you access the series through a streaming service like Hulu or Netflix, treat the streaming service as a secondary container and include a URL for the episode.

59. DVD or Blu-ray

Follow the format for films, but include the version information if applicable (such as *director's cut*).

> *No Country for Old Men*. Directed by Joel Coen and Ethan Coen, performances by Tommy Lee Jones, Javier Bardem, and Josh Brolin, director's cut, Paramount Pictures, 15 Apr. 2011.

60. Online video

Videos posted online on sites like YouTube may not list a creator. If they do, begin with this person's name. If not, begin the entry with the video's title, enclosed by quotation marks, and follow this with the site name (in italics), the words *uploaded by,* and the name (or screen name) of the person or organization who posted the video. Include the name of the site in italics and the date the video was posted.

> "*Dangerous Minds* Clip." *YouTube,* uploaded by byakuya20, 6 May 2008, youtu.be/DhTo79xuEk.
> Wesch, Michael. "A Vision of Students Today." *YouTube*, 28 May 2013, youtu.be/dGCJ46vyR9o.

AUDIO SOURCES

61. Musical composition

For a published musical score, follow the format for a book.

> Gershwin, George. *An American in Paris*. Gershwin 50th Anniversary ed., Warner Brothers, 1987.

62. Sound recording

> Thompson, Richard. "1952 Vincent Black Lightning." Performance by Del McCoury. *Del and the Boys*, Ceili Music, 2001.

63. Podcast

Give the name of the episode inside quotation marks and the name of the series in italics.

> Carlin, Dan. "King of Kings II." *Hardcore History*, 20 Mar. 2016, www.dancarlin.com/hardcore-history-57-kings-kings-ii/.

64. Musical, dramatic, dance, or artistic performance

> Marcus, Greil. *Lipstick Traces*. Adapted by Kirk Lynn, directed by Shawn Sides, performances by Lana Lesley and Jason Liebrecht, 31 Aug. 2000, Off Center, Austin.

65. **Speech, debate, mediated discussion, or public talk**

Indicate the venue and city. If the city is part of the venue name, there is no need to list it twice.

> Clinton, Hillary Rodham. "Frontlines and Frontiers: Making Human Rights a Human Reality." 6 Dec. 2012, Dublin City University.

23i Other Sources

GOVERNMENT DOCUMENTS

66. **Government documents other than the *Congressional Record***

If you are citing a congressional document other than the *Congressional Record*, be sure to identify the congress and, when necessary, the session.

> Malveaux, Julianne. "Changes in the Labor Market Status of Black Women." *A Report of the Study Group on Affirmative Action to the Committee on Education and Labor*. Government Printing Office, 1987. 100th Congress, 1st session, House Report 100-L, pp. 231-55.

67. ***Congressional Record***

> Congressional Record. 8 Feb. 2000, pp. 1222-46.

68. **Government publication**

Government publications are issued in many formats. If you cannot locate the author of the document, give the name of the government and the agency that published it.

> United States, Department of Health and Human Services, Center for Disease Control and Prevention. "Investigation of Outbreak of Infections Caused by *Salmonella* Saintpaul." *Salmonella,* 3 July 2008, www.cdc.gov/salmonella/saintpaul/jalapeno/archive/070308.html.

69. **Legal case from a library database**

> Bilski v. Kappos. 561 US 08-964. Supreme Court of the United States, 28 June 2010. Legal Information Institute/Cornell University Law, www.law.cornell.edu/supct/cert/08-964.

BROCHURES, PAMPHLETS, AND LETTERS

70. **Brochure or pamphlet**

> Watkins Health Center. *The Common Cold*. Univeristy of Kansas, 2013.

71. **Published letter**

Wilde, Oscar. "To Lord Alfred Douglas." 17 Feb. 1895. *The Complete Letters of Oscar Wilde,* edited by Merlin Holland and Rupert Hart-Davis, Henry Holt, 2000, pp. 632-33.

72. **Unpublished letter**

Welty, Eudora. Letter to Elizabeth Bowen. 1 May 1951, Harry Ransom Humanities Research Center.

73. **Personal interview**

Bieber, Justin. Personal interview. 5 Mar. 2013.

74. **Broadcast interview**

Fey, Tina. Interview by Terry Gross. *Fresh Air*, National Public Radio, 25 Jan. 2013.

DISSERTATIONS AND PUBLISHED CONFERENCE PROCEEDINGS

75. **Published dissertation or thesis**

Mason, Jennifer. *Civilized Creatures: Animality, Cultural Power, and American Literature, 1850-1901*. Dissertation, U of Texas at Austin, 2000. UMI, 2000.

76. **Unpublished dissertation or thesis**

Schorn, Susan. "The Merciful Construction of Good Women: Actresses in the Marriage-Plot Novel." Dissertation, U of Texas at Austin, 2000.

77. **Published proceedings of a conference**

Abadie, Ann, and Robert Hamblin, editors. *Faulkner in the 21st Century: Proceedings of the 27th Faulkner and Yoknapatawpha Conference, Aug. 10-16, 2000*. U of Mississippi P, 2003.

COMPANY REPORT

78. **Company report from a library database**

Nike, Inc. SWOT Analysis. 2016, pp. 1-8. *Business Source Complete*, proxy.wexler.hunter.cuny.edu/ebscohost.com/direct=true&db= bth&AN=115360677&site=ehost-live.

23j Informational Notes

MLA style makes no recommendations about formatting or inclusion of notes. It is designed to avoid the need for either footnotes or endnotes. Documentation should be handled using in-text citations and a list of works cited. However, two kinds of notes sometimes appear in MLA style. Notes may be placed at the bottom of the page or at the end of the paper.

Content notes supply additional information that would interrupt the flow of the text, yet may be important to provide the context of a source.

> Much speculation has blamed electronic media, especially television, for an alleged decline in literacy, following Newton N. Minow's famous 1961 description of television as a "vast wasteland."[1]

The note explains who Minow was and why the remark was newsworthy.

> 1. Minow, the newly appointed chairman of the Federal Communications Commission, told the assembled executives of the National Association of Broadcasters in May 1961 that "[w]hen television is bad, nothing is worse" (Adams). Minow's efforts to upgrade programming were met with cries of censorship from the television industry, and Minow resigned two years later.

You need to include any sources you use in notes in the list of works cited.

> ### Work Cited
>
> Adams, Val. "F.C.C. Head Bids TV Men, Reform 'Vast Wasteland.'" *The New York Times*, 10 May 1961, p. 11.

Bibliographic notes give either evaluative comments about sources or additional references.

> "Fordism" is a summary term for the system of mass production consolidated by Henry Ford in the early decades of the twentieth century.[1]

The note gives the origin of the term "Fordism."

> 1. The term "Fordism" was first used by Italian political theorist Antonio Gramsci in his prison notebooks, written while he was jailed under Mussolini's fascist dictatorship.

Work Cited

Gramsci, Antonio. *Selections from the Prison Notebooks of Antonio Gramsci.* Edited and translated by Quintin Hoare and Geoffrey Nowell Smith, International Publishers, 1971.

23k Sample Research Paper with MLA Documentation

Chapters 17 through 22 discuss how to plan and write a research paper. The following research paper, written by Gabriella Lopez, makes a proposal argument. The paper is annotated to show specific features of MLA style and to show how the works-cited page is organized.

FORMATTING A RESEARCH PAPER IN MLA STYLE

If your teacher has specific requirements for formatting, follow them. If not, here are general guidelines for formatting a research paper.

- **Use white, 8½-by-11-inch paper.** Don't use colored or lined paper.
- **Double-space everything—the title, headings, body of the paper, quotations, and works-cited list.** Set the line spacing in your program for double spacing and leave it there.

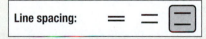

- **Put your last name and the page number at the top of every page, aligned with the right margin,** one-half inch from the top of the page. Most programs have a header command that will automatically put a header with the page number on every page.
- **Specify 1-inch margins.** One-inch margins are the default setting for most programs.
- **Do not justify (make even) the right margin.** Justifying the right margin throws off the spacing between words and makes your paper harder to read. Use the left-align setting instead.

- **Indent the first line of each paragraph one-half inch.** Set the paragraph indent command or the tab on the ruler on your screen at one-half inch.

- **Use the same readable typeface throughout your paper.** Use a standard font such as Times New Roman, 12 point.

- **Use block format for quotations longer than four lines.** See page 237, example #8.

- **Include your name, course information, and date.** Unless your instructor asks for a separate title page, put 1 inch from the top of the page your name, your instructor's name, the course, and the date on separate lines. Center your title on the next line. Do not underline your title or put it inside quotation marks.

⬛eck with your ⬛structor to find ⬛t whether you ⬛ed a separate ⬛e page.

1″

1/2″

Lopez 1

Include your last name and page number as page header, beginning with the first page, 1/2″ from the top.

Gabriella Lopez

Professor Kimbro

English 1102

6 May 2016

⬛nter the title. ⬛ not underline ⬛e title, put it ⬛side quotation ⬛arks, or type it ⬛all capital ⬛ters. It should ⬛e no special ⬛matting.

1/2″

Establishing a Campus Garden

◄► When high school seniors begin to look at colleges and universities, they consider many factors: location, academics, and the quality of campus life, including food service. Now prospective students are also considering sustainability. Sustainability has become a buzzword in many fields, including

1″

architecture, energy, urban planning, and nutrition. And it seems to have a particular popularity on college campuses (Egan). According to a 2006 article in *USA Today*, students are increasingly interested in schools with "green" practices, which offer local, sustainable, and organic options in their food service (Horovitz). In 2009, the *Princeton Review* found that 66% of high

1″

1″

Specify 1"
margins all
around.
Double-space
everything.

school–age college applicants and parents surveyed "would find information about a college's dedication to the environment useful in their college selection process" (Klinck).

Higher education is responding. Not only do colleges and universities lead other institutions and industries with 3,850 LEED (Leadership in Energy and Environmental Design) certified buildings (Klinck), and show commitment to recycling and waste-reduction programs, but schools are also increasingly devoting at least a portion of food budgets to buying from local farms and producers (Pino). And this trend should only grow: representatives from the Association for the Advancement of Sustainability in Higher Education worked with Food Alliance to create *A Guide to Developing a Sustainable Food Purchasing Policy*, which helps colleges develop policies that will suit their campuses and communities (Buck et al.). Some schools, most notably Yale University, have even established farms and gardens on or near campus that serve as living classrooms for environmental studies and provide food for students as well as the community.

Indent each
paragraph 1/2".

"Going green" is not easy, nor is it inexpensive. For those reasons, many schools, including our own, are finding it difficult to move beyond campus-wide recycling programs to other initiatives such as increasing the amount of local organic foods in the dining halls. The fact that many colleges contract with

Lopez 3

outside food service vendors makes this goal even more difficult. An alternative approach, however, can provide both fresh, healthy food and hands-on experience in environmental stewardship. Establishing a small organic campus garden is a low-cost, high-yield way to support our school's mission, our students, the local community, and the global environment.

Our school in particular has a stated commitment to creating a campus in which students feel safe and sustained in an environment that is, according to the Web page, "contingent on the every-day learning process." One of the immediate benefits to establishing a campus organic garden is promoting a healthy relationship to food. According to a survey of 2,200 American college students, a significant number of women and a smaller group of men have "major concerns about eating and food with respect to both weight and health" (Rozin et al. 132). The negative feelings about food that result from these concerns can lead to eating disorders, primarily in young women (140). In short, Americans have become neurotic about eating. Michael Pollan attributes this anxiety to "nutritionism": the belief, fueled by food scientists and the food industry, that nutrients and the energy (or calorie) count is more important than actual food, and since nutrients exist at the molecular level, we believe we need to eat "scientifically," under the direction of the experts (8). This promotion

Lopez's thesis appears here, at the end of her third paragraph.

Cite publications within the text by the name of the author (or authors).

Lopez 4

of discrete nutrients over whole food has led to the industrialization of food production—more processed foods, more artificial grains, more chemicals to raise animals and vegetables in vast "monocultures," more sugars and fats, and less variety in our diet that has been reduced to a glut of wheat, corn, and soy (10). Thus, not only is our industrialized diet making us physically sick; in fact, it is also making us emotionally unhealthy. Pollan observes that food concerns much more than nutrition: "Food is all about pleasure, about community, about family and spirituality, about our relationship to the natural world, and about expressing our identity" (8).

Colleges are becoming increasingly aware of the relationships among individual, social, and environmental health, and that projects like campus farms and gardens serve not only students, but also the local population, and even the planet (Pino). The Dartmouth Organic Farm Web site points to these connections:

> The very nature of an agricultural enterprise lies in the intersection of culture and the environment, to identify and respond to the needs of a society while recognizing the limits and demands of the immediate, local ecosystem. A farm is one of the last institutionalized vestiges of our direct connection to the natural world that surrounds and supports us. ("Dartmouth")

Do not include a page number for items without pagination, such as Web sites.

Quotations of more than four lines should be indented 1/2". Do not use quotation marks. Introduce block quotations rather than just dropping them into the text.

Lopez 5

There is evidence to support these claims. A study in the United Kingdom found that people with the highest levels of "ecoliteracy" (accumulated ecological knowledge) acquired that knowledge through direct experience and talking with others rather than from schooling and television (Pilgrim et al.).

One of the missions of our school, as stated on our Web site, is "the development of men and women dedicated to the service of others." Establishing a campus organic farm that could immediately serve as a model of sound nutritional and environmental practices, and perhaps one day provide food for local relief organizations, certainly supports this mission.

Another benefit to establishing a campus organic garden is that it would provide educational opportunities to students who are interested in the growing field of sustainability. As concern about the environment grows, colleges and universities are beginning to incorporate sustainability into their programs. Environmental studies classes and majors are growing and diversifying. Students can now get MBAs in sustainable-business practices and train to build and operate wind turbines, among other things (Berman). In the area of public policy, a major in this field is also becoming more valuable. *The New York Times Magazine* notes this cultural trend: "Time was, environmental-studies majors ran campus recycling programs. Now they run national campaigns" ("Learn").

Sources not identified with an author are referenced by a shortened title.

Lopez 6

Because our school is much smaller and has fewer resources than Yale or most of the other schools with well-known and successful sustainable food projects including Dartmouth, Rutgers, Dickinson, Boston College, Colby, Columbia, Wisconsin-Madison, Iowa State, UCSD (University of California, San Diego), UCLA, and the University of Nebraska, establishing a farm or a large garden seems improbable. I propose that we establish a campus garden following the very simple principles of organic "square-foot" gardening. Square-foot gardening is raised-bed gardening that takes place in 6- to 12-inch-deep frames that have been segmented into a grid (see fig. 1). The size of each square in the grid depends on what plants are planted there; certain plants require larger and deeper grids (Bartholomew 15-16). The main benefit of square-foot gardening is that one can grow the same amount of produce in a 140-square-foot grid that is typically grown in the average 700-square-foot, single-row garden (42). Thus, a garden—or multiple gardens, placed strategically according to the sunlight needs of the plants—can be fitted into small spaces around campus. We don't need to find one large, dedicated space. Another benefit is that since the beds are filled with a high-nutrient mix of compost, peat moss, and vermiculite, the quality of soil the beds are built on top of does not matter (30-31). Thus, no money needs to be spent on testing the soil, as Yale and other schools had to do when

Give page numbers for paraphrases as well as direct quotations.

Lopez 7

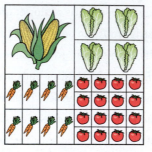

Fig. 1. The grid in a square-foot gardening plot is divided according to the mature size of each plant.

they chose the land for their farms. In fact, the beds can be placed on pavement, a patio, or even a roof (51). The main considerations are sunlight and water drainage. The frames can even be built to be portable—again, requiring no dedication of a large space for the garden.

Another great benefit to the square-foot garden is that the smaller beds are easily adapted to grow seasonal crops, making it easier to recognize and explore the foods within our foodshed, or regional food chain, as the locavore movement encourages (Maiser). The smaller size of the beds also means that crops and harvests can be staggered. Regular row planting replicates the same kinds of yields as industrial farming, meaning that an entire row of the same item is harvested all at once, which can lead to waste. Staggering crops ensures that only what is needed is grown and harvested (Bartholomew 18), and staggering maximizes use of the space. For example, planting fast-growing plants that

Lopez 8

mature quickly between rows of slower growing plants means that early crops can be harvested and plants removed before the slower growers need the space (Damiano). Finally, the smaller beds and loose soil reduce the amount of labor needed. There is no need for tilling, and weeding is much easier. Also, the high-quality soil mixture requires no fertilizer, and planting pest-resistant plants, such as marigolds, alongside the produce and herbs eliminates the need for pesticides. In short, square-foot gardening is ideal for a small group of beginning gardeners (Bartholomew 13). Those who worry about overcrowding their garden can use gardening templates, as amateur gardeners like TheOldWoodworker show in their *YouTube* videos (00:02:13-00:05:00).

Gardening is still a fickle enterprise, and beginners (as most student volunteers will be) will have difficulty assessing the right amount to plant and anticipate harvesting. In *All New Square Foot Gardening: Grow More in Less Space*, Mel Bartholomew says that it is best to start small in the spring season, with a garden about one-third of the ideal size. For phase two, the summer season, more beds can be added as needed or beds can be relocated or reconfigured. For phase three, the fall season, beds can again be added, relocated, or reconfigured as needed (Bartholomew 44).

Even though our campus organic garden will not be built on the same scale as at the larger schools, much can still be learned from them, especially regarding how they gain support and how they

Lopez 9

maintain interest in their project. The key to both
Yale's Sustainable Food Project and Dartmouth's
Organic Farm is activist students. Unlike student
activists of the past, however, today's students
are working with school administrators to make
change possible. And school administrators are seeing
the surge in green activism on campus as something
that could appeal to prospective freshmen and alumni
alike (Lewington). Establishing a core group of
students responsible for shepherding the project is
essential; these students can then start finding allies
on campus. Other successful activist student groups are
a good possibility, as are like-minded faculty, and food
service administration and staff.

Once support is gained from students, faculty,
staff, and administration, the logistics of building
the gardens can get under way. Little space and few
resources and tools are necessary for square-foot
gardening, but supplies such as building materials,
ingredients for the soil mixture, and seeds will still
have to be gathered. Frames for the beds can be made
from discarded building materials as long as wood is
not painted or treated (Bartholomew 57). Compost for
the soil mixture can be made from existing kitchen
waste. Seeds, peat moss, vermiculite, and small tools
are not expensive and can be bought with donated
funds. Partnering with a community organic gardening
organization or individuals in the community may
yield not only donated or discounted supplies but also

training for student volunteers and a tie to the local community, which can help maintain support for the project in the long term.

Maintaining interest is important to keeping support, getting volunteer labor, and allowing for future growth. Holding events is one way to keep the excitement going. Yale's Sustainable Food Project offers cooking classes, uses a pizza oven installed on the farm to bake pizzas every Friday to thank volunteers, and even hosts an annual pig roast to celebrate the end of classes (Samadzadeh). Events of this scale are probably not an option for a smaller garden, but working with food service to create theme menus, such as Colby's "Garlic Fest," can attract attention (Jacobs). In addition, highlighting the farm or garden during student orientation and during parent weekends not only helps garner financial support, but also attracts new volunteers. Finally, inviting members of the community to visit and donating produce to local organizations will publicize the garden and gain further support.

As sustainability becomes increasingly important in society, colleges and universities have increased responsibility not only to be models of sustainable practices, but also to train students for jobs in an economy and environment informed by sustainability. The Sustainable Endowments Institute urges, "Colleges and universities, as leaders of innovation in our society, have the potential to demonstrate

Lopez 11

sustainable principles in their campus operations and
endowment policies. Their examples can provide a
road map for others to follow" ("Frequently"). For our
college to remain competitive with other schools, we
need to increase our commitment to these important
ideas. Establishing a campus garden should be the
first step.

If a source consists of a single page, do not give the page number in the citation.

Lopez 12

Works Cited

Bartholomew, Mel. *All New Square Foot Gardening: Grow
  More in Less Space*. Cool Spring Press, 2006.

Berman, Jillian. "Sustainability Could Secure a Good
  Future: College Students Flock to 'Green' Degrees,
  Careers." *USA Today*, 3 Apr. 2009, p. 7D. *LexisNexis
  Academic*, www.lexisnexis.com/lnacui2api/auth/
  checkbrowser.do.

Buck, Matthew, et. al. *A Guide to Developing a
  Sustainable Food Purchasing Policy*. 2007,
  www.sustainablefoodpolicy.org/.

Damiano, Jessica. "Growing Vegetables in Small Spaces:
  Train Them up Trellises and Plant Crops in Succession."
  Newsday, 2 May 2010, www.newsday.com/services/
  test/2.811/2.1167/growing-vegetables-in-small-
  spaces-1.1883928.

"Dartmouth Organic Farm." *Dartmouth Group Directory*.
  Dartmouth College, 2012, dgd.dartmouth.edu/
  group/202.

Center "Works Cited" on a new page.

Double-space all entries. Indent all but the first line in each entry 1/2".

Alphabetize entries by the last names of the authors or by the first important word in the title if no author is listed.

Italicize the titles of books and periodicals.

Lopez 13

Egan, Timothy. "The Greening of America's Campuses."

   The New York Times, 8 Jan. 2008, www.nytimes.com/

   2006/01/08/education/edlife/egan_

   environment.html.

"Frequently Asked Questions." *The College Sustainability*

   Report Card. Sustainable Endowments Institute,

   2007-2011, www.greenreportcard.org/about/

   faq.html.

Horovitz, Bruce. "More University Students Call for

   Organic, 'Sustainable' Food." *USA Today*, 26 Sept.

   2006, usatoday.com/money/food/2006-09-26-

   college-food-usat_x.htm.

Jacobs, Ruth. "Organic Garden Gives Back." *Colby Magazine*,

   vol. 97, no. 3, 2008, issuu.com/colbycollegelibrary/

   docs/2008_v097_n3/10.

Klinck, Betty. "Find a Green College: Check! Princeton

   Review Helps Applicants Who Seek Sustainability."

   USA Today, 20 Apr. 2010, p. 7D. *LexisNexis Academic*,

   www.lexisnexis.com/lnacui2api/api/version1/

   getDocCui?lni=7Y8S-GW20-Y9M0-51MP&csi=

   270944,270077,110598411&hl=t&hv=t&hnsd=

   f&hns=t&hgn=t&oc=00240&perma=true.

"Learn." *The New York Times Magazine*, 20 Apr. 2008,

   www.nytimes.com/2008/04/20/magazine/

   20Learn-btext.html.

Lewington, Jennifer. "Students Are at the Forefront of

   the Campus Green Revolution." *The Globe and Mail*,

   22 Aug 2012, www.theglobeandmail.com/news/

   national/education/students-at-the-forefront-of-

   the-campus-green-revolution/article4192784/.

Lopez 14

Maiser, Jennifer. "10 Reasons to Eat Local Food." *Life Begins @ 30*, 29 Aug. 2005, www.lifebeginsat30.com/jen/2005/08/10_reasons_to_e.html.

Pilgrim, Sarah, et al. "A Cross-Regional Assessment of the Factors Affecting Ecoliteracy: Implications for Policy and Practice." *Ecological Applications*, vol. 17, no. 6, 2007, pp. 1742-51.

Pino, Carl. "Sustainability on the Menu: College Cafeterias Are Buying Local and Going Organic." *E-The Environmental Magazine,* Mar.-Apr. 2008, www.emagazine.com/includes/print-article/magazine-archive/6625/.

Pollan, Michael. *In Defense of Food: An Eater's Manifesto*. Penguin Books, 2008.

Rozin, Paul, Rebecca Bauer, and Dana Catanese. "Food and Life, Pleasure and Worry, among American College Students: Gender Differences and Regional Similarities." *Journal of Personality and Social Psychology*, vol. 85, no. 1, 2003, pp. 132-41. *PsycARTICLES*, doi:10.1037/0022-3514.85.1.132.

Samadzadeh, Nozlee. "Farm Update: The Third Annual Jack Hitt Annual Last Day of Classes Pig Roast." *Yale Sustainable Food Project Student Blog*, 3 May 2010, yalesustainablefoodproject.wordpress.com/2010/05/03/farm-update-the-third-annual-jack-hitt-annual-last-day-of-classes-pig-roast/.

TheOldWoodworker. "Square Foot Gardening Templates." *YouTube*, 22 Feb 2016, youtu.be/LzhR66qY46I.

Go through your text and make sure all the sources you have used are in the list of works cited.

FORMATTING THE WORKS CITED IN MLA STYLE

- **Begin the works-cited list on a new page.** Insert a page break before you start the works-cited page.

- **Center "Works Cited" on the first line at the top of the page.**

- **Double-space all entries.**

- **Alphabetize each entry by the last name of the author** or, if no author is listed, by the first content word in the title (ignore *a, an, the*).

- **Indent all but the first line in each entry one-half inch.**

- **Italicize the titles of books and periodicals.**

- **If an author has more than one entry,** list the entries in alphabetical order by title. Use three hyphens in place of the author's name for the second and subsequent entries.

  Murphy, Dervla. *Cameroon with Egbert*. Overlook Press, 1990.

  ---. *Full Tilt: Ireland to India with a Bicycle*. John Murray, 1965.

- **Go through your paper to check that each source you have used is in the works-cited list.**

APA, CMS, and CSE

24 APA Documentation

QUICK*TAKE*

After reading this chapter, you should be able to . . .

- Recognize in-text citations in APA style (24a)
- Recognize reference list entries in APA style (24b)
- Construct in-text citations (24c)
- Construct reference list entries (24d)
- Create citations for print periodical sources (24e)
- Create citations for print books and nonperiodical sources (24f)
- Create citations for online sources (24g)
- Create citations for visual and multimedia sources (24h)
- Format a paper in APA style (24i)

APA DOCUMENTATION MAP

1 | Collect the right information

For every source you need to have

- the name of the author or authors,
- the full title, and
- complete publication information.

For instructions go to the illustrated examples in 24d of the four major source types:

- **PERIODICAL SOURCES**
- **BOOKS AND NONPERIODICAL SOURCES**
- **ONLINE SOURCES**

For other kinds of sources such as visual and multimedia sources, see the index of references at the end of 24d and the examples in 24h.

2 | Cite sources in two places

Remember, this is a two-part process.

To create citations

(1) in the **body of your paper**, go to 24c.
(2) in a **list of references at the end of your paper**, go to 24d.

Social sciences disciplines—including government, linguistics, psychology, sociology, and education—frequently use the American Psychological Association (APA) documentation style. The APA style is similar to the MLA style in many ways. Both styles use parenthetical citations in the body of the text, with complete bibliographical citations in the list of references at the end. Both styles avoid using footnotes for references.

If you have questions that the examples in this chapter do not address, consult the *Publication Manual of the American Psychological Association*, sixth edition (2010).

3 | Find the right model citations

You'll find **illustrated examples of sources** in 24d.

Once you match your source to one of those examples, you can move on to more specific examples:

- **PERIODICAL SOURCES;** go to 24e.
- **BOOKS AND NONPERIODICAL SOURCES;** go to 24f.
- **ONLINE SOURCES;** go to 24g.

A complete list of examples is found in the index of references at the end of 24d.

4 | Format your paper

You will find a **sample research paper in APA style** and instructions on formatting the body of your paper and your references list in 24i.

A note about footnotes:
APA style does not use footnotes for documentation. Use in-text citations instead (see 24c).

Writer at Work

Jacob Pietsch chose to make a proposal argument that policymakers in the United States should consider high-speed rail as a sound investment in infrastructure. He wanted to argue that public support now exists for high-speed rail that policymakers could leverage. You can read the complete paper in 24i at the end of this chapter.

How to quote and cite a source in the text of an APA-style paper

Jacob searched for articles on the library database *Academic Search Complete* using the search terms "high-speed rail" and "investments." He found the article below and printed a copy using the PDF option, which shows the article in its original format.

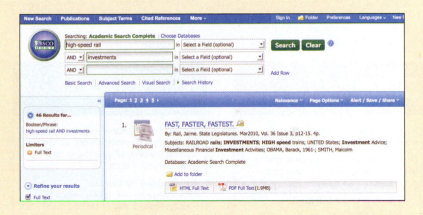

To support his argument that many Americans favor high-speed rail, he wanted to quote the statistic that the states collectively submitted $57 billion in funding requests for the first $8 billion of federal money designated for high-speed rail.

Jacob can either (1) mention author Jaime Rall in the text of his paper, followed by the date of publication (see page 312), or (2) place the author's name and date of publication inside parentheses following the quotation. At the end of the sentence, he must include the page number where he found the quotation inside parentheses.

Author's name in signal phrase

Jaime Rall (2010) reports that "for the initial $8 billion in federal stimulus money, states submitted 259 applications for a total of $57 billion" (p. 13).

OR

Author's name in parenthetical citation

State-level interest in securing federal funding for rail projects was also evidenced by 259 applications (totaling a value of $57 billion requested) for the initial $8 billion in federal stimulus money (Rall, 2010, p. 13).

If Jacob includes a quotation that is forty words or longer, he must double-space and indent the quotation in his paper one-half inch (see example on p. 311).

Include in-text citations for summaries and paraphrases

To argue that the public support for high-speed rail remains untapped, Jacob points out how limited high-speed rail technologies are in the United States. He used information from an article by Tim De Chant, who is a journalist and creator of *Per Square Mile*. The wording was not especially important, so Jacob summarized De Chant's reflections.

With such interest in high-speed rail systems, it is surprising that the only true high-speed rail currently operating in the United States is the Acela Express in the Northeast Corridor (De Chant, 2011).

24b Creating the List of References

Writer at Work

Jacob was ready to create an entry for the list of references at the end of his paper. Jacob kept a copy of this screenshot from his library's online journals and made notes about the proper information to create the entry. He used the instructions in 24d to format the citation.

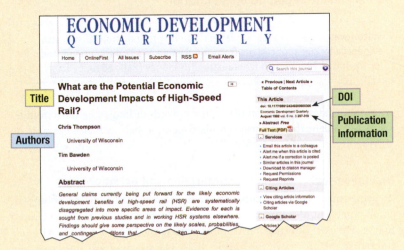

Jacob asked a series of questions to create an entry for this source in his list of references.

1. What information do I need to pull from this screenshot?

For a source like this article from an online database, he needs to know five things: (1) what type of source it is; (2) the author(s); (3) the title; (4) the publication information; and (5) the DOI.

2. I know this is from my library's online database, but that could be one of several different types of sources. What kind of source is this?

The kinds of sources you'll find in a database are an article from a periodical (newspaper or a scholarly journal), a business or financial report, a legal case, or an abstract. Jacob's source type is an article.

3. Now how do I find the author's name?

If the author's name is not under the title, look for a bold heading that says something like "AUTHOR" or "BYLINE." If more than one author is listed, take note of all names listed.

4. What is the title of my source?

If the title is not immediately evident, look for a heading that says "TITLE" or "HEADLINE."

5. Where do I find the publication information?

The name and date of the periodical are usually listed at the top of the page but sometimes are found at the bottom. In this case the page number is listed under "This Article."

6. Where do I find the DOI?

The DOI is often listed along with information on the publisher at the top of the page, but sometimes it may be located at the bottom or in a side bar. In Jacob's case, the DOI for the article by Thompson and Bawden is located in the right-hand navigation column along with the article's publication information.

Jacob listed the required information.

Authors	Thompson, C., & Bawden, T.
Date of Publication	1992
Title of article	What are the potential economic development impacts of high-speed rail?
Publication information	
Name of journal	*Economic Development Quarterly*
Volume and number	6(3)
Pages	297–319
DOI	10.1177 /08912424920060306

Then he used the instructions in 24d to format his citation. You can see Jacob's complete list of references in the sample paper at the end of this chapter (24i).

Thompson, C., & Bawden, T. (1992). What are the potential economic development impacts of high-speed rail? *Economic Development Quarterly, 6*(3), 297–319. doi:10.1177/08912424920060306

24c In-Text Citations in APA Style

APA style emphasizes the date of publication. When you cite an author's name in the body of your paper, always follow it with the date of publication. Notice too that APA style includes the abbreviation for page (p.) in front of the page number. A comma separates each element of the citation.

> Zukin (2004) observes that teens today begin to shop for themselves at age 13 or 14, "the same age when lower-class children, in the past, became apprentices or went to work in factories" (p. 50).

If the author's name is not mentioned in the sentence, the reference looks like this:

> One sociologist notes that teens today begin to shop for themselves at age 13 or 14, "the same age when lower-class children, in the past, became apprentices or went to work in factories" (Zukin, 2004, p. 50).

The corresponding entry in the references list would be

> Zukin, S. (2004). *Point of purchase: How shopping changed American culture.* New York, NY: Routledge.

Paraphrase, summary, or short quotation

In APA style a short quotation has fewer than forty words.

> "The appeal of a shopping spree," one sociologist comments, "is not that you'll buy a lot of stuff; the appeal is that, among all the stuff you buy, you'll find what you truly desire" (Zukin, 2004, p. 112).

The author's name is provided in the parenthetical reference.

In this example, the author's name is provided inside the parentheses at the end of the sentence. Put the author's name in a signal phrase in your sentence when you want to give an affiliation or title to indicate the authority of your source. See the following example.

"The appeal of a shopping spree," noted sociologist Sharon Zukin (2004) comments, "is not that you'll buy a lot of stuff; the appeal is that, among all the stuff you buy, you'll find what you truly desire" (p. 112).

Put the page number in parentheses after the quotation. Note that the period comes after the parentheses.

When the author of the quotation is clearly named in the sentence, add the date in parentheses after the author's name.

Quotations forty words or longer

Orlean (2001) has attempted to explain the popularity of the painter Thomas Kinkade:

> People like to own things they think are valuable. . . . The high price of limited editions is part of their appeal; it implies that they are choice and exclusive, and that only a certain class of people will be able to afford them. (p. 128)

The sentence introducing the quotation names the author.

Note that the period appears before the parentheses in an indented "block" quote.

The date appears in parentheses immediately following the author's name.

Index of in-text citations

1. Author named in your text 288
2. Author not named in your text 288
3. Work by a single author 288
4. Work by two authors 288
5. Work by three to five authors 288
6. Work by six or more authors 288
7. Work by a group or organization 288
8. Work by an unknown author 289
9. Two works by one author published in the same year 289
10. Parts of an electronic source 289
11. Two or more sources within the same sentence 289
12. Work cited in another source 289

See also entries 48, 49, 50, 53, 60.

Sample in-text citations

1. Author named in your text

The influential sociologist Daniel Bell (1973) noted a shift in the United States to the "postindustrial society" (p. 3).

2. Author not named in your text

In 2012, the Gallup poll reported that 56% of adults in the United States think secondhand smoke is "very harmful," compared with only 36% in 1994 (Saad, 1997, p. 4).

3. Work by a single author

(Bell, 1973, p. 3)

4. Work by two authors

List both authors' last names, joined with an ampersand.

(Suzuki & Irabu, 2013, p. 404)

When you cite the authors' names in a sentence, use *and* in place of the ampersand.

Suzuki and Irabu (2013) report . . .

5. Work by three to five authors

The authors' last names follow the order of the title page.

(Francisco, Vaughn, & Romano, 2012, p. 7)

Subsequent references can use the first author's name and *et al.*

(Francisco et al., 2012, p. 17)

6. Work by six or more authors

Use the first author's last name and *et al.* for all in-text references.

(Swallit et al., 2014, p. 49)

7. Work by a group or organization

Identify the group in the text and place the page number in parentheses.

The National Organization for Women (2001) observed that this "generational shift in attitudes towards marriage and childrearing" will have profound consequences (p. 325).

If you use the name of the group in an in-text citation, the first time you cite the source put its acronym (if there is one) in brackets.

> (National Organization for Women [NOW], 2001)

Use the acronym in subsequent in-text citations.

> (NOW, 2001)

8. Work by an unknown author

Use a shortened version of the title (or the full title if it is short) in place of the author's name. Capitalize all key words in the title. If it is an article title, place it inside quotation marks.

> ("Derailing the Peace Process," 2013, p. 44)

9. Two works by one author published in the same year

Assign the dates letters (*a*, *b*, etc.) according to their alphabetical arrangement in the references list.

> The majority of books written about coauthorship focus on partners of the same sex (Laird, 2007a, p. 351).

10. Parts of an electronic source

If an online or other electronic source does not provide page numbers, use the paragraph number preceded by the abbreviation *para.*

> (Robinson, 2013, para. 7)

11. Two or more sources within the same sentence

Place each citation directly after the statement it supports.

> Some surveys report an increase in homelessness rates (Alford, 2004) while others chart a slight decrease (Rice, 2006a) . . .

If you need to cite two or more works within the same parentheses, list them in the order in which they appear in the references list.

> (Alford, 2004; Rice, 2006a)

12. Work cited in another source

> Saunders and Kellman's study (as cited in Rice, 2006a)

24d Illustrated Samples and Index of References in APA Style

Periodical sources

Entry in references list

Resnik, L., Gray, M., & Borgia, M. (2011). "Measurement of community reintegration in sample of severely wounded servicemembers." *Journal of Rehabilitation Research and Development 48*(2), 89–102. doi:10.1682/JRRD.2010.04.0070

Elements of the citation

Author's Name

The author's last name comes first, followed by the author's initials.

Join two authors' names with a comma and an ampersand.

Date of Publication

Give the year the work was published in parentheses.

Newspapers and popular magazines are referenced by the day, month, and year of publication.

Title of Article

- Do not use quotation marks. If there is a book title in the article title, italicize it.

- Titles of articles in APA style follow standard sentence capitalization.

Publication Information

Name of journal

- Italicize the journal name. Note the use of capitalization.

- Put a comma after the journal name.

Volume, issue, and page numbers

- Italicize the volume number.

- If each issue of the journal begins on page 1, give the issue number in parentheses, followed by a comma.

- If the article has been assigned a DOI (digital object identifier), list it after the page numbers but without a period at the end. APA now recommends listing DOIs as URLs. Use the new format if available: http://dx.doi.org/10.XXXX/JXXXX

Find the right example as your model (you may need to refer to more than one model)

What type of article do you have?

A scholarly journal article or abstract?

- For an article in a journal with continuous pagination, see example #19.
- For an article in a journal paginated by issue, see example #20.
- For a weekly, biweekly, or monthly publication, see examples #21–#22.
- For an abstract, see examples #23–#24.

A newspaper article, review, or letter to the editor

- For a newspaper article, see example #25.
- For a review, see example #26.
- For a letter to the editor or editorial, see example #27.

A government document?

See examples #48–#49.

How many authors are listed?

- One, two, or more authors: see examples #13–#15.
- Unknown author: see example #17.

Books and nonperiodical sources

Title of book → FIVE MINDS FOR THE
FUTURE

Author's name → Howard Gardner

HARVARD BUSINESS SCHOOL PRESS
BOSTON, MASSACHUSETTS

↑ Publisher and place of publication

Entry in references list

Gardner, H. (2007). *Five minds for the future.* Boston, MA: Harvard
Business School Press.

Elements of the citation

Author's or Editor's Name

The author's last name comes first, followed by a comma and the author's initials.

For an editor, put the abbreviation *Ed.* in parentheses after the name. **Kavanagh, P. (Ed.).**

Year of Publication

- Give the year the work was copyrighted in parentheses.
- If no copyright year is given, write *n.d.* ("no date") in parentheses.

Book Title

- Italicize the title.
- Titles of books in APA style follow standard sentence capitalization: Capitalize only the first word, proper nouns, and the first word after a colon.

Publication Information

Place of publication

- For all books, list the city with a two-letter state abbreviation (or full country name) after the city name.
- If more than one city is given on the title page, list only the first.

Publisher's name

Do not shorten or abbreviate words like *University* or *Press*. Omit words such as *Co.*, *Inc.*, and *Publishers*.

Find the right example as your model (you may need to refer to more than one model)

How many authors are listed?

- One, two, or more authors: see examples #28–#31.
- Unknown or group author: see examples #33–34.

Do you have only a part of a book?

- For a chapter written by the same author as the book, see example #40.
- For a chapter in an edited collection, see example #41.

Do you have a printed document other than a book or article?

- For a technical or research report, see example #44.
- For a dissertation or thesis, see example #47.
- For a government document, see example #48.

Do you have an e-book?

- For an e-book with a DOI, see example #38.
- For an e-book with no DOI assigned, see example #39.

Online sources

Journal title

Title of article

Author

Date

Volume, page, and DOI

Entry in references list

Tenenbaum, D. J. (2005). Global warming: Arctic climate: The heat is on. *Environmental Health Perspectives*, 113, A91. doi:10.1289/ ehp.113–a91a

TITLES AND URLS IN APA-STYLE REFERENCES

If you are citing a page or an article that has a title, treat the title like an article in a periodical.

Heiney, A. (2004). A gathering of space heroes. Retrieved from the National Aeronautics and Space Administration Web site: http://www.nasa.gov/missions/

Otherwise, treat the name of the Web site itself as you would a book. No retrieval date is necessary if the content is not likely to be changed or updated. If no DOI is assigned, provide the home or entry page for the journal or report publisher.

Elements of the citation

Author's Name or Organization

- Authorship is sometimes hard to discern for online sources. If you do have an author or creator to cite, follow the rules for periodicals and books.
- If the only author you find is a group or organization, list its name as the author.

Dates

Give the date the site was produced or last revised (sometimes the copyright date) after the author.

Title of Page or Article

- Web sites are often made up of many separate pages or articles. Each page or article on a Web site may or may not have a title.

URL and DOI

- If the article has a DOI (digital object identifier), give the DOI in numeric or URL form after the title.
- If the article does not have a DOI, copy the Web address exactly as it appears in your browser window. You can even copy and paste the address into your text for greater accuracy.
- Break a URL at the end of a line *before* a mark of punctuation. Do not insert a hyphen.

Find the right example as your model (you may need to refer to more than one model)

What kind of publication do you have?

- For a document in a database, see example #53.
- For an article with a DOI assigned, see example #61.
- For an article with no DOI assigned, see example #62.
- For an article in a newspaper or magazine, see examples #63–#64.
- For a government publication, see example #60.

Who is the author?

- For a known author, see example #56.
- For a group or organization as the author, see example #57.

Do you have a source that is posted by an individual?

- For a *Facebook* update or a *Twitter* post, see examples #65–#66.
- For a blog entry, see example #67.
- For an e-mail , see example #69.

Index of References Entries

24e Periodical Sources in APA-Style References

JOURNAL AND MAGAZINE ARTICLES

13. **Article by one author**

> Goolkasian, P. (2012). Research in visual pattern recognition: The enduring legacy of studies from the 1960s. *American Journal of Psychology*, *125*, 155–163.

14. **Article by two authors**

> McClelland, D., & Eismann, K. (2013).

15. **Article by three or more authors**

List last names and initials for up to seven authors, with an ampersand between the last two names. For works with eight or more authors, list the first six names, then an ellipsis, then the last author's name.

> Andis, S., Franks, D., Gee, G., Ng, K., Orr, V., Ray, B., . . . Tate, L.

16. **Authors listed with the word *with***

> Bettinger, M. (with Winthorp, E.).

17. **Article by an unknown author**

> The green gene revolution [Editorial]. (2004, February). *Scientific American*, *291*, 8.

18. **Article by a group or organization**

Smithsonian Institution. (2003). The player. *Diamonds are forever: Artists and writers on baseball.* San Francisco, CA: Chronicle Books.

19. **Article in a journal with continuous pagination**

Include only the volume number and the year, not the issue number.

Engen, R., & Steen, S. (2000). The power to punish: Discretion and sentencing reform in the war on drugs. *American Journal of Sociology, 105,* 1357–1395.

20. **Article in a journal paginated by issue**

If each issue of the journal begins on page 1, give the issue number in parentheses (not italicized) after the volume number.

Bunyan, T. (2010). Just over the horizon—the surveillance society and the state in the EU. *Race and Class, 51*(3), 1–12.

MONTHLY, WEEKLY, AND BIWEEKLY PERIODICALS

APA does not abbreviate any month.

21. **Weekly or biweekly periodicals**

Hurtley, Stella. (2004, July 16). Limits from leaf litter. *Science, 305,* 311–313.

22. **Monthly publications**

Barth, A. (2010, March). Brain science gets squishy. *Discover,* 11–12.

ABSTRACTS

23. **Abstract from an original source**

de Watteville, C. (1904). On flame spectra [Abstract]. *Proceedings of the Royal Society of London, 74,* 84.

24. **Abstract from a printed secondary source**

Van Schaik, P. (1999). Involving users in the specification of functionality using scenarios and model-based evaluation. *Behaviour and Information Technology, 18,* 455–466. Abstract obtained from *Communication Abstracts,* 2000, *24,* 416.

NEWSPAPERS

25. **Newspaper article**

> Olsen, E. (2010, June 22). A campaign for M&Ms with a salty center? Sweet. *The New York Times*, p. B6.

If an article has no author, list and alphabetize by the first significant word in the title of the article.

> Incorrect cancer tests can be costly. (2004, December 16). *USA Today*, p. 8D.

REVIEWS AND LETTERS TO THE EDITOR

26. **Review**

> Henig, R. N. (2010, June 27). The psychology of bliss [Review of the book *How Pleasure Works* by Paul Bloom]. *The New York Times Book Review*, p. 6.

27. **Letter to the editor or editorial**

> Wilkenson, S. E. (2001, December 21). When teaching doesn't count [Letter to the editor]. *The Chronicle of Higher Education*, p. B21.

24f Books and Nonperiodical Sources in APA-Style References

BOOKS

28. **Book by one author**

The author's last name comes first, followed by a comma and the first initial of the author's first name and middle initial, if any.

> Gladwell, M. (2011). *Outliers: The story of success.* New York, NY: Back Bay Books.

For a book with an editor (instead of an author), put the abbreviation *Ed.* in parentheses after the name.

> Rasgon, N. L. (Ed.). (2006). *The effects of estrogen on brain function.* Baltimore, MD: Johns Hopkins University Press.

29. Two or more books by the same author

Arrange according to the date, with the earliest publication first, or alphabetically according to the names of additional authors.

Jules, R. (2003). *Internal memos and other classified documents*. London, England: Hutchinson.

Jules, R. (2004). *Derelict cabinet*. London, England: Corgi-Transworld.

30. Book by two authors

Hardt, M., & Negri, A. (2000). *Empire*. Cambridge, MA: Harvard University Press.

31. Book by three or more authors

List last names and initials for up to seven authors, with an ampersand between the last two names. For works with eight or more authors, list the first six names, then an ellipsis, then the last author's name.

Anders, K., Child, H., Davis, K., Logan, O., Orr, J., Ray, B., . . . Wood, G.

32. Authors listed with the word *with*

Bettinger, M. (with Winthorp, E.).

33. Book by an unknown author

Survey of developing nations. (2003). New York, NY: Justice for All Press.

34. Book by a group or organization

Centers for Disease Control and Prevention. (2003). *Men and heart disease: An atlas of racial and ethnic disparities in mortality*. Atlanta, GA: Author.

35. Translated book

Freud, S. (2010). *Three contributions to the theory of sex* (A. A. Brill, Trans.). Las Vegas, NV: IAP Publishing. (Original work published 1909)

36. Revised or later edition of a book

Weintraub, A. (2004). *Yoga for depression: A compassionate guide to relieve suffering through Yoga* (2nd ed.). New York, NY: Broadway Books.

37. Multivolume book

Schwarzer, M., & Frensch, P. A. (2010). *Personality, human development and culture: International perspectives on psychological science* (Vol. 2). London, UK: Psychology Press.

38. E-book with DOI

Chaffe-Stengel, P., & Stengel, D. (2012). *Working with sample data: Exploration and inference.* doi:10.4128/9781606492147

39. E-book with no DOI assigned

Burton, R. (1832). *The anatomy of melancholy.* Retrieved from http://etext.library.adelaide.edu.au/b/burton/robert /melancholy

40. Chapter written by the same author as the book

Add the word *In* after the chapter title and before the book title. Include inclusive page numbers for the chapter inside parentheses.

Savage, T. (2004). Challenging mirror modeling in group therapy. In *Collaborative practice in psychology and therapy* (pp. 130–157). New York, NY: Haworth Clinical Practice Press.

41. Chapter in an edited collection

Boyaton, D. (2010). Behaviorism and its effect upon learning in schools. In G. Goodman (Ed.), *The educational psychology reader: The art and science of how people learn* (pp. 49–66). New York, NY: Peter Lang.

42. Chapter in a volume in a series

Jackson, E. (1998). Politics and gender. In F. Garrity (Series Ed.) & M. Halls (Vol. Ed.), *Political library: Vol. 4. Race, gender, and class* (2nd ed., pp. 101–151). New York, NY: Muse.

43. Selection reprinted from another source

Thompson, H. S. (1997). The scum also rises. In K. Kerrane & B. Yagoda (Eds.), *The art of fact* (pp. 302–315). New York, NY: Touchstone. (Reprinted from *The great shark hunt*, pp. 299–399, by H. S. Thompson, 1979, New York, NY: Simon & Schuster)

RESEARCH REPORTS, CONFERENCE PROCEEDINGS, AND DISSERTATIONS

44. Technical and research reports

Austin, A., & Baldwin, R. (1991). *Faculty collaboration: Enhancing the quality of scholarship and teaching* (ASCHE-ERIC Higher Education Report 7). Washington, DC: George Washington University.

45. Published conference proceedings

Abarkan, A. (1999). Educative physical planning: Housing and the emergence of suburbia in Sweden. In T. Mann (Ed.), *Power of imagination. Proceedings of the 30th annual conference of the Environmental Design Research Association* (pp. 24–32). Edmond, OK: Environmental Design Research Association.

46. Unpublished paper presented at a symposium or meeting

Kelly, M. (2004, November). *Communication in virtual terms.* Paper presented at the annual meeting of the National Communication Association, Chicago, IL.

47. Dissertation or thesis

Tzilos, G. K. (2010). *A brief computer-based intervention for alcohol use during pregnancy* (Doctoral dissertation). Available from ProQuest Dissertations and Theses database. (UMI No. 3373111)

GOVERNMENT AND LEGAL DOCUMENTS

48. Government document

When the author and publisher are identical, use the word *Author* as the name of the publisher.

U.S. Environmental Protection Agency. (2002). *Respiratory health effects of passive smoking: Lung cancer and other disorders* (EPA Publication No. 600/6–90/006 F). Washington, DC: Author.

In-text

(U.S. Environmental Protection Agency [EPA], 2002)

49. *Congressional Record* (Senate resolution)

> S. Res. 103, 107th Cong., 147 Cong. Rec. 5844 (2001) (enacted).

In-text

> (S. Res. 103, 2001)

RELIGIOUS TEXTS, PAMPHLETS, AND INTERVIEWS

50. **Religious or classical texts**

Reference entries are not required for major classical works or the Bible, but in the first in-text citation, identify the edition used.

> John 3.16 (Modern Phrased Version)

51. **Bulletins or pamphlets**

> University Health Center. (2001). *The common cold* [Brochure]. Austin, TX: Author.

52. **Published interview**

> Bush, L. (2001, April). [Interview with P. Burka]. *Texas Monthly*, pp. 80–85, 122–124.

24g Online Sources in APA-Style References

LIBRARY DATABASES AND ENCYCLOPEDIAS

53. **Document from a database**

APA no longer requires listing the names of well-known databases. Include the name of the database only for hard-to-find books and other items.

> Holloway, J. D. (2004). Protecting practitioners' autonomy. *Monitor on Psychology, 35*(1), 30.

54. **Electronic copy of an abstract retrieved from a database**

> Putsis, W. P., & Bayus, B. L. (2001). An empirical analysis of firms' product line decisions. *Journal of Marketing Research, 37*(8), 110–118. Abstract retrieved from PsycINFO database.

55. Online encyclopedia

> Swing. (2013). In *Britannica Online*. Retrieved April 29, 2013, from
> http://www.britannica.com/

ONLINE PUBLICATIONS

56. Online publication by a known author

> Carr, A. (2003, May 22). *AAUW applauds Senate support of title IX
> resolution*. Retrieved from http://www.aauw.org/about
> /newsroom/press_releases/030522.cfm

57. Online publication by a group or organization

> Girls Inc. (2013). *Girls' bill of rights*. Retrieved from
> http://www.girlsinc.org/about/girls-bill-of-rights/

58. Online publication with no known author or group affiliation

Begin the reference with the title of the document.

> *Halloween costumes from my warped mind*. (n.d.). Retrieved from
> http://home.att.net/~jgola/hallow01.htm

59. Online publication with no copyright or revision date

If no copyright or revision date is given, use *(n.d.)*, as shown in entry 58.

60. Online government publication

> U.S. Public Health Service. Office of the Surgeon General.
> (2001, March 11). *Women and smoking*. Retrieved from
> http://www.surgeongeneral.gov/library/womenandtobacco/

In-text

(U.S. Public Health Service [USPHS], 2001)

ONLINE PERIODICALS

Because URLs frequently change, many scholarly publishers have begun to use a DOI, a unique alphanumeric string or URL that is permanent. If a DOI is available, use the DOI instead of the URL.

61. Article with DOI assigned

You may need to click on a button such as "Article" or "PubMed" to find the DOI. There is no need to list the database or the retrieval date if the DOI is listed.

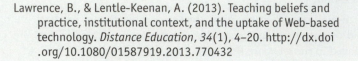

Lawrence, B., & Lentle-Keenan, A. (2013). Teaching beliefs and practice, institutional context, and the uptake of Web-based technology. *Distance Education, 34*(1), 4–20. http://dx.doi .org/10.1080/01587919.2013.770432

62. **Article with no DOI assigned**

Brown, B. (2004). The order of service: The practical management of customer interaction. *Sociological Research Online, 9*(4). Retrieved from http://www.socresonline.org.uk/9/4 /brown.html

63. **Article in an online newspaper**

King, M. (2013, January 25). Council preview. *Austin Chronicle*. Retrieved from http://www.austinchronicle.com/

64. **Article in an online magazine**

Resnikoff, N. (2010, June 22). Media ignores Gulf tragedy: Focuses on campaign narrative. *Salon*. Retrieved from http://www.salon.com/

UNEDITED ONLINE SOURCES

65. **Social media (e.g., *Facebook*) update**

The Daily Show. (2013, March 18). Political speeches contain much more than empty promises. [Facebook page]. Retrieved July 29, 2013, from https://www.facebook.com/thedailyshow

66. ***Twitter* update or tweet**

Collins, F. S. (2013, April 30). Check out my NPR interview this afternoon with Marketplace's @kairyssdal about #NIH research [Tweet]. Retrieved from https://twitter.com/NIH

67. **Blog entry**

Spinuzzi, C. (2010, January 7). In the pipeline [Blog post]. Retrieved from http://spinuzzi.blogspot.com/search ?updated-max=2010-01-25T12%3A35%3A00-06%3A00

68. **Wiki entry**

Mount Everest. (n.d.). In *Wikipedia*. Retrieved November 12, 2013, from http://en.wikipedia.org/wiki/Mt._Everest

69. E-mail

E-mail sent from one individual to another should be cited as a personal communication. Personal communication is cited in text but not included in the reference list.

(D. Jenkins, personal communication, July 28, 2013)

24h Visual and Multimedia Sources in APA-Style References

MULTIMEDIA

70. Television program

Winter, T. (Writer), & Van Patten, T. (Director). (2012). Resolution [Television series episode]. In T. Winter (Producer), *Boardwalk empire*. New York, NY: HBO.

71. Film, video, or DVD

Boal, M. (Writer), & Bigelow, K. (Director). (2012). *Zero dark thirty* [Motion picture]. United States: Columbia Pictures.

72. Musical recording

Waits, T. (1980). Ruby's arms. On *Heartattack and vine* [CD]. New York, NY: Elektra Entertainment.

73. Audio or video file or podcast

Horne, E. (Producer). (2013, July 9). *Radiolab* [Audio podcast]. Retrieved from http://www.radiolab.org/series/podcasts/

74. Photograph or work of art

American Heart Association. (2009). *Hands-only CPR graphic* [Photograph]. Retrieved from http://handsonlycpr.org /assets/files/Hands-only%20me.pdf

75. Map, chart, or graph

Information Architects. (2010). Web Trend Map 4 [Map]. Retrieved from http://www.informationarchitects.jp/en/wtm4/

24i Sample Research Paper with APA Documentation

Major kinds of papers written in APA style include the following.

Reports of research

Reports of experimental research follow a specific organization in APA style.

- **The abstract** gives a brief summary of the report.
- **The introduction** identifies the problem, reviews previous research, and states the hypothesis that was tested. Because the introduction is identified by its initial position in the report, it does not have to be labeled "introduction."
- **The method section** describes how the experiment was conducted and how the participants were selected.
- **The results section** reports the findings of the study. This section often includes tables and figures that provide statistical results and tests of statistical significance. Tests of statistical significance are critical for experimental research because they give the probability that the results could have occurred by chance.
- **The discussion section** interprets the findings and often refers to previous research.

Case studies

Case studies report material about an individual or a group that illustrates some problem or issue of interest to the field.

Reviews of literature

Reviews of literature summarize what has been published on a particular subject and often evaluate that material to suggest directions for future research.

Thesis-driven arguments

Thesis-driven arguments are similar to reviews of research, but they take a particular position on a theoretical or a real-life issue. The APA paper that follows by Jacob J. Pietsch is a thesis-driven proposal argument that advocates a particular course of action.

FORMATTING A RESEARCH PAPER IN APA STYLE

APA offers these general guidelines for formatting a research paper.

- **Use white, 8½-by-11-inch paper.** Don't use colored or lined paper.

- **Double-space everything—the title page, abstract, body of the paper, quotations, and list of references.** Set the line spacing on your word processor for double spacing and leave it there.

- **Include a running head aligned with the left margin on every page.** The running head is an abbreviated title set in all caps with a maximum of 50 characters. Include a page number for every page, aligned with the right margin.

- **Specify 1-inch margins.** One-inch margins are the default setting for most computers.

- **Do not justify (make even) the right margin.** Justifying the right margin throws off the spacing between words and makes your paper harder to read. Use the left-align setting instead.

- **Indent the first line of each paragraph one-half inch.** Set the paragraph indent command or the tab on the ruler at one-half inch.

- **Use block format for quotations longer than forty words.** See page 4 of the student paper in 24i.

- **Create an abstract.** The abstract appears on a separate page after the title page. Insert and center "Abstract" at the top. Do not indent the first line of the abstract. The abstract should be a brief (120 words or under) summary of the paper.

- **Create a title page.** Follow the format below for your title page. It should have

  1. a running head beginning with the words "Running head:" followed by a short title in ALL CAPS at the top left and a page number at the top right,
  2. a descriptive title that is centered in the top half of the page with all words capitalized except *a*, *an*, *the*, prepositions, and conjunctions under four letters,
  3. your name centered on a separate line, and
  4. your school centered on a separate line.

Running head: OPPORTUNITIES FOR HIGH-SPEED RAIL   1

nclude a running ead, consisting f a short version f your title in LL CAPS and he page num- er. This header hould be about ½" from the top f the page. Set he margins of our paper to 1".

Opportunities for Developing High-Speed

Rail in the United States

Jacob J. Pietsch

The University of Texas at Austin

Center your title in the top half of the page. The title should clearly describe the con- tent of the paper and should be no longer than 12 words. If the title runs to 2 lines, double-space it.

On the line below the title, include your name, also centered. On the next line below, include the name of your school. Double-space between these lines.

OPPORTUNITIES FOR HIGH-SPEED RAIL   2

Continue the running head.

Abstract

Policymakers in the United States must consider the impact of continued population growth and correspond- ing freight requirements on underfunded transportation systems. Proactive investments in transportation systems such as high-speed rail provide these policymakers with an opportunity to build additional capacity to move peo- ple and freight. In light of public support for developing high-speed rail, careful investments in systems that will likely succeed can lead to deeper government investments in the future. Although policymakers may face political challenges in providing funding for high-speed rail, the need for transportation systems that can support popula- tion growth will only become more pressing over time.

The abstract appears on a separate page with the title *Abstract* cen- tered at the top.

Do not indent the first line of the abstract.

The abstract should be a brief (120 words or fewer) sum- mary of your paper's argument.

Opportunities for Developing High-Speed Rail
in the United States

Many Americans may consider the limits of transportation systems only when they sit in traffic on their daily commutes, forgetting how easily they can access most modern conveniences thanks to previous generations' investments in highways, subways, ferries, light rail, railroads, and air systems. On the one hand, the networks of transportation that connect America's cities and weave them into the global economy have facilitated unprecedented economic growth; on the other, failing transportation systems have the potential to inhibit economic progress. As stress continues to build on America's current infrastructure, "the nation's roads, rails, ports, and airports will require huge new investments to accommodate an estimated 120 million additional Americans by 2050" (PennDesign, 2011, p. 199).

In addition to meeting the needs of a growing population, transportation systems must also carry material resources and commodities along an extensive transportation network. The Federal Railroad Administration estimates that for each American, freight transportation systems must carry "40 tons of freight . . . annually" (U.S. Department of Transportation, 2010, p. 4). The movement of people and goods places significant strain on the current transportation systems, most evident in phenomena such as traffic congestion and deteriorating roadways. A public relations consultant for Amtrak and Boeing, Joseph Vranich, points to the crux issue, "Every

Center your title at the beginning of the body of your paper. If it runs to 2 lines, double-space it.

All quotations should be cited by author, date, and page number.

OPPORTUNITIES FOR HIGH-SPEED RAIL   4

municipal, state and federal transportation official has to deal with the question: How am I going to get more transportation capacity?" (Kaderbeck & Peterson, 1992, 56). By making proactive investments in transportation systems, policymakers can take a role in directing economic development rather than reacting to it.

Public transportation plays an important role in alleviating some of the burden on overcrowded highways. Beyond providing affordable transportation and reducing the environmental impact of commuting, public transportation systems actually create savings for non-riders as well:

> If public transportation service had been discontinued and the riders traveled in private vehicles in 2010, the 439 urban areas would have suffered an additional 796 million hours of delay and consumed 300 million more gallons of fuel. The value of the additional travel delay and fuel that would have been consumed if there were no public transportation service would be an additional $16.8 billion, a 17% increase over current congestion costs in the 439 urban areas. (Eisele, Schrank, & Lomax, 2011, p. 14)

Policymakers at all governmental levels should consider these savings derived from investment in public transportation and weigh the upfront costs of such investments against their returns over time and not simply compared to short-term gain from eliminating expenditures.

Quotations of more than 40 words should be indented ½" from the margin. Include citations from the original text, but do not list those works in your references unless you cite them again elsewhere in the paper.

For block quotations, parenthetical citations go outside closing punctuation.

OPPORTUNITIES FOR HIGH-SPEED RAIL   5

Alongside other popular options for increasing capacity (such as expanding roadways), policymakers should especially consider investing in high-speed rail systems. Advances in rail "can [allow policymakers to] reuse existing rights-of-way, engage new tunneling technologies, and minimize the need for land acquisition" (PennDesign, 2011, p. 199). These emerging high-speed rail technologies offer the opportunity to revitalize the rail industries that were once regarded as "the world's most extensive passenger rail system" before federal infrastructure funding shifted more heavily to establishing the interstate highway system and, in recent decades, air travel (Yaro, 2011, p. 253). That is not to say that policymakers should favor rail exclusively over other, established transportation systems; rather, they should consider high-speed rail as a complement to those systems.

Public interest in high-speed rail is currently high; as of 2010, "88 percent of [survey] respondents support development of a national HSR system" (Yaro, 2011, p. 253). Jaime Rall (2010) reports that "for the initial $8 billion in federal stimulus money, states submitted 259 applications for a total of $57 billion" (p. 13). With such interest in high-speed rail systems, it is surprising that the only true high-speed rail currently operating in the United States is the Acela Express in the Northeast Corridor (De Chant, 2011). Some policymakers may be concerned with advancing infrastructure spending in the wake of the recession; however, they can benefit from current public support for high-speed rail.

If you include the author's name in the text, include the publication year in parentheses immediately after it. If necessary, include the page number in parentheses with the abbreviation p. following the citation.

OPPORTUNITIES FOR HIGH-SPEED RAIL   6

Investments from the federal government played a key role in fostering every major transportation system in the United States, "from the construction of canals in the 18th century, to the 19th-century transcontinental railroad and the national rail system, to the 20th-century interstate highway and aviation systems" (PennDesign, 2011, p. 201). When President Obama signed the American Recovery and Reinvestment Act in 2009, the federal government came to the table with $8 billion in funding specifically for high-speed rail (Todorovich, Schned, & Lane, 2011, pp. 55–56). However, cuts to funding for high-speed rail in 2011 threatened the tenuous advances in high-speed rail development because the necessary long-term planning is difficult to maintain under conditions of "unpredictable appropriations" (Todorovich, Schned, & Lane, 2011, p. 55–56). To avoid wasted dollars on incomplete projects and make thoughtful infrastructure investments, policymakers need to implement more stable funding mechanisms for high-speed rail.

While high-speed rail systems are high-cost initiatives, different types of high-speed rail can be tailored to meet the unique needs of each region (Todorovich & Hagler, 2011, p. 3). When state and local governments use federal funds for rail programs, they can "meet important transportation needs while building markets for passenger rail" (Todorovich & Hagler, 2011, p. 3). Policymakers can identify and prioritize projects in corridors based on regional qualities such as "density,

> In a parenthetical citation, use *&* instead of *and* when listing more than one author.

economic activity, and existing travel markets to support strong ridership on these new services" (Hagler & Todorovich, 2009, p. 1). If these projects are successful, they can set a precedent for future investments in high-speed rail.

Over the next 50 years, the need for infrastructure spending is projected to further increase. However, justifying the nation's first heavy spending projects in high-speed rail presents a challenge for policymakers, especially considering that "predicting the internal transportation effects of new infrastructure or a change in regulatory regime is remarkably difficult . . . due to inadequate knowledge of causal linkages [and] a lack of appropriate dynamic data" (Button & Reggiani, 2011, p. 10). These challenges for policymakers are exacerbated by the fact that infrastructure issues do not often have the same sense of immediacy to constituents as competing policy needs (Benner & Pastor, 2011, p. 315). When high-speed rail development does manage to capture regional attention, "the policy levers are likely to be local, state, and federal" (Benner & Pastor, 2011, p. 315). As of 2005, half of the states still did not have transportation departments with rail offices, which draws attention to the need for states to participate in regional planning dialogues concerning high-speed rail (Rall, 2010).

Despite the challenges policymakers face in adding transportation capacity, the key to success for developing high-speed rail systems in the United States

OPPORTUNITIES FOR HIGH-SPEED RAIL   8

lies in "constructing an open and participatory decision-making process capable of securing optimal social and economic development outcomes from any public funding of high-speed rail" (Thompson & Bawden, 1992, p. 316). If policymakers make well-planned, incremental investments in high-speed rail with available funding, then these successes can secure support for more stable, long-term sources of funding. Although policymakers may face political challenges pursuing long-term investment for high-speed rail, the need for new infrastructure that can support population growth will only become more pressing over time.

OPPORTUNITIES FOR HIGH-SPEED RAIL   9

References

Benner, C., & Pastor, M. (2011). Moving on up? Regions, megaregions, and the changing geography of social equity organizing. *Urban Affairs Review*, *47*(3), 315–348. doi:10.1177/1078087410391950

Button, K., & Reggiani, A. (2011). *Transportation and economic development challenges*. Retrieved from http://uar.sagepub.com/content/47/3/315 .full.pdf

De Chant, T. (2011, May 27). U.S. not dense enough for high speed rail? Think again. Retrieved from http://persquaremile.com/2011/05/27/u-s-not -dense-enough-for-high-speed-rail-think-again/

Center *References* at the top.

Alphabetize entries by last name of the first author.

Indent all but the first line of each entry.

Double-space all entries.

OPPORTUNITIES FOR HIGH-SPEED RAIL   10

Eisele, B., Schrank, D., & Lomax, T. (2011, September).
    2011 congested corridors report. Retrieved from
    the Texas Transportation Institute Web site:
    http://d2dtl5nnlpfr0r.cloudfront.net/tti.tamu
    .edu/documents/corridors-report-2011.pdf

Hagler, Y., & Todorovich, P. (2009, September). Where
    high speed rail works best. *America 2050*. Retrieved
    from http://www.america2050.org/pdf/2050
    _Report_Where_HSR_Works_Best.pdf

Kaderbeck, S., & Peterson, T. (1992). High-speed rail.
    American City and County, 101(11), 56.

PennDesign. (2011). *High-speed rail in the northeast
    megaregion: From vision to reality*. Retrieved from
    University of Pennsylvania School of Design Web site:
    http://www.design.upenn.edu/city-regional-planning
    /high-speed-rail-northeast-megaregion-vision-reality

Rall, J. (2010). Fast, faster, fastest. *State Legislatures,
    36*(3), 12–15.

Thompson, C., & Bawden, T. (1992). What are the
    potential economic development impacts of high-
    speed rail? *Economic Development Quarterly, 6*,
    297–319. doi: 10.1177/089124249200600306

Todorovich, P., & Hagler, Y. (2011, January). High speed
    rail in America. *America 2050*. Retrieved from
    http://www.america2050.org/pdf/HSR-in
    -America-Complete.pdf

Todorovich, P., Schned, D., & Lane, R. (2011). *High
    speed rail: International lessons for U.S. policy
    makers*. Retrieved from Lincoln Institute of Land

OPPORTUNITIES FOR HIGH-SPEED RAIL 11

Policy Web site: https://www.lincolninst.edu/pubs
/dl/1948_1268_High-Speed%20Rail%20PFR
_Webster.pdf

U.S. Department of Transportation. Federal
Railroad Administration. (2010, September).
National rail plan: Moving forward. Retrieved from
http://www.fra.dot.gov/eLib/Details/L02696

Yaro, R. D. (2011). Moving forward: The promise of
megaregions and high speed rail. In E. Seltzer &
A. Carbonell (Eds.), *Regional planning in America:
Practice and prospect* (pp. 243–268). Cambridge,
MA: Lincoln Institute of Land Policy.

Go through your text and make sure that everything you have cited, except for personal communication, is in the list of references.

FORMATTING THE REFERENCES IN APA STYLE

- Begin the references on a new page. Insert a page break before you start the references page.
- Center "References" on the first line at the top of the page.
- Double-space all entries.
- Alphabetize each entry by the last name of the author or, if no author is listed, by the first content word in the title (ignore *a*, *an*, *the*).
- Indent all but the first line in each entry one-half inch.
- Italicize the titles of books and periodicals.
- Go through your paper to check that each source you have used (except personal communication) is in the list of references.

25 | CMS Documentation

QUICK*TAKE*

After reading this chapter, you should be able to . . .

- Use in-text citations in CMS (25a)
- Create citations for books and nonperiodical sources (25b)
- Create citations for periodical sources (25c)
- Create citations for online sources (25d)
- Create citations for multimedia sources (25e)
- Use correct formatting for a paper in CMS (25f)

Writers who publish in business, social sciences, fine arts, and humanities outside the discipline of English often use *The Chicago Manual of Style* (CMS) method of documentation. CMS guidelines allow writers a clear way of using footnotes and endnotes (rather than MLA and APA in-text citations) for citing the sources of quotations, summaries, and paraphrases. If you have questions after consulting this chapter, you can consult *The Chicago Manual of Style*, sixteenth edition (2010), or visit the Web site (www.chicagomanualofstyle.org).

25a In-Text Citations in CMS Style

In-text citations

CMS describes two systems of documentation, one similar to APA and the other a style that uses footnotes or endnotes, which is the focus of this chapter. In the footnote style, CMS uses a superscript number directly after any quotation, paraphrase, or summary. Notes are numbered consecutively throughout the essay, article, or chapter. This superscript number corresponds to either a footnote, which appears at the bottom of the page, or an endnote, which appears at the end of the text.

> In *Southern Honor: Ethics and Behavior in the Old South*, Wyatt-Brown argues that "*paradox, irony,* and *guilt* have been three current words used by historians to describe white Southern life before the Civil War."[1]

Note

> 1. Bertram Wyatt-Brown, *Southern Honor: Ethics and Behavior in the Old South* (Oxford: Oxford University Press, 1983), 3.

Bibliography

Wyatt-Brown, Bertram. *Southern Honor: Ethics and Behavior in the Old South*. Oxford: Oxford University Press, 1983.

Footnote and endnote placement

Footnotes appear at the bottom of the page on which each citation appears. Begin your footnote four lines from the last line of text on the page. Double-space footnotes and endnotes.

Endnotes are compiled at the end of the text on a separate page entitled *Notes*. Center the title at the top of the page and list your endnotes in the order they appear within the text. The entire endnote section should be double-spaced—both within and between each entry. Even with endnotes it's still possible to include explanatory footnotes, which are indicated by asterisks or other punctuation marks.

CMS bibliography

Because footnotes and endnotes in CMS format contain complete citation information, a separate list of references is often optional. This list of references can be called the *Bibliography*, or if it has only works referenced in your text, *Works Cited, Literature Cited*, or *References*.

THE *CHICAGO MANUAL OF STYLE* AND PUBLISHING

The *Chicago Manual of Style* is the favorite of the publishing industry because it is far more comprehensive than either the *MLA Handbook* or the *Publication Manual of the American Psychological Association*. The sixteenth edition has been updated to include instructions on how to create and edit electronic publications, including Web sites and e-books. Because many businesses and organizations now produce electronic publications, a basic knowledge of the electronic publishing process could be a valuable item on your résumé.

The *Chicago Manual* also gives advice on copyright law, such as how a work is granted copyright, what may constitute copyright violation, and what is fair use.

In addition, writers and publishers turn to the *Chicago Manual* for the fine points of writing. For example, there are two kinds of dashes: a longer dash called an *em dash* (discussed in Chapter 41) and a shorter dash called an *en dash*. If you want to know when to use an en dash, the *Chicago Manual* is the place to look.

Index of CMS Documentation

25b Books and Nonperiodical Sources in CMS Style

Note

1. Nell Irvin Painter, *Creating Black Americans: African-American History and Its Meanings, 1619 to the Present* (New York: Oxford University Press, 2006), 5.

Bibliography

Painter, Nell Irvin. *Creating Black Americans: African-American History and Its Meanings, 1619 to the Present.* New York: Oxford University Press, 2006.

AUTHOR'S OR EDITOR'S NAME

In a note, the author's name is given in normal order.

In the bibliography, give the author's last name first. If an editor, put *ed.* after the name.

BOOK TITLE

Use the exact title, as it appears on the title page (not the cover).

Italicize the title.

Capitalize all nouns, verbs, adjectives, adverbs, and pronouns, and the first word of the title and subtitle.

PUBLICATION INFORMATION

In a note, the place of publication, publisher, and year of publication are in parentheses.

Place of publication

- Add the state's postal abbreviation or country when the city is not well known (Foster City, CA) or ambiguous (Cambridge, MA, or Cambridge, UK).

- If more than one city is given on the title page, use the first.

Publisher's name

- You may use acceptable abbreviations (e.g., *Co.* for *Company*).

- For works published prior to 1900, the place and date are sufficient.

YEAR OF PUBLICATION

- If no year of publication is given, write *n.d.* ("no date") in place of the date.

- If it is a multivolume edited work published over a period of more than one year, put the span of time as the year.

Sample citations for books and nonperiodical sources

BOOKS

1. **Book by one author**
   In a note the author's name is given in normal order.

   > 1. Thomas Friedman, *The World Is Flat: A Brief History of the Twenty-first Century* (New York: Farrar, Straus and Giroux, 2005), 9.

   In subsequent references, cite the author's last name only:

   > 2. Friedman, 10.

   If the reference is to the same work as the preceding note, you can use the abbreviation *Ibid.*:

   > 3. Ibid., 10.

   In the bibliography, give the author's name in reverse order.

   > Friedman, Thomas. *The World Is Flat: A Brief History of the Twenty-first Century*. New York: Farrar, Straus and Giroux, 2005.

   For edited books, put *ed.* after the name.

   > Chen, Kuan-Hsing, ed. *Trajectories: Inter-Asia Cultural Studies*. London: Routledge, 1998.

2. **Book by multiple authors**
   For books with two or three authors, in a note, put all authors' names in normal order. For subsequent references, give only the authors' last names:

   > 4. Taylor Hauser and June Kashpaw, *January Blues* (Foster City, CA: IDG Books, 2003), 32.

   In the bibliography, give second and third names in normal order.

   > Hauser, Taylor, and June Kashpaw. *January Blues*. Foster City, CA: IDG Books, 2003.

   When there are more than three authors, in a note, give the name of the first author listed, followed by *et al*. List all of the authors in the bibliography.

3. **Book by an unknown author**
   Begin both the note and the bibliography entries with the title.

   Note

   > 6. *Remarks upon the Religion, Trade, Government, Police, Customs, Manners, and Maladys of the City of Corke* (Cork, 1737), 4.

   Bibliography

   > *Remarks upon the Religion, Trade, Government, Police, Customs, Manners, and Maladys of the City of Corke*. Cork, 1737.

4. **Book by a group or organization**

Treat the group or organization as the author of the work.

Note

> 7. World Health Organization, *Advancing Safe Motherhood through Human Rights* (Geneva, Switzerland: World Health Organization, 2001), 18.

Bibliography

> World Health Organization. *Advancing Safe Motherhood through Human Rights*. Geneva, Switzerland: World Health Organization, 2001.

PARTS OF BOOKS

5. **Single chapter by the same author as the book**

Note

> 1. Ann Ardis, "*The Lost Girl, Tarr,* and the Moment of Modernism," in *Modernism and Cultural Conflict, 1880-1922* (New York: Cambridge University Press, 2002), 78–113.

Bibliography

> Ardis, Ann. "*The Lost Girl, Tarr,* and the Moment of Modernism." In *Modernism and Cultural Conflict, 1880-1922*. New York: Cambridge University Press, 2002.

6. **Selection in an anthology or a chapter in an edited collection**

Note

> 2. Renato Constantino, "Globalization and the South," in *Trajectories: Inter-Asia Cultural Studies*, ed. Kuan-Hsing Chen (London: Routledge, 1998), 57–64.

Bibliography

> Constantino, Renato. "Globalization and the South." In *Trajectories: Inter-Asia Cultural Studies*, edited by Kuan-Hsing Chen, 57–64. London: Routledge, 1998.

7. **Article in a reference work**

Publication information is usually omitted from citations of well-known reference volumes. The edition is listed instead. The abbreviation *s.v.* (*sub verbo* or "under the word") replaces an entry's page number.

Note

> 4. *Encyclopaedia Britannica*, 2009 ed., s.v. "mercantilism."

8. **Introduction, foreword, preface, or afterword**

When citing an introduction, foreword, preface, or afterword written by someone other than the book's main author, the other writer's name comes first, and the main author's name follows the title of the book.

Note

> 5. Edward Larkin, introduction to *Common Sense*, by Thomas Paine (New York: Broadview, 2004).

Bibliography

Larkin, Edward. Introduction to *Common Sense*, by Thomas Paine, 1–16. New York: Broadview, 2004.

REVISED EDITIONS, VOLUMES, AND SERIES

9. **Revised or later edition of a book**

Note

> 1. Fred S. Kleiner, *Gardner's Art through the Ages: A Global History*, 13th ed. (Boston: Wadsworth, 2010), 85.

Bibliography

Kleiner, Fred S. *Gardner's Art through the Ages: A Global History*. 13th ed. Boston: Wadsworth, 2010.

10. **Work in more than one volume**

Note

> 1. Oscar Wilde, *The Complete Works of Oscar Wilde*, vol. 3 (New York: Dragon Press, 1998), 1024.

Bibliography

Wilde, Oscar. *The Complete Works of Oscar Wilde*. Vol. 3. New York: Dragon Press, 1998.

EDITIONS AND TRANSLATIONS

11. **Book with an editor**

Note

> 1. Thomas Hardy, *Jude the Obscure*, ed. Norman Page (New York: Norton, 1999), 35.

Bibliography

Hardy, Thomas. *Jude the Obscure*. Edited by Norman Page. New York: Norton, 1999.

12. Book with a translator

Follow the style shown in entry 11, but substitute *trans.* for *ed.* in the note and *Translated* for *Edited* in the bibliographic entry.

GOVERNMENT DOCUMENTS

13. Government document

Note

> 5. US Congress House Committee on Armed Services, *Comptroller General's Assessment of the Iraqi Government's Record of Performance* (Washington, DC: Government Printing Office, 2008), 40.

Bibliography

> US Congress House Committee on Armed Services. *Comptroller General's Assessment of the Iraqi Government's Record of Performance.* Washington, DC: Government Printing Office, 2008.

14. *Congressional Record*

For legal documents including the *Congressional Record*, CMS now follows the recommendations in *The Bluebook: A Uniform System of Citations* issued by the Harvard Law Review Association. The *Congressional Record* is issued in biweekly and permanent volumes. If possible, cite the permanent volumes.

Note

> 6. 156 Cong. Rec. 11,265 (2010).

RELIGIOUS TEXTS

15. Religious texts

Citations from religious texts appear in the notes but not in the bibliography. Give the version in parentheses in the first citation only.

Note

> 4. John 3:16 (King James Version).

LETTERS

16. Published letter

Note

> 5. Oscar Wilde to Robert Ross, 25 November 1897, in *The Complete Letters of Oscar Wilde*, ed. Merlin Holland and Rupert Hart-Davis (New York: Holt, 2000), 992.

Bibliography

Wilde, Oscar. *The Complete Letters of Oscar Wilde*. Edited by Merlin Holland and Rupert Hart-Davis. New York: Holt, 2000.

17. **Personal letter to author**

Personal communications are not usually listed in the bibliography because they are not accessible to the public.

Note

7. Ann Williams, letter to author, May 8, 2013.

DISSERTATIONS AND CONFERENCE PROCEEDINGS

18. **Unpublished dissertation**

Note

7. James Elsworth Kidd, "The Vision of Uncertainty: Elizabethan Windows and the Problem of Sight" (PhD diss., Southern Illinois University, 1998), 236.

Bibliography

Kidd, James Elsworth. "The Vision of Uncertainty: Elizabethan Windows and the Problem of Sight." PhD diss., Southern Illinois University, 1998.

19. **Published proceedings of a conference**

Note

8. Joyce Marie Jackson, "Barrelhouse Singers and Sanctified Preachers," in *Saints and Sinners: Religion, Blues, and (D)evil in African-American Music and Literature: Proceedings of the Conference held at the Université de Liège* (Liège: Société Liègeoise de Musicologie, 1996), 14–28.

Bibliography

Jackson, Joyce Marie. "Barrelhouse Singers and Sanctified Preachers." In *Saints and Sinners: Religion, Blues, and (D)evil in African-American Music and Literature: Proceedings of the Conference held at the Université de Liège*, 14–28. Liège: Société Liègeoise de Musicologie, 1996.

25c Periodical Sources in CMS Style

Note

> 1. Michael Hutt, "A Nepalese Triangle: Monarchists, Maoists, and Political Parties," *Asian Affairs* 38 (2007): 11–22.

Bibliography

> Hutt, Michael. "A Nepalese Triangle: Monarchists, Maoists, and Political Parties." *Asian Affairs* 38 (2007): 11–22.

AUTHOR'S OR EDITOR'S NAME

In a note, the author's name is given in normal order.

In a bibliography, give the author's last name first.

TITLE OF ARTICLE

- Put the title in quotation marks. If there is a title of a book within the title, italicize it.
- Capitalize nouns, verbs, adjectives, adverbs, and pronouns, and the first word of the title and subtitle.

PUBLICATION INFORMATION

Name of journal

- Italicize the name of the journal.
- Journal titles are normally not abbreviated in the arts and humanities unless the title of the journal is an abbreviation (*PMLA*, *ELH*).

Volume, issue, and page numbers

- Place the volume number after the journal title without intervening punctuation.
- For journals that are paginated from issue to issue within a volume, do not list the issue number.

DATE

- The date or year of publication is given in parentheses after the volume number, or issue number, if provided.

Sample citations for periodical sources

JOURNAL ARTICLES

20. Article by one author

Note

1. Sumit Guha, "Speaking Historically: The Changing Voices of Historical Narration in Western India, 1400–1900," *American Historical Review* 109 (2004): 1084–98.

In subsequent references, cite the author's last name only:

2. Guha, 1085.

If the reference is to the same work as the reference before it, you can use the abbreviation *Ibid.*:

3. Ibid., 1087.

Bibliography

Guha, Sumit. "Speaking Historically: The Changing Voices of Historical Narration in Western India, 1400–1900," *American Historical Review* 109 (2004): 1084–98.

21. Article by two or three authors

Note

3. Pamela R. Matthews and Mary Ann O'Farrell, "Introduction: Whose Body?" *South Central Review* 18, no. 3–4 (Fall–Winter 2001): 1–5.

All authors' names are printed in normal order. For subsequent references, give both authors' last names.

4. Matthews and O'Farrell, 4.

Bibliography

Matthews, Pamela R., and Mary Ann O'Farrell. "Introduction: Whose Body?" *South Central Review* 18, no. 3–4 (Fall–Winter 2001): 1–5.

22. Article by more than three authors

Note

Give the name of the first listed author, followed by *et al.*

5. Michael J. Thompson et al., "The Internal Rotation of the Sun," *Annual Review of Astronomy and Astrophysics* 41 (2003): 602.

Bibliography

List all the authors (inverting only the first author's name).

Thompson, Michael J., Jorgen Christensen-Dalsgaard, Mark S. Miesch, and Juri Toomre. "The Internal Rotation of the Sun." *Annual Review of Astronomy and Astrophysics* 41 (2003): 599–643.

23. **Article by an unknown author**

Note

6. "Japan's Global Claim to Asia," *American Historical Review* 109 (2004): 1196–98.

Bibliography

"Japan's Global Claim to Asia." *American Historical Review* 109 (2004): 1196–98.

DIFFERENT TYPES OF PAGINATION

24. **Journals paginated by volume**

Note

4. Susan Welsh, "Resistance Theory and Illegitimate Reproduction," *College Composition and Communication* 52 (2001): 553–73.

Bibliography

Welsh, Susan. "Resistance Theory and Illegitimate Reproduction." *College Composition and Communication* 52 (2001): 553–73.

25. **Journals paginated by issue**

For journals paginated separately by issue, list the issue number after the volume number.

Note

5. Tzvetan Todorov, "The New World Disorder," *South Central Review* 19, no. 2 (2002): 28–32.

Bibliography

Todorov, Tzvetan. "The New World Disorder." *South Central Review* 19, no. 2 (2002): 28–32.

POPULAR MAGAZINES

26. Magazines

For a weekly or biweekly popular magazine, give both the day and month of publication as listed on the issue. (For a monthly magazine, the month suffices.)

Note

> 5. Malcolm Gladwell, "Pandora's Briefcase," *New Yorker*, May 10, 2010, 72–78.

Bibliography

> Gladwell, Malcolm. "Pandora's Briefcase." *New Yorker*, May 10, 2010, 72–78.

27. Regular features and departments

Do not put titles of regular features or departments of a magazine in quotation marks.

Note

> 3. Conventional Wisdom, *Newsweek*, May 14, 2007, 8.

REVIEWS AND EDITORIALS

28. A review

Provide the title, if given, and name the work reviewed. If there is no title, just name the work reviewed.

Note

> 1. Jeff Severs, review of *Vanishing Point,* by David Markson, *Texas Observer*, February 2, 2004.

Bibliography

> Severs, Jeff. Review of *Vanishing Point,* by David Markson. *Texas Observer*, February 2, 2004.

29. A letter to the editor or an editorial

Add *letter* or *editorial* after the name of the author (if there is one). If there is no author, start with the descriptor.

Note

> 2. Mary Castillo, letter to the editor, *New York Magazine*, May 14, 2007, 34.

Bibliography

> Castillo, Mary. Letter to the editor. *New York Magazine*, May 14, 2007, 34.

NEWSPAPERS

30. Newspaper article

Note

> 1. Melena Ryzik, "Off the Beaten Beat," *New York Times*, May 11, 2007, late edition, sec. E.

- The month, day, and year are essential in citations of materials from daily newspapers. Cite them in this order: Month–Day–Year (November 3, 2016).
- For an item in a large city newspaper that has several editions a day, give the edition after the date.
- If the newspaper is published in sections, include the name, number, or letter of the section after the date or the edition (sec. C).
- Page numbers are usually omitted. If you put them in, use *p.* and *col.* (column) to avoid ambiguity.

25d Online Sources in CMS Style

ONLINE PUBLICATIONS

31. **Document or page from a Web site**

To cite original content from within a Web site, include as many descriptive elements as you can: author of the page, title of the page, title and owner of the Web site, and the URL. Include the date accessed only if the site is time-sensitive or is frequently updated. If you cannot locate an individual author, the owner of the site can stand in for the author.

Note

> 11. National Organization for Women, "NOW History," accessed October 8, 2016, http://www.now.org/history/history.html.

Bibliography

> National Organization for Women. "NOW History." Accessed October 8, 2016. http://www.now.org.history/history.html.

32. **Online book**

Note

> 12. Angelina Grimké, *Appeal to the Christian Women of the South* (New York: New York Anti-Slavery Society, 1836), accessed November 2, 2016, http://history.furman.edu/~benson/docs /grimke2.htm.

CITING ONLINE SOURCES IN CMS STYLE

CMS advocates a style for citing online and electronic sources that is adapted from its style for citing print sources. Titles of complete works are italicized. Quotation marks and other punctuation in citations for online sources should be used in the same manner as for print sources.

Access dates: List the date of access before the URL or DOI.

Revision dates: Due to the inconsistency in the practice of Internet sites stating the date of last revision, CMS recommends against using revision dates in citations.

DOIs and URLs: If the book or article has a digital object identifier (DOI) assigned, list it and not the URL. Otherwise, list the URL. If a URL has to be broken at the end of a line, the line break should be made before a slash (/) or other mark of punctuation. CMS does not use angle brackets (<>) to enclose URLs.

For details not covered in this section, consult *The Chicago Manual of Style*, sixteenth edition, sections 14.4–14.13.

Bibliography

Grimké, Angelina. *Appeal to the Christian Women of the South.* New York: New York Anti-Slavery Society, 1836. Accessed November 2, 2016. http://history.furman.edu/~benson /docs/grimke2.htm.

33. Online article

Note

13. Margaret Cohen, "Literary Studies on the Terraqueous Globe." PMLA 125, no. 3 (2010): 657–62, doi:10.1632/pmla .2010.125.3.657.

Bibliography

Cohen, Margaret. "Literary Studies on the Terraqueous Globe." *PMLA* 125, no. 3 (2010): 657–62. doi:10.1632/pmla .2010.125.3.657.

OTHER ELECTRONIC SOURCES

34. Posting to a discussion list or group

To cite material from archived Internet forums, discussion groups, MOOs, or blogs, include the name of the post author, the name of the list

or site, the date of the posting, and the URL. Limit your citation to notes or in-text citations.

Note

16. Jason Marcel, post to U.S. Politics Online Today in Politics Forum, April 4, 2004, http://www.uspoliticsonline.com/forums/forumdisplay.php?f=24.

35. E-mail

Because personal e-mails are not available to the public, they are not usually listed in the bibliography.

Note

11. Erik Lynn Williams, "Social Anxiety Disorder," e-mail to author, August 12, 2016.

25e Multimedia Sources in CMS Style

36. Musical recording

Note

8. Judy Garland, "Come Rain or Come Shine," *Judy at Carnegie Hall: Fortieth Anniversary Edition*, recorded 1961. Capitol B000059QY9, compact disc.

Bibliography

Garland, Judy. "Come Rain or Come Shine." *Judy at Carnegie Hall: Fortieth Anniversary Edition*. Recorded 1961. Capitol B000059QY9, compact disc.

37. Film or video

Note

9. *Invictus*, directed by Clint Eastwood (2009; Hollywood, CA: Warner Home Video, 2009), DVD.

Bibliography

Invictus. Directed by Clint Eastwood. Hollywood, CA: Warner Home Video, 2009. DVD.

38. Speech, debate, mediated discussion, or public talk

Note

16. Ellen Arthur, "The Octoroon, or Irish Life in Louisiana" (paper presented at the 2001 Annual Convention of the American Conference for Irish Studies, New York, June 2001).

Bibliography

Arthur, Ellen. "The Octoroon, or Irish Life in Louisiana." Paper presented at the 2001 Annual Convention of the American Conference for Irish Studies, New York, June 2001.

39. Interview

Note

15. Gordon Wood, interview by Linda Wertheimer, *Weekend Edition,* National Public Radio, May 14, 2005.

Bibliography

Wood, Gordon. Interview by Linda Wertheimer. *Weekend Edition.* National Public Radio. May 14, 2005.

40. Illustrations, figures, and tables

When citing figures from sources, use the abbreviation *fig.* However, spell out the word when citing tables, graphs, maps, or plates. The page number on which the figure appears precedes any figure number.

Note

16. Christian Unger, *America's Inner-City Crisis* (New York: Childress, 2003), 134, fig. 3.4.

25f Sample Pages with CMS Documentation

Jason Laker

American History 102

February 28, 2017

The Electoral College: Does It Have a Future?

Until the presidential election of 2000, few Americans thought much about the Electoral College. It was something they had learned about in civics class and had then forgotten about as other, more pressing bits of information required their attention. In November 2000, however, the Electoral College took center stage and sparked an argument that

continues today: Should the Electoral College be abolished?

The founding fathers established the Electoral College as a compromise between elections by Congress and those by popular vote.[1] The College consists of a group of electors who meet to vote for the president and vice president of the United States. The electors are nominated by political parties within each state, and the number each state gets relates to the state's congressional delegation. The process and the ideas behind it sound simple, but the actual workings of the Electoral College remain a mystery to many Americans.

The complicated nature of the Electoral College is one of the reasons why some people want to see it abolished. One voter writes in a letter to the editor of the *New York Times* that the elimination of the Electoral College is necessary "to demystify our voting system in the eyes of foreigners and our own citizenry."[2] Other detractors claim that it just does not work, and they cite the presidential elections of 1824, 1876, 1888, and, of course, 2000 as representative of the failures of the College. Those who defend the Electoral College, however, claim that the failures of these elections had little to do with the Electoral College itself.[3]

According to Gary Gregg, director of the McConnell Center for Political Leadership, a new study shows that much of what Americans think we know about the Electoral College is wrong. Consequently, we should actively question the wisdom of those who want to see it abolished.[4]

Laker 6

Notes

1. Lawrence D. Longley and Neal R. Peirce, *The Electoral College Primer 2000* (New Haven: Yale University Press, 1999).

2. William C. McIntyre, "Revisiting the Electoral College," *New York Times*, November 17, 2001, late edition, sec. A.

3. Avagara, *EC: The Electoral College Webzine*, accessed January 21, 2017, http://www.avagara .com/e_c/.

4. Gary Gregg, "Keep the College," *National Review Online*, November 7, 2001, accessed January 19, 2017, http://www.lexisnexis.com/universe/.

Laker 7

Bibliography

Avagara. *EC: The Electoral College Webzine*. Accessed February 21, 2017. http://www.avagara.com/e_c/.

Gregg, Gary. "Keep the College." *National Review Online*, November 7, 2001. Accessed February 19, 2017. http://www.lexisnexis.com/universe/.

Longley, Lawrence D., and Neal R. Peirce. *The Electoral College Primer 2000*. New Haven: Yale University Press, 1999.

McIntyre, William C. "Revisiting the Electoral College." *New York Times*, November 17, 2001, late edition, sec. A.

26 CSE Documentation

After reading this chapter, you should be able to . . .

- Use in-text references in CSE style (26a)
- Create references for books and nonperiodical sources (26b)
- Create references for periodical sources (26c)
- Create references for online sources (26d)
- Format a paper in CSE style (26e)

Within the disciplines of the natural and applied sciences, citation styles are highly specialized. Many disciplines follow the guidelines of particular journals or style manuals within their individual fields. Widely followed by writers in the sciences is the comprehensive guide published by the Council of Science Editors: *Scientific Style and Format: The CSE Manual for Authors, Editors, and Publishers*, eighth edition (2014).

The preferred documentation system in CSE places references in the body of the text using a superscript number, which is preceded by a space and placed inside punctuation. For example:

> Cold fingers and toes are common circulatory problems found in most heavy cigarette smokers [1].

This number corresponds to a numbered entry on the CSE source list, titled *References*.

The CSE References page lists all sources cited in the paper. To create a CSE References page, follow these guidelines:

1. Title your page "References" and center this title at the top of the page.
2. Single-space within citations and double-space between citations.
3. List citations in the order they appear in the body of the paper. Begin each citation with its citation number, followed by a period, flush left, and do not indent any lines that follow.
4. Authors are listed by last name, followed by initials. Capitalize only first words and proper nouns in cited titles. Book titles are not underlined or italicized, and article titles are not placed between quotation marks. Names of journals should be abbreviated where possible.
5. Cite the publication year and volume or page numbers if applicable.

26a In-Text References in CSE Style

CSE documentation of sources does not require the names of authors in the text but only a number that refers to the References list at the end.

> In 1997, the Gallup poll reported that 55% of adults in the United States think secondhand smoke is "very harmful," compared to only 36% in 1994 [1].

The superscript [1] refers to the first entry on the References list, where readers will find a complete citation for this source.

What if you need more than one citation in a passage?

If the numbers are consecutive, separate them with a hyphen. If nonconsecutive, use a comma.

> The previous work [1,3,5-8,11]

Index of CSE Documentation

26b Books and Nonperiodical Sources in CSE-Style References

1. Nance JJ. What goes up: the global assault on our atmosphere. New York: W Morrow; 1991.

AUTHOR'S OR EDITOR'S NAME

The author's last name comes first, followed by the initials of the author's first name and middle name (if provided). If the source has an editor instead of an author, put the word *editor* after the name.

BOOK TITLE

- Do not italicize or underline titles.
- Capitalize only the first word and proper nouns.

PUBLICATION INFORMATION

Year of publication

- The year comes after the other publication information. It follows a semicolon.
- If it is a multivolume edited work published over a period of more than one year, give the span of years.

Page numbers

- When citing part of a book, give the page range for the selection: *p. 60–90.*

Sample references

BOOKS

1. Book by a single author/editor

   2. Wilson EO, The social conquest of earth. New York (NY): Liveright; 2012.

2. Book by two or more authors/editors

   3. O'Day DH, Horgen PA, editors. Sexual interactions in eukaryotic microbes. New York (NY): Academic Press; 1981.

3. Book by a group or organization

   4. IAEA. Manual on radiation haematology. Vienna (Austria): IAEA; 1971.

4. Two or more books by the same author

Number the references according to the order in which they appear in the text.

> 5. Gould SJ. The structure of evolutionary theory. Cambridge (MA): Harvard University Press; 2002.

> 8. Gould SJ. Wonderful life: the Burgess Shale and the nature of history. New York (NY): Norton; 1989.

PARTS OF BOOKS

5. Single chapter written by the same author as the book

> 6. Ogle M. All the modern conveniences: American household plumbing, 1840–1890. Baltimore: Johns Hopkins University Press; 2000. Convenience embodied; p. 60-92.

6. Selection in an anthology or chapter in an edited collection

> 7. Kraft K, Baines DM. Computer classrooms and third grade development. In: Green MD, editor. Computers and early development. New York (NY): Academic; 1997. p. 168-179.

REPORTS

7. Technical and research reports

> 9. Austin A, Baldwin R, editors. Faculty collaboration: enhancing the quality of scholarship and teaching. ASCHE-ERIC Higher Education Report 7. Washington (DC): George Washington University; 1991.

26c Periodical Sources in CSE-Style References

1. Bohannon J. Climate change: IPCC report lays out options for taming greenhouse gases. Science. 2007;316(5826): 812–814.

AUTHOR'S NAME

The author's last name comes first, followed by the initials of the author's first name and middle name (if provided).

TITLE OF ARTICLE

- Do not place titles inside quotation marks.
- Capitalize only the first word and proper nouns.

PUBLICATION INFORMATION

Name of journal

- Do not abbreviate single-word titles. Abbreviate multiple-word titles according to the National Information Standards Organization (NISO) list of serials.
- Capitalize each word of the journal title, even if abbreviated.

Date of publication, volume, and issue numbers

- Include the issue number inside parentheses if it is present in the document. Leave no spaces between these items.

JOURNAL ARTICLES

8. Article by one author

1. Board J. Reduced lodging for soybeans in low plant population is related to light quality. Crop Science. 2001;41:379-387.

9. Article by two or more authors/editors

2. Simms K, Denison D. Observed interactions between wild and domesticated mixed-breed canines. J Mamm. 1997;70:341-342.

10. Article by a group or organization

4. Center for Science in the Public Interest. Meat labeling: help! Nutrition Action Health Letter: 2. 2001 Apr 1.

11. **Article with no identifiable author**

If you cannot find an indentifiable author or organization, begin the entry with the article title.

12. **Journals paginated by issue**

Use the month or season of publication (and day, if given) for journals paginated by issue. Include the issue number in parentheses after the volume number.

> 8. Barlow JP. Africa rising: everything you know about Africa is wrong. Wired. 1998 Jan; 142-158.

26d Online Sources in CSE-Style References

Include the DOI at the end if available.

13. **Online journal articles**

> 2. Schunck CH, Shin Y, Schirotzek A, Zwierlein MW, Ketterle W. Pairing without superfluidity: the ground state of an imbalanced fermi mixture. Science. 2007 [accessed 2013 June 15]; 316(5826):867-870. http://www.sciencemag.org/cgi/content /full/3165826/867/DC1. doi:10.1126/science.1140749.

14. **Scientific databases on the Internet**

> 3. Comprehensive Large Array-data Stewardship System. Release 4.2. Silver Spring (MD): National Environmental Satellite, Data, and Information Service (US). 2007-[updated 2015 Nov 25; cited 2016 May 14]. www.class.noaa.gov/saa/products/welcome.

15. **E-Books**

> 18. Chen A. Celebrating 30 years of the space shuttle program. Washington (DC): National Aeronautics and Space Administration; 2012 [accessed 2016 May 14]. https://www.nasa.gov/connect /ebooks/shuttle_retrospect_detail.html.

26e Sample Pages with CSE Documentation

Do 1

Thuydung Do

BIO 206L Fall 2016

November 13, 2016

The Preference of Home Soil over Foreign Soil in

Pogonomyrmex barbatus

Abstract

Tests were conducted to see whether or not harvester ants of the species *Pogonomyrmex barbatus* can actually distinguish home soil from foreign soil. These ants were exposed to different types of soils, and the time they spent on each soil was recorded. The Wilcoxon Signed Rank test was performed to analyze the collected data. It was observed that *Pogonomyrmex barbatus* does show preference for home soil over foreign soil.

Introduction

Pieces of food are sometimes seen surrounded by hundreds of ants a while after they were dropped on the table or on the ground. There are also trails of ants that line up in an orderly fashion leading from the food to the nests. How do these ants know to follow each other in a line instead of scattering all over? The main method is through releasing pheromones [1]. The pheromones allow the ants to trail after one another, but where will they go? What makes these different ant mounds unique from one another? Based on research

Do 2

done by Wagner and her group, soil biota and soil chemistry of each nest can set themselves apart [2]. Can the harvester ants detect these differences in the soils at all, or are all soils the same to them? In this experiment, the null hypothesis that harvester ants *Pogonomyrmex barbatus* cannot distinguish home soil from foreign soil and neutral soil was tested in attempt to find the answer to this question.

Do 3

References

1. Holldobler B, Morgan ED, Oldham NJ, Liebig J. Recruitment pheromone in the harvester ant genus *Pogonomyrmex*. J Insect Phys. 2001;47:369-374.

2. Wagner D, Brown M, Gordon D. Harvester ant nests, soil biota and chemistry. Oecologia. 1997;112:232-236.

PART 7 Effective Style and Language

STYLE AND LANGUAGE MAP

| **Understand how to write with impact** | • Active verbs give your writing force. Go to 27a and 27b.
• Putting the focus on people and other actors makes your writing come alive. Go to 27c. |

| **Understand how to write concisely** | • Eliminate unnecessary words and wordy phrases. Go to 28a and 28b.
• Eliminate empty words like very and totally. Go to 28a.
• Simplify tangled sentences. Go to 28c. |

| **Understand how to write with emphasis** | • Know where to place main ideas. Go to 29a.
• Recognize and correct faulty parallelism. Go to 29c, 29d, and 29e. |

| **Find the right words** | • Be aware of levels of formality. Go to 30a.
• Use precise and accurate words. Go to 30c.
• Write to be inclusive. Go to Chapter 31. |

27 | Write with Power

QUICK*TAKE*

After reading this chapter, you should be able to . . .

* **Recognize the power of verbs** (27a)
* **Make your writing active** (27b)

  Passive: The snowboard was invented by Sherman Poppen.
  Active: Sherman Poppen invented the snowboard.

* **Use agents in your writing** (27c)

  No agent: It was made as a plaything for his daughter.
  With agent: Poppen made the first snowboard as a plaything for his daughter.

* **Vary your sentences** (27d)

  Choppy and repetitive: It was called the Snurfer. The name was a combination of snow and surfer. It was a skateboard without wheels. It was manufactured as a toy the next year.
  Variety: Poppen named his snowboard the Snurfer, which was a combination of snow and surfer. Essentially a skateboard without wheels, the Snurfer was manufactured as a toy the next year.

Keeping a few principles in mind can make your writing a pleasure to read instead of a boring slog.

In visuals

You imagine actions when subjects are captured in motion.

In writing

Your readers expect actions to be expressed in verbs: *gallop, canter, trot, run, sprint, dash, bound, thunder, tear away*.

In visuals

Viewers interpret the most prominent person or thing as the subject—what the visual is about.

In writing

Readers interpret the first person or thing they meet in a sentence as what the sentence is about (the jockey, the horse). They expect that person or thing to perform the action expressed in the verb.

345

27a Pay Attention to Verbs

A teacher may once have told you that verbs are "action words." Where are the action words in the following paragraph?

> Red hair flying, professional snowboarder and skateboarder Shaun White became a two-time Olympic gold medalist with a record score of 48.4 at the 2010 Winter Olympics. White was a skier before he was 5, but became a snowboarder at age 6, and by age 7 he had become a professional, receiving corporate sponsorships. At age 9, White became friends with professional skateboarder Tony Hawk, who became White's mentor in becoming a professional skateboarder. White is known for accomplishing several "firsts" in snowboarding, including being the first to land back-to-back double corks and to master a trick called a Cab 7 Melon Grab. He is also the holder of record for the highest score in the men's halfpipe at the Winter Olympics.

No action words here! The paragraph describes a series of actions, yet most of the verbs are *is, was,* and *became.* These sentences typify writing that uses *be* verbs (*is, are, was, were*) when better alternatives are available. Think about what the actions are and choose powerful verbs that express those actions.

> Red hair flying, professional snowboarder and skateboarder Shaun White **scored** a 48.4 during the 2010 Winter Olympics and **won** his second gold medal. White **skied** before he was 5, but **switched** to snowboarding at age 6, and by age 7 **received** corporate sponsorships. At age 9, White **befriended** professional skateboarder Tony Hawk, who **mentored** White and **helped** him become a professional skateboarder. White **has accomplished** several "firsts" in snowboarding, including landing back-to-back double corks and mastering a trick called a Cab 7 Melon Grab. He also **holds** the record for the highest score in the men's halfpipe at the Winter Olympics.

STAYING ON TRACK

Express actions as verbs

Many sentences contain words that express action, but those words are nouns instead of verbs. Often the nouns can be changed into verbs. For example:

> The arson unit ~~conducted an investigation of~~ **investigated** the mysterious fire.

> The committee ~~had a debate over~~ **debated** how best to spend the surplus funds.

Notice that changing nouns into verbs also eliminates unnecessary words.

27b Stay Active

When you were a very young child, you learned an important lesson about language. Perhaps you can remember the day you broke the cookie jar. Did you tell Mom, "I knocked over the jar"? Probably not. Instead, you might have said, "The jar got broken." This short sentence accomplishes an amazing sleight of hand. Who broke the jar and how the jar was broken remain mysterious. Apparently, it just broke.

"Got" is often used for "was" in informal speech. In written language, the sentence would read, "The jar was broken," which is an example of the passive voice. Passives can be as useful for adults as for children to conceal who is responsible for an action:

> The laptop containing our customers' personal information
> **was misplaced**.

Who misplaced the laptop? Who knows?

Sentences with transitive verbs (labeled "TV" below; verbs that need an object; see 35c) can be written in the active or passive voice. In the active voice, the subject of the sentence is the actor. In the passive voice, the subject is being acted upon.

Active   ┌───── SUBJ ─────┐┌─TV─┐
             Leonardo da Vinci **painted** *Mona Lisa* between 1503 and 1506.

Passive ┌─SUBJ─┐┌───TV───┐
            Mona Lisa **was painted** by Leonardo da Vinci between 1503 and 1506.

The passive is created with a form of *be* and the past participle of the main verb. In a passive voice sentence, you can either name the actor in a *by* phrase following the verb or omit the actor altogether.

Passive   *Mona Lisa* was painted between 1503 and 1506.

STAYING ON TRACK

Prefer the active voice

To write with power, consider different ways of saying the same thing. The extra effort will bring noticeable results.

Passive   A request on your part for special consideration based on your experience working in the profession **will be reviewed** by the admissions committee.

STAYING ON TRACK *(Continued)*

Active   If you ask for special consideration because you have worked in the profession, the graduate admissions committee **will review** your request.

27c Find Agents

The **agent** is the person or thing that does the action. The most powerful writing usually highlights the agent in a sentence.

Focus on people

Read the following sentence aloud.

> Mayoral approval of the recommended zoning change for a strip mall on Walnut Street will negatively impact the traffic and noise levels of the Walnut Street residential environment.

It sounds dead, doesn't it? Think about the meaning of the sentence for a minute. It involves people—the mayor and the people who live on Walnut Street. Putting those people in the sentence makes it come alive.

With people

> If the **mayor** approves the recommended zoning change to allow a strip mall on Walnut Street, **people who live on the street** will have to endure much more noise and traffic.

Identify characters

If people are not your subject, then keep the focus on other types of characters.

Without characters

> The celebration of Martin Luther King Day had to be postponed because of inclement weather.

With characters

> A severe **ice storm** forced the **city** to postpone the Martin Luther King Day celebration.

STAYING ON TRACK

Include people

Including people makes your writing more emphatic. Most readers relate better to people than to abstractions. Putting people in your writing also introduces active verbs because people do things.

Without people

Remembering that the ghosts in the arcade game Pac-Man move directly in response to the player's movements can aid greatly in winning the game.

With people

If **you** remember that the ghosts in the arcade game Pac-Man move directly in response to the player's movements, **you** increase your chances of winning the game.

27d Vary Your Sentences

Read the following passage.

> On the first day Garth, Jim, and I paddled 14 miles down Johnstone Strait. The morning was moist and deceptively calm. We stopped to watch a few commercial fishing boats net salmon on the way. Then we set up camp on a rocky beach. We headed down the strait about 5 more miles to Robson Bight. It is a famous scratching place for orcas. The Bight is a small bay. We paddled out into the strait so we could see the entire Bight. There were no orcas inside. By this time we were getting tired. We were hungry. The clouds assumed a wintry dark thickness. The wind was kicking up against us. Our heads were down going into the cold spray.

The subject matter is interesting, but the writing isn't. The paragraph is a series of short sentences, one after the other, that have a thumpety-thump, thumpety-thump rhythm. When you have too many short sentences one after the other, try combining a few of them. The result of combining some (but not all) short sentences is a paragraph whose sentences match the interest of the subject.

Revised

> On the first day Garth, Jim, and I paddled 14 miles down Johnstone Strait **on a moist and deceptively calm morning.** We stopped to watch a few commercial fishing boats net salmon before we set up camp on a rocky beach and headed down the strait about 5 more miles to Robson Bight, a small bay known as a famous scratching place for orcas. We paddled out into the strait so we could see the entire Bight, but there were no orcas inside. **By this time we were tired and hungry, the clouds had assumed a wintry dark thickness, and the wind was kicking up against us—our heads dropped going into the cold spray.**

Ahead of us we heard what sounded like a series of distant shotgun blasts, and when it happened again, we could see the fins of a pod of orcas. We stopped paddling. **The orcas were feeding on the salmon, surfacing at 6- to 8-second intervals, coming straight at us, swimming in twos and threes, at least twelve of them, a mix of the long fins of the bulls and the shorter, more rounded fins of the cows, the noise of their exhaling becoming louder and louder.**

27e Give Your Writing Personality

Nobody likes listening to the voice of a robot. Good writing—no matter what the genre—has two unfailing qualities: a human personality that bursts through the page or screen and a warmth that suggests the writer genuinely wishes to engage the readers.

From age eleven to age sixteen I lived a spartan life without the usual adolescent uncertainty. I wanted to be the best swimmer in the world, and there was nothing else.

—Diana Nyad

You don't choose your family. They are God's gift to you, as you are to them.

—Desmond Tutu

Sentences like these convince your readers that you are genuinely interested in reaching out to them.

28 | Write Concisely

After reading this chapter, you should be able to . . .

- **Eliminate unnecessary words** (28a)

  Wordy: I was fourteen years of age when my friends and I happened upon the totally abandoned house in the exact middle of the woods.
  Less wordy: I was fourteen when my friends and I happened upon the abandoned house in the middle of the woods.

- **Reduce wordy phrases** (28b)

  Wordy: At that point in time, I was of the opinion that I alone amongst all the people in my family of origin recognized the hypocrisy of a bourgeois, middle-class existence.
  Less wordy: At that time, I believed that in my family I alone recognized the hypocrisy of middle-class life.

- **Simplify tangled sentences** (28c)

  Wordy: There were no words exchanged by us as we surveyed the unsettling array of stuff left behind by the house's former occupants.
  Less wordy: Nobody said a word as we surveyed the unsettling array of stuff that the house's former occupants had left behind.

Clutter creeps into our lives every day.

Clutter also creeps into our writing in the form of unnecessary words, inflated constructions, and excessive jargon.

In **regards to** the Web site, the content is **pretty** successful **in consideration of** the topic. The site is **fairly** good **writing-wise** and is **very** unique in telling you how to adjust the rear derailleur one step at a time.

The words in **burgundy** are clutter. Get rid of the clutter. You can say the same thing with half the words and gain more impact as a result.

The well-written Web site on bicycle repair provides step-by-step instructions on adjusting your rear derailleur.

28a Eliminate Unnecessary Words

Empty words resemble the foods that add calories without nutrition. Put your writing on a diet.

Redundancy

Some words act as modifiers, but when you look closely at them, they repeat the meaning of the word they pretend to modify. Have you heard expressions such as *red in color, small in size, round in shape, several in number, past history, attractive in appearance, visible to the eye,* or *honest truth?* Imagine *red* not referring to color or *round* not referring to shape.

Legalese

Legal language often attempts to remove ambiguity through repetition and redundancy. For example, think about what a flight attendant says when your plane arrives.

Please remain seated, with your seatbelt fastened, until the airplane has come to a full and complete stop; when you deplane from the airplane, be sure to take with you all your personal belongings.

Is there a difference between a *full* stop and a *complete* stop? Can you *deplane* from anything but an airplane? Would you have any *nonpersonal* belongings?

Some speech situations like the flight attendant's instructions may require redundancy to ensure that listeners understand, but in writing, say it once.

COMMON ERRORS

Empty intensifiers

Intensifiers modify verbs, adjectives, and other adverbs, and they often are overused. One of the most overused intensifiers is *very*.

> The new copper roof was **very bright** on a sunny day.

A new copper roof reflects almost all light. *Very bright* isn't an accurate description. Another adjective would be more accurate.

> The new copper roof was **blinding** on a sunny day.

Very and *totally* are but two of a list of empty intensifiers that usually can be eliminated with no loss of meaning. Other empty intensifiers include *absolutely*, *awfully*, *definitely*, *incredibly*, *particularly*, and *really*.

Remember: When you use *very*, *totally*, or another intensifier before an adjective or adverb, always ask yourself whether there is a more accurate adjective or adverb you could use instead to better express the same thought.

28b Reduce Wordy Phrases

We acquire bad writing and speaking habits because we read and hear so much wordy language. Many inexperienced writers use phrases like "It is my opinion that" or "I think that" to begin sentences. These phrases are deadly to read. If you find them in your prose, cut them. Unless a writer is citing a source, we assume that the ideas are the writer's. (See "When to use I" on p. 366.)

Coaches are among the worst in using many words for what could be said in a few:

> After much deliberation about Brown's future in football with regard to possible permanent injuries, I came to the conclusion that it would be in his best interest not to continue his pursuit of playing football again.

The coach might have said simply:

> Because Brown risks permanent injury if he plays football again, I decided to release him from the team.

Perhaps the coach wanted to sound impressive, authoritative, or thoughtful. But the result is the opposite. Speakers and writers who impress us are those who use words efficiently.

STAYING ON TRACK

Replace wordy phrases

Certain stock phrases plague writing in the workplace, in the media, and in academia. Many wordy phrases can be replaced by one or two words with no loss in meaning.

Wordy   **Within the time period of no more than** the past decade, *Twitter* has become one of the ten most visited Web sites on the Internet.

Concise   **In** the past decade, *Twitter* has become one of the ten most visited Web sites on the Internet.

Wordy	Concise
at this point in time	now
at that point in time	then
due to the fact that	because
for the purpose of	for
have the ability to	can
in spite of the fact that	although
in the event that	if
in the modern world of today	today
in the neighborhood of	about
it is possible that there might be	possibly
make an attempt	try
met with her approval	she approved
The great writer by the name of Henry David Thoreau	Henry David Thoreau

28c Simplify Tangled Sentences

Long sentences can be graceful and forceful. Such sentences, however, often require several revisions before they achieve elegance. Too often long sentences reflect wandering thoughts that the writer did not bother to go back and sort out. Two of the most important strategies for untangling long sentences are described in Chapter 27: using active verbs (Section 27a) and naming your agents (Section 27c). Here are some other strategies.

Revise expletives

Expletives are empty words that can occupy the subject position in a sentence. The most frequently used expletives are *there is*, *there are*, and *it is*.

> **Wordy**   **There is** another banking option that gives you free checking.

To simplify the sentence, find the agent and make it the subject.

> **Revised**   Another **banking option** gives you free checking.

> **Wordy**   **There were** several important differences between their respective positions raised by the candidates in the debate.

> **Revised**   The **candidates** raised several important differences between their respective positions in the debate.

A few kinds of sentences—for example, *It is raining*—do require you to use an expletive. In most cases, however, expletives add unnecessary words, and sentences usually read better without them.

Use positive constructions

Sentences become wordy and hard to read when they include two or more negatives such as the words *no*, *not*, and *nor* and the prefixes *un-* and *mis-*. For example:

> **Difficult**   A **not un**common complaint among employers of new college graduates is that they **cannot** communicate effectively in writing.

> **Revised**   Employers frequently complain that new college graduates cannot write effectively.

> **Even simpler**   Employers value the rare college graduate who can write well.

Phrasing sentences positively usually makes them more economical. Moreover, it makes your style more forceful and direct.

Simplify sentence structure

Long sentences can be hard to read, not because they are long, but because they are convoluted and hide the relationships among ideas. Consider the following sentence.

> Some historians are arguing that World War II actually ended with German reunification in 1990 instead of when the Japanese surrendered in 1945, after which time the Cold War got in the way of formal legal settlements amongst the involved nations and Germany was divided between the Western powers and the Soviet Union, meaning that no comprehensive peace treaty was signed.

This sentence is hard to read. To rewrite sentences like this one, find the main ideas and then determine the relationships among them.

After examining the sentence, you decide there are two key ideas:

1. Some historians argue that World War II actually ended in 1990 with German reunification, not when the Japanese surrendered in 1945.
2. The Cold War and the division of Germany between the Western powers and the Soviet Union hindered formal legal settlements amongst the involved nations.

Next ask what the relationship is between the two ideas. When you identify the key ideas, the relationship is often obvious; in this case (2) is the cause of (1). Thus the word you want to connect the two ideas is *because*.

> **Because** the Cold War and the division of Germany between the Western powers and the Soviet Union hindered formal legal settlements amongst the involved nations, some historians argue that World War II actually ended in 1990 with German reunification rather than with the Japanese surrender in 1945.

The revised sentence is both clearer and more concise, reducing the number of words from sixty-one to forty-seven.

29 | Write with Emphasis

QUICK*TAKE*

After reading this chapter, you should be able to . . .

- **Manage emphasis in your sentences** (29a)

  Main idea unclear: Pluto was once classified as a planet. Now it is classified as a dwarf planet. It does not meet the IAU's official definition of a planet.

  Main idea made clear: Pluto's classification changed from planet to dwarf planet **because** it does not meet the IAU's official definition of a planet.

- **Construct links across sentences** (29b)

- **Use parallelism correctly** (29c)

  Not parallel: To be a planet, a celestial body must be in orbit around the Sun, **mass must be sufficient** to assume a nearly round shape, and **enough gravitational force to have** no other comparably sized objects in its orbit must be shown.

  Parallel: To be a planet, a celestial body must **orbit around the Sun**, **have sufficient mass** to assume a nearly round shape, and **show enough gravitational force** to have no other comparably sized objects in its orbit.

29a Manage Emphasis in Sentences

Put your main ideas in main clauses

Emphasize your most important information by placing it in main clauses and your less important information in subordinate clauses (for a description of main and subordinate clauses, see 32c).

In the following paragraph all the sentences are main clauses:

> Lotteries were common in the United States before and after the American Revolution. They eventually ran into trouble. They were run by private companies. Sometimes the companies took off with the money. They didn't pay the winners.

This paragraph is grammatically correct, but it does not help the reader understand which pieces of information the author wants to emphasize. Combining the simple sentences into main and subordinate clauses and phrases can significantly improve the paragraph.

First, identify the main ideas.

Lotteries were common in the United States before and after the American Revolution. They eventually ran into trouble.

These ideas can be combined into one sentence.

Lotteries were common in the United States before and after the American Revolution, but they eventually ran into trouble.

Now think about the relationship of the three remaining sentences to the main ideas. Those sentences explain why lotteries ran into trouble; thus, the word you want to use to connect the ideas is *because*.

Lotteries were common in the United States before and after the American Revolution, but they eventually ran into trouble **because** they were run by private companies that sometimes took off with the money instead of paying the winners.

Put key ideas at the beginning and end of sentences

Read these sentences aloud.

1   The **Cottingley Fairies**, a series of five photographs taken in 1917 by Elsie Wright and Frances Griffiths, depicts the girls interacting with what seem to be fairies.

2   A series of photographs showing two girls interacting with what seem to be fairies, known as the **Cottingley Fairies**, was taken by Elsie Wright and Frances Griffiths in 1917.

3   The series of photos Elsie Wright and Frances Griffiths took in 1917 showing the two girls interacting with what seem to be fairies is called the **Cottingley Fairies**.

Most readers put the primary emphasis on words at the beginning and end of a sentence. The front of a sentence usually gives what is known: the topic. At the end is the new information about the topic. Subordinate information is in the middle. If a paragraph is about the Cottingley Fairies, we would not expect the writer to choose sentence 2 over 1 or 3. In sentence 2 the reference to the Cottingley Fairies is buried in the middle.

Photographs and writing gain energy when they emphasize key ideas.

In visuals

Photographers create emphasis by composing the image to direct the attention of the viewer. Putting people and objects in the foreground and making them stand out against the background gives them emphasis.

In writing

You have many tools for creating emphasis. Writers can design a page to gain emphasis by using headings, white space, type size, color, and boldfacing. Just as important, learning the craft of structuring sentences will empower you to give your writing emphasis.

29b Forge Links Across Sentences

When your writing maintains a focus of attention across sentences, the reader can distinguish the important ideas and how they relate to each other. To achieve this coherence, control which ideas occupy the positions of greatest emphasis. The words and ideas you repeat from sentence to sentence act as links.

Link sentences from front to front

In front-to-front linkage, the subject of the sentence remains the focus from one sentence to the next. In the following sequence, sentences 1 through 5 are all about Arthur Wright. The subject in each of sentences 2–5 refers to the first sentence by using the pronouns *he* and *his*.

1   **Arthur Wright** was one of the first electrical engineers in England.

2   **He** loaned his camera to his daughter Elsie, who took the fairy pictures in the yard behind their house.

3   **His** opinion was that the pictures were fake.

4   However, **his** wife Polly was convinced that they were real.

5   Nevertheless, **he** banned Elsie from ever using his camera again.

Each sentence adds more information about the repeated topic, Arthur Wright.

Link sentences from back to front

In back-to-front linkage, the new information at the end of the sentence is used as the topic of the next sentence. Back-to-front linkage allows new material to be introduced and commented on.

1   By the summer of 1919, the girls and their photographs had become so well known that author Sir Arthur Conan Doyle even wrote an article for a leading magazine claiming that the photos and the fairies were **real**.

2   Not everyone believed that the Cottingley Fairies were **authentic**, however, and other public figures wrote the papers calling the photographs a **hoax**.

3   The **hoax** continued until the 1980s when both Elsie and Frances finally admitted that all but one of the pictures were fake.

Back-to-front linkage is useful when ideas need to be advanced quickly, as when you are telling stories. Rarely, however, will you use either front-to-front linkage or back-to-front linkage for long. You will mix them, using front-to-front linkage to add more information and back-to-front linkage to move the topic along.

STAYING ON TRACK

Check links across sentences

Where in the following paragraph is your attention disrupted?

> In February 1888 Vincent van Gogh left cloudy Paris for Arles in the sunny south of France. Later that year he persuaded fellow painter Paul Gauguin to join him. Gauguin, who had traveled in the tropics, did not find Arles colorful and exotic. Critics hail this period as the most productive in van Gogh's brilliant but short career.

The last sentence connects distantly with what has come before by mentioning art and van Gogh, but it jars you when you read it because new information, "critics," comes where we expect to find known information. Adding a clause provides a bridge between the old and new information.

> In February 1888 Vincent van Gogh left cloudy Paris for Arles in the sunny south of France. Later that year he persuaded fellow painter Paul Gauguin to join him. Gauguin, who had traveled in the tropics, did not find Arles colorful and exotic. **Although van Gogh and Gauguin argued and soon parted company,** critics hail this period as the most productive in van Gogh's brilliant but short career.

29c Use Parallel Structure with Parallel Ideas

What if Patrick Henry had written "Give me liberty or I prefer not to live"? Would we remember those words today? We do remember the words he did write: "Give me liberty or give me death." Writers who use parallel structure often create memorable sentences.

Use parallelism with *and, or, nor, but*

When you join elements at the same level with coordinating conjunctions, including *and, or, nor, yet, so, but,* and *for,* use parallel grammatical structure.

Awkward

In today's global economy, **the method of production and where factories are located** have become relatively unimportant in comparison with **the creation of new concepts and marketing those concepts**.

Parallel

In today's global economy, **how goods are made and where they are produced** have become relatively unimportant in comparison with **creating new concepts and marketing those concepts.**

COMMON ERRORS

Faulty Parallel Structure

When writers neglect to use parallel structure, the result can be jarring. Reading your writing aloud will help you catch problems in parallelism. Read this sentence aloud.

> At our club meeting, we identified problems in **finding** new members, **publicizing** our activities, and **maintenance** of our Web site.

The end of the sentence does not sound right because the parallel structure is broken. We expect to find another verb + *ing* following *finding* and *publicizing*. Instead, we run into *maintenance*, a noun. The problem is easy to fix: Change the noun to the *-ing* verb form.

> At our club meeting, we identified problems in finding new members, publicizing our activities, and **maintaining** our Web site.

Remember: Use parallel structure for parallel ideas.

Use parallelism with *either/or, not only/but also*

Make identical in structure the parts of sentences linked by correlative conjunctions: *either . . . or, neither . . . nor, not only . . . but also,* and *whether . . . or.*

Awkward

Purchasing the undeveloped land **not only gives us a new park but also is something that our children will benefit from in the future.**

Parallel

Purchasing the undeveloped land **not only will give our city a new park but also will leave our children a lasting inheritance.**

The more structural elements you match, the stronger the effect.

Correct

Either **we find** a way to recruit new members or **we settle** for the current number of sailboats.

Improved

Either **we find a way to recruit new members** or **we drop the plan to increase our fleet.**

The first sentence is correct but still clunky. The parallelism is limited to *we find/we settle*. The second sentence delivers more punch by extending the parallelism: *we find a way to recruit new members/we drop the plan to increase our fleet*. Matching structural elements exactly—verb for verb, article for article, adjective for adjective, object for object—provides the strongest parallelism.

29d Use Parallel Structure with Lists

Lists are frequently used in visual aids for oral presentations and in announcements, brochures, instructions, and other kinds of writing. The effectiveness of a bulleted list is lost, however, when the items are not in parallel form. In a list of action items, such as a list of goals, beginning each item with a verb emphasizes the action. See the example below.

Sailing Club Goals

- Increase the membership by 50% this year
- Compete in all local regattas
- Offer beginning and advanced classes
- Purchase eight new Flying Juniors
- Organize a spring banquet
- Publicize all major events

29e Use Parallel Structure in Paragraphs

Use parallelism to create rhythm

Parallel structure does not have to be used in rigid, mechanical ways. Repeating elements of structure can build a rhythm that gives your prose a distinctive voice.

If you don't like my book, write your own. If you don't think you can write a novel, that ought to tell you something. If you think you can, do.

—Rita Mae Brown, from *A Note*

Use parallel structure to pair ideas

Parallel structure is also useful to pair ideas. The closer the similarity in structure, the more emphasis you will achieve.

> Being a grown-up means assuming responsibility for yourself, for your children, and—here's the big curve—for your parents. In other words, you do get to stay up later, but you want to go to sleep sooner.

> —Wendy Wasserstein, from *Bachelor Girls*

■ Parallel structure in images also creates emphasis. Notice how the horse and the groom have a parallel stance—both tense, both with knees bent, both looking away—connected only by the hand on the rein.

30 | Find the Right Words

QUICK*TAKE*

After reading this chapter, you should be able to . . .

- **Choose the right level of formality** (30a)

  Informal: The reporter was all up in Senator Grimes's face about the scandal.

  Formal, college writing: The reporter confronted Senator Grimes about the scandal.

- **Recognize denotation and connotation** (30b)

- **Use the right words** (30c)

  Imprecise and incorrect: The senator said he had received bad council from someone.

  More precise and correct: Senator Grimes admitted accepting bad counsel from his financial advisor.

- **Use figurative language effectively** (30d)

  Literal: Senator Grimes was very nervous under the scrutiny of the press.

  Figurative: Senator Grimes melted under the scrutiny of the press.

30a Be Aware of Levels of Formality

Colloquialisms

Colloquialisms are words or expressions that are used informally, often in conversation but less often in writing.

> I'm not happy with my grades, but that's **the way the cookie crumbles.**

> I've **had it up to here** with all of Tom's complaining.

> Liz is always **running off at the mouth** about something.

Aside from carrying meanings that aren't always obvious to your reader, colloquialisms usually indicate a lack of seriousness that runs counter to what you'll be trying to accomplish in most academic and professional writing. Colloquialisms can suggest a flippant attitude, carelessness, or even thoughtlessness.

College writing does not mean, however, that you should try to use big words when small ones will do as well or that you should use ten words instead of two.

Slang

The most conspicuous kind of language to be avoided in most college writing is slang. The next time a friend talks to you, listen closely to the words he or she uses. Chances are you will notice several words that you probably would not use in a college writing assignment. Slang words are created by and for a particular group—even if that group is just you and your friend.

> Keesha's new earrings were **on fleek**.

> Quit **throwing shade** at me.

Aside from being a fun way to play with language, slang asserts a sense of belonging to a group. But because slang excludes those who are not members of the group, it is best avoided in college writing.

STAYING ON TRACK

When to use *I*

You may have been taught to avoid the first person (*I, we*) in academic and professional writing. Some instructors feel that first-person references reflect a self-indulgence that is inappropriate outside of autobiography. Sentences beginning with *I* refer to the author and make him or her the subject. In a sentence such as *I think Florida's west coast beaches are better in every way than those on the east coast*, the reader's attention is divided between the beaches and the person evaluating the beaches.

Another reason some instructors prohibit use of the first person is the tendency of writers to overuse it. Some writers feel that nothing can be invalidated as long as each potentially arguable assertion starts with *I think* or *I feel*. *I* becomes a shield, which the writer uses to escape the work of building an argument.

Occasionally, the use of *I* is redundant. In the following sentence, the nature of the assertion clearly indicates that it's the writer's opinion:

Redundant *I* I think the Panama Canal is the greatest engineering achievement of the United States.

Here you can safely drop *I think* without changing the sentence's meaning. Sometimes, however, you will want to indicate plainly that an assertion is tentative. *I* is critical to the meaning of this sentence:

Tentative *I* I thought that the dim, distant light was a planet.

If you're unsure whether or not first-person references are permissible, ask your instructor.

30b Be Aware of Denotation and Connotation

Words have both literal meanings, called **denotations**, and associated meanings, called **connotations**. The contrast is evident in words that mean roughly the same thing but have different connotations. For example, some people are set in their opinions, a quality that can be described positively as *persistent*, *firm*, and *steadfast* or negatively as *stubborn*, *bull-headed*, and *close-minded*.

In college and professional writing, writers are expected not to rely on the connotations of words to make important points. For example, the statement *It's only common sense to have good schools* carries high positive connotations but is not precise enough for college writing. Most people believe in common sense, and most people want good schools. What is common sense for one person, however, is not common sense for another; how a good school is defined varies greatly. You have the obligation in college writing to support any judgment with evidence.

30c Use Specific Language

Be precise

Effective writing conveys information clearly and precisely. Words such as *situation*, *sort*, *thing*, *aspect*, and *kind* often signal undeveloped or even lazy thinking.

> **Vague** The violence aspect determines how video games are rated.
>
> **Better** The level of violence determines how video games are rated.

When citing numbers or quantities, be as exact as possible. A precise number, if known, is always better than slippery words like *several* or *many*, which some writers use to cloak the fact that they don't know the quantity in question. If you know an approximate quantity, indicate the quantity but qualify it: *about twenty-five* tells readers much more than *many*.

Use a dictionary

There is no greater tool for writers than the dictionary. When you write always have a dictionary handy—either a book or an online version—and get into the habit of using it. In addition to checking spelling, you can find additional meanings of a word that perhaps you had not considered, and you can find the etymology—the origins of a word. In many cases knowing the etymology of a word can help you use it to better effect. For example, if you want to argue that universities as institutions have succeeded because

they bring people together in contexts that prepare them for their lives after college, you might point out the etymology of *university*. *University* can be traced back to the late Latin word *universitas*, which means "society or guild," thus emphasizing the idea of a community of learning.

COMMON ERRORS

Words often confused

Words with different meanings that are pronounced in the same way are called **homonyms**. Be particularly careful that you select the correct one. These pairs can cause confusion.

bare—unadorned
bear—(1) an animal; (2) to carry

capital—(1) government seat; (2) material wealth; (3) uppercase letter
capitol—a building housing a government seat

cite—(1) to make mention of; (2) to quote as an example
sight—something seen
site—place, location

coarse—rough
course—plotted-out site or matter; an academic class

counsel—(1) advice; (2) lawyer; (3) to advise
council—a deliberative body

complement—to go with, as in *That tie complements that suit.*
compliment—to flatter

fair—(1) just; (2) carnival
fare—(1) ticket price; (2) to get along

hear—to listen to
here—location

passed—went by
past—time before the present

patience—the state of calmly waiting
patients—people receiving medical care

peace—serenity
piece—a part of

plain—(1) simple; (2) level land
plane—(1) short for airplane; (2) level surface; (3) carpenter's tool

principal—(1) head of an organization; (2) a sum of money
principle—a basic law or guideline

wear—(1) to don clothes; (2) to erode
where—location

weather—climatic condition
whether—if

Other words do not sound exactly alike, only similar. The words in the following pairs are frequently confused:

accept—to receive
except (as preposition)—excluding

advice—a suggestion
advise—to suggest

affect—to act upon or to have an effect on something or somebody
effect (as noun)—a change caused by an action

allude—to make reference to
elude—to evade

allusion—an indirect reference
illusion—a false impression

conscience—moral compass
conscious—aware

continually—(1) consistently; (2) regularly
continuously—without stopping

desert—(1) geographical feature; (2) to abandon
dessert—sweet snack

elicit—to bring out
illicit—unlawful

loose—not tight
lose—(1) to misplace; (2) to fail to win a game

personal—(1) individual; (2) private
personnel—staff

presence—opposite of absence
presents—(1) gifts; (2) introduces

respectfully—demonstrating respect
respectively—in the given order

Remember: Use a dictionary to check that you are using the right word.

30d Use Effective Figurative Language

Figurative language—figures of speech that help readers get a more vivid sense of an object or idea—is what you use when literal descriptions seem insufficient.

Literal   The prosecutor presented a much stronger legal case than did the defense attorney.

Figurative   The prosecutor took the defense attorney apart like a dollar watch.

The two most common figures of speech are the simile and the metaphor. A **simile** usually begins with *as* or *like* and makes an explicit comparison.

In the past talking about someone's children was **like** talking about the weather.

Metaphor is from a Greek term that means "carry over," which describes what happens when you encounter a metaphor: You carry over the meaning from one word to another. Metaphor makes a comparison without using *like* or *as*.

She reached the **pinnacle** of her profession.

[highest point ———————▶ best]

Two other forms of figurative language are **synecdoche**, in which the part is used to represent the whole (a hood ornament that represents a car) and **metonymy**, in which something related stands in for the thing itself (*White House* for the executive branch; *brass* for military officers).

If not used imaginatively, figurative language merely dresses up a literal description in fancy clothes without adding to the reader's understanding of the object or idea. The purpose of figurative language is to convey information vividly to help the reader grasp your meaning.

You'll want to avoid **clichés**, which are relics of figurative language, phrases used so often that they have become tired and stripped of meaning. Among countless others, the following expressions have hardened into clichés.

better late than never	out like a light
blind as a bat	playing with fire
easier said than done	pride and joy
hard as a rock	thin as a rail
ladder of success	water under the bridge
nutty as a fruitcake	wise as an owl

STAYING ON TRACK

Think fresh

You might find yourself resorting to clichés when you're low on inspiration or energy. Read your drafts aloud to yourself to identify clichés, listening for the phrases that you've used or heard before. Make a note of them and either change the clichés to literal descriptions or, better still, create fresh new phrases to convey what you were trying to say with the clichés.

Cliché

When we entered the old café with the screen door banging behind us, we knew **we stood out like a sore thumb.**

Specific

When we entered the old café with the screen door banging behind us, we knew **we stood out like our hybrid Prius in the parking lot full of pickup trucks.**

---

31 | Write to Be Inclusive

QUICK*TAKE*

After reading this chapter, you should be able to . . .

- **Avoid stereotypical assumptions** (31a)
  Stereotype: Like all Southern men, the author was fiercely loyal to his mother.
  Stereotype avoided: The author was fiercely loyal to his mother.

- **Be inclusive about gender** (31b)
  Not inclusive: Who will be manning the information booth this year?
  More inclusive: Who will be staffing the information booth this year?

- **Be inclusive about race, ethnicity, and other differences** (31c)
  Not inclusive: He was raised in the usual large Irish Catholic family.
  More inclusive: He was raised in a large family.

While the conventions of language change continually, three guidelines for inclusive language toward all groups remain constant.

- Do not point out people's differences unless those differences are relevant to your argument.
- Call people whatever they prefer to be called.
- When given a choice of terms, choose the more accurate one.

31a Be Aware of Stereotypes

Reject stereotypes

A **stereotype** makes an assumption about a group of people by applying a characteristic to all of them based on the knowledge of only a few of them. The idea that Asian women are submissive, for instance, is a stereotype; it tries to apply one personality trait to many individuals whose only shared characteristics are their gender and ethnicity. Such a stereotype is just as ridiculous as a belief that all Idahoans are potato farmers.

Of course you want to avoid obviously harmful (not to mention inaccurate) stereotypes such as *People on welfare are lazy*, *gays are effeminate*, or *NASCAR fans are rednecks*. More subtle stereotypes, however, may be harder to identify and eliminate from your writing. If you want to offer an engineer as an example, will you make the engineer a man? If you want your reader to envision a child living in subsidized housing, will you describe the child as an African American? Instead of using these examples that perpetuate stereotypes, try to choose cases that go against them.

Watch for assumptions about what's "normal"

Assumptions about what's "normal" or "regular" can create bias. Calling one person or group "normal" implies that others are abnormal.

Problematic norm

Gloria Nuñez isn't like the regular sprinters at the Greater Detroit Meet; while other runners gingerly settle their feet into the blocks, Nuñez plants her prosthetic foot in the block and waits for the starting gun.

Better

Gloria Nuñez is one sprinter at the Greater Detroit Meet who might surprise you; while other runners gingerly settle their feet into the blocks, Nuñez plants her prosthetic foot in the block and waits for the starting gun.

31b Be Inclusive About Gender

Avoid exclusive nouns and pronouns

Don't use masculine nouns and pronouns to refer to groups that are not exclusively male. *He*, *his*, *him*, *man*, and *mankind* are outmoded and inaccurate terms for all genders.

- Don't say *boy* when you mean *child*.
- Use *people* instead of *men*.
- Use *humanity* or *humankind* in place of *mankind*.

Eliminating *he*, *his*, and *him* when referring to an individual (representative or hypothetical) who is not necessarily male is more complicated. (Although it is grammatically incorrect, in an effort to respect gender identifications beyond "he" and "she," an increasing number of instructors now permit students to use "they" as a singular noun in select situations.) In most cases, try one of the following approaches.

- Make the noun and its corresponding pronoun plural. The pronoun will change from *he*, *him*, or *his* to *they*, *them*, or *theirs*.

  #### Biased masculine pronouns

  An **undercover agent** won't reveal **his** identity, even to other agents, if **he** thinks it will jeopardize the case.

  #### Better

  Undercover agents won't reveal **their** identities, even to other agents, if **they** think it will jeopardize the case.

- Replace the pronoun with another word.

  #### Biased masculine pronoun

  Anyone who wants to rent scuba gear must have **his** certification.

  #### Better

  Anyone who wants to rent scuba gear must have **diver** certification.

Use gender-neutral names for professions

Professional titles that indicate gender—*chairman*, *waitress*—falsely imply that the gender of the person doing the job changes the essence of the job being done. Terms like *woman doctor* and *male nurse* imply that a woman working as a doctor and a man working as a nurse are abnormal. Instead, write simply *doctor* and *nurse*.

Biased, gender-specific	Better, gender-neutral
chairman	chair, chairperson
clergyman	member of the clergy
congressman	representative or senator
fireman	firefighter
foreman	supervisor
hostess	host
mailman	mail carrier
manpower	personnel, staff
policeman	police officer
salesman	salesperson
stewardess	flight attendant
waitress	server
weatherman	meteorologist
workmen	workers

Eliminate bias when writing about sexual orientation

Sexual orientation refers to a person's identification as bisexual, heterosexual, homosexual, transsexual, or other. *Heterosexual* and *homosexual* carry a somewhat clinical connotation. Referring to people who are homosexual as *gays* can lead to confusion: It sometimes connotes men and women, sometimes just men. Instead, use *gay men* and *lesbians*. Again, the principle is to use terms that individuals in specific groups prefer, and this continues to evolve.

31c Be Inclusive About Race and Ethnicity

Use the terms for racial and ethnic groups that the groups use for themselves. Use *black* to write about members of the Black Coaches' Association and *African American* to write about members of the Society for African American Brotherhood. Avoid outdated terms like *Negro*.

If you are still in doubt, err on the side of specificity. For instance, while *Latino(a)*, *Hispanic*, and *Chicano(a)* are all frequently accepted terms for many people, a term that identifies a specific country (*Mexican* or *Puerto Rican*) would be more accurate. *Asian* is currently preferred over *Oriental*; however, terms like *Vietnamese* and *Japanese* are even more specific. Also, *English* and *British* are different. The people who live in England are English, but people from elsewhere in Great Britain—Scotland, Wales, Northern Ireland—will be quick to tell you that they are not English. Call people from Wales *Welsh* and those from Scotland *Scots*.

When discussing an American's heritage, often the best term to use is the country of origin plus the word *American*, as in *Swedish American* or *Mexican American* (note that these terms are not hyphenated). Currently, *black* and *African American* are acceptable. In the United States, both *American Indians* and *Native Americans* refer to indigenous peoples, but recently indigenous activists have preferred *American Indian* because of its familiarity and long use. In Canada the preferred name for indigenous peoples is either *First Nations* or *First Peoples* (or *Inuit* for those who live in the eastern Canadian Arctic and *Inuinnaq* for those in the central Canadian Arctic). If you are writing about specific people, use the name of the specific American or Canadian indigenous group (*Cree, Hopi, Mi'kmaq, Ute*).

31d Be Inclusive About Other Differences

Writing about people with disabilities

The *Publication Manual of the American Psychological Association* (6th ed.) offers good advice about putting people first, not their disability. (For more information, see section 3.15, "Disabilities," in the *Publication Manual*.) Write *people who are deaf* instead of *the deaf* and *a student who is quadriplegic* instead of *a quadriplegic student*. Discuss *a woman who uses a wheelchair*, not *a wheelchair-bound woman*. Don't reduce people to their deficiencies.

Writing about people of different ages

Avoid bias by choosing accurate terms to describe age. If possible, use the person's age rather than an adjective, like *elderly* or *older*, which might offend. *Eighty-two-year-old Adele Schumacher* is better than *elderly Adele Schumacher* or *Adele Schumacher, an older resident*.

Writing about people of different religions

Avoid making assumptions about someone's beliefs or practices based on religious affiliation. Even though the Vatican opposes capital punishment, many Roman Catholics support it. Likewise, not all Jewish men wear yarmulkes. The tremendous variation within religions and among individual practitioners makes generalizations questionable.

31e Recognize International Varieties of English

English today comes in various shapes and forms. Many applied linguists now speak of "World Englishes" in the plural, to highlight the diversity of the English language as it is used worldwide. English has long been established as the dominant language in Australia, Canada, New Zealand, the

United Kingdom, and the United States, although many people in those countries also speak other languages at home and in their communities. Englishes used in these countries share many characteristics, but there also are differences in sentence structures, vocabulary, spelling, and punctuation. For example:

British English	**Have you got** your ticket?
U.S. English	**Do you have** your ticket?

British English	What's the price of **petrol** (petroleum) these days?
U.S. English	What's the price of **gas** (gasoline) these days?

Newer varieties of English have emerged outside of traditionally English-speaking countries. Many former British and U.S. colonies—Hong Kong, India, Malaysia, Nigeria, Papua New Guinea, the Philippines, Singapore, and others—continue to use a local variety of English for both public and private communication. Englishes used in many of these countries are based primarily on the British variety, but they also include many features that reflect the local context.

Indian English	**Open** the air conditioner.
U.S. English	**Turn on** the air conditioner.

Indian English	They're **late** always.
U.S. English	They're always **late.**

Philippine English	You don't **only know.**
U.S. English	You just don't **realize.**

Philippine English	I **had seen** her yesterday.
U.S. English	I **saw** her yesterday.

Singaporean English	I was **arrowed** to lead the discussion.
U.S. English	I was **selected** to lead the discussion.

Singaporean English	I am not sure **what is it.**
U.S. English	I am not sure **what it is.**

Remember that what is correct differs from one variation of English to another.

UNDERSTANDING GRAMMAR MAP

Understand the basics of the classes of words and sentences

- Recognize word classes. Go to 32b.
- Understand the kinds of clauses and phrases. Go to 32c and 32d.
- Understand the types of sentences. Go to 32e.

Identify major sentence errors and learn how to correct them

- Recognize and fix sentence fragments, run-ons, and comma splices. Go to Chapter 33.

Identify subject-verb agreement problems and other problems with verbs

- Recognize and fix subject-verb agreement errors. Go to Chapter 34.
- Recognize and fix common verb errors. Go to Chapter 35.

Identify pronoun problems and learn how to correct them

- Recognize and fix problems with pronoun case and agreement. Go to 36a and 36b.
- Identify and correct vague pronoun references. Go to 36d.

Identify problems with modifiers and learn how to correct them

- Choose the correct modifiers and place them carefully. Go to 37a–37c.
- Identify and correct dangling modifiers. Go to 37e.

32 | Grammar Basics

QUICK*TAKE*

After reading this chapter, you should be able to . . .

- **Identify the parts of a sentence** (see below)

  Subject: Hippopotamuses (noun)
  Predicate: kill (main verb) more humans (direct object) than any other African wild mammal (prepositional phrase).

- **Recognize word classes:** Hippo (noun), it (pronoun), kills (verb), fat (adjective), easily (adverb), to (preposition), and (conjunction), the (article), oh (interjection) (32b)

- **Identify clauses** (32c)

  Clause: Hippos will open their mouths wide

- **Identify phrases and distinguish them from clauses** (32d)

  Phrase: to warn other creatures to stay away.

- **Identify the types of sentences** (32e)

  Simple: Hippos are vegetarian.
  Compound: Hippos are vegetarian, but they will attack other animals.
  Complex: Hippos attack other animals when they feel threatened.
  Compound-complex: Hippos may look fat and slow when they are on land, but a fully grown hippo can easily outrun a person.

32a Sentence Basics

Sentences are the basic units in writing. Many people think of a sentence as a group of words that begins with a capital letter and ends with a period, but that definition includes grammatically incomplete sentences called **fragments** (see 33a).

Subjects and predicates

Regular sentences must have a subject and a predicate that includes a main verb. Typically the subject announces what the sentence is about, and the predicate says something about that subject or conveys the action of the subject.

Subject	Predicate
I	**want** a new iPhone.
By 1910, 26 million Americans	**were going** to the movies at nickelodeon theaters every week.

377

The exception to this rule is a class of sentences called **imperatives,** in which the subject is usually implied. In these sentences, we know that the subject is *you* without stating it.

Quit bothering me.

Help me carry in the groceries.

Sentence patterns

Sentences can be classified into four major patterns according to function.

- **Declaratives.** Declarative sentences make statements.

  The house on the corner was built in 2001.

- **Interrogatives.** Interrogatives are usually referred to as questions.

  Who will be the first to volunteer?

- **Imperatives.** Imperatives request or demand some action.

  Stop complaining.

- **Exclamations.** Exclamations are used to express strong emotion.

  What an incredible performance you gave!

Sentences can be classified as either **positive** or **negative**. A sentence can be made negative by inserting a negative word, usually *not* or a contracted form of *not* (*can't, isn't*).

Positive	Juanita has worked here for a year.
Negative	Juanita has **not** worked here for a year.

Sentences with transitive verbs (see 32c) can be considered as **active** or **passive** (see 27b). Sentences can be made passive by changing the word order.

Active	The House of Representatives selected Thomas Jefferson as president in 1800 when the electoral vote ended in a tie.
Passive	Thomas Jefferson **was selected** president by the House of Representatives in 1800 when the electoral vote ended in a tie.

Exercise 32.1 Identify whether each sentence is active or passive. If the sentence is passive, rewrite it to make it active.

> **Example** There are so many places in the United States where supernatural creatures are reported to roam that it would take a lifetime to visit them all. (passive)
>
> **Revised** You could spend a lifetime traveling across the United States and still not visit all of the places where supernatural creatures are rumored to roam. (active)

1. Do you know the phone number for the shrieking "Donkey Lady" in San Antonio, Texas?
2. Disagreements have arisen over whether the "Mothman" of Point Pleasant, West Virginia, simply warns about or actually causes disasters.
3. Stay away from the tall, green "Grinning Man" of Elizabeth, New Jersey, if you don't want to have nightmares.
4. "Wendigo psychosis," a craving for human flesh, was named after the malevolent Wendigo of the Algonquin people.
5. Victims of the goat-like "Pope Lick Monster" of Kentucky are attacked with a blood-stained axe!

32b Word Classes

Like players in a team sport who are assigned to different positions, words are classified into parts of speech. The different positions on a team have different functions. The parts of speech also serve different functions in sentences. And just as individuals can play more than one position on a team, so too can individual words belong to more than one part of speech. *Try* is a noun in *The third try was successful* but a verb in *I would not try it.*

Nouns

A noun is the name of a person, place, thing, concept, or action. Names of particular persons, places, organizations, companies, titles, religions, languages, nationalities, ethnicities, months, and days are called **proper nouns** and are almost always capitalized. More general nouns are called **common nouns** and are seldom capitalized unless they begin a sentence (46a). Most common nouns can be made plural, and most are preceded by articles (*a, an, the*).

Nouns can be **possessive** (indicating ownership: *cat's*, *Ivan's*), **collective** (referring to a group: *family*, *jury*), **concrete** (referring to people, places, and things: *girl*, *truck*), and **abstract** (referring to qualities and states of mind: *humor*, *belief*). Multilingual writers should see Chapter 49 for more on count and noncount nouns.

Pronouns

Pronouns are a subclass of nouns and are generally used as substitutes for nouns. Pronouns themselves are divided into several subclasses.

- **Personal pronouns:** *I, you, he, she, it, we, they, me, him, her, us, them*

  I gave my old racquet to **her. She** gave **me** a used iPad in return.

- **Possessive pronouns:** *my, mine, his, hers, its, our, ours, your, yours, their, theirs*

  My old racquet is now **hers**.

- **Demonstrative pronouns:** *this, that, these, those*

  Those are the mittens I want.

- **Indefinite pronouns:** *all, any, anyone, anybody, anything, both, each, either, everyone, everything, many, neither, no one, none, nothing, one, some, someone, somebody, something*

  Everyone was relieved that the driver's injuries were minor.

- **Relative pronouns:** *that, which, what, who, whom, whose, whatever, whoever, whomever, whichever*

  The house, **which** hung off a steep ridge, had a stunning view of the bay.

- **Interrogative pronouns:** *who, which, what, where*

  What would you like with your sandwich?

- **Reflexive pronouns:** *myself, ourselves, yourself, yourselves, himself, herself, itself, themselves*

  The twins behaved **themselves** around their grandfather.

- **Reciprocal pronouns:** *each other, one another*

  The brothers didn't like **each other**.

See Chapter 36 for more on pronouns.

Exercise 32.2 The underlined words in the following paragraph are pronouns. Identify the function of each. Does it serve as a personal, possessive, demonstrative, indefinite, relative, interrogative, reflexive, or reciprocal pronoun?

Example   On November 20, 1820, a sperm whale rammed and sank *POSS* the whaleship *Essex*, but all the sailors escaped with <u>their</u> lives.

The ramming was no accident; after the whale hit the *Essex* once, <u>it</u> turned around to hit the ship a second time. The sailors found <u>themselves</u> adrift in three whaleboats, 1,200 miles from the nearest islands. However, the crew feared that <u>those</u> were populated by cannibals. After a month starving at sea, the sailors found a small island, <u>which</u> offered little to eat. Crushed by hunger, the crew convinced <u>each other</u> to eat a fellow sailor who had died of starvation. <u>Who</u> could say that <u>anybody</u> would act differently if placed in similar circumstances? <u>Their</u> chances of survival weakened with each passing day. Yet, first mate Owen Chase navigated <u>his</u> whaleship for eighty-eight days until the crew was rescued by a merchant ship.

Verbs

Verbs indicate actions, states of mind, occurrences, and states of being. Verbs are divided into two primary categories: **main verbs** and **auxiliaries**. A main verb must be present in the predicate. The main verb may be the only word in the predicate.

> She **slept**.

> When he heard the starting gun, Vijay **sprinted**.

Auxiliaries (often called *helping verbs*) include forms of *be, have,* and *do*. A subset of auxiliaries are **modals**: *can, could, may, might, must, shall, should, will, would.*

> You **will be** satisfied when you see how well they painted your car.

> She **might have been** selected for the lead role in the ballet if her strained muscle **had** healed.

See Chapters 34 and 35 for more on verbs.

Verbals

Verbals are forms of verbs that function as nouns, adjectives, and adverbs. The three kinds of verbals are infinitives, participles, and gerunds.

- **Infinitives:** An infinitive is the base or *to* form of the verb. Infinitives can be used in place of nouns, adjectives, or adverbs.

  ┌NOUN┐
  To fly has been a centuries-old dream of people around the world.

  ┌ADJECTIVE┐
  Keeping your goals in mind is a good way **to succeed**.

- **Participles:** Participles are either present (*flying*) or past (*defeated*). They always function as adjectives.

  The **flying** insects are annoying.

  Napoleon's **defeated** army faced a long march back to France.

- **Gerunds:** Gerunds have the same form as present participles, but they always function as nouns.

  Flying was all that she wanted to do in life.

Adjectives

Adjectives modify nouns and pronouns. Some adjectives are used frequently: *good, bad, small, tall, handsome, green, short.* Many others are recognizable by their suffixes: *-able* (*dependable*), *-al* (*cultural*), *-ful* (*hopeful*), *-ic* (*frenetic*), *-ive* (*decisive*), *-ish* (*foolish*), *-less* (*hopeless*), *-ous* (*erroneous*).

> The **forgetful** manager was always backed up by her **dependable** assistant.

Adjectives often follow linking verbs.

> That drumbeat is **relentless**.

Numbers are considered adjectives.

> Only **ten** team members showed up for practice.

See Chapter 37 for more about adjectives and adverbs.

Adverbs

Adverbs modify verbs, other adverbs, adjectives, and entire clauses. The usual suffix for adverbs is *-ly*. Many adverbs do not have suffixes (*then, here*), and others have the same form as adjectives (*fast, hard, long, well*).

> That drummer plays **well**. [modifies the verb *plays*]

> That drummer plays **very** well. [modifies the adverb *well*]

That answer is **partly** correct. [modifies the adjective *correct*]

Frankly, I couldn't care less. [modifies the clause *I couldn't care less*]

Conjunctive adverbs often modify entire clauses and sentences. Like coordinating conjunctions, they indicate the relationship between two clauses or two sentences. Commonly used conjunctive adverbs include *also, consequently, furthermore, hence, however, indeed, instead, likewise, moreover, nevertheless, otherwise, similarly, therefore, and thus.*

The Olympics brings together the best athletes in the world; **however**, the judging often represents the worst in sports.

Exercise 32.3 The underlined words in the following paragraph are modifiers. Label each modifier as adjective or adverb and write which word it modifies.

Example

ADV   ADJ MOD WOMAN ADJ MOD WOMAN
MOD LIVING

After <u>initially</u> living the life of an <u>average</u> <u>middle-class</u>

ADV MOD BECAME

woman, Dorothy Parker <u>ultimately</u> became one of the

ADV MOD INFAMOUS ADJ MOD WITS ADJ MOD CENTURY

most <u>infamous</u> wits of the <u>twentieth</u> century.

Parker's father encouraged her to pursue "<u>feminine</u> arts" such as piano and poetry, but <u>just</u> following his death in 1913, she rushed into what turned out to be a <u>profitable</u> foray into the world of literature. <u>Almost</u> <u>immediately</u>, *Vanity Fair* purchased one of her poems, leading her into a <u>full-time</u> writing position with *Vogue*. It was <u>life-changing</u>, as Parker's flair for <u>clever</u> prose <u>swiftly</u> led her into the <u>inner</u> sanctum of New York <u>literary</u> society. Parker was fired from *Vanity Fair*'s editorial board in 1919 after <u>harshly</u> panning an advertiser's film. Despite her <u>early</u> departure from magazines, Parker gained <u>lasting</u> fame as a <u>prolific</u> writer and critic.

Prepositions

Prepositions indicate the relationship of nouns or pronouns to other parts of a sentence. Prepositions come before nouns and pronouns, and in this sense prepositions are "prepositioned." The noun(s) or pronoun(s) that follow them are called the objects of prepositions.

PREP OBJ   PREP OBJ

She took the job **of** speechwriter **for** the president.

Here are some common prepositions.

about	behind	from	than
above	below	in	through
across	beside	inside	to
after	between	of	toward
against	but	off	under
among	by	on	until
around	despite	out	up
as	down	over	upon
at	during	past	with
before	for	since	without

Some prepositions are compounds.

according to	due to	in front of	next to
as well as	except for	in spite of	out of
because of	in addition to	instead of	with regard to

Exercise 32.4   Underline the prepositional phrases in the following paragraph and circle the prepositions.

> **Example**   (In)2009 scientists exploring the extinct volcano Mount Bosavi(on)the Pacific island of Papua New Guinea found forty new animal species.

Until recently the hard-to-reach land inside Mount Bosavi had been a "lost world" because of the forbidding walls of the volcano. Among the species discovered by the science team are the giant Bosavi wooly rat and a fish that makes a grunting sound with its swim bladder. During their exploration of the volcano, the scientists also found over fifteen kinds of frogs, including one with fangs! High above these other fascinating creatures lives the newly discovered silky cuscus, which dines upon fruits and leaves. Despite the disruption caused by their human visitors, both the giant rat and the cuscus seem to be friendly and without fear, following closely beside the teams as they made their way through the rainforest.

Conjunctions

Conjunctions indicate the relationship between words or groups of words. The two classes of conjunctions are **coordinate**, indicating units of equal

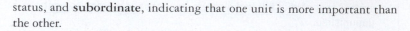

status, and **subordinate**, indicating that one unit is more important than the other.

- **Coordinating conjunctions:** The seven coordinating conjunctions are *and, but, or, yet, for, so,* and *nor.*

  Do you want cake **or** ice cream?

  I graduated a semester early, **but** I had to go to work immediately to pay off loans.

- **Subordinating conjunctions:** Subordinating conjunctions introduce subordinate clauses. Common subordinating conjunctions are *after, although, as, because, before, if, since, that, unless, until, when, where, while.*

  Although the word *earwig* is Anglo-Saxon for "ear-creature," earwigs do not actually crawl into people's ears.

Articles

There are two classes of articles:

- **Definite article:** *the*
- **Indefinite article:** *a, an*

Multilingual speakers should see 49d for more on articles.

Interjections

Interjections are words like *oops, ouch, ugh,* and *ah.* They are usually punctuated separately, and they do not relate grammatically to other words.

Exercise 32.5 Each underlined word in these paragraphs represents one of the word classes explained in this section. Identify nouns, pronouns, verbs, verbals, adjectives, adverbs, prepositions, conjunctions, articles, and interjections.

> **Example** In 1874 Colonel George Armstrong Custer announced
> PREP   NOUN   VERB
>
> the discovery of gold on French Creek near present-day
> NOUN   ADJ
>
> Custer, South Dakota.

Gold! This discovery not only triggered the Black Hills gold rush but also gave rise to the lawless town of Deadwood, which reached a population of around 5,000 within the next two years. Many scheming businesspeople flocked to Deadwood, hoping to strike it rich by offering supplies and entertainments, many of them illegal, to the gold miners. Deadwood also quickly gained a reputation as a place where murders,

such as that of <u>Wild Bill Hickok</u>, were frequent <u>and</u> murderers <u>went</u> unpunished.

<u>As</u> the gold vein <u>became</u> the property of <u>mining</u> companies, Deadwood lost <u>its</u> rough and rowdy <u>character</u> and <u>gradually</u> settled down into a <u>prosperous</u> town. <u>However</u>, a fire on <u>September 26</u>, <u>1879</u>, devastated the town, destroying <u>over</u> 300 buildings. <u>Without</u> the opportunities that <u>characterized</u> the town's early days, many of <u>those</u> who had lost their belongings <u>in</u> the fire left town <u>to try</u> their luck elsewhere.

32c Clauses

Clauses are the grammatical structures that underlie sentences. Each clause has a subject and a predicate, but not all clauses are sentences. The variety of clauses is nearly infinite because phrases and other clauses can be embedded within them in a multitude of ways. Nevertheless, a few basic patterns are central to English clause structure.

Subject-verb-object

On the predicate side of a clause, you always find a main verb and often a direct object that is affected by the action of the verb.

┌—S—┐ ┌—V—┐ ┌—DO—┐
Ahmad **kicked** **the ball.**

This basic pattern, called **subject-verb-object** or **S-V-O**, is one of the most common in English. Verbs that take objects (*kick, revise*) are called **transitive verbs**. Some transitive verbs can take two objects: a **direct object** that completes the sentence and an **indirect object**, usually a person, indirectly affected by the action.

┌—S—┐ ┌V┐ ┌IO┐ ┌—DO—┐
Ahmed **gave** **Sally** **the ball.**

Clauses without objects

Not all clauses have objects.

┌—S—┐ ┌—V—┐
Maria **slept.**

┌———S———┐ ┌—V—┐
The engine **runs** rough. [*Rough* is an adverb, not an object.]

┌———S———┐ ┌———V———┐
The staff **cannot work** on weekends. [*On weekends* is a prepositional phrase.]

This clause pattern is **subject-verb** or **S-V**. Verbs that do not require objects are called **intransitive verbs**. Many verbs can be both transitive and intransitive.

Intransitive   Ginny **runs** fast.

Transitive   Ginny **runs** the company.

For more on the verbs *lay/lie, set/sit,* and *raise/rise,* see 35c.

Linking-verb clauses

A third major pattern links the subject to a noun or an adjective that follows the verb and restates or describes the subject. The most commonly used verbs for this pattern are forms of *be.*

McKinley was president in 1900.

Rosalia Fernandez is the assistant manager.

The results of the MRI **were negative.**

What follows the verb is the subject complement, either a noun or noun phrase (*president, assistant manager*) or a predicate adjective describing the subject (*negative*).

Other linking verbs besides *be* are *appear, become, feel, look, remain,* and *seem.* These linking verbs often refer to people's perceptions or senses.

Jennifer felt nervous when she accepted the award.

Main versus subordinate clauses

All the examples of clauses we have looked at up to now can stand by themselves as sentences. These clauses are called **main** or **independent clauses**. Other clauses have the necessary ingredients to count as clauses—a subject and a main verb—yet they are incomplete as sentences.

Where you choose to go to college

Which was the first to be considered

As fast as my legs could pedal

These clauses are examples of **subordinate** or **dependent clauses**. They do not stand by themselves but must be attached to another clause:

I rode my bike **as fast as my legs could pedal**.

Subordinate clauses as modifiers

- **Adjective clauses:** Adjective clauses modify nouns and pronouns. They are also called **relative clauses** and usually begin with a relative pronoun.

Steroids that are used to increase muscle density have many harmful side effects.

The site where the fort once stood was washed away by a hurricane.

- **Adverb clauses:** Adverb clauses function as adverbs, modifying verbs, other adverbs, adjectives, and entire clauses. They begin with a subordinating conjunction such as *after, although, as, because, before, if, since, that, unless, until, when, where,* or *while.*

Modifies verb	She **arrived** after we had carried all of our furniture into our new apartment.
Modifies adverb	Jeff laughed **nervously** whenever the boss came around.
Modifies adjective	The forward was not as **tall** as the media guide stated.
Modifies clause	When you see a person faint, **you** should call 911.

Exercise 32.6 Identify which of the three main clause patterns each of the following sentences exemplifies: subject-verb-object, subject-verb, or subject-linking verb.

Example   In 1954 the United States Supreme Court ordered school desegregation. (Subject-verb-object)

1. Arkansas Governor Orval Faubus refused to obey the order.
2. The Arkansas militia seemed impenetrable.
3. Nine African American students retreated from the school.
4. President Eisenhower sent the National Guard to escort the students.
5. The guardsmen were successful.

32d Phrases

Phrases add to a sentence groups of words that modify or develop parts of the sentence. Some phrases can be confused with clauses, but phrases lack either a subject or a main verb.

Prepositional phrases

Prepositional phrases consist of a preposition and its object, including modifiers of the object. They can modify nouns, verbs, or adjectives.

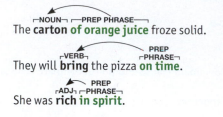

┌NOUN┐ ┌—PREP PHRASE—┐
The **carton of orange juice** froze solid.

┌—VERB┐   ┌ PREP
┌PHRASE┐
They will **bring** the pizza **on time**.

┌ADJ┐ ┌PHRASE┐ PREP
She was **rich in spirit**.

Verbal phrases

Each of the three kinds of verbals—infinitives, participles, and gerunds—can be used to create phrases.

- **Infinitive phrases:** Infinitive phrases can function as nouns, adverbs, and adjectives. As nouns they can be subjects, objects, or complements.

  ┌————SUBJECT————┐
  To succeed where others had failed was her goal.

- **Participial phrases:** Participial phrases are formed with either present participles (*flying*) or past participles (*defeated*); they function as adjectives.

  The freighter, **listing noticeably to the port side**, left the port without balancing the load.

- **Gerund phrases:** Gerund phrases formed from the present participle (*-ing*) function as nouns.

  ┌———SUBJECT———┐
  Feeding stray cats became my next-door neighbor's obsession.

Appositives

Appositive phrases modify nouns and are often set off by a pair of commas. They usually follow the noun they modify. They are quite useful as identifying tags for nouns.

Andy, **my old linguistics teacher**, became one of my best friends.

Absolutes

Absolute phrases are nearly clauses because they include a noun or pronoun and a verb; however, the verb is a participle ending in *-ing* or *-ed* and not a main verb. Absolute phrases can appear anywhere in a sentence and are set off by commas.

He struggled at the beginning of his speech, **his voice trembling**.

32e Sentence Types

Simple sentences

A simple sentence consists of one main clause and no subordinate clauses.

>   ⌐SUBJ⌐ ⌐VERB⌐
> The two toy **figures spun** together.

Simple sentences can become quite long if phrases are added.

> ⌐————————MAIN CLAUSE————————⌐
> **The two toy figures spun together**, standing on top of their round metal pedestal, teetering back and forth in a jerky, clockwise motion, slowing gradually.

Compound sentences

Compound sentences have two or more main clauses and no subordinate clauses. The main clauses are connected in one of three ways: (1) by a semicolon, (2) by a comma and a coordinating conjunction (*and, but, or, for, so, nor, yet*), or (3) by punctuation and a conjunctive adverb (*furthermore, however, indeed, nevertheless, therefore*).

> ⌐————MAIN CLAUSE————⌐   ⌐————MAIN CLAUSE————⌐
> Mike walked to his car, **and** he opened the trunk.

> ⌐————————MAIN CLAUSE————————⌐   ⌐————MAIN CLAUSE————
> The theater enjoyed record attendance; **however**, rising costs took
> ⌐————————⌐
> all the profits.

Complex sentences

Complex sentences have one main clause and one or more subordinate clauses.

> ⌐————MAIN CLAUSE————⌐ ⌐————SUBORDINATE CLAUSE————⌐
> Mike walked to his car **when** he got out of class.

Compound-complex sentences

Compound-complex sentences have at least two main clauses and at least one subordinate clause.

> ⌐————MAIN CLAUSE————⌐ ⌐————SUBORDINATE CLAUSE————⌐   ⌐————MAIN CLAUSE————
> Mike walked to his car when he got out of class, **but** he had to go back
> ⌐————————⌐
> for his briefcase.

Exercise 32.7   The following are simple sentences. Rewrite each as compound, complex, and compound-complex sentences.

Simple example Baseball, America's national pastime, has endured decades of poor attendance, scandals, and players' strikes.

Compound	Baseball has endured decades of poor attendance, scandals, and players' strikes, yet it is still America's national pastime.
Complex	Baseball, which many consider America's national pastime, has endured decades of poor attendance, scandals, and players' strikes.
Compound-complex	While it has been called America's national pastime for over a century, baseball has endured many trials, yet the game has survived decades of poor attendance, scandals, and players' strikes.

1. Philip K. Wrigley, chewing gum entrepreneur, founded the All-American Girls Professional Baseball League in 1943, bolstering waning interest in baseball during World War II.
2. The league attracted women from all over, providing them with a national venue to showcase their athletic talents.
3. The league peaked in 1948 with ten teams and over 900,000 paying fans.
4. Promoting an image of femininity among female athletes, the league insisted on strict regulations regarding dress and public behavior.
5. Lacking audience interest, the league folded in 1954.

33 | Fragments, Run-ons, and Comma Splices

QUICK*TAKE*

After reading this chapter, you should be able to . . .

- **Identify and correct fragments** (33a)

  Error: Early traveling salesmen once literally drummed up business. **Beating drums and ringing bells.**
  Correct: Early traveling salesmen once literally drummed up business by beating drums and ringing bells.

- **Identify and correct run-on or "fused" sentences** (33b)

  Error: The first deadbeats were "debt beaters" they left their debts behind.
  Correct: The first deadbeats were "debt beaters." They left their debts behind.

- **Identify and correct comma splices** (33c)

  Error: Dressed to the nines doesn't refer to the 1–10 scale, it's slang for "dressed to thine eyes."
  Correct: Dressed to the nines doesn't refer to the 1–10 scale. It's slang for "dressed to thine eyes."

33a Fragments

Fragments in speech and writing

Fragments are incomplete sentences. They are punctuated to look like sentences, but they lack a key element—often a subject or a verb—or else are a subordinate clause or phrase. In spoken language we usually pay little attention to fragments.

Missing subject; missing verb	**Nothing like a hot shower when you're cold and wet.**
Missing subject	**I was completely hooked on the game. And played it constantly.**
Missing verb	**You too?**
Subordinate clause	**If you think so.**

In writing, however, fragments usually interrupt the reader. Consider another example of a full sentence followed by a fragment:

The university's enrollment rose unexpectedly during the fall semester. **Because the percentage of students who accepted offers of admission was much higher than previous years and fewer students than usual dropped out or transferred.**

Such fragments compel a reader to stop and reread. When a sentence starts with *because*, we expect to find a main clause later. But here, the *because* clause refers back to the previous sentence. The writer no doubt knew that the fragment gave reasons why enrollment rose, but a reader must stop to determine the connection.

In formal writing you should avoid fragments. Readers expect words punctuated as a sentence to be a complete sentence. They expect writers to complete their thoughts rather than force readers to guess the missing element.

Basic strategies for turning fragments into sentences

Incorporate the fragment into an adjoining sentence.   In many cases you can incorporate the fragment into an adjoining sentence.

She saw him coming. ~~And~~ *a*nd looked away.

I was hooked on the ~~game. Playing~~ *game, playing* day and night.

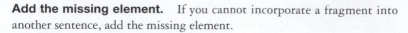

Add the missing element. If you cannot incorporate a fragment into another sentence, add the missing element.

He *is* studying more this semester.

When aiming for the highest returns, ~~and~~ also ~~thinking~~ about the possible losses.
investors should think

COMMON ERRORS
Recognizing fragments

If you can spot fragments, you can fix them. Grammar checkers can find some of them, but they miss many fragments and identify other sentences wrongly as fragments. Ask these questions when you are checking for sentence fragments.

- **Does the sentence have a subject?** Except for commands, sentences need subjects:

  Jane spent every cent of credit she had available. **And then applied for more cards.**

- **Does the sentence have a complete verb?** Sentences require complete verbs. Verbs that end in *-ing* must have an auxiliary verb to be complete.

  Ralph keeps changing majors. **He trying to figure out what he really wants to do after college.**

- **If the sentence begins with a subordinate clause, is there a main clause in the same sentence?** A good test to determine if a subordinate clause is a fragment is to say "I think that" before a possible fragment.

  Even though Seattle is cloudy much of the year, no American city is more beautiful when the sun shines. **Which is one reason people continue to move there.**

Remember:

  1. A sentence must have a subject and complete verb.

  2. A subordinate clause cannot stand alone as a sentence.

Watch for these fragments

1. Pay close attention to sentences that begin with transitional words, coordinating conjunctions, and subordinating conjunctions. Among the most common fragments are those that begin with a

transitional word (*also, therefore, however, consequently*), a coordinating conjunction (*and, but, or*), or a word indicating a subordinate clause (*although, because, if, since*). Prepositional or verbal phrase fragments are also common.

Transitional words and phrases such as *also, however,* and *therefore* mark movement from one idea to another, such as introducing another example, a change in direction, or a conclusion. Writers often produce fragments when trying to separate these shifts with a period.

> Susan found ways to avoid working during her shift. ~~T,~~ therefore making more work for the rest of the employees.

Compound predicates are linked by a coordinating conjunction such as *and, but,* or *or*. Because compound predicates share the same subject, the solution for a coordinating conjunction fragment is to incorporate it into the sentence with the subject.

> Heroin use among urban professionals is on the rise in the United States. ~~A~~ and also in Europe, after several decades during which cocaine was the preferred drug among this group.

2. Look for subordinate clause fragments.

Subordinate clauses resemble sentences because they contain subjects and verbs. But subordinate clauses cannot stand alone as sentences because their meaning is dependent on another clause. Subordinate clauses begin with words such as *although, after, before, despite, if, though, unless, whether, while, when, who,* and *that*. Subordinate clause fragments often follow the sentence to which they actually belong. You can fix the subordinate clause fragment by incorporating it into the preceding sentence.

> A recent scientific study showed that wives of soldiers who were deployed to wars in Afghanistan and Iraq were more frequently diagnosed with sleep disorders, depression, and anxiety. ~~W,~~ while wives whose husbands were not deployed suffered fewer problems.

Or you can fix the subordinate clause fragment by turning it into a sentence.

> A recent scientific study showed that wives of soldiers who were deployed to wars in Afghanistan and Iraq were more frequently diagnosed with sleep disorders, depression, and anxiety. In comparison, the study also showed that wives whose husbands were not deployed suffered fewer problems.

3. Look for phrase fragments.

Phrases also cannot stand alone as sentences because they lack either a subject, a verb, or both. There are many kinds of phrase fragments. Prepositional phrase fragments are easy to spot and fix.

As Helen looked over the notes for her autobiography, she mused about how much her life had changed. ~~I,~~ **i**n ways she could not have predicted.

Andrew accepted the university's award for outstanding dissertation. ~~W,~~ **w**ith great dignity and humility.

Appositive phrases, which rename or describe a noun, are often fragments.

For his advanced history course, Professor Levack assigned J. J. Scarisbrick's *Henry VIII*. ~~A,~~ **a**n older text historians still regard as essential when studying sixteenth-century English history and politics.

Verbal phrase fragments are sometimes difficult to spot because verbals look like verbs. But remember: They function as adjectives, nouns, or adverbs.

On their last trip to Chicago, Greta went to the Art Institute, but Roger didn't go. ~~Roger,~~ having visited that museum twice already.

4. Watch for list fragments.   Do not isolate a list from the sentence that introduces it. Words or phrases such as *for example, for instance, namely,* and *such as* often introduce lists or examples. Make sure these lists are attached to a sentence with a subject and verb.

Several Ben and Jerry's ice cream flavors are puns. ~~S,~~ **s**uch as Cherry Garcia, Phish Food, and The Full VerMonty.

Exercise 33.1   Revise each of the following to eliminate sentence fragments.

Example   Certain mammals, like flying squirrels and sugar gliders, are varieties that actually ~~glide. Which~~ *glide, which* enables them to survive when they are being hunted by nimble predators.

1. Flying squirrels, like typical squirrels except they have flaps of skin that allow them to glide.
2. Flying squirrels glide gracefully. From tree to tree with surprising ease.
3. To gain speed and momentum, flying squirrels often free-fall for several feet. Then to turn in midair, lower one arm.
4. One of the largest known varieties the Japanese giant flying squirrel. Two feet long from its head to its furry tail.
5. Gliding escaping predators and gathers food quickly.

Exercise 33.2 Find the fragments in the following paragraph and revise the paragraph to eliminate them.

Barton Springs still seems like a place not in Texas for those who come from elsewhere. Surrounding hills covered by live oaks and mountain juniper. And ground around the pool shaded by pecan trees whose trunks are a dozen feet in circumference. Banana trees and other tropical plants grow in the roofless dressing areas of the pool. With grackles whistling jungle-like sounds outside. The pool is in a natural limestone creek bed. Which is an eighth of a mile long. Fed by 27 million gallons of 68° water bubbling out of the Edwards Aquifer each day.

33b Run-on Sentences

Run-on sentences (also called "fused sentences") are the opposite of sentence fragments. While fragments are incomplete sentences, run-ons jam together two or more sentences, failing to separate them with appropriate punctuation. And while fragments are sometimes acceptable, especially in informal writing, run-on sentences are never acceptable.

Fixing run-on sentences

Take three steps to fix run-on sentences: (1) identify the problem, (2) determine where the run-on sentence needs to be divided, and (3) choose the punctuation that best indicates the relationship between the main clauses.

1. Identify the problem. When you read your writing aloud, run-on sentences will often trip you up, just as they confuse readers. You can also search for subject and verb pairs to check for run-ons. If you find two main clauses with no punctuation separating them, you have a run-on sentence.

        ┌──────SUBJ──────┐ ┌──────VERB──────┐
Online businesses are not **bound** to specific locations or old ways

         ┌S┐┌V┐
of running a business **they are** more flexible in allowing employees

to telecommute and to determine the hours they work.

2. Determine where the run-on sentence needs to be divided.

Online businesses are not bound to specific locations or old ways of running a business **|** they are more flexible in allowing employees to telecommute and to determine the hours they work.

COMMON ERRORS

Recognizing run-on sentences

When you read the following sentence, you realize something is wrong.

I do not recall what kind of printer it was all I remember is that it could sort, staple, and print a packet at the same time.

The problem is that the two main clauses are not separated by punctuation. The reader must look carefully to determine where one main clause stops and the next one begins.

I do not recall what kind of printer it was **|** all I remember is that it could sort, staple, and print a packet at the same time.

A period should be placed after *was*, and the next sentence should begin with a capital letter:

I do not recall what kind of printer it wa**s. A**ll I remember is that it could sort, staple, and print a packet at the same time.

Run-on sentences are major errors.

Remember: Two main clauses must be separated by correct punctuation.

---

3. Determine the relationship between the main clauses.   You will revise a run-on more effectively if you determine the relationship between the main clauses and understand the effect or point you are trying to make. There are several punctuation strategies for fixing run-ons.

- **Insert a period.** This is the simplest way to fix a run-on sentence.

  Online businesses are not bound to specific locations or old ways of running a business**. T**hey are more flexible in allowing employees to telecommute and to determine the hours they work.

However, if you want to indicate the relationship between the two main clauses more clearly, you may want to choose one of these strategies.

- **Insert a semicolon (and possibly a transitional word indicating the relationship between the two main clauses).**

Online businesses are not bound to specific locations or old ways of running a business**; therefore,** they are more flexible in allowing employees to telecommute and to determine the hours they work.

- **Insert a comma and a coordinating conjunction** (*and, but, or, nor, for, so, yet*).

Online businesses are not bound to specific locations or old ways of running a business**, so** they are more flexible in allowing employees to telecommute and to determine the hours they work.

- **Make one of the clauses subordinate.**

Because online businesses are not bound to specific locations or old ways of running a business, they are more flexible in allowing employees to telecommute and to determine the hours they work.

Exercise 33.3   Correct the following run-on sentences.

Example   Japanese Kabuki theater surfaced in the early ~~1600s its~~ *1600s. Its* origins are often linked to the public, improvised performances of Izumo Grand.

1. The original Kabuki troupes were mostly composed of female dancers however male performers replaced them after the art became associated with prostitution.
2. Performances included several thematically linked elements such as dance, history, and domestic drama they lasted up to 12 hours.
3. In the 1700s choreographers and special schools became commonplace Kabuki dance became more complex.
4. Kabuki costumes are often quite elaborate actors sometimes need assistance preparing for performances.
5. Since World War II, Western influences have altered the social position of Kabuki ticket prices have risen, making performances more accessible to tourists, but not the average Japanese citizen.

33c Comma Splices

Comma splices are a kind of run-on sentence. They do include a punctuation mark—a comma—but it is not a strong enough punctuation mark to separate two main clauses. Comma splices often do not cause the same

problems for readers as run-ons. The following sentence can be read aloud with no problem.

> Most of us were taking the same classes, if someone had a question, we would all help out.

On the page such sentences may cause confusion because commas are used to distinguish between elements within sentences, not to mark the boundary between sentences. Most readers see comma splices as errors, which is why you should avoid them.

Fixing comma splices

You have several options for fixing comma splices. Select the one that best fits where the sentence is located and the effect you are trying to achieve.

1. Change the comma to a period.   Most comma splices can be fixed by changing the comma to a period.

> It didn't matter that I worked in a windowless room for 40 hours a
> *week. Online*
> ~~week, online~~ I was exploring and learning more about distant people
>
> and places than I ever had before.

2. Change the comma to a semicolon.   A semicolon indicates a close connection between the two main clauses.

> It didn't matter that I worked in a windowless room for 40 hours a
> *week;*
> ~~week,~~ online I was exploring and learning more about distant people
>
> and places than I ever had before.

3. Insert a coordinating conjunction.   Other comma splices can be repaired by inserting a coordinating conjunction (*and, but, or, nor, so, yet, for*) to indicate the relationship of the two main clauses. The coordinating conjunction must be preceded by a comma.

> Digital technologies have intensified a global culture that affects us daily in large and small ways, **yet** their impact remains poorly understood.

4. Make one of the main clauses a subordinate clause.   If a comma splice includes one main clause that is subordinate to the other, rewrite the sentence using a subordinating conjunction.

> *Because community*
> ~~Community~~ is the vision of a great society trimmed down to the size of a small town, it is a powerful metaphor for real estate developers who sell a mini-utopia along with a house or condo.

COMMON ERRORS

Recognizing comma splices

When you edit your writing, look carefully at sentences that contain commas. Does the sentence contain two main clauses? If so, are the main clauses joined by a comma and a coordinating conjunction (*and, but, for, or, not, so, yet*)?

Incorrect The **concept** of "nature" **depends** on the concept of human "culture," the **problem is** that "culture" is itself shaped by "nature."
[Two main clauses joined by only a comma]

Correct Even though the concept of "nature" depends on the concept of human "culture," "culture" is itself shaped by "nature."
[Subordinate clause plus a main clause]

Correct The concept of "nature" depends on the concept of human "culture," but "culture" is itself shaped by "nature."
[Two main clauses joined by a comma and coordinating conjunction]

Treating the word *however* as a coordinating conjunction produces some of the most common comma splice errors. *However* does not function grammatically like the coordinating conjunctions *and, but, or, nor, yet, so,* and *for* (see 32b).

Incorrect The White House press secretary repeatedly avowed the Administration was not choosing a side between the two countries embroiled in conflict, however the developing foreign policy suggested otherwise.

Correct The White House press secretary repeatedly avowed the Administration was not choosing a side between the two countries embroiled in conflict; however, the developing foreign policy suggested otherwise.
[Two main clauses joined by a semicolon]

Remember: Do not use a comma as a period.

5. Make one of the main clauses a phrase. You can also rewrite one of the main clauses as a phrase.

Community—**the vision of a great society trimmed down to the size of a small town**—is a powerful metaphor for real estate developers who sell a mini-utopia along with a house or condo.

Exercise 33.4 The following sentences all contain comma splices. Eliminate the splices using the methods indicated in parentheses.

Example Accused Nazi propagandist Leni Riefenstahl was born in Germany in ~~1902, her~~ *1902. Her* films *Triumph of the Will* and *The Olympiad* are said to have captured the essence of the Nazi era. (Change comma to a period.)

1. Riefenstahl spent her early days performing in Germany as a dancer, a 1924 knee injury derailed her dance career, this accident led her to a successful, scandal-ridden life in film. (Insert a coordinating conjunction; change comma to a period.)
2. Early editing work prepared her to direct her first film, *The Blue Light*, however, national recognition was slow to come. (Change the comma to a semicolon.)
3. The year 1935 saw the release of Riefenstahl's film *Triumph of the Will*, which stunningly captured a Nazi Party rally, to be sure, this film forever cast a shadow over the director's career. (Change comma to a period.)
4. Her pioneering techniques such as the underwater camera in her documentary of the 1936 Berlin Olympics, *The Olympiad*, captured the spirit of athletics, her place in film history was solidified. (Make one of the main clauses a subordinate clause; insert a coordinating conjunction.)
5. The French imprisoned Riefenstahl because her films were considered Nazi propaganda, she was not an active member of the Nazi Party, her film career was forever damaged by such insinuations. (Make one of the main clauses a phrase; change comma to a period.)

34 | Subject-Verb Agreement

QUICKTAKE

After reading this chapter, you should be able to . . .

- **Identify agreement in the present tense** (34a)
- **Decide whether a subject is singular or plural** (34b)

  Singular: **Neither curling nor diving is** considered an extreme sport.
  Plural: Ernest Hemingway is believed to have said that **bullfighting, motor racing, and mountaineering are** the only real sports.

- **Choose the right verb for indefinite pronouns** (34c)

  Indefinite pronouns: Some say that this statement implies that a sport must involve peril. (plural)

- **Select the right verb for collective nouns** (34d)

  Collective nouns: This **generation seems** to like sports that involve peril. (singular)

- **Recognize inverted word order** (34e)
- **Choose the correct verb for subjects that describe amounts, numbers, and pairs** (34f)

  Treat as singular: Two decades was all the time extreme sports needed to become mainstream.
  Treat as plural: Mirrored sunglasses are the choice of many extreme athletes.

34a Agreement in the Present Tense

When your verb is in the present tense, agreement in number is straight-forward: The subject takes the base form of the verb in all but the third person singular. For example, the verb *walk* in the present tense agrees in number with most subjects in its base form.

First person singular	I walk
Second person singular	You walk
First person plural	We walk
Second person plural	You walk
Third person plural	They walk

Third person singular subjects are the exception to this rule. When your subject is in the third person singular (*he, it, Fido, Lucy, Mr. Jones*), you need to add an *s* or *es* to the base form of the verb.

Third person singular (add *s*)	He walks. It walks. Fido walks.
Third person singular (add *es*)	Lucy goes. Mr. Jones goes.

34b Singular and Plural Subjects

Sometimes it will be difficult to determine whether your subject is singular or plural, especially when subjects joined by *and* refer to the same thing or idea (*toast and jam, peace and quiet*) or when subjects are linked by *either . . . or* or *neither . . . nor*.

Subjects joined by *and*

When two subjects are joined by *and*, treat them as a compound (plural) subject.

> **Omar and Jane are** leaving for New York in the morning.

Some compound subjects are treated as singular. These kinds of compounds generally work together as a single noun. Although they appear to be compound and therefore plural, these subjects take the singular form of the verb.

> **Rock and roll remains** the devil's music, even in the twenty-first century.

Also, when two nouns linked by *and* are modified by *every* or *each*, these two nouns are likewise treated as one singular subject.

> **Each night and day brings** no new news of you.

An exception to this rule arises when the word *each* follows a compound subject. In these cases usage varies depending on the number of the direct object.

> **The army and the navy each have** their own air forces.

> **The owl and the pussycat each has** a personal claim to fame.

Subjects joined by *or, either . . . or*, or *neither . . . nor*

When a subject is joined by *or, either . . . or,* or *neither . . . nor*, make sure the verb agrees with the subject closest to the verb.

> ⌐SING⌐　　⌐PLURAL⌐　⌐PL⌐
> Is it **the sky or the mountains** that **are** blue?

> ⌐PLURAL⌐　⌐SING⌐　　⌐SING⌐
> Is it **the mountains or the sky** that **surrounds** us?

> ⌐PLURAL⌐　　⌐SING⌐⌐SING⌐
> **Neither the animals nor the zookeeper knows** how to relock the gate.

> ⌐SING⌐　⌐PLURAL⌐⌐PL⌐
> **Either a coyote or several dogs were** howling last night.

Subjects along with another noun

Verbs agree with the subject of a sentence, even when a subject is linked to another noun with a phrase like *as well as, along with,* or *alongside.* These modifying phrases are usually set off from the main subject with commas.

┌──────────IGNORE THIS PHRASE──────────┐
Chicken, alongside various steamed vegetables, **is** my favorite meal.

Multilingual writers can find more on singular and plural subjects in 49c.

COMMON ERRORS

Subjects separated from verbs

The most common agreement errors occur when words come between the subject and verb. These intervening words do not affect subject-verb agreement. To ensure that you use the correct verb form, identify the subject and the verb. Ignore any phrases that come between them.

┌──────IGNORE THIS PHRASE──────┐
Incorrect   **Students** at inner-city Washington High **reads** more than suburban students.

Correct   **Students** at inner-city Washington High **read** more than suburban students.

Students is plural and *read* is plural; subject and verb agree.

Incorrect   **The whale shark,** the largest of all sharks, **feed** on plankton.

Correct   **The whale shark,** the largest of all sharks, **feeds** on plankton.

The plural noun *sharks* that appears between the subject *the whale shark* and the verb *feeds* does not change the number of the subject. The subject is singular and the verb is singular. Subject and verb agree.

Remember: When you check for subject-verb agreement, identify the subject and verb. Ignore any words that come between them.

Exercise 34.1 Underline the subject in the following sentences and decide whether it should be treated as singular or plural. Next, circle the verb. If the verb doesn't agree in number with the subject, revise so that it agrees.

Example   Various <u>regions</u> in Italy—including Tuscany,

possess

Lazio, and Umbria—~~possesses~~ rich cultures that

revolve around food preparation and meals.

["Regions" is plural, so the verb needs to be changed to "possess."]

1. Some cite Rome's Marcus Gavius Apicius as the author of the first cookbook, written in the first century.
2. Each Italian city and town in Italy possess a historical rationale for the gastronomical traditions of today.
3. People in central Italy enjoy eating many types of meat, but neither beef nor liver outshine the popularity of the region's top meat, pork.
4. Cheese, as well as foods such as balsamic vinegar and olive oil, is sometimes named for the region where it is produced.
5. Almost every man and woman in America know spaghetti hails from Italy, but many fail to learn about the rich and varied Italian tradition of food.

34c   Indefinite Pronouns as Subjects

The choice of a singular or plural pronoun is determined by the **antecedent**—the noun that a pronoun refers to. For instance, the sentence *My friend likes soup* might be followed by another sentence, *She makes a new kind daily*. The pronoun must be singular because *she* refers to the singular noun *friend*.

Indefinite pronouns, such as *some, few, all, someone, everyone,* and *each,* often do not refer to identifiable subjects; hence they have no antecedents. Most indefinite pronouns are singular and agree with the singular forms of verbs. Some, like *both* and *many*, are always plural and agree with the plural forms of verbs. Other indefinite pronouns are variable and can agree with either singular or plural verb forms, depending on the context of the sentence.

COMMON ERRORS

Agreement errors using *each*

The indefinite pronoun *each* is a frequent source of subject-verb agreement errors. If a pronoun is singular, its verb must be singular. This rule holds true even when the subject is modified by a phrase that includes a plural noun.

(Continued on next page)

COMMON ERRORS   *(Continued)*

A common stumbling block to this rule is the pronoun *each*. *Each* is always treated as a singular pronoun in college writing. When *each* stands alone, the choice is easy to make:

Incorrect   Each **are** an outstanding student.
Correct   Each **is** an outstanding student.

But when *each* is modified by a phrase that includes a plural noun, the choice of a singular verb form becomes less obvious:

Incorrect   Each of the girls **are** fit.
Correct   Each of the girls **is** fit.

Incorrect   Each of our dogs **get** a present.
Correct   Each of our dogs **gets** a present.

Remember: *Each* is always singular.

Exercise 34.2   Identify the underlined indefinite pronoun in each sentence as singular or plural. Then circle the verb and correct it if it does not agree in number with the pronoun.

Example   *plural   have*
Many ⟨has⟩ heard of the curse that strikes down those who enter the tomb of Tutankhamen.

1. A newspaper article about the discovery of the tomb in 1922 by Howard Carter stated that an inscription cursed <u>all</u> who enters to a certain death.
2. <u>Everyone</u> believed in the curse, though, because writers such as Sir Arthur Conan Doyle and Marie Corelli had planted the seed of a "terrible curse" in the minds of the press.
3. <u>Both</u> was inspired by earlier writers, such as Louisa May Alcott and Jane Loudon Webb.
4. <u>Each</u> had published a mummy story prior to the discovery of the tomb.
5. <u>No one</u> have done more to perpetuate the myth than Webb, however, whose novel *The Mummy* (1828) invented the story of a mummy coming back to life to seek revenge.

34d Collective Nouns as Subjects

Collective nouns refer to groups (*administration, audience, class, committee, crew, crowd, faculty, family, fleet, gang, government, group, herd, jury, mob, public, team*).

When members of a group are considered as a unit, use singular verbs and singular pronouns.

> The **audience was** patient with the novice performer.

> The **crowd is** unusually quiet at the moment, but **it** will get noisy soon.

When members of a group are considered as individuals, use plural verbs and plural pronouns.

> The **faculty have their** differing opinions on how to address the problems caused by reduced state support.

Sometimes collective nouns can be singular in one context and plural in another. Writers must decide which verb form to use based on sentence context.

> The **number** of people who live downtown **is** increasing.

> A **number** of people **are** moving downtown from the suburbs.

> **Sports is** one of the four main buttons on the newspaper's Web site.

> **Sports are** dangerous for children under 5.

Exercise 34.3 The following paragraph contains collective nouns that can be considered either singular or plural depending on the context. Select the form of the verb that agrees with the subject in the context given.

Example The jury (<u>is</u>/are) ready to deliberate.

[*Jury* is considered singular.]

The jury (<u>believe</u>/believes) that they will resolve their differences in judgment.

[*Jury* is considered plural.]

The administration usually (try/tries) to avoid responsibility for issues concerning students living off campus but also (listen/listens) when the city government (complain/complains) about student behavior. The public (is/are) upset about large parties that last into the morning. The university formed a committee of students, faculty, and neighborhood residents to investigate the problem. Unfortunately, the committee (disagree/disagrees) about the causes of excessive noise.

34e Inverted Word Order

Writers use inverted word order most often in forming questions.

Cats are friendly.

Are cats friendly?

Writers also use inverted word order for added emphasis or for style considerations. Do not be confused by inverted word order. Locate the subject of your sentence and then make sure your verb agrees with that subject.

34f Amounts, Numbers, and Pairs

Subjects that describe amounts of money, time, distance, or measurement are singular and require singular verbs.

Three days is never long enough to unwind.

Some subjects, such as courses of study, academic specializations, illnesses, and even some nations, are treated as singular subjects even though their names end in *-s* or *-es*. For example, *economics, news, ethics, measles*, and *the United States* all end in *-s* but are all singular subjects.

Economics is a rich field of study.

News keeps getting more and more commercial.

Other subjects require a plural verb form even though they refer to single items such as *jeans, slacks, glasses, scissors*, and *tweezers*. These items are all pairs.

Your **jeans look** terrific.

My **glasses are** scratched.

35 | Verbs

After reading this chapter, you should be able to . . .

- **Identify basic verb forms** (35a)
- **Use regular and irregular verb forms correctly** (35b)

  Regular: We **entered** a film contest last year.
  Irregular: We **made** a short, low-budget version of a popular movie.

- **Use transitive and intransitive verbs correctly** (35c)

  Transitive: In the movie, the Scottish warriors refuse to **lay** their **weapons** down.
  Intransitive: At the end, the hero **lies** in agony on the torturer's table.

- **Avoid shifts in tense** (35d)

  Incorrect: After Starkiller Base **destroyed** the Republic capital and fleet, First-Order stormtroopers **surrounds** Han, Chewbacca, and Finn.
  Correct: After Starkiller Base **destroyed** the Republic capital and fleet, First-Order stormtroopers **surrounded** Han, Chewbacca, and Finn.

- **Use indicative, imperative, and subjunctive verbs correctly** (35e)

  Indicative: *Zero Dark Thirty* **depicts** how the CIA found Osama bin Laden.
  Imperative: See *Zero Dark Thirty* to decide if it is pro- or anti-torture.
  Subjunctive: If the use of torture **were** not at the heart of the movie, *Zero Dark Thirty* would be much less controversial.

Multilingual writers can find more on verbs in Chapter 50.

35a Basic Verb Forms

Almost all verbs in English have five possible forms. The exception is the verb *be*. Regular verbs follow this basic pattern.

THE BASIC PATTERN OF REGULAR VERBS				
Base form	Third person singular	Past tense	Past participle	Present participle
jump	jump	jumped	jumped	jumping
like	likes	liked	liked	liking
talk	talks	talked	talked	talking
wish	wishes	wished	wished	wishing

Irregular verbs do not follow this basic pattern. See 35b for the forms of irregular verbs.

Base form

The base form of a verb is the one you find listed in the dictionary. This form indicates an action or condition in the present.

> I **like** New York in June.

> We **talk** often on weekends.

Third person singular

The base form of the verb changes when used with third person singular subjects. Third person singular subjects include *he, she, it* and the nouns they replace, as well as other pronouns, including *someone, anybody,* and *everything.* (See 34c.) Present tense verbs in the third person singular end with an *s* or an *es.*

> Ms. Nessan **speaks** in riddles.

> He **watches** too much television.

Past tense

The past tense describes an action or condition that occurred in the past. For most verbs, the past tense is formed by adding *d* or *ed* to the base form of the verb.

> I **called** at nine, but no one **answered**.

> She **inhaled** the night air.

Many verbs, however, have irregular past tense forms. (See 35b.)

COMMON ERRORS

Missing verb endings

Verb endings are not always pronounced in speech, especially in some dialects of English. It's also easy to omit these endings when you are writing quickly. Spelling checkers will not mark these errors, so you have to find them while proofreading.

Incorrect	Jeremy **feel** as if he's catching a cold.
Correct	Jeremy **feels** as if he's catching a cold.

Incorrect	Sheila **hope** she would get the day off.
Correct	Sheila **hoped** she would get the day off.

Remember: Check verbs carefully for missing *s* or *es* endings in the present tense and missing *d* or *ed* endings in the past tense.

Past participle

The past participle is used with *have* to form verbs in the perfect tense, with *be* to form verbs in the passive voice (see 27b), and to form adjectives derived from verbs.

Past perfect	They **had gone** to the grocery store prematurely.
Passive	The book **was written** thirty years before it **was published**.
Adjective	In the eighties, **teased** hair was all the rage.

Present participle

The present participle functions in one of three ways. Used with an auxiliary verb, it can describe a continuing action. The present participle can also function as a noun, known as a **gerund**, or as an adjective. The present participle is formed by adding *ing* to the base form of a verb.

Present participle	Wild elks **are competing** for limited food resources.
Gerund	**Sailing** around the Cape of Good Hope is rumored to bring good luck.
Adjective	We looked for shells in the **ebbing** tide.

Exercise 35.1 Write the correct form of each underlined verb using the clues given in parentheses.

Example Although it sound*s* (third person singular) simple, noodle*ing* (present participle-gerund), or catch*ing* (present participle-gerund) fish by using only your bare hands, is complicate*d* (past participle-adjective).

Flathead catfish are the <u>choose</u> (past participle-adjective) prey for <u>noodle</u> (gerund) because they <u>lives</u> (base form) sedentary lifestyles in holes or under brush. A noodler <u>begin</u> (third person singular) by <u>go</u> (gerund) underwater to depths ranging from only a few feet to a <u>daunt</u> (present participle-adjective) 20 feet. Placing his or her hand inside a <u>discover</u> (past participle-adjective) catfish hole, a noodler <u>use</u> (third person singular) his or her arm as bait to <u>luring</u> (base form) the fish. If all <u>go</u> (third person singular) as <u>plan</u> (past participle-adjective), the catfish will swim forward and <u>fastened</u> (base form) itself onto the noodler's hand and arm.

> Because catfish often weigh up to 50 to 60 pounds, many a noodler has <u>need</u> (past participle) help <u>lift</u> (gerund) their catch out of the water.

35b Irregular Verbs

A verb is **regular** when its past and past participle forms are created by adding *ed* or *d* to the base form. If this rule does not apply, the verb is considered an **irregular** verb. Here are common irregular verbs and their basic conjugations.

COMMON IRREGULAR VERBS		
Base form	**Past tense**	**Past participle**
arise	arose	arisen
be (is, am, are)	was, were	been
bear	bore	borne or born
beat	beat	beaten
become	became	become
begin	began	begun
bend	bent	bent
break	broke	broken
bring	brought	brought
buy	bought	bought
choose	chose	chosen
cling	clung	clung
come	came	come
cost	cost	cost
creep	crept	crept
deal	dealt	dealt
dig	dug	dug
dive	dived or dove	dived
do	did	done
draw	drew	drawn
drink	drank	drunk
drive	drove	driven
eat	ate	eaten
fall	fell	fallen
feed	fed	fed
feel	felt	felt
fight	fought	fought
fling	flung	flung

COMMON IRREGULAR VERBS (*Continued*)		
Base form	**Past tense**	**Past participle**
fly	flew	flown
forbid	forbade or forbad	forbidden
forget	forgot	forgotten or forgot
forgive	forgave	forgiven
freeze	froze	frozen
get	got	got or gotten
give	gave	given
go	went	gone
grow	grew	grown
hang	hung	hung
have	had	had
know	knew	known
lay	laid	laid
lend	lent	lent
lie	lay	lain
make	made	made
read	read	read
run	ran	run
say	said	said
see	saw	seen
send	sent	sent
shine	shone	shone
show	showed	shown or showed
sit	sat	sat
sleep	slept	slept
speak	spoke	spoken
spring	sprang or sprung	sprung
swim	swam	swum
take	took	taken
teach	taught	taught
tell	told	told
think	thought	thought
understand	understood	understood
wear	wore	worn
write	wrote	written

COMMON ERRORS

Past tense forms of irregular verbs

The past tense and past participle forms of irregular verbs are often confused. The most frequent error is using a past tense form instead of the past participle with *had*.

Incorrect	**PAST TENSE** She had never **rode** a horse before.
Correct	**PAST PARTICIPLE** She had never **ridden** a horse before.
Incorrect	**PAST TENSE** He had **saw** many alligators in Louisiana.
Correct	**PAST PARTICIPLE** He had **seen** many alligators in Louisiana.

Remember: Change any past tense verbs preceded by *had* to past participles.

Exercise 35.2   Underline the correct form of the irregular verbs.

Example   Until recently historians (see/<u>saw</u>) the Dark Ages as a period of cultural, social, and economic stagnation, but new research (<u>shows</u>/shown) that a great deal of economic growth happened during that period.

The Dark Ages are (understand/understood) to have (took/taken) place between the decline of the Roman Empire and the 1500s. Historians (think/thought) that little or no trade happened during the Dark Ages because spices, which (come/came) to Europe from the East, are not (written/wrote) about in documents from that time period. However, evidence that there (be/was) trade between Europe and the East has been found in the bones of rats. Bones (dug/dig) up in Italy and (knew/known) to be from the Dark Ages (is/are) from rats born in Egypt. Since rats (do/did) not travel by foot more than 100 feet from where they are born, the Egyptian rats probably (ride/rode) to Europe on ships. Thus, historians (felt/feel), we should (begin/begun) to rethink what we believe about this misunderstood period.

35c Transitive and Intransitive Verbs

Lay/lie, set/sit, and *raise/rise*

Do you know whether you raise or rise from bed in the morning? Do your house keys lay or lie on the kitchen table? Does a book set or sit on the shelf?

Raise/rise, lay/lie, and *set/sit* are transitive and intransitive verbs that writers frequently confuse. Transitive verbs take direct objects, nouns that receive the action of the verb. Intransitive verbs act in sentences that lack direct objects. Chickens *lay* eggs, but people *lie* down.

The following charts list the trickiest pairs of transitive and intransitive verbs and the correct forms for each verb tense. Pay special attention to *lay* and *lie*, which are irregular.

	lay (put something down)	lie (recline)
Present	lay, lays	lie, lies
Present participle	laying	lying
Past	laid	lay
Past participle	laid	lain

Transitive   Once you complete your test, please **lay** your pencil (direct object, the thing being laid down) on the desk.

Intransitive   The *Titanic* **lies** upright in two pieces at a depth of 13,000 feet.

	raise (elevate something)	rise (get up)
Present	raise, raises	rise, rises
Present participle	raising	rising
Past	raised	rose
Past participle	raised	risen

Transitive   We **raise** our glasses (direct object, the things being raised) to toast Uncle Han.

Intransitive   The sun **rises** over the bay.

	set (place something)	sit (take a seat)
Present	set, sets	sit, sits
Present participle	setting	sitting
Past	set	sat
Past participle	set	sat

Transitive   Every morning Stanley **sets** two dollars (direct object, the amount being set) on the table to tip the waiter.

Intransitive   I **sit** in the front seat when it's available.

Exercise 35.3 Decide whether each of the sentences in the following paragraph calls for a transitive or intransitive verb and underline the correct choice.

Example   The eastern diamondback rattlesnake (will set/<u>will sit</u>) immobile for hours, sometimes coiled and sometimes stretched to its full length of 7 feet.

A rattlesnake will often (lay/lie) in wait for its favorite meal: a rat. When you encounter one of these poisonous snakes, (set/sit) aside your assumptions about aggressive snakes; many are timid. You can tell a rattlesnake feels threatened if its tail (rises/raises) and you hear a sharp rattling sound. If you are hiking in the desert in the southwestern United States, do not (sit/set) down without carefully surveying the ground. To (rise/raise) your chances of avoiding a rattlesnake bite, make noise when you are hiking in wilderness areas.

35d Shifts in Tense

Appropriate shifts in verb tense

Changes in verb tense are sometimes necessary to indicate a shift in time.

Present to past
  PRESENT TENSE   PAST TENSE
I never **shop** online anymore because I **heard** that
  PRESENT PERFECT TENSE
hackers **have stolen** thousands of credit card

numbers used in Internet transactions.

Past to future
  PAST TENSE   FUTURE TENSE
Because Oda **won** the lottery, she **will quit** her job
       PRESENT TENSE
at the hospital as soon as her supervisor **finds** a

qualified replacement.

Inappropriate shifts in verb tense

Be careful to avoid confusing your reader with unnecessary shifts in verb tense. Once you reach the proofreading stage of your writing, dedicate one careful reading of your text to finding inappropriate tense changes.

Incorrect
  PRESENT TENSE
While Brazil **looks** to ecotourism to fund rainforest
       PAST TENSE
preservation, other South American nations **relied**

on foreign aid and conservation efforts.

The shift from present tense (*looks*) to past tense (*relied*) is confusing. The sentence attempts to compare Brazil with other South American

countries, but the shift in tenses muddles the comparison. Correct the mistake by putting both verbs in the present tense.

Correct   PRESENT TENSE
While Brazil **looks** to ecotourism to fund rainforest
PRESENT TENSE
preservation, other South American nations **rely** on

foreign aid and conservation efforts.

Exercise 35.4 Read the paragraph and underline the correct verb tenses.

Example   The American Indian Movement (AIM) (originated/originates) in Minneapolis in 1968.

Native American activists, including Dennis Banks and Russell Means, (created/create) AIM, a militant organization that fights for civil rights for American Indians. AIM members (participate/participated) in a number of famous protests, including the occupation of Alcatraz Island (1969–1971) and the takeover of Wounded Knee (1973). The group (has helped/helps) Indians displaced by government programs, (will work/has worked) for economic independence for Native Americans, and (agitates/has agitated) for the return of lands (seize/seized) by the U.S. government. In his book *Agents of Repression: The FBI's Secret War against the Black Panther Party and the American Indian Movement*, Ward Churchill (documented/documents) how the FBI (infiltrated/infiltrates) AIM in an attempt to destroy it. While most local chapters of AIM (have disbanded/disband), Native American activists today still (fight/fought) for their autonomy and for compensation for centuries of oppression and economic injustice.

COMMON ERRORS

Unnecessary tense shift

Notice the tense shift in the following example.

Incorrect   PAST TENSE
In May of 2000, the "I Love You" virus **crippled** the

computer systems of major American companies and
PAST TENSE
irritated millions of private computer users. As the
PRESENT TENSE   PRESENT TENSE
virus **generates** millions of e-mails and **erases** millions of

computer files, companies such as Ford and Time
PRESENT TENSE
Warner **are** forced to shut down their clogged e-mail systems.

(Continued on next page)

> ### COMMON ERRORS   *(Continued)*
>
> The second sentence shifts unnecessarily to the present tense, confusing the reader. Did the "I Love You" virus have its heyday several years ago, or is it still wreaking havoc now? Changing the verbs in the second sentence to the past tense eliminates the confusion.
>
> **Correct**   In May of 2000, the "I Love You" virus **crippled** the computer
> PAST TENSE
> systems of major American companies and **irritated** millions
> PAST TENSE
> of private computer users. As the virus **generated** millions
> PAST TENSE
> of e-mails and **erased** millions of computer files, companies
> PAST TENSE
> such as Ford and Time Warner **were** forced to shut down
> their clogged e-mail systems.
>
> **Remember: Shift verb tense only when you are referring to different time periods.**

35e   Shifts in Mood

Indicative, imperative, and subjunctive verbs

Verbs can be categorized into three moods—indicative, imperative, and subjunctive—defined by the functions they serve.

Indicative verbs state facts, opinions, and questions.

Fact   Many activists in the United States **are fighting** to end the death penalty.

Opinion   Ending the death penalty **will undermine** the criminal justice system.

Question   Why **do** some people **support** the death penalty?

Imperative verbs make commands, give advice, and make requests.

Command   **Tell** me why you support the death penalty.

Advice   **Try** to think of the death penalty as a civil rights issue.

Request   **Could** you please **explain** how the death penalty is cruel and unusual punishment?

Subjunctive verbs express wishes, unlikely or untrue situations, hypothetical situations, requests with *that* clauses, and suggestions.

Wish	We **wish** that the prison system **were** better at rehabilitating offenders.
Unlikely or untrue situation	**If** the death penalty **were** an effective deterrent, there would be far fewer murders in this country.
Hypothetical situation	**If** the death penalty **were** abolished, states could save millions of dollars every year.

The subjunctive in past and present tenses

Subjunctive verbs are usually the trickiest to handle. In the present tense, subjunctive clauses call for the base form of the verb (*be, have, see, jump*).

> It is essential that children **be** immunized before they enter kindergarten.

In the past tense, they call for the standard past tense of the verb (*had, saw, jumped*), with one exception. In counterfactual sentences the *to be* verb always becomes *were*, even for subjects that take *was* under normal circumstances.

Indicative	I **was** surprised at some of the choices she made.
Subjunctive	If I **were** in her position, I'd do things differently.
Indicative	The young athletes found that gaining muscle **was** not easy.
Subjunctive	If being muscular **were** easy, everyone would look like Arnold Schwarzenegger.

Exercise 35.5 Replace the underlined verb with a verb in the correct mood using the clues in the brackets.

Example Nitrogen Narcosis <u>result</u> ^s [indicative] when nitrogen
levels in the bloodstream <u>became</u> *become* [indicative] elevated
because of pressure.

This phenomenon is called "rapture of the deep" because the increase in nitrogen makes a diver feel as if she <u>is</u> [subjunctive] invincible. <u>Being</u> [imperative] very careful, however; this situation is dangerous. Often the combination of nitrogen and excessive oxygen <u>overwhelm</u> [indicative] the diver, causing her to wish that she could <u>got</u> [subjunctive] free of the breathing

apparatus. A diver above the surface of the water <u>experience</u> [indicative] one atmosphere of pressure. How much <u>do</u> the pressure <u>increase</u> [indicative] if the diver is 100 feet below the surface? <u>Imagining</u> [imperative] having a 300-pound weight on your chest. That's right—the pressure <u>triple</u> [indicative]. It is crucial that a diver <u>prepares</u> [subjunctive] for the possibility of rapture occurring during a dive. Often divers <u>would</u> inhale [indicative] nitrous oxide to see how they would handle themselves if they <u>was</u> [subjunctive] in the throes of rapture of the deep.

36 | Pronouns

QUICK*TAKE*

After reading this chapter, you should be able to . . .

- **Choose the correct pronoun case** (36a)

  Incorrect: She and **me** gave a better presentation than **him**.
  Correct: **She and I** gave a better presentation than **he** did.

- **Identify and correct errors in pronoun agreement** (36b)

  Incorrect: **Everybody** in the class had a chance to give **their** opinions.
  Correct: **All students** had a chance to give **their** opinions.

- **Identify and correct problems with pronouns and gender** (36c)

- **Identify and correct vague pronoun references** (36d)

  Vague: Tom thought he could run a marathon after he finished a 10K race. **This** was a mistake. [*This what*?]
  Better: Tom thought he could run a marathon after he finished a 10K race. **This overconfidence** was a mistake.

36a Pronoun Case

Subjective pronouns function as the subjects of sentences. **Objective pronouns** function as direct or indirect objects. **Possessive pronouns** indicate ownership.

Subjective pronouns	Objective pronouns	Possessive pronouns
I	me	my, mine
we	us	our, ours
you	you	your, yours
he	him	his
she	her	her, hers
it	it	its
they	them	their, theirs
who	whom	whose

People who use English regularly usually make these distinctions among pronouns without thinking about them.

> S   O   P   S   O O   S   O
> I let him use my laptop, but he lent it to her, and I haven't seen it since.

Nonetheless, choosing the correct pronoun case sometimes can be difficult.

Pronouns in compound phrases

Picking the right pronoun sometimes can be confusing when the pronoun appears in a compound phrase.

> If we work together, you and **me** can get the job done quickly.

> If we work together, you and **I** can get the job done quickly.

Which is correct—*me* or *I*? Removing the other pronoun usually makes the choice clear.

> **Incorrect**   **Me** can get the job done quickly.

> **Correct**   **I** can get the job done quickly.

Similarly, when compound pronouns appear as objects of prepositions, sometimes the correct choice isn't obvious until you remove the other pronoun.

> When you finish your comments, give them to her or **I.**

> When you finish your comments, give them to her or **me.**

Again, the choice is easy when the pronoun stands alone.

Incorrect   Give them to **I**.

Correct   Give them to **me**.

We and *us* before nouns

Another pair of pronouns that can cause difficulty is *we* and *us* before nouns.

Us friends must stick together.

We friends must stick together.

Which is correct—*us* or *we*? Removing the noun indicates the correct choice.

Incorrect   **Us** must stick together.

Correct   **We** must stick together.

Exercise 36.1   Underline the pronoun in each sentence of the following paragraph and replace the pronoun if it is incorrect.

Example   You and ~~me~~ should pay more attention to what we eat.

If you and a friend go on a road trip, the ADA suggests that you and her limit your stops at fast-food restaurants. The association suggests us snack in the afternoon, provided we choose foods that are healthy for you and I. If your friend wants a cheeseburger for lunch, you should respond that you and her could split the meal. For your sake and me, it is not a good idea to snack after dark.

Who versus *whom*

Choosing between *who* and *whom* is often difficult, even for experienced writers. When you answer the phone, which do you say?

1. To **whom** do you wish to speak?
2. **Who** do you want to talk to?

Probably you chose sentence 2. However, *"To whom do you wish to speak?"* may sound stuffy but is technically correct. The reason it sounds stuffy is that the distinction between *who* and *whom* is disappearing from spoken language. *Who* is more often used in spoken language, even when *whom* is correct.

COMMON ERRORS

Who or *whom*

In writing, the distinction between *who* and *whom* is still often observed. *Who* and *whom* follow the same rules as other pronouns: *Who* is the subject pronoun; *whom* is the object pronoun. If you are dealing with an object, *whom* is the correct choice.

Incorrect   **Who** did you send the letter to?
                   Who did you give the present to?

Correct   To **whom** did you send the letter?
                   To **whom** did you give the present?

Who is always the right choice for a subject pronoun.

Correct   **Who** gave you the present?
                   Who brought the cookies?

If you are uncertain, try substituting *she* and *her* or *he* and *him*.

Incorrect   You sent the letter to **she** [who]?
Correct   You sent the letter to **her** [whom]?

Incorrect   **Him** [Whom] gave you the present?
Correct   **He** [Who] gave you the present?

Remember: *Who* = subject   *Whom* = object

Whoever versus *whomever*

With the same rule in mind, you can distinguish between *whoever* and *whomever*. Which is correct?

> Her warmth touched **whoever** she met.

> Her warmth touched **whomever** she met.

In this sentence the pronoun functions as a direct object: Her warmth touched everyone she met, not someone who touched her. Thus *whomever* is the correct choice.

Exercise 36.2   In the following sentences, fill in the blank with the correct pronoun: *who, whom, whoever,* or *whomever.*

Example   Kids _who_ have depression, attention-deficit/hyperactivity disorder, or social phobia are more likely than their peers to become addicted to the Internet.

1. Past research suggests that 1.4 percent to 17.9 percent of adolescents are addicted to the Internet, most of _____ live in Eastern nations rather than in Western nations.

2. Although there is no official diagnosis for Internet addiction, _____ uses the Internet so much that it interferes with everyday life and decision-making ability may be an addict.

3. Boys are more likely to become addicted to the Internet than girls, except for those for _____ depression and social phobias are a problem, but boys _____ use the Internet for more than twenty hours a week are at highest risk of all.

4. _____ suspects his or her child has an Internet addiction should monitor that child's Internet usage.

5. There is one residential treatment center for Internet addiction in the United States available for _____ has been diagnosed with this illness.

Pronouns in comparisons

When you write a sentence using a comparison that includes *than* or *as* followed by a pronoun, usually you will have to think about which pronoun is correct. Which of the following is correct?

> Vimala is a faster swimmer than **him**.

> Vimala is a faster swimmer than **he**.

The test that will give you the correct answer is to add the verb that finishes the sentence—in this case, *is*.

> **Incorrect**   Vimala is a faster swimmer than **him is**.

> **Correct**   Vimala is a faster swimmer than **he is**.

Adding the verb makes the correct choice evident.

In some cases the choice of pronoun changes the meaning. Consider the following examples.

> She likes ice cream more than **me**. [A bowl of ice cream is better than hanging out with me.]

> She likes ice cream more than **I**. [I would rather have frozen yogurt.]

In such cases it is better to complete the comparison.

> She likes ice cream more than **I do**.

Possessive pronouns

Possessive pronouns are confusing at times because possessive nouns are formed with apostrophes, but possessive pronouns do not require apostrophes. Pronouns that use apostrophes are always **contractions**.

It's = It is
Who's = Who is
They're = They are

The test for whether to use an apostrophe is to determine whether the pronoun is possessive or a contraction. The most confusing pair is *its* and *it's*.

Incorrect	**Its** a sure thing she will be elected.
Correct	**It's** a sure thing she will be elected. [**It is** a sure thing.]

Incorrect	The dog lost **it's** collar.
Correct	The dog lost **its** collar. [Possessive]

Whose versus *who's* follows the same pattern.

Incorrect	**Who's** bicycle has the flat tire?
Correct	**Whose** bicycle has the flat tire? [Possessive]

Incorrect	**Whose** on first?
Correct	**Who's** on first? [**Who is** on first?]

Possessive pronouns before -*ing* verbs

Pronouns that modify an -*ing* verb (called a *gerund*) or an -*ing* verb phrase (*gerund phrase*) should appear in the possessive.

Incorrect	The odds of **you** making the team are excellent.
Correct	The odds of **your** making the team are excellent.

Exercise 36.3   The following sentences include all the pronoun uses explained in this section. Underline the correct pronoun in each sentence.

Example   Phineas Gage was a railroad foreman (whom/<u>who</u>), in 1848, became a medical miracle.

1. (We/Us) students knew him as the man (who's/whose) head was pierced with a tamping iron and he survived.
2. (Him/His) surviving was due to one of the first neurosurgeries ever, which was nothing like surgeries you or (me/I) have ever heard about.
3. (Whomever/Whoever) knew Phineas before the accident, knew a different version of (his/him) after.
4. (Its/It's) shocking to see Phineas's skull and life mask in the Warren Anatomical Museum.
5. However, a recently discovered photo of Phineas showing (his/him) holding the iron is possibly more interesting than (them/they).

36b Pronoun Agreement

Because pronouns usually replace or refer to other nouns, they must match those nouns in number and gender. The noun that the pronoun replaces is called its **antecedent**. If pronoun and antecedent match, they are in **agreement**. When a pronoun is close to the antecedent, usually there is no problem.

> **Maria** forgot **her** coat.

> The band **members** collected **their** uniforms.

When pronouns and the nouns they replace are separated by several words, sometimes the agreement in number is lost.

> When the World Wrestling Federation (WWF) used **wrestlers** [PLURAL] to represent nations, there was no problem identifying the **villains**. **He** [SING] was the enemy if **he** [SING] came from Russia. But since the Cold War, **wrestlers** [PLURAL] can switch from **good guys** to **bad guys**. We don't immediately know how **he** [SING] has been scripted—good or bad.

Careful writers make sure that pronouns match their antecedents.

Collective nouns

Collective nouns (such as *audience, class, committee, crowd, family, herd, jury, team*) can be singular or plural depending on whether the emphasis is on the group or on the particular individuals.

> **Correct**   The **committee** was unanimous in **its** decision.

> **Correct**   The **committee** put **their** opinions ahead of the goals of the unit.

Often a plural antecedent is added if the sense of the collective noun is plural.

> **Correct**   The individual committee **members** put **their** opinions ahead of the goals of the unit.

COMMON ERRORS

Indefinite pronouns

Indefinite pronouns (such as *anybody, anything, each, either, everybody, everything, neither, none, somebody, something*) refer to unspecified people or things. Most take singular pronouns.

> **Incorrect**   **Everybody** can choose **their** roommates.

| Correct | **Everybody** can choose **his or her** roommate. |
| Correct alternative | **All students** can choose **their** roommates. |

A few indefinite pronouns (*all, any, either, more, most, neither, none, some*) can take either singular or plural pronouns.

| Correct | **Some** of the shipment was damaged when **it** became overheated. |
| Correct | **All** thought **they** should have a good seat at the concert. |

A few are always plural (*few, many, several*).

| Correct | **Several** want refunds. |

Remember: Words that begin with *any, some,* and *every* are usually singular.

COMMON ERRORS

Pronoun agreement with compound antecedents

Antecedents joined by *and* take plural pronouns.

| Correct | **Moncef and Driss** practiced **their** music. |

Exception: When compound antecedents are preceded by *each* or *every,* use a singular pronoun.

| Correct | **Every male cardinal and warbler** arrives before the female to define **its** territory. |

When compound antecedents are connected by *or* or *nor,* the pronoun agrees with the antecedent closer to it.

Incorrect	**Either the Ross twins or Angela** should bring **their** games.
Correct	**Either the Ross twins or Angela** should bring **her** games.
Better	**Either Angela or the Ross twins** should bring **their** games.

When you put the plural *twins* last, the correct choice becomes the plural pronoun *their.*

Remember:

1. Use plural pronouns for antecedents joined by *and.*

2. Use singular pronouns for antecedents preceded by *each* or *every.*

3. Use a pronoun that agrees with the nearest antecedent when compound antecedents are joined by *or* or *nor.*

Exercise 36.4 In the following sentences, pronouns are separated from the nouns they replace. Underline the antecedent and fill in the pronoun that agrees with it in the blank provided.

> **Example** Ironically, <u>greyhounds</u> are rarely gray; *their* fur can be all shades of red, brown, gray, and brindle.

1. Canine experts disagree on the origin of the name "greyhound," but many believe _____ derives from "Greek hound."
2. For over 5,000 years, greyhounds have been prized for _____ regal bearing and grace.
3. Greyhounds were introduced into England by the Cretans around 500 BC, but _____ are best known as the mascot for America's number-one bus line.
4. King Cob was the first notable greyhound sire recorded after England began documenting canine pedigrees in 1858, and _____ fathered 111 greyhounds in three years.
5. Each greyhound King Cob fathered was of the purest pedigree, even though _____ great-grandfather was a bulldog.

Exercise 36.5 Underline the indefinite pronouns, collective nouns, and compound antecedents in the paragraph that follows. Circle the related pronouns and, if necessary, revise them to agree with their antecedents. In some cases you may have to decide whether the emphasis is on the group or individuals within the group.

> **Example** <u>Many stories</u> attempt to explain why the number 13 is
>
> considered unlucky, but (they) provide no evidence that
>
> Friday is a particularly unlucky day. In fact, if <u>everyone</u>
>   *he or she*
> were to follow stories from Greek history, (they) might be
>
> avoiding ladders and sidewalk cracks on Tuesday the 13th.

Although few would admit it, he or she often take(s) extra precautions on Friday the 13th. Some are so paralyzed by fear that they are simply unable to get out of his or her bed when Friday the 13th comes around. The Stress Management Center and Phobia Institute estimate(s) that more than 17 million people admit to being extra careful as they drive and go about their business on this day. Perhaps they are right to be concerned! A team writing for a British medical journal has shown that there is a significant increase in traffic accidents on Friday the 13th. However, this fear seems to be directed toward cars.

> According to representatives from both airlines, neither Delta nor United Airlines suffer from any noticeable drop in travel on Friday the 13th.

36c Problems with Pronouns and Gender

English does not have a neutral singular pronoun for a group of mixed genders or a person of unknown gender. Referring to a group of mixed genders using male pronouns is unacceptable to many people. Unless the school in the following example is all male, many readers would object to the use of *his*.

Sexist **Each student** must select **his** courses using the online registration system.

Some writers attempt to avoid sexist usage by substituting a plural pronoun. This strategy, however, produces a grammatically incorrect sentence that also risks putting off some readers.

Incorrect **Each student** must select **their** courses using the online registration system.

One strategy is to use *his or her* instead of *his*.

Correct **Each student** must select **his or her** courses using the online registration system.

Often you can avoid using *his or her* by changing the noun to the plural form.

Better **All students** must select **their** courses using the online registration system.

In some cases, using *his or her* may be necessary. Use this construction sparingly.

COMMON ERRORS

Problems created by the pronoun *one* used as a subject

Some writers use *one* as a subject in an attempt to sound more formal. At best this strategy produces writing that sounds stilted, and at worst it produces annoying errors.

Sexist **One** can use **his** brains instead of a calculator to do simple addition.

Incorrect **One** can use **their** brains instead of a calculator to do simple addition. [Agreement error: *Their* does not agree with *one*.]

(Continued on next page)

COMMON ERRORS *(Continued)*

Incorrect	When **one** runs a 10K race for the first time, **you** often start out too fast. [Pronoun shift error: *One* changes to *you*.]
Correct	**One** can use **his or her** brains instead of a calculator to do simple addition.
Correct	**One** can use **one's** brains instead of a calculator to do simple addition.

You're better off avoiding using *one* as the subject of sentences.

Better	**Use your brain** instead of a calculator for simple addition.

Remember: Avoid using the pronoun *one* as a subject.

Exercise 36.6   The following sentences contain examples of gender bias. Rewrite the sentences using subject and pronoun formations that are unbiased. Try to avoid using "his or her" constructions.

Example	When an American turns 18, he is bombarded with advertisements that market easy credit.
Revised	When **Americans** turn 18, **they** are bombarded with advertisements that market easy credit.

1. When someone is financially overextended, he often considers credit cards as a way of making ends meet.
2. One might begin to convince himself that credit is the only way out.
3. But each adult must weigh the advantages and disadvantages of her own credit card use.
4. Eventually, one may find himself deep in debt because of high credit rates and overspending.
5. Then, one option might be for the individual to find a debt consolidator to assist him.

36d Vague Reference

Pronouns can sometimes refer to more than one noun, thus confusing readers.

The **coach** rushed past the injured **player** to yell at the **referee**. **She** was hit in the face by a stray elbow.

You have to guess which person *she* refers to—the coach, the player, or the referee. Sometimes you cannot even guess the antecedent of a pronoun.

> The new subdivision destroyed the last remaining habitat for wildlife within the city limits. **They** have ruined our city with their unchecked greed.

Whom does *they* refer to? the mayor and city council? the developers? the people who live in the subdivision? or all of the above?

Pronouns should never leave the reader guessing about antecedents. If different nouns can be confused as the antecedent, then the ambiguity should be clarified.

Vague   Mafalda's pet boa constrictor crawled across Tonya's foot. **She** was mortified.

Better   When Mafalda's pet boa constrictor crawled across Tonya's foot, **Mafalda** was mortified.

If the antecedent is missing, then it should be supplied.

Vague   Mafalda wasn't thinking when she brought her boa constrictor into the crowded writing center. **They** got up and left the room in the middle of consultations.

Better   Mafalda wasn't thinking when she brought her boa constrictor into the crowded writing center. **A few students** got up and left the room in the middle of consultations.

COMMON ERRORS

Vague use of *this*

Always use a noun immediately after *this, that, these, those,* and *some.*

Vague   Enrique asked Meg to remove the viruses on his computer. **This** was a bad idea.

Was it a bad idea for Enrique to ask Meg because she was insulted? Because she didn't know how? Because removing viruses would destroy some of Enrique's files?

Better   Enrique asked Meg to remove the viruses on his computer. **This imposition** on Meg's time made her resentful.

Remember: Ask yourself "*this* what?" and add the noun that *this* refers to.

37 | Modifiers

QUICK*TAKE*

After reading this chapter, you should be able to . . .

- **Use comparatives and superlatives correctly** (37a)

  Incorrect: The Great Seattle Fire of 1889 that destroyed twenty-five city blocks was the **most large** fire in the city's history.
  Correct: The Great Seattle Fire of 1889 that destroyed twenty-five city blocks was the **largest** fire in the city's history.

- **Use adjectives carefully and correctly** (37b)
- **Use adverbs carefully and correctly** (37c)
- **Place modifiers near the words or phrases they modify** (37d)

  Incorrect: After decreeing that all new buildings had to be made of stone or brick, **the streets and sidewalks** were raised one or two stories higher than before, leaving a system of tunnels and rooms under the city.
  Correct: After decreeing that all new buildings had to be made of stone or brick, **Seattle's leaders** raised the streets and sidewalks one or two stories higher than before, leaving a system of tunnels and rooms under the city.

- **Identify and correct dangling modifiers** (37e)

37a Choose the Correct Modifier

Modifiers come in two varieties: adjectives and adverbs. The same words can function as adjectives or adverbs, depending on what they modify.

Adjectives modify

nouns—*iced* tea, *power* forward
pronouns—He is *brash*.

Adverbs modify

verbs—*barely* reach, drive *carefully*
adjectives—*truly* brave activist, *shockingly* red lipstick
other adverbs—*not* soon forget, *very* well
clauses—*Honestly*, I find ballet boring.

Adjectives answer the questions *Which one? How many?* and *What kind?* Adverbs answer the questions *How often? To what extent? When? Where? How?* and *Why?*

Use the correct forms of comparatives and superlatives

As kids, we used comparative and superlative modifiers to argue that Superman was *stronger* than Batman and recess was the *coolest* part of the day. Comparatives and superlatives are formed differently; all you need to know to determine which to use is the number of items you are comparing.

Comparative modifiers weigh one thing against another. They either end in *er* or are preceded by *more*.

> Road bikes are **faster** on pavement than mountain bikes.

> The **more courageous** juggler tossed flaming torches.

Superlative modifiers compare three or more items. They either end in *est* or are preceded by *most*.

> April is the **hottest** month in New Delhi.

> Wounded animals are the **most ferocious**.

When should you add a suffix instead of *more* or *most*? The following guidelines work in most cases.

Adjectives

- For adjectives of one or two syllables, add *-er* or *-est*.
  redder, heaviest
- For adjectives of three or more syllables, use *more* or *most*.
  more viable, most powerful

Adverbs

- For adverbs of one syllable, use *-er* or *-est*.
  nearer, slowest
- For adverbs with two or more syllables, use *more* or *most*.
  more convincingly, most humbly

Some comparatives and superlatives are irregular. The following list can help you become familiar with them.

FREQUENTLY USED COMPARATIVES AND SUPERLATIVES		
Adjective	**Comparative**	**Superlative**
good	better	best
bad	worse	worst
little (amount)	less	least
many, much	more	most
Adverb	**Comparative**	**Superlative**
well	better	best
badly	worse	worst

Do not use both a suffix (*-er* or *-est*) and *more* or *most*.

Incorrect   The service at Jane's Restaurant is **more slower** than the service at Alphonso's.

Correct   The service at Jane's Restaurant is **slower** than the service at Alphonso's.

Be sure to name the elements being compared if they are not clear from the context.

Unclear comparative   Mice are **cuter**.
Clear   Mice are **cuter than rats**.

Unclear superlative   Nutria are the **creepiest**.
Clear   Nutria are the **creepiest rodents**.

Absolute modifiers cannot be comparative or superlative

Absolute modifiers are words that represent an unvarying condition and thus aren't subject to the degrees that comparative and superlative constructions convey. How many times have you heard something called *very unique* or *totally unique*? *Unique* means "one of a kind." There's nothing else like it. Thus something cannot be *very unique* or *totally unique*. It either is unique or it isn't. The United States Constitution makes a classic absolute modifier blunder when it begins, "We the People of the United States, in Order to form a more perfect Union. . . ." What is a *more perfect Union*? What's more perfect than perfect itself? The construction is nonsensical.

Absolute modifiers should not be modified by comparatives (*more* + modifier or modifier + *-er*) or superlatives (*most* + modifier or modifier + *-est*). Note the following list.

COMMON ABSOLUTE MODIFIERS		
absolute	impossible	unanimous
adequate	infinite	unavoidable
complete	main	uniform
entire	minor	unique
false	perfect	universal
fatal	principal	whole
final	stationary	
ideal	sufficient	

Exercise 37.1   Decide whether each word in parentheses should be comparative or superlative. Rewrite the word, adding either the correct suffix (*-er* or *-est*) or *good, best, bad, worst, more, most, less,* or *least.* If you find an absolute modifier (a word that should not be modified), underline it.

> *best*
> **Example** Volkswagen's Beetle is the (good) selling car in history
> even though it had the same body for sixty years and had
> undergone only <u>minor</u> mechanical changes.

1. The Model T is ranked second in sales, but it is perhaps (important) historically than the Beetle because it was the first car to be mass produced, paving the way for cars to be built (cheaply) and (quickly) than ever before.

2. Selling for about $300, the Model T wasn't the (expensive) car on the market in the 1920s, however; that unique honor belongs to the 1922 Briggs & Stratton Flyer, which sold for $125 to $150.

3. With a top speed of over 250 mph and a price well over $1.7 million the Bugatti Veyron 16.4 is currently the (expensive) and (powerful) car in the world, but it is not the (fast). The SSC Ultimate Aero is (fast) than the Bugatti.

4. Although fast "muscle cars," such as the Camaro, the Corvette, the Firebird, and the Mustang, are (fast) than the Aero, that they are also (expensive) makes them (attractive) to young drivers and therefore (dangerous), too.

5. The (safe) car in history, the 1957 Aurora, is also the (rare); the one Aurora that was ever built was considered a complete failure.

Double negatives

In English, as in mathematics, two negatives equal a positive. Avoid using two negative words in one sentence, or you'll end up saying the opposite of what you mean. The following are negative words that you should avoid doubling up:

barely	nobody	nothing
hardly	none	scarcely
neither	no one	

Incorrect, double negative	**Barely no one** noticed that the pop star lip-synched during the whole performance.
Correct, single negative	**Barely anyone** noticed that the pop star lip-synched during the whole performance.
Incorrect, double negative	When the pastor asked if anyone had objections to the marriage, **nobody** said **nothing**.
Correct, single negative	When the pastor asked if anyone had objections to the marriage, **nobody** said **anything**.

COMMON ERRORS

Irregular adjectives and adverbs

Switch on a baseball interview and you will likely hear numerous modifier mistakes.

> Manager: We didn't play **bad** tonight. Martinez hit the ball **real good**, and I was glad to see Adamski pitch **farther** into the game than he did in his last start. His fastball was on, and he walked **less** hitters.

While this manager has his sports clichés down pat, he makes errors with five of the trickiest modifier pairs. In three cases he uses an adjective where an adverb would be correct.

Adjectives	Adverbs
bad	badly
good	well
real	really

[*Bad*, an adjective modifying the noun *call.*] The umpire made a **bad** call at the plate.

[*Badly*, an adverb modifying the verb *play.*] We didn't play **badly**.

[*Good*, an adjective modifying the noun *catch.*] Starke made a **good** catch.

[*Well*, an adverb modifying the verb *hit.*] Martinez hit the ball **well**.

Exception: *Well* acts as an adjective when it describes someone's health: Injured players must stay on the disabled list until they feel **well** enough to play every day.

[*Real*, an adjective modifying the noun *wood.*] While college players hit with aluminum bats, the professionals still use **real** wood.

[*Really*, an adverb modifying the adverb *well.*] Martinez hit the ball **really** well.

The coach also confused the comparative adjectives *less* and *fewer,* and the comparative adverbs *farther* and *further.*

Adjectives

less—a smaller, uncountable amount
fewer—a smaller number of things

Less	Baseball stadiums with pricey luxury suites cater **less** to families and more to business people with expense accounts.
Fewer	He walked **fewer** hitters.

Adverbs

farther—a greater distance
further—to a greater extent, a longer time, or a greater number

Farther	Some players argue that today's baseballs go **farther** than baseballs made just a few years ago.
Further	The commissioner of baseball curtly denied that today's baseballs are juiced, refusing to discuss the matter **further**.

Remember: *Bad, good, real, less* (for uncountables), and *fewer* (for countables) are adjectives. *Badly, well, really, farther* (for distance), and *further* (for extent, time, or number) are adverbs. *Well* is an adjective when it describes health.

Exercise 37.2   Revise the following paragraph to eliminate double negatives. More than one answer may be correct in each case.

Example   One ~~can't~~ *can* hardly survey the history of the American film industry without encountering the story of the Hollywood Ten, a group of artists targeted as communists.

After the creation of the House Un-American Activities Committee (HUAC), Cold War paranoia could not barely hide itself in post–World War II America. HUAC followed on the coattails of the 1938 Special Committee on Un-American Activities. This earlier committee did not focus not solely on communists; extremists from both the far left and the far right were targeted. By the 1940s, however, HUAC focused not on neither white supremacist nor pro-Nazi groups, but instead on the supposed communist infiltration of Hollywood. Scarcely no one could escape the grasp of HUAC; actors, producers, and directors all came under scrutiny. By the end of the proceedings, not hardly nobody remained unscathed. Hundreds in the entertainment industry were either fired or appeared on the infamous HUAC blacklist.

Exercise 37.3 The following words in parentheses are tricky adjective-adverb pairs. Underline the word(s) being modified in the sentence and circle the correct adjective or adverb from the pair.

Example   To ensure the success of their missions, NASA has

tackled the challenge of enabling astronauts <u>to eat</u>

(healthy/(healthily)) in space so that <u>they</u> can stay

(good/(well)).

In the early days of manned space missions, NASA had (fewer/less) problems feeding astronauts. But the (further/farther) astronauts traveled, the (further/farther) NASA had to go to ensure healthy eating in space. For example, the Mercury missions of the early 1960s took (fewer/less) time than an actual meal, so NASA's (real/really) challenge didn't come until crews were in space for longer periods of time. However, these shorter trips worked (good/well) as tests for experimental astronaut foods. By the mid-1960s, the astronauts on the Gemini missions were offered better ways to prepare and enjoy food in space. Engineers eventually discovered that packaging food in an edible liquid or gelatin container would prevent it from crumbling and damaging the equipment (bad/badly). By the time of the Space Shuttle expeditions in the 1980s and 1990s, (real/really) headway had been made in terms of (good/well) dining technology, and crew members could devise their own menus.

37b Place Adjectives Carefully

As a general rule, the closer you place a modifier to the word it modifies, the less the chance you will confuse your reader. This section and the next elaborate on this maxim, giving you the details you need to put it into practice. Most native speakers have an ear for many of the guidelines presented here, with the notable exception of the placement of limiting modifiers, which is explained in 37c.

Place adjective phrases and clauses carefully

Adjective clauses frequently begin with *when*, *where*, or a relative pronoun like *that*, *which*, *who*, *whom*, or *whose*. An adjective clause usually follows the noun or pronoun it modifies.

Adjective clause modifying *salon*: The **salon where I get my hair styled** is raising its prices.

Adjective clause modifying *stylist*: I need to find a **stylist who charges less**.

Adjective phrases and clauses can also come before the person or thing they modify.

Adjective phrase modifying *girl:* **Proud of her accomplishment**, the little **girl** showed her trophy to her grandmother.

Adjective phrases or clauses can be confusing if they are separated from the word they modify.

Confusing   **Watching from the ground below**, the kettle of broadwing hawks circled high above the observers.

Is the kettle of hawks watching from the ground below? You can fix the problem by putting the modified subject immediately after the modifier or placing the modifier next to the modified subject.

Better   The kettle of broadwing hawks circled high above the **observers who were watching from the ground below**.

Better   **Watching from the ground below**, the **observers** saw a kettle of broadwing hawks circle high above them.

See dangling modifiers in 37e.

Place one-word adjectives before the modified word(s)

One-word adjectives almost always precede the word or words they modify.

Pass the **hot** sauce, please.

When one-word adjectives are not next to the word or words being modified, they can create misunderstandings.

Unclear   Before his owner withdrew him from competition, the **fiercest** rodeo's bull injured three riders.

Readers may think *fiercest* modifies *rodeo's* instead of *bull*. Placing the adjective before *bull* will clarify the meaning.

Better   Before his owner withdrew him from competition, the rodeo's **fiercest** bull injured three riders.

Exception: predicate adjectives follow linking verbs

Predicate adjectives are the most common exception to the norm of single-word adjectives preceding words they modify. Predicate adjectives follow linking verbs such as *is, are, was, were, seem, feel, smell, taste,* and *look*. Don't be fooled into thinking they are adverbs. If the word following a linking verb modifies the subject, use a predicate adjective. If it modifies an action verb, use an adverb. Can you identify the word being modified in the following sentence?

I feel **odd**.

Odd modifies the subject *I*, not the verb *feel*. Thus, *odd* is a predicate adjective that implies the speaker feels ill. If it were an adverb, the sentence would read *I feel oddly*. The adverb *oddly* modifying *feel* would imply the speaker senses things in unconventional ways. Try the next one.

> The bruise looked **bad**.

Since *bad* modifies *bruise*, *bad* is a predicate adjective implying a serious injury. *Looked* is the linking verb that connects the two. If we made the modifier an adverb, the sentence would read *The bruise looked badly*, conjuring the creepy notion that the bruise had eyes but couldn't see well. You can avoid such bizarre constructions if you know when to use predicate adjectives with linking verbs.

37c Place Adverbs Carefully

For the most part, the guidelines for adverb placement are not as complex as the guidelines for adjective placement.

Place adverbs before or after the words they modify

Single-word adverbs and adverbial clauses and phrases can usually sit comfortably either before or after the words they modify.

> Dimitri **quietly** **walked** down the hall.

> Dimitri **walked** **quietly** down the hall.

Conjunctive adverbs—*also, however, instead, likewise, then, therefore, thus,* and others—are adverbs that show how ideas relate to one another. They prepare a reader for contrasts, exceptions, additions, conclusions, and other shifts in an argument. Conjunctive adverbs can usually fit well into more than one place in the sentence. In the following example, *however* could fit in three different places.

Between two main clauses

Professional football players earn exorbitant salaries; **however,** they pay for their wealth with lifetimes of chronic pain and debilitating injuries.

Within second main clause

Professional football players earn exorbitant salaries; they pay for their wealth, **however,** with lifetimes of chronic pain and debilitating injuries.

At end of second main clause

Professional football players earn exorbitant salaries; they pay for their wealth with lifetimes of chronic pain and debilitating injuries **however**.

Subordinating conjunctions—words such as *after, although, because, if, since, than, that, though, when,* and *where*—often begin **adverb clauses**. Notice that we can place adverb clauses with subordinating conjunctions either before or after the word(s) being modified:

After someone in the audience yelled, he **forgot** the lyrics.

He **forgot** the lyrics **after someone in the audience yelled**.

While you have some leeway with adverb placement, follow the advice in 37d: Avoid distracting interruptions between the subject and verb, the verb and the object, or within the verb phrase. A long adverbial clause is usually best placed at the beginning or end of a sentence.

COMMON ERRORS

Placement of limiting modifiers

Words such as *almost, even, hardly, just, merely, nearly, not, only,* and *simply* are called limiting modifiers. Although people often play fast and loose with their placement in everyday speech, limiting modifiers should always go immediately before the word or words they modify in your writing. Many writers have difficulty with the placement of *only*. Like other limiting modifiers, *only* should be placed immediately before the word it modifies.

Incorrect   The Gross Domestic Product **only** gives one indicator of economic growth.

Correct   The Gross Domestic Product gives **only** one indicator of economic growth.

Remember: Place limiting modifiers immediately before the word(s) they modify.

Exercise 37.4 Rewrite each of the following sentences, moving the adverb to eliminate possible confusion. Place adverbs where they make the most logical sense within the context of the sentence. Underline the adverbs in your revised sentences.

Example In the mid-1800s, Father Gregor Mendel developed experiments ingeniously examining the area of heredity.

Revised In the mid-1800s, Father Gregor Mendel <u>ingeniously</u> developed experiments examining the area of heredity.

1. Mendel's work focused on initially hybridizing the Lathyrus, or sweet pea.
2. The Lathyrus possessed variations conveniently composed of differing sizes and colors.
3. Hybridizing the plants easily allowed Mendel to view the mathematical effects of dominant and recessive trait mixing.
4. By crossing white-flowered pea pods with red-flowered pea pods, Mendel proved successfully existing pairs of hereditary factors determined the color characteristics of offspring.
5. Though published in 1866, Mendel's theory of heredity remained unnoticed mostly by the biological community until the early 1900s.

37d Revise Disruptive Modifiers

The fundamental way readers make sense of sentences is to identify the subject, verb, and object. Modifiers can sink a sentence if they interfere with the reader's ability to connect the three. Usually, single-word modifiers do not significantly disrupt a sentence. However, avoid placing modifying clauses and phrases between a subject and a verb, between a verb and an object, and within a verb phrase.

Disruptive The forest fire, **no longer held in check by the exhausted firefighters**, jumped the firebreak.
[Separates the subject from the verb]

Better **No longer held in check by the exhausted firefighters**, the forest fire jumped the firebreak.
[Puts the modifier before the subject]

Disruptive The fire's heat seemed to melt, **at a temperature hot enough to liquefy metal**, the saplings in its path.
[Separates the verb from the object]

Better **At a temperature hot enough to liquefy metal**, the fire's heat seemed to melt the saplings in its path.
[Puts the modifier before the subject]

WRITING SMART

Split infinitives

An infinitive is *to* plus the base form of a verb. A split infinitive occurs when an adverb separates *to* from the base verb form.

Infinitive = *To* + Base verb form

    Examples: to feel, to speak, to borrow

Split infinitive = *To* + Modifier + Base verb form

    Examples: to strongly feel, to barely speak, to liberally borrow

The most famous split infinitive in recent history occurs in the opening credits of *Star Trek* episodes: "to boldly go where no man has gone before." The alternative without the split infinitive is "to go boldly where no man has gone before." The writers in *Star Trek* no doubt were aware they were splitting an infinitive, but they chose *to boldly go* because they wanted the emphasis on *boldly*, not *go*.

Nevertheless, many split infinitives are considered awkward for good reason.

Awkward	You have to get away from the city lights **to better appreciate** the stars in the night sky.
Better	You have to get away from the city lights **to appreciate** the stars in the night sky **better**.
Awkward	**To, as planned, stay** in Venice, we need to reserve a hotel room now.
Better	**To stay** in Venice **as planned**, we need to reserve a hotel room now.

When a sentence would sound strange without the adverb's splitting the infinitive, you can either retain the split or, better yet, revise the sentence to avoid the problem altogether.

Acceptable	When found by the search party, the survivors were able **to barely whisper** their names.
Alternative	When found by the search party, the survivors **could barely whisper** their names.

37e   Revise Dangling Modifiers

Some modifiers are ambiguous because they can apply to more than one word or clause. Dangling modifiers are ambiguous for the opposite reason; they don't have a word to modify. In such cases the modifier is usually an introductory clause or phrase. What is being modified should immediately follow the phrase, but in the following sentence it is absent.

> **After bowling a perfect game**, Surfside Lanes hung Marco's photo on the wall.

Neither the subject of the sentence, *Surfside Lanes,* nor the direct object, *Marco's photo,* is capable of bowling a perfect game. Since a missing noun or pronoun causes a dangling modifier, simply rearranging the sentence will not resolve the problem. You can fix a dangling modifier in two ways.

1. Insert the noun or pronoun being modified immediately after the introductory modifying phrase.

   > After bowling a perfect game, **Marco** was honored by having his photo hung on the wall at Surfside Lanes.

2. Rewrite the introductory phrase as an introductory clause to include the noun or pronoun.

   > After **Marco** bowled a perfect game, Surfside Lanes hung his photo on the wall.

Exercise 37.5   Each of the following sentences contains a dangling modifier. Revise the sentences to eliminate dangling modifiers according to the methods described in 37e. More than one way of revising may be correct.

Example   Though it preceded Woodstock, popular music history often obscures the Monterey Pop Festival.

Revised   Though the Monterey Pop Festival preceded Woodstock, it is often obscured by popular music history.

1. Lasting for three days in June of 1967, over thirty artists performed.
2. The largest American music festival of its time, attendance totaled over 200,000.
3. With artists such as Ravi Shankar, Otis Redding, and The Who, the fans encountered various musical genres.
4. Performing live for the first time in America, fans howled as Jimi Hendrix set his guitar on fire.
5. Establishing a standard for future festivals, Woodstock and Live Aid would eventually follow suit.

PART 9

Understanding Punctuation and Mechanics

UNDERSTANDING PUNCTUATION AND MECHANICS MAP

Understand when to use and where to place commas

- Know what parts of sentences need to be set off with commas. Go to 38a and 38b.
- Avoid unnecessary commas. Go to 38b and 38i.
- Know when to use commas with long modifiers. Go to 38c

Understand the correct uses of semicolons and colons

- Use semicolons with closely related main clauses. Go to 39a.
- Know when to use and when not use colons with lists. Go to 39c and 39d.

Understand the correct uses of hyphens and dashes

- Know when to use hyphens correctly. Go to Chapter 40.
- Know when to use dashes to set off information. Go to 41b.
- Know how to type a dash. Go to 41d.

Understand the correct uses of apostrophes

- Know when to use apostrophes to indicate possession and omitted letters. Go to 42a and 42b.
- Understand when to use *its* versus *it's*. Go to 42a.

Understand the correct uses of quotation marks

- Know when to use quotation marks to set off direct quotations and for certain titles. Go to 43a and 43b.
- Know how to use other punctuation with quotation marks. Go to 43e.

Understand the correct uses of other punctuation marks

- Know how to use periods, question marks, exclamation points, brackets, ellipses, and slashes. Go to Chapter 44.

38 | Commons

QUICK*TAKE*

After reading this chapter, you should be able to . . .

- **Set off parts of a sentence correctly with commas** (38a)

  Incorrect: Although bears have a better sense of smell than bloodhounds there are reasons why the military cannot fly them into dangerous areas **,** and have them sniff out enemy combatants.

  Correct: Although bears have a better sense of smell than bloodhounds **,** there are reasons why the military cannot fly them into dangerous areas and have them sniff out enemy combatants.

- **Use commas correctly with compound clauses** (38b)
- **Use commas correctly with long modifiers** (38c)

  Restrictive: Anyone **who thinks bears could be trained to carry out a military mission** hasn't really thought the idea through.

  Nonrestrictive: The Pentagon **,** **which recently added a virtual suggestion box to its Web site** **,** has been receiving some unusual ideas.

- **Use commas correctly in a series** (38d)
- **Use commas correctly with coordinate adjectives** (38e)
- **Use commas correctly with quotations** (38f)

  Incorrect: "Bears are the best sniffers" **,** wrote someone.

  Correct: "Bears are the best sniffers **,**" wrote someone.

- **Use commas correctly with dates, names, titles, and addresses** (38g)
- **Use commas effectively to avoid confusion** (38h)
- **Avoid unnecessary commas** (38i)

  Incorrect: Bears look clumsy **,** but can run as fast as a horse.

  Correct: Bears look clumsy **•** but can run as fast as a horse.

38a Commas with Introductory Elements

Introductory elements usually need to be set off by commas. Introductory words or phrases signal a shift in ideas or a particular arrangement of ideas; they help direct the reader's attention to the writer's most important points.

Common introductory elements

Conjunctive adverbs	Introductory phrases
however	of course
therefore	above all
nonetheless	for example

Conjunctive adverbs	Introductory phrases
also	in other words
otherwise	as a result
finally	on the other hand
instead	in conclusion
thus	in addition

When a conjunctive adverb or introductory phrase begins a sentence, the comma follows.

> **Therefore,** the suspect could not have been at the scene of the crime.

> **Above all,** remember to let water drip from the faucets if the temperature drops below freezing.

When a conjunctive adverb comes in the middle of a sentence, set it off with commas preceding and following.

> If you really want to prevent your pipes from freezing, **however,** you should insulate them before the winter comes.

Conjunctive adverbs and phrases that do not require commas

Occasionally the conjunctive adverb or phrase blends into a sentence so smoothly that a pause would sound awkward.

Awkward	Of course, we'll come.
Better	Of course we'll come.

Awkward	Even if you take every precaution, the pipes in your home may freeze, **nevertheless.**
Better	Even if you take every precaution, the pipes in your home may freeze **nevertheless.**

Exercise 38.1   Underline conjunctive adverbs, introductory phrases, and long introductory modifiers in the following sentences. Then set off those elements with commas when necessary.

Example   <u>Although king cobras have small fangs,</u> one bite is poisonous enough to kill an elephant.

1. King cobras in fact have a poisonous bite from the moment they are born.
2. Even though king cobras carry lethal venom, women in Thailand's King Cobra Club dance with the snakes' heads in their mouths.
3. Also, many Southeast Asian countries worship the king cobra.

4. Above all, avoid provoking king cobras; they are not aggressive animals if left undisturbed.

5. An antidote is available however, if you are bitten by a cobra.

COMMON ERRORS

Commas with long introductory modifiers

Long subordinate clauses or phrases that begin sentences should be followed by a comma. The following sentence lacks the needed comma.

Incorrect   Because teens and younger adults are so comfortable with and reliant on cell phone devices texting while driving does not immediately seem like an irresponsible and possibly deadly act.

When you read this sentence, you likely had to go back to sort it out. The words *cell phone devices* and *texting* tend to run together. When the comma is added, the sentence is easier to understand because the reader knows where the subordinate clause ends and where the main clause begins:

Correct   Because teens and younger adults are so comfortable with and reliant on cell phone devices, texting while driving does not immediately seem like an irresponsible and possibly deadly act.

How long is a long introductory modifier? Short introductory adverbial phrases and clauses of five words or fewer can get by without the comma if the omission does not mislead the reader. Using the comma is still correct after short introductory adverbial phrases and clauses.

Correct   In the long run stocks have always done better than bonds.
Correct   In the long run, stocks have always done better than bonds.

Remember: Put commas after long introductory modifiers.

38b Commas with Compound Clauses

Two main clauses joined by a coordinating conjunction (*and, or, so, yet, but, nor, for*) form a compound sentence (see 32e). Writers sometimes get confused about when to insert a comma before a coordinating conjunction.

Use a comma to separate main clauses

Main clauses carry enough grammatical weight to be punctuated as sentences. When two main clauses are joined by a coordinating conjunction, place a comma before the coordinating conjunction in order to distinguish them.

Sandy borrowed Martin's iPad on Tuesday, **and** she returned it on Friday.

Very short main clauses joined by a coordinating conjunction do not need commas.

> She called **and** she called, but no one answered.

Do not use a comma to separate two verbs with the same subject

Incorrect   Sandy borrowed Martin's video camera on Tuesday **,** **and** returned it on Friday.

Sandy is the subject of both *borrowed* and *returned*. This sentence has only one main clause; it should not be punctuated as a compound sentence.

Correct   Sandy borrowed Martin's video camera on Tuesday **and** returned it on Friday.

Exceptions to this rule occur when there is a lapse of time or after *said*.

> He did not study, and failed.

> "That's fine," he said, and went on reading.

COMMON ERRORS

Commas in compound sentences

The easiest way to distinguish between compound sentences and sentences with phrases that follow the main clause is to isolate the part that comes after the conjunction. If the part that follows the conjunction can stand on its own as a complete sentence, insert a comma. If it cannot, omit the comma.

Main clause plus phrases

Mario thinks he lost his passport while riding the bus or by absentmindedly leaving it on the counter when he checked into the hostel.

Look at what comes after the coordinating conjunction *or*:

by absentmindedly leaving it on the counter when he checked into the hostel

This group of words is not a main clause and cannot stand on its own as a complete sentence. Do not set it off with a comma.

Main clauses joined with a conjunction

On Saturday Mario went to the American consulate to get a new passport **,** but the officer told him that replacement passports could not be issued on weekends.

Read the clause after the coordinating conjunction *but*:

the officer told him that replacement passports could not be issued on weekends

This group of words can stand on its own as a complete sentence. Thus, it is a main clause; place a comma before *but*.

Remember:

1. Place a comma before the coordinating conjunction (*and, but, for, or, nor, so, yet*) if there are two main clauses.

2. Do not use a comma before the coordinating conjunction if there is only one main clause.

Do not use a comma to separate a main clause from a restrictive clause or phrase

When clauses and phrases that follow the main clause are essential to the meaning of a sentence, they should not be set off with a comma.

Incorrect	Sandy plans to borrow Felicia's HBO login **,** while Felicia is on vacation.
Correct	Sandy plans to borrow Felicia's HBO login while Felicia is on vacation.
Incorrect	Sandy plans to borrow Felicia's HBO login while Felicia is on vacation **,** in order to catch up on her favorite shows.
Correct	Sandy plans to borrow Felicia's HBO login while Felicia is on vacation in order to catch up on her favorite shows.

COMMON ERRORS

Do not use a comma to set off a *because* clause that follows a main clause

Writers frequently place unnecessary commas before *because* and similar subordinate conjunctions that follow a main clause. *Because* is not a coordinating conjunction; thus it should not be set off by a comma unless the comma improves readability.

(Continued on next page)

COMMON ERRORS *(Continued)*

Incorrect   I struggled to complete my term papers last year,
because I had a full-time job along with my course load.
Correct   I struggled to complete my term papers last year because
I had a full-time job along with my course load.

But do use a comma after an introductory *because* clause.

Incorrect   Because Danny left his jersey at home Coach benched him.
Correct   Because Danny left his jersey at home, Coach benched him.

Remember: Use a comma after a *because* clause that begins a sentence. Do not use a comma to set off a *because* clause that follows a main clause.

Exercise 38.2   Decide which of the coordinating conjunctions in the following sentences should be preceded by commas and add them.

Example   Most people are familiar with the usual five senses,
but there are four more accepted senses.

1. Thermoception is the sense of heat or its absence.
2. Because of the fluid-containing cavities of our inner ear we have a sense of balance, or equilibrioception.
3. Nociception is the perception of pain from the skin, joints, and body organs yet this does not include the brain.
4. Headaches do not originate from the brain because the brain has no pain receptors.
5. Proprioception is also known as "body awareness" and it refers to our unconscious knowledge of where our body parts are.

38c Commas with Nonrestrictive Modifiers

Imagine that you are sending a friend a group photo that includes your aunt. Which sentence is correct?

In the back row the woman wearing the pink hat is my aunt.

In the back row the woman, wearing the pink hat, is my aunt.

Both sentences can be correct depending on what is in the photo. If there are three women standing in the back row and only one is wearing a pink hat, this piece of information is necessary for identifying your aunt. In this case the sentence without commas is correct because it identifies your aunt as the woman wearing the pink hat. Such necessary modifiers are **restrictive** and do not require commas.

If only one woman is standing in the back row, *wearing the pink hat* is extra information and not necessary to identify your aunt. The modifier in this case is **nonrestrictive** and is set off by commas.

Distinguish restrictive and nonrestrictive modifiers

You can distinguish restrictive and nonrestrictive modifiers by deleting the modifier and then deciding whether the remaining sentence is changed. For example, delete the modifier *once synonymous with the Internet* from the following sentence.

> The proliferation of gadgets with downloadable apps including Twitter, Facebook, Skype, online games, and streaming movies have cannibalized the World Wide Web **,** **once synonymous with the Internet ,** and have challenged the Web browser as the center of the Internet world.

The result leaves the meaning of the main clause unchanged.

> The proliferation of gadgets with downloadable apps including Twitter, Facebook, Skype, online games, and streaming movies have cannibalized the World Wide Web and have challenged the Web browser as the center of the Internet world.

The modifier is nonrestrictive and should be set off by commas.

In contrast, deleting *who left work early* does change the meaning of the following sentence.

> The employees **who left work early** avoided driving home in the blizzard.

Without the modifier the sentence reads

> The employees avoided driving home in the blizzard.

Now, it sounds as if all the employees avoided driving home in the blizzard instead of just the ones who left early. The modifier is clearly restrictive and does not require commas.

Recognize types and placement of nonrestrictive modifiers

Nonrestrictive modifiers are used frequently to add details. You can add several kinds of nonrestrictive modifiers to a short, simple sentence (see 32c and 32d).

> The student ran across campus **,**

> which left him panting when he got to class. [adjective clause]
> his backpack swaying back and forth. [absolute phrase]
> weaving his way down the crowded sidewalks. [participial phrase]

Nonrestrictive modifiers can be placed at the beginning of sentences.

> When he realized his watch had stopped **,** [adverb clause]
> With his thoughts on the intramural championship later that afternoon **,** [prepositional phrase]
> Rushing to get to class **,** [participial phrase]
>
> the student ran across campus.

They also can be placed in the middle of sentences.

> The student **,**
>
> who had woken up only 15 minutes before class **,** [adjective clause]
> my old roommate **,** [appositive]
> wearing a ripped black trenchcoat **,** [participial phrase]
> with one arm in a cast and the other clutching a stack of books **,** [prepositional phrase]
>
> ran across campus.

Pay special attention to appositives

Clauses and phrases can be restrictive or nonrestrictive, depending on the context. Often the difference is obvious, but some modifiers require close consideration, especially appositives. An **appositive** is a noun or noun phrase that identifies or adds information to the noun preceding it.

Consider the following pair.

1   Apple's tablet the iPad introduced a class of devices between smartphones and laptops.

2   Apple's tablet, the iPad, introduced a class of devices between smartphones and laptops.

Which is correct? The appositive *the iPad* is not essential to the meaning of the sentence and offers additional information. Sentence 2 is correct.

Use commas around nonrestrictive clauses within a *that* clause

Restrictive clauses beginning with *that* sometimes have a nonrestrictive clause embedded within them.

> **Incorrect**   I want you to know that **despite all the arguments we have had over the past few months** I still value your advice.

Correct   I want you to know that **,** **despite all the arguments we have had over the past few months ,** I still value your advice.

Use commas to mark off parenthetical expressions

A **parenthetical expression** provides information or commentary that is usually not essential to the sentence's meaning.

Incorrect   My mother much to my surprise didn't say anything when she saw my pierced nose.

Correct   My mother **,** much to my surprise **,** didn't say anything when she saw my pierced nose.

Some parenthetical expressions are essential to the point of the sentence, especially ones that make contrasts, but they too are set off by commas.

Incorrect   The candidate's conversational skills not her résumé landed her the job.

Correct   The candidate's conversational skills **,** not her résumé **,** landed her the job.

However, do not use a comma when the parenthetical expression is one word and its function is not obviously parenthetical.

Incorrect   The First Year Studies course is **,** fundamentally **,** an introduction to writing arguments.

Correct   The First Year Studies course is fundamentally an introduction to writing arguments.

COMMON ERRORS

Commas with *that* and *which* clauses

Writers often confuse when to use commas to set off modifying phrases beginning with *that* and *which*. *That* clauses follow a hard-and-fast rule: They are used only as restrictive modifiers.

A *that* clause is a restrictive modifier: Omit commas

Two other women were wearing the same dress **that Sherice bought specifically to wear to the awards banquet**.

Which clauses are usually used as nonrestrictive modifiers. While *which* clauses can also function as restrictive modifiers, careful writers observe the difference and change *which* to *that* if the clause is restrictive.

(Continued on next page)

COMMON ERRORS   *(Continued)*

A *which* clause is a nonrestrictive modifier: Use commas

A student government committee is recommending the allocation of an additional $10,000 for Black History Month festivities **, which take place in February ,** in order to bring a nationally known speaker to campus.

When a *which* clause acts as a restrictive modifier, change *which* to *that*

Incorrect   The uncertainty **which** surrounded the selection of the new coach was created by the sudden and unexpected resignation of her predecessor.

Correct   The uncertainty **that** surrounded the selection of the new coach was created by the sudden and unexpected resignation of her predecessor.

Remember:

1. *That* clauses are restrictive modifiers and do not take commas.

2. *Which* clauses can be either restrictive or nonrestrictive, but careful writers use them as nonrestrictive modifiers and set them off with commas.

Use commas to mark off absolute phrases

An **absolute phrase** contains at least one noun or pronoun and at least one participle (see 32d). Absolutes can modify a noun or a whole sentence.

Incorrect   Her project completed Marianne decided to splurge on a beach vacation.

Correct   Her project completed **,** Marianne decided to splurge on a beach vacation.

Exercise 38.3   The underlined portions of the following paragraph are modifiers. Identify each modifier as either restrictive or nonrestrictive. Then set off the nonrestrictive modifiers with commas.

Example   Marcus Ulpius Traianus ‸ a successful governor and soldier ‸ became the Roman emperor in the year AD 98.
    (Nonrestrictive modifier)

Trajan decided to use the Empire's coffers <u>which were brimming with war booty</u> to begin a massive building program. He commissioned the market <u>Mercati Traianei</u> and a lush new forum. In AD 113 he also

built a column <u>still on display in Rome today</u> adorned with reliefs depicting his military victories. But the conditions <u>that many Romans faced from day to day</u> stood in stark contrast to the splendor Trajan created. <u>Living in cramped apartment buildings</u> people coped with dark, dirty, and sometimes cold homes.

38d Commas with Items in a Series

In a series of three or more items, place a comma after each item except the last one. The comma between the last two items goes before the coordinating conjunction (*and, or, nor, but, so, for, yet*).

> Health officials in Trenton **,** Manhattan **,** and the Bronx have all reported new cases of meningitis.

Exercise 38.4 Insert commas to separate items in a series, following the academic convention. Some sentences may not require commas.

Example   Suburban residents unknowingly spread diseases among deer by feeding them salt ⌃ corn ⌃ and pellets.

1. White-tailed deer ground squirrels gray squirrels foxes raccoons coyotes opossums and armadillos often wander across my back yard.
2. White-tailed deer and coyotes are among the animals that have adapted best to urban habitats.
3. Deer find cover in urban green belts and thrive on young trees shrubs and flowers that homeowners plant.
4. White-tailed deer reproduce quickly because they have always been prey animals for wolves coyotes mountain lions bobcats and bears.
5. Elimination of predators curtailment of hunting and a high birth rate have led to deer overpopulation in many urban areas.

38e Commas with Coordinate Adjectives

Coordinate adjectives are two or more adjectives that independently modify the same noun. Coordinate adjectives that are not linked by *and* must be separated by a comma.

> After the financial crisis of 2007–2010, the creators of credit-default swaps and other risky investments are no longer the **fresh-faced , giddy** kids of Wall Street.

Distinguish coordinate adjectives

You can recognize coordinate adjectives by reversing their order; if their meaning remains the same, the adjectives are coordinate and must be

linked by *and* or separated by a comma. In the following example, when the order of the adjectives changes, the description of *lifestyles* retains the same meaning.

> Because border collies are bred to herd sheep, their energetic temperaments may not suit city dwellers' more **sedentary, staid** lifestyles.

> Because border collies are bred to herd sheep, their energetic temperaments may not suit city dwellers' more **staid, sedentary** lifestyles.

Do not use commas to link cumulative adjectives

Commas are not used between cumulative adjectives. Cumulative adjectives are two or more adjectives that work together to modify a noun: *deep blue sea, inexpensive mountain bike*. If reversing their order changes the description of the noun (or violates the order of English, such as *mountain inexpensive bike*), the adjectives are cumulative and should not be separated by a comma.

The following example doesn't require a comma in the cumulative adjective series *massive Corinthian*.

> Visitors to Rome's Pantheon pass between the **massive Corinthian** columns flanking the front door.

We know they are cumulative because reversing their order to read *Corinthian massive* would alter the way they modify *columns*—in this case, so much so that they no longer make sense.

Exercise 38.5 | Identify each underlined adjective series as either coordinate or cumulative. Then insert commas to separate coordinate adjectives.

Example   Krampus is a furry, demon-like creature that accompanies Santa Claus on his rounds during Christmastime. (*Coordinate*)

In Austrian and Hungarian holiday folklore, Krampus punishes the naughty children, while Santa rewards the good. The naughtiest most unrepentant children are carted away by Krampus in a large basket or bag to be cast into the dark fiery pits of Hell. On nineteenth-century postcards, Krampus is often depicted with sharp curling horns, hooves, and a long red tongue. Menacing leering eyes flash as he threatens his charges with rough birch switches and rusty chains. More modern postcards show a well-dressed well-groomed devil. This dapper human-like Krampus is shown either flirting with or being bested by pretty young women. Krampus is still celebrated today around December 5 or 6 with

raucous community festivals and parades. During these events, young men dressed as the dark forbidding figure accost adults, especially attractive single women.

38f Commas with Quotations

Properly punctuating quotations with commas can be tricky unless you know a few rules about when and where to use commas.

When to use commas with quotations

Commas set off signal phrases that attribute quotations to a speaker or writer, such as *he argues, they said,* and *she writes.*

"When you come to a fork in the road **,**" said Yogi Berra **,** "take it!"

If the attribution follows a quotation that is a complete sentence, replace the period that normally would come at the end of the quotation with a comma.

Incorrect	"Simplicity of language is not only reputable but perhaps even sacred **.**" writes Kurt Vonnegut.
Correct	"Simplicity of language is not only reputable but perhaps even sacred **,**" writes Kurt Vonnegut.

When an attribution is placed in the middle of a quotation, put the comma preceding the attribution within the quotation mark just before the phrase.

Incorrect	"Nothing is at last sacred **"**, wrote Emerson in his 1841 essay, "but the integrity of your own mind."
Correct	"Nothing is at last sacred **,**" wrote Emerson in his 1841 essay, "but the integrity of your own mind."

When not to use commas with quotations

Do not replace a question mark or exclamation point with a comma.

Incorrect	"Who's on first **,**" Costello asked Abbott.
Correct	"Who's on first **?**" Costello asked Abbott.

Not all phrases that mention the author's name are attributions. When quoting a term or using a quotation within a subordinate clause, do not set off the quotation with commas.

"Stonewall" Jackson gained his nickname at the First Battle of Bull Run when General Barnard Bee shouted to his men that "Jackson is standing like a stone wall."

Even a quotation that is a complete sentence can be used in a subordinate clause. Such quotations should not be set off with commas. Pay special

attention to quotations preceded by *that, which*, and *because*; these words are the most common indicators of a subordinate clause.

> It was Benjamin Franklin's conviction that ●"[t]hose who would give up essential liberty to purchase a little temporary safety deserve neither liberty nor safety."

Exercise 38.6   Read the following paragraph for errors in comma usage with quotations. Some are used correctly. Cross out unnecessary commas, move misplaced commas, and add omitted commas.

Example   When inspecting a painting for authenticity, try looking for an angle that catches the glare of lights. "You will not be able to see what the paintings show⌃" asserts author James Elkins⌃ "but you'll get a good look at the *craquelure*."

Craquelure is, "the fine network of cracks that scores the surface of . . . paintings" (Elkins 20). Elkins explains that "few museum visitors realize how many paintings have been seriously damaged" and goes on to list possible hazards, such as damage by, "fire, water, vandalism, or just the wear and tear of the centuries" (20). Not all cracks are signs of legitimate age; indeed "Counterfeiters have faked cracks by putting paintings in ovens, and they have even rubbed ink in the cracks to make them look old" (Elkins 22). Though cracks often happen with mishandling, Elkins explains that, "most cracks in paintings that are not caused by accidents are due to the flexing of the canvas or the slow warping of the wood" (22). If you are serious about art history, you may want to learn how to read the cracks in artwork. "*Craquelure* is not a hard-and-fast method of classifying paintings," admits Elkins "but it comes close" (24).

38g Commas with Dates, Numbers, Titles, and Addresses

Some of the easiest comma rules to remember are the ones we use every day in dates, numbers, personal titles, place names, direct address, and brief interjections.

Commas with dates

Use commas to separate the day of the week from the month and to set off a year from the rest of the sentence.

> March 25 , 1942

> Monday , November 18 , 2014

On July 27 **,** 2015 **,** the opening ceremony of the World Scout Jamboree will be televised.

Do not use a comma when the month immediately precedes the year.

12 June 1988

April 2016

Commas with numbers

Commas mark off thousands, millions, billions, and so on.

16 **,** 500 **,** 000

However, do not use commas in street addresses or page numbers.

page 1542

7602 Elm Street

Commas with personal titles

When a title follows a person's name, set the title off with commas.

Zoe Hart **,** MD

Jackie Hart **,** Vice President for Operations, reported that her company's earnings were far ahead of projections.

Commas with place names

Place a comma between street addresses, city names, state names, and countries.

Poughkeepsie **,** New York

Lima **,** Peru

Write to the president at 1600 Pennsylvania Avenue **,** Washington **,** DC 20500.

Commas in direct address

When addressing someone directly, set off that person's name in commas.

I was happy to get your letter yesterday **,** Jamie.

Yes **,** Virginia **,** there is a Santa Claus.

Commas with brief interjections

Use commas to set off brief interjections like *yes* and *no*, as well as short questions that fall at the ends of sentences.

The director said that, no, the understudy would not have to stand in for the lead tonight.

Have another piece of pie, won't you?

Exercise 38.7 The fictitious business letter that follows is missing commas with dates, numbers, personal titles, place names, direct addresses, and brief interjections. Insert commas where they are needed.

Mazaces' Headquarters
Cairo Egypt
December 13 332 BC

Parmenio
Commander of Syria
Damascus Syria

Dear Parmenio:

Thank you for your latest correspondence dated December 9 332 BC. I am pleased to hear the streets of Damascus remain quiet since our arrival in October 333 and that mighty Syria has adjusted herself to our presence.

To other matters. I write to request 4,000 of your most rested troops be sent to Egypt to arrive no later than January 1 331 BC. The fighting in Gaza was bitter and our enemy merciless; my soldiers are tired and need to recuperate before marching westward.

I busy myself with the construction of the city of Alexandria. Address future correspondence to 12 Conquest Avenue Alexandria where I will soon move in order to oversee the construction directly. Deinocrates head architect has seen to every detail, but of course detail requires time. I remain here until the spring when I intend for our armies to reunite and travel west to Thapsacus Mesopotamia where we will meet Darius King of Persia and secure his defeat for our mutual triumph and to the glory of Greece.

Sincerely,
Alexander the Great (Alex)

38h Commas to Avoid Confusion

Certain sentences can confuse readers if you do not indicate where they should pause within the sentence. Use a comma to guide a reader through these usually compact constructions.

Unclear	With supplies low prices of gasoline and fuel oil will increase.

This sentence could be read as meaning *With supplies, low prices will increase.*

Clear	With supplies low, prices of gasoline and fuel oil will increase.

Exercise 38.8   Some of the sentences in the following paragraph are confusing because they lack clarifying commas. Add commas where readers need more clues about how to read the sentences.

Example	Using new ways of dating, scientists can now apply multiple techniques to determine an object's age.

Because geologists used both radiometric and fossil dating we now know that the Colorado River started carving the Grand Canyon only five or six million years ago. Scientists were able to accurately date the Shroud of Turin believed by many Catholics to be Christ's burial covering to between AD 1260 and 1390. This particular example of carbon dating challenged some believers to weigh faith against science. The mysterious Sphinx stands before the pyramid of Khafre dated using the "star method." Scientists determined that the Sphinx and its host pyramid are approximately seventy years younger than was originally believed.

38i   Unnecessary Commas

Do not place a comma between a subject and a predicate

Incorrect	American children of immigrant parents, often do not speak their parents' native language.

Correct	American children of immigrant parents often do not speak their parents' native language.

However, you do use commas to set off modifying phrases that separate subjects from verbs.

Incorrect	Steven Pinker author of *The Language Instinct* argues that the ability to speak and understand language is an evolutionary adaptive trait.

Correct	Steven Pinker, author of *The Language Instinct*, argues that the ability to speak and understand language is an evolutionary adaptive trait.

Do not use a comma with a coordinating conjunction unless it joins two main clauses

Incorrect	Susana thought finishing her first novel was hard , but soon learned that getting a publisher to buy it was much harder.
Correct	Susana thought finishing her first novel was hard but soon learned that getting a publisher to buy it was much harder.
Correct	Susana thought finishing her first novel was hard , but **she** soon learned that getting a publisher to buy it was much harder.

Do not use a comma after a subordinating conjunction such as *although, despite,* or *while*

Incorrect	Although , soccer is gaining popularity in the States, it will never be as popular as football or baseball.
Correct	Although soccer is gaining popularity in the States, it will never be as popular as football or baseball.

Do not use a comma before *than*

Some writers mistakenly use a comma with *than* to try to heighten the contrast in a comparison.

Incorrect	Any teacher will tell you that acquiring critical thinking skills is more important , than simply memorizing information.
Correct	Any teacher will tell you that acquiring critical thinking skills is more important than simply memorizing information.

Do not use a comma before a list

Placing a comma after *such as* or *like* before introducing a list is a common mistake.

Incorrect	Many hourly workers, such as , waiters, dishwashers, and cashiers, do not receive health benefits from their employers.
Correct	Many hourly workers, such as waiters, dishwashers, and cashiers, do not receive health benefits from their employers.

39 Semicolons and Colons

QUICKTAKE

After reading this chapter, you should be able to . . .

- **Use semicolons to link related ideas** (39a)

  Incorrect: The first reports of an elephant arriving in the United States are from 1796 **;** which may have been an elephant named Old Bet.

  Correct: The first reports of an elephant arriving in the United States are from 1796 **;** they may have been referring to an elephant named Old Bet.

- **Use semicolons correctly with commas** (39b)

- **Use colons correctly in sentences** (39c)

  There is one elephant behavior that keepers look out for as a warning of possible aggression **:** rocking.

- **Use colons correctly with lists** (39d)

  Elephants need a few things to keep them healthy and happy **:** fresh food, plenty of water, room to roam, and the companionship of other elephants.

39a Semicolons with Closely Related Main Clauses

Why use semicolons? Sometimes we want to join two main clauses to form a complete sentence in order to indicate their close relationship. We can connect them with a comma and a coordinating conjunction like *or, but,* or *and.* However, using those constructions too often can make your writing cumbersome. Instead, you can omit the comma and coordinating conjunction, and insert a semicolon between the two clauses.

Semicolons can join only clauses that are grammatically equal. In other words, they join main clauses only to other main clauses, not to phrases or subordinate clauses. Look at the following examples.

Incorrect
————————————MAIN CLAUSE————————————
Gloria's new weightlifting program will help her recover

—————————————————PARTICIPIAL PHRASE—————————————
from knee surgery **;** doing a series of squats and presses

with a physical therapist.

Incorrect
————————————MAIN CLAUSE————————————
Gloria's new weightlifting program will help her regain

————————————————SUBORDINATE CLAUSE————————————
strength in her knee **;** which required surgery after she

injured it skiing.

Correct

MAIN CLAUSE
Gloria's new weightlifting program will help her recover

MAIN CLAUSE
from knee surgery **;** a physical therapist leads her through a

series of squats and presses.

COMMON ERRORS

Main clauses connected with transitional words and phrases

Closely related main clauses sometimes use a conjunctive adverb (such as *however, therefore, moreover, furthermore, thus, meanwhile, nonetheless, otherwise*; see the list in 38a) or a transition (*in fact, for example, that is, for instance, in addition, in other words, on the other hand, even so*) to indicate the relationship between them. When the second clause begins with a conjunctive adverb or a transition, a semicolon is needed to join the two clauses. This sentence pattern is frequently used; therefore, it pays to learn how to punctuate it correctly.

Incorrect **(comma splice)**	No one doubts that exercise burns calories **,** however, few people can lose weight by exercise alone.
Correct	No one doubts that exercise burns calories **;** however, few people can lose weight by exercise alone.

The semicolon separates the second main clause from the first. Note that a comma is also needed to separate *however* from the rest of the second clause.

Incorrect **(comma splice)**	The poster design left much to be desired **,** for example, the title was printed in garish red, orange, and green.
Correct	The poster design left much to be desired **;** for example **,** the title was printed in garish red, orange, and green.

Note that in addition to the semicolon, a comma separates *for example* from the rest of the second clause.

Remember: Main clauses that use a conjunctive adverb or a transitional phrase require a semicolon to join the clauses.

Do not use a semicolon to introduce quotations

Use a comma or a colon instead.

Incorrect   Robert Frost's poem "Mending Wall" contains this line**;** "Good fences make good neighbors."

Correct   Robert Frost's poem "Mending Wall" contains this line**:** "Good fences make good neighbors."

Do not use a semicolon to introduce lists

Incorrect   William Shakespeare wrote four romance plays at the end of his career**;** *The Tempest, The Winter's Tale, Cymbeline,* and *Pericles.*

Correct   William Shakespeare wrote four romance plays at the end of his career**:** *The Tempest, The Winter's Tale, Cymbeline,* and *Pericles.*

39b Semicolons Together with Commas

When an item in a series already includes a comma, adding more commas to separate it from the other items will only confuse the reader. Use semicolons instead of commas between items in a series that have internal punctuation.

Confusing   The church's design competition drew entries from as far away as Gothenberg**,** Sweden**,** Caracas**,** Venezuela**,** and Athens**,** Greece.

Clearer   The church's design competition drew entries from as far away as Gothenberg, Sweden**;** Caracas, Venezuela**;** and Athens, Greece.

Exercise 39.1   Decide where semicolons should go in the following paragraph. Add any semicolons that would repair run-on sentences, fix comma splices, or clarify a list. Also eliminate any incorrectly used semicolons and insert the correct punctuation.

Example   In the summer of 1947, a flying object crashed in eastern New Mexico**;** the incident feeds speculation that the government hides evidence of UFOs.

The media reported that the wreckage of a flying saucer had been discovered on a ranch near Roswell, military spokespeople

came up with another explanation. They asserted that the flying saucer was actually a balloon, people stationed at the base, however, reported seeing unidentifiable bodies removed from the wreckage. Initially even UFO enthusiasts believed the government's reports; which seemed plausible at the time. The Air Force has declared the case closed they stated that the bodies at the crash sites were test dummies. Roswell, New Mexico, joins the list of rumored UFO hot spots that includes Delphos, Kansas, Marshall County, Minnesota, Westchester, New York, and Gulf Breeze, Florida.

39c Colons in Sentences

Like semicolons, colons can join two closely related main clauses (complete sentences). Colons indicate that what follows will explain or expand on what comes before the colon. Use a colon in cases where the second main clause interprets or sums up the first.

> Anthrozoology, the study of how animals and people relate to one another, sheds light on larger issues in human psychology **:** people's interactions with animals illustrate concepts of altruism, ethics, and taboo.

You may choose to capitalize the first word of the main clause following the colon or leave it lowercase.

Colons linking main clauses with appositives

A colon calls attention to an appositive, a noun, or a noun phrase that renames the noun preceding it. If you're not certain whether a colon would be appropriate, put *namely* in its place. If *namely* makes sense when you read the main clause followed by the appositive, you probably need to insert a colon instead of a comma. Remember, the clause that precedes the colon must be a complete sentence.

> I know the perfect person for the job, **namely** me.

The sentence makes sense with *namely* placed before the appositive. Thus, a colon is appropriate.

> I know the perfect person for the job **:** me.

Never capitalize a word following a colon unless the word starts a complete sentence or is normally capitalized (see Chapter 46).

Colons joining main clauses with quotations

Use a colon to link a main clause and a quotation that interprets or sums up the clause. Be careful not to use a colon to link a phrase with a quotation.

WRITING SMART

Punctuation following quotations

Writing often requires quoting someone else's words. Use the correct sequence of punctuation marks when sharing a quotation with readers.

Place semicolons and colons outside quotation marks

Commas and periods that come after a quotation sit inside the quotation marks. The rule is different, however, for semicolons and colons: They sit outside the quotation marks. Because commas and periods always appear inside the quotation marks, semicolons and colons may seem incorrectly placed if you don't know that they follow a different rule.

Put commas and periods inside the quotation marks
"The length of a film," said Alfred Hitchcock, "should be directly related to the endurance of the human bladder."

Put semicolons outside quotation marks
Chicago mayor Richard Daley said, "The police are not here to create disorder. They're here to preserve disorder"; his misstatement hit at the truth underlying the violent treatment of protestors at the 1968 Democratic Convention.

Put colons outside quotation marks
"I believe, absolutely, that if you do not break out in that sweat of fear when you write, then you have not gone far enough": Dorothy Allison reassures would-be writers that they can begin on guts alone.

Remember: Little dogs (commas, periods) sleep in the house. Big dogs (semicolons, colons) sleep outside.

For more on using quotation marks correctly, see Chapter 43.

Incorrect: noun phrase–colon–quotation

President Roosevelt's strategy to change the nation's panicky attitude during the Great Depression: "[T]he only thing we have to fear," he said, "is fear itself."

Correct: main clause–colon–quotation

President Roosevelt's strategy to end the Great Depression was to change the nation's panicky attitude: "[T]he only thing we have to fear," he said, "is fear itself."

Also, a colon is often used after a main clause to introduce an indented block quotation (see 21d).

39d Colons with Lists

Use a colon to join a main clause to a list in a sentence. Remember that a colon cannot join a phrase or an incomplete clause to a list.

Incorrect: noun phrase–colon–list

Three ingredients for soup: chicken stock, peeled shrimp, and chopped tomatoes.

Correct: main clause–colon–list

You can make a tasty soup with just three ingredients: chicken stock, peeled shrimp, and chopped tomatoes.

Incorrect: incomplete clause–colon–list

Volunteers aid biologists in: erosion control, trail maintenance, tree planting, and cleanup.

Correct: main clause without a colon

Volunteers aid biologists in erosion control, trail maintenance, tree planting, and cleanup.

COMMON ERRORS

Colons misused with lists

Some writers think that anytime they introduce a list, they should insert a colon. Colons are used correctly only when a complete sentence precedes the colon.

Incorrect	Jessica's entire wardrobe for her trip to Cancun included: two swimsuits, one pair of shorts, two T-shirts, a party dress, and a pair of sandals.
Correct	Jessica's entire wardrobe for her trip to Cancun included two swimsuits, one pair of shorts, two T-shirts, a party dress, and a pair of sandals.

Correct   Jessica jotted down what she would need for her trip**:** two swimsuits, one pair of shorts, two T-shirts, a party dress, and a pair of sandals.

Remember: A colon should be placed only after a clause that can stand by itself as a sentence.

Exercise 39.2 Decide where colons should go in the following sentences; add any that are necessary. Eliminate any incorrectly used colons and insert the correct punctuation.

Example   In the Philippines, you flirt with danger when you sing one song**:** "My Way," by Frank Sinatra.

1. Authorities do not know exactly how many people have been killed in the past few years in the Philippines for singing "My Way," but the number has been high enough to cause people to ask some questions, can the killings be blamed on violent culture? Or, is there something about the song that drives people to irrational anger?

2. One witness to many incidents of karaoke-related violence offers up an explanation for why Sinatra's song seems to make tempers flare, "Everyone knows it, and everyone has an opinion."

3. Karaoke-related assaults and killings have happened recently in countries other than the Philippines, however, including: Malaysia, Thailand, and the United States.

4. The prevalence of karaoke in the culture of the Philippines makes related violence statistically much more likely social gatherings almost always involve karaoke, and stand-alone karaoke machines can be found everywhere, including remote rural locations.

5. Karaoke singers everywhere can prevent violence by: showing respect to other singers, not hogging the microphone, and choosing songs that have not already been sung.

40 | Hyphens

QUICK*TAKE*

After reading this chapter, you should be able to . . .

- **Hyphenate compound modifiers correctly** (40a)

  Incorrect: His apartment was on the second-story.
  Correct: He had a second-story apartment.

- **Hyphenate compound nouns correctly** (40b)

  Incorrect: self awareness, city state
  Correct: self-awareness, city-state

- **Use hyphens to divide words at line breaks** (40c)

- **Use hyphens to improve clarity** (40d)

  Less clear: He tried to recreate the atmosphere of Greenwich Village during the 1960s.
  Clearer: He tried to re-create the atmosphere of Greenwich Village during the 1960s.

Hyphens (-) are frequently confused with dashes (—), which are similar but longer. Dashes are used to separate phrases. Hyphens are used to join words.

40a Hyphens with Compound Modifiers

When to hyphenate

Hyphenate a compound modifier that precedes a noun.

When a compound modifier precedes a noun, you should usually hyphenate the modifier. A compound modifier consists of words that join together as a unit to modify a noun. Since the first word modifies the second, compound modifiers will not make sense if the word order is reversed.

middle - class values   best - selling novel
self - fulfilling prophecy   well - known musician

Hyphenate a phrase when it is used as a modifier that precedes a noun.

step - by - step instructions   all - or - nothing payoff
all - you - can - eat buffet   over - the - counter drug

Hyphenate the prefixes *pro-, anti-, post-, pre-, neo-,* and *mid-* before proper nouns.

pro - Catholic sentiment

mid - Atlantic states

neo - Nazi racism

pre - Columbian art

Hyphenate a compound modifier with a number when it precedes a noun.

eighteenth - century drama

one - way street

tenth - grade class

47 - minute swim

When not to hyphenate

Do not hyphenate a compound modifier that follows a noun.

Avoid using hyphens in compound modifiers when they come after the noun.

The instructor's approach is student centered.

Among serious video game players, *Mass Effect* and its sequels are well known.

Do not hyphenate compound modifiers when the first word is *very* or ends in *ly.*

newly recorded data

very cold day

Do not hyphenate chemical terms.

calcium chloride base

hydrochloric acid solution

Do not hyphenate foreign terms used as adjectives.

a priori decision

post hoc fallacy

Exercise 40.1   In the following sentences, decide where hyphens should be placed. Some sentences may require more than one hyphen, and some sentences may need hyphens deleted.

Example   Since there are few clear enemies of the state in the post‸Soviet era, political parties lack a galvanizing issue.

1. Some people consider the Electoral College to be un-democratic.
2. Independent candidates are often viewed as fly by night long shots with little or no hope of winning positions of power.
3. The tension surrounding the five week wait for the 2016 presidential election results was palpable.
4. Mostly-negative political ads are becoming more common.

5. Local candidates' political debates are rarely considered important enough to interrupt regularly-scheduled programming.
6. Candidates with free market economic policies are often popular with large corporations, which in turn make substantial donations to the candidates with favorable platforms.

40b Hyphens with Compound Nouns

A compound noun is made up of two or more words that work together to form one noun. You cannot change the order of words in a compound noun or remove a word without altering the noun's meaning. No universal rule guides the use of hyphens with compound nouns; the best way to determine whether a compound noun is hyphenated is to check the dictionary.

Some hyphenated compound nouns

T - shirt	heart - to - heart	play - by - play
sister - in - law	great - grandfather	speed - reading

Some compound nouns that are not hyphenated

oneself	heartland	speed of light
time zone	open house	playbook

While there's no set rule for all cases of compound nouns, some prefixes and suffixes that commonly require hyphens are *ex-*, *all-*, *self-*, and *-elect*.

All - American	president - elect
self - conscious	ex - employee

COMMON ERRORS

Hyphens with numbers

Whole numbers between twenty-one and ninety-nine are hyphenated when they are written as words.

Incorrect	twentysix
Correct	twenty - six
Incorrect	sixteen - hundred
Correct	sixteen hundred

40c Hyphens That Divide Words at the Ends of Lines

A hyphen can show that a word is completed on the next line. Hyphens divide words only between syllables.

> The Jackson family waited out the tor-
> nado in their storm cellar.

Unless you have a special reason for dividing words at the ends of lines, avoid doing it. One special situation might be the need to fit as much text as possible on each line of a narrow column. Another might be the need to fit text inside the cells of a table. But in MLA-style and APA-style papers, do not hyphenate words at the ends of lines.

40d Hyphens for Clarity

Certain words, often ones with the prefixes *anti-*, *re-*, and *pre-*, can be confusing without hyphens. Adding hyphens to such words will show the reader where to pause to pronounce them correctly.

> The courts are in much need of **repair**.

> The doubles final will **re-pair** the sister team of Venus and Serena Williams.

> **Reform** in court procedure is necessary to bring cases quickly to trial.

> The thunderclouds **re-formed** after the hard rain, threatening another deluge.

41 | Dashes and Parentheses

QUICK*TAKE*

After reading this chapter, you should be able to . . .

- **Identify when to use dashes and parentheses rather than commas** (41a)

  Regular emphasis: Marie set her pie, a lemon meringue, on the table.
  More emphasis: Mother scowled (after telling Marie in advance that she hated meringue).
  Greatest emphasis: Mother—who had planned this party for months—was about to lose her temper.

- **Use dashes and parentheses to set off information** (41b)
- **Use other punctuation correctly with parentheses** (41c)

  Incorrect: Seattle gets less rain than its reputation suggests (38 inches per year versus over 41 inches for every city on the eastern seaboard **.)**
  Correct: Seattle gets less rain than its reputation suggests (38 inches per year versus over 41 inches for every city on the eastern seaboard **).**

- **Use other punctuation correctly with dashes** (41d)

41a Dashes and Parentheses vs. Commas

Like commas, parentheses and dashes enclose material that adds, explains, or digresses. However, the three punctuation marks are not interchangeable. The mark you choose depends on how much emphasis you want to place on the material. Dashes indicate the most emphasis. Parentheses offer somewhat less, and commas offer less still.

Commas indicate a moderate level of emphasis

Bill covered his new tattoo **,** a pouncing tiger **,** because he thought it might upset our mother.

Parentheses lend a greater level of emphasis

I'm afraid to go bungee jumping **(**though my brother tells me it's less frightening than a roller coaster **)**.

Dashes indicate the highest level of emphasis and, sometimes, surprise and drama

Christina felt as though she had been punched in the gut; she could hardly believe the stranger at her door was really who he claimed to be **—** the brother she hadn't seen in twenty years.

474

Exercise 41.1 Look at the modifying phrases that are underlined in the following paragraph. Use commas, parentheses, or dashes to set them off, based on the level of emphasis you want to create.

Example Coffee, one of the most significant crops of all time,

has its origins in Africa (like so many other

cornerstones of civilization).

Coffea arabica the official name for the bean was made popular in Yemen. The Shadhili Sufi used coffee to inspire visions and to stimulate ecstatic trances making coffee drinking a spiritual experience. The use of the beverage spread largely through other Muslims the Sufi had contact with, and by 1500 it was well known throughout the Arab world. Cafés originated in the Middle East. These early cafés one of the few secular public spaces Muslims could congregate were seen as subversive.

41b Dashes and Parentheses to Set Off Information

Dashes and parentheses call attention to groups of words. In effect, they tell the reader that a group of words is not part of the main clause and should be given extra attention. Compare the following sentences.

When Shanele's old college roommate, Traci, picked her up at the airport in a new car, a Porsche Boxster, she knew that Traci's finances had changed for the better.

When Shanele's old college roommate, Traci, picked her up at the airport in a new car (a Porsche Boxster), she knew that Traci's finances had changed for the better.

When Shanele's old college roommate, Traci, picked her up at the airport in a new car— a Porsche Boxster— she knew that Traci's finances had changed for the better.

The Porsche Boxster is weighted differently in these three sentences because of punctuation. In the first, it is the name of the car. But in the third, it's as if an exclamation point were added—a Porsche Boxster!

The lesson here is simple enough. If you want to make an element stand out, especially in the middle of a sentence, use parentheses or dashes instead of commas.

Dashes with final elements

A dash is often used to set off an element at the end of a sentence that offers significant comments about the main clause. This construction is a favorite

of newscasters, who typically pause for a long moment where the dash would be inserted in writing.

> The *Titanic* sank just before midnight on April 14, 1912, at a cost of over 1,500 lives ▬ a tragedy that could have been prevented easily by reducing speed in dangerous waters, providing adequate lifeboat space, and maintaining a full-time radio watch.

Dashes can also anticipate a shift in tone at the end of a sentence.

> A full-sized SUV can take you wherever you want to go in style ▬ if your idea of style is a gas-guzzling tank.

Parentheses with additional information

Parentheses are more often used for identifying information, afterthoughts or asides, examples, and clarifications. You can place full sentences, fragments, or brief terms within parentheses.

> Some argue that ethanol **(**the pet solution of politicians for achieving energy independence**)** costs more energy to produce and ship than it produces.

Exercise 41.2 Insert dashes and parentheses in the following sentences to set off information.

Example Naples⌃founded by the Greeks, enlarged by the Romans, and ruled later by the Normans, Hohenstaufen, French, and Spanish⌃is one of the few European cities where the links to the ancient world remain evident.

1. Naples is a dirty and noisy metropolis in a spectacular setting a city that sprawls around the Bay of Naples with Mount Vesuvius at its back facing out to the islands of Procida, Ischia, and Capri.
2. The most famous eruption of Mt. Vesuvius the eruption that destroyed Pompeii and Herculaneum occurred in AD 79.
3. Some of the inhabitants of Pompeii decided to flee as the eruptions began, but they ran into several obstacles, such as darkness, unbreathable ash-filled air, and a continuous rain of pumice and *lapilli* small round droplets of molten lava.
4. The minor details in Pompeii graffiti scrawled on the walls give the city a living presence.
5. Herculaneum also known as Ercolano to the west of Pompeii was buried by a mudslide in the same eruption.

COMMON ERRORS

Do not use dashes as periods

Do not use dashes to separate two main clauses (clauses that can stand as complete sentences). Use dashes to separate main clauses from subordinate clauses and phrases when you want to emphasize the subordinate clause or phrase.

Incorrect: main clause–dash–main clause

I was one of the few women in my computer science classes— most of the students majoring in computer science at that time were men.

Correct: main clause–dash–phrase

I was one of the few women in computer science— a field then dominated by men.

Remember: Dashes are not periods and should not be used as periods.

41c Other Punctuation with Parentheses

Parentheses with numbers or letters that order items in a series

Parentheses around letters or numbers that order a series within a sentence make the list easier to read.

Angela Creider's recipe for becoming a great novelist is to **(1)** set aside an hour during the morning to write, **(2)** read what you've written out loud, **(3)** revise your prose, and **(4)** repeat every morning for the next thirty years.

Parentheses with abbreviations

Abbreviations made from the first letters of words are often used in place of the unwieldy names of institutions, departments, organizations, or terms. In order to show the reader what the abbreviation stands for, the first time it appears in a text the writer must state the complete name, followed by the abbreviation in parentheses.

The University of California, Santa Cruz **(UCSC),** supports its mascot, the banana slug, with pride and a sense of humor. And although it

sounds strange to outsiders, UCSC students are even referred to as "the banana slugs."

Parentheses with in-text citations

The various documentation styles require that information quoted, paraphrased, or summarized from an outside source be indicated with a research citation. In several of the styles, including MLA (see Chapter 23) and APA (see Chapter 24), the citation is enclosed in parentheses.

> E. B. White's advice on writing style is to use your natural voice **(** Strunk and White 70 **).**

COMMON ERRORS

Using periods, commas, colons, and semicolons with parentheses

When an entire sentence is enclosed in parentheses, place the period before the closing parenthesis.

Incorrect	Our fear of sharks, heightened by movies like *Jaws,* is vastly out of proportion with the minor threat sharks actually pose. **(** Dying from a dog attack, in fact, is much more likely than dying from a shark attack **).**
Correct	Our fear of sharks, heightened by movies like *Jaws,* is vastly out of proportion with the minor threat sharks actually pose. **(** Dying from a dog attack, in fact, is much more likely than dying from a shark attack **.)**

When the material in parentheses is part of the sentence and the parentheses fall at the end of the sentence, place the period outside the closing parenthesis.

Incorrect	Reports of sharks attacking people are rare **(** much rarer than dog attacks **.)**
Correct	Reports of sharks attacking people are rare **(** much rarer than dog attacks **).**

Place commas, colons, and semicolons after the closing parenthesis.

Incorrect	Although newspaper editors generally prize concise letters to the editor, **(** the shorter the better **)** they will occasionally print longer letters that are unusually eloquent.

Correct	Although newspaper editors generally prize concise letters to the editor (the shorter the better), they will occasionally print longer letters that are unusually eloquent.

Remember: When an entire sentence is enclosed in parentheses, place the period inside the closing parenthesis; otherwise, put the punctuation outside the closing parenthesis.

Exercise 41.3 Decide where to add parentheses in the following sentences. Be careful to place them correctly in relation to other punctuation marks.

Example *Saturday Night Live* (SNL) is a weekly late-night comedy-variety show based in New York City.

1. *SNL* has been broadcast live by the National Broadcasting Company NBC on Saturday nights since October 11, 1975.
2. The show was called *NBC's Saturday Night* until 1976 a short-lived variety show hosted by Howard Cosell was also called *Saturday Night Live*.
3. On Saturdays that the show is broadcast live, the cast and crew have to 1 run through the show with props 2 do a full dress rehearsal 3 reorder the script if any sketches are cut and 4 get ready to go live at 11:30 p.m. EST.
4. The premature deaths of a few well-known cast members John Belushi, Gilda Radner, Phil Hartman, Chris Farley, and Danitra Vance have given rise to a superstition known as the "*Saturday Night Live* Curse."
5. Critics claim that talk of the show's being under a curse is ridiculous, because a few untimely deaths are inevitable when a show has had a cast of over 100 people "*SNL* is *Saturday Night Live* on NBC" par. 14.

41d Other Punctuation with Dashes

Dashes with a series of items

Dashes can set off a series. They are especially appropriate when the series comes in the middle of a sentence or when the series simply elaborates on what comes before it without changing the essential meaning of the sentence. Normally commas enclose nonessential clauses; however, placing commas around items separated by commas would confuse readers about where the list begins and ends.

Rookie Luke Scott became the first player in Major League Baseball history to hit for the reverse cycle — a home run, a triple, a double, and a single in that order — in last night's game against the Diamondbacks.

Dashes with interrupted speech

Dashes also indicate that a speaker has broken off in the middle of a statement.

> "Why did everybody get so quiet all of a —"; Silvia stopped in her tracks when she noticed that the customer had a pistol pointed at the clerk.

COMMON ERRORS

The art of typing a dash

Although dashes and hyphens look similar, they are actually different marks. The distinction is small but important because dashes and hyphens serve different purposes. A dash is a line twice as long as a hyphen. Most word processors will create a dash automatically when you type two hyphens together. Or you can type a special character to make a dash.

Do not leave a space between a dash or a hyphen and the words that come before and after them. Likewise, if you are using two hyphens to indicate a dash, do not leave spaces before and after the hyphens.

Incorrect   A well - timed effort at conserving water may prevent long - term damage to drought - stricken farms -- if it's not already too late.

Correct   A well-timed effort at conserving water may prevent long-term damage to drought-stricken farms —if it's not already too late.

Remember: Do not put spaces before or after hyphens and dashes.

42 | Apostrophes

QUICKTAKE

After reading this chapter, you should be able to . . .

- **Use apostrophes to show possession** (42a)

  Jimmy's collar, alumni's donations, states' rights, passerby's, Jim and Victoria's office, Sanjay's and Cho's performances *BUT* Aristophanes's plays, Moses's death

- **Use apostrophes to show omitted letters and numbers** (42b)

  No omissions: Do not tease me for liking 1970s rock and roll.
  Omissions: Don't tease me for liking '70s rock 'n' roll.

- **Omit apostrophes when making nouns plural** (42c)

  Incorrect: Her three goal's registered her first hat trick.
  Correct: Her three goals registered her first hat trick.

42a Possessives

Nouns and indefinite pronouns (e.g., *everyone, anyone*) that indicate possession or ownership are in the **possessive case**. The possessive case is marked by attaching an apostrophe and an *-s* or an apostrophe only to the end of a word.

Singular nouns and indefinite pronouns

For singular nouns and indefinite pronouns, add an apostrophe plus *-s: -'s*. Even singular nouns that end in *-s* usually follow this principle.

> Iris**'s** coat
>
> everyone**'s** favorite
>
> a woman**'s** choice

Official names of certain places, institutions, and companies may or may not add *-'s* for singular nouns: *Governors Island, Teachers College of Columbia University, Mothers Café, Saks Fifth Avenue, Walgreens Pharmacy.* Note, however, that many companies do include the apostrophe: *Denny**'s** Restaurant, Macy**'s**, McDonald**'s**, Wendy**'s**.*

Plural nouns

For plural nouns that do not end in *-s*, add an apostrophe plus *-s: -'s.*

> media**'s** responsibility
>
> children**'s** section

For plural nouns that end in *-s*, add only an apostrophe at the end.

> attorney**s'** briefs
>
> the Kennedy**s'** legacy

Compound nouns

For compound nouns, add an apostrophe plus *-s* to the last word: *-'s*.

> my mother-in-law**'s** house
>
> mayor of Cleveland**'s** speech

Two or more nouns

For joint possession, add an apostrophe plus *-s* to the final noun: *-'s*.

> mother and dad**'s** yard
>
> Ben & Jerry**'s** Ice Cream

When people possess or own things separately, add an apostrophe plus *-s* to each noun: *-'s*.

> Roberto**'s** and Edward**'s** views are totally opposed.
>
> Dominique**'s**, Sally**'s**, and Vinatha**'s** cars all need new tires.

COMMON ERRORS

Possessive forms of personal pronouns never take the apostrophe

Incorrect   *her's, it's, our's, your's, their's*

The bird sang in **it's** cage.

Correct   *hers, its, ours, yours, theirs*

The bird sang in **its** cage.

Remember: It's = It is

Exercise 42.1   The apostrophes have been omitted from the following paragraph. Insert apostrophes in the appropriate places to indicate possession.

> **Example**   Pompei**'s** ruins were excavated during the past two centuries.

Its destruction was caused by an eruption of Mount Vesuvius in AD 79. Survivors stories contain accounts of tunneling through up to 16 feet of debris after the disaster. The Naples Museums collection contains painted stuccos and other art objects from Pompeii that illustrate the delicate nature of the artisans techniques. More than 500 residents bronze seals were found, and these helped identify the occupants of many destroyed homes. Pompeiis ruins provide the worlds most accurate snapshot of Hellenistic and Roman times.

42b Contractions and Omitted Letters

In speech we often leave out sounds and syllables of familiar words. In writing these omissions are noted with apostrophes.

Contractions

Contractions combine two words into one, using the apostrophe to mark what is left out.

I am	→ I'm	we are	→ we're
I would	→ I'd	they are	→ they're
you are	→ you're	cannot	→ can't
you will	→ you'll	do not	→ don't
he is	→ he's	does not	→ doesn't
she is	→ she's	will not	→ won't
it is	→ it's		

Omissions

Using apostrophes to signal omitted letters is a way of approximating speech in writing. They can make your writing look informal and slangy, but overuse can become annoying in a hurry.

rock and roll ———→ rock 'n' roll
the 1960s ———→ the '60s
neighborhood ———→ 'hood

42c Plurals of Letters, Symbols, and Words Referred to as Words

When to use apostrophes to make plurals

The trend is away from using apostrophes to form plurals of letters, symbols, and words referred to as words. In a few cases, adding the apostrophe plus -*s* is still used, as in this old saying:

Mind your p's and q's.

Words used as words are italicized, and their plural is formed by adding an -*s* not in italics, not an apostrophe and -*s*.

> Take a few of the **_ands_** out of your writing.

Words in quotation marks, however, typically use apostrophe and -*s*.

> She had too many "probably**'s**" in her letter for me to be confident that the remodeling will be finished on schedule.

When not to use apostrophes to make plurals

Do not use an apostrophe to make family names plural.

> **Incorrect**   You've heard of keeping up with the Jones**'s.**
>
> **Correct**   You've heard of keeping up with the Jones**es.**

Do not use apostrophes for indicating plurals of numbers and acronyms. Add only -*s*.

1890**s**	four CEO**s**	several DVD**s**
eight**s**	these URL**s**	the images are all JPEG**s**

COMMON ERRORS

Do not use an apostrophe to make a noun plural

Incorrect   The two government**'s** agreed to meet.

Correct   The two government**s** agreed to meet.

Incorrect   The video game console**'s** of the past were one-dimensional.

Correct   The video game console**s** of the past were one-dimensional.

Remember:

Add only -*s* = plural

Add apostrophe plus -*s* = possessive

Exercise 42.2   In the following sentences, some apostrophes were placed correctly, some were placed incorrectly, and others were omitted altogether. Cross out incorrectly used apostrophes and add apostrophes where necessary.

> **Example**   Americans have often loved their presidents‸ nicknames
>
> *presidents*
> more than they loved the‸president's themselves.

1. Texas VIP's and international diplomats alike affectionately referred to Lyndon B. Johnson as "Big Daddy."
2. There were no *ifs*, *ands*, or *buts* when the "Rough Rider," Theodore Roosevelt, rode into town.
3. Similarly, when old "Give, Em Hell," also known as Harry Truman, was on the Hill, congressmen could never catch up on their Z's.
4. Jimmy Carters staff learned quickly of his attention to small details, down to the dotting of is and crossing of ts.
5. The last thirty years has seen two George Bush's in the White House.
6. In the 1990's, George H. W. Bush was known as "No New Taxes."

43 Quotation Marks

QUICK*TAKE*

After reading this chapter, you should be able to . . .

- **Correctly incorporate words from sources** (43a)

  Direct quotation: Warren Zevon's final piece of advice was to "enjoy every sandwich."

  Paraphrase: Warren Zevon's final piece of advice was to enjoy it all, even the small things.

- **Recognize when to use quotation marks with titles** (43b)
- **Identify other uses of quotation marks** (43c)
- **Identify and correct misused quotation marks** (43d)
- **Use periods and commas with quotation marks** (43e)

  Incorrect: Groucho Marx once said, "I was married by a judge; I should have had a jury".

  Correct: Groucho Marx once said, "I was married by a judge; I should have had a jury."

  Correct: Groucho Marx once said, "I was married by a judge; I should have had a jury" (Kanfer 45).

- **And use colons and semicolons with quotation marks** (43e)

  Incorrect: As Flannery O'Connor wrote in 1955, "the truth does not change according to our ability to stomach it;" many today would do well to heed these words.

  Correct: As Flannery O'Connor wrote in 1955, "the truth does not change according to our ability to stomach it"; many today would do well to heed these words.

43a Direct Quotations

Use quotation marks to enclose direct quotations

Enclose direct quotations—someone else's words repeated verbatim—in quotation marks.

> Michael Pollan, the author of *Food Rules* and *The Omnivore's Dilemma*, argues that industrial agriculture uses too much fossil fuel to grow food: "We need to reduce the dependence of modern agriculture on oil, an eminently feasible goal—after all, agriculture is the original solar 'technology.'"

Even brief direct quotations, such as the repetition of someone else's original term or turn of phrase, require quotation marks.

> Michael Pollan, the author of *Food Rules* and *The Omnivore's Dilemma*, argues that reducing the amount of oil used to grow food is "an eminently feasible goal."

Do not use quotation marks with indirect quotations

Do not enclose an indirect quotation—a paraphrase of someone else's words—in quotation marks. However, do remember that you need to cite your source not only when you quote directly but also when you paraphrase or borrow ideas.

> Michael Pollan, the author of *Food Rules* and *The Omnivore's Dilemma*, argues that reducing the amount of oil used to grow food would make food cheaper in hungry nations and lessen the impacts of global warming.

Do not use quotation marks with block quotations

When a quotation is long enough to be set off as a block quotation, do not use quotation marks. MLA style defines long quotations as more than four lines of prose or more than three lines of poetry. APA style defines a long quotation as one of more than forty words. In the following example, notice that the long quotation is indented one-half inch—the same as a paragraph indent—and quotation marks are omitted. Also notice that the parenthetical citation for a long quotation comes after the period.

> Complaints about maintenance in the dorms have been on the rise ever since the physical plant reorganized its crews into teams in August. One student's experience is typical:
>> When our ceiling started dripping, my roommate and I went to our resident director right away to file an emergency maintenance request. Apparently the physical plant felt that "emergency" meant they could get around to it in a week or two.

By the fourth day without any word from a maintenance person, the ceiling tiles began to fall and puddles began to pool on our carpet. (Trillo)

The physical plant could have avoided expensive ceiling tile and carpet repairs if it had responded to the student's request promptly.

Set off quotations in dialogue

Dialogue is traditionally enclosed within quotation marks. Begin a new paragraph with each change of speaker.

> Before Jim and Lester walk 50 yards on a faint animal trail, they hear the brush rattle in front of them and the unmistakable snorting of a rhino. Jim crouches and looks through the brush. Lester watches Jim, wondering why he isn't retreating, then scrambles up a nearby tree. "Come on back," he yells to Jim, who is now out of sight.
>
> After a few minutes Jim reappears. "I got right next to it but I never did get a good look. I was so close I could even smell it."
>
> "The other one is still out there in the grass. And I heard a third one behind us toward the river."
>
> "We better get out of here before it gets dark. Are you going to spend the night in the tree?"
>
> "I'm thinking about it."

Exercise 43.1   The following sentences contain direct quotations (underlined) and paraphrases from Tony Horowitz's *Confederates in the Attic: Dispatches from the Unfinished Civil War* (Pantheon Books, 1998). Add, delete, or move quotation marks as needed and correct the placement of citations and the setting of quotes if set incorrectly.

Example   After completing his wild and often contradictory ride through two full years, fifteen states, and the contemporary landscape of what he terms the "South's Unfinished Civil War," award-winning journalist and cultural historian Tony Horowitz concluded: "the pleasure the Civil War gave me was hard to put into words" (387).

1. Horowitz's difficulty was finding words that might make sense, as he puts it, to anyone other than a fellow addict (387).

2. There are, Horowitz allows, clear and often-cited reasons why one might develop a passion for the Civil War, however. Everywhere, people spoke of family and fortunes lost in the war (384), Horowitz writes.

3. Horowitz notes that many Southerners, nostalgic for old-time war heroism, still revere men like Stonewall Jackson, Robert E. Lee, and Nathan Bedford Forrest—"figures that he refers to as the marble men of Southern myth (385)."

4. Civil War heroes were, after all, human. And these men, who for some command the status of gods, were also, in Horowitz's words, petty figures who often hurt their own cause by bickering, <u>even challenging each other to duels.</u> (385)

5. The Civil War was also unique because it marked the first war in which the rural landscape of the nineteenth-century United States met a new kind of war technology. Horowitz states: "It was new technology that <u>made the War's romance and rusticity so palpable. Without photographs,</u> <u>rebs and Yanks would seem as remote to modern Americans as</u> Minutemen and Hessians. Surviving <u>daguerreotypes from the 1840s and</u> <u>1850s were mostly stiff studio portraits. So the Civil War was as far back</u> <u>as we could delve in our own history and bring back naturalistic images</u> <u>attuned to our modern way of seeing</u> (386)."

43b Titles of Short Works

While the titles of longer works such as books, magazines, and newspapers are italicized or underlined, titles of shorter works should be set off with quotation marks. Use quotation marks with the following kinds of titles.

Short stories	"Light Is Like Water," by Gabriel García Márquez
Magazine articles	"Race against Death," by Erin West
Newspaper articles	"Cincinnati Mayor Declares Emergency," by Liz Sidoti
Short poems	"We Real Cool," by Gwendolyn Brooks
Essays	"Self-Reliance," by Ralph Waldo Emerson
Songs	"Purple Haze," by Jimi Hendrix
Speeches, lectures, and sermons	"Zero to Web Page in Sixty Minutes," by Jean Lavre
Chapters	"Last, Best Hope of Earth," Chapter 8 of *The Civil War*, by Shelby Foote
Episodes of television and radio shows	"Treehouse of Horror," an episode of *The Simpsons*

The exception.   Don't put the title of your own paper in quotation marks. If the title of another short work appears within the title of your paper, retain the quotation marks around the short work. The title of a paper about Jimi Hendrix, for instance, might read:

The History of Hendrix: Riffs on "Purple Haze"

43c Other Uses of Quotation Marks

Quotation marks to indicate the novel use of a word

Quotation marks around a term can indicate that the writer is using the term in a novel way, often with skepticism, irony, or sarcasm. The quotation marks indicate that the writer is questioning the term's conventional definition. Notice the way quotation marks indicate skepticism about the conventional definition of *savages* in the following passage.

> In the early days of England's empire building, it wasn't unusual to hear English anthropologists say that conquered native people were savages. Yet, if we measure civilization by peacefulness and compassion for fellow humans, those "savages" were really much more civilized than the British.

Quotation marks to indicate that a word is being used as a word

Italics are usually used to indicate that a word is being used as a word, rather than standing for its conventional meaning. However, quotation marks are correct in these cases as well.

> Beginning writers sometimes confuse "their," "they're," and "there."

43d Misuses of Quotation Marks

Do not use quotation marks for emphasis

It's becoming more and more common to see quotation marks used to emphasize a word or phrase. Resist the temptation in your own writing; it's an incorrect usage. In fact, because quotation marks indicate that a writer is using a term with skepticism or irony, adding quotation marks for emphasis will highlight unintended connotations of the term.

> **Incorrect**   "fresh" seafood

By using quotation marks here, the writer seems to call into question whether the seafood is really fresh.

> **Correct**   fresh seafood

> **Incorrect**   Enjoy our "live" music every Saturday night.

Again, the quotation marks unintentionally indicate that the writer is skeptical that the music is live.

> **Correct**   Enjoy our live music every Saturday night.

You have better ways of creating emphasis using your word-processing program: **boldfacing**, <u>underlining</u>, *italicizing*, and using color.

Do not use quotation marks around indirect quotations or paraphrases

Incorrect   The airport security guard announced that "all bags will be searched and then apologized for the inconvenience to the passengers."

Correct   The airport security guard announced, "All bags will be searched. I apologize for the inconvenience." [direct quotation]

Correct   The airport security guard announced that all bags would be searched and then apologized for the inconvenience to the passengers. [indirect quotation]

Avoid using quotation marks to acknowledge the use of a cliché

You may have seen other writers enclose clichés in quotation marks. Avoid doing this; in fact, avoid using clichés at all. Clichés are worn-out phrases; fresh words engage readers more.

Incorrect   To avoid "letting the cat out of the bag" about forthcoming products, most large companies employ security experts trained in preventing commercial espionage.

Correct but stale   To avoid letting the cat out of the bag about forthcoming products, most large companies employ security experts trained in preventing commercial espionage.

Correct and effective   To prevent their savvy competitors from peeking at forthcoming products, most large companies employ security experts trained in preventing commercial espionage.

43e   Other Punctuation with Quotation Marks

The rules for placing punctuation with quotation marks fall into three general categories.

Periods and commas with quotation marks

Place periods and commas inside closing quotation marks.

Incorrect   "The smartest people", Dr. Geisler pointed out, "tell themselves the most convincing rationalizations".

Correct	"The smartest people," Dr. Geisler pointed out, "tell themselves the most convincing rationalizations."

Exceptions occur when a parenthetical citation follows a short quotation. In MLA and APA styles, the period follows the closing parenthesis.

Incorrect	"The smartest people," Dr. Geisler pointed out, "tell themselves the most convincing rationalizations." (52)

Correct	"The smartest people," Dr. Geisler pointed out, "tell themselves the most convincing rationalizations" (52).

Colons and semicolons with quotation marks

Place colons and semicolons outside closing quotation marks.

Incorrect	"From Stettin in the Baltic to Trieste in the Adriatic, an iron curtain has descended across the Continent;" Churchill's statement rang through Cold War politics for the next fifty years.

Correct	"From Stettin in the Baltic to Trieste in the Adriatic, an iron curtain has descended across the Continent"; Churchill's statement rang through Cold War politics for the next fifty years.

Exclamation points, question marks, and dashes with quotation marks

When an exclamation point, question mark, or dash belongs to the original quotation, place it inside the closing quotation mark. When it applies to the entire sentence, place it outside the closing quotation mark.

In the original quotation

"Are we there yet?" came the whine from the back seat.

Applied to the entire sentence

Did the driver in the front seat respond, "Not even close"?

Exercise 43.2 The following sentences use a variety of punctuation marks with quotations. Some are used correctly, and some are not. Move the punctuation marks that are incorrectly placed in relation to the quotation marks.

Example	In her essay "Survival Is the Least of My Desires," the novelist Dorothy Allison describes herself as being "born poor, queer, and despised."

1. What does Allison mean when she tells gay and lesbian writers, "We must aim much higher than just staying alive if we are to begin to approach our true potential?"

2. She elaborates, "I want to write in such a way as to literally remake the world, to change people's thinking as they look out of the eyes of the characters I create" (212.)

3. "I believe in the truth"; this declaration forms the cornerstone of the philosophy Allison wants to pass on to gay and lesbian writers.

4. According to Allison, "I write what I think are "moral tales." That's what I intend, though I grow more and more to believe that telling the emotional truth of people's lives, not necessarily the historical truth, is the only moral use of fiction." (217)

5. "I believe the secret in writing is that fiction never exceeds the reach of the writer's courage", says Allison.

COMMON ERRORS

Quotations within quotations

Single quotation marks are used to indicate a quotation within a quotation. In the following example, single quotation marks clarify who is speaking. The rules for placing punctuation with single quotation marks are the same as the rules for placing punctuation with double quotation marks.

Incorrect   When he showed the report to Paul Probius, Michener reported that Probius "took vigorous exception to the sentence "He wanted to close down the university," insisting that we add the clarifying phrase "as it then existed"" (Michener 145).

Correct   When he showed the report to Paul Probius, Michener reported that Probius "took vigorous exception to the sentence 'He wanted to close down the university,' insisting that we add the clarifying phrase 'as it then existed'" (Michener 145).

Remember: Single quotation marks are used for quotations within quotations.

44 | Other Punctuation Marks

QUICK*TAKE*

After reading this chapter, you should be able to . . .

- **Use periods correctly** (44a)

  Incorrect: A group of artists and computer hackers wondered if there was a way to draw with the eyes**?** [a period should be used here]

  Correct: A group of artists and computer hackers wondered, "Is there a way to draw with the eyes**?"**

- **Use question marks correctly** (44b)

- **Use exclamation points correctly** (44c)

- **Use brackets correctly** (44d)

  Incorrect: Describing the Battle of Tarawa, World War II photographer Norman Hatch said, "They (the Japanese) were just mown down."

  Correct: Describing the Battle of Tarawa, World War II photographer Norman Hatch said, "They **[**the Japanese**]** were just mown down."

- **Use ellipses correctly** (44e)

  Full quotation: Author Seth Grahame-Smith explains how he equates slaveholders with vampires in *Abraham Lincoln: Vampire Hunter*: "Both creatures, basically slaveholders and vampires, steal lives—take the blood of others—to enrich themselves."

  Shortened quotation: Author Seth Grahame-Smith explains how he equates slaveholders with vampires in *Abraham Lincoln: Vampire Hunter*: "Both creatures **. . .** steal lives **. . .** to enrich themselves."

- **Use slashes correctly** (44f)

44a Periods

Periods at the ends of sentences

Place a period at the end of a complete sentence if it is not a direct question or an exclamatory statement. As the term suggests, a direct question asks a question outright. Indirect questions, on the other hand, report the asking of a question.

Direct question	Mississippi opponents of the Confederate-themed state flag wonder, "Where does the state's pride in its heritage end and its respect for those offended begin**?"**
Indirect question	Mississippi opponents of the Confederate-themed state flag wonder where the state's pride in its heritage ends and its respect for those offended begins**.**

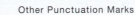
Periods with quotation marks and parentheses

When a quotation falls at the end of a sentence, place the period inside the closing quotation marks.

> Although he devoted decades to a wide range of artistic and political projects, Allen Ginsberg is best known as the author of the poem "Howl."

When a parenthetical phrase falls at the end of a sentence, place the period outside the closing parenthesis.

> Mrs. Chen, a grandmother in Seneca Falls, is training for her first 10K race (6.2 miles).

When parentheses enclose a whole sentence, place the period inside the closing parenthesis.

> Computer science researchers have been able to identify people in anonymous databases, including Netflix's, by collecting information on services such as Facebook, Flickr, and Twitter. (Even more unsettling to privacy advocates, researchers have been able to predict individual Social Security numbers by using publicly available information.)

Periods with abbreviations

Many abbreviations require periods; however, there are few set rules. Use the dictionary to check how to punctuate abbreviations on a case-by-case basis.

> John F. Kennedy   Mr.   misc.   a.m.

The rules for punctuating two types of abbreviations do remain consistent: Postal abbreviations for states and most abbreviations for organizations do not require periods.

> OH for Ohio   ACLU for the American Civil Liberties Union
> CA for California   NRA for the National Rifle Association

When an abbreviation with a period falls at the end of a sentence, do not add a second period to conclude the sentence.

> **Incorrect**   Her flight arrives at 6:22 p.m..
>
> **Correct**   Her flight arrives at 6:22 p.m.

Periods in citations of poetry and plays

Use a period to separate the components of the following kinds of literary citations. MLA style uses the following conventions.

A poem divided into sections such as books or cantos

book.lines   *The Inferno* 27.79-84

A prose play

act.scene   *Beyond Therapy* 1.4

A verse play

act.scene.lines   *Twelfth Night* 3.4.194-98

Periods as decimal points

Decimal points are periods that separate integers from tenths, hundredths, and so on.

99.98% pure silver   98.6° Fahrenheit
on sale for $399.97   2.6 liter engine

Since large numbers with long strings of zeros can be difficult to read accurately, writers sometimes shorten them using decimal points. Notice how the decimal points make the second sentence easier to read than the first.

> When the national debt rose over **$13,000,000,000,000** in 2010, the United States Congress passed legislation to limit the debt ceiling to **$14,300,000,000,000**.

> When the national debt rose over **$13 trillion** in 2010, the United States Congress passed legislation to limit the debt ceiling to **$14.3 trillion**.

Exercise 44.1 Periods have been omitted from the paragraph that follows. You can see how confusing writing becomes without proper period placement. Add periods and capitalize the first words of sentences correctly to clear up the confusion.

Example   Mr. Clarence Saunders worked most of his life to develop the modern supermarket.

Mr Saunders started working as a grocer when he was sixteen moving through various jobs in the field, including wholesale, he realized that grocers lost money by selling on credit at the age of twenty-six he formed Saunders-Blackburn Co, which dealt only in cash and urged its retail customers to do the same in 1916, on Jefferson St in Memphis, Tennessee, he opened the first self-service grocery store in the US, Piggly Wiggly by 1922, there were 1,200 stores in 29 states in 1923, however, Saunders went bankrupt and lost not only the enormous pink marble mansion he was building but also the rights to his own name

> trying to rebuild, he went on to create the Clarence Saunders Sole Owner of My Name Stores chain, which went into bankruptcy during the Great Depression in order to promote these stores Saunders founded a professional football team called the Clarence Saunders Sole Owner of My Name Tigers in 1930, the team, usually just called the Tigers, was invited by the NFL to join their organization, but Saunders refused

44b Question Marks

Question marks with direct questions

Place a question mark at the end of a direct question. A direct question is one that the questioner puts to someone outright. In contrast, an indirect question merely reports the asking of a question. Question marks give readers a cue to read the end of the sentence with rising inflection. Read the following sentences aloud. Hear how your inflection rises in the second sentence to convey the direct question.

> **Indirect question**
>
> Desirée asked whether Dan rode his motorcycle without a helmet**.**

> **Direct question**
>
> Desirée asked, "Does Dan ride his motorcycle without a helmet**?"**

Question marks with quotations

When a quotation falls at the end of a direct question, place the question mark outside the closing quotation mark.

> Did Abraham Lincoln really call Harriet Beecher Stowe "the little lady who started this big war**"?**

Place the question mark inside the closing quotation mark when only the quoted material is a direct question.

> Slowly scientists are beginning to answer the question, "Is cancer a genetic disease**?"**

When quoting a direct question in the middle of a sentence, place a question mark inside the closing quotation mark and place a period at the end of the sentence.

> Market researchers estimate that asking Burger World's customers "Do you want fries with that**?"** was responsible for a 15 percent boost in their french fries sales.

Question marks to indicate uncertainty about dates or numbers

Place a question mark in parentheses after a date or number whose accuracy is in question.

> After his escape from slavery, Frederick Douglass (1817**?-**95) went on to become a great orator and statesman.

Exercise 44.2 Periods and question marks have been omitted from the paragraph that follows. Add periods and question marks where needed and capitalize the beginnings of sentences.

> **Example** What was so earth-shattering about Friedan's naming of the "problem with no name"**?**
>
> Betty Friedan's *The Feminine Mystique* addressed the question, "Is this all" She examined why millions of women were sensing a gnawing feeling of discontent Friedan asked, "Can the problem that has no name somehow be related to the domestic routine of the housewife" and examined women's shifting place in postwar America What were women missing In asking these questions, Friedan legitimized the panic and uneasiness of many women who found the roles of mother and wife not wholly satisfying However, did this naming solve the "problem with no name"

44c Exclamation Points

Exclamation points to convey strong emotion

Exclamation points conclude sentences and, like question marks, tell the reader how a sentence should sound. They indicate strong emotion. Use exclamation points sparingly in formal writing; they are seldom appropriate in academic and professional prose.

Exclamation points with emphatic interjections

Exclamation points can convey a sense of urgency with brief interjections. Interjections can be incorporated into sentences or stand on their own.

> Run**!** They're about to close the doors to the jetway.

Exclamation points with quotation marks

In quotations, exclamation points follow the same rules as question marks. If a quotation falls at the end of an exclamatory statement, place the exclamation point outside the closing quotation mark.

The singer forgot the words of "America the Beautiful"**!**

When quoting an exclamatory statement at the end of a sentence that is not itself exclamatory, place the exclamation point inside the closing quotation mark.

Jerry thought his car would be washed away in the flood, but Anna jumped into action, declaring, "Not if I can help it**!"**

When the quotation of an exclamatory statement does not fall at the end of a sentence, place the exclamation point inside the closing quotation mark and place a period at the end of the sentence.

Someone yelled "Loser**!"** when the candidate walked on stage.

44d Brackets

While brackets (sometimes called *square brackets*) look quite similar to parentheses, the two perform different functions. Brackets have a narrow set of uses.

Brackets to provide clarification within quotation marks

Quoted material sometimes requires clarification because it is removed from its context. Adding clarifying material in brackets can allow you to make the quotation clear while still accurately repeating the exact words of your source. In the following example, the writer quotes a sentence with the pronoun *they,* which refers to a noun in a previous, unquoted sentence. The material in brackets clarifies to whom the pronoun refers.

The Harris study found that "In the last three years, they **[**Gonzales Junior High students**]** averaged 15% higher on their mathematics assessment tests than their peers in Northridge County."

Brackets within parentheses

Since parentheses within parentheses might confuse readers, use brackets to enclose parenthetical information within a parenthetical phrase.

Representative Patel's most controversial legislation (including a version of the hate crimes bill **[**HR 99-108**]** the house rejected two years ago) has a slim chance of being enacted this session.

44e Ellipses

Ellipses let a reader know that a portion of a passage is missing. You can use ellipses to keep quotations concise and direct readers' attention to what is

important to the point you are making. Ellipses consist of a string of three periods with spaces separating the periods.

Ellipses to indicate an omission from a prose quotation

When you quote only a phrase or short clause from a sentence, you usually do not need to use ellipses.

> Mao Tse-tung first used "let a hundred flowers blossom" in a Beijing speech in 1957.

Except at the beginning of a quotation, indicate omitted words with ellipses. Type a space between each ellipsis dot and between the ellipses and the words preceding and following them.

The original source

> "The female praying mantis, so named for the way it holds its front legs together as if in prayer, tears off her male partner's head during mating. Remarkably, the headless male will continue the act of mating. This brutal dance is a stark example of the innate evolutionary drive to pass genes onto offspring; the male praying mantis seems to live and die only for this moment."

An ellipsis indicates omitted words

> "The female praying mantis ... tears off her male partner's head during mating."

Note: Retain any punctuation mark falling before the omitted passage if it clarifies the sentence. In this case the comma before the omitted passage would not make the sentence any clearer, so it was not retained.

Ellipses to indicate the omission of a whole line or lines of poetry

Using more than three periods is appropriate in just one instance: to signal the omission of a full line or lines of poetry in the middle of a poetry quotation. In such instances, use an entire line of spaced periods.

Original

> My Shakespeare, rise; I will not lodge thee by
> Chaucer or Spenser, or bid Beaumont lie
> A little further, to make thee a room;
> Thou art a monument, without a tomb,

And art alive still, while thy book doth live,
And we have wits to read, and praise to give.

—Ben Jonson, "To the Memory of My Beloved,
the Author, Mr. William Shakespeare" (1623)

Omitted lines of poetry

My Shakespeare, rise;

. . . .

Thou art a monument, without a tomb,
And art alive still, while thy book doth live,
And we have wits to read, and praise to give.

Ellipses to indicate a pause or an interrupted sentence

Ellipses can provide a visual cue that a speaker is taking a long pause or that a speaker has been interrupted.

"And the winner is ... David Goldstein."

"That ball is going, going, ... gone!"

"Be careful that you don't spill ..."

44f Slashes

Slashes to indicate alternative words

Slashes between two words indicate that a choice between them is to be made. When using slashes for this purpose, do not put a space between the slash and words.

| Incorrect | Maya was such an energetic baby that her exhausted parents wished she had come with an on / off switch. |
| Correct | Maya was such an energetic baby that her exhausted parents wished she had come with an on/off switch. |

The following are common instances of the slash used to indicate alternative words:

either/or	and/or	pass/fail
player/coach	win/lose	on/off

Slashes to indicate line breaks in short quotations of verse

Line breaks—where the lines of a poem end—are artistic choices that affect how we understand a poem. Thus, it is important to reproduce them

accurately when quoting poetry. The task is not difficult in MLA style when the quotation is four or more lines long: Simply indent the quoted lines 1 inch and mimic the line breaks of the original verse. When you quote three or fewer lines of poetry, however, and must integrate the quotation into the paragraph rather than setting it off in a block, use slashes to indicate line breaks. Type a space on either side of the slash.

> Wilfred Owen, a veteran of World War I trench warfare, makes a counterargument to those who believe along with the poet Horace that *"dulce et decorum est pro patria mori"*—that it is sweet and fitting to die for one's country. After describing the horrors of men dying from a poison gas attack, he concludes his poem with these lines: "My friend, you would not tell with such high zest **/** To children ardent for some desperate glory, **/** The old lie: *Dulce et decorum est* **/** *Pro patria mori.*

Slashes with fractions

Place a slash between the numerator and the denominator in a fraction. Do not put spaces around the slash.

Incorrect	3 **/** 4
Correct	3**/**4

Slashes with dates

In informal writing, slashes divide the month, day, and year in a date. A longer format is appropriate for formal academic and professional writing. Omit the slashes, spell out the month, and place a comma after the day.

Informal	Javy, save **1/14/16** on your calendar; I reserved two tickets for the talent show.
Formal	It was a pleasure to meet you during my December 14 interview for Universal Oil's marketing internship. As we discussed, I will not be available for full-time employment until my graduation on **May 12, 2017**. However, I am hopeful that we can work out the part-time arrangement you suggested until that date.

Exercise 44.3 Take a look at the way the following paragraph uses all the punctuation marks discussed in this chapter: periods, question marks, exclamation points, brackets, ellipses, and slashes. Some are used correctly, and others are used incorrectly or omitted altogether. Correct any punctuation mistakes that you find and add any necessary marks that have been omitted.

Example Many ask, "Why have snakes become a symbol of religious devotion?"

In 1996 alone, over sixty deaths occurred due to religious snake handling. Mark 16.18 in the King James version of the Bible states, "They shall take up serpents and if they drink any deadly thing it shall not hurt them . . ."! This passage instigated the formation of a religion that thrives among the Irish and English descendants living in Appalachia. (In the 1990s over 2,000 snake handlers lived in Appalachia alone.)

Snake handling has been investigated by both practitioners of the fine arts (Romulus Linney's *Holy Ghosts* (1971) examines snake handling in the South) and news media. One controversial case examined Rev Glenn Summerford who attempted to kill his wife by forcing her to handle rattlesnakes. The general public often sees snake handling as a frightening act of fundamentalism practiced by congregations (often assumed to be undereducated)

45 | Write with Accurate Spelling

QUICK*TAKE*

After reading this chapter, you should be able to . . .

- **Use spelling checkers cautiously** (45a)

  Incorrect: Mini people believe **their** able **two** think **four** themselves, but a few experiments **half** shown that this is often **knot** the case.
  Correct: Many people believe **they're** able **to** think **for** themselves, but a few experiments **have** shown that this is often **not** the case.

- **Distinguish between words that sound alike but have different meanings** (45b)

  Incorrect: Your right **too** try **two** think **four** yourself.
  Correct: You're right **to** try **to** think **for** yourself.

45a Know the Limitations of Spelling Checkers

Spelling checkers do help you to become a better speller. But spelling checkers are quite limited and miss many errors. If you type *ferry tail* for *fairy tale*, your spelling checker will not catch the errors.

WRITING SMART

Electronic dictionaries

Many reputable dictionaries are available online. For a list, check your school library's Web site. *The Merriam-Webster Dictionary* is available to everyone online at www.merriam-webster.com/dictionary/. Additionally, many word-processing programs and computers offer dictionaries, such as the Dashboard dictionary/thesaurus included with Apple products; these programs have the advantage of being available offline, too.

How do you look up a word if you have no idea how to spell it?

Use *Google* as a quick way to check if you have the right spelling. If your guess is incorrect, *Google* will suggest the correct spelling. Also, you can find definitions by using the "define:" operator in *Google*; for example, "define: crepuscular."

Exercise 45.1 The author of the following paragraph ran it through a spelling checker and took all of the checker's advice. The checker missed some errors and created a few new errors. Correct all the spelling mistakes in the paragraph.

Example
~~Its~~ *It's* indicative of ~~Despond~~ *Desmond* Tutu's feelings of solidarity

with his parishioners that he opted to live in ~~Sowed~~ *Soweto*,

a poor black neighborhood, rather than in Houghton,

a rich suburb.

Archbishop Despond Tutu's message to the peoples of South Africa is that all are "of infinite worth created in the image of god" and "to be treated . . . with reverence" (Wepman 13). Tutu maintains that this is true fore whites as well as blacks, a position that isn't popular wit some South African. It can be scene from the many awards tutu has received, not least among them the Nobel Peace Prize in 1984, that his commitment to morality and human freedom have had an effect the world over. Archbishop Despond Tutu is a ban who does not waist the potential of hiss powerful role as religious leader. On the contrary, the Archbishop seas many political problems as moral ones and speaks out frequently on human rights issues.

45b Distinguish Homonyms

Homonyms are pairs (*your, you're*) and trios (*their, there, they're*) of words that sound alike but have different spellings and meanings. They are tricky words to spell because we don't learn to distinguish them in spoken language, and spelling checkers don't flag them as errors because they correctly spell other words in their databases. It's easy to type *there* for *their* or *Web sight* for *Web site* and not catch the error when you proofread.

Exercise 45.2   Circle the correct homonyms in the paragraph that follows.

Example   The pitch drop experiment is a long-term experiment measuring the flow of a (peace/piece) of pitch, or bitumen, over many years.

This famous experiment was started in 1927 (by/buy) Professor Thomas Parnell of the University of Queensland to demonstrate that (sum/some) substances that (seem/seam) to be solid are actually (vary/very) (hi/high)-viscosity fluids. Parnell's first step was to (pour/poor) a heated sample of pitch into a sealed funnel. The pitch was then (aloud/allowed) to settle until 1930, at (which/witch) time the seal was cut. Over the (past/passed) seventy years, only (ate/eight) drops have fallen. To date, no (won/one) has ever (seen/scene) a drop fall. After Parnell (died/dyed) in 1948, John Mainstone became the (hair/heir) to the experiment. Although scientists now (no/know) that pitch has a viscosity more than 230 billion times that of water (do/due) to (there/their) work, Parnell and Mainstone (one/won) the 2005 Ig Nobel Prize in Physics, a parody of the well-known Nobel Prize.

COMMON ERRORS

Commonly misspelled words

Is *accommodate* spelled with one *m* or two? Is *harass* spelled with one *r* or two? Use your online dictionary to check for common misspellings.

Remember: Always check a dictionary when you are unsure of how a word is spelled.

46 | Capitalization and Italics

QUICK*TAKE*

After reading this chapter, you should be able to . . .

- **Capitalize words properly** (46a)

  Incorrect: Some **a**mericans are surprised to learn that most **s**outh **a**fricans are **p**rotestants, and while no sect has the majority, there are more **p**entecostals than any other denomination.

  Correct: Some **A**mericans are surprised to learn that most **S**outh **A**fricans are **P**rotestants, and while no sect has the majority, there are more **P**entecostals than any other denomination.

- **Use italics correctly** (46b)

  Incorrect: An English major doesn't "have" to read Herman Melville's novel **"Moby-Dick"** or read any of his short stories, such as ***Bartleby, the Scrivener***, but it couldn't hurt.

  Correct: An English major doesn't "have" to read Herman Melville's novel *Moby-Dick* or read any of his short stories, such as **"Bartleby, the Scrivener,"** but it couldn't hurt.

46a Capital Letters

Capitalize the initial letters of proper nouns and proper adjectives

Capitalize the initial letters of proper nouns (nouns that name particular people, places, and things), including the following.

Names	Sandra Day O'Connor	Bill Gates
Titles preceding names	Dr. Martin Luther King, Jr.	Mrs. Fields
Place names	Grand Canyon	Northwest Territories
Institution names	Department of Labor	Amherst College
Organization names	World Trade Organization	American Cancer Society

Company names	Motorola	JoJo's Café and Bakery
Religions	Protestantism	Islam
Languages	Chinese	Swahili
Months	November	March
Days of the week	Monday	Friday
Nationalities	Italian	Indonesian
Holidays	Passover	Thanksgiving
Departments	Chemistry Department	Department of the Interior
Historical eras	Enlightenment	Middle Ages
Regions	the South	the Midwest
Course names	Eastern Religions	Microbiology
Job title when used with a proper noun	President Nelson Mandela	

Capitalize the initial letters of proper adjectives (adjectives based on the names of people, places, and things).

African American bookstore	Avogadro's number	Irish music

Avoid unnecessary capitalization

Do not capitalize the names of seasons, academic disciplines (unless they are languages), or job titles used without a proper noun.

Seasons	fall, winter, spring, summer
Academic disciplines (except languages)	chemistry, computer science, psychology, English, French, Japanese
Job titles used without a proper noun	The vice president is on maternity leave.

Capitalize titles of publications

In MLA and CMS styles, when capitalizing titles, capitalize the initial letters of all first and last words and all other words except articles, prepositions, and coordinating conjunctions. Even if it is one of those, capitalize the initial letter of the first word in the subtitle following a colon.

James and the Giant Peach

The Grapes of Wrath

The Writing on the Wall: An Anthology of Graffiti Art

COMMON ERRORS

Capitalizing with colons, parentheses, and quotations

Capitalizing with colons

Except when a colon follows a heading, do not capitalize the first letter after a colon unless the colon links two main clauses (which can stand as complete sentences). If the material following the colon is a quotation, a formal statement, or consists of more than one sentence, capitalize the first letter. In other cases capitalization is optional.

Incorrect   We are all being integrated into a global economy that never sleeps: **A**n economy determining our personal lives and our relationships with others.

Correct   We are all being integrated into a global economy that never sleeps: **W**e can work, shop, bank, and be entertained 24 hours a day.

Capitalizing with parentheses

Capitalize the first word of material enclosed in parentheses if the words stand on their own as a complete sentence.

> Beginning with Rachel Carson's *Silent Spring* in 1962, we stopped worrying so much about what nature was doing to us and began to worry about what we were doing to nature. (**S**cience and technology that had been viewed as the solution to problems suddenly became viewed as their cause.)

If the material enclosed in parentheses is part of a larger sentence, do not capitalize the first letter enclosed in the parentheses.

> Beginning with Rachel Carson's *Silent Spring* (**f**irst published in 1962), we stopped worrying so much about what nature was doing to us and began to worry about what we were doing to nature.

(Continued on next page)

COMMON ERRORS *(Continued)*

Capitalizing with quotations

If the quotation of part of a sentence is smoothly integrated into a sentence, do not capitalize the first word. Smoothly integrated quotations do not require a comma to separate the sentence from the rest of the quotation.

> It's no wonder the *Monitor* wrote that Armand's chili was "the best in Georgia, bar none"; he spends whole days in his kitchen experimenting over bubbling pots.

But if the sentence contains an attribution and the quotation can stand as a complete sentence, capitalize the first word. In such sentences a comma should separate the attribution from the quotation.

> According to Janet Morris of the *Monitor,* "The chili Armand fusses over for hours in his kitchen is the best in Georgia, bar none."

Remember: For elements following colons or within parentheses or quotation marks, capitalize the first letter only if the group of words can stand as a complete sentence.

Exercise 46.1   Nothing in the paragraph that follows has been capitalized. Revise it as necessary.

Example   _C courses in _A american history often disregard the

founding of the ~~fbi~~ *FBI*.

the federal bureau of investigation (fbi) has long been considered an american institution that was fathered by president theodore roosevelt. during the early 1900s, the united states was going through what some referred to as the progressive era. (during this period, the american people believed government intervention was synonymous with a just society.) roosevelt, the president during part of this era, aided in the creation of an organization devoted to federal investigations. prior to 1907, federal investigations were carried out by agents-for-hire employed by the department of justice. on wednesday, may 27, 1908, the u.s. congress passed a law prohibiting the employment of agents-for-hire and enabling the establishment of an official secret service directly affiliated with the department. that spring, attorney general charles bonaparte appointed ten agents who would report to a chief examiner. this action is often considered to be the birth of the fbi.

46b Italics

The titles of entire works (books, magazines, newspapers, films) are italicized in print. The titles of parts of entire works are placed within quotation marks.

Books	*The Brief Wondrous Life of Oscar Wao*
Magazines	*Make*
Journals	*Journal of Fish Biology*
Newspapers	*The Commercial Appeal*
Feature-length films	*Avatar*
Long poems	*Beowulf*
Plays, operas, and ballets	*Hamilton*
Television shows	*Game of Thrones*
Radio shows and audio recordings	*The Fame Monster*
Paintings, sculptures, and other visual works of art	*Cloud Gate*
Pamphlets and bulletins	*Surrealist Manifesto*

Also italicize the names of ships and aircraft.

Spirit of St. Louis	*Challenger*
Titanic	*Pequod*

The exceptions. Do not italicize the names of sacred texts in the body of your paper.

The text for our course, *Sacred Texts from Around the World,* contains excerpts from the New English Bible, the Qur'an, the Talmud, the Upanishads, and the Bhagavad Gita.

Exercise 46.2 Underline any words in the following paragraph that should be italicized.

Example Both controversial in their own right, the famed clothing designer Coco Chanel and the painter of <u>Guernica</u>, Pablo Picasso, are listed by <u>Time</u> magazine as two of the "Most Interesting People of the Twentieth Century."

Many think Coco Chanel is to fashion what the Bible is to religion. Consequently, various types of media have been used to try to capture the essence of this innovative designer. Films such as Tonight or Never preserve Chanel's designs for future generations,

while the failed Broadway musical Coco attempts to embody her life's work. More recently, print and small screen have attempted to encapsulate the impact of the designer in specials like A&E Top 10: Fashion Designers and books such as Chanel: Her Style and Her Life. Chanel was as monumental and self-destructive as the Titanic. She almost single-handedly redefined women's clothing through the popularization of sportswear and the jersey suit. But she also sympathized with Hitler after the release of his book Mein Kampf and the relocation of the Jews, and her image was further tarnished by her wartime romance with a Nazi officer. However, after her initial success waned during World War II, magazines such as Vogue and Life welcomed her back. She reinvented herself and her clothing line in the 1950s, and today she stands as one of the most influential fashion designers in history.

47 Abbreviations, Acronyms, and Numbers

QUICK*TAKE*

After reading this chapter, you should be able to . . .

- **Use abbreviations correctly** (47a)

  Incorrect: Although he demands to be called "Dr. Hastings," Robert's **Dr. of Phil.** degree is strictly honorary.

  Correct: Although he demands to be called "Doctor Hastings," Robert's **PhD** is strictly honorary.

- **Use acronyms correctly** (47b)

- **Know when to spell out numbers** (47c)

  Incorrect: There are about **20,000,000,000** chickens in the world, which is about **3** chickens for every person.

  Correct: There are about **20 billion** chickens in the world, which is about **three** chickens for every person.

47a   Abbreviations

Abbreviations are shortened forms of words. Because abbreviations vary widely, you will need to look in the dictionary to determine how to abbreviate words on a case-by-case basis. Nonetheless, there are a few patterns that abbreviations follow.

Abbreviate titles before and degrees after full names

Ms. Ella Fitzgerald	**Dr.** Suzanne Smith	Driss Ouaouicha, **PhD**
Prof. Vijay Aggarwal	San-qi Li, **MD**	Marissa Límon, **LLD**

Write out the professional title when it is used with only a last name.

Professor Chin	**Doctor** Rodriguez	**Reverend** Ames

Conventions for using abbreviations with years and times

BCE (before the common era) and CE (common era) are now preferred for indicating years, replacing BC (before Christ) and AD (*anno Domini* ["the year of our Lord"]). Note that all are now used without periods.

479 **BCE** (or BC)

1610 **CE** (or AD, but AD is placed before the number)

The preferred written conventions for times are a.m. (*ante meridiem*) and p.m. (*post meridiem*).

9:03 **a.m.**

3:30 **p.m.**

An alternative is military time.

The morning meal is served from **0600** to **0815**; the evening meal is served from **1730** to **1945**.

Latin abbreviations

Some writers sprinkle Latin abbreviations throughout their writing, apparently thinking that they are a mark of learning. Frequently these abbreviations are used inappropriately. If you use Latin abbreviations, make sure you know what they stand for.

cf.	(*confer*)	compare
e.g.	(*exempli gratia*)	for example
et al.	(*et alia*)	and others
etc.	(*et cetera*)	and so forth
i.e.	(*id est*)	that is
N.B.	(*nota bene*)	note well
viz.	(*videlicet*)	namely

COMMON ERRORS

Making abbreviations and acronyms plural

Plurals of abbreviations and acronyms are formed by adding -*s*, not -'*s*.

> Technology is changing so rapidly these days that many **PCs** become obsolete husks of circuits and plastic in only a few years.

Use -*s* only to show possession.

> The **NRA's** position on trigger locks is that the government should advocate, not legislate, their use.

Remember: When making abbreviations and acronyms plural, add -*s*, not -'*s*.

In particular, avoid using *etc.* to fill out a list of items. Use of *etc.* announces that you haven't taken the time to finish a thought.

Lazy	The contents of his grocery cart described his eating habits: a big bag of chips, hot sauce, frozen pizza, **etc.**
Better	The contents of his grocery cart described his eating habits: a big bag of chips, a large jar of hot sauce, two frozen pizzas, a twelve-pack of cola, three Mars bars, and a package of Twinkies.

Conventions for using abbreviations in college writing

Most abbreviations are inappropriate in formal writing except when the reader would be more familiar with the abbreviation than with the words it represents. When your reader is unlikely to be familiar with an abbreviation, spell out the term, followed by the abbreviation in parentheses, the first time you use it in a paper. You may then use the abbreviation in subsequent sentences.

> The **Office of Civil Rights (OCR)** is the agency that enforces Title IX regulations. In 1979, **OCR** set out three options for schools to comply with Title IX.

Exercise 47.1   The following is a paragraph from a research paper in which every word is spelled out. Decide which words would be more appropriate as abbreviations and write them correctly. Remember, this is formal academic writing; be sure to follow the conventions for using abbreviations

in papers. When you have more than one abbreviation style to choose from, select the one recommended in this section. Note: The term "dense rock equivalent" is abbreviated DRE.

Example Peter Francis, ~~Doctor of Philosophy~~, is among the scholars who have written introductory texts on volcanoes.

PhD

The unpredictable, destructive nature of volcanoes has attracted the interest of both scholarly and lay circles. Though it erupted in anno Domini 79, Mount Vesuvius is still famous because of its violent decimation of the city of Pompeii. Second to Vesuvius in destructive power is Mount Pelée, which in 1902 killed nearly thirty thousand people (id est, all but four of the citizens of Saint Pierre). Scholars like Professor George Walker have attempted to quantify and predict the effects of volcanoes. Professor Walker developed a system whereby volcanic eruptions are judged by magnitude, intensity, dispersive power, violence, and destructive potential. Walker began using a measurement called dense rock equivalent to measure unwitnessed eruptions. The actual volume of a volcano is converted into dense rock equivalent, which accounts for spaces in the rocks. Walker et alia have continued to perform research that will aid in the study of volcanoes.

47b Acronyms

Acronyms are abbreviations formed by capitalizing the first letter in each word. Unlike other abbreviations, acronyms are pronounced as words.

AIDS for Acquired Immunodeficiency Syndrome
NASA for National Aeronautics and Space Administration
NATO for North Atlantic Treaty Organization

A subset of acronyms is initial-letter abbreviations that have become so common that we know the organization or thing by its initials.

WAC for writing across the curriculum
ATM for automated teller machine
HIV for human immunodeficiency virus
LCD for liquid crystal display
rpm for revolutions per minute
URL for uniform resource locator

Familiar acronyms and initial-letter abbreviations such as CBS, CIA, FBI, IQ, and UN are rarely spelled out. In a few cases, such as *radar* (radio

*d*etecting *a*nd *r*anging) and *laser* (*l*ight *a*mplification by *s*timulated emission of *r*adiation), the terms used to create the acronym have been forgotten by almost all who use them.

Unfamiliar acronyms and abbreviations should always be spelled out. Acronyms and abbreviations that are familiar in particular fields should be spelled out on first use. For example, MMPI (Minnesota Multiphasic Personality Inventory) is a familiar abbreviation in psychology but is unfamiliar to those outside that discipline. Even when acronyms are generally familiar, few readers will object to your giving the terms from which an acronym derives on the first use.

> The **National Association for the Advancement of Colored People (NAACP)** is the nation's largest and strongest civil rights organization. The **NAACP** was founded in 1909 by a group of prominent black and white citizens who were outraged by the numerous lynchings of African Americans.

COMMON ERRORS

Punctuation of abbreviations and acronyms

The trend now is away from using periods with many abbreviations. In formal writing you can still use periods, with certain exceptions.

Do not use periods with

1. **Acronyms and initial-letter abbreviations:** AFL-CIO, AMA, HMO, NAFTA, NFL, OPEC
2. **Two-letter mailing abbreviations:** AZ (Arizona), FL (Florida), ME (Maine), UT (Utah)
3. **Compass points:** NE (northeast), SW (southwest)
4. **Technical abbreviations:** kph (kilometers per hour), SS (sum of squares), SD (standard deviation)

Remember: Do not use periods with postal abbreviations for states, compass points, technical abbreviations, and established organizations.

47c Numbers

In formal writing, spell out any number that can be expressed in one or two words, as well as any number, regardless of length, at the beginning of a sentence. In general, spell out words from one through ninety-nine. Also, hyphenate two-word numbers from twenty-one to ninety-nine.

My office is **twenty-three** blocks from my apartment—too far to walk but a perfect bike riding distance.

When a sentence begins with a number that requires more than two words, revise it if possible.

Correct but awkward

Twenty-three thousand six hundred runners left the Hopkinton starting line at noon in the Boston Marathon.

Better

At the start of the Boston Marathon, **23,600** runners left Hopkinton at noon.

The exceptions. In scientific reports and some business writing that requires the frequent use of numbers, using numerals more often is appropriate. Most styles do not write out in words a year, a date, an address, a page number, the time of day, decimals, sums of money, phone numbers, rates of speed, or the scene and act of a play. Use numerals instead.

In **2011** only **33**% of respondents said they were satisfied with the City Council's proposals to help the homeless.

The **17** trials were conducted at temperatures **12–14°C** with results ranging from **2.43** to **2.89** mg/dl.

When one number modifies another number, write one out and express the other in numeral form.

In the last year, all **four 8th** Street restaurants have begun to donate their leftovers to the soup kitchen.

Only after Meryl had run in **12 fifty**-mile ultramarathons did she finally win first place in her age group.

Exercise 47.2 All of the numbers in the following paragraph are spelled out. Decide where it would be more appropriate to use numerals instead and revise. Remember to add hyphens where necessary.

Example A form of temporomandibular joint dysfunction (TMJ) was

identified in ~~nineteen hundred thirty-four~~ *1934* by Doctor

Costen.

Five hundred sixty is the number of times you heard a popping sound resonating from the jaw of the woman sitting next to you on

the plane. She may be one of over nine point five million people suffering from TMJ, a condition that often causes symptoms such as popping, swelling, and aching in the jaw. At least one study has shown that women on hormone treatments are seventy seven percent more likely to develop TMJ symptoms. The disorder goes by at least six names, most of which include the initials TM, for temporomandibular: Costen's Syndrome, TMJ, TMD, TMJDD, CMD, and TMPD. Doctors currently prescribe at least forty nine different treatments for the disorder, ranging from one-dollar-and-fifty-cent mouth guards to prevent tooth grinding to a myriad of treatments which could cost thousands of dollars.

IF ENGLISH IS NOT YOUR FIRST LANGUAGE MAP

Understand the expectations of writing in the American style

- Know what is expected in college writing in English. Go to 48a.
- Know what resources can help you write in English. Go to 48c and 48d.

Understand English nouns and articles

- Know the different kinds of English nouns. Go to 49a–49c.
- Know when to use definite and indefinite articles in English. Go to 49d.
- Know how to select the correct English preposition. Go to 49e.

Understand English verbs

- Know the different kinds of English verbs. Go to 50a–50e.
- Know how to write a conditional sentence. Go to 50f.
- Know how to use English phrasal verbs. Go to 50g.

Understand English sentence structure

- Recognize the subject of a sentence. Go to 51a.
- Understand word order in sentences in English. Go to 51b.
- Know where to place modifiers. Go to 51c.

48 | Writing in a Second (or Third or Fourth) Language

QUICK*TAKE*

After reading this chapter, you should be able to . . .

- **Understand the demands of writing in English** (48a)
- **Use other languages as resources** (48b)
- **Use dictionaries effectively** (48c)
- **Use English idioms correctly** (48d)

  Incorrect: Did he **kick the calendar**? [literal translation of Polish *kopnąć w kalendarz* with the same idiomatic meaning as "kick the bucket" in English]

  Correct: Did he **kick the bucket**?
- **Identify and avoid plagiarism** (48e)

48a Understand the Demands of Writing in English

If English is not your first language, you may have noticed some differences between writing in English and writing in your native language. Some of the differences are relatively easy to identify, such as the direction of writing (left to right instead of right to left or top to bottom), the uses of punctuation (€2,500.00 instead of €2.500,00), and conventions of capitalization and spelling. Other differences are more subtle and complex, such as the citation of sources, the uses of persuasive appeals, and the level of directness expected in a given situation.

Talk with other writers

When you write in an unfamiliar situation, it may be helpful to find a few examples of the type of writing you are trying to produce. If you are writing a letter of application to accompany a résumé, for example, ask your friends to share similar letters of application with you and look for the various ways they present themselves in writing in that situation. Ask them to read their letters out loud and to explain the decisions they made as they wrote and revised their letters.

Recognize the American style of writing

No simple generalizations can be made for every kind of writing in the United States, but writers who have been educated in other cultures often

become aware of differences in style, especially in the workplace and in college. The fast pace of American life and the increasing use of fast digital technologies encourage a style of writing that values brevity.

The American style of writing is typically

- **more concise** than that of cultures where the rich profusion of words is valued;
- **more direct** in announcing the topic at the beginning rather than leading up to the topic;
- **more topic focused**, keeping on the main idea rather than introducing digressions;
- **more explicit** in setting out reasons and evidence;
- **less conscious of politeness** in the desire to get to the main point;
- **more careful to distinguish the words of others** with the use of quotation marks;
- **more insistent that all writing is original**, with serious consequences for plagiarism;
- **more conscious of giving the sources** of facts, figures, and the ideas of others.

Know what is expected in college writing

Understanding what is expected in college writing is as important as understanding English language conventions. College writers are expected to meet the expectations listed below. You will find detailed information on these expectations in other parts of this book.

WRITING SMART

A guide to expectations for writing in college

Address the specific demands of the assignment.	See 2a and 2b for general assignment analysis.
	See 17a for analyzing research assignments.
Use the appropriate format and sources for particular disciplines.	See Chapters 11 and 12.
Pay close attention to document design.	See Chapter 14 for multimedia design and Chapter 15 for design presentation.

Follow specific formatting rules.	See 23k for MLA style. See 24i for APA style.
Understand and avoid plagiarism. The expectations are different in the United States from many other countries.	See Chapter 21.
Incorporate the words and ideas of others into your writing.	See Chapter 21.
Choose words carefully and connect ideas clearly.	See Part 7.
Use accepted grammatical forms.	See Part 8. See Chapters 49, 50, and 51 for specific explanations of English grammar and mechanics for multilingual speakers.
Spell and punctuate correctly.	See Part 9.
Use your instructor's and peers' comments to revise and improve your writing.	See Chapter 4.

48b Use Your Native Language as a Resource

As you continue to develop your ability to write in English, you will find that many of the strategies you developed in your native language are useful in English as well. The ability to think critically, for example, is important in any language, although what it means to be "critical" may differ from one context to another. Imagery, metaphors, and expressions adapted from your native language may make your writing culturally richer and more interesting to read.

You can also use your native language to develop your texts. Many people, when they cannot find an appropriate word in English, write down a word, a phrase, or even a sentence in their native language and consult a dictionary or a handbook later; it helps to avoid interrupting the flow of thought in the process of writing. Incorporating key terms from your native language is also a possible strategy. For example, a term from Japanese can add flavor and perspective to a sentence: "Some political leaders need to have *wakimae*—a realistic idea of one's own place in the world."

48c Use Dictionaries

You can use regular English dictionaries for definitions, but most English dictionaries designed for native English speakers do not include all of the information that many multilingual English speakers find useful. For example, you may know the word *audience* but not whether and when *audience* can function as a count noun. Learner's dictionaries, such as the *Longman Dictionary of American English*, include information about count/noncount nouns and transitive/intransitive verbs (see Chapters 49 and 50). Many of them also provide sample sentences to help you understand how a word is used.

Some multilingual English speakers also find a bilingual dictionary useful. Bilingual dictionaries are especially useful when you want to check your understanding of an English word or when you want to find equivalent words for culture-specific concepts and technical terms. Some bilingual dictionaries also provide sample sentences. When sample sentences are not provided, check the usage in another dictionary or by searching for the word or phrase online.

48d Understand English Idioms

Idioms are nonliteral expressions that gain a set meaning when they are used again and again. In the United States, for example, if someone has to "eat crow," he or she has been forced to admit being wrong about something. When people "walk a fine line," they are being careful not to irritate or anger people on different sides of an argument. Simpler examples of idiomatic usage—word order, word choice, and combinations that follow no obvious or set rules—are common even in the plainest English.

The way certain prepositions are paired with certain words is often idiomatic. It might be possible to use a preposition other than the one usually used, but the preferred combination is accepted as correct because it sounds "right" to longtime English speakers. Any other preposition sounds "wrong," even if it makes sense.

"Incorrect" idiom   Here is the answer *of* your question.

Accepted idiom   Here is the answer *to* your question.

Note that the second sentence is no more logical than the first. But to first-language English speakers, that first sentence sounds imprecise and strange. See 49e for more information on English preposition usage.

Placement order for modifiers is often idiomatic in English—or at least the rules are arbitrary enough that it may make more sense to memorize

certain patterns than to try to place modifiers entirely by logic. Say you want to modify the noun *dogs* with three adjectives:

> brown
> three
> small

In English, all these adjectives will be placed before the noun they are modifying. But in what order should they go? There are a number of possibilities:

> Small three brown dogs
> Three brown small dogs
> Small brown three dogs
> Three small brown dogs
> Brown small three dogs
> Brown three small dogs

Only two of these options may sound at all correct to first-language English speakers: "Three brown small dogs" and "Three small brown dogs." To put the adjective for number anywhere but first sounds wrong. The other two adjectives, describing size and color, also have a correct order to the ears of English speakers. Thus, "three small brown dogs" sounds more natural than "three brown small dogs."

Though idioms may be frustrating, you can take comfort in the fact that many first-language English speakers struggle with them, especially when using prepositions. Because idioms are not governed by a single set of rules, you can only learn idioms one example at a time. Thus, the more you speak, read, and hear English, the better your grasp of idioms will become.

WRITING SMART

Research English idioms online

Many combinations of English words don't follow hard-and-fast rules but simply sound right to native speakers of English. If you are unsure whether you should write *disgusted with* or *disgusted for*, use *Google* or another search engine to find out how they are used.

Put the words inside quotation marks in the search box. You'll get many hits for both *disgusted with* and *disgusted for*, but you'll see about ten times more for *disgusted with*. You'll also notice that many of the hits for *disgusted for* will be examples of *disgusted* at the end of one sentence and *For* at the beginning of the next sentence. You can use this method to determine that *disgusted with* is the better choice.

Exercise 48.1 Choose the idiom commonly used in English. If you are unsure, check a dictionary, *Google*, or another search engine to test the idiom.

1. The actor (suicided/committed suicide) after his wife's death.
2. He will be here (of/on) Sunday.
3. I have a question (for/of) you about your job.
4. Those (red, long/long, red) peppers are too hot (for/to) eat.
5. We were (drive/driving) as fast as we could.
6. (Knowing/To know) her is (to love/loving) her.
7. (A/The) last thing we want (do/to do) is (to make/making) trouble (on/for) you.
8. All he wants (do/to do) is (watching/to watch) television.
9. The cage held (five yellow fuzzy/five fuzzy yellow) chicks.
10. Her apartment is (on/at) the third floor.
11. The baby (borned/was born) healthy.
12. I am responsible (to/for) choosing a location (of/for) the party.

49 | Nouns, Articles, and Prepositions

QUICK*TAKE*

After reading this chapter, you should be able to . . .

- **Use different types of nouns correctly** (49a)

  Incorrect: When we landed in Memphis International Airport, we asked for **informations** about transportation to Graceland, Elvis Presley's former **H**ome.

  Correct: When we landed in Memphis International Airport, we asked for **information** about transportation to Graceland, Elvis Presley's former home.

- **Identify count and noncount nouns** (49b)
- **Identify singular and plural forms** (49c)
- **Use articles correctly** (49d)

  Incorrect: A mother of **a** soldier held **the** picture of him up to **a** camera.

  Correct: The mother of **the** soldier held **a** picture of him up to **the** camera.

- **Use prepositions correctly** (49e)

  Incorrect: Please leave the keys **of** the car **to** the hook.

  Correct: Please leave the keys **for** the car **on** the hook.

49a Kinds of Nouns

There are two basic kinds of nouns. A **proper noun** begins with a capital letter and names a unique person, place, or thing: *Theodore Roosevelt, Russia, Eiffel Tower*. In the following list, note that each word refers to someone or something so specific that it bears a name.

Proper nouns

Beethoven	Yao Ming	South Korea
Empire State Building	New York Yankees	Africa
Honda	Picasso	Stockholm
Thanksgiving	Queen Elizabeth	Lake Michigan

The other basic kind of noun is called a **common noun**. Common nouns do not name a unique person, place, or thing: *man, country, tower*. Note that the words in the following list are not names and so are not capitalized.

Common nouns

composer	athlete	country
building	baseball team	continent
company	painter	city
holiday	queen	lake

Common nouns can also refer to abstractions, such as *grace, love*, and *power*. In English, proper nouns are names and are always capitalized while common nouns are not names and are not capitalized.

Exercise 49.1   Underline the common nouns in the following paragraph once and underline the proper nouns twice. Correct any errors in capitalization.

Example   In 1903, a fire in̲ c̲hicago led to the new safety̲ l̲aws.

In 1903, Chicago opened the new Iroquois theater on West Randolph street. Around christmas, the Theater held a performance of "Mr. blue beard" starring eddie Foy. Shortly after the play started, a light sparked causing a curtain to catch on fire. Elvira Pinedo said the crowd panicked after a giant Fireball appeared. This panic led to the deaths of more than 600 people, many of whom died because bodies were pressed against doors that opened inward. Shortly after the Tragedy, Mayor Carter H. Harrison was indicted and new laws demanded Theaters have doors that open outward, toward the lobby.

49b Count and Noncount Nouns

Common nouns can be classified as either *count* or *noncount*. **Count nouns** can be made plural, usually by adding -*s* (*finger, fingers*) or by using their plural forms (*person, people; datum, data*). **Noncount nouns** cannot be counted directly and cannot take the plural form (*information*, but not *informations*; *garbage*, but not *garbages*). Some nouns can be either count or noncount, depending on how they are used. *Hair* can refer to either a strand of hair, when it serves as a count noun, or a mass of hair, when it becomes a noncount noun.

Correct usage of *hair* as count noun

I carefully combed my few **hairs** across my mostly bald scalp.

Correct usage of *hair* as noncount noun

My roommate spent an hour this morning combing his **hair**.

In the same way, *space* can refer to a particular, quantifiable area (as in *two parking spaces*) or to an unspecified open area (as in *there is some space left*).

If you are not sure whether a particular noun is count or noncount, consult a learner's dictionary. Count nouns are usually indicated as [C] (for "countable") and noncount nouns as [U] (for "uncountable").

Exercise 49.2   The following sentences include various types of plural nouns: count, noncount, and those that can be either, depending on how they are used. Underline the correct plural form from the choices provided.

Example   The first (animal/<u>animals</u>) in space were fruit flies.

1. In 1946 these tiny (astronaut/astronauts) were launched on an American rocket with some (corns/corn) to test the (effect of radiation/effect of radiations) at high (altitude/altitudes).
2. Fruit (fly/flies) match three-(quarter/quarters) of human disease (gene/genes), sleep every (night/nights), and reproduce very quickly, so replacing them does not cost a lot of (monies/money).
3. After fruit flies, scientists sent (moss/mosses) and then (monkeys/monkey).
4. The first (monkeys/monkey) to return from space safely was Albert IV, which was accompanied by eleven (mouses/mice) on his journey.
5. The Russian space program launched more than ten (dog/dogs) into space before launching (people/peoples).
6. Although (scientist/scientists) argue that the (information/informations) gathered from space missions using (animal/animals) has saved (life/lives), (activist/activists) argue that these (experiment/experiments) were cruel and unnecessary.

49c Singular and Plural Forms

Count nouns usually take both singular and plural forms, while noncount nouns usually do not take plural forms and are not counted directly. A count noun can have a number before it (as in *two books, three oranges*) and can be qualified with adjectives such as *many* (*many books*), *some* (*some schools*), *a lot of* (*a lot of people*), *a few* (meaning several, as in *I ate a few apples*), and *few* (meaning almost none, as in *few people volunteered*).

Noncount nouns can be counted or quantified in only two ways: either by general adjectives that treat the noun as a mass (*much* information, *little* garbage, *some* news) or by placing another noun between the quantifying word and the noncount noun (two *kinds* of information, three *piles* of garbage, a *piece* of news).

COMMON ERRORS

Singular and plural forms of count nouns

Count nouns are simpler to quantify than noncount nouns. But remember that English requires you to state both singular and plural forms of nouns consistently and explicitly. Look at the following sentences.

Incorrect   The three **bicyclist** shaved their **leg** before the big race.

Correct   The three **bicyclists** shaved their **legs** before the big race.

In the first sentence, readers would understand that the plural form of *bicyclist* is implied by the quantifier *three* and that the plural form of *leg* is implied by the fact that bicyclists have two legs. (If they didn't, you would hope that the writer would have made that clear already!) Nevertheless, correct form in English is to indicate the singular or plural nature of a count noun explicitly, in every instance.

Remember: English requires you to use plural forms of count nouns even when a plural number is clearly stated.

Exercise 49.3   The following paragraph includes many examples of singular/plural inconsistency. Correct any incorrect versions of nouns.

Example   In the history of fashion, many ~~word~~ *words* have lost their original ~~meaning~~ *meanings*.

Every year, thousands of bride and groom don traditional attire while attending their wedding. One garment associated with many of these traditional wedding is the groom's cummerbund or decorative waistband. This garment dates back many century to Persia where they were known as a "kamarband" or "loinband." The cummerbunds was first adopted by a few British military officer in colonial India and later by civilians. These cummerbund were traditionally worn with the pleats facing up to hold ticket stubs and other item. These day, however, cummerbunds are usually worn just for decoration.

49d Articles

Articles indicate that a noun is about to appear, and they clarify what the noun refers to. There are only two kinds of articles in English, definite and indefinite.

1. **the:** *The* is a **definite article**, meaning that it refers to (a) a specific object already known to the reader, (b) one about to be made known to the reader, or (c) a unique object.
2. **a, an:** The **indefinite articles** *a* and *an* refer to an object whose specific identity is not known to the reader. The only difference between *a* and *an* is that *a* is used before a consonant sound (*man, friend, yellow*), while *an* is used before a vowel sound (*animal, enemy, orange*).

Look at these sentences, identical except for their articles, and imagine that each is taken from a different newspaper story.

Rescue workers lifted **the** man to safety.

Rescue workers lifted **a** man to safety.

By use of the definite article *the*, the first sentence indicates that the reader already knows something about the identity of this man and his needing to be rescued. The news story has already referred to him. The sentence also suggests that this was the only man rescued, at least in this particular part of the story.

The indefinite article *a* in the second sentence indicates that the reader does not know anything about this man. Either this is the first time the news story has referred to him or there are other men in need of rescue. When deciding whether to use the definite or indefinite article, ask yourself whether the noun refers to something specific or unique, or whether it refers to something general. *The* is used for specific or unique nouns; *a* and *an* are used for nonspecific or general nouns.

A small number of conditions determine when and how count and noncount nouns are preceded by articles.

1. *A* or *an* is not used with noncount nouns.

Incorrect   The crowd hummed with **an** excitement.

Correct   The crowd hummed with excitement.

2. *A* or *an* is used with singular count nouns whose particular identity is unknown to the reader or writer.

Detective Johnson was reading **a** book.

3. *The* is used with most count and noncount nouns whose particular identity is known to the reader.

The noun may be known for one of several reasons:

- The basic rule is that *a* or *an* is used on the first mention of a noun and *the* is used for every subsequent mention.

  I bought a book yesterday. **The** book is about Iraq.

- The noun is accompanied by a superlative such as *highest, lowest, best, worst, least interesting,* or *most beautiful* that makes its specific identity clear.

  This is **the most interesting book** about Iraq.

- The noun's identity is made clear by its context in the sentence.

  The book I bought yesterday is about Iraq.

- The noun has a unique identity, such as *the moon*.

  This book has as many pages as **the Bible**.

4. *The* is not used with noncount nouns meaning "in general."

Incorrect   **The** war is hell.

Correct   War is hell.

COMMON ERRORS

Articles with count and noncount nouns

Knowing how to distinguish between count and noncount nouns can help you decide which article to use. Noncount nouns are never used with the indefinite articles *a* and *an*.

Incorrect   Maria jumped into **a** water.

Correct   Maria jumped into **the** water.

(Continued on next page)

COMMON ERRORS *(Continued)*

No articles are used with noncount and plural count nouns when you wish to state something that has a general application.

Incorrect   **The** water is a precious natural resource.

Correct   Water is a precious natural resource.

Incorrect   **The** soccer players tend to be quick and agile.

Correct   Soccer players tend to be quick and agile.

Remember:
1. **Noncount nouns are never used with** *a* **and** *an*.
2. **Noncount and plural nouns used to make general statements do not take articles.**

Exercise 49.4   Underline the correct definite or indefinite articles for the nouns in the following paragraph.

Example   (A/An/<u>The</u>) First Earth Battalion was (<u>a</u>/an/the) secret military unit established in 1979 by Lieutenant Colonel Jim Channon, (<u>a</u>/an/the) U.S. soldier who had served in (a/an/<u>the</u>) Vietnam War.

Channon wanted to establish (a/an/the) new military based on New Age teachings. Members of the First Earth Battalion believed that their first loyalty was to (a/an/the) planet, so they sought nondestructive methods of conflict resolution. Channon referred to members of (a/an/the) First Earth Battalion as "warrior monks" because they would ideally have (a/an/the) dedication of (a/an/the) monk and (a/an/the) skill of (a/an/the) warrior. (A/An/The) warrior monk would learn different martial arts for self-defense, using (a/an/the) attacker's strength against himself or herself. To promote universal healing, (a/an/the) warrior monk would also use (a/an/the) number of methods like yoga, qigong, and reiki. After training, (a/an/the) warrior monk would also be able to become invisible, bend metal with (a/an/the) mind, walk through walls, calculate without (a/an/the) computer, and kill (a/an/the) goat just by staring at it. In short, Channon imagined (a/an/the) army made up of enlightened warriors who would promote peace and make (a/an/the) Earth whole.

49e Prepositions

Prepositions are positional or directional words like *to, for, from, at, in, on,* and *with*. They are used before nouns and pronouns, and they also combine with adjectives and adverbs. Each preposition has a wide range of possible

meanings depending on how it is used, and each must be learned over time in its many contexts.

Some of the most common prepositional phrases describe time and place, and many are idiomatic.

Incorrect	**On** midnight
Correct	**At** midnight
Incorrect	**In** the counter
Correct	**On** the counter
Incorrect	**In** Saturday
Correct	**On** Saturday
Incorrect	**On** February
Correct	**In** February

Over time, you may notice patterns that help you determine the appropriate preposition. For example, *at* precedes a particular time, *on* precedes a day of the week, and *in* precedes a month, year, or other period of time.

COMMON ERRORS

Misused prepositions

The correct use of prepositions often seems unpredictable to multilingual speakers of English. When you are not sure which preposition to use, consult a dictionary.

Of for *about*	The report on flight delays raised criticism ~~of~~ **about** the scheduling of flights.
On for *into*	The tennis player went ~~on~~ **into** a slump after failing to qualify for the French Open.
To for *in*	Angry over her low seeding in the tournament, Amy resigned her membership ~~to~~ **in** the chess club.
To for *of*	The family was ignorant ~~to~~ **of** the controversial history of the house they purchased.

Remember: When you are uncertain about a preposition, consult a learner's dictionary intended for nonnative speakers of English. See Chapter 48 on the use of learner's dictionaries.

Exercise 49.5 Underline the proper preposition in parentheses in the following paragraph.

Example (<u>In</u>/On/At) the 1940s, several dozen pilots died trying to break Mach 1, the speed of sound.

(In, On, At) that time, pilots were familiar (with/in/on) the "wall of air" that existed (in/on/at) the speed of sound. Many airplanes shattered (into/onto/from) a million pieces because of this "wall of air." Pilots were especially afraid (for/on/of) a condition called "compressibility," which would make them lose control (in/of/on) the plane. Air Force pilot Chuck Yeager tried to break the sound barrier (from/with/on) *Glamorous Glennis*, a plane named (from/for/to) his wife. (In/On/At) October 14, 1947, Yeager made an attempt to reach Mach 1. The ground crew heard a boom (from/at/in) the distance and feared that *Glamorous Glennis* had crashed. They cheered (with/from/in) joy when they heard Yeager say (with/in/on) the radio a few moments later that he had broken the sound barrier.

Exercise 49.6 The following paragraph contains adjective-preposition phrases. Choose the correct preposition.

Example The Statue of Liberty was (full for/<u>full of</u>) significance for the millions of immigrants.

The United States remains (grateful to/grateful with) the people of France for the gift of the Statue of Liberty. France supported the colonists during the American Revolution and continues to be (proud for/proud of) its role in creating the United States. Although many Americans today are not (aware of/aware with) the importance of French support in the founding of their country, they are nonetheless (interested in/interested with) French culture and (fond of/fond with) its cuisine.

50 | Verbs

QUICK*TAKE*

After reading this chapter, you should be able to . . .

- **Understand the use of different kinds of verbs** (50a)
  Incorrect: She **intending to learn** several skills that **would help** her **becoming** a superhero.
  Correct: She **intends to learn** several skills that **will help** her **to become** a superhero.
- **Use** *be* **verbs correctly** (50b)
- **Use modal auxiliary verbs correctly** (50c)
- **Use verbs and infinitives correctly** (50d)
- **Use verbs and** *-ing* **verbals correctly** (50e)
- **Write conditional sentences correctly** (50f)
  Incorrect: If she **had talked** with me in private, I **would not become** so angry.
  Correct: If she **had talked** with me in private, **I would not have become** so angry.
- **Use phrasal verbs correctly** (50g)
  Incorrect: She **made out** the story.
  Correct: She **made up** the story.

50a Types of Verbs

The verb system in English can be divided between simple verbs like *run*, *speak*, and *look* and verb phrases like *may have run, have spoken*, and *will be looking*. In the verb phrases, the words that appear before the main verbs—*may, have, will*, and *be*—are called **auxiliary verbs** (also called **helping verbs**). Helping verbs, as their name suggests, exist to help express something about the action of main verbs: for example, when the action occurs (tense), whether the subject acted or was acted upon (voice), or whether or not an action occurred.

50b *Be* Verbs

Indicating tense and voice with *be* verbs

Like the other auxiliary verbs *have* and *do, be* changes form to signal tense. In addition to *be* itself, the **be verbs** are *is, am, are, was, were*, and *been*.

To show ongoing action, *be* verbs are followed by the present participle, which is a verb with an *-ing* ending.

Incorrect	I **am think** of all the things I'd rather **be do**.
Correct	I **am thinking** of all the things I'd rather **be doing**.
Incorrect	He **was run** as fast as he could.
Correct	He **was running** as fast as he could.

To show that an action is being done to, rather than by, the subject, follow *be* verbs with the past participle (a verb usually ending in *-ed, -en*, or *-t*).

Incorrect	The movie **was direct** by John Woo.
Correct	The movie **was directed** by John Woo.
Incorrect	The complaint **will be file** by the victim.
Correct	The complaint **will be filed** by the victim.

Verbs that express cognitive activity

English, unlike Chinese, Arabic, and several other languages, requires a form of *be* before the present or past participle. As you have probably discovered, however, English has many exceptions to its rules. Verbs that express some form of cognitive state rather than a direct action are not used as present participles with *be* verbs. Examples of such words include *know, like, see,* and *believe*.

Incorrect	You **were knowing** that I would be late.
Correct	You **knew** that I would be late.

But here's an exception to an exception: A small number of these verbs, such as *considering, thinking,* and *pondering,* can be used as present participles with *be* verbs.

I **am considering** whether to finish my homework first.

Exercise 50.1   The following paragraph is filled with *be* verbs. In each case, underline the correct verb form from the choices provided in parentheses.

Example   Rosh Hashanah, one of the religious High Holy Days, (is celebrated/is celebrating) beginning on the second day of the seventh month of the Jewish calendar, Tishri.

Though many think it marks only the Jewish New Year, those who celebrate Rosh Hashanah (understand/are understanding) that it has many other meanings as well. Rosh Hashanah (is also called/are also called) the day of the blowing of the Shofar, the day of remembrance, and the day of judgment. It long (has been consider/has been considered) the only High Holy Day that warrants a two-day celebration; those who (observe/are observing) the holiday consider the two-day period one extended 48-hour day. Families (feast/are feasting) on foods that (are sweetened/are sweetening) with honey, apples, and carrots, symbolizing the sweet year to come. Challah, the bread that (is eating/is eaten) on the Sabbath, is reshaped into a ring, symbolizing the hope that the upcoming year will roll smoothly.

50c Modal Auxiliary Verbs

Modal auxiliary verbs—*will, would, can, could, may, might, shall, must,* and *should*—are helping verbs that express conditions like possibility, permission, speculation, expectation, obligation, and necessity. Unlike the helping verbs *be, have,* and *do,* modal verbs do not change form based on the grammatical subject of the sentence (*I, you, she, he, it, we, they*).

Two basic rules apply to all uses of modal verbs. First, modal verbs are always followed by the simple form of the verb. The simple form is the verb by itself, in the present tense, such as *have,* but not *had, having,* or *to have.*

Incorrect   She should **studies** harder to pass the exam.

Correct   She should **study** harder to pass the exam.

The second rule is that you should not use modals consecutively.

Incorrect   If you work harder at writing, you **might could** improve.

Correct   If you work harder at writing, you **might** improve.

Ten conditions that modals express

- **Speculation:** If you had flown, you **would** have arrived yesterday.
- **Ability:** She **can** run faster than Jennifer.
- **Necessity:** You **must** know what you want to do.
- **Intention:** He **will** wash his own clothes.
- **Permission:** You **may** leave now.
- **Advice:** You **should** wash behind your ears.
- **Possibility:** It **might** be possible to go home early.
- **Assumption:** You **must** have stayed up late last night.
- **Expectation:** You **should** enjoy the movie.
- **Order:** You **must** leave the building.

Exercise 50.2 The following sentences contain modal auxiliary verbs. Some are used properly and some improperly. Identify the conditions they express (speculation, ability, necessity, and so on) and correct any incorrect modal usage.

Example	Donnie is a Doberman Pinscher dog who can arranges his plush toys in geometric forms.
Revised	Donnie is a Doberman Pinscher dog who **can arrange** his plush toys in geometric forms. (ability)

1. His owner rescued him from an animal shelter knowing that it might could take him a long time to bond with her, but it was a job she must be doing.
2. The producers of National Geographic Channel's *Dog Genius* show must have been impressed, or they would not have been featuring Donnie arranging his toys into circles, triangles, and parallel lines.
3. You should watch a video of the show so you can see Donnie arrange his toys to look like they are hugging and holding hands, as if he would be liking to communicate something.
4. Donnie also creates arrangements in which he matches toys that are like each other, as if he thinks monkeys might should always be with monkeys and frogs might should always be with frogs.
5. Scientists who study dogs like Donnie must to make sure that the dogs are not being coached, so they will often use remote video cameras and film the dogs when no humans are around.

50d Verbs and Infinitives

Several verbs are followed by particular verb forms. An **infinitive** is *to* plus the simple form of the verb. Here are common verbs that are followed by an infinitive.

afford	expect	promise
agree	fail	refuse
ask	hope	seem
attempt	intend	struggle
claim	learn	tend
consent	need	wait
decide	plan	want
demand	prepare	wish

Incorrect	You **learn playing** the guitar by practicing.
Correct	You **learn to play** the guitar by practicing.

Some verbs require that a noun or pronoun come after the verb and before the infinitive.

advise	instruct	require
cause	order	tell
command	persuade	warn

Incorrect I would **advise to watch** where you step.

Correct I would **advise you to watch** where you step.

A few verbs, when followed by a noun or pronoun, take an *unmarked infinitive*, which is an infinitive without *to*.

have	let	make

Incorrect I will **let** her **to plan** the vacation.

Correct I will **let** her **plan** the vacation.

Exercise 50.3 Complete the following sentences by choosing the proper verb, pronoun, and infinitive combinations from those provided in parentheses. Underline the correct answer.

Example Because reality television producers (to struggle/ struggle to) attract and keep a wide audience, they have developed many different formulas for their shows.

1. Shows in which a camera (follows/to follow) a person or a group of people around during their everyday life (refer to you/are referred to) as "documentary style."
2. The best known type of documentary style show (forces strangers living/ forces strangers to live) together, (causing them to face/causing to face) a variety of conflicts.
3. Other documentary shows follow a professional or group of professionals as they (try completing/try to complete) a project, such as (opening/to open) a restaurant.
4. The extreme competition on some reality shows (causes to cheat participants/ causes participants to cheat) each other so that they will not be (chosen to leave/chosen leaving) the show.
5. A more positive type of show is the improvement or make-over show in which experts (advise to improve someone/advise someone to improve) his or her clothes, home, or overall life.

50e Verbs and *-ing* Verbals

Other verbs are followed by **gerunds**, which are verbs ending in *-ing* that are used as nouns. Here are common verbs that are followed by a gerund.

admit	discuss	quit
advise	enjoy	recommend
appreciate	finish	regret
avoid	imagine	risk
consider	practice	suggest

Incorrect   She will **finish to grade** papers by noon.

Correct   She will **finish grading** papers by noon.

A smaller number of verbs can be followed by either gerunds or infinitives (see 50d).

begin	hate	love
continue	like	start

With gerund   She **likes working** in the music store.

With infinitive   She **likes to work** in the music store.

Exercise 50.4   The following sentences include verbs that should be followed by either gerunds or infinitives. Underline the correct gerund or infinitive from the options provided in parentheses. If both options are correct, underline both.

Example   Children enjoyed (to watch/<u>watching</u>) Pecos Bill in Disney's 1948 animated feature *Melody Time*.

1. Historians risk (misidentifying/to misidentify) actual origins when stories have been passed down simply by word of mouth.
2. Though some like (to believe/believing) that Edward O'Reilly found the story of Pecos Bill circulating among American cowboys, it is hard to prove.
3. The story of little Bill, who was raised by coyotes, fails (to go/going) away despite its ambiguous origins.
4. Despite the confusion, stories about Bill's bride Slue-Foot Sue and his horse Widow Maker continue (to spread/spreading) as part of Americana.
5. Because of the debate over authenticity, however, some consider (to call/calling) the story popular culture rather than folklore.

50f Conditional Sentences

Conditional sentences express *if-then* relationships: They consist of a **subordinate clause** beginning with *if, unless,* or *when* that expresses a condition, and a **main clause** that expresses a result. The tense and mood of the verb in the main clause and the type of conditional sentence determine the tense and mood of the verb in the subordinate clause.

┌ SUBORDINATE CLAUSE ┐ ┌──── MAIN CLAUSE────┐
When the wind stops, the sea becomes calm.

Conditional sentences fall into three categories: **factual, predictive,** and **hypothetical.**

Factual conditionals

Factual conditional sentences express factual relationships: If this happens, that will follow. The tense of the verb in the conditional clause is the same as the tense of the verb in the result clause.

Incorrect	When it rains, the ground **would become** wet.
Correct	When it rains, the ground **becomes** wet.

Predictive conditionals

Predictive conditional sentences express predicted consequences from possible conditions. The verb in the conditional clause is in the present tense, and the verb in the result clause is formed with a modal (*will, would, can, could, may, might, shall, must,* and *should*) plus the base form of the verb.

Incorrect	If you **take** the long way home, you **enjoy** the ride more.
Correct	If you **take** the long way home, you **will enjoy** the ride more.

Hypothetical conditionals

Hypothetical conditional sentences express events that are either not factual or unlikely to happen. For hypothetical events in the past, the conditional clause verb takes the past perfect tense. The main clause verb is formed from *could have, would have,* or *might have* plus the past participle.

Incorrect	If we **had fed** the dog last night, he **would not run** away.
Correct	If we **had fed** the dog last night, he **would not have run** away.

For hypothetical events in the present or future, the conditional clause verb takes the past tense and the main clause verb is formed from *could, would,* or *might* and the base form.

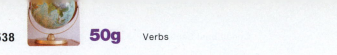
Incorrect	If we **paid** off our credit cards, we **can** buy a house.
Correct	If we **paid** off our credit cards, we **could** buy a house.

Exercise 50.5   Rewrite the following sentences to reflect the conditional category represented in the parentheses following the sentence.

Example	If you **were to show** irrational fear toward a common object or situation, you **would be diagnosed** with a phobia. (predictive)
Rewrite	If you **show** irrational fear toward a common object or situation, you **will be diagnosed** with a phobia.

1. If a child was terrified whenever he or she saw a clown, that child had coulrophobia. (factual)
2. If you were ever attacked by birds, you developed ornithophobia. (hypothetical)
3. If someone had claustrophobia, he would not be comfortable in a small cave. (factual)
4. If you develop heliophobia, you do not enjoy sunbathing. (predictive)
5. If a dentist has dentophobia, she has to find a new job. (hypothetical)

50g Phrasal Verbs

The liveliest and most colorful feature of the English language, its numerous idiomatic verbal phrases, gives many multilingual speakers the greatest difficulty.

Phrasal verbs consist of a verb and one or two **particles**: either a preposition, an adverb, or both. The verb and particles combine to form a phrase with a particular meaning that is often quite distinct from the meaning of the verb itself. Consider the following sentence.

I need to **go over** the chapter once more before the test.

Here, the meaning of *go over*—a verb and a preposition that, taken together, suggest casual study—is only weakly related to the meaning of either *go* or *over* by itself. English has hundreds of such idiomatic constructions, and the best way to familiarize yourself with them is to listen to and read as much informal English as you can.

Like regular verbs, phrasal verbs can be either transitive (they take a direct object) or intransitive. In the preceding example, *go over* is transitive. *Quiet down*—as in *Please quiet down*—is intransitive. Some phrases,

like *wake up*, can be both: *Wake up!* is intransitive, while *Jenny, wake up the children* is transitive.

In some transitive phrasal verbs, the particles can be separated from the verb without affecting the meaning: *I made up a song* is equivalent to *I made a song up*. In others, the particles cannot be separated from the verb.

Incorrect	You shouldn't **play** with love **around**.
Correct	You shouldn't **play around** with love.

Unfortunately, there are no shortcuts for learning which verbal phrases are separable and which are not. As you become increasingly familiar with English, you will grow more confident in your ability to use phrasal verbs.

51 | English Sentence Structure

QUICK*TAKE*

After reading this chapter, you should be able to . . .

- **Use subjects of sentences correctly** (51a)
  Incorrect: Is my favorite flavor of ice cream.
  Correct: Pistachio is my favorite flavor of ice cream.
- **Use correct patterns for English sentences** (51b)
  Incorrect: The server brought her.
  Correct: The server brought her **a whole salmon.**
- **Use modifiers correctly** (51c)
  Unclear: After eating a few bites, **the salmon** was not fully cooked.
  Clear: After eating a few bites, **she** realized that the salmon was not fully cooked.

51a Subjects

With the exception of **imperatives** (commands such as *Be careful!* and *Jump!*) and informal expressions (such as *Got it?*), sentences in English usually contain a subject and a predicate. A **subject** names who or what the sentence is about; the **predicate** contains information about the subject.

⌐SUBJECT¬ ⌐PREDICATE¬
The lion is asleep.

Many languages allow the writer to omit the subject if it's implied, but formal written English requires that each sentence include a subject, even when the meaning of the sentence would be clear without it. In some cases, you must supply an **expletive** (also known as a *dummy subject*), such as *it* or *there*, to stand in for the subject.

Incorrect	**Is** snowing in Alaska.
Correct	**It is** snowing in Alaska.
Incorrect	**Won't** be enough time to climb that mountain.
Correct	**There won't** be enough time to climb that mountain.

Both main and subordinate clauses within sentences require a subject and a predicate. A main clause can stand alone as a sentence, while subordinate clauses can only be understood in the context of the sentence of which they're a part. Still, even subordinate clauses must contain a subject. Look at the underlined subordinate clauses in the following two correct sentences.

We avoided the main highway <u>because **it** had two lanes blocked off</u>.

We avoided the main highway, <u>**which** had two lanes blocked off</u>.

In the first example, the subject of the subordinate clause is *it,* a pronoun representing the highway. In the second sentence, the relative pronoun *which*—also representing the highway—becomes the subject. When you use a relative pronoun, do not repeat the subject within the same clause.

Incorrect	We avoided the highway, which **it** had two lanes blocked off.

In this sentence, *it* repeats the subject *which* unnecessarily.

Exercise 51.1   Underline all of the subjects in the following sentences. Some sentences may have more than one subject; some may appear to have none. If the sentence appears to have no subject, supply the needed expletive.

Example   Though <u>you</u> may have heard of Lee Harvey Oswald and John Wilkes Booth, many lesser-known <u>individuals</u> have put <u>presidents</u> in harm's way.

1. Though some assassins are widely known, Charles Guiteau and Leon Czolgolsz are relatively obscure.
2. Guiteau shot President James Garfield in 1881, and was little doubt he would be hanged for the murder.
3. Twenty years later, Czolgolsz stood face-to-face with his victim, President William McKinley.

4. History books are littered with the names of would-be assassins such as Giuseppe Zangara, Samuel Byck, and Sarah Jane Moore.
5. You should protect your leaders because there is no way to tell what the future will bring.

Exercise 51.2 In the following sentences, underline main clauses once and subordinate clauses twice. Circle the subjects in each.

Example   When scientists explain phenomena such as volcanoes and earthquakes, they often use the theory of plate tectonics.

1. Geologists based the theory on an earlier one that had observed that the continents fit together like pieces of a puzzle.
2. In the 1950s and 1960s, scientists found evidence to support the earlier theory, so they were able to confirm its hypothesis regarding continental drift.
3. Although water and earth appear to be distinctly separate, they share a similar underlayer called the asthenosphere.
4. This layer possesses high temperatures and high pressure, and these conditions allow for fluid rock movement.
5. As plates move around, they can create volcanoes or increase and decrease the size of oceans and mountains.

51b English Word Order

All languages have their own rules for sentence structure. In English, correct word order often determines whether or not you succeed in saying what you mean. The basic sentence pattern in English is subject + predicate. A **predicate** consists of at least one main verb (see Section 32a). Although it is possible to write single-verb sentences such as *Stop!*, most English sentences consist of a combination of several words. A simple English sentence can be formed with a noun and a verb.

   Birds fly.

In the above sentence, the subject (birds) is taking the action *and* receiving the action. There is no other object after the verb. The type of verb that can form a sentence without being followed by an object is called an **intransitive verb**. If the verb is intransitive, like *exist,* it does not take a direct object.

Some verbs are **transitive**, which means they require a **direct object** to complete their meaning. The direct object receives the action described by the verb.

Incorrect   The bird saw.

Correct   The bird saw a cat.

In this sentence, the subject (the bird) is doing the action (saw) while the direct object (a cat) is receiving the action. A sentence with a transitive verb can be transformed into a passive sentence (*A cat was seen by the bird*). See Chapter 27 for active and passive sentences.

Some verbs (*write, learn, read,* and others) can be both transitive and intransitive, depending on how they are used.

Intransitive   Pilots fly.

Transitive   Pilots fly airplanes.

Most learner's dictionaries and bilingual dictionaries indicate whether a particular verb is transitive or intransitive. See 48c on the use of dictionaries.

In another simple pattern, the transitive verb is replaced by a linking verb that joins its subject to a following description.

The tallest player was the goalie.

Linking verbs like *was, become, sound, look,* and *seem* precede a *subject complement* (in this example, *the goalie*) that refers back to the subject.

At the next level of complexity, a sentence combines a subject with a verb, direct object, and indirect object.

INDIRECT   DIRECT
OBJ   OBJ
The goalie passed her the ball.

Passed is a transitive verb, *ball* is the direct object of the verb, and *her* is the indirect object, the person for whom the action was taken. The same idea can be expressed with a prepositional phrase instead of an indirect object.

DIRECT   PREP
OBJ   PHRASE
The goalie passed the ball to her.

Other sentence patterns are possible in English. (See Chapter 32.) However, it is important to remember that altering the basic subject + verb + object word order often changes the meaning of a sentence. If the meaning survives, the result may still be awkward. As a general rule, try to keep the verb close to its subject and the direct or indirect object close to its verb.

Exercise 51.3 Label the parts of speech in the following sentences: subject (S), transitive or intransitive verb (TV or IV), linking verb (LV), direct object (DO), indirect object (IO), subject complement (SC), and prepositional phrase (PP). Not all sentences will contain all of these parts, but all will contain some.

Example

$$\overset{\text{S}}{\text{Hinduism}} \overset{\text{TV}}{\text{includes}} \overset{\text{DO}}{\text{several gods and heroes}} \overset{\text{PP}}{\text{in its system}}$$

$$\overset{\text{PP}}{\text{of beliefs.}}$$

1. Ganesh is the god of good luck.
2. Young Ganesh stood at the doorway to his mother's house.
3. He denied his father entry.
4. His father beheaded him.
5. His mother replaced his head with the head of an elephant.

51c Placement of Modifiers

The proximity of a modifier—an adjective or adverb—to the noun or verb it modifies provides an important clue to their relationship. Modifiers, even more than verbs, will be unclear if your reader can't connect them to their associated words. Both native and nonnative speakers of English often have difficulty with misplaced modifiers.

Clarity should be your first goal when using a modifier. Readers usually link modifiers with the nearest word. In the following examples, the highlighted words are adjective clauses that modify nouns.

| Unclear | Many pedestrians are killed each year by motorists **not using sidewalks**. |
| Clear | Many pedestrians **not using sidewalks** are killed each year by motorists. |

| Unclear | He gave an apple to his girlfriend **on a silver platter**. |
| Clear | He gave an apple **on a silver platter** to his girlfriend. |

An **adverb**—a word or group of words that modifies a verb, adjective, or another adverb—should not come between a verb and its direct object.

| Awkward | The hurricane destroyed **completely** the city's tallest building. |
| Better | The hurricane **completely** destroyed the city's tallest building. |

While single-word adverbs can come between a subject and its verb, you should avoid placing adverbial phrases in this position.

> **Awkward**   Galveston, **following the 1900 hurricane that killed thousands**, built a seawall to prevent a future catastrophe.
>
> **Better**   **Following the 1900 hurricane that killed thousands**, Galveston built a seawall to prevent a future catastrophe.

As a general rule, try to avoid placing an adverb between *to* and its verb. This is called a **split infinitive**.

> **Awkward**   The water level was predicted **to not rise**.
>
> **Better**   The water level was predicted **not to rise**.

Sometimes, though, a split infinitive will read more naturally than the alternative. Note also how the sentence with the split infinitive is more concise.

> **Without split infinitive**   Automobile emissions in the city are expected **to increase by more than two times** over the next five years.
>
> **With split infinitive**   Automobile emissions in the city are expected **to more than double** over the next five years.

Certain kinds of adverbs have special rules for placement. Adverbs that describe how something is done—called **adverbs of manner**—usually follow the verb.

> The student listened **closely** to the lecture.

These adverbs may also be separated from the verb by a direct object.

> She threw the ball **well**.

Adverbs of frequency are usually placed at the head of a sentence, before a single verb, or after an auxiliary verb in a verb phrase.

> **Often**, politicians have underestimated the intelligence of voters.

> Politicians have **often** underestimated the intelligence of voters.

It's common practice in English to combine two or more nouns to form a compound noun. Where two or more adjectives or nouns are strung together, the main noun is always positioned at the end of the string:

> 12-speed road **bike**, tall oak **tree**, computer **table**

Exercise 51.4 The following sentences include confusing modifiers. Underline the confusing modifiers, identify the broken rule (far away from modified word; adverb between verb and direct object; adverbial phrase between subject and verb; split infinitive), and rewrite the sentence clearly.

Example Awareness of autism has increased through the life story of Temple Grandin <u>worldwide</u>. **(Far away from modified word)**

Revise Awareness of autism has increased worldwide through the life story of Temple Grandin.

1. Doctors, seeing a bleak future for Grandin, told her parents that she should be institutionalized.
2. However, Grandin's mother was determined to not give up on her daughter.
3. Called often "weird" by her classmates, Grandin excelled in school and earned eventually a PhD in animal science.
4. Grandin has used her ability unique to think visually to design facilities humane for livestock.
5. She has also to other people with autism become a hero.

Exercise 51.5 Underline all the adjectives and adverbs in the following sentences. Label adverbs of manner or adverbs of frequency, and correct improper word order where you find it.

adverb of frequency

Example Americans associate <u>often</u> cards and dice with <u>shady</u> gamblers <u>Las Vegas</u>.

Revise Americans often associate cards and dice with shady Las Vegas gamblers.

1. By the fourteenth century, cards playing were used widely for gambling.
2. The invention of the printing press directly connects to the proliferation of card games standardized.
3. Ancient dice directly can be traced to Tutankhamen's tomb.
4. Gamblers hollowed frequently the center of an illegally rigged die.
5. These classic games have withstood well the test of time.

COMMON ERRORS

Dangling modifiers

A **dangling modifier** does not seem to modify anything in a sentence; it dangles, unconnected to the word or words it presumably is intended to modify. Frequently, it produces funny results.

When still a girl, my father joined the army.

(Continued on next page)

COMMON ERRORS *(Continued)*

It sounds like *father* was once a girl. The problem is that the subject, *I*, is missing.

> **When I was still a girl**, my father joined the army.

Dangling modifiers usually occur at the head of a sentence in the form of clauses, with a subject that is implied but never stated.

Incorrect   After lifting the heavy piano up the stairs, the apartment door was too small to get it through.

Correct   After lifting the heavy piano up the stairs, **we discovered** the apartment door was too small to get it through.

Whenever you use a modifier, ask yourself whether its relationship to the word it modifies will be clear to your reader. What is clear to you may not be clear to your audience. Writing, like speaking, is an exercise in making your own thoughts explicit. The solution for the dangling modifier is to recast it as a complete clause with its own explicit subject and verb.

Remember: Modifiers should be clearly connected to the words they modify, especially at the beginning of sentences.

Exercise 51.6   The following sentences include dangling modifiers. Rewrite the sentences so that the relationship between subject, verb, and modifier is clear.

Example   In his early thirties, France was dealt a hefty blow by Maximilien Robespierre.

Revise   In his early thirties, Maximilien Robespierre dealt France a hefty blow.

1. His philosophical role model, Robespierre followed the writings of Jean Jacques Rousseau.
2. Elected on the eve of the French Revolution, the people were enthralled by his skillful oratory.
3. Gaining further power in the following years, his influence over domestic affairs was unmistakable.
4. A bloodbath known as the Reign of Terror, Robespierre ordered a rash of executions of members of the aristocracy and his political enemies.
5. After they tired of his aggressive tactics, he was overthrown by his own political party.

Glossary of Grammatical Terms and Usage

The glossary gives the definitions of grammatical terms and items of usage. The grammatical terms are shown in blue. Some of the explanations of usage that follow are not rules, but guidelines to keep in mind for academic and professional writing. In these formal contexts, the safest course is to avoid words that are described as *nonstandard*, *informal*, or *colloquial*.

a/an   Use *a* before words that begin with a consonant sound (*a train*, *a house*). Use *an* before words that begin with a vowel sound (*an airplane*, *an hour*).

a lot/alot   *A lot* is generally regarded as informal; *alot* is nonstandard.

absolute   A phrase that has a subject and modifies an entire sentence (see 32d).

The soldiers marched in single file, their rifles slung over their shoulders.

accept/except   *Accept* is a verb meaning "receive" or "approve." *Except* is sometimes a verb meaning "leave out," but much more often, it's used as a conjunction or preposition meaning "other than."

She accepted her schedule except for Biology at 8 a.m.

active   A clause with a transitive verb in which the subject is the doer of the action (see 27b). See also **passive**.

adjective   A modifier that qualifies or describes the qualities of a noun or pronoun (see 32b, 37a, and 37b).

adjective clause   A subordinate clause that modifies a noun or pronoun and is usually introduced by a relative pronoun (see 32c). Sometimes called a *relative clause*.

adverb   A word that modifies a verb, another modifier, or a clause (see 32b, 37a, and 37c).

adverb clause   A subordinate clause that functions as an adverb by modifying a verb, another modifier, or a clause (see 32c).

advice/advise   The noun *advice* means a "suggestion"; the verb *advise* means to "recommend" or "give advice."

affect/effect   Usually, *affect* is a verb (to "influence") and *effect* is a noun (a "result"):

Too many pork chops affect one's health.

Too many pork chops have an effect on one's health.

Less commonly, *affect* is used as a noun and *effect* as a verb. In the following examples, *affect* means an "emotional state or expression," and *effect* means "to bring about."

The boy's affect changed when he saw his father.

The legislators will attempt to effect new insurance laws next year.

agreement   The number and person of a subject and verb must match—singular subjects with singular verbs, plural subjects with plural verbs (see Chapter 34). Likewise, the number and gender of a pronoun and its antecedent must match (see 36b).

all ready/already   The adjective phrase *all ready* means "completely prepared"; the adverb *already* means "previously."

> The tour group was all ready to leave, but the train had already departed.

all right/alright   *All right*, meaning "acceptable," is the correct spelling. *Alright* is nonstandard.

allude/elude   *Allude* means "refer to indirectly." *Elude* means "evade."

> He alluded to the fact that he'd eluded capture.

allusion/illusion   An *allusion* is an indirect reference; an *illusion* is a false impression.

> The painting contains an allusion to the *Mona Lisa*.

> The painting creates the illusion of depth.

among/between   *Between* refers to precisely two people or things; *among* refers to three or more.

> The choice is between two good alternatives.

> The costs were shared among the three participating companies.

amount/number   Use *amount* with things that cannot be counted; use *number* with things that can be counted.

> A large amount of money changed hands.

> They gave him a number of quarters.

an   See a/an.

antecedent   The noun (or pronoun) that a pronoun refers to (see 36b). *Jeff* is the antecedent of *his* in the following sentence.

> Jeff stopped running when his knee began hurting.

anybody/any body; anyone/any one   *Anybody* and *anyone* are indefinite pronouns and have the same meaning; *any body* and *any one* are usually followed by a noun that they modify.

> Anybody can learn English, just as anyone can learn to bicycle.

> Any body of government should be held accountable for its actions.

anymore/any more   *Anymore* means "now," while *any more* means "no more." Both are used in negative constructions.

> No one goes downtown anymore.

> The area doesn't have any more stores than it did in 1960.

anyway/anyways   *Anyway* is correct. *Anyways* is nonstandard.

appositive   A word or a phrase placed close to a noun that restates or modifies the noun (see 32d).

> Dr. Lim, my physics professor, is the best.

articles   The words *a*, *an*, and *the* (see 32b and 49d).

as/as if/as though/like   Use *as* instead of *like* before dependent clauses (which include a subject and verb). Use *like* before a noun or a pronoun.

Her voice sounds as if she had her head in a barrel.

She sings like her father.

assure/ensure/insure   *Assure* means "promise," *ensure* means "make certain," and *insure* means to "make certain in either a legal or financial sense."

Ralph assured the new client that his company would insure the building at full value, but the client wanted higher approval to ensure Ralph was correct.

auxiliary verb   Forms of *be*, *do*, and *have* combine with verbs to indicate tense and mood (see 32b). The modal verbs *can*, *could*, *may*, *might*, *must*, *shall*, *should*, *will*, and *would* are a subset of auxiliaries.

bad/badly   Use *bad* only as an adjective. *Badly* is the adverb.

He was a bad dancer.

Everyone agreed that he danced badly.

being as/being that   Both constructions are colloquial and awkward substitutes for *because*. Don't use them in formal writing.

beside/besides   *Beside* means "next to." *Besides* means "in addition to" or "except."

Does anyone, besides your mother, want to sit beside you when you're coughing like that?

between   See among/between.

bring/take   *Bring* describes movement from a more distant location to a nearer one. *Take* describes movement away.

Bring me the most recent issue. You can take this one.

can/may   In formal writing, *can* indicates ability or capacity, while *may* indicates permission.

If I may speak with you, we can probably solve this problem.

case   The form of a noun or pronoun that indicates its function. Nouns change case only to show possession: the dog, the dog's bowl (see 32b). See **pronoun case** (36a).

censor/censure   To *censor* is to edit or ban on moral or political grounds. To *censure* is to reprimand publicly.

The Senate censored the details of the budget.

The Senate censured one of its members for misconduct.

cite/sight/site   To *cite* is to "mention specifically"; *sight* as a verb means to "observe" and as a noun refers to "vision"; *site* is most commonly used as a noun that means "location," but is also used as a verb to mean "situate."

He cited as evidence the magazine article he'd read yesterday.

Finally, he sighted the bald eagle. It was a remarkable sight.

The developers sited the houses on a heavily forested site.

clause   A group of words with a subject and a predicate. A main or independent clause can stand as a sentence. A subordinate or dependent clause must be attached to a main clause to form a sentence (see 32c).

collective noun A noun that refers to a group or a plurality, such as *team, army,* or *committee* (see 34d).

comma splice Two independent clauses joined incorrectly by a comma (see 33c).

common noun A noun that names a general group, person, place, or thing (see 32b and 49a). Common nouns are not capitalized unless they begin a sentence.

complement A word or group of words that completes the predicate (see 32c). See also **linking verb**.

Juanita is my aunt.

complement/compliment To *complement* something is to complete it or make it perfect; to *compliment* is to flatter.

The chef complemented their salad with a small bowl of soup.

The grateful diners complimented the chef.

complex sentence A sentence that contains at least one subordinate clause attached to a main clause (see 32e).

compound sentence A sentence that contains at least two main clauses (see 32e).

compound-complex sentence A sentence that contains at least two main clauses and one subordinate clause (see 32e).

conjunction See **coordinating conjunction; subordinating conjunction**.

conjunctive adverb An adverb that often modifies entire clauses and sentences, such as *also, consequently, however, indeed, instead, moreover, nevertheless, otherwise, similarly,* and *therefore* (see 32b and 37c).

continual/continuous *Continual* refers to a repeated activity; *continuous* refers to an ongoing, unceasing activity.

Tennis elbow is usually caused by continual stress on the joint.

Archaeologists have debated whether Chaco Canyon was inhabited intermittently or continuously.

coordinate A relationship of equal importance, in terms of either grammar or meaning (see 29c).

coordinating conjunction A word that links two equivalent grammatical elements, such as *and, but, or, yet, nor, for,* and *so* (see 32b).

could of Nonstandard. See **have/of**.

count noun A noun that names things that can be counted, such as *block, cat,* and *toy* (see 49b).

dangling modifier A modifier that is not clearly attached to what it modifies (see 37e).

data The plural form of *datum*; it takes plural verb forms.

The data are overwhelming.

declarative A sentence that makes a statement (see 32a).

Dover is the capital of Delaware.

dependent clause   See **subordinate clause**.

determiners   Words that initiate noun phrases, including possessive nouns (*Pedro's violin*); possessive pronouns (*my, your*); demonstrative pronouns (*this, that*); and indefinite pronouns (*all, both, many*).

differ from/differ with   To *differ from* means to "be unlike"; to *differ with* means to "disagree."

Rock music differs from jazz primarily in rhythm.

Miles Davis differed with critics who disliked his rock rhythms.

different from/different than   Use *different from* where possible.

Dark French roast is different from ordinary coffee.

direct object   A noun, pronoun, or noun clause that names who or what receives the action of a transitive verb (see 32c).

Antonio kicked the ball.

discreet/discrete   Both are adjectives. *Discreet* means "prudent" or "tactful"; *discrete* means "separate."

What's a discreet way of saying "Shut up"?

Over the noise, he could pick up several discrete conversations.

disinterested/uninterested   *Disinterested* is often misused to mean *uninterested*. Disinterested means "impartial." A judge can be interested in a case but disinterested in the outcome.

double negative   The incorrect use of two negatives to signal the same negative meaning.

We don't have no money.

due to the fact that   Avoid this wordy substitute for *because*.

each other/one another   Use *each other* for two; use *one another* for more than two.

effect   See **affect/effect**.

elicit/illicit   The verb *elicit* means to "draw out." The adjective *illicit* means "unlawful."

The teacher tried to elicit a discussion about illicit drugs.

emigrate from/immigrate to   *Emigrate* means to "leave one's country"; *immigrate* means to "settle in another country."

ensure   See **assure/ensure/insure**.

enthused   Nonstandard in academic and professional writing. Use *enthusiastic* instead.

etc.   Avoid this abbreviation for the Latin *et cetera* in formal writing. Either list all the items or use an English phrase such as *and so forth*.

every body/everybody; every one/everyone   *Everybody* and *everyone* are indefinite pronouns referring to all people under discussion. *Every one* and *every body* are adjective-noun combinations referring to all members of a group.

Everyone loves a genuine smile.

Every one of the files contained a virus.

except   See **accept/except**.

except for the fact that   Avoid this wordy substitute for *except that*.

expletive   The dummy subjects *it* and *there* used to fill a grammatical slot in a sentence.

> It is raining outside.

> There should be a law against it.

explicit/implicit   Both are adjectives; *explicit* means "stated outright," while *implicit* means just the opposite, "unstated."

> Even though we lacked an explicit contract, I thought we had an implicit understanding.

farther/further   *Farther* refers to physical distance; *further* refers to time or other abstract concepts.

> How much farther is your home?

> I don't want to talk about this any further.

fewer/less   Use *fewer* with what can be counted and *less* with what cannot be counted.

> There are fewer canoeists in the summer because there is less water in the river.

flunk   In formal writing, avoid this colloquial substitute for *fail*.

fragment   A group of words beginning with a capital letter and ending with a period that looks like a sentence but lacks a subject or a predicate or both (see 33a).

further   See **farther/further**.

gerund   An *-ing* form of a verb used as a noun, such as *running, skiing,* or *laughing* (see 32b).

good/well   *Good* is an adjective and is not interchangeable with the adverb *well.* The one exception is health. Both she feels *good* and she feels *well* are correct.

> The Yankees are a good baseball team. They play the game well.

hanged/hung   Use *hanged* to refer only to executions; *hung* is used for all other instances.

have/of   *Have,* not *of,* follows *should, could, would, may, must,* and *might.*

> I should have [not *of*] picked you up earlier.

he/she; s/he   Try to avoid language that appears to exclude either gender (unless this is intended, of course) and awkward compromises such as *he/she* or *s/he.* The best solution is to make pronouns plural (the gender-neutral *they*) wherever possible (see 36c).

helping verb   See **auxiliary verb**.

hopefully   This adverb is commonly used as a sentence modifier, but many readers object to it.

> I am hopeful [not *Hopefully*] we'll have a winning season.

illusion   See **allusion/illusion**.

immigrate   See **emigrate from/immigrate to**.

imperative   A sentence that expresses a command (see 32a). Usually the subject is implied rather than stated.

> Go away now.

implicit   See **explicit/implicit**.

imply/infer   *Imply* means to "suggest"; *infer* means to "draw a conclusion." The ad implied that the candidate was dishonest; I inferred that the campaign would be one of name calling.

in regards to   Avoid this wordy substitute for *regarding*.

incredible/incredulous   *Incredible* means "unbelievable"; *incredulous* means "not believing." Their story about finding a stack of money in a discarded suitcase seemed incredible; I was incredulous.

independent clause   See **main clause**.

indirect object   A noun, pronoun, or noun clause that names who or what is affected by the action of a transitive verb (see 32c). Antonio kicked the ball to Mario.

infinitive   The word *to* plus the base verb form: *to believe, to feel, to act*. See also **split infinitive**.

infinitive phrase   A phrase that uses the infinitive form of a verb (see 32d). To get some sleep is my goal for the weekend.

interjection   A word expressing feeling that is grammatically unconnected to a sentence, such as *cool, wow, ouch,* or *yikes*.

interrogative   A sentence that asks a question (see 32a). Where do you want to go?

intransitive verb   A verb that does not take an object, such as *sleep, appear,* or *laugh* (see 32c and 35c).

irregardless   Nonstandard for *regardless*.

irregular verb   A verb that does not use either *-d* or *-ed* to form the past tense and past participle (see 35b).

it is my opinion that   Avoid this wordy substitute for *I believe that*.

its/it's   *Its* is the possessive of *it* and does not take an apostrophe; *it's* is the contraction for *it is*. Its tail is missing. It's an unusual animal.

-ize/-wise   The suffix *-ize* changes a noun or adjective into a verb (*harmony, harmonize*). The suffix *-wise* changes a noun or adjective into an adverb (*clock, clockwise*). Some writers are tempted to use these suffixes to convert almost any word into an adverb or verb form. Unless the word appears in a dictionary, don't use it.

kind of/sort of/type of   Avoid using these colloquial expressions if you mean *somewhat* or *rather*. *It's kind of hot* is nonstandard. Each is permissible, however, when it refers to a classification of an object. Be sure that it agrees in number with the object it is modifying. This type of engine is very fuel-efficient. These kinds of recordings are rare.

lay/lie   *Lay* means "place" or "put" and generally takes a direct object (see 35c). Its main forms are *lay, laid, laid. Lie* means "recline" or "be positioned" and does not take an object. Its main forms are *lie, lay, lain.*

> He lays the papers down. He laid the papers down.

> He lies down on the sofa. He lay down on the sofa.

less   See **fewer/less.**

lie   See **lay/lie.**

linking verb   A verb that connects the subject to the complement, such as *appear, be, feel, look, seem,* or *taste* (see 32c).

lots/lots of   Nonstandard in formal writing; use *many* or *much* instead.

main clause   A group of words with a subject and a predicate that can stand alone as a sentence (see 32c). Also called an *independent clause.*

mankind   This term offends some readers and is outdated. Use *humans, humanity,* or *people* instead.

may/can   See **can/may.**

may be/maybe   *May be* is a verb phrase; *maybe* is an adverb.

> It may be time to go.

> Maybe it's time to go.

media   This is the plural form of the noun *medium* and requires a plural verb.

> The media in this city are biased.

might of   See **have/of.**

modal   A kind of auxiliary verb that indicates ability, permission, intention, obligation, or probability, such as *can, could, may, might, must, shall, should, will,* or *would* (see 32b).

modifier   A general term for adjectives, adverbs, phrases, and clauses that describe other words (see Chapter 37).

must of   See **have/of.**

noncount noun   A noun that names things that cannot be counted, such as *air, energy,* or *water* (see 49b).

nonrestrictive modifier   A modifier that is not essential to the meaning of the word, phrase, or clause it modifies and should be set off by commas or other punctuation (see 38c).

noun   The name of a person, place, thing, concept, or action (see 32a). See also **common noun** and **proper noun** (see 49a).

noun clause   A subordinate clause that functions as a noun (see 32c).

> That the city fails to pick up the garbage is ridiculous.

number   See **amount/number.**

object   Receiver of the action within the clause or phrase (see 32c and 32d).

OK, O.K., okay   Informal; avoid using in academic and professional writing. Each spelling is accepted in informal usage.

owing to the fact that   Avoid this wordy, colloquial substitute for *because.*

parallelism   The principle of putting similar elements or ideas in similar grammatical form (see 29c, 29d, and 29e).

participial phrase   A phrase formed either by a present participle (for example, *racing*) or by a past participle (for example, *taken*). (See 32d.)

participle   A form of a verb that uses *-ing* in the present (*laughing, playing*) and usually *-ed* or *-en* in the past (*laughed, played*). See 35a. Participles are either part of the verb phrase (*She had played the game before*) or used as adverbs and adjectives (*the laughing girl*).

parts of speech   The eight classes of words according to their grammatical function: nouns, pronouns, verbs, adjectives, adverbs, prepositions, conjunctions, and interjections (see 32b).

passive   A clause with a transitive verb in which the subject is being acted upon (see 27b). See also **active**.

per   Try to use the English equivalent of this Latin word except in technical writing or familiar usages like *miles per gallon*.

The job paid $20 an hour.

As you requested [not *per your request*], I'll drive up immediately.

phenomena   This is the plural form of *phenomenon* ("observable fact" or "unusual event") and takes plural verbs.

The astronomical phenomena were breathtaking.

phrase   A group of words that does not contain both a subject and a predicate.

plenty   In academic and professional writing, avoid this colloquial substitute for *very*.

plus   Do not use *plus* to join clauses or sentences. Use *and, also*, *moreover*, *furthermore*, or another conjunctive adverb instead.

It rained heavily, and it was also [not *plus it was*] bitterly cold.

precede/proceed   Both are verbs, but they have different meanings: *precede* means "come before," and *proceed* means "go ahead" or "continue."

In the United States, the national anthem precedes every major league baseball game.

We proceeded to the train station.

predicate   The part of the clause that expresses the action or tells something about the subject. The predicate includes the verb and all its complements, objects, and modifiers (see 32a).

prejudice/prejudiced   *Prejudice* is a noun; *prejudiced* is an adjective.

The jury was prejudiced against the defendant.

She knew about the town's history of racial prejudice.

preposition   A class of words that indicate relationships and qualities (see 32b and 49e).

prepositional phrase   A phrase formed by a preposition and its object, including the modifiers of its object (see 32d).

principal/principle   *Principal* means first in importance (*school principal, principal reason*). *Principle* applies to beliefs or understandings (*It goes against my principles*).

pronoun   A word that stands for another noun or pronoun. Pronouns have several subclasses, including personal pronouns, possessive pronouns, demonstrative pronouns, indefinite pronouns, relative pronouns, interrogative pronouns, reflexive pronouns, and reciprocal pronouns (see 32b and Chapter 36).

pronoun case   Pronouns that function as the subjects of sentences are in the **subjective** case (*I, you, he, she, it, we, they*). Pronouns that function as direct or indirect objects are in the **objective** case (*me, you, him, her, it, us, them*). Pronouns that indicate ownership are in the **possessive** case (*my, your, his, her, its, our, their*) (see 36a).

proper noun   A noun that names a particular person, place, thing, or group (see 32b and 49a). Proper nouns are capitalized.

raise/rise   The verb *raise* means "lift up" and takes a direct object. Its main forms are *raise, raised, raised*. The verb *rise* means "get up" and does not take a direct object. Its main forms are *rise, rose, risen*.

The workers carefully raised the piano onto the truck.

The piano slowly rose off the ground.

real/really   Avoid using *real* as if it were an adverb. *Really* is an adverb; *real* is an adjective.

The singer was really good.

What we thought was an illusion turned out to be real.

reason is because   Omit either *reason is* or *because* when explaining causality.

The reason he ran is that he thought he was late.

He ran because he thought he was late.

reason why   Avoid using this redundant combination.

The reason he's so often late is that he never wears a watch.

relative pronoun   A pronoun that initiates clauses, such as *that, which, what, who, whom,* or *whose* (see 32b).

restrictive modifier   A modifier that is essential to the meaning of the word, phrase, or clause it modifies (see 38c). Restrictive modifiers are usually not set off by punctuation.

rise/raise   See **raise/rise**.

run-on sentence   Two main clauses fused together without punctuation or a conjunction, appearing as one sentence (see 33b).

sentence   A grammatically independent group of words that contains at least one main clause (see 32a).

sentence fragment   See **fragment**.

set/sit   *Set* means "put" and takes a direct object (see 35c); its main forms are *set, set, set. Sit* means "be seated" and does not take a direct object; its main forms are *sit, sat, sat. Sit* should not be used as a synonym for *set*.

Set the bowl on the table.

Please sit down.

shall/will *Shall* is used most often in first person questions, while *will* is a future tense helping verb for all persons. British English consistently uses *shall* with first person: *I shall, we shall.*

Shall I bring you some water?

Will they want drinks, too?

should of See **have/of.**

sit/set See **set/sit.**

some time/sometime/sometimes *Some time* means "a span of time," *sometime* means "at some unspecified time," and *sometimes* means "occasionally."

Give me some time to get ready.

Let's meet again sometime soon.

Sometimes, the best-laid plans go wrong.

somebody/some body; someone/some one *Somebody* and *someone* are indefinite pronouns and have the same meaning. In *some body*, *body* is a noun modified by *some*, and in *some one*, *one* is a pronoun or adjective modified by *some.*

Somebody should close that window.

"Some body was found on the beach today," the homicide detective said.

Someone should answer the phone.

It would be best if some one person could represent the group.

sort of See **kind of/sort of/type of.**

split infinitive An infinitive with a word or words between *to* and the base verb form, such as *to boldly go, to better appreciate* (see 37d).

stationary/stationery *Stationary* means "motionless"; *stationery* means "writing paper."

subject A noun, pronoun, or noun phrase that identifies what the clause is about and connects with the predicate (see 32a and 32c).

subject-verb agreement See **agreement.**

subordinate A relationship of unequal importance, in terms of either grammar or meaning (see 29a).

subordinate clause A clause that cannot stand alone but must be attached to a main clause (see 32c). Also called a *dependent clause.*

subordinating conjunction A word that introduces a subordinate clause. Common subordinating conjunctions are *after, although, as, because, before, if, since, that, unless, until, when, where,* and *while* (see 32b).

such Avoid using *such* as a synonym for *very*. It should always be followed by *that* and a clause that contains a result.

It was a very [not *such a*] hot August.

sure A colloquial term used as an adverb to mean "certainly." Avoid using it this way in formal writing.

You were certainly [not *sure were*] correct when you said August would be hot.

sure and/sure to; try and/try to   *Sure to* and *try to* are correct; do not use *and* after *sure* or *try*.

Be sure to [not *sure and*] take out the trash this morning.

Try to [not *try and*] finish first.

take   See **bring/take**.

that/which   *That* introduces a restrictive or essential clause. Restrictive clauses describe an object that must be that particular object and no other. Though some writers occasionally use *which* with restrictive clauses, it is most often used to introduce nonrestrictive clauses. These are clauses that contain additional nonessential information about the object.

Let's listen to the CD that Clarence bought.

Clarence's favorite music, which usually puts me to sleep, is too mellow for me.

transition   A word or phrase that notes movement from one unit of writing to another.

transitive verb   A verb that takes a direct object (see 32c and 35c).

unique   *Unique* means one of a kind. Things cannot be "very unique" or "more unique." They are either unique or not.

verb   A word that expresses action or characterizes the subject in some way. Verbs can show tense and mood (see 32b and Chapter 35).

verbal   A form of a verb used as an adjective, adverb, or noun (see 32b). See also **gerund**, **infinitive**, **participle**.

well/good   See **good/well**.

which/that   See **that/which**.

who/whom   *Who* and *whom* follow the same rules as other pronouns: *Who* is the subject pronoun; *whom* is the object pronoun (see 36a).

Sharon's father, who served in the Korean War, died last year.

Sharon's father, whom several of my father's friends knew, died last year.

will/shall   See **shall/will**.

-wise/-ize   See **-ize/-wise**.

would of   See **have/of**.

you   Avoid indefinite uses of *you*. It should only be used to mean "you, the reader."

The [not *your*] average life span in the United States has increased consistently over the past 100 years.

your/you're   The two are not interchangeable. *Your* is the possessive form of "you"; *you're* is the contraction of "you are."

Your car can be picked up after 5 p.m.

You're going to need money to live in Manhattan.

Index

G

Gale Virtual Reference Library, 163
Gender
  inclusiveness and, 373–374, 429–430
  pronouns and, 373, 429–430
General keywords, 173
General OneFile, 179
Generalizations
  hasty, 49
  transitional words and, 28
Genres of academic writing
  case studies, 122–123, 307
  choosing, 6–7
  disciplines, 104–105, 117–119
  essay exams, 115–116
  informative writing, 69–80
  lab reports, 124–125
  literary analysis, 105–114
  observations, 120–121
  position arguments, 81–90
  proposal arguments, 81–90
  rhetorical analysis, 56–68
Geography, evidence in writing in, 119
Geology, evidence in writing in, 119
Gerund phrases, 389
Gerunds, 382, 411, 425, 532, 536, 552
Goals
  collaborative writing and, 20
  planning and, 9–10
  presentation planning, 146
  for revisions, 36–39
good/well, 552
Google, 172, 180, 181, 185, 186
  spelling assistance, 503
Google Earth, 186
Google Scholar, 179
Government sources
  APA in-text citations, 302, 304
  APA References list, 302–303, 304
  CMS documentation, 325
  evidence in, 119
  finding, 173
  MLA Works Cited list, 263
  online, 182–183, 263, 304
  print, 263, 325
Grammar. *See individual parts of grammar*
Grant proposals, 131–132
Graphic narratives, MLA Works Cited list, 256–257
Graphics. *See* Images; Visual texts
Graphs
  APA References list, 306
  citation requirements, 221
  line, 143, 145
  misleading, 54
  MLA Works Cited list, 260
  as sources for research, 186
Groups
  APA in-text citations, 288–289
  APA References list, 298, 300, 304
  CMS documentation, 323
  CSE documentation, 339, 341
  MLA in-text citations, 236
  MLA Works Cited list, 255, 259

H

hanged/hung, 552
hardly, 441
Hasty generalization, 49
have, 381, 411
have/of, 552
he, 380
Headings
  APA-style paper, 308
  MLA-style paper, 266
Health Reference Center, 177
Health sciences, academic writing and, 118
hear/here, 368
he/his/him, 373
Helping verbs. *See* Auxiliary verbs
here/hear, 368
her/hers/herself, 380, 429
he/she; s/he, 373, 552
him/his/himself, 380
his, 429
History, writing on, evidence in, 104, 105
Home page. *See also* Internet; Web sources
  evaluating, 200, 201–202
  library, 163, 175, 183
  MLA Works Cited list, 249
Homonyms, 368–369, 503–504
hopefully, 552
however, 400, 440
HTML format, database source texts, 177
Humanities. *See also* CMS documentation; MLA documentation
  evidence in, 104–105
  writing in, 103–116
Humor, in presentations, 150
hung/hanged, 552
Hyphens, 470–473, 514–515. *See also* Dashes
  for clarity, 473
  with compound nouns, 472
  dashes *versus*, 480
  to divide words at end of line, 473
  with numbers, 472–473
Hypothetical conditional sentences, 537–538

I

I, 380, 421–422
Ibid, CMS documentation, 322, 328
-ic suffix, 382
IceRocket, 185
Idea maps, 12–13
Ideas
  development of, 35
  parallelism and, 364
Idioms, 520–521, 538
i.e. (that is), 511
if, 388, 441
illicit/elicit, 369, 551
illusion/allusion, 369, 548
Illustrated books, MLA Works Cited list, 256–257
Illustrations. *See also* Photo essays
  citation requirements, 221
  CMS documentation, 334

Credits

Text Credits

Page 8, © Union of Concerned Scientists. Used with permission.

Page 174, LexisNexis Academic screen shot reprinted with the permission of Lexis Nexis, a division of Reed Elsevier Inc.

Page 175, Used with permission, The University of Kansas Libraries.

Page 178, Courtesy of EBSCO. Used with permission.

Page 189, Courtesy of EBSCO. Used with permission.

Page 242, Courtesy of EBSCO. Used with permission.

Page 246, © JSTOR. Used with permission.

Page 282, Courtesy of EBSCO. Used with permission.

Page 284, Courtesy of EBSCO. Used with permission.

Page 284, Courtesy of EBSCO Publishing. Used with permission.

Image Credits

Parts 1 through 10 dividers, Lester Faigley

Page 13, nyul/123rf

Page 24, Lester Faigley

Page 30, Lester Faigley

Page 53, Library of Congress Prints and Photographs Division [LC-USZ62-55378]

Page 54, Lester Faigley

Page 57 top left, Library of Congress Prints and Photographs Division

Page 57 top right, Library of Congress Prints and Photographs Division [LC-DIG-ppmsca-11724]

Page 57 bottom, Library of Congress Prints and Photographs Division [LC-DIG-ppmsca-19926]

Page 67, Lester Faigley

Pages 134–138, Lester Faigley

Page 139, ajr_images/Fotolia

Page 148, Lester Faigley

Page 152, Lester Faigley

Page 154, doctor bass/Shutterstock

Page 157, Lester Faigley

Page 185, G. Bacon/ESA/NASA

Page 189, Lester Faigley

Page 203, Bryan Trandem/Quayside Publishing Group

Page 217, Library of Congress Prints and Photographs Division [LC-USZC4-6144]

Page 244, Penguin Press

Page 248 top, NASA's Kennedy Space Center, Florida/ NASA

Page 248 bottom, NASA

Page 345, Lester Faigley

Page 351, Lester Faigley

Page 359, Lester Faigley

Page 364, Lester Faigley

All images without crediting appear courtesy of Lester Faigley.

REVISION GUIDE

Commonly used editing and proofreading symbols are listed here, along with references to the relevant chapters and sections of this handbook. See Chapter 4 for general advice on rewriting, editing, and proofreading.

Words, Sentences, and Paragraphs

abbr	Abbreviation problem: 47a	*num*	Number problem: 47c
adj	Adjective problem: 37a-b	*p*	Punctuation problem: 38-44
adv	Adverb problem: 37a, 37c	*pass*	Passive voice misused: 27a
agr	Agreement problem, either subject-verb or pronoun-antecedent: 34, 36b	*pl*	Plural form misused or needed: 49c
		pron	Pronoun problem: 36
apos	Apostrophe missing or misused: 42	*ref*	Reference of a pronoun unclear: 36d
art	Article is missing or misused: 49d	*run-on*	Run-on sentence problem: 33b
cap	Capitalization is needed: 46a	*sexist*	Sexist language: 31b
case	Case of a pronoun is incorrect: 36a	*sp*	Spelling needs to be checked: 45
coh	Coherence lacking in a paragraph: 3c	*sub*	Subordination is faulty: 29a
cs	Comma splice occurs: 33c	*trans*	Transition needed, use transitional terms: 3c
dm	Dangling modifier appears: 37e	*vb*	Verb problem: 35
		w	Wordy: 28
frag	Fragment instead of complete sentence: 33a	*ww*	Wrong word: 30
		¶	Paragraph break needed: 3
ital	Italics missing or misused: 46b	*no* ¶	No paragraph break needed: 3
lc	Lower case needed: 46a	//	Parallelism needs to be checked: 29c-e
mm	Misplaced modifier: 37b-c		

Punctuation and Mechanics

⋏	Comma needed: 38	( )	Parentheses needed: 41
⋎	Apostrophe needed: 42	[ ]	Brackets needed: 44d
⋎ ⋎	Quotation marks needed: 43	#	Add a space
⊙	Period needed: 44a	⊃	Close up a space
?	Question mark needed: 44b	⌣	Delete this
!	Exclamation point needed: 44c	⋀	Insert something
—	Dash needed: 41	∿	Transpose (switch the order)
· · ·	Ellipses needed: 44e		

Detailed Contents

i

Contents

Symbol	Meaning
or	Faulty abbreviation **64**
	Misused adjective or adverb **56**
-	Problem with subject-verb or pronoun agreement **53, 55a**
or	Inappropriate word or phrase **47**
	Incorrect or missing article **69b**
k	Awkward
	Faulty capitalization **63**
e	Error in pronoun case **55d, e**
he	Overused expression **48d**
	Problem with coherence **7f**
ᴎ	Incomplete comparison **39c**
rd	Problem with coordination **44**
	Comma splice **52**
	Diction problem **47, 48**
	More development needed **6b, c**
	Dangling modifier **43e**
	Documentation problem APA **31, 32**; Chicago **35, 36**; CSE **37**; MLA **26, 27**
h	Problem with emphasis **44**
ct	Inexact word **48**
n	Example needed **6b**
	Sentence fragment **51**
	Fused (or run-on) sentence **52**
ɑ	Problem with hyphen **67**
	Incomplete construction **39**
	Stronger introduction needed **6c**
	Italics or underlining needed **66**
	Jargon **47c**
	Lowercase letter needed **63**
	Mixed construction **40**
	Misplaced modifier **43a–d**
	Meaning not clear
d	Error in mood **54j**
	Error in manuscript form **8** APA **33**; Chicago **36**; MLA **29**
	Error in number style **65**
	Paragraph **6c**

Symbol	Meaning
p	Punctuation error
‸	Comma **57a–j**
no ,	Unnecessary comma **57k–o**
;	Semicolon **58**
:	Colon **59**
ꞌ	Apostrophe **60**
" "	Quotation marks **61**
. ? !	Period, question mark, exclamation point **62a–c**
— ( ) [ ] . . . /	Dash, parentheses, brackets, ellipses, slash **62d–h**
para	Problem with a paraphrase **24c, e**
pass	Ineffective use of passive voice **46b**
pn agr	Problem with pronoun agreement **55a**
quote	Problem with a quotation **24e, 61b, g**
ref	Problem with pronoun reference **55b**
rep	Repetitious words or phrases **38b**
run-on	Run-on (or fused) sentence **52**
sexist	Sexist language **47e, 55a**
shift	Shift in point of view, tense, mood, or voice **41**
sl	Slang **47a**
sp	Misspelled word **68**
sub	Problem with subordination **44**
sv agr	Problem with subject-verb agreement **53**
t	Verb tense error **54f**
trans	Transition needed **7f**
usage	See Glossary of Usage **50**
var	Vary your sentence structure **45**
vb	Verb problem **54**
w	Wordy **38**
ww	Wrong word **48f**
//	Parallelism needed **42**
#	Add a space
^	Insert
⌒	Close up space
x	Obvious error
??	Unclear

Quick Guide to Key Resources

TIPS FOR MULTILINGUAL WRITERS

THE MOST COMMON ERRORS

SECTIONS OF VISUAL RHETORIC

Tab 2: © Stapleton Collection/Corbis; **p. 35:** Courtesy of the Peace Corps; **p. 39:** Courtesy of the Peace Corps; **p. 56:** © Stockbyte/PunchStock RF; **p. 57 (top):** © Erica Simone Leeds RF; **p. 57 (bottom):** Courtesy of adbusters.org; **p. 60:** © Hulton Archive/Getty Images; **p. 61:** © Jamie Kingham/cultura/Corbis; **p. 62:** Library of Congress Prints and Photographs Division [LC-DIG-fsa-8b29516]; **p. 64:** © Corbis RF; **p. 66 (left):** © John Foxx/Stockbyte/Getty Images RF; **p. 66 (middle left):** © Brand X Pictures/PunchStock RF; **p. 66 (middle right):** © Ingram Publishing RF; **p. 66 (right):** © Ingram Publishing/Fotosearch RF; **p. 91:** Library of Congress Prints and Photographs Division [LC-DIG-fsa-8b29516]

Tab 3: © Philadelphia Museum of Modern Art/Corbis; **p. 140:** Courtesy of adbusters.org; **p. 165 (top):** © Photographer's Choice/Getty Images; **p. 165 (bottom):** © Glowimages RF; **p. 175** © Nichole Sobecki/AFP/Getty Images; **p. 176:** © Franco Fojanini/Getty Images RF

Tab 4: © John Lamb/Getty Images RF; **p. 191:** © Yagi Studio/Getty Images RF; **p. 192 (hallway):** © Vstock LLC/Getty Images RF; **p. 192 (computer):** © Gregor Schuster/Getty Images RF; **p. 192 (boy):** © Stockdisc RF; **p. 192 (phone):** © McGraw-Hill Education; **p. 192 (girl):** © Thinkstock/Getty Images RF; **p. 193:** © PSL Images/Alamy RF

Tab 5: NASA/J. J. Hester, Arizona State University

Tab 6: © Toño Labra/age fotostock

Tab 7: © Justin Kerr

Tab 8: © Glen Allison/Getty Images RF

Tab 9: © Uyen Le/Getty Images RF

Tab 10: © Mimmo Jodice/Corbis

Tab 11: © David Malan/Getty Images RF

Tab 12: © Tom Bonaventure/Getty Images RF

Tab 13: © De Agostini/Getty Images; **FR-1** © Philip Colla Natural History Photography; **FR-3** © Bettmann/Corbis; **FR-4** © Hulton-Deutsch Collection/Corbis; **FR-6** © Bettmann/Corbis